NORTH
AMERICA

ATLANTIC
OCEAN

AFRICA

AHMEDABAD
BOMBAY

OCEAN

NORTHERN CIRCARS

MADRAS

PACIFIC
OCEAN

SOUTH
AMERICA

ST. HELENA

FORT YORK

AUSTRALIA

INDIAN
OCEAN

ANTARCTICA

NORTH
SEA

EUROPE

BLACK SEA

GREAT
BRITAIN

IRELAND

USHANT
ISLAND

FRANCE

MINORCA

MEDITERRANEAN SEA

SPAIN

GIBRALTAR

OCEAN

AFRICA

ST. LOUIS

FORT JAMES

GOLD
COAST

The Fate of the Day

The Fate
of the Day

The War for America,
Fort Ticonderoga to Charleston, 1777–1780

Volume Two
of the Revolution Trilogy

Rick Atkinson

CROWN
NEW YORK

CROWN
An imprint of the Crown Publishing Group
A division of Penguin Random House LLC
1745 Broadway
New York, NY 10019
crownpublishing.com
penguinrandomhouse.com

Maps © 2025 by Gene Thorp

Library of Congress Cataloging-in-Publication Data is on file with the publisher.

Hardcover ISBN 978-0-593-79918-5
Signed edition ISBN 979-8-217-08662-7
Ebook ISBN 978-0-593-79919-2

Editors: John Sterling and Gillian Blake
Editorial assistants: Amy Li and Jess Scott
Production editor: Natalie Blachere
Text designer: Andrea Lau
Production: Heather Williamson
Copy editor: Bonnie Thompson
Proofreaders: Chuck Thompson, Janet Renard, and Andrea Connolly Peabbles
Indexer: Elise Hess
Publicist: Dyana Messina
Marketer: Julie Cepler

Manufactured in Canada

1 3 5 7 9 8 6 4 2

First Edition

The authorized representative in the EU for product safety and compliance is
Penguin Random House Ireland, Morrison Chambers, 32 Nassau Street,
Dublin D02 YH68, Ireland, https://eu-contact.penguin.ie.

To Penny, Wren, Luca, Whit, and Nico.

Our conflict is not likely to cease so soon as every good man would wish. . . . Our cause is noble. It is the cause of mankind, and the danger to it springs from ourselves.

—*George Washington, March 31, 1779*

Contents

LIST OF MAPS xi

MAP LEGEND xii

LIST OF ILLUSTRATIONS xiii

PROLOGUE, *France, February–April 1777* 1

    The Monarchs 1

    The Diplomat 11

    The Adventurer 20

Part One

1. THE MARCH OF ANNIHILATION 29
    Fort Ticonderoga, New York, July–August 1777

2. THIS CURSED, CUT-UP LAND 55
    New York, July 1777

3. FELLOWS WILLING TO GO TO HEAVEN 76
    Little Neshaminy Creek, Pennsylvania, August 1777

4. THINE ARROWS STICK FAST IN ME 96
    Oriskany, New York, and Bennington, Vermont, August 1777

5. A BARBAROUS BUSINESS IN A BARBAROUS COUNTRY 118
    Brandywine, Pennsylvania, September 1777

6. THESE ARE DREADFUL TIMES 144
    Philadelphia and Paoli, Pennsylvania, September 1777

7. BORN UNDER A FIERY PLANET 163
    Germantown, Pennsylvania, October 1777

8. TO RISK ALL UPON ONE RASH STROKE 182
    Saratoga, New York, September 1777

9. HOW ART THOU FALLEN 201
    Saratoga, New York, October 1777

10. THE ELEMENTS IN FLAMES 233
    Philadelphia, October–December 1777

Part Two

11. THE KING'S WAR 257
    London, November 1777–February 1778

12. BLESSED IS HE THAT EXPECTS NOTHING 278
    Paris, December 1777–March 1778

13. THE VORTEX OF SMALL FORTUNES   292
Valley Forge, Pennsylvania, January–June 1778

14. I WOULD RATHER LOSE THE CROWN   321
London and Portsmouth, England, April–June 1778

15. THE FRENCH FLAG IN ALL ITS GLORY   338
Paris and the English Channel, February–July 1778

16. FLYING FROM A SHADOW   356
Monmouth Court House, New Jersey, June 1778

17. FORTUNE IS A FICKLE JADE   384
New York and Newport, Rhode Island, July–August 1778

18. A STAR AND A STRIPE FROM THE REBEL FLAG   411
New York and Savannah, Georgia, October 1778–February 1779

19. THE UNCERTAINTY OF HUMAN PROSPECTS   428
Philadelphia, December 1778–February 1779

Part Three

20. A SUMMONS TO THE QUEEN'S HOUSE   447
London, January–July 1779

21. I DETEST THAT SORT OF WAR   465
Hampton Roads, Virginia, and Stony Point, New York,
March–July 1779

22. THE VALLEY OF BONES   485
The American Frontier, June–September 1779

23. EVERYTHING IS NOW AT STAKE   508
British Home Waters, July–September 1779

24. THE GREATEST EVENT THAT HAS HAPPENED   536
Savannah, Georgia, September–October 1779

25. ETERNITY IS NEARER EVERY DAY   557
Morristown, New Jersey, December 1779–February 1780

26. SHE STOOPS TO CONQUER   579
Charleston, South Carolina, February–June 1780

EPILOGUE, *Britain and America, June 1780*   608

AUTHOR'S NOTE   619

NOTES   621

SOURCES   771

ACKNOWLEDGMENTS   823

INDEX   829

Maps

1. The British Empire, *1777* — Endpapers
2. The North American Theater, *June 1777–May 1780* — 28
3. Hudson Valley Battleground, *July–August 1777* — 31
4. Battle of Hubbardton, *July 7, 1777* — 45
5. New York City, *Summer 1777* — 57
6. Fort Stanwix and the Battle of Oriskany, *August 5–6, 1777* — 99
7. Battle of Bennington, *August 16, 1777* — 109
8. Battle of Brandywine, *Morning–3 p.m., September 11, 1777* — 121
9. Battle of Brandywine, *3 p.m.–9 p.m., September 11, 1777* — 133
10. Attack at Paoli, *September 20–21, 1777* — 148
11. Battle of Germantown, *October 4, 1777* — 165
12. The Battle of Saratoga at Freeman's Farm, *September 19, 1777* — 185
13. Battle for the Hudson Highlands, *October 1777* — 203
14. The Battle of Saratoga at Bemus Heights, *October 7, 1777* — 209
15. Philadelphia and the Battle for the Delaware, *October–November 1777* — 235
16. Approach to Monmouth, *June 19–28, 1778* — 359
17. Battle of Monmouth, *Afternoon, June 28, 1778* — 365
18. Battle for Newport, *July–August 1778* — 393
19. Attack on Hampton Roads, *May 1779* — 469
20. Assault on Stony Point, *July 15–16, 1779* — 478
21. War on the American Frontier, *1778–1779* — 487
22. British Home Waters, *August–September 1779* — 513
23. Assault on Savannah, *October 9, 1779* — 540
24. Siege of Charleston, *February–April 1780* — 583
25. Fall of Charleston, *April–June 1780* — 589

Legend

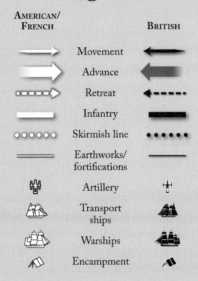

AMERICAN/ FRENCH		BRITISH
→	Movement	←
⇒	Advance	⬅
▭▭▭▭▷	Retreat	◄- - - -
▬▬▬▬	Infantry	▬▬▬▬
०००००००	Skirmish line	••••••
═══════	Earthworks/ fortifications	───────
ᛦ	Artillery	⊥
⛵	Transport ships	⛴
⛵	Warships	⛴
⛺	Encampment	⛺

FEATURES

○	City/Town	═══	Road
◉	Capital	───	River
🏠	House	─ ─ ─	Boundary
🏠	Tavern	‑ ‑ ‑	Fence
⛪	Church	‑×‑×‑	Rail fence
🏛	Hall/Meetinghouse/ Prison/Theater/ College	∿∿∿∿	Stone wall
🏭	Mill	▢	Body of water
✦	Fort	▨	Woods
†✿	Cemetery	∴	Orchard
⊔	Bridge	▨	Marsh
⋯	Ford	▨	Mudflat
‿	Pass	▨	Beach
□	Other feature	▨	Terrain
✸	Clash	◣	Highlighted terrain
✕	Previous engagement		
🔥	Burned		

Boundaries and geographic labels generally reflect British cartographic surveys from the mid-eighteenth century. Borders often were disputed.

Illustrations

FIRST INSERT

1. Antoine-François Callet, *Louis XVI,* oil on canvas, 1778–79. (© Photographic Archive Museo Nacional del Prado, Madrid)
2. Anonymous artist, after Élisabeth-Louise Vigée Le Brun, *Marie-Antoinette,* oil on canvas, after 1783. (Courtesy National Gallery of Art, Washington, DC, Timken Collection)
3. Louis Carrogis De Carmontelle, *Benjamin Franklin,* drawing, c. 1780–81. (Courtesy National Portrait Gallery, Smithsonian Institution; bequest of Mrs. Herbert Clark Hoover)
4. Nicolas Pérignon, *The Potager of the Hôtel de Valentinois in Passy,* gouache over graphite on linen, c. 1780. (Courtesy National Gallery of Art, Washington, DC, Samuel H. Kress Collection)
5. Sylvester Harding, *Portrait of David Murray; 2nd Earl of Mansfield,* drawing, c. 1760–1809. (© Trustees of the British Museum)
6. Charles Clément Bervic, *Charles Gravier, Count of Vergennes,* etching, aquatint, 1780. (Courtesy Metropolitan Museum of Art, New York; gift of William H. Huntington, 1983)
7. Joseph Boze (?), *Marquis de Lafayette,* oil on canvas, c. 1780–90. (Courtesy Mount Vernon Ladies' Association)
8. Charles Willson Peale, *Arthur St. Clair,* oil on canvas, 1782–84. (Courtesy Independence National Historical Park)
9. Jacob Lazarus Hart, *General Philip Schuyler,* oil on canvas, c. 1881. (New York State Office of Parks, Recreation & Historic Preservation, Schuyler Mansion State Historic Site, Albany, NY)
10. Joshua Reynolds, *General John Burgoyne,* oil on canvas, c. 1766. (Frick Collection, New York; Image © The Frick Collection)
11. John Vanderlyn, *The Murder of Jane McCrea,* oil on canvas, 1804. (Photograph, Allen Phillips, Wadsworth Atheneum Museum of Art, Hartford, CT)
12. Charles Willson Peale, *George Washington,* oil on canvas, c. 1779–81. (Courtesy Metropolitan Museum of Art, New York; gift of Collis P. Huntington, 1897)
13. Attributed to Andrea Soldi, *Portrait of General Sir Henry Clinton,* oil on canvas, c. 1762–65. (American Museum & Gardens, Bath, UK)
14. Richard Purcell (H. Fowler, Charles or Philip Corbutt), *William Howe, 5th Viscount Howe,* mezzotint, published May 1778. (© National Portrait Gallery, London)
15. Henry Singleton, *Richard Howe, 1st Earl Howe,* oil on canvas, before 1799. (© National Portrait Gallery, London)
16. William Augustus West, Viscount Cantelupe, *The Battery of the Rebels opened on Brandywine heights the 11th of September 1777 in the county of Birmingham,* sketch, 1777. (Reproduced by permission of Durham University Library and Collections and Lord Howick Estate)

17. Samuel Arlent Edwards, after Charles Willson Peale, *Gen. Nathaniel* [sic] *Greene,* color mezzotint, 1900. (Courtesy Anne S. K. Brown Military Collection, Brown Digital Repository, Brown University Library)

18. Charles Willson Peale, *General Henry Knox,* watercolor on ivory, 1778. (Courtesy Metropolitan Museum of Art, New York; gift of J. William Middendorf II, 1968)

19. Charles Willson Peale, *Portrait of Major General Anthony Wayne,* oil on canvas, 1783–84. (Courtesy Philadelphia Museum of Art; gift of the McNeil Americana Collection)

20. Joseph Collyer, after Thomas Lawrence, *Sir Charles Grey, K.B.,* stipple-engraving, published May 1797. (Courtesy Anne S. K. Brown Military Collection, Brown Digital Repository, Brown University Library)

21. Xavier della Gatta, *Battle of Paoli,* gouache on paper, 1782. (Museum of the American Revolution)

22. Edward Lamson Henry, *The Attack on Chew's House during the Battle of Germantown, 1777,* oil on canvas, 1878. (Art Institute of Chicago / Art Resource, NY, George F. Harding Collection)

23. John Francis Eugene Prud'homme, *Peter Gansevoort,* stipple engraving, date uncertain. (Courtesy Print Collection, New York Public Library)

24. Charles Willson Peale, *Joseph Brant [Thayendanegea],* oil on canvas, 1797. (Courtesy Independence National Historical Park)

25. Leroy Williams, *Battle of Bennington,* oil painting, 1938. (Bennington Museum, Bennington, VT)

26. Johann Heinrich Schröder, *Portrait of Friedrich Adolph Riedesel, Baron of Eisenbach,* pastel, c. 1795. (Courtesy National Museum in Warsaw)

27. *Friederike* [sic] *Charlotte Luise Riedesel.* (Courtesy Library of Congress)

28. Unidentified artist after Thomas Sully, *Patrick Henry,* oil on canvas, before 1878. (Courtesy Independence National Historical Park)

29. *Brig. Gen. Daniel Morgan.* (Courtesy Print Collection, New York Public Library)

30. Julian Rys, after unidentified source, *Tadeusz Kosciuszko,* oil on canvas, 1897. (Courtesy Independence National Historical Park)

31. Alonzo Chappel, *Battle of Saratoga: Gen. Arnold wounded in the attack on the Hessian redoubt,* engraving, 1860. (Courtesy Print Collection, New York Public Library)

32. John Graham, artist, William Nutter, engraver. *To the Right Honourable the Earl of Warrington this plate, of the burial of General Fraser is dedicated,* engraving, 1794. (Courtesy Society of the Cincinnati, Washington, DC)

33. James Peale, *Horatio Gates at Saratoga,* oil on canvas, c. 1800. (Courtesy Maryland Center for History and Culture, 1890.2.1; gift of Mrs. William S. G. Baker)

34. John Trumbull, *The Surrender of General Burgoyne at Saratoga, October 16, 1777,* oil on canvas, c. 1822–32. (Courtesy Yale University Art Gallery, Trumbull Collection)

35. William Russell Birch, *Second Street north from Market St. with Christ Church, Philadelphia,* hand-colored engraving, 1828. (Courtesy Library Company of Philadelphia)

36. Johann Heinrich Tischbein, *Carl Aemil Ulrich von Donop,* oil on canvas, 1765, Museum für Kunst und Kultur, Münster. (Courtesy Wikimedia Commons)
37. Irwin John Bevan, *Lord Howe's Fleet in the Delaware River, October 1777,* drawing, watercolor. (Mariners' Museum and Park, Newport News, Virginia)
38. Unidentified British naval officer, *Destruction of HMS Augusta in the Delaware River, 23 October 1777,* oil painting, before 1779. (Courtesy Naval History and Heritage Command)

SECOND INSERT

39. Benjamin West, *George III,* oil on canvas, 1779. (© Royal Collection Enterprises Limited 2024 | Royal Collection Trust)
40. Benjamin West, *Queen Charlotte,* oil on canvas, 1779. (© Royal Collection Enterprises Limited 2024 | Royal Collection Trust)
41. Thomas Sutherland, engraver, and William Westall, illustrator, *Buckingham House,* illustration, aquatint, 1819. (Courtesy Print Collection, New York Public Library)
42. Johann Jacobé, after George Romney, *Lord George Germain,* mezzotint, c. 1780–97. (© Trustees of the British Museum)
43. John Singleton Copley, *Study for Lord North,* drawing, 1779–80. (Courtesy Boston Athenæum)
44. Thomas Gainsborough, *John Montagu, 4th Earl of Sandwich, 1st Lord of the Admiralty,* painting, 1783. (National Maritime Museum, Greenwich, London, Greenwich Hospital Collection)
45. Valentine Green, after Nathaniel Dance, *Martha Ray,* mezzotint, 1777. (© National Portrait Gallery, London)
46. William Brooke Thomas Trego, *The March to Valley Forge, December 19, 1777,* oil on canvas, 1883. (Museum of the American Revolution, conserved with funds provided by the Society of the Descendants of Washington's Army at Valley Forge)
47. Ellen Sharples, after James Sharples, Sr., *Benjamin Rush,* pastel on paper, 1805. (Courtesy Independence National Historical Park)
48. Ralph Earl, *Major General Friedrich Wilhelm Augustus, Baron von Steuben,* oil on canvas, c. 1786. (Courtesy Yale University Art Gallery; gift of Mrs. Paul Moore in memory of her nephew Howard Melville Hanna, Jr., B.S., 1931)
49. John Singleton Copley, *Henry Laurens,* oil on canvas, 1782. (Courtesy National Portrait Gallery, Smithsonian Institution)
50. Charles Willson Peale, *John Laurens,* watercolor on ivory, 1780. (Courtesy National Portrait Gallery, Smithsonian Institution)
51. Jean Laurent Mosnier, *Portrait of John Graves Simcoe,* oil painting, 1791. (Courtesy Toronto Public Library, Baldwin Collection of Canadiana)
52. Pierre Ozanne, *Le vaisseau le Languedoc démâté par le coup de vent dans le nuit du 12' attaqué par un vaisseau de guerre Anglois l'après midy du 13 Aoust 1778.* (Courtesy Library of Congress)

53. Benjamin West, *The Death of Chatham,* oil on canvas, 1778. (Courtesy Yale Center for British Art, Paul Mellon Fund, in honor of Professor Jules David Prown)

54. Robert Sayer, *An English jack-tar giving monsieur a drubbing,* cartoon, mezzotint, published May 1779. (Courtesy Library of Congress)

55. John Rising, after Joshua Reynolds, *The Hon. Charles James Fox MP,* oil on canvas, after 1782. (© National Trust, Petworth House, Egremont Collection)

56. *Charles Henry Comte D'Estaing,* n.d. (Courtesy Print Collection, New York Public Library)

57. Pompeo Girolamo Batoni, *Don José Moñino y Redondo, Conde de Floridablanca,* oil on canvas, c. 1776. (The Art Institute of Chicago / Art Resource, NY; Charles H. and Mary F. S. Worcester Collection)

58. John Trumbull, after Gilbert Stuart, *John Adams,* oil on canvas, 1793. (Courtesy National Portrait Gallery, Smithsonian Institution)

59. Joseph Skelton, after Théodore Gudin, *Combat Naval d'Ouessant (Naval Battle of Ushant),* engraving, n.d. (Courtesy Yale University Art Gallery)

60. Joshua Reynolds, *Admiral Augustus Keppel,* painting, 1779. (National Maritime Museum, Greenwich, London, Greenwich Hospital Collection)

61. William T. Ranney, *Recruiting for the Continental Army,* oil on canvas, 1857–59. (Munson Museum, Utica, NY / Art Resource, NY; gift of T. Proctor Eldred)

62. John Trumbull, *Alexander Hamilton,* oil on canvas, 1832. (Courtesy Yale University Art Gallery, Trumbull Collection)

63. *Major John André, from a miniature by himself,* n.d. (Courtesy Print Collection, New York Public Library)

64. Joshua Reynolds, *Captain the Honourable John Byron,* painting, 1759. (National Maritime Museum, Greenwich, London, Caird Collection)

65. George Romney, *Major-General Sir Archibald Campbell,* oil on canvas, 1790–92. (Courtesy National Gallery of Art, Washington, DC, Timken Collection)

66. *Sir George Collier Knt. Vice Admiral of the Blue,* stipple engraving, 1814. (Courtesy Print Collection, New York Public Library)

67. William Dickinson, after George Romney, *Sir Charles Hardy,* mezzotint, published January 1781. (© National Portrait Gallery, London)

68. Jean Michel Moreau, *John Paul Jones,* engraving, 1781. (Courtesy Library of Congress)

69. Charles Grignion, *Captain Sir Richard Pearson,* painting, 1780. (National Maritime Museum, Greenwich, London, Caird Collection)

70. Thomas Mitchell, *Battle between Continental Ship Bonhomme Richard and HMS Serapis, 23 September 1779,* oil on canvas, 1780. (Courtesy Naval History and Heritage Command)

71. Bass Otis, *William Alexander,* oil on canvas, c. 1858. (Courtesy Independence National Historical Park)

72. Charles Willson Peale, *Henry Lee,* oil on canvas, c. 1782. (Courtesy Independence National Historical Park)

73. Julian Rys after unidentified source, *Casimir Pulaski,* oil on canvas, c. 1897. (Courtesy Independence National Historical Park)

74. Richard Morrell Staigg, after John Trumbull, *John Sullivan,* oil on canvas, 1876. (Courtesy Independence National Historical Park)

75. Charles Willson Peale, *Benjamin Lincoln,* oil on canvas, c. 1781–83. (Courtesy Independence National Historical Park)

76. Diana Dietz Hill, *Charles Cornwallis, 1st Marquess Cornwallis,* watercolor on ivory, 1786. (Courtesy Mount Vernon Ladies' Association; gift of Katherine Merle-Smith Thomas, 2010)

77. Henry Bryan Hall, *Admiral Marriot Arbuthnot,* 1874. (Courtesy Print Collection, New York Public Library)

78. Alonzo Chappel, *Siege of Charleston,* engraving by Johnson, Fry & Co., 1862. (Courtesy Anne S. K. Brown Military Collection, Brown Digital Repository, Brown University Library)

79. James Heath, engraver, Francis Wheatley, artist, *The riot in Broad Street on the seventh of June 1780,* engraving, 1790. (Courtesy Society of the Cincinnati, Washington, DC)

The Fate of the Day

Prologue

The Monarchs

As the Parisian social season drew to a close in February 1777, few courtiers could guess that the queen of France was eager for the gaiety to end. Week after week, Marie-Antoinette had flitted from one grand ball to another, at the Palais-Royal, the Opéra on the rue de Richelieu, or her own stupendous palace at Versailles. When she was not dancing, she could be found at the theater, the racetrack, or high-stakes gambling tables, where her losses from faro, *lansquenet,* and other ruinous card games now approached half a million livres. The king's brother privately had begun calling her "Madame Deficit."

No matter. There was always another ball to attend somewhere, usually beginning at midnight and lasting until daybreak, with dance floors so crowded that spurs and canes were forbidden. Rarely did her husband, Louis XVI, accompany her, although, as she would write in mid-February to her mother, the empress Maria Theresa of Austria, she went out only "after telling the king and making sure he would not be displeased." He invariably replied that "I could go there as long as it amused me."

The queen particularly adored the masquerades so popular during Carnival, the raucous festival gripping Paris for more than a month before the arrival of Lent, that season of ostensible sacrifice and reflection preceding Easter. Often she wore a silk domino to cover the upper half of her face, arriving in a plain carriage without the royal coat of arms and sitting on a stool rather than the fine chair reserved for royalty. "She fancied she was never recognized," one nobleman wrote, "but she always was." Masks and costumes allowed the wellborn and the lowborn to mingle in a way that was otherwise unthinkable, creating a mélange said to include "great ladies, kept girls, one-night stands, professional gamblers, great lords, actresses, and high-flying crooks."

Masked or unmasked, the queen was stunning. Ash-blond tresses framed her oval face and luminous blue eyes, and her alabaster skin was "so translucent that it allowed no shadows," an admirer wrote. Despite the wide hoops and long train of her gowns, she had perfected the "Versailles glide," an ability to cross a room so that it seemed her feet never touched the ground, wearing gloves scented with jasmine provided by her personal perfumer. A smitten observer invoked Virgil's *vrea incessu patuit Dea*: "in her movement the true goddess was revealed." When one varlet suggested that she seemed to lack rhythm on the dance floor, a chivalrous defender snapped, "Then the music must be wrong."

Some thought she had lost weight during the winter, a disappointment to those who had already waited seven years for her to produce a royal heir. Others grumbled that she paid too much attention to visiting English noblemen—known for their graceful dancing—despite portents of a drift toward war between France and Britain, a hereditary enmity newly rekindled by clandestine French help for American rebels. In truth, she was simply a coquette given to banter with handsome gallants, and caught up in the recent French enthusiasm for all things English, from horse racing and tea drinking to Shakespeare. Politics bored her and, she told one confidant, "I am terrified of being bored."

"My fate," Marie-Antoinette would later write, "is to bring misfortune." She was the fifteenth of Maria Theresa's sixteen children and, as a fourteen-year-old archduchess, had been bundled off from Vienna to Paris in 1770 to cement a Franco-Austrian alliance, following three centuries of hostility. Two days after she met the fifteen-year-old dauphin, they married in an extravaganza that included a matrimonial supper of two hundred dishes, the most spectacular fireworks ever seen at Versailles, and the illumination of the vast gardens with a clever network of wicks that permitted sixteen thousand lanterns to be lighted in three minutes. Another fireworks demonstration in central Paris went badly wrong when a premature explosion triggered a stampede that killed 132 people. "Their wedding," one historian would write, "was a state occasion that remained stigmatized by tragedy." Four years later, with the death of Louis XV from smallpox, her husband became king and she a queen at age nineteen. For the rest of their lives, he called her simply "Madame."

Despite a lingering Viennese accent, she had become so French that she needed German lessons to remain proficient in her mother tongue. Life at Versailles was elegant and stupefyingly excessive. Couturiers routinely descended, providing her with three yards of new ribbon each morning to tie the royal peignoir, and four new pairs of shoes a week. Three times a year, thirty-six new costumes were ordered for her wardrobe—velvets and furs in winter, satins and silks in spring, and gauzes in summer, with count-less lace mantelets, embroidered swags, and riding habits. Her jewelry chest, big as a sepulchre and lined with crimson velvet, held trays of dia-monds and other priceless gems by the fistful, plus a collar of pearls, the smallest the size of a filbert nut. Monsieur Léonard, the queen's hairdresser, drove his six-in-hand the twelve miles from Paris to Versailles almost every morning. He grew more inventive with each passing season, amass-ing horsehair, gauze, and surplus human locks to create coiffures so tall it was said that the door lintels of the palace would have to be raised. This year the French court's enthusiasm for the American rebellion could be seen in the *coiffure de la liberté*, with dozens of curls powdered as if rimed stiff with frost.

When Carnival at last drew to a close on Shrove Tuesday, February 11, the queen hosted a final dance in the Hall of Mirrors, the most renowned room in Europe: 240 feet long, with seventeen arched windows reflected in seventeen enormous mirrors, and a vaulted ceiling forty feet above the parquet floor. Murals depicted French battlefield triumphs against the Dutch in the seventeenth century, although the solid silver chairs and ta-bles that had once furnished the hall had been melted down to pay for other military adventures. After supper she headed for the Opéra ball, her carriage lured by the glow of Parisian lights to the northeast. By tradition, street crowds burned an effigy to end the season, and Paris wobbled back into sobriety. "Thus ended the Carnival," wrote Count Florimond de Mercy-Argenteau, the Austrian ambassador to France. "The queen confessed to me that after all she had been very little amused."

She returned to the palace early Wednesday morning and ascended the Queen's Staircase, her Versailles glide reduced to a trudge. Allegorical vir-tues decorated the ceiling of her bedchamber—*Charity, Abundance, Fidel-ity, Prudence*—all suitable for Lent. New candles, made of costly beeswax rather than tallow to avoid smoke stains, flickered in their sconces; her ladies-in-waiting replaced them whenever she left the room, then sold the used stubs in the market. Nineteen babies had been born to monarchs in the apartments she now occupied, none of them hers. She changed for Mass and walked to the palace chapel, then returned to sleep in the canopy bed. The first signs of spring would appear in a few weeks, and the queen could resume her daily walks among the chestnuts and pruned hornbeams on the palace grounds. To provide privacy, a new Queen's Grove had just been in-stalled, with four long paths planted with Virginia tulip trees, chokeberries, and other exotic flora brought back from North America. An aqueduct, pumps, and fourteen waterwheels lifted water vertically five hundred feet from the Seine bottomlands to irrigate the beds and fill the fountains.

All the while commissions would continue to fly from the palace for furniture and objets d'art fit for a queen: oriental porcelain, wallpapers, armchairs upholstered in white brocade, console tables embellished with bronze mounts and tortoiseshell inlay, marquetry commodes in mahogany and maple, and more Japanese lacquer boxes to add to her huge collection. Marie-Antoinette would not be bored.

As his vivacious, convivial wife was to Carnival, so the pious, solitary Louis XVI was to Lent. She was capricious; he was prudent. She was extravagant; he was thrifty. She was lovely; he was not, with his beaky nose, watery blue eyes, and big ears poking from beneath his wig. Stout and awkward, he "was heavy and unmajestic" in his movements, a courtier wrote, "his person greatly neglected." He always seemed to be "embarrassed by his sword, while never knowing what to do with his hat." Sophisticates sneered at his virtues, at his incapacity for small talk and his juvenile penchant for practical jokes, such as turning on the garden sprinklers to soak unsuspecting strollers. An aunt once urged him to discard his chronic diffidence. "Exclaim, bawl out, make a noise," she told him. "Dash my china to pieces and make yourself talked about."

"My greatest fault," he conceded, "is a sluggishness of mind." Yet he had been a precocious student, with a knack for mathematics, physics, geography, and Latin. He was proficient in Italian, Spanish, and English. Despite his mother's warning that English was "a language full of dangers," he translated Milton into French, devoured David Hume's *History of England*—the beheading of Charles I unnerved him—and understood parliamentary politics better than any of his ministers. His private rooms were jammed with telescopes, barometers, and sextants, as well as locks he made himself under the tutelage of a skilled smith, grinding, filing, and oiling in a palace workshop until his hands were black with grime.

A fine equestrian and an excellent shot, he was obsessed with hunting. Three years earlier he had begun keeping a journal, and as it grew to eight hundred pages, he diligently recorded bagging 189,251 birds and 1,274 stags while riding 128 horses, most of them cited by name. "Stag hunting. Got one. Have had a fit of indigestion," one typical entry read, although he also tallied his days spent traveling to other royal châteaus—eighty-three in 1776—and his charitable gifts, including 240 livres to a priest at Notre-Dame. He trimmed his own household expenses by reducing the number of horses in his stables from six thousand to eight hundred and reducing the carriages following the royal hunt from twenty to two. He was known, not entirely sardonically, as "Louis the Desired."

He was an accidental monarch, placed on the throne after the death of his grandfather in 1774 only because of the premature deaths of his father and two older brothers. "The power of the throne is absolute," he had written a few years earlier. "Nothing can check it, but it must be founded on justice and reason." Yet late in life he would cite only two occasions when being king made him happy. The first was his coronation, in June 1775, when in the cathedral at Reims, wearing an ermine cape and cradling a six-foot scepter, he vowed to "extirpate heretics"; as the crown of Charlemagne, encrusted with rubies, sapphires, and emeralds, was placed on his head, he wept. After being anointed with the holy oil of Clovis, he followed tradition by touching more than two thousand scrofula sufferers and making the sign of the cross over their lesions. It was said that four were cured, miraculously.

The second happy moment would not come until June 1786, when he made a state visit to celebrate the construction of a new Atlantic harbor at Cherbourg. Here was a royal irony. Since boyhood Louis had been transfixed by ships and all things nautical, studying ocean charts, vessel design, tides, rigging, and naval artillery until he reportedly knew as much as could be known without being a sailor. Now, in the spring of 1777, he was pondering whether to wager his kingdom by rebuilding the French navy to confront Britain, whose fleet was the greatest the world had ever known. Yet that brief trip to Normandy a decade hence would be the first and only time in his life that he ever saw the sea.

Versailles had been the political, administrative, and social capital of the kingdom for nearly a century, ever since the Sun King, Louis XIV, built the palace on the site of a hunting lodge and then required attendance by his nobles, on the presumption that those not at court were plotting sedition. Twelve thousand aristocrats, officials, servants, and idlers now crowded the château and adjacent precincts in a daily jostle for status and privilege. The tang of chimney soot scented the air, and, a visitor wrote, "the passages, the courtyards, the wings, and the corridors were full of urine and fecal matter," which "made one retch." Anyone with a proper hat and a sword, which could be rented from the gate porter, was allowed entry, and the antechambers swarmed with curious commoners, including women who could not afford rouge and instead tinted their cheeks with red wine.

The king and queen were described as "martyrs to decorum." Among the Versailles rituals was the *grand couvert*, typically on Sunday, when any visitor deemed to be "cleanly dressed" could watch the royal family dine.

More than forty dishes were brought from the kitchen in a procession and arranged symmetrically on a large table as musicians played on tiered steps. Tasters first nibbled at the veal, partridge, and hare before the king and queen lifted their forks, to the delight of the gawking provincials who packed the dining salon.

Even emptier ceremonies began and ended each day. The *lever*—the rising—started with the king's awakening at seven a.m. as his doctors, a priest, and a score of favored courtiers surrounded the bed to remove his white silk nightshirt and sleeping cap. This was followed by a larger ceremony attended by as many as 150 men, with those of the highest rank helping him don his breeches, shirt, dress coat, and that embarrassing sword. The king then sprinkled himself with holy water, murmured a prayer, and marched out to meet the day. After supper, during the *coucher*—bedtime—the routine was reversed, putting Louis back in his nightclothes and under the blankets.

Amid the relentless rituals, Louis devoted himself to the demands and duties of the throne. Every vital decision of state came through him, the absolute if often indecisive monarch. In a kingdom of twenty-eight million people, more than double the population of Britain and Ireland combined, a crisis always seemed to be erupting somewhere. Two years earlier, for instance, a poor harvest had caused bread prices to soar, triggering violent riots. The king deployed twenty-five thousand troops, who fired on the hungry mobs. Several rioters were hanged from a Paris gallows.

Of immediate concern was his nation's role in the world. France and England had fought each other in four coalition wars over the past century. The first three ended inconclusively, but the fourth—the Seven Years' War, known in America as the French and Indian War—ended with catastrophe for France in 1763, leaving the country humiliated, deeply in debt, and stripped of Canada, much of India, and an enormous tract between the Appalachian Mountains and the Mississippi River. Happily, France kept several islands in the West Indies, notably Martinique, Guadeloupe, and St. Lucia, which together provided roughly 40 percent of French imports. Acre for acre, a Caribbean sugar island was second in profit only to New World gold or silver mines. Hundreds of ships continued to haul not only mountains of sugar and coffee back to French ports, but also thousands of tons of indigo, cotton, and cocoa.

In the past decade, French prosperity had rebounded smartly. Overseas commerce—including a large share of the African slave trade—was now greater than ever. France had retained almost all of her allies from the last war, while Britain stood alone, also deeply in debt, with the added burden of an empire that stretched from Central America to the Arctic, and eastward to the Bay of Bengal. As Versailles in 1777 informed Spain, the kingdom's closest confederate, "France possesses colonies that suffice for its population and its economy. More would be a liability."

Losing the last war had forced France to adopt reforms and efficiencies at home. Not only was the army again among Europe's largest, with 170,000 infantry and 46,000 cavalry troops in 235 regiments, but military improvements ranged from a better musket to renovations in artillery, supply, recruiting, and naval affairs. When the government's finance chief advised against another war, warning that "the first gunshot will drive the state to bankruptcy," Louis sacked him, hiring in his place a Protestant banker from Geneva whose mission was to borrow enough money to rebuild the French navy and keep Versailles solvent without raising taxes.

Habitually cautious, Louis would move with small steps—his version of the Versailles glide. A year earlier he had reluctantly agreed to clandestine military support for American insurgents, despite doubts about a king encouraging republican rebels against another king. French commoners and young aristocrats alike vibrated with enthusiasm for the American cause, but Louis believed that a secret subsidy to the rebels was morally dubious, even if the initial amount—a million livres—was less than Marie-Antoinette spent on entertainment in a year.

Yet he knew that England remained his inveterate foe, regardless of Milton's sublime poetry and Hume's entrancing histories. It was necessary, he told Spain, to "humiliate this power which is the natural enemy and rival of our house." Otherwise British imperial strength would soon stifle France's economic resurgence and prevent Versailles from regaining its rightful place at the apex of European powers.

Since the end of the last war, French agents abroad had closely tracked British political and military developments, trying to detect weaknesses not only in the home islands but as far afield as the Baltic, Africa, and America. The king's ministers collected secret dispatches about Britain's troop movements, command changes, coastal defenses, and parliamentary debates. French naval engineers, covertly dispatched to southern England, studied ports, shipbuilding, and maritime trade. A clerk in London's colonial office provided inside information for 500 guineas a year. Another spy received £17 a month to "live, travel, and bribe." Agents pilfered British industrial secrets in wool, cloth, and steelmaking, while covertly studying paper mills, Newcastle coal mines, the use of salt in glazing and tanning, and Royal Navy experiments in bolting copper sheaths to warship hulls for improved efficiency.

And all the while, the king told his ministers, France intended "to meddle adroitly in the affairs of the British colonies [and] to give insurgent colonists the means of obtaining supplies of war, while maintaining the strictest neutrality."

When trumpets announced Louis's return to Versailles from the hunt, a heavyset, graying functionary often watched the mud-spattered cavalcade from his office window overlooking the palace courtyard. Charles Gravier, the Comte de Vergennes, served not only as French foreign minister, but as the king's chief strategist and closest adviser. Having allowed himself this brief distraction, he would return to his rosewood desk, with its gold-leaf inlay, where he usually could be found from eight a.m. until ten p.m., plotting Britain's decline and France's ascent. Sometimes he slipped up an inner staircase to the king's apartments for an evening chat or to deliver yet another tedious memorandum stressing two themes: that Britain was a "restless and greedy nation" and that another war appeared inevitable if France was to regain her former glory.

A deft, loyal monarchist, both prudent and audacious, Vergennes had served his nation since his first diplomatic posting, in Lisbon in 1739. Assignments had followed in Trier and Stockholm, where he had helped organize a coup that restored the Swedish monarchy. A stint in Constantinople damaged his career when he fell for Anne Viviers, a widowed commoner—"a woman of the people," one courtier sneered—who bore him two sons before they married in 1767. "It is a rare occurrence in this century for a wife and husband to love each other," Vergennes wrote, "and, what is more, to dare profess it." As a new king, Louis had elevated him to the ministry because of his broad experience, circumspection, and temperance. Avoiding what Vergennes called "the dissipations and frivolous amusements" of court life, he installed Anne and their boys in "La Solitude," a charming house away from the palace on the Avenue de Paris, where she would be insulated from aristocratic snubs.

France did not wish to crush Britain, Vergennes told the king. Such aggression would alarm other European powers, including the Prussians, the Dutch, and the Russians. Rather, the task at hand was to weaken London enough to restore French prestige as first among equals on the Continent, with "the right to influence all great affairs." The American rebellion, now entering its third year, provided a perfect vehicle for sapping British strength, giving France time to brace for war and to enlist Spain's military assistance under the Family Compact, which bound the Bourbon dynastic regimes in Versailles and Madrid and required them to provide mutual support.

Timing was critical, of course. In recent months the Americans had pressed for a formal commercial and military treaty with France, even offering assistance in capturing British sugar islands in the West Indies. Yet French war preparations remained incomplete, and the American rout from New York the previous summer had revealed troubling battlefield shortcomings. On the other hand, delay could lead to reconciliation between Britain and the rebellious colonies, perhaps resulting in their combined assault on Bourbon possessions in the New World.

After pondering these complexities, Vergennes prepared still another *mémoire*. Secret aid to the Yankees—cannons, muskets, gunpowder—helped the rebels, but greater assistance was needed to resolve the deadlocked struggle, liberate the American colonies, and thus ensure Britain's enfeeblement. Otherwise France's sugar wealth and Spain's mother lodes in Peru and Mexico would be in peril. "The time has come to decide," he wrote. "We must either abandon America to its own devices, or courageously and effectively come to its side."

Courage would be useless without a navy capable of confronting perfidious Britain, and this hard truth now preoccupied the king and his men. Not since the seventeenth century had France enjoyed naval superiority over the Royal Navy, and in the last war Britain had all but destroyed the French fleet. By late 1758 nearly twenty thousand French seamen were languishing in English jails. Versailles was so strapped for cash that some ships were built of inferior fir rather than oak, and dockyards were forced to stop buying food for the cats needed to keep the rats away.

With Louis's wary support, the naval budget had nearly tripled since he took the throne; in 1778 it would exceed 100 million livres, equivalent to more than £4 million sterling. He instructed his ministers "to develop actively, but noiselessly, the navy," as if "to get everything ready for an invasion of England." Three major shipyards had been remodeled, with contracts placed from Scandinavia to Albania for hemp, masts, sailcloth, pitch, and oak. Led by the chemist Antoine Lavoisier, whose scientific achievements included the study of oxygen and combustion, the French gunpowder industry had been transformed to produce a thousand tons annually. Cannon production was overhauled this spring at a cost of two million livres, with a British expert hired to direct operations and to overcome iron ore shortages by melting down old French, Spanish, and Dutch guns. Ten thousand naval gunners were in training.

Improvements took root in shipboard discipline, signaling, and ship design, considered by some seafarers to be superior to English design. France now had a rational system for registering mariners and drafting them into the navy as needed, rather than resorting to Britain's impressment method, a form of legal kidnapping. French naval officers, mostly sons from the minor nobility who could prove their aristocratic blood with a certified family genealogy, received extensive instruction in navigation, hydrography, astronomy, naval architecture, and gunnery before ever joining the fleet.

Each month dockyards in Toulon, Brest, and other ports turned out at least one ship of the line, the largest and most vital vessels for blue-water combat, plus shoals of frigates, brigs, schooners, and cutters. Donations from patriotic French towns and citizens helped underwrite construction and repairs. "The king," Vergennes wrote on April 12, "now has forty-two ships of the line in readiness," with more on the stocks. Madrid this spring reported that by late 1778 fifty-nine Spanish ships of the line should be afloat, which, when combined with the French fleet, would exceed the Royal Navy in combat heft. All the Bourbon navies lacked, as one naval historian observed, was "a tradition of victory."

None of this went unseen by ubiquitous British spies, who knew about the ships, the guns, and those stockpiles of oak, pitch, and powder. They knew, as well, of French munitions shipments to America and even a cheeky American proposal to swap British sugar islands for eight French men-of-war to bolster the weak rebel navy. No less galling was the cordial reception given by French ports to American marauders, both Continental Navy cruisers and Yankee privateers—government-authorized pirates who in recent months had captured or destroyed scores of British merchantmen, driving up shipping and insurance rates.

The task of protesting these insults from the French fell to David Murray, the seventh Viscount Stormont and Britain's ambassador to Versailles, whose long diplomatic career included stints in Dresden, Warsaw, and Vienna. Handsome and pompous, with a nose for sniffing out intrigues and a flair for theatrical tantrums, Lord Stormont appeared in Vergennes's office at all hours to pound on the rosewood desk and complain in flawless French that "your conduct is neither peace nor war." Some speculated that he had been unhinged by the premature death of his wife; it was said that he had carried her embalmed heart across France in his luggage.

When Stormont complained that a 1713 treaty prohibited French ports from sheltering Britain's enemies, Vergennes issued sonorous, toothless decrees and closed a harbor or two, requiring American vessels to seek refuge in others surreptitiously. French mariners meanwhile purchased captured British brigs and schooners from rebel privateers along the Atlantic coast, disguising them with paint, French names, and clever carpentry that included new figureheads. When Stormont confronted the minister with precise details about French ships carrying war matériel to Boston or Charleston or Philadelphia, Vergennes replied, "There is an unaccountable enthusiasm in favor of the Americans." When Stormont protested that platoons of French military officers had crossed the Atlantic to join the insurrection, Vergennes answered, "Yes, the French nation has a turn for adventure." And when Stormont railed against the senior American diplomat in Paris, the conniving Dr. Franklin, declaring, "He will lie, he will promise, and he will flatter with all the insincerity and subtlety that are natural to him," Vergennes merely shrugged.

Stormont "has a talent for giving much importance to very small matters," the foreign minister privately observed. But when the British announced that the Royal Navy would extend patrols into the Bay of Biscay to intercept American commerce, Versailles ordered a French ship of the line and three frigates on station to safeguard free trade. For now peace obtained, held in place by duplicity and calculated self-interest. Louis XVI, anxious but resolved, waited for the moment to ripen.

"If we are forced to make war on England," the king wrote, "it must be solely with the aim of trying to ruin her commerce and undermining her strength by supporting the revolt and the separation of her colonies." French aid to the American cause, if artfully managed, would draw Britain "deeper and deeper into that war. And the more they fight, the greater their mutual destruction."

The Diplomat

The lying, flattering, insincere, subtle Benjamin Franklin could often be found on spring afternoons atop a white barge shaded with canvas and anchored in the Seine opposite the Tuileries Garden, in central Paris. Here he soaked in heated mineral water to treat the psoriasis, gout, and boils that vexed him. Despite such afflictions, he had recently described himself to a friend as "strong and hearty . . . very plainly dressed, wearing my thin, grey, straight hair that peeps out under my only coiffure, a fine fur cap, which comes down to my forehead almost to my spectacles. Think how this must appear among the powdered heads of Paris."

The "fat old fellow"—also his description—still had the burly shoulders and strong back of a printer who had once manhandled eighty-pound forms of lead type for a living. After taking the waters, a half smile on his pursed lips and a knowing glint in his hazel eyes, he might ramble down the rue Saint-Honoré with his crab-tree walking stick to the Café de la Régence or into the Académie Royale des Sciences, to which he had been elected in 1772 as the celebrated author of *Experiments and Observations on Electricity.* "Such a person was made to excite the curiosity of Paris," an acquaintance wrote. "The people clustered around as he passed and asked, 'Who is this old peasant who has such a noble air?'"

Paris itself was a tonic for a man who had turned seventy-one in January, a month after arriving from Philadelphia on a mission for the Second Continental Congress to make common cause with the Versailles regime. Franklin adored what he called the city's "prodigious mixture of magnificence and neglect." The stink of open sewers mingled with the fragrance of lilacs, baking bread, and innumerable cheeses. Bells pealed incessantly from church steeples and the Hôtel de Ville clock tower, as men and women alike carried parasols along the Pont Neuf on sunny days to preserve their fashionable pallors. Minstrels strolled the boulevards, singing, for a coin or two, of courtship, seduction, or even the struggle for freedom in faraway America.

Each morning hundreds of wagons rumbled toward Les Halles and other markets with butchered meat, fish, and produce fertilized with manures, animal and human, that had been swept up from Parisian streets and carted to outlying farms. Barges towed by a dozen or more horses worked up the river with cargoes of Norman grain, timber, and fruit. Twenty thousand carriers lugged pails of mineral water door to door for those wary of drinking from the Seine. Each evening lanternmen for hire roamed the streets crying "Here's your light" and offering protection against footpads and other ne'er-do-wells. Streetwalkers strutted with breasts bared or stood on iron chairs in the Tuileries to lift their skirts for prospective customers. Medieval Paris lay very near the surface of the modern city—in the popular belief in witches and enchantments, for example, or in the beggars seen this spring collecting the charred bones of a convicted murderer who had been broken on the rack and then publicly burned alive. Even his teeth were believed to bring good luck, like the knuckles of martyred saints brought back to France by the cartful during the Crusades.

Franklin was a frequent visitor to the Bibliothèque Nationale, which had an immense collection of books, maps, and postage stamps. As an enlightened man of letters, he could hardly endorse the French government's repression of public speech: only funeral and wedding announcements could be printed without permission. Every manuscript proposed for publication was reviewed by censors, who decided whether to allow even a handbook for governesses or a text on Mexican cures for venereal disease. The city's first daily newspaper had appeared just a few months earlier, but it carried little more than lurid accounts of accidents and purported medical miracles. Still, French publishers had discovered a lucrative market for books about America, many of them wildly inaccurate. Franklin's own *Poor Richard's Almanack*, first published in 1732 under the pseudonym Richard Saunders, had been translated as *The Science of Good Richard, or the Easy Way to Pay Taxes.* At four sous a copy, it was selling well.

Paris fully reciprocated Franklin's affection. The American war against Britain had inflamed French imaginations as a primordial struggle for liberty, equality, and fraternity. Franklin was both emblematic of rebel audacity and "the model of human virtues—antique simplicity, good faith, and sincerity," a French writer observed. The son of a chandler, grandson of a blacksmith, he had risen in the commercial world on merit and pluck before devoting himself to science, civic advancement, and practical invention, including those bifocals on his nose. "People repeated in all societies what they had heard him say," wrote the Marquis de Condorcet, a prominent mathematician and philosopher. "Every house where he consented to go gained him new admirers who became so many partisans of the American Revolution." As his Virginia colleague Thomas Jefferson would later write, Franklin was "America itself when in France."

Demands for his image had only intensified this spring, in oil or pastel, miniature or life-size, sculpted, painted, or etched on vases, matchboxes, or Sèvres teacups. Some 150 engravings of him would be published, often depicting a savvy, purposeful tamer of lightning; he complained of a stiff neck from posing so often. "The clay medallion of me," he wrote his daughter, Sarah, in Philadelphia, "was the first of the kind made in France. A variety of others have been made since of different sizes . . . some so small as to be worn in rings, and the numbers sold are incredible." Poets competed to laud him in verse, including one line censored as blasphemous: "Can he who has disarmed the gods fear the power of kings?"

He kept a hornbook in his pocket to record hundreds of invitations and obligations—dinners, concerts, lectures, soirees. Exquisite women, an ecclesiastical friend wrote, "flocked to see him, to speak to him for hours on end without realizing that he did not understand much of what they said because of his scant knowledge of our language." His spoken French was indeed patchy and ungrammatical if fearless. "If you Frenchmen would only talk no more than four at a time," he declared, "I might understand you." Regardless, he knew the value of keeping his own counsel and could sit for hours as "silent as midnight." Even his occasional faux pas—he preferred to bite the heads from asparagus stalks rather than use a fork—added to his charm. Franklin had also become adept at the French custom of kissing women on the neck to avoid smudging their rouged cheeks.

In late February he had moved from a Paris inn to the Hôtel de Valentinois, a castellated hilltop château in Passy, a village on the city's western fringe. The owner, an enthusiast for the American cause whose great wealth derived from fisheries, ceramics, mining, and weaving uniforms for the French army, installed Franklin in a spacious pavilion two hundred yards from the main house. A walled garden featured linden trees, chestnuts, and an orangerie. He who had disarmed the gods promptly installed a lightning rod on the roof, and recommended the same for Strasbourg Cathedral and the Paris powder magazine.

Frugality, Franklin admitted, was "a virtue I never could acquire myself." His domestic staff now included a cook, a maître d'—who laid in chamber pots, a coffee roaster, and a feather duster for Franklin's desk— and a liveried coachman with a carriage, hired for five thousand livres a year. On his rare evenings at home, he enjoyed a joint of beef or mutton, followed by rabbit or wild duck with fruit; his wine cellar soon grew to more than a thousand bottles, notably red and white Bordeaux, Madeira, and five brands of champagne. "I think the French cookery agrees with me better than the English," he wrote his sister Jane. "Upon the whole I live as comfortably as a man can well do, so far from his home and his family."

In fact his household included a pair of family companions who had sailed with him from Philadelphia: his grandsons Temple, who served as his secretary, and Benjamin, who was often at school in Geneva. Much as Franklin cherished their company, the boys reminded him of two recent bereavements that had darkened his life. Deborah, his common-law wife of forty-four years, had died in December 1774, "and I every day become more sensible of the greatness of that loss, which cannot now be repaired," Franklin had written in March. No less searing was the bitter estrangement from his son William, the father of Temple, who, as the royal governor of New Jersey, had remained defiantly loyal to the British Crown and was now locked up in a rebel jail in Connecticut.

Life went on. From Passy he consulted with fellow scientists at the nearby royal physics laboratory, where a large telescope had been built to search for planets beyond Saturn. At the Académie Royale his interests ranged from potato cultivation and the aurora borealis to the weight of air and how to design a better bread oven. It was rumored that he had concocted a potion to "smooth the waves of the sea in one part of the globe and raise tempests and whirlwinds in another." He dined, he wined, he kissed necks and soaked in his tubs.

Occasionally he clambered into his coach for the nine-mile jaunt up the road to Versailles for diplomatic receptions or to privately press the American case. The French police watched him almost as closely as British agents did, perhaps near enough to see him perched naked in an open window at the Hôtel de Valentinois, for his famous "air bath," or as he pulled up to a table for another game of chess, his favorite pastime.

"There hardly ever existed such a thing as a bad peace or a good war," Franklin would assert in an oft-quoted aphorism. Yet having committed himself to this particular war, he remained bellicose and relentless. The avuncular public man who swanned through Parisian salons masked a zealous revolutionary.

As the representative in London for several American colonies from 1766 to 1775, he had honed his diplomatic skills, preferring patience and perseverance to confrontation and importunity. The first shots at Lexington and Concord in April 1775 had radicalized him. Each subsequent episode in the struggle stiffened his defiance against what he saw as British oppression: the siege of Boston; the burning of Charlestown, Falmouth, and Norfolk; the disastrous American invasion of Canada and the failed enemy incursions in the Carolinas; the loss of Long Island and New York City; and the British lunge across New Jersey before General George Washington's brilliant, desperate counterstrokes at Trenton and Princeton. The past two years of bloodshed, pillage, and terror had put a hard edge on the old man. The war was now a grudge match.

In Paris he served as his country's preeminent gunrunner. With help from the two other American commissioners serving in France, the Connecticut merchant Silas Deane and the Virginian Arthur Lee, he made covert purchases of war stuff, organized an intricate transatlantic smuggling network, arranged secret military and financial aid from European powers, waged a nimble propaganda campaign, and orchestrated the naval attacks against British shipping.

In April the first ships carrying munitions secretly transferred from French government arsenals had arrived in Portsmouth, New Hampshire, and Martinique, a Caribbean way station en route to the American coast. The bounty included fifty-six tons of gunpowder, fifty-two brass cannons on wheeled carriages, a quarter million gun flints, twelve tons of musket balls, tents, spades, surgical instruments, thousands of muskets and bayonets, and a case of sherry.

Many more vessels were on the high seas or loading out in Bordeaux, Le Havre, or other ports with gunlocks, shoes, five hundred pairs of pistols trimmed in copper, and ten thousand uniforms—half the coats blue and half brown—plus breeches made of double-milled white cloth. Forty workmen in a Nantes warehouse had been hired to dismantle, clean, and reassemble tens of thousands of surplus French firelocks at two livres per gun. The *Hardi* sailed from Marseille disguised as a funeral vessel, trimmed in black with tears painted on her sails, supposedly carrying a dead Polish nobleman to the Baltic; beyond Gibraltar she swung west toward Charleston, her hold packed with munitions.

Amsterdam had become Europe's busiest market for military stores, and thousands of muskets made in Liège, some stamped with PRO LIBERTATE, had been shipped through the North Sea to America via ports in the French and Dutch West Indies. Dutch gunpowder mills now produced seventy-five tons a month, a fair portion of it packed in tea chests and rice barrels for America in exchange for tobacco, indigo, and naval stores. Huge profits lured even some British commercial ships into the trade, causing London's ambassador to The Hague to warn, "We run the risk of seeing half the merchant marine of Great Britain employed to make war on the other half." The Spanish government publicly rebuffed Arthur Lee when he sought to visit Madrid, but discreetly ordered eleven thousand pairs of shoes, eighteen thousand blankets, and thirty thousand uniforms sent to the Continental Army. The Royal Arms Factory also delivered a thousand muskets and a hundred tons of saltpeter—the critical ingredient in gunpowder—to Bilbao for shipment to New England. Other supplies, including surplus powder from Mexico and quinine from Peru to treat malaria, were routed to the Americans through Havana and New Orleans. Spanish bankers in Holland provided rebel purchasing agents with a line of credit.

Versailles had rejected the American request for eight large warships. Each would have cost nearly a million livres and diverted French shipyards feverishly rebuilding the king's navy. Foreign Minister Vergennes also ignored a subsequent congressional proposal, tendered in March, for a full-throated military alliance in exchange for Grenada and other British sugar islands, as well as Newfoundland fishery rights.

Franklin shrugged off the rejections and instead organized his own cockleshell navy to carry the war into European waters. His appetite for seizing British merchantmen had been whetted aboard the black-hulled, eighteen-gun *Reprisal* during his voyage from Philadelphia when Captain Lambert Wickes took two brigs off the French coast. After putting Franklin ashore, Wickes and his Continental Navy crew set off on a longer predatory cruise around Ireland; they returned to Lorient with almost eighty prisoners and five prizes, including *Polly & Nancy*, carrying dried cod from Liverpool to Cadiz, and *Betty*, bound for Londonderry with barrel hoops and claret.

Franklin dispatched Wickes again in April, this time joined by the brig *Lexington* and the sloop *Dolphin*, all three vessels flying Union Jacks as a deception. In a month the squadron captured eighteen British merchantmen in the Irish Sea, and Franklin delighted in reciting the spoils: flour from Ireland, brandy from Bristol, fish from Poole, more prisoners. At the end of the voyage, *Reprisal* avoided capture by the ship of the line *Burford* only by tossing her eighteen guns overboard and stealing away at night through shoal water to Saint-Malo, in Brittany.

Such rebel marauding panicked British coastal towns. Marine insurance spiked. The great trade fair at Chester was canceled for fear of seaborne raiders. Four Royal Navy men-of-war patrolled the Irish Sea. Ambassador Stormont again pounded Vergennes's desk, and a Swedish diplomat reported that Britain and France were in a state of "half war." To appease London and forestall a complete rupture, Wickes would be sent back across the Atlantic at French insistence, but that voyage ended badly: caught in a storm off Newfoundland, *Reprisal* foundered in mountainous seas and went down with all hands except for the cook, who was rescued while clinging to a scrap of gangway ladder.

A gallant captain and 129 shipmates had been lost, but others took up the fight. American privateers, calling themselves "brethren of the coast," were spotted this spring in Solway Firth and the Firth of Clyde, near Dublin and Penzance, and among the Channel Islands. "The sea is overspread with privateers," the British Admiralty conceded. Rarely did a day pass without a merchantman's capture or destruction. Three brigantines dispatched by the Massachusetts Board of War—*Freedom*, *Tyrannicide*, and *Massachusetts*—took more than twenty prizes among them by early summer. Other cruisers plagued British merchant shipping in the West Indies, driving several firms out of business.

Franklin also found a worthy successor to Wickes in Gustavus Conyngham, an Irish-born Philadelphian whom he had commissioned in March as a captain in the Continental Navy. Posing as a smuggler in a ten-gun lugger named *Surprize*, Conyngham captured the packet *Prince of Orange* on May 3, then the brig *Joseph*. Shifting to the swift cutter *Revenge*, he sailed out of Dunkirk on a rampage from the Baltic to the Mediterranean. In less than eighteen months Conyngham would be credited with sixty enemy prizes, captured, burned, or ransomed. Posters in England depicted him as a piratical cutthroat with a brace of pistols in his belt. More than two dozen Royal Navy warships chased after him, futilely. A British officer in Cadiz reported that the American came "swaggering in with his thirteen stripes, saluted the Spanish admiral, had it returned," and took on fresh provisions before again making for the open sea.

* * *

Supplicants by the hundreds beat a path to Franklin's door in Passy seeking contracts, cash, introductions, advice, and preferment. A visitor one morning counted thirteen carriages in the drive, "the owners of which were making proposals of every kind." The front hallway grew crowded with samples of uniform cloth. "Gunpowder is made nearby. I should be glad to assist American ships if you will send them here," a man from La Rochelle wrote, adding, "Our brandy is almost as good as that of Cognac." Quacks and cranks offered secret inks, healing powders, a cannon that could fire twelve times in a minute, a sort of Trojan horse, and an automatic chess-playing machine. Franklin was not displeased when British newspapers reported that he was collaborating with French artisans in Calais to position "a great number of reflecting mirrors . . . to burn and destroy the whole navy of Great Britain in our harbors."

More than four hundred volunteers sought military commissions to join *les insurgents*, including Russians, Italians, Walloons, Poles, three Peruvians, a former French galley slave, a Capuchin monk seeking a chaplaincy, and a fellow from Lille who proposed to serve as "a musician, an accountant, or a bad poet." Franklin complained of being "fatigued with their applications and offers"; before the year was out he would write that "the noise of every coach now that enters my court terrifies me." But in one eight-day period he sent four letters to General Washington with thirteen recommended names. Most applicants were soldiers of fortune—"mere Caesars," in Franklin's phrase. Yet a few combined military experience, status, and republican ideals, like Charles François Sevelinges, the self-styled Marquis de Brétigney, who crossed the Atlantic with nine comrades at his own expense, carrying arms and uniforms for 130 men. He would fight until the end of the war.

Telling the truth, Franklin advised a French neighbor, "is my only cunning." Such balderdash was also part of his cunning. Sometimes diplomacy and prevarication were two sides of the same coin. "We have ordered no prizes into the ports of France," he told Vergennes—a flagrant untruth. When grim reports reached Versailles about the loss last November of three thousand Americans at Fort Washington in New York, plus the British capture of Newport, Rhode Island, and the slow collapse of Continental currency, Franklin dismissed the dispatches as exaggerated. He instead stressed those American victories at Trenton and Princeton, and the soaring principles in the Declaration of Independence.

In April, when Franklin wrote Lord Stormont to propose a prisoner exchange, the letter was returned unopened with a note scribbled on the envelope: "The king's ambassador receives no letters from rebels but when they come to implore His Majesty's mercy." Franklin responded by turning the man's name into a verb, *stormonter*, a pun on the French *mentir*, meaning "to lie." And when a Parisian asked about the ambassador's claim that six Continental regiments had surrendered, Franklin converted the name back to a noun. "No, monsieur," he answered. "It is not a truth. It is only a Stormont." The witticism circulated widely.

"There is no little enemy," *Poor Richard's Almanack* advised. Britain was a large enemy indeed, and Franklin's contempt increased week by week. He kept meticulous track of enemy atrocities, including the desecration of American towns and the incitement of Indians and slaves. "Of all the wars in my time," he wrote his friend and fellow scientist Joseph Priestley, "this on the part of England appears to me the wickedest, having no cause but malice against liberty." Among his reported dining companions in Paris that spring was Edward Gibbon, the British scholar and parliamentarian whose first volume of *The History of the Decline and Fall of the Roman Empire* had been published to acclaim the previous year. Franklin confided that when the historian prepared to document the decline and fall of the British Empire, he would happily provide source materials.

Meanwhile he drew strength from his cause—"the greatest revolution the world ever saw" and "a miracle in human affairs." He could only agree with a recent article, published by the French foreign ministry no less, that the emergence of his new nation in the New World was "one of the major events of modern history." As always, he counseled patience with the French. "Let them take their own time," he advised Congress. If diplomacy was often "prancing without advancing," in the phrase of the French statesman Talleyrand, Franklin was certain that he was moving, if sometimes imperceptibly, in the right direction.

"We shall be stronger the next campaign than we were in the last," he told Priestley, "better armed, better disciplined, and with more ammunition. . . . This war must end in our favor." He and Silas Deane wrote Congress in April, "All Europe is for us. . . . We are fighting for the dignity and happiness of human nature. . . . Every nation in Europe wishes to see Britain humbled, having all in their turn been offended by her insolence."

And in his Passy sanctuary, studying the rooks, pawns, and bishops arranged on the board before him, he would write, "Life is a kind of chess in which we have often points to gain and competitors or adversaries to contend with, and in which there is a vast variety of good and ill events that are in some degree the effects of prudence, or the want of it."

He played often, he played to win, and he was a poor loser.

The Adventurer

Three hundred miles southwest of Passy, Bordeaux was booming. Skiffs and coasters glided among the larger barks and brigs along a waterfront so vibrant that sightseers rented chairs to watch the ships unload their cargoes. All arriving merchandise was taxed by weight, and two-wheeled drays hauled kegs, casks, and barrels to scales hung from overhead timbers in the old customs house. Porters in knee breeches and tricorn hats bent double under bundles and bales, and packhorses with panniers lashed across their rumps clopped up from the quays. High railings kept smugglers from evading inspection. Bordeaux was an inland port, linked by the river Garonne to the Bay of Biscay, sixty miles northwest; into the holds of outbound merchantmen, stevedores hoisted sacks of salt stamped with the royal fleur-de-lis and oak wine barrels girdled with chestnut hoops. Much of the town's wealth derived from slaving—some four hundred slave-trafficking expeditions departed Bordeaux over the years, second only to Nantes among French ports. But these days money could be made carrying contraband, and more than a few vessels anchored in the stream were bound for America.

On Wednesday, March 19, two strangers arrived in Bordeaux by road, red-eyed and exhausted after their long trip from Paris in a muddy cabriolet. After cleaning up and reporting to the king's military commandant on the rue Vital Carles, beneath the soaring bell tower of the Basilique Saint-Michel, they strolled down to the docks for the embarkation certificates required of all travelers leaving France. Both attested that they were Roman Catholics rather than absconding Huguenots, and that they were bound for Cap-Haïtien, on the West Indies island of Saint-Domingue, "on business."

A clerk recorded the older man's name as Baron de Caune, a reasonable approximation of Baron Johann de Kalb. The burly, teetotaling, dimple-chinned Bavarian, now fifty-five years old, had awarded himself a barony and the noble prefix "de" upon becoming a French infantry captain during the War of Austrian Succession, in the 1740s. Distinguished combat service in the Seven Years' War had brought legitimate honors, including promotion to lieutenant colonel and the enameled, eight-pointed cross of the Royal and Military Order of St. Louis. Several details of Kalb's biography went undisclosed: he did not reveal his Protestant faith; nor did he mention that, having obtained a two-year leave of absence from the French army, he now held a major general's commission in the American Continental Army, signed by rebel diplomats in Paris.

His younger companion was even more circumspect, listing his age as twenty (he was still nineteen), his hair as blond (it was quite red), and his name as Gilbert du Motier, a technically accurate truncation, although he once quipped that he had been "baptized like a Spaniard with the name of every conceivable saint who might offer me more protection in battle." More to the point, he was far better known as the Marquis de Lafayette and was among the wealthiest men in France. He, too, was a newly minted major general, as he had written his father-in-law after secretly leaving Paris without an adieu to his pregnant wife and young daughter: "You will be astonished, my dear Papa. . . . I have found a unique opportunity to distinguish myself. . . . I am a general officer in the army of the United States of America. My zeal for their cause and my frankness won their confidence."

Their business in town concluded, the two aspiring warlords hoisted their baggage into a hired longboat at the Saint-Michel docks and headed downstream on the broad, muddy river, past farmers plowing, women hoeing, and fishermen selling hakes and skates from their dories; past flocks of sheep and ancient estates; past convents and parish churches and greening vineyards spreading up the south-facing hills. Halfway to the sea, in a reedy, left-bank roadstead at Pauillac, they found a 278-ton former freighter named *Clary*, which Lafayette had purchased for 112,000 livres, outfitted with a few deck guns, and renamed *La Victoire*. Thirty crewmen and a dozen other officers, ranging in rank from lieutenant to colonel, had also found their way to Pauillac and now waited for a fair wind to board ship.

He seemed an unlikely hero, this Gilbert du Motier, this boy marquis. Taller than average for his day, he stood five feet, nine inches, with a high, receding brow beneath his shock of auburn hair, "his nose large and long, eyebrows prominent and projecting over a fine, animated hazel eye," as one acquaintance wrote. He was a bit ungainly, perhaps still growing into his long limbs. "He danced without grace and sat badly on his horse," a courtier sniffed. Napoleon Bonaparte, then just seven years old, would later dismiss him as "just another nitwit"; the Marquis de Mirabeau, a prominent economist, decried "the idiocy of his character and the smallness of his head." The Vicomte de Chateaubriand, a writer and future foreign minister, concluded that he "had only one idea, and fortunately for him it was the idea of the century." He was "a righter of wrongs," a subsequent biographer wrote. "Freedom was his mistress, and he was faithful to her until his last breath." John Stuart Mill, an English philosopher and economist who half a century later struck up a friendship with Lafayette, wrote, "His was not the influence of genius, not even of talents. It was the influence of a heroic character."

He had been born in remote, rugged Auvergne, in south-central France, in a slate-roofed château tower built of local volcanic cobbles. His forefathers included noble swordsmen who had served alongside King Louis IX in the dismal Sixth Crusade in 1250, against the English at Poitiers in 1356, and against them again with Joan of Arc at the siege of Orléans in 1428. An English bullet had killed his father, Michel, a colonel in the king's grenadiers, at the Battle of Minden in northern Germany in 1759, a month before Gilbert's second birthday. The boy remained for a decade in Auvergne—peasant playmates imprinted him with an egalitarian bias—until his mother, Jolie, the scion of wealthy Breton nobility, moved him to Paris. At age thirteen, "burning with the desire to have a uniform," as he later wrote, he was admitted into the Black Musketeers, the king's guard, with training at the royal riding school in Versailles. More conventionally, he studied Cicero, Virgil, and Herodotus, winning a prize in Latin composition and finding much to admire, through Plutarch, in republican Rome.

Misfortune made him a rich orphan at age twelve. The abrupt deaths of his mother and maternal grandfather in 1770 left him with an estate worth three million livres and an annual income from his Brittany and Auvergne estates exceeding 120,000 livres, at a time when an unskilled laborer might earn a thousand livres in a lifetime. Marriage made him richer still. Jean Paul François de Noailles, the Duc d'Ayen, was a chemist and prominent grandee with five daughters who needed husbands. In April 1774, the archbishop of Paris married Lafayette and Adrienne de Noailles, sixteen and fourteen years old, respectively. The newlyweds lived on the rue Saint-Honoré in the Noailles family palace, built with two wings, each more than a hundred feet long, and appointed with masterworks by Rubens, Rembrandt, and Leonardo.

Lafayette joined a Freemason lodge, attracted by the organization's Enlightenment creed of tolerance, virtue, and social meritocracy. He was further rescued from the dissipated life of the idle rich by his military bent: promoted to captain in the French dragoons, he joined his regiment at Metz in eastern France in 1775 and found both a calling and a cause. The American insurrection, so alluring to the French, soon infected Captain Lafayette. He conceived of an expedition to the New World as a way to affirm his political convictions, correct the insults of the Seven Years' War, and avenge his father's death at British hands. He secured a secret American commission and discreetly inquired about buying a ship.

With the end of Carnival this February, he had accepted an invitation to travel to London, where Adrienne's uncle, the Marquis de Noailles, was the French ambassador. He was introduced at court to King George III, attended a ball at the home of Lord George Germain, the secretary of state for the American Department, and chatted at the opera with General Henry Clinton, who was about to return to New York as second-in-command of the British expeditionary army. "London is a delightful city," he wrote Adrienne. "We dance all night. . . . We never retire here before five a.m." Yet nothing he had seen or heard lessened his "desire to debase England." He now was certain that "to injure England is to serve my country."

Then word had arrived from Bordeaux: *Victoire* was ready to sail. As he hurried with Kalb to the marshy anchorage at Pauillac, he pondered his family's ancient coat of arms and concluded that it failed to convey the audacity, the *passion* now animating him. He added a two-word motto that captured his impulse for the flamboyant gesture: *Cur non?* Why not?

It was not to be quite so simple. On Tuesday, March 25, just as Lafayette stepped into a launch to be rowed to *Victoire*, a courier brought him a letter from a friend in Paris. As oarsmen pulled through the river weeds, he tore open the wax seal to find disturbing news. His father-in-law, the Duc d'Ayen, having finally received the "dear Papa" note, was outraged at his abrupt departure. Foreign Minister Vergennes, after learning of Lafayette's plan, also worried that if the British captured Lafayette on the high seas, he would be treated "with a harshness which is not unknown to that nation." The king himself was said to be mortified at the marquis's foolery, and was considering a *lettre de cachet*, a royal arrest order.

Hoisting himself onto *Victoire*'s main deck, Lafayette pondered his course. The letter "reminded me of the grief I was causing my pregnant, loving wife," he later wrote. He had also provoked "the authority and anger of the government." Kalb, who watched him agonize, wrote his wife, "If that letter had not been handed to him after we were already settled in the rowboat, I believe he would have chosen to turn back immediately." But that night they raised anchor, unfurled the canvas, and—"in the most glorious weather," Kalb recorded—glided downstream. By noon on Wednesday they had reached the river's mouth at Pointe de Grave and swung south through a heavy swell across the Bay of Biscay. Kalb was further astonished when his young companion disclosed that he had not discussed the American scheme with Adrienne or her father. "My advice," the Bavarian wrote, "was to abandon his plan, and return immediately to Paris. . . . I advised him to give way to his family and to avoid a rupture with them."

Instead, on Friday, March 28, after sailing past the Pyrenees foothills,

Victoire's crew pulled into a narrow inlet flanked by shoals at Los Pasajes, a dozen miles beyond the Spanish border. "I have given my word," Lafayette wrote Adrienne, "and I would rather die than go back on it."

An assiduous contriver of his own myth, the marquis, over the next half century, would embellish the story of his flight to America with melodramatic flourishes. Louis XVI had indeed forbidden French officers from serving in British colonies without permission, but the edict was widely ignored without consequences. There certainly would be no *lettre de cachet*. Many court officials, although sympathetic to his family's alarm, were unperturbed, if not supportive of Lafayette's gambit.

As for the Noailles clan, his in-laws' primary concern was to avoid public embarrassment and to disavow responsibility for such an impetuous scheme. "I presented him at court! What is he trying to do to me?" the Marquis de Noailles complained from London, adding, "His age may excuse his thoughtlessness. . . . He concealed his intentions . . . from me and from everybody." At least some of Lafayette's elders seemed to have known of his plans: under French law he was still a minor and had required authorization from his family—precisely who remained unclear—to purchase the *Victoire*. Regardless, the Duc d'Ayen was plainly miffed at the abrupt abandonment of his daughter, even if Adrienne appeared to take her husband's caprice in stride. "I was pregnant," she later said, "and loved him deeply."

On Monday, March 31, a courier from the military authorities in Bordeaux arrived in Los Pasajes with another letter: Lafayette, as directed by Versailles in deference to d'Ayen, was to travel overland to Toulon, in southern France, to rendezvous with his father-in-law for a grand tour of Italy, apparently on the presumption that months of staring at Renaissance frescoes would bring him to his senses. Lafayette told Kalb that he would obey this command; after dinner with the marquis in nearby San Sebastian, Kalb wrote his wife on April 1 that he had advised selling *Victoire* at a loss:

> This is the end of his expedition to America to join the army of the insurgents. He is at this moment leaving for Bordeaux. . . . This folly will cost him dearly. . . . Time will hang heavy on my hands here in the meantime. I do not believe he will be able to rejoin me.

After three days of brooding in a coach traveling north on the post road, Lafayette reported to the Bordeaux commandant, who insisted that he follow orders and continue on to the south of France. He took rooms above the bustling Cours du Chapeau-Rouge, roamed the promenades, and brooded some more. Ambassador Stormont, who had been following the imbroglio with glee, was cheered by rumors that Lafayette had been tossed into a Bordeaux dungeon. "Lafayette's expedition has been a short one indeed," Stormont crowed at Versailles.

Lafayette had nearly resigned himself to an Italian fate when a close comrade, the Marquis de Mauroy, galloped into town with authoritative reports from Versailles: permission to sail, if not precisely granted, would at least not be denied. The government was indifferent, and so too the king. The Duc d'Ayen would forgive him, eventually. Word had spread through Paris and the provinces about the *drame de Lafayette*, arousing great sympathy and enthusiasm. All France wanted him to go.

He went. Boarding a chaise to Toulon under the commandant's watchful eye, he waited until the coachman changed horses at a posthouse, then disguised himself in a courier's togs and rode southwest on a borrowed mount as Mauroy followed in another carriage. At nine a.m. on April 17, after hiding in a Bayonne stable and with help from an innkeeper's daughter in Saint-Jean-de-Luz, he trotted down to the Los Pasajes waterfront to loud huzzahs from his shipmates. "At this moment," Kalb wrote, "the marquis has arrived."

Lafayette wrote to the American diplomats in Paris that he was ready to sail, "full of joy, hope, and zeal for our common cause. . . . Altogether this affair has produced the *éclat* that I desired, and at this moment everybody has his eyes on us. I will try to justify the celebrity." To Adrienne he wrote, "Dear heart . . . Having to choose between the slavery that everyone believes he has the right to impose upon me and the liberty that called me to glory, I departed."

On Sunday, April 20, *Victoire* again nosed into the Bay of Biscay. "My companions on board," Mauroy wrote, "were in a visible state of enthusiasm." That ardor might have been tempered had they known that Lafayette, aware that his lightly armed vessel was no match for even a small British man-of-war, had resolved that if captured he would blow up the ship rather than surrender. He advised the captain that they would bypass Cap-Häitien, steering instead for South Carolina. "The sea is so dismal and I believe we sadden each other, she and I," he told Adrienne. "Always the sky, always the water, and again, the next day, the same thing."

Rumors would arise in their wake: that he had landed in Boston with four thousand French troops, or that he had come ashore in Providence to raise an army of three hundred thousand American patriots. That such a high-born aristocrat had thrown in his lot with republican insurgents titillated Parisian salons. Even the queen was said to applaud, although one grand dame, forgetting that he was an orphan, said, "How I pity his mother." The Prussian ambassador at Versailles kept Frederick the Great informed, as did the Russian ambassador for Catherine the Great. "He is exceedingly beloved," Franklin told Congress. "Those who censure it as imprudent in him do nevertheless applaud his spirit."

Shipmates passed around Abbé Raynal's recent history of European colonization in the New World to learn something about their destination. They practiced their English—Lafayette had a fine ear for the language, and Kalb was fluent—and talked together of their dreams and ambitions. "The happiness of America is intimately connected with the happiness of mankind," the marquis wrote in another letter to Adrienne. "She is destined to become the safe and venerable asylum of virtue, of honesty, of tolerance, of equality, and of peaceful liberty. . . . Night coming on obliges me to stop, for I have lately forbidden the use of lights about the ship."

Night fell. The darkened boat beat on. His destiny lay west, over the horizon, where eventually his name would adorn some six hundred towns, counties, schools, mountains, and other American landmarks. He had chosen to risk everything—for glory, for adventure, for an idea. Why not?

Part One

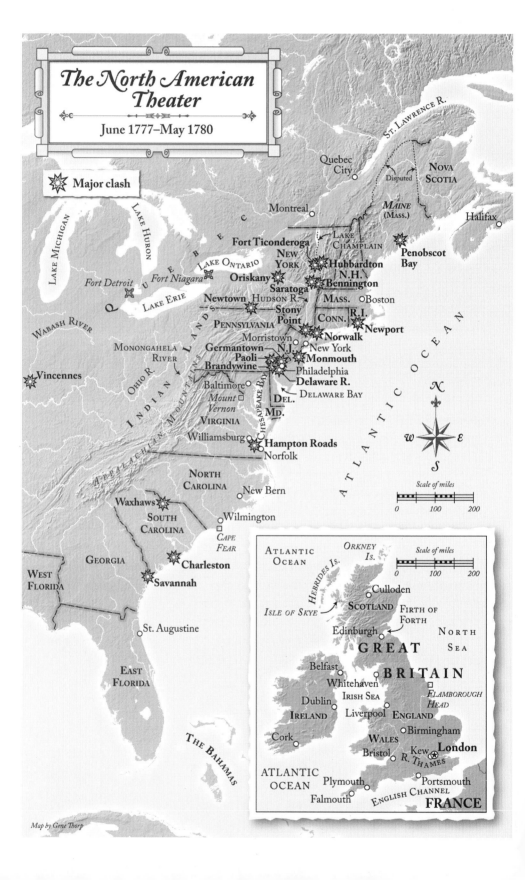

The North American Theater
June 1777–May 1780

✦ Major clash

ST. LAWRENCE R.

Quebec City

Disputed

NOVA SCOTIA

Halifax

Montreal

MAINE (MASS.)

Penobscot Bay

LAKE MICHIGAN

LAKE HURON

LAKE ONTARIO

Fort Detroit

Fort Niagara

LAKE ERIE

LAKE CHAMPLAIN

Fort Ticonderoga

NEW YORK

Hubbardton

N.H.

Oriskany

Saratoga

Bennington

MASS.

Boston

Newtown

HUDSON R.

Stony Point

CONN.

R.I.

Newport

PENNSYLVANIA

Morristown

Norwalk

WABASH RIVER

MONONGAHELA RIVER

OHIO R.

INDIAN LANDS

Germantown

Paoli

Brandywine

N.J.

New York

Monmouth

Philadelphia

Delaware R.

Baltimore

Mount Vernon

CHESAPEAKE BAY

DEL.

DELAWARE BAY

MD.

Vincennes

VIRGINIA

Williamsburg

Hampton Roads

Norfolk

APPALACHIAN MOUNTAINS

NORTH CAROLINA

New Bern

ATLANTIC OCEAN

N
W   E
S

Scale of miles
0   100   200

Waxhaws

SOUTH CAROLINA

Wilmington

CAPE FEAR

GEORGIA

Charleston

WEST FLORIDA

Savannah

St. Augustine

EAST FLORIDA

THE BAHAMAS

ATLANTIC OCEAN

ORKNEY IS.

Scale of miles
0   100   200

HEBRIDES IS.

Culloden

ISLE OF SKYE

SCOTLAND

FIRTH OF FORTH

Edinburgh

NORTH SEA

GREAT

Belfast

BRITAIN

Whitehaven

IRISH SEA

FLAMBOROUGH HEAD

Dublin

Liverpool

ENGLAND

IRELAND

Birmingham

WALES

Cork

Bristol

Kew

London

R. THAMES

ATLANTIC OCEAN

Plymouth

Portsmouth

Falmouth

ENGLISH CHANNEL

FRANCE

Map by Gene Thorp

1.

———◦———

The March of Annihilation

A rattle of drums at four a.m. on July 1, 1777, roused the British encampment at Crown Point, on the western lip of Lake Champlain. Soldiers stumbled from their tents, shrugged on their uniform coats, and gobbled down a cold breakfast with the indifference of men who expected no better. For the past fortnight the invasion force of eight thousand troops had sailed and rowed south for a hundred miles, from the Richelieu River in Quebec to within fifteen miles of the American stronghold at Fort Ticonderoga. Through mischance and rebel defiance, many of these same redcoats had failed to capture the fortress eight months earlier, despite standing at the gates. Now the prize again lay within grasp, and this time they intended to win through. "We are to contend for the king and the constitution of Great Britain, to vindicate law and to relieve the oppressed," orders issued the previous evening proclaimed. "This army must not retreat."

By five a.m., the sun had crested the great shoulders of the Green Mountains to the east, gilding the craggy Adirondacks in the west. Platoon after platoon scuffed down to the shoreline to clamber aboard gunboats, longboats, and six-oared, flat-bottomed bateaux. Shouted orders carried across the lake, along with the creak of capstans and oarlocks. Soon the first vessels pulled away from the anchorage, to assemble mid-lake in battle formation. Army musicians caught the moment and struck up martial airs. "The music and drums of the different regiments were continually playing," a Royal Artillery lieutenant wrote, "and contributed to make the scene and passage extremely pleasant."

More than a hundred birch-bark canoes led the flotilla. Each carried twenty to thirty warriors, mostly Iroquois sporting nose rings, slitted earlobes, and feathers in tufted topknots, their eyelids and cheeks daubed with vermilion paint. Some wore knife sheaths made from lynx skins and, a British officer recorded, an "arse clout, or covering for the privities."

Arrayed across the mile-wide lake behind the Indian vanguard came the main battle force, "the most complete and splendid regatta you can possibly conceive," a witness reported: the three-masted frigate *Royal George*, built by shipwrights in Canada during the winter and carrying 26 guns, and smaller vessels named *Inflexible, Carleton, Maria,* and *Royal Convert,* as well as 44 gunboats, 23 longboats, 26 cutters, 260 bateaux, and a wallowing ninety-one-foot radeau, or raft, the *Thunderer,* ferrying barreled gunpowder and heavy cannons intended to blast Ticonderoga's walls to rubble. A brig, a gundalow, and a sloop—*Washington, Jersey,* and *Lee*—had been captured in October from the rebel general turned commodore Benedict Arnold, whose gallant, forlorn rearguard fight in these very waters had helped delay the earlier British attack until winter forced the invaders back to Canada. All told, this squadron carried 133 naval guns to complement the army's 130 field cannons, mortars, and howitzers, each barrel stamped with the king's monogram or other symbols of possession. Storeships and lake transports continued to arrive at Crown Point from the north, laden with almost five thousand tons of salt pork, hard biscuits, and other rations, along with siege tools, ammunition, rum, cattle, and civilian camp followers, whose numbers officially included 225 women and 500 children, although some hyperbolists would claim that the combined figure actually approached two thousand.

"It looked," wrote Corporal Roger Lamb of the 9th Regiment of Foot, "like some stupendous fairy scene of a dream." By late afternoon, many troops had disembarked on either shore to join the advance regiments moving toward Ticonderoga, now just a few miles ahead. Bullfrogs croaked in the shallows, and white elderberry blossoms brightened the conifer thickets, "the birthplace of every biting insect," one miserable chaplain wrote. Some men smeared cedar sap on their faces in a vain effort to repel mosquitoes and deerflies.

On the left, to the east, four thousand mercenaries plodded through the underbrush. Known collectively as Hessians, since most Germans hired by London to fight in America came from Hesse-Kassel, this contingent was largely from the small, impoverished duchy of Brunswick, whose ruling family had intermarried with the British royal family. Brunswick's duke collected £7 a year for each rented soldier, plus a blood-money bounty for every man killed or captured and an equivalent stipend for every three wounded. The troops earned the same eight pence a day as their British comrades, minus deductions for food and uniforms. Most of the German troops had spent an agreeable winter in isolated bivouacs along the St. Lawrence and Richelieu Rivers, developing a taste for beaver tail, salted sturgeon, and maple sugar.

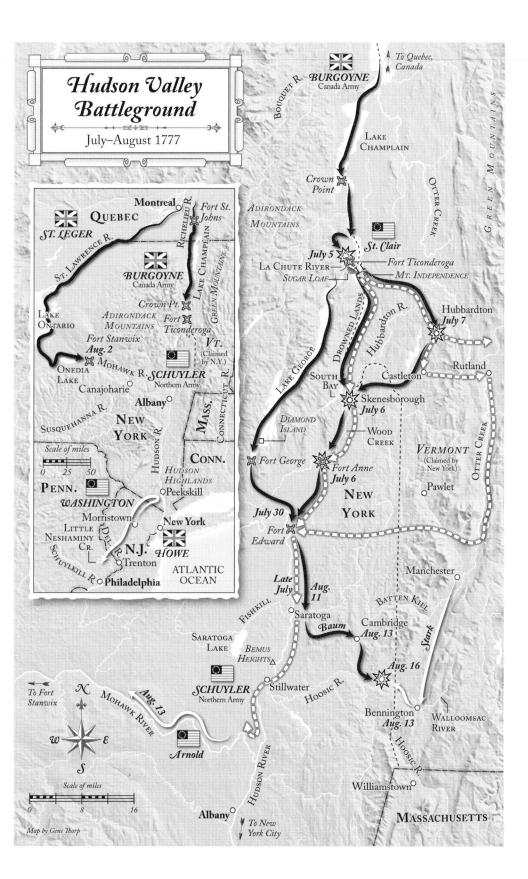

Hudson Valley Battleground

July–August 1777

Map by Gene Thorp

Jäger scouts—professional hunters—led the column, distinctive in their green coats trimmed in crimson and black hats decorated with pom-poms. Dragoons followed in leather breeches and woolen gaiters, dismounted for the moment but hopeful of finding American horses ahead. Armed with short carbines and three-foot broadswords, many cultivated horizontal waxed mustaches and wore their hair in a queue down the back "like a Chinese mandarin," an admirer wrote. Grenadiers, artillerymen, musicians, gunsmiths, servants, and sutlers filled out the procession, prodded forward by blue-coated officers wearing silver sashes and wielding canes or pointed spontoons. During the voyage down the lake, some men had stripped to the waist to bask in the warm sun and, a surgeon reported, "have been badly sunburned, large blisters developing on their skin."

The Germans were led by Major General Friedrich Adolph Riedesel. Thirty-nine years old, with a moon face and a ramrod bearing, he had forsaken his law studies in Marburg to take up soldiering, soon demonstrating a hussar's valor at Minden during the Seven Years' War. Fluent in French and conversational English, Riedesel considered the opportunity to command in North America to be "sent by Providence." He had sworn allegiance to George III, like each of his Brunswickers, and had predicted in a dispatch to his duke that "this campaign will finish the war." Although British officers could be insufferably supercilious toward their German allies, he got on well with the redcoats, even if they stumbled over the pronunciation of his name, calling him "General Red Hazel."

Those redcoats could now be seen across the lake, moving south in a snaking column parallel to the Germans. Brawny grenadiers, often used to lead assaults, had exchanged their tall bearskin hats for more practical felt caps trimmed in horsehair. Each foot soldier carried a ten-pound musket, a sixteen-inch bayonet, a tin canteen, a linen haversack, and his own blanket—a battlefield luxury, since in peacetime five men typically shared two blankets. British infantrymen were among the finest soldiers in the world, but most of these troops were green; only the 47th Regiment of Foot had seen extensive combat, at Lexington and Bunker Hill, among other clashes. They were led nonetheless by an exceptional cadre of junior officers, thirty of whom would become generals, including eighteen destined to be full generals, the army's highest rank. In addition, another six future general officers could be found among the twenty-two Royal Artillery officers in the column.

Squinting at both shorelines through his spyglass from the pitching deck of the *Royal George*, Lieutenant General John Burgoyne was as pleased with his invasion force as he was with himself. At fifty-four, he had endured a long and arduous climb to high command, and he intended to return to London to claim the laurels owed every victorious commander. Educated at Westminster School, where even mathematics was taught in Latin and boys were birched for the slightest transgression, he had joined the army at fifteen, earned a reputation as both a swordsman and a card sharp, then wrecked his career by eloping with Charlotte Stanley, the youngest daughter of a very angry earl. Effectively banished to France and forced to sell his commission, Burgoyne lived modestly with Charlotte on the Seine for seven years, growing vegetables, traveling the Continent, and making a living at whist and twenty-one.

At last all was forgiven, and a belated reconciliation brought the couple back to England. Burgoyne returned to duty as an aging dragoon captain, just in time to win fame at the cannon's mouth in the Seven Years' War, notably in Normandy and Brittany against the French, and on the Tagus River near Lisbon against the Spanish. The king of Portugal gave him a diamond ring in gratitude, and he emerged from the struggle as a British war hero.

Burgoyne's ascent continued in peacetime. Elected to the House of Commons, he was a diligent, independent military reformer. His insights from an inspection tour of Continental armies impressed George III, as did his parliamentary investigation of East India Company corruption. He and Charlotte shuttled between fine houses in Lancashire and Surrey and on Hertford Street, in tony Mayfair, an easy stroll from the London gambling tables at Brooks's club. An aspiring playwright, he also became a regular in the Green Room at Drury Lane Theater, where in 1774 the actor and impresario David Garrick directed Burgoyne's *The Maid of the Oaks*, a triumphant success.

As a military thinker he was progressive and admired. "On every occasion," one officer wrote, "he was the soldier's friend." He advocated higher pay for the ranks and the recruitment of Irish Catholics, traditionally excluded from the army. British soldiers were to be treated as "thinking beings" to be led, not as livestock to be cursed. He endorsed the injunction "Never beat your men. It is unmanly." Effective officers must seek "insight into the character of each particular man" while mastering the nitty-gritty of military life, including how to properly shoe a horse.

War with America brought new chances for glory. "I look upon America as our child," he told the Commons, "which we have already spoilt by too much indulgence." The king agreed. Burgoyne was posted to Boston weeks after the shooting erupted, and then to Canada as second-in-command under General Guy Carleton, whose decision not to assault, or at least challenge, the American garrison at Ticonderoga in late autumn had left Burgoyne disgruntled enough to criticize his superior upon returning to London. The government concurred: Carleton had been too passive, allowing thousands of rebels to shift south and reinforce the Continental Army before its stunning midwinter attacks at Trenton and Princeton.

Burgoyne had reappeared on the St. Lawrence in late spring with a sheaf of blunt orders from the American Department in Whitehall. Carleton was to remain in Quebec as an administrator and logistician. Burgoyne would command the new Canada Army in the invasion of New York, an appointment "particularly directed by the king." Furious at this censure, Carleton sent an insolent, twenty-two-page reply and his resignation. But a replacement would not arrive for a year; until then, always the good soldier, he pledged that Burgoyne "shall have every assistance in my power." Carleton would support the expedition, he added, "as if I was to command it myself."

"The king relies upon your zeal," Lord Germain, secretary of the American Department, told his generals in Canada, and Burgoyne was nothing if not zealous. The invasion plan was largely his, conceived in "Thoughts for Conducting the War from the Side of Canada," which he wrote during the winter while taking the cure at Bath. He found that the waters there were the best treatment for two catastrophes that had forever smudged his bright soul: the death, more than a decade earlier, of his ten-year-old daughter and only child, and then Charlotte's passing last summer. Mourning her loss, he called her "that truest friend, amiable companion, tenderest, best of women and wives. . . . She is hourly before my eyes."

"Thoughts" was bold, complex, and ultimately incoherent. The Canada Army would besiege and overrun Ticonderoga, then push on fifty miles to Fort Edward, where the Hudson River—also known as the North River—became navigable, then tramp south another fifty miles to Albany. To confuse and disperse the rebels, a diversionary force under brevet Brigadier General Barrimore Matthew St. Leger was now traveling west from Montreal to Lake Ontario, with instructions to pivot south into the Mohawk River valley in New York before rejoining the Canada Army on the Hudson. Burgoyne's intent was to dismember the thirteen rebellious colonies, effectively amputating New England—the beating heart of the rebellion—from the rest. The king himself had approved the plan after studying his maps and offering canny comments about the terrain south of Lake Champlain.

Upon reaching Albany, the Canada Army would fall under the senior British commander in North America, General Sir William Howe, now at his headquarters in New York City. "It is become highly necessary that the most speedy junction of the two armies should be effected," Burgoyne's orders declared. He and St. Leger "must never lose view of their intended junction with Sir William Howe as their principal objects." Yet—and here the scheme's brilliance dimmed—in April Howe had explicitly informed London and his colleagues in Canada that he intended to march south this summer, perhaps to seize Philadelphia. Only a small rump force would remain behind to secure Manhattan, too weak to advance upriver through the Hudson Highlands for a rendezvous in Albany.

With remarkable nonchalance, both the government and Burgoyne shrugged off this inconvenient wrinkle. No attempt was made to ensure that the "junction with Sir William Howe" was more than notional, or to assess how the Canada Army, if forced to spend the next winter in Albany, would supply itself across more than 200 wilderness miles from Montreal or 150 miles upriver from New York City. While conceding that "extraordinary physical difficulties" lay ahead, Burgoyne exuded the high-spirited complacency obligatory at the beginning of every military calamity. To General Edward Harvey, the army's adjutant general in London, he wrote, "I have reason to be exceedingly satisfied with all that has been done."

He had complaints, of course, even as the stubby profile of Ticonderoga first loomed into view from the *Royal George* on Wednesday, July 2. The Canada Army was a third smaller than the eleven-thousand-man force he had recommended. He had hoped for a thousand Indians, but only four hundred had joined the expedition. Instead of two thousand Canadians, just 150 had enlisted, "awkward, ignorant, disinclined to the service, & spiritless," as he informed London. Some had been locked in a Montreal monastery in a bootless attempt to prevent desertions. Carleton had ordered another five hundred peasants marched south under guard from Quebec as a *corvée*—an unpaid, forced-labor detachment—but many of them had also run off, having "imbibed too much of the American spirit of licentiousness and independence," Burgoyne concluded.

He had ample artillery, but what about ammunition? For each 6-pounder—so called for the weight of the cannonball fired—his gunners carried only 124 rounds. And what about food? The army devoured eighteen tons each day. A thousand horses and a hundred oxen required fourteen tons of forage a day. Not until early June had he asked his quartermaster to calculate the number of wagons needed to carry enough provisions to feed ten thousand mouths on the Hudson. Even now carpenters were struggling to assemble the requisite 1,125 carts, but fewer than half would be completed, most of them two-wheeled variants built of flimsy green wood and able to carry just eight hundred pounds. Not least among the general's worries, a Montreal newspaper had published "the whole design of the campaign almost as accurately as if it had been copied from the secretary of state's letter." Burgoyne suspected a leak from the government's opponents in England.

For all that, over the past two weeks the Canada Army had traveled as far as Carleton had in four months the previous year—in part because a small fleet had already been built for Burgoyne. The army's two wings now stood three miles from rebel outposts. Bell tents popped up among the trees, and blue smoke from a thousand campfires curled into the summer sky. *Royal George, Inflexible,* and the rest of the fleet came to anchor just beyond enemy cannon range; a floating boom encircled the larger vessels as protection against fire rafts. "With our glasses we could distinguish everything they were about in the fort," wrote a lieutenant in the 53rd Foot. "It was entertaining enough . . . and its novelty made it amusing."

Scouts had given Burgoyne sketches of the American fortifications. Prisoners snatched from isolated sentry posts or rebel patrols provided intelligence about the defenders, their weaponry, and their plight. Hour by hour these American positions were being outflanked by Germans to the east and British troops to the west. The last of Burgoyne's heavy artillery had been delayed briefly by contrary winds, but soon the bombardment would begin. He took a moment to scratch out a dispatch to General Howe, wherever he was. "The army is in the fullest powers of health and spirit," Burgoyne wrote. "The enemy do not appear to have the least suspicion of the king's real instructions relative to the campaign after the reduction of Ticonderoga."

No man standing on Ticonderoga's parapets could doubt his peril. Bonfires gleamed on both lake shores, redcoat skulkers could be seen darting in the rear of the American fortifications, and an enemy armada had appeared out of the mist, including three-masted warships bristling with cannons. Random gunshots echoed in the woods. "The scene thickens fast," a Continental officer wrote.

For more than two decades a fortress had stood on this rocky promontory, hard by the narrow strait through which the waters of Lake George, four miles away, spilled into Lake Champlain via the tumbling La Chute River. First the French, then the British, and now the Americans had occupied the site: hewing timber, slaking lime, hauling rocks, setting palisades, and erecting stone barracks and parapets of oak, hemlock, and chestnut. Most of the outer walls were wooden; two rows of massive timbers had been laid, one huge log atop another, the open space between the rows packed with earth and stones.

Over the past two years the Americans had added trenches, log breastworks, redoubts, and an abatis—a tangled barricade of felled trees with sharpened branches—along the northwestern defenses known as the Old French Lines. They had raised extensive works, including a star-shaped fort with gun embrasures, barracks, blockhouses, and a hospital on Mount Independence, a 350-acre tableland summit half a mile southeast of Ticonderoga. To link the two forts across the spillway, engineers had been building the "Great Bridge," a floating span four hundred yards long and twelve feet wide, supported by sunken piers. Until it was finished, a temporary span crossed the water. To prevent British men-of-war from sailing south, a boom stretched across the strait, with timbers riveted together by a double chain of iron links an inch and a half square. The bridge and its defenses, an American officer boasted, "does honor to the human mind and power." More than a hundred iron guns protected the entire stronghold.

To command the "Gibraltar of the North," as some insisted on calling this outpost, Major General Arthur St. Clair had arrived in mid-June on orders from Congress. Born in the Scottish Highlands and educated at the University of Edinburgh, St. Clair briefly studied medicine before joining the British Army and subsequently scaling the cliffs of Quebec in September 1759 under a young Colonel William Howe. Marriage to an American heiress with a £14,000 dowry provided wealth and independence. St. Clair sold his commission, immigrated to western Pennsylvania, and a decade later returned to uniform in the Continental Army, serving with distinction at Trenton and Princeton. Tall and graceful, with chestnut hair and blue-gray eyes, he sprinkled his correspondence with Latin quotations from Horace and allusions to ancient military campaigns.

Ticonderoga horrified him. The powder magazines leaked, not a single room in the hospital was ready, segments of the abatis had been burned for firewood, and the fortifications remained unfinished. Row galleys intended for Lake George still stood on the stocks, a new fourteen-gun schooner lacked guns and rigging, and the nearby forest, an officer warned, was "so infested with savages as to render it exceedingly hazardous" for reconnaissance or hunting parties.

Far worse was the shortage of men. Some ten thousand American troops had occupied these fortifications the previous fall, enough to send General Carleton retreating into Canada, and experienced officers agreed that at least ten thousand were again needed to withstand a British assault, plus two thousand more to secure the Hudson and Mohawk valleys. A meticulous tally on June 28 found barely two thousand enlisted men present and fit for duty in ten depleted Continental regiments, plus perhaps a hundred officers and three hundred gunners and artificers. Two Massachusetts militia regiments on Mount Independence intended to leave when their enlistments expired, on July 5.

Except for a few natty officers and some men in captured British tunics, "none of the troops have uniforms & consequently make a very awkward appearance," a soldier wrote. Shoes were so precious that scouts sometimes had to borrow footwear from men remaining within the walls. Many lacked proper weapons, despite the recent arrival from New Hampshire of contraband French muskets. Only a few hundred bayonets could be found, and pleas were sent to Philadelphia for cartridge paper, even if it required tearing pages from old books. Some regiments had been enfeebled by a measles outbreak, which, a doctor reported, had "left many of them languid, with coughs." St. Clair estimated that if he evenly spaced the available men around his extensive lines, "they would have been scarcely within the reach of each other's voices." Some officers hoped that, if attacked, the Ticonderoga garrison could hold out atop Mount Independence. St. Clair disagreed. Among other shortcomings, troops there had to clamber down the steep slopes almost to the lake for water.

"I am in a situation," St. Clair wrote, "where I . . . have captivity or death before my eyes." On June 29 he sent his eleven-year-old son to Albany for safety. In a note to Congress he added, "No army was ever in a more critical situation than we are in."

Now the wolf was at the door. General Washington had been cocksure that another British descent down Lake Champlain "is against all probability." As recently as June 16 the commander in chief had asserted that the Canada Army was likely traveling down the St. Lawrence to join Howe by sea in New York rather than risk a blooding at the Gibraltar of the North. Eight New England regiments originally designated for Ticonderoga had been diverted by Washington to Peekskill, two hundred miles south, to protect the Hudson Highlands.

On July 4, a day that passed without particular jubilation inside the fortress, another nine hundred New England militiamen arrived. "A great number were mere boys," St. Clair noted, and they intended to remain for only a few days. Still, the defenders steeled themselves with brave talk. A soldier just off the sick roll wrote his father that he had "hopes of announcing to you in a few days welcome news of the total defeat of the enemy." Colonel Ebenezer Francis of Massachusetts scratched out a letter to his wife and enclosed a thirty-dollar bill. He wrote:

You may be sure it is not counterfeit for it came immediately from ye Congress. Our garden grows finely & we live very well. . . . Don't let it give you any trouble because the enemy are near us. Our cause is just & good.

An American bombardment of both wings on July 4 accomplished little against an enemy tucked among the trees. British soldiers seized Mount Hope, a green knob west of the Old French Lines, cutting the road to Lake George and forcing rebel firebrands to burn blockhouses and a sawmill along the La Chute to prevent their capture. American grapeshot—small iron balls packed in oiled canvas that flew from a cannon like a shotgun blast—shattered a rash Iroquois charge across open ground. "The Indians were so much in liquor that I found it impossible to bend them to obedience," a British officer wrote. Yet the noose tightened on the Yankee left. So, too, the right, where Germans flanking Mount Independence crashed through thickets so dense that "nobody can see his hand in front of his own eyes," a Brunswicker wrote. "Our people trip on top of each other."

A careful inspection with his spyglass of the American works "convinces me that they have no men of military science," Burgoyne wrote in a dispatch to Carleton. He remained aboard the *Royal George*, so command ashore of the British wing fell to his deputy, Major General William Phillips, an artilleryman who resembled one of his fieldpieces in appearance and temperament. To hurry cannons into the battle at Minden, Phillips reportedly had broken fifteen canes over the haunches of horses pulling the gun carriages. Here he was no less impatient while sailors used block and tackle to lower deck guns onto the shore from *Thunderer* after the radeau proved too unwieldy to maneuver in the shallows below Ticonderoga. Rebel gunfire offended him, and Phillips was keen to answer loud disloyalty with his own cannonade.

By the small hours of Saturday, July 5, a forty-man British patrol had reached the crest of Sugar Loaf, a humpback ridge a mile south of Ticonderoga across the La Chute. An American map drawn the previous summer had labeled this terrain "Inaccessible Hill," but officers soon recognized that it was both accessible and close enough to threaten Ticonderoga and Mount Independence. Yet American proposals to fortify the site had gone nowhere—too few men were available to occupy too much hill. General Phillips would not make the same mistake.

At two p.m. a young British engineer, Lieutenant William Twiss, reported from the summit that all rebel movements not only could be clearly seen, "even having their numbers counted," but also were indeed within artillery range. Four hundred axmen gashed a narrow roadbed with astounding speed, despite suffocating heat and "almost a perpendicular ascent." A tarred hawser, an iron hook, and an enormous team of oxen hauled a pair of 12-pounders, each weighing a ton and a half, up the hill. The ring of ax blows and a dust cloud rising from Sugar Loaf caused unease in the American camp, where the surgeon's mate James Thacher told his diary, "A few days, it is expected, will decide our fate."

In the event, that fate would be settled in just a few hours. As the sun slid toward the Adirondacks, St. Clair convened a council of senior officers to review his predicament. The garrison food supply was sufficient but not inexhaustible: quartermasters reported a two-month provision of salt beef and pork, supplemented by eighty cows and a herd of sheep brought in the previous day by the New England militiamen. The appearance of redcoats on Sugar Loaf was disturbing, although no barrage of cannonballs had begun yet. But St. Clair had no doubt that simultaneous attacks against Ticonderoga and Mount Independence by an enemy with three times his strength would quickly overrun the garrison. He faced an agonizing decision, as his deputy quartermaster later recounted: "If he remained there he would save his character and lose the army. If he went off, he would save the army and lose his character."

Quickly and unanimously, the council voted to save the army by fleeing south "as soon as possible." At six p.m., orders went out for every soldier to pack up four days' provisions and forty-eight musket rounds. As twilight faded after eight p.m., troops swarmed east across the temporary floating bridge and over Mount Independence. Most would march toward Castleton, Vermont, on the only road still open. Several hundred others were ordered to the South Bay boat docks at the foot of the hill. Here a half dozen small vessels remained from Arnold's shattered squadron, along with seventy bateaux still watertight enough to float. St. Clair ordered the craft divided up to carry food casks, tools, a hundred barrels of gunpowder, the sick, and his military chest containing the garrison payroll. "A retreat with an inferior army from before a superior one," he later observed, "never will be effected without prudence, fortitude, and secrecy."

None of that obtained here. Men blundered about in the dark in "the greatest disorder," an officer wrote—a crescent moon would not rise until early morning—and panicky militiamen were "exceedingly insubordinate and seditious." A stiff northeast wind rocked the boats and impeded loading. Lieutenant Thomas Blake of the 1st New Hampshire Regiment found "clothing chests all broke open, the clothing thrown about and carried off by all that were disposed to take it, and everything in great confusion." St. Clair galloped to the head of the mob on the Castleton road in a vain effort to form a military column. The mob swept past him. "Such a retreat," another New Hampshire soldier wrote, "was never heard of since the creation of the world."

Fires broke out, first in an officer's house, then on Mount Independence. Long, garish shadows of scurrying men stretched across the hillside. A British lieutenant in the 47th Foot wrote of seeing "a very uncommon smoke within their works and many fires during the night." Deserters at first light confirmed the wholesale evacuation. On the *Royal George*, Burgoyne "had but time to drink one glass of wine," a staff officer noted, before ordering his army forward in full pursuit.

By midmorning on Sunday, July 6, British and Brunswick flags were flapping above Fort Ticonderoga and Mount Independence, respectively. Abandoned livestock grazed on the parade grounds. The king's men were astonished to find a bakery and brewery intact, along with stocks of sugar, coffee, butter, and cheese, as well as a handsome standard embroidered with gold and silver thread. "The privates in our army have got a considerable amount of booty," a Brunswicker noted in his diary. Quartermasters put the value of captured stores at £150,000, including 1,768 barrels of flour, 72 tons of beef and pork, 31 bushels of salt, 120 gallons of rum, and 93 cannons, just a third of them spiked with nails pounded into their touchholes.

A few shots from British gunboats severed the chain boom "with great dexterity," and within half an hour gunners had also blasted a fifty-foot segment from the temporary bridge. At Burgoyne's direction, British grenadiers and light infantry hurried toward Castleton in pursuit of those rebels retreating afoot, to be followed by Riedesel and several regiments of Germans. After taking aboard three other redcoat regiments, the British men-of-war eased one by one through the broken span, led by *Washington*, *Carleton*, and ten gunboats. Each carried a 24-pounder or an 8-inch howitzer. *Royal George* and *Inflexible* followed with Burgoyne and his staff.

Below Ticonderoga the water passage narrowed to a thin neck known as the Drowned Lands. Choked with marsh grass and glacial deposits, the channel then widened again into South Bay, the lower appendage of Lake Champlain, which petered out twenty-five miles south at Skenesborough, a tidy hamlet of seventy-three families. Using the town's sawmill, cooperage, and forge, Arnold had built his mosquito fleet here a year earlier, and here the waterborne contingent of fleeing Americans arrived at three p.m.

on Sunday afternoon. Wood ducks and herons took flight from the bulrushes.

No sooner had the fugitives dropped anchor than the boom of gunfire echoed along the steep ridgeline above the docks. Redcoats had disembarked three miles north to outflank the village, while *Royal George, Inflexible*, and the gunboats surged ahead to catch the American rear. Crimson flame spurted from the bow chasers, and white plumes leaped from the lake where cannonballs fell wide. "Burgoyne himself was at our heels," Thacher later wrote. He opened his bulky medical chest, grabbed a few instruments and potions, then fled along the waterfront.

The schooner *Liberty* and galley *Trumbull* promptly struck their flags in surrender. But defiant Yankee crews set fire to the cutter *Enterprise*; she burned to the waterline. *Revenge* and *Gates*, reportedly carrying fifteen tons of gunpowder, exploded in two thunderous blasts unlike anything ever heard in this rustic backwater. Debris rained down as firebrands ignited the mills, the stockade, and several storehouses before racing into the woods when the redcoats drew near. Orange sheets of flame danced through the village.

Burgoyne's men took thirty prisoners, but the rest escaped. A hundred-yard hike led to Wood Creek, where some refugees found rowboats; most walked all night through the forest, glancing furtively over their shoulders. Ten miles ahead lay decrepit Fort Anne, and thirteen miles beyond that stood Fort Edward, on the Hudson. Behind lay debacle and shame.

In Skenesborough the fires gradually winked out. The king's men used grappling hooks to drag the harbor for crates, chests, and weapons tossed overboard by the rebels. The scavengers found "so many tents, shirts, pieces of clothing, and other items that they held a kind of country fair with them the next day," a witness reported. Burgoyne placed his headquarters in a huge stone manor house, shaded with oaks and maples, belonging to Philip Skene, a retired British officer granted almost thirty thousand acres on Lake Champlain in 1765 for his faithful service to the Crown in North America. Skene, ever loyal, agreed to join the Canada Army as a political fixer. More pleased with himself than ever, Burgoyne sent his aide-de-camp back to England via Quebec with dispatches "important to the king's service," as well as a copy of his bombastic warning to American insurgents that "the messengers of justice & of wrath await thee in the field." His full, orotund account of Ticonderoga's capture would be printed in a special edition of the *London Gazette*, prompting cynics to dub him Julius Caesar Burgonius.

After a night's rest, the 9th Regiment of Foot requisitioned a week's worth of provisions, dragged fifty bateaux across the portage to Wood

Creek, and resumed the chase. The entire 1st Brigade would soon follow. "The British bayonet," Captain Sir Francis Carr Clerke, Burgoyne's secretary, told a friend in England, "will ever make its way."

General St. Clair and most of his disorderly, knackered men had fled twenty-seven miles to Castleton on the "military road"—no more than a rutted cart track—built the previous year to link Mount Independence with southern Vermont and the Connecticut River valley. Aware that more British bayonets undoubtedly followed close behind, St. Clair detached some of his best Continental troops to slow them down. Late Sunday afternoon, twelve hundred soldiers from the 2nd New Hampshire and Vermont's Green Mountain Boys converged on Hubbardton, a hardscrabble crossroads abandoned that morning by the nine families who lived there.

The rearguard leader, a Bunker Hill veteran named Colonel Seth Warner, had intended to press on this evening to Castleton, seven miles south, but too many sick, injured, and exhausted men at the end of their tether needed a few hours' rest. Troops scraped out firing positions in a half-moon formation across a hillside and threw up hasty log breastworks on farms barely wrenched from primeval forest. Stumps and girdled trees still dotted small fields bordered with wild carrot, staghorn sumac, and frosted hawthorn.

The distant crackle of musketry at five a.m. on Monday brought the bivouac to life. Pickets watching the road from a saddle on Sargent Hill, to the north, had fired on the shadowy vanguard of a redcoat column before scrambling back to Sucker Brook, where New Hampshire and Massachusetts troops behind a makeshift abatis had begun boiling water with a few shavings of chocolate for breakfast. As morning sunlight filtered through the hardwoods, 850 British soldiers drew near, weary, thirsty, and vengeful after a twenty-one-hour march from Mount Independence. Brigadier General Simon Fraser, a Highlander whose long career had included service in Germany, Canada, and Gibraltar, directed his column to fan out in a line for several hundred yards on either side of the road. After debating whether to wait for Riedesel and his Brunswickers, who were plodding several miles behind, Fraser gave the order to attack at six-thirty a.m. "I was then," he later wrote, "in the most disaffected part of America."

The dim early light brightened yellow flashes from hundreds of muzzles. Volley answered volley, and banks of gray smoke rolled across the creek. Shouts and shrieks carried above the roaring gunfire, along with curses at frequent misfires—perhaps one for every four trigger pulls from damp powder, dull flints, or ill fortune—and the awful thud of a one-ounce lead ball hitting human flesh. "Every man was trying to secure himself behind girdled trees," rebel fifer Ebenezer Fletcher wrote. Eyes watered from the sharp stink of burned powder. Men tore open cartridges with their teeth, blackening lips and chins, before sprinkling a few grains into the priming pan and tamping home another round. The greasy powder residue on metal ramrods soon blackened hands as well.

Major Robert Grant of the 24th Foot was among the first to fall, shot dead before he crossed the creek. Twenty-one comrades fell near him, killed or wounded. But Fraser's superior numbers soon told, and the Yankees fell back to what would be called Monument Hill, sheltering behind a log-and-stone fence among the other New England musketeers. Fraser ordered ten grenadier companies to swing wide to the right to turn Colonel Warner's left flank and cut the Castleton road. Weathering "such a fire sent amongst them as not easily conceived," as a British officer boasted, the Americans holding the high ground bent but then stiffened, answering with "showers of balls mixed with buckshot"; the latter were intended to blind, sting, and annoy. On the British left, Fraser led his light infantry in an uphill charge at seven-thirty a.m., troops bellowing. A British lieutenant fell dead, shot through both eyes, and the brawl surged back and forth at ranges under thirty yards. Smoke blanketed the slope now strewn with inert bodies and men writhing in pain. Sensing that his left flank was about to be turned, and convinced that he faced at least two thousand enemies—nearly twice the rebel strength—Fraser sent a courier to Riedesel, pleading for reinforcements.

The faint, familiar roar of battle surprised General Red Hazel, who had assumed that no British attack would begin until his Brunswick troops arrived. Spurring his horse into a trot, he reached a clearing on Sargent Hill and through his *Fernglas* could plainly see the British predicament even before Fraser's winded messenger came racing up. Most Brunswickers lagged at least two miles behind, but Riedesel ordered his van of eighty grenadiers and one hundred *Jäger* to attack immediately with fixed bayonets. Belting out a German hymn while accompanied by drummers, the Brunswickers slammed into the American right wing.

The day turned. "Smoke was so thick on the hill we did not see the enemy until they fired," an American soldier reported. Blue grenadier uniforms also confused some men. The rebel right buckled abruptly, then the left. Colonel Francis, who had sent his wife the new thirty-dollar bill and soothing assurances, took a musket ball in the right arm and then, a captain reported, "the fatal wound through his body, entering his right breast. He dropped on his face." He would leave behind his widow and five children.

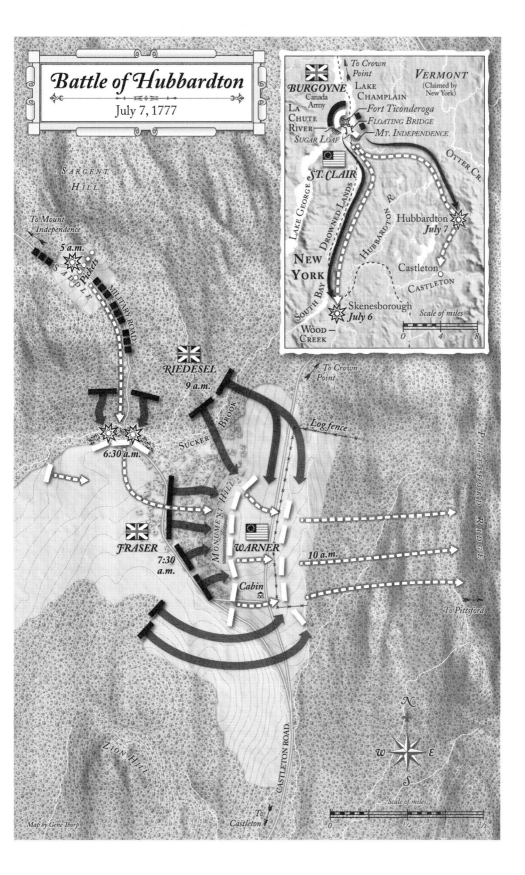

Battle of Hubbardton
July 7, 1777

SARGENT HILL

To Mount Independence

5 a.m.

Pickets

SADDLE

MILITARY ROAD

RIEDESEL
9 a.m.

SUCKER BROOK

6:30 a.m.

Log fence

To Crown Point

PITTSFORD RIDGE

MONUMENT HILL

FRASER
7:30 a.m.

WARNER

10 a.m.

Cabin

To Pittsford

ZION HILL

CASTLETON ROAD

To Castleton

N
W E
S

Scale of miles
0   1/4   1/2

Map by Gene Thorp

Inset map

To Crown Point

BURGOYNE
Canada Army

VERMONT
(Claimed by New York)

LA CHUTE RIVER

LAKE CHAMPLAIN

Fort Ticonderoga

Floating Bridge

Mt. Independence

Sugar Loaf

ST. CLAIR

LAKE GEORGE

DROWNED LANDS

NEW YORK

Hubbardton R.

Hubbardton
July 7

Otter Cr.

Castleton

CASTLETON

South Bay

Skenesborough
July 6

Wood Creek

Scale of miles
0   4   8

Alone or in small bands, the Americans scuttled across the Castleton road, hurrying through grain fields and into the forest below Pittsford Ridge, to the east, "popping away from behind trees," a soldier recalled. Colonel Warner "poured out a torrent of execrations upon the flying troops," then shouted for his men to "scatter and meet me in Manchester," fifty miles south. By ten a.m., the Battle of Hubbardton was over. A thousand Continentals, now twice routed, picked their way through the wilderness. "Our men have no blankets," Captain Moses Greenleaf told his diary. "Nothing but the heavens to cover them, and not a mouthful of meat or bread."

The morning had proved dire for both sides. The king's losses included almost 40 British dead and 130 wounded, one in five of Fraser's troops, plus 10 Brunswickers killed and 15 wounded. Warner's rear guard suffered 40 dead, nearly 100 wounded, and 240 captured, a third of his force. Those who survived the bloodletting blinked with incredulity at their good fortune. Major Alexander Lindsay, the twenty-five-year-old Earl of Balcarres, counted five bullet holes in his uniform, including one ball deflected by a gun flint in his pocket. "You may observe on this occasion I am not born to be shot," he wrote his sister, "whatever may be my fate." Wolves would dig up the shallow graves of men less lucky, and human bones littered the landscape until 1784, when locals interred them properly.

The redcoats had "discovered that neither were they invincible, nor the rebels all poltroons," a British officer wrote. Guarded by two grenadier companies, American prisoners were sent back to Ticonderoga in a pelting rain, along with an urgent request for surgeons. Fraser and Riedesel then led their columns on to Skenesborough, leaving the injured under lean-tos built from branches and tree bark. Contemporary medical texts divided wounds into four categories—incised, punctured, lacerated, and contused— all of which could be found at Hubbardton. The wounded, a British lieutenant wrote, "were in a very bad situation." Medicos did their inadequate best: pressing extruded intestines back into the viscera with two forefingers; enlarging bayonet wounds in the chest to allow pooling blood to drain; and amputating compound fractures with a screw tourniquet, a bone saw, and ligatures of waxed shoemaker's thread. A bullet boring through soft tissue often left a red stripe on the skin, helping surgeons find the ball and clean the wound of uniform cloth and shirt threads before infection could set in, since a common, if feckless, treatment for tetanus was to throw a pail of water on the patient.

"It happened in the most unfortunate place in the world," wrote John McNamara Hayes, a British surgeon who reached the battlefield on July 8. He noted that his hands were soon "imbrued in blood, my face as dirty, &

my beard as long as a Capuchin friar." Most of the sentient wounded rejected a proposal that they be wheeled in handbarrows twenty miles back
to Mount Independence. Those capable of sitting or being lashed to a saddle "are being brought away as fast as they are capable of being removed on
horseback," General Phillips wrote on July 16. But scores would remain in
their leaky bowers for weeks, or until they died and their bones joined
other bones.

"Riedesel rages with anger because [Fraser] had gotten himself into
trouble completely needlessly, which we had to pay for with much blood,"
a Brunswicker recorded. Riedesel himself wrote to his duke in mid-July
that Fraser had incurred heavy casualties "only because he did not want to
wait for me." Even so, he added, "I would never have thought that the rebels fought so stubbornly."

Fugitives from Ticonderoga began arriving at Fort Edward on the night
of July 8, bedraggled and dispirited. Enos Hitchcock, a Harvard-educated
army chaplain, listed the possessions he had abandoned, including two
blankets, a coat, shoes, "one looking glass," saddlebags, and, most lamented, "15 gallons best rum, 5 gallons best brandy." Despite also losing
his Bible and Psalter, Hitchcock preached a sermon from Nehemiah 4:14
in a copse along the Hudson. "Be not ye afraid of them," he implored. "Remember the Lord, which is great and terrible, and fight for your brethren,
your sons and your daughters, your wives and your houses."

Such divine fortitude would be needed in this isolated place. A stockade had stood at the head of North River navigation since 1709, protecting the overland portages to Lakes Champlain and George. Here the river
bent in from the west over cataracts and then swept south for its long,
majestic journey to New York Harbor and the Atlantic. Early in the French
and Indian War, as many as fifteen thousand British and provincial troops
had camped here, making Fort Edward—named for the Duke of York,
George III's younger brother—the third-largest town in America, as well
as Britain's northernmost outpost on the continent. With the French defeat, Britons shifted north, and the settlement declined. American pioneers
built mills for lumber, grain, gunpowder, and snuff, but the fort fell into
such disrepair that a galloping horse could clear the crumbling palisade.

St. Clair arrived on July 12, after nearly a week of dodging the British.
"On the whole," he wrote, "I think myself very happy to make my retreat
from under their nose." The two thousand Continentals who tumbled in
after him would provide the core of a new Northern Army, reinforced by
ranks from the south and militia regiments. But he quickly learned that

Congress and most of his countrymen were outraged at the loss of the Gibraltar of the North without a fight. "I think we shall never defend a post until we shoot a general," John Adams of Massachusetts, president of the Board of War, told his wife, Abigail. St. Clair noted, with some justification, "Although I have lost a post, I have eventually saved a state." Still, he lamented the "heavy load of obloquy" now heaped on him, and not for a year would a court-martial clear him of malfeasance.

St. Clair's immediate superior also came in for condemnation, although he had known nothing in advance of the evacuation. Major General Philip Schuyler had spent much of the spring fending off accusations that he had botched the previous year's invasion of Canada, as well as scurrilous allegations that he was a secret loyalist and an embezzler. A lanky patrician with vast land holdings from the Hudson to Detroit, Schuyler had demonstrated conspicuous talents during both the last war and this one in organizing supply and transportation operations, as well as in fruitful Indian negotiations. No sooner had he cleared his name during a congressional investigation and returned to his Albany headquarters in June than he faced new charges of complicity in the Ticonderoga disaster.

"The spirit of malevolence knows no bounds," he wrote General Washington, "and I am considered a traitor." A perfectionist and sometime martinet—he acknowledged being as "crusty as an old woman"—Schuyler had long been ensnared in the violent dispute between New York and New England over control of the New Hampshire Grants, territory that would soon become the state of Vermont. Yankees considered his Dutch pedigree particularly suspect. "My crime," he told a friend, "consists in not being a New England man."

Wobbling between despair and defiance as he arrived at Fort Edward, he ordered a thousand troops with felling axes north of the compound to delay the British by dropping bridges, destroying causeways, diverting streams to create swamps, and toppling enormous trees like jackstraws across Wood Creek. In a scorched-earth campaign designed "to leave nothing but a wilderness to the enemy," his men herded away cattle, arrested loyalists, and burned sawmills, standing crops, and, at the foot of its eponymous lake, Fort George.

A brigade of Continental reinforcements from Massachusetts included only 575 rank and file fit for duty, Schuyler told Washington on July 15. "Several of these are Negroes," he added with evident scorn, "and many of them young, small, and feeble boys. Desertion prevails and disease gains ground." Schuyler had collected thirty cannons, but all were immobile; he sent several carpenters to build gun carriages, using the forge and mills at his country estate in Saratoga, with timber pried from a covered bridge.

The magazine at Fort Edward held fifteen tons of gunpowder but only enough lead for three extra bullets per soldier, some of whom had no ammunition at all. His skittish neighbors in Albany stripped lead weights from clocks and window sash cords for the army even as they hid their furniture and silver plate from the approaching British.

Schuyler was gratified to hear that General Arnold was hurrying up the Hudson; he had witnessed "that gentleman's military abilities, and his arrival will afford me great satisfaction." Still, he told the New York Council of Safety, "our affairs in this quarter daily put on a more gloomy aspect." To prevent all militiamen from deserting, half had been permitted to go home to harvest their fields, leaving his Northern Department with just under five thousand Continentals of all ranks and sixteen hundred militia. "Nothing shall be left undone," he promised Washington, "to prevent the enemy from penetrating farther in the country."

"If we act vigorously, we save the country," Schuyler added in a note to Colonel Seth Warner. "Greater misfortunes have happened and have been retrieved."

On Burgoyne's orders, the king's men on July 13 celebrated a thanksgiving service for "the fortunate progress of our army," even as they lamented another thirty-nine casualties suffered when the 9th Foot was attacked near Fort Anne. ("The enemy came pouring down upon us like a mighty torrent," a survivor reported.) As if to answer Nehemiah, a German chaplain preached a sermon from Psalm 92, verse 12: "The righteous shall flourish like the palm tree." Late in the day, thousands of soldiers fired three rapid volleys in a *feu de joie* salute while listening for rattlesnakes in the underbrush. Some had developed a taste for snake soup, and the skins could be used to cover bayonet scabbards. But rumors spread among Brunswick troops that rattlers grew twelve to sixteen feet long, could kill with a glance, and that within an hour a bitten victim's body "will have taken the color of the snake."

Pacing the fine parlor of his headquarters mansion in Skenesborough, Burgoyne had more on his mind than reptiles. Two routes could take his army to the Hudson. The first, more than ninety miles long, required returning north to Ticonderoga, portaging four uphill miles along the La Chute River, sailing south across Lake George, then following a decent road along the Great Carrying Place to Fort Edward. The alternative route was shorter, just twenty-seven miles, but no army had ever ventured from Skenesborough along boggy Wood Creek, where Schuyler's vandals were briskly laying obstructions.

Burgoyne chose both approaches. Heavy baggage and the forty-three field guns he intended to move south would take "the more commodious route by Lake George." But the four brigades already concentrating at Skenesborough would bull down Wood Creek to avoid "the impressions which a retrograde movement often occasions in the minds of foes and friends," as he wrote Carleton in Quebec.

Advancing roughly a mile a day, work gangs built what a witness denounced as "the meanest, worst, and most desolate road I ever saw." Rebel axmen made it meaner. Felled trees were "as thick as the lamps upon Westminster Bridge," a British officer wrote, and the crash of more falling trees beyond the next hill became the "leit-motif of the resistance." Wood Creek grew so narrow that bateaux men could touch both banks simultaneously. Engineers had to build forty bridges and a two-mile log causeway across a morass. Scouts roaming near the Hudson, a German lieutenant wrote, found that "all the fields of standing corn were laid waste, the cattle driven away, and every particle carefully removed."

American prisoners toiled on the La Chute portage "from daybreak to sunset," General Phillips wrote on July 16. But half of Burgoyne's eight hundred Canadian laborers had already deserted, and each day a dozen more disappeared. The two-wheeled carts broke down continually—each general's baggage filled six of them—and only a third of the horses promised from Canada had arrived.

In an eight-page letter marked "private," Burgoyne in mid-July told Germain in London that malicious rebels were trying "to make a desert of the country." However, he expected hundreds of armed loyalists to rally to his standard so that he could pit "provincial against provincial." Burgoyne had considered diverting the expedition eastward to intimidate New England and gather provisions, but reports of growing enemy strength on the Hudson persuaded him to push on to Fort Edward and then Albany. As he finished the dispatch, his tidy handwriting grew jittery from fatigue, or perhaps anxiety, yet he managed a closing note of assurance: "Upon the whole of my situation, my lord, I am confident of fulfilling the object of my orders."

Burgoyne had also described for Germain the efforts to restrain his Indian allies. "Were they left to themselves," he wrote, "enormities too horrid to think of would ensue." Even before leaving Lake Champlain he had gathered the Iroquois and other native chiefs along the Bouquet River for a war feast, followed by his windy harangue regarding battlefield conduct and the need to avoid atrocities. On July 17, another canoe flotilla arrived at Skenesborough, with 170 Canadian volunteers and 400 additional warriors from several western nations, including Ottawa, Fox, and Winnebago.

Resplendent in his finest dress uniform, Burgoyne settled into a large chair placed within a hastily erected bower. As his officers and the Indians sat on logs and pine boughs, he invoked "the great king, our common father," whose favor they must all beseech.

"It may be permissible that you scalp those whom you have killed in battle," he said in French as interpreters translated. "But in the name of my king, I forbid you to practice this on any prisoner or wounded. . . . Regard all old people, women, and children as holy, and do them no harm." The warriors answered with a great shout, a war song, and a spirited dance. Burgoyne shook hands, then distributed provisions, a barrel of rum, and medallions bearing the image of George III before striding back to his headquarters.

The killing began promptly. Some warriors observed Burgoyne's strictures; others ignored them. On July 21, Indians ambushed three dozen Continentals, leaving "eight killed and fifteen wounded on our side," a Massachusetts captain reported at Fort Edward. Several days later, a war party massacred and scalped an ardent loyalist, John Allen, and his wife, sister-in-law, three young children, and two slaves as they sat down to dinner after a long day of harvesting wheat a few miles southeast of the fort. Neighbors buried the victims beneath an apple tree in two graves, one for whites, the other for blacks. On July 26, Indians struck a Continental picket just a few hundred yards north of the fort, killing five soldiers and their lieutenant, whose hands were chopped off. The same marauders then seized a young white woman in a nearby house and, during a quarrel over who owned the hostage, shot and scalped her while she was still alive. They then buried a tomahawk in her chest as a finishing blow and partly stripped off her chintz gown and calamanco petticoat.

If obscure in life, Jane McCrea in death would become one of the most famous American women of her century. Known as Jenny, she was the daughter of a Presbyterian divine in New Jersey and the fiancée of a loyalist American lieutenant serving in the Canada Army. A later forensic exhumation revealed that she was petite, barely five feet tall, and in her mid-twenties. Lurid fabrications would claim that she had knee-length blond hair and was wearing her wedding dress when she died.

The murder outraged Burgoyne. "The news I have just received of the savages having scalped a young lady, their prisoner, fills me with horror," he told General Fraser at eight p.m. on July 26. The next morning he summoned several chiefs, excoriated them for "such unheard of barbarities," and demanded that the killer, a young Ottawa warrior, be put to death. He relented only after being warned that if he persisted, the Indians would "retire in a body, massacring whatever defenseless people lay in their path" on the return to Canada. "If he had not pardoned the man, which he did," a grenadier captain wrote, "I believe the total defection of the Indians would have ensued."

Burgoyne had intended to instill fear in the rebels, and fear there was. But newspaper accounts of the atrocity, published over the coming weeks in Boston, Philadelphia, and elsewhere, also fueled American contempt for the British and rage at the Indians. One wild-eyed report claimed that Burgoyne paid $10 for each scalp and that King George was "counting the scalps sent in bales to him."

As for Jenny McCrea, although buried not far from where she perished, she lived on and on, in mawkish fiction, in bad poetry, in a circus act titled "The Death of Miss McCrea," and in paintings, including a *tableau d'histoire* accepted by the Paris salon in 1804 and a re-creation featured on a calendar issued in the twentieth century by the Glens Falls Insurance Company. "O cruel Britons! / Who no pity feel!" the Reverend Wheeler Case wrote in a ballad of innumerable stanzas. "Where did they get the knife, the cruel blade? / From Britain it was sent, where it was made."

By late July, American troops had forsaken Fort Edward and the benighted borderland between the Hudson and Lake Champlain. Outnumbered and outgunned, with no hope of holding the derelict outpost, Schuyler crossed to the North River's west bank with most of his men and fell back to Saratoga. They arrived "dirty, hungry, weary and wet," a captain reported, harassed every step of the way by hundreds of warriors on both sides of the river. One dead soldier was found not only scalped but with the soles of his feet sliced off. General Arnold, who arrived in time to help direct the retreat, wrote Washington, "We are daily insulted by the Indians." Most regiments lacked blankets, tents, camp kettles, and salt meat. In a letter to his wife, Major James McClure requested linen to make an extra shirt, since he told her, "I have none, old or new, except the won I have on."

On July 30, Burgoyne's advanced corps camped on the heights above Fort Edward. It had taken them nearly three weeks to move twenty-three miles. "Our tents were pitched in a large field of as fine wheat as I ever saw, which in a few minutes was all trampled down," Lieutenant William Digby wrote. Raspberries and blueberries ripened in the summer sun, and Digby admired "the most romantic prospect of the Hudson's river, interspersed with small islands."

Departing rebels had smashed the fort's doors and windows but otherwise left the shabby buildings and three bastions intact. The imperial bureaucracy quickly took root. Military clerks scratched out receipts for wagons, livestock, wood, and candles, written in a fine copperplate hand on brown scraps of paper: "This is to certify that Thomas Pointer at Fort Anne has delivered one cow for the use of the regiment dragoons. August 2, 1777." Loyalist Pointer made his mark to collect £2.

Burgoyne moved into a snug two-story house, painted red and yellow, with a gambrel roof. Staff officers and couriers tramped around the yard at all hours. Indian scouts brought in seven prisoners and four scalps on the morning of August 3, and eleven more scalps in the afternoon. To discourage desertion, Burgoyne authorized the Indians to shoot absconders on sight. To reinforce the point, a German deserter apprehended near Skenesborough was marched to Fort Edward and shot by a firing squad.

"Our general is really a fine, agreeable, manly fellow," Fraser wrote of Burgoyne, "but hates lines of resistance when they interrupt his projects. And they will occur here frequently." With a supply line stretching 185 miles to Montreal, Burgoyne estimated that for every hour devoted to strategic issues, he spent another twenty hours calculating how to feed his army. The shortage of boats, wagons, and draft animals meant it would take nearly a month to build up the army's magazines before advancing south. Just to meet daily consumption needs, sixty-five carts would have to reach Fort Edward each day.

And then what? In another private letter to Germain in London, Burgoyne reported that he had sent ten messengers by different routes to General Howe in New York and "not one is returned to me. I am in total ignorance of the situation or intentions of that general." Burgoyne had told no one, not even General Riedesel, of Howe's stated proposal to take his army south toward Philadelphia. He once again wrote Howe, blithely predicting that he expected to reach Albany around August 23 and looked forward to giving battle—if the rebels could be forced to make a stand. The American efforts to denude the land of livestock, crops, and loyalists "seems to me an act of desperation & folly," he told Germain. "It cannot finally impede me."

Except for two regiments and an artillery company left to garrison Ticonderoga and protect the supply route, the remaining German and British troops arrived on the Hudson. The hurried American withdrawal, an unwitting Riedesel wrote, "would be the last effort of the rebels" before Howe blocked further retreat—an anvil to Burgoyne's hammer. Once the Canada Army had gathered itself, he added, "the march of annihilation should be continued southward."

*　*　*

A boy fleeing south with his father, a teamster, later wrote, "Our procession of flying inhabitants wore a strange and melancholy appearance. A long cavalcade of wagons filled with all kinds of furniture stretched along the road." Some refugees sat two to a horse. A large gaggle on foot tried to keep up with their mounted neighbors, he added, but "everyone for himself was the constant cry."

Some Americans wondered if the king's legions were the instrument of a wrathful God. "Our sins are so great that we have reasons to expect severe correction," wrote William Williams, a delegate to Congress from Connecticut. "God will accomplish his own design." Chaplain Hitchcock recorded two suicides, including a woman who cut her own throat.

"The cursed war whoop makes the woods ring for miles," a Continental officer noted, and each whoop, each gunshot, each severed scalp "strikes a panic on our men." Private Samuel Smith wrote his wife, "I am tired of marching with my back to the enemy." Smith's march would end soon enough: in a few weeks he would be dead.

On August 3, as the army's rear guard prepared to abandon Saratoga for another forced march down the Hudson, Major Henry B. Livingston, Schuyler's aide-de-camp, wrote a friend, "We are busy at packing to move off, and of course in confusion. Destruction & havoc mark our steps. . . . With these men, are we to oppose an army superior in number, flushed with success, well-officered & disciplined?"

With a final yelp of despair, he added, "God only knows where we shall stop retreating."

2.

This Cursed, Cut-Up Land

Two hundred miles downriver from Fort Edward, New York had again become precisely what London promised for all of America whenever the rebels returned to their senses: a prosperous, peaceable outpost of the world's greatest empire. The city's population of twenty-five thousand before the war had dwindled to five thousand during Britain's violent eviction of Washington and his army in August 1776. Now the number had climbed back above twelve thousand, with hundreds more returning each week to revive their businesses, seek work, or help the king's men crush the insurrection.

Loyalists—called Tories by contemptuous patriots—wore long red ribbons as a token of fidelity to the Crown; some of the enslaved even bedecked their caps with scarlet rags. Refugees and returning residents were advised to formally record their allegiance on the rolls kept at Scott's Tavern, near city hall, where they might find propaganda pamphlets like *The Duty of Honoring the King*. Engravers, clockmakers, cobblers, and blacksmiths set up their shops, happy to be paid in British pounds rather than chaffy Continental dollars. Milliners, glovers, perukers, and silversmiths were again swamped with orders, and housewrights, bricklayers, masons, and glaziers had more work than they could handle. "Flying machines"— public coaches—rattled up and down the city streets. Everyone seemed in a hurry.

Hundreds of ships filled the great harbor each month. Sailors in tarred breeches and fearnought jackets swarmed along the East River waterfront, jamming gin mills, dram shops, and alehouses. (New York had one liquor retailer for every thirteen adult males, and heavy drinkers were classified as "one, two, or three bottle men.") Stevedores unloaded European cargo worthy of the town's ambitions: yellow flannels, Irish linen, umbrellas, and carpets for Alexander Leckie's emporium on Hanover Square; ivory combs, saddles, sealing wax, and silk knee garters for Neil Jamieson's general store;

wall hangings, French raspberry brandy, and gentlemen's dress frocks for the Cane & Walking Stick Warehouse. Other shops advertised Durham mustard, crates of Madeira, "superfine broadcloths," and "very elegant pictures of the king and queen in gold burnished frames." *The American Military Pocket Atlas*, intended "for the use of the military gentleman," included a helpful map of Lake Champlain.

British regulars had been posted here since 1664, and each morning stiff-legged redcoats drilled on the Common, wheeling left and wheeling right, often to applause from red-ribboned admirers. Rebels controlled most of the terrain encircling the city, including Connecticut, the lower Hudson, much of Westchester County, and nearly all of New Jersey. The surprise attack at Trenton in December made the king's troops skittish and the Americans bold. Loyalists with spyglasses kept watch over Long Island Sound for the double-prowed whaleboats of Connecticut raiders intent on stealing hogs or kidnapping prominent Tories. Even on the northern knuckle of Manhattan Island, military couriers required an escort of fifty dragoons. "All traveling between the posts is hazardous," a British soldier warned.

Yet within the city a "Rule, Britannia" swagger obtained. The king's birthday, on June 4, had been commemorated with twenty-one-gun salutes from Fort George and four hundred vessels, all flying Union Jacks. That night every house was illuminated with spermaceti candles, and celebratory musket fire persisted past midnight. During these long summer days, redcoats amused themselves with saltwater bathing, foot races, and "knock-chops," a contest between two men sitting on a fence and trying to knock each other's hat off. Two cricket teams, Brooklyn and Greenwich, played on the Bowling Green for fifty-guinea wagers, and the ponies ran at Ascot Heath, five miles east of the Brooklyn ferry. Boats raced in the harbor for prizes awarded by Vice Admiral Lord Richard Howe, commander of the North American station, and every fortnight a dance was held at Hicks's or Roubalet's Tavern. Officers drank toasts "to a long and moderate war."

Martial law still prevailed in New York, and although residents paid no taxes, they also had no elections, judges, jury trials, or civil courts. British officers controlled all aspects of municipal life, from lamp lighting and street sweeping to murder investigations. Bakers were required to put their initials on each bread loaf. Every cartman needed a license, with an assigned number painted in red on his vehicle. Any pub serving soldiers or sailors after eight p.m. risked having the furniture confiscated. Any traveler to New Jersey after sunset risked "military execution."

New York City
Summer 1777

NEW JERSEY
HUDSON RIVER
MANHATTAN I.
EAST RIVER
NEW YORK
Detail
New York
LONG ISLAND
Paulus Hook
Brooklyn
UPPER BAY
STATEN ISLAND
Scale of miles
0   2   4

HUDSON RIVER

NEW YORK

MANHATTAN ISLAND

Wetlands

COLLECT POND

CHAPEL ST.
CHURCH ST.
CHAMBERS ST.
WARREN ST.
King's College
BROADWAY
Bridewell
Negro Burial Ground
Almshouse
New Gaol (Provost)
COMMON
BOWERY LANE

Canvas Town
St. Paul's Chapel
Area burned in 1776 fire
Brick Presbyterian Church
Rhinelander's
Jews' Burial Ground
Theatre Royal
New Lutheran Church
CROWN ST.
Friends meetinghouse
NASSAU ST.
North Dutch Church
Van Cortlandt's
Methodist meetinghouse
Middle Dutch Church
Trinity Church
Livingston's
City Hall
WATER STREET
QUEEN STREET
CROWN STREET
WILLIAM ST.
Shipyards
BROADWAY
BROAD ST.
WALL ST.
BOWLING GREEN
George III statue (site)
No. 1 (British H.Q.)
BEAVER ST.
BEAVER ST.
HANOVER SQUARE
Long Island ferry
DOCK ST.
Area burned in 1776 fire
Fort George
Queen's Head Tavern
Grand Battery
Whitehall slip

EAST RIVER

N
W   E
S

Scale of feet
0   600   1,200

Map by Gene Thorp

No rules were enforced more rigorously than those intended to prevent fire, including mandatory monthly chimney inspections. An inferno the previous September had destroyed more than five hundred houses, a quarter of the city's total, plus many other structures. Rumors persisted that arsonists—said to include a shoemaker, a saddler, and a milkman—were plotting another conflagration. The housing shortage had pushed rents up 400 percent in the past year. Many officers and their servants slept seven or more to a room in confiscated rebel houses marked with the initials "G.R.," for George Rex. The king's troops, packed like sprats in a tin, filled King's College, two breweries, various warehouses, three Dutch churches, a half dozen Quaker and Presbyterian meetinghouses, and sundry buildings on Staten and Long Islands, although parts of the latter still reeked from unburied rebels killed last summer.

For many civilians, finding a decent place to live was even worse. An English visitor who arrived in mid-May wrote, "I took lodgings at a little dirty pot-house, the only one we can get." The burned district from Broadway to the Hudson was now known as Canvas Town for the sailcloth shelters erected among charred walls, chimneys, and cellars. "Fireships"— prostitutes with venereal disease—toiled in an open-air brothel, and the sprawling slum had become a demimonde of swindlers, beggars, astrologers, and banditti, "wretches who turned highwaymen in despair," by one account.

New York was also a haven for rebel deserters, who received £3 for defecting, plus a bounty of twenty-five shillings for each musket surrendered and £15 for each horse. Of the deserters, Lieutenant Loftus Cliffe wrote, "This town swarms with them." Two years of war had only deepened British contempt for the Americans, "a leveling, underbred, artful race of people," in the opinion of one British marine captain, who hoped that the pardon now offered to any turncoat Continental officer "will save our people the trouble of putting them to death."

Deserters and loyalists alike were encouraged to take up arms in the king's cause. London sent military kit for thousands of provincial troops, and recruiters offered blandishments over free rum and in newspaper advertisements that invariably ended with "God save the King!" Any recruit who enlisted for three years in the Prince of Wales's Loyal American Volunteers, for instance, was promised a £5 bonus, a Brown Bess musket, a smart uniform, and "100 acres of land on the Mississippi" after the war. Many found such offers irresistible. According to the historians Samuel Eliot Morison and Henry Steele Commager, the state of New York ultimately provided more fighting men for loyalist units—some twenty-three thousand—than for the Continental Army.

*   *   *

Two other groups crowded the city in the summer of 1777. A census counted 1,951 blacks, 16 percent of New York's population. Free or enslaved, they worked as foragers, fiddlers, teamsters, and woodcutters at six pence a day, handling much of His Majesty's loading, hauling, and road building. Black women made musket cartridges or worked as nurses, cooks, and laundresses. A "Negro barracks" stood near the army's wagon yard in Brooklyn. Other blacks camped in a field west of Broadway, only to be decimated by smallpox; the dead were interred in the Negro Burial Ground above Chambers Street.

Royal Navy raids along Chesapeake Bay and the Carolina coast brought back ever more escaped slaves, and so many runaways arrived from New Jersey that Hudson River ferry operators were ordered to stop transporting them without authorization. Many blacks viewed Great Britain as a liberating force, a notion encouraged by some royal officials eager to undermine the American economy. New York was a refuge. Here blacks could worship, marry, have their children baptized at the Anglican church, and enjoy "Ethiopian balls," where women of color danced with white men.

Even so, slaves belonging to New York loyalists remained enslaved, and on Manhattan's docks auctions of human chattel continued. "For sale, a fine Negro boy and a billiard table," read one newspaper ad. Another advised, "To be sold, a young Negro wench who has had the smallpox. Can cook very well. . . . Lowest price £70." The enslaved who fled from loyalist or British owners were considered malefactors. One Caspar Springsteen advertised a $10 reward for the return of "Charles, a Negro of yellowish cast"; the 17th Dragoons on Long Island offered five guineas for a runaway identified only as "a Negro boy."

The second group in New York also arrived in numbers. More than eighteen thousand German soldiers had reached North America in 1776, including the Brunswickers now massing on the upper Hudson. Many hundreds subsequently perished. The causes of death listed for a single Hessian regiment during two years of expeditionary warfare included drowning, gunshots, typhus, typhoid, cannonballs, consumption, dysentery, gangrene, suicide, and unspecified misadventures. Hundreds of others had been captured and now worked, often in Pennsylvania, as prisoner farmhands, tailors, and shoemakers. Their replacements, required by contract between their sovereigns and King George, arrived mostly aboard British transports in New York.

Those who trudged across the East River docks in June and July were described by Captain Johann von Ewald, a Hessian *Jäger*, as comprising "deserters of all nations . . . failed officers and aristocrats who had misfortune, students of all faculties, bankrupts, merchants, and all sorts of adventurers." Ewald was not far wrong: the troops included a haberdasher from Hannover, a monk from Würzburg, and a wandering poet from Jena. The journey to America for thirteen hundred recruits from Bayreuth and Ansbach had begun badly on the river Main in a mutiny suppressed only with horsewhips and a two-hour gunfight that caused thirty casualties.

Some Hessians offered by their princes were rejected for physical deficiencies, including epilepsy, too few teeth to bite open a musket cartridge, and old age—sixty or above. But the king's recruiters usually took what they could get. After inspecting 437 Hessians, a British officer reported, "There are some of them with but one eye, though otherwise serviceable." The three-month voyage to America in overcrowded ships improved no one's health: the men slept six to a bunk in "places of repose," and many suffered lost teeth and bleeding gums from scurvy, a wasting disease caused by insufficient vitamin C. Despite efforts to purify the ships' holds with vinegar and fireballs made of beaten gunpowder, tobacco, and more vinegar, typhus and other diseases typically killed at least 8 percent of all passengers on transatlantic crossings. Each dead German was laced up in a linen hammock with a cannonball at his feet, then tossed overboard. Frederick the Great, whose Prussians did not participate in the soldier trade with Britain, would write in October, "I never think of the present war in America without being struck by the eagerness of some German princes to sacrifice their troops in a quarrel which does not concern them."

"We have seen a true paradise," Sergeant Johann Ernst Prechtel told his diary after disembarking in New York in June. A closer look tempered such enthusiasm, particularly after a shortage of barracks rooms forced Hessian troops to sleep in a churchyard. Britain had hired German regiments since 1715, but collaboration in America at times grew brittle. One Hessian officer wrote home to complain of "the confounded pride and arrogant bearing of the English, who treat everyone who was not born on their ragamuffin island with contempt." A British officer conceded that "differing as we do in language, manners, and ideas, English and Hessian did not coalesce into one corps." Desertion and death from battle wounds or disease meant that more than a third of those sent across the sea to make war on the Americans would never see Germany again.

For now these newcomers tried to lose their sea legs and steady themselves for battle. "The English keep their clothing very clean," a Bayreuth private observed in his diary, "and have only the vices of cussing, swearing, drinking, whoring, and stealing."

* * *

On Saturday, July 5, almost at the very hour the Americans decided to abandon Ticonderoga, three Royal Navy men-of-war threaded the Narrows from the open sea into New York Bay. Six merchantmen followed in their wake, trailed by another eleven armed victuallers from Ireland with enough casked salt meat, flour, butter, oatmeal, and other staples to keep the garrison fed into the fall—a welcome bounty, since some food prices had soared eightfold in the city.

The guns at Fort George boomed in salute as a barge from the frigate *Liverpool* nosed toward shore with a paunchy, balding lieutenant general aboard, queasy as always when required to leave solid ground. His bright blue eyes took in the familiar Dutch stepped gables, the Georgian brick row houses, and the cobbled streets leading to the docks. Henry Clinton had been here before. His father, a British admiral, had served as governor of New York for a decade, and Henry's boyhood in New York had included a stint in the local militia before he'd returned to England, at nineteen, for a commission in the Coldstream Guards. The military life suited him and he prospered, serving gallantly in battle during the Seven Years' War and with distinction as an aide to two celebrated generals, until he was badly wounded in Germany in 1762. The stultifying heat in high-summer America would, he knew, aggravate that old scar.

Peace in 1763 brought an opportunity for an officer of ambition and high intellect to study military theory while visiting European battlefields and analyzing the generalship of Scipio, Marlborough, and other great captains. Clinton married for love, won a seat in Parliament in 1772 through the patronage of the Duke of Newcastle, a cousin, and was promoted to major general the same year. When his wife died after bearing five children in as many years, Clinton was as unhinged as his friend and fellow widower John Burgoyne would be a few years later.

The American war revived him. Placing his children with relatives, he arrived in Boston shortly after the shooting started and spent eighteen months as a subordinate to General Howe, demonstrating more tactical prowess than any other British general in the field. He had proposed seizing Dorchester Heights, in Boston, before Washington actually did it. He also argued for a flank attack at Bunker Hill rather than the calamitous frontal assault; successfully planned the British rout of rebel forces on Long Island; led the victory at Kip's Bay that resulted in New York's capture; and commanded the force that seized Newport and Narragansett Bay. Only at Charleston had he failed, after miscalculating the tenacity of the American defenses on Sullivan's Island.

As always with Clinton, insecurity, grievance, and a congenital lack of tact smudged his achievements. Given to morbid introspection and pessimism, he could be querulous, thin-skinned, and neurotic—or, as he preferred, "warm." One colleague considered him "inconstant as a weather-cock," and by the time he returned to England, in early 1777, he and Howe were hardly speaking.

Yet with few successful generals emerging from America, his star re-mained ascendant in London. He declined to campaign for command of the Canada Army, declaring that "Burgoyne knew better what to do and how to do it," then brooded at his own diffidence after seeing the coveted post given away. The government instead asked him to return to New York, again as Howe's deputy and potential successor. Among other credentials, Clinton's service in the last war and fluency in German made him popular with the Hessians, who called him "Klington."

He agreed but insisted on a "mark of royal approbation," which, he told a friend, was also "recompense for an injury already done me"; he still seethed at the halfhearted government support for his actions at Sullivan's Island. And so, in early April, after George III touched him with a sword at St. James's Palace and draped a red ribbon over his right shoulder, the newly knighted General Sir Henry Clinton kissed his sovereign's hand and once more boarded ship for America. "I am perfectly satisfied with your conduct," the king told him. "Leave your honor to me. It will be in good hands."

An avid violinist who had given performances in Boston during the occupation, Clinton carried several fiddles and bass viols in his baggage. The long voyage to New York had afforded him time to practice and to contemplate the task ahead. During a final conversation at Whitehall with Lord Germain, the American secretary had asserted that the rebels grew "less able every day." With the temerity that so vexed his superiors, Clinton replied, "Was, is, or will their inability be greater than ours? Certainly no." Nonetheless, he believed that the American cause was likely doomed un-less buttressed by foreign intervention, from the French or others.

The insurrectionists were said to be "deep into principles," and he con-sidered the British Army a poor blunt instrument for restoring the king's authority in such a political struggle. Perhaps Clinton's shrewdest insight was that this war required figuring out how "to gain the hearts & subdue the minds of America." Some four thousand British officers would serve here, but too many focused on simply thumping the rebels in battle with-out contemplating the political, economic, and geographic warp of the struggle. He also believed that London overstated loyalist strength and underrated how ardently the colonists intended to shape their own destiny, irrespective of an imperial government intent on subjugating its dependencies from India to the Ohio territory.

"Very sulkily I shall go," Clinton had written before leaving England, and sulky he was as he made his way through New York's streets, past haggling merchants and guttersnipe children and artisans in leather aprons, past the charred ruins of Trinity Church and clerks darting in and out of countinghouses, past lobsterback soldiers sweating in their red wool coats and makeshift jails chockablock with rebel prisoners. He was back where he had started his soldiering life more than three decades earlier, and back once again under the command, as Clinton would write, of "a man I neither esteem as an officer or a man."

General Sir William Howe, that very man, was waiting for him at No. 1 Broadway. His headquarters stood across from the Bowling Green, where only the stone plinth remained from an equestrian statue of King George pulled down a year earlier and melted into bullets by a frisky rebel mob following a public reading of the new Declaration of Independence. The grand house of yellowish brick and ornate cornices at No. 1 featured a Greek pediment and Palladian windows on the second floor. A massive front door opened to a wide foyer, a banquet hall, a staircase said to be "as grand as any in the city," and a parlor fifty feet long with grace notes of Dutch tile. The large garden out back ran along the cut-stone glacis of Fort George to the water's edge, offering a panoramic view of the bay.

Dark and thickset, Howe looked the part of an imperial viceroy. His siblings still called him "the Savage," from his roughhewn appearance after bitter combat in Canada during the last war. But now he cut "a fine figure, full six feet high and well proportioned," as an American diarist noted. "His manners were graceful and dignified." It was widely believed, with scant evidence, that he was cavorting in New York with Elizabeth Loring, the wife of a Boston loyalist who served as the British commissary of prisoners. One gossip insisted that Betsy Loring "is the very Cleopatra to this Antony of ours," and the loyalist Thomas Jones, a former provincial supreme court judge, claimed that Howe spent his days "feasting, gunning, banqueting, and in the arms of Mrs. Loring," when he was not nuzzling her at the faro table. Ignoring such calumny, Howe displayed devotion to his wife, Fanny, writing her letters up to twenty pages long so frequently that other officers' wives in England grew envious.

Otherwise he was famously taciturn. "It's the Howe fashion to be silent," a family friend explained. Those silences could irk his government. Lord Germain had complained several weeks earlier that Howe frustrated the American Department "by not communicating his ideas more frequently and more explicitly." Yet after nearly two years of command in America, Howe had little left to say. Before becoming commander in chief in 1775, he was among the least senior of 119 British generals considered candidates for the post; now he was among the most blooded. Despite his successes at Long Island, White Plains, and Fort Washington, it was whispered in some London drawing rooms that he was deliberately moderate in his warmaking out of sympathy for the rebels—a baffling canard to Americans whose men were bayoneted, whose women were raped, and whose towns were burned.

He had hoped to finish the war this year, but now had grave doubts despite commanding the greatest army Britain had ever sent overseas: forty-one thousand men scattered from Halifax to Florida, almost half of the king's land forces globally. Years of war had seared him, starting with the mortal wounding of his eldest brother, George, from French gunfire near Ticonderoga in 1758, and the deaths of 40 percent of his regimental comrades in 1762 at Havana, mostly from disease. More recently he had seen the abyss in the bloodbath at Bunker Hill and in rebel ferocity at Trenton. He no longer underestimated the complexity of this war, and he no longer was certain of his ability to win it.

"No man in the world can be more cautious than he is," his aide-de-camp had written in June, "which is unavoidably necessary in this cursed, cut-up land." Some subordinates found his generalship a mystifying sequence of delays, missed opportunities, faulty planning, and, again, long silences. "I readily concede that Howe is no Caesar," a *Jäger* captain would write, "but for an American war he is a good enough general." Yet Howe himself was unsure of that. "The war," he wrote Germain in early July, "is now upon a far different scale with respect to the increased power & strength of the enemy than it was last campaign." He suspected that nothing better could be wrenched from the Americans than "an equivocal neutrality." In America, he would tell Parliament, "the happiest commander will be he who escapes with the fewest blots." William Howe, perhaps more determined to avoid losing the war than to winning it, was trying to escape without more blots.

Howe and Clinton held three long conversations the next week, all too often shoving aside vital military questions to dwell on their personal grudges and mutual antipathy. "They raked over all their disagreements with the humorless candor of adolescents, while the fate of the war hung in the balance," wrote William Willcox, Clinton's biographer. Had Clinton at White Plains disparaged Howe's generalship, telling others that he "could not bear to serve" under him any longer? Well, yes, but why had Howe botched the landings at Frog's Neck, overextended his lines in New Jersey, and rudely criticized Clinton's command decisions in Rhode Island? Howe "feared it would be impossible for us to live together in that harmony so necessary for chiefs composing this army," Clinton recorded in a long memorandum, scratched out in a jagged hand made all the more indecipherable by his roiling emotions. "We never had agreed upon any single question. . . . By some cursed fatality we could never draw together." Just before the third and final conversation, he wrote the Duke of Newcastle, "I wish to go home and never desire to serve again."

But serve he must, and Clinton soon grasped how the war had grown more convoluted during his months in England. Admiral Howe, the general's elder brother, now commanded eighty fighting ships in North American waters, almost a third of the Royal Navy's total, plus a quarter of all British tars. Blockades of both Delaware and Chesapeake Bays had tightened, but without strangling American commerce. Since January, Admiral Howe's men-of-war had captured more than two hundred prizes, seizing cargoes ranging from indigo and tobacco to rum and ammunition. Yet along the vast seaboard, cruisers caught only an estimated one in nine American smugglers, and it was a rare day when the rebels failed to take at least one British merchantman in return.

Ashore the struggle was equally dire, despite insistent rumors that Washington had been killed, wounded, or captured, or had declared himself dictator with the title "Lord Protector." A British spy claimed that he "appeared much agitated in his countenance, was very incoherent in his discourse, his eyes sunk and dejected," and that his maid "frequently caught him in tears about the house." This was hardly credible, particularly since royal troops in just the first three months of the year had suffered nearly a thousand casualties inflicted by the incoherent, dejected, weepy American commander, with many more incapacitated by sickness.

The king himself encouraged amphibious raids against New England, and in late April eighteen hundred redcoats under Major General William Tryon, the former royal governor of New York, had descended on Danbury, Connecticut. They burned almost two hundred structures—houses, barns, mills, and churches—and the flames consumed five thousand barrels of flour and salt meat, five thousand pairs of shoes, and seventeen hundred tents. The American dead included Major General David Wooster, commander of the state militia, shot fatally through the groin.

But the day had turned with the arrival of the ubiquitous Benedict Arnold, who had been visiting his family in nearby New Haven before receiving the order to join Schuyler and the Northern Army. By the time the raiders had marched the more than twenty miles back to the coast, fighting for every yard, the rebel force had swelled to twenty-five hundred or more. Four bayonet charges were needed to hold the Americans at bay before Tryon's men could scramble back aboard their ships. General Arnold lost two horses to gunfire but was unscathed other than a bullet through his coat collar; the British put their losses at 172 dead and wounded, while claiming rebel casualties were more than twice that. "As the rascals are skulking about the whole country," a Scottish officer observed dryly, "it is impossible to move with any degree of safety without a pretty large escort."

Ambushes, firefights, and raids also plagued New Jersey, where British troops held only a toehold in the northeast corner of the state. In mid-June, Howe marched eighteen thousand men with a thousand wagons southwest, as if to cross the Delaware into Pennsylvania. Washington refused to take the bait, keeping his much smaller army on impregnable high ground in the Watchung Mountains, to the north. Howe loitered near Princeton for a week, ransacked a few dissident churches, burned a few farmhouses, then returned to Perth Amboy, on the coast, only to lunge again, this time to the northwest, in a vain effort to catch the Continentals off guard. Washington danced away, and Howe ordered his troops ferried two hundred yards across Arthur Kill to Staten Island, where they received an extra rum ration and were now encamped in a great arc, much as they had been a year earlier.

Another month of the fighting season had been squandered to no purpose. The armies were back almost to the same positions held in mid-November. "I can scarce hear a man speak on the subject but in passion or despair," wrote Ambrose Serle, Admiral Howe's secretary. Except for a small garrison at Paulus Hook, across the Hudson from lower Manhattan, all of New Jersey had been abandoned. Also forsaken were thousands of Jersey loyalists, who were filled with "mortification and resentment" at being left alone to fend off rebel retaliation, as one wrote. The withdrawal, he added, "made our brave fellows almost gnaw their own flesh out of rage."

The forfeiture of the New Jersey granary further stressed British logistics. "There is no dependence for supplies for the army from this continent," a commissary official in New York told London. Nearly all food, forage, and other provisions would have to continue crossing three thousand miles of open ocean. That required, at great expense, a substantial portion of the six thousand vessels in Britain involved in foreign trade, as well as Royal Navy protection against rebel buccaneers. The Treasury Board calculated that feeding 40,000 soldiers for the next year would take 7,300 tons of flour and 4,500 tons of salt meat, among other foodstuffs. Also, 4,000 army horses would consume 20,000 tons of hay and oats annually; Howe was told that 15,000 tons could be purchased in Rhode Island, but to date he had received barely a hundred. The frantic search for forage had "kept the army the whole winter in perpetual harassment," an officer reported.

Not since the time of the Romans had an expeditionary legion attempted such a stupendous supply effort. Too often shipments arrived like the barrels of bread recently received aboard the *Providence Increase*, a brigantine from Cork, the preeminent British supply depot for Atlantic operations. "The whole cargo appears to us to have been made of bad stuff," supply officers wrote, "weevil-eaten, full of maggots, moldy, musty & rotten & entirely unfit for men to eat." Contractors quibbled over a government request that they spend an extra sixpence to put a fourth iron hoop on each food cask to lessen leakage and spoiling. As partial compensation for such shabby fare, this spring Howe had also signed a contract with Mure, Son & Atkinson, merchants on Nicholas Lane in London, for 350,000 gallons of rum, to be shipped directly to the New York garrison from Jamaica.

Nothing chafed the fraying relationship between Howe and Clinton more than the question of how to fight the Americans in 1777. Since the previous November, Howe had proposed three successive plans, each quite different. His first scheme, intended "to finish the war in one year," would have attacked New England from Newport with ten thousand troops, sent another ten thousand up the Hudson to meet a royalist force marching south from Canada, and left fifteen thousand in New Jersey and New York to pin down Washington's army before swinging south in the winter.

Even before learning from London that only a fraction of the fifteen thousand reinforcements he requested would be available, Howe changed his mind. Pennsylvania loyalists persuaded him that capturing Philadelphia and its surrounding counties—said to be overwhelmingly supportive of the Crown—would end the rebellion by subduing the middle colonies rather than trying to cleave New England from its neighbors. Small garrisons would remain in New York and Rhode Island. With hardly a second thought, Howe had tossed aside the centerpiece of British strategy for the past two years.

In his third plan, dated April 2, Howe wrote, "I propose to invade Pennsylvania by sea, and from this arrangement must probably abandon the Jerseys." Marching overland from New York risked a devastating ambush at the Delaware, and resupplying his army across New Jersey was too precarious. By attacking Philadelphia from the south after an amphibious landing, he would force Washington to give battle in defense of the city.

"The defeat of the rebel regular army," he added, "is the surest road to peace." He regretted that shortages of dragoons, artillery, and campaign kit had so delayed his expedition that "my hopes of terminating the war this year are vanished." Moreover, he could offer "little assistance" to the Canada Army.

London endorsed each scheme in turn. "The king entirely approves of your proposed deviation from the plan which you formerly suggested," Germain wrote in March after receiving the second iteration. The proposal to attack by sea was also endorsed with little debate shortly after its receipt in May, although that confirmation would not reach Howe until late summer. Despite the commanding general's glum prediction of a protracted war, Germain hoped "this campaign will put an end to the unhappy contest." He also suggested that the army might complete its triumph in Philadelphia in time to turn north and assist Burgoyne before winter arrived, but he did not press the point. In none of the eight previous letters the American secretary sent to his commander in chief between early March and mid-April had he mentioned the Canada Army or the advance from Quebec into New York.

This muddle appalled Clinton. "I totally disapprove of the present plan of operations," he wrote Newcastle on July 11. "I have taken the liberty of saying so."

To Howe he predicted "the hazard of a miscarriage." A sea voyage to Philadelphia in summer would likely be impaired by contrary southerly winds and sickness in the ranks. "The time of year is bad," he warned. Better to wait until cooler weather before going south. Far better to sail upriver now, cuff aside rebel defenders in the Hudson Highlands, and join hands with Burgoyne in Albany. Otherwise British forces would be fragmented, allowing the Americans to concentrate where they pleased, against Burgoyne, or Howe, or the isolated garrisons at Newport or New York. The king's forces would be on the defensive, and "no rebellion could be quelled by armies on the defensive." Threatening Philadelphia was unlikely to force Washington into giving battle against the king's army. The American commander would be "a fool if he did," Clinton insisted, and an occupation of the city would immobilize Howe's army, precluding assistance to Burgoyne. When Howe asserted that Pennsylvania loyalists were tired of war and ready for a reconciliation, Clinton indelicately observed that Howe had "thought the same of Jersey" before the Trenton debacle.

Round and round they went. Clinton acknowledged that his arguments were "repeated perhaps oftener than was agreeable." Howe shrugged and parried and refused to budge.

On July 14 American deserters confirmed rumors that Ticonderoga had fallen; additional reports in the coming days suggested that the Canada Army was well on its way to Albany. "The strength of General Burgoyne's army," Howe wrote Germain, "is such as to leave no room to dread the event." He would proceed toward Philadelphia, leaving Clinton in New York with seven thousand men, mostly German and provincial troops but surely sufficient to defend the city.

Clinton's pessimism now spiraled into despondence. The fortifications around New York extended for a hundred miles, giving him an average of one defender for every twenty-five yards—hardly an invincible force if Washington chose to "murder us," and certainly insufficient to help Burgoyne if necessary. Glum news from Newport underscored his vulnerability: forty-four rebel raiders in five whaleboats, led by Lieutenant Colonel William Barton, a former Providence hatmaker, had snatched Major General Richard Prescott, the British commander in Rhode Island, from his bed early on July 11 without a shot fired, despite thirty-five hundred redcoats and a Royal Navy squadron in the vicinity. Prescott was quoted as pleading with his captors, "For God's sake, let me get my clothes."

"Liable to General Howe's caprices, I serve in dread," Clinton wrote his family in England on July 15. The commander in chief's plans seemed built on "false principles," including his baffling desire to have the entire Continental Army confront Burgoyne in the Hudson Valley, on the premise that Washington would be unable to provision his troops there through the harsh winter. How a besieged Burgoyne was supposed to do so was unclear. "I almost doubt," Clinton told General Harvey, the adjutant general in London, "whether the northern army will penetrate as far as Albany."

Determined to stay busy, Clinton inspected British defenses from the Narrows and Staten Island to King's Bridge, on the northern tip of Manhattan. He placed his headquarters in the nineteen-room Roger Morris mansion above Harlem, where Washington had lived for five weeks in the fall. There, gazing at the lovely vistas of the Hudson, Harlem, and East Rivers, he was struck by an epiphany: Howe had designed an elaborate ruse. The expedition to Philadelphia was only a deception to confuse the enemy, a feint to the south before he pivoted upriver to merge his army with Burgoyne's, the proper and obvious military course.

Pulling out quill, ink, and paper, Clinton scratched an urgent note, certain that he had smoked out Howe's clever stratagem. "As second in command I should not suppose you meant to deceive me," he wrote. "You nevertheless do mean to deceive us all. . . . You will go up the North River to the Highlands. You can mean nothing else." Howe's reply came quickly.

"If I was ever so much inclined, I could not do so," he answered. "For I have sent my plan home, and it has been approved."

Dumbfounded, Clinton eventually sent General Harvey an appropriate postscript: "Should I serve with him twenty years, I fear we shall not agree."

On July 16 General Howe hosted a dinner for his senior officers in a tavern near No. 1 Broadway. Fifty-six men sat at a long table, drinking toasts to the king, to the empire, and to their imminent journey, although, as Captain William Dansey of the 33rd Foot wrote his wife, "Where we are going to, Lord knows." Some suspected a move up the Hudson; others guessed New England, Savannah, or Charleston. "Everything is secret & mysterious," a loyalist volunteer reflected. The Howe brothers had recruited ship pilots for nearly every segment of the Atlantic coast to further obscure their destination. A few anticipated Philadelphia, but as Major Charles Stuart wrote his father, Lord Bute, a former prime minister, "What our chiefs think to gain by possessing that town, I cannot judge."

That evening, Howe's battle staff boarded the *Britannia*, a former East India brig featuring lacquered white staterooms with mahogany paneling and large green portholes. The commanding general joined his brother aboard the flagship *Eagle*, a sixty-four-gun warship anchored in the lee of Staten Island amid a congregation of more than two hundred other vessels. Each of the king's warships saluted the Howes by manning the yards—several thousand Jack Tars perched like seabirds on the spars—and then roaring out three cheers. *Eagle* alone carried forty-one pilots to confound any spy trying to guess her destination.

For more than a week troops had been shuttled to their transports from four ferry landings on Staten Island. As ordered, each regiment struck its tents, delivered all baggage to the beach for loading into long-boats, then formed snaking queues to await embarkation. Manifests listed twenty-seven British and eight German regiments—the rank-and-file strength of each ranged from 256 to 565 men—plus light dragoons, 550 artillerymen, four pioneer companies, British and German riflemen, loyalist units, staff officers, servants, and camp followers. The July sun brightened the distinctive uniform facings of each redcoat foot regiment: philamot yellow, pale yellow, deep yellow, gosling green, willow green, popinjay green, purple.

Twenty-three brigs, schooners, and sloops had stalls fitted to carry nearly a thousand horses. Flatboats capable of landing six thousand men in shallow water were stowed with "the greatest care," as instructed, and every regiment was permitted four heavy wagons. Each man-of-war shipped three hundred rounds per gun, each transport carried three months' provisions, and each British and Hessian regiment could purchase three pipes of Madeira—almost four hundred gallons—at Wills's Wharf for £28 each, payment on delivery. Several tons of medical supplies were hoisted into the ships' holds, including 172 medications—camphor, Peruvian bark, ipecac, packets of James's Powders—plus thirty-six dozen lancets, six dozen stump caps for amputees, and twenty-four sets of trepanning instruments. Final letters home were collected in sacks for a Royal Mail packet boat bound for England.

Red, white, yellow, blue, and striped signal pendants flew from various masts and yardarms, summoning adjutants, brigade majors, and other officers for conferences or orders. On July 19, *Eagle* hoisted a signal to set sail, but the wind died and the anchors fell with a dejected splash. Day followed night followed day. Fresh provisions dwindled. "No one seems to be able to figure out why we are waiting here so long," a general's aide wrote. The sun hammered each weather deck, and the stink of unwashed men, their hair pomaded with hog's lard, rose from every hold. "Never shall I forget the stench emanating from so many filthy heads crowded together in the low rooms," an officer later recalled. Captain James Murray of the 57th Foot had spoken for many in telling his sister, "The only blessing which indulgent heaven has granted as a recompense for all the hardships of a military life is a total exemption from the necessity of thinking."

For several days the vessels caught just enough air to slide through the Narrows to the anchorage at Sandy Hook, outside the bay. But the wind came foul again, and then the tide was spent, and a harsh storm blew through. Finally the weather faired, and at six-thirty a.m. on Wednesday, July 23, the order came to crowd on sail. Rebel sentinels stared agog from the high ground above the New Jersey coast as sailors shuffled onto the yards to unfurl their canvas and strained at the capstans to weigh anchor. Like a thing alive, the fleet began to move, among the greatest fleets ever seen in American waters, 280 vessels led by the frigate *Liverpool*. Then came *Eagle*, then a multitude of victuallers and hospital ships, transports carrying horses, and transports carrying eighteen thousand men. Three additional warships bracketed each flank, followed astern by the sixty-four-gun *Nonsuch*, the fireship *Vulcan*, and four row galleys. A British officer found the sight "undescribably noble."

As he watched the armada beat for the open sea, a man left behind with his demons scribbled a letter to an army friend in England. "It bears heavy on Burgoyne," wrote Henry Clinton. "If this campaign does not finish the war, I prophesy that there is an end of British dominion in America."

Just as Clinton had predicted earlier in the month, the short voyage south was miserable, beset for a week with contrary winds and stifling heat. "I don't know whether there be anything new upon the face of the earth," Captain Murray wrote his sister, "but I am very sure there is nothing new upon the face of the water." In dense fogs, Admiral Howe ordered signal guns fired every half hour to keep the fleet formation intact. When thunderstorms approached, he ordered the ships dispersed to avoid collisions. "The transports with the poor soldiers were tossed about exceedingly & exposed at times to much danger in running afoul of each other," wrote Serle, the admiral's secretary. A passenger aboard the brig *Edward*, which departed New York in a convoy for England at the same time the fleet sailed, described spiteful weather in Long Island Sound:

> The sea a-roaring, the ship a-rolling, the rigging breaking, the masts a-bending, the sail a-rattling, the captain swearing, the sailors grumbling, the boys a-crying, the hogs a-grunting, the dog a-barking, the pots and glasses breaking . . . I am confoundedly sick.

One hundred and fifty miles south of Sandy Hook, just off Cape Henlopen at the mouth of Delaware Bay, Captain Andrew Snape Hamond had been on station since April aboard the frigate *Roebuck*, in command of a small squadron trying to deter smugglers. The son of a London merchant, Hamond occasionally sent armed marines ashore to buy cattle and other provisions with counterfeit Continental currency. Three months in the bay had worn both ships and crews. The *Thames* alone, patrolling near Cape May, had a sick captain and forty-nine sick sailors, including a dozen reportedly "now in a dying state"; sixteen others had died since the frigate took station. Such losses deepened Captain Hamond's contempt for the Americans. "They seem to place their entire dependence on their being able to hold out longer than we can," he had written. "They are daily practicing every kind of art, treachery, & cruelty to destroy us."

Shortly after dawn on Wednesday, July 30, the dull tedium of blockade duty was dispelled by the abrupt appearance from the southeast of several hundred ships, including men-of-war flying the Royal Navy's white ensign. At ten a.m., summoned by signal flag to *Eagle*, Hamond climbed to the flagship's quarterdeck and was escorted below to a compact cabin, made to seem larger and brighter with white walls, mirrors, gold skirt boards, and copper engravings. The Howe brothers, dark and regal in their uniforms, wasted no time in requesting "every information collected respecting General Washington's army" and the state of rebel defenses along the Delaware River south of Philadelphia.

Relying on information received the previous day "from persons who had never deceived me," Hamond reported that the Continental Army had crossed the Delaware and was marching toward Wilmington, thirty miles southwest of Philadelphia. Rebel river defenses were "strong," with fifty vessels or more, including row galleys and xebecs, at Darby, at Mud Creek, and in the mouth of the Schuylkill River. Travel on the Delaware could be exacting—"I do not know of any river so difficult of navigation," Hamond would later assert—because of shifting channels, mud banks, and a $3^1/_2$-knot tidal run. Even so, he believed a landing was possible at New Castle, six miles below Wilmington, or farther south at Reedy Island. Philadelphia's negligible defenses to the south and west, away from the Delaware, would be no match for an army attacking the city's landward flank. With a brisk northeast wind now blowing, he noted, "a finer opportunity of running up the river never offered."

General Howe listened intently, his face inscrutable as usual, before sharply disagreeing. "Great opposition" must be expected at Wilmington or New Castle, he said. Rebel fire rafts and small attack vessels on the narrow Delaware could "do great damage among the transports," making the attempt "extremely hazardous." Troops advancing on causeways across marshy, malarial Reedy Island could be cut down by enemy fire from the riverbank.

Asking Hamond to remain in the cabin, the admiral steered his brother into the stern gallery—a windowed balcony overhanging the water—for a private, nose-to-nose conversation. When they returned, General Howe announced that he was determined to land his army in Maryland "at Head of the Elk in the Chesapeake," a few miles east of where the Susquehanna River emptied into that bay. Troops could come ashore there "without any molestation," and horses would recover from the sea voyage in safety before the expedition moved on. The Americans "no doubt" knew his intent to capture Philadelphia, he added, and this deviation would surprise them.

Certainly this plan surprised Captain Hamond. He swallowed his astonishment and pointed out "the great length of time it would take to make such a detour with so large a fleet." They would have to sail 130 miles southwest just to enter the Chesapeake at Cape Charles, Virginia, then another 200 miles north to Head of Elk, which still lay 50 miles from Philadelphia.

The bay, the largest estuary in North America, with an intricate, eleven-thousand-mile coastline, could also be "most hazardous." Narrowing in places to less than three miles, it had an average depth of only twenty-one feet. A quarter of the bay was less than six feet deep.

Hamond's surprise only grew when Admiral Howe took him aside and confidentially disclosed that "the general's wishes and intentions were first to destroy the magazines at York and Carlisle before he attacked the rebel army or looked towards Philadelphia." Those strongholds, more than a hundred miles west of Philadelphia, would require a forced march across almost half of Pennsylvania.

An army quartermaster was summoned and asked about "the state of the forage" still available on the horse transports. Enough for fourteen days, he answered. Hamond thought that the admiral seemed ready to force the Delaware, but his brother dug in his heels, declaring that he had been "from the beginning for making the landing in Chesapeake Bay." Hamond was surprised yet again to learn that none of the forty-one pilots reportedly aboard *Eagle* knew the Chesapeake north of Annapolis well enough to guide the army ashore with confidence. Having often sailed those waters, he offered to buoy the channels and steer clear of shoal water. That offer was promptly accepted. Another riotous flutter of signal flags alerted the fleet: prepare to sail.

A decision had been made, but it was predicated on flawed intelligence, as the historian Michael C. Harris would write. Hamond's information was fundamentally incorrect. Washington was *not* marching toward Wilmington. He and his army remained a hundred miles north, thoroughly baffled about where the king's men had gone. The shore defenses on the Delaware below Philadelphia were badly undermanned, with barely two hundred militiamen at two of the forts, none at a third, and no gunners yet assigned to the city's floating batteries.

A signal gun barked from the *Eagle*. Rebel lookouts squinting through their telescopes atop the octagonal seventy-foot Cape Henlopen lighthouse gazed with mouths agape as a thousand white sails billowed. The fleet wheeled about in a languid turn and made for the southern horizon. By four p.m. every ship had vanished into the summer haze.

William Howe chose not to inform London of this diversion, since the government was perfectly aware that Philadelphia was his ultimate goal. Not for another two months and six days would the king and his ministers hear from their field commander. Most of the troops, once again sweltering in the pitching holds, also remained ignorant of their new destination. "His Excellency General Howe is very secretive about his undertakings," a Hessian officer wrote his family.

Those who knew could hardly be happy. "The hearts of all men were struck with this business, everyone apprehending the worst," Secretary Serle told his journal. "We are bound to the Chesapeake. . . . May God defend us from the fatality of the worst climate in America at this worst season of the year to experience it. I can write no more. My heart is full."

3.

———

Fellows Willing to Go to Heaven

B y midmorning even the shaded woodlands above the pretty creek had grown "melting hot," in one description, and "like the breath of an oven," in another. Local farmers agreed that not for a generation had a warmer August been felt in Bucks County, twenty miles north of Philadelphia. Goldenrod and orange jewelweed wilted in the heat, and flotillas of fallen leaves from the black walnuts and Norway maples swept downstream past soldiers scrubbing themselves in the tannic riffles with the five ounces of lye soap issued to each man. Acrid smoke from green firewood hung over the wetlands, and the ring of felling axes echoed against Carr's Hill, where eleven thousand men from the Continental Army had pitched their tents a week earlier to await the reappearance of their vanished enemy.

For more than a month the Americans had marched this way and that after leaving their winter quarters in Morristown, New Jersey, accomplishing little, as one critic grumbled, except "to wear out stockings, shoes, and breeches." Intelligence that General Howe intended to sail up the Hudson sent the Americans chuffing north toward West Point, only to reverse course upon learning that the British fleet had instead sailed south. Each day gallopers on lathered horses with heaving flanks and flaring nostrils arrived carrying news of enemy sightings off the Jersey coast. "They keep our imaginations constantly in the field of conjecture," General Washington admitted.

A report of the fleet dropping anchor near Cape Henlopen sent the army pelting westward across the Delaware in such haste that men drowned, horses collapsed from the heat, and wagons lost wheels or broke axles. No sooner had the army swung south toward Germantown, six miles above Philadelphia, than another messenger brought news of the fleet leaving Delaware Bay. Guessing that the Howes had again sailed north, perhaps to attack New England or to join Burgoyne, Washington put his men in motion back toward northern New Jersey. "Marching and counter-marching," an officer complained, "and often not knowing which."

"We are yet entirely in the dark as to the destination of the enemy," Washington told a subordinate on August 7. "The fleet has neither been seen or heard of since they left the capes of the Delaware." At nine p.m. on August 10, with the exhausted army resting for the night along Little Ne-shaminy Creek before crossing into New Jersey, an urgent message from Congress reported that the British finally had been spotted sailing south, fifty miles below Cape Henlopen. Frustrated and confused, Washington ordered his troops to hold here until the enemy's course became clear. "I am now as much puzzled about their designs as I was before," he wrote, "being unable to account upon any plausible plan for General Howe's con-duct."

A week passed without further march orders, then most of another week. The footsore army regained its swank and the camp took on a settled look, with musket racks, kitchen tents, and bake ovens. Sentries stood grass-guard to watch the horses grazing in the fens. Farmwives from the nearby hamlet called Cross Roads brought fresh vegetables for sale, and slaughter pens were built away from the creek, with pits for the butchered cattle and hog carcasses. Each regiment dug its latrine vaults at a remove behind the tents, but a stench hung in the torrid woods and the army could be smelled long before it was seen. Sunstroke, dysentery, and other afflic-tions killed a few men; they were interred in a Presbyterian churchyard half a mile upstream, their graves marked by common stones without in-scriptions.

Martial noises filled the camp, from the reveille cannon at dawn to the hammering of armorers at their forges repairing broken muskets and the incessant *tap, tap, tap* of knappers chipping blocks of chert to make gun flints. Boxwood fifes squealed, and boys with heavy sticks pounded their sheepskin drumheads in a sound one officer described as "forcibly grand." When musicians finished practicing their camp and duty calls, they enter-tained the troops with jigs, reels, and a tune called "God Save the Con-gress." To prevent promiscuous firing, muskets by order were to remain unloaded "until we are close to the enemy and there is a moral certainty of engaging them." Still, occasional gunshots rang out, and a Virginia officer was slightly wounded when an accidental discharge "struck the lower part of his testicles, I think but skin-deep," a soldier recorded. "I hope he will soon get well without damage to his reputation."

"We have the most respectable body of Continental troops," Brigadier General Henry Knox, the army's artillery chief, wrote his wife, Lucy, at home in Boston. "Hardy, brave fellows who are as willing to go to heaven by the way of a bayonet or sword as any other mode." Elijahs, Solomons, Ephraims, and Jacobs filled the ranks, as well as one Hate-evil, a private in the 6th Massachusetts who, despite his pious name, would be convicted of theft and sentenced to receive "one hundred lashes on his bare back, well laid on." This biblical multitude included, according to an enumeration by John Adams, "Roman Catholics, English Episcopalians, Scotch and American Presbyterians, Methodists, Moravians, Anabaptists, German Lutherans, German Calvinists, Universalists, Arians, Priestleyans, Socinians, Independents, Congregationalists, Horse Protestants and House Protestants, deists and atheists."

Knox and his fellow generals wore rank sashes across their chests. Hat cockades denoted the ranks of lesser officers by color, while sergeants and corporals wore red and green cloth swatches, respectively, on their right shoulders. A few units looked smart, like the light dragoons who rode dapple-gray mounts and covered their pistol holsters with black bearskin. But they were the exception. "The troops are barefooted, bare-legged, and almost bare-assed," a Connecticut colonel wrote on August 12, and a Rhode Island officer advised his governor that civilians along the line of march had dubbed his troops "the ragged, lousy, naked regiment." Shoes remained scarce, and Washington had recently complained to his clothier general that a shipment of five thousand pairs were "good for nothing. They are thin French pumps that tear to pieces whenever they get wet." So many men needed shoes, he added, that "if we had 50,000 pair it would not be too many."

As they formed ranks to practice the manual of arms, some wore fringed linen hunting shirts, dyed yellow, brown, black, or purple. Others turned out in blue coveralls or buckskin breeches laced tight in the back, with coats of a decidedly civilian cut, described as "light-colored, snuff-colored, dark serge, dark drab, brown broadcloth, and blue sagathy." Hats might be round, felt, wool, beaver, slouched, or cocked. One dragoon officer outfitted his soldiers in scarlet coats captured from a British transport, until Washington warned that "our people will be destroying themselves" in fratricidal gunplay; the men were ordered to cover the coats under brown smocks.

Knox, a bulky, twenty-seven-year-old former Boston bookseller, had won Washington's confidence with his leadership moxie and aptitude for gunnery, not to mention his remarkable feat eighteen months earlier in transporting British cannons captured at Ticonderoga to Boston, forcing the enemy to abandon the city. "We are well supplied with arms and ammunition," Knox wrote Lucy. "But—I am sorry to say it—we seem to be increasing most rapidly in impiety. . . . This is a bad omen." Despite orders prohibiting blasphemy, the troops "are remarkably expert in swearing ways," an army doctor agreed. A chaplain's department had been formed in May in hopes that militant men of the cloth could "suppress the horrid sins of cursing, swearing, and other vices," while instilling the spirit of Jeremiah: "Cursed be he that keepeth back his sword from blood." Congress had also planned to print thirty thousand Bibles to encourage rank-and-file godliness, until the cost of paper and binding quashed the project.

For now the army would enforce discipline and piety with brute force. Officers periodically assembled the men to hear the articles of war read aloud, all 102 of them, including sixteen capital offenses, such as plundering or striking a superior officer. At Washington's insistence, Congress had raised the maximum number of lashes to be administered for misdemeanors from thirty-nine to one hundred. A whipping post, dubbed "the adjutant's daughter," was erected across York Road near the stone bridge spanning the Neshaminy, and frequent courts-martial guaranteed that she stayed busy. Americans had 225 expressions for drunkenness, according to a glossary compiled by Benjamin Franklin, and all too many soldiers were found jagged, jambled, juicy, fishy, catching the cat, or going to Jerusalem by imbibing wring-jaw cider or stinking whiskey—known as "the creature"—still warm from the still.

Through "a signal act of mercy," Washington pardoned seventeen dragoons convicted of mutiny or desertion—capital offenses—in exchange for "a full return of fidelity, submission, and obedience." But he let stand the conviction of a quartermaster charged with stealing his colonel's horse. The defendant, with his coat turned inside out, was led around his jeering regiment while sitting backward on a nag. Drummer boys and tootling fifers played "The Rogue's March" to escort him from camp and out of the army's sight, forever.

The merciful George Washington occupied a two-story, shingle-roofed farmhouse perched a hundred paces up from the Little Neshaminy. The summer retreat of a Philadelphia widow, the brown stone house with brown shutters had two chambers on the first floor, now crowded with sweating aides and staff officers. A small room adjacent to the kitchen served as the commander in chief's office. A window faced the creek, providing Washington with the water view he cherished, whether in the grand panorama of the Potomac at Mount Vernon or the bucolic vistas from the headquarters he had occupied in Cambridge and New York.

Twenty-six months in command had etched furrows in his brow and crow's-feet around his slate-blue eyes. Gray streaked his hair, and long days in the saddle this summer had bronzed his face, obscuring the faint small-pox scars, noticeable only with the sort of close inspection that he hardly encouraged. Now forty-five, he remained as physically imposing as ever in his brushed blue coat with buff facings, towering over most men with a commanding presence that made it possible to "distinguish him to be a general from among 10,000 people," as the physician Benjamin Rush declared. Admirers sought to excel one another with encomiums and laudatory descriptions of His Excellency, as he was known. "He is well-made and exactly proportioned, his physiognomy mild and agreeable," a French officer would write. "He has neither a grave nor a familiar air. His brow is sometimes marked with thought, but never with inquietude." A family friend who had seen him at Morristown during the winter described casual moments when "General Washington throws off the hero and takes on the chatty, agreeable companion. He can be downright impudent sometimes." Chaplain Israel Evans allowed that simply seeing Washington bolstered his courage. He prayed for legions of angels to safeguard him.

Some worried that he had grown too large, too elevated for a nascent republic. John Adams regretted the "superstitious veneration" accorded Washington by many of his fellow congressmen. A toast now heard at banquet tables—"God save great Washington"—carried deplorable royalist overtones. "We can allow a certain citizen to be wise, virtuous, and good without thinking him a deity or a savior," Adams wrote to his wife, Abigail. Others noted the ferocious temper lurking beneath Washington's normally placid countenance; as Thomas Jefferson observed, he could be "most tremendous in his wrath."

"I never see that man laugh to show his teeth," recalled a Mount Vernon slave, among nearly six hundred who would toil at the plantation during the master's lifetime. "He done all his laughing inside." Twenty years of dental miseries kept Washington tight-lipped; he would eventually wear dentures made out of cow and human teeth—some of the latter purchased from the enslaved—as well as from elephant and hippo ivory set in a lead frame. Although remote and occasionally dour, he had an earthy sense of humor, enjoying the company of certain scapegraces as well as attractive women. "It is assuredly better to go laughing than crying thro' the rough journey of life," he would tell an old friend after the war.

No one doubted that his journey now was exacting. "The weight of the whole war may justly be said to lay upon his shoulders," Lieutenant Colonel Tench Tilghman, among the thirty-two aides who would serve the commanding general, had written his father a few months earlier. He could strike a necessary pose, as both the hardened commander and the peaceable civilian whose beloved husbandry had been interrupted, alas, by his nation's call to arms. Each day, each hour seemed to bring alarms, startlements, jolts. He was confounded by the loss of Ticonderoga, "an event of chagrin & surprise not apprehended, nor within the compass of my reasoning," as he had written General Schuyler. "This stroke is severe indeed, and has distressed us much." There was nothing for it but to soldier on, he told Schuyler. "Our situation before has been unpromising and has changed for the better, so, I trust, it will again."

Washington could be impenetrably reserved and opaque. One portraitist noted his "remarkable dead eye" when he chose to hide the inner man or discourage familiarity. Yet his virtues were transparent. From his officers, as from himself, he expected courage, virtue, and "a defense of all that is dear & valuable in life"—the American cause being foremost. Jefferson believed that his mind was "slow in operation, being aided little by invention or imagination, but sure in conclusion." Since July 1775, when he took command, his generalship had been a medley of misfortune and miscalculation—at Long Island, Kip's Bay, and Fort Washington—along with bold aggression at Dorchester Heights, Trenton, and Princeton. Good luck attended him, in providential fogs, stumbling enemies, and bullets that barely missed. John Adams conceded that his "great, manly, warlike virtues" reassured the public, as did his rectitude and readiness to sacrifice self-interest for a greater good.

"For attention to business, perhaps he has no equal," his adjutant general, Colonel Timothy Pickering, concluded. An adhesive memory, a passion for details, and a mind organized for executive action served him and his army well. Washington had once taken fencing lessons to become more nimble; generalship kept him nimble intellectually, able to handle complex tasks simultaneously, from supply and recruitment minutiae to tactical dispositions, strategic planning, and a correspondence, mostly with subordinates and his political masters, now averaging three hundred letters a month. His constitution, like his will, seemed built from iron. Other than occasional intestinal distress and infrequent touches of malaria, he remained robust and durable.

Like most mortals, he craved admiration and affirmation. To Governor Patrick Henry of Virginia he had written that every officer ought to have "the character of a gentleman, a proper sense of honor, and some reputation to lose." That reputation, which was paramount to Washington, still hung in the balance. From the day of his appointment by Congress, two years earlier, he had recognized that his "abilities & military experience may not be equal to the extensive & important trust" placed in him, without fully anticipating quite how perilous his task would be. As he had recently confided to his stepson, John Parke Custis, "I do not think that any officer since the creation ever had such a variety of difficulties & perplexities to encounter as I have."

Washington would use more than a hundred names for a supreme being, as tallied by later scholars. He often invoked Providence, less frequently God, and almost never Jesus Christ, although he wanted each man to act like "a Christian soldier." In acknowledging "the uncertainty of human things," he sometimes echoed the classical Stoics, notably Seneca, a first-century Roman who advised, "It is a rough road that leads to the heights of greatness."

The road had surely been rough for these two years, with some five hundred military and naval engagements, and more than eight thousand American casualties. American ambitions had changed markedly since Lexington and Concord, from a demand to be fully British in rights and privileges to not being British at all but, rather, a free, independent people. What form this new entity should take was still uncertain, as seen in the many metaphors used to describe the United States: a flight of birds, a flock of sheep, a swarm of fish, or, as depicted on the Continental six-dollar bill, a beaver gnawing down a large tree. Some Americans thought of themselves as an alligator, a wildcat, a swarm of angry hornets, or a coiled rattlesnake. Loyalists suggested that the insurgency instead resembled a mongrel dog, a long-eared ass, or a zebra with thirteen stripes, each named for a state, with troublesome Massachusetts at the rump.

Whatever the nation would become, the army must be the transformational agent in the ascent from colonial backwater to sovereign power. Rebellion still streamed from a thousand pulpits and a hundred printing presses, but precisely how to convert that defiance into a war-winning military philosophy remained elusive. This was the essence of Washington's mission. When he later ordered busts of prominent generals to decorate Mount Vernon, he chose the likes of Alexander the Great and Julius Caesar, audacious, risk-taking commanders celebrated for their battlefield brio. Yet these two years of combat had forced him to restrain his intrinsic, swashbuckling aggression and to move with unwonted caution.

His Excellency now believed that the struggle was existential, not only for the United States but also for Britain. "Her very existence as a nation depends now upon her success," he had written a friend in April. "For should America rise triumphant in her struggle for independency, she must fall." That made the enemy all the more dangerous: this would be a fight to the death. He also knew that his generalship must be as politically savvy as it was militarily sound; hence those hundreds of letters to Congress, state officials, committees of safety, and others vital to shoring up the cause and supporting the army.

He would continue to watch for opportunities to give the foe "a fatal stab" in a titanic, decisive battle that settled all. But stinging defeats by a better-equipped, better-disciplined adversary had revealed the necessity of defensive war—bobbing, weaving, retreating. "We should on all occasions avoid a general action, or put anything to the risk unless compelled by a necessity into which we ought never to be drawn," Washington had advised Congress in September. His intention was to bleed the British, to corrode their will in America and at home, "to take advantage of favorable opportunities, and waste and defeat the enemy by piecemeal," as described by his new aide, Lieutenant Colonel Alexander Hamilton, a twenty-two-year-old artillery officer who considered himself field marshal material. To sustain this patient, protracted way of war, Washington told Congress in December, "let us have a respectable army, and such as will be competent to every contingency."

Of roughly two hundred thousand American men who would bear arms in the patriot cause, about half served in the Continental Army and half in militia regiments manned by part-time citizen soldiers. More than seven hundred skirmishes during the war would be fought by militiamen alone. They also gathered intelligence, set ambushes, guarded prisoners, and served as a partisan constabulary, intimidating Crown loyalists and coercing the uncommitted.

Washington never stopped carping about the militia, which he considered unreliable and poorly trained, with officers often pulled from "the lowest class of people, and instead of setting a good example to their men are leading them into every kind of mischief." But he had grudgingly come to acknowledge that militia regiments were "more than competent to all the purposes of defensive war." This month he would even praise their "spirit and fortitude." Defeating the British Empire, however, required a professional, permanent army, competent indeed to every contingency. Building such an insuperable force continued to occupy his every waking hour on the Little Neshaminy.

Nudged by the commander in chief, Congress had finally set aside its fears that a standing army would become a tool of tyranny. Men who enlisted for three years or the duration would receive a twenty-dollar bounty and a hundred acres of frontier land if they survived the war. As many as 110 regiments could be formed, plus artillery, cavalry, and support units, providing a force of at least seventy-six thousand men. Exclusive of the small Northern Army under Schuyler, Washington had reorganized his "main army" into ten brigades, each with four or five regiments and, ostensibly, with 738 officers and men in each regiment. Two brigades made up a division.

This neat construct proved a pipe dream. Ranks had been so slow to fill this summer that enlistees were said by one congressman to "take the field tardily, as if they were going to be hanged." Although a military manual suggested that recruits should be seventeen to twenty-five years old and free of "ruptures, scald heads, convulsion fits, or other extraordinary complaints," recruiters were rarely so selective. Yet regiments typically mustered at half strength. Only thirty-five thousand Continentals would serve in 1777, a number that declined in subsequent years. Of 2.5 million Americans, only about half a million were not women, enslaved, infirm, inveterate loyalists, or outside a reasonable military age—a modest pool from which to build a mighty host year after year.

Moreover, this was an altered army. Rabid enthusiasm for the cause had faded since 1775, when the ranks had been filled with propertied freeholders and tradesmen. Many soldiers had returned to their farms, tanneries, shops, or countinghouses. Some hoped to make money from the war or to find quick riches on a privateer. Others had families they could no longer ignore. Few from their ilk would commit to three years in uniform. "I am very mad," John Adams wrote Abigail in April. "The gloomy cowardice of the times is intolerable."

Instead the army increasingly derived from the landless young, the poor, the desperate, and sometimes the shiftless. These ranks included unemployed laborers, apprentices, farmhands, servants, drifters, and recent immigrants, notably Irish Protestants driven to America by crop failures and the collapse of the weaving industry. Fewer than one in five enlistees was married. None would get rich on a private's $6.66 monthly salary or the $9 a sergeant earned, but for many the bonus paid was the most cash they had ever held in hand. Of almost ninety thousand Continental veterans who would file pension applications long after the war, few claimed to have enlisted out of patriotic zeal. Although most were patriots by political affiliation, the need for a modest income and a hope for personal betterment now motivated men more than ideology or contempt for overbearing Britain.

Several New England states this year began resorting to conscription, sometimes with names drawn from a hat. But they also permitted the hiring of substitutes for Continental service or buying exemption with a fine. In New Jersey, drafted masters enrolled slaves or indentured servants in their stead, and as many as 40 percent of the state's Continental soldiers were substitutes. One New Jersey officer described new soldiers as "mostly foreigners" with "no attachment to the country except what accrues from the emoluments of the service." Maryland would soon force vagrants into the ranks, and also offer pardons to loyalists "that were arrested or hereafter shall be arrested," in exchange for a three-year enlistment. A Boston barber who was drafted cursed his bad luck and told his two apprentices, "If either of you had the spunk of a louse, you would offer to go for me."

Still, the numbers fell short, far short. All nine North Carolina regiments had joined the main army in July, but instead of 7,000 authorized men, they collectively included only 131 officers and 963 enlisted troops. With Manhattan and Long Island in British hands, New York reduced its regiments from seven to five. The 2nd Maryland mustered 147 men—less than a quarter of its nominal strength—plus four officers, three of them lieutenants; the rest had resigned in a dispute over rank. Washington's native Virginia, the largest state, sent a dozen regiments to the army but with barely 2,500 soldiers fit for duty, one-fourth the requested total. "Enlistments go badly," Governor Henry admitted. "Indeed they are almost stopped."

Desertion made things worse, despite a prodigal use of the adjutant's daughter and occasional firing squads. Washington had studied Frederick the Great's *Instructions for His Generals*, which offered a dozen tips for thwarting deserters, including frequent roll calls and doubling the number of sentries at dusk. Congress offered five dollars for each absconder arrested, and Delaware's sole regiment ordered all desertion courts-martial moved to the head of the docket "that they may be punished as soon as possible." "Our army is shamefully reduced by desertion," Washington wrote John Hancock, president of the Congress. "We shall be obliged to detach one-half of the army to bring back the other."

For officers, the army remained a place to obtain station and status, especially for those of humble birth. Ambitious, capable men with a knack for leading other men could ascend, such as the Rhode Island anchorsmith Nathanael Greene, the Virginia teamster Daniel Morgan, and the Boston bookseller Henry Knox. Nine of ten New Jersey officers derived from the wealthiest one-third of the state's population, yet an elite pedigree was neither required nor a guarantee of success in this martial world. "For many," the historian John Shy would write, "military service in the Revolution deflected life not only outward but upward."

A Maryland colonel might grumble that new junior officers coming into camp were "perfect novices and but few removed from idiots," but they would be critical in helping Washington weld this heterogeneous horde into a disciplined national force. New Englanders still called Virginians

"Buckskins" or "Eye Gougers"—they reputedly grew long fingernails to scratch opponents in a fight—while Yankees were known as "Pumpkin Heads." As many as a quarter of the Continentals were Irish; they were given many nicknames, none of them flattering.

"For posterity I bleed," one regimental banner proclaimed, and this was true, regardless of a man's provenance or motive for serving. More than a hundred divines would join the new chaplains' corps, and they did their utmost to build esprit with an injunction from 2 Samuel: "Be of good courage, and let us play the men for our people and for the cities of our God."

Washington had vowed "by every means in my power [to] keep the life and soul of this army together," as he wrote Congressman Robert Morris. That would require further tightening the bond between the commander in chief and the men he commanded—a covenant fashioned from his personal charisma, a shared commitment to revolutionary ideals, and the practical application of an insight he had voiced earlier this year, that "a people unused to restraint must be led, they will not be drove."

Keeping the army together would also require, as Washington had long recognized, his attention to every detail of army administration. Sentries were reminded to face outward when on guard duty and not "to sleep a single moment." He insisted that drummers and fifers needed more practice, "the music of the army being in general very bad." Ferrymen on the Delaware had been accused of price gouging, and so too some farmers. The Navy Board wanted ropemakers released from the army's ranks to ply their trade. What color horses, he asked a dragoon officer, should be ridden by reconnaissance scouts if white and near white seemed too conspicuous? To standardize salutes, junior officers encountering superiors were to remove their hats with the right hand and make a sweeping motion to the left side.

There was more, always more. Slaughterhouse offal, he declared, must be buried deeper. The widow of a captain killed at Princeton deserved $50. To deter theft, every tool and firelock belonging to the army was to be stamped with "U.States" or "U.S." In an eighteen-paragraph letter sent to General Howe in New York, Washington proposed, without success, a prisoner exchange. A new personal guard for the commander in chief would be formed of "sober, young, active, & well-made men," each between five feet nine and five feet ten inches tall, preferably Virginians "of some property" to encourage loyalty. As his own spymaster, Washington sent $500 to one Nathaniel Sacket "for secret services," adding, "It runs in my head that I was to correspond with you by a fictitious name. If so, I have forgot the name and must be reminded of it again."

An army needed maps beyond those sketched by Washington himself, and in late July Congress appointed a Continental geographer, the Scottish-born engineer Robert Erskine. He and his surveyors would produce 275 topographical and sketch maps, many on the scale of a mile to the inch. An army needed bread, and in early summer Congress appointed a superintendent of bakers, the German-born Christopher Ludwick, who had studied gingerbread and the confectionary arts in London. He and his journeymen built eleven ovens in six locations and were baking loaves by the ton each day. An army needed a flag, and on June 14 Congress resolved that the American standard would carry thirteen alternating red and white stripes with thirteen white stars in a blue field. An army needed money, and Congress appointed Michael Hillegas as treasurer of the United States to print more.

Dire shortages of guns and gunpowder had eased a bit. Washington hoped to acquire two hundred brass cannons—3-, 6-, and 12-pounders— plus larger-caliber weapons for sieges and defense. Foundries, powder laboratories, air furnaces, and boring mills were ordered built. After identifying gunners sufficiently schooled in geometry and square-root tables to calculate distance and elevation, Henry Knox instructed them to aim at redcoat infantry formations to break up bayonet charges, rather than, as the British often preferred, targeting enemy gun batteries. But copper and nickel, critical elements in casting guns, were rare enough in America that most artillery would have to come from France, like the fifty-two brass guns recently arrived aboard the *Amphitrite*. Twenty-one of those were "exceedingly heavy and unmanageable," Washington decided, and would be recast so that each bulky French gun became three mobile 6-pounders. Over the past several months, French royal armories had also shipped sixty thousand muskets with bayonets, allowing Continental troops to discard fowling pieces and other long guns ill-suited for shooting men.

Every state except Delaware would build at least one gunpowder mill, but only a third of the powder burned by American troops in the past two years had been made domestically, and much of that required imported saltpeter, the critical ingredient. Happily, resourceful smugglers from Holland, Spain, and France slipped through the British cordon to stock American magazines, including seven tons recently brought into Boston aboard the sloop *Republic* and another fifty tons from Nantes that arrived in New Hampshire in mid-May, aboard *Mercure*. Each month powder brigs, schooners, and sloops from St. Eustatius, Curaçao, Guadeloupe, and other transshipment ports in the West Indies sailed up the James, York, or Rappahannock Rivers in Virginia.

Washington also knew that the army's health was paramount. Even in benign seasons a couple thousand soldiers were typically unfit for duty with dysentery, intractable diarrhea, or other maladies. Dr. Rush, now working on the Little Neshaminy as surgeon general of the army's Middle Department, had recently written "Preserving the Health of Soldiers," an essay printed across the entire front page of the *Pennsylvania Packet*. Rush urged close-cropped hair, temperance, frequent changes of small clothes, bathing at least twice weekly, ample vegetables in the daily ration, and washing utensils after every meal. Despite such precautions, typhus had ripped through military hospitals in early May.

Among the most consequential decisions Washington would ever make was to reverse his earlier resistance to inoculating soldiers against smallpox, a disease he acknowledged as "the greatest of all calamities." Outbreaks had devastated the army, including regiments retreating from Canada the previous summer, despite efforts to quarantine the sick. Crude inoculation, which required smearing active viral pus in a small incision on the arm or thigh, typically resulted in a mortality rate of less than 2 percent, and often much lower, compared to 15 percent, and often much higher, for those sickened naturally. Yet inoculation required two weeks of preparation with purgatives and a proper diet, and then a month of isolation while the patient recovered. Reluctant to sequester large portions of his army, a year earlier Washington had ordered any officer "who shall suffer himself to be inoculated" to be cashiered as "an enemy and traitor to his country."

But additional outbreaks in Virginia, New York, and elsewhere caused him to change his mind while the army was still in winter quarters. A witness to a smallpox ward in Morristown wrote:

> More frightful and pitiable human beings I have never seen. The heads of some of them were swelled to nearly double their natural size, their eyes closed, and their faces were black as coal. The most of these died.

Pressed by both his medical staff and common soldiers, Washington relented, telling a physician in February, "We should have more to dread from it than the sword of the enemy. You will without delay inoculate all the Continental troops." Churches served as quarantine centers, and new recruits headed to the army were first diverted for mandatory inoculation and isolation.

Washington's abrupt conversion encouraged inoculation in states that had sharply restricted the practice, particularly in the North. In a letter to his brother, written in June, he advocated "a law to compel the masters of families to inoculate every child born within a certain limited time, under severe penalties." At the same time, in defiance of Virginia law, he ordered the inoculation of his family and all slaves at Mount Vernon.

Throughout the spring and early summer, physicians had notched the arms of thousands of soldiers and swabbed them with smallpox pus, under "constant pressure from Washington to do it faster," as one historian later wrote. Few died, many were saved, and the threat subsided. "The camp is thought to be entirely clear of infection," the commander in chief had recently written, "and the country pretty much also."

On Thursday morning, August 21, day eleven of the Little Neshaminy encampment, the commander in chief convened a war council to consider the army's next move. Thirteen generals tromped into the front parlor of the farmhouse headquarters, including Knox, Greene, and Anthony Wayne, a Pennsylvanian. "His Excellency," Greene observed, "is exceedingly impatient." They chatted in low murmurs, shifting from foot to foot while waiting for Washington to begin. Among them stood a lanky redheaded newcomer wearing a major general's sash beneath his elegant French uniform tunic. Gilbert du Motier, the Marquis de Lafayette, already known to his American comrades simply as "the markwiss," had arrived.

He had made landfall in South Carolina aboard the *Victoire* in mid-June after a tedious fifty-four-day crossing. The landscape and people immediately beguiled him. "Nature adorns everything with an age of youth and majesty. . . . All citizens are brothers. In America there are no poor, and none that one could even call peasants," he wrote his wife, Adrienne, ignoring half a million black slaves. The enchantment dulled a bit during the month-long overland trek to Philadelphia and the frosty reception initially given him by Congress. Yet his ardor and his charming, fractured English soon won over the skeptics, aided by an introductory letter from Franklin, in Paris, who urged, "The civilities and respect that may be shown to him will be serviceable to our affairs here, as pleasing not only to his powerful relations and to the court, but the whole French nation." After agreeing to serve without pay or to claim a field command, Lafayette received his rank sash, outfitted himself with horses, a carriage, weapons, and camp equipage, then trotted north to join his new army.

"About eleven thousand men, ill-armed and still worse clothed, presented a strange spectacle," he later wrote. He quickly won friends in the officer corps, including Greene, who called him "a most sweet-tempered young gentleman," and Colonel Hamilton, who became his close ally even as he mocked "the thousand little whims" that seemed to buffet Lafayette. Perhaps surprisingly, he also won the affection of Washington, a fellow Mason whom the marquis described to Adrienne as an "intimate friend" and "excellent man," the embodiment of fortitude, incorruptibility, and other classical virtues he had read about in Plutarch and Livy.

Washington had developed a fine disdain for most of the foreign officers beating a path to his door. "You cannot conceive what a weight these kind of people are upon the service and upon me in particular," he wrote Hancock. "This evil, if I may call it so, is a growing one. . . . They are coming in swarms." Many were simply "hungry adventurers" who were "entirely useless as officers from their ignorance of the English language." Others he considered "so many spies in our camp."

The matter had come to a head in June with the arrival of another Frenchman, Philippe Charles Tronson du Coudray, waving a major general's commission, signed by the commissioner Silas Deane in Paris, that gave him command of all American artillery and engineers. Said to have survived thirty duels, as vain and querulous as he was capable—his competence extended to cannon metallurgy and gunpowder manufacturing—Coudray soon alienated everyone he met. On July 1, Knox, Greene, and Major General John Sullivan wrote letters threatening resignation if the interloper was made senior to them. Congress denounced this "extremely displeasing" insolence, threatened to dismiss or even arrest the trio, and insisted that Washington extract an apology from them. His Excellency ignored the demand, fearing the loss of three esteemed officers. The imbroglio subsided only when Congress grudgingly disavowed Deane's promise, instead appointing Coudray to a sinecure as "inspector general of ordnance and military manufactories." In September, Coudray would further resolve matters by drowning when his horse tumbled into the Schuylkill River—*"peut être un heureux accident,"* Lafayette observed. Perhaps a happy accident. He was buried in a Roman Catholic graveyard at public expense.

Lafayette clearly seemed a different creature. His unpretentious modesty appealed to Washington, but the commander in chief was uncertain what to do with a boy whose military experience consisted of peacetime summer maneuvers in faraway Metz. "What the designs of Congress respecting this gentleman were," he had written a Virginia delegate on August 19, "I know no more than the child unborn & beg to be instructed." For now he would keep the "Marquis de le Fiatte" close by his side.

The first question Washington put to his generals when they assembled that Thursday regarded the British: "What is the most probable place of their destination?" Intelligence from New York revealed that horse stalls with sheepskin padding had been built on some transports, suggesting a long sea voyage, but nothing had been seen of the fleet in a fortnight. Washington conceded that "the amazing advantage the enemy derive from their ships and the command of the water keeps us in a state of constant perplexity." Coffeehouse wits joked that the British had sailed to Bermuda for refuge, but Washington believed that Howe's "abandoning General Burgoyne is so unaccountable a matter that till I am fully assured it is so, I cannot help casting my eyes continually behind me."

The council unanimously concurred that the Howes had sailed south and that "Charleston, from a view of all circumstances, is the most probable object of their attention." Washington had come to the same conclusion, despite doubting the sense of transporting an army to the South Carolina lowlands during malaria season.

If this was so, he persisted, "will it be advisable for this army . . . to march that way?" No, his men replied, since the Continentals "could not possibly arrive at Charleston in time to afford any succor." In that case, Washington asked, how should the army "be employed? Shall it remain where it now is, or move towards Hudson's River?" The answer was prompt and again unanimous, formally signed by all thirteen generals, including Lafayette: "The army should move immediately towards the North River," either to confront Burgoyne or perhaps to attack New York.

"We have perhaps not a moment to lose," Washington informed Congress. "I shall move the army to the Delaware tomorrow morning." But no sooner had Hamilton galloped off to Philadelphia with this dispatch than a breathless courier from Hancock arrived in camp with news from Virginia: the British fleet had been seen veering around Cape Charles into Chesapeake Bay. Confusion followed. In general orders on Friday, Washington declared, "The army is to march tomorrow morning." A few hours later he countermanded himself: "The army is not to march tomorrow morning." At ten p.m. he reversed course again: "The army is to march tomorrow morning at 4 o'clock precisely, if it should not rain, towards Philadelphia." An additional report from Maryland had confirmed "two hundred sail of Mr. Howe's fleet being at anchor in Chesapeake Bay."

Aides settled the commanding general's account at the farmhouse, paying cash for the butter, beets, milk, eggs, and beef tongue consumed, plus a few dollars more to have the kitchen scrubbed. Before first light on Saturday, August 23, the ranks filed from the Neshaminy meadows, past the whipping post, and onto York Road. Thirty men on horseback followed the baggage wagons to sweep up stragglers.

A sixteen-mile southward march brought the column to Germantown.

Washington put his headquarters for the night in Stenton, a two-story brick mansion on a loyalist estate. There he and twenty officers dined on fresh mutton at three p.m. "They behaved civil, were very quiet," a local diarist recorded. "Washington appeared extremely grave & thoughtful."

Certainly the moment was grave enough. After months of indecisive sparring, the opposing armies seemed headed for a collision. With the enemy fleet approaching the northern rim of the Chesapeake, not only was Philadelphia at risk, but also Reading, the army's biggest supply depot in the middle states. Congress had ordered military stores evacuated from two other Pennsylvania towns, York and Lancaster, where dozens of mills, ironworks, and gunsmithies stood in jeopardy.

No doubt the war would grow darker in the coming weeks. Fire and sword, heartbreak and slaughter were about to sweep the land. Yet beneath his furrowed brow the commander in chief also had a glint in his eye. Peril here brought opportunity elsewhere, to the north. "As there is not now the least danger of General Howe's going to New England," he wrote a subordinate in the Hudson Valley, "I hope the whole force of that country will turn out, and . . . entirely crush General Burgoyne."

Gusty thunderstorms soaked the ranks during a night split open with lightning bolts. The sodden army struck its tents at three a.m. on Sunday, August 24, then heaved them onto the baggage wagons. Washington had carefully choreographed a show of force through Philadelphia, as he told Hancock, "that it may have some influence on the minds of the disaffected there." With a clatter of drums the regiments stepped off, shoes squelching for those who were shod. Two hours later they crossed Cohoquinoque Creek to reach Front Street, then continued past the Delaware River wharves, warehouses, and ship chandlers' shops.

Washington led the column, magnificently mounted and dressed in his finest blue-and-buff, with Lafayette riding at his side. Prancing cavalry followed them, trailed by a pioneer company carrying axes as if to hew open a road. Then came brigade after brigade, the men marching twelve abreast with muskets shouldered and green sprigs in their hats. Gun carriages and ammunition wagons separated the regiments, the iron rims grating across the cobblestones. Four hundred field musicians played a quickstep, as instructed, "but with such moderation that the men may step to it with ease and without dancing along."

Across High Street they tramped before pivoting right on Chestnut Street, away from the river. Thousands of spectators lined the brick and flagstone sidewalks: Irish craftsmen, Welsh milkmaids, African pepper-pot women selling soup, and Quaker merchants, known snidely as "Broad-brims" or "Thees and Thous." Five blocks west, the brigades paraded past the grand statehouse, with its distinctive keystone archways, belltower, and steeple. Beaming congressmen stood outside for two hours as the host marched by. John Adams judged the army to be well armed, "pretty well-clothed, and tolerably disciplined." In a letter to Abigail that afternoon, he praised "this fine spectacle," but added:

> Much remains to be done. Our soldiers have not yet quite the air of soldiers. They don't step exactly in time. They don't hold up their heads quite erect, nor turn out their toes so exactly as they ought. They don't all of them cock their hats.

For many of the rank and file, this was their first glimpse of Philadelphia, that "great and noble city," as a British officer had written before the war, when it was the empire's fourth-largest metropolis, after London, Edinburgh, and Dublin. With five thousand houses of sand-scrubbed floors and whitewashed walls, and three thousand other buildings, the city had long been America's commercial center and largest port. Artisans sewed shoes, boiled soap, and laid bricks. Hundreds of the enslaved worked the ropewalks, tanneries, and shipyards. Farmers and trappers in market stalls sold eggs, fruit, bear bacon, and possum meat. Furniture makers turned out bespoke chairs, chests, and tables. Residents in one ward alone practiced seventy different trades, from porter and skinner to crier, glazier, and goat keeper.

At least a third of the city's retailers were women, toiling as bakers, braziers, mantua makers, innkeepers, tinkers, and distillers. Philadelphia was also an emblem of American aspiration, a town of learning and science. It was Franklin's town, the keyhole through which the Enlightenment had entered the colonies. Not quite classless nor fully democratic, but more of both than most eighteenth-century societies, it offered broad enfranchisement, social mobility, and tolerance.

War now tested these admirable virtues. Week by week the cultured city of thirty-eight thousand took on a militant mien. Lead downspouts were melted for bullets. Pick-and-shovel laborers worked on river defenses, including men pressed from the streets to help dig trenches and build fire rafts. Eight hundred invalids had formed a corps for sentry duty and other non-combat tasks. Anticipating a British assault, some affluent revolutionaries had decamped to their country homes. Most Quakers remained, defiantly neutral; Adams, never neutral, found them "dull as beetles." A British agent and former clerk in the mayor's office, James

Molesworth, had been hanged before an immense throng of spectators for offering three pilots £50 to guide Royal Navy ships through the Delaware obstructions. Ardent loyalists stayed indoors, fearful of detention, or worse.

New men-of-war stood abuilding on dockyard stocks. Some mills made gunpowder, while others turned out paper for musket cartridges, orderly books, and, inevitably, Continental currency. A foundry on the waterfront opposite Old Swedes Church produced brass cannons. Notices in the *Pennsylvania Evening Post* offered rewards for deserters, including $10 for "a certain Peter Bommont, a Frenchman born," who jumped ship from the Continental xebec *Champion*: "Speaks but indifferent English. Chunky, fat, and pockmarked."

The Pennsylvania assembly had passed a law in June requiring residents to take an oath renouncing allegiance to George III or risk a loss of suffrage and the right to buy or sell land. A month later, Congress recommended seizing all former Crown officials and others with "a disposition inimical to the cause of America." In the coming days houses would be searched for weapons and dozens arrested for suspected disloyalty, mostly Quakers who denounced rebel zealots as "the warm people." Some of the detained were jailed in the Masonic lodge on Second Street. Others were banished to rural Virginia and forced to pay their confinement costs.

"This civil war has rendered the minds of our governors desperate & savage," the Quaker loyalist James Allen told his diary. "Hard is the fate of those poor people whose only crime is thinking differently from their oppressors."

Late in the morning Washington and his aides peeled away from the parade for a brief stop at City Tavern on Second Street, Philadelphia's most fashionable public house. A staff officer soon settled the bill—£12 for punch, seven shillings sixpence for grog, and £1 for hay and oats to feed a dozen horses—and the commander in chief again cantered south. He had specifically insisted that to preserve an image of stolid masculinity "not a woman belonging to the army is to be seen with the troops on their march through the city." Artillery molls and other camp followers had been shunted with the baggage wagons onto byways west of town, where they now hurried to catch the receding column. A disapproving Philadelphia man reported seeing "their hair flying, their brows beady with the heat, their belongings slung over one shoulder, chattering and yelling in sluttish shrills as they went, and spitting in the gutters." The army and these auxiliaries were reunited near a rickety pontoon-and-plank bridge over the

Schuylkill before halting for the evening in Darby. Behind them, anxious Philadelphians continued to scavenge lead for bullets while keeping an ear cocked for distant cannon fire.

Tomorrow the Continentals would march twenty miles to Wilmington and then camp on the high ground west of that town. Another twenty miles to the southwest lay Head of Elk and the upper reaches of the Chesapeake. Somewhere between here and there, in an anonymous field or on some nameless hill, they would likely confront their enemy.

None could be certain of God's favor, or of the triumph of their cause, or even of living until the end of the week. For every man who had seen combat, another had yet to hear a shot fired in anger and could only ponder his own mettle. "Having never been in action, I know not what would be my feelings," a Massachusetts officer wrote his wife. "But I trust in God I shall not disgrace myself, nor dishonor you."

4.

———◦———

Thine Arrows Stick Fast in Me

A hundred miles west of Albany and barely beyond musket range from the Mohawk River, American sentries peered toward the distant tree line from their ramparts late in the afternoon on Friday, August 1, watching for the attack they knew was coming.

Omens had accumulated all summer. Two Continentals had been ambushed while pigeon hunting a mile from the fort; the British paid a Seneca chief $10 for each scalp, although one of the victims, a captain, had survived both a bullet in the back and the bloody knife. Five men cutting sod had been captured by Indians, with a sixth killed and scalped. The previous Sunday three farm girls picking raspberries were attacked just five hundred yards outside the main gate. One escaped, but the other two were tomahawked and scalped. Now friendly Oneida scouts warned of a large British column with Indian allies approaching.

Only this forlorn outpost could stop them from reaching the Hudson Valley. Fort Stanwix, built in 1758 and named for an otherwise forgotten British general from the last war, stood at the threshold between the Atlantic world to the east and the virgin frontier in the west. In 1776, Congress had ordered the dilapidated structure rebuilt; although redesignated as Fort Schuyler, the new name was widely ignored. If remote, the stronghold now seemed almost as formidable as Ticonderoga, 140 miles northeast. Four stout bastions stood at the corners, more than a hundred yards apart and connected by a sloping glacis, a wide ditch, and ramparts fraised with pointed stakes. A triangular ravelin protected the front gate, approached across a drawbridge raised with a counterweight. Cannons on wooden platforms pointed in all directions, and a sally port in the east wall led to Spring Brook, fifty yards away. Built for 400 men, the compound now held 550 Continentals. A southeast casemate served as a barracks for soldiers, who often slept sitting up in straw-filled cribs because it was believed to be healthier than lying down.

Colonel Peter Gansevoort, whose family had lived in this region for a century, commanded both the 3rd New York Regiment and the fort. Sensible and composed, a tall, florid, twenty-eight-year-old veteran of the Canada invasion in 1775, he had worked tirelessly for months: replacing rotted timbers, stacking sod against the outer walls as a cushion against cannonballs, erecting sentry boxes, sending women and children east to safety, and sewing a makeshift flag from scraps of red cloth, a white shirt, and a blue camlet cloak. But in dispatches to General Schuyler in Albany, Gansevoort privately lamented his "great deficiency of cannon shot"; he also reported that too many lead bullets did not fit his musket barrels and that the garrison's supply of beef, much of it already spoiled, was dwindling. "All my fear," his fiancée had written him, "is that you will be blocked up in the fort and will be forced to surrender for the want of provision and left to the mercy of those brutes." Gansevoort answered with bravado: "I think myself as safe in this fort as I would in any part of America."

At five p.m., as shadows stretched across the Mohawk a few hundred yards to the south, the garrison huzzahed at the sight of five bateaux carrying ammunition, food, and two hundred reinforcements, Massachusetts Continentals among them. No sooner had the baskets, crates, and troops been bundled into the fort than campfires were spotted to the northwest, flickering among the trees like fireflies.

By Saturday morning Fort Stanwix was surrounded. Eight hundred redcoats, German *Jäger*, Canadians, and loyalists swarmed out of the forest, along with a comparable number of warriors from a dozen tribes, including Seneca in calico-print shirts with silver wheels dangling from their earlobes and large black dots painted on chins and cheeks. A few Indian daredevils darted from bush to bush and ran through the garrison potato patch near the fort walls with "the most horrid yelling," an American officer wrote. Musket balls and German rifle fire whistled over the parapets, killing one Continental sentry and wounding seven. An occasional gout of smoke eventually spurted from a hummock six hundred yards to the northeast, followed by a hollow boom and a cannonball smacking into a sod-upholstered bastion wall or skipping in great bounds past the glacis.

At three p.m. a British captain strutted forward under a truce flag to demand the fort's surrender. Any resistance or "phrenzy of hostility," he warned, would result in the Indians being unshackled to massacre every man. Colonel Gansevoort rejected the ultimatum with contempt.

Here, then, was the other wing of Burgoyne's invasion, the diversion that had been sent up the St. Lawrence from Montreal and then along Lake

Ontario before turning southeast toward the Mohawk. The last stretch of the three-hundred-mile trek had been particularly troublesome, requiring axmen to cut a sixteen-mile road and clear an obstructed creek. "I have tortured myself for three days and nights with 15 bateaux laden with 142 barrels of provisions," a *Jäger* lieutenant wrote. Indians wrapped the blistered, bleeding feet of their German comrades in alder-leaf poultices.

Brigadier General Barry St. Leger's orders from Burgoyne were succinct: to reach the Hudson and rejoin him near Albany after drawing rebel defenders away from the Canada Army. Irish-born and educated at Eton and Cambridge, with a devotion to strong drink, St. Leger quickly realized that his intelligence about Fort Stanwix was "the most erroneous that can be conceived," as he wrote General Carleton in Quebec. Despite reports from captured Americans of strong fortifications and a robust garrison, he had instead relied on obsolete accounts of a flimsy, undermanned outpost in disrepair. One look at the walls revealed that his paltry artillery train of four light guns and four mortars would hardly pound the fort into submission. The defenders standing shoulder to shoulder along the parapets also contradicted Burgoyne's blithe assurance that "it is not to be imagined that any detachment of such force as that of Schuyler can be supplied by the enemy for the Mohawk."

St. Leger would have to rely on his Indian accomplices to win through. Since early summer the British had implored the Six Nations of the Iroquois—also known as the Haudenosaunee—to take up the war belt against American rebels, plying the tribes with ostrich feathers, brass kettles, bells, guns, scalping knives, and a "flood of rum," as one Indian recorded. But the civil war between whites threatened to fracture the Great Peace that had endured within the confederation for generations in the north woods. If few Haudenosaunee tribes fully understood the politics of the rebellion, all recognized the utility of supporting the winning side. The Oneida and Tuscarora now aligned with the Americans; the Seneca, Mohawk, Cayuga, and Onondaga fought for the British. One civil war had ignited another.

Perhaps St. Leger's most charismatic Indian ally was Thayendanegea, also known as Joseph Brant, a Mohawk who had straddled two cultures since boyhood. Brant had been educated at an Indian charity school in Connecticut, where he'd been described as a "sprightly genius" who studied English, Hebrew, Greek, and Latin, and helped an Anglican priest translate the Gospel of Saint Mark into Mohawk. Having led war parties against the French in the Seven Years' War, Brant was sent to England in November 1775 to discuss Indian matters with the king's government. Billeted at the Swan with Two Necks near St. Paul's Cathedral, he was

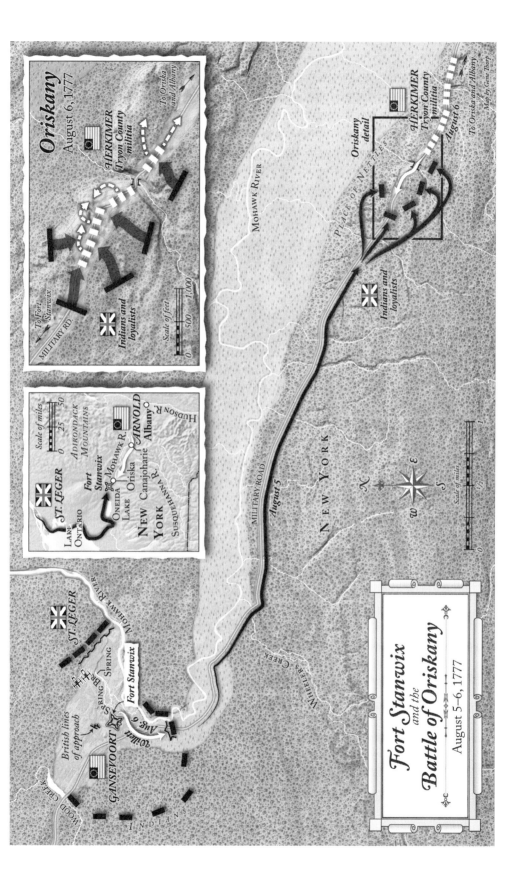

Oriskany

August 6, 1777

HERKIMER
Tryon County
militia

Indians and
loyalists

To Fort
Stanwix

MILITARY RD

To Oriska
and Albany

Scale of feet
0   500   1,000

ADIRONDACK
MOUNTAINS

Scale of miles
0   25   50

ST. LEGER

LAKE
ONTARIO

Fort
Stanwix

ONEIDA
LAKE   Oriska

Mohawk R.

NEW
YORK

Canajoharie

ARNOLD

Albany

Hudson R.

Susquehanna R.

MOHAWK RIVER

PLACE OF NETTLES

Oriskany
detail

HERKIMER
Tryon County
militia

August 6

Indians and
loyalists

To Oriska and Albany

Map by Gene Thorp

NEW YORK

N
W   E
S

Scale of miles
0   1/10   1/4

Scale of miles
0   1/2   1

MILITARY ROAD

August 5

WHEELER'S CREEK

ST. LEGER

MOHAWK RIVER

SPRING

British lines
of approach

Bue Spring

Fort Stanwix

To Willet
Aug. 6

GANSEVOORT

WOOD CREEK

I N D I A N S

Fort Stanwix
and the
Battle of Oriskany

August 5–6, 1777

presented in Mohawk dress to George III, who gave him a watch. He then chatted up Lord Germain, had his portrait painted by George Romney while wearing a ruffled shirt and clutching a tomahawk, sat for an interview with James Boswell for the *London Magazine*, and attended a masquerade ball in full warrior regalia. One admirer wrote that "he conversed well, possessed polished manners, and . . . had a manly and intelligent cast of countenance."

Now in his mid-thirties, Brant had urged all Indians to defend their "lands & liberty against the rebels," whose appetite for territory belonging to others seemed insatiable. On the late afternoon of Tuesday, August 5, as the siege tightened around Fort Stanwix, he received an urgent message from his older sister, Molly, who lived in the Mohawk valley village of Canajoharie: eight hundred rebel militiamen were marching up the river to reinforce Gansevoort and his garrison.

After a quick conference, St. Leger detached more than five hundred men, mostly loyalists and Indians who had set up separate camps half a mile east of Fort Stanwix. Brant knew of an excellent spot for a horseshoe ambush, a shallow ravine called the Place of Nettles, six miles downstream from the fort. The warriors, including the Seneca war chiefs Cornplanter and Old Smoke, slipped away from the cordon in five single-file columns. Tonight they would eat cold rations and sleep without campfires, tormented by mosquitoes. Tomorrow would be a killing day. "The Indians," a *Jäger* lieutenant advised his diary, "do not allow themselves either to be commanded or restrained."

By midmorning on August 6 the column of militia reinforcements stretched for a mile along the narrow road just south of the Mohawk, near the Oneida village of Oriska, later renamed Oriskany. Tiny dust devils boiled up from each footfall, as men rambling three abreast prattled about the summer harvest and this latest threat to their family homesteads by invaders said to have invested Fort Stanwix. Cicadas churred in the hemlocks and sugar maples, counterpoint to jingling bridles and the whipcrack of teamsters driving fifteen heavy wagons pulled by oxen. The road veered away from the river to descend into a deadfall bottomland of arroyo willow and yellow birch. A bridge crossed a sluggish stream running south to north, and here the boggy trace had been corduroyed with logs for almost three hundred yards. Butterflies danced among purplestem aster and Allegheny blackberry.

They were led by a slender, dark-haired man on a white mare who three days earlier had issued a summons for "every male person, being in health, from sixteen to sixty years of age" to muster at a stockade thirty miles downstream from Fort Stanwix with musket, powder horn, two dozen lead balls, and an edge weapon, preferably a bayonet or tomahawk. Brigadier General Nicolas Herkimer, commander of the Tryon County militia, had more to lose than most of those marching behind him. A fortune derived from two thousand acres of wheat, hemp, and flax, tended by thirty slaves, had given him a fortified Georgian mansion with a gambrel roof overlooking the Mohawk, on which he rowed to church each Sunday. Moneylending, portage services, and rum sales paid for the imported Chinese porcelain and other fine things filling the house.

Herkimer preferred to speak German, like many of his neighbors, but the farmers and tradesmen in work smocks, waistcoats, and linsey-woolsey breeches who heeded his summons also spoke Dutch, French, Gaelic, English, or, for the sixty Oneida warriors among them, an Iroquoian language. Early this morning a polyglot dispute had broken out when Herkimer had proposed delaying their march until further news arrived from Colonel Gansevoort. Several subordinates had accused him of timidity. "High words" followed, a witness reported, until an angry Herkimer relented, barking in English, "March on." The column had surged forward with a jubilant shout.

The general and his vanguard had nearly emerged from the ravine when crackling musketry erupted from both sides of the road. Several bullets hit Colonel Ebenezer Clark, at the head of the column; he tumbled from his saddle, dead before he hit the ground, and his terrified horse galloped ahead. Two captains also fell dead in the first volley, and a ball through the heart killed a sergeant and wounded the lieutenant behind him. Fire raked the column before Mohawk and Seneca warriors burst from the thickets to fall on the militia with melee weapons—tomahawks, knives, ball clubs, spears—dashing out brains and cutting the throats of the wounded before stripping them of their coats and breeches. The fusillade targeted the teamsters and their teams, and ox carcasses soon blocked the road like great black stones. An officer sprinted down the column, screaming in Dutch, "Run, boys, run! You are all dead!" The lagging rear guard turned and hurtled toward the river, chased by both whooping Indians and their loyalist neighbors.

Shouting orders in German, Herkimer had wheeled around when a musket ball slammed through his left calf six inches below the knee, fracturing the tibia and fibula and killing his mare. Comrades dragged him up the northern slope to a beech tree, propped him against his saddle, and knotted a tourniquet around his thigh. The general pulled a tobacco pipe and tinderbox from his pocket and continued issuing orders, wreathed in fragrant blue smoke and pointing out enemies with the pipe stem.

Fathers and sons died together. Neighbor killed neighbor. Iroquois killed Iroquois. Parched men scraped holes in the bog and used their brogans to scoop out a few ounces of muddy drinking water. Gunsmoke settled in a dense fog over the road, and drumfire subsided to the heckling of sniper shots.

An abrupt, violent thunderstorm at midday dampened powder and further cut visibility, halting the carnage for an hour. Pulling on his pipe, Herkimer, from his beech tree redoubt, positioned the surviving militiamen in a defensive circle beneath the brow of a hill, organizing them into fighting pairs—one man to load and the other to shoot. Corpses were stripped of canteens and ammunition.

The rain stopped. Musket fire resumed. But by midafternoon, after six hours of mayhem, the ambushers had begun to leak away, dragging their wounded. Herkimer's men—the living, the dead, and those not quite either—still held the Place of Nettles when the last shot faded to silence, except for birdsong and the wounded men mewing like lost children.

The butcher's bill was appalling. Estimates of the Tryon County militia dead ranged from two hundred to more than double that; total militia casualties likely exceeded five hundred, more than half of Herkimer's force. Several dozen captives were marched away, some to be ransomed in Canada, others to be slaughtered by Indians in a retributive rage, including a captain who reportedly had both legs severed at the knees with a hatchet and a half dozen others clubbed to death after being forced to run a Seneca gauntlet. "In the valley homes was great mourning," a local history noted. "For such a small population, the losses were almost overwhelming. In some families the male members were wiped out." Oriskany would be among the war's bloodiest battles.

The king's losses included eleven whites and thirty-three Indians killed, including nine chiefs, mostly Seneca. A *Jäger* lieutenant wrote of the returning ambushers, "Every Indian had a few and most had four to eight scalps as trophies hanging from their belts. Many donned the coats of the dead men and ran around thus clad." They were stunned, however, to find that their camps east of Fort Stanwix had been plundered and burned during the battle. Although unaware of the Oriskany ambush, Colonel Gansevoort earlier in the day had dispatched 250 raiders under Lieutenant Colonel Marinus Willett, a reputed "street brawler" from Long Island who one day would serve as mayor of New York City. They returned with twenty-one wagonloads of booty from the empty camps, including blankets, deerskins, brass kettles, enemy battle flags—promptly hoisted on the Fort Stanwix flagpole—and scalps believed to belong to the raspberry-picking girls murdered a few days earlier.

A final casualty from Oriskany was carried on a litter through the front door of his riverfront house on August 8. For a week General Herkimer smoked his pipe and chatted from his bed with condolatory neighbors. But the wounded leg mortified, and of necessity was taken off. After lingering in great pain for several days, Herkimer called for his Bible and read aloud the 38th Psalm: "O Lord, rebuke me not in thy wrath, neither chasten me in thy hot displeasure. For thine arrows stick fast in me." That night, after thirty drops of laudanum—triple the usual dose—he crossed over. "We cannot always parry death," his surgeon said. "So there is an end of it."

St. Leger resumed his siege with a barrage that had "not the least effect upon the sodwork of the fort," he admitted. One disdainful Indian likened the British shelling to "apples that children were throwing over a garden fence." At five p.m. on August 8, three British officers approached the fort under another truce flag. Blindfolded, they were led into Gansevoort's candlelit dining room before being unmasked and offered wine, cheese, and crackers. Burgoyne and the Canada Army had reached Albany, the emissaries claimed, falsely. Unless Fort Stanwix surrendered, enraged Indians would murder women and children throughout the Mohawk valley. "Their blood will be on your head," Gansevoort replied, "not ours." He intended to "defend this fort to the last extremity in behalf of the United American States."

By August 15, 137 cannonballs and shells had been fired, but to so little effect that a German officer wrote, "The defenders loudly scold and laugh at us." Gansevoort ordered all provisions shifted from bastions to the parade ground in case a shell burst set the magazines ablaze. When the enemy dammed Spring Brook, the Continentals dug two wells inside the walls for drinking water. Sniping and a few rounds of grapeshot discouraged British attempts to carve a siege trench 150 yards from the glacis.

The garrison's predicament had not gone unremarked by General Schuyler, even as he pondered how to halt Burgoyne's further advance down the Hudson. On August 13, the dauntless Benedict Arnold volunteered to lead nine hundred Continentals up the Mohawk in relief of Fort Stanwix. Schuyler quickly consented.

Arnold was aware of the Oriskany calamity, and he moved west with deliberation. He also seethed at another of those personal insults that so often bedeviled him. In February, without consulting General Washington,

Congress had appointed five new major generals, all less senior than Arnold and his inferior in ability. The commander in chief regretted this snub, advising Congress that "a more spirited and sensible officer fills no department in your army." But delegates were determined to distribute high rank evenly among the states regardless of merit, and Arnold's native Connecticut already had two Continental major generals. "I confess this is a strange mode of reasoning," Washington wrote Arnold, while urging him "not to take any hasty step." Arnold, predictably, viewed the omission as "an implicit impeachment of my character," as he told Washington, and "a very civil way of requesting my resignation."

He quit, but held his resignation in abeyance when trouble flared in the north. Congress, reminded by his spontaneous valor at Danbury that no finer battle captain fought for either side, belatedly promoted him to major general in May but without restoring his seniority over the five officers elevated earlier. So here he was, as dark and graceful as a raven, the combat commander most feared by the British, again marching toward the sound of the guns but wrapped in pique, umbrage, and grievance as if they were threads in a second uniform. "You will hear of my being victorious," he wrote when the column was thirty-five miles from Fort Stanwix, "or no more."

With militia reinforcements, Arnold's corps approached fifteen hundred men. But before confronting St. Leger, he agreed to a ruse involving a Mohawk valley loyalist named Hanjost Schuyler, a distant relation to the Continental general, who had been arrested for treasonous support of the king's invaders. Some would later describe him as "misty-minded" or a half-wit, but he had wits enough to propose a clever gambit and a clemency deal that would spare him a hundred lashes, if not the scaffold.

At dawn on Friday, August 22, Hanjost stumbled into St. Leger's camp in a meadow near Fort Stanwix. Wild-eyed and babbling, with bullet holes in his clothing to suggest hot pursuit, he warned of at least two thousand Continentals fast approaching with a powerful artillery train. Two panting Oneidas followed on his heels, raising the same dire alarm.

Weary of the ineffectual siege and grieving over losses at Oriskany, St. Leger's Indian confederates needed little encouragement to break camp. "Huts and tents were set on fire," a *Jäger* diarist wrote. "Wine and brandy kegs were smashed open." Drunken whites and Indians alike "lay on the ground like cattle" or bickered over muskets, bayonets, and scraps of clothing.

A British deserter told Gansevoort that the invaders were "retreating with great precipitation" toward Oneida Lake, twenty miles to the west. Scouts creeping from Fort Stanwix found the enemy campsite deserted except for two Indians dining at St. Leger's table. A search of the British commander's escritoire discovered his journals, correspondence with Burgoyne, and other revelatory documents. Abandoned camp kettles, wagons, frying pans, milch cows, and additional plunder would be confiscated by the army or auctioned outside the main gate at Fort Stanwix.

Informed by Gansevoort of the enemy's flight—"I am at a loss to judge their real intentions," the colonel added—Arnold ordered a forced march up the Mohawk. In crossing the Oriskany killing fields, his men covered their noses against the unspeakable stench. They could not, however, cover their eyes. "As the dead had not been buried and the weather was warm, they were much swollen and of a purple color, which represented the frailty of man," an officer wrote. "We must have marched over and very near about four hundred dead bodies."

Arnold's arrival at Stanwix was greeted with a booming salute from thirteen cannons and three lusty cheers. He ordered five hundred men to chase the enemy, but the pursuers soon returned to report seeing a few final bateaux crossing Oneida Lake in a heavy rain as the invaders fled toward Lake Ontario and then on to the St. Lawrence. Arnold denounced St. Leger as "the head of a banditti of robbers, murderers, and traitors" and vowed condign punishment for loyalists who refused to declare allegiance to the American cause.

American sovereignty on the Mohawk had been preserved, but not the peace. As Arnold reassembled his men and wheeled the column back toward the Hudson, rebels and their Oneida allies plundered Mohawk villages, driving off livestock and carting away grain, squash, and beans. A Church of England chapel downriver from General Herkimer's estate was turned into a tavern, then, later, a stable. Recalcitrant loyalists were trussed and horsewhipped, their homes ransacked. Several hundred fled to Canada for sanctuary, there to nurse grudges and plot reprisals. Here, too, was the frailty of man.

The Canada Army remained fifty miles north of Albany, struggling in this hostile land to build up sufficient strength for a final lunge down the Hudson. Burgoyne exaggerated the damage he was inflicting on Schuyler's forces, but not his troubles with Indian allies and supplies. "I have detachments of seventeen different nations," he wrote Howe. "There is infinite difficulty to manage them. My effort has been to keep up their terror and avoid their cruelty." Quartermasters needed nearly a month to move provisions from St. Johns, near the northern end of Lake Champlain, to army magazines on the Hudson. Portaging ammunition, rations, and bateaux the eighteen miles from Lake George to Fort Edward was complicated by heavy rains and a shortage of draft animals.

"It was often necessary to employ ten or twelve oxen upon a single bateau," Burgoyne told Germain. Fifteen days of backbreaking effort in August had yielded only an extra four days of stockpiled provisions. Forage remained in short supply, even in harvest season; a single eight-hundred-pound wagonload of oats, a necessary staple for working horses, had reached Fort Edward. Not least among his aggravations, Burgoyne issued multiple orders for officers to reduce their personal baggage until finally, in a fit of anger, he condemned the "enormous mismanagement . . . in respect to the king's carts."

A partial solution to the army's woes beckoned from the east, where American settlements were flush with horses, wagons, and grain. Burgoyne embraced a proposal by General Riedesel, the Brunswick commander, to send several hundred German dragoons, American loyalists, Canadian volunteers, and Indians into the Connecticut River valley to procure more than a thousand mounts and other army needs. The expedition would be led by Lieutenant Colonel Friedrich Baum, a dragoon commander who had risen through the ranks from corporal without ever leading an independent command or learning any language other than German—even though his new command included men who spoke only English, French, Algonquin, or Iroquois. Under "Instructions for Lieutenant Colonel Baume"—the British high command misspelled his name—the detachment had marched south ten miles from Fort Edward, waded the waist-deep Batten Kill, and had bivouacked due east of Saratoga on August 11 when Burgoyne himself trotted up to announce an abrupt change of plans.

Rather than heading northeast toward Manchester, Baum was to angle southeast for thirty miles to Bennington, a village on the edge of the Green Mountains in a self-proclaimed republic that would become the state of Vermont. The place contained "a very considerable magazine," according to loyalist informants, including large herds of bullocks and horses said to be lightly guarded by a few hundred militiamen and "very easy to surprise." This bounty would bolster the Canada Army's move down the Hudson. The thrust into southern Vermont would also discourage the rebels from further reinforcing Fort Stanwix—a diversion to aid St. Leger's diversion, which at the moment had yet to retreat toward Canada.

Riedesel, returning from an inspection trip to Lake George, was "much astonished" at this alteration, as he later wrote. He "pointed out the risk incurred": Bennington stood "at too great a distance and the enemy too near it." A loyalist guide advised the high command that no fewer than three thousand men should accompany Colonel Baum.

Burgoyne brushed aside this naysaying. The expedition, now grown to 760 men with two field guns, would be able to live off the land for a couple weeks before rejoining the Canada Army in Albany. Baum had been warned "not to incur the danger of being surrounded or having a retreat cut off." He could expect to seize so many horses that they "must be tied together by strings of ten each in order that one man may lead ten horses." Skene, the loyalist grandee with the vast estate on Lake Champlain, would accompany Baum to help "distinguish the good subjects from the bad" as he neared Vermont.

On Wednesday, August 13, the expedition set out on a "one-rod road"—a route typically just over sixteen feet in width, enough for two wagons to pass abreast. Packhorses carried sacks of flour but no tents, and all women, children, and military colors had been left on the Hudson. Baum's dragoons, ever hopeful of finding mounts just over the next hill, clumped along in their flamboyant cocked hats, broadsword scabbards trailing on their hips. The road wound through fields of maize, rye, and flax, abandoned in mid-harvest. Troops stepped from the ranks to filch pumpkins and potatoes from garden plots while peering into every barn and stable for livestock. Baum struggled to prevent his Indian allies from slaughtering confiscated cattle for both meat and the bells around their necks. As instructed by Skene, loyalists rallying to the column swore allegiance to the Crown after close examination for political deviancies, then stuck white paper strips in their hats as ensigns of the king's favor.

Gallopers crisscrossed the countryside, banging on farmhouse doors and shouting, "Prepare yourselves with bullets!" Some patriots tossed pewter spoons, cabinet clock weights, and jewelry into melting pots for musket balls. Others armed themselves with scythes, pitchforks, axes, and clubs. William Gilmore left his oxen in the field to help set fire to a bridge on Baum's approach route. Families piled feather beds and household duffle into their wagons and hied east. Sarah Rudd, the wife of a militia lieutenant, later described "my flight on horseback and in feeble health, with my babe and two other small children, and my eldest daughter running on foot by the side of me from Bennington to Williamstown."

Burgoyne had apparently forgotten that thousands of armed, vindictive New Englanders had rapidly assembled during the April 1775 skirmishes at Lexington and Concord, and that nine thousand American provincials had rallied to the British when French invaders threatened this region in 1758. British intelligence also failed to recognize that Bennington was defended by far more than a few hundred feeble militiamen, or that just the right man had appeared to take command for the Americans.

John Stark and his New Hampshire regiment had fought valiantly from Bunker Hill to Princeton before he resigned his Continental commission when Congress declined to promote him to brigadier general. His native state gave him that rank and command of much of New Hampshire's militia, praising his "noble disposition of mind." In less than a week, fifteen hundred men flocked to his standard, more than a tenth of all New Hampshire males sixteen or older—farmers and sawyers, teamsters and millers, loggers and smiths. Some walked out of church to enlist. To finance this force, local authorities pledged $3,000 in specie, an equal amount in silver and pewter, and the cash raised from selling seventy hogsheads of Tobago rum.

Just shy of forty-nine, Stark was sinewy, weather-beaten, and splenetic, a man who had survived capture and torture by Indians, ambuscade by the French, and the abattoir of Bunker Hill. A devotee of Charles XII, Sweden's abstemious warrior-king, Stark carried a copy of his memoir on campaign. When General Schuyler ordered all militia to march to the Hudson valley, Stark ignored him, choosing not to be "under the command of those officers on whose account I quitted the army, lest the remedy should prove worse than the disease." More succinctly he declared, "Stark chooses to command himself." A Continental officer told Schuyler, "He seems to be exceedingly soured."

Schuyler was shrewd enough not to force the issue, and Stark promised to "throw away all private resentment when put in balance with the good of my country." On August 8, by great good fortune for the rebel cause, he had repositioned his brigade south by marching twenty-five miles from Manchester to Bennington, unaware that Burgoyne would target the village for despoliation. Additional militiamen from Vermont and Massachusetts hurried to the camp, a picturesque legion in flax shirts, homespun coats, cowhide shoes with buckles, and round-crowned hats. Although French muskets now armed some Continental regiments, many militiamen kept their New England fowling pieces, which tended to be more accurate than muskets, including the British Brown Bess. By August 13, two thousand men had pitched their tents around Bennington, sipping branch water tinted with rum and chewing on lead bullets out of the conviction that it reduced thirst. When fleeing settlers reported Indians in Cambridge, New York, eighteen miles to the northwest, Stark dispatched Lieutenant Colonel William Gregg and 220 men to "make discoveries."

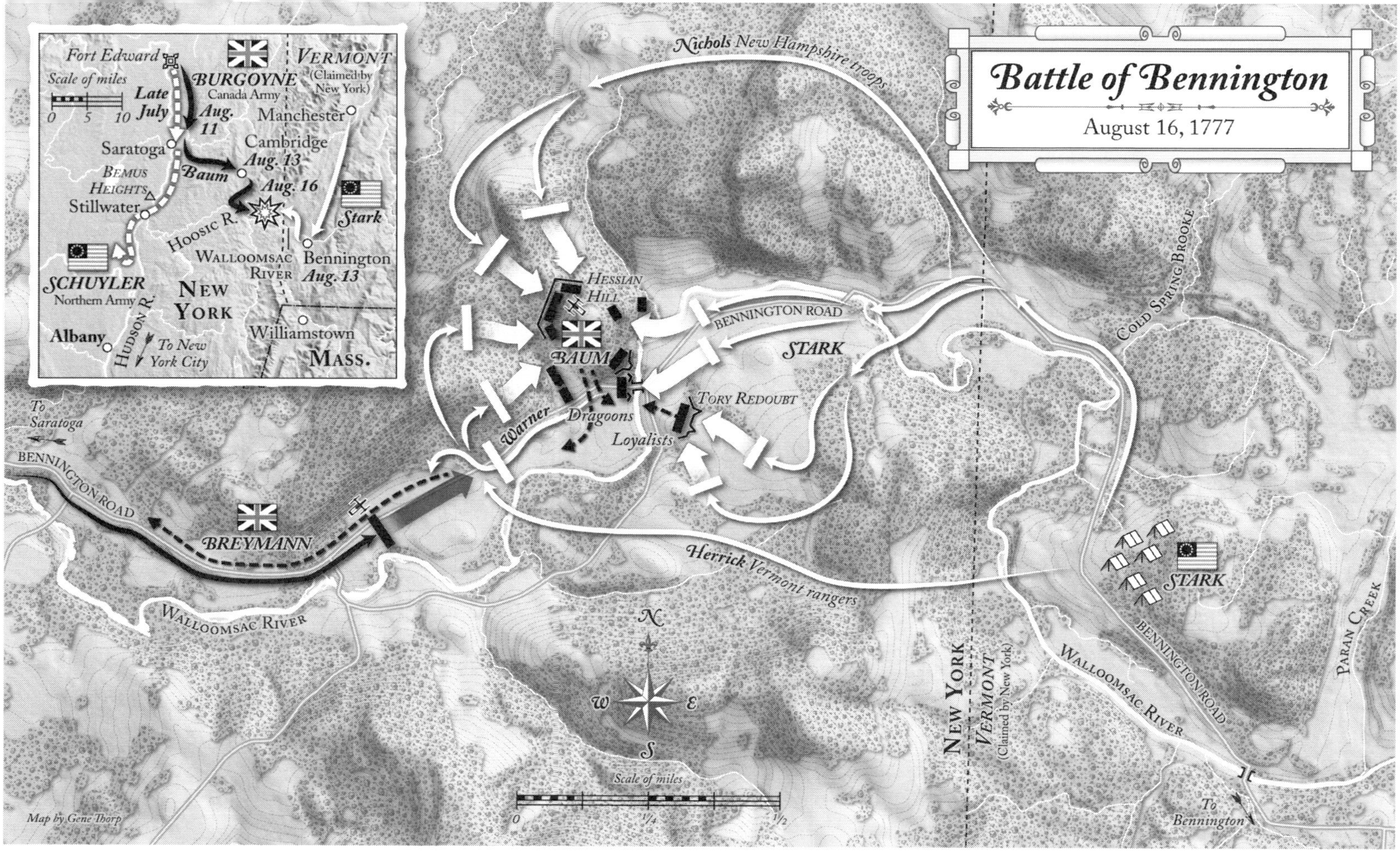

Battle of Bennington
August 16, 1777
Fort Edward
BURGOYNE
Canada Army
VERMONT
(Claimed by New York)
Scale of miles
0 5 10
Late July
Aug. 11
Manchester
Saratoga
Cambridge
Aug. 13
Baum
BEMUS HEIGHTS
Aug. 16
Stillwater
Stark
HOOSIC R.
WALLOOMSAC RIVER
Bennington
Aug. 13
SCHUYLER
Northern Army
NEW YORK
HUDSON R.
Albany
Williamstown
To New York City
MASS.
Nichols New Hampshire troops
HESSIAN HILL
BAUM
BENNINGTON ROAD
STARK
TORY REDOUBT
Dragoons
Loyalists
Warner
COLD SPRING BROOKE
To Saratoga
BENNINGTON ROAD
BREYMANN
Herrick Vermont rangers
STARK
PARAN CREEK
WALLOOMSAC RIVER
N
W
E
S
NEW YORK
VERMONT
(Claimed by New York)
BENNINGTON ROAD
WALLOOMSAC RIVER
Scale of miles
0 1/4 1/2
To Bennington
Map by Gene Thorp

*   *   *

Baum himself arrived in Cambridge at four p.m. on August 13 to learn that at least eighteen hundred rebel gunmen had massed at Bennington. "I will be particularly careful on my approach to that place," he wrote Burgoyne through a translator. Loyalists "are flocking hourly, but want to be armed," he subsequently added. "The savages cannot be controlled. They ruin and take everything they please. P.S. Beg Your Excellency to pardon the hurry of this letter. It is written on the head of a barrel." Burgoyne replied that Baum's progress had been "very satisfactory," but if he found the enemy "too strongly posted at Bennington," he should fortify himself in a strong redoubt "till you receive an answer from me."

Baum edged forward on Thursday, August 14, and soon bumped into Colonel Gregg's detachment near a mill. A few excited volleys sent the rebels flitting eastward, and Baum was pleased to find seventy-eight barrels of "very fine flour," twenty barrels of salt, and a thousand bushels of wheat. Captured militiamen advised him that Stark was simply awaiting more reinforcements before attacking. When a French Canadian suggested falling back to await his own reinforcements, Baum agreed in principle but argued that his orders precluded retreat.

At noon the invaders reached the Walloomsac River, high and fast after recent rain. A trestle bridge with a timber deck spanned the flood, and two families preparing to cross with wagons pulled by six oxen apiece were ordered to dismount, unharness the teams, and unload the furniture piled in the beds. Gunners muscled a pair of brass 3-pounders up to emplacements above the bridge. Rebel militia could be seen lining a ridge a thousand yards to the east, but Stark had pulled most of his brigade back toward Bennington to contemplate his next move.

Still on the New York side of the border, Baum halted to organize his defenses; he sent another courier to Burgoyne with a plea for reinforcements. The Brunswick dragoons camped behind a hasty breastworks built from fallen timber on a bald, arrow-shaped knoll, to be known as Hessian Hill, three hundred feet above the bridgehead. Old-growth forest loomed behind the bastion, and the east face dropped sharply over shaly talus and bedrock outcrops to the river. Baum ordered almost three hundred men in the Queen's Loyal Rangers and other American loyalists across the Walloomsac to high ground—soon called the Tory Redoubt—between rows of flax and a cornfield overlooking the bridge. "We felt perfectly safe," one defender later said, but this poor tactical decision left Baum's divided forces too far apart for mutual reinforcement. Dawn on Friday brought leaden skies and rain that fell like bird shot, forcing both little armies to shelter for the day, except for skulking detachments sent by Stark "to try the enemy's temper." Militia skirmishers returned with silver ornaments stripped from two Indians killed in a gunfight.

Baum's men spent a wet, miserable night without campfires, listening to occasional gunshots and stray Indian whoops. "We were all impressed with a powerful sense of impending danger," a German officer later wrote. But a serene dawn on Saturday, August 16, brought fields newly washed and a promise of summer sunshine. The swollen Walloomsac swept past the redoubt before plunging under the bridge. Foraging parties looked for livestock. "This morning we took possession of many horses," Julius Friedrich Wasmus, a Brunswick surgeon, told his diary. "If this continues, the regiment will soon be mounted."

More militiamen had arrived during the stormy night, giving Stark nearly a three-to-one advantage over his foe. The next morning he splintered three detachments from his force, including two hundred New Hampshire men ordered to circle several miles to the north on a wide flanking movement under Colonel Benjamin Nichols, and three hundred Vermont rangers sent south under Colonel Samuel Herrick. They moved at a dog trot, slurping from pails of water offered by farm women standing near their wells, then cautiously forded the tumbling river. A third force of three hundred, partly obscured by trees and broken ground, pressed toward the trestle bridge on both sides of the Bennington road.

From his command post on a hillside near the bridge, Baum watched rebels darting to and fro through his spyglass and briefly wondered if the Americans were abandoning their lines. Dragoons in the redoubt, seeing men in waistcoats and shirtsleeves on their distant flanks, were said to conclude that more loyalists were approaching to join the two hundred who had already thrown in with the expedition. Skene, whose task was to distinguish the good Americans from the bad, had left Baum's side and ridden west to watch for reinforcements from the Canada Army.

Two musket shots in rapid succession at three p.m. signaled the attack. "Our officers said, 'Now, my boys, is our time,'" Private Benjamin Bean later wrote. "Every man ran as fast as he can and made all the noise he can." The Tory Redoubt fell quickly. Rebels concealed in the corn rushed forward, some with husks in their hats as camouflage. Others attacked frontally against the southeast corner of a fence-rail fieldworks stuffed with flax or up a ravine parallel to the river that gave onto the loyalist flank. "They all came jumping in upon us with such a noise," a loyalist recalled. "We scattered in all directions."

If brief, the assault was nasty. Militiaman William Clement reported parrying a loyalist bayonet before thrusting his own into the assailant's eye with such force that the blade "came off and remained in the Tory's head. . . . The body was buried in that condition." Lieutenant Colonel John Peters, who would lose more than half of his Queen's Loyal Rangers that afternoon, described hearing a man yell:

> "Peters, you damned Tory, I have got you." He rushed on me with his bayonet which entered just below my left breast, but was turned by the bone. . . . I saw that it was a rebel captain, an old school fellow & play-mate, and a cousin of my wife's. Though his bayonet was in my body, I felt regret at being obliged to destroy him.

On Hessian Hill, the flankers led by Colonels Herrick and Nichols hid in the dense woods after encircling the dragoons. Stark ordered a hundred militiamen across the bridge as a frontal diversion. Brunswickers peering east from the redoubt then heard "a sudden tramping of feet in the forest on our right," a German officer wrote. "We were surrounded." Gunfire built to a roar, and smoke hung like a dirty halo over the rocky knoll. "The battle became general and desperate immediately," wrote militiaman David Holbrook.

One of the German 3-pounders positioned within the perimeter barked and barked again, but the case shot—iron balls packed into a cylindrical tin canister—had a lethal range of only eighty yards. Of greater anxiety for Baum was that dragoon cartridge boxes held just ten rounds. These troops had been trained to fight from horseback with swords and firelocks, and an effort to stand and fire a simultaneous volley proved disastrous. "As soon as they rose up to take aim, bullets went through their heads," wrote Wasmus, the surgeon. "In a short time, our tallest and best dragoons were sent into eternity."

As the battle intensified, emboldened attackers began to leap over the breastworks where the enemy defenses seemed thinnest. "The bayonet, the butt of the rifle, the saber, [and] the pike were in full play," a survivor wrote. The lieutenant commanding Baum's 3-pounders was wounded above the eye and captured, along with his gunners and guns. "There was no regular battle," recalled Captain Peter Clark. "All was confusion." In describing his confrontation with a German defender, militiaman Leonard Robinson wrote, "I prayed the Lord to have mercy on his soul, and then took care of his body." Wasmus placed a dressing station in the rear behind a towering oak, and there he tried to treat his wounded compatriots. "The bullets were dreadful, whistling over and beyond me," he wrote. "I remained lying on the ground until the enemy urged me rather impolitely to get up." He would spend his next three years in America as a prisoner of war.

Almost two hours into the battle, with casualties climbing, ammunition scarce, and General Stark advancing on the bridge with a thousand reinforcements, Baum ordered his dragoons to draw their swords and hack an escape path through the perimeter. Some broke in panic, skittering down the steep front slope and into the river, only to drown or be shot dead, their bodies swept downstream like blue rafts. Baum and a few comrades hobbled across a field southwest of the bridge; there the Brunswick commander abruptly crumpled into a furrow. Wasmus, while being led away with other prisoners, came upon him moments later "lying completely naked on a cart. He was shot through the abdomen and was crying and begging that the cart should go slow, but the men did not understand our language." At last the makeshift ambulance stopped at a farmhouse, where Baum was carried inside and laid on the dirt floor to die.

No sooner had the shooting ebbed than nearly seven hundred Brunswick reinforcements approached from the west, led by teams pulling a pair of 6-pounders. Washboard roads, heavy rain, upended ammunition carts, a befuddled guide, underfed dray horses, and the congenital delinquency of the commander, Lieutenant Colonel Heinrich Breymann, had kept the relief column from moving more than half a mile an hour since receiving Burgoyne's urgent order the previous morning. Breymann was greeted on the road at four-thirty p.m. by Skene, who reported that Baum was entrenched several miles ahead. He neglected to mention, through ignorance or neglect, that the expedition was fighting to avoid annihilation.

As the column plodded forward, men appeared along a distant rail fence, some with white feathers or scraps of paper in their hats. Breymann later wrote:

> I perceived a considerable number of armed people, some in jackets & some in shirts, who were endeavoring to gain a height which was on my left. . . . I showed these people to [Skene] who assured me they were royalists and rode up toward them and called out, but received no answer than a discharge of firearms. . . . Then began the attack.

Skene's horse fell dead beneath him. A Bennington militiaman who was among those shooting from the hillside declared, "It was like firing into a flock of sheep." Breymann ordered his light infantry to attack the hill as he moved forward with grenadiers. The two 6-pounders raked the slope with case shot; rebel gunners answered with the captured 3-pounders before bounding from tree to tree toward a log fence in the lee of Hessian Hill. "My gun barrel was by this time too hot to hold," Private Thomas Mellen recalled, "so I seized a musket from a dead Hessian." General Stark, mounted on a spirited five-year-old mare with a doeskin saddle, barked orders and encouragement while trotting around the edge of what he would call "the hottest engagement I have ever witnessed, resembling a continual clap of thunder." Another officer hollered, "Fight on, boys. Reinforcements close by."

Breymann had closed to within ninety yards of the faltering rebel line when the day swung against him. From the east came 150 long-striding Green Mountain Boys under Colonel Seth Warner, summoned from Manchester by Stark, who had urged them to "come in with all speed." More gunfire thunderclaps echoed in the woodlands. The Americans aimed at enemy muzzle flashes and cannoneers, edging around Breymann's left flank.

Surviving German gunners began creeping west. "Our ammunition was all expended and the artillery in consequence ceased firing," Breymann wrote. "The horses either were dead or in a condition which prevented them from moving." Skene found at least one serviceable mount, slashed the traces to the gun carriage, and rode away.

Abandoning the cannons and their eight brass drums, the Germans at last took to their heels, hurrying toward the setting sun. Breymann followed, a flesh wound oozing from his left leg and several bullet holes ventilating his coat. "We pursued them till dark, when I was obliged to halt for fear of killing our own men," Stark reported. "Had daylight lasted one hour longer, we should have taken the whole body of them." At least some of his men had broken into captured German liquor stocks and were in no condition to pursue. Breymann and his enfeebled survivors reached Cambridge at midnight for a few hours' sleep under the stars before pressing on to the Hudson at dawn on August 17.

The Americans had won their first undisputed victory in the northern theater since General Richard Montgomery's seizure of St. Johns, Chambly, and Montreal, in Quebec, almost two years earlier. "The bells were rung, guns fired, the people shouted in the street," Lucy Knox wrote Henry from Boston. "Every man you saw, from the fine gentleman to the porter, were as happy as liquor could make them." Congress would belatedly reward Stark with a Continental brigadier general's commission.

Yet it was the small domestic stories that held the eye and filled the heart. "Most affectionate husband, after my kind respects to you, hoping you are yet in the land of the living," Elizabeth Gage wrote her husband, David, a militiaman from Pelham, New Hampshire. "I have heard of the battle that General Stark has had with the enemy, and I expect that you and the rest of our Pelham men was in the battle, which makes me feel very melancholy, expecting every day to hear bad news from you." A few days later he replied:

> Loving wife, I have this time an opportunity to write and do gladly improve it to inform you that I am in the land of the living and in perfect health and bless be God for it. . . . I am your kind and loving husband, David Gage.

More than half a century later, Hannah Wheeler, at age ninety-two, would recall hearing that four men had been killed at Bennington from her husband David's Massachusetts militia company. "It was rumored that *he* was killed and when he returned I cried, and he asked me if I was sorry, but I told him I was crying for joy." The news kindled different emotions in others. Ann Peters, wife of the loyalist commander routed at the Tory Redoubt, received an erroneous report that he and their oldest son had been killed at Bennington. "My calamities are very great," she said before hearing that they were in fact safe in Burgoyne's camp. "But thank God they died doing their duty to their king and country. I have six sons left, and as soon as they shall be able to bear arms, I will send them against the rebels."

Burgoyne would need them promptly. Bennington had cost him 207 dead and 750 captured, including 30 officers, without the expedition ever leaving New York. Stark put his casualties at 30 killed and 40 wounded. The only British troops to march with Baum, 50 sharpshooters from the Company of Marksmen, had been all but exterminated; only 8 made it back to the Hudson. German losses included not only 70 percent of the men engaged on August 16 but also four field guns, a thousand muskets and rifles, and nine hundred swords, some of which would be distributed to American cavalrymen. "This affair in its consequences," a captured German officer wrote, "has caused us much damage."

The battle's aftermath held the usual horror. A woman named Sally Kellogg described wounded Germans being carted from the battlefield, including "men with broken legs, some with balls shot through their bodies, some with their heads done up, some men on litters." A rebel soldier later wrote, "One Tory with his left eye shot out was led by me, mounted on a horse who had also lost his left eye. It seems to me cruel now. It did not then." Militiaman Peter Clark wrote his wife in late August that scouts had found "twenty-six of the enemy lying dead in the woods. They stank so they would not bury them. . . . The wounded Hessians die three or four in a day. They are all in Bennington meeting house, which smells so it is enough to kill anyone in it."

Women on the streets of Bennington heckled ambulatory German prisoners. Bound with ropes two by two, they scuffed into makeshift jails soon infested with "tribes of vermin." Officers were locked in the second-floor room of a tavern. Uncounted privates crowded a church, where a sudden commotion caused jumpy guards to fire through the door, killing two men and wounding five.

At three a.m. on August 17 couriers arrived with the bad news from the Walloomsac at Burgoyne's new headquarters south of Fort Edward. After consulting Riedesel, the British commander prepared to lead the entire army east to rescue the expedition. But as exhausted and wounded men streamed back into camp, he put aside that impractical notion in favor of simply blaming his allies. The Germans were too slow, too encumbered with their broadswords, too *German*.

"Colonel Baum was induced to proceed without sufficient knowledge of the ground," Burgoyne wrote Germain. "His design was betrayed. The men who had taken the [loyalty] oaths were the first to fire upon him." To Riedesel he added, "The march of Mr. Breymann was very slow. It would have been better if he had left his artillery to follow after him under an escort." In a crowning hallucination, he told London that the rebels "have small cause for exaltation, their loss in killed and wounded being more than double to ours."

In general orders, Burgoyne advised his troops that "the attempt having failed of success through the chances of war, the troops must necessarily halt some days for bringing forward the transport of provisions." Failure to collect livestock and provisions in Vermont would require remaining on the Hudson indefinitely to continue accumulating supplies from Lake George. This pleased no one, given the sweltering heat, which British officers compared to Madras, in India. "One could hardly breathe when sitting in the tents," a German soldier wrote. "Dysentery raged among us." Meals had grown scanty and monotonous: "pork at noon, pork at night, pork cold, pork hot."

Still, their objective lay near. One final push would win through. Despite this setback, since Ticonderoga six weeks earlier, the rebels had demonstrated little capacity to halt the king's drive down the Hudson. "We shall soon be in a position to move on toward Albany," a Brunswick soldier wrote. "The unhappy occurrence has not dispirited us."

Burgoyne also put on a brave face, although two catastrophic intelligence failures, at Fort Stanwix and Bennington, had whittled away both his force and his confidence. New Englanders were rallying to the rebel cause by the thousands. The Continental Army downriver grew stronger by the day. His supply system seemed to be teetering.

But his orders were clear, at least in his own mind: to "force a junction with Sir William Howe." Whatever chances of war befell him and his Canada Army, he wrote, "I am not at liberty to remain inactive."

5.

———

A Barbarous Business in a Barbarous Country

The great British fleet carrying the two Howe brothers had traveled only thirty miles from the Delaware Bay in late July when the fair wind turned foul. Prevailing summer southwesterlies acted as a sea anchor, and by the time the *Eagle* and her consorts finally turned north at Cape Charles into Chesapeake Bay on August 9, most of the eighteen thousand troops had spent a month on their ships since boarding in New York, with two more weeks to go before reaching Head of Elk.

"The weather is insufferably hot," Captain Francis Downman, a Royal Artillery officer, wrote aboard *Brilliant*. A seaman who had sailed the coast of equatorial Africa swore he had never felt "such an intense, suffocating heat." A Hessian lieutenant aboard *Martha* informed his diary, "Anyone who has a desire to experience misery and misfortune should go aboard a ship. . . . The meat is miserable and frightfully salted so that it can hardly be eaten, and then one nearly dies of thirst. The entire ship is full of lice." *Martha*'s mate died on August 10 and was buried at sea, lashed to a board weighted with a dozen cannonballs. Men who slept on deck to escape the torrid compartments below awoke to find their skin black from pitch melting in the ship's seams.

Where the bay was wide, the land could be smelled in loamy whiffs but not seen. Swans and sea eagles circled the ships, and blue crabs swarmed by the many thousands near the surface. Where the bay narrowed, the resourceful Captain Hamond, as agreed, placed pilot vessels to mark the channel. In shoal water near Poole's Island, the largest ships churned up bottom mud, and small boats sailed two cable lengths—twelve hundred feet—ahead of each vessel, reporting the depth with signal flags. To avoid groundings, Admiral Howe sailed only by day. At sunset the ships dropped anchor, each displaying two lights side by side to starboard and two more, one atop the other, to port. Nine frigates protected the flotilla; one of them, the *Sphynx*, captured a heedless James River brig carrying 150 hogsheads of tobacco, which the admiral ordered distributed to his sailors.

Thunderstorms "as has never been seen in Europe," in one Hessian's description, battered the expedition almost daily. A storm struck early in the evening of August 3 with "indescribably frightful thunder and lightning," a Mirbach Regiment lieutenant wrote, shredding sails and laying a sloop on beam-ends; seven men and a woman who sought safety in a skiff were lost when the painter snapped and the boat capsized. On August 8 lightning killed the ship's carpenter on the *Jenny Hamilton*, and subsequent strikes destroyed ten horses and shivered the masts of several transports, knocking down yards and igniting fires as the wind in the rigging rose to a shriek. Major General Earl Charles Cornwallis and Major General James Grant were aboard *Isis* when lightning bolts splintered the topgallant mast, shattered the mainmast, and burned the shrouds. "Lord Cornwallis and I were reading in the cabin when it happened," Grant wrote, "which was filled in a moment with a sulfurous smell." The generals shifted their berths to the *Charming Nelly*, and *Isis* limped back to New York for refitting.

Between tempests, some officers enjoyed "sailing up the most beautiful bay, perhaps, in the world," as Lieutenant Loftus Cliffe wrote his brother. A French cook, a German harpist, and ample claret made the voyage pleasant enough aboard *Aeolus*, despite the heat and the tedium. "All were healthy and merry. We played shilling whist every evening," Henry Strachey, another aide to Admiral Howe, wrote aboard *Eagle*. "I am grown somewhat fatter."

Alarm guns and signal fires along the shoreline tracked the fleet. Loyalist farmers—white and black—rowed out to sell melons, milk, and other staples, preferably for payment in salt, and to retail the latest war news. It was said that frightened rebel merchants in Wilmington had sent their wares to Chester County in Pennsylvania for safekeeping; that some Chesapeake families had fled to Lancaster and points west; that on Washington's order, livestock had been driven deep into the marshes; and that runners—millstones—had been removed to "render the mills useless" to the British. It was also said that confiscations of wheat, flour, and cheese by rebel troops from Quaker farm wagons were recorded in the Friends' Book of Sufferings. A rumor heard outside Annapolis claimed that General Burgoyne had "given the rebels a severe thrashing near Albany."

If the voyage was hard on men, it went harder on the horses. Each tethered mount typically needed a stall with light and good ventilation, sixteen pounds of hay and oats daily, six gallons of fresh water, and perhaps a little vinegar for wetting mouths and nostrils. None of that was available as the voyage dragged on, and almost hourly dead horses were swayed up in slings from the holds to be tossed over the side with a sad splash. Forage grew so short that horses were heaved overboard and drowned as a humane alternative to starvation. Their carcasses washed up on Maryland beaches like mileposts. By late August, 170 horses were dead and 150 more were either dying or crippled beyond useful service. This equicide, as General Howe recognized, would impair the army's mobility once he regained solid ground.

The commanding general was often seasick in his cabin aboard the *Eagle*—"this wooden cage," in Strachey's phrase—but that did not stop him from eating hearty breakfasts of cold meat, mutton chops, or broiled chicken. In a resurgence of optimism, he and his brother agreed that if Washington could be forced to fight in the next few weeks "the whole may be finished this year," Strachey recorded. On August 16, a Royal Navy courier had finally tracked down the general to deliver a dispatch from Lord Germain dated three months earlier, giving the king's formal consent for the plan to capture Philadelphia by sea—"trusting, however," Germain added, "that whatever you may meditate, it will be executed in time for you to cooperate with the army ordered to proceed from Canada and put itself under your command." Germain confided that his anxiety about the 1777 campaign "is in a great degree diminished" by intelligence reports that the rebels were struggling to fill their own ranks.

Beginning at five a.m. on August 23, both Howe brothers explored the upper reaches of the bay in search of landing spots. The admiral personally took soundings in the Elk River with a lead line from a small boat. At four a.m. on Monday, August 25, the shallow-draft *Sphynx, Apollo,* and *Senegal* weighed anchor to stand upstream. Admiral Howe hoisted his flag on the fore-topmast head of the *Vigilant*, and at ten a.m. the two brothers stepped ashore at Turkey Point, a Hessian captain reported, to "boisterous shouts of joy" from troops following in fifty-man flatboats. Wave after wave landed behind them—infantry, artillery, supply wagons, and cavalry with a few crowbait horses. The voyage from New York had taken as long as a trip to England, and the army was still sixty miles from Philadelphia, almost as far as when it occupied Perth Amboy, New Jersey, in June.

Few residents could be found when redcoats walked into Head of Elk, a village of forty brick and stone houses. "The women fled to avoid barbarities, which they imagined must be the natural attendants of a British army," Lieutenant William Hale of the 45th Foot wrote to his father, an admiral, in England. But the Continental Army storehouses were full of

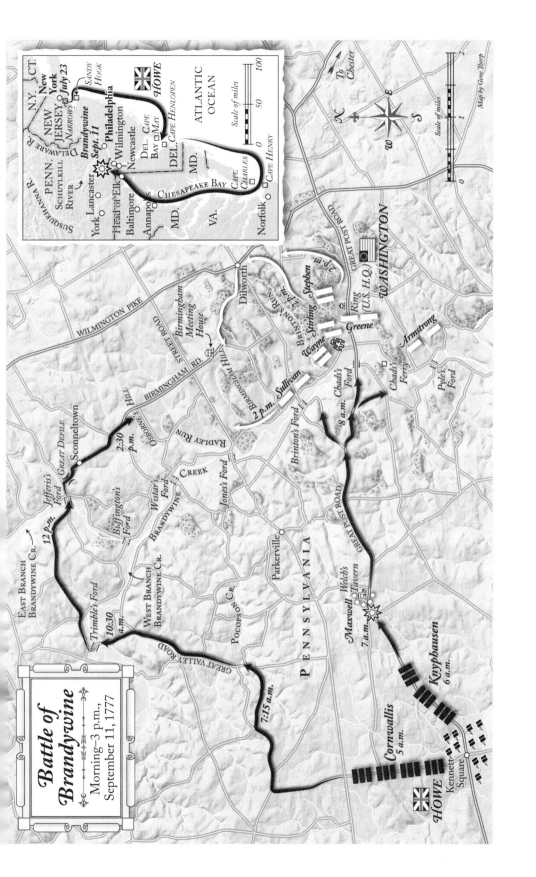

Battle of Brandywine
Morning–3 p.m., September 11, 1777

Map by Gene Thorp

Inset map labels:

N.Y. | CT.
New York
NEW JERSEY
Sandy Hook *July 23*
Narrows *July 23*
PENN.
Schuylkill River
Susquehanna R.
Lancaster
York
Head of Elk
Baltimore
Annapolis
Brandywine *Sept. 11*
Philadelphia *Sept. 11*
Wilmington
Newcastle
DEL.
Del. Bay
Cape May
Cape Henlopen
ATLANTIC OCEAN
HOWE
MD.
VA.
Norfolk
Cape Charles
Cape Henry
Chesapeake Bay
Scale of miles — 0 50 100

Main map labels:

To Chester
GREAT POST ROAD
WASHINGTON
Ring (U.S. H.Q.)
2 p.m.
Stephen
Stirling
Wayne
Greene
Armstrong
Chadds Ferry
Pyle's Ford
Chadds Ford *8 a.m.*
BRINTON'S RUN
2 p.m. Sullivan
Brinton's Ford
Birmingham Meeting House
Dilworth
BIRMINGHAM STREET ROAD
BIRMINGHAM RD.
BIRMINGHAM HILL
RADLEY RUN
WILMINGTON PIKE
Sconneltown
2:30 p.m.
OSBORNE'S HILL
GREAT DEFILE
Jefferis's Ford
12 p.m.
EAST BRANCH BRANDYWINE CR.
Trimble's Ford *10:30 a.m.*
Wistar's Ford
Buffington's Ford
BRANDYWINE CREEK
Jones's Ford
WEST BRANCH BRANDYWINE CR.
Parkerville
Pocopson Cr.
GREAT VALLEY ROAD
7:15 a.m.
PENNSYLVANIA
GREAT POST ROAD
Maxwell's Welch's Tavern
7 a.m.
Cornwallis *5 a.m.*
Knyphausen *6 a.m.*
Kennett Square
HOWE

Scale of miles — 0 1 2

molasses, Indian corn, tobacco, pitch, flour, rum, and a hundred butts of porter. A Continental agent who had been told to remove all cattle to the east instead sold a hundred head to British commissaries. Two dozen abandoned coasters held more grain, sugar, and indigo.

Tents had been left aboard the ships, and thunderstorms drenched the ranks night after night. The Guards alone had sixteen thousand cartridges ruined by rain, a quarter of their ammunition. "We have lived like beasts," Hale wrote. "No plates, no dishes, no tablecloth."

Yet for all the hardships of the past six weeks, this was a formidable, ferocious host gathering itself like a clenched fist. Most troops here had joined a peacetime army for a lifelong career, unaware that they would be swept up in a violent revolutionary drama three thousand miles from home. (More recent recruits were promised a discharge after three years, unless the rebellion ended sooner.) Few had been compelled to join; by law each man attested before a magistrate that his service was voluntary. Recruiters were instructed that no "stroller, vagabond, or sailor" need apply, or men with "rupture, broken bones, or king's evil running sores on any part of his body." A prohibition against any applicant "who is not a Protestant" had been eased in 1775 to permit the recruitment of Roman Catholics. Even papists could be taught to shoot rebels.

About half the enlisted troops were at least literate enough to sign their names, as the historian Don N. Hagist later established. More than half had been tradesmen before taking up soldiering, and they were as varied in their civilian professions—weavers, tailors, coopers, bricklayers, butchers, barbers—as they were in their ethnicity: English, Scottish, Welsh, German, Swedish, Swiss, Polish, Dutch, Danish, and the odd American. They had been lured to the colors for the pound sterling a month in pay, for the chance to see the world, to "be freed from the clamours of a wife," as one wrote, or, in the words of another, for "the glory of victory, the comforts of a pension in old age, and the pleasure of recounting my adventures to others." Each man was told to be "master of his person" by carrying himself properly—chin up, shoulders back, stomach in. Their officers derived mostly from the upper classes to ensure loyalty to the Crown; commissions were bought and sold, perhaps £2,000 for a captaincy and twice that for a lieutenant colonel's billet. Collectively, they gave General Howe one of the finest armies in the world, and at the moment they were keen to drub the faithless insurgents who had brought them to this obscure spot on the earth's far edge.

Howe was determined to punish indiscipline, and no sooner had the army settled into camp than two soldiers were hanged and five others severely whipped for plundering. British officers often blamed their German comrades for bad behavior. "The Hessians are more infamous & cruel than any," wrote Ambrose Serle, the admiral's secretary. "It is a misfortune that we ever had such a dirty, cowardly set of contemptible miscreants."

Yet it was a redcoat drummer in the 27th Foot who was given five hundred lashes a week later, again for plundering. On August 31, Major Charles Stuart wrote his father of "plundering and irregularity of every kind." The same day, two soldiers from the 71st Foot were found not far from camp with their throats cut. "It is supposed they were plundering and were set upon by some lurking rebels," an officer wrote. Several gunners also went missing, and two grenadiers were found "hanged by the rebels with their plunder on their backs," Lieutenant John Peebles told his diary. Captain John André later estimated that "at the Head of Elk we lost two hundred men in a very few days, and most probably the greatest number in excursions for plunder." As a captain in the 57th Foot wrote his sister on September 1, "It is a barbarous business and in a barbarous country."

On Wednesday, September 3, the army heaved itself forward in two columns under General Cornwallis and General Wilhelm von Knyphausen, the Hessian commander. Five miles to the east, across the Delaware state line, the columns reunited. Howe sent invalids and extra baggage back to Head of Elk to reboard the fleet, which his brother would guide down the Chesapeake and up Delaware Bay for an eventual rendezvous with the army in Philadelphia. Each officer's field equipage was reduced to weapons, two shirts, a blanket, and a canteen.

Summer was gone. One Hessian commander feared that too much of the fighting season had been frittered away with it. "The outcome will show whether I am mistaken," Colonel Carl von Donop wrote his prince in Germany in early September. "We have allowed the rebels too much time in which to become soldiers."

After a short, sharp scrap with Continentals at Cooch's Bridge, the army pivoted north toward Pennsylvania, led by two hundred pioneers in leather aprons and heavy gloves who groomed the rain-mired byway with shovels, picks, and axes. "The roads heavy and the horses mere carrion," wrote Captain John Montrésor, the army's chief engineer. The column soon stretched for ten miles through sassafras groves and orchards saggy with fruit. Droves of lowing cattle and bleating sheep moved with the troops and a provision train of 276 wagons. Flankers traipsed half a mile on either side of the column to confiscate more livestock and nail amnesty offers to the doors of vacant farmhouses, even as they spared "neither friend nor foe, burning, robbing, stealing all the way they went," a Pennsylvanian named John Miller reported.

Howe soon recognized that he had few friends here, despite issuing "a free and general pardon" to insurgents, who "voluntarily come and surrender themselves." The robust loyalist support that he had expected failed to appear. In a dispatch to London, Howe reported that most Americans here "are strongly in enmity against us, many having taken up arms" or vanished into the hinterlands. Rebel newspapers claimed a stunning victory over Burgoyne at a place called Bennington. In reply to Germain's recent letter, Howe said he hoped that his campaign in Pennsylvania would "be finished in time for me to cooperate with the [Canada] army," but "I cannot flatter myself I shall be able to act upon the king's expectations in this particular."

For the moment, the task was to find Washington and force him to give battle. "Otherwise," wrote Captain Friedrich Ernst von Münchhausen, Howe's German aide-de-camp, "this war will not end for a long time."

The elusive General Washington had spent the end of August in a makeshift headquarters at Quaker Hill, on the southwest fringe of Wilmington. When reports arrived of British landings near Head of Elk, he rode with Lafayette, General Greene, Lieutenant Colonel Hamilton, and most of his cavalry on a thirty-six-mile reconnaissance gallop to Iron Hill, on the Maryland border. Here he pulled out his three-draw mahogany-and-brass spyglass, made with a flared eyecup by a London optician. Even extended to its full thirty-three inches, the glass revealed little of an enemy still tucked behind hills and in thick woodlands. The traveling party spent a stormy night in the vacant house of a loyalist lawyer before returning to Wilmington. A day later, Howe claimed the house for his headquarters.

Washington's army had nearly doubled in size in the past month: it now numbered almost nineteen thousand troops, including five thousand militiamen. As usual, he was disappointed by the militia turnout, but of more immediate concern was a shortfall of guns and ammunition. In letters to the commissary of military stores in Philadelphia, he requested five hundred to a thousand muskets and bayonets, as well as "all the rifles in your hands," since "the bad weather has damaged many of late." The commissary replied that he had "very few" firelocks but would send fifty wagons to Wilmington with more than eight hundred thousand musket cartridges. In a further search for paper to make cartridges, couriers visited mills near Lancaster, where printers donated several carts stacked with loose pages ready for the bindery of John Foxe's *Book of Martyrs*, a lurid account of Catholic oppression of Protestants. This, Washington's staff announced, would provide "literary ammunition."

When the king's men began to move north, Washington moved with them. To protect Philadelphia, he would put aside his strategy of defensive war, but only in hopes of baiting the British into attacking him on favorable ground. He created a new light infantry corps of five hundred men to hector the enemy and "to know as exactly as possible how and where they lie, where their several guards are stationed and the strength of them, and everything necessary to be known," as he wrote on September 3. "Be prepared," he told the grizzled corps commander, Brigadier General William Maxwell, "to give them as much trouble as you possibly can." Refugees fled from the path of both armies with a few sticks of furniture piled on their wagons in "the most distressing scenes imaginable," Greene wrote to his wife, Caty. "The country all resounds with the cries of the people." In general orders on September 5, Washington told his men that the enemy appeared intent on capturing Philadelphia, but if defeated "they are utterly undone—the war is at an end. . . . The eyes of all America and Europe are turned on us. . . . Glory waits to crown the brave."

Howe refused, for the moment, to be undone. Marching through deserted Newark, Delaware, a village described by one British officer as "remarkable for sedition & Presbyterian sermons," the column slid past Washington's right. The American commander had intended to make a stand on Red Clay Creek, a couple miles above the Delaware border, but Howe threatened to cut off the Continentals from the extensive supply magazines in Lancaster, to the northwest, and perhaps even from Philadelphia, thirty miles to the northeast. On Tuesday morning, September 9, Washington ordered his army to reposition at Chads's Ford, where the Great Post Road connecting Philadelphia and Baltimore crossed Brandywine Creek.

This rugged, vertical ground in Chester County provided precisely the sort of defensible position the commander in chief had envisioned. Embraced by steep banks and hardwood thickets, the creek flowed fast and often nose-deep northwest to southeast for twenty-two miles before emptying into the Delaware River near Wilmington. Captain Montrésor, the British engineer, described the terrain as "an amazing strong country, being a succession of large hills, rather sudden with narrow vales." The Continental geographer, Robert Erskine, had compiled a map of the roads around the Brandywine. Washington also knew that several other fords were interspersed for six miles upstream from Chads's, each called by one or more local names—Brinton's, Painter's, Jones's, Buffington's—which soon confused the Continentals assigned to defend them. Scouts assured the commanding general that no usable crossings existed for twelve miles above Buffington's Ford.

This was incorrect, but Washington failed to examine the countryside himself or ensure that trusted lieutenants did so, just as a year earlier he had failed to use his experienced surveyor's eye to good advantage at Long Island, White Plains, and Fort Washington. Nor, apparently, did he consult the soldiers now entrenching along the Brandywine, who might know this landscape, including local militia battalions and two Continental regiments from Pennsylvania. Of the seventeen thousand American troops assembled near the creek, at least seven hundred were mounted, but they would not be effectively used to reconnoiter the potential battlefield or to track enemy movements.

Washington placed his headquarters in the home of a Quaker farmer, Benjamin Ring, who had sent his family away as the armies drew near. The fieldstone house with white shutters stood on a steep slope among sycamores and oaks a mile east of Chads's Ford. Aides assembled the commanding general's long camp bed, built of beech and red oak with tapering posts, a rectangular headboard, and hinged rails for easy storage. Washington issued a flurry of orders prohibiting promiscuous gunfire and the destruction of farm fences. The commissary general was to have at least three days' provisions within a few miles of the army's rear, while the troops "are to be provided with cooked provisions for tomorrow." Hundreds of pickets were to be posted. The enemy army, he notified Congress, was said to be "in a tolerably compact body" to the west. "Maneuvering appears to be their plan," he added. "I hope we shall be able to find out their real, intended route, & to defeat their purposes."

Late in the afternoon of Wednesday, September 10, the Reverend Joab Trout delivered a sermon on the hillside above Washington's headquarters. "Soldiers and countrymen," he said in a loud, strong voice. "We have met in the peaceful valley on the eve of battle while the sunlight is dying away." He continued:

> They may conquer us tomorrow. Might and wrong may prevail, and we may be driven from this field. But the hour of God's own vengeance will come. . . . Eternal God fights for you. He rides on the battle cloud. He sweeps onward with the march of the hurricane charge. God the awful and the infinite fights for you, and will triumph.

The chaplain paused before concluding, "The doom of the British is near."

Apples and peaches now ready for picking would instead rot on the ground. Buckwheat ripening for harvest in a month would be trampled, along with the Indian corn and fields fertilized with wood ash for the winter wheat and rye scheduled for planting later in September. Thursday was baking day on many farms, perfuming the air with the scent of burning brushwood, but most ovens in the Brandywine valley remained cold on September 11. Nearly half of the county's residents were Quakers, although some had been expelled from the Society of Friends for owning a slave, keeping a tavern, marrying outside the faith, or paying taxes to support the rebellion. War would bring calamity to believer and nonbeliever alike. It also brought the suspicious contempt of both belligerent sides. "The villainous Quakers are employed upon every quarter to serve the enemy," wrote General Greene, a disaffected Quaker himself. "Some of them are confined and more deserve it."

Greene's division, the largest in the Continental Army, with twenty-five hundred men, anchored the American line on the Brandywine, straddling the Great Post Road—hardly more than a cart path, despite the ostentatious name. A four-gun battery pointing west overlooked both Chads's Ford and a ferry landing. Two Pennsylvania militia brigades covered the army's southern flank to Greene's left; to his right two thousand Pennsylvania Continentals in Anthony Wayne's division had dug in with more artillery. Reserve forces waited on the high ground a thousand yards back from the creek. To feel for the approaching enemy, eight hundred men under General Maxwell—known as Scotch Willie for his thick brogue—had forded the creek to edge westward as early light filtered through the tree canopy.

Washington's right wing had been entrusted to Major General John Sullivan, a litigious, barrel-shaped New Hampshire lawyer with a peptic ulcer and eyes almost as dark as his curly black hair. For the past two years, whenever the rebel army had faced a crisis on the battlefield, Sullivan had seemed to be the man of the hour—with decidedly mixed results in Canada and at Long Island, where he'd been captured and later exchanged. In August he had commanded a misbegotten raid against the British on Staten Island, which had ended in a disorderly retreat. More than two hundred of his men were taken prisoner and paraded past "a multitude of insulting spectators" in New York, a disgusted captain reported. "He has his wants and he has his foibles," Washington acknowledged, among them tippling, self-pity—"I am the butt against which all the darts are leveled," Sullivan wrote—and hypochondria. A few weeks earlier he had informed Washington that he had been bled four times during a recent illness, from which "I shall never perfectly recover." The commanding general had also rebuked him for "imaginary slights. . . . No other officer of rank in the whole army has so often conceived himself neglected, slighted, and ill-treated as you have."

A skeptical Dr. Benjamin Rush dismissed Sullivan as "weak, vain, without dignity, fond of scribbling [and], in the field, a madman." Yet Washington rarely turned on his senior lieutenants, and Sullivan, vain, mad, or otherwise, was once again in the field. At Brinton's Ford, two miles upstream from Chads's, he commanded eighteen hundred men and was responsible for defending the creek and its crossings to the north.

General Howe had placed his command post in a tavern at Kennett Square, a crossroads six miles west of the Brandywine. By paying local loyalists up to twenty guineas to act as guides, he had gained a better grasp of the terrain than Washington had, and a few captured Continentals provided details about American positions.

At six a.m., General Knyphausen surged east with almost seven thousand British and German troops. His vanguard—ninety British riflemen and the Queen's Rangers, both outfitted in green uniforms—had traveled only three miles when gunfire cackled around Welch's Tavern, where 150 of Maxwell's light infantrymen manned an outpost. After several volleys that left the forest floor littered with green-jacketed bodies, the Americans fell back on the Great Post Road to a fence behind a clearing, where they again ambushed the king's men. Knyphausen ordered dragoons and Highlanders to outflank the rebel left, and four teams of horses jangled down the road pulling field guns.

The weight of numbers soon told. By midmorning Maxwell had pulled his rear guard back across the Brandywine as the king's men muscled 12-pounders and howitzers along the western ridge above Chads's Ford. Musketry sputtered and died away, overwhelmed by the boom of artillery from both sides. Pennsylvania gunners mixed liquor and a dash of gunpowder into their water cask "to make them resolute," according to a fifteen-year-old gunner, then aimed at enemy muzzle flashes a few hundred yards away. Before noon cannon roars echoed up the creek bed like something caged and angry. British and German foot soldiers swarmed down swales and behind hills without attempting to cross the Brandywine.

The Americans had reason to be pleased with their morning, having suffered fifty casualties to eighty for the king's men. Among those badly wounded, by a bullet that shattered his right elbow, was Captain Patrick Ferguson, commander of the British riflemen and inventor of a patented breech-loading rifle capable of firing six highly accurate rounds a minute—double the rate for a conventional musket, as demonstrated to King George the previous fall. Ferguson's injury would result in his unit being disbanded before the new weapon could prove its value on the battlefield.

Still, Washington sat his horse above the ford and wondered why the British assault seemed halfhearted. "The firing of the field artillery by the enemy is merely to amuse," Colonel Timothy Pickering, the adjutant general, suggested while on horseback next to him. "The main body must be marching to cross at some other place."

William Howe would not need Captain Ferguson's rifles on Thursday morning, for he had indeed stolen a march on the Americans while they were distracted by Knyphausen's noisy sortie. At five a.m., eighty-two hundred men led by Howe and Cornwallis had wheeled away from Kennett Square, concealed by the morning fog as they tramped north on the Great Valley Road, which ran roughly parallel to the Brandywine. Led by loyalists, including a local blacksmith and a clockmaker, the column had swung onto Greave Valley Road and, by ten-thirty a.m., reached Trimble's Ford, a mile above Buffington's Ford and unknown to the American high command. The fog burned off and the day warmed. The column waded waist-deep through the creek's west branch before angling east with the intention of looping behind the unwitting Americans.

As the morning slipped past, Washington was thoroughly confused. A vague report at eight a.m. of a flanking column across the Brandywine caused him to send Major John Jamison from his light dragoons to investigate. At nine-thirty a.m., Sullivan informed the commanding general that Jamison had reported "there was no enemy there." A second officer sent to Buffington's, where the two branches merged into a single creek, agreed that "no enemy had passed that way." But still another officer, Colonel Moses Hazen, reported British troops on the Great Valley Road a mile west of the forks. Shortly after eleven a.m., Washington scribbled a note to his dragoon commander, Colonel Theodorick Bland:

> I earnestly entreat continuance of your vigilant attention to the movements of the enemy. . . . I wish you to gain satisfactory information of a body confidently reported to have gone up to a ford seven or eight miles above this. It is said the fact is certain.

Yet nothing was certain. At the same hour, Lieutenant Colonel James Ross of the 8th Pennsylvania wrote Washington from the Great Valley Road that at least five thousand enemy soldiers "with 16 or 18 field pieces marched this road just now. . . . We are close in their rear with about 70 men." Ross's troops had even exchanged volleys with the redcoats. This suggested that the bulk of Howe's army had moved upstream, leaving Knyphausen's wing at Chads's Ford isolated and vulnerable. Washington hastily drafted orders for Sullivan, Greene, and Maxwell to lunge across the creek in a sudden counterattack. No sooner had Continentals tromped to the water's edge than Washington countermanded his order, in response to another confounding report, this one from Major Joseph Spear of the Chester County militia, who told Sullivan that he had "heard nothing of the enemy about the forks of the Brandywine & is confident they are not in that quarter." Perhaps Howe had sent a feint up the Great Valley Road; he could be doubling back to rejoin Knyphausen and trap the Americans as they crossed the Brandywine.

Howe had no such trickery in mind. By early afternoon his column was splashing through crystalline Jefferis's Ford, on the Brandywine's eastern branch. Dust billowed above the regiments, powdering red and blue uniforms as they swung southeast onto Birmingham Road and up the Great Defile, a steep, twisting ascent past empty farmhouses and neatly fenced meadows. Pairs of *Jäger* scouts led them, two hundred paces apart, under the command of Captain Johann von Ewald, an exceptionally competent officer who as young man had lost his left eye in a duel and would spend eight years in America fighting the insurgents. Ewald was already considered a military intellectual, and his accumulated aphorisms included several pertinent on this Thursday afternoon, notably "Never think yourself fully secure" and "Demoralize the enemy, then annihilate him." Finishing his climb away from the creek bottom, Ewald was astonished to find no trace of rebel troops guarding the narrow ravine. "A hundred men," he later wrote, "could have held up the army the whole day."

As lathered teams pulled the last of the gun carriages and creaking ammunition wagons to the top, Howe ordered a brief rest on Osborne's Hill for the winded men and beasts, who had marched twelve miles in eight hours. Troops pulled food and canteens from their haversacks. Their commander rode to an open clearing where "with a most cheerful countenance [he] convened with his officers & invited several to a light refreshment on the grass," a lieutenant wrote. A mile to the south stood Birmingham Meeting House, evacuated that morning by Quaker worshippers when rebel troops seized the building for a hospital. An anonymous entry in the Friends' meeting book for September 11 noted simply, "Today there was much confusion outside."

While many of his neighbors scattered, curiosity kept a twenty-one-year-old Quaker named Joseph Townsend from fleeing the king's men. "In a few minutes the fields were literally covered with them," he wrote. "Their arms and bayonets being raised, shone as bright as silver." German troops "wore their beards on their upper lips, which was a novelty in that part of the country." British officers asked Townsend "where Mr. Washington was to be found." An officer in boots and spurs "mounted on a large English horse much reduced in flesh" proved to be General Howe, "a large, portly man of coarse features."

The British commander scrutinized the rolling terrain to the south with his spyglass. Rebel troops had begun to scurry around the meeting-house and into fighting formations on the broad hillside beyond it. Howe ordered his army forward.

Washington had returned to his headquarters at the Ring house for a midday dinner when a dispatch sent at one-fifteen p.m. by Colonel Bland, the dragoon commander, at last caused the scales to fall from his eyes. "I have discovered a party of the enemy on the heights," Bland wrote, "about half a mile to the right of the meeting house (Birmingham)." This was followed by a brief, anguished note from General Sullivan: "The enemy are in the rear of my right." These warnings, although estimating enemy strength on Osborne's Hill at two brigades—less than half of Howe's actual strength—sparked an uproar in the American camp. "Never was men more surprised, from private to His Excellency, than we were," wrote Lieutenant Colonel Adam Hubley, Jr., commander of the 10th Pennsylvania Regiment.

His Excellency ordered his reserve divisions to hurry the two miles toward Birmingham from their positions above the Brandywine. Commanded by Major Generals Adam Stephen and William Alexander—known as Lord Stirling because of his disputed claim to a Scottish earldom—they moved "in a trott," one officer wrote, their wagons "all kicking up thick clouds of dust." Sullivan followed with two Maryland brigades from his division, under orders to take command of the new defensive position to the north even though, as he wrote, "I neither knew where the enemy were or what route the other two divisions were to take."

As regiments arrived from the Brandywine, an improvised forward line formed behind the three-foot stone wall of the Birmingham Meeting House cemetery and in a nearby woodlot. Generals Stephen and Lord Stirling deployed the bulk of their four brigades across Birmingham Hill, half a mile south of the meetinghouse. On a knoll between the two divisions, five French fieldpieces were unlimbered, each inscribed near the muzzle with the Latin motto ULTIMA RATIO REGUM: "the final argument of kings."

And then the king's men were on them. Three columns a quarter mile apart and parallel to Birmingham Road swept down Osborne's Hill, sluicing through apple orchards and over split-rail fences. Cornwallis led them. "He was on horseback, appeared tall and sat very erect," Joseph Townsend reported. "His rich scarlet clothing loaded with gold lace [and] epaulettes . . .

occasioned him to make a brilliant and martial appearance." Musket barrels scoured with wet brick dust glinted in the afternoon sun, and hooves churned more dust below the horses' bellies. The first spatter of gunfire from skirmishers soon built to a roar. Tongues of flame licked from the muzzles, followed by the rattle of steel ramrods as another cartridge was teased down each smoking barrel.

A blood-smeared Dr. Rush was treating patients in the Birmingham Meeting House, where sick and injured men lay on wooden benches. A door lifted from its hinges served as a makeshift surgical table, and a large pit dug in the adjacent burying ground was intended as a receptacle for amputated limbs and a common grave for the newly dead. Several soldiers' wives bustled about, filling canteens. Rebel resistance around the meeting-house stiffened to allow Rush and a colleague, Dr. Lewis Howell, to evacuate their patients amid "the heaviest firing I ever heard," as Howell reported after fleeing without his coat, hat, or horse.

The 170 men in the 3rd Virginia Regiment under Colonel Thomas Marshall fought valiantly "long enough to save the army from utter ruin," an admiring officer later wrote. Only when British light infantry enveloped both his flanks at the stone wall did Marshall retreat south, despite two bullets in his horse and losses that included two lieutenants killed and seventy-three enlisted casualties.

Scorching American fire forced Captain Ewald and his *Jäger* to fall back two hundred paces. "We have learned from the rebels to cover our bodies if there's a tree or a rail near us," a captain had written his mother that spring. Ewald clambered up a wooded rise to his right, where he was astonished to see rebel forces on Birmingham Hill, a quarter mile away— "an entire line deployed in the best order, several of whom waved to me with their hats."

Howe saw the same enemy disposition, and with the meetinghouse secured by four p.m., he ordered Cornwallis to attack up the hill. Quickly the king's men spread into open order two ranks deep: almost nine thousand troops at arm's length from one another, extending nearly a mile across the lower slope. Just west of Birmingham Road, the British grenadier commander bellowed, "Put on your caps! For damned fighting and drinking, I'll match you against the world." His men plucked off their red cloth forage hats and drew the black bearskins from their packs, smoothing the fur before pulling them on, adding another foot in height to men who were already the army's tallest. "I would not exchange those three minutes of rapture to avoid ten thousand times the danger," Lieutenant William Hale, a grenadier officer in the 45th Foot, subsequently wrote his parents. *Jäger* and British light infantry troops fanned out two hundred yards ahead of

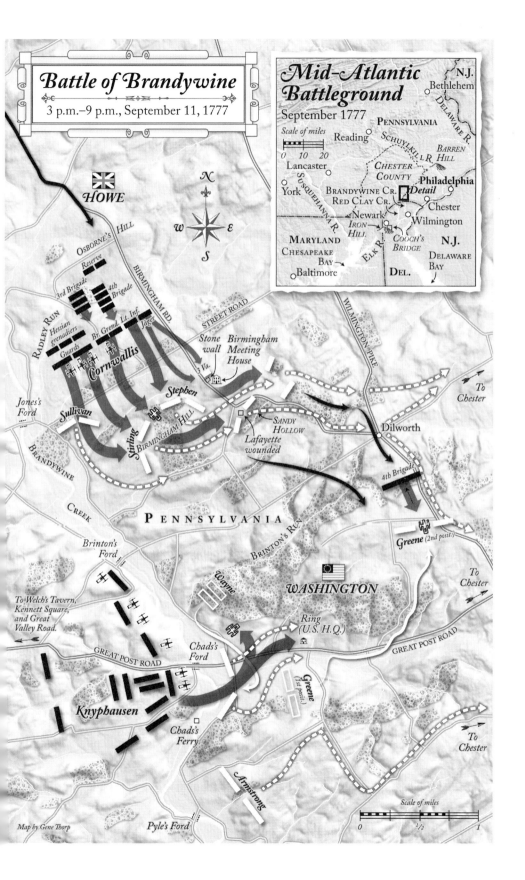

Battle of Brandywine
3 p.m.–9 p.m., September 11, 1777

Mid-Atlantic Battleground
September 1777

Scale of miles
0   10   20

N.J.
Bethlehem

PENNSYLVANIA

DELAWARE R.

Reading

SCHUYLKILL R.

BARREN HILL

CHESTER COUNTY

Lancaster

Philadelphia
Detail

York

SUSQUEHANNA R.

BRANDYWINE CR.
RED CLAY CR.

Chester

Newark

Wilmington

MARYLAND
CHESAPEAKE BAY

IRON HILL

ELK R.

COOCH'S BRIDGE

N.J.

Baltimore

DEL.

DELAWARE BAY

HOWE

Osborne's Hill

Reserve

3rd Brigade

4th Brigade

BIRMINGHAM RD.

RADLEY RUN

Hessian grenadiers

Guards

Br. Grend. Lt. Inf.

Jäger

Cornwallis

STREET ROAD

Stone wall

Birmingham Meeting House

3 Va.

WILMINGTON PIKE

To Chester

Stephen

Jones's Ford

Sullivan

Stirling

BIRMINGHAM HILL

SANDY HOLLOW

Lafayette wounded

Dilworth

BRANDYWINE

CREEK

PENNSYLVANIA

4th Brigade

Brinton's Ford

BRINTON'S RUN

Greene (2nd positn.)

To Chester

Wayne

WASHINGTON

To Welch's Tavern,
Kennett Square,
and Great
Valley Road.

Ring
(U.S. H.Q.)

GREAT POST ROAD

GREAT POST ROAD

Chad's Ford

Greene (1st positn.)

Knyphausen

Chad's Ferry

To Chester

Armstrong

Scale of miles
0   ½   1

Pyle's Ford

Map by Gene Thorp

the Guards, grenadiers, foot regiments, and Hessians. Drummers and fifers struck up "The Grenadiers March." A shrill racket of whistles, trumpets, and brass hunting horns also erupted as the line surged forward, "the most grand and noble sight imaginable," a British officer wrote.

"The infantry that can load the fastest will always defeat those who are slower to reload," advised Frederick the Great, an apostle of raw firepower. But roughly a third of battle casualties in this war came from the bayonet, and the king's men moved swiftly in hopes of closing to within stabbing distance. Trained to be quick and violent, each redcoat was advised to "fix with his eye the attention of his opponent"—mesmerizing the victim—rather than looking at the bayonet. The drum cadence increased from 75 paces per minutes to 120, a quickstep dubbed the "English gallop." Covering a hundred yards per minute, the redcoats soon outpaced thirteen hundred Hessian grenadiers clumping behind in their brass mitre caps.

"Now the battle began which proved excessive severe," Ebenezer Elmer, a surgeon's mate in the 2nd New Jersey, told his journal. "The enemy came on with fury." Outnumbered two to one, Stephen's division, on the American right, and Stirling's, on the left, braced for the assault on good ground, although a northerly breeze blew black smoke into their faces. Continental cannonballs skipped down the slope in a flat trajectory, bouncing and taking flight again for another hundred yards after the "first graze" ricochet, followed by a second and even a third graze, each a threat to shear off arms, legs, or heads wearing bearskin bonnets.

When the enemy drew closer, American gunners switched to grapeshot and case—those iron balls in their tin containers—to keep the bayonets at bay. The Royal Artillery answered with 6- and 12-pounders. "A cannonball went through Captain Stout and through a sergeant that stood behind him, killing them both," a New Jersey lieutenant recorded. A bullet in the thigh sent Colonel Israel Shreve, commander of the 2nd New Jersey, off the field in excruciating pain. "Cannons roaring, muskets cracking, drums beating, bombs flying all around, men a-dying & wounded," an American gunner wrote. "Horrid groans." A British officer recalled:

> There was the most infernal fire of cannon and musketry, the most incessant shouting. Incline to the right! Incline to the left! Halt! Charge! . . . The balls plowing up the ground, the trees cracking over one's head, the branches riven by artillery, the leaves falling as in autumn by the grapeshot.

General Sullivan and his two Maryland brigades had arrived after a march from the Brandywine on a rude lane through pinched ravines. These reinforcements gave the Americans fifty-three hundred men on Birmingham Hill. Yet no sooner had his men begun to occupy a wooded knob on the western edge of the battlefield than Sullivan realized that Stirling and Stephen were half a mile to his right, leaving a yawning hole in the American line. Riding to the crest of the hill to confer with the two generals, he ordered all Continental regiments to shift east to tighten the formation and prevent enemy *Jäger* from enveloping his right flank. "Small arms roared like the rolling of a drum," wrote Captain Enoch Anderson, a Delaware officer. "The word was again given: 'March, march to the right! The enemy wants to turn our right!'"

Sullivan's left proved even more vulnerable. British guardsmen swept up the western flank of Birmingham Hill and smashed into the 1st Maryland Brigade as it began to reposition. Panicky troops farther uphill fired wildly at the Guards, spraying the Marylanders with errant musket balls. "We were in confusion," wrote Colonel John Hoskins Stone, a future Maryland governor. "In a few minutes we were attacked in front and flank, and by our people in the rear. . . . The enemy pushed on and soon made us all run off." The 2nd Maryland Brigade also bolted; Sullivan watched from the hilltop as his command pelted through grain fields and into the trees, chased by salvos from British 12-pounders that caromed among the branches.

The collapse of the American left exposed Stirling's flank. "The firing while the action lasted was the warmest I believe that has been in America since the war began," a staff officer wrote. With Birmingham Hill now "disputed muzzle to muzzle," in Sullivan's account, British and German troops moved in short rushes to seize the crest five times, only to be driven off five times. Although fewer than 1 percent of musket balls fired in combat typically hit their target, a British regiment arrayed in two ranks across a frontage of 150 yards could fire a thousand to fifteen hundred rounds per minute, enough to wreak havoc even if only one bullet in a hundred struck home. The "disorder of the nervous system" of a man hit with a one-ounce lead ball, a witness reported, resembled "the flutterings of a wounded bird."

Men fell, rose, and fell again, fluttering. As he waved his sword, Lieutenant Colonel William Medows, commanding the 1st British Grenadiers, took a bullet through the arm and out his back; blown from his saddle, he also broke a collarbone in the fall. Officers and enlisted ranks in the 64th Foot began to fall, and would continue falling through the rest of the day. Among the Americans, Private John Francis of the 3rd Pennsylvania had both legs "much shattered by grapeshot." A musket ball struck Private Adam Koch of the 9th Pennsylvania below the right eye before exiting under his right ear. Captain John Brady of the 12th Pennsylvania and his fifteen-year-old son were both wounded. Private John Malone lost his right eye and was captured. A bullet removed all of Sergeant Banks Dudley's upper teeth, an insult that plagued him for the rest of his life.

Despite Stirling's shouted encouragement while "whipping and spurring down the road at full gallop," his line buckled. "We broke and rallied and rallied and broke, from height to height," a soldier in the 3rd New Jersey said. Major Joseph Bloomfield of the same regiment wrote, "About sunset we made a stand when I was wounded, having a ball with the wad shot through my left forearm, & the fuse set my coat and shirt on fire." He joined hundreds of Pennsylvania and New Jersey troops as they streamed south, exposing Stephen's left flank and his two Virginia brigades, the last American units left on Birmingham Hill. As Hessians shouted *"Allons! Allons!"* in imitation of Frederick the Great—"Let's go!"—artillerymen positioned three guns to enfilade the Virginians with grapeshot. "After a steady, stubborn fight from hill to hill," in Ewald's description, Stephen's men also fell back at six p.m., ceding the hill to Howe, Cornwallis, and their sovereign. "The valley was filled with smoke," a New Jersey diarist wrote. "The sun was set when I left the hill, from whence I saw the fate of the day."

Battered but not yet beaten, the Americans formed another line along a sunken farm lane known as Sandy Hollow. Among those rallying here was Major General Lafayette, who had persuaded Washington, at the Ring house, to let him ride to the sound of the guns. Having turned twenty a few days earlier and now under fire for the first time, Lafayette "dismounted and did his utmost to make the men charge with fixed bayonets," another French officer reported, to the point of even "pushing them in the back."

But more retreating men stumbled into the hollow, pursued by redcoats, who closed to within twenty yards. "Confusion became extreme," Lafayette acknowledged. Just then a British ball punched through his left calf. He doubled over in pain as blood filled his boot. Comrades tied a hasty bandage over the wound, hoisted him onto his horse, and sent him trotting toward Chester, fourteen miles southeast. For the young marquis, the Battle of Brandywine was over.

Washington arrived at a gallop, accompanied by Knox, Hamilton, and the rest of the command retinue with sufficient light left in the afternoon to see his entire right wing collapse at Birmingham Hill. As ordered, Greene also arrived with his panting division, the lead brigade trotting almost four miles on the Great Post Road from the Brandywine in forty-five minutes. "I found the whole of the troops routed and retreating precipitately," Greene wrote, "and in the most broken and confused manner."

Dusk began to sift over the landscape as he hurried his regiments—predominantly Virginians—onto the gentle reverse slope of plowed fields a mile south of Dilworth, a crossroads hamlet. They formed a wedge between their retreating Continental comrades and the pursuing enemy, whose advance had been slowed by broken terrain and exhaustion after thirteen hours on the march. As fourteen hundred weary, unknowing redcoats in Brigadier General James Agnew's 4th Brigade approached, Greene's men rose and lashed them with sleeting musket fire and grapeshot from two of Knox's guns.

"We had no sooner reached the hill than . . . there was a terrible firing and nearly all of the officers of these regiments were slain," Ewald wrote. He exaggerated, but only slightly. The British 46th and 64th Regiments suffered 130 casualties between them, with seven officers in the latter killed or wounded. A light infantry captain in the 17th Foot recalled, "We were compelled to throw ourselves on our knees and bellies, and keep up a fire from the slope of the hill." Royal Artillery gunners urged their spavined draft teams forward, and for twenty minutes a trio of 12-pounders roared back at Knox's muzzle flashes.

The light faded, transmuting men into shadows. Ammunition ran short for both sides and gunplay subsided to a mutter. On orders from Washington, who watched from horseback two hundred yards behind the firing line, Greene's men withdrew to join the column of fugitives shuffling southeast. Greene estimated his losses at "upwards of a hundred men killed and wounded" in the hour-long brawl.

The battle ended where it began, at Chads's Ford. As planned, General Knyphausen had listened for the intensifying gunfire to the north late that afternoon, then ordered his six thousand redcoats, Hessians, and loyalists to plunge across the creek, led by the 4th Foot—known as the King's Own—the 5th Foot, and the Queen's Rangers. British batteries pummeled rebel parapets and gun positions, but Continental return fire frothed the Brandywine, "playing upon us with grapeshot, which did much execution," a ranger sergeant reported. "The water took us up to our breasts and was much stained with blood. . . . Many poor fellows fell in the river and were swept away with the current." Seventy-two rangers were killed or wounded, a quarter of the force.

Yet Knyphausen's weight of numbers told again. With most of Washington's army diverted to the right wing, only Maxwell's light infantry and Wayne's two thousand Pennsylvanians, thinly arrayed south of the Great Post Road, held the ford and adjacent ferry landing, plus a couple thousand militiamen entrenched farther downstream. After scrambling up the creek bank and across a bogland, guardsmen and Welch Fusiliers pressed

Wayne's right flank, with Highlanders and rangers hemming in his left. "Our artillery made a clear lane through them as they mounted the works," an American gunner reported, "but they filled up the ranks again." Some rebels rallied in an orchard behind the Ring house, where fighting was described as "bayonet to bayonet." On the rebel left, a single British cannon-ball grazed a lieutenant, broke a sergeant's shoulder, and struck a third soldier in the head, knocking him "over on the ground for near two rods"—eleven yards. A major who had his horse shot out from under him was mounting another when mortally wounded.

With their draft horses killed or maimed, rebel artillerymen spiked several guns and fled. Redcoats captured other fieldpieces and turned them on the retreating Americans. At six-thirty p.m. Wayne pulled his men back into the gloaming on the Chester Road to join the retreating tide. A militiaman from Philadelphia described marching "over the dead and dying, I saw many bodies crushed to pieces beneath the wagons. . . . We were bespattered with blood."

"Our army was something broke," a New Jersey Continental added. "It was necessary to leave the field of action. . . . I came off with a heart full of distress."

"The rebels stood a considerable smart battle, more than usual," a British lieutenant told his diary. "But they soon run." By nine p.m., another officer noted, the king's men "were able to sit down and refresh ourselves with some cold pork and grog on the ground the enemy had first posted themselves." As Lieutenant Cliffe of the 46th Foot wrote his brother, "The fatigues of this day were excessive. . . . Had we even daylight we could not make anything of a pursuit."

Little imagination was required to envision avenging cavalrymen sabering the vulnerable Yankee column. Howe's host included three squadrons of the 16th Light Dragoons plus a hundred mounted *Jäger*; but the wretched state of their mounts after the voyage from New York now precluded a chase. Once again, as on Long Island and elsewhere, the British failed to convert a tactical battlefield whipping into a decisive strategic triumph. Some officers also privately fretted over the troubling news from Bennington. General Howe "never pursues his victories," wrote Captain Montrésor, the chief engineer. "Why not go up the North River first and join Burgoyne? . . . The bane of the British Army throughout America has been the subdividing of it." Still, as Captain Downman observed while searching for horses to pull captured American cannons and other booty,

"Washington is retiring as fast as we advance. He beats us in running, but in nothing else."

That seemed fair enough. Scattered across fields and down drove lanes, the Americans shuffled through the night. A few surviving artillery carriages jolted along as fast as tired horses could plod. Teamsters urged on their wagon teams with oaths and whipcracks, shouting for footsore men to move aside. "I was famishing with drought," wrote Jacob Nagle, a gunner still three days shy of his sixteenth birthday. "Coming to a well, [I] could not get near it for the mob of soldiers." A sergeant major whose knapsack vanished during the battle made an inventory of his lost world: "1 uniform coat, brown faced with white; 1 shirt; 1 pair stockings; 1 sergeant's sash; 1 pair knee buckles; $^1/_2$ lb. soap; 1 orderly book. . . . I likewise lost my hat but recovered it again." A Virginia regiment that had lost its colors wobbled into Chester with a red bandanna tied to a ramrod.

"The sun had for some time disappeared," Colonel Pickering, the adjutant general, wrote of riding east next to Washington. "As we proceeded in retiring, the general said to me, 'Why, 'tis a perfect rout.'" 'Twas indeed. As fatigued men collapsed in fields and vacant lots around Chester, open wagons packed with casualties continued on to hospitals in Philadelphia and Trenton. The wounded included Major Bloomfield, the New Jersey officer whose coat had caught fire when he was shot in the arm and who would finally be treated by a doctor "53 hours after I was wounded, 20 hours of which it bled." Lafayette, attended in Chester by a French-speaking Virginia captain named James Monroe, was loaded onto a Delaware River scow and shipped upstream for recuperation in Philadelphia's Indian Queen Hotel. He quoted Washington as telling his personal physician, "Treat him as if he were my son," instructions perhaps contrived in Lafayette's fecund imagination. To Adrienne in Paris he wrote without sentimentality on September 12, "This battle will, I fear, have unpleasant consequences for America."

Very early that Friday morning, the commanding general made a hasty bivouac in Chester. He ordered a gill of rum or whiskey—five ounces—for every soldier. The countryside was to be combed for deserters, and a straggler line in town should "examine every house." Officers must carefully inspect muskets to be sure each had a good flint and that "the inside of them [is] washed clean."

Once again Washington found himself sending bad news to a Congress so unsettled at the approach of Howe's army—barely twenty-five miles from Philadelphia—that some delegates had packed their bags and ordered their horses newly shod. Pickering helped write the midnight dispatch, which began, "I am sorry to inform you that in this day's engagement we have been obliged to leave the enemy masters of the field." Although hundreds of men had tossed away their blankets during the retreat, and some had also discarded their muskets, by foresight the army's baggage had been packed and moved away before the battle, salvaging both wagons and matériel.

After reading the draft, Washington asked Pickering to insert "some words of encouragement." Before sending the dispatch by courier to Philadelphia, the adjutant general added, above the commander in chief's name, "Notwithstanding the misfortune of the day, I am happy to find the troops in good spirits, and I hope another time we shall compensate for the losses now sustained."

The extent of those losses would take weeks to parse. Howe eventually put the king's casualties at 587, including 93 killed, a figure considered reasonably accurate despite higher numbers cited by Captain Ewald and others. Washington likely lost eleven hundred to thirteen hundred, including as many as three hundred killed and four hundred captured, plus eleven cannons seized. "I am happy in being able to inform you that I still exist," Dr. Howell wrote his father. "With all my misfortunes, I think myself happy."

At daybreak on September 12, each of Howe's regiments sent a surgeon's mate in a wagon to prowl the countryside for wounded men. Four women from each brigade served as nurses in the provisional hospital at Dilworth, and more wagons hauled injured Hessians to Wilmington, now under British occupation. Medicos operated without anesthesia, handing terrified men a strip of leather or lead bullets to bite during surgery; teeth marks recorded their agony. For hopeless cases, including gunshots to the gut, Madeira and laudanum were given to "smooth the path of death," as one physician put it. The watchful Quaker Joseph Townsend looked on at Birmingham Meeting House as a British surgeon tightened a brass clamp high on a mangled leg, which he then lopped off with a bone saw—another ruined limb for the pit in the burying ground next door.

At Howe's request, Washington sent Dr. Rush with an American medical contingent to help search ditches, woodpiles, and thickets for wounded rebels, who were then treated in an improvised surgery at the Turk's Head tavern, a few miles east of the upper Brandywine. In a report to John Adams, Rush praised the competence of the British physicians while conceding that "they hate us in every shape we appear to them."

*   *   *

War in Chester County had raked over patriot, loyalist, and neutral alike, including victims such as Gideon Gilpin, who tried to abide by Quaker "peace testimony" tenets but whose farm above Chads's Ford had been plundered of four thousand fence rails, ten milch cows, forty-eight sheep, twenty-eight swine, twelve tons of hay, a clock, a gun, fifty pounds of bacon, and a history book. Seed for spring planting had been filched for miles around, along with livestock and millstones. Tax rolls revealed that five years would pass before prosperity returned to this region.

Brandywine justly burnished William Howe's military reputation. As usual, he had displayed heedless courage in battle where bullets and balls flew thickest. If his generalship was imperfect—by one account only half of his troops and a third of his guns had gotten into the fight—he had been deft in outflanking Washington yet again. "Howe surely deserves great credit for the move," Major General Grant wrote General Harvey, the adjutant general in London. "His disposition was masterly, & he executed his plan with ability."

As for the Americans, the battle was "the most severe action that has been fought in this war," Henry Knox wrote Lucy in Boston. "Heaven frowned on us to a degree." But divine displeasure satisfied few of his countrymen as an explanation. No sooner had a courier brought details from Brandywine to the public house at the Indian Queen in Philadelphia than Congress and ordinary citizens began apportioning culpability and reproach.

Some blamed Pennsylvania for a poor showing by the local militia, particularly compared to their militant counterparts in New England, who had rallied to oppose the enemy at Lexington, Concord, and Bennington. "Upwards of 65,000 men are enrolled in the militia of Pennsylvania," Pickering wrote his brother, "yet we have not 2,000 in the field and these are of little worth and constantly deserting." Washington agreed that "the conduct of the militia is much to be regretted." Even Major General John Armstrong, the state's militia commander, conceded that many of his men were a "scandal to the military profession."

Yet Congress found more fault in the Continental Army. Many "principal officers are incompetent," one delegate complained, "and I fear it is an evil that cannot be remedied." General Sullivan, already in bad odor, made a convenient scapegoat. "The fortune of the day was injured by miscarriages where you commanded," a North Carolina congressman told him directly. "Your duty as a general was not well performed. My objection to you is want of sufficient talent." Sullivan defended himself with deflection and self-pity, telling John Hancock, "It was ever my opinion that the enemy would come round on our right flank. This opinion I often gave the general." That general—Washington—declined to censure Sullivan, perhaps aware that excessive scrutiny of his lieutenants would reveal his own shortcomings. "I never blamed you," Washington wrote Sullivan with faint praise a month later. "No part of your conduct preceding the action was, in my judgment, reprehensible."

As was sometimes his wont, the commander in chief tried to sidestep both the magnitude of the defeat and his own responsibility, telling the army in general orders on September 13 that "the enemy's loss greatly exceeded ours." He also announced that Congress, "in consideration of the gallant behavior of the troops," would provide the ranks with thirty hogsheads of rum—more than fifteen hundred gallons. Yet Brandywine was "probably Washington's worst battlefield performance of the war," as the historian Edward G. Lengel concluded. Some men closest to the commanding general's elbow, Pickering among them, believed that he had reacted, hesitantly, rather than seizing the initiative as a great captain must. The ground should have been scouted, men familiar with that ground interrogated, and Howe's maneuvers anticipated. Major General Baron de Kalb, Lafayette's companion in the voyage from Bordeaux, had come to his own conclusions about Washington in a month of observing the Continental Army. "He is the most amiable, kind-hearted, and upright of men," Kalb wrote his wife. "But as a general he is too slow, too indolent, and far too weak. . . . Whatever success he may have will be owing to good luck and to the blunders of his adversaries." He also added, shrewdly, that for the American cause "one obstacle remains which exceeds all others—the absence of a navy. Without assistance from abroad, they will never get one."

Good luck and an opponent's blunders perhaps counted for more than Kalb reckoned; they had long contributed to Washington's success as a commander. So, too, did the dogged optimism of an army "panting to have at the enemy again," as Lieutenant Colonel Hubley of the 10th Pennsylvania wrote. A Delaware officer added, "We had our solacing words always ready for each other: 'Come, boys, we shall do better another time.'" Even Colonel Stone, whose Maryland brigade had been sent flying ignominiously from the field, told Congress, "Upon the whole, I do not think we have lost anything but the day. . . . We ought to attack them everywhere we meet them."

Perhaps the most lyrical exposition came from the quill of the man the troops called Common Sense, after the incandescent pamphlet he had published as a rallying cry in 1776. Thomas Paine, recently appointed secretary to Congress's Committee of Foreign Affairs, considered himself "a farmer of thoughts" whose task was to teach Americans—"in language as plain as the alphabet"—the "manly doctrine of reverencing themselves" by embracing their native simplicity, rusticity, and social virtues. In *The American Crisis, Number IV*, dated "Philadelphia, September 12, 1777," he wrote, "Those who expect to reap the blessings of freedom must, like men, undergo the fatigues of supporting it." In the course of twelve hundred words arranged in ten paragraphs, he added:

> It is not a field of a few acres of ground but a cause that we are defending, and whether we defeat the enemy in one battle, or by degrees, the consequences will be the same. . . . The glow of hope, courage, and fortitude will, in a little time, supply the place of every inferior passion and kindle the whole heart into heroism.

Paine closed with an admonition for General Howe. "You have yet scarce began upon the war, and the further you enter, the faster will your troubles thicken," he warned. "We are sure that we are right, and we leave to you the despairing reflection of being the tool of a miserable tyrant."

6.

These Are Dreadful Times

Philadelphia took fright. The *Pennsylvania Evening Post* reported that General Howe "has invaded this state," then added, "God save the people." All shops and stores were to "be immediately shut up, except those only where workmen are employed in making or repairing the public arms." Bell-ringing criers hurried through the streets summoning "every man who can carry a gun" to report for mustering. Books and documents removed from the state library, as well as court records and cash reserves, were trundled up the Delaware River to Easton for safekeeping; the shallop *Sturdy Beggar* also sailed north carrying the state assembly papers and a printing press. The *Pennsylvania Journal* published a half-sheet edition that included Washington's official account of Brandywine and editorial assurances that "our army is but little the worse for the late engagement."

Even so, Congress ordered flour, sugar, iron, and other commodities removed from the city by wagon or on sloops and flatboats. Cattle were driven off, all decked boats shifted from the Pennsylvania shoreline to New Jersey, and the Schuylkill River bridge at High Street was dismantled. Blankets, shoes, and clothing would be collected, forcibly if necessary, for the troops. Philadelphians agreed in a meeting at the Pennsylvania State House to organize night fire patrols, given rumors that arsonists had hidden tarred fagots in various outhouses. Hundreds of Hessian and British prisoners were to be moved from Lancaster to Carlisle and other less vulnerable towns. The approach of redcoat liberators emboldened the unfree. "Ran away on Sunday night, a Negro man named Hero, about 25 to 30 years of age," read an *Evening Post* advertisement placed by Congressman Robert Morris. "Whoever secures the Negro so that his master gets him again shall have twenty dollars reward."

Apprehension turned to panic at one a.m. on Friday, September 19, when a dispatch arrived from Lieutenant Colonel Hamilton for John Hancock, warning, incorrectly, that Howe's legions had forded the Schuylkill to begin marching on the city. "If Congress have not yet left Philadelphia," Hamilton urged, "they ought to do it immediately without fail." The word spread faster than any fire. "The confusion, as you may suppose, was great," Paine reported in a letter to Benjamin Franklin. "It was a beautiful, still, moonlit morning, and the streets as full of [fleeing] men, women, and children as on a market day." Roads to the north and ferries headed east were jammed with refugees; the road to Reading was said to be "the most travelled in America." Sarah Logan Fisher, whose Quaker royalist husband had been exiled to Virginia, told her diary, "A great knocking at people's doors & desiring them to get up. . . . Wagons rattling, horses galloping, women running, children crying, delegates flying." Congressman Henry Laurens, whose son John had recently joined Washington's staff as an aide-de-camp, wrote a friend, "Fright sometimes works lunacy."

"When morning came," Sarah Fisher noted dryly, "it proved a false alarm." Hamilton had misread British intentions after a brief skirmish with dragoon raiders, sounding his tocsin without Washington's knowledge. But panic was not easily headed. The state government fled to Lancaster. Congress followed, "chased like a covey of partridges," in John Adams's phrase. One unnerved delegate rode off without bothering to saddle his horse, while in the tumult another had his pocket picked of $260 and a couple dozen lottery tickets. After reaching Lancaster, the delegates would keep going west, crossing the Susquehanna at Wright's Ferry on canoes and flatboats for a sixpence fee. They finally stopped in York, the new provisional capital; a sleepy market town without enough beds, it stood more than eighty crow-flying miles from Philadelphia.

As the government bustled west, eighteen of the city's largest bells traveled north to avoid capture and smelting, including those from Christ and St. Peter's Churches, temporarily concealed in heaps of manure and hay. Carpenters recorded the diameter of each at the lip for identification. The bronze statehouse steeple bell—four feet wide, weighing just over a ton, and inscribed with the biblical admonition "Proclaim liberty throughout all the land"—arrived in Bethlehem, sixty miles north of Philadelphia, where the transport wagon broke down in the street. Unloaded from the bed with much grunting, the bell and her sisters were subsequently hidden in the cellar of Zion Reformed Church in nearby Northampton Towne.

The procession of refugees had just begun for Bethlehem, a compact village founded in 1741 where Monocacy Creek flows into the Lehigh River. Here peaceable German-speaking Moravians had built America's first pumped municipal waterworks; they had also established thriving trades that included a brass foundry, a tannery, shops for clockmaking, and mills for lumber, grist, and soap—all of which would now be upended by war. Wagons carrying military stores from Philadelphia and Reading began arriving the night of September 18 in "a scene of wild confusion," a Moravian diarist noted, including guards firing their muskets into the air to no obvious purpose.

Sulfur and gunpowder were stored at the flaxseed house, and soldiers set up a munitions laboratory for making cartridges. Rum and other provisions went into the dye house or to the tile kilns, half a mile northwest of town. Congressional archives arrived with an escort of a hundred Continental troops, plus several delegates taking a circuitous route to York; they included Hancock, John and Samuel Adams, and a Virginian driving General Washington's borrowed phaeton, which, he admitted, was "much dirtied and in some places torn."

Before long, nine hundred wagons carrying war matériel and the army's heavy baggage, Washington's included, had parked along the Lehigh or in fields behind the genteel Sun Inn, demolishing seventeen thousand fence rails and crushing thirty-two acres of buckwheat and Indian corn. "With them came a crowd of low women and thieves," the diarist James Allen complained, as well as loyalist prisoners chained in pairs. A well-attended Moravian church sermon dilated on a theme from the Gospel of Saint Matthew: "He that is not with me is against me." Continental authorities warned that as many as two thousand wounded and sick soldiers were also en route. "These are dreadful times," they explained.

Broken boys from Brandywine soon flooded Bethlehem, jamming the Sun Inn, private houses, and particularly the Single Brethren's House, a three-story limestone building with a double-hipped roof and a belvedere offering splendid views of the Lehigh valley. More than five hundred American soldiers would die of disease and battle wounds in Bethlehem during the war, most to be buried anonymously in "Strangers' Row" on a hillside along Market Street.

Among the arriving invalids was Lafayette, who had been evacuated by boat from Philadelphia to Bristol and then driven to Bethlehem in Congressman Laurens's coach. With his wounded leg still suppurating, unable to wear a boot, he was carried into the Sun Inn to be nursed by Moravian brethren, one of whom wrote, "We found him a very intelligent and pleasant young man." He spent his days reading an English-language history of Moravian missions in Greenland and writing letters to Vergennes and others at Versailles, urging an alliance with America and all-out war against Britain, including French attacks in the Caribbean, Canada, and India.

It was said that street minstrels in Paris now sang ballads extolling Lafayette's valor and that even Voltaire had taken notice of his intrepid commitment to the American cause. In letters to Adrienne the marquis confessed to both homesickness and impatience to rejoin General Washington. As for the bullet wound in his left calf, he told her, it was only an excuse "to give myself airs and to make myself interesting."

General Howe had loitered near Brandywine for several days of recuperation before pushing north to White Horse Tavern, twenty-five miles from Philadelphia. Here the two armies again drew close on September 16, until a late afternoon thunderstorm with gale winds—"the heaviest downpour in this world," a Hessian officer said—ended any prospect of a battle. "We were drenched and sank in mud to our calves," another Hessian reported. Lieutenant Colonel John Laurens complained that "the dye washed out of my hat," but of much greater concern were shoddy Continental cartridge boxes that failed to repel the rain. "Nearly all the musket cartridges of the army that had been delivered to the men were damaged, consisting of about 400,000," Knox wrote Lucy. "This was a most terrible stroke to us." Worse yet, another quarter million cartridges evacuated from Philadelphia magazines disappeared, apparently scattered willy-nilly or dumped into the Delaware.

After missing an opportunity to confront Washington at White Horse Tavern, Howe consoled himself with a full-throated raid on Continental magazines at an ironworks and mill complex called Valley Forge, on the south bank of the Schuylkill. Before Americans could evacuate their stores, dragoons and three companies of light infantry struck on September 18, confiscating 3,800 barrels of flour, 25 barrels of horseshoes, wagonloads of tomahawks, soap, and candles, plus 150 horses. On the same day, the king's army, fifteen thousand strong, moved in two columns on Swedes Ford Road through a long, shallow hollow running west to east and known as the Great Valley. Again the heavy footfalls of hard men sounded across Chester County. Here, intending to stage for a final lunge at Philadelphia, Howe, Cornwallis, and Knyphausen bedded their troops in dells and woodlands across a two-mile encampment near the General Paoli Tavern, improbably named for a Corsican nationalist, Pasquale Paoli, whose Mediterranean island had been ruled for two centuries by Genoa until, in 1755, he led a successful revolt. Known to Corsicans as *Il Babbù*—Daddy—he would be revered by Napoleon Bonaparte as a family friend, a reforming statesman, and a benevolent despot.

Washington ordered a countermove to disrupt the British advance. This time he chose a field commander who knew the local terrain intimately. Brigadier General Anthony Wayne's farm and tannery stood three miles south of the British bivouac. Now thirty-two, with his regiments

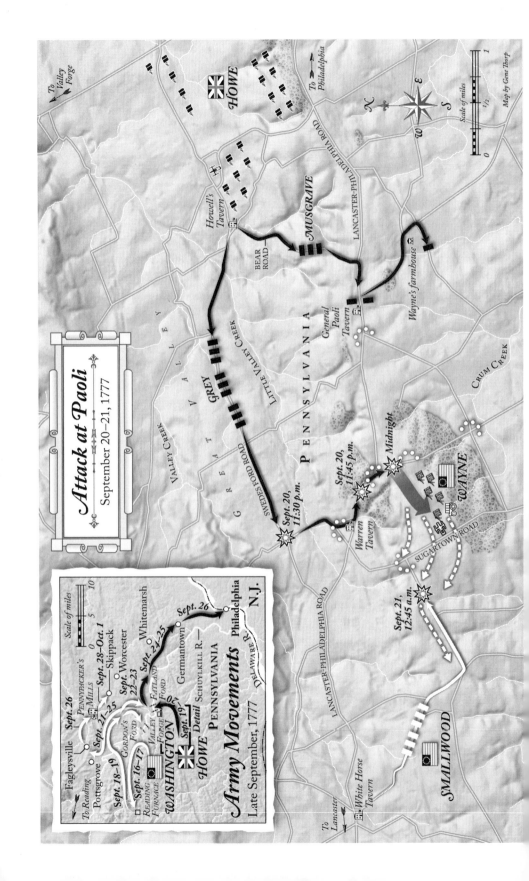

Attack at Paoli
September 20–21, 1777

Map by Gene Thorp

HOWE

MUSGRAVE

Howell's Tavern

Bear Road

LANCASTER-PHILADELPHIA ROAD

To Philadelphia

N
E
W
S

Scale of miles
0   1/2   1

Wayne's farmhouse

GREY

LITTLE VALLEY CREEK

General Paoli Tavern

VALLEY CREEK

GREAT VALLEY

SWEDES FORD ROAD

PENNSYLVANIA

To Valley Forge

CRUM CREEK

Sept. 20, 11:30 p.m.

Sept. 20, 11:45 p.m.

Midnight

Warren Tavern

WAYNE

SUGARTOWN ROAD

Sept. 21, 12:45 a.m.

LANCASTER-PHILADELPHIA ROAD

SMALLWOOD

White Horse Tavern

To Lancaster

Army Movements
Late September, 1777

Scale of miles
0   5   10

Fagleysville   Sept. 26

To Reading

Pottsgrove

PENNYPACKER'S MILLS   Sept. 28–Oct. 1

Sept. 21–25   Skippack

Sept. 22–23   Worcester

GORDON'S FORD

Sept. 18–19

Sept. 16–17

READING FURNACE

Sept. 24–25   Whitemarsh

FATLAND FORD

VALLEY FORGE

Sept. 19

Sept. 20   Germantown   Sept. 26

Detail

Schuylkill R.

Philadelphia

WASHINGTON

HOWE

PENNSYLVANIA

Delaware R.   N.J.

To Lancaster

largely intact after Brandywine, Wayne was described by an admirer as "a caged leopard, an entire stranger to repose." A former surveyor with an aptitude for mathematics, he indulged a fondness for bespoke broadcloth suits, ruffled wristbands, and tricorn beaver hats that had earned him the nickname "Dandy Wayne"; during the harrowing retreat from Canada, where he was among the few American commanders to distinguish himself, he insisted that each company appoint a barber to maintain soldierly appearances. The exigencies of war forced Wayne to give up white cravats, although his Philadelphia tailor continued to sew him lambskin breeches. More to the point, by one comrade's account, he was known as an officer who "could fight as well as brag" and who "entertained the most sovereign contempt for the enemy."

Under a full harvest moon on the misty night of Thursday, September 18, Wayne led twenty-two hundred men with four field guns through the Great Valley, a few hours after Howe's legions had passed that way. Seizing ten fat cows to butcher for his men, he chose to camp in a secluded glade just west of the British. His orders from the commander in chief were to "harass & distress" the enemy rear guard as they crossed the Schuylkill. "The cutting of the enemy's baggage would be a great matter," Washington wrote from Reading Furnace, twenty miles northwest, but he instructed Wayne to avoid "ambuscades" and any other "disagreeable situation." After looping northwest, the main army would swing east across the Schuylkill to guard the river fords leading toward Philadelphia.

Early Friday morning, Wayne wrote Washington that after scouting Howe's perimeter, he found that the enemy "lay too compact to admit of an attack" by his small detachment. He instead urged the army to hurry forward. "There never was, nor never will be a fairer opportunity of giving the enemy a fatal blow than the present," Wayne added. "For God sake, push on as fast as possible." Three hours later he wrote, "The enemy are very quiet, washing & cooking. . . . I believe he knows nothing of my situation, as I have taken every precaution to prevent any intelligence getting to him."

Wayne was deluded. The glare of cook fires had alerted the British, along with gunshots from Continentals who violated orders by firing their muskets to clear them of jammed cartridges. British intelligence could hardly have been better informed. At least one order from Washington fell into Howe's hands on September 19, revealing the American plan. Captain von Münchhausen, Howe's German aide, wrote in his journal, "General Wayne . . . is only three miles behind us. We are informed that his 2,000 men are not militia. . . . Wayne intends to attack our rear guard and our baggage."

The Americans laagered in a rolling farm field surrounded by stands of oak and maple. Major Cromwell Pearce, who owned this land, was away, but his wife, Margaret, was home with at least two of her six children—Cromwell Jr., age five, and Marmaduke, thirteen months old. Lacking tents, Wayne's men built "booths"—wigwams—from brush and tree branches. His nine regiments, distributed in two brigades, comprised mainly Pennsylvania farmers, shopkeepers, and frontiersmen, many from northern Ireland or Germany. The cannons and two dozen supply wagons were parked near the southern tree line.

Wayne intended to pounce on Howe's tail as soon as the British broke camp, but since two p.m. he had also been waiting for twenty-one hundred Maryland militiamen marching from the west to join him, doubling the size of his force. With rain threatening, he ordered his troops to shelter in the crude booths to keep their muskets and cartridges dry. Loitering less than an hour's march from an enemy force many times larger unsettled some Continental officers. "This division is now in the post of danger," Colonel Thomas Hartley, commander of the 1st Pennsylvania Brigade, wrote at six p.m. on Saturday, September 20. "I understand General Howe means to have us attacked tomorrow morning."

Darkness spread across the camp like a blanket. Men wrapped their firelocks under their coats. Crickets sang in counterpoint to the low murmur of human voices. Again Wayne pulled out his watch and peered west, scanning the Lancaster road for Marylanders.

Tall and spare, with a narrow chest and close-set eyes in a vulpine face, Major General Charles Grey had served the Crown well for most of his forty-seven years. The son of a Northumberland baronet, he had helped smash the Jacobites at Culloden in 1746 before being twice wounded in the West Indies and again at Minden, while fighting the French. After a stint as aide-de-camp to George III, he had arrived in New York this June as a colonel—leaving a wife and five children in London—and had soon been promoted to major general in command of Howe's 3rd Brigade. Just a few weeks in America were enough to sharpen his skepticism about the king's cause. "The difficulties to encounter in this contest are great," he wrote a friend in July. "The people, to a man, [are] against us."

Grey had no hesitation, however, about the task Howe assigned him on September 20. At ten p.m. on Saturday night, guided by loyalists and a troop of the 16th Light Dragoons, he led three regiments of more than twelve hundred men back through the Great Valley on Swedes Ford Road. The ranks included Highland Scots in the 42nd Regiment, known as the

Black Watch, who had swapped their plaid kilts for more practical trousers but kept their feathered bonnets and short red coats trimmed in blue. Two additional regiments with six hundred men under Lieutenant Colonel Thomas Musgrave swung south on Bear Road to take up a blocking position at the Paoli Tavern, just above General Wayne's farmhouse. They marched "in dead silence," an officer recorded, and every redcoat was told to remove the flint from his musket. Only edged weapons would be used in the night assault. "By not firing," explained Grey's aide, Captain John André, "we knew the foe to be wherever fire appeared."

Wayne had deployed six picket posts around the Continental camp during the evening, each with nineteen sentries, supplemented by a dozen mounted sentinels called videttes. Just before midnight, two of these horsemen spotted shadowy figures approaching on Swedes Ford Road. After three shouted challenges went unanswered, one vidette fired his carbine. Both then turned and raced for camp, a mile south.

Grey's column followed, the pace quickening. An alert picket commanded by Lieutenant Edward Randolph of the 4th Pennsylvania shouted another challenge, then fired at only fifteen yards' range but managed to hit nothing. Ferocious redcoats fell on the sentries with swords and bayonets, killing several as the rest fled, including Randolph, now missing an eye. With the Continental camp just ahead, Grey yelled, "Dash, light infantry!" Guided by the scattered fire of retreating pickets, hundreds of men swarmed past their commander with a guttural cheer that tore open the night.

Alerted by a galloping vidette, Wayne had bellowed for his troops to form under arms. "I was waked by the noise of a person calling, 'Turn out, turn out, the enemy is coming!'" Colonel Richard Humpton, commander of the 2nd Pennsylvania Brigade, later recounted. Wide-eyed men spilled into the open field, now glistening in a light rain. Distant gunshots from Lieutenant Randolph's pickets echoed in the trees, and more cries sounded. "Up, men, the British are on you!" On Wayne's command, artillerymen hitched their teams to the four gun carriages and ammunition wagons, grabbed the reins, and rattled west across the field toward Sugartown Road, at the rear of the camp, followed in train by commissary wagons pulled by oxen.

Wayne ordered two hundred men from the 1st Pennsylvania Regiment into a battle line to slow the redcoats now appearing along the eastern and northern tree lines. "Stand like a brave soldier," he told Captain James Wilson, "and give them a fire." But as pickets fleeing before the British skittered through the trees, the Americans fired on one another in fratricidal confusion. "Then followed a dreadful scene of havoc," a British officer wrote. "The shrieks, groans, shouting, imprecations, deprecations, the clashing of swords & bayonets."

Five hundred baying light infantrymen charged across the encampment as the Americans scattered. "The light infantry bayoneted every man they came up with," Lieutenant Martin Hunter of the 52nd Foot told his journal. A trumpet signaled a second wave of attackers, including saber-wielding dragoons and three hundred soldiers from the 44th Foot, thrusting and slashing with their bayonets in what Hunter, a future senior general who was shot in the right hand, called "the most dreadful scene I ever beheld. Every man that fired was instantly put to death."

Some Continentals hid in their flimsy booths or submerged themselves in a nearby bog. "All the noise and yells of hell," wrote Colonel Hartley, the 1st Brigade commander. "The carnage was very great." A drum major lost his left eye and all the fingers on his left hand. Private William Lear of the 11th Pennsylvania suffered a bayonet thrust in the right leg, a sword wound to the hand, and a broken jaw from a musket butt. Captain Andrew Irvine of the 7th Pennsylvania had seventeen wounds; his fife major was stabbed thirteen times and captured. An examination of one survivor found "forty-six bayonet wounds," mostly nicks said to have been inflicted by a dozen redcoats "in sport." Major Marien Lamar, commanding the 4th Pennsylvania, called to his fleeing men, "Halt, boys. Give these assassins one fire." Enemy soldiers bayoneted him to death in his saddle. "The annals of the age cannot produce such a scene of butchery," Colonel Samuel Hay would write. "All was confusion, the enemy among us."

Terrified men, some firing wildly over their shoulders as they ran, careered north and west, chased by Highlanders, dragoons, and light infantrymen. Darkness, dense woods, and fast legs allowed most to escape. The cavalcade of guns and wagons stalled momentarily when one carriage lost a wheel on the rutted track, blocking an opening through the fence. Soldiers manhandled the wreckage aside, and the procession clattered into the night.

Just west of the bloodletting at Paoli, the Maryland militia finally approached under Brigadier General William Smallwood, a Continental officer and the pompous scion of a wealthy planter family. Unsettling noises ahead and reports of British bushwhackers caused Smallwood's guides to balk at leading him farther; as he halted the column and pulled back to high ground, gunshots from British stragglers ignoring Grey's no-fire stricture killed one Marylander and panicked two thousand others. "Many flung down their guns & run off, & have not been heard of since," Smallwood reported, "the artillery men and wagoneers cutting their horses loose & running off with them." He ordered a five-mile retreat, which, he added, "was the only well-executed order of the night." Half of the Maryland brigade deserted, completing the American debacle.

On Sunday morning, local farmers scuffed through the toppled booths and detritus of a battle lost. Finding a few suffering souls pleading for water, they used their broad-brimmed hats to scoop at puddles or dipped tree leaves from broken branches into muddy wheel ruts to soak up a little moisture. Fifty-two dead American soldiers would be buried on the field in two rows at the bottom of a long trench.

Captain André put total American casualties from the "prodigious slaughter" at two hundred, including seventy-one prisoners, forty of whom were wounded badly enough to be deposited in various farmhouses. On Sunday Howe sent Washington another of his courteous victor's notes. "There being some wounded officers & men of your army at Howell's Tavern & the neighboring houses," he wrote, "I am to request you will lose no time in sending whom you shall think proper for this purpose." Grey's marauders, André wrote, "returned to camp before daybreak with eight or ten wagons & thirty or forty horses borrowed of General Wayne, & having refreshed the men with some good gin with which our friends the Dutch had supplied these gentlemen." André was dismissive of the Continentals. "Moving & pushing distracts & demolishes these people," he added.

Distracted if not demolished, Washington found himself uncertain whether the British intended to seize Philadelphia, twenty-five miles east of the British legion, or the extensive supply depots in Reading, thirty-five miles west. With Continentals spread for nine miles along the Schuylkill's north bank, he concluded that Howe had designs on Reading, "the loss of which must have proved our ruin," he later told his brother. On Monday morning, September 22, he shifted west, leaving the fords downstream unprotected.

Before sunset on Monday, Howe had sent three hundred Hessians over Gordon's Ford. They found, as an American officer conceded, that the Schuylkill had fallen in recent days and "is fordable at almost any place." At eleven p.m., the bulk of the king's army began to wade across Fatland Ford, near Valley Forge, three feet deep and three hundred paces wide. Forming a picket line a hundred yards beyond the riverbank, the vanguard kindled blazing fires to dry their shoes and uniforms. Three British brigades followed at three a.m., trailed by Hessian grenadiers, *Jäger*, livestock, and the wagon train. Loyalist troops and the final redcoats waded across at four p.m. on Tuesday, September 23. In general orders, Howe averred that his soldiers' triumph at Paoli "without firing a shot not only proves their spirit and discipline, but also their evident superiority over the enemy." Dry-shod again, the army swung toward Philadelphia in high spirits.

As his foemen tramped east, Washington convened a war council of fourteen generals at Pottsgrove, eighteen miles southeast of Reading, now quite secure. Reviewing the sorry events of the past few days, he reported the British lunge across the Schuylkill and conceded that his troops were in "no condition to make a forced march, as many of them were barefooted and all excessively harassed with their great fatigue." To a man, his lieutenants agreed they ought not pursue Howe. In a note to Hancock, the commander in chief reported that the Continental Army could no longer protect a city that Congress had already abandoned. "General Howe's situation in Philadelphia will not be the most agreeable," he predicted, since British supplies could only come up the Delaware River. "I am not without hope that the acquisition of Philadelphia may, instead of his good fortune, prove his ruin," he added.

The savagery of the Paoli massacre, as rebels soon called it, left some British officers uneasy at the prospect of American retaliation. "I don't think our battalion slept very soundly after that night for a long time," wrote Lieutenant Hunter, who noted that his 52nd Foot was now known as "the Bloodhounds." Another officer in the regiment, Lieutenant Richard St. George, added, "They threaten retaliation, vow that they will give no quarter. . . . My ear is susceptible to the least noise." Their commander carried from the battlefield a nickname he would keep into posterity: "No-Flint" Grey.

The long-suffering John Adams lamented in his diary that the mood was "gloomy, dark, melancholy, and dispiriting. When and where will the light spring up?" Washington had been "out-generaled" again. "Oh, heaven! Grant us one great soul!" he wrote. "One leading mind would extricate the best cause from that ruin which seems to await it. . . . One active masterly capacity would bring order out of this confusion and save this country." But there would be no official castigation for the misadventure at Paoli. A court-martial convened in late October and chaired by General Sullivan acquitted Wayne "with the highest honor," concluding that he "did everything that could be expected from an active, brave, and vigilant officer."

On September 25, a mild, sunny Thursday, General Howe and the king's men marched into Germantown in two columns. "There was no violence and no offense. Men occasionally dropped out of the line and asked for milk or cider," a twelve-year-old witness reported. With their tents still on Admiral Howe's ships, the troops built shelters from fence rails covered with straw, sod, or cornstalks. Rain laid the dust that night, and early the next morning an advance guard of three thousand British and German grenadiers set off for Philadelphia as the day faired, their hair powdered, mustaches waxed, buckles polished, and leather cartridge boxes blackened. Redcoat cap badges bore the motto NEC ASPERA TERRENT: "Undaunted by difficulties."

On Friday, the city usually swarmed with country people, livestock, and hundreds of wagons arriving for Saturday market, with boats on the Delaware bringing fish from the deep and produce from New Jersey. But on this day the streets and docks remained quiet, except for loyalists and other gawkers lining the walkways. At ten a.m., two hundred dragoons in black leather caps with bearskin crests led the procession across Vine Street, their sabers drawn and held vertically at the right shoulder. Sixty fifers and drummers followed, beating a deliberate sixty-four steps per minute, sticks raised to eye level. Bandsmen played "God Save the King." Behind them came six 12-pounders and four howitzers, the iron rims on the carriage wheels grating over the cobbles and green garlands threaded through the horses' traces. Captain Montrésor, the engineer, recorded the "acclamation of some thousands of the inhabitants, mostly women and children."

Howe had ridden halfway to Philadelphia, then let Cornwallis take the honors while he returned to Germantown, where most of the army would wait until the pacified city was prepared for a full occupation. Cornwallis's command group, with aides and staff officers, trotted down Second Street beneath the massive Palladian window and two-hundred-foot octagonal spire of Christ Church, the tallest structure in North America. The column swung west on Chestnut—mimicking the route taken by Washington and his Continentals a month earlier—then halted at the statehouse, now bell-less. "No wanton levity or indecent mirth," Sarah Fisher noted in her journal. "Baggage, wagons, Hessian women, & horses, cows, goats, & asses brought up the rear. . . . Everything appeared still & quiet." Elizabeth Drinker, whose Quaker royalist husband had been banished to Virginia along with Mrs. Fisher's, observed, "Well, here are the English in earnest."

Within hours they made the town their own. British grenadiers occupied the Bettering House on Spruce Street and a shipyard to the south, with the Royal Artillery housed along Chestnut Street, Hessians arrayed on the city's northern edge, and the main guard post placed in the statehouse. Officers reserved fine houses for themselves with proprietary chalk marks. Montrésor's engineers immediately built three artillery batteries on the riverfront; other guns were wheeled to the city's perimeter. Forage yards sprang up near the Delaware and next to the potter's field. Local laborers willing to work for the Crown could earn eight shillings a day, plus meals. Informants got rewards for pointing out hidden rum, wagons, and other contraband wanted by the army. Farmers with grain to sell received payment in gold or silver. A night watch of 120 men called out not only the hour but also the weather.

An estimated twelve thousand Philadelphians had fled the city, but twice that number remained. The *Evening Post*, switching allegiance with astounding celerity to support the king's army, detected "a joy in the countenances of the well-affected." Loyalists soon rounded up several hundred rebel sympathizers and herded them into the new Walnut Street jail, behind stone walls twenty feet high. Most were quickly released; British jailers needed the cells for prisoners from Brandywine and Paoli. Yet suddenly loyalists were ascendant, if not quite in charge.

Here, indeed, was the place to launch a counterrevolution, to affirm the British government's strategic thesis that loyalty to the Crown remained strong in the American colonies beyond New York. If two of every three Yankees were at least tacitly loyal, as some of the king's most fervent advisers maintained, the army's task now was to "assist the good Americans to subdue the bad ones," in one British official's phrase. William Howe had argued that Pennsylvania was the right place to roll back the rebellion, and many rebels feared that he was correct. "Here is more Toryism, I suggest, than in all the states besides," General Smallwood told Maryland's governor. Traditional Pennsylvania elites—Quakers and Anglicans—who had been swept aside by militant radicals resented their diminished status and awaited restoration of previous privileges. Hardly had Cornwallis arrived than taverns again resounded with roaring toasts to King George, and armed units began to organize, such as the 1st Battalion of Pennsylvania Loyalists, commanded by William Allen, Jr., a Continental Army lieutenant colonel who defected to the king's cause.

Foremost among influential Philadelphia loyalists was lawyer Joseph Galloway, a former speaker of the Pennsylvania Assembly and a former congressman, to whom Franklin, upon departing for France, had entrusted his papers, including the only copy of his work-in-progress *Autobiography*. As the rift with the mother country had grown, Galloway had turned his coat, defecting to the British in late 1776. If petty and vain, he was "too valuable to be neglected," in one loyalist clergyman's estimation, and he proved his worth by organizing reconnaissance teams at Brandywine and helping to guide British troops across those fatal upstream fords.

Although Howe would eventually condemn Galloway as "a nugatory informer" and a "visionary"—neither term a compliment—he now appointed him police supervisor, port superintendent, and chief spymaster, with eighty agents and twenty counterintelligence operatives, all for a generous annual income of £770. Galloway helped provision British forces, administered oaths of allegiance, collected military maps, organized a census to identify military-age males for the king's cause, regulated import prices, and drafted a scheme to kidnap both Congress and the governor of New Jersey. He insisted that "more than four-fifths of the people would prefer a union with Great Britain . . . to that of independence." A rebel editorial denounced him as a "Lucifer of earth."

Yet Galloway and his masters in London consistently overestimated the potency of loyalist support in America, a political chimera that distorted British military decisions for years. Later scholarship would conclude that about 16 percent of the total American population throughout the war— just over half a million of more than three million—were committed loyalists. (If five hundred thousand black slaves were excluded from that total, the proportion rose to almost 20 percent.) At least thirty thousand loyalists would fight for the Crown, from drummer boys to field-grade officers, and perhaps almost twice that number, according to historian Wallace Brown. But that cadre proved insufficient for sustained battlefield or political success, particularly since hundreds—and eventually thousands—of loyalists would flee to Canada, England, or the West Indies. The fate of a counter-rebellion in rural eastern Maryland by 250 armed Tories earlier this year was typical; two thousand rebel militiamen and Continentals swiftly crushed the uprising, chasing the loyalists into the Chesapeake wetlands or out to remote islands in the bay. A Tory farmer, John Tims, was sentenced in the Talbot County courthouse to be hanged and "cut down alive that his entrails be taken out and burned before his face, and his head cut off and his body divided into four quarters." Presumably chastened, Tims repented and was later pardoned.

Loyalists lacked national leaders, effective propaganda, and self-sufficiency without massive British support. None of the thirteen states remained under loyalist control, despite pockets of strength along the western frontier from New York to Georgia and in maritime regions of the middle states, including southeastern Pennsylvania and southern Delaware. Rebel success in the past two and a half years had derived less from military triumphs, of which there were few, than political victories, of which there were many. Virtually all levers of power, from municipal committees of safety to state governments and the national Congress, remained under insurrectionist control.

Local patriot agencies recruited soldiers, collected weapons, and enforced revolutionary orthodoxy by identifying, threatening, and punishing those hesitant to support the cause. In New York, a parent whose son fought for the British was subject to an annual tax. South Carolina divided loyalists into four classes, with varying degrees of reprisal, depending on the extent of alignment with the enemy. Refusal to accept Continental currency—"rag money," as the loyalist New York newspaper *Rivington's Gazette* called it—was a crime in many states and a means of identifying inimicals. Mandatory oaths renouncing allegiance to the Crown also distinguished friend from foe; those who refused to swear could be disarmed, fined, deprived of legal rights, exiled, or jailed without bond. This fracturing of the body politic foreshadowed the Civil War, nearly a century later, not in the causes of the schism but in internecine malignancy and the bitter estrangement of American from American.

"In politics the middle way is none at all," John Adams asserted, and civil war bred immoderation and, sometimes, terror. Judicial procedures, with court hearings and legal representation for the accused, were usually observed in rebel jurisdictions, but justice could be ferocious and unsparing. Loyalists in Virginia were whipped until they shouted, "Liberty forever." A loyalist who died in New Jersey earlier this year while serving as a British guide was punished in the afterlife by having his farm, woodlot, livestock, and three slaves confiscated, leaving his widow and eleven children to the mercy of "an unfeeling world."

"A Tory is an incorrigible animal," Governor William Livingston of New Jersey wrote Washington, "and nothing but the extinction of life will extinguish his malevolence against liberty." The corpses of two New Jersey loyalists captured and hanged after a skirmish were reportedly "drawn on a sled from under the gallows & thrown into the room" where other loyalists "are confined in irons." In May, New York's assembly had advised the state militia to uncover all "emissaries of the enemy" and "immediately execute them." The criminalization of loyalty to the Crown could be seen in vigorous "Tory hunting": expropriation, exile, and occasional executions, including the likes of Moses Dunbar, captured with a commission from William Howe in his pocket while enlisting Connecticut men for a loyalist regiment. Before his hanging in Hartford on March 19—it was said that his patriot father offered to provide hemp for the noose—his pregnant young wife was forced to sit beside him as he rode in the tumbrel to the gallows.

Brutal as Britain's treatment of American prisoners could be, the king's government prosecuted few insurrectionists for treason, sedition, or rebellion. A loyalist newspaper, sniffing hypocrisy among the patriots, versified: "The cry was for liberty / Lord, what a fuss! / But pray, / How much liberty left they for us?" Yet if, as the radical British politician John Wilkes asserted, "*successful* resistance is revolution, not a rebellion," the Americans were making a revolution. Some citizens, of course, were simply trying to avoid being swept away by turbulent historical forces they hardly understood. But many loyalists were condemned, as the historian George Otto Trevelyan would write, "to stand by, idle and powerless, while the two nations which they equally loved, were tearing at each other's vitals."

General Howe had more immediate concerns than the welfare of his loyalists. Philadelphia had been seized from the Americans but was not yet useful to the king's forces. His brother's fleet, again harrowed by bad weather and contrary winds, would not reach the Delaware River from Head of Elk until early October. When the admiral arrived, he would find the river blocked by rebel defenders for at least ten miles south of the city, precluding the delivery of food, ammunition, and other necessities, given the vulnerability of overland transport to ambush in Chester County and New Jersey. For now, a flatboat hugging the western shoreline on dark nights occasionally slipped through with provisions for Philadelphia, but the trip was so exacting that crews required strong drink to steel themselves before setting out.

American efforts to prevent British engineers from fortifying Philadelphia's docklands began badly. Commodore John Hazelwood, commanding a small Continental river squadron bolstered by Pennsylvania Navy vessels, had ordered Captain Charles Alexander, aboard the sleek new frigate *Delaware*, to "do everything in your power to annoy the enemy." At ten a.m. on September 27, Alexander closed to within three hundred yards of a recently erected Royal Artillery battery at Reed Street, a mile southeast of the statehouse. The sloop *Fly* accompanied *Delaware*, and several row galleys took positions in the shallows to rake the adjacent wharves and cross streets. Hundreds of spectators crowded the waterfront at a prudent distance, but no sooner had a spirited cannonade erupted than *Delaware* ran aground on a Windmill Island mudflat. A British howitzer shell struck the cookhouse, decapitating the cook and setting the frigate on fire. After another shell exploded in the bow, Alexander struck his colors. The entire crew of 152 men surrendered and were marched into the Walnut Street jail, except for those who agreed to switch sides. *Fly* beat for the Jersey shore with her main mast shivered and ten sailors dead or wounded. British tars soon extinguished the flames on *Delaware* and eased her back into the channel, now flying a Union Jack.

In an hour, Hazelwood had lost his biggest warship. The remaining Delaware River flotilla would hardly intimidate the Royal Navy. It included a pair of three-masted xebecs with triangular lateen sails, a two-masted shallop called *Black Dick*, several fireships with names like *Blast* and *Aetna*, and thirteen poorly manned flat-bottomed galleys, each fifty feet long and thirteen feet wide, painted black and yellow, with a single large cannon in the bow and propelled by twenty oars.

Thomas Paine had read of ancient fire arrows, and he took the initiative in designing a crossbow that, he claimed, could shoot an arrow across the Delaware at enemy positions with flame encased "in a bulb near the top." Washington and Congress preferred more practical river defenses that would not incinerate America's largest city. To that end, three forts stood along the banks below Philadelphia. French engineers favored the southernmost, at Billingsport, where the Delaware was narrowest. But on October 1, two redcoat regiments crossed the river from Chester to Raccoon Creek in New Jersey, then attacked through a cornfield. The hundred-man garrison burned the Billingsport barracks and escaped in small boats, firing over the gunwales with the six muskets they'd managed to salvage.

The two remaining river strongholds hardly seemed formidable. Fort Mercer, named for a martyr from the Battle of Princeton, was still under construction at Red Bank, on the New Jersey side of the Delaware, with weak exterior walls encircling a stout interior redoubt. Nineteen hundred yards due west, near the mouth of the Schuylkill, sat Mud Island, now renamed Fort Mifflin, to honor the Continental Army's adjutant general. As a keystone of rebel defenses, this was "a burlesque upon the art of fortification," in an American surgeon's description, or, as an experienced European officer later wrote, "the worst that I have ever seen."

Lieutenant Colonel Samuel Smith, ordered by Washington to reinforce Fort Mifflin with his 4th Maryland Regiment, arrived in late September to find "everything in the utmost confusion." Only sixty militiamen manned the bastion, some from the aptly named Invalid Corps; none knew how to fire their shore guns, which hardly mattered since artillery ammunition was not "sufficient for an hour" of combat. Separated from the mainland by a shallow channel six hundred yards wide, the island was an insalubrious bog of muskrat holes, cattails, and thickets of whortleberry and sumac. After work gangs had driven tree trunks into the mud as a foundation, the first stone and earthen fortifications had been built in 1771 by none other than Captain Montrésor as a British redoubt against the French during the last war. Philadelphians had resumed work on the unfinished citadel in 1775, digging drainage ditches, building blockhouses, and mounting 18-pounders to command the river. But high tides still flooded the parade ground, and the wooden palisades on three sides were too low to prevent a determined enemy from firing into the compound. As Cornwallis would observe, "'Twas a cursed little mud island."

The most formidable American defenses near Philadelphia were the least visible. Submerged on the Delaware's silty bottom were chevaux-de-frise, originally invented to impede enemy cavalry charges in northern Europe. Architect Robert Smith, who had designed several prominent buildings in Philadelphia and Nassau Hall, in Princeton, had adapted the concept to thwart hostile ships sailing upriver. Over two years, with support from a municipal committee headed by Benjamin Franklin, more than two hundred of the obstructions had been built at a cost of £8,000, four times the original estimate.

Huge timbers formed frames thirty feet square, floored with plank hoppers to hold up to sixty tons of stone ballast. Chained together for stability, the frames were sunk in the Delaware using sea anchors. Each cheval-de-frise was fitted with two or three long iron spears called "pricks," pointing downstream and positioned just below the river surface to disembowel any vessel headed upstream. Similar contraptions had failed on the wide, deep Hudson the previous summer, but in the shallow Delaware, alive with shoals and shifting channels, they were lethal. Ten patriot river pilots, sworn to secrecy, earned £6 a month for guiding friendly vessels through the twisting maze created by the double row of chevaux at the Billingsport narrows and the triple row farther north, between Forts Mercer and Mifflin.

These rebel nuisances—the mosquito fleet, the two surviving forts, and the sunken obstacles, which the British called "stackadoes"—would have to be swept aside before Philadelphia's port could open. In early October, Captain Montrésor, on orders from General Howe, crossed to Province Island, which sat in the mouth of the Schuylkill like a cork in a bottle. The engineer confirmed that the island, site of the city's pesthouse since the 1740s, was dry enough for them to build artillery batteries that could range Fort Mifflin. Wagons escorted by the 23rd Royal Welch Fusiliers began hauling cannons from Chester.

Upon reaching the Delaware with his fleet, Admiral Howe sent *Pearl*, *Camilla*, *Liverpool*, and *Roebuck* upstream to Billingsport. Naval officers cautiously examined the lower rows of stackadoes, only to find themselves under attack at night from darting row galleys and oil-soaked fire rafts, engulfed in flame and drifting south on the tide until frantic tars in small boats snagged the pyres with grappling hooks and towed them toward shore. For now the warships fell back to Chester. Both Howes agreed that no channels could be opened through the stackadoes until the shorelines had been cleared, the forts subdued, and the pesky gunboats driven off.

Food stocks in the city diminished quickly. The days grew shorter and the nights colder. Farmers dismantled and hid their fences before soldiers could snatch them for firewood. "Much drunkenness & irregularity among the men, which occasions frequent courts-martial and punishments," Lieutenant John Peebles wrote. Redcoats and loyalists alike grew uneasy. Sarah Logan Fisher summed up the predicament in her diary:

> Not a barrel of good flour to be bought at any price. . . . Scarcely any meat in market, nor a pound of butter or an egg. . . . Not any wood to be had at any price. . . . As the English have neither the command of the river nor the country, provisions cannot be brought in.

Reports of such difficulties pleased Washington. Not long before, he had feared that "the loss of Philadelphia would prove an irreparable injury" to the American cause. Now, as the commander in chief wrote to the exiled state government in Lancaster, "Without the free navigation of the Delaware, I am confident that General Howe will never remain in Philadelphia."

7.

———

Born Under a Fiery Planet

The Continental Army collected itself in late September at Pennypacker's Mills on Perkiomen Creek, twenty-five miles northwest of Philadelphia. Every regiment was instructed to keep busy making musket cartridges using powder, paper, and lead balls supplied by General Knox. Marauding troops also plundered fence rails for campfires, hayricks for forage, and chicken coops for cook pots.

While contemplating his next move, Washington sat for an ivory miniature portrait by Captain Charles Willson Peale, commander of a Pennsylvania militia company. Trained as a saddler and a silversmith, Peale had taught himself painting by studying other artists; his admirers had financed a two-year stay in London so that he could train under the expatriate master Benjamin West before opening a studio in Philadelphia. He would paint General Washington fourteen times from life, but His Excellency admired him as much for his revolutionary fervor as for his brushstrokes. Captain Peale so loathed loyalists that he proposed painting their houses black, much like "the Turks used to designate the residences of liars." After finishing the Washington portrait at Pennypacker's Mills, he set aside his palette to cast 176 lead bullets, which he donated to the cause.

No less belligerent, the commander in chief, by October 2, had decided to make another thrust at the enemy. Spies and intercepted letters revealed that General Howe had halved his army in Germantown to eight thousand men, with the other half—including most of his best grenadiers and Highland regiments—deployed to Philadelphia, Wilmington, and Chester. Reinforced by militia from three states, Washington could muster sixteen thousand troops fit for immediate combat, sorted into six divisions and four independent brigades. His intricate plan, drafted in just two days and approved by all sixteen subordinate generals, called for a surprise attack on Germantown by four columns marching through the night over backwoods roads before converging to strike simultaneously at dawn across a five-mile front.

At noon on Friday, October 3, after the army had sidled to within sixteen miles of Howe's encampment, invalids were carted to a safe haven in Bethlehem—a sure sign of imminent trouble. "This serves to inform you that we are still in the land of the living," Captain James Cox, a former tailor, wrote to his wife and five children in Baltimore. "We are still advancing down towards the enemy and expect very soon to be foul of each other. . . . May heaven protect us all." That night each man was to carry forty rounds and two days' of cooked rations. There would be no noise, no lights, and no talk. With a mild, moonless evening ahead, every soldier was again given a scrap of white paper to wear in his hatband for mutual recognition. In general orders, Washington implored the ranks to rouse themselves:

> Will you suffer the wounds given to your country to go unrevenged? General Howe has . . . left us no choice but conquest or death. . . . Our dearest rights, our dearest friends, our own lives, honor, glory, and even shame urge us to the fight. And, my fellow soldiers, when an opportunity presents, be firm, be brave, show yourselves men, and victory is yours.

At six p.m., New Jersey and Maryland militiamen, who had the farthest to march, on the left flank, stepped off. They were followed by five thousand Continentals under General Greene, also veering to the left, then General Armstrong's Pennsylvania militia regiments, assigned to the right flank. Washington rode southeast down Skippack Road at eight p.m. with the fourth and final column: thirty-seven hundred Continentals, including seven Maryland regiments commanded by General Sullivan, who was still seething over what he called "the very unjust censure cast upon me" for his performance at Staten Island and at Brandywine.

No men shared the commander in chief's appetite for revenge more than those who had survived Paoli two weeks earlier. "Dawn is big with the fate of thousands," Anthony Wayne wrote his wife, Polly, before riding into the night with the final column. "We cannot fear. My heart sets lightly in its mansion. Every artery beats in unison, and I feel unusual ardor."

Founded a century earlier by Rhineland émigrés, Germantown stretched for two miles along a single street lined with stone houses. White cedar shingles, quaint gables, and shaded front stoops lent the village a tidy uniformity. Palings and picket fences enclosed orchards, paddocks, and

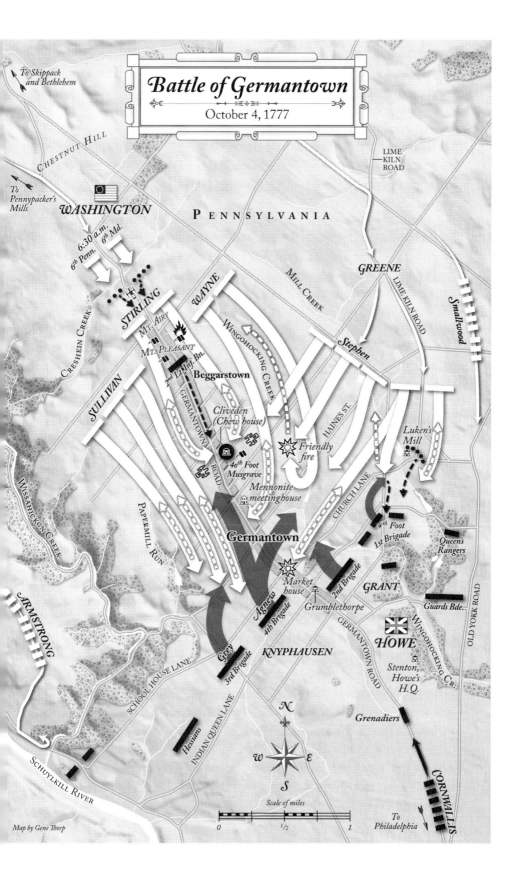

Battle of Germantown
October 4, 1777

To Skippack and Bethlehem

CHESTNUT HILL

LIME KILN ROAD

To Pennypacker's Mills

WASHINGTON

6:30 a.m. 6th Penn. 6th Md.

PENNSYLVANIA

GREENE

LIME KILN ROAD

Smallwood

MILL CREEK

STIRLING

WAYNE

Stephen

MT. AIRY

MT. PLEASANT

WINGOHOCKING CREEK

CRESHEIM CREEK

2nd Lt. Inf. Bn.

Beggarstown

SULLIVAN

Cliveden
(Chew house)

HAINES ST.

Luken's Mill

GERMANTOWN ROAD

40th Foot
Musgrave

Friendly
fire

4th Foot
1st Brigade

WISSAHICKON CREEK

Mennonite
meetinghouse

CHURCH LANE

Queen's
Rangers

PAPERMILL RUN

Germantown

2nd Brigade

GRANT

Market
house

Agnew
4th Brigade

Grumblethorpe

Guards Bde.

ARMSTRONG

Grey
3rd Brigade

KNYPHAUSEN

GERMANTOWN ROAD

HOWE

WINGOHOCKING CR.

OLD YORK ROAD

Stenton,
Howe's
H.Q.

SCHOOL HOUSE LANE

Hessians

INDIAN QUEEN LANE

N

W   E

S

Grenadiers

SCHUYLKILL RIVER

Scale of miles

0   1/2   1

CORNWALLIS

To
Philadelphia

Map by Gene Thorp

vegetable gardens. Local tradesmen produced goods in "quantity and perfection," a visitor reported, including wagons for the Continental Army and hospital supplies, stored in the vinegar house.

General Howe deliberately avoided entrenchments and other conspicuous defenses in Germantown, to demonstrate "the acknowledged superiority of the king's troops over the enemy," he asserted. Instead he arranged ten regiments under General Knyphausen to the left, or west, of the high street—closest to the Schuylkill—and six more under General Grant to the right, plus dragoons, the Guards, the 1st Light Infantry, and the Queen's Rangers. All troops faced northwest, the presumed vector of danger, where 350 men in the 2nd Light Infantry occupied a trip-wire outpost two miles from town on Mount Pleasant. Howe placed his headquarters in Stenton, the Georgian manor house on the road into Philadelphia where Washington had spent the night after leaving the Little Neshaminy six weeks earlier.

The king's men were aware of the American "vow that they will give no quarter to any of our battalions," as one officer wrote. Yet most believed that Brandywine and Paoli "had dispirited the enemy to such a degree that it would be utterly impossible for Washington to give us any further trouble for some time at least," according to Captain Richard Fitzpatrick. Vague rumors on Friday of rebel stirrings "were very little credited," Captain André told his journal. Portents and omens in the small hours of October 4 were acknowledged by some, ignored or dismissed by others. At two a.m., pickets on Lime Kiln Road seized a lost rebel flanker, who initially admitted that two Continental brigades were advancing on Germantown; under further interrogation in the guardhouse, he confessed that Washington's entire army was on the move. Senior officers woke General Grant, who ordered troops roused and Howe warned.

Yet if an alarm to "alert and accouter" reached some regiments—Howe later told Lord Germain that the army had been "immediately ordered under arms"—a drowsy nonchalance persisted in much of the force. "We knew nothing of all these movements of the enemy . . . until after daybreak," Knyphausen later wrote his prince. Captain Fitzpatrick admitted being surprised "in every sense of the word." Lieutenant Martin Hunter, recovered from the gunshot wound he suffered at Paoli, would claim, "The first that General Howe heard of General Washington's marching against us was the attack upon us at daybreak."

Swirling fog muted the first orange glow seeping from the east at five a.m. as the 6th Pennsylvania Regiment crept down Chestnut Hill on the Germantown road. Ordered to use bayonets and sabers to silence the British pickets, they were instead discovered throwing down fence rails to open a corridor for the serried column following behind them. Squinting sentries spotted the Continentals, fired several volleys into the fog, then fell back six hundred yards to the light infantry tents and wigwams on Mount Pleasant. Small red tongues of flame soon licked back and forth across the front, punctuated by concussive booms from a pair of British 6-pounders. The 6th Maryland extended the Pennsylvania line to the left, filing across the road and into the fields. More Continentals followed, including Wayne's two Pennsylvania brigades.

Sunrise at precisely six a.m. hardly brightened the day. Gunsmoke and burning wheat stubble, ignited by muzzle flashes, thickened into "the most horrid fog I ever saw," wrote Brigadier General George Weedon. Wounded redcoats stumbled toward the rear, including a sentry with his hand all but severed by a bullet through the wrist. The 52nd Foot surged forward, adding another 350 muskets to the British line, and for a few unnerving minutes the Americans buckled and the attack stalled. A 6-pound cannonball ripped a leg below the knee from Private Abraham Best of the 6th Pennsylvania, his blood freckling the men around him. Another ball ricocheted off a signpost, blew through the withers of the horse carrying Brigadier General Francis Nash, commander of the North Carolina Continentals, cut a furrow across Nash's left thigh, then virtually decapitated Major James Witherspoon, the eldest son of Reverend John Witherspoon, a signer of the Declaration and the president of the College of New Jersey, in Princeton. Sprawled in the dirt next to his dead horse and his dead aide, Nash covered the terrible wound to his leg with both hands and called to his men, "Never mind me. I have had a devil of a tumble. Rush on, my boys."

More Continentals pressed into the brawl, including Sullivan's Marylanders from the northwest, lapping at the redcoats' flanks. "A devil of a fire upon our front & flank came ding-dong about us," wrote Lieutenant Loftus Cliffe of the 46th Foot. "All sides of us was the hottest fire I ever heard." Lieutenant Hunter of the 52nd Foot heard Wayne's vengeful Pennsylvanians invoke his regiment's nickname from Paoli as they howled, "Have at the Bloodhounds!" With some volleys exchanged at barely ten yards' range, Captain Enoch Anderson of the 1st Delaware wrote, "My men were falling very fast. I now took off my hat and shouted as loud as I could, 'Charge bayonets, and advance!'"

At length the brag of a trumpet sounded withdrawal, and the British drew back toward the village, stabbing their gun-carriage horses rather than giving them into rebel hands. "This was the first time we had ever retreated from the Americans," Hunter added, "and it was with great difficulty we could get the men to obey our orders." General Grant ordered two more regiments, the 5th and 55th Foot, to confront Wayne's Pennsylvanians;

both soon fell back in disarray, the 5th reporting ten dead and forty-six wounded. Wayne later wrote Polly:

> Our officers exerted themselves to save many of the poor wretches who were crying for mercy, but to little purpose. The rage and fury of the soldiers were not to be restrained for some time, at least not until great numbers of the enemy fell by our bayonets.

An officer in the 10th Pennsylvania observed, "Our people showed them no quarter . . . and put their bayonets through all ye came across."

In Beggarstown, a hamlet just north of Germantown, retreating redcoats found Howe straddling his horse beneath a towering chestnut tree. The commanding general "got into a great passion, exclaiming, 'For shame, light infantry! I never saw you retreat before,'" Hunter recorded. "'Form! Form! It's only a scouting party.'" At that moment, the van of Sullivan's column swarmed into view, led by three field guns firing grapeshot. Howe and his entourage abruptly galloped for the rear, past gaping schoolboys watching the battle from their rooftops. "We really all felt pleased," Hunter added sardonically, "to hear the grape rattle about the commander in chief's ears."

Washington also felt pleased as he trailed Sullivan's division on the Germantown road. By seven a.m. the enemy had been driven back to the edge of the British bivouac. Marylanders seized the two abandoned 6-pounders, although the drag ropes had been cut and "we could do nothing with them," an officer lamented. The smoke and fog "made such a midnight darkness that a great part of the time there was no discovering friend from foe but by the direction of the shot," a Continental officer wrote. Sullivan later reported that "the enemy were routed yet they took advantage of every yard, house, & hedge in their retreat, which kept up an incessant fire through the whole pursuit."

Washington sent orders for General Lord Stirling's two reserve brigades to hurry forward, giving Sullivan's men time to replenish their dwindling ammunition. The day seemed all but won. "We had full possession of the enemy's camp, which was on fire in many places, dead and wounded men laying strewed about," wrote Brigadier General John Lacey, commanding the Pennsylvania militia on the far right wing of the American assault. Private Ephraim Kirby, a mounted courier for the Continentals, would tell his father that while carrying messages that morning he rode "over the dead bodies where they lay as thick as the stones in a stony fallow field. Shocking to behold."

*   *   *

A mile and a half south of where the morning's clash had begun stood Cliveden, the most elegant house in Germantown and among the finest in eastern Pennsylvania. Built of Wissahickon schist fieldstone, with glinting flecks of mica, the mansion displayed perfect Georgian symmetry, including twelve-over-twelve windows and two wide brick chimneys above opposing gables. A pair of sculpted lions on the entry stoop guarded the French front doors. An open-air colonnade led to a large kitchen dependency behind the house, matched in size and shape by a washhouse on the other side. Five huge stone urns imported from England sat on brick plinths at the corners and peak of the roof, and grounds that spread across fifty-five acres displayed four life-size marble statues perched on pedestals in the classical style. Servants lived in a hayloft above the stables, hard by the carriage house. Master masons, metalsmiths, stone carvers, and carpenters had given the house many grace notes, from brass doorknobs and the fluted Doric columns in the entry foyer to jack arch lintels and keystones above the windows.

Cliveden was the summer home of Benjamin Chew, a Quaker jurist who had studied law at the Middle Temple in London before serving his native state in various legal posts, including registrar of wills and chief justice. Chew also owned a courtly house on Third Street in Philadelphia and nine plantations, tended by more than two hundred slaves, on both sides of the Chesapeake in Maryland, Virginia, and Delaware. Dismayed by British colonial policies, he nonetheless opposed rebellion, which had led Congress in late summer to order his arrest as "dangerous to the public liberty." Jailers confined him in the Union Iron Works in New Jersey, quarters considerably less comfortable than Cliveden.

The British now made good use of Chew's vacant house, despite General Lacey's assertion that the enemy had been overrun. The 40th Foot had pitched camp behind Cliveden, near the kitchen garden and a cobble-stoned washboard used to clean carriages. The ranks remained diminished by losses suffered at Princeton in January, where the regiment had barricaded itself inside Nassau Hall, to bad effect; eighty-five soldiers were captured. Forty-year-old Lieutenant Colonel Thomas Musgrave, the only surviving heir of the fourth Baronet of Hayton Castle, commanded the 40th, replacing an officer killed on Long Island. Musgrave had had his own brush with mortality at White Plains, where he had taken a bullet in the face that left him disfigured with a hole through one cheek.

Fleeing redcoats warned that the Americans were bayoneting every

British soldier within reach, and Musgrave ordered more than a hundred of his men inside the mansion. "It was tenable," an American officer later conceded, a perfect stronghold. Musketeers manned every window, from cellar to garret, locking the heavy black wooden shutters on the ground floor and bolting all three entrances. Musgrave climbed the U-shaped staircase to place his command post on the second floor, near lawyer Chew's empty bedchamber at the front of the house. Pleased to find excellent fields of fire in all directions, he informed his men, as one recalled, that their "only safety was in the defense of that house, that if they let the enemy get into it, they would undoubtedly every man be put to death. . . . They must sell themselves as dear as possible."

Wayne's Pennsylvanians and Sullivan's Marylanders streamed past Cliveden on two sides, squeezing off a few volleys before hurrying south toward the market house in the center of Germantown. Trailing rebel regiments formed a cordon along a low stone wall and around cherry trees lining the front drive. The gunfire slackened briefly, then became general. After picking up a British Brown Bess he'd found leaning against a fence, Private Philip Ludwig said brightly, "This is much better than mine." He then fell dead from a bullet through the forehead. "The balls seemed to come in showers," recalled Ensign John Markland of the 6th Pennsylvania, whose shoulder was shattered. A surgeon snipped away his bloody right sleeve, then cut off the left to use as a bandage; Markland would wear the sleeveless remnant for three weeks, picking bone slivers from his wound with a penknife. The redcoats "commenced a brilliant & incessant firing from the windows," another officer recorded. "The fog was very thick & kept the smoke down so low that the battle was fought without the adverse parties scarcely seeing each other."

Washington and his staff halted on the high road two hundred yards north of Cliveden's front door. Listening to the drumfire ahead, His Excellency told Colonel Pickering, "I am afraid General Sullivan is throwing away his ammunition. Ride forward and tell him to preserve it." The adjutant general trotted past the mansion into the village, delivered the message, and returned within a hundred yards of the great house, astonished to hear musket balls whizzing above, behind, and in front of him as muzzle flashes winked from every second-story window. Rejoining Washington at a fast clip, he found the commanding general in fervid conversation with Brigadier General Knox, who straddled a large horse able to carry his nearly three hundred pounds. The two men dismounted to climb onto a carriage block with their spyglasses, in vain hopes of a better view of Cliveden. Knox, dressed in a blue-and-buff uniform with a handkerchief discreetly covering his left hand—the fingers had been maimed in a youthful hunting accident—would write Lucy that "it absolutely became impossible to see an object at twenty yards' distance."

Squinting, they debated whether to bypass this vexing fortress or besiege it with artillery if the British refused a surrender ultimatum. Knox favored the latter course, declaring with some heat, "It would be unmilitary to leave a castle in our rear." A Massachusetts lawyer with a full fund of military opinions, Pickering disagreed. "Doubtless that is a correct general maxim," he said, "but it does not apply here." He suggested leaving a single regiment to encircle the house, and if the British should "sally, such a regiment will take care of them." Any move "to summon them to surrender will be useless," Pickering added. "They will fire on your flag." Several eavesdropping junior officers concurred with the adjutant, Hamilton and Captain Henry Lee of the light dragoons among them.

Washington had no more experience with this sort of tactical conundrum than Knox had, and he sided with his artillery chief. Lieutenant Colonel William Smith, Pickering's deputy, volunteered to carry a truce flag forward to demand a surrender, but got no further than the front gate when he was mortally wounded. "In a few minutes Mr. Smith was brought back with his leg broken and shattered by a musket ball fired from the house," Pickering wrote.

Rebel soldiers had at last managed to manhandle the two abandoned British 6-pounders onto the western verge of the Germantown road, joined by a pair of Pennsylvania field guns. The first shot, at a range of 120 yards, blew Cliveden's front doors from their hinges. Succeeding blasts perforated the black shutters, smashed the plaster walls inside, fractured the front steps, and dismembered the delicate lawn statuary. Stone fragments, wood splinters, and glass shards lacerated the British defenders, who tried to rehang the doors or at least shove chairs and tables into the yawning entryway. American grapeshot, aimed at the upper floors, chipped window frames and the stone urns on the roof.

But Wissahickon schist walls two feet thick proved obdurate. Musgrave bounded between rooms, consoling his wounded and shouting, "Hurrah to the king! Hurrah to the English!" Washington and his lieutenants ordered the house stormed while gunners continued to pepper the upper floors and roofline with grape. Officers from the 1st and 3rd New Jersey Regiments led their cheering men up the driveway, but bullets swept the column. British defenders bayoneted several men trying to force the front hall. "My horse was shot under me . . . within about three yards of the corner of the house," wrote Colonel Elias Dayton, who commanded the 3rd

New Jersey. "About this time came on perhaps the thickest fog known in the memory of man, which together with the smoke brought on almost midnight darkness."

Several officers now proposed to burn out the British by setting fire to the shutters and window frames. Lieutenant Colonel Laurens, a French captain named Thomas-Antoine de Mauduit, the Chevalier du Plessis, and two aides to General Sullivan, Majors John White and Edward Sherburne, dashed into the stable, scooped up armloads of straw, and crept past the kitchen. Mauduit du Plessis pried open a shutter and climbed onto the sill, only to be confronted by a British officer with a pistol. Another redcoat inside fired, wounding his officer by mischance as the Frenchman ran to safety. Laurens neared the front stoop with drawn sword, but a spent ball slammed into his side, aggravating a flesh wound in his right shoulder suffered earlier in the morning. He, too, took to his heels, and would fashion an arm sling from the green sash he wore as Washington's aide. Major White was shot dead trying to ignite a window frame. Major Sherburne reportedly was bayoneted in the mouth while prying open a ground-floor window; also shot, he staggered back into his lines and would die the next day.

Continental artillery continued to rake the walls, with great noise but little effect. For more than an hour Musgrave and his men halted or disrupted the attack of five brigades, roughly four thousand Continentals. And still the British held the house.

Washington's plan at Germantown was similar to his surprise attack against the Hessian garrison at Trenton on Christmas night ten months earlier. In both battles he divided his force to slam into the enemy from two converging angles. Now, as the roaring standoff at Cliveden unfolded, General Greene barreled into the village from due north with five additional brigades. A guide had taken a wrong turn, angling the column more than two miles away from Sullivan's spearhead, rather than the intended mile, and putting Greene's arrival forty minutes behind schedule. Fog, creeks, broken terrain, and countless rail fences had further disrupted his tight march formation.

Nonetheless, several thousand additional Continentals, mostly Virginians led by a brigade of New Englanders, swarmed toward Howe's right flank. "Our orders were not to fire till we could see the buttons upon their clothes," wrote Private Joseph Plumb Martin of the 8th Connecticut, a sixteen-year-old preacher's son. Smoke obscured the enemy "before we had either time or leisure to examine their buttons," he added, but three overmatched British light infantry companies fell back from Luken's Mill, across a buckwheat field. The 4th Regiment of Foot—veterans of Concord, Bunker Hill, Long Island, and Brandywine—moved forward into a maelstrom. One redcoat company hurried along a sunken lane, unaware that Virginia riflemen were waiting in ambush with their rifle barrels steadied on fence rails. The point-blank volley "knocked them down fifty men," a captain reported. Dead soldiers and the writhing wounded filled the lane, darkening the dust with British blood.

"The enemy were driven quite through their camp," Martin wrote. "They left their kettles, in which they were cooking their breakfasts, on the fires." Brigadier General George Weedon, a former Virginia tavern keeper now commanding Greene's 2nd Brigade, later recalled, "Victory was declaring in our favor."

But victory could be capricious, and the elation soon faded. Neither Greene nor his lieutenants could see where they were going or who was on their flanks; one senior officer estimated the visibility at under ten yards. Bypassed pockets of British soldiers stirred alarm in the rear. No one seemed to know whether Sullivan's attack had succeeded or where Washington was. Another Virginia brigade, under Brigadier General William Woodford, swept west off Lime Kiln Road and blundered into the brawl at Cliveden. Approaching the carriage house behind the mansion, Woodford's gunners unlimbered four fieldpieces and battered the back of the mansion, blowing open the rear door and sending a 6-pound ball through a large window above the grand staircase. Other rounds overshot the roof, landing beyond the front driveway among New Jersey and Pennsylvania Continentals, who concluded that Musgrave's defenders were firing round shot and grape from the second floor.

Disorder spiraled toward chaos, minute by minute. General Wayne's Pennsylvanians had battled a quarter mile or more past Cliveden when an intensifying din from the estate caused hundreds of his men, suspecting an enemy in their rear, to countermarch north. Seeing these wraiths approaching through the fog, more Virginians, under Major General Adam Stephen, fixed their bayonets and fired a volley, igniting a frenzied, fratricidal gunfight that ended only when the Pennsylvanians, unaware that "it was our own people," as Wayne told his wife, fled the field. Wayne took "a touch on my left hand" from a musket ball and his left foot was "a little bruised by one of their cannon shot." Bullets in the flank and neck killed his splendid roan.

Major General Grey—the notorious "No-Flint"—pushed two redcoat brigades north along the high street from their encampments near Indian Queen Lane and School House Lane. Soldiers of both armies scuttled in and out of houses and through back gardens, exchanging volleys at twenty paces or less. The crescendo of musketry and cannon fire reminded a Connecticut officer of "the crackling of thorns under a pot and incessant peals of thunder." Artillery could be heard not only in Philadelphia but even in Bethlehem, fifty miles away, the historian Thomas J. McGuire would write. The spirited 9th Virginia, from Greene's corps, had reached the market house, ransacking an enemy bivouac and rounding up a hundred prisoners, when the surging British counterattack trapped and annihilated the regiment, killing, wounding, or capturing 185 officers and men, four-fifths of the unit's strength. British prisoners were freed and rebel captives locked inside a church, including the 9th Virginia commander, Colonel George Mathews, bleeding from bayonet wounds. A witness reported that American faces as well as those of their British guards bore the telltale stigma of heavy combat: "well-blackened about their mouths with gunpowder, in biting off their cartridges."

By nine a.m. the American attack on Germantown had come unstitched. Ammunition grew short. Some companies edged forward to find that others, ostensibly protecting their flanks, had instead removed to the rear. Gunfire felled more officers, including Major Uriah Forrest of the 3rd Maryland, whose splintered femur would require amputation of the leg, and a captain in the same regiment, shot through the mouth with a ball that split his tongue and blew through the back of his jawbone. Sullivan later described Washington "exposing himself to the hottest fire of the enemy . . . [which] obliged me to ride to him & beg him to retire." His Excellency withdrew "a small distance, but his anxiety . . . soon brought him up again where he remained till our troops had retreated."

That retreat had already started. Half a dozen men could be seen helping a slightly wounded mate as an excuse to leave the field. Drove lanes and trampled cropland soon thickened with fugitives bearing tales of a flank turned, or of two flanks turned, or of friends firing on friends. Such rumors "like an electrical shock seized some thousands who fled in confusion," an officer reported. Absconding men scooted around saber-wielding Continental cavalrymen sent to prevent their withdrawal, or even darted under the horses' bellies. "I threw my squadron of horse across the road, by order of General Washington, repeatedly, to prevent the retreat of the infantry," Major Benjamin Tallmadge reported. "But it was ineffectual."

Brigadier General James Agnew, whose 4th Brigade had been badly lashed by Greene's ambushers in the twilight at Brandywine, now led the British counterattack toward Cliveden. He had just passed the Mennonite meetinghouse when scores of rebels rushed out from behind a stone building and opened fire. Agnew wheeled around and put spurs to his horse, but one ball passed through his right hand and a second struck him in the lower back, severing his spine before punching through his chest. Aides carried him into Grumblethorpe, a large stone house used as the brigade headquarters. Before he died "he could only turn his eyes and look steadfastly on me with seeming affection," Private Alexander Andrew, his manservant, wrote Agnew's widow. After removing the brigadier's watch and a purse containing four guineas, Andrew added, "I then had him laid out and decently dressed with some of his clean and best things, and had a coffin made, the best the place could produce."

At Cliveden, Colonel Musgrave heard British fifes and drums from the approaching 44th Foot, and he watched the last Continentals scamper up the road toward Mount Airy. Musgrave and his men shouldered aside the furniture barricading the front entrance and emerged, filthy, blood-spattered, and exhilarated. Of the hundred or so defenders, he would report four dead, twenty-nine wounded, and three missing.

General Lord Stirling's reserves held open the Germantown high road long enough for Wayne and Sullivan to extract their commands under Washington's baleful eye. Greene, with his own assault thoroughly deranged and exposed to counterattack, also ordered a hasty retreat north to Skippack Road. "For marching and expedition, I give them all possible merit," a captain in the 4th Foot wrote. "It is hardly possible to catch them."

General Cornwallis tried. Hastening from Philadelphia with British and Hessian grenadier reinforcements—the latter "smoking their pipes & marching at a steady pace," a witness noted—he arrived in Germantown to find the battle over. Generals Grey and Grant joined the chase, sweeping up stragglers and dogging the American rear guard several miles past Mount Airy to Whitemarsh and Wissahickon Creek before turning back. "They took such care of their cannon & are so well supplied with horses that we could not catch them," Grant wrote General Harvey in London. Once again, the Americans had outrun Howe's pursuit.

Thomas Paine had followed the army at a safe distance toward Germantown early that morning, and he waited by the road until the day was decided. "I met several of the wounded in wagons, on horseback, and on foot," he reported in a letter to Franklin, in Paris. Among them was General Nash, borne on a litter made of poles, his left thigh destroyed by a cannonball. The troops, Common Sense added, "appeared to me to be only sensible of a disappointment, not a defeat." He noted:

> Nobody hurried themselves. Everyone marched his own pace. The enemy kept a civil distance behind, sending every now and then a shot

after us, and receiving the same from us. . . . The enemy came within three-quarters of a mile and halted.

As for the unfortunate turn of events, Paine wrote, "I believe no man can inform truly the cause of that day's miscarriage."

By nine p.m. most rebel troops had staggered back into Pennypacker's Mills, their eyelids as heavy as storm shutters. "I had previously undergone many fatigues, but never any that so much overdone me as this," wrote Lieutenant James McMichael. "I had marched in twenty-four hours forty-five miles, and in that time fought four hours. . . . It was almost an unspeakable fatigue." Tormented by thirst and hunger, some troops settled for foraged turnips and walnuts or flour mixed with water and scorched on a hot, flat rock. A quartermaster appeared with a hogshead of whiskey on a wagon, measuring out a pint for every four men. "Our stomachs being empty, the whiskey took rank hold," Private Martin wrote.

Only now did many men realize, from campfire scuttlebutt or simply the absence of familiar faces, that some comrades were missing and gone forever—"the children of misfortune, born under a fiery planet," as Captain Anderson of the Delaware regiment called them. Those who survived could only shrug at fate's mystery. "Got my breeches cut just by the knees with a bullet," Lieutenant Joseph Blackwell of the 3rd Virginia wrote home. "Nothing more at present, but give my love to sister, family, & all other asking friends." Even those too exhausted to eat wondered what had gone wrong. "Some bad management on our side obliged us to retreat," Captain William Beatty of Maryland told his journal. No soldier could dispute him.

Once again every regiment was ordered to draw powder, ball, and paper from the artillery park magazine to make cartridges, forty per man, plus a dozen from the army's ready-made cache to be issued as emergency ammunition if British pursuers arrived in the night. Straggler lines were set up outside Pennypacker's Mills to discourage desertion.

"Fortune smiled on us for a full three hours," wrote General Wayne. "Confusion ensued, and we ran away from the arms of victory open to receive us."

On Sunday, October 5, Captain Ewald of the *Jäger* rode across the Germantown battlefield. At Cliveden he found splintered woodwork, the windows stove in, and the roof holed. "I counted seventy-five dead Americans, some of whom lay stretched in the doorways, under the tables and chairs, and under the windows, among whom were seven officers," he wrote. "The rooms of the house were riddled by cannonballs and looked like a slaughterhouse because of the blood spattered around." Hundreds of curious sightseers made their way from Philadelphia to poke about. Even ardent loyalists could pity the seventeen rebels buried under a cherry tree near the front gate. Another thirty went into a single pit by the northwest corner of the house. Still others were interred here and there. A redcoat who found a speechless dying man urged him, "Pray now for your soul." As a British burial detail collected the enemy dead from orchards and woodlots and bullet-perforated houses, an officer advised them not to "cast dirt in their faces, for they are also mothers' sons."

Washington initially estimated his casualties at "upwards of three hundred." Alas, as he later acknowledged, the actual number was more than triple that amount: 1,073, including 152 dead—30 officers among them— and 400 captured. The king's losses were half as many: 520 total, of whom 80 were killed, plus 24 Hessian casualties. The Continentals lost a capable general when Nash of North Carolina, described by an admirer as "brave, modest, sensible, attentive, and good-tempered," died after bleeding through two feather mattresses in a farmhouse on Forty Foot Road. Siblings who came to collect his body found it too corrupted, and instead settled for a lock of his hair. "Unrelenting war, that without distinction layest in the same dust the coward and the brave," Lieutenant Samuel Shaw, a Massachusetts artillery officer, wrote his father.

The usual agonies attended the wounded, including those who spent a cold October night alone in the open. "I extracted four balls by cutting in the opposite side from where they went in," Jonathan Todd, a surgeon's mate in the 7th Connecticut, wrote his family on October 6. "My clothes are all bloody. Have none clean to put on. . . . None of you know the hardships of a soldier's life." Luck had danced across the battlefield alongside misfortune, and among the lucky were John Geyer, an eleven-year-old drummer wounded in the heel, and his father, Peter, who survived a bayonet to the groin and a bullet in the leg. Both recovered after three months' recuperation, nursed by the boy's mother, Mary Geyer, who also worked as a washerwoman in Peter's Pennsylvania company.

Uncovered, springless wagons hauled hundreds to Bethlehem in a jolting procession. "Many wounded were brought hither," the Moravian war diary recorded, "attired in rags swarming with vermin." They joined other invalids from Brandywine and Paoli in the jammed Single Brethren's House, in fifty tents erected in the rear garden, in a nearby fulling mill normally used for making woolen cloth, or in Strangers' Row, the burying ground on Market Street.

British physicians converted a Germantown stable into an operatory. "The surgeons were beginning to arrange long tables made out of doors, on which to lay the wounded, friends and foes alike, for amputation," a witness recorded. In Philadelphia, three Presbyterian and two Lutheran churches were confiscated for hospital wards, along with a sugar refinery, the town playhouse, and private houses. More amputations occurred in Pennsylvania Hospital, a large brick structure at Eighth and Pine Streets, where basement cells confined the insane. Meat from a drove of cows killed during the battle sold on the street for a half dollar per pound.

Dozens of captured Continental officers were jailed in the Golden Swan tavern or the second-floor Long Room of the statehouse after the windows had been nailed shut. Prisoners by the hundreds jammed the Walnut Street jail, under the jurisdiction of the British provost, Captain William Cunningham, an inveterate sadist described by one writer as "a villainous dog." Here battlefield consequences would continue to cascade as typhus, transmitted by lice, ripped through filthy, crowded cellblocks. "It swept off in the course of three months 400 men, who were all buried in one continued grave, three deep upon another," Lieutenant James Morris of the 5th Connecticut wrote. "Death was so frequent it ceased to terrify." Known as jail fever, camp fever, hospital fever, ship's fever, and spotted fever, typhus by any name had been the great destroyer of armies for millennia. A medical text noted that the disease first presented as "a languor of the whole body and the feeling that the head was compressed in a hoop." In later stages it caused a black crust on the tongue, "thick as the blade of a knife," and could cause gangrene of the fingers, nose, ears, and genitals. Typhus killed another three hundred men in Bethlehem and sickened not only ten of eleven surgeons there but also every orderly and nurse.

One especially unfortunate prisoner on Walnut Street was Ensign Martin Hurley of the 1st New Jersey. Wounded and captured near Cliveden, he was recognized by a British corporal as a former redcoat who had deserted from the 44th Foot in Boston two years earlier. Court-martialed and convicted of "enlisting with the rebels," he was hanged along with three looters on October 8 in the Royal Artillery compound.

General Howe's lieutenants were irate enough at local citizens for not warning them of Washington's imminent attack that they threatened to order "the country for twelve miles round Germantown to be destroyed." The threat passed, not least because so much harm had already been inflicted; an assessor would calculate that 119 Germantown houses suffered more than £26,000 in damage. Howe's men voiced grudging admiration for the American sally, "the most spirited I believe they ever made on the

British troops," one officer wrote. Captain von Münchhausen told his journal, "Everyone admits that Washington's attack was very well planned."

Not everyone conceded that in the American camp, where puzzlement and vexation prevailed. "We most certainly were drubbed," Dr. James Wallace wrote from army headquarters on October 12. "The whole of this affair appears a mystery to me." Brigadier General Weedon wrote a friend in Virginia, "So sportive is fortune, and the chances of war so uncertain, that when victory was in our hands we had not grace to keep it."

"Remember the mistakes of that day," the chaplain presiding at General Nash's burial advised the officers standing at his grave. Yet there was disagreement on what those mistakes were and who was culpable. The complexity of the attack came in for criticism. "To execute such a plan requires great exactness in the officers conducting the columns, as well as punctuality in commencing the march," wrote Colonel Pickering. The two flanking columns, made up of three thousand militiamen, had been particularly hapless. Armstrong's desultory Pennsylvanians, on the far right, missed a chance to fall on the enemy rear despite a two-to-one advantage over Knyphausen's Hessians along the Schuylkill. On the far left, Brigadier General Smallwood's Marylanders—joined by a New Jersey regiment regrettably wearing captured red British coats—made little headway against guardsmen and the Queen's Rangers before retreating in disorder. "The weakness of the human heart prevailed," a Maryland officer told a friend.

In a dispatch to the Massachusetts Council, Knox blamed the fog, neglecting to mention his fatuous advice at Cliveden. "In most countries which have been invaded, one or two battles have decided their fate," he added. "But America rises after a defeat." To Lucy he blamed heaven. "God who orders all things for the best gave us not the final victory," he wrote on October 6. "Perhaps He will the next time."

Paine confided to Franklin that after following the army back to Pennypacker's Mills, "I breakfasted next morning at General Washington's quarters." The commander in chief "was at the same loss, with every other, to account for the accidents of the day." Paine suggested that "a new army once disordered is difficult to manage, the attempt dangerous." A French officer would later tell Washington, "Your Excellency in that instance really conquered General Howe, but his troops conquered yours."

For a man proverbially incapable of mendacity, Washington could be disingenuous in his dispatches to Congress after an unsuccessful action, and Germantown was no exception. He failed to reveal the rococo intricacy of the plan or the misstep at Cliveden, preferring to cite "the extreme haziness of the weather" and insisting that the "day was rather unfortunate than injurious." He claimed that British losses were double if not triple his own, that Howe required two hundred wagons to cart away his wounded, and that the enemy army was so beset with "tumult, disorder, & even despair" that Howe had intended to retreat twenty miles to Chester. In general orders to his own troops, he declared, with some legitimacy, that the battle had demonstrated "the enemy are not proof against a vigorous attack, and may be put to flight when boldly pushed. This they will remember." Eager to turn the page, he told his brother simply, "In a word, it was a bloody day."

Beset by urgent army business, he advised Hancock that his cash strongbox was down to $10,000, with many troops unpaid since July. "Our distress for want of shoes & stockings is amazingly great," he added. The clothier general, in recent months, had provided fifteen thousand coats, nineteen thousand vests, thirty-six thousand pairs of shoes, and eighty-five hundred blankets, but the army still needed many thousands of everything, including sixty-five hundred more pairs of shoes and twenty-four hundred hats.

Privately, Washington's spirits had reached a low ebb. Rumors of Congress meddling with general officer promotions without his advice infuriated him. The resignation of twenty officers in less than a week threatened "a train of evils unforeseen and irredeemable," as he wrote Richard Henry Lee, a congressman from Virginia. He added a threat:

> I have been a slave to the service. I have undergone more than most men are aware of to harmonize so many discordant parts. But it will be impossible for me to be of any further service if such insuperable difficulties are thrown in my way.

The repulse at Germantown, following Brandywine, Paoli, and the loss of Philadelphia, all within a month, brought inevitable recriminations. Samuel Adams decried "a miserable set of general officers. . . . How was the victory snatched out of our hands at Germantown?" Upon visiting the Continental camp a few days after the battle, Dr. Rush found the troops "dirty, undisciplined, & ragged." He told John Adams, "Be not deceived, my friend. Our army is no better than it was two years ago."

But that was untrue, and Adams was closer to the mark in writing Abigail, on October 7, "Our people will and do fight, and although they make a clumsy hand of it, yet they do better and better." As a palliative, a scapegoat was found: Major General Stephen, who had commanded part of Greene's wing. A former British naval surgeon who had immigrated to Virginia, fought against the French in the last war, and now owned a gun factory with thirty workers, Stephen was described by Rush, a former advocate, as a "sordid, boasting, cowardly sot." A court-martial concluded that although he had not been drunk at Germantown, as accused, he was nevertheless guilty of "unofficerlike behavior in the retreat [and] . . . has been frequently intoxicated while in the service." He was cashiered, opening a command position for Lafayette once he finished his recuperation in Bethlehem.

The war moved on. The army, shod or shoeless, would move on, too. Congress chose to laud Washington's bravery and struck a medal in his honor. Wayne reconsidered his glum image of the army lumbering away from victory's laurels, telling Polly, "Upon the whole, it was a glorious day." General Stirling, who also had a fine horse shot from under him at Germantown, wrote that "the enemy will find that after every battle our army will increase and theirs diminish."

That curious American buoyancy obtained in the ranks. So did a seething wrath. "Vengeance burns in every breast," wrote Colonel Charles Webb of the 2nd Connecticut, "and we shall undoubtedly very soon be at them again."

8.

—◆—

To Risk All upon One Rash Stroke

Late summer in the Hudson valley had been pleasant enough for John Burgoyne. In mid-August the British commander shifted his headquarters eight miles south from Fort Edward into a stately confiscated house on a bluff above the river. Built in 1770 by a British émigré turned rebel whose fortune derived from Caribbean plantations and an antebellum contract to provide the Royal Navy with masts and spars, the oak-timbered mansion was more than fifty feet wide, with a square wing on either end and bowed windows on the second floor. Four broad steps led to the front door. Burgoyne and his senior officers enjoyed convivial evenings on the two-story veranda. A German officer remarked that it was "the first house built in good taste that we had seen in a long time."

Camp social life was much enhanced by the improbable arrival of General Riedesel's baroness wife and their three daughters, ages five and under, accompanied by two maids. Now thirty-one and the daughter of a Prussian general, Frederika Charlotte von Riedesel had been depicted by the German portrait painter Johann Tischbein as "Spring," a beautiful, undaunted young woman draped in silk and lace with a basket of pink flowers. She had passed the transatlantic voyage to Canada knitting a nightcap for her husband, tending to the children, and singing Italian arias, to which she was partial. The Riedesels occupied a single room in a gambrel-roofed house in Fort Edward. Servants slept in the entrance hall. Frau Riedesel quickly developed a taste for grilled bear, particularly the paws, eaten in a nearby barn on a table improvised with boards laid across two barrels. Cedar logs burned in a campfire to repel mosquitoes. "The evening was spent by the gentlemen in playing cards and myself in putting the children to bed," she later wrote. "We passed very happily three weeks together." When her husband suggested that she and the girls return to Canada, she convinced him to allow them to follow a day's march behind the Canada

Army in a carriage. Burgoyne warned her, as he had warned his troops, "Britons never retreat."

By mid-September the hour had approached for Britons and their German allies to advance down the Hudson, despite the setbacks at Fort Stanwix and Bennington, despite the difficulty in amassing supplies, and despite inveterate American hostility. "The great bulk of the country is undoubtedly with Congress in principle and zeal, and their measures are executed with secrecy and dispatch that are not to be equaled," Burgoyne wrote Lord Germain. The rebel scorched-earth tactics had intensified. "All the fields of standing grain were laid waste," a German officer wrote. "The cattle were driven away, and every particle of grain, as well as morsel of grass, carefully removed." Four hundred loyalists and Canadians remained with the army "but not half of them armed," Burgoyne reported. He found them "a tax upon time and patience."

Except for the occasional bear paw, the army often ate salt meat from Canada in an effort to keep its modest herd of livestock on the hoof as long as possible. To discourage deserters, officers took roll three times a day. Captured absconders were shot or given a thousand lashes, well laid on. Indians in the king's service received twenty dollars for each deserter's scalp, although all but eighty warriors had decamped for Canada to help with tribal harvests. Not since early August had any word been heard from General Howe, wherever he was now, and an American turncoat claimed on September 7 that fourteen thousand Americans had massed on defensible ground twenty miles downriver.

Burgoyne would write that he never anticipated encountering "such a tract of country and hosts of foes without any cooperation from New York." That was disingenuous. Orders from London had made clear that the Canada Army was an independent command, untethered from royal forces to the south. Burgoyne had even assured the government that his large artillery train would allow him to defend Albany should he "winter there, without communication with New York."

Yet lack of reinforcements from Canada posed a quandary for the Canada Army. In Quebec, General Carleton continued to send matériel south across Lakes Champlain and George, but he rejected Burgoyne's request for more soldiers to garrison Ticonderoga and guard the overland supply route. Germain's orders, he wrote, precluded sending any of the king's forces still remaining in Canada below Île aux Noix, where Champlain emptied into the Richelieu. Such instructions "must be obeyed," Carleton explained, although "indeed to me they appear incomprehensible." To protect his lines of communication, Burgoyne sent back more than nine hundred men, which "drained the life blood" from the army and left barely seven thousand able-bodied troops to press on to Albany. "I must do as well as I can," he told Carleton, adding:

> But I am sure Your Excellency, as a soldier, will think my situation a little difficult. . . . A breach into my communications must either ruin my army entirely or oblige me to return in force.

Burgoyne vowed to press on. "I yet do not despond," he wrote. "I rest in confidence that whatever decision may be passed upon my conduct, my good intent will not be questioned." Countless tasks required his attention. Each brigade was told to brew spruce beer as a prophylaxis against scurvy, which, along with dysentery, was gaining ground in the ranks. An effort to muscle a gunboat overland on rollers from Lake George to the Hudson failed—the road was too steep and rocky—but scores of bateaux were brought by wagon from Fort George and Fort Anne, a jolting journey that made extensive recaulking of the boats necessary. Enough cartridges were fashioned to provide each army musketeer with a hundred rounds. Quartermasters continued to search for carts, since the army never had more than two hundred, enough to transport only four days' provisions.

Two-thirds of the Canada Army's big guns had been left at Ticonderoga, but Burgoyne still carried forty-six cannons, mortars, and howitzers, out of a belief that "artillery was extremely formidable to raw troops," particularly Americans, who preferred to fight from entrenchments rather than in the open. Four horses were required to pull each of the eighteen 6-pounders and accompanying ammunition carts, with smaller teams for smaller guns and larger teams for the half dozen 12- and 24-pounders. All told, the artillery park alone needed 237 draft horses, and forage remained a troubling worry.

High water from heavy rains washed away the first bridge built across the Hudson. The construction of a replacement, supervised by Royal Navy officers, was completed in late August below the Saratoga rapids, using bateaux as pontoons, roped and chained together, then overlaid with plank flooring. Men, guns, and supplies would be transferred from the east bank to the west, where the only road south traced the river shoreline.

If some of the king's liege men had begun to curse "this evil, mountainous, and watery continent," as one Brunswicker wrote, others felt a sense of high purpose and camaraderie. "None but stupid mortals can dislike a lively camp, good weather, good claret, good music, and the enemy near," Captain Sir Francis Carr Clerke, a baronet and Burgoyne's secretary, told a friend in England on September 10. "I believe now we shall soon have

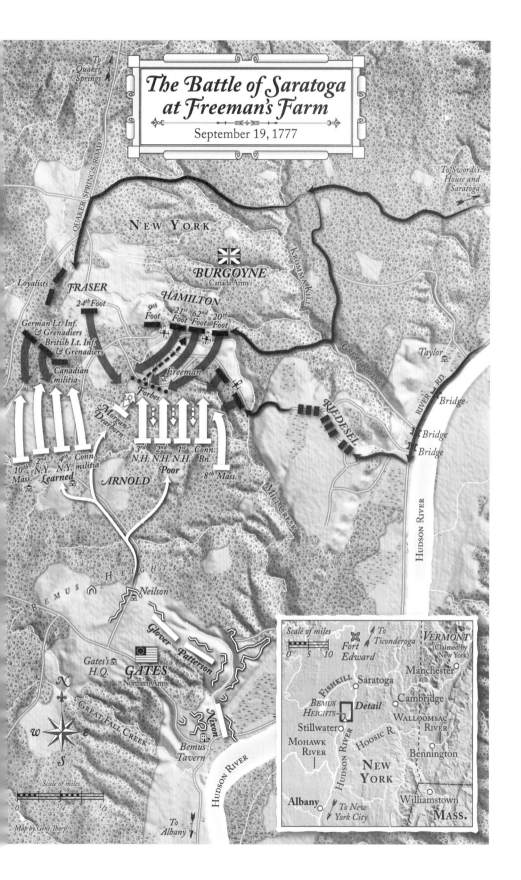

The Battle of Saratoga at Freeman's Farm

September 19, 1777

To Quaker Springs

To Swords's House and Saratoga

NEW YORK

Loyalists

FRASER
24th Foot

BURGOYNE
Canada Army

HAMILTON

German Lt. Inf.
& Grenadiers

9th Foot

21st Foot
62nd Foot
20th Foot

British Lt. Inf.
& Grenadiers

Canadian militia

Freeman

Forbes

Taylor

RIEDESEL

Bridge

Morgan Dearborn

Bridge

Bridge

3rd N.H. 2nd N.H. 1st N.H.
Poor

Conn. Bn.

2nd N.Y. 4th N.Y. Conn. militia

10th Mass.

Learned

8th Mass.

ARNOLD

MILL CREEK

HUDSON RIVER

BEMUS HEIGHTS

Neilson

Glover Patterson

Gates's H.Q.

GATES
Northern Army

N

W   E

S

GREAT FALL CREEK

Nixon

Bemus Tavern

To Albany

HUDSON RIVER

Scale of miles

0   1/4   1/2

Map by Gene Thorp

Scale of miles

0   5   10

Fort Edward

To Ticonderoga

VERMONT
(Claimed by New York)

Manchester

FISHKILL

Saratoga

Cambridge

BEMUS HEIGHTS

Detail

WALLOOMSAC RIVER

Stillwater

Hoosic R.

Mohawk River

Bennington

NEW YORK

HUDSON RIVER

Albany

To New York City

Williamstown

MASS.

KROMMA KILL

GREAT RAVINE

RIVER RD.

something to do. . . . We set our faces forward, and mean to bite hard if anything dares to show itself."

Three days later, at seven on a crisp, gorgeous Saturday morning, Burgoyne sat his horse by the bridge as his army began crossing to the western shore. The green river reflected blue sky and white clouds torn to rags by the wind. Reds and oranges tinted the towering trees along the Hudson, and a scent of decay rose from the water, reminders of the advancing season. Drums beat and battle flags stirred on the breeze as the serpentine line of troops—cherry red for the British, blue and green for the Germans—tramped to the far bank and swung south. After the last carts, bateaux men, and camp followers reached solid ground, including General Riedesel's family, British tars broke the bridge into segments that would float downriver parallel to the marching army. "Further communication with Canada was now cut off," Riedesel observed dryly. The Hudson had become a Rubicon.

The long column halted for the evening in Saratoga, a Dutch hamlet on the Fishkill, a swift tributary of the Hudson where Burgoyne put his headquarters in General Schuyler's fine country house. A dispatch from William Howe had finally found him, the only one in many weeks, since other couriers had been thwarted or captured. Written in tiny characters on two narrow strips of paper hidden in a small silver egg, the laconic message read: "My intention is for Pennsylvania where I expect to meet Washington. . . . After your arrival at Albany, the movements of the enemy will guide yours. . . . Success be ever with you."

At noon on September 15, the army lurched south again to the tootling strains of march music but advanced only three miles to Dovegat, a manor house on an ancient Hudson oxbow. Scouts reported a half dozen small bridges wrecked and trees felled across the road ahead. Brunswickers bivouacked along the river, on mown fields with enough abandoned wheat and rye sheaves to provide camp straw for the entire army. Burgoyne and Riedesel trotted off on a reconnaissance ride at one p.m. the next day with grenadiers, light infantry, and pioneer detachments shouldering entrenching tools to groom the roads and repair the bridges. They returned to Dovegat at dusk. "We saw nothing of the enemy," a German officer noted.

On Wednesday morning, September 17, drummers beat the signal to break camp, and the army eased forward another three miles before stopping near Swords's House, owned by a loyalist arrested several months earlier and now commandeered for Burgoyne's newest headquarters. The king's legions had covered barely fifteen miles in almost a week, but British sentries could hear distant rebel camp sounds to the south. Enemy scouts flitted among the trees across the river. By Thursday afternoon two small bridges on the river road had been repaired, and a larger span, known as "Number 1," was completely rebuilt, with two hundred Germans posted to guard it.

If uncertain of the precise disposition, strength, and intent of the American force ahead, Burgoyne knew that a substantial army lay somewhere across the Great Ravine, a steep crevasse cut by a creek called Kromma Kill. Any doubts that the enemy was near had been erased Thursday when rebel ambushers fell on an unarmed British foraging party that, without authorization, had wandered five hundred yards beyond the outer redcoat pickets to root for potatoes. Several dozen gleaners had been killed, wounded, or captured, no doubt providing the Americans with detailed intelligence.

Burgoyne was furious. "The life of a soldier is the property of the king," he declared in scathing general orders. "The first soldier caught beyond the advance sentries of the army will be instantly hanged." Success be ever with you.

After pummelings at Ticonderoga, Hubbardton, and Fort Edward, the fag end of the Northern Army in August had retreated down the Hudson to a constellation of rocky islands in the Sprouts, where the Mohawk flowed into the larger river, ten miles above Albany. Ten Continental regiments arrived as reinforcements from the Hudson Highlands, and the enemy incursion from the north encouraged New England townships to muster thousands of additional militiamen, who were summoned by church bell, signal cannon, and, in one village, conch shell.

Every day more armed New Englanders joined the encampment around the Sprouts. Continental and militia officers drilled and inspected, poked and prodded. Troops eventually dug a deep, wide trench across the river road and emplaced artillery to discourage British sorties from the north. A nine-hundred-foot bridge built from rafts would soon span the Hudson near Stillwater, a dozen miles north of the confluence of the Hudson and the Mohawk, permitting drovers to bring sheep and cattle to the west bank to feed the growing host. Chaplains preached on the righteousness of the cause, including a popular sermon derived from a passage in Exodus: "The Lord is a man of war."

General Schuyler also was a man of war, but the "very mysterious" abandonment of Ticonderoga, in John Hancock's words, had permanently stained his reputation. Despite General St. Clair's public acknowledgment of his own responsibility for the loss, Schuyler's adversaries were "relentless and bent on your destruction," a friend in Philadelphia warned him.

New Englanders who had long disliked the patrician Dutch New Yorker spread ludicrous rumors that he had deliberately ordered Ticonderoga's heavy artillery replaced with worthless light guns, and that he had been paid to betray the fort with British gold and silver hidden inside hollow cannonballs and fired across American lines. Even Lieutenant Colonel Hamilton, who would become Schuyler's son-in-law, considered him "inadequate to the important command with which he has been entrusted," as he wrote a friend. "There seems to be a want of firmness in all his actions."

Schuyler advised Washington that he intended to "go on smiling with contempt on the malice of my enemies." But smiles would not save him. New Englanders hinted that they might refuse to defend New York unless Schuyler was removed as commander of the Northern Army; by a vote of eleven states to one, with one abstention, Congress appointed Major General Horatio Gates to replace him. "Gates is the man of my choice," wrote Samuel Adams. "He is honest and true."

Gates appeared on the evening of August 19 at Northern Army headquarters on Van Schaick Island, in the Sprouts. Gracious if humiliated, Schuyler meticulously reviewed the disposition of his forces with the new commander and offered to remain in Albany as an administrator and logistician, tasks at which he had always excelled. "I have done all that could be done," Schuyler added before riding away. "The palm of victory is denied me and it is left to you, General."

Victory hardly seemed inevitable. As Schuyler had disclosed, only four brigades were fit for duty at the moment, plus a few hundred artillerymen and engineers. Albany storehouses held just thirty barrels of flour. Munition supplies included a dozen ammunition wagons, twelve tons of lead for musket balls, and twenty tons of grapeshot, a paltry supply. A quartermaster return showed an inventory of 187 blankets and 600 pairs of shoes—the Continental Army's bête noire—plus 300 pairs of French pumps "not fit for campaign purposes." Still, the change of command lifted spirits. "From a miserable state of despondency and terror, Gates's arrival raised us, as if by magic," Colonel Udney Hay wrote George Clinton, the newly elected governor of New York. "We began to hope and then to act."

As Samuel Adams observed, Gates had "the art of gaining the love of his soldiers." Gladsome and convivial, he was given to ribald stories and profanity so voluble that "it made a New Englander's hair almost stand on end," an acquaintance wrote. He was fifty but looked older. A stooped posture, a ruddy complexion, and spectacles perched on the end of his nose all contributed to the nickname "Granny." He often tossed out sardonic epigrams, including "Bipeds have a strange propensity to evil" and "The world will do its own business." Dr. Rush found that "his conversation abounded in anecdotes and was entertaining upon all subjects."

Gates described himself as having "grown old under a helmet." Born in England to a customs collector and a duke's housekeeper, he received enough schooling to be adept in French and Latin before joining the British Army. As a soldier he evinced both a staff officer's organizational skills and luck on the battlefield, surviving a gunshot wound to the chest during Major General Edward Braddock's catastrophic defeat by the French in western Pennsylvania in 1755; an even luckier comrade in that slaughter pen was a young Virginia militia officer named Washington, who emerged unscratched. Bored, financially strapped, and stymied from further promotion after the peace of 1763, Major Gates sold his commission six years later and immigrated to America "to find," as he wrote, "asylum from the various disappointments of a life too much diversified by care."

He adored his adopted country, becoming a self-described "red-hot republican" and buying Traveler's Rest, an eight-hundred-acre plantation in western Virginia, which he worked with half a dozen slaves. "I was such a fool to stay so long in England," he told a friend, "vainly hoping for what I never obtained." War with Britain brought him back into uniform as the Continental Army's first adjutant general, despite chronic dysentery. His competence, including his skill in reviving the battered American invasion force expelled from Canada a year ago, so impressed Washington that he had pleaded with Gates to return to his staff "as the only means of giving form and regularity to our new army." Ever ambitious, Gates told Congress he deserved better. Now he had his own army.

Not only did that army expand every day; most troops filling the ranks had combat experience, unlike Burgoyne's Canada Army. On August 31, Major General Arnold returned to Van Schaick's Island with a thousand men from his successful relief mission at Fort Stanwix. Around the same time, eight companies of riflemen from Virginia and Pennsylvania also arrived, sent by Washington as "a good counterpoise to the Indians." Dressed in fringed hunting shirts and leggings, with tomahawks and sheathed scalping knives tucked into their belts, these "shirtmen" could reputedly shoot a man dead at two hundred yards or more, unnerving some British officers in America sufficiently to prompt them to hide identifying symbols of rank that might draw a sniper's attention. Although there were fewer than five hundred of them, Washington advised, "It will answer a good purpose if you give out that they are double that number."

Commanding this Detached Rifle Battalion was a tall, blue-eyed frontiersman with ropy muscles and gray streaks in his auburn hair. Born in the 1730s—even he was uncertain which year—Colonel Daniel Morgan had worked as a sawyer, a teamster, and an Indian fighter; a bullet through the cheek two decades earlier had knocked out several teeth and left an angry scar on his upper lip where it exited his mouth. "From my youth I have been a soldier," he would declare late in life. Yes, but also a pugnacious brawler, a convicted horse thief, an accused arsonist, a slave-owning planter, an officeholder, and a litigant hauled into court at least twenty-two times for reneging on his debts. Marriage to Abigail Curry improved his behavior as well as his reading, writing, and ciphering. Accompanying Arnold through the Maine wilderness into Canada two years earlier, Morgan had been captured during the failed assault on Quebec and spent eight months in General Carleton's dungeon before being exchanged. Even now no man was deemed faster on horseback or on foot. It was later claimed that he signaled his troops with a turkey call made from a seashell. "Exactly fitted for the toils and pomp of war," as an admirer wrote, he was just what Gates needed.

Meticulous tests made by British weapons experts confirmed what every redcoat in the north woods knew: the American rifle was superior in accuracy to a smoothbore flintlock musket, particularly beyond a hundred yards' range. But the rifle had its limitations. Loading took longer. Spiral grooves cut inside the barrel provided stability to the fired bullet, and thus greater precision, but ramming home a rifle ball wrapped in an oiled cloth patch required greater effort. Also, most rifle barrels were octagonal and unsuited for a bayonet, leaving riflemen vulnerable to charging redcoats.

To remedy these defects, Gates improvised. Five companies totaling 340 New England light infantry musketeers were assigned on September 11 to join Morgan's corps, complementing and protecting the riflemen. These "vigorous young men selected from the line" were commanded by Major Henry Dearborn of New Hampshire, who had also been captured at Quebec. This amalgamated Continental unit—seemingly a better solution than Washington's plan to provide the riflemen with five hundred spears for close combat—would anchor the Northern Army's left wing under General Arnold. Among other sharpshooter duties once the battle was joined, the shirtmen were expected to dispatch as many enemy officers as possible into the next world.

Another officer in Gates's ranks would not fire a shot at Saratoga, but he surely was as valuable as any gunman. Colonel Thaddeus Kościuszko had been born to minor Polish nobility in 1746, educated by priests near Pinsk, then learned fort construction, mapmaking, and other engineering skills in Warsaw. Several more years of schooling in France, including architecture and art studies at the Royal Academy of Painting and Sculpture, in Paris, exposed him to Enlightenment principles. Political upheaval in Poland—and his thwarted elopement after an angry nobleman snatched back his daughter—led him to Philadelphia, despite a shipwreck on a Martinique reef en route. A Congress desperate for engineers commissioned him as a Continental colonel. Washington, who would misspell his name eleven different ways, described "Cosieski" as "a gentleman of science & merit . . . deserving of notice."

Gates noticed. In the past year, Kościuszko had worked on Delaware River defenses before traveling to Ticonderoga, where his warnings of blockhouses "erected in the most improper places" and the fort's vulnerability to enemy bombardment from Sugar Loaf came too late to avert disaster. Now he cautioned Gates that the Northern Army encampment on the river plain would likewise be exposed if enemy troops gained the encroaching hills. "They may take aim at your shoe buckles," he said. With Gates and Arnold at his side, Kościuszko rode north to look for better ground.

They found it three miles above Stillwater at Bemus Heights, where the Hudson bent west, squeezing the river road to Albany through a narrow, swampy bottleneck. Dense woodland covered bluffs to the west. Rills running toward the Hudson had carved ravines like natural moats, perpendicular to any British line of advance. Several small farms linked by narrow lanes had been cleared across this rolling upland. The heights were named for Jotham Bemus, a cattle drover and tavern keeper recently arrested for alleged espionage and confined in the fleet prison, a floating rebel jail anchored eighty miles south. "This is the spot," Kościuszko declared. A British column would be canalized between the high ground and the river. Pulling paper and pencil from his portfolio, he sketched positions for the army brigades perpendicular to the Hudson and along a ridge parallel to the river.

On Friday, September 12, the day before Burgoyne crossed the river, the Northern Army settled onto the heights. Now more than eight thousand strong, they soon "entrenched to their eyes," a witness reported, demonstrating that no combatant was more ardent than an American soldier with a shovel. Directed by Kościuszko, who carried a Spanish sword inscribed "Do not draw me without reason, do not sheath me without honor," they swiftly built breastworks, redoubts, and abatis. Twenty-two cannons, including some salvaged by Schuyler from Fort George, defended a mile-long line on rising ground. Hundreds of new tents arrived to replace those lost at Ticonderoga. Gates placed his headquarters in an abandoned red farmhouse with brass door handles—rare in these parts—and a barn suitable for a field hospital.

Six hundred yards north, Arnold shared another farmhouse with Brigadier General Enoch Poor, a brigade commander from New Hampshire. Also abandoned, the John Neilson house had a cedar-shingle roof and a narrow front porch; unfired brick lined the interior walls to keep out both drafts and vermin. Still limping from the gunshot wound suffered at Quebec, and still seething at the refusal of Congress to restore his rank seniority, Arnold took time to draft a new will. As always, the prospect of combat stirred his blood; he referred to Burgoyne's men as "infernals."

Patrols captured a few careless infernals, who provided useful intelligence under interrogation at Gates's quarters. A New Hampshire officer sent to climb a tree on the Hudson's eastern bank reported that enemy troops had struck most of their tents on the river plain and appeared to be moving toward the American lines. On September 17 Gates sent another plea for reinforcements from New England, explaining that Burgoyne had drawn up the Canada Army just seven miles north of his own. "It is evident the general designs to risk all upon one rash stroke," Gates wrote. "Without one moment's delay, the militia from every part should be ordered here."

The American ranks braced for battle, confident if anxious. "I have not the least doubt of beating or compelling Mr. Burgoyne to return back at least to Ticonderoga, if not to Canada," wrote Brigadier General John Glover, whose brigade of four Massachusetts regiments and several New York militia regiments helped anchor the rebel center. "His situation is dangerous, which he must see & know, if he is not blind."

On September 18 commissary officers distributed bread rations and a half gill of rum for each soldier. Troops were ordered to lay on their arms rather than undressing at night. Campfires dwindled to embers. Dreaming men tossed fitfully under the new tents, muttering in their sleep.

At dawn on Friday, September 19, a thick mist "which you could actually grasp with your hands" rose from the river, a German officer wrote, but it soon burned off as a warm sun climbed above the trees. Seventy-two hundred of the king's men broke camp. Crown troops fixed bayonets. Each carried a hundred rounds in pouches, boxes, or knapsacks made of goatskin, cowhide, or painted linen. Their linen haversacks bulged with three days' rations. Royal Artillery ammunition chests held seventy round shot and thirty case shot for each 6-pounder. Hospital tents and other baggage were loaded onto packhorses or the rickety carts. Servants carried their officers' tin canteens.

Burgoyne split the Canada Army into three columns, and at eleven a.m. a single hollow *crack* from a signal gun put the force in motion. On the right, Brigadier General Simon Fraser led twenty-four hundred men, followed by five hundred Germans in reserve, from Swords's House to Quaker Springs Road, two miles west of the river, then pivoted south. In the center, led by Brigadier General James Inglis Hamilton and accompanied by Burgoyne, another seventeen hundred descended on a cart path into the crepuscular Great Ravine and across Kromma Kill before trudging up the steep southern slope.

On the left, sixteen hundred of Riedesel's Brunswickers in striped linen trousers edged south on the river road, trailed by a thousand reserves guarding the army's heavy artillery, baggage, and a squadron of bateaux, laden with supplies, beating along the shoreline. Dragoons and infantrymen crossed the rebuilt Number 1 bridge and marched eight hundred paces to a marshy ravine where engineers, protected by a pair of 12-pounders, toiled to repair Number 2. Scouts scurried back to advise Riedesel that Number 3, another six hundred yards ahead, also had been wrecked by rebel vandals.

The distant crackle of musket fire carried from the west. Every man along the river abruptly looked up and cocked an ear.

Goaded by the aggressive Arnold, Gates had ordered Morgan's corps to venture north in search of Burgoyne's vanguard, to "observe their direction and harass their advance." At twelve-thirty p.m., just over a mile from the Neilson house, seven hundred men arrived on the southern edge of a farm worked by John Freeman, a loyalist who had packed up with his wife and ten children to trail the British forces as refugees. Golden uncut wheat and rye stood high around a scattering of girdled trees in a field eight hundred yards long and half as wide, partly enclosed with split-rail fences. Fifteen minutes later, a hundred redcoat skirmishers under Major Gordon Forbes stepped from the northern tree line and surrounded Freeman's log house and barn. Peering across the field, the redcoats spotted men approaching in hunting shirts and wide-brimmed hats. A ragged British volley at long range clipped wheat stalks and tree branches.

A stupendous roar from several hundred long rifles answered. Gunsmoke rolled over the field as whooping rebels charged through the grain. The fusillade wounded Major Forbes and killed or injured all but one of his officers. The skirmishers melted back into the woods, pursued by riflemen who outran Major Dearborn's light infantrymen assigned to protect them.

That was a mistake. Reinforcements from General Fraser's column to the northwest, including two companies from the 24th Foot, swept onto the farm, blistering the scattered shirtmen in the left flank and chasing them deep into the forest. Dearborn herded his men to a hill on the southern lip of the farm while Morgan reportedly rode through the woods with his turkey-call shell, trying to reassemble his corps.

The battle was joined. At two p.m., General Hamilton appeared on the northern edge of Freeman's farm with four British regiments. The redcoats shrugged their knapsacks, blankets, haversacks, and water flasks into a pile, then formed a line of battle, the men eighteen inches apart. Leaving the 9th Foot in reserve—the only regiment among the four with recent combat experience—Hamilton positioned four 6-pounders to provide covering fire. With a bawl of orders from junior officers, most of the brigade surged past the Freeman farmhouse toward Dearborn's musketeers, clinging to their hilltop.

The king's troops were abruptly intercepted by Colonel Joseph Cilley's 1st New Hampshire Regiment, which emerged shooting from the woods. For twenty minutes the Hampshire men exchanged volleys with the redcoats, then tumbled back into the underbrush, shot to ribbons. With authority from Gates, Arnold fed more regiments onto the farm, beginning with the 3rd New Hampshire, led by Colonel Alexander Scammell, a tall, thin, Harvard-educated teacher, who persuaded Cilley's bloodied troops to reverse course and rejoin the firefight along a perimeter fence. A Connecticut militia battalion took post on their right flank, eventually followed by the rest of General Poor's New Hampshire brigade and Morgan's riflemen, turkey-called back into coherence. Two New York regiments and more Connecticut militia bracketed Dearborn's hill to the west, confronting Fraser's grenadiers and foot regiments. The 8th Massachusetts moved up on the right, and the crescent-shaped American line spit sheets of flame from more than two thousand muzzles. "Such an explosion of fire I never had any idea of before," wrote Lieutenant William Digby of the 53rd Foot.

A large share of the carnage amid the trampled grain and the girdled trees fell on the 62nd Foot, outfitted in round black caps with an upturned visor and a sagittal plume. Advancing in the center of General Hamilton's line and ordered to attack with "the national weapon"—the bayonet—the regiment surged across the field, drums pounding, driving the rebels into the trees, only to be driven back in turn. Redcoats who had been "the most forward in the pursuit were the first to fall," a British captain wrote. Burgoyne, Hamilton, and their aides watched through the billowing gun smoke as the struggle surged this way and that, shouts and shrieks rising above the percussive battle din. "The dead bodies of friends and enemies covered each other," a redcoat reported.

Much of the British fire flew high, a common flaw among callow troops. Severed twigs and autumnal leaves showered the American line, and a piney scent from gashed conifers perfumed the air. As Morgan's men moved against the British left, Burgoyne noted "a great number of marksmen armed with rifle-barrel pieces." The toll among the king's officers was frightful—more than a third of those leading the 62nd were killed or wounded. Losses in the 20th Foot were nearly as severe, including the regiment's lieutenant colonel, who was twice wounded. "Several of the Americans placed themselves in high trees, and as often as they could distinguish a British officer's uniform, took him off by deliberately aiming at his person," wrote Corporal Roger Lamb of the 9th Foot. The four Royal Artillery gun crews also bled freely. By one count, thirty-six of forty-eight gunners were casualties; the detachment captain was shot dead, along with every horse needed to pull the carriages. Two 6-pounders were captured, then recaptured. Heavier fieldpieces were hauled from the river road to Freeman's farm, but round shot fired into the distant tree line just brought down more leaves and bigger twigs.

By four-thirty p.m. the fighting had spilled into adjacent farm fields and woodlands. With the New Hampshire brigade exhausted from hours of fighting and low on ammunition—cartridges scavenged from dead redcoats would not fit most American muskets—Arnold assembled three hundred volunteers from the rear into a provisional regiment under Major William Hull. After an exchange of volleys at fifty yards' range and a sudden American bayonet charge, Hull's men captured a sergeant major and nineteen privates sheltering in a log house.

The shadows grew long as Arnold rode his gray charger to Gates's headquarters. He had shoved his last regiment into the fight, the 10th Massachusetts, but wanted more firepower to knock the enemy back into the Great Ravine. Gates shook his head. All afternoon he had expected an enemy attack down the river road against the American right wing, and had even ordered the army's "tents struck and baggage loaded . . . to secure a retreat if it was necessary." He had already eyed a potential defensive line along the Mohawk, fourteen miles south.

Arnold pressed his case, urging, perhaps demanding, that more troops be shunted to the left wing. The battlefield had changed hands three times, four times, maybe six times, usually in increments of a hundred yards or so. Enemy cannons had been seized, although not kept. Morgan's riflemen were lacerating Burgoyne's flank and rear on the farm. The British line was close to collapse. Another regiment or two could win the day.

Gates's usual amiability vanished. Cheeky insubordination offended him. He "drew his sword," a witness reported, "and said he commanded and would be obeyed."

Arnold turned on his heel, swung into the saddle, and rode off at a full gallop.

General Riedesel had no intention of attacking the American right wing, because he couldn't. Since noon his column had moved barely a thousand yards along the river, delayed by pernicious rebel sabotage to bridges and the roadbed. The heckle of musketry and cannon fire from the west had not shifted in hours, suggesting that Burgoyne had made little progress. As the afternoon light began to fade, a rider pulled up with a message from the British commander: "Come to my assistance and endeavor to attack the enemy on the right flank." Riedesel was to bring as many German troops as could prudently be spared.

Within minutes, the German commander had collected more than seven hundred blue-coated Brunswickers and set off through the forest on a lateral lane away from the Hudson. Captain Georg Päusch followed with a pair of 6-pounders, ammunition carts, and tools to groom gun positions. Shortly before the sun set, at six p.m., the Germans neared the farm's eastern edge. Riedesel ordered drummers to beat a quick march, alerting the beleaguered redcoats ahead. "They bellowed one hurrah after another," a German officer wrote, "and we replied with a *vivat!*" As his reinforcements crested a hill and emerged from the woods, Riedesel saw scores of carcasses—human and equine—sprawled in the grain; he estimated that the three redcoat regiments floundering in the farm field ahead had been "thinned down to one-half."

Brunswickers pressed forward on the double quick "with loud war cries." Päusch unlimbered his guns on a slope, aided by redcoats hauling on the drag ropes and lugging flannel ammunition cartridges up the steep terrain, despite showers of rebel bullets. He ignored a cowering German surgeon, "drunk as a beast," and ordered his gunners to open fire with case shot at hardly more than pistol-shot range. Twilight brightened the ruby-red muzzle flashes, and artillery thunderclaps echoed along the ridgeline to the west.

Now it was the Americans who were struck in the flank. Scores of small iron balls tore through the line, lashing tree trunks, rye stalks, and men trying to make themselves as small as possible. After a dozen rounds fired in brisk succession, the rebel ranks slid away through the tree line to seek shelter in the woods.

As at Hubbardton, Riedesel's timely arrival revived the teetering British fortunes. In minutes Freeman's farm, or its wreckage, had been ceded to the king's men. The last magenta fingers of light faded in the west. The guns fell silent.

"The fire never ceased from the time it began till after sundown, which was six or seven hours," wrote Ensign Samuel Armstrong, who fought with Dearborn's light infantry. "All the skirmish happened within the circumference of seventy acres." Burgoyne held those seventy acres and more at the end of the day—"masters of the field," as he told London—but the terrain was rich only in bullet-riddled tree stumps. He never saw Bemus Heights, and his men never came within a mile of the American defensive line built there by Kościuszko. As the historian Eric H. Schnitzer would observe, the Canada Army was weaker strategically at sunset than it had been at dawn. Victory was at best pyrrhic.

Fraser convinced Burgoyne that the exhausted ranks were incapable of resuming the battle without rest, and an attack scheduled for Saturday morning was postponed until three p.m. and then canceled indefinitely. The rebels had given Burgoyne's troops "a pretty good bruising," wrote Colonel Scammell, the 3rd New Hampshire commander, who escaped the day with a musket ball through his coveralls and another that smashed his musket.

Some 150,000 lead bullets had been fired by both sides, and although barely a thousand hit a living target, they did damage enough. The "good bruising" cost the British 566 men killed, wounded, missing, or captured. The 62nd Foot alone suffered more than 200 casualties, including Lieutenant Stephen Harvey, the mortally wounded sixteen-year-old nephew of the British Army's adjutant general in London. "Tell my uncle I died like a soldier," he said, then reportedly accepted a surgeon's advice to avoid the "most exquisite torture" by taking a massive dose of opium. He shared a grave with two other lieutenants, neither older than seventeen. The losses were severe enough that Burgoyne took the unusual step of permitting 120 American loyalists "of tried bravery and fidelity" to enlist as British infantry regulars.

American battle losses totaled about 325, killed, wounded, and captured. Almost thirty officers were among the dead or severely wounded, including two lieutenant colonels killed. Temperatures plummeted in the evening, and "we heard the cries and groans of the wounded all night," Captain Benjamin Warren of the 6th Massachusetts told his diary. A few Indians loitering in Burgoyne's camp crossed the battlefield at night to scalp rebel corpses for the bounties paid by the British. Scavengers and burial parties from both armies stripped the dead of arms and clothing; sometimes, unwittingly, they stripped the merely unconscious, like Captain Daniel Clark, who was found Saturday morning "entirely naked," Warren wrote. "He was wounded in the head. They gave him drink in a spoon."

Damaged redcoats were trundled on ammunition carts to a makeshift hospital in a stable and large tents along the Hudson. "It is an unpleasant sight for all soldiers," Captain Päusch said. Damaged Americans were evacuated to the two-story hospital in Albany, where thirty surgeons could handle up to five hundred patients. "Many of them must be subjected to capital operations," observed James Thacher, the surgeon's mate, who noted that a ward crammed with battle injuries "is a fine field for professional improvement." Among those treated was Private Thomas Haines of the 1st New Hampshire, credited with using his bayonet to kill two Britons before a bullet in the right cheek carried away eleven teeth and part of his tongue. Left for dead, he eventually recuperated in Albany, reenlisted in 1781, and lived until 1847, when he passed before his ninetieth birthday.

"I trust we have convinced the British butchers that the cowardly Yankees can, and when there is a call for it, *will* fight," Major Dearborn wrote in his journal a few hours after the battle. None could gainsay American courage, even if tactical prowess at times was wanting—notably in the failure of Morgan's riflemen and Dearborn's light infantry to fight together as intended. Arnold again proved his skill as a battle captain, feeding regiments into the fight with deliberation, mostly on favorable ground away from the rebel camp. Coolly competent, he directed the action from a suitable, effective distance rather than rushing into the fight.

Gates later faced condemnation from historians who were partisans for Schuyler or Washington. He was accused of timidity for remaining two miles from the action at his headquarters and refusing Arnold's plea for further reinforcement. Yet Gates demonstrated prudence and skill in fortifying Bemus Heights, in positioning his Northern Army athwart the enemy's route to Albany, and in allocating firepower on September 19 without risking the sort of flank attack that had undone Washington at Long Island and Brandywine. Few Americans had been captured, evidence of an orderly fighting withdrawal. His confrontation with Arnold at the end of the day evinced reasonable, if theatrical, professional disagreement. In a slaughterhouse, passions ran high. "The two generals complemented each other," historian John F. Luzader would conclude, "and achieved a strategic victory."

Gates also sensed that his success was incomplete. The Americans had held their own, but the day ended in a draw. Burgoyne still occupied the field of battle; worse, the Canada Army remained intact and no doubt was keen to avenge this setback. The bloodletting along the Hudson had not ended.

The clang of picks, shovels, and felling axes soon carried along the valley as both camps deepened and widened their entrenchments. Burgoyne's men muscled their guns across Freeman's farm to a new battery on the southern perimeter of the blood-drenched clearing. Two redoubts a quarter mile apart also rose on the western flank of the king's position. The larger of the two, an extended rectangle, stretched for four hundred yards, enclosing Freeman's farmhouse and barn within an abatis, earthen walls, sally ports, eight artillery embrasures, and vertical posts braced with river cobbles hauled up from the Hudson.

Yet as the days grew shorter and the nights grew colder, such revetments provided little comfort for the king's men. "No vegetables, no tobacco, no brandy," Johann Bense, a Brunswick grenadier, complained in his journal on September 20. As often occurred after eighteenth-century battles, the effects of officers killed in action were auctioned off to their comrades, and the dead again moved among the living, at least in a fine hat here, a silver gorget there, or a brace of pistols, a set of shoe buckles, a spyglass. Heavy autumn rains also brought back the dead. "Many bodies not buried deep enough in the ground appeared . . . and caused a most dreadful smell," wrote Lieutenant Digby.

Since leaving Skenesborough in July, the Canada Army had traveled just 50 miles. Albany remained another 30 miles south, and New York 150 miles beyond that. Yet one bit of encouraging news arrived on September 21 when a courier slipped into camp with a coded message for Burgoyne from General Sir Henry Clinton, still commanding the king's forces around Manhattan Island during Howe's absence. "You know my good will & are not ignorant of my poverty of troops," Clinton had written from New York on September 11. He intended to sail fifty miles upriver into the Hudson Highlands to overwhelm the rebel stronghold at Fort Montgomery:

If you think 2,000 men can assist you effectually, I will make a push at Montgomery in about ten days. But ever jealous of my flanks, if they make a move in force on either of them, I must return to save this important post. . . . Let me know what you would wish.

Burgoyne ordered a cannon crew at midnight to fire eight rounds toward several rebel outposts as a diversion, allowing the messenger to creep through the lines and scuttle back downriver. He carried an answer for Clinton: "An attack, or the menace of an attack upon Montgomery must be of great use. . . . Do it, my dear friend, directly."

As rumors about this exchange circulated in whispered conversations among the king's officers, hope and elation vied with skepticism and despair. "It must be owned," wrote Lieutenant Digby, "General Burgoyne was too ready to believe any report in our favor."

9.

———

How Art Thou Fallen

*D*o it, my dear friend, directly.

The secret courier carrying Burgoyne's plea for help took more than a week to reach British headquarters in New York, but by then General Clinton had already anticipated the need to act. Other desperate messages disclosed the Canada Army's peril. A British captain who traveled incognito from Saratoga reported that at least twelve thousand rebels—twice the number of redcoats and Brunswickers still fit to fight after the September 19 battle—had entrenched hardly a mile south of Burgoyne's fortifications. More were assembling north to block any retreat toward Ticonderoga. Food and other supplies dwindled by the day. Burgoyne wanted both advice and a secure corridor from Albany to New York, but Clinton's avowed goodwill had limits: in a stiff, third-person reply he declared, "Sir H. Clinton cannot presume to give any orders to General Burgoyne. General Burgoyne could not suppose that Sir H. Clinton had an idea of penetrating to Albany."

Not to Albany, but perhaps far enough up the Hudson to draw away part of Gates's Northern Army. Clinton's legion in New York numbered just under seven thousand, including three thousand armed provincials. That was barely enough to defend the hundred-mile perimeter that looped around Manhattan, Staten, and Long Islands. Sir H. Clinton knew that he needed to strike a fine balance. Emboldened by rebel successes at Bennington and Fort Stanwix, enemy detachments had launched several disquieting attacks near New York. But Burgoyne's predicament seemed too fateful to ignore.

Reinforcements from Britain had been expected for months, and on September 24 a squadron finally dropped anchor in New York Harbor with seventeen hundred troops after a tedious passage from England. Clinton swiftly organized an amphibious expedition he would personally lead, with three thousand of his best men organized in three divisions aboard flatboats, bateaux, and river transports under Royal Navy escort. Sailing north on a rising tide on the evening of October 3, the flotilla feinted at Tarrytown to confuse the enemy before reaching Verplanck's Point, fifteen miles farther north on the Hudson's east bank, at noon on October 5.

The abrupt appearance of this river apparition spooked the small rebel garrison, which bolted inland. Spaced along the gorge ahead stood three American forts, the heart of the Hudson defenses. Beyond that, far upstream, lay Albany and then the besieged Canada Army at Saratoga. Without instructions from General Howe, now presumably settling into Philadelphia for the winter, Clinton was uncertain of his course. This sortie was already two weeks later than the date he had proposed to Burgoyne in his September 11 offer of help. He would improvise, using his best judgment, for king and country.

A band of Precambrian granite ten miles wide formed the Hudson Highlands. Scarps, tors, and crags rose fourteen hundred feet above the glacier-carved river valley. A Continental Army chaplain described the land here as "majestic, solemn, wild, and melancholy." Five of Washington's most trusted generals, including Greene, Knox, and Wayne, had assured him a few months earlier that if the Hudson could be obstructed "the enemy will not attempt to operate by land—the passes through the Highlands are so exceedingly difficult."

One proposal for clogging the Hudson called for thousands of soldiers to roll boulders into the river from the sheer precipice known as Anthony's Nose so that no British man-of-war larger than a sloop could sail upstream. This scheme died aborning when planners realized that the Hudson here was 150 feet deep. Instead, a star-shaped fort was built on the western riverbank at the mouth of Popolopen Creek and named for Governor George Clinton, who took post here as both a brigadier general in the Continental Army and the commander of New York militia. A thirty-five-ton chain stretched 1,650 feet across the river from Anthony's Nose to Fort Montgomery, a rough-hewn earthen enclosure on the Popolopen's north bank named for the patriot martyr of Quebec. With 850 links forged mostly at iron furnaces in New Jersey and hauled by ox teams into the Highlands, the chain, which cost $12,000, had snapped twice under the force of the sixty-five million gallons of water rushing through the river channel each minute. Successfully repaired with cables, anchors, and hundreds of pine-log floats, the barrier was considered a marvel of military engineering.

A third, smaller redoubt, Fort Constitution, stood six miles upriver. All three were undermanned, particularly since many garrison troops were

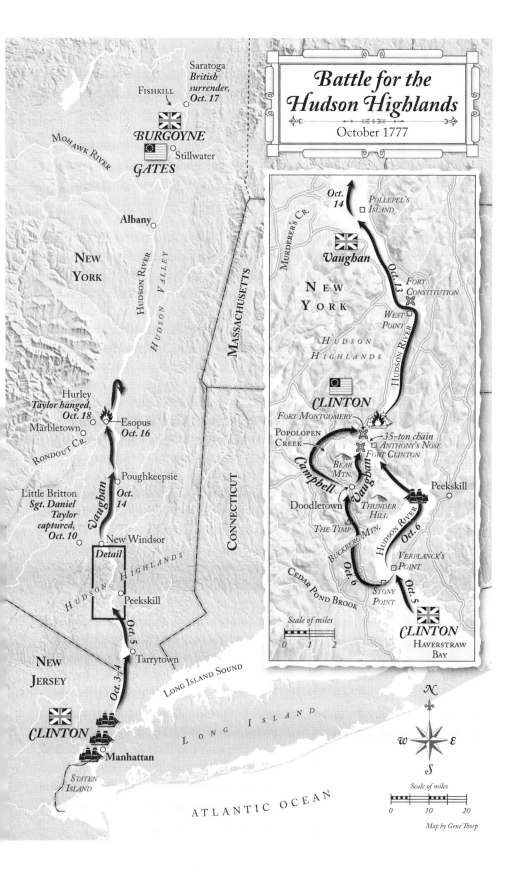

Battle for the Hudson Highlands

October 1777

Map by Gene Thorp

said to be home "getting in their winter grain." A chain of alarm posts crowned the highest hills up the Hudson from New York City; large pyramidal beacons fifteen miles apart, made of split wood and dry brush, they were to be ignited whenever trouble appeared to be coming upstream. Finally, a river squadron also stood vigil, including two new frigates, *Congress* and *General Montgomery*, launched at Peekskill and now anchored just above the great chain.

None of this deterred Henry Clinton for a moment. At daybreak on Monday, October 6, he left four hundred men at Verplanck's Point, then crossed the river to land unopposed at Stony Point. The warships tacked toward the chain to bombard rebel fortifications as a diversion while nine hundred troops under Lieutenant Colonel Mungo Campbell marched seven miles west, past Thunder Hill and Bear Mountain, to approach Fort Montgomery from the rear. Brushing aside a rebel outpost, the attackers rushed the fortifications at five p.m. At the same hour, across Popolopen Creek, twelve hundred additional assault troops under Major General John Vaughan struck Fort Clinton, clawing through an abatis and into the gun batteries.

Ferocious fighting spilled across both forts. Colonel Campbell was killed in the first exchange, and a cannonball blew apart Vaughan's horse. Rebel case shot grew so savage that "we thought heaven was falling," a German survivor recalled. But with fewer than six hundred defenders between the two redoubts—half the necessary strength, and many of them unarmed militia—the Americans were doomed. Naval artillery battered the eastern faces of both bastions, gouging walls and gunports. Governor Clinton escaped from his eponymous fort by bounding down the scree to the river and into an overloaded boat. His brother, Brigadier General James Clinton, in command at Fort Montgomery, survived when an orderly book in his pocket deflected a bayonet thrust. Sliding down a hundred-foot slope into the ravine between the forts, he too scampered to safety.

By eight p.m. the king's men held both strongholds. The assault cost them 183 casualties, including 42 dead. The Americans counted 70 killed, 40 wounded, and 240 captured; they also lost sixty-seven field guns, six tons of powder, sundry provisions, and four hundred thousand musket and cannon cartridges. Many of their dead were tossed into a nearby pond.

The debacle continued on the river. The Continental frigates *Congress* and *General Montgomery*, undermanned with novice crews, hoisted sail to stand upstream at ten p.m. but could make no headway against a foul wind and an ebb tide. Both captains ordered their men ashore in small boats before setting the ships ablaze. The row galley *Shark* did the same. "As every sail was set, the vessels soon became magnificent pyramids of fire," a

British officer wrote. "The long train of ruddy light that shone upon the water for a prodigious distance had a wonderful effect." When flames reached the loaded cannons belowdecks, pyrotechnic explosions rocked the Hudson glens.

A day later Royal Navy tars easily severed the chain and log boom at Fort Montgomery. Fifteen hundred redcoats sailed north to assault Fort Constitution, a battlement with thirty-six guns on an island facing the promontory called West Point. They found it abandoned and burning. The Hudson Highlands belonged to the king and his men. An officer hoisted a Union Jack on a staff above a blockhouse to make the point.

Henry Clinton took a moment to write Burgoyne a secret dispatch from Fort Montgomery. "*Nous y voilà*," he began. Now we are here. "Nothing now between us but Gates. I sincerely hope this little success may facilitate your operation. . . . I heartily wish you success." He gave the message to Sergeant Daniel Taylor, a loyalist serving in a royal provincial regiment but currently disguised in a blue camlet coat with silver epaulets.

This buoyant epistle never reached Burgoyne. The confluence of Clintons—three generals of the same surname from two different armies—now confounded Sergeant Taylor. The morning after slipping away from Fort Montgomery, he blundered into soldiers wearing faded red coats with yellow facings who told him their commander's name was Clinton. Taylor, manifestly confused, asked to see him and was escorted to a frame house set amid locust and balm of Gilead trees. Here he learned that the redcoats were in fact Connecticut Continentals wearing captured British uniforms and now serving under Governor George Clinton, who had made the house his headquarters.

A search disclosed that the courier carried not only personal letters written by British officers to friends in the Canada Army but a small silver ball sealed with a tiny screw. Taylor promptly swallowed the capsule. A dose of tartar emetic administered by a rebel physician brought it back up. He swallowed it again. When Taylor refused another emetic, Governor Clinton—already enraged by his rout along the Hudson—threatened to open his stomach with a scalpel. The silver ball reappeared, the note to Burgoyne tucked inside was discovered, and Taylor confessed. After condemnation by a hasty court-martial, and a hastier farewell letter scribbled to his family, he was hanged from an apple tree. "He did not appear to be either a political or a gospel penitent," a witness recorded.

Unaware of this sad muddle, Henry Clinton had returned to New York, where he assembled six months of supplies to provision the Canada Army if Burgoyne could reach Albany. Sailing back to the Highlands, Clinton ordered General Vaughan to continue north with two thousand troops, again escorted by the Royal Navy in a half dozen shallow-draft warships.

Led by the brig *Diligent*, the squadron squeezed past unfinished chevaux-de-frise sunk between Pollepel's Island and Murderer's Creek above West Point. Forty miles upriver on Thursday, October 16, they approached the Dutch village of Esopus, also called Kingston, which stood on the Hudson's west bank and currently served as New York's state capital. Vaughan, who was described by a subordinate as "ill-tempered and capricious, ever censuring the conduct of others," intended to reach Albany in hopes of a rendezvous with Burgoyne. But, as he told Henry Clinton, "Esopus being a nursery for almost every villain in the country," he would first stop here.

"We are hellishly frightened," a rebel wrote a friend as word spread of an armada approaching with thirty galleys, flatboats, naval vessels, and transports, including the inaptly named *Friendship*. The state assembly and senate, meeting respectively in a tavern and a cramped shop, sent the treasury and official records to Rochester, then fled and eventually reconvened in Poughkeepsie. Women buried their china and other household treasures before grabbing their children and heading west in a cavalcade of wagons. Shouted snatches of Dutch doggerel could be heard in Esopus: *"Loop, jongens, de Rooje komme."* Run, boys, the redcoats are coming. Scores of loyalists held in the local jail and aboard the fleet prison—three anchored ships described by one inmate as "fetid cesspits of disease, suffering, and privation"—were marched off to Hartford under militia guard. The prison ships were scuttled and burned on Rondout Creek, along with the galley *Lady Washington* and other rebel vessels.

Ignoring a few wild shots from militia cannons, Vaughan and his minions fell on the village like demons of castigation. Outnumbered ten to one, militiamen spiked their guns, hopped from the breastworks, and ran, chased by bayonets. Redcoat incendiaries dashed from house to house with burning fagots. "I pray the Lord will support me under so heavy a trial," a resident told his diary. Black smoke soon spiraled above the streets, and by late Thursday afternoon 116 houses, 103 barns, 17 shops and storehouses, the courthouse, and a church with stained glass windows had been reduced to ash and charred stone. Esopus joined Charlestown, Falmouth, Norfolk, and other American communities immolated by the king's men. Upon hearing the news, General Lord Stirling called Vaughan "a little piratical destroyer," adding, "I have no doubt he will receive some punishment from heaven worthy of such villainous cruelty." The *New York Packet* paraphrased the book of Isaiah: "Britain, how art thou fallen!"

Vaughan reboarded *Friendship* and pressed on another twelve miles, burning mills and manor houses up the Hudson until his river pilots refused to proceed farther. Loyalist intelligence reported five thousand rebels massing on the east bank under Major General Israel Putnam and fifteen hundred more under Governor Clinton on the west bank. Albany still lay forty-five miles ahead. No sign of Burgoyne could be seen, heard, sniffed, or imagined. Vaughan concluded that it was "impractical" to give the Canada Army further help.

Moreover, Henry Clinton had directed him to turn back. A sloop-of-war from Philadelphia had brought orders from General Howe, who needed reinforcements to help force open the Delaware River against stubborn rebel defenses. Clinton was to dispatch four thousand troops from New York "without delay," including three British and two German regiments, plus the 17th Dragoons. Any hope of securing the Hudson valley had vanished, and Burgoyne likely would have to make his way back to Canada. "From my heart I pity him," Clinton told Vaughan.

No doubt, but Clinton pitied himself more. "Still stronger reasons every day determine me to quit this mortifying service," he wrote General Harvey in London. Later in October he requested leave to return to England, unaware that on October 22 Howe also asked to be relieved of command. "I was obliged to submit to the mortification of enduring my situation somewhat longer," Clinton would write.

General Vaughan's expedition hoisted sail for Manhattan. Fort Clinton, which had been renamed Fort Vaughan, was demolished and abandoned. So, too, Fort Montgomery. Rebel regiments once again took title to the Hudson Highlands—the key to the continent, Henry Clinton had called it. As a souvenir of his fleeting triumph, he packed up the great chain for shipment to Britain. From there it would be sent on to Gibraltar and stretched around the harbor as protection against Barbary pirates, French freebooters, and others who wished ill to the empire.

In early October the Canada Army woke each morning to find every tent white with hoarfrost. Eight hundred wounded and ailing men crowded the hospital compound, with additional invalids consigned to regimental infirmaries. Brewers continued to make spruce beer by fermenting boiled conifer needles with maple sugar, but scurvy and other ills persisted. Foraging details protected by more than two hundred soldiers searched for hay around Dovegat and east of the Hudson; another bridge across the river was laid on bateaux near the mouth of Kromma Kill. But emaciated horses now died as routinely as men. A quart of rum cost eight shillings, if it could be found. For want of tobacco even officers smoked dried leaves or sassafras root. Salt pork, a Brunswicker recorded, "was disgusting even to touch the meat, not to mention its bad smell."

Desertion grew so promiscuous that General Riedesel doubled his pickets—"one is to keep close watch on the other"—and offered a ten-guinea reward for every captured absconder, or five guineas for those shot dead. Burgoyne ordered bonfires lighted at night a hundred yards beyond his advanced sentries to illuminate infiltrators, runaways, and renegade foragers. Hardly an hour passed without rebels shooting up an outpost or snatching men trying to fetch water from the river. "All is hostile and dangerous in an alarming degree," a British officer wrote.

Burgoyne required all mariners and bateaux men to drill several hours each day as infantrymen in preparation for battle. In two weeks a thousand men felled a thousand trees for a fort above the Hudson dubbed the Great Redoubt, built on high ground just north of Kromma Kill and overlooking the Canada Army's artillery park and hospital. Others cleared fields of fire around the new works on Freeman's farm. Campfire rumors circulated: that St. Leger's corps would circle down from the north to provide reinforcements, and that Henry Clinton was advancing up the Hudson's eastern shore to encircle Gates. Frau Riedesel, worried for the fate of her three daughters, privately discharged her resentment onto Burgoyne's head. "General Burgoyne was very fond of indulging," she later wrote in a calumnious accusation. "He spent half the night in singing and drinking. . . . He was very fond of champagne."

With food stocks down to a two-week supply, rations were cut by a third on October 3. Each soldier would receive two pounds of bread and bad meat a day instead of three, with a few pence reimbursed in his pay for the shortfall. On Saturday, October 4, Burgoyne summoned Major Generals Riedesel and Phillips for a war council. The commanding general reviewed the alarming state of supplies in the Canada Army. Winter was fast approaching. No further word had been heard from Clinton. "What should be undertaken under the present circumstances?" he asked. Should the army mass to attack the American left and rear, forcing a decision now?

Riedesel and Phillips balked. Too little was known about Gates's positions. The British camp would be vulnerable to a devastating counterattack if left exposed when most of the king's fighting force moved forward to attack. Riedesel believed that unless the enemy's left flank was found to be weak, the Canada Army should retract across the Hudson to Batten Kill, a tributary twelve miles below Fort Edward. If they were forced back to Ticonderoga, this would be a critical first step.

Burgoyne pondered the dilemma for another day, then reconvened his

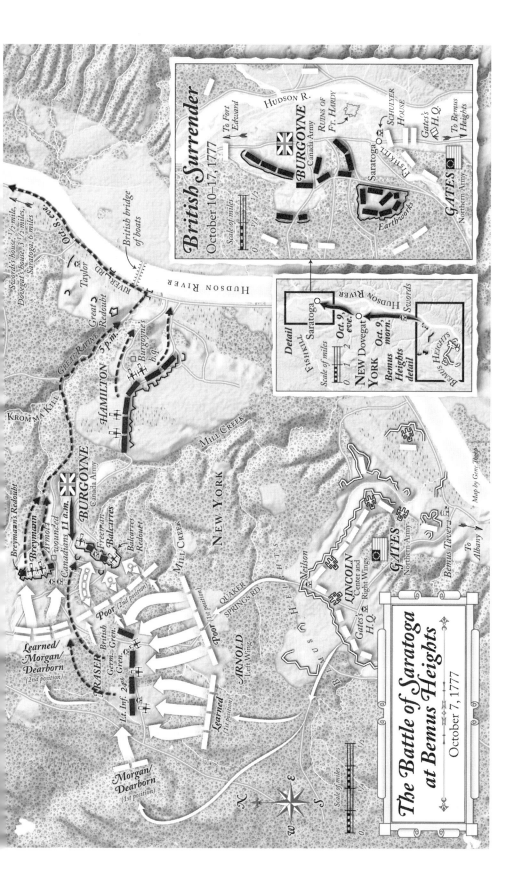

The Battle of Saratoga at Bemus Heights

October 7, 1777

Map by Gene Thorp

British Surrender

October 10–17, 1777

Scale of miles

HUDSON R.

To Fort Edward

RUINS OF FT. HARDY

SCHUYLER HOUSE

BURGOYNE
Canada Army

Gates's H.Q.

To Bemus Heights

FISHKILL

Saratoga

Earthworks

GATES
Northern Army

Detail

Scale of miles

FISHKILL

Saratoga

Oct. 9, eve.

NEW DOVEGAT
YORK

Oct. 9, morn.

Swords

HUDSON RIVER

Bemus Heights detail

BEMUS HEIGHTS

Swords's house, 1/2 mile
Dovegat's house, 3 1/2 miles
Saratoga, 6 miles

Oct. 8, eve.

Taylor

GREAT RAVINE

KROMMA KILL

Great Redoubt

British bridge of boats

RIVER RD.

HUDSON RIVER

HAMILTON 3 p.m.

Burgoyne's h.q.

Breymann's Redoubt

BURGOYNE
Canada Army

Breymann

Arnold wounded

Canadians 11 a.m.

Freeman

Balcarres

Balcarres Redoubt

MILL CREEK

NEW YORK

MILL CREEK

FRASER

British Germ. Gren.

1st Inf. 24th Gren.

Poor (2nd position)

Learned/
Morgan/
Dearborn
(2nd position)

Learned (1st position)

ARNOLD
Left Wing

Poor (1st position)

QUAKER SPRINGS RD.

Neilson

MUS HEIGHTS

LINCOLN
Center and Right Wings

Gates's H.Q.

GATES
Northern Army

Bemus Tavern

To Albany

Morgan/
Dearborn
(1st position)

Scale of miles

generals on the evening of October 5, with Brigadier General Fraser joining them. Habitually reluctant to retreat, the British commander "looked upon a retrograde movement as too hard," the Brunswick war diary recorded. Instead, he proposed leading a large reconnaissance force along the ridgeline to the west to seek "any possible means of forcing a passage" around Gates's left wing. If not, they could then fall back to Batten Kill as a last resort. No one but the four of them was to know of this gambit.

The next day, to boost morale, Burgoyne ordered a dozen barrels of rum distributed to his army, including three barrels for the Brunswick rank and file and another for German officers. At midnight, a Royal Artillery 12-pounder fired once. Three signal rockets followed, chasing one another brilliantly into the night like tiny comets, just in case General Clinton was close enough to see them.

Any potential retreat to the north had been complicated, as Burgoyne well understood, by American countermoves in the past fortnight. General Carleton's refusal to garrison the lines of communication below Canada had forced Burgoyne to post detachments from his army north of the Hudson, notably around Ticonderoga, where a thousand British and German troops, under Brigadier General Henry Watson Powell, stood guard, plagued by malaria, dysentery, and boredom.

More than twice that number of rebel militia, mostly Massachusetts men on three-month enlistments, had congregated at Pawlet, forty miles north of Bennington. They were commanded by Continental Major General Benjamin Lincoln, a stout church deacon and malt house proprietor whom Washington had praised as "an excellent officer," despite his lack of combat experience. With approval from Gates, Lincoln organized three detachments of five hundred men each and ordered them to harass the enemy's rear posts with sneak attacks. Traveling without tents or baggage other than "one shift of clothes only," the first force easily seized Skenesborough, at the southern tip of Lake Champlain. The second crept close to Mount Independence and skirmished with the German garrison.

The third detachment followed game trails through the wilderness to Lake George under Colonel John Brown, then infiltrated the lower slopes of Sugar Loaf, listening for rattlesnakes and redcoat patrols. A Yale-educated lawyer, Brown so loathed Benedict Arnold, with whom he'd quarreled bitterly during the retreat from Canada eighteen months earlier, that he had printed handbills warning, "Money is this man's God, and to get enough of it he would sacrifice his country." Brown resigned his Continental commission during the dispute but remained at war with both Arnold and the British after receiving command of a Massachusetts militia regiment.

At first light on September 18, Brown's men burst from their thickets. Within hours they overran the battery atop Sugar Loaf; after capturing a gun crew and a Canadian work detail, they lobbed 12-pound balls at Ticonderoga. Four British companies from the 53rd Foot were seized along the La Chute portage, and 118 American prisoners set free. "They come out of their holes and cells with wonder and amazement," Brown wrote. "I immediately armed them." Nearly three hundred of the king's troops were captured, and more than two hundred bateaux and other lake craft destroyed. "I have been favored with good success," Brown wrote General Lincoln.

Good, if imperfect. Militiamen attacked the approaches to Mount Independence with war whoops and musketry but failed to evict the Germans, who were bolstered by swarms of grapeshot fired from *Maria* and *Carleton* on the lake below. More captured British field guns cannonaded Ticonderoga but without forcing the gates. General Powell answered a surrender demand with defiance: "The garrison entrusted to my charge I shall defend to the last." Brown assembled a small flotilla to attack the king's stores on Diamond Island, near the foot of Lake George, but two assault landings were thrown back and the marauders returned to shore before burning their boats.

Yet the weeklong sequence of attacks further tipped the scales against Burgoyne. To hold the fortifications around Ticonderoga would require at least two thousand troops, Powell advised Carleton. The raiders had killed or snatched most of his oxen and horses. In late September, when St. Leger finally arrived with his bedraggled corps after the looping retreat from Fort Stanwix via the St. Lawrence, he was unable to reinforce Burgoyne for want of carts and draft animals to transport provisions and baggage. By contrast, Lincoln and most of his raiders hied south to join Gates.

News of the pummeling given Powell's rear guard "produced universal joy in the camp," the Northern Army reported. Gates now believed that Burgoyne could retreat only by abandoning much of his kit. "Perhaps his despair may dictate him to risk all upon one throw," he wrote Governor Clinton on October 4. "He is an old gamester and in his time has seen all chances. I will endeavor to be ready to prevent his good fortune." To a subordinate on the same day he declared himself prepared to "put a finishing stroke to this campaign. The enemy are at their last gasp in every question."

*   *   *

During the fortnight since the Battle of Freeman's Farm, hundreds of additional New England and New York militia had arrived in the rebel camp almost daily. Nearly thirteen thousand soldiers now carpeted Bemus Heights, half of them militiamen. Staff officers toiled to organize bivouac assignments, ammunition and ration supplies, and the integration of more than fifty regiments into the Northern Army's battle structure. The newcomers included 150 Oneida and Tuscarora warriors, who were given red wool caps to identify them as Indian allies. Each day they brought in British, German, and Canadian prisoners, sometimes with their faces painted red or black by their captors or with nooses around their necks. One loyalist was buried to his chin beside a bonfire with Indians "hooting & hollowing round him," a witness wrote. "Then he was handcuffed & sent to Albany jail." Gates offered a $20 bounty for each prisoner but refused to pay for scalps.

Commissary officers collected writing paper in Albany to make musket cartridges and lead weights in Schenectady for bullets. Washington had written Gates suggesting the return of Colonel Morgan and his riflemen to Pennsylvania "if his services can be dispensed with. . . . I do not mention this by way of command, but leave you to determine upon it." Gates replied deftly on October 5, "Your Excellency would not wish me to part with the corps the army of General Burgoyne are most afraid of."

The prospect of another bloody brawl on this same ground caused reflective men to consider their mortality and their families at home. "Remember my love to the children according to their capacity," Adjutant Nathanial Bacheller, a New Hampshire militia officer, wrote his wife, Susanna, after riding into camp on his old mare. "I went into the service out of principle, & I am well-contented & hope through the divine blessing to return to you & our children in God's time." Captain James Bancroft of the 8th Massachusetts wrote his wife that he was "prepared for a better meeting in a better world, where we shall be separated no more by wars and commotion." A sense of common purpose and exuberant well-being took deep root. After reaching Bemus Heights on October 4 to join the 15th Massachusetts, Colonel Timothy Bigelow, a blacksmith who had left five young children at home, wrote to a friend in Worcester, "It is the happiest camp I ever was in."

There were unhappy corners, to be sure. The relationship between Gates and Arnold, once warm and collaborative, had frayed. Although Arnold's performance at Freeman's farm embodied "the very genius of war," as an admirer wrote, Gates's dispatch to Congress about the battle gave no credit to him or his men, who'd shouldered most of the fighting. That shabby oversight enraged Arnold, who on the evening of September 22 had confronted Gates in his farmhouse headquarters. "Matters were altercated in a very high strain," a witness reported. "Both were warm." Arnold returned to the Neilson house and wrote the commander an intemperate letter—"I am thought of no consequence in this department"—then requested permission to travel south to rejoin Washington. Gates agreed. Arnold thought better of leaving on the eve of battle, and a petition from most of his fellow generals entreated him to stay. But he again complained of being treated with "indignity" by Gates, adding, "I know of no reason for your conduct unless I have been traduced by some designing villain."

Congenitally thin-skinned, Arnold pressed his grievances. "I have every reason to think your treatment proceeds from a spirit of jealousy," he wrote in another carping letter. Gates was sensible enough not to reply, although he privately told his wife, "The fatigue of body and mind which I continually undergo is too much for my age and constitution." Supporters of both men stoked the spat. Lieutenant Colonel James Wilkinson, the army's deputy adjutant general and a varlet ever keen to promote dissension, wrote General St. Clair, "Generals Gates and Arnold have differed beyond reconciliation."

Fortunately for the American cause, that was untrue. When General Lincoln arrived in camp, Gates gave him command of the center and right divisions of the Northern Army, leaving intact Arnold's division on the left wing. "I think this campaign," Gates wrote on October 4, "will have a happy issue for the cause of freedom & America."

Sunrise at five forty-four on Tuesday, October 7, brought a splendid day after overnight showers had laid the dust. Migrating geese oared south through a blue sky. Birdsong filled the woods—warblers, thrushes, trilling woodpeckers—and herons stalked the banks of Kromma Kill.

Burgoyne and his generals, each gorgeously uniformed, spent two hours in a tent reviewing the morning's expedition. To forestall betrayal by deserters, no written orders had been drafted. Fifteen hundred chosen men, British and German, were instructed to leave their haversacks and blankets in camp; it should take only a few hours to probe the rising ground on the American left wing. If the rebel defenses seemed porous, more troops and artillery would mass to force a passage south the next day, following the geese toward Albany.

Three columns stepped off at eleven a.m., silent but for footfalls and the jingling harnesses of gaunt horses pulling ten fieldpieces. Traveling southwest under a canopy of trees for nearly a mile and onto what one German called "the damned crooked road," the men then pivoted into two adjacent fields of standing wheat connected by a narrow cow path. The hump of a wooded hill loomed to the west. With sickles and knives some rank and file began cutting the grain with short, swift strokes, piling the stalks on carts to be wheeled back to a hungry camp.

British grenadiers and light infantry sidled off to the left and right flanks, respectively, as Germans and the 24th Foot filled most of the center. This thin line, red and blue, soon stretched for nearly half a mile in two ranks along a worm fence. Adjutants, engineers, and quartermasters climbed to the roof of an abandoned farm cabin; there they gazed through their glasses at the impenetrable tree line to the south where *Jäger* had chased away rebel pickets with a fusillade of rifle shots. Gunners positioned a pair of British 12-pounders in front of the cabin. Three pairs of 6-pounders took post elsewhere along the line, with two howitzers in reserve next to a dilapidated barn.

Burgoyne sat his horse near the field guns, scanning the terrain and conferring in low tones with Generals Riedesel, Phillips, and Fraser. Tranquil harvesting sounds filled the clearing. The sheaves of cut wheat grew higher. Officers on their rooftop parapet strained at their eyepieces, seeing nothing. More American sentries, concealed astride a ridge on the nearby Jesse Chatfield farm, watched as the king's men, awaiting orders, sat on the ground or shifted from foot to foot in the fields below.

A mile and a half south, Horatio Gates and a small coterie of Continental officers crowded around a table in the commander's red farmhouse headquarters to share a midday dinner of broiled ox heart. Gates and Arnold had patched over their earlier spat: they were not only sitting together but conversing in civil tones. Cutlery clattered on pewter plates. Water pitchers and a wine decanter circled the table. Once again the discourse turned to the question of whether, as one officer recorded, "we should commence the attack or receive General Burgoyne behind our breastwork" if the Canada Army ventured down the Hudson.

Dark eyes agleam, his purple rank sash stretched diagonally across his chest, Arnold predictably favored the former option. An attacker, he argued, retained "the advantage, for he can always take his own time and choose the point of attack," then retire into his own lines if repulsed. Gates was more circumspect. He countered that, if repulsed, "undisciplined militia would keep on retiring," deranging the Northern Army.

The *pock pock pock* of distant gunshots interrupted this colloquy. "We all rose from table," Lieutenant Colonel John Brooks of the 8th Massachusetts later recorded, "and General Arnold, addressing General Gates, said,

'Shall I go out and see what is the matter?'" Gates said nothing, then replied, "I am afraid to trust you, Arnold." More gunshots carried from the north. "I will be careful," Arnold persisted, "and if our advance does not need support, I will promise not to commit you." Gates paused again. "Well, then," he said at length, "order on Morgan to begin the game." Arnold bolted through the door, swung into the saddle, and galloped away on his dark Spanish bay.

The seven hundred men in Morgan's corps had returned to Bemus Heights a few hours earlier, following a stealthy, fraught patrol around the British encampment on Monday night. After tramping seven miles north to the outskirts of Saratoga and seizing several prisoners, "we got bewildered in the woods & stayed all night long," huddled together against the cold rain, Major Dearborn admitted. Arnold, unsympathetic and in high feather, ordered Morgan to "file to the left and ascend the eminence." The riflemen and Dearborn's accompanying musketeers were to protect the American left flank by denying redcoats the high ground to the west.

From the excited, wheezing pickets who had raced back to camp after trading shots with Burgoyne's *Jäger*, Gates now knew that a sizable enemy contingent occupied farm clearings almost within cannon range of the American entrenchments. He ordered Colonel Scammell's 3rd New Hampshire to press northward, then rode half a mile north to the Neilson house to advise Arnold that more Continentals were headed his way, and that Morgan should be forewarned to avoid fratricide. Arnold was away, reconnoitering British positions, but "soon returned & told General Gates that the enemy's design was to take possession of a hill about a quarter of a mile to the west of our lines," wrote Nathanial Bacheller, the New Hampshire militia adjutant who was waiting for orders on the Neilson porch. In a letter to his wife two days later, Bacheller—who called himself an "eye & earwitness"—continued:

> General Arnold says to General Gates, "It is late in the day, but let me have men & we will have some fun with them before sunset." Upon which the [Continental and militia] brigades began to march at the lower lines, three-quarters of a mile from us, but in plain sight. . . . Soon a very heavy fire began both with cannon & small arms.

With Gates's permission, Arnold dispatched several more New Hampshire, Connecticut, and New York regiments from General Poor's brigade to attack Burgoyne's left with sixteen hundred troops. More than twenty-five hundred in Brigadier General Ebenezer Learned's brigade swarmed toward the enemy center. Militiamen from Massachusetts, New York, and

New Hampshire also pressed forward, loading their firelocks with two to four buckshot—"Yankee peas"—in addition to lead musket balls. Some soldiers from both sides scored the balls with knives to make them fragment in flight, causing savage wounds.

By four p.m. the fire was "violent and incessant," a Connecticut officer wrote. Six thousand men grappled in a smoking, shrieking death struggle. Arnold reportedly rode back and forth, waggling a sword above his head and shouting, "We'll have them all in hell before night." British 12-pounders fired blindly into the tree line beyond the wheat fields. Burgoyne shifted the 24th Foot to support beleaguered British grenadiers on his far left; 6-pounders initially kept the Americans at bay, but dogged rebels captured two of the guns. Captain Päusch, the Hessian artillery officer, ordered two more dragged to safer ground near the farm cabin, where he could rake the American ranks with case shot. The barrels grew hot enough to blister any hand that touched them.

Captain John Money, the Canada Army quartermaster general who would outlive the day to become a major general, later wrote that a British soldier "becomes, in a scarlet coat, a complete target to riflemen." The bright facings and polished gun barrels might also betray them, Money added, but it was the distinctive coats that allowed an enemy to gauge British strength "at a great distance, even if they are posted in a wood."

Those red coats now fell in alarming numbers. Morgan and Dearborn, this time working hand in glove, had climbed onto a wooded rise several hundred yards behind the British right flank. Riflemen braced against tree trunks to squeeze off rounds aimed at officers, gunners, and the rank and file. Then with a great shout—no voice louder than Morgan's howl—they "poured down like a torrent from the hill," a witness wrote. Musketeers hurdled a fence and slammed into the light infantry, who buckled and broke. Dearborn found Captain Clerke, Burgoyne's secretary, gravely wounded on the ground next to his dying horse. Evacuated to Gates's headquarters, the man who a month earlier had celebrated "good weather, good claret, good music, and the enemy near" would not live to see his twenty-ninth birthday, later in the month.

Overwhelmed grenadiers on the British left also crumpled. Lieutenant Colonel Wilkinson wrote of witnessing several "in the agonies of death" and of finding their commander, Major John Acland, lying in an angle of the worm fence. Upon being wounded Acland had supposedly offered fifty guineas to any redcoat who would carry him to safety, but the grenadier who hoisted him on his back was overtaken and both men were captured. "Very inconveniently," Acland told Wilkinson, "I am shot through both legs." He, too, was taken on horseback to the American camp.

With rebels enveloping both his flanks, Burgoyne recognized his peril. After ordering a retreat—"draw as soon as possible back to the camp"—he rode toward the Hudson with Phillips and Riedesel. Those still in the wheat fields sought to extricate themselves amid "the greatest possible disorder," in one German officer's description. Captain Päusch attempted to wheel his remaining guns away but concluded that "it was impossible to save anything. I called to my few remaining men to save themselves." He scooted through a fence and into the underbrush, where, he recounted, "I met all the different nationalities of our division running pell-mell."

General Fraser had lingered to organize a rear guard. Halfway between the battlefront and Freeman's farm, he halted his big gray under a basswood tree and watched the light infantry and 24th Foot moving northeast at a double-quick pace behind Riedesel's Brunswickers. Morgan later asserted that he ordered a sharpshooter up a tree to take aim at a mounted British officer and "pooh, he was gone." Whether Fraser was the target would never be certain, but he abruptly doubled over in the saddle with a bullet through his left side. Blood seeped across his white breeches. An aide caught the general before he tumbled to the ground, then hurried him away through the smoke and the shouts and the swirling tumult.

By five p.m. none of the king's men remained in the wheat fields except for corpses sprawled across the half-harvested stubble. Burgoyne in two hours had suffered more than four hundred casualties—a quarter of his detachment. Every fieldpiece was lost. Most survivors retreated into the enormous fortification that had been erected across Freeman's farm, later known as the Balcarres Redoubt after Major Alexander Lindsay, the Earl of Balcarres, whose light infantry defended the works. Musketeers clambered onto fire steps behind the earthen berms. Artillerymen manned six cannons and two howitzers mounted on gun platforms, their barrels poking through embrasures in the log walls. Women, children, sutlers, and other camp followers scrambled through the woods back toward the Great Ravine.

The pursuing Americans "attacked with as much fury as the fire of small arms can admit," Balcarres later reported. More reinforcements poured into the battle, bringing rebel strength to more than eight thousand men. But all twenty-two American cannons remained back on Kościuszko's fortifications at Bemus Heights, and lead bullets would not win through against fieldworks with twelve-foot log walls. General Poor's brigade lunged toward the redoubt, only to be driven back by unforgiving gunfire.

A better prospect lay several hundred yards to the northwest. A fortified camp, later dubbed Breymann's Redoubt for the Brunswick officer sent without success to rescue Colonel Baum at Bennington two months earlier, was poorly designed, badly built, and defended by only two hundred Germans—including Breymann himself—with two 6-pounders. As the sun slid behind the western hills, Learned's men overran two nearby log cabins occupied by a few terrified Canadian draftees. The 5th and 6th Massachusetts Regiments, with Morgan's corps, then fell on the redoubt as Arnold galloped inside through an opening on the left, followed by a dozen riflemen. "It was, 'Come on, boys!' Not, 'Go on, boys!'" a Yankee soldier recalled. "He didn't care for nothin'. He'd ride right in."

Defenders fired one erratic volley before abandoning the breastworks and fleeing through their tent bivouac in the rear. Lieutenant Colonel Breymann was not with them. "A constant tyrant to his grenadiers," Lieutenant Julius von Papet later wrote, he was "struck down by a ball from one of his own men after the fiend had sabered four of his command" while trying to halt their retreat.

As a bellowing Arnold demanded surrender, a shot from a Brunswick grenadier shattered his left leg near the ankle—a few inches from the wound he had suffered in Quebec—also killing his Spanish bay and pinning him beneath the carcass. "I assisted in extricating him from it by removing the horse," Dearborn later wrote. "I asked him if he was badly wounded. He replied, 'In the same leg,' and wished the ball had passed his heart." Comrades knotted a tourniquet from strips of his breeches, then loaded him onto a litter fashioned from sapling poles to carry him back to Bemus Heights. Four agonizing days would pass before he reached the Albany hospital. This time Gates effusively praised "the gallant Major General Arnold" in his official dispatch.

Darkness rolled over the battlefield like a lid. "Drove them from their camp & took it with their tents standing & pots boiling," Oliver Boardman, a Connecticut militiaman, told his diary. Capture of the Breymann outworks exposed not only the larger Balcarres Redoubt to attack from behind, but also the road that angled through the Great Ravine to the Canada Army's main encampment on the Hudson. Burgoyne ordered Balcarres to evacuate the fortifications before dawn to consolidate all defenses around the Great Redoubt. With campfires left burning, the column slipped through the woods at midnight, carrying the wounded through the ravine and across Kromma Kill to momentary safety.

*   *   *

"The fields are strowed with the dead," Captain Benjamin Warren of the 6th Massachusetts had written in his diary after the shooting ebbed on Tuesday night. First light on Wednesday proved it so. Years later, as the land was cleared, woodcutters would find tree trunks embedded with bullets and case shot. Farmers plowed up cannonballs, uniform buttons, musket barrels, and bones, so many bones. It was not unusual to see five or ten exhumed skulls stacked on tree stumps around the fields, as if watching where it had ended badly for them on that October day long ago.

Northern Army casualties totaled about 150 of all ranks killed, wounded, or missing, more than thirty of them officers. Lumber wagons hauled injured American, British, and German soldiers to the improvised hospital in the barn by Gates's headquarters, "wretches pale and lifeless, with countenances of an expression peculiar to gunshot wounds," a witness recorded. Private Ezra Tilden, a Massachusetts militiaman, described seeing men "shot almost through ye body & crying to God, to Jesus, &c., to take away their lives. Poor miserable creatures indeed." With the barn full, many were laid in a circle on the cold ground as surgeons probed, extracted, stitched, sawed, and trepanned. Private Samuel Woodruff of the Connecticut militia wrote that "about seventy of them died of their wounds during the night."

Among the last Continental casualties was General Lincoln. Trotting down a cart path while scouting the enemy withdrawal, he blundered into a picket. "I was checking and spurring my horse," he later recalled. "I saw two in British uniforms present & fire." As he turned to race away, he called to an aide, "The rascals have struck me. . . . In my hip, I believe." A lieutenant corrected him: "It is your ankle, sir." Like Arnold, he was evacuated to Albany, where doctors would struggle to save his right leg. Gates had abruptly lost both of his major generals.

Three miles north, this new day brought misery, heartache, and more death to the Canada Army. British losses included 450 killed or badly injured, plus 180 captured. The Germans counted 94 dead, 67 wounded, and 102 captured. Frau Riedesel had planned to dine on Tuesday with her husband and three British generals. Instead Fraser, with a bullet in his gut, was bundled into the cabin north of the Great Redoubt where she and her daughters had been listening for hours to the distant din of battle. The table settings were removed and the pine table carried away to be replaced by a bed for Fraser. The baroness heard his febrile patter—"Oh, fatal ambition. Poor General Burgoyne! My poor wife"—as he tumbled in and out of consciousness. Other wounded men soon crowded the cabin, apologizing for causing her trouble. After wrapping the children in a blanket, she slept with them in the hallway. "Don't conceal anything from me," Fraser told a doctor. "Must I die?"

Yes, he must. At eight a.m. on Wednesday, Fraser crossed over. His body was washed, wrapped in a winding sheet, and returned to the bloody bed while the baroness and the girls looked on. At six p.m., as Fraser had requested, he was carried to a grave in the Great Redoubt, where he had admired the river view. Burgoyne joined the cortege, eulogizing Fraser as a soldier "devoted to glory and prodigal of life, earnest for the general success of the campaign." A chaplain read the Church of England's burial office as cannonballs whizzed above the knot of mourners—"a real military funeral," General Riedesel said dryly. Rebel gunners firing the Royal Artillery 12-pounders captured in the wheat field on Tuesday were unaware of who had gathered on the ridgeline at dusk, or why. The scene, wrote Lieutenant Digby, seemed "big with the fate of many."

"I never saw so affecting a sight," another officer agreed. The moment also drew out the dramatist in Burgoyne, who would write:

> The incessant cannonade during the ceremony, the steady attitude and unaltered voice with which the chaplain officiated—though frequently covered with dust which the shot threw up on all sides of him—[and] the growing darkness added to the scenery. . . . The whole would make one of the finest subjects for the pencil of a master.

"Everything might go very badly," Riedesel had told his wife while Fraser lay dying in bed. He was not wrong. The dead brigadier had hardly been in his grave an hour when the Canada Army, now squeezed into a narrow, half-mile shelf along the river, abandoned the Great Redoubt and trudged north after dismantling the floating bridge. "Our calashes were ready and waiting," the baroness wrote. "Fires were left burning everywhere. . . . Little Frederika was very much frightened . . . and I had to hold my handkerchief over her mouth to prevent our being discovered." Her exhausted husband fell asleep in the carriage with his head on her shoulder, their three girls curled around them. Cold rain pelted the column as crowbait horses pulled baggage carts and artillery carriages with thirty salvaged guns.

Americans swiftly overran the forsaken encampment to discover more than four hundred enemy sick and wounded left behind. Sprawled on dirty straw, dozens were "terribly mangled," a Connecticut militiaman observed. British medicos who had remained with the patients hardly looked up from their extractions and amputations. A note from Burgoyne for Gates read, "I recommend them to the protection which I feel I should show an enemy in the same case."

A gray, wet dawn on Thursday, October 9, found the king's fugitives only to Dovegat, less than five miles from the Great Redoubt. After a brief rest, Burgoyne had them moving again. Orders and counterorders swept up and down the lurching column. Vengeful redcoats burned houses along the river road and, a soldier from the 47th Foot reported, seventy-two barrels of rum to keep the liquor from rebel gullets. Several dozen deserters stole away, including Brunswickers with their wives. Rebels following on the river road would find scores of dead draft horses. Some had collapsed from hunger; others were put down whenever a British cart threw a wheel or broke an axle. The debris trail included barrels of gunpowder, flour, and salt pork. "Roads strowed with wagons, baggage, dead carcasses, ammunition, tents, etc.," a Continental officer noted in his diary.

Early that evening the column closed on Saratoga. Rebels had demolished the bridge, so soldiers waded across the icy Fishkill and entrenched on the heights away from the river. Pick-and-shovel men in the German bivouac could hardly dig deeper than a foot in the rocky ground. It was whispered in the ranks that St. Leger would soon arrive with nine hundred reinforcements and that Henry Clinton was coming with even more; only the desperately credulous now put stock in such latrine rumors. Rebel snipers across the Hudson fired all night through the rain, shooting up bateaux brought upstream from the disassembled bridge. A north wind brought more rain and a hard freeze. "Heavy hoarfrost," a Brunswick grenadier wrote in his journal. "We were thoroughly wet and camped in open air."

Burgoyne again moved into Schuyler's country house, admiring the formal garden and two dozen outbuildings on both sides of the Fishkill, including a gristmill, a linen mill, and sawmills. He sent the 47th Foot with other troops and a squad of artificers to scout the road and repair bridges up the Hudson's west bank. But Fort Edward, to the north, had been stoutly occupied by rebel militia, blocking that escape route. Loyalists guarding the repair crew took fright at American skirmishers and ran off, leaving the artificers to "escape as they could." Burgoyne ordered the entire detachment back to Saratoga.

Convinced that Gates intended an all-out assault, the British commander crossed the Fishkill and joined his dwindling legion on the rocky heights. He left Schuyler's house, barns, sheds, and mills convulsed in flames to prevent the enemy from occupying them, sparing only a sawmill on the upper creek and the privy. Rebels soon "swarmed around the little adverse army like birds of prey," wrote Corporal Lamb of the 9th Foot. "Whistling of bullets from their rifle pieces were heard constantly by day and night."

Thousands of American Continentals and militia enveloped the king's bridgehead on both sides of the Hudson. Gates, who had begun referring to his adversary as "Brother Burgoyne," occupied a small wooden house a mile south of the Fishkill before moving his headquarters into a marquee. Worried that the Canada Army had begun edging north upriver to escape, Gates ordered two brigades and the Rifle Corps to jump the creek and strike from the south on the foggy Saturday morning of October 11. A Continental detachment attacked the anchorage at the mouth of the Fishkill, routing British sailors, seizing their bateaux, and capturing several dozen men from the 62nd Foot. But Brigadier Generals Glover and John Nixon found redcoats still heavily entrenched, with artillery raking the creek crossings. A ball blew apart an American soldier's skull, and bone fragments lacerated the face of fifer Nicholas Stone, standing beside him. After hearing a British deserter's warning that "the whole army is now in camp," Gates canceled the assault.

Even so, the Canada Army's predicament worsened hour by hour. "It is as bad as possible," a senior officer told Burgoyne, who could only agree when a cannonball fired across the Hudson "discomposed" his dinner table while he sat eating with subordinates. Without fodder, horses ate oak leaves, branches, and bark. Then, a German officer recorded, "they ate the saddles off their backs and died miserably, one after another." Lieutenant Digby of the 53rd Foot wrote on October 11, "Our cattle began to die fast and the stench was very prejudicial in so small a space." Campfires were forbidden at night after American gunners aimed at the flames and killed several men. A soldier in the 47th Foot reported living on four biscuits a day and crude flour dumplings. The sole entry in Lieutenant Lord Francis Napier's journal for October 12 read, "The cannonade still kept up."

"All things in this camp became sadder and sadder for us," a German officer wrote. Frederika Riedesel and her family sheltered in the stinking cellar of a house used as the army's hospital. Three wounded British officers lay near them, including an aide to General Phillips who had been shot in the face. A soldier's wife braved sniper fire to fetch water from the river; she received twenty guineas for her courage. "Eleven cannonballs flew through the house and we could distinctly hear them rolling about over our heads," the baroness wrote. A wounded soldier lying on a table to have his leg amputated had the other leg torn off when shot blew through the wall. He crawled into a corner in agony.

Brother Burgoyne estimated that sixteen thousand Americans "extended three parts in four of a circle around us," with the final quadrant—including the road north—about to close. At three p.m. on Sunday, October 12, he convened a war council with Generals Phillips, Riedesel, and James Hamilton, their faces gray with exhaustion. Their provisions might last another week, Burgoyne told them. No rum or spruce beer remained. All bateaux had been destroyed or captured. To escape north with carts or gun carriages required rebuilding at least one substantial bridge while under enemy fire, a task that would take at least fourteen hours.

He listed five options: remain stationary and wait for "favorable events"; attack the besiegers; retreat toward a Hudson River ford above Fort Edward, repairing the damaged bridges; retreat at night after abandoning all guns and baggage, in hopes of looping around the western shore of Lake George; or reverse course "to march rapidly for Albany." The conference minutes recorded their decision: "The fourth proposition is the only recourse," a night flight without encumbrances, requiring "the utmost secrecy and silence."

The Canada Army's last rations were distributed to the ranks. As darkness fell and word spread of their departure, "a certain joy took hold of both the officers and privates," a Brunswick officer wrote. Joy turned to ashes at eleven p.m. Returning scouts reported Americans now dug in along the march route. A retreating column would be "immediately discovered" and smashed, they added. "It is too late," Burgoyne told his lieutenants.

At seven p.m. on Monday, after another tedious day of cannonading, Burgoyne reconvened his generals while also inviting officers ranked captain and higher, in order that "a full representation of the army" could consider the dire matters at hand. The stench of dead animals draped the camp. Booming field guns and the sharp *ping* of rifle bullets punctuated the night. "Are there examples in military history," Burgoyne asked, "that an army has capitulated in the situation in which ours now finds itself?" To a man, they answered yes. Is an army with thirty-five hundred rank and file still fit to fight justified, he continued, "upon the principles of national dignity and military honor, in capitulating in any possible situation?" Again, they concurred.

Burgoyne posed his final question: "Is the present situation of that nature?" Yes, they told him, certainly. Before his lieutenants shuffled from the room for a few hours of fitful sleep, he summarized aloud their assent: "The present situation justifies a capitulation upon honorable terms."

* * *

Only sketchy details had reached Gates about the battle at Forts Clinton and Montgomery, 130 miles south, and the British immolation of Esopus, forty miles closer. Yet the threat of Henry Clinton bulling up the Hudson valley to trap the Northern Army against Burgoyne's rump force gnawed at him. When a white flag—carried by a twelve-year-old British ensign, according to one account—brought Burgoyne's request for negotiations on Monday evening, Gates immediately consented.

An eerie calm sifted over the river at ten a.m. on Tuesday, October 14, as Lieutenant Colonel Robert Kingston, the British deputy adjutant general, rode slowly through a ford near the creek's mouth, downstream of the wrecked Fishkill bridge. On the south bank he was blindfolded with his own handkerchief and led by the elbow to Gates's marquee. Kingston carried a truculent note from Burgoyne, which nevertheless acknowledged "the superiority of your numbers" and proposed a ceasefire. Gates, spectacles perched on the tip of his nose, pulled out a sheet of paper listing seven conditions for surrender.

The endgame at Saratoga had begun, although negotiations during the next two days at times resembled an opéra bouffe, with more blindfolds, more histrionic postures, more war councils, more delays, more declamations. Burgoyne sent a cheeky ten-point counterproposal; it included a request for "free passage to be granted to this army to Great Britain upon condition of not serving again in North America during the present contest." He also insisted that the word "capitulation" be replaced by "convention," implying not a battlefield surrender by vanquished to victor but, rather, an accord between equal opponents.

Gates agreed, looking over his shoulder toward Esopus, although when Burgoyne demanded that British officers inspect the Northern Army to confirm its strength, the American commander threatened to resume his attacks with "the most stringent measures." Instead, he enclosed an abstract showing that the American host now exceeded twenty thousand men, fourfold the king's force. The deal was done. The final "articles of convention" contained thirteen clauses, including an agreement that the Canada Army would sail home from Boston.

"The grand army of Gen. Burgoin capillelated & agreed to be prisoners," an American soldier wrote. At eight a.m. on Friday, October 17, Riedesel gathered his Brunswickers and told them, in a voice cracking with emotion, "It was no lack of courage on your part by which this awful fate has come upon you." To his prince he wrote, "I consider myself the most unfortunate man on earth." He handed the baroness a stack of regimental colors and tassels to be secretly sewn inside a mattress. Burgoyne declared upon his honor that battle flags had been left in Canada, but similar acts of duplicity occurred across the encampment, where officers were ordered to conceal their silk colors "so as not to surrender any trophies to the enemy which were too beautiful for them." Thirty sets were hidden away, including colors from the 9th Foot that would be presented to George III four years later. Burgoyne also surreptitiously distributed the remaining gold and silver in his military chest to paymasters and senior officers, to be distributed through the ranks. "Not a shilling" fell into rebel hands, Colonel Kingston later assured Parliament.

As the morning fog burned off, Burgoyne appeared from his quarters in a dress uniform, "as if going to assist in some gala occasion," a Brunswick journal noted. "He looked like a dandy rather than a warrior." The defeated general had already scratched his signature with an inked quill on the capitulation document, and the Canada Army orderly book noted simply, "Treaty of convention signed." Some veteran troops "sobbed like children," while others smashed their muskets in rage or stomped holes in their drumheads. Lieutenant Digby, among those who wept, wrote, "Thus ended all our hopes of victory, honor, glory, &c., &c., &c."

At ten-thirty a.m. the king's men filed from their fetid entrenchments and gathered at Fort Hardy, a decrepit French and Indian War relic at the mouth of the Fishkill. Here they stacked their muskets or laid them on the ground while American troops moved forward to occupy the vacant lines, "stepping off with a tolerable good grace [to] the old favorite tune of 'Yankee Doodle,'" a witness recorded. "This was truly pleasing." A British officer wrote that for rebels the melody was "esteemed as warlike as 'The Grenadier's March.' It is the lover's spell, the nurse's lullaby."

"The greatest conquest ever known," Major Dearborn wrote in his journal with pardonable hyperbole. The Canada Army would yield 6 generals, 350 other officers, 5,900 enlisted men, and about 600 women and children. Another 500 Canadians, teamsters, Indians, and American loyalists were permitted to walk north to Canada. Since leaving Montreal four months earlier, Burgoyne had lost more than 8,000 men. The captured booty included 30 brass artillery pieces, 60 wagons, 4,600 shoulder weapons, 149 cavalry swords—"very strong & heavy"—and other war matériel. The fine artillery "is an acquisition America could have got no other way . . . a loss Great Britain cannot for some long time repair," a British officer told his brother in England. Captain Joseph Hodgkins, a cobbler from Massachusetts who had fought since Lexington, wrote his wife, Sarah, "We have had a very fatiguing campaign, but we have done the business we came here for."

So had Horatio Gates. Wearing a plain blue coat, his lank hair poking in gray strands from under his hat, he rode slowly up the river road and halted at the simple Dutch Reformed Church, a few hundred yards south of the charred rubble that had been Schuyler's house. Burgoyne, Riedesel, and their senior lieutenants clopped on their scrawny mounts across the Fishkill ford, then through two long lines of rebel soldiers bracketing the road. "No laughing or marks of exultation were to be seen among them," a Massachusetts colonel said of the American troops. "They had fortitude of mind to bear prosperity without being too much elated."

Gates plucked the hat from his head and extended his hand. Burgoyne shook it and said, "The fate of war has put me into your hands." Gates replied, according to an American chaplain, "If enterprise, courage, and perseverance would have given you success, victory would have been yours." They dismounted and walked to a marquee fashioned from river-craft canvas. Two planks laid across empty salt-meat barrels held platters of ham, goose, beef, and boiled mutton, to be washed down with New England rum. Only two glasses could be found, so subordinates drank from ceramic saucers.

As the meal ended, Gates "filled a bumper and, in a most polite and liberal manner, drank His Britannic Majesty's health," a witness reported. Burgoyne answered with a toast to George Washington, then offered his sword in its scabbard to Gates, who, in a chivalrous gesture, promptly returned it. The king's lieutenant general had surrendered to a former half-pay major. Burgoyne would describe the moment as "calamitous," adding, "It was an awful, but it was an honorable hour."

At three-thirty p.m. the king's men formed columns and waded the Fishkill, the muddy water further soiling their filthy trousers—"the most agreeable sight that ever my eyes beheld," Colonel Jeduthan Baldwin noted in his diary. Then south they marched, between more rows of Continentals and American militia, who stood with muskets in hand, bayonets fixed, colors flying, and the gunners next to their guns. "They remained so perfectly quiet that we were utterly astounded," a German soldier wrote. "None of them evinced the least sign of hate or malicious joy as we passed by." Lieutenant Lord Napier later told his journal, "They behaved with the greatest decency and propriety, not even a smile appearing in any of their countenances, which circumstance I really believe would not have happened had the case been reversed."

By sunset the last echelons of the defeated army had shambled past. They would camp for the night at Freeman's farm, then begin the two-hundred-mile trek toward Boston. "Thus we witness the incalculable reverse of fortune," wrote James Thacher, "and the extraordinary vicissitudes of military events, as ordained by divine Providence." Gates took a moment at the end of the day to scratch a note to his wife:

Burgoyne and his whole army have laid down their arms, and surrendered themselves to me and my Yankees. Thanks to the Giver of all victory for this triumphant success. . . . If Old England is not by this lesson taught humility, then she is an obstinate old slut, bent upon her ruin.

Thousands of prisoners crossed the Hudson at Stillwater on Saturday morning. "The world seemed to be full of troops, and all in motion," a fifteen-year-old boy helping to guard them later wrote. The Germans were ferried first, he added, "with their baggage on horses that were mere skeletons, not able apparently to bear the weight of their own carcasses." General Glover, who commanded the evacuation, sent the British eastward via Northampton, Massachusetts, and the "foreign troops" via Springfield. Collectively they were now known as the Convention Army.

Yankee families drove up in their wagons to gawk at the plodding columns or to trade drams of liquor for cartridge pouches; a few encouraged desertion, plundered the prisoners, or stole the wretched horses. Trudging through the Berkshires, a German wrote, "we got so covered with frost during the night, we looked like great sugar dolls." By the time they staggered into Cambridge in November, a Massachusetts woman reported, they were "a sordid set of creatures in human figure—poor, dirty, emaciated men, [and] great numbers of women who seemed to be the beasts of burden, having a bushel basket on their back by which they were bent double."

Burgoyne and a score of his senior officers had an easier time of it. By invitation they spent ten days at Schuyler's mansion outside Albany, a house built "in elegant ancient style and fancifully ornamented," an American physician wrote. Frau Riedesel and her daughters also joined them, after traveling from Saratoga in Schuyler's carriage, nibbling smoked tongue, bread, and butter. Burgoyne toiled on a sixty-paragraph dispatch to his government, attempting to explain the inexplicable. When he apologized to Schuyler for burning his country estate, the American replied, "That is the fate of war. . . . Let us say no more about it." He had already begun planning to rebuild the manor house on the same foundations, using British prisoners for masonry work and other skilled labor. Burgoyne plucked a pair of rhinestone buckles from his shoes for one of Schuyler's daughters as a token of thanks, then he and his entourage decamped for Boston on October 27.

They left behind a town heaving with misery. At least a thousand sick and wounded soldiers, many of them British or German, jammed Albany churches, private houses, and the large wooden hospital, with its cupola and stockade fence. Thirty physicians, surgeons, and other medicos "all are constantly employed," Thacher wrote—dressing jagged injuries, trepanning fractured skulls, and applying tincture of myrrh to wounds infested with maggots. One witness would recall late in his life the "horror and sickness of heart" the sufferings from Saratoga had caused, adding, "The remembrance cannot be effaced."

Two American major generals lay near each other in the hospital. Lincoln demonstrated a cheerful stoicism despite both a gunshot wound that would shed bone fragments for years and a more private injury: he had learned that his youngest daughter had died at home in September, while his wife had narrowly survived smallpox. Arnold's wound and compound fracture seemed "less dangerous in the beginning than Lincoln's," a physician wrote, but was slower to heal. "He abuses us for a set of ignorant pretenders," Dr. James Browne reported. Arnold, the former apothecary, knew enough medicine to ridicule the bloodletters hovering around his bed and to dismiss talk of amputating his purulent leg as "damned nonsense."

With the limb immobilized in a wooden fracture box, he suffered bedsores and pain so intense he had difficulty holding a pen. "He is very peevish and impatient under his misfortune," Thacher wrote, "and required all of my attention during the night." Even a belated authorization by Congress to restore Arnold's seniority over five lesser major generals failed to revive his spirits. He brooded and seethed, cultivating a saturnine contempt for Congress and the small men who bullyragged him. Weeks and then months would pass before he could regain his feet, only to find his left leg two inches shorter than his right.

"The malice of this man," an aide to Gates reported, "is so bitter."

If Arnold was miserable, his countrymen were giddy at the news from Saratoga. Shore batteries and ships fired salutes, bonfires blazed, states declared a day of thanksgiving, and celebratory doggerel included such timeless couplets as "Burgoyne unmindful of impending fates / Could cut his way through woods but not through Gates." Dancing couples in Pennsylvania invented the "Burgoyne's Surrender." A note describing the American victory was baked inside a loaf of bread delivered to rebel prisoners in New York. "As soon as that was read in the Congress Room"—a detention cell—"the whole prison resounded with three cheers," an inmate reported. Jailers insisted "it was a damned rebel lie."

Washington congratulated Gates on a "signal success . . . that does the highest honor to the American arms." For many Americans, victory "confirmed God's superintending Providence," a historian would write. Gamblers willing to wager that the war would last longer than another five months could command five-to-one odds. Burgoyne was lampooned as "Jack Brag," and his name promptly became a verb: "to burgoyne" an enemy was to lure him into a fatal trap.

Loyalists stood with mouths agape. Gobsmacked British and German officers in New York, Philadelphia, and Newport could scarcely credit accounts from the upper Hudson. "Burgoyne's disaster has greatly changed the face of affairs in this country," General Cornwallis conceded. "God only knows how this business will end." Henry Clinton and his staff braced for a rebel assault on New York City. "Everyone is disgusted here," one of his officers wrote. "There has been such a series of blunders." Some of General Howe's senior commanders recognized their culpability in Burgoyne's demise. "The loss of his army was unavoidable from the moment we sailed from New York," Colonel William Harcourt wrote his brother in England. Others blamed London. "This unfortunate event, it is to be hoped, will in future prevent ministers from pretending to direct operations in a country at three thousand miles distance, of which they have so little knowledge," Carleton wrote Burgoyne in a consolatory letter.

The strategy of using Canada as a springboard for plunging into the American interior, which had dominated British thinking for two years, was now defunct; a new strategy would be needed. But first the remnants of the Canada Army must be extracted. On November 8, General Powell and his sixteen hundred men, two-thirds of them German, abandoned Ticonderoga, Mount Independence, and other outposts to avoid being trapped by winter ice. Gunners used hammers to whack off the trunnions of cannons that could not be evacuated, then tossed the barrels into Lake Champlain. *Flexible*, *Maria*, *Carleton*, and other vessels made ready to sail as firebrands dashed through the works.

"We saw all the log houses, the store houses, the hospital, all the huts and cottages, everything which could be ruined by fire, in flames," a German adjutant wrote. "The floating bridge was also cut down and burned. We embarked and departed." Then fifty barrels of gunpowder stacked in the cellars under Ticonderoga detonated with a monstrous roar, shattering the fortress. "Carthage had probably not been reduced to ashes as quickly," Ensign Friedrich von Hille noted. The flotilla passed Crown Point at noon and was dusted with snow that evening. But the return voyage to Canada proved perilous. Green Mountain Boys harried the expedition, snatching forty-nine prisoners and nearly a hundred horses. The radeau *Thunderer*, converted into a hospital ship to carry 150 sick and wounded men, struck a rock off Windmill Point and sank, drowning an unknown number of invalids. In mid-November the numb refugees reached St. Johns on the Richelieu, where, Hille wrote, "we made extremely big fires, similar to the drawings of hell."

To evacuate the Convention Army from Boston, the Royal Navy staged twenty-five transport ships at Newport, victualed for an eight-week transatlantic voyage with two thousand barrels of flour. Yet Congress now balked, recognizing that the indulgent terms granted by Gates would allow Britain to use these returning troops for garrison duty in Ireland and other imperial locales, freeing soldiers at those outposts for combat service in America. Moreover, the haul from Saratoga more than doubled the number of the king's men in rebel custody, providing leverage to demand better treatment for American prisoners now held in deplorable conditions.

Intent on forcing London to recognize American sovereignty, Congress would suspend embarkation of the Convention Army late in the year, pending "explicit ratification" of the treaty by George III and Parliament. Such an agreement would be an "acknowledgement of our capacity to treat as a nation," wrote Henry Laurens, who had replaced Hancock as president of Congress. London refused, squawking loudly. "This flagrant breach of faith will at last convince the British nation that the rebel chiefs are a set of unprincipled scoundrels," Captain Frederick Mackenzie told his diary.

Yet bad faith cut both ways. William Howe covertly planned to keep many of Burgoyne's troops in America, ostensibly because Washington had failed to follow through on a previous prisoner exchange. In a secret note on November 16, he ordered Burgoyne to have the transports sent not to England after they were loaded in Boston, but to New York. "Conceal from the captains and troops the intention of such orders," Howe commanded. "Use every possible precaution to keep the enemy ignorant of my intentions."

The Americans indeed remained ignorant of this duplicity until after the war, but suspicions and mistrust had been aroused. "Without great precaution & very delicate management," Washington warned, "we shall have all these men, if not the officers, opposed to us in the spring." And so the Convention Army would remain in Massachusetts for a year, living in crude barracks, dying of scurvy, or deserting, and every Thursday parading for Generals Riedesel and Phillips while oboists played airs that evoked happier days. "We generally live in a sad loneliness," a German soldier wrote, although the British government spent almost £30,000 to supply rations, firewood, and other amenities. In November 1778, as commanded by Congress, the Convention Army marched from Massachusetts in the same threadbare uniforms the troops wore at Saratoga, traveling more than six hundred miles to Charlottesville, in western Virginia, beyond the reach of British raiders tempted to liberate them.

Here they would remain for years in crowded cabins infested with termites and rats. Some escaped to rejoin royal forces; others deserted and settled permanently in America. Officers who could afford better quarters rented plantation houses from the local gentry. They also built a "Comedy House" to stage theater productions twice a week behind a curtain decorated with a painted harlequin who pointed his wooden sword at the phrase, "Who would have expected this here?" The Riedesels made the best of their confinement, making friends with a charming local planter named Jefferson, who provided garden seeds and a piano for the baroness to play. London tried to keep the prisoners sedated by paying for eighty pipes of wine—more than ten thousand gallons—to be shipped from New York to Virginia.

John Burgoyne followed a different fate. Even before leaving Albany he had sharpened his quill to complain, expound, and accuse. "I have been surrounded with enemies, ill-treated by pretended friends, abandoned by a considerable part of my own army, totally unassisted by Sir William Howe," he told his nieces. To Howe he wrote, "Had all my troops been British, I should have made my way through Mr. Gates's army." To Lord Germain he confessed, "I am sunk in mind and body." Perhaps, he suggested, it might have been better had he died on the battlefield.

In truth, he was overmatched. A field general of modest talents, Burgoyne was unprepared for adversity, incapable of adapting, unlucky, and unwilling to cut his losses while he still could. Failing to recognize the explosive power of a revolutionary movement until it was too late, he also forgot that the lifeline of every British army, as the historian George Athan Billias would write, "rested upon its communication with the sea." The Canada Army had surrendered far, far from the smell of salt water.

Upon arriving in Boston on November 8, Burgoyne drew such a curious throng that "the streets were filled, the doors, windows, the tops of the houses and fences crowded," reported Major General William Heath, the American commander. Through the winter, a local woman wrote, he could be seen riding down Queen Street "followed by as great a number of spectators as ever attended a pope." In a letter from Cambridge he told a friend, "The value of life has been for some time over with me." After swearing to Congress, "under God," that his health depended on returning to England to take the waters, he sailed from Newport aboard the *Grampus*, without a farewell salute, in mid-April 1778, arriving in Portsmouth a month later.

He had predicted that "ministerial ingratitude will be displayed," and in this he was prescient. The king refused to grant an audience. The government both ignored and reproved him. He requested a court-martial to clear his name, but a panel of generals ruled that as a prisoner on parole he was ineligible for such a proceeding. A parliamentary inquiry devolved into bickering between Burgoyne and Germain. With the king's consent, he was ordered back into captivity in America but refused, pleading ill health, and once again immersed himself in the palliative waters at Bath. This, he again predicted accurately, was the "suicide of my professional existence." Accused of disobedience, he was stripped of various honors and sinecures, including the governorship of Fort William in Scotland, which was given to General Vaughan, the despoiler of Esopus.

In 1780 he would return to the theater, achieving greater success as a playwright than he ever did as a general. His light opera *The Lord of the Manor* had a fine run at Drury Lane, and *The Heiress* was a comic stage sensation, described by an admirer as "one of the most pleasing in our language." After his death in 1792, at the age of seventy, he was buried in the north cloister of Westminster Abbey beneath a bare slab. The precise location was soon forgotten, but a century later he would be immortalized, after a fashion, by George Bernard Shaw in *The Devil's Disciple*. "Burgoyne's surrender at Saratoga," Shaw wrote, "made him that occasionally necessary part of our British system, a scapegoat."

As for Saratoga, Henry Clinton succinctly summed up the campaign as "the height of impropriety and bad policy." The battle shattered British pretensions in New England, weakened the empire in Canada, and in all thirteen states demoralized loyalists and inspirited rebels. Perhaps most telling, the American victory commanded admiration in Versailles and other European capitals.

"Thus ended a campaign which at the beginning was attended with every appearance of success," Lieutenant Lord Napier wrote in his journal as he headed to prison. "We had conceived the idea of our being irresistible. What afterwards followed plainly evinced we were not more than mortals."

10.

The Elements in Flames

PHILADELPHIA, OCTOBER–DECEMBER 1777

Before dawn on Tuesday, October 21, a tall, graying man in a silver-laced blue coat watched with approval as fifteen hundred scruffy German troops sorted themselves into a compact column on Arch Street in Philadelphia. A silver gorget hung round his neck, inscribed with a Hessian motto—NESCIT PERICULA: "No fear of danger"—and a crimson thread had been worked through the silver sword sash on his hip. A portrait painted a decade earlier by Johann Tischbein the Elder had depicted him as lean and cocksure in hunting togs, holding a rifle and pointing to a rabbit he had just shot, with a spaniel at his side and "C.E.U.," the initials of his Christian names, embroidered on his collar. Colonel Carl Emil Ulrich von Donop, as overbearing and arrogant as he was ardent and refined, had assembled his brigade along the Delaware River this morning. Together they intended to hunt down rebel rabbits.

He had pleaded for this chance to redeem German honor after what he called the "eternal disgrace to our nation" ten months earlier: Washington's obliteration of the garrison at Trenton, for which he, as the senior Hessian officer in southern New Jersey, was not entirely blameless. "Tell your general," Donop had recently advised General Howe's aide, "that Germans are not afraid to face death." Desperate to open the Delaware to British shipping, Howe relented, assigning three Hessian grenadier regiments, with *Jäger*, artillery, and the Mirbach Regiment, to seize Fort Mercer at Red Bank, on the Jersey side of the river. That would allow the Royal Navy to finish extracting from the Delaware mud the stackadoes—chevaux-de-frise—still thwarting efforts to bring into Philadelphia the ammunition, medical supplies, and six-month stockpile of bread, flour, and salt meat now marooned on more than two hundred victuallers and other vessels below Chester. Soon the river would freeze solid, and a hungry city would become a starving city.

At sunrise soldiers, horses, and gun carriages began filing from a wharf onto fourteen flatboats captured from the Americans. Across the olive-green river the first vessels nosed toward Cooper's Ferry, sailors squinting into the morning glare as they peered upstream for rebel row galleys. The previous day, all of the king's men had heard celebratory gunfire from American pickets outside the city. "They say that General Burgoyne was taken prisoner," Ambrose Serle, Admiral Howe's secretary, had noted. "Their leaders often make triumphs or imaginary victories to keep up the spirits of the deluded people."

Regardless of the Canada Army's fate, Donop knew that Howe was still struggling to make Philadelphia his own a month after the city's capture. Fourteen perimeter redoubts had been built, all anchored on the Delaware and the Schuylkill. The bulk of the army had marched down from Germantown two days earlier, giving the city a military population of eighteen thousand, plus twenty-five thousand civilians, each of whom needed to eat. Jack Tars had finally made a hundred-foot gap in the stackadoes downriver at Billingsport, but the larger reef of obstructions upstream between the two strongholds on either side of the Delaware, Forts Mercer and Mifflin, remained intact, protected by rebel shore guns and two floating batteries—named *Arnold* and *Putnam*—with sixteen 18-pounders between them. An October 11 attempt to bombard Fort Mifflin into submission had failed when a surprise rebel sortie against Province Island, in the mouth of the Schuylkill, drove two hundred redcoats helter-skelter from a shore battery. "Come along, my lads," a rebel officer had yelled, "and you shall be well used." More than fifty grenadiers, 10th Foot troops, and gunners surrendered. A court-martial this week would convict a British major and a captain of misbehaving before the enemy, cashiering them from the service.

Such craven malfeasance would not be tolerated by C.E.U. von Donop. He had once believed, as he told his prince, that the mighty British would "show us the way to glory." Now he had doubts. Howe's dawdling march across the Pennsylvania countryside "could have been done better by an ensign," Donop had complained, and Province Island, although soon reclaimed, was a sorry fiasco. How could such things happen when so many American officers were lowborn merchants, barbers, and innkeepers? A Hessian lieutenant colonel later wrote that Donop "made enemies of General Howe and all the English generals with the sarcastic letters and sharp tongue." But capturing Fort Mercer would set things right, demonstrating to the British how vital their German allies could be. Howe had told him to "improvise" in his attack, and Donop intended to do just that.

The autumn sun had passed the meridian when the last artillery cart was unloaded on the Jersey shore, eight miles upriver from Fort Mercer.

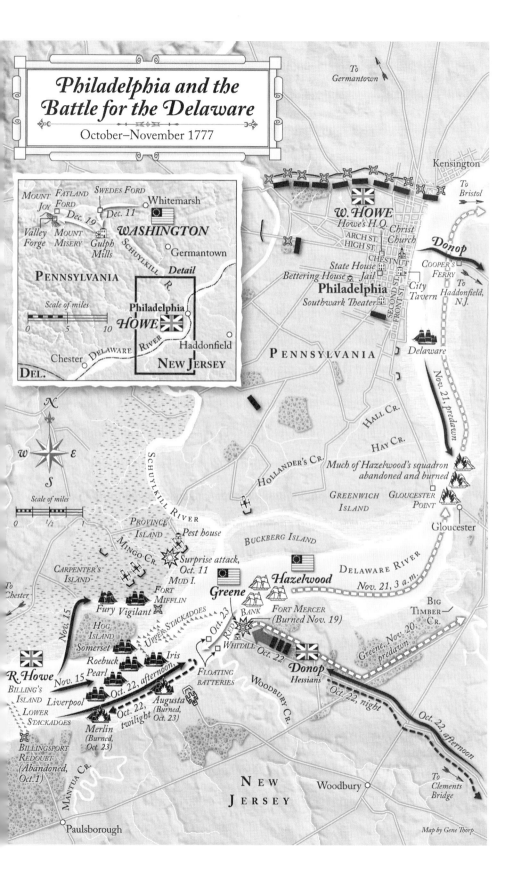

Philadelphia and the Battle for the Delaware

October–November 1777

Detail map (inset):

Mount Joy • Fatland Ford • Swedes Ford • Whitemarsh
Dec. 19 • Dec. 11
Valley Forge • Mount Misery • Gulph Mills • **WASHINGTON**
PENNSYLVANIA • Germantown
Schuylkill R.
Detail
Philadelphia
HOWE
Scale of miles
0 5 10
Chester • DELAWARE RIVER • Haddonfield
DEL. • **NEW JERSEY**

Main map labels:

To Germantown
Kensington
To Bristol
W. HOWE
Howe's H.Q. • Christ Church
ARCH ST. • HIGH ST. • CHESTNUT
Donop
State House • COOPER'S FERRY
Bettering House • Jail • City Tavern • To Haddonfield, N.J.
Philadelphia
Southwark Theater
SECOND ST. • FRONT ST.
Delaware
Nov. 21, predawn

PENNSYLVANIA

HALL CR.
HAY CR.
HOLLANDER'S CR.
Much of Hazelwood's squadron abandoned and burned
GREENWICH ISLAND • GLOUCESTER POINT • Gloucester

N
W E
S

Scale of miles
0 1/2 1

SCHUYLKILL RIVER
PROVINCE ISLAND • Pest house
MINGO CR.
Surprise attack, Oct. 11
Mud I.
CARPENTER'S ISLAND
BUCKBERG ISLAND
Hazelwood
DELAWARE RIVER
Nov. 21, 3 a.m.
Fort MIFFLIN
Greene
BANK
To Chester
Fury Vigilant
UPPER STACKADOES
Oct. 23
BIG TIMBER CR.
HOG ISLAND
Somerset
RED
FORT MERCER (Burned Nov. 19)
WHITALL Oct. 22
Roebuck • Iris
Pearl
Nov. 15
FLOATING BATTERIES
Donop
Hessians
Greene, Nov. 20, predawn
R. Howe
Nov. 15
BILLING'S ISLAND
Liverpool
Oct. 22, afternoon
Augusta (Burned, Oct. 23)
Oct. 22, twilight
WOODBURY CR.
Oct. 22, night
Oct. 22, afternoon
LOWER STACKADOES
Merlin (Burned, Oct. 23)
BILLINGSPORT REDOUBT (Abandoned, Oct. 1)
MANTUA CR.
NEW JERSEY
Woodbury
To Clements Bridge
Paulsborough

Map by Gene Thorp

The column heaved forward at three p.m. toward Haddonfield, five miles inland, where they apprehended rebel sympathizers identified by ardent loyalists, then camped for the night in a square formation. At four a.m. on October 22 they set out again with two local guides, who led them roundabout to Clements Bridge since militiamen had destroyed the span at Buck Tavern. Occasional potshots "disquieted our march on all sides," a Hessian officer wrote, but a Rhode Island captain and six Continentals in a hunting party blundered into the brigade. They assured Donop that Fort Mercer's defenders remained unaware of their jeopardy.

At midday the Germans reached Red Bank. The fort stood six hundred yards distant on a forty-foot bluff above the Delaware. As gunners unlimbered two English howitzers and eight 3-pounders, Donop ordered Captain Ewald, who had served with valor at Brandywine, to creep forward from the forest's edge to scout the defenses. "The *Jäger* had to crawl out on their stomachs up to the abatis," a lieutenant wrote. "Many from the garrison were walking about outside the fort and were joking, and knew nothing about us." An American flag flew from a hickory tree. Ewald reported seeing "a breastwork twelve feet high, palisaded and dressed with assault stakes."

The gate was open. Apparently it was wash day. Laundry lay draped over the ramparts.

War had come to the ninety-acre farm of James and Ann Whitall, despite their best attempts to fend it off. Married since 1739, with issue that included six sons, three daughters, and grandchildren, they had made a good life in Red Bank, even if Ann inclined to humorless severity. "Our Lord pronounces a woe against them that laugh," she had informed her diary, and when her boys went ice-skating after Quaker meeting she decried "the wormwood and the gall. . . . Oh, this wicked world!"

American soldiers had also brought woe after arriving on the farm in April to build Fort Mercer a hundred paces from their doorstep. When the Whitalls declined to sell a portion of their land, the Continentals took it. They then dismantled the Whitall barn for stockade timber, confiscated three thousand oak staves and forty-seven sheep, and cut down almost three hundred apple and peach trees to make a double abatis. Officers bivouacked in the two-story brick Whitall house and its fieldstone wing on the south end. A son, Job, recorded in his journal on October 10 that soldiers "turned us out of the kitchen, ye largest room upstairs, and ye shop." Two days later they "took 15 tons of hay, 60 bushels of wheat, 1,000 cedar boards, 85,000 rails, etc."

On Wednesday morning, October 22, Job wrote, "Day pleasant and fair. . . . Father and I hung the gate and finished the stacks." But when a neighbor alerted him to blue-coated soldiers approaching from Philadelphia, Job loaded his wife and children into a wagon, along with a sugar barrel, cider cask, and mahogany tea table. Herding twenty-one cows before him, he drove to an uncle's farm for refuge. James and Ann remained in their house, waiting for trouble.

Contrary to Colonel Donop's delusion, the Americans knew that he was coming. A patriot backwoodsman had run ten miles to inform the fort of Hessians on the march from Cooper's Ferry. "This evening we received certain intelligence that the enemy was a-coming to attack us, which obliged us to work all night long," a Continental officer wrote late Tuesday. Colonel Christopher Greene, a cousin of Nathanael Greene's and a veteran of both Bunker Hill and the Quebec campaign, left the Whitall house and moved back into the stockade, along with his officers, the expropriated sheep, and other livestock. Weapons were inspected, and even drummers and fifers received firelocks. Gunners sighted and primed their fourteen fieldpieces with double loads of grapeshot. The open gate, the nonchalant soldiers strolling outside the walls, the flapping laundry—all were a ruse.

Donop had also been misinformed about the fort. "The post with which you are now entrusted," Washington had written Greene on October 8, "is of the utmost importance to America. . . . The whole defense of the Delaware absolutely depends on it, and consequently all the enemy's hope of keeping Philadelphia." With guidance from Captain Mauduit du Plessis, the French engineer who had vainly tried to set fire to Cliveden during the Germantown battle, soldiers reduced the fort from a thousand feet long to a third of that in order to better fit a garrison of only five hundred men from the 1st and 2nd Rhode Island Continentals. Double-boarded walls built with Whitall lumber formed the new stockade, with fire steps on the parapet, an outer ditch fifteen feet wide, and those abatis of Whitall fruit trees. The original walls remained standing; that, too, was a ruse. "Unfortunately," a British officer later acknowledged, "our intelligence was bad."

Four hours after arriving in Red Bank, Donop was ready. Each regiment had been ordered to make a hundred fascines, cylindrical bundles of sticks that would be dumped in the outer ditch to build causeways. Yet some German officers had misgivings. The walls looked too stout for their small field guns. No one had thought to bring scaling ladders or tools to hack through the abatis. Rebel row galleys lurked nearby, but Royal Navy men-of-war were slow to warp close to Red Bank to provide naval gunfire. *Jäger* venturing near the fort had drawn cannon fire. The rebels were alert.

Donop waved off the doubters. At four p.m., as shadows began to stretch, he ordered a drummer to beat the signal for a parley. Major Charles Stuart, among the few Britons with the expedition, marched under a white flag to within two hundred feet of the gate to warn that "no quarter will be given" unless "the soldiers of Congress" surrendered immediately. Told that the fort would be defended to the "last extremity," Stuart marched back into the trees and told Donop, "Colonel Greene, who commands the fort, sends his compliments. He shall await Colonel Donop." A Hessian artillery captain told Ewald, "We have let luck slip through our fingers. . . . We will get a good beating."

Ten minutes later flame spurted from the Hessian gun line, and for a quarter of an hour balls rained down on Fort Mercer. "It made the gravel and dust fly from the top of our fort," wrote Captain Stephen Olney, "and took off all the heads that happened to be in the way." Then the cannonade stopped, more drums pounded, and the Hessian regiments surged forward—"rushed on very rash," a Rhode Islander noted—with *Jäger* marksmen covering their flanks. Greene watched with his pocket spyglass, then hopped down from the rampart. "Fire low, men," he said. "They have a broad belt just above their hips. Aim at that."

Fascines filled the ditch. Mustachioed grenadiers in tall brass hats chopped at the abatis with swords and knives, then stood on one another's shoulders to scale the outer wall. Encountering little resistance, they gave a great shout—"*Victoria!*"—and rushed toward the second abatis, clawing and hacking with a guttural roar.

Then hundreds of muskets appeared above the inner parapet, and a scorching volley blasted the grenadiers off their feet. "We began a smart fire with our artillery & our small arms . . . as smart as ever was known," wrote Sergeant John Smith of the 1st Rhode Island. Greene hoisted signal flags to summon reinforcements from Commodore Hazelwood's riverine squadron. Two row galleys advanced south through the shoreline reeds to pour grapeshot into the Hessian flanks, calling to the fort through brass speaking trumpets for advice on where to shoot.

Caught in a cross fire from the fort and the Delaware, Donop's men fell in heaps. Some were shot at such close range that gun wadding scorched them. A few timid Continentals kept their heads down and fired over the parapet "by guesswork," a witness reported, but an officer walked the line, "thrashing them with his hanger" to encourage fortitude and better marksmanship. Bodies piled up at the barred gate. Others tumbled down the riverbank, shot trying to escape the maelstrom. "There was nothing to do," a German lieutenant wrote, "but die or retire."

Many died. Others retired "in the most precipitated manner" back over the outer wall, an American officer reported, grapeshot and musket balls swarming around their ears. Forty minutes after it began, the "great slawter" ended. Donop had been hit in the upper left thigh. His adjutant lay near him, mortally wounded. "Both of his legs were shot to pieces and another bullet entered his mouth and came out through his cheek," a German major recorded. One grenadier regimental commander lay dead near the gateposts; another was wounded in both legs.

While leading a patrol to inspect the outer defenses, Captain Mauduit du Plessis found Donop behind a scrub pine. Six Continentals carried him on a blanket into the fort. "I am in your hands," he told them in French. "You may revenge yourselves." As night fell, survivors retreated "all in bustle and disorder" into the forest, then sloughed back toward Cooper's Ferry. No casualty wagons had accompanied the expedition, and shattered officers were laid across artillery carriages, the guns having been tossed into a creek. "I lost five of my oldest friends," Ewald wrote, "and four of my best friends were severely wounded. As long as I have served, I have not yet left a battlefield in such deep sorrow." Captain Francis Downman, commanding the two British howitzers, later wrote:

> This night's march was as melancholy and as disagreeable a one as ever I experienced. It was dark and excessively cold. The roads were deep and narrow and enclosed with wood. We lost our way twice. . . . Add to this the groans of the wounded.

Those unable to hobble away would lie on the battlefield until dawn. Skim ice formed on puddled blood. American soldiers carried the wounded one by one to the Whitall house, where doors lifted from their hinges served as surgical tables. Donop was also lugged from the fort to the house. "I am content," he was quoted as saying. "I die in the hands of honor itself." Ann Whitall proved to be a capable nurse while reminding the Hessians that they had "no one else to blame but themselves." The long night confirmed her instincts: there was ample wormwood and gall in this wicked world.

For the Royal Navy, worse was to come. On Admiral Howe's orders, a small squadron led by *Augusta*, a sixty-four-gun warship, had eased through the gap in the lower stackadoes near Billingsport at midday on Wednesday before gliding upriver toward Red Bank on light airs with topsails unfurled. Treacherous tides, a persistent north wind, a narrow river channel, and cannon fire from American shore batteries and gunboats bedeviled the pilots. Three ships had run aground earlier in the week, heaved off only with hawsers and expletives. By the time the men-of-war reached the upper stackadoes late Wednesday afternoon, five hundred yards from Fort Mercer, Colonel Donop's cause was lost. After a few truculent if ineffectual broadsides, the squadron turned back downstream at twilight.

The sloop-of-war *Merlin* promptly stuck fast near the mouth of Mantua Creek. As the flood tide ebbed, *Augusta* also "took the ground," in the phrase of her captain, Francis Reynolds. Admiral Howe would conclude that the stackadoes had altered the river's current enough to dislocate both the channel and its muddy bars. Stuck the ships remained through the night, despite efforts to pull off *Augusta*, despite dumping all drinking water to lighten her tonnage, and despite more curses. The north wind increased before dawn, flattening the next flood tide. "We hove without any effect," Reynolds reported.

Dawn on Thursday brought Royal Navy reinforcements up the Delaware but also a dozen rebel row galleys downriver, guns blazing. The floating batteries *Arnold* and *Putnam* joined in bombarding the stranded vessels. Gunners at Fort Mifflin fired heated shot, and glowing red pellets hissed as they skipped across the water. Four blazing fireships drifted south—*Comet*, *Hellcat*, *Volcano*, and *Aetna*—causing little damage but much chaos. Cannonballs hulled the forty-four-gun *Roebuck* several times and forced her downstream with six dead and ten wounded. With her keel embedded in the mud, *Augusta* continued flinging broadsides from an awkward angle. Spectators clustered on high ground above the Schuylkill. "The elements seemed to be in flames," one reported.

Captain Reynolds was pacing his quarterdeck at eleven a.m. when, he recounted, "I heard an odd crackling kind of noise." An officer sent to investigate returned to announce that the ship was on fire. Moments later, flames licked aft along the hull and through the captain's cabin. Americans would claim credit, but more likely wads from her own guns had ignited a pile of seamen's hammocks. Fire climbed the shrouds as seamen leaped into the river. Rescuers in barges and longboats plucked some to safety, including Reynolds; others sank, flailing, beneath the surface. A witness described *Augusta* "laying broadside-to aground, and the flames issuing through every port she had." From his flagship downriver, Admiral Howe ordered all vessels to stand away. *Merlin* was to be abandoned and burned.

Just past noon the inferno reached *Augusta*'s powder magazine. "I cannot think an eruption of Vesuvius could exceed it," Henry Strachey, the admiral's aide, wrote his wife. Spars, decking, and other debris rained across the Delaware. Shock waves sent concussion ghosts fluttering over sail canvas up and down the river. Washington's camp, sixteen miles northwest, heard the detonation. "We were stunned with a report as loud as a peal of a hundred cannon at once," Paine wrote Franklin. "I saw a thick smoke rising like a pillar and spreading from the top, like a tree." Howe would obscure his casualty figures, but Captain Montrésor wrote that "the chaplain, one lieutenant, and sixty men perished," some of them forsaken in the ship's sick bay. Several hours later, the abandoned *Merlin* also blew up.

Roebuck and *Isis* anchored near *Augusta*'s wreckage in a futile effort to fend off rebel scavengers, who soon recovered more than two dozen 24-pounders, twenty-seven silver watches, and some uncharred linen. The hulk would remain a menace to navigation for nearly a century, until her timbers were salvaged for furniture and woodwork in the headquarters of the Daughters of the American Revolution.

In two days rebels had caused the destruction of four Hessian regiments and a pair of Royal Navy warships. The remnants of Donop's brigade reached Cooper's Ferry at eleven a.m. on Thursday, just before *Augusta* exploded. More than twenty wounded men had died during the return march. Two British regiments with thirty wagons escorted the survivors across the river and into Philadelphia before midnight. Since setting out on Tuesday morning, wrote Captain Downman, "We had marched about forty-two miles and been well thrashed into the bargain."

Hessian losses from Fort Mercer approached four hundred killed, wounded, and captured, compared to thirty-seven Americans. In Red Bank, Colonel Greene's men could hardly keep up with stripping the German dead and interring them in mass graves, since more died hour by hour. The Mirbach Regiment, accustomed to drowsy garrison duty except for the forty sanguinary minutes at Fort Mercer, lost its colonel and ninety-five others dead or injured. "Poor Lieutenant Schotten's right arm was amputated," a Hessian officer wrote. "He has been practicing writing with the left and it's going well." Nicholas Collin, a Swedish pastor whose church was nearby, hurried to the Whitall house to find wounded Germans sprawled from cellar to attic. A few read from little Lutheran prayer books. Collin told his journal:

> About 200 were lying on straw in two large rooms, some without arms and legs. Outside the house lay two piles of arms and legs. . . . Some floated in blood and told me that others had died for lack of something to bandage their wounds with. While I was there several men died in great agony and convulsions.

Colonel Donop was moved to a more commodious farmhouse on Woodbury Creek. "I did my duty as a soldier," he told one of his officers. "But as a brigadier, I behaved like an ensign." He made a dying bequest to General Knyphausen of his favorite horse, "a chestnut with the finest saddle and equipment." Captain Mauduit du Plessis quoted him as saying, "I die a victim of my own ambition and my sovereign's avarice."

He crossed over at eight-thirty p.m. on October 29. "Now he is with his ancestors," a comrade observed. "It is too bad that he was so loud and ambitious. Otherwise he was a good fellow." Donop was buried near the fort, feet facing the river, with the honors of war provided by four hundred Continentals. Musketmen fired three volleys. Grave robbers would find him soon enough, chipping away the sandstone tomb marker, stealing his bones as relics, and imbedding his teeth in the handles of walking sticks. For some time a New Jersey physician kept his skull.

"How German bones are scattered around in this war," Ewald wrote. Since leaving the fatherland, the Hessian Corps, the largest of the German contingents, had lost an estimated twenty-two hundred of fourteen thousand men. Surviving officers sent detailed accounts of Red Bank to Landgraf Friedrich II, softening the news by including acorns from ten varieties of American oak trees, sewn in linen pouches, for the prince's foresters to plant. But Fort Mercer, following the severe losses at Trenton and Bennington, would prove a turning point for the Germans. Except for a few elite units like the *Jäger*, their future contributions to King George's war would be modest, if not marginal. "We have lost our desire to serve the English," an officer wrote.

The Whitall family reclaimed their bloodied house, yet no peace came to the farm. At a Continental Army court-martial on October 31, a loyalist scout and a black slave were convicted of "conducting ye enemy through the country [and] for being spies & traitors." With Greene's garrison attending under arms, the defendants were hanged the next morning on a scaffold fifty yards from the Whitalls' front door. The bodies dangled in their nooses until dusk as an admonition to opponents of the cause. During the next month, British foragers further pillaged the farm, snatching not only livestock but, as Job Whitall wrote on November 21, "our bread, pie, milk, cheese, meat dishes, cups, spoons."

James and Ann would submit an invoice to the state of New Jersey, asking £5,760 as compensation for damages that included "one barn and hay house totally destroyed," along with "an orchard [of] near three hundred grafted trees." Authorities ignored the request. The bill was never paid.

*   *   *

The disaster at Red Bank forced the Howe brothers to redouble their efforts to take Fort Mifflin, just south of Philadelphia. "We are just now an army without provisions," Captain Montrésor confided to his diary on November 1. Shortages extended beyond rations to firewood, ammunition, winter clothing, and cash, although somehow fifty hogsheads of rum had reached the Schuylkill from Delaware Bay on eight flatboats. Horses had little forage "so that they are all perishing," Captain Münchhausen, General Howe's aide, wrote on November 3. Confirmation of Burgoyne's surrender left the army "somewhat dejected," Montrésor added. Knyphausen was among the crestfallen. "I believe that the ability to make progress in this campaign is gone," the Hessian commander wrote. "We will have to act defensively."

The bombardment of Fort Mifflin began in a gusty rain on Monday morning, November 10. Heavy guns on Province and Carpenter's Islands fired eighty rounds each, bolstered by howitzers and mortars. Teamsters drove thirty-five wagons of ammunition from the statehouse lawn to replenish British batteries. Cannonballs slammed into the fort's blockhouses, buildings, and palisade. Captain Samuel Treat, the garrison artillery chief, was among the casualties. "A slight squeeze of the hand and he expired," reported Lieutenant Colonel Samuel Smith, Fort Mifflin's commander. "No wound was apparent." To General Washington, Smith wrote, "The fort will be laid open and everything destroyed if they continue to cannonade and bombard us. . . . Our men, already half-jaded to death with constant fatigue, will be unfit for service." From Whitemarsh, northwest of the city, the commander in chief urged Smith to stand fast "till the latest extremity." Soon, surely, the river would freeze, immobilizing enemy ships and forcing Howe from Philadelphia.

For now, autumn rains flooded the Fort Mifflin parade ground under two feet of water. The barrage resumed early Tuesday and continued Wednesday. A British ball punched through a barracks chimney before striking Smith in the left hip and dislocating his wrist. Covered in brick dust, he was evacuated across the river to Fort Mercer. American hopes tumbled, rose, and tumbled again. A hundred reinforcements arrived from Red Bank late Wednesday night under Major Simeon Thayer of the 2nd Rhode Island, bringing the beleaguered garrison to over three hundred men, each of them miserable. "It was utterly impossible to lie down to get any rest or sleep on account of the mud," wrote Joseph Plumb Martin. Defenders used splinters from the smashed palisades to build campfires. Lookouts cried "A shot!" whenever they spotted a British muzzle flash; the men dived for cover, then burned their hands retrieving red-hot British cannonballs to fire back.

But there was no dodging the British onslaught. "I saw men who were stooping to be protected by the works—but not stooping low enough—split like fish to be broiled," Martin wrote. Some of the seventy men killed were interred in graves scooped from the mud wall on the western flank. The capable garrison engineer, Major François Louis Teisseydre, the Marquis de Fleury, prodded shirkers with his cane to patch the shattered fortifications with planks, "rammed earth," and even discarded sentry boxes. Fires ignited by incendiary mortar rounds were smothered with wet rawhides. "We will defend the ground inch by inch," Fleury told his diary on November 14, "and the enemy shall pay dearly for every step."

The end came a day later, on Saturday, November 15, the sixth day of bombardment. That morning the *Grand Duchess of Russia*, an old East Indiaman refurbished in New York as a shallow-draft gunship and renamed *Vigilant*, crept on a rising tide along the Delaware's western bank before dropping anchor forty yards from the back side of Fort Mifflin. With marine marksmen in her tops protected by large bags of cotton, *Vigilant* opened fire with fourteen 24-pounders on the starboard side of her upper deck, joined by three more big guns aboard the sloop *Fury*. The men-of-war *Roebuck*, *Isis*, *Liverpool*, *Pearl*, and *Somerset*, brandishing more than two hundred guns among them, raked both the front of the fort and another American battery across the river. "Such a thunder of cannon never was heard in America before," wrote Colonel Israel Angell, who watched the spectacle from Fort Mercer.

One Continental officer estimated that at the height of the bombardment more than a thousand artillery rounds were fired in twenty minutes. Fort Mifflin's surviving guns soon fell silent. Grapeshot, musket fire, and grenades showered the fort from *Vigilant*'s upper works "so that it was almost impossible for a man to move without being killed," a witness reported. Commodore Hazelwood's river squadron closed to within four hundred yards of *Vigilant*, but a British cross fire drove away the boats, damaging eleven of twelve row galleys and killing or wounding almost forty sailors.

"The whole area of the fort was as completely plowed as a field," Martin wrote, "and the guns all dismounted. . . . If ever destruction was complete, it was here." Major Thayer could only agree, writing, "We have lost a great many men today. . . . We shall be obliged to evacuate the fort this night." After dark the garrison rowed with muffled oars across the river to Fort Mercer, leaving Thayer and a rear guard of forty volunteers to set the ruins on fire at midnight before also stealing away. "We were all surprised to see the fort in flames," Captain Downman wrote. "It burnt very fiercely all night."

Daybreak on Sunday showed the tattered Stars and Stripes still flying. As the Howe brothers and General Cornwallis stood in spitting snow to watch from the Pennsylvania shore, boats from Carpenter's Island carried two hundred of the king's men to claim the fort. Seamen tore down the rebel colors and ran up a Union Jack. "In almost every place you see blood and brains dashed about," Downman wrote. Redcoats stripped the dead of their shoes, he added, then tossed the bodies into a ditch "with as little concern or feeling as a butcher shows in killing or cutting up an ox."

Still, a grudging admiration obtained. "The Americans," Serle wrote, "defended it with a spirit they have shown nowhere else." Henry Knox concurred, telling Lucy, "The defense of Fort Mifflin is as gallant as to be found in history."

With the loss of Fort Mifflin, other American defenses on the Delaware were doomed. At William Howe's command, Cornwallis led two thousand British troops across the river from Chester to approach Fort Mercer from the south. The redcoats moved swiftly toward Red Bank, crossing streams on a portable bridge hinged with copper plates and transported in a heavy wagon; unlike Colonel Donop's star-crossed expedition, this column carried siege guns and scaling ladders. On the night of November 19, Colonel Greene and his garrison, outnumbered five to one, scattered gunpowder across the stockade, struck a spark, then bolted from the burning fort across Big Timber Creek, to the northeast. Cornwallis found only charred ruins.

At three o'clock the next morning, Commodore Hazelwood led thirteen row galleys and a dozen guard boats undetected along the Jersey shoreline toward safe haven in Bristol, twenty-five miles upstream on the Pennsylvania side of the river. But contrary north winds gripped the squadron's sailing vessels, and British shore batteries spotted them drifting on the tide in the moonlight early on November 21. The frigate *Delaware*, now flying the king's white ensign, chased a schooner aground, where she burned to her ribs. A few small craft escaped north, but the rest of the squadron was abandoned and set ablaze, including the brigantine *Andrew Doria*, the xebecs *Repulse* and *Champion*, a pair of sloops, and the two floating batteries. Their crews fled toward Burlington. Another crowd gathered along the Philadelphia docklands to gape at the flaming masts and sails mirrored in the black water. "There was never a more beautiful fireworks than the one caused by fifteen burning ships during the dark night," wrote Captain Münchhausen. "As soon as the fire reached the powder magazines, they blew up with loud explosions. It was the most spectacular sight I have ever seen."

Howe completed the inferno by ordering almost a dozen large country manors torched, along with barns and outbuildings, ostensibly to keep rebel snipers from firing out the windows at British pickets. Philadelphians counted the blazes from their rooftops; most of the houses, they soon realized, belonged to loyalists. The king's men, an American major wrote, "seem to have given up the thoughts of conquering by force of arms and are determined to frighten the people into submission by their ravages & burnings."

On Sunday, November 23, nearly two months after the city's capture, the first sloops and small merchantmen carrying British wares berthed along Philadelphia's wharves. Within four days, as sailors ripped more stackadoes from the river bottom to open the channel, sixty vessels rode at anchor off the city, with many more working upstream from Delaware Bay. "The Delaware never had near the number of ships on it as are at present," the *Pennsylvania Evening Post* reported, "there being supposed to be upwards of four hundred." But Robert Morton, a sixteen-year-old Quaker boy, was unimpressed. "A British army of 12,000 men and a fleet of 300 sail," he told his diary, "had been detained in their operations near seven weeks by a power far inferior to theirs."

As his army settled in around him for the winter, General Howe commandeered a large house on the south side of High Street with fluted columns, mahogany balusters, and walls three bricks thick. The British commander considered his work in America to be finished. His brother had advised London that William now believed crushing the rebellion was "of greater compass than he feels himself able to direct." He was weary, discouraged, and at odds with the ministry over the forces needed to win. In a dispatch to Lord Germain, the general formally asked the king's permission to resign. "I am led to hope I may be relieved from this very painful service, wherein I have not had the good fortune to enjoy the necessary confidence of my superiors," he wrote. Without an additional ten thousand reinforcements by late spring, "there is no prospect of terminating the war," and he wanted no part of it. Meanwhile, he needed another £300,000 to cover the "extraordinary expenses of the forces."

Until hearing a reply from his government, he would tighten his grip on eastern Pennsylvania and make the army comfortable. Few officers complained about spending the winter in Philadelphia. "The only hardships I endure are being obliged to sleep in my bed, to sit down to a very good dinner every day, to take a gentle ride for appetite's sake or to exercise my horses," wrote Captain John André, who now occupied Dr. Franklin's vacant home. Gambling tables could be found at the Indian Queen and the Bunch of Grapes, and cockfights in Moore's Alley drew wagers as high as a hundred guineas. Tutors advertised instruction in the violin, clarinet, and German flute, or three months of French lessons for $21.

Officers hosted balls at City Tavern on Thursday nights. They formed supper clubs with names like the Friendly Brothers and the Society of Journeymen Tailors, and they advertised for servants capable of both dressing their hair and grooming their horses. Howe's Strolling Players settled into the Southwark Theater, on Cedar Street. With a stage illuminated by oil lamps and box seats selling for a dollar, the first comedies would open to a full house in January—*No One's Enemy but His Own* and *The Deuce Is in Him.* Captain André was lauded for his skill as a scenery painter—his "foliage was uncommonly spirited and graceful," a theater patron wrote—and Howe himself could be found in his stage box at most Monday performances, a twinkle in those usually impenetrable eyes.

Hessian officers admired Philadelphia's broad streets and handsome public buildings. "A wide stone pavement in front of the houses makes walking very easy," a captain wrote, "and I must admit that this is better than in Göttingen." Runaway slaves, rebel deserters, and loyalist refugees soon flooded the town. Howe ordered five thousand uniforms to outfit provincial troops willing to fight for their king; he failed to fill more than a quarter of them, despite recruitment posters that offered loyalist enlistees a bonus of fifty acres "where every gallant hero may retire and enjoy his bottle and lass."

Even so, taverns echoed with the roar of loyalists belting out "Britons, Strike Home" or "God Save the King." Transport ships brought merchants and artisans in long leather aprons from New York and Halifax to open new shops on Water, Front, and Second Streets. An occupation newspaper, the *Royal Pennsylvania Gazette*, advertised cricket bats, a haberdasher on Third Street offered to clean "officer's epaulettes . . . with as much elegance as any in London or Paris," and Henry Johns, on Second Street, peddled ivory forks, tea trays, and candle snuffers. Dr. Anthony Yeldall touted his "Anti-Venereal Essence," which not only cured disease "but will also effectually prevent catching the infection. . . . No questions need to be asked. Two dollars."

Auctions of household furniture—some of it looted—were held on Tuesdays. The *Evening Post* regularly promoted a different commodity: "To be sold, a mulatto girl, about 13 or 14 years of age, who has had the smallpox." Handbills invited farmers to bring their wares to market on Wednesdays and Saturdays for payment in sterling, although reports circulated that those whom the rebels caught trading with the British would be branded on the forehead with the initials "WH"—William Howe. Yet all in all, a Hessian captain wrote, "we are well-supplied with all that is necessary and superfluous. Assemblies, concerts, comedies, clubs, and the like make us forget there is any war."

WH was not likely to forget the war, or the twenty thousand Continental soldiers lurking somewhere just to the west. A thousand British and German troops now manned redoubts on the city's perimeter; the guard changed every two days. Howe had increased the civilian night watch from 17 to 120 men, but burglary, rape, and theft spiked during the occupation. "These are sad times for thieving & plundering," Elizabeth Drinker wrote in her diary on December 11. "'Tis hardly safe to leave the door open a minute." Drunken misbehavior also increased, and in mid-December Howe ordered restrictions on "public houses, dram shops, and retailers of strong liquors."

Ice had begun to obstruct the Delaware, giving rebel marauders opportunities for plunder. "We have dilly-dallied and shilly-shallied till the river is frozen up," wrote Captain Downman, "by which means several of our ships have been caught, stripped of their cargo, and then set on fire." Stackadoe remnants also continued to plague navigation, even sinking luckless vessels like the *Juliana*, carrying peas, raisins, and bread for the garrison. Three thousand horses required twenty-four tons of hay each day, and in December Howe launched two modestly successful foraging expeditions into the countryside, one that he led personally, with seven thousand men, and another under Cornwallis, with five thousand. Yet firewood was already scarce; redcoats who volunteered as woodcutters could earn five shillings a cord.

Food, ammunition, and blankets had been stockpiled in warehouses, but provisioning more than forty thousand soldiers and civilians through the winter would bedevil British supply officers. "We cannot with safety go a hundred yards beyond our lines without a large escort," the new commissary general, Daniel Wier, warned in late November. "We can expect no supplies or assistance from this country, but must place our whole dependence on what we receive from the other side of the water."

With the fourth year of war soon to begin, William Howe was not the only officer to sour on the endeavor, notwithstanding City Tavern balls and occasional guffaws at the Southwark Theater. "I grow every day more and more disgusted with the folly & iniquity of the cause in which I am condemned to serve," Captain Richard Fitzpatrick, a Guards officer and member of Parliament, wrote his brother, the Earl of Upper Ossory. Brigadier General James Pattison, who had recently arrived from England to command the Royal Artillery detachments, also wrote his brother in December. "All the efforts that Great Britain can make will never effectively conquer this great continent," he warned, adding:

> We have not only armies to combat, but a whole country, where every man, woman, and even child is your enemy. . . . Ministers have been deceived and have never known the true state of this country. If they had, they never would have entered into a war with it.

At six p.m. on December 11, the Continental Army crossed the Schuylkill at Swedes Ford on two bridges built by French engineers—one fashioned from rafts and the other from planks laid across thirty-six wagons. For some veterans, this was their thirteenth crossing of the river during the fall campaign, which had begun more than three months earlier on Little Neshaminy Creek. When the last oxcart reached the southern bank at sunrise, the army pressed on to Gulph Mills, sixteen miles northwest of Howe's mansion on High Street. Five brigades from the Northern Army had arrived, along with a limping Lafayette—"the marquis is determined to be in the way of danger," General Greene observed—giving Washington more than nineteen thousand troops, plus four hundred women and children. This host would loiter for a week at Gulph Mills while the high command plotted its next move.

"The leaves and ground were as wet as water could make them," wrote Joseph Plumb Martin. "We were starved and as cross and ill-natured as curs." Often only gunpowder ignited on sodden kindling could start a campfire. On December 14, after a supper of thin soup "full of burnt leaves and dirt," Dr. Albigence Waldo, a surgeon in the 1st Connecticut, told his diary, "Poor food. Hard lodging. Cold weather. Fatigue. Nasty clothes. Nasty cookery. Vomit half my time. Smoked out of my senses. The devil's in it. I can't endure it. Why are we sent here to starve and freeze?"

Camp scuttlebutt swirled along with the smoke and snow flurries: General Howe had been wounded; he was tearing up paving stones in Philadelphia; most of New York had burned down; the British were deflowering virgins and kidnapping young boys. Also, Franklin had been assassinated in Paris, or had fled France for Prussia, or was negotiating peace terms with King George.

Amid the lurid rumors, scraps of news also circulated, some good, some disheartening. A French ship had arrived in New Hampshire with forty-eight brass cannons, eighteen mortars, and thirty tons of sulfur. A tent fire had badly burned five men sorting musket cartridges and incinerated six thousand rounds. Maryland troops in Wilmington had seized several sloops and an armed brig carrying a thousand enemy stand of arms. Soldiers were ripping the leather from cartridge boxes to wrap their bare feet, despite a $10 reward offered by Washington to any man who could "produce the best substitute for shoes made of raw hides."

Congress honored the victory at Saratoga by proclaiming Thursday, December 18, a national day of "thanksgiving and praise." Chaplains preached from Exodus 15—the triumphant song of Moses at the Red Sea—or Deuteronomy 23:14: "for the Lord thy God walketh in the midst of thy camp to deliver thee and to give up thine enemies before thee." Yet after three days of heavy rain, without flour, bread, or decent meat, Thursday's dinner for Washington's troops was hardly more than a half gill of rice and a tablespoon of vinegar, believed to ward off scurvy. Major Dearborn, who had rejoined the main army after surviving the battles at Freeman's farm and Bemus Heights, advised his journal, "All we have to be thankful for is that we are alive & not in the grave with many of our friends."

Where "thy camp" should be located for the winter had preoccupied Washington for weeks. Castrametation—the art of laying out a military bivouac—was considered vital to preserving an army's security, health, and morale. No less an authority than Frederick the Great declared that it was "one of the primary studies that a general should make." Congress had pressed Washington to unite the Continental Army and militia for an attack on Philadelphia, but when he surveyed his senior lieutenants in early December, all twenty-one of them opposed such a move as imprudent. Greene wrote twenty-three paragraphs to explain his misgivings, and Knox invoked Frederick's maxim that "the first object of winter quarters is tranquility." Some of the commander in chief's officers recommended wintering at Wilmington; others suggested Lancaster or Reading. Congress, although a hundred miles from danger, wanted the army interposed between Howe's legions and the temporary capital in York.

At ten a.m. on December 19, the army set forth again, nineteen thousand men headed west. "The sun shone out this morning, being the first time I had seen it for seven days, which seemed to put new life into everything," wrote Lieutenant Samuel Armstrong of the 8th Massachusetts. Sunshine soon yielded to a snow squall. "We marched all the day without provisions," Colonel Israel Angell noted in his diary. "The roads was excessive bad and our horses very poor and weak." As the winter sun set, at just past four-thirty, the column halted for a paltry supper of raw corn. The Continental Army was home.

Here then was Valley Forge, a thirty-five-hundred-acre triangular swatch of wooded uplands, sparsely peopled by Welsh Quakers. Overnight it would become the fourth-largest town in America. Dominated by Mount Joy—named by William Penn a century earlier—and its topographical twin, the presciently dubbed Mount Misery, much of the forest primeval endured in thickets of ash and black birch, poplar and sugar maple, hickory and chestnut oak. Viburnum and dogwood limned the meadows, and frosted hawthorn brightened thickets with brilliant red fruit that resembled beads of blood.

Washington had chosen this rugged place as near enough to Philadelphia—twenty-four miles—to harass loyalists and the king's men, yet sufficiently remote to allow his army what he hoped would be a placid winter while girding for the spring campaign. Three creeks provided clean water, and a gristmill had survived a British raid earlier in the fall. Fatland Ford, on the adjacent Schuylkill, offered an escape route to the north, as needed. Continental magazines in Reading and Pottsgrove were accessible by river, and Congress was close enough—eighty miles west, across the Susquehanna. "The general seems resolved to keep us together," Brigadier General Jedediah Huntington wrote his brother in Connecticut on December 20. "I wish I could tell you I was coming home to see you. Instead I am going to build me a house in the woods."

Castrametation began in earnest that morning in twenty-five-degree weather. Within an eight-mile perimeter, engineers marked out fifteen brigade laagers, which would be further carved up for individual regiments. Timbering squads were told how to cut tree trunks for huts, of which hundreds would be built in the coming weeks.

Yet Valley Forge was ghastly from the start. A survey of the army, General Sullivan told Washington, revealed "the whole of them without watch coats, one-half without blankets, & more than a third without shoes, stockings, or breeches . . . & not a few without shirts." Washington tallied 2,898 privates "unfit for duty because they are barefoot and otherwise naked," including all but eighteen men in a New York regiment. "To add to this miserable tale," that regiment's commander added, "we are becoming exceedingly lousy. I am myself not exempted." Although Congress had promised winter uniforms, "it is as yet upon paper only," a colonel wrote. "I wish the army could see something real." Clothier General James Mease, a Philadelphia merchant, was so overmatched that Anthony Wayne complained bitterly of soldiers perishing "of a disorder called the Meases, i.e., for want of clothing."

They were perishing of other afflictions, too. Dr. Rush, now surgeon general for the Middle Department, disclosed in mid-December that he had believed that the thirteen army hospitals in Pennsylvania, New Jersey, and Maryland housed three thousand patients, including men wounded at Brandywine, Germantown, and the Delaware forts. "I have discovered that they now amount to five thousand," Rush wrote, plus thousands of others in the care of regimental medicos. Almost a third of the army was sick. "A great majority of those who die under our hands perish with fevers caught in our hospitals," Rush added. Hundreds more, while not incapacitated, were tormented by scabies, better known as Scotch fiddle or simply "the itch," caused by a burrowing mite and treated, often ineffectually, with a paste of sulfur and hog's lard.

Despite these troubles, Washington had secretly decided to ignore his generals' caution and attack Philadelphia. Spies told him that half of Howe's army had marched toward Chester and into southern New Jersey on another foraging sortie; the commander in chief intended to strike the remaining garrison on Christmas Day with two assault wings bolstered by militia and Continental troops summoned from Wilmington. But the plan collapsed before Washington could even issue preliminary orders: an alarming report from the commissary on December 22 revealed that not a single cow could be found for slaughter—the army normally consumed eight hundred a week—and that no more than twenty-five barrels of flour remained on hand, far short of the two hundred needed each day. Warehouses in Lancaster, York, and Head of Elk contained provisions, but the army lacked enough wagons and pull teams to bring adequate supplies to camp, since each round-trip to those depots over dreadful winter roads took an average of twelve days.

"His Excellency amazed and highly offended at this failure," noted Lieutenant Colonel Charles Stewart, the deputy quartermaster general. Another officer quoted Washington as saying, "Damn it." The officer then commented, "This is language that His Excellency is by no means accustomed to use and you may judge of the provocation when he is obliged to adopt it." Aide-de-camp John Laurens wrote, "I could weep tears of blood."

An urgent meeting of general officers in Washington's marquee confirmed that mass insubordination in the ranks threatened to spiral into mutiny. Soldiers ordered into formation chanted, "No meat, no meat" and sullenly imitated the calls of owls and crows. The lucky ones might scavenge a small pumpkin to roast on a hot rock or an ear of corn to pound into porridge. "Hunger will break through a stone wall," Brigadier General James Mitchell Varnum warned, paraphrasing Shakespeare in *Coriolanus*. "The men must be supplied or they cannot be commanded." To Henry Laurens in York, Washington wrote on December 23, "Unless some great and capital change suddenly takes place . . . this army must inevitably be reduced to one or other of these three things: starve, dissolve, or disperse. . . . This is not an exaggerated picture." Laurens, in turn, wrote Governor William Livingston of New Jersey, "Our whole system is tottering, & God only knows whether we shall be able to prop it up."

Earlier in the fall, Congress had granted Washington authority to seize needed provisions from Pennsylvanians, "leaving such quantities only as he shall judge necessary for the maintenance of their families." He had been reluctant to alienate his civilian neighbors, lest they turn against both the army and the larger cause. But now he set aside such scruples. Detachments from each brigade were to collect livestock, grain, salt, and other provisions in exchange for receipts to be redeemed by Congress, someday. All farmers within a seventy-mile radius were ordered to thresh their stored wheat and rye or risk having it confiscated as mere straw.

"We have hardly been here six days and are already suffering for want of everything," Major General Kalb wrote a friend in France. "What will be done when the roads grow worse and the season more severe?" On Christmas Eve, Continental rustlers brought in seven hundred head of cattle and enough other foodstuffs to carry the army through the year's end. Yet a supply officer admitted, "What will be the fate of tomorrow, I know not. . . . Our case is bad."

The holy day came and went. "We have not so merry a Christmas," Major Dearborn wrote in his journal. Sergeant John Smith of the 1st Rhode Island recorded, "Nothing remarkable except it snowed a little at night." The year straggled to a close, ending what would remain the war's bloodiest in terms of American combat casualties, exclusive of deaths from disease or in British prisons. In 266 military engagements and 42 naval skirmishes, 1777 had left 1,517 dead in battle and nearly 5,000 wounded, captured, or missing.

Yet the aggregate tally hardly conveyed the anguish that was measured, as always in war, by individual calamity and private, bottomless suffering. Sergeant Oliver Reed, a thirty-one-year-old veteran in the 4th Connecticut, had served since the earliest days of the war. At Fort Mifflin he had seen his captain shot dead by a musket ball through the neck. Then a letter from his wife, Betty, at home in Pomfret, reported that typhus had killed three of their four children, all under the age of six. "I never see nobody die in such distress as he did," she wrote of their son Chester, not yet three. "He had his senses till the last, and the last words he said was, 'I am a-coming, I am a-coming, I am a-coming.'"

Sergeant Reed, heartsick beyond comprehension, would follow his duty at Valley Forge, but he, too, was coming. Death claimed him before he had given another year to the cause. And Betty, now widowed with but one surviving child, would inform Oliver's family, "Bone of your bone and flesh of your flesh is gone and is no more among the living, but is congregated with the dead."

Part Two

11.

———◦———

The King's War

War brought Britain's animal spirits to a roar. A dispatch from Brandy-wine had arrived at Plymouth in early November and was printed in the *London Chronicle* to widespread jubilation. The king's ministers and courtiers "received this news with transports of joy," one diarist noted, although cynics suspected a ruse to manipulate the stock market, which indeed went up. Subsequent reports of Philadelphia's capture caused another "wild tumult of joy."

War was what great powers did in pursuit of commercial wealth, if not hegemony, and between 1695 and 1815 Britain was at war more often than at peace. She now laid fair claim to being the world's largest shipbuilder, with the world's greatest navy and merchant fleet, as well as a global center for international trade, banking, and insurance. War contracts benefited merchants, shippers, smelters, and makers of munitions, textiles, shoes, medical supplies, and a hundred other commodities. Opticians around St. Paul's churchyard sold brass spyglasses to army and naval officers, and the seaport of Poole, in Dorset, specialized in making the sails needed by several thousand British ships. Not coincidentally, of forty-six major contractors providing the government with war matériel and services in America, eighteen were members of Parliament and eighteen others had close ties to members.

Trade with rebellious America had been prohibited since 1775, but new European customers compensated for that loss. "The orders from Russia and Germany are greater than ever were known," *Lloyd's Evening Post* reported. English velvets found new markets in Naples and Messina. Pig-iron production was doubling every eight years, and advances like Richard Arkwright's water frame and James Hargreaves's spinning jenny brought enormous gains in cloth manufacturing. "The age," lexicographer Samuel Johnson observed with pride, "is running mad after innovation."

The author Daniel Defoe had divided the British people into seven groups: "the great, the rich, the middle sort, the working trades, the country people, the poor, and the miserable." Prosperity was hardly spread evenly. Blue bloods dined on turtle and malmsey—a fortified, sweet Madeira—and quarreled in French so that eavesdropping servants could not understand them. A typical laborer, by contrast, earned £27 a year, a tradesman perhaps £40. Life remained hard if not brutish for a chambermaid required to know the nine steps in washing lace or for the two thousand Britons jailed for unpaid debts, despite palliative efforts by the Society for the Relief of Persons Imprisoned for Small Sums.

War came with costs of course, and not just for the amputees periodically seen hobbling down a gangplank at Portsmouth on vessels newly arrived from New York or Philadelphia. Roughly £8 of every £10 of public money was spent on military purposes. The first year of the American war had added another £3.5 million to government debt, still swollen from the £100 million accrued during the Seven Years' War. The country gentry grumbled about taxes, since almost a quarter of the Crown's revenue derived from the land tax. Excise taxes also went up and up. A foreign visitor wrote that "the English are taxed in the morning for the soap that washes their hands, at nine for coffee, tea, and the sugar they use at breakfast, at noon for the starch that powders their hair, at dinner for the salt that savors their meat, and for the beer they drink."

But if thirteen Crown colonies were in rebellion, fourteen others—mostly Caribbean islands—remained a loyal, docile source of wealth. Some 1,800 West Indies plantations provided a hundred thousand hogsheads of sugar annually for British jams, gingerbread, chocolate, and tea—Britons consumed more sugar and rum per capita than anyone on earth. This white gold made the rich richer, although it, too, brought complications. Troops were needed to protect the 50,000 planters from uprisings by 275,000 black slaves. Provisions to feed chattel, masters, and soldiers no longer came from nearby America, and this year several thousand of the enslaved had died of malnutrition and related diseases on Antigua, St. Kitts, and other islands in the Leeward chain. That required diverting some cane fields to cropland while also shipping salt meat and other provender to the islands from Britain; this, in turn, required armed convoys to fend off rebel privateers and to escort home the sugar, rum, molasses, and coffee.

Running an empire had never been simple.

The sounds of imperium were loudest in London, heard in the squeal of wooden axles and iron-shod wagon wheels rolling over the granite setts along Thames Street from Puddle Dock, and in the bellow of carters and sedan-chair carriers crying, "By your leave, sir!" as they eased through the crowds around the city's forty-two markets. Butchers in their stalls urged, "Rally up! Rally up!," and bawling vendors offered Yarmouth herrings, Essex mutton, and ham trimmed thin enough to read a newspaper through the slices. It was said that two hundred thousand rural families worked to provide London with bread, and countless others fed a city that annually consumed seven hundred thousand sheep and lambs, eighteen hundred tons of butter and cheese, and twenty million gallons of rum, brandy, wine, and gin, which also was known as cock-my-cap, poverty, heart's-ease, and strip-me-naked.

Women sold milk from pails on a yoke, sometimes enhanced with chalk and water scooped from a horse trough. Mountebanks on street corners touted nostrums: fried mice for whooping cough or incontinence, a broth made of puppies and a stewed owl for bronchitis, or a bit of powdered human skull in William Lowther's Medicinal Compound for epilepsy and memory loss. (An inventive dentist advised using one's own urine for toothbrushing, with a few grains of gunpowder to "give your teeth an inconceivable whiteness.") Bells clanged on the river wherries and pealed from St. Martin-in-the-Fields and St. Margaret's, in Westminster, answered by the infernal racket of dice boxes in Fleet Street coffeehouses. Petty criminals sat in the stocks at Charing Cross to be pelted with ordure by passersby—no rocks permitted—while royal proclamations were read out nearby. Profanity and execration floated through the London air like coal smoke. "Englishmen are mighty swearers," a foreign visitor observed. "I consider this another of their defects."

For every sound there was a sight, and for every sight a smell. Mackerel boats, produce victuallers, barges, colliers, and three-masters from the wide world plied the pungent, briny Thames. The city was so crowded that physicians urged their patients to loiter on the river bridges for a whiff of fresh air. Streetlamps were lighted at sunset regardless of the moon's phase; it was claimed that more lamps glowed along Oxford Road alone than in all of Paris, although wary pedestrians had to dodge dripping oil. The aggrieved and insulted fought duels with rapiers or pistols in Hyde Park, in Kensington Gardens, and particularly in the Field of Forty Footsteps, behind Montague House. Crowds flocked to cockfights and dog fights, badger and bull baiting, and bare-knuckle boxing matches lasting thirty rounds. A female pugilist known as Bruising Peg drew particular acclaim.

The broad-shouldered town made as much as it consumed, thanks to the skinners, tanners, and glue makers in Southwark; the brewers, distillers, and coopers in Lothbury; and the tinware makers in Crooked Lane, flax dressers in Moorgate, curriers at London Wall, whalebone boilers in Whalebone Court, and horners making lanthorns in Inkhorn Court. No city was more vivid, or as chockablock with diversions and oddities. Mrs. Salomon's Waxworks, in Fleet Street, displayed Antony and Cleopatra, King Charles I on the scaffold, and the Turkish sultan's seraglio. Bethlehem Hospital—Bedlam—earned up to £400 a year by charging visitors admission to gape at the lunatics. Rackstraw's Museum of Anatomy featured stuffed crocodiles, a whale skeleton, and a "reproductive organ department." The curious could spend a shilling to watch a man eat stones, a "Learned Pig" tell time, or a family of porcupines imported from the New World mostly sleep. Theater tickets at Drury Lane or Covent Garden ranged from a shilling to four and sixpence. The inestimable David Garrick had retired the previous year at age fifty-nine; in his last performance as Lear, the actresses playing Goneril and Regan sobbed openly at his departure from the stage.

"When a man is tired of London," Samuel Johnson had famously observed in September, "he is tired of life." Perhaps so, although the city was also notorious as the world's suicide capital, despite the enduring medieval custom of burying the self-murdered at a crossroads with a stake through the heart.

Dr. Johnson was contemptuous of American rebels and spoke of them "with sulfurous vapor," according to James Boswell, his biographer. For most of London's 750,000 denizens, the war remained remote, half a world away. Yet a certain anxiety obtained, even among those who swaggered with imperial pride. British and German casualties in North America now totaled roughly fifteen thousand, and the war had already cost at least £20 million, making more taxes inevitable. American privateers in 1776 had captured or spoiled twenty-five thousand hogsheads of sugar, contributing to the collapse of four West Indies merchant companies in London, according to the historian Andrew Jackson O'Shaughnessy. Now rebel raiders often took two or three merchantmen a day in the Windward Islands and had captured valuable vessels in the Jamaica fleet. Privateers snatched additional prizes in European and American waters, causing freight rates to triple; for the first time, convoys were needed to protect the Irish linen trade. Insurance premiums on some cargoes had jumped from 2 to 28 percent. Opportunities for plunder also infected Caribbean islanders, particularly those from French, Dutch, Spanish, and Danish colonies. "The genius of all West Indians, without distinction, seems turned to piracy and freebooting," the governor of Grenada had written Lord Germain in late October.

Despite the distraction of porcupines and learned pigs, reminders of the war could be seen in the exiled American loyalists who clustered at the New England Coffee House, in Threadneedle Street. Over ale from their armchairs they plotted campaigns on how to subdue Massachusetts or South Carolina, and how to spur the king's ministry to greater ferocity. The British Treasury had allocated £58,000 in pensions for "American sufferers," but the stipend amounted to only about £100 each in the ruinously expensive city that one exile called "a sad lickpenny." The sufferers passed their time wandering as tourists through Stonehenge, Blenheim, and medieval cathedrals because, as one British historian would write, "in England they were nobodies."

Year by year, the civil war in America unsettled more Britons. Josiah Wedgwood, whose brilliant innovations helped industrialize European pottery manufacturing, decried the "wicked and preposterous war"; he produced intaglio medals featuring a rattlesnake with the rebels' "Don't tread on me" admonition. Clergyman and philosopher Richard Price sold sixty thousand copies of *Observations on the Nature of Civil Liberty*, which argued that American virtue would triumph over British turpitude. "From one end of North America to the other they are fasting and praying," Price wrote. "We are running wild after pleasure. . . . Which side is Providence likely to favor?"

No one asked more uncomfortable questions about America than Horace Walpole, the astringent, fitfully reliable son of a former prime minister and the prince of British epistolary writers. "Can you conquer them without beating them? Can you maintain the country when you have conquered it?" he wrote on November 7. "Will a destroyed country maintain your army?" Described by an acquaintance as "long and slender to excess," with a high forehead, dark eyes, and a peculiar gait—"as though crossing a wet street"—Walpole filled Strawberry Hill, his country house in Twickenham, with dogs, cats, goldfish, lilacs, and bric-a-brac, including the spurs worn by King William III at the Battle of the Boyne in 1690. He foresaw disaster in the American quarrel, in which "we shall molder piecemeal into our insignificant islandhood. . . . The term *Great Britain* will be a jest." Lamenting the time it took to get news across the Atlantic—"people should never go to war above ten miles off"—in late fall he informed a British diplomat and confidant in Italy:

Impatience is very high, and uneasiness increases with every day. There is no sanguine face anywhere, but many alarmed ones. . . . How the war should end but in ruin, I am not wise enough to conjecture. France suspends the blow to make it more inevitable.

By custom and obligation, the king opened each new session of Parliament, and the dutiful George III would do precisely that on Tuesday, November 18. He rose as usual at six a.m. in the Queen's House—later called Buckingham Palace—and shaved himself, seeing in the mirror a robust thirty-nine-year-old with ruddy cheeks, thick lips, protruding eyes, a high forehead balanced by a dimpled chin, and, as one countess observed, "extremely fine teeth." Not quite six feet tall, he had a regal, erect bearing that made him appear larger. It was said that he considered it effeminate to have a carpet in his bedroom, and he often took to his horse for exercise early in the morning, regardless of the weather, then worked on his correspondence before a frugal breakfast. "I only prefer eating plain and little," he once explained, describing himself as "a good-mutton man" who preferred a jug of barley water to wine but was not averse to the occasional roasted pike or pork neck with gooseberry sauce.

Before noon he traveled the six hundred yards to St. James's Palace by sedan chair, to dress for the ceremony. Twice this year he had been attacked: once while riding in Hyde Park, by a man who seized his reins, and the second time while en route to the theater in the Haymarket, by a woman who smashed the glass of his chair. Both assailants had been adjudged insane, but George kept his eyes open, mindful that particularly in London he was more liked than loved.

Dressers, courtiers, and retainers flitted about St. James's, swaddling him in silk and ermine until he was as bejeweled, bestarred, and besceptered as any potentate. No one spoke unless spoken to, and, needless to say, no one sat in His Majesty's presence. Such court rituals pleased him; decorum and protocol affirmed his cosmology. His views on the monarchy had matured, not to say ossified, in the seventeen years since he'd first donned the crown, and a few guiding precepts shaped his reign. The monarch's preeminent task was to preserve the British constitution, enshrined in documents like the Magna Carta and the Act of Settlement. He believed that much of Europe was shackled by popery, despotism, or both, evils he abhorred no less than runaway democracy. A wise king heeded Parliament, the cabinet ministry, and public opinion, even while restraining change. Maritime power and colonial policy should promote commerce, the bedrock of national affluence. France, "that dangerous and faithless nation," was, as ever, the hereditary enemy. The king's powers included the authority to appoint and dismiss ministers, and to make war or peace. For almost three years now he had chosen war, and it was on the drear subject of the American rebellion that he would again speak today to Parliament. "I am born for the happiness or misery of a great nation," he had explained, a bit obscurely, "and consequently must often act contrary to my passions."

In midafternoon the gilded, four-ton state coach, pulled by eight matched horses and preceded by horse guards and trumpeters, drew up to the sovereign's entrance under the Victoria Tower in Westminster. Guns saluted the monarch's arrival at the medieval palace that since the fourteenth century had served as the House of Lords, said by one writer to be "overcrowded, insanitary, and damp" with "the haphazard accretions of a long and vigorous history." After donning the robe of state and the imperial state crown, encrusted with hundreds of diamonds, rubies, sapphires, and emeralds, George strode in full regalia through the royal gallery and into the chamber. Some 230 lords awaited him in crimson robes and coronets, including two dozen bishops in their lawn sleeves and surplices of white cambric with square caps trimmed in black silk. Dukes wore five gold bands on each sleeve, from shoulder to elbow. Earls displayed three bands, viscounts and barons two. The elect few belonging to the Order of the Garter wore golden collars. Several hundred members summoned from the House of Commons stood in the rear, drab by comparison in their coats and boots.

The king ascended a low platform and took his seat on a canopied throne. For the nearsighted monarch, the faces before him were blurred, but he knew that he was among friends, mostly. Roughly a third of those in the Commons were placemen beholden to the Crown: civil servants, court officials, government contractors. More than forty were serving military officers, and a similar number held sinecures, often for life. To keep the right men in office, the king secretly diverted £1,000 a month from his privy purse to influence elections, and no one kept a closer eye on critical votes to be sure that recipients of the Crown's largesse did their duty. In the Lords, most of the ancient peerage and the so-called Bench of Bishops resolutely backed the government on matters of war and peace. Church of England pulpits across the realm echoed that support, although rarely with the vigor of the Reverend John Butler, who declared of the Americans, "If they were all put to the sword, I will not condemn the severity."

The king's ministers had been of mixed minds in drafting this speech for him. "How shall we mention America?" Lord North, the prime minister, had asked. "Shall we be very stout? Or shall we take advantage of the flourishing state of our affairs to get out of this damned war?" William Eden, an undersecretary of state who ran the secret service, believed "the supposition of goodish news" should drive the rhetoric. But the goodish news of Brandywine and Philadelphia earlier this month had been eclipsed by baddish accounts of Bennington, Fort Stanwix, and even unconfirmed reports that General Burgoyne's march down the Hudson had been checked after a scrap at a place called Freeman's farm.

George still regretted giving concessions to the colonists during the Stamp Act crisis, more than a decade earlier. "Too great lenity of this country," he had told North in early summer, "increased their pride and encouraged them to rebel." He had believed then that "the Americans will treat before winter." Now such optimism seemed misplaced. Still, if the United Kingdom was not quite winning the war, at least it was not losing. The king continued to embrace several articles of faith: that "a majority of the people of America" would rather be his subjects than cut loose from the empire; that American independence would mean economic disaster for the mother country, while encouraging insurrections in Ireland, Canada, India, and the West Indies; and that recalcitrant rebels "must be flogged into obedience" before their monarch could extend forgiveness to the remorseful.

Perched on his throne, the king held his address in both hands. "My lords and gentlemen," he began, his voice rising to the rafters. "The continuance of the rebellion in North America demands our most serious attention." Rebel obstinacy required "pursuing the proper measures for keeping my land forces complete to their present establishment." No doubt "the spirit and intrepidity of my forces, both by sea and land, will . . . be attended with important success. . . . I rely on your zeal and public spirit."

He paused, studying the script, written on goatskin vellum. "I receive repeated assurances from foreign powers of their pacific dispositions," he said upon resuming. Yet, given that "the armaments in the ports of France and Spain continue, I have thought it advisable to make a considerable augmentation of my naval forces." In truth, as he privately knew, British intelligence had damning evidence of European perfidy. There had been eighty-five sailings of supply ships to the rebels from French ports this fall and at least twenty more from Bilbao, in northern Spain. The Americans had reportedly received at least two hundred brass field guns and thirty thousand muskets from French royal magazines. Three thousand barrels of Spanish gunpowder were routed through Havana and New Orleans, and saltpeter, sulfur, four million flints, and a thousand brace of cavalry pistols had been shipped from various continental ports, including Prussian uniform cloth sent from Hamburg via Amsterdam. Ten thousand shipwrights, riggers, sailmakers, and other artificers now gathered in Brest, along with thousands of French sailors assembled from Dunkirk to Bayonne, all of them reportedly "arming and equipping every ship that is fit for service."

Every eye in the hall remained fixed on the king's face as he finished. "I shall ever be watchful for an opportunity of putting a stop to the effusion of the blood of my subjects," he said. "I still hope that the deluded and unhappy multitude will return to their allegiance, and . . . rekindle in their hearts a spirit of loyalty to their sovereign and of attachment to their mother country." That, he added, would allow "what I shall consider as the greatest happiness of my life, and the greatest glory of my reign—the restoration of peace, order, and confidence to my American colonies."

He stood and swept from the hall, past bowed heads and bent knees. Clambering back into his enormous coach, he was alone with his thoughts as the procession swayed back toward St. James's. Increasingly, he knew, this conflict was known as "the king's war." So be it. Earlier this year, as the nation's captain general, he had designed the so-called Windsor uniform as a new court costume to signal discipline and duty.

So much about this war baffled him, including how his reign had become entangled in a squalid brawl in the empire's most distant marchlands. Or how more than fifty thousand of the king's soldiers, supported by the greatest navy ever to ply the world's seas, should be stymied by fewer than three million provincials. Was Britain not the nation that in the Seven Years' War had trounced the Bourbon powers of France and Spain, which together had a population tenfold larger?

Rebellion posed the mortal threat of disorder, of this he was certain. Rebellion also demonstrated intolerable contempt for a sovereign Parliament, as well as the sovereign himself. George was personally wounded by the rebels' erasure of his name from American streets and buildings, and by the mock trials that impugned his authority.

There was nothing for it but to soldier on. His ministers would run the war, of course, albeit with his bully advice. Modesty prevented him from concurring with Dr. Johnson's assertion that "the king can do no wrong." He would contribute as he could, encouraging fortitude and scrutinizing every particular of this contest, from officer promotions to victualling plans to the number of blankets needed by each regiment. A military band now played marches whenever he spent the night at Windsor Castle. "Firmness," he would tell Lord North, "is the characteristic of an Englishman."

Wild rumors swept London in late fall: that General Arnold had surrendered with twelve thousand rebel soldiers; that Washington had died of typhus; that the Continental Army was reduced to seven hundred men. The official government periodical, the *Gazette*—known to cynics as the

Royal Lying Gazette—published its share of balderdash, including reports that hungry American troops had turned to cannibalism. A few newspapers reliably supported the North ministry out of conviction, including *Lloyd's Evening Post*, although one reader called the periodical a "motley medley of soporific dullness." Others could be bought, notably the *Morning Post*, a harsh government critic that abruptly pivoted to become a fervid booster after publisher Henry Bate, a vicar who also wrote comic operas, received a £200 annual pension and vague promises of a peerage. His paper now assured readers that the American uprising was all but quashed, even if the Howe brothers, as one published letter asserted, had converted to Quakerism.

Yet bad news traveled on long legs, and the truth from America would soon arrive in stride. Howe's dispatch of late October came on Monday, December 1, disclosing the Red Bank debacle, the losses of *Augusta* and *Merlin*, and the commanding general's resignation request. Worse yet, at nine o'clock the next evening, John Montagu, the fourth Earl of Sandwich and first lord of the Admiralty, sent the king an urgent message from his offices in Whitehall. Captain John Moutray of the fifty-gun warship *Warwick* had just reached London from the anchorage at Spithead, off Portsmouth, after sailing from Quebec five weeks earlier. "Lord Sandwich will come with him to the Queen's House immediately," the message advised.

The news was bad indeed, carried to Governor Carleton in Canada by survivors who had escaped from Saratoga. Burgoyne and his army had surrendered. General Fraser was dead, and so, too, many others. Five thousand or more had been captured. "The king fell into agonies on hearing this account," Walpole later asserted. If so, he recovered quickly, assuring Lord North in a note written from the Queen's House that this "present misfortune" was "very serious but not without remedy."

Finding that remedy would fall first to Lord George Germain, the American secretary and the king's most ardent warlord. A substantial part of the largest army Britain had ever dispatched from this sceptered isle was imprisoned, a development sure to embolden the French, the Spanish, the Americans, and the opposition in Parliament. On Wednesday morning, December 3, Germain scribbled a note to a subordinate—his jagged handwriting prodding the paper with the quill—asking for thoughts on "any expedient for extricating this country out of its distress." Then he headed for the House of Commons, steeling himself.

He had been through worse trials. A tall, muscular man with a long face and penetrating blue eyes, Germain at age sixty-one still had remarkable eyesight, able to see with a glance who was present on the opposition benches and how the session would likely unfold. Fluent and meticulous in debate, with a tenacious memory and a knack for precision, "no man better understood the management of Parliament," an acquaintance declared. Yet he was "perhaps the most traduced of English statesmen," the historian Piers Mackesy would write. In an earlier, luckier life he had been a celebrated lieutenant general. But confusion at the Battle of Minden against the French in 1759 led to his court-martial for disobeying orders, dismissal from the army with imputations of cowardice, and disgrace that never quite faded, despite George III's recognition that he deserved rehabilitation.

A devoted husband with five children, he was widely suspected of bisexuality, considered both a sin and a crime, and to his vindictive detractors he remained the "Minden buggering hero." In private, over a pint of claret with friends, he could be "one of the very best companions of the age," an admirer wrote. "He had such power of seeing into the heart of hypocrisy." Yet in public he often seemed wary and saturnine, given to sarcasm, melancholy, and, a biographer wrote, "an excess of dogmatic self-confidence, impatient of any plan but his own." The wounds never fully closed.

Appointed American secretary two years earlier as the most junior of three British secretaries of state, he had quickly become the first among equals by making destruction of the rebel insurrection his obsession, empowered by a king whose obdurate views he shared. "I can think and speak of nothing but America," Germain told a colleague. With two deputies and half a dozen clerks toiling in a four-room Whitehall suite, he spent his days and many nights poring over military dispatches marked "Secret," "Most Secret," or "Most Secret and Confidential," trying to direct a war three thousand miles away on a continent he had never seen. No detail seemed too trivial for his attention, including his request that correspondence to and from America be encased in oilskin bags and thrown overboard as needed to preclude capture. His myriad responsibilities included annually buying £20,000 worth of hatchets, firelocks, war paint, and sundry gifts to retain the loyalty of Indians from Florida to Quebec. Also: getting Hessian troops from Germany to the New World despite an obstinate refusal by Frederick the Great to let some detachments sail down the Rhine; relaying the king's pleasure to fleet commanders in America, although he and Admiral Howe reportedly had not been on speaking terms since 1758; and making sense of an asinine British system that splintered responsibility for transporting troops and supplies across the Atlantic among the Ordnance Board, the Navy Board, the Victualling Board, and the Treasury, depending on whether the cargo to be shipped was a gun, a man, a horse, camp equipage, food, or other war stuff.

Germain referred to himself as "a man-of-war," and he kept as a souvenir the bloody uniform he had worn at Fontenoy in 1745 when, as a twenty-nine-year-old colonel, he had been shot in the chest and captured by the French. That he was brave, durable, and tenacious was beyond doubt. He believed "the whole power of the state should be exerted" to crush the rebellion, which derived from "a tumultuous and riotous rabble" that had cowed the majority of loyal Americans. The time had come, he would tell the House of Commons, "to treat America no longer as a child that was to be reclaimed by gentle correction, but as an enemy that was to be forced into peace by dint of arms."

Many sheets of foolscap fluttered from his office with directives and schemes, but no document laid out a coherent concept for winning the war. Like many in the government—and, indeed, like his monarch—he never grasped the power of a determined revolutionary ideology that demanded liberty, equality, and the consent of the governed. Germain's acute eyesight was bereft of any vision other than brute force and imperious demands for submission; he saw no profit in negotiating with rebels, or even trying to understand why they were rebellious.

He, more than anyone, was responsible for the calamity at Saratoga by failing to recognize that the divergent, incompatible campaigns unspooling in America required coordination and a supervisory intelligence. Instead, a scheme now being drafted in his office to crush the insurgency— "Considerations on the Great Question: What Is Fit to Be Done with America?"—proposed replacing the thirteen American states with eight provinces, each confined to the Atlantic seaboard. Americans would be prohibited from bearing arms, building shipyards, or forming militias. Each landowner would swear fealty to the king and Parliament or forfeit his property. The Crown would appoint all officials and clergymen, and the colonies would pay at least £300,000 annually to help underwrite imperial defenses. A newly anointed colonial aristocracy would counterbalance democratic pretensions in a society so badly "tinctured with republicanism."

Germain urged "Roman severity" as the proper answer to American insolence, and his colleagues in the government could only hope he was right. "If it is possible to bring us out of our present confusion," one British diplomat said of Germain, "I am confident he will do it."

On the afternoon of Wednesday, December 3, the House of Commons buzzed with expectation. It was said that dispatches had arrived from Quebec with fell tidings. Members strolled from the drafty chamber for another cup of wine or a handful of nuts, then strolled back in, some wearing greatcoats, hats, or even spurs. They clucked at dullards who stood to speak and encouraged the silver-tongued with cries of "Hear him! Hear him!" Germain settled onto the Treasury bench next to Lord North and was listening to a tedious debate about troop numbers in North America when a staunch opponent of the war, Colonel Isaac Barré, demanded that the American secretary "declare upon his honor what was become of General Burgoyne and his brave troops."

Germain rose to his feet. Yes, he admitted, the government had received "expresses from Quebec with a piece of very unhappy intelligence." Official confirmation had yet to reach London, but it appeared that "General Burgoyne and his army were surrounded by a force greatly superior . . . and forced to capitulate." This was indeed "a most unfortunate affair," but he hoped the Commons would "not be over-anxious in condemnation," instead suspending "judgment both on the conduct of the general and of the minister." A careful inquiry, he added, would show that both he and Burgoyne were "free from guilt."

Jaws dropped. Eyes widened. This disclosure "occasioned great consternation and some warm altercation," one correspondent wrote. Another noted that "the friends of government were much confounded and staggered by such a shock," while opposition members began "roaring like so many bulldogs."

Barré barked first. How shameful to suggest that "Burgoyne failed through his own misconduct," he told Germain. "The man who planned the expedition was to blame. . . . Does the noble lord know the extent of his criminality?" Others joined the baying. Dublin-born Edmund Burke, among Parliament's most gifted orators, voiced disbelief at "a whole army compelled to lay down their arms." Such a calamity was unknown "in the annals of our history," he charged. "Ignorance stamped every step taken during the course of the expedition, but it was the ignorance of the minister for the American Department."

The worst pummeling came from a plump, untidy twenty-eight-year-old with shaggy eyebrows and such a knack for getting under his monarch's skin that he had become the undisputed leader of the government opposition. Burke called Charles James Fox "the greatest genius that perhaps this country has produced"; a bibliophile adept in Spanish, French, and Italian, he each year reread *The Odyssey* and *The Iliad* in Greek, and he broadened his knowledge of military matters by spending weeks in the royal dockyards living aboard warships with naval officers. Elected to the Commons at age nineteen, he had been best known for dissipation and spectacular gambling losses that were said to cost his wealthy, indulgent father a thousand guineas a week for three years. When not playing whist or faro, Fox could often be found at the racetrack, "whipping, spurring, and blowing" in the grandstand as the ponies, including some owned by him, came down the stretch.

Even adversaries acknowledged his incandescence in debate. "It is impossible for me to describe with what fire and persuasion he spoke," a German visitor said. The glamorous duchess of Devonshire observed, "His conversation is like a brilliant player at billiards. The strokes follow one another, piff, paff!" In the Commons he often wore blue and buff in homage to the Continental Army, and his attacks on Germain—"an ill-omened and inauspicious character, unfit to serve the Crown"—had grown ever more vitriolic. "Bleeding has been his only prescription," Fox had declared earlier this week. "More blood! More blood! Still more blood!" After one particularly lacerating attack, North had turned to him and said, in an audible whisper, "Charles, I am glad you did not fall on me today, for you was in full feather."

Now he was again in full feather, admittedly seething with "rage and indignation." Wheeling on Germain, North let the accusations fly, piff, paff:

> An army of ten thousand men destroyed by the ignorance—the obstinate, willful ignorance—and incapacity of the noble lord. . . . A gallant general sent like a victim to be slaughtered . . . under the direction of a blunderer, which circumstance alone was the cause of his disgrace.

Parliament had been "imposed on and deceived." Did this not call "loudly for vengeance" and an investigation, beginning with a public review of all government papers regarding the Canada expedition and instructions given to General Howe?

Fox sat, his face flushed, his eyebrows twitching. In recent years he had moderated his gambling, but one wager recorded in the betting book at Brooks's club loomed large. A year ago General Burgoyne had bet him fifty guineas "that he will be home victorious from America by Christmas Day 1777." Fox had warned the general, "Be not over-sanguine." Now the admonition seemed prescient.

The house adjourned.

The search for scapegoats began immediately. Parliament blamed ministers, ministers blamed generals, generals blamed one another, or ministers, or admirals. The *Public Ledger* noted that the king had opened three consecutive sessions of Parliament with promises of imminent success in America, revealing himself to be "a very lying prophet." The Howe brothers' mother, an aged dowager, even berated Germain during a reception at his Pall Mall town house for allegedly suborning the libel of her sons in the newspapers. "Her ladyship added that she wished she was a man," the *Evening Post* reported, presumably to demand satisfaction in the Field of Forty Footsteps.

Advent came and went, and so did Christmas, the Feast of St. Stephen, Twelfth Night, and Epiphany. The new year began with the king in ill humor when the annual ode composed for recitation in the royal presence irked him; he instructed a retainer to "convey to the poet laureate the strong expressions of his displeasure" for invoking God's help in reconciling with the American rebels. "I consider it impious to convert a joyous ode into an anthem or a psalm," George added. "Let me not know it repeated."

London merchants, ever hopeful of making a shilling from misfortune, stockpiled goods to ship to America in anticipation of a reconciliation and the resumption of trade. Much of the nation, however, rallied behind the government's bellicose demand that the rebels be brought to heel. Manchester agreed to raise a battalion of more than a thousand men. Liverpool, Glasgow, and Edinburgh followed in step. Precisely how best to employ these troops and the forces already deployed across the Atlantic continued to vex the king and his ministers. In a note to North on January 13, 1778, at "2 min. past 8 p.m.," George wrote, "Perhaps the time may come when it would be wise to abandon all North America but Canada, Nova Scotia, and the Floridas. . . . But to treat with independence can never be possible."

The confusion intensified when Lord Germain vanished behind a veil of bereavement: Diana, his wife of twenty-three years, died suddenly of measles on January 15. Wearing black crepe, the grieving American secretary secluded himself at Knole, his country house southeast of London, an enormous former archbishop's palace with more than four hundred rooms sprawling across four acres. "A man at my time of life, depressed by misfortunes, will make but a bad figure in an office that requires full vigor of mind," he wrote his deputy the day after her death.

The king and Lord North privately hoped he would quit. The American secretary's resignation would be "a most favorable event," George wrote, since he "has so many enemies." But allies urged Germain to pull round. "Avail yourself of the best relief from private affliction—public business," wrote Henry Howard, Lord Suffolk, another secretary of state. "We can't go far without your assistance." The government dishevelment was made evident when William Barrington, the secretary at war, told the king that "the administration was not equal to the times" and proposed inviting Prince Ferdinand of Brunswick, the victorious German general at Minden, to become Britain's commander in chief. This odd suggestion found no favor, and Barrington would soon resign, pinching from his office two silver inkstands and a pair of taper-pots as the spoils of service.

As Germain pondered his course, North convened a cabinet meeting on January 17 at his home on Downing Street, a pleasant location by Horse Guards Parade, notwithstanding the cheeky beggars camped near the green front door with its lion's-head knocker. Facing St. James's Park and built on Thames wetlands, the house was perpetually sinking and required repeated repairs; not until the twentieth century would it contain any bathrooms, forcing the prime minster to bathe in a tin hip tub set on an oilcloth.

In a spacious ground-floor room with five large windows looking onto the garden, the ministers stroked their chins and scratched their heads. Conquering America in a land campaign seemed unlikely without another thirty thousand troops, but only three or four thousand could be spared. What to do about General Howe remained unresolved. Lord Sandwich of the Admiralty doubted the importance of the North American theater, given the threat at home.

"As soon as France determines to make war, a squadron will be sent to attack us," Sandwich argued in a memo to North. "They are, at bottom, our inveterate enemies, and are only waiting for the favorable moment to strike a blow." Admiral Howe had ninety vessels on station, which should "have made it very difficult for the Americans. . . . The contrary however has been the case." Maritime warmaking in America ought to mainly blockade ports and disrupt smuggling, he insisted. The Admiralty this month had issued secret orders that all vessels suspected of carrying aid to the rebels be stopped on the high seas, even if escorted by French naval ships. The Royal Navy now had forty-two large ships of the line in home waters, each typically with sixty-four guns or more. But the combined Bourbon fleets certainly had that number already, with "many more ready to receive men." A year would be required to put another twenty-five British capital ships into service. If Britain was "in imminent danger of a foreign war, which in my opinion is the case," Sandwich added, "a day ought not be lost."

More chin stroking, more head scratching, more palaver. The king's men came to their feet and shuffled out through the green door to their carriages in Downing Street. No decisions had been reached. A week passed, and then another. Germain set aside his grief and agreed to return to his post. Parliament reconvened. On February 2, a chirpy crowd jostled through the House of Commons doors and into the galleries to hear Fox speak for two hours and forty minutes, delivering what the *London Chronicle* described as the "most striking proofs of judgment, sound reasoning, and astonishing memory." Insisting that the war had been mismanaged and that an independent America would not enfeeble British interests, he moved that no more army regiments be permitted to cross the Atlantic. "Not one of the ministers knew what to say and so said nothing," Walpole recorded. Fox's motion was defeated, but newspapers condemned the king's men for declining to "answer a single syllable."

Frederick, Lord North, detested being a war minister. Good news from the American battlefield in the fall had briefly lifted his spirits. "The war seems to be taking a more decisive turn than I thought a little while ago," he wrote in October. But recent tidings left him complaining of depression, lassitude, and memory loss. Now forty-five, he wanted nothing more than to lay down the premiership he had held for eight years and retire among the horse chestnuts and linden trees at Bushy Park, his home in an elbow of the Thames outside London. "You may now and then be inclined to despond," the king acknowledged in a note on January 31, but "you have too much personal affection for me and sense of honor to allow such a thought to take any hold on your mind." The thought certainly had hold of North, but he continued to toil for country and for king—they had been friends since boyhood—and, not least, for the emoluments that came with the job. He had a wife and six children to support, and lacked independent wealth.

He was amiable, gracious, and conciliatory, with a self-deprecating wit that charmed political allies and adversaries alike. Once, when an opponent in the Commons castigated the prime minister for letting his country go to ruin while he napped on the Treasury bench, North opened an eye and replied, "I wish to heaven that I was." He feigned indolence, "concealing a first-class mind behind his bland and corpulent exterior," a biographer wrote. "In North there was a lovable quality which set him apart from contemporaries." Walpole noted his "deep, untuneable voice" and a "void of affectation"; he also postulated that North believed difficult questions would vanish if ignored long enough.

Among the prime minister's admirers was a spindly, red-haired backbencher who consistently supported the government, despite doubts about a war "from whence no reasonable man entertains any hope of success." Edward Gibbon was at work in his Bentinck Street study on the second volume of his history of Rome's fall, and the daily drama in the Commons affirmed his conviction that history was "little more than the register of the crimes, follies, and misfortune of mankind," a grand pageant of civilization and barbarism. He considered North "a statesman of spotless integrity" to whom he would dedicate his fourth and final volume. But Fox, ever quick, first penned his own snatch of doggerel: "King George in a fright / Lest Gibbon should write / The story of England's disgrace."

North was leader of the Commons, finance minister, head of the cabinet, and chief progenitor of government policy. His "labors are immense," a colleague wrote, "and such as few constitutions could bear." With Parliament again in session, he was often on the floor three days a week, occasionally past midnight, sometimes still wearing the blue sash and Garter star of his court dress, having attended the king at St. James's. Expert at gauging the temper of the chamber, "he took the trouble to understand men's motives and ambitions," another writer noted. As head of the Treasury Board, he missed only 23 of 670 formal meetings in seven years, orchestrating, in partnership with the Bank of England and London financiers, Britain's sophisticated system of revenue, expenditure, and borrowing, which successfully paid for wars and national growth. No one better understood how to raise loans and invent taxes—including a new duty this year on male servants—in order to underwrite the military, supply the army, and keep the government solvent.

"Curse his virtues," one adversary said, paraphrasing Joseph Addison's *Cato*. "They've undone his country." Even the king suspected there was something to that. While admiring North's happy marriage, Anglican piety, and parliamentary skills, George had doubts about his "natural good nature and love of indecision." Susceptible to bullying and blandishment, he could be rattled and irresolute in a crisis; in recent correspondence his handwriting skittered across the page as if the words were windblown, with frequent smudges, blots, and cross-outs. He acknowledged ignorance of military affairs and North American geography, and even disliked the title "prime minister," which was, perhaps, indicative of his effort to shrug off his burdens. Yet a colleague believed he "only wanted one quality to make him a great and distinguished statesman—despotism and violence of temper." As a successor in Downing Street later asserted, "The first essential for a prime minister is to be a good butcher."

Good or otherwise, he was the butcher George had. There was no obvious replacement whom the king trusted. Alerted to the prime minister's financial straits by a cabinet subminister, the king suggested to North that perhaps cold cash might "set your affairs in order" and ease his perturbations. "If £20,000 is necessary, I am resolved you shall have no other person concerned in freeing them but myself," George wrote. "I love you as well as a man of worth as I esteem you as a minister." North accepted most of the sum, although Parliament remained unaware that tax money from the secret service fund was subsidizing the prime minister's personal debts.

So he remained at the helm, despite his misgivings about the war and his own capacity, despite opposition charges of "timidity and procrastination," despite unkind whispers that he was "a weak old man." With a great sigh he wrote, "I am under such obligations to the king that I can never leave his service while he desires me to remain in it."

In late January, North had insisted to the Commons that Britain was fighting "a constitutional war, a popular war." Yet there were signs that the popularity was brittle: opposition in Parliament remained fractured, but the government majority on American matters had diminished from a dependable 150-vote margin in the Commons to less than two-thirds of that. On February 6, four days after Fox's stem-winder, Burke delivered a three-and-a-half-hour floor speech that excited so much applause that a colleague wanted it printed and "affixed to all the church doors."

More alarming, "an approaching war with France and Spain appears now almost out of doubt," North wrote the king. The newspapers increasingly disparaged "perfidious Gaul," and coffeehouse bookmakers offered four-to-one odds that war would be declared by June. A false report in February that French troops had attacked the Malabar coast, in southwest India, caused a 4 percent drop on the London stock exchange. The *Morning Post* informed readers that the "old arch-rebel," Benjamin Franklin, had offered Florida to Spain and Canada to France in exchange for military aid, and that he had moved to Vienna to woo additional allies.

Britain had no allies in Europe other than little Portugal. North knew that in the past, waging war successfully against Versailles had required blockading French fleets in their home ports while attacking overseas colonies to wreck France's maritime commerce. How this could be accomplished while simultaneously throwing fifty thousand troops and half the Royal Navy at the Americans remained unclear.

Desperate times required desperate measures. On Tuesday, February 17, the prime minister took the floor in the Commons, apologizing for "the intended length" of his speech. Then for two hours, with eloquence and some penitence, he laid out what he called "conciliatory propositions." The Coercive Acts of 1774, which North had written to punish the Americans and compel their submission, had obviously failed to work. He confessed himself "extremely disappointed" that the subsequent "war in America had turned out very differently" from his expectations. Methodically reviewing the Stamp Act, the tea tax, and other measures imposed by Britain, North now proposed "to remove all fears, real or pretended, of Parliament's ever attempting to tax them again" and to repeal all repressive acts passed since 1763. A British commission, to be appointed by the king, would have "very large powers" to grant pardons and to negotiate with Congress, state assemblies, and "General Washington or any other officer." The king's government would not concede independence but, rather, would offer broad concessions, including autonomy and reparations, to forestall "protracting the war, the effusion of blood, and the immoderate expense." This, he hoped, would lead to a "lasting bond of union" with America.

North eased back onto his bench. "A dull, melancholy silence for some time succeeded to this speech," the *Annual Register* reported. "Astonishment, dejection, and fear overclouded the whole assembly." These concessions exceeded even those initially demanded by the Continental Congress. On the government benches, "mortification was evident."

Fox popped to his feet, hardly bothering to conceal a smirk as he congratulated the prime minister on his "conversion." The terms outlined "did not materially differ from those" proposed by Burke three years earlier. Fox only wished "that this concession had been made more early." Others from the opposition piled on, rebuking the government for the thousands of lives lost and the millions of pounds squandered. "What reparation could the noble lord make to the fatherless children and widows, and a great country which he has made desolate and oppressed?" one member declaimed. On and on it went, with North accused of deception, of execrable policy, of putting "the existence of the empire to the hazard merely to try the mettle of the Americans."

Late in the evening the king wrote North from the Queen's House to assure him that "I sincerely rejoice the measures proposed by you this day," although another fortnight would be required for the Conciliatory Acts to pass both houses. Germain complained to a friend that North's gambit "has been carried on not only without consulting me, but without the smallest degree of communication. . . . I cannot doubt but that my services are no longer acceptable." Yet if the war widened to include the Bourbon foe, surely Germain's star would again ascend. Someone would be needed to direct this larger, more dangerous conflict. The king's warlord would have to step forward.

The conciliation measures would continue to provoke scorn and ridicule from both supporters and opponents of the government. "Such a bundle of imbecility never disgraced a nation," Dr. Johnson thundered. A *Morning Post* writer asked why such "terms of humiliating reconciliation" should be offered to a "race of unnatural and ungrateful bastards." Walpole, always ready with a diatribe, waxed on in scathing letters to various friends:

> The nation has leaped from outrageous war to a most humiliating supplication for peace. . . . Such accommodating facility had one defect—it came too late. . . . How one blushes to be an Englishman.

To this he would add, "Children break their playthings to see the inside of them. . . . We have been like babies smashing an empire to see what it was made of."

12.

———⋆———

Blessed Is He That Expects Nothing

The old arch-rebel had offered neither Canada nor Florida in exchange for Bourbon help; nor had he moved to Vienna. Instead, Dr. Franklin was enjoying a fine winter in Paris, attending the opera to see *Alceste*, dickering with arms merchants who trotted out to Passy in their phaetons, and flirting with beautiful women whose powdered curls were piled up in a new coiffure called *les Insurgents*.

French police lurking outside the Hôtel de Valentinois continued to watch him closely. One surveillance report concluded that "Franklin seems to have lost a great deal of his exuberance, and appears much preoccupied." The dreary news from Brandywine had certainly dampened his spirits, as did claims by Viscount Stormont, the British ambassador, that Burgoyne had captured Albany to control both the Hudson and Mohawk valleys, even as General Howe advanced on Philadelphia, Franklin's hometown.

A year had passed since his arrival in France as the senior American commissioner, and Versailles still showed no readiness to support the rebel cause with a formal alliance. Franklin took solace in continuing to orchestrate privateer attacks on British shipping and in sending munitions to kill redcoats in America. *Le Brune* had sailed from Lorient, ostensibly for the French West Indies, with forty-six field guns hidden in her hold under a load of salt. The *Duchesse de Grammont* was scheduled to sail soon from Nantes with pistols, carbines, thirteen thousand uniforms, and fifteen hundred rampart fusils, heavy muskets fired on a swivel fork. Some shipments went awry, like the *Lady Elizabeth*, captured while sailing from Guadeloupe to South Carolina with uniforms and a thousand stand of arms. But Franklin tried to heed his own advice from *Poor Richard's Almanack*: "Blessed is he that expects nothing, for he shall never be disappointed."

On the morning of Thursday, December 4, in the rear Valentinois pavilion, behind the barren linden trees, he met with his fellow commission-ers, Silas Deane and Arthur Lee, to discuss further shipments and await a courier believed to be on the final leg of his journey from America. They were joined by a tall, slender Frenchman who for the past year had been their chief gunrunner and advocate in Versailles, Pierre-Augustin Caron, a former watchmaker widely known as Beaumarchais, although Franklin called him Figaro, after the likable rogue who was his most enduring liter-ary invention. *The Barber of Seville* had first appeared onstage in February 1775, taking France and then the Continent by storm; Beaumarchais was now writing a sequel, *The Marriage of Figaro*, restoring much of the scath-ing sarcasm about the French aristocracy that he had been forced to excise from the first play. The heraldic device Beaumarchais had adopted for himself included a drum with the motto *Non sonat nisi percussus*: "It does not sound unless I bang it."

An intriguer "with every finger in a pie," as one admirer wrote, he was a playwright, publisher, financier, inventor, polemicist, and forger, as well as an adviser to kings and, more than once, a prison inmate. At the mo-ment he was in danger of also becoming a bankrupt. Roderigue Hortalez & Cie, the front company he ran in the rue Vieille du Temple, operated with a dozen or more vessels sailing from Bordeaux, Nantes, Le Havre, and Marseille; in the past year they had carried at least five million livres' worth of covert war matériel to America from French government arsenals and other suppliers. Beaumarchais had expected to be reimbursed with return shipments of tobacco to defray his expenses and pay for more arms. But except for a small cargo of rice and indigo that recently arrived from America aboard the *Amphitrite*, he had received nothing because of Brit-ain's blockade of ships trying to leave rebel ports and confusion over whether his arms shipments were a secret gift from Versailles or a loan. An American agent ostensibly helping him in Nantes "is drunk at least twenty-two hours out of twenty-four," an associate reported, "and never without one or two whores in company." Indignant British protests over his activi-ties periodically resulted in ostentatious crackdowns by Versailles, forcing Beaumarchais to unload his contraband under police supervision, then secretly reload it again after paying lavish bribes.

As Figaro, his alter ego, explained from the stage, "I hasten to laugh at everything for fear of being obliged to weep." Only an emergency subsidy from the Comte de Vergennes, the foreign minister, had kept Beaumarchais afloat. "I have exhausted my money and credit," he would write Congress this month. "I was counting on receiving goods in return, as was promised on many occasions."

This confusion was not close to resolution when, at eleven-thirty a.m.

that Thursday, the sound of hoofbeats echoed outside. Franklin and his companions hurried into the courtyard to greet Jonathan Austin, secretary to the Massachusetts Board of War, who had crossed the Atlantic from Boston in just thirty-one days. Before the courier could alight from his coach, Franklin called out, "Sir, is Philadelphia taken?"

"Yes, sir," Austin replied. Franklin clasped his hands together in despair and turned to go back inside. "But, sir," Austin continued, "I have greater news than that. General Burgoyne and his whole army are prisoners of war." Moreover, General Washington had boldly attacked the British camp at Germantown. Although the assault had ultimately been repulsed, the foray had displayed the army's fighting spirit in full measure. Austin handed his dispatches to the jubilant Franklin as huzzahs filled the courtyard. "Mr. Austin," Franklin said, "you have brought us glorious news." Beaumarchais raced back to Paris—perhaps to exploit this intelligence in his stock market investments—but urged on the postillion with such a frenzy that the carriage overturned on the rue des Petits-Champs. "The violence of the fall made me bleed profusely at the nose and mouth," he would write the next day. "Nevertheless," he added, "the charming news from America is a balance to my soul."

Franklin and his colleagues composed long dispatches to Versailles, Madrid, and Berlin, exaggerating only slightly "the total reduction of the force under General Burgoyne" with losses that exceeded ten thousand men and included four members of Parliament captured. In their letter to Vergennes, they asked for Louis XVI "to resume the consideration" of a treaty, since American success would secure an "increase in the commerce, wealth, and strength of France and Spain." Beaumarchais, bandaged and bruised, assured Vergennes that Washington had permitted Howe to enter Philadelphia in order to surround him. "Brave, brave people!" he told an associate. "Their warlike conduct justifies my esteem."

Word spread quickly among Parisians, provoking "great demonstrations of joy, as if it had been a victory gained by their own arms," wrote Temple, Franklin's elder grandson. Anne-Louise Brillon de Jouy, a neighbor of Franklin's in Passy, told him, "My dear Papa, we share your joy as fully as we love you. . . . I am about to compose a triumphal march to enliven the way of General Burgoyne and his men, wherever they may be heading."

On December 6, at nine a.m., Vergennes's first secretary, Conrad-Alexandre Gérard, a sobersided, English-speaking Alsatian lawyer, appeared at the Hôtel de Valentinois carrying official congratulations from the court, as well as a pledge of three million livres. Since there now was "no doubt of the ability and resolution" of the United States to prosecute the war, Gérard added, an alliance seemed all but certain. Just before noon on Friday, December 12, the American commissioners arrived by coach outside the east wing of the Versailles palace, where an usher bundled them into another hackney for the half-mile ride to Vergennes's country house. Suave and dignified despite the poundage accumulated during decades of sedentary diplomacy, the foreign minister greeted them warmly and applauded "the present prosperous state of our affairs."

"All this seems to bring us closer to the moment of crisis which I have always foreseen," Vergennes had written earlier in the week to his ambassador in London. The French merchant and fishing fleets were home safely for the winter from the far reaches of the Atlantic and no longer vulnerable to British depredations. French shipwrights had just launched the fleet's fifty-second ship of the line, giving the combined Bourbon navies more than eighty of the largest warships; for the first time since 1690, France was close to parity with Britain at sea. Vergennes now referred to the Americans fulsomely as "our friends." New rumors from London had suggested that the British might consider reconciliation with the rebels, leaving France at risk of confronting a united Anglo enemy bent on snatching away the French sugar islands and parts of Spanish America. Would it be "more expedient to have war against England and America united," he had written, "or with America for us against England?" The king took the point and, in an order written on his pale blue quartered notepaper, authorized Vergennes to begin negotiating a Franco-American alliance. Louis added the royal imprimatur: *"Approuvé le 6 décembre 1777."*

But first, as Vergennes now told the commissioners, a treaty must await word from Madrid. Under the *Pacte de Famille* of 1761, Louis XVI and his uncle Charles III were required to assist each other in war and peace, acting in concert when facing a common enemy and providing certain forces in any conflict, including at least twenty ships of the line. Without Spanish concurrence, "nothing could be done." The conversation swung round to fishery rights off Canada, the sugar islands—America would guarantee all French and Spanish possessions in North America—and the proper western boundary of the United States. The commissioners thought the Mississippi River a suitable demarcation.

The discussion ended with bows, handshakes, and pledges of secrecy. Aware of French anxiety about facing a unified Anglo-American foe, Franklin urged a quick decision by Versailles "if reconciliation with Britain was to be prevented." He and his comrades sped back to Passy in their coach, quite pleased with themselves.

*   *   *

British officials had been steaming open intercepted mail since at least the Tudor dynasty three centuries earlier, sometimes with warrants signed by a secretary of state and sometimes without. A "Secret Office," managed by a director known as the "Secret Man," examined foreign correspondence in three rooms next to the Foreign Office on Lombard Street; an adjacent "Private Office" read domestic letters. When the mailbags were especially full, eight openers, decipherers, translators, and engravers might work until three a.m., using special fluids to reveal invisible inks on diplomatic dispatches and suspicious epistles, particularly from French, Prussian, Russian, Spanish, and American senders trusting enough to use the British postal service. The king received copies, marked "Private and Most Secret," and wax-seal replicas were meticulously engraved before the letters were resealed and sent on to the addressee.

This operation was financed by the British secret service fund, which also paid for bribes in foreign capitals and a network of spies across the Continent, including bankers in Rotterdam and Amsterdam. British agents in French ports provided detailed intelligence about shipbuilding and other naval developments, as well as contraband shipments to America from the likes of Beaumarchais; London was "far better informed of American activities than was Congress," one historian would later assert. Supervising the spies was Paul Wentworth, a loyalist lawyer from New Hampshire who now lived in London in a flamboyant style financed by plantation income from South America and a generous stipend from William Eden, the secret service chief. Wentworth carried his own private cipher and recipes for secret ink. He used at least twenty identities—most of them known to French authorities—and threw lavish parties at the home of his Parisian mistress for French friends who believed him to be simply a *bon vivant* banker. Aware of his chicanery, Beaumarchais considered Wentworth the cleverest man in England. "He speaks French as well as you," Figaro told Vergennes, "and better than I."

Wentworth's prize agent in Paris, given the nom de guerre "Dr. Edwards," was the Massachusetts-born Edward Bancroft, who as a young physician hired by plantation masters in South America had once cared for a thousand or more slaves in Dutch Guiana. Bancroft had published both a three-volume epistolary novel and a well-regarded natural history that included chapters on electric eels and the poisons local Indians used on their arrowheads. His treatise on vegetable dyes, particularly those derived from the inner bark of the black oak, led to his election by both the Royal Society and the Medical Society of London.

Silas Deane, who as a young Yale graduate had tutored Bancroft when the boy lived in Connecticut, had persuaded him in July 1776 to come to Paris to serve as an assistant and translator, even though the doctor privately seemed ambivalent about American independence. About the same time, Wentworth recruited Bancroft, whom he had first met in South America. For his espionage he would receive a £500 annual stipend—later doubled—plus a £400 bonus and a lifetime pension. Franklin liked the convivial, urbane Bancroft—a fellow scientist—and promoted him in March 1777 to commission secretary; he lived in Passy with access to all documents regarding privateers, treaty proposals, arms shipments, congressional correspondence, and French war preparations. "I have papers of the first consequence," Bancroft told Wentworth, "and there are now no secrets kept from me." From his apartments in the rue de Richelieu, the spymaster arranged a dead drop for "Dr. Edwards" to deliver his dispatches: written in invisible ink, they would be concealed inside an empty bottle that on Tuesday evenings was placed within a hollow boxwood trunk on the south terrace of the Tuileries Garden. Retrieved by Ambassador Stormont's chaplain, the reports then were sent on to London. Sometimes Bancroft used a numerical code: 136 for Spain, 57 for England, 122 for Paris, and so on.

"Three may keep a secret if two of them are dead," Franklin had written in *Poor Richard*. Despite repeated warnings of snoops and spies in Paris, he ignored such admonitions and his own aphorism. He instead claimed that his guiding principle was "to be concerned in no affairs that I should blush to have made public, and to do nothing but what spies may see." This feckless insouciance was damaging to his cause and ruinous to mariners intercepted by well-informed British men-of-war. Unaware of Bancroft's treachery, Franklin also showed little circumspection about other agents lurking in his orbit, including a Maryland-born sea captain named Joseph Hynson, who in October had been entrusted with months of confidential correspondence to be sent to Philadelphia from Le Havre. Hynson instead slipped blank paper into the dispatch case and sent the originals to Eden, who described him as "an honest rascal & no fool though apparently stupid," then rewarded him with a lifetime £200 annual stipend.

A man pretending to be an American merchant named George Lupton occasionally dined with Franklin; he was actually a British spy, Jacobus Van Zandt, who provided London with details about clandestine American shipping in Nantes, Bordeaux, and Dunkirk and also snuck into Deane's closet to rifle through his correspondence. The congenitally suspicious Arthur Lee, who often complained about lax security, nevertheless hired two consecutive personal secretaries, John Thornton and the

Reverend Hezekiah Ford, both of whom worked as British agents. More-over, in June, while Lee sought Prussian support for the American cause, his hotel desk in Berlin was jimmied by another British operative, who sent copies of the stolen papers to London. These betrayals aside, Frank-lin's majordomo at the Valentinois was embezzling from him.

Damage from the intrusions would have been much worse had not George III disparaged Bancroft as "entirely an American and that every word . . . was to deceive." The king, who carefully vetted foreign intelli-gence, doubted that the £60,000 spent by the secret service so far during his reign was worth the expense; he considered one agent in Paris no more trustworthy than the newspapers, "those daily productions of untruths." As for Wentworth, "an avowed stockjobber," the king wrote, "I have read through the very voluminous and undigested letters from Mr. Wentworth, whose productions I confess it is hard to labor through."

The stockjobber appeared in Paris on December 12 under orders from Eden to assess whether the Americans would accept a settlement on terms other than full independence. In an anonymous note to Deane, Wentworth suggested a rendezvous at Pot de Vin's Bathing Machine, on the Seine. The son of a Connecticut blacksmith, wary of British skullduggery, Deane re-plied that he could be found in his lodgings at the Hôtel de Coislin, on the rue Royale. Over a subsequent dinner and conversation at the Café Saint-Honoré, Wentworth outlined a reconciliation plan based on amnesty and an armistice. Cooperative American leaders would be showered with knighthoods, governorships, and baronies. Deane, whom Wentworth de-scribed as "vain, desultory, and subtle," told him to talk to Franklin.

Days passed. Wentworth was closely shadowed by both French police and agents for Beaumarchais, who warned Vergennes, "Be sure that the English ministers are working seriously to make peace with America." Fearing assassination or arrest, the spymaster grew so anxious at this re-lentless surveillance that he burned his secret papers. At last Franklin agreed to see him, and on January 6 he received Wentworth with disarm-ing charm at the Hôtel de Valentinois.

The charm soon vanished. In his dispatch to Eden, composed partly in numeric code, Wentworth would write, "I called on 72 [Franklin] yester-day and found him very busy." The old man grew waspish and "worked himself up into passion and resentment," denouncing "the barbarities in-flicted on his country . . . the regular system of devastation and cruelty which every general had pursued. Here he lost breath in relating the burning of towns, the neglect or ill-treatment of prisoners." He insisted on "107" [independence] from "64" [England], before finally agreeing to listen as Wentworth read aloud an unsigned letter from the British government—written by Eden—asking how America would respond to concessionary proposals, such as ending imperial taxation and resuming transatlantic trade.

"He said it was a very interesting, sensible letter," Wentworth related. "Pity it did not come a little sooner." But if "64" was prepared to fight for another decade, as the letter asserted, "7" [America] would fight for half a century. After two hours of inconclusive talks, Franklin rang a small bell. Deane and Bancroft joined them for an affable dinner before Wentworth returned to Paris. "I never knew him so eccentric," he told Eden. "He was diffuse and unmethodical." Although 72 had consented to another conversation, Wentworth added, "on reflection I do not see any good end it can answer, and therefore I shall not go."

Precisely as the tamer of lightning had intended, police reports of the meeting between a British spymaster and America's chief diplomat had a galvanic effect in Versailles. The next day, January 7, the king met Vergennes and other senior ministers in the Council Room, next to his bedchamber. A porphyry bust of Alexander the Great stood on the marble fireplace mantel next to a door that opened into the Hall of Mirrors. Blue-and-gold brocade covered the walls, and the carved wood paneling depicted small sprites offering advice in times of war and peace.

In a reply received on December 31, Spain had rejected the French proposal for a joint treaty with the Americans. Madrid was not ready for war, at least on behalf of republican rebels; the annual treasure fleet bringing bullion from Mexico and South America would not return until summer, a key factor in whether Spain could afford another clash with Britain. But at Versailles the risk of a rapprochement between Britain and her colonies had forced the issue. Some hotspurs in the French court were eager to fight immediately. "Seeing as we are ready, why wait for the English to be so as well?" wrote one courtier, who proposed sailing up the Thames and burning the Chatham Dockyard.

This found no favor with Vergennes, who made it clear that France would not alarm other European states by completely prostrating the British and deranging the continental balance of power. "Even if I could destroy England, I would abstain from doing so, as from the wildest folly," he said. Britain must be seen as the aggressor, with France as the aggrieved, noble defender of the American underdog, the powerful protecting the weak. In a dispatch to Madrid, he urged Spain to reconsider. "Nothing can justify," he wrote, "letting slip through our fingers the only opportunity in many centuries to put England in its place." The moment had come for France to again ascend. Eventual victory over Britain would bring "glory and inestimable advantages," he argued in the Council Room. "In separating the United States from Great Britain," he later wrote, "it was above all their commerce which we wanted."

Louis listened, perhaps both to his councillors and to those fairies flitting across the wall. War seemed inevitable. The radiant news from Saratoga, the alarming reports from Passy and London, and the opportunity to restore France to preeminence in Europe, fifteen years after the humiliation of the last war, had finally persuaded him to move ahead. At the end of the meeting he approved a long document detailing why France favored twin treaties with the Americans: a military alliance and a commercial pact that recognized independence. "Now or never," Vergennes had asserted. The king agreed: now.

At six p.m. on January 8, Gérard met the American commissioners in Deane's apartment. After extracting pledges of secrecy from the three men, he told them that the king was prepared to move ahead without Spain, but he had two questions: What must Versailles do to make Franklin and his *confrères* turn a deaf ear to any British peace offer short of full independence? And what guarantees would Congress and the American public require? Gérard left them to discuss the matter in private; an hour later, he returned to find Deane and Lee bickering as Franklin scratched an answer to the first query. Signing "a treaty of amity and commerce," he wrote, would allow the commissioners "to firmly reject all propositions made to them of peace from England." The second question would take several days to sort out, since no timely guidance from Congress was possible. But the commissioners suggested that an ironclad guarantee of French support to evict Britain from North America, plus a gift of "six or eight" large capital ships, should suffice.

"The Doctor," Gérard subsequently told Vergennes, "observed that this was what they had been proposing and soliciting in vain for a year. . . . We parted very satisfied with each other."

Louis wrote Charles III to explain his decision to press ahead. "The destruction of the army of Burgoyne, and the very confined state in which Howe finds himself, have totally changed the face of things," he told his uncle. "America is triumphant and England beaten." Louis would later claim, when life had taken a darker turn, that as a callow young king he had been manipulated by his advisers. That charge was unpersuasive, even if not wholly untrue. As Vergennes wrote in mid-March, "The supreme decision was taken by the king. The influence of his ministers was not decisive." In fact, the foreign minister added, "His Majesty has given courage to us all."

On Friday evening, February 6, Franklin dressed with particular care, choosing a suit of Manchester velvet with ribbing an eighth of an inch wide. He had worn this very attire in London four years earlier when he was publicly berated like a common pickpocket before King George's Privy Council for his role in disclosing confidential correspondence from a Crown official. That humiliation still gnawed at him, and he selected the suit for tonight's occasion, he told a friend, "to give it a little revenge."

He disembarked from his coach onto the rue Royale and climbed the wide stone staircase to Deane's apartment in the Hôtel de Coislin, where Gérard and the other commissioners awaited him. On a table near the marble fireplace lay the two treaties, inscribed in copperplate script on parchment, the English and French versions aligned side by side. After some nervous patter about fine-print minutiae, Gérard signed first, then Franklin. They chatted by the blazing fire as Deane and Lee stepped forward to sign. Wax seals were affixed, and by nine p.m. the deed was done. Clutching the documents against that vengeful velvet coat, Franklin rode back to Passy to have them copied.

The French had been remarkably generous. Versailles demanded no commercial privileges or territorial acquisitions, although France could keep any British island in the West Indies seized by French forces. The thirty-three articles in the "treaty of amity and commerce" committed "the most Christian king" to protect American ships; privateers would also be permitted to openly bring captured prizes into French ports. "If war should break out between France and Great Britain," the thirteen-article "treaty of alliance" obligated Versailles and the United States to "make it a common cause." Article 8 confirmed that "neither of the two parties shall conclude either truce or peace with Great Britain without the formal consent of the other," nor "lay down their arms until the independence of the United States" was formally conceded by Britain in an accord "that shall terminate the war."

"The treaties with France are at length completed and signed," the proud commissioners wrote Congress. They praised "the king's magnanimity and goodness" and the "good will of this court and the nation in general." A secret clause would admit Spain into the alliance upon request, "and there is no doubt of the event." Once France and Britain moved closer to war, the pacts would be made public and surely "encourage other powers in Europe to ally themselves with us."

Word of Lord North's conciliatory proposals soon reached France. In hopes of outrunning the British gambit, a French frigate, the *Nymphe*, carried copies of the treaties westward from Brest on February 27, but she would require two months to reach Boston. A duplicate set also left Brest aboard the *Sensible* on March 8. London learned of the pacts much sooner. Within hours of the signings in the Hôtel de Coislin, Bancroft instructed a business associate in London to sell stocks, which would undoubtedly fall; he also provided Wentworth with extensive details, and in less than three days the British ministry knew of the alliance. Yet without a public declaration or a violent act of aggression from France, the treaties remained little more than a troublous rumor.

"Preparations for war are carried on with immense activity," Franklin told Congress. So they were. On March 7, Louis approved sending naval vessels to escort merchant ships back from the West Indies, bringing both sugar and trained sailors to man the French fleet. Seamen on coasters and fishermen also were conscripted. Naval officer leaves were canceled and port fortifications strengthened. Shipwrights and repair gangs were to toil at night, and "the work must not be interrupted for holidays or Sunday," wrote Gabriel de Sartine, a former Paris police chief who now served as the French naval minister. In orders marked *"pour vous seul"*—"for you only"—Sartine urged an admiral in Toulon to finish preparing his squadron for sea; four American pilots, recruited by Silas Deane, would join him shortly. Brest was ordered to fit out more ships of the line, including two leviathans, the 90-gun *Ville de Paris* and the 110-gun *Bretagne*. Matériel shipped to America included not only a thousand tons of brass cannons but also snare drums, horse combs, belt buckles, wagon harnesses, amputation instruments, opium, silk for regimental colors, tools for shoemakers, and sheep shears.

With France hurtling toward the precipice, Vergennes, who more than anyone had put his country on this path, harbored private moments of doubt, if not remorse. "I have only a feeble confidence in the energy of the United States," he told his ambassador in Madrid. Congress often seemed beset by "habitual inertia," with its share of *"mauvaises têtes et coeurs peu honnêtes"*—bad heads and dishonest hearts. But on March 13, upon his order, the French envoy in London delivered to the British government a copy of the commercial treaty with its formal recognition of the United States of America. (The military pact remained secret.) Three days later, Stormont was recalled. Packing up at the Hôtel des Deux-Ponts, he posted a public notice: "As the English ambassador is about to leave Paris, he begs all those who have any claims against him to call at once at the embassy."

As for the Americans, Stormont could only grumble, "They play us off against one another. Franklin's natural subtlety gives him a great advantage in such a game."

On Friday morning, March 20, the courtyard at Versailles bustled as usual with tourists, hucksters, and porters renting the ceremonial swords necessary for admission to the palace. Sedan chairs swayed across the cobbles, and carriages rolled in and out bearing noblemen, pretenders, and princes of the church. Royal troops marched with a heavy footfall, including Gardes Françaises in blue coats with red vests and Gardes Suisses in red coats with blue vests. Officers strutted about, the white plumes in their chapeaux fluffing in the breeze on this first day of spring. It was whispered that of late the king and queen had been carnal with unwonted frequency, and the court's hopes for an heir had soared. The royal obstetrician prayed for a princeling, since girls were debarred from the French throne and he would receive an annual reward of forty thousand livres for safely delivering a baby boy.

Shortly before noon a procession of coaches wheeled up the avenue de Paris between the Great Stables and the Small Stables. A murmur in the crowd grew to a shout. *"Vive Franklin! Vive l'Amérique!"* Drums beat as the commissioners stepped one by one from separate vehicles and walked unhurriedly toward Vergennes's apartments. Franklin "wore a russet velvet coat, white stockings, his hair hanging loose, his spectacles on his nose, and a white hat under his arm," a witness reported. White ruffles peeked from his cuffs, and a buckle sat atop each shoe like a silver butterfly. A Paris newspaper reported that he had chosen to appear unwigged after a *perruquier* summoned to Passy could not produce a periwig that fit. "It is true that Franklin does have a fat head," a commentator added. "But it is a great head." The court painter thought he resembled "a stocky farmer."

Vergennes served a light meal and chatted easily, betraying no sense of unease about the future. Then he led the delegation up the Queen's Staircase, feet scuffing across the polychrome marble, and through the Salle des Gardes, where bodyguards and a few favored dogs ate and slept. They paused in the Salon de l'Oeil-de-Boeuf, the bull's-eye, named for an oval window set within a ceiling frieze depicting a ring of gamboling children. Paintings by Veronese and other Venetian artists hung on the walls, and ticking could be heard from one of the palace's two hundred clocks. An usher scratched on an inner door. The Swiss guards stepped aside as "the ambassadors of the thirteen united provinces" were announced, and the group walked into the king's bedchamber.

A carved allegory titled *France Watching over the Sleeping King* stood above an alcove lined with crimson velvet embroidered in gold and containing the royal bed. On a marble mantel stood a bust of Louis XIV, the Sun King, who had died in this room in 1715 after a seventy-two-year reign. His great-great-great-grandson, the current king, "had been in prayer, stopped, and assumed a noble posture," noted Emmanuel, the Duc de Croÿ, a courtier and distinguished soldier who was present. Louis had grown stout, and his physicians recommended that he drink Vichy water to forestall obesity. Yet he moved with grace to greet his visitors. "He had his hair undressed, hanging down on his shoulders, no appearance of preparation to receive us, nor any ceremony in doing it," Lee later wrote. "The king appeared to speak with manly sincerity." Vergennes presented the commissioners to his monarch and other ministers, including Sartine.

"Please assure Congress of my friendship," Louis said. "I hope this will be for the good of the two nations." Franklin nodded and murmured his thanks. "Your Majesty may count on the gratitude of Congress and its faithful observance of the pledges it now takes," he replied. Vergennes fairly purred in adding, "It is certain, sire, that no conduct could be wiser or more reserved than that of these gentlemen here."

Then they were done. The monarch known as the Silent King turned and strode from the room. "We have judged them free people," he would later write. "We have given them existence as a nation." Vergennes led the visitors from the palace and through a rambunctious crowd on the streets to his town house. With Franklin at his side and "a grand company of nobility" round the table, as Lee recorded, the foreign minister and Gérard hosted an elegant dinner to commemorate the day. "It is the fate of you who discovered electricity to electrify the two ends of the world," de Croÿ told Franklin. Privately he wondered if this spring day presaged both "an implacable war and perhaps the creation of a country larger than our own, which could one day subjugate Europe."

Later Marie-Antoinette sent an invitation to the Americans to join her as she played faro. They found a large table with golden piles of louis d'or before each gambler. Some spectators sat in low chairs with a carved armrest on the backs, designed to be straddled by women wearing huge hoop dresses. The queen, her long blond hair piled high and her alabaster complexion slightly flushed, gestured to Franklin to stand behind her in the post of honor. She was amused by his nickname—*"l'ambassadeur électrique"*—and turned to chat whenever there was a break in the betting.

This year alone she would lose 180,000 livres at cards; perhaps the electrical ambassador would change her luck.

"It looks as if our navy will soon be active," she had written her mother, the empress Maria Theresa, two days earlier. "The king sleeps with me three or four nights a week." Regardless of her fortunes at the gaming table, it was later believed that she and Louis finally conceived their first child on this very night. The baby would be born on December 19 and christened Marie-Thérèse Charlotte, a girl.

13.

———•———

The Vortex of Small Fortunes

From the quartzite citadel of Mount Joy, the armed camp in the limestone valley below looked "like some grand city," a Massachusetts ensign wrote. Two thousand huts stood along tidy streets arrayed in parallel lines around the makeshift parade ground. By late January entrenchments and earthworks had connected five redoubts in a semicircle extending from the Schuylkill, with an abatis, a sloped earthen glacis, and a six-foot ditch. Four dozen guns perched on the fortifications, pointing east and south—the likely direction of any British attack from Philadelphia. Ox teams plodded through mud to their fetlocks, dragging logs from distant woodlots. Although the winter was blessedly mild for eastern Pennsylvania, with only ten days of falling snow recorded during the six-month encampment, ten thousand cords would be needed for heat, and nearly every tree for miles had already been felled. Smoke from unseasoned green wood billowed out of the kitchens behind each regiment, wafting across wash benches and laundry lines.

Grunting men swung billhooks and axes, splitting the logs with iron frows. Others straddled rooflines, nailing wood shingles or repairing thatch in a futile effort to patch leaks. The huts were alike by regulation: sixteen feet long and fourteen feet wide, gabled, with tiered bunks for a dozen soldiers and a stone fireplace at one end—"little shanties which are scarcely gayer than dungeon cells," Lafayette wrote Adrienne. A slurry of wood chips, stones, and clay daubed the cracks between the logs. Some huts displayed homely grace notes, perhaps a bookshelf or oiled paper covering a window—none had glass—or an oilcloth tacked over the door to block drafts. Every day a musket cartridge was burned inside each cabin to clear the miasma of close living. That, too, was futile.

Muddy Forge, as soldiers called this place, was symmetrical, bucolic, and wretched. Barefoot sentries stood on old hats in an attempt to keep frostbite from their toes. Tatterdemalion officers appeared at reveille in coats made from threadbare blankets or bedspreads. A Delaware officer asked his wife to rip up her white linen tablecloths to make him breeches. Men yoked themselves to carts and wagons because so many draft horses were dead. "For breakfast we have bacon and smoke," wrote Dr. Bodo Otto. "For dinner, smoke and bacon. For supper, smoke." Homesickness was another miasma that never cleared away. An officer who heard a violin playing sweetly in a nearby hut confessed, "I wished to have the music cease, and yet dreaded its ceasing."

Surgeon Albigence Waldo recorded a standard greeting between the troops: "Good morning, brother soldier, how are you?" "All wet, I thankee. Hope you are so." Less droll was his diary entry after finding a man dead in his bunk. "There the poor fellow lies, not superior to a clod of earth, his mouth open, his eyes staring," Waldo wrote. "What a frail, dying creature is man. We are certainly not made for this world." Sixty soldiers a week were dying by early February; the cumulative number in late spring would reach two thousand or more in the camp and at nearby hospitals, not counting hundreds more among camp followers, teamsters, and artisans. Often they were buried in an unmarked section of the Valley Meeting House yard, at times three to a grave. "Hope the many deaths that happen around us may serve to prepare us for a dying hour," a surgeon's mate from Connecticut wrote his father. Private Elijah Fisher, who had fought at Bunker Hill after enlisting in a New Hampshire regiment at age sixteen, noted in his diary on February 8, after a serious illness, "I gits better but a number dyed."

The wonder was that any recovered. Almost a third of the country's thirty-five hundred physicians served with the Continental Army, but only a hundred had medical degrees. One New England medico observed that treatment for all ailments typically involved "bleeding, vomiting, blistering, purging. . . . If the illness continued, there was *repetendi*," often leading to "death by physician." Some surgeons sprinkled burning gunpowder to cauterize wounds. Remedies included poultices of cow dung, rotten apples, or rabbit fat. Therapies for dysentery—endemic in army bivouacs—included castor oil, butter with beer, hot lard with boiled eggs inserted between the buttocks, and, of course, more bleeding. If those failed, a folk remedy called for whirling a black cat with a white spot around the patient's head three times. Inspectors found that the mortality rate of soldiers admitted to army hospitals in Pennsylvania and New Jersey reached 20 percent, not least because eighteenth-century medicine was a "cul-de-sac of therapeutic nihilism."

Warm clothing would have helped the cause. By mid-February four thousand men were unfit for duty for want of winter apparel; many could not even leave their quarters. General Enoch Poor told New Hampshire authorities that for each one hundred soldiers in his brigade he had but one coat, six waistcoats, four pairs of breeches, and two blankets; two of every three men lacked shoes. The Royal Navy's tightened blockade on Chesapeake and Delaware Bays forced the diversion of uniforms and other vital supplies from Europe to distant ports in northern New England or to Ocracoke Island, off the North Carolina coast. Ice on the Susquehanna blocked other shipments, and at one point a shortage of buttons made new wool uniforms unwearable. A camp census found 219 former tailors in the ranks, and many were put to work with needle and thread, repairing rags. Medical officers also collected clothing from the dead to dress the living.

Misery could be found in every corner of the camp. "The place I am in at present is very bad," Isaac How Davenport, a Massachusetts Continental, wrote his brother in mid-January. Lack of forage killed so many horses—fifteen hundred by one count—that sanitation squads could not keep pace with the carcasses that littered Valley Forge. Joseph Joslin, an eighteen-year-old teamster from Connecticut, wrote, "Now we have about 30 oxen gone to the hospital and sent 13 more today—Abigail, Lucy, Anne, Peggy. . . . Well, I need not name them all." To provide 42,000 rations each day, commissaries needed 250 wagons to carry barreled provisions from magazines in Pennsylvania and New Jersey; instead, the army barely had 30 still functioning. Impassable roads made even those useless at times, and the most bountiful harvest Virginia had reaped in years proved of little benefit to the Continental Army because of an inability to transport grain and other provender. Supply officers also reported shortages of barrels and casks—many staves were fed into campfires—as well as almost every commodity. "Not a candle to write by," a commissary noted, "even for His Excellency." Salt to preserve slaughtered meat grew grievously short, notwithstanding efforts at saltworks along the coast to boil down seawater in kettles; bushel prices had jumped fifteen-fold in the past year.

Resignations by army administrators further crippled the supply system. Quartermaster General Thomas Mifflin had quit in early October on grounds of poor health, and five months would elapse before Congress replaced him. The wagonmaster general also resigned in October; the post remained unfilled for months in part because Congress insisted on capping payment for a wagon, driver, and four horses at thirty shillings a day, less than half of what teamsters could earn elsewhere. Joseph Trumbull, the competent commissary general, had quit in August after Congress foolishly curtailed his authority and imposed nonsensical regulations; his lethargic replacement, William Buchanan, was said to be "as incapable as a child" and "paralyzed by his adversities." A deputy commissary general was given to hysterics and "resigned repeatedly, regularly, and monotonously."

"What are Congress doing? Why this torpor? Why this supineness?" Brigadier General Wayne demanded. From the beginning of the war Congress had struggled to create effective administrative machinery to support the army, and by early 1778 that incapacity had crippled the ability to feed, clothe, and otherwise sustain nineteen thousand troops in their winter cantonment. "No person knows how to act or what to do," a commissary officer complained, with only slight exaggeration. A visiting New York official wrote a Virginia congressman in February, "All prospect of keeping the army together is now at an end, and you may expect every moment to hear of its dissolution."

"We should give much to be out of this truly horrible place, but I don't think anyone feels the hardships more than General Washington," a French officer wrote his mother from Valley Forge. "He must have hours of terrible discouragement."

Yes, he did: hours, days, weeks, and eventually months of discouragement, if not despondency. In February, despite the shortage of candles, Washington sent dozens of letters to Congress, governors, and military commanders at all points of the compass, pleading for food and other necessities in correspondence so hurried that often the salutation was abbreviated to "Dr sr" and the signature simply "G. W—n."

Washington had occupied thirty different dwellings and campsites in the five months before he moved into Isaac Potts's two-story fieldstone house along Valley Creek. Here he would live for half a year, sharing the same small lodging with at least fifteen others. A front room on the ground floor with window seats, crown molding, and twelve-inch-plank floors housed half a dozen aides, with their quills, inkwells, and sanders; all officers were instructed to "set their watches by the tall case clock" against the wall. Washington's adjacent office featured a Queen Anne desk by the plastered fireplace and a Chippendale drop-leaf table. A covered archway known as a dogtrot led to the detached kitchen. The commanding general slept in a second-floor bedroom with three south-facing windows overlooking a stable, a carriage house, and distant huts housing his Life Guard, all Virginians. Many of those not named W—n but working for him lived in the Potts garret, including the enslaved manservant William Lee and his free black wife, Margaret Thomas. The house, a visitor observed, was "exceedingly pinched for room."

Martha Washington arrived at dusk on February 5, her coach loaded with hams, cheeses, nuts, and dried fruit from Mount Vernon. A short, plump woman with animated brown eyes, she would spend her third consecutive winter in a Continental camp, "steady as a clock, busy as a bee, and as cheerful as a cricket," as she later described herself. "Mrs. Washington is excessive fond of the General and he of her," wrote General Greene. "They are very happy in each other." On February 22 she arranged a dinner of chicken and boiled parsnips for her husband's forty-sixth birthday; she also paid fifteen shillings to have the 4th Continental Artillery band serenade him outside the Potts house in a biting wind, then served rum and well water to the musicians. Week by week the household scrounged as it could, collecting seven pounds of sealing wax from Boston, a half dozen lemons from a seized British brig, and writing paper wherever it could be found. From other captured enemy vessels Washington bought forty-two pounds of sugar, four canisters of Hyson tea, a dozen white kid gloves, and twelve pounds of the "best hair powder."

As always, the commanding general found distraction and comfort when he could steal an hour to devote to Mount Vernon. He considered himself "banished from home . . . during these troubles," as he wrote to Lund Washington, his cousin and overseer. No detail of husbandry was too trivial for his attention from afar: how young saplings were to be planted; how mares should be bred with a stud named Steady; how Potomac shad could be salted and sold to the army; how oyster shells could pave the estate walkways; whether the enslaved Silla should be parted from her spouse, Jack, an enslaved cooper who, Lund reported, "cries and begs, saying he had rather be hanged than separated." Despite Jack's pleas, Silla was apparently shipped to Fredericksburg for at least a year to help care for Washington's aging mother.

Martha also paid $56 to the sedulous Captain Peale for a portrait and two miniatures of her husband. The full visage showed a strapping man with shrewd eyes and a face aged beyond his forty-six years by cares and anxieties. On paper he commanded ninety-seven regiments, but the nine from North Carolina, as a sad example, comprised fewer than six hundred rank and file fit for duty. Since late summer, "near a thousand officers" had resigned from the Continental Army, by Greene's count, including ninety from Virginia who would leave the army by early spring, seven colonels among them. Washington cajoled or shamed still others into withdrawing their resignations. He acknowledged "great inconveniences from the service. But are we to quit?"

The fate of the army, and thus the nation, seemed to hang in the balance at Valley Forge. By mid-February the commissary department had completely collapsed in a "fatal crisis," as Washington termed it. "The skeleton of an army presents itself to our eyes in a naked, starving condition, out of health and out of spirits," wrote Gouverneur Morris, a visiting congressman from New York. Daily rations were halved, and at least two brigades grew mutinous, "making his excellency the most unhappy man in the world," a staff officer reported. An officer in the 4th Massachusetts wrote, "The beef we draw would hardly be eat by a New England dog."

The army was forced to rely on confiscation. "Exert yourself," Hamilton wrote one colonel in an order from the Potts house. "Our distress is infinite." Foragers sought livestock, grain, fodder, wagons, and harnesses as far south as the Potomac River, searching barns, mills, corncribs, and stalls, beating the woods and swamps, taking whatever they could find in exchange for scribbled chits. "Have to break open stable doors, windows, &c.," an officer reported. "Very disagreeable."

Greene, Wayne, and Captain Henry Lee led several thousand men through southeast Pennsylvania, southern New Jersey, and Delaware, respectively. "The inhabitants cry out and beset me from all quarters," Greene wrote Washington, "but like Pharaoh I harden my heart." Despite vows to "forage the country naked," he found that "the country is very much drained," with barely enough provisions to "prevent the army from disbanding," as Greene told Knox. Wayne hoped to find at least 3,000 head of livestock but rounded up only 130 while skirmishing with British patrols and recalcitrant loyalists. "The army, you know, is the vortex of small fortunes," a dragoon wrote from New Jersey.

In trying to feed his own men, Washington also sought to interdict farmers carrying goods to General Howe on the five roads into Philadelphia. A thousand Pennsylvania militiamen were supposed to patrol the crescent between the Schuylkill and the Delaware, but by February that force had "dwindled away to nothing," Washington complained—fewer than a hundred armed men. A Continental colonel writing from Old York Road estimated that enough flour slipped into the city every day "to maintain eight or ten thousand men." Apprehended smugglers were punished savagely: Thomas Butler, a flour merchant, received 250 lashes across his bare back, and the sheep drover Daniel Williamson got 200. Lesser miscreants were pelted with their own eggs. Washington rejected a proposal to forcibly evict all residents east of the Schuylkill as more "desirable than practicable," but he encouraged Brigadier General John Lacey to confront loyalist Quakers and seize their horses. Lacey complied, telling his cavalry that "if they refuse to stop when hailed, fire upon them and leave their corpses laying in the road."

Like most civil wars, this one intensified day by day in a brutal cycle of violence and retribution. "Everywhere distrust, fear, hatred, and abominable selfishness," wrote Nicholas Collin, the Lutheran pastor who had ministered to dying Hessians at Red Bank. "Parents and children, brothers and sisters, wife and husband were enemies to one another."

In desperation, Washington in February asked his most trusted and competent lieutenant to become quartermaster general, effectively serving as his chief of staff and principal victualler. Nathanael Greene resisted. While he toiled as a supply officer, Greene told a fellow general, "all of you will be immortalizing yourselves in the golden pages of history." To Washington he lamented, "Nobody ever heard of a quartermaster in history." Congress sweetened the offer by allowing Greene to retain his field command as a major general—in "the line of splendor," he called it—and to split a 1 percent commission on all army purchases with two able assistants. He also could appoint forage masters, wagon masters, and other vital department officers. In the end he relented out of devotion to the patriot cause and to Washington. "There is no other man upon earth could have brought me into the business but you," Greene told the commander in chief.

He was precisely the right man for the job. Now thirty-five, with the burly shoulders of someone who'd once forged anchors for a living, he had an ambling gait from a crick in one knee and the chronic wheeze of a severe asthmatic; a dusty camp bed might keep him awake half the night, gasping for breath. Personally fearless, he was as aggressive as Washington—always ready for "fisty cuffing"—yet he also sensed when to urge restraint, recently having told the commanding general, "The cause is too important to be trifled with [just] to show our courage." Greene had been cast out of the Quaker assembly in Rhode Island, ostensibly for embracing the profession of arms and violating the prohibition against spiritous liquor, but he still quoted the Bible frequently. As an autodidact, he was such a voracious reader that a friend remarked, "Nobody could get the substance out of a book as he could." Sometimes petulant, he could be sensitive to slights, including Washington's failure to publicly acknowledge his adroit rearguard actions at Brandywine. He embraced both homespun remedies, such as removing an infant's birthmark by washing it in port and then giving the child a few sips, and portentous bromides, including "Human life is checkered with evils. . . . It is the business of a soldier and a philosopher to be prepared for whatever may happen." His luck for good or ill, he believed, was recorded in "the book of fate."

Not least among Greene's assets was his wife, Caty, who arrived at Valley Forge in February after depositing their young children, George Washington Greene and Martha Washington Greene, with relatives in Rhode Island. "I feel a blank in my heart which nothing but your presence can fill up," her husband had written. Described as "a handsome, elegant, and accomplished woman," with violet eyes and glossy black hair, she had many admirers in the officer corps, including the commander in chief. Though devoted to "my dear angel," Greene at times could be overbearing. "Remember when you write to Mrs. Knox you write to a good scholar," he told Caty. "Therefore mind and spell well. You are defective in this matter, my love. A little attention will soon correct it."

The new quartermaster soon recognized that his department was "very much out of order in almost every part of the continent." The items for which he was responsible included iron spoons, wooden pails, stew pans, cannon shot (double-headed, grape, langrage, round), shoes, shot pouches, dung forks, saddles, ice skates, calfskins, compasses, tents (bell, common, horsemen's, marquee, walled), forage, three types of adzes, five types of axes, eleven types of saws, and fourteen types of vessels, from barges to whaleboats and xebecs. Within hours of taking office on Saturday, March 28, he sought wagons in Virginia, sent work details to repair the roads from various depots, calculated whether teamsters were worth £10 a month, and wondered how to reduce equine mortality.

He organized a flotilla of shallow-draft vessels to haul hay and other supplies down the Schuylkill from Reading. Two tons of iron were sent to a New Jersey forge to make eighteen hundred camp kettles, and a supplier in Boston agreed to make fifty thousand cedar canteens. A farm across the river from Valley Forge became a storage site for flour by the barrel, rice by the tierce, and cattle by the drove. Storerooms were set aside for vinegar, mutton, soap, tongues, and barreled pork. Greene proved that even if only one victualing scow in four eluded the forty Royal Navy ships on blockade duty, it was still more efficient for the army to move supplies by water than overland. A cavalry colonel received $50,000 in early March to buy six hundred horses in Virginia and North Carolina, "sound and clean made," as Washington instructed. Slowly the horse yard began to fill up again, each animal branded on the left rear haunch with "CA," for Continental Army. Wagon masters would assemble three hundred jolt-wagons by May. "General Greene desires you'd hurry," one teamster was told, "and drive as if the devil was in you."

Greene's desk at Moore Hall, a confiscated loyalist estate three miles west of the Potts house, was soon piled high with statistical sheets, bills, contracts, complaints, and inventories of everything from bridles and tar barrels to tomahawks. For every problem solved, two more appeared: three hundred hats proved much too small for American heads; a lead mine in

Juniata, Pennsylvania, had leaky shafts and a shortage of experienced miners; a merchant contracted to provide thirty thousand yards of linen for shirts and coveralls delivered only thirteen hundred yards of shoddy material; prices rose while Continental currency values plummeted.

But slowly the camp, the army, and the cause eased back from the brink. Meticulous and indefatigable, Greene would spend $4 million by late spring, admitting that "it seems to be but a breakfast for the department." The organization he was building would eventually include three thousand agents, regional deputies, assistants, clerks, accountants, auditors, messengers, foragemasters, teamsters, artificers, and boatmen; as quartermaster general he would write twenty-five hundred letters. With each passing day his thoughts turned to the summer campaign ahead. Knox's artillery arsenal now included 170 guns and 21 mortars, for which he wanted 215,000 shot and shell, plus 500 covered ammunition carts. Washington wanted a thousand tons of gunpowder stockpiled and four hundred musket cartridges for every soldier in the line. The arsenal in Lebanon alone, seventy miles west, was turning out six thousand cartridges a day, each with a one-ounce lead ball and three buckshot. Women made a third of them.

After Caty went home to Rhode Island, Greene wrote her from Valley Forge:

> I am here in the usual style—writing, scolding, eating & drinking. But there is no Mrs. Greene to retire to spend an agreeable hour with. . . . Kiss the sweet little children over and over again for their absent Papa. You must make yourself as happy as possible.

Another indispensable man arrived at Muddy Forge on Tuesday, February 24. Barrel-chested, slab-cheeked, and toting both a brace of enormous horse pistols and a silver-headed swagger stick, he wore a splendid scarlet uniform trimmed in blue and adorned with the Star of Fidelity, an eight-pointed gaud of gold and silver. Knee-high riding boots, a fine cloak, and a black beaver bicorne—set just so atop his powdered, graying head—completed the ensemble. "He seemed to me," a sixteen-year-old American private wrote, "the perfect personification of Mars." His attendants included two aides as vividly costumed as he was, a French cook, a valet, two lesser servants, and Azor, a skittish Italian greyhound. He spoke barnyard German, capable French, and not a syllable of English. In his portmanteau he carried effusive letters of endorsement from both Franklin and Congress identifying "this illustrious stranger" as Baron Friedrich Wilhelm von Steuben, "a lieutenant general in foreign service" and former aide-de-camp to Frederick the Great.

Washington trotted out to escort him into camp over the new nine-pillared bridge spanning the Schuylkill at Fatland Ford. Through Steuben's English-speaking secretary, the commander in chief soon learned of their eventful journey: how they had sailed from Marseille in late September aboard *Flamand*, a French ship chartered by Monsieur Beaumarchais and disguised as a merchantman bound for Martinique; how after surviving a stupendous storm, three fires in the forecastle, and a mutiny—the mutineers were shot—the ship arrived in New Hampshire on December 1 with forty-eight brass 4-pounders, four thousand muskets, thirty tons of sulfur, and nine tons of gunpowder; how several thousand welcoming New Englanders appeared on the Portsmouth waterfront "as if to look at a rhinoceros," providing Steuben with wagons, packhorses, and "five Negroes given me as grooms and drivers." He had come to Valley Forge as a volunteer rather than risk provoking discontent among Washington's generals by demanding high rank. Having been misinformed in France about the preferred color of American uniforms, Steuben intended, first thing, to find a dyer who could transmute his red tunic to blue. "He appears to be much of a gentleman," Washington wrote Congress, "a man of military knowledge and acquainted with the world."

In fact, he was not what he seemed. Born in Magdeburg in 1730, the son of a Prussian army engineer, Steuben had enlisted at sixteen. He fought in the War of the Austrian Succession and then, as an infantry captain, in the Seven Years' War, during which he was wounded twice and captured by the Russians. Later he served briefly as a junior aide to the great Frederick before peace returned to Europe. Sociable, witty, and well-read in both tactical military manuals and Enlightenment literature—he revered *Don Quixote*—Steuben became the court chamberlain for a penurious, obscure prince in southwestern Germany. His services and "irreproachable conduct" earned him that Fidelity star and the honorific title of *Freiherr*—"baron." But an accusation in August 1777 that he had "taken familiarities with young boys" sent Steuben hastening to Paris, possibly to avoid prosecution. Described by an otherwise admiring biographer as "a systematic, circumstantial, and deliberate liar," Steuben met the ubiquitous Beaumarchais, who introduced him to the American commissioners in Passy.

Apparently unaware of the malfeasance allegations but impressed by Steuben's experience and bearing, Franklin recommended his "true zeal for our cause" to Washington. Either deceived by the baron or in cahoots with him, Franklin enhanced his credentials by asserting that he had served Frederick "in all his campaigns" for twenty years, including as the

Prussian quartermaster general; the former captain was also transformed into a former lieutenant general—a promotion of six grades. Before buying his bespoke scarlet uniform and leaving for Marseille, Steuben requested compensation only for his expenses and for the loss of his European income, declining to mention that he had none. More than a decade later, Steuben would write that if he had used "illicit stratagems to gain admission into the service of the United States, I am sure I have obtained my pardon of the army."

That much, at least, was true. During his first fortnight at Valley Forge he dined ten times with Washington and swiftly beguiled the aides Hamilton and Laurens, who carried on long conversations with him in French on topics ranging from infantry tactics to Cervantes and Voltaire. Given the title of inspector and the authority to teach the army soldiering techniques, Steuben rose at three o'clock each morning, drank his coffee and smoked his pipe as a servant dressed his hair, then set off on horseback for the Grand Parade, a mile-long meadow in a sheltered valley. "He has undertaken the discipline of the army," a colonel wrote, "and shows himself to be a perfect master of it, not only in the grand maneuvers but in the most minute details."

No defect plagued the Continental Army more than an incapacity for close-order drill, the coordination among units maneuvering under fire. As demonstrated at Brandywine, Germantown, and elsewhere, "it was almost impossible to advance or retire in the presence of the enemy without disordering the line and falling into confusion," a veteran officer conceded. Steuben opened what he called his "military school" by choosing a company of 120 fit men and drilling them intensely in the manual of arms: marching, firing by platoons, bayonet assaults, and other battlefield skills. He increased the American march rate to 75 paces per minute, up from the British 60, and quick time to 120 paces, or "about as quick as a common country dance." The troops learned to shift from a march column into a line of battle, allowing the army to move and deploy with alacrity. As companies were trained, they returned to their brigades to provide drill instructors for the other regiments.

American officers were astonished to see a decorated nobleman of the Holy Roman Empire—a high-ranking intimate of Frederick the Great's, no less—personally barking drill orders while tromping through the mud. "In our European armies a man who has been drilled for three months is called a recruit," Steuben explained. "Here, in two months, I must have a soldier." When frustrated or irate "he began to swear in German, then in French, and then in both languages together," his secretary, Peter Du Ponceau, reported. If that failed to bring results, he would tell Du Ponceau,

"Come and swear for me in English." He soon learned two syllables in English—"Goddamn!"—and then a complete sentence: "I can curse dem no more." Americans, he soon recognized, were unaccustomed to blind obedience. To a Prussian friend he wrote, "You say to your soldier, 'Do this,' and he does it. But I am obliged to say, 'This is the reason why you ought to do that.' And then he does it."

Steuben continued to dine often with Washington and to pay evening calls at the Potts house for discussions about discipline, supply, army administration, and such nettlesome issues as how to prevent lost or pilfered muskets. He demonstrated wry humor by organizing a dinner at his own quarters and inviting only young officers who no longer had an intact pair of breeches; he fed the *sans culottes*, as he called them, tough beef and potatoes, with a dessert of hickory nuts and "salamanders"—a liquor-filled glass that was set on fire and quaffed, flame and all. Some commanders found him tactless and abrasive, but they never knew when Steuben would appear—poking, prodding, scrutinizing, correcting. A colonel who was told by an unlettered clerk that his brigade was due for inspection by "the honorable Bang Stubang," was also advised, "It would be needless to inform you that he will be very particular." Washington was pleased enough with his performance that in May he endorsed Steuben's appointment as inspector general of the Continental Army, with a major general's rank and pay.

By the time Steuben confessed to John Laurens that he had never been a Prussian lieutenant general, no one cared. "Baron Steuben is making sensible progress with our soldiers," Laurens said in breaking the news to his father, Henry, the president of Congress. "He is exerting himself like a lieutenant anxious for promotion," young Laurens added, "and the good effects of his labor are visible."

On April 5 another poseur arrived in camp. Major General Charles Lee, second in command of the Continental Army, had been in British custody for sixteen months after being captured by dragoons in New Jersey. Released on parole pending his imminent exchange for Richard Prescott, the British general snatched last summer from his bedroom in Newport, Lee made his way out from Philadelphia at two p.m. to a hero's welcome, a noisy pack of dogs gamboling at his heels as usual. A corporal and eight privates collected his baggage, and on Washington's order, Greene sent "two of the best horses" from the Continental yard as his personal mounts. Officers in double ranks formed an honor guard along the road east of the Valley Forge redoubts as fifes and drums played martial airs. A witness recorded the commander in chief's welcoming embrace:

> All the music of the army attended. The General, with a great number of principal officers and their suites, rode about four miles on the road towards Philadelphia and waited till General Lee appeared. General Washington dismounted & received General Lee as if he had been his brother.

Captivity had not improved Lee's appearance. His narrow shoulders sat on a frame so thin and spindly that he hardly seemed to cast a shadow. Hobbled by gout, his complexion sallow, he had a receding chin and an enormous nose variously described as "disagreeable" and "a real deformity." Much of his flamboyant wardrobe had vanished at the time of his capture: a bone-white uniform faced in blue, a black hussar's tunic trimmed in fox pelts, his silver epaulets, five fine waistcoats, and a cherished pair of steel pistols inlaid with gold. Now more conventionally uniformed, he was, as ever, a bit slovenly.

No matter. He was back with the army he had served well, from Cambridge to Charleston. Washington escorted him through an exuberant cordon of soldiers around the Potts house, where he was toasted many times at a dinner in his honor before retiring for the night in Lady Washington's sitting room. When he emerged late the next morning, Colonel Elias Boudinot reported, "he looked as dirty as if he had lain in the street all night."

He would forever remain a riddle to both his detractors and his admirers. Among the most eccentric figures to serve the American cause, he described himself as "a courtier" and "a vagabond," with "a most canine, insatiable appetite attended with weakness and low spirits." The son of a colonel, commissioned as a British Army subaltern at age eleven, he considered himself "born in the army," although an education in Switzerland developed his fluency in Latin, Greek, the Romance languages, and mathematics, along with a fondness for Plutarch and Rousseau. He had retired as a half-pay British lieutenant colonel after more than three decades of service, including an improbable stint as a Polish major general, before resigning his commission and immigrating to America in 1773. His fiery rhetoric and his contempt for the king and his army enchanted American rebels. Dr. Rush found him "eloquent and at times witty and brilliant in conversation." He considered prudence "a rascally virtue," and Rush observed that "a troupe of dogs, which he permitted to follow him everywhere, seemed to engross his whole heart." Lee agreed, explaining, "When

my honest quadruped friends are equaled by the bipeds in fidelity, gratitude, or even good sense, I will become . . . a philanthropist." Upon accepting a major generalship when the war began, he soon became Washington's
capable right hand.

"His brain was lucid and incisive," a sympathetic biographer, John
Richard Alden, later wrote. "Vain and ambitious, yet conscious of his
defects . . . he was looked upon by many [patriots] as the ablest officer in
the Continental Army during the first nineteen months of its existence."
Yet even before Lee's capture, certain character flaws had leaked through:
he could be erratic, disloyal, and intemperate, traits that contributed to his
careless apprehension by an enemy patrol. While conceding that he was
"an original genius," James Thacher saw "a malignant, sordid passion for
personal satire and invective. . . . He could descend to the level of a querulous clown." But now he was ready to help command the army he had not
seen for nearly a year and a half.

He disliked what he saw. Within hours of arriving at Valley Forge, he
confided to Colonel Boudinot, the Continental commissary of prisoners,
that he "found the army in a worse situation than he expected and that
General Washington was not fit to command a sergeant's guard." Even before leaving British custody, he had proposed that Congress build a strong
fortress in Pittsburgh as a refuge for "all the old men, women, and children," as well as "all the riches of the country"; if that citadel still seemed
vulnerable, Congress could "row down the Ohio to Spanish territory for
protection."

He now outdid this silly chimera with "Plan of an Army," which he
described to Washington as "a hobby horse [that] runs away with me. Indeed I am so infatuated with it that I cannot forbear boasting its excel-
lences." Any suggestion that the Continental Army was "equal to the British
in discipline, officers, and even ardor or numbers . . . is talking nonsense,"
he wrote in his windy treatise. The only hope for success was "a plan of
defense," wearing down the British by avoiding them. In a note to Congress he requested promotion to lieutenant general—a rank held only by
Washington—asserting that he "cannot do without me."

Lee knew that skeptics in Congress and in the army nurtured doubts
about Washington's competence. A furor earlier in the year had exposed the
commanding general's vulnerability when an Irish-born, French-trained
brigade commander named Thomas Conway wrote defamatory remarks
that reached Washington's ear, allegedly including the charge that "a weak
general and bad counselors" were undermining the patriot cause. Conway
had served capably at Brandywine and Germantown, and Congress promoted him to major general over twenty-three more senior brigadiers—"as

unfortunate a measure as ever was adopted," in Washington's lament—then appointed him inspector general with sweeping powers that undercut the commander in chief. Factions formed. Horatio Gates, inflated by his Saratoga success and recently named by Congress to be president of the Board of War and Ordnance, seemed to fancy himself a suitable candidate if a new army chief was required. The commanding general's aides led a counterattack against Conway, whom Hamilton called a "villainous calumniator" and "vermin bred in the entrails."

Although Greene suspected a "cabal" and John Laurens detected a "pernicious junto," no organized conspiracy threatened Washington's leadership. Always sensitive to criticism, he deftly let proxies argue his case, including loyal generals with political clout and Henry Laurens, a stalwart champion who told Lafayette that the contretemps "amounts to little more than tittle tattle." A strong majority in Congress recognized that Washington, if imperfect, was capable and indispensable. The fracas subsided. The commanding general "is out of reach of his enemies, if he has an enemy, a fact which I am in doubt of," the senior Laurens added. Gates meekly pledged his fealty. Washington, aware of Gates's ambitions, agreed to bury their differences "in silence and, as far as future events will permit, oblivion," although he would never completely trust him again. Conway, in a theatrical snit, submitted his resignation in mid-April, only to be stunned when Congress accepted it, opening the inspector generalship for Steuben—albeit under Washington's chain of command. An indignant Washington partisan, Brigadier General John Cadwalader, challenged Conway to a duel, then put a bullet through his jaw and out the back of his neck, which "stopped his lying mouth." From what he assumed was his deathbed, Conway wrote Washington, acknowledging, "You are in my eyes the great and good man." He in fact recovered and returned to France. "The determinations of Providence," Washington mused, "are always wise, often inscrutable."

Whether Charles Lee saw in this ruction a path to fulfill his own overweening ambition was unclear. Regardless, he was harboring a secret that would likely have led to his arrest had it not remained undiscovered until the 1850s, when a researcher found an incriminating document in the papers of Henry Strachey, Admiral Howe's aide. Dated March 29, 1777, and titled "Mr. Lee's Plan," the eight pages in Lee's handwriting offered the Howe brothers a "scheme for putting an end to the war." Written while he was jailed in New York, the proposal asserted that America could not win on the battlefield and "must in the end, after great desolation, havoc, and slaughter, be reduced to submit." To hasten that day, Lee urged the Howes to send two thousand redcoats in transports up the Potomac to Alexandria, Virginia, and another two thousand up the Chesapeake to Annapolis. This "will unhinge and dissolve the whole system of defense. . . . Many inhabitants will lay down their arms and welcome the liberators." The rebellion, he confidently predicted, would collapse in two months.

In late 1776 Lee had publicly declared that "for the salvation of the state" it might be necessary to commit a "brave, virtuous kind of treason." Whether this proposal was that sort of perfidy would never be known; nor was it certain that the British high command had reviewed his plan, much less acted on it. Lee may have been trying to save his skin—some Britons wanted to hang him as a turncoat—or perhaps he hoped to mislead the Howes into taking a false step. The gambit appeared to do him no good in captivity, since he subsequently spent six months in the insalubrious confines of the *Centurion*, a British warship anchored in New York Harbor. If it was a ruse, he never disclosed the matter to Washington. However ineffectual, and whatever his motive, Mr. Lee's Plan was a betrayal.

For now, Lee headed west from Valley Forge to briefly consult with Congress in York and then south to visit his estate in western Virginia. Upon the formal completion of his exchange for General Prescott, he intended to be back in camp by mid-May, dogs at his heels, in time for the next campaign. "I shall most cordially and sincerely congratulate you on your restoration to your country and to the army," Washington told him. After his return, Lee would also take the new oath required by Congress of all Continental officers, swearing on his honor to "acknowledge the United States of America to be free, independent, and sovereign states," and to "renounce, refuse, and abjure any allegiance or obedience" to the British Crown.

Greening grass and the croak of frogs in their marshes heralded the return of spring to eastern Pennsylvania in late April, along with peach, cherry, and apple blossoms. Yet dull winter seemed to cling to York, a dreary German village with 286 houses, a dozen inns, three churches, and several Virginia regiments camped on the common. For eight months Congress had made this "small, inconvenient, and uncomfortable" place the seat of government, and delegates carped about "the worst roads I ever travelled over," as Richard Henry Lee wrote Patrick Henry, as well as the "very bad fare," which James Lovell asserted had "torn out the bowels" of his colleagues. Others were peeved by the exorbitant price of beer charged by a local brewer—half a dollar for a gallon. Worse still, wrote the concupiscent Gouverneur Morris, "there are no fine women here at York."

Printing money seemed to be York's principal industry. A Hall & Sellers press, once owned by Franklin, had been installed on the second floor of a gambrel-roofed building at Market and Beaver Streets. Using rag paper stippled with blue fibers and mica flakes, it had turned out $25 million in denominations ranging from $2 to $40. Each Continental bill, inked with a pigment called Frankfort black, was supposed to be signed by two witnesses—one in black ink and the other in red—although the Treasury Office soon would hire boys for a pittance to do the job. In a vain attempt to forestall counterfeiters, various engraved seals were used, including an ornate hog on the $4 bill, as well as inspiriting Latin mottoes, such as POST NUBILA PHOEBUS—"After dark clouds comes the sun"—later printed on $55 notes.

Printers could hardly meet the demand. "'Tis impossible for the press to turn out money as fast as 'tis wanted," Colonel Timothy Pickering wrote on May 1. Despite the plunging value of Continental currency, now $6 to a dollar in silver or specie, Congress resisted shoring up the nation's revenue system with taxation. "Do you think, gentlemen, that I will consent to load my constituents with taxes when we can send to our printer and get a wagonload of money?" one delegate asked. The treasury consequently sent cash in great stacks to the army, along with shears to cut individual bills from the sheets of money.

Since shortly after the first shots were fired at Lexington, Congress, by default, had served as the country's supreme executive, legislative, and judicial authority. Henry Laurens urged states to send "no frolickers, no jolly fellows, or you will be despised," adding, "We want genius, insight, foresight, fortitude, and all the virtuous powers of the human mind." He would be largely disappointed. No more than three dozen of the eighty-eight elected congressmen were ever present in York simultaneously; often less than twenty appeared. Few were exalted as statesmen. "Debates were perplexed, inconclusive, and irksome," a congressman from North Carolina complained. Another delegate concluded that the only time Congress moved swiftly was "when it was ignorant of the subject." Much of the work was done by committees, now 253 in number and often preoccupied with minutiae, such as whether to appropriate $16.39 for ferry fees and how to dispose of goods abandoned by the British if they should evacuate Philadelphia. An exasperated Laurens suggested that it would be better "to catch the bear before you sell his skin."

At three p.m. on Saturday, May 2, a courier named Simeon Deane arrived in town to find that Congress had adjourned for the week. In a pub on Centre Square, Deane announced that he had come from Paris bearing treaties with France signed by the American commissioners—including his brother Silas and Dr. Franklin—and a proxy for His Most Christian

Majesty, Louis XVI. The cupola bell above the brick courthouse soon clanged, and chattering delegates pushed through the double doors from George Street to reassemble in the meeting hall. While pawing over the documents, they learned that the French frigate *Sensible* had deposited Deane on the Maine coast three weeks earlier. Traveling by horseback through Boston, Providence, and the Continental Army encampment at Fishkill, New York, he had spread the joyful news to cannon salutes and riotous celebrations. "America," a jubilant soldier wrote, "is at last saved by almost a miracle."

Congress agreed, and unanimously ratified both treaties at three p.m. on May 4. Three hundred copies were printed for distribution to the states. Six vessels would each carry a set of the certified documents across the Atlantic to ensure that at least one copy reached Versailles. Courier Deane received $3,000 in freshly printed bills for his trouble.

The tidings triggered jubilation at Valley Forge. "No event was ever received with a more heartfelt joy," Washington wrote Henry Laurens. The commander in chief had admittedly been "among those few who never built much upon a French war," suspecting that France "never meant more than to give us a kind of underhand assistance." He hoped that this generosity from Europe would cause the states to "shake off their languor and be stimulated to complete their battalions." The news also helped counter a grim dispatch from General Lacey, north of Philadelphia, where eight hundred British raiders had attacked a militia camp at Crooked Billet before dawn on May 1, killing thirty men and capturing almost twice that number. "Several were inhumanly butchered after they had surrendered," Lacey wrote. Others were tossed into a raging buckwheat fire and burned alive. "This," Washington had replied sternly, "will ever be the consequence of permitting yourself to be surprised."

At nine a.m. on Wednesday, May 6, each brigade assembled to hear their chaplains read a formal announcement of the Franco-American alliance. Rebel propagandists were already spinning explanations for this abrupt covenant between Protestant America—of three thousand religious congregations, only sixty were Roman Catholic—and French papists. France, it was said, acted solely from magnanimity and was but moderately Catholic; the danger of popery was overblown, and moreover God himself had arranged this collaboration.

A cannon shot at ten-thirty signaled the beginning of the grand review. The entire army marched to the parade ground in bright sunshine, silent but for squealing fifes and the rap of drums. "Triumph beamed in every countenance," John Laurens wrote. Steuben strutted through the ranks, the jeweled star agleam on his uniform coat. Inspecting a bayonet here and a firelock there, he announced one by one to the brigade commanders that their men passed muster. Thirteen field guns each fired three salvos, the thunderous booms rattling up the slope of Mount Joy and down the Schuylkill. Troops raised their muskets and, on signal, running fire crackled down the line from right to left, then left to right. Smoke draped the ranks as the men cried in unison, "Huzzah! Long live the king of France!" Additional shouts acclaimed "the friendly European powers" and "the American states." The celebratory gunfire, a diarist wrote, was "more agreeable to a soldier's ear than the most finished piece of your favorite Handel."

"The officers of each brigade then walked thirteen abreast," Captain Peale recorded. "His Excellency went along with his retinue . . . each regiment saluting him as he passed." Another witness applauded "the brilliancy and good order of their arms, and the remarkable animation with which they performed the necessary salute as the general passed along." Tears streaked Lafayette's cheeks as he stood on the right of the line in the post of honor, his white sash emblematic of Bourbon France. He wept in pride and in sorrow: a letter had just arrived from Adrienne telling him that their elder daughter, Henriette, had died before her second birthday. "My heart is tormented with my own grief and with yours," Lafayette would write his wife. "And while my heart was consumed with sorrow, I had to receive and take part in public celebrations."

The review ended, and the troops dispersed to collect a dipper of rum. Some played cricket or long bullet, a game to see who could roll a cannonball farthest. Fifteen hundred officers and guests, including Martha Washington, Lucy Knox, and other wives, sat at tables under canvas stretched across poles for a feast of "fat meat, strong wine, and other liquors." Washington pardoned two condemned deserters and ordered other military prisoners released from confinement. A New York officer declared this to be "the greatest day ever yet experienced in our independent world of liberty." When the commander in chief mounted his horse at five p.m. to return to the Potts house, thousands clapped and cheered and tossed their hats. He turned and huzzahed several times in reply, then rode on. It was said that "never had men seen Washington's face so radiant."

He had survived the hardest season of his life. No doubt more hard seasons lay ahead, as Henry Laurens cautioned in a note a few days later. "There is blood, much blood, in our prospect," he wrote. "Britain will not be hummed by a stroke of policy. She will be very angry." But for the moment, with the applause of his men still ringing in his ears, Washington would breathe easy. "Providence has a just claim to my humble and grateful thanks for its protection & direction of me," he wrote a friend in Virginia, "and for its constant interposition in our behalf when the clouds were heaviest." He added:

> To paint the distresses & perilous situation of this army in the course of last winter . . . would require more time and an abler pen than mine. Nor, since our prospects have so miraculously brightened, shall I attempt it, or even bear it in remembrance further than as a memento.

A day after the Valley Forge merriment, the twenty-eight-gun British frigate *Greyhound* nosed up the Delaware River, concluding a placid voyage from New York. Barefoot seamen perched on the yards to furl her topgallant sails as she dropped anchor with a great splash in the crowded roadstead off Philadelphia. From the quarterdeck Major General Clinton scrutinized the city's skyline, the waterfront, and the two rebel forts—Mifflin and Mercer—that had caused so much trouble. In a fortnight this world would be his to command: the government had finally acceded to William Howe's request to come home, and Clinton—"our trusty and well-beloved Sir Henry Clinton," in the king's phrase—was to replace him. "The power, reputation, and future welfare of this nation," Lord Germain had told him, now depended on his success in America. His cousin the Duke of Newcastle added, "You have established yourself as the best officer we have, in the opinion of everybody. . . . For God's sake, bear it."

Bearing it was not Clinton's forte. He was ever querulous, tetchy, and tactless, resentful of superiors but doubtful of his own capacity. He had never led a large army or even fought a big battle, much less directed a campaign. "This command," he had written, "cannot fall upon my shoulders." After the Saratoga calamity, Clinton had devoted much of the winter in New York to sending self-exculpatory letters to London with copies of his correspondence to Burgoyne and Howe. He peppered the ministry with requests, remonstrances, and explanations, while writing private memoranda bemoaning the war as "hopeless" and critiquing government decisions. Lord North had been skeptical of his appointment. "It is certainly not desirable, if it can be avoided, to employ any general who . . . complains of slights and ill-treatment," the prime minister told the king. But for lack of an obvious alternative, Clinton got the job as commander in chief of "all the king's forces lying upon the Atlantic," such as they were.

Only love brightened his life, and Clinton the widower had fallen hard for his Irish housekeeper, Mary O'Callaghan Baddeley, the wife of a British sergeant major. Finding her "honest, attentive, and diligent," Clinton ceded "total management" of his household in New York to her even as he pursued greater intimacy. "I never for many months could gain an inch," he later wrote, until "she detected her husband in an intrigue with a common strumpet." She then "attached herself to me" and became his mistress; her husband, Thomas Baddeley, stood aside after Clinton secured him an officer's commission in a loyalist regiment. Mary would remain his lifelong companion, bearing several of his children and making him happy as few things ever did.

Clinton had been ashore in Philadelphia but for a day, with barely time to pay courtesy calls on the Howe brothers, when the sloop *Porcupine* arrived from England carrying two sets of instructions from Germain. The first, dated March 8, informed Clinton of the new conciliatory measures passed by Parliament. A three-man Commission for Quieting Disorders in America, led by Frederick Howard, the Earl of Carlisle, would be sent to the rebel capital from London to negotiate a reconciliation with the Americans. "There can be no room to doubt," Germain wrote, "that the generous terms now held out to them will be gladly embraced." Another campaign would probably be unnecessary.

The second sheaf, marked "Most Secret" and dated March 21, superseded the hallucinatory first instructions. London had just confirmed France's recognition of American independence. An alliance had been formed, treaties signed. War was inevitable, probably against both Bourbon powers. The king intended to avenge this insult, Germain advised, "by an immediate attack upon the French possessions in the West Indies." Clinton was to seize St. Lucia, in the Windward Islands, with five thousand men before the fall hurricane season set in. Another three thousand were to be sent to St. Augustine and Pensacola in defense of Florida. Should a French fleet appear in American waters, Admiral Howe should "attack, defeat, and utterly destroy the said squadron."

Finally, Germain continued, "it is our will and pleasure that you do evacuate Philadelphia." No reinforcements for America were likely, and the army would have to consolidate its combat strength. If Clinton could not hold New York, he must shift his headquarters to Rhode Island or even Halifax. Perhaps the munificent terms in the Conciliatory Acts, soon to be explained by Lord Carlisle, would bring the Americans to their senses and back into the imperial fold. Regardless, Germain added, the king would rely upon "your zeal and ability."

"I am directed to evacuate Philadelphia," Clinton wrote in a private note to himself. "My fate is hard. Forced to an apparent retreat with such an army is mortifying."

* * *

At three-thirty p.m. on Monday, May 18, under fair skies with gusty winds from the west, the most extravagant gala ever seen in America began at Knight's Wharf, on the Delaware. More than four hundred guests filed onto three row galleys and twenty-seven barges, each gaily draped with bunting and flags. One hundred and eight musicians filled three more barges, and the Howe brothers, accompanied by Clinton, took seats on the galley *Hussar* as the regatta drifted downriver past spectators lining the Philadelphia shoreline. Near Market Place the bargemen laid on their oars long enough for the floating orchestra to play "God Save the King" at a somber tempo before the procession came ashore at Walnut Grove, near the shipyards in Southwark.

Here then was the *Mischianza*—the neologism had been coined by Captain John André, who defined it as "a variety of entertainments"—a tribute to the departing commander, who had led them for two and a half years, since Bunker Hill. On a broad greensward sloping up from the river, two squads of British officers appeared, tricked out as medieval knights, half in black satin costumes and half in white, their horses caparisoned in matching colors. A trumpet sounded and mock jousting began, first with lances in the lists, then with pistols fired in the air and pantomime sword blows that simulated war the way every wellborn Briton would prefer: as a lofty crusade fought by men of breeding according to certain civil rules.

At length the tournament ended to applause from appreciative spectators, who, Captain Downman surmised, "did not expect to see anything so ridiculous." The guests made their way to a makeshift ballroom decorated with eighty-five mirrors, where musicians played minuets and reels until ten p.m. Then the windows were flung open to view fireworks organized by Captain Montrésor, the engineer: Chinese fountains, firepots, rockets, and, as a finale, an illuminated arch with a mannequin of Fame blowing a trumpet above the encomium "Thy laurels shall never fade."

Supper was served at midnight on tables arranged in a canvas salon nearly two hundred feet long and brightened by eighteen chandeliers and a hundred three-branch candelabras. Black slaves dressed in white shirts, blue turbans, and silver collars carried out twelve hundred dishes, including lamb, Yorkshire pies, veal, chicken, buttered ham, West Indies fruit, and "fine green turtle, just arrived from New Providence" in the Bahamas. Later the drinking and dancing resumed, gamblers found the faro table, and the last celebrants wobbled home at seven a.m. André, who had served as chief impresario, put the cost of the spectacle at 3,314 guineas, donated by staff officers. The evening, he told a friend, was "beyond description magnificent."

Skeptics disagreed. "Our enemies will dwell upon the folly & extravagance of it with pleasure," wrote Serle, the admiral's secretary. "Every man of sense . . . was ashamed." To others it was a "ridiculous farce" or "a shameful scene of dissipation" or, as the *Gentleman's Magazine* opined, "dancing at a funeral."

Hardly had the final toast been offered to General Howe than the army pounded north after intelligence reports placed General Lafayette and more than two thousand Continentals at Barren Hill on the Schuylkill, just outside Germantown. Ordered by Washington to "use every possible precaution" in gathering intelligence about British "motions and designs," this reconnaissance force had sidled eastward from Valley Forge on May 18, unaware that spies were watching intently. Howe and Clinton led eight thousand men and fifteen field guns in three hastily assembled columns, notwithstanding the bleary eyes and throbbing heads in the British officer ranks. But scouts warned Lafayette of his peril, and his men splashed back safely across the river at Matson's Ford before the dawdling redcoats could cinch the noose. "The water was up to our middle," a Continental private wrote, "and run very swift so that we were obliged to hold each other." The exasperated British columns returned to the city in the evening on May 20, Major Carl Baurmeister recorded, after "a fruitless march totaling forty English miles." Ambrose Serle told his journal, "Follies and blunders without end."

Barren Hill would be William Howe's last military adventure in America. Shortly after noon on May 24, Clinton escorted him to a wharf where Admiral Howe waited in a barge to transport his brother to the man-of-war *Andromeda*, anchored at Billingsport. The artillery park in Philadelphia fired a nineteen-gun salute, and it was said that officers wept while bidding him farewell. "Whether you can send a better general than Sir William Howe I know not," a lieutenant in the 45th Foot wrote his father. "One more beloved will with difficulty be found."

Upon reaching England in early July, Howe would find fewer accolades and more invective. "Every error committed at home has been improved upon by a certain commander in America," the *General Evening Post* declared. A member of Parliament suggested that he "deserves to be brought home in chains." The Philadelphia loyalist James Allen told his diary, "His conduct has given little satisfaction either here or in England. . . . Though a good-natured, worthy man in private life, he is no politician & has very moderate abilities."

His battlefield successes at Long Island, Kip's Bay, and Brandywine had no doubt been overshadowed by shortcomings and missteps, including a failure to destroy the Continental Army in 1776 and his neglect of the loyalists, who were vital to any British hope for victory in America. His way of war tended to be plodding, pessimistic, and incremental, an incoherent combination of coercion and conciliation that often left him at odds with his king and his government. Like most other senior British commanders in America, he was capable more often than he was inept, but that was insufficient for the task at hand. A soldier of great experience who surely understood war, he did not understand *this* war. "The situation demanded a great man," his biographer Troyer Steele Anderson would write. "Sir William Howe was just a competent man."

Before the competent man left for home, his successor purchased from him a gelding for £73 and various pantry delicacies that Sir William would no longer need: twelve pounds of almonds, six quarts of Spanish olives, a thirty-eight-pound block of cheese, and two dozen wineglasses. As he watched Howe vanish down the Delaware, Clinton wrote, "My command is now very unenviable indeed."

The Commission for Quieting Disorders arrived in Philadelphia aboard the *Trident* in a downpour on June 6, after being "insulted by a party of riflemen who fired several shots at us" as the ship sailed up the Delaware, Lord Carlisle reported. He and his two colleagues—the secret service chief William Eden and George Johnstone, a former governor of West Florida—were astounded to find the army packing up to leave the city; no one in London had thought to inform them that it was to be evacuated, even though the order had been sent to Clinton three weeks before their departure. This abandonment of the rebel capital was "most prejudicial to the conduct of our negotiation," they wrote Germain, and reduced their mission to "a mixture of ridicule, nullity, and embarrassments." They were further dismayed to learn that Congress had already agreed to an alliance with France and that Britain commanded nothing between New York and Florida except, for the moment, four square miles along the Delaware. Noting the enormous size of America, Carlisle wrote a friend, "We have nothing on a great scale with us but our blunders."

Carlisle, barely thirty years old, hardly had the stature to impress flinty rebels who for more than three years had been fighting for life and liberty.

Known mostly for cavorting with like-minded macaronis at his Pall Mall clubs and for losing stupendous sums at Almack's gaming tables, he confessed to loving cricket and dancing "till I can scarcely crawl." Even Eden considered Carlisle a "bepowdered fop." A London newspaper claimed that his baggage aboard *Trident* included ninety wardrobe cases, forty boxes of tooth powder, half a dozen opera glasses, two portable billiard tables, and a pianoforte.

Despite such ridicule, he was determined to plunge ahead. A letter to Congress, embossed with the image of a fond mother caressing her children, explained the generous terms of the Conciliatory Acts, guaranteeing the Americans great autonomy, exemption from taxes, and the manifold benefits of empire. Flyers outlining Lord North's proposals were distributed publicly but to bad effect: in Providence the town hangman burned a copy under the gallows, and the governor of New Jersey folded the sheet into a kite for his son. "Can they raise our cities out of their ashes?" wrote George Mason of Virginia. "Can they replace, in ease & affluence, the thousands of families whom they have ruined? . . . We can never again trust a people who have thus used us." Reports spread that the king's government had hinted at a £10,000 bribe for Congressman Joseph Reed of Pennsylvania and a dukedom for Washington if they could arrange a peace. "They are," the commander in chief wrote of the overtures, "meant to poison the minds of the people and detach the wavering, at least, from our cause."

"The common people hate us in their hearts, notwithstanding all that is said of their secret attachment to the mother country," Carlisle wrote his wife. Congress unanimously rejected the conciliation measures as "utterly inadmissible [and] derogatory to the honor of an independent nation." Congressman William Henry Drayton told Carlisle, "The great powers of Europe smile upon us. We rely upon our own virtue and the favor of heaven. . . . Farewell." The disheartened commissioners soon prepared to make their way to New York.

So did the army. After consultations with Admiral Howe, Clinton had decided to travel overland. The navy lacked sufficient tonnage to move thirty-four thousand people, five thousand horses, munitions, baggage, and provisions in a single voyage. Women, children, loyalists, rebel prisoners, and a few regiments would travel by sea, while the rest marched the hundred miles through New Jersey. Attacking St. Lucia and sending troops to Florida would have to wait, despite Germain's orders. Perhaps Washington would be bold enough to confront the king's men on their passage north. "Should W. put himself in my way," Clinton wrote in a private memo, "something may come of it. *Nous verrons.*" We shall see.

1. Louis XVI was an accidental king, placed on the throne in France after the death of his grandfather in 1774 only because of the premature deaths of his father and two older brothers. An absolute monarch, he would decide whether covert French aid to the American rebels expanded into a full military and diplomatic alliance.

2. Marie-Antoinette, an Austrian archduchess, became queen of France four years after her marriage at the age of fourteen to Louis. Capricious and extravagant, she was privately known among courtiers in Versailles as "Madame Deficit" for her enormous gambling debts. "My fate," she wrote, "is to bring misfortune."

3. Benjamin Franklin—a "fat old fellow," in his own description—worked assiduously as the senior American diplomat in France to enlist support for the rebellion from both the court at Versailles and the French people, with whom he was wildly popular. "Every house where he consented to go gained him new admirers who became so many partisans of the American Revolution," one French writer observed.

4. Beginning in February 1777, Franklin and his two grandsons lived at the Hôtel de Valentinois, a hilltop château in Passy, on the road from Paris to Versailles. With a domestic staff that included a cook, a maître d', and a liveried coachman, Franklin acknowledged, "Upon the whole I live as comfortably as a man can well do."

5. With a flair for theatrical tantrums, David Murray, the Viscount Stormont and Britain's ambassador to Versailles, complained that Franklin "will lie, he will promise, and he will flatter with all the insincerity and subtlety that are natural to him."

6. Charles Gravier, the Comte de Vergennes, served Louis XVI not only as foreign minister but also as the king's chief strategist. Vigorous support for American rebels, he argued, was the best way to weaken archrival Britain and restore French prestige in Europe, with "the right to influence all great affairs."

7. Gilbert du Motier, the Marquis de Lafayette, among the wealthiest men in France but with modest military credentials, was nineteen years old when he defied his king and his family to sail from Bordeaux to America. Accepting a major general's commission in the Continental Army, he would serve as both a capable combat leader and a vital link to the French regime. Of the Americans he wrote, "My zeal for their cause and my frankness won their confidence."

8. Major General Arthur St. Clair had studied medicine in his native Scotland and served in the British Army before immigrating to Pennsylvania. Given command of Fort Ticonderoga in northern New York, he chose to abandon the vital citadel in July 1777 when confronted by a superior British invasion force from Canada. "Although I have lost a post," he argued, "I have eventually saved a state."

9. Blame for the loss of Ticonderoga fell hardest on Major General Philip Schuyler, a patrician New Yorker who commanded the American Northern Army. "I am considered a traitor," he wrote, but his swift actions helped stall the enemy advance down the Hudson River.

10. Lieutenant General John Burgoyne was an admired combat leader, military reformer, and playwright when he led his Canada Army into New York as part of a scheme to separate New England from the other rebellious states. A British government official wrote to him from London, "The king relies upon your zeal."

11. Jane McCrea was engaged to an American loyalist serving as a lieutenant with the British invasion force when she was captured and murdered by Indians allied with the Crown, as depicted in this melodramatic 1804 painting. The killing, which fueled rebel rage, "fills me with horror," Burgoyne conceded.

12. George Washington's commanding presence made it possible to "distinguish him to be a general from among 10,000 people," an admirer wrote, although after several years of struggle against the British Empire, one aide declared that "the weight of the whole war may justly be said to lay upon his shoulders." This portrait, a copy by Charles Willson Peale of an original he painted in Philadelphia in 1779, shows Washington in a blue rank sash after his capture of the Hessian garrison in Trenton on Christmas night 1776.

13. Major General Henry Clinton, who became commander in chief of British forces in North America in 1778, had spent part of his childhood in New York when his father served as royal governor of the colony. An officer of ambition and high intellect, Clinton also was beset with insecurity, grievance, and a congenital lack of tact.

14. As the British commanding general for nearly three years early in the war, Major General William Howe cut "a fine figure, full six feet high and well proportioned," an American diarist wrote. Despite battlefield victories at New York, Brandywine, and Germantown, his failure to destroy the rebel army brought mounting criticism. In America, he told Parliament, "the happiest commander will be he who escapes with the fewest blots."

15. Known as "Black Dick" for his dark complexion, Vice Admiral Lord Richard Howe, William's older brother and commander of the Royal Navy in North America, was among Britain's greatest fighting sailors and naval innovators. "The greater his difficulties," an admiring captain observed, "the more he seems to rise above them."

16. At the Battle of Brandywine on September 11, 1777, depicted here in a watercolor by British ensign William Augustus West, the king's troops stole a march around the right flank of American forces, then routed them from the battlefield and into a headlong retreat toward Philadelphia. "Our army was something broke," a New Jersey Continental wrote. "I came off with a heart full of distress."

17. Nathanael Greene of Rhode Island had ascended from private to major general by virtue of his competent leadership and administrative abilities. But as the Continental Army approached collapse at Valley Forge, General Washington pressed him to relinquish battlefield command in order to become quartermaster general. "Nobody ever heard of a quartermaster in history," Greene complained.

18. A former Boston bookseller who commanded the Continental Army's artillery, Brigadier General Henry Knox lauded the steady improvement he saw in the ranks. "Hardy, brave fellows who are willing to go to heaven by the way of a bayonet or sword as any other mode," he wrote.

19. Brigadier General Anthony Wayne, a Pennsylvanian, was described by one admirer as "a caged leopard, an entire stranger to repose." Although he "entertained the most sovereign contempt for the enemy," he found himself outwitted when the British attacked his Paoli bivouac, near Valley Forge, at midnight on September 20, 1777.

20. Major General Charles Grey had served the Crown in uniform for three decades when he led the surprise attack at Paoli. But he was skeptical about ultimately defeating the Americans. "The difficulties to encounter in this contest are great," he wrote. "The people, to a man, [are] against us."

21. Guided by loyalists and ordered not to alert the sleeping Continentals by firing muskets, British dragoons and infantry troops fell on the Paoli encampment with bayonets, swords, and knives. "All the noise and yells of hell," an American colonel wrote. "The carnage was very great."

22. The abrupt American attack against the British at Germantown on October 4, 1777, stalled when redcoats fought stubbornly from Cliveden, the stone mansion shown in this scene painted a century later. Despite hours of relentless cannonading by Continental artillery, the defenders held fast until the Americans retreated.

23. Colonel Peter Gansevoort commanded both the 3rd New York Regiment and Fort Stanwix on the Mohawk River. Besieged by redcoats, loyalists, and Indians in August 1777, Gansevoort brushed off surrender demands by announcing his intent to "defend this fort to the last extremity in behalf of the United American States."

24. Joseph Brant, also known by his Mohawk name of Thayendanegea, was among the most charismatic Indian allies of the British in central New York. Educated at an Indian charity school, where he had studied English, Hebrew, Greek, and Latin, he helped organize the ambush of a militia column at Oriskany in August 1777. The attack left five hundred rebels dead, wounded, or captured.

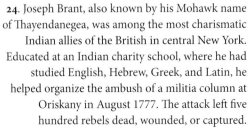

25. A foraging expedition to Bennington, Vermont, by German dragoons, American loyalists, Canadian volunteers, and Indians did not make it out of New York State before militiamen under Brigadier General John Stark surrounded and annihilated the intruders on August 16, 1777. This 1938 painting shows the mortally wounded Lieutenant Colonel Friedrich Baum, in a blue uniform coat, being carried into a farmhouse while his captured German troops are escorted to prison.

26. Major General Baron Friedrich Riedesel commanded the detachment of four thousand German troops who joined the invasion of New York from Canada in 1777. Known to his British comrades as "General Red Hazel," he believed that the chance to fight in North America had been "sent by Providence."

27. The indomitable Frederika Charlotte Riedesel, daughter of a Prussian general, crossed the Atlantic with her three young daughters to join her husband in the Canada Army's advance down the Hudson River. Captured at Saratoga, the Riedesel family would eventually be interred in a prison camp in Charlottesville, Virginia, where a local planter named Thomas Jefferson befriended them.

28. As a Virginia firebrand and the state's governor, Patrick Henry in late 1777 authorized an expedition under Lieutenant Colonel George Rogers Clark to seize the Illinois country bordering the Mississippi River. By ending British hegemony in the region, he hoped to also open trade routes to the Spanish in St. Louis and New Orleans, and discourage predatory Indian raids.

29. "From my youth I have been a soldier," Colonel Daniel Morgan would declare, although he had also been a sawyer, teamster, brawler, convicted horse thief, slave-owning planter, and frequent court litigant. As commander of a rifle corps at Saratoga, he was "exactly fitted for the toils and pomp of war," one acquaintance wrote.

30. Born to minor Polish nobility and educated in France, Colonel Thaddeus Kościuszko had already proved his value as a skilled engineer when he supervised the Northern Army's fortifications along the Hudson River near Saratoga. Pointing to rising ground known as Bemus Heights, where American troops were to build their breastworks and redoubts, he declared, "This is the spot."

31. Major General Benedict Arnold had fought with valor from Quebec to Connecticut before taking command of the Northern Army's left wing at Saratoga. Still limping from a gunshot wound suffered in Canada, seething with grievances and resentments, he was again badly wounded in the same leg and briefly trapped under his dying horse during the decisive attack against an enemy position on October 7, 1777.

32. As General Burgoyne, seen at left with his hand raised to his chin, looks on, Brigadier General Simon Fraser is lowered into his grave after being shot by an American sniper in the battle for Bemus Heights. During the funeral, rebel gunners—unaware of who had gathered on the ridgeline, or why—cannonaded the burial party with captured British 12-pounders. Burgoyne later called the dramatic scene "one of the finest subjects for the pencil of a master."

33. A former British Army officer, Horatio Gates had immigrated to Virginia, joined the American cause, and risen to major general by the time he took command of the Northern Army shortly before the epic battle at Saratoga. Nicknamed "Granny" because of his gray hair, stooped posture, and spectacles often perched on the end of his nose, he had "the art of gaining the love of his soldiers," one congressman wrote.

34. After his defeat at Saratoga, General Burgoyne, flanked by the British artillery commander, Major General William Phillips, offers his sword to the victorious General Gates on October 17, 1777. The observant American officers include Daniel Morgan, dressed in white buckskin. "Burgoyne and his whole army have laid down their arms," Gates wrote his wife that night, "and surrendered themselves to me and my Yankees."

35. As the largest port and commercial center in North America, Philadelphia was also an emblem of American aspiration, a city of learning and science. This peaceful scene of Second Street and Christ Church with its white steeple would soon be overshadowed by frantic, futile efforts to keep the British Army from capturing the town and the adjacent Delaware River.

36. Hessian colonel Carl von Donop had pleaded with the British high command for a chance to redeem German honor after what he called the "eternal disgrace to our nation"—the capture of the garrison at Trenton in late 1776. Ordered to assault Fort Mercer on the New Jersey side of the Delaware River, he found the American stronghold stoutly defended. Mortally wounded, Donop lamented on his deathbed, "I die a victim of my own ambition and my sovereign's avarice."

37. Even after capturing Philadelphia in September 1777, British forces struggled for almost two months to open the city to shipping by defeating rebel defenses on the Delaware River. Sunken obstacles, riverside strongholds, and a small but intrepid flotilla of American warships plagued the Royal Navy until late November. "A British army of 12,000 men and a fleet of 300 sail," a Quaker boy wrote, "had been detained in their operations near seven weeks by a power far inferior to theirs."

38. The Royal Navy's most devastating loss in the battle for the Delaware occurred when the sixty-four-gun frigate *Augusta* ran aground on mud shoals while battling American gunboats. As depicted in this painting by an anonymous British naval officer, fire in the ship's powder magazine sparked a devastating explosion on October 23, 1777, killing at least sixty sailors. "I cannot think an eruption of Vesuvius could exceed it," an eyewitness wrote.

General Howe had intended to abandon Philadelphia's loyalists, after advising them to make peace with rebel leaders. "Now a rope, as it were, [is] about their necks," the loyalist leader Joseph Galloway warned, "and all their property subject to confiscation." Some sent toast and butter to American prisoners in the Walnut Street jail in a pathetic attempt to curry favor. "The distress of the inhabitants in general [is] inexpressibly great," Ambrose Serle wrote. Clinton reversed Howe's policy and offered passage to those who wanted to leave. Three thousand accepted, along with some of the 4,347 American deserters who, by one British tally, had allegedly absconded since September and risked hanging if caught.

By mid-June, hundreds of baggage wagons had been ferried across the Delaware from the Upper Coal Yard Wharf. Flatboats manned by five hundred sailors carried soldiers, livestock, and forty-six field guns, each with 150 rounds, to a bridgehead at Cooper's Point, on the New Jersey shore. By Clinton's order, horses incapable of hard work were shot and tossed into the river, along with damaged cannons and muskets. Two dozen unfinished vessels on shipyard stocks were set ablaze, enshrouding the waterfront in a gray pall. Hessian desertions grew so persistent that one commander locked troops in their barracks at night and ordered roll call taken hourly during the day; to forestall further defections, two German regiments embarked for New York on horse transports. Guards escorted American prisoners from their cells to nine vessels at Penrose Wharf. Six hundred sick and wounded redcoats boarded *Active* and *Webb*. Another hospital transport, *America*, carried army invalids to England but would founder nine days out; the passengers were rescued, narrowly, and a government investigation condemned "such shameful inattention to the safety of men who have suffered in His Majesty's service."

Wheelbarrows, drays, and jolt-wagons pulled by hand shuttled baggage to the wharves in what one witness called "a continual scene of terror, hurry, & confusion." Loyalists auctioned their furniture on the sidewalks, and departing shopkeepers sold their wares for a song—much of it purchased surreptitiously for the Continental Army. British troops would leave local merchants holding £10,000 in unpaid debts. Limited shipping space meant that the provisions abandoned in Philadelphia included thirteen tons of flour, eight tons of salt pork, twelve thousand bushels of salt, and almost forty thousand gallons of rum. More than two hundred ships had assembled on the Delaware from the city docks to Reedy Island, below Wilmington; a bobbing squadron of chairs, tables, cupboards, and other heirlooms too bulky for the holds floated on the tide. "Imagine this river covered with vessels . . . [and] crowded with people leaving the city where they have been born and bred," a loyalist woman wrote. "Leaving their whole property and all their fortune but what they carry with them. It is indeed a most melancholy scene."

An embittered, end-of-days mood took root. "The soldiers indulged in a scene which was cruel and ridiculous," a Hessian sergeant noted. "Everything in the rooms was thrown out of the windows." Or stolen. Captain André, serving as an aide to General Grey, pinched a portrait of Franklin from his dining room; painted by Benjamin Wilson in 1759, the canvas would hang in No-Flint Grey's ancestral seat for more than a century. "I am sure you will pity us here," Captain Nesbit Balfour wrote a friend, "insulted & ridiculed by the Americans, disgusted & unhappy amongst ourselves." Captain Montrésor told his diary before crossing the river, "The whole has been a comedy of errors. . . . Now comes on the farce."

On June 16, Clinton reported that his entire army was out of Pennsylvania except for a rear guard. He crossed the next day with Knyphausen and other senior commanders. At least Mrs. Baddeley would be waiting for him in New York.

The last grenadiers and light infantry slunk from their redoubts in Philadelphia at dawn on Thursday, June 18, marching south for two miles. They demolished the bridge across the marshes behind them before crossing the river to Gloucester Point, just above the charred ruins of Fort Mercer. *Vigilant* briefly ran aground near Mud Island before pulling free and working downstream with the rest of the fleet, including Admiral Howe aboard *Eagle* and the Commission for Quieting Disorders aboard *Trident*.

"This morning when we arose there was not one red coat to be seen in town," Elizabeth Drinker wrote that Thursday. Another Philadelphian added, "They did not go away. They vanished."

As Continental cavalrymen swept into town later in the day, an elderly Quaker called out, "If Uncle Howe was still there, thee would not be going so fast." They rode on, clattering past the Bettering House to the Dock Creek bridge, near the river, and rousting a few British deserters from their bolt-holes. The horsemen "had drawn swords in their hands," Drinker wrote. "Galloped about the streets in a great hurry."

"I found many lean faces," wrote Captain Peale, who rode into Philadelphia the same afternoon. Some six hundred houses had been destroyed. Many others were plundered, not only of furniture but also doors, windows, and even roofs. Redcoats had chopped holes in floors to deposit rubbish and feces in the cellars. "Lucy and I went in," General Knox would write his brother regarding the town, "but it stunk so abominably that it was impossible to stay there, as was her first design."

Fences, palings, and thousands of fruit trees had been splintered for firewood. Every church linked to the rebel cause was desecrated, with tombstones toppled, windows smashed, and pews and pulpits burned. Old Pine Street Church, home to a Presbyterian congregation, had been used as a British hospital, then as a stable, then as a burying ground for a hundred dead Hessians. Eighteen Windsor chairs and other furnishings in the statehouse were pillaged, and the stench from horse carcasses and human corpses interred nearby in shallow trenches would force Congress to reconvene instead at a local college; meanwhile, delegates ordered another $20 million printed and awarded $45 to a bell ringer for services rendered in York. Notices soon appeared around town, including one that advised, "Ran away the morning the British army left Philadelphia, a Negro boy named Tony. . . . Ten pounds reward." Also: "Whereas my wife, Elizabeth Martin, hath eloped from me and gone off with the British army, I will pay no debts of her contracting."

The realization that the British had whisked away three thousand loyalists brought solace. "Our city," Dr. Rush wrote, "had undergone some purification." By Friday morning, carriages and wagons clogged the roads into Philadelphia as exiled residents made their way home. They gave way to Massachusetts troops escorting an open barouche pulled by two matched bays and carrying a Continental major general in an immaculate blue broadcloth uniform with one leg propped up on the opposite seat. Cheers went up as Benedict Arnold stepped gingerly onto the pavement at Second Street outside the double-winged Slate Roof House, former home of William Penn and more recently occupied by Henry Clinton.

Arnold's arrival at Valley Forge in mid-May, after months of recuperation from the gunshot wound to his left leg, had proved "a great joy to the army," a comrade wrote. Still in pain and limping badly despite a special shoe with a thickened heel, he also suffered from what an aide described as "a violent oppression" in his stomach, possibly from ulcers. Washington, delighted to see one of his favorite officers back on duty, appointed him military governor of Philadelphia until he could remount a horse and take a field command. Before leaving Valley Forge, Arnold had signed the required oath of allegiance, witnessed by Knox, to "support, maintain, and defend the said United States."

Within hours of reaching Philadelphia he was hard at work, declaring martial law and closing all private shops until inventories could be completed, thus permitting the army to seize goods abandoned by the British. Pennsylvania authorities had ordered Captain Peale to confiscate the property of departed loyalists, but Washington, wary of vindictive reprisals, instructed Arnold "to preserve tranquility and order in the city, and give security to individuals of every class and description." Protecting loyalists from "persecution, insult, or abuse," as the commander in chief insisted, would be difficult, given the prevailing vengeful mood. The *Evening Post* warned "traitors and Tories who have taken active part with the enemy . . . [that] the day of trial is close at hand when you shall be called upon to answer for your impertinence." An army colonel observed that Arnold "was much crowded with business."

Twenty miles northwest of the city, the Continental Army had abandoned fetid Valley Forge on June 13 for a temporary bivouac across the Schuylkill. At two a.m. on Saturday, June 20, more than sixteen thousand soldiers struck their tents, broke camp, and headed for Coryell's Ferry on the Delaware, above Trenton. At a council of war with fifteen of his generals earlier in the week, Washington had raised seven questions regarding the army's proper course of action. Almost to a man his lieutenants had urged caution, believing, as Knox told him, "that it would be the most criminal degree of madness to hazard a general action." Some preferred to seek refuge in the Hudson valley or to linger in Pennsylvania until Clinton's intentions became clear.

But after six months of inactivity, Washington was ready for a confrontation. Emboldened by both the news from France and his army's resurgent strength, he ordered a pursuit of the enemy on a vector most likely to intercept the king's column as it ambled north through New Jersey. General Lee led the vanguard toward the Delaware, followed by brigade after brigade, tramping through a warm summer rain.

"We shall proceed towards Jersey & govern ourselves according to circumstances," Washington wrote Congress. His assistant secretary, Dr. James McHenry, noted succinctly in his diary: "The whole army in motion."

14.

———◆———

I Would Rather Lose the Crown

Englishmen went about their business even as they braced for war with France. Farmers sowed their fields, merchants sold their wares, and on a single day in early April the public executioner hanged six convicted footpads on the Kingston Hill gallows. Dreadful storms struck Birmingham a day later, splitting trees, unroofing houses, and destroying a windmill with a bolt of lightning said by a witness to be shaped like a weaver's shuttle. Another bolt threw a fireball down the kitchen chimney of the Blue Boar tavern, filling the rooms with reeking sulfur. Some saw auguries of a hard spring ahead.

The confirmation of an American alliance with the Catholic regime in Versailles further cooled British sympathy for the rebels, who had entered "into a league with our ancient, inveterate, and perfidious foes," as one newspaper charged. A taunt in the *General Evening Post* asked, "Say, Yankees, don't you feel compunction / At your unnatural, rash conjunction?" A martial anthem, "Rouse, Britain's Warlike Throng," was sung with fervor at Vauxhall Pleasure Gardens, on the Thames bankside. Such pugnacity unnerved the many Frenchmen working in London's luxury trades as dressmakers, confectioners, hairdressers, and fencing masters.

A brushfire war in North America had abruptly threatened to become a global struggle from the Caribbean to the Indian subcontinent, as well as in British waters. No man in the kingdom rued this more than the despondent prime minister, whose requests to resign not only resumed but became frantic. "Lord North feels that both his mind and body grow every day more infirm," he had written the king from Downing Street in March. He later added, "Your Majesty's service requires a man of great abilities. . . . I am certainly not such a man." And: "Let me not go to the grave with the guilt of having been the ruin of my king and country." The job had become "capital punishment itself." Ministers grumbled about his procrastination, vacillation, and failure to even prepare cabinet agendas. "I am not my own master," he explained. "I am tied to a stake and can't stir."

The king urged him to spend a restful week in April at Bushy Park so "that you may recruit your mind." Although George privately told a courtier that North must "cast off his indecision and bear up, or no plan can succeed," he remained solicitous and generous, giving the prime minister both wardenship of the Cinque Ports—a sinecure that yielded £4,000 annually—and a promise of the first tellership of the exchequer, worth at least another £10,000. Royal messengers wearing oval gilt medals with a silver greyhound as a badge of office regularly sped from the king's study with notes urging North to buck up, stand fast, be brave.

"Peace with America and a change in the ministry," the prime minister replied, "are the only steps which can save this country." He believed, with increasing conviction, that he had identified a candidate who could solve both matters. Why not ask the greatest living Briton to lead the government? True, the best days of William Pitt, now the first Earl of Chatham, were behind him. But as the preeminent architect of British victories in the Seven Years' War, he had treated American colonists as compatriots rather than vassals or refractory children, for which they had raised statues and named towns in his honor. Revered as "the Great Commoner," he later served young King George as prime minister. Popular enthusiasm for Chatham still approached adoration; bludgeoning the French was the highest possible attainment for an Englishman.

His fame, eloquence, and effulgent patriotism evoked imperial glory. He had demonstrated, as one admirer wrote, "how one great man, by his superior ability, could raise his drooping country from the abyss of despair." Recent poor health had kept him from Parliament for two years, but last fall he returned to the House of Lords with his old vigor to give four memorable addresses. "A dawn of joy breaks in upon my mind," the Duke of Grafton wrote after hearing him speak. "May he act once more the part of the savior of his country." In recent months, a public clamor had grown for his return to high office, a sentiment now endorsed by North. Perhaps there was still some magic in the man. No doubt the French dreaded such a resurrection.

So, too, did George III. He had raised Chatham to the peerage but now loathed him more than any public figure in England, with the possible exception of Charles James Fox. That "extraordinary brain," the king told North, "contains nothing but specious words and malevolence." In his recent floor speeches, Chatham had excoriated Crown policy in America as a "labyrinth of imbecility, cruelty, and horror." He denounced German hirelings as "mercenary sons of rapine and plunder" and considered the war "unjust in its principles, impracticable in its means, and ruinous in its consequences." In a voice so thunderous it could be heard in the Westminster lobbies outside the Lords' chamber, he warned:

> You cannot conquer America. . . . Your efforts are forever vain and impotent. . . . If I were an American, as I am an Englishman, while a foreign troop was landed in my country I never would lay down my arms. Never, never, never!

No doubt Chatham had "the scent of office in his nostrils again," as one biographer wrote. The king refused to meet with him but reluctantly approved an oblique approach to see if he might lend his prestige to the government in exchange for a nominal seat in the cabinet. When Chatham's partisans insisted that he replace North and be given sweeping powers, George slammed the door against "that perfidious man" and his acolytes. To North he wrote, "I would rather lose the crown I now wear than bear the ignominy of possessing it under their shackles." When North again suggested drawing some opposition leaders into the government for a display of national unity, another royal messenger flew from the Queen's House.

"Whilst any ten men in the kingdom will stand by me, I will not give myself up into bondage," George replied. If Britons would not abet him, he added, "they shall have another king."

Both the upper galleries and the drafty chamber floor in the House of Lords were crowded to capacity on Tuesday, April 7, when a man who looked older than his sixty-nine years stepped into the chamber. Tall and gaunt, with gleaming eyes and a raptor's beak, he was dressed in black velvet with both legs wrapped in flannels and a large wig spilling down his narrow skull. Two young men—his son and son-in-law—helped him shuffle to the earls' bench. "He looked like a dying man," a witness recorded, "yet never was seen a figure of more dignity. He appeared like a being of a superior species." He bowed to the peers, who stood in respect and made a lane for him to reach his seat.

Lord Chatham had endured debilitating physical and mental infirmities for much of his life. Crippling gout first afflicted him as a schoolboy at Eton. Depression and insomnia incapacitated him for weeks at a time, often succeeded by a manic "streak of frenzy." During one bleak period when he was prime minister, meals were passed to him through a hatch in the door of his darkened room. But today he had roused himself to debate the great issues of the moment.

He rose slowly, leaning on a crutch. "The stillness in the house was such that a falling handkerchief would have been heard," a biographer wrote. Chatham lifted a hand toward heaven. "I am old and infirm, have one foot—more than one foot—in the grave," he said. "I have risen from my bed to stand up in the cause of my country, perhaps never again to speak in this house." Hardly more than a whisper at first, his voice grew stronger as he recounted events that had led to the disastrous rupture with America. Refusing to concede independence—he aligned with the king on this issue—he nonetheless had long supported concessions and indulgences for the colonies. Now a much larger threat loomed, with the risk of dismemberment for the empire—the empire he had helped fashion. To avoid humiliation and decline, the nation must rally, just as it had rallied to win the last war. He continued:

> Shall a people that seventeen years ago was the terror of the world now stoop so low as to tell its ancient, inveterate enemy, "take all we have, only give us peace?" My lords, any state is better than despair. . . . If we must fall, let us fall like men.

He sat down after ten minutes and listened, a frown creasing his brow, as the Duke of Richmond argued that Britain must prepare for war with the Bourbon powers by letting America break away. When Richmond sat, Chatham rose, sat, then struggled to rise again. Abruptly clutching his chest, he staggered and tumbled backward. Colleagues caught him in their arms as alarmed cries rippled through the chamber. Windows were flung open and the galleries cleared. Someone waved reviving salts under the stricken man's nose.

He was indeed dying, although he lived long enough to be carted home to Hayes, his beloved estate in Kent, with its twenty-four bedrooms, stables for sixteen horses, brewhouse, peachery, and grounds that reflected his passion for landscape gardening. As the end came, he asked to hear the passage from *The Iliad* recounting Hector's death at the hands of Achilles outside the walls of Troy.

Parliament appropriated £20,000 to settle his many debts. But the House of Lords rejected by a single vote a proposal that all peers attend his funeral together, a churlish snub influenced by George, who also told North that a unanimous decision by the House of Commons to fund a public funeral in Westminster Abbey was "an offensive measure to me personally." Few of the king's men would attend rather than insult the monarch, prompting Gibbon's tart observation that "the government ingeniously contrived to secure the double odium of suffering the thing to be done, and of doing it with an ill grace." Newspaper hirelings secretly paid by the government continued to ridicule the Great Commoner, as if abusing his corpse.

He lay in state at Westminster, in the Painted Chamber, for two days, beneath black drapery and a tapestry depicting the defeat of the Spanish Armada two centuries earlier. Eight halberdiers and ten torchbearers stood sentinel as large crowds paid their final respects and "Chathamania" inspired valedictory odes said to "revive all the colors of popularity." Then the funeral procession crossed New Palace Yard through ranks of foot guards to the Abbey's western door, led by the high constable, six conductors carrying black staves capped with an earl's coronet, and seventy indigents in dark cloaks, one for every year of his life. Physicians, divines, and sundry esquires followed in close mourning. Crimson velvet and a black pall covered the coffin, affixed with a silver plate identifying him as "the most noble and puissant William Pitt, Earl of Chatham." Above his grave an allegorical monument would depict Prudence, Fortitude, and Britannia seated on a rock as if listening to the statue of Chatham in parliamentary robes, his right hand thrust forward in a gesture of declamation. The inscription credited him with raising "Great Britain to a height of prosperity and glory unknown to any former age."

Now he was gone, and with him a certain antique splendor. The king would only look forward, hoping for new heights of prosperity and glory on the horizon. To North he wrote, "May not the political exit of Lord Chatham incline you to continue at the head of my affairs?"

George rarely traveled beyond the bounds of greater London. Never in his long life would he see his realms in Scotland, Ireland, or Wales, much less Hannover, Jamaica, Bengal, or Quebec. Nor would he ever visit a coal mine or an iron foundry. But at one p.m. on Friday, April 24, he boarded the royal yacht *Princess Augusta* in Greenwich and headed down the Thames, the captain general intent on preparing his kingdom for war.

Past Woolwich he sailed, home of the Royal Artillery, which saluted with twenty-one guns from the riverbank. Fifteen hundred workers, many of them boys, made cannons and ammunition in the ordnance factory, while women in town sewed canvas gunpowder cartridges. More salutes followed from Tilbury Fort, Gravesend, and warships cruising near the Nore, where the Thames estuary swirled into the North Sea. Here the last invasion of England had occurred in June 1667, when Dutch raiders stormed several river citadels and destroyed much of the English fleet before towing the eighty-gun *Royal Charles* back to Holland as a war trophy and tourist attraction.

George was determined that no such humiliation would ever again befall this sceptered isle. War with France, he believed, could rally Britain even as war with America had divided it. To encourage patriotic fervor "against our natural and insidious enemy" he had recently ordered a special performance at Drury Lane of *Judas Maccabaeus*, written by George Frideric Handel in honor of England's victory at Culloden in 1746. He even directed army officers to abstain from claret and other French wines, and he applauded aristocrats like the Earl of Dunmore and the Duke of Gordon, who were raising new regiments; plucky individuals and stalwart towns would muster fifteen thousand troops this year. Most came from Scotland, although Oxfordshire offered six guineas to each army volunteer and Liverpool spent £3,000 to form the 79th Regiment of Foot. A review of the new Northamptonshire militia reportedly drew a jubilant crowd despite drenching rain. "There is quite a military rage just now," one enthusiast wrote.

After sailing three miles up the Medway, a serpentine tributary of the Thames, *Augusta* dropped anchor at eight-thirty a.m. on Saturday at the Royal Navy dockyard in Chatham. Artificers cheered and waved their tools as the king stepped ashore. He spent the day poking about here and there: viewing repairs aboard *London* and *Namur*; watching shipwrights build *Suffolk*, *Leander*, and *Alfred*, designed to carry almost two hundred guns among them; and visiting the forge, the mast pond, and shops making rope, anchors, and beer. Officers pledged their "inviolable attachment to your sacred person" and workers sang "God Save Great George Our King" before a barge returned him to the yacht for the night. Stars above wheeled in their courses, reflected in the dark river like sprinkled silver.

An easterly breeze on Sunday carried him to his newest ship of the line. The Royal Navy had just begun painting names across warship sterns, and this one would be forever celebrated: *Victory*. Moored in eleven fathoms near Sheerness at the Medway's mouth, she had been commissioned a month earlier and was just a fortnight away from making for the open sea. Six thousand oak trees—a hundred acres of woodland—had made her "the largest and finest ship ever built," the *Public Advertiser* proclaimed, and no one who saw her would dispute it. Everything about the vessel was majestic, from the 110-foot bowsprit to the three octagonal lanterns along the taffrail. She boasted thirty miles of rigging; thirty-six sails, sewn from four acres of canvas; a hull two feet thick at the waterline; bower anchors each weighing four tons, with eight-inch cables raised on capstans turned by two hundred grunting men; and, not least, a hundred guns on three decks—twenty-one of which welcomed the king as he prepared to come aboard. For weeks shipwrights, riggers, carpenters, caulkers, and seamen had swarmed over *Victory*. They tarred the rigging, trimmed the iron ballast, slung the yards, stowed spare masts, holystoned the deck, polished the brightwork, and hoisted four hundred barrels of gunpowder—twenty-one tons—into magazines lined with copper to prevent sparks.

George adored this wooden world, with its smells of pitch and tar, paint and varnish, sawn oak, elm, pine, and fir. He scrutinized "with great attention every part of the ship," a witness reported. He saw how walls in the gun decks were painted Venetian red to reduce the shock of seeing blood spattered in combat, while those below the waterline were whitewashed with lime and fish glue to suppress vermin and enhance the dim light. Each of the largest guns, ship-smashing 32-pounders, required a crew of thirteen. At sea with a fair wind, he was assured, she could make eight knots or more despite her girth. Of some eight hundred crewmen, almost a quarter would man the tops, and for his benefit they practiced reefing the sails a hundred feet above the deck—reminding one another of the ancient adage "One hand for the ship and the other for yourself." A lieutenant bawled through a speaking trumpet, "Topmen lay aloft. Throw off the buntlines. Ease the clewlines." For a life of danger and discomfort, an ordinary seaman earned nineteen shillings a month and an able seaman twenty-four, pay that had not increased since 1653.

At length the king took his leave, confident that no adversary could stand against this magnificent machine and her fell sisters. Select officers kissed the royal hand. Another twenty-one guns saw him off, and *Augusta* glided back up the Thames on a fair wind and a making tide, arriving in Greenwich at midnight on Monday. A carriage with a cavalry escort waited to carry him home. So gratified was George by what he had seen on the Medway that he ordered a bonus of £5 for every able seaman and half that for ordinary seamen. "I trust in the justness of my cause," he would write North, "and the bravery of the nation."

No one was more pleased by the king's pleasure than the tall, weathered man who had been at his elbow throughout the excursion. John Montagu, the fourth Earl of Sandwich and first lord of the Admiralty, had long nurtured George's maritime enthusiasms by sending elegant models of warships to the Queen's House and arranging tutorials in naval design. The royal dockyards were easily Britain's biggest employer, and the Royal Navy, the western world's largest industrial organization, protected both the home islands and the nation's global commerce, the font of wealth and power. Like his monarch, Lord Sandwich resolved that it must ever be thus. "Our navy," he had recently assured Parliament, "is more than a match for the whole house of Bourbon."

"No man in the administration was so much a master of the business, so quick, or so shrewd," Walpole wrote of Sandwich. Orphaned young, he had inherited his earldom at age ten in 1729. After Eton and Cambridge, where he became a proficient versifier in Greek and Latin, he toured the Mediterranean for two years, returning with a pair of mummies and eight embalmed ibises from the Memphis catacombs before having his portrait painted while wearing a Turkish turban, a red silk sheath, and a pasha's blue cloak. Described by James Boswell as a "jolly, hearty, lively man," he had such a shambling gait that an acquaintance said he appeared to be "walking down both sides of the street at once." Sandwich admitted, with self-deprecation, that a former dancing master had requested that he "never tell anyone of whom you learned to dance." His passions ranged from linguistics and history to astronomy, numismatics, and cricket. A fellow of the Royal Society, he belonged to the Egyptian Club, the Royal Academy of Arts, the Concerts of Antient Music, and the Sublime Society of Beefsteaks, which assembled in Covent Garden with the battle cry "Beef and Liberty." For years he staged elaborate Christmas oratorios at Hinchingbrooke, his estate in Cambridgeshire, during which he played the kettledrums with dogged exuberance.

He had more experience than any other man in government. At age twenty-nine Sandwich had headed the Admiralty for the first time, followed over the years by appointments as secretary of state (twice), postmaster, first lord again in 1763, and this third stint, beginning in 1771. Energetic and canny, with a superb executive mind, he was impoverished by the standards of British aristocrats and needed the jobs. The king's personal affection enhanced his authority—they shared both musical and nautical tastes—as did as his control over naval patronage and seventeen seats in the Commons, a small but influential voting bloc. "He was a hard man to surprise. He thought ahead and took precautions," the naval historian N.A.M. Rodger would write. "Though he did not betray others, he was always alert to the possibility that they might betray him."

Some considered him a rascal, if not a rakehell. "Vices, more than years, have marked him gray," a disapproving poet wrote. One social club expelled him for blasphemy, and it was said that he took "ladies of pleasure" on long trout-fishing vacations. His libertine antics included a passionate affair with his sister-in-law. "I have never pretended to be free from indiscretion," Sandwich conceded. Worse still, he befriended actors, gave appointments to capable men of obscure birth, and demonstrated professional expertise, a déclassé attribute suggestive of tradesmen. (The *Gentleman's Magazine* once sneered at an accomplished chancellor of the exchequer for his "clerk-like knowledge of finances.")

His wife, the daughter of an Irish viscount, bore him five children before mental illness crushed her. Tucked away in a Windsor Castle apartment, she was declared legally insane in 1767. Long before that Sandwich had met Martha Ray, a beautiful sixteen-year-old mantua maker almost three decades his junior. He hired instructors to teach her dancing, deportment, singing, French, and the harpsichord. As his consort, though never his social equal, Martha often took the female lead in Hinchingbrooke musical productions, shared his apartment in Whitehall, and gave birth to nine more of his children, five of whom survived. An acquaintance described "a perpetual smile on her countenance, which rendered her agreeable to every beholder."

From six a.m. until nightfall, Sandwich could often be found in his Admiralty offices, a stone's throw from Whitehall Stairs, on the Thames. Working at his desk through meals, he sometimes ate sliced meat between two pieces of bread, which he held in one hand while he wrote with the other—the eponymous sandwich. "My business," he asserted, "is always my pleasure." He made it his business to know the royal dockyards better than anyone ever had, conducting annual inspections to correct inefficiencies and to root out supine, incompetent, and corrupt officers. "A man is never so much convinced of what is right or wrong as when he sees it with his own eyes," he asserted.

To build a durable fleet, he insisted on a three-year stockpile of seasoned oak—green wood could cut a ship's longevity at sea by half or more—and comparable supplies of pitch, tar, iron, hemp, and pulley blocks (of which a ship like *Victory* needed fourteen hundred in the rigging and gun rooms). He built sheds for timber storage, supplemented the king's dockyards by shifting some repairs and shipbuilding to private yards, and bought masts from Riga and Gothenburg to compensate for the loss of the best, biggest sticks from New England. His patronage of Royal Navy exploratory expeditions had led Captain James Cook earlier this year to name a newly discovered Pacific archipelago the Sandwich Islands, later known as Hawaii.

At times he could be smug and prideful, so immersed in niggling details that he lost sight of the horizon. Sandwich had dismissed rebellious Americans as "raw, undisciplined, cowardly men"; as late as November 1776 he had insisted that "the very sound of cannon" would scatter them "as fast as their feet could carry them." But the disastrous defeat at Saratoga and the Franco-American pact stunned him. The Royal Navy had almost four hundred vessels of all sizes, including ships under construction, undergoing repairs, or "in ordinary," a form of reserve. But the fleet now needed to grow quickly, with frigates and ships of the line launched from the yards as never before.

That would require all of the first lord's skill. Because North had wanted a quick, cheap war against the Americans, and had hoped to avoid provoking France with an ostentatious naval buildup, the government had resisted Sandwich's pleas for full mobilization until this January. The navy was badly dispersed and overworked. Almost all frigates and other light, maneuverable warships—virtually the entire cruiser strength of the Royal Navy—had ended up in American coastal waters, from Newfoundland to Jamaica. Yet even that had been insufficient to blockade rebel ports or crush the insurrection. The fleet was simply too small for all the demands made on it, including support of the king's army, protecting British merchantmen from privateers, and, now, confronting powerful Bourbon squadrons.

Shipyards had been ordered to pick up the pace by working double shifts and also on Sundays. No strategic principle was considered more imperative than to keep the Royal Navy stronger than the combined naval power of France and Spain. But it took nine months to build a frigate and three years for a big ship of the line; a shortage of skilled shipwrights, sailmakers, and smiths exacerbated delays. Sandwich's difficulties were compounded by squabbling among admirals over promotions, appointments, and prize money. Meanwhile American privateers continued to wreak havoc from the West Indies to the English Channel. A survey by the House of Lords in February had disclosed that 733 merchant vessels had been captured in the past two years, of which more than three-quarters were neither ransomed nor retaken. Those net losses would reach almost 2,400 before the war ended, equivalent to more than a third of all British merchant vessels trading abroad when the shooting began.

Manning the fleet remained particularly difficult. In the course of this war, of 171,000 Royal Navy seamen, 1,240 would be killed in action, 18,500 would die of disease, and 42,000 would desert. Navy vessels on average lost 7 percent of their crews to desertion each year, with those gone missing marked "r"—for "run"—in the ships' rosters. In 1776 alone, 16 percent of all sailors had absconded, such flight reflecting the low pay and spartan conditions at sea, including "the confined, birdcage-like space which seamen are obliged to live in," as one captain acknowledged.

Britain's traditional remedy for manpower was the press-gang, and on

March 16, the Admiralty had ordered a general press to cover a shortfall that otherwise would amount to tens of thousands of sailors. Authority for forcible conscription derived from the powers of arrest recorded in the *Black Book of the Admiralty* during the fourteenth-century reign of Richard II; by this century only enslaved Africans exceeded impressed sailors as the empire's largest source of forced laborers. A thousand officers and sailors from the navy's Impress Service manned forty-nine stations around Britain, mostly in ports, where apprehended swabs could be detained in alehouse "lock-up rooms" until they were marched to their ships, occasionally in fetters. Another thousand worked aboard tenders to grab crewmen from homebound merchantmen, and in May the Admiralty would temporarily halt outbound sailings from English harbors to cull the crews for still more sailors. Only seafarers were supposed to be pressed, but press-gangs swept up so many unlucky landsmen that a third of a warship's company might consist of lubbers. The navy's penchant for pressing seamen from army victualing vessels proved particularly self-defeating, since hundreds of transport ships would be immobilized in British waters for lack of crewmen.

Despite his bravado in assuring Parliament that the king's navy could defeat the Bourbons, Sandwich was privately less sanguine. On April 13 he had written that war against France, Spain, and America "is, I fear, more than we are equal to." How to simultaneously safeguard the home islands and British interests elsewhere around the globe was an insuperable dilemma that now caused bitter divisions in the cabinet.

Sandwich argued that Britain could overcome the loss of America and other colonies, including the sugar islands, but would not survive a destruction of the fleet that left England open to invasion. Keeping most warships concentrated along the English Channel was prudent until French intentions became clear, particularly since the enemy fleet was divided between Brest, on the Atlantic coast, and Toulon, in the Mediterranean.

Abandoning America altogether to fight a larger, more dangerous foe made sense to Sandwich, but the king balked at such a radical realignment. Without America, would Britain even have an empire? Clinton had been told to abandon Philadelphia and withdraw to New York to prepare for an assault on the French at St. Lucia. Pending the outcome of Lord Carlisle's dubious negotiations, Germain favored continuing to give battle against the rebels while also attacking the French squadron in the Mediterranean before it could slip past Gibraltar, into the Atlantic. But on April 27, the day George returned from the Medway, intelligence from Paris confirmed that twelve French capital ships and five frigates had sailed from Toulon with four thousand troops and nine months of provisions under Vice Admiral Charles Hector, the Count d'Estaing. "I never can sufficiently lament the not having sent a fleet to Gibraltar to prevent the Toulon squadron passing the straits," Germain wrote. "The risk of that measure was trifling in comparison to what we may suffer by leaving such a fleet at liberty to attack us." Two days later, in "A Protest from Lord George Germain," he urged sending a squadron to reinforce Admiral Howe in America. He told the cabinet:

> If we are not able to resist France in this, its first offensive operation, what have we not to dread when it shall be joined by the land and sea forces of the revolted provinces? . . . In all military operations of importance, some risk must be run.

The greater risk, Sandwich countered, was in weakening the home fleet. D'Estaing's destination was unknown. Sending a substantial British force across the Atlantic would prove disastrous if the Toulon ships sailed not west but north to join more than two dozen ships of the line at Brest. "We cannot for certain say where he is going," the first lord wrote, "and therefore our dilemma is very great, particularly as we are not able to make any detachments from home consistent with the security of this island." Yet the king disagreed, writing Sandwich from the Queen's House on April 29: "I have not the smallest doubt that d'Estaing's fleet is . . . to attack Philadelphia or New York. . . . We must strengthen Lord Howe."

The decision was made. Thirteen capital ships would soon sail for North America, confronting d'Estaing wherever he could be found. George wrote North that he was "convinced of the propriety" of this action. Sandwich, however, was *not* convinced. He had organized another naval inspection for the king, even grander than the excursion down the Thames. Perhaps the captain general could be persuaded to change his mind.

"Left the Queen's House at 57 minutes past five," George wrote in a memorandum to himself on Saturday, May 2. "Arrived at Portsmouth at 57 minutes past twelve." The royal chaise had fairly flown from London, averaging twelve miles per hour despite three changes of horse teams along the route and such heavy rain near the coast that the king could not see the Spithead anchorage from Portsdown Hill. Boisterous crowds cheered him with "every demonstration of joy," he noted, and a delegation of ropemakers escorted the coach the final four miles to the dockyard commissioner's house. An earsplitting cannonade and a chorus of "God Save the King" announced the monarch's arrival. Sandwich met him at the front door.

Five years had passed since George last visited the largest and most vital of the royal dockyards, during a commemoration of Britain's victory in the Seven Years' War a decade earlier. Since then thousands of soldiers had embarked here for America, with loyal pensioners lining the streets to thwart desertion as regiments marched onto the wharves, where "they rolled us down the hatchways like so much lumber," as a soldier in the 33rd Foot had written in February. This visit, in the midst of one war and on the eve of another, would be more sober.

Servants hauled several wagonloads of furniture into the commissioner's house, including the royal bed. For solace and companionship George had brought Charlotte—"the queen of my heart," as he called her. It was said, unkindly, that the king had winced the first time he saw his homely, seventeen-year-old German bride, chosen in part by thumbing through the *New Berlin Almanac* for a suitable princess. But their marriage in 1761 proved happy and bountiful, producing a dozen children so far, with three more to come. She shared his piety as well as his affection for Handel, country dances, and the theater; he indulged her enthusiasms for jewelry, dogs, and snuff, slipping her another £6,000 this year atop an annual allowance of £50,000. She was fluent in English and French, but in private they spoke German. Charlotte's "excellent qualities appear stronger to me every hour," he would write, and in these exacting times he needed her stability and reassurance. In another year they would send their third son, William, not yet thirteen, into the Royal Navy. "I speak, I hear, and I dream only of war," Charlotte wrote her brother. "I am becoming political despite myself."

At three p.m. the king dined with Sandwich and eight admirals, raising a glass of champagne to the success of the fleet, despite his avowed disapproval of both French wines and "the bad custom of toasting." He then retired upstairs for coffee with the queen and a chance to take his spyglass to the rooftop. The skies had cleared, and late afternoon sunshine glistened brilliantly on forty-two ships of the line anchored at Spithead and St. Helen's Road, along the Isle of Wight. Other vessels beyond counting—sloops, tenders, East Indiamen, bumboats, jolly boats—slid across the Solent and Portsmouth Harbour, each wake etched in sapphire.

By five p.m. he was in the dockyard and then on the water aboard *Augusta* as three thousand artificers serenaded him with "Britons, Strike Home!" For the next four days he rose before dawn to poke about, as he had on the Medway, inspecting the marine barracks, the new powder magazine, the hemp house, the Gun Wharf, and what one visitor called the

House of Vulcan, where dozens of men black with coal dust hammered at a huge forge. Outside the charred, thousand-foot Great Double Rope House, he saw where the arsonist James Aitken, better known as John the Painter, had been hanged from a mizzenmast fourteen months earlier in front of twenty thousand witnesses. He watched ships building—*Crocodile, Eurydice, St. George*—and ships refitting—*Vigilant, Lion, Marlborough, Centaur.* Others loaded provisions from the three Great Storehouses into their holds, including, for a single large warship, 31 tons of salt pork and beef, 35 tons of bread, 38 tons of beer, 184 tons of water, 50 tons of coal, and 2 tons of vinegar. Ratcatchers set traps on every vessel headed to sea.

Nothing intrigued George more than the small frigate he saw stranded in a dry dock. *Fox* had been captured by rebel brigands off Newfoundland last June, then retaken by the Royal Navy a month later. Now workmen meticulously sheathed her hull with thin copper plates, an innovation one captain called "the finest invention in the world" and another naval expert deemed "the most noteworthy design improvement of the century." Wooden ships began to deteriorate from the moment they touched salt water; a seventy-four-gun man-of-war typically spent fifteen months in the dockyard for repairs out of every five years in service. Barnacles, sea-weeds, and a parlous boring mollusk, *Teredo navalis*, known simply as "worm," impaired speed and maneuvering, requiring the frequent careen-ing of fouled hulls.

For centuries mariners had experimented with countermeasures, but the navy had finally found a masterly solution. Britain mined half of the world's copper, mostly in Cornwall and Wales, and in late 1775 sheets of the metal had been bolted below the waterline on several small naval ves-sels. Coppered ships often gained a knot in speed—a substantial tactical advantage—and required far less hull maintenance, leaving them at sea longer and freeing up dockyards for major repairs. A chemical reaction poorly understood at the time caused underwater copper to corrode the iron bolts holding together a ship's keel, sternpost, and rudder; ingenious modifications eventually solved this problem, including the creation of a watertight seal between the two metals. The king and Sandwich would agree this year to copper all warships, despite the expense: *Fox* alone cost almost £4,000, and a ship of the line required fifteen tons of copper, ap-plied in three hundred pliant sheets. But within two years most of the fleet would be sheathed, making the navy faster, nimbler, and more durable.

The king reboarded *Augusta*, this time with Charlotte at his side. On Tuesday, so many salutes thundered from the ramparts and the anchorage that their ears rang constantly. (To conserve powder, in another month most salutations between ships would be limited to cheers and flags.) Fifty yawls and barges carrying the eight admirals and every ship's captain trailed the yacht in four columns as their Royal Highnesses sailed through the fleet to triple hurrahs from crews assembled on decks and in the rigging. Later George visited both *Sandwich* and *Prince George*, each carrying ninety guns and redolent of those shipboard scents he cherished. He had intended to return to London on Wednesday, but instead announced that he and Charlotte would extend their stay to a full week. "This has put great alacrity into all of them," he wrote North. "I have no object but to be of use. If that is answered, I am completely happy."

The monarch and his queen at last clambered back into their chaise on Saturday morning, May 9. The king rewarded his hosts with honors and gratuities, including promotions, knighthoods, and at least two baronetcies. Throngs in Petersfield and Godalming cheered the royal couple as they passed, reassuring George that his popularity remained robust, at least outside London.

"I know very well I have a difficult time to steer the helm," he told his two eldest sons, George and Frederick, but he intended to "do my duty to the best of my abilities." He was gratified that the royal visit seemed to provide "universal comfort" in Portsmouth and that he had chivied the navy enough to take "every step necessary to quicken the sailing."

Yet the fleet did not sail, not quickly and not for the next month. After whispering in the king's ear for a week, Sandwich had persuaded him to countermand the cabinet order dispatching a squadron to America, at least until Admiral d'Estaing's destination was known with certainty. On May 13 Sandwich sent a courier "to stop the sailing . . . till further orders." The sailing stopped.

Finally on June 2 the frigate *Proserpine*, which had shadowed d'Estaing from Gibraltar, swooped into Falmouth to confirm that the French flotilla was indeed headed west across the Atlantic under "a great press of sail." There would be no merger of the Toulon and Brest men-of-war into a single armada of evil intent. Again the cabinet convened, this time with a consensus. Two Royal Navy fleets were to sortie, one for America, the other for France. Events that had moved uncertainly in fits and starts for six months now began to hurry headlong.

The fleet bound for America had assembled in Plymouth, on the south coast of Devon. Orders to "put to sea without one moment's loss of time" reached Vice Admiral John Byron at three a.m. on June 7. After two days of contrary winds, a frigate and thirteen capital ships—including *Royal Oak*, *Invincible*, and the ninety-gun flagship *Princess Royal*—swung wide of Land's End for the open ocean, bound for New York. War with France, Byron wrote a friend, "might be a lucky circumstance for me."

That was unlikely. Few English sea dogs had more experience than Byron, and even fewer had less meteorological luck, as implied by his nickname, "Foul-Weather Jack." After joining the navy at age nine, he had subsequently been serving as a seventeen-year-old midshipman aboard *Wager*, a converted East Indiaman, when a ferocious storm off Cape Horn wrecked the frigate on the southern coast of Chile. Surviving as a castaway on shellfish, cress, and the ship's dog, Byron and several shipmates would not return to London for more than five years; he later wrote an acclaimed narrative of his ordeal. An excellent seaman, he soon ascended to post captain and married a first cousin, the Cornish beauty Sophia Trevanion, who wrote of her husband: "Though trained in boisterous elements, his mind / Was yet by soft humanity refined."

That was sweet nonsense—he was a notorious rake—but in the following twenty years he commanded many ships in war and in peace. Cruising the Gulf of St. Lawrence in 1760, Byron destroyed a French squadron of more than twenty vessels trying to relieve Montreal. On voyages of exploration for his government, he claimed the Falkland Islands for George III, circumnavigated the globe, and reported, oddly, that Patagonia was populated by civilized giants over seven feet tall. War with America brought him promotion to admiral.

The Romantic poet George Gordon, Lord Byron, his grandson, would immortalize him in *Don Juan* while also writing, "He had no rest at sea, nor I on shore." The memoirist Nathaniel Wraxall agreed that "all the tempests of the deep seemed to have conspired against him," since he "seemed to be always under the influence of an unlucky planet"—perhaps Neptune. So it was hardly a shock when a colossal gale struck Foul-Weather Jack after he left Plymouth, badly damaging most of his ships, scattering the fleet, and forcing him to bear away to Halifax in *Princess Royal*, alone. His confrontation with d'Estaing would have to wait.

The other British fleet, now preparing to sail for the French coast, was commanded by a short, corpulent man with a broken nose, a bad back, and, as a consequence of scurvy, very few teeth. Vice Admiral Augustus Keppel, the son of an earl, had also gone to sea as a boy, eventually building a distinguished record that included successful attacks against the French at Senegal and Quiberon Bay, and against the Spanish at Havana, where he earned twenty-five thousand guineas in prize money. Elected to Parliament from Windsor, popular in the navy and, as one writer observed, "well fitted to become the national hero," he had refused on grounds of conscience to fight the Americans. Despite opposing the North government politically, despite not having been to sea in fifteen years, and despite being plagued with "bad nerves and a worse constitution," he was chosen by dint of seniority to lead the Channel fleet, the beating heart of the Royal Navy. *Victory*, now moored at Spithead, became his flagship.

Between entertainments for the king and queen around Portsmouth the previous month, he found that the ships assigned to him had been ransacked of sailors, sails, cordage, and other provisions in order to outfit Byron's fleet. Intrinsically gloomy, Keppel also convinced himself, without evidence and contrary to Sandwich's assurances, that he was to be a scapegoat should the navy fail. "If this fleet is soon to be brought to action against those of France and Spain," he wrote Sandwich, "I should feel some anxiety concerning a situation in which the security of my country and my own reputation are at stake." Several unkind ministers suspected that his overriding ambition was not victory at sea but embarrassment of the government.

Regardless, the moment had come for both his reputation and his country. Keppel would sail toward the French coast, although to preserve Dutch neutrality and to keep Spain peaceable as long as possible, France must appear the aggressor. On Friday, June 12, *Victory*'s decks were swabbed with vinegar a final time and scrubbed with holystones shaped like Bibles. Those grunting men at the capstans won their anchors, and the loud clap of billowing canvas could be heard as topmen loosed the sheets. With precision and grace, the Channel fleet crowded on sail, beating away from the Isle of Wight like a flock of mythical white birds.

By dusk England was a faint green ribbon astern. Twenty-one British ships of the line made for Brest, two hundred miles to the southwest, determined to make the French fire first.

15.

———◦◦◦———

The French Flag in All Its Glory

No event in early 1778 enchanted France more than the return to Paris on Tuesday, February 10, of the eighty-three-year-old François-Marie d'Arouet, better known as Voltaire, after almost three decades of exile in Switzerland. Perhaps the greatest voice of the Enlightenment, he was the author of more than two hundred volumes of plays, poems, stories, and philosophical tracts, some of which had been burned by the public hangman as a signal of official disfavor. His reformist campaigns against fanaticism, aristocratic pretension, and ecclesiastical prerogative—"Crush the infamy," Voltaire urged—had led to banishment, but now he was permitted to come home to die. Adoring mobs thronged the quai des Théatins to glimpse "the king of thought" or, failing that, to kiss the horses pulling his coach. "We are come to beg you, sir, to breathe upon us," a worshipful group of actors pleaded. It was said that in his prime he drank fifty cups of coffee a day, but now that he was, admittedly, "ancient and unwell," coughing up blood, the doctors recommended ass's milk instead.

It was only fitting that this continental apotheosis of rationalism, tolerance, and irony should meet his Yankee counterpart, whom Voltaire had called "the worthiest man in America, and perhaps in Europe." He and Benjamin Franklin met briefly in the Frenchman's bedroom, where Voltaire offered a brief benediction in English—"God and liberty"—to Franklin's eight-year-old grandson, Benny. A more public encounter occurred on April 29 at the Académie Royale des Sciences. "There presently arose a general cry that Monsieur Voltaire and Monsieur Franklin should be introduced to each other," a witness recorded. "The two aged actors . . . then embraced each other by hugging one another in their arms and kissing each other's cheeks." Yelps of approval filled the hall. "Someone said that Solon was embracing Sophocles," wrote the Marquis de Condorcet. All Paris kept a death watch a month later to see if the anticlerical Voltaire would request rites of absolution as the end approached. He did not, and it was claimed, apocryphally, that when urged to renounce the devil he replied, "Is this a time to make enemies?" In the event, he reportedly rebuffed the priest with a succinct "Leave me to die in peace."

Franklin lived on, now allied with another new arrival in *la Ville Lumière*. Silas Deane had been recalled to Philadelphia in late March— he would spend years answering charges of embezzlement and war profiteering—to be replaced in April by a plump, erect man with bright blue eyes, a balding pate, and the calloused hands of someone who split his own firewood. After a tempestuous crossing from Boston, a thirteen-gun salute followed by thirteen toasts had welcomed John Adams to Bordeaux, although some mistook him for *le fameux* Adams—his cousin Samuel. More gunfire and toasts saw him off to Paris, where he arrived at nine p.m. on April 8. Franklin insisted that he and his ten-year-old son, John Quincy, join him in Passy at the Hôtel de Valentinois, and their unsteady diplomatic partnership began the next day.

"I am but an ordinary man," Adams would write after a year in Paris. "The times alone have destined me to fame." He called himself "John Yankee," and as a young lawyer, standing before a mirror to practice Cicero's orations against Catiline, he had wondered what was required to become "a great man." Diligence, service in a noble cause, and constructive self-criticism, certainly; toward that end he rebuked himself for sleeping late. Dr. Rush admired his ability to see "the whole of a subject at a single glance," and the historian Bernard Bailyn would assert that he wrote with "a vividness and an accuracy of phrasing that makes his prose the most alive and readable of any written in eighteenth-century America."

Yet he could be caustic and irascible, with a molten temper. He looked as awkward as he felt; his cannonball torso inspired the rude nickname "His Rotundity." Two decades earlier he had written, "My motions are stiff and uneasy, ungraceful, and my attention is unsteady and irregular." A spectacular marriage in 1764 made him a better man, at times a great one, although he and the witty, candescent Abigail had been apart for half of their conjugal lives. Their intimacy and partnership would be cultivated in part through more than eleven hundred letters they wrote each other over the course of forty years. Five months earlier she had described living in an age of armed rebellion as "one continued scene of anxiety and apprehension. . . . Must I cheerfully comply with the demand of my country?"

For the moment, yes, as must her husband. John Adams in Paris was "quite out of his element," a friend wrote. "He cannot dance, drink, game, flatter, promise, dress, swear with the gentlemen, and talk small talk or flirt with the ladies." He both admired and despised French wealth and sophistication; upon seeing Marie-Antoinette at Versailles, he described her as "an object too sublime and beautiful for my dull pen." France was "one great garden," he told Abigail. "Everything that can soothe, charm and bewitch is here," although "luxury, dissipation, and effeminacy are pretty much at the same degree of excess." Yet he had no doubt that this ancient kingdom was vital to America. "The more I consider our affairs," he told a friend in Boston, "the more important our alliance with France appears to me. It is a rock upon which we may safely build." Ever dutiful, he reported that he was "studying French like a schoolboy"; he sometimes attended the theater to read the text of a play while listening to the actors pronounce their lines.

He was surprised to find turmoil and rancor in the American legation, notwithstanding the recent triumph of the French treaties. "This is an ugly situation," he wrote his cousin Samuel. Commissioner Arthur Lee, dubbed "the Wasp" by one adversary, "has confidence in nobody," Adams told his diary. "He believes all men selfish and no man honest or sincere." Deane's recall owed much to scurrilous allegations sent by Lee to Congress. The scion of prominent Virginia planters, a graduate of Eton who had studied both medicine in Edinburgh and law at the Inns of Court in London, Lee was thin-skinned, dyspeptic, and captious. His disposition was not improved by his failures as an envoy to Madrid, Vienna, and Berlin. The French had quickly come to distrust "the bilious Arthur Lee, with his yellow skin, green eyes, yellow teeth, and hair always in disorder," in Beaumarchais's arch description.

With Deane's departure Lee concentrated his vitriol on Franklin, whom he called "the most corrupt of all corrupt men." To his brother Richard Henry Lee, he wrote, "The old doctor is concerned in the plunder. . . . In time we shall collect the proofs." In a written riposte to Lee's calumny, Franklin this month had condemned "your sick mind, which is forever tormenting itself with its jealousies, suspicions, and fancies"; he then decided not to send the note, opting instead for a disdainful silence. Adams found himself "an umpire between two bitter and inveterate parties," as he wrote on May 2. Finding the legation's financial affairs in a "state of confusion and darkness," with "no books of account or any documents," Adams sought to impose administrative discipline, even as he regretted "more animosity among the Americans here than I remember to have seen anywhere else."

Adams, to be sure, disapproved of Franklin's epicurean habits: the nine liveried servants, the thousand-bottle wine cellar, the parade of women wanting to kiss Papa on the cheek. ("The ladies of this country," he wrote, "have an unaccountable passion for old age.") No doubt he envied a man considered Voltaire's equal. "Franklin's fame was universal," Adams wrote years later.

> His name was familiar to government and people, to kings, courtiers, nobility, clergy, and philosophers, as well as plebeians, to such a degree that there was scarcely . . . a scullion in a kitchen who was not familiar with his name, and who did not consider him as a friend of human-kind. When they spoke of him, they seemed to think he was to restore the golden age.

But Adams wondered if Franklin was too indolent, too taciturn to press America's cause with sufficient ardor among the European powers. A New England Puritan, marinated in piety and stiff-necked virtue, he privately called Franklin "the old conjuror," a sybarite who "loves his ease, hates to offend, and seldom gives any opinion till obliged to do it." He also suspected Franklin of "backstairs intrigues" and even of hiring a secretary to spy on him. For his part, Franklin wrote that Adams "means well for his country, is always an honest man, often a wise one, but sometimes and in some things, absolutely out of his senses."

Their mutual love of country and scathing contempt for the enemy allowed them to make common cause despite such differences. Adams recognized that Franklin "has as determined a soul as any man" in opposing Britain's tyranny. Both men agreed that the French fleet dispatched from Toulon would be vital in securing naval ascendancy in American waters. But the enemy must also feel the lash of war at home—in British waters, on British soil, at British hearths. Adams was delighted to learn that Franklin had found just the man for the task.

Abigail Adams would describe Captain John Paul Jones as "a most uncommon character . . . small of stature, well-proportioned, soft in his speech, easy in his address, polite in his manner, vastly civil. . . . He is said to be a man of gallantry and a favorite amongst the French ladies." Those who had seen him swinging a cutlass in battle or roaring curses from the quarterdeck drew a less genteel portrait. As he put to sea from Brest on April 10, two days after Commissioner Adams arrived in Paris, Jones paraphrased *Paradise Lost* in a letter to a friend: "The world lays all before me."

The son of a gardener from Solway Firth, on Scotland's southwest coast, John Paul had gone to sea at age thirteen; after killing a mutinous crewman in the West Indies, he added a new surname to cover his tracks and fled to

America. Short and wiry, with prominent cheekbones, a cleft chin, and hazel eyes, he found purpose and opportunity in war, having won a commission in the nascent Continental Navy. He had a heraldic seal cut, featuring a stag and the motto *Pro Republica*, and drafted his will, leaving a modest estate to his mother and sisters in Scotland. A few sharp scraps enhanced his reputation as a resourceful brawler; he was seen as a turbulent, prideful sailor given to feuds and sentimental verse, which he both read and wrote. Ranked only eighteenth of twenty-four captains in seniority, he complained bitterly of the higher status given to men "altogether illiterate and utterly ignorant of marine affairs." Perhaps weary of his irascibility, Congress sent him to France, where he appeared at the Hôtel de Valentinois in a dark blue captain's coat with white linings, lapels, and breeches, a black cockade skewering his tricorn hat and epaulets on his shoulders, said to make short men look taller. The uniform closely resembled that of a Royal Navy officer, a useful subterfuge in close encounters on the open ocean.

Dr. Franklin, charmed by "the strange magnetism of his presence," ordered the thirty-year-old swashbuckler to wreak havoc "as you shall judge best for distressing the enemies of the United States." Jones also took to heart the suggestion, perhaps from Franklin, that he improve his French by acquiring "a sleeping dictionary"—a local mistress. Even before returning to his ship in Brittany he caught the attention of Britain's highest circles, thanks to the usual spies flitting around Passy. "One Captain Jones . . . will soon insult some part of the coast of Great Britain," North warned Sandwich. "My informer could not say exactly what his destination was."

"Fresh gales, close weather," Jones's log recorded on April 15 as the Continental Navy sloop-of-war *Ranger* plunged "with a bone in her teeth" through St. George's Channel, between Wales and Ireland. Built a year earlier, she was square-rigged, painted black topside with a broad yellow stripe round the hundred-foot hull, a crew of 150, eighteen 9-pounders, and a Union Jack flapping from the fore-topmast head. Jones had made her a better sailor by cutting down her masts and spars and shifting twenty-eight pigs of lead ballast. With difficulty he had replaced some of the original bread-bag sails, made from heavy hemp and jute, rather than the superior Russia duck or English canvas, preferred for catching light breezes.

Those shabby fabrics were characteristic of a navy plagued with a shortage of shipwrights, crewmen, and proper materials. Congress too often assigned shipbuilding to states as a result of political influence rather than capability. Even after vessels were launched, they sometimes waited a year or more for enough sailors, guns, and rigging to leave port. During the entire war the Continental fleet would include only sixty-four vessels bigger than a lugger; collectively they carried thirteen hundred cannons, compared to the almost seven thousand guns now deployed by the Royal Navy (and less than a tenth the number of guns eventually carried by some two thousand American privateers). Half of the new warships built by Congress, at a cost exceeding $12 million, would never get to sea. Others got there slowly—notably, the frigate *Trumbull*, which drew too much water to clear the shoals at the mouth of the Connecticut River and would be trapped at her moorings upstream for years. She was among thirteen new Continental frigates, of which nine, by the end of 1778, would be destroyed or seized by the British. None of the remaining four survived the war.

This spring was particularly catastrophic for the navy. *Alfred* and *Virginia* had been captured. *Columbus* breached off Narragansett Bay trying to elude the enemy. *Independence* wrecked on the Ocracoke bar while sailing home from France, and British raiders burned *Effingham* and *Washington* north of Philadelphia. No fate was bleaker than that of the thirty-two-gun frigate *Randolph*, which on March 7 had been cruising sixty leagues east of Barbados when a sail appeared as a distant speck. When the vessel drew near at nine p.m. under a dim crescent moon, Captain Nicholas Biddle realized that she was not the small British man-of-war he had misidentified, but *Yarmouth*, a sixty-four-gun ship of the line. Gunport lids were triced up, and for fifteen minutes *Randolph* gave better than she got, shooting away the larger ship's mizzen topmast and bowsprit. Badly wounded in the thigh by a splinter, Biddle continued to command from a chair brought on deck from his cabin. Then he and *Randolph* abruptly vanished in a staggering explosion, evidently triggered by a spark in the magazine that blew spars, planks, cordage, and human limbs across the sea. "Our ship was in a manner covered with parts of her," the British captain wrote. Days later four sailors from a quarterdeck gun crew were found on a flotsam raft, the only survivors from a complement of 315 men.

"Our naval affairs have been conducted shockingly," a Continental Army officer lamented. Not least among the consequences, hundreds of captured American sailors from naval crews and privateers now jammed filthy cells in southern England, where they were treated more like pirates than prisoners of war. Those caught trying to escape might be consigned to the Black Hole, "forty days, half starved, allowed neither bed nor bedding," a diarist in Forton Prison, outside Portsmouth, reported. An inmate at Mill Prison, near Plymouth, wrote, "Many are strongly tempted to pick up the greens in the yard and eat it. . . . Some will pick up snails, boil and eat them, and drink the broth. . . . Rats have been eat in this prison before." English sightseers gawked at "the American monsters."

Various retaliatory schemes had been proposed to further damage British commercial interests, including attacks on Bermuda, the North Atlantic fishing fleet, Hudson Bay merchant vessels, or East Indiamen laying over at St. Helena in the South Atlantic during the return voyage to England from Asia. "A sudden blow may be struck which will alarm & shake Great Britain," Deane wrote Congress before leaving Paris. "The plundering and burning of Liverpool & Glasgow would be a most glorious revenge." Captain Jones, keen to avenge Charlestown, Falmouth, Esopus, and other immolated American towns, disclosed his own thoughts in a dispatch to the Paris commissioners. "We cannot yet fight their navy, as their numbers and force is so far superior to ours," he wrote. "Therefore it seems to be our most natural province to surprise their defenseless places."

Such a place lay in Whitehaven, a port on England's northwest coast that had grown prosperous from coal exports and trade with the Americas. Jones knew it well: from here he had first shipped out as a cabin boy eighteen years earlier. In the small hours of April 23, he and thirty-one volunteers stepped from *Ranger* into two cutters and headed for shore, rowing against the tide. They carried bundles of pine fagots dipped in pitch and brimstone. To encourage mayhem, the captain, wrapped in a boat cloak, promised his men that they would be rewarded for each English ship burned, just as if the vessels had been captured.

The first apricot glow of dawn appeared in the east as the boats grounded outside the harbor. Climbing on one another's shoulders, the raiders scaled a waterside parapet, seized the sentinels found asleep in a guardhouse, spiked three dozen cannons in the south battery by driving nails into their touchholes, then did the same along the north battery. Jones strode down to the harbor, expecting to see some of the two hundred colliers and other vessels in flames, but instead found that his squad of incendiaries had broken into a tavern "to make very free with the liquor." Worse still, a turncoat Irish seaman had slipped away to bang on doors along Marlborough Street and raise the alarm. Jones tossed a burning fagot down a hatchway on the collier *Thompson*, followed by a barrel of tar. Flames soon licked up the masts and into the rigging "with great violence," a witness reported. By now hundreds of bewildered townsfolk were hurrying toward the waterside. Jones held them off with a brandished pistol and a curled lip, then dashed into a waiting boat. Oarsmen rowed for their lives, a few wild gunshots from the parapets plumped the sea, and the raiders sculled back to *Ranger*.

"Had it been possible to land a few hours sooner," Jones later mused, "not a single ship out of more than two hundred could have possibly escaped." Instead only *Thompson* was burned. But the captain had made his point. "The town is much alarmed," a dispatch to the Admiralty advised. The *Gazetteer and New Daily Advertiser* was more explicit: "Two-thirds of the people are bordering on insanity, the remainder on idiotism." Couriers carried warnings to "all the capital seaports in the kingdom."

No tocsin could reach St. Mary's Isle, across Solway Firth, faster than *Ranger*, and by eleven a.m. Jones and a dozen armed men were again ashore. Hiking up a path toward a brick mansion, they proclaimed themselves to be a Royal Navy press-gang seeking recruits; in a heartbeat every able-bodied man in the harbor had disappeared. At the front door of the manor house, the Americans were chagrined to hear from a remarkably poised Helen Hamilton, the Countess of Selkirk, that her husband, the earl, was away taking the waters at Buxton, in Derbyshire. Jones had intended to snatch him as a hostage to be exchanged for imprisoned Yankee seamen. When the captain ordered his grumbling men back to the ship, they refused, insisting on looting the mansion. Abashed at this mutinous behavior—"plunder rather than honor was the object of the *Ranger*'s officers and crew," he later complained—Jones agreed that a delegation led by two officers could demand the Selkirk silver in lieu of the earl. Eager to be shut of these "horrid-looking wretches," the countess complied, handing over 250 ounces of plate, spoons, tureens, and the morning teapot. "I must say," she subsequently wrote her husband, "they behaved civilly."

With this booty safely stowed below, *Ranger* crossed the Irish Sea on light airs. At daybreak the next morning the ship stood in toward Kilroot Point, along the northern lip of Belfast Lough. Here the twenty-gun British sloop-of-war *Drake*, cruising near ancient Carrickfergus Castle, dispatched a gig with an officer and six tars to investigate the stranger flying a Union Jack. Jones kept his crew concealed and invited the delegates on deck before arresting them at gunpoint and ordering them below with the stolen silver.

Aboard *Drake*, Captain George Burdon, a superannuated Royal Navy officer on the eve of retirement, grew impatient and ordered his sloop to stand out against a freshening northeast wind. When the British ship had closed to within pistol range, Jones ordered the Stars and Stripes unfurled. A broadside of 9-pounders ripped through *Drake*'s bow and down her weather deck in a searing cone of flame and metal. Captain Burdon pitched over dead with a shot in the brain, and his senior lieutenant fell mortally wounded. For sixty-five minutes "the action was warm, close, and obstinate," Jones later wrote, before the British sailing master, now in command, bellowed, "Quarter! Quarter!" and struck his colors. *Ranger* suffered three dead, including the lieutenant of marines. "Our low rigging much shattered," the log recorded, "and most ye running rigging cut away." *Drake* was hurt worse: two dozen casualties, various yards shot to stubs, and the hull "very much galled."

A fortnight later, at seven p.m. on May 7, *Ranger* sailed into the Brest roadstead with an inverted Royal Navy white ensign beneath the American flag, two hundred prisoners in the hold, and *Drake* trailing in her wake. Franklin now had British tars to trade, although not for another year would London agree to an exchange of naval prisoners. A patrol that accomplished little more than purloining some tableware and battering a minor warship nevertheless reverberated: Whitehaven was the first English town to endure such an insult since the Dutch scourged the Medway in 1667.

The *Morning Chronicle and London Advertiser* reported panic in Scotland and northern England, so that "a general intimidation discovers itself on every appearance of a sail." The *Morning Post*, which published a blow-by-blow account from Whitehaven, demanded a squadron of frigates to defend the Channel Islands and the Irish Sea. The *London Courant* told Lord North that the American raid "hath stripped you naked, and . . . exposed your negligence and incapacity." An enormous headline in the *Cumberland Chronicle* declared "Unparalleled Impudence!" in reporting that the American brigand captain had given a swatch of *Drake's* mainsail to three Irish fishermen with the suggestion that it be used by the local governor to make himself a pair of trousers.

Bankers packed up their gold to be carted inland. London stocks fell. Shipping insurance premiums on the Irish Sea quadrupled. The *Morning Chronicle* published a primer on coastal artillery, noting that "the charge of powder for every cannon is allowed as one-third the weight of the ball it carries." The government agreed to erect coastal batteries to defend coalfields on the Firth of Clyde. Forty thousand Protestant volunteers enrolled in an Irish coastal militia led by, among others, a fighting bishop. The Admiralty surmised, incorrectly, that the buccaneer was again at sea, this time with a flotilla under orders "to plunder and destroy the leaching grounds" in northern Ireland where valuable linen was spread out to bleach for weeks or months.

"Not all their boasted navy can protect their own coast," Jones declared. British newspapers printed his identity, making him instantly infamous. Chapbook illustrations depicted him as a cruel cutthroat. Mothers spooked their children into good behavior by invoking his name. Among several ballads describing his exploits, one asked:

You have heard o' Paul Jones, have you not, have you not?
A rogue and a vagabond, is he not, is he not?

Lionized in Paris, he became a regular guest at the Hôtel de Valentinois as he supervised the conversion of a French merchant ship, the *Duc de Duras*, into a forty-two-gun frigate. He would rename her *Bonhomme Richard* to honor Franklin, whose compendium of proverbs and advice from his annual *Poor Richard's Almanack* had been published this year in a French edition titled *La science du bonhomme Richard*.

Jones also sent the Countess of Selkirk a fourteen-paragraph letter explaining himself. "I have drawn my sword in the present generous struggle for the rights of men," he wrote. "I profess myself a citizen of the world." He urged her to "use your soft persuasive arts with your husband to endeavor to stop this cruel and destructive war." And, as a gallant gesture, he bought the pilfered silver at auction—personally paying almost three thousand livres to compensate *Ranger's* crew—and sent it back to her. It was said that when she received the teapot, the leaves from her breakfast tea were still inside.

The French soon had their own hero to celebrate. No declaration of war had yet been issued by Versailles or London, but war edged closer, hour by hour. The *Stamford Mercury* and other British periodicals published tables listing Royal Navy and French ships likely to give battle, along with their locations, number of guns, and captains' names. French army encampments popped up in Brittany, Normandy, and Picardy to keep Britain anxious and focused on the English Channel, even as Admiral d'Estaing sailed from the Mediterranean for America. Each adversary was eager to have the other seen as an aggressor in hopes of cultivating European sympathy once the shooting began.

After leaving Portsmouth, Admiral Keppel and his fleet had reached the mouth of the English Channel, southwest of Cornwall, with secret orders to seize any French cruiser attempting to shadow them and to give battle if the Brest fleet emerged. On Wednesday morning, June 17, lookouts spotted a pair of French frigates and two smaller vessels on the horizon. Aboard *Victory*, Keppel hoisted signals for a general chase to at least interrogate the intruders. His ships beat to quarters: drums pounded out "Heart of Oak," boarding parties readied cutlasses and pikes, surgeons laid out lancets and bone saws, and powder monkeys fetched cartridges from the magazines for gun crews preparing to sponge, worm, load, and run out the heavy cannons through open ports.

The French scattered, but by six p.m. the newly coppered, thirty-two-gun *Arethusa*—a former French man-of-war, captured in the last war—had pulled even with the thirty-gun *Belle Poule* and ordered her to come about. Lieutenant Jean Isaac Chadeau de la Clocheterie refused. At fifty yards' range, *Arethusa* opened fire and was immediately answered with a French broadside. For five hours, in winds so feeble the ships could barely keep steerageway, they traded point-blank salvos, each gouging the other as they drifted toward the Breton coast. Shortly before midnight, exhausted and blood-drenched, they separated. *Arethusa* suffered 8 dead and 36 wounded from a crew of almost 200; she required towing to rejoin Keppel's fleet. *Belle Poule* crept through the coastal shallows to safety at Plouescat with 45 dead and 57 wounded from a complement of 230.

A ten-gun French schooner was captured, and the other French frigate, *Licorne*, also came to grief. Cornered by the frigate *Milford* and the seventy-four-gun *Hector*, she was being escorted to Keppel's flagship when her captain made a futile attempt to sail away, fired one broadside at the sixty-four-gun *America*, then surrendered. A third French frigate, *Pallas*, was spotted by the British fleet and was captured without gunplay after being chased down by two coppered cruisers.

With nearly four dozen French sailors dead, three ships captured, and hundreds of sailors headed to Forton Prison, Versailles had its casus belli, although each adversary would cast the other as the aggressor. Cries of "*La guerre! La guerre!*"—War! War!—echoed through the palace and across the land. The king gave Lieutenant de la Clocheterie a triumphant welcome, a promotion to captain, and command of a seventy-four-gun man-of-war. Widows and orphaned children received pensions; the wounded got stipends. Fashionable ladies in Paris adopted the *coiffure Belle Poule*, featuring a small model of the frigate tucked among their powdered curls.

"The insult done to my flag by a frigate of the king of England," Louis wrote in a furious dispatch to his naval commander in Brest, "[has] forced me to put an end to the moderation that I was proposing to myself." The fleet should make for the open sea as soon as a fair wind allowed. The renaissance of the French navy was almost complete; not since the reign of Louis XIV had it been this large, this capable, this eager for glory. The king's admirals still lacked a tradition of victory, but the king convinced himself that French ships could triumph quickly, in a single campaign, even without Spain's assistance. On July 10, Louis authorized mass reprisals against British shipping and declared France to now be at war. "My chief confidence," he told his admirals, "is in the protection of the God of battles."

From captured French officers and papers discovered aboard *Licorne* and *Pallas*, Keppel concluded that the Brest fleet had twenty-seven ships of the line ready for combat, with five more soon to join them—significantly more than his twenty. To the puzzlement of his monarch, he sailed back up the Channel for reinforcements, anchoring off Portsmouth. "I cannot conceal that I am much hurt at the resolution taken by Admiral Keppel of instantly returning," George wrote Sandwich from the Queen's House. "I fear this step will greatly discourage the ardor of the country." An invasion alert was sent to military commanders in southern England, with plans for a scorched-earth campaign if French marauders came ashore. Dragoons would patrol the coast while reserve forces massed inland, ready to protect London and to counterattack from camps in Kent and astride the Thames in Essex.

Sandwich hastened to Portsmouth to prod Keppel. The admiral resented being prodded and complained at not receiving public praise for his sensible, cautious conduct. "Nothing has yet happened," Sandwich replied coolly, "that has furnished such an opportunity." As Britain and France had been slow to come to blows, both now were in a hurry—Britain to win decisively before Spain joined her Bourbon partner, France to win decisively before the British could fully mobilize Royal Navy seamen and bring more men-of-war from the shipyards.

On July 9, Keppel once again set sail, this time with twenty-four ships of the line and a promise of at least five more to follow quickly, giving him parity with the French. The Brest fleet, he soon learned, had put to sea the previous day.

Ushant was a craggy, fogbound speck of rock twenty miles off the western tip of Brittany. Measuring five miles by two miles and shaped like a crab's claw, the island boasted a single fishing village and more short-tailed sheep than people. Here—or, rather, twenty leagues west of here—the two fleets first spied each other emerging from the Atlantic mist like canvas-shrouded wraiths on Thursday afternoon, July 23.

Keppel's Channel fleet by now had thirty ships of the line plus nine smaller vessels, enough to stretch for nine miles across the sea when arrayed for battle. The French fleet numbered twenty-nine ships of the line and nine frigates, manned by twenty-two thousand men and commanded by Vice Admiral Louis Guillouet, the Comte d'Orvilliers. Now sixty-eight, d'Orvilliers had begun his military life in French Guiana, where his father was governor, before spending most of his long career training several generations of naval officers. Although one writer considered him "crabbed and despondent," he was generally admired as a competent, creditable officer. He kept a grand table on the flagship *Bretagne*—his shipboard cellar included a thousand bottles of Margaux and Sauternes—and the crew included his son and two nephews.

Sartine, the naval minister, had told the admiral that "the eyes of Europe" were on his fleet, and a gorgeous sight it was: chalk-white sails billowing in the thick weather; brown hulls breasting the dark sea; squadron pennants and signal flags flapping madly; gold trim on forecastles carved with figurehead unicorns, gargoyles, and dragons. D'Orvilliers had been instructed to cruise for a month, to "show the French flag in all its glory" while scourging enemy merchantmen, but to engage Keppel only under propitious conditions. He well understood that he could lose the war in an afternoon. "If I know him to be too superior," the admiral acknowledged, "I will avoid a disproportionate action as well as I can."

Friday morning dawned with Keppel between D'Orvilliers and Brest, although the French held the weather gage—an advantageous wind that allowed initiative in maneuver. But during the night two French men-of-war had been separated from the fleet and chased back to Brittany, leaving D'Orvilliers with 1,950 guns in twenty-seven large ships, compared to 2,280 Royal Navy guns, a slight if worrisome advantage in weight of metal for the British. Uncertain of his prospects and reluctant to give battle, the French admiral beat westward into the Atlantic for three days, keeping six to ten miles between his force and his pursuers. Vessels in both fleets struggled to hold station with their sisters, through fog, tempests, and inky nights. A single poor performance—sailing "like a haystack," in seaman's jargon—could disrupt the formation, causing anarchy if not collisions, and giving the enemy an opening for attack.

That opening came on Monday, July 27. A shift in the wind from west to south favored the British, but a brief, violent squall at ten a.m. caused the forces to lose sight of each other for nearly an hour. When the storm cleared, d'Orvilliers had come about, reversing his sailing order to prevent the British vanguard from picking off French stragglers. Basic naval tactics had changed little in the past century, requiring warships to give mutual support in a compact line of the largest vessels—ships of the line—to preclude enemy broadsides from directly ahead or astern, where men-of-war were most vulnerable.

Tempestuous seas and the French maneuver seemed to momentarily disarrange d'Orvilliers's fleet. "Large body of his fleet appeared in great confusion," *Victory*'s log recorded. Confusion also beset the British, for the two lines were so suddenly upon each other, passing in opposite directions, that neither had time to even hoist their national colors. At eleven-twenty a.m. Keppel ordered a red flag aloft from *Victory*'s deck—the signal for battle—and at that moment the French opened fire.

Tongues of flame stabbed back and forth, reflected in the sea below and from low clouds above. Shouts and shrieks were swallowed by the throaty roar of cannons and the splintering crunch of shattered oak. A single broadside from a large ship might burn three hundred pounds or more of powder, and within minutes thick smoke swaddled both fleets, blinding many gunners. Gun captains bellowed commands above the din: "Cast off the tackles and breeching!" "Bruise the priming!" "Fire!" "Sponge the gun!" Then more powder bags were rammed down the sponged barrel, followed by round shot or grape, chain, or langrage—metal junk—for shredding sails, rigging, and sailors. Thick breaching ropes prevented a fired gun from recoiling across the deck, and block and tackle winched each wooden-wheeled carriage back into position for another go. Nimble crews could fire a broadside every three to five minutes, usually at ranges under three hundred yards; a superior rate of fire, combined with a heavier weight of metal, typically told in battle. On this violent Monday, as the ships wallowed through heavy seas with canvas clapping, French gunners most often fired on the upward roll to rake enemy masts and rigging, while the British fired on the downward roll, aiming between railing and waterline to sweep decks and perforate hulls.

As the largest vessel in the Channel fleet and positioned in the center of the British line, *Victory*, in her first fight, drew ample attention from French gunners. Half a dozen ships of the line pumped broadsides at her, but *Victory*'s gunners held their fire until coming abreast of the three-deck, 110-gun *Bretagne*. Back and forth they traded roaring blows, gouts of smoke spurting from their gun decks. D'Orvilliers's flagship was hulled several times, and one severe broadside made a single gaping wound in *Bretagne*'s side where three gun ports had been. *Victory* swaggered down the French line, firing at six more enemy ships, including the ninety-gun *Ville de Paris*, and taking a severe cudgeling in return. "Our ships greatly damaged in the rigging & sails," the *Victory* log acknowledged after a cursory survey of the British fleet. Her own damage included a large hole through the mainmast eight feet above the deck and more holes through the bowsprit, mizzenmast, and several yards. Rigging, blocks, stays, shrouds, braces, and sails were mangled. Among the casualties were eleven dead and twenty-six wounded. King George would have been hard-pressed to recognize the beautiful new ship he had admired three months earlier.

By one p.m. she had cleared the French line. Ten ships in the British van came about to chase the French rear guard, but now turmoil and disarray, those handmaidens of battle, took hold. "We passed through a very heavy fire from five & twenty of the enemy's ships, which shattered our masts, rigging, and sails all to pieces," wrote Lieutenant Edward Bowater aboard *Terrible*, sailing behind *Victory*. "We have ten men killed and twenty-one wounded. . . . Most of our wounded have lost either legs or arms."

Victory, which had been sailing in the middle of the fleet formation, was so discomposed that she took an hour to wear round away from the wind while seamen frantically spliced the rigging and carpenters jury-rigged masts and yards. Even in the best of times signaling at sea was difficult, but now thick smoke, scattered ships, and damage aloft meant that signals were unseen, misread, or ignored. Five British ships were pummeled too badly to make headway and drifted south. D'Orvilliers, seeing a chance for easy prey, directed his ships to cut them off, but dishevelment also plagued the French and the order was not heeded promptly. Peering through his spyglass, Keppel recognized the enemy admiral's intent and replaced the red battle flag with a signal for the fleet to form a line of battle to intercept the French.

Confusion now devolved into chaos. The squadron of ten ships bringing up the rear of the Channel fleet was commanded by Vice Admiral Sir Hugh Palliser, comptroller of the navy, a member of Parliament, and an Admiralty board commissioner. A self-made seaman from Yorkshire, Palliser was still tormented by injuries suffered in the West Indies thirty-five years earlier when an arms chest had exploded aboard *Sunderland*, spraying shot through his right shoulder and torso. Today, in the initial exchange against the French, his ships had taken the brunt of enemy fire, including his own flagship, *Formidable*, now battered and nearly immobile.

By four p.m. Keppel had managed to get most of the fleet in line, but a third of his firepower remained two miles upwind, milling around *Formidable*. An hour later, Keppel dispatched a frigate to advise Palliser, an old friend and comrade, that "he was only waiting for him to renew the action." This command brought no more response than the flutter of signal flags had. Keppel and his staff fretted and fumed on *Victory*'s quarterdeck, periodically squinting north before fuming some more. The fleet admiral, with "extraordinary—if not culpable—forbearance," as the naval historian William Laird Clowes later wrote, waited until seven p.m. to bypass Palliser by summoning the rear ships into his line individually.

By then daylight had faded, the French had drawn off, and no chance remained to renew the fight before darkness fell. From *Victory* several French lamps could be seen burning through the night nearby, presumably to keep d'Orvilliers's three squadrons aligned. But at dawn on Tuesday these were seen to be stay-behind decoys, fast-sailing ships now headed southeast in the wake of the French fleet, already twenty miles away and making for Brest, like ghosts at cockcrow.

No ships had been sunk or captured in the inconclusive Battle of Ushant, the first fleet action between these implacable enemies since 1759. Both navies evinced courage but also inexperience, particularly in ship-to-ship communication and the balletic handling required to synchronize large flotillas in combat.

If indecisive, the fray had hardly been bloodless. D'Orvilliers suffered 161 dead and 513 wounded; Keppel counted 133 dead and 373 wounded. Broken men were lugged down to the orlop in the hold of each ship, a netherworld dimly lit by purser's glims—sputtering candles in tin sconces—and thick with the briny stink of bilgewater, the precise odor of despair. Here surgeons hacked and patched and occasionally used hot pitch to seal a stump, following amputations on patients stupefied with rum and muted by a leather gag between the teeth. Loblolly boys carried away the severed limbs to feed the sharks.

Each side claimed a victory neither had won. "That I have beat the French there cannot be any doubt, and their retreat in the night is shameful and disgraceful to them as a nation," Keppel wrote Sandwich. That judgment was disputed even aboard his own flagship. "The French behaved more like seamen and more officer-like than was imagined they would do," a lieutenant on *Victory* wrote. "Their ships were in very high order, well-managed, well-rigged, and . . . much more attentive to order than our own." French gunnery so devastated British spars, sails, and rigging that the Channel fleet could barely crawl into Plymouth for repairs. "They have crippled the fleet in that respect beyond any degree I ever saw," Keppel admitted. Four ships required dry-docking, including *Egmont*, found to have seventy shot holes in her hull, five below the waterline. Several had apparently come from a broadside fired by a confused Royal Navy sister.

Even the king acknowledged the "great havoc" suffered by his navy. Dockyard mast houses, chronically short of skilled artificers, would require months to repair or replace all of the long sticks damaged in barely two hours of mayhem. Keppel's champions, of whom there were many in the parliamentary opposition, made the best of the equivocal battle results. "You have saved us twice in one summer," Edmund Burke told him, "once by retreating and once by fighting." If disappointed at the Channel fleet's missed opportunity, Sandwich affected equanimity. "It is unfortunate that the affair was not more decisive," he wrote, "but I am persuaded it was out of our power to make it so."

The first news of Ushant had been carried to Versailles by the Duc de Chartres, a cousin of the king's who commanded one of the French squadrons. His breathless account briefly incited jubilation; closer questioning revealed that he had exaggerated both the Brest fleet's triumph and his own dubious contribution. The king soon relieved Chartres of command and transferred him to the army. Still, as one historian wrote, the French "enjoyed the unusual experience of bringing home all their ships after an encounter with the Royal Navy." D'Orvilliers was acclaimed a hero who had restored national pride and redressed the disgrace of the Seven Years' War. Yet crowing would go only so far, especially if the fighting season were to end this year without a decisive victory. Foreign Minister Vergennes, gimlet-eyed as always, recognized the difficulty of confronting the Royal Navy without naval allies. France, he concluded, needed Spain's help, and soon.

Both fleets were patched up enough to return to sea in a few weeks. Keppel arrived off Ushant but found no French to fight: d'Orvilliers was instead on a month-long cruise across the Bay of Biscay toward Cape Finisterre, in northwest Spain. The Channel fleet would put in at Spithead in late October with fourteen hundred sick sailors, potentially enough to imperil naval operations the following spring. Even *Victory* "has the distemper in a degree," Keppel advised in a note to Sandwich. He was not well himself. "Our chief has at times been very much afflicted with his disorder," a subordinate wrote, "and appears to be much chagrined by his bad luck."

Few shipboard maladies were as noxious as the political disorder that would now roil the navy and the nation. On the day the fleet anchored after the battle, Admiral Palliser went ashore at Portsmouth, where he was shown an anonymous article in an opposition newspaper, the *General Advertiser and Morning Intelligencer*, implying that his disobedience, if not his cowardice, had cost Keppel a victory. Furious, Palliser demanded that Keppel disavow the allegations. Keppel refused, evidently believing them to be true. Palliser published a lengthy rebuttal, asserting that he had not seen certain signals, that his *Formidable* was too badly damaged to continue the fight, and that the battle had been mismanaged by the fleet admiral. He demanded, unwisely, that Keppel be court-martialed for misconduct and neglect of duty.

The controversy caught fire. Factions formed. Friends fell out. Captain John Jervis, whose eighty-gun *Foudroyant* had sailed just behind *Victory* during the battle, took a moment to describe the dire developments in a letter to his close friend Henry Clinton, in America. "Terrible schisms and distractions must arise in the fleet and the nation at large," Jervis wrote. "The times are fevered to a high degree."

Accusations flew like cannon shot. The Admiralty, unable to shrug off Palliser's charges, made plans to stage a trial of Keppel in Portsmouth. Ushant was over, but the bloodletting had just begun.

16.

———◆———

Flying from a Shadow

No place in America had been more routinely despoiled by war than New Jersey, and for the fourth time in eighteen months a British host was again on the march through Jersey fields and woodlands, like a scarlet dragon. If the state's commitment to the patriot cause had once seemed doubtful—a former governor, William Franklin, remained in jail for unyielding loyalty to the Crown—these repeated intrusions stiffened resistance and hardened allegiances. A British officer now classified New Jersey as "an enemy's country, universally hostile," and a German lieutenant told his diary, "We have to be more careful of the farmers than of the enemy soldiers. . . . Their malice and hatred toward us can be seen." Joseph Clark, a carpenter's apprentice from Elizabethtown who taught himself Latin to win admission to the college at Princeton, wrote, "Never did the Jerseys appear more universally unanimous to oppose the enemy. They turned out, young and old, great and small, rich and poor. Scarcely a man that could carry a musket was left at home."

General Clinton's "noble little army," as he chose to describe it, tramped northeast from the Delaware beginning on June 19 in two parallel columns that stretched for "near twelve miles," the commanding general told Lord Germain. The procession comprised twenty-one thousand soldiers, armed loyalists, teamsters, and refugees, as well as five thousand horses, fifteen hundred wagons, and almost four dozen field guns. Also: ammunition carts, private rigs, mobile blacksmith shops, portable bridges, bakeries, and what one skeptical observer called "every kind of useless stuff." Under an order issued soon after leaving Philadelphia, "the women of the army are constantly to march upon the flanks of the baggage"; violators were drummed from the columns. Each soldier carried two days' worth of cooked rations in his haversack, and commissary drays hauled provisions for sixteen more, to be supplemented by produce and meat on the hoof purchased or seized en route to New York. Redcoats were advised to shave at least every third morning and to care for their marching feet by wearing linen stockings dipped in oil. Frequent rain fell like buckshot, and each late June day was hotter than the day before. In its wake the noble army left burned houses, smashed furniture, dead cows with steaks cut from their flanks, and cherry trees, heavy with fruit, chopped to flinders.

Rebels, in turn, "destroyed every bridge on the road," Clinton recorded, requiring "a full corps of engineers" to repair spans over Cooper's Creek, Moore's Creek, Ballybridge Creek, Bird Creek, and more. Other saboteurs filled in wells, demolished causeways, and blocked up stream sluices to mire the roadbeds. Boys with hickory switches herded cattle, hogs, and sheep away from the invaders' path. Scattered leaflets warned the king's men that they risked "being Burgoyned." Snipers fired from thickets, barns, and hilltops, although always at their peril: of seven men taking potshots from a house in Mount Holly, two were captured, three killed, and two others "ran into the cellar and fastened it so that we were obliged to burn the house and consume them in it," noted Andrew Bell, Clinton's secretary. At Crosswicks Creek, eight miles southeast of Trenton, eight hundred New Jersey Continentals and militiamen on June 23 battled light dragoons and Queen's Rangers for six hours before falling back at dusk to fight another day.

By June 25 the torrid summer heat had become harrowing. Men who collapsed on the road were hoisted onto their officers' horses "to be carried along with us," one Hessian reported. Captain Ewald, the *Jäger* officer, told his journal, "I lost over 60 men out of 180 foot *Jäger* and 30 horsemen, among which may well be some 20 men who dropped dead from the great heat and fatigue." A British grenadier officer wrote his parents in England:

> Such a march may I never again experience . . . the sun beating on our heads with a force scarcely to be conceived in Europe, and not a drop of water. . . . The whole road, strewed with miserable wretches wishing for death, exhibited the most shocking scene I ever saw.

Desertion also thinned the ranks. Most skedaddlers were German, perhaps encouraged by a recent offer from Congress, printed on a thousand broadsheets, of eight hundred acres of good woodland, plus hogs, cows, and a bull for any Hessian captain who turned his coat with at least forty men in tow. British deserters included Sergeant Thomas Sullivan, a light infantryman who had married an American during the Philadelphia occupation. He and a dozen disaffected comrades stole away while on picket duty; Sullivan made his way back to the city, sold his musket and tomahawk for $24, and soon found work as a Continental quartermaster.

Clinton discouraged such disloyalty with severity. Drummer John Fisher had deserted from the 28th Foot a year earlier and joined the New Jersey militia. Badly injured in a skirmish and captured by his erstwhile redcoat comrades, he was recognized, convicted after a drumhead court-martial, and hanged on June 22, his saber wounds still bleeding. Fisher's body remained dangling from a roadside tree branch as an admonition. Even so, during just the first week of the march, an estimated five hundred of the king's men absconded, according to the historians Mark Edward Lender and Garry Wheeler Stone.

On Friday morning, June 26, the sweating, footsore column came to a halt at Monmouth Court House, a remote crossroads hamlet sometimes called Freehold. The previous day, Clinton had decided to begin the long last leg of his New Jersey anabasis by swinging farther east, despite wash-board roads described by a British staff officer as "remarkably bad." Wrongly informed that General Gates was barreling down the Hudson to join Washington at New Brunswick—Gates actually was headed to White Plains, sixty miles north—Clinton took a road fork to the right, toward the Navesink River and, ultimately, Sandy Hook, where Admiral Howe could ferry the army across New York Bay.

By this decision, war sank its sharp talons into Monmouth. General Knyphausen led one column into an encampment just east of the village while General Cornwallis settled the other on high ground to the west. Here they would loiter for two days, sheltering from the scorching sun, resting their blown horses, and foraging for fresh food. From Longstreet's Hill, two miles north, American sentinels watched several thousand tents sprout like mushrooms; cook fires at sunset flickered along a four-mile crescent, spewing orange sparks into the heavens. Spies told Clinton that rebels were thickening on his left flank. "They are determined to attack our rear and aim at the baggage," Secretary Bell wrote in his journal.

Monmouth consisted of little more than a wooden courthouse built in 1715, a shingle-roofed Anglican church, two taverns, a tanyard, blacksmith and wheelwright shops, and a couple dozen houses. The Atlantic lay four-teen miles due east. To the northwest three shallow ravines, known locally as "morasses," cut across a rolling terrain of hay meadows, woodlots, and flax, rye, and corn fields. Three years of civil strife had already scarred this obscure corner of New Jersey, settled in the previous century by Scottish and Dutch families; before the rebellion ended, more than a hundred bloody frays would be fought in the surrounding county. In April, loyalist raiders had razed the sprawling Union saltworks nearby, and a "noted hanging place" outside Monmouth would tally at least thirteen executions. The prevailing malevolence was evinced by a loyalist freebooter named

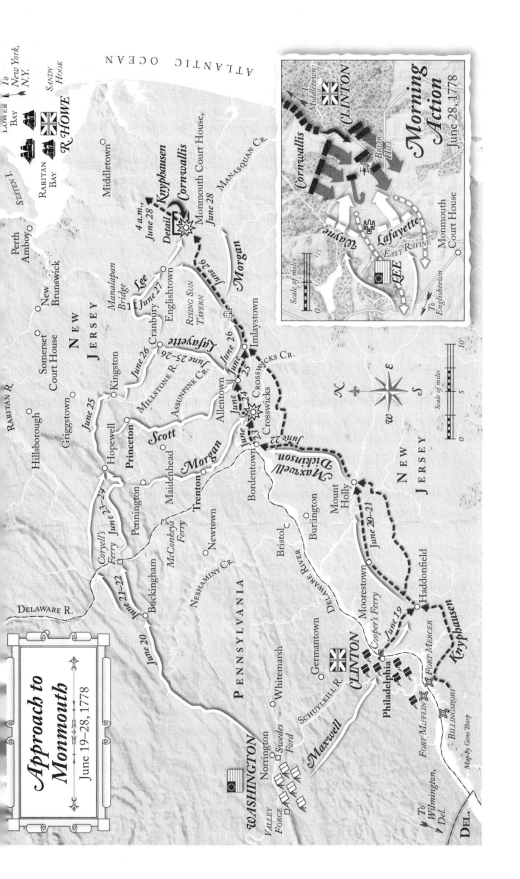

Approach to Monmouth
June 19–28, 1778

ATLANTIC OCEAN

To New York, N.Y.

LOWER BAY

SANDY HOOK

R. HOWE

STATEN I.

RARITAN BAY

Perth Amboy

New Brunswick

Middletown

4 a.m., June 28

Knyphausen

Cornwallis

Monmouth Court House, June 28

MANASQUAN CR.

Detail

Morning Action
June 28, 1778

To Middletown

CLINTON

BRIAR HILL

Cornwallis

Lafayette

Wayne

EAST RAVINE

Monmouth Court House

LEE

To Englishtown

Scale of miles

Lee
June 27

Englishtown

Manalapan Bridge

Cranbury
June 26

RISING SUN TAVERN

Morgan

June 26

NEW JERSEY

Somerset Court House

Kingston

Lafayette
June 25–26

MILLSTONE R.

ASSUNPINK CR.

Imlaystown

Allentown

CROSSWICKS CR.

Griggstown

June 25

Scott

Princeton

Hopewell

Maidenhead

Morgan

Crosswicks

NEW JERSEY

Hillsborough

RARITAN R.

Pennington

Coryell's Ferry June 23–24

Trenton

Bordentown

Maxwell/ Dickinson
June 22

Scale of miles

Buckingham

McConkey's Ferry

Newtown

NESHAMINY CR.

June 21–22

PENNSYLVANIA

June 20

Bristol

DELAWARE RIVER

Burlington

Mount Holly

June 20–21

Haddonfield

June 19

Knyphausen

DELAWARE R.

Whitemarsh

Germantown

SCHUYLKILL R.

Moorestown

Cooper's Ferry

FORT MERCER

Norrington

Swedes Ford

WASHINGTON

VALLEY FORGE

Maxwell

CLINTON

Philadelphia

FORT MIFFLIN

BILLINGSPORT

To Wilmington, Del.

DEL.

Map by Gene Thorp

Lewis Fenton, who warned a local tailor after robbing him, "I am coming to burn your barns and houses, and roast you all like a pack of kittens."

Clinton's men also brought violence to Monmouth. "Every place here was broken into and plundered by the English soldiers," a German sergeant recorded in his journal. Troops demolished the church steeple and yanked the bell from the courthouse belfry. Foraging parties, British and German, looted farms and silenced protests with an occasional butt stroke from a musket. "Contrary to orders and notwithstanding all the precautions," Lieutenant John Peebles told his diary, "a good deal of plundering going on." A fusilier officer admitted being "mortified at observing the great irregularity and excesses that have been committed." Clinton detested indiscipline and threatened "immediate execution" of soldiers caught committing acts "so disgraceful to the army." But the depredations continued. Major Carl Baurmeister, a Hessian adjutant, acknowledged, "It has made the country people all the more embittered rebels."

On both Friday and Saturday nights, violent thunderstorms swept Monmouth with lightning and more buckshot rain. "We again got wet through," a discouraged Hessian wrote. The deluges only seemed to intensify the heat. From his temporary headquarters in the house of aged Elizabeth Covenhoven—she, too, would be plundered before the British marched away—Clinton ordered his army to prepare to break camp at three a.m. on Sunday. Sandy Hook and the Royal Navy lay twenty-five miles ahead. The commander in chief was uncertain what the Continental Army intended, but he hoped that "Mr. Washington might yet afford me an opportunity of having a brush with him."

Even Washington was uncertain of his own intentions. After leaving the Schuylkill bivouac early on Saturday, June 20, the Continental host had swiftly marched eastward to the Delaware. At three p.m. on Sunday, Washington crossed Coryell's Ferry to spend the night with his aides in a cut-stone house on a hillside overlooking the river. While waiting for the rest of his troops to cross into New Jersey the next day in what a Rhode Island soldier described as "wraining wether," he issued a flurry of orders: each brigade was to submit a tally of men "actually on the spot fit for duty"; arms and ammunition were to be "well-cleaned and afterwards carefully inspected"; tents and heavy baggage would be sent off in wagons, making the army more agile; soldiers must avoid "injuring themselves by drinking cold water." He paid his host £10 for thirty-eight meals and "trouble, etc., made in the house." Then, with the sound of cracking whips, creaking wagons, and jingling harnesses, they set off at four a.m. on June 23 across New Jersey to find the enemy. Few doubted, as one officer wrote, that the campaign now underway seemed "big with the fates of Britain and America."

In their frayed shirts and threadbare breeches, much of the Continental Army still resembled a legion of plowmen and barkeeps. Perhaps one in five lacked shoes, although a late consignment of two thousand muskets and bayonets from New England ensured that every man was armed, if not shod. In the final weeks at Valley Forge, Washington had prepared for the summer fighting season with his usual exhaustive attention to detail. Twenty coopers made casks to carry salt pork, fish, and other provisions, and an inventory of war matériel provided precise numbers for 111 crucial items, from shovels, knapsacks, and water buckets to reams of writing paper and, for reasons unclear, three petticoats.

Washington split the army into two wings, with Charles Lee on the right, commanding almost five thousand men in six brigades, and Lord Stirling on the left, with just under four thousand in five brigades. Lafayette led a reserve of thirty-seven hundred. Scouts traveled three hundred yards in front of the main column, and each regiment posted an officer and eighteen men as flank guards, a hundred yards to the left or right. Quartermaster General Greene, no less meticulous than His Excellency, had organized depots at fifteen-mile intervals up the western spine of New Jersey, stocked with two hundred thousand bushels of grain, one hundred thousand rations, rum, hay, and spare wagons; troops arrived at their encampments to find latrines, firewood, bedding straw, and barrels of vinegar—Greene's all-purpose answer to intestinal disorders and other ailments. Masons had even walled some campsite springs with stone to keep the water limpid.

At nine a.m. on June 24, Washington summoned a dozen generals to his temporary headquarters in Hopewell, seven miles northwest of Princeton. They gathered in the wood-paneled southeast room of a hilltop house just as a total eclipse darkened the landscape, so that for an hour it was impossible to read without candlelight. Ignoring this portent, the commanding general gave a brisk status report, shadows deepening the furrows on his face. The enemy was plodding in two columns northeast across New Jersey at roughly five miles a day. Clinton appeared to have nine to ten thousand rank and file, slightly fewer than Washington's own army around Hopewell. Another twelve hundred Continentals under Brigadier General Maxwell—Scotch Willie—were harassing the king's column "by hanging on their flanks and rear." More than a thousand militiamen from nine counties had joined them in demolishing bridges, felling trees, and rounding up deserters; over the next two days Washington would exchange eleven dispatches about these tasks and more with Major General Philemon Dickinson, the capable militia commander in New Jersey.

Here, Washington told his generals during the conference, was the issue. "Will it be advisable for us, of choice, to hazard a general action?" he asked. "What precise line of conduct will it be best for us to pursue?" Should a full attack be launched? A fragmentary attack? If that was too risky, what measures could be taken "to annoy the enemy in their march"?

In the crepuscular room, the generals furrowed their brows and shuffled their feet. Lee spoke "very eloquently," Lafayette later reported, and with his usual certitude. If the two armies were of comparable strength, Lee argued, it would be reckless to risk an all-out attack. Even a limited assault would ineluctably spiral into a full-fledged battle against an enemy eager for just such a clash. If Clinton intended to abandon Pennsylvania and New Jersey, he added, why not "erect a bridge of gold for the enemy" to encourage his flight? One by one Greene, Knox, Stirling, Steuben, and the rest agreed unanimously that an attack "will not be advisable." Instead, another fifteen hundred men should be dispatched to join Generals Maxwell and Dickinson in nipping at the enemy's heels.

Washington adjourned the meeting, and his lieutenants tromped back to their commands as the missing sun reappeared. Almost instantly several officers had second thoughts. Lafayette believed it "would be disgraceful for the leaders and humiliating for the troops to allow the enemy to cross the Jerseys with impunity." In a febrile note he told Washington he would wager "my fortune, all what I possess in the world" in guaranteeing that "no harm shall arise" by launching a bold strike at the enemy's flank with at least two thousand men. Greene also wrote the commanding general:

> If we suffer the enemy to pass through the Jerseys without attempting anything upon them, I think we shall ever regret it. . . . People expect something from us & our strength demands it. . . . I think we can make a very serious impression without any great risk.

No one was more agitated at what he called "the characteristic imbecility of a council of war" than Lieutenant Colonel Hamilton, who had served as notetaker during the dim-lit conference. The generals collectively resembled a "society of midwives," he complained in a letter to his friend Colonel Boudinot.

Lee's prudence was more sensible than either he or Hamilton realized. Washington had badly underestimated Clinton's strength, which approached eighteen thousand soldiers of all ranks, more than his own Continentals. But emboldened by the newfound aggression of his most trusted deputies, the commanding general decided to dispatch shock troops to discomfit the king's columns. Colonel Morgan was to join General Dickinson with more than eight hundred men to gnaw "the enemy's right flank and give them as much annoyance as possible." This detachment included Morgan's notorious riflemen, most of Washington's Life Guard, two North Carolina infantry companies, and a couple dozen marksmen from each brigade. They were followed by another fifteen hundred commanded by Brigadier General Charles Scott and a thousand under the ever-pugnacious Anthony Wayne.

Washington chose Lafayette to lead a vanguard that had abruptly swelled to more than four thousand Continentals. "You are to use the most effectual means for gaining the enemy's left flank and rear," the commanding general told him on June 25, "giving them every degree of annoyance . . . as will cause the enemy most impediment & loss in their march." Eager as a puppy, Lafayette galloped off to Cranbury, thirteen miles west of Monmouth, arriving at nine-thirty p.m. Here he was joined by his temporary aide, Colonel Hamilton, his junior in rank but senior in age, by a year, at twenty-one. "The young Frenchman in raptures with his command & burning to distinguish himself," noted Dr. McHenry, Washington's assistant secretary.

Less enraptured was Major General Lee, who had declined an offer to command the detachment when it was a mere fifteen hundred men. Now that the force had tripled in size, second only to the main army in heft and prestige, he regretted his demurral. "My ceding it would of course have an odd appearance," he wrote Washington as Lafayette cantered across the sandy New Jersey byroads. "I must entreat therefore, after making a thousand apologies for the trouble my rash assent has occasioned to you, that if this detachment does march that I may have the command of it."

Although Hamilton later denounced this gambit—"General Lee's conduct with respect to the command of this corps was truly childish," he wrote Boudinot—the request was hardly unreasonable, given the prevailing conventions on seniority, status, and personal honor. Washington recognized Lee's prerogative, yet worried about "wounding the feelings of the Marquis de Lafayette." After pondering the matter, he proposed "an expedient" solution in his reply to Lee. He would further enlarge the vanguard with another thousand troops, "giving you the command of the whole," which would equal almost half of the entire Continental Army and certainly warrant a commander of Lee's stature. But Lafayette was to proceed with whatever harassing attacks he had already planned "as if no change had happened, and you will give him every assistance and countenance in your power." Washington would follow with his remaining brigades—roughly seven thousand men—prepared to reinforce as necessary. He signed the order, "Your most obedient & affectionate servant."

This solution may have been too clever by half. Lafayette's difficulties had compounded from the moment he set out with his detachment, swinging south, then east to feel for Clinton's left flank. He lacked rations to feed his large force—"we are schort of provisions," he wrote Washington—and reliable intelligence about both enemy and American positions had been difficult to obtain. He was ready to obey Lee, "cheerfully . . . not only out of duty but out of what I owe to that gentleman's character." Yet rain, brutal heat, and the unfamiliar terrain confounded every movement. After getting reports from the other Continental forces trailing the British, Hamilton warned Washington of "the extreme distress of the troops for want of provisions. General Wayne's detachment is almost starving and seems both unwilling and unable to march further. . . . If the [main] army is totally out of supporting distance, we risk the total loss of the detachment in making an attack." In a dispatch written to the commanding general at ten-thirty p.m. on June 26, Lafayette conceded, "I have given up the project of attacking the enemy, and I only wish to join General Lee."

This mare's nest awaited Lee on Saturday, June 27, upon his arrival in Englishtown, a hamlet hemmed in by woodlands five miles northwest of Monmouth. More than five thousand troops were now under his command here, drawn from thirty-one infantry regiments, but he knew few of his subordinates and had never set foot in this part of New Jersey. Seven hundred militiamen had seized the crossroads at the Tennent meetinghouse, a white clapboard Presbyterian church perched on a prominent knuckle above the road, midway between Englishtown and Monmouth. Even in the shade, if shade could be found, by midday temperatures had climbed toward one hundred degrees Fahrenheit. Soldiers panted under huckleberry bushes or in crude brush huts. Officers sipped vinegar and water to remain erect; one considered paying $30 for a drink of cold water.

Troops felled by the heat and other maladies lay on pews inside the meetinghouse, now converted into a field hospital. Overhead a nine-pane window in the stubby octagonal steeple afforded a panoramic view to the southeast, across the three ravines toward the courthouse, where the king's army made ready to break camp in a few hours. Lee could not quite see them, other than wisps of their camp smoke, but he had no doubt that Clinton and his horde were there in force, alert and vengeful.

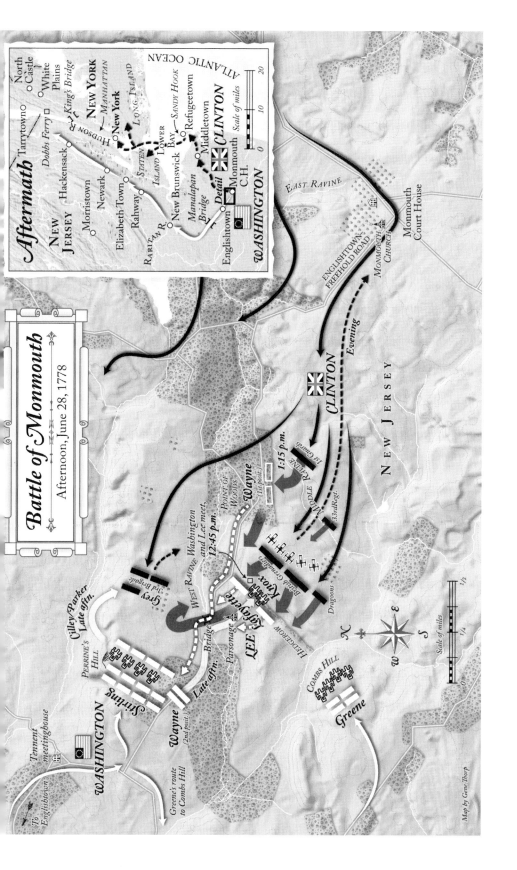

Battle of Monmouth
Afternoon, June 28, 1778

Aftermath

NEW YORK

North Castle
White Plains
Tarrytown
Dobbs Ferry
King's Bridge
Hackensack
Morristown
Newark
Elizabeth Town
Rahway
New Brunswick
Raritan R.
Mamalapan Bridge
Englishtown
Staten Island
Lower Bay
Sandy Hook
Refugeetown
Middletown
Monmouth C.H.

NEW JERSEY

NEW YORK
Manhattan
Hudson R.
Long Island

ATLANTIC OCEAN

CLINTON

WASHINGTON

Detail

Scale of miles
0   10   20

East Ravine

Englishtown-Freehold Road

Monmouth Church

Monmouth Court House

Evening

CLINTON

1:15 p.m.

1st Guard

Middle Ravine

33rd Regt.

NEW JERSEY

Point of Woods

Wayne (1st posit.)

Washington and Lee meet, 12:45 p.m.

West Ravine

Grey 3rd Brigade

British Grenadiers

Dragoons

Knox

Lafayette

LEE

Bridge

Hedgerow

Parsonage

Cilley/Parker late aftn.

Perrine's Hill

Stirling

Wayne (2nd posit.)

Late aftn.

Combs Hill

Greene

Tennent meetinghouse

WASHINGTON

Greene's route to Combs Hill

To Englishtown

Scale of miles
0   1/4   1/2

N   E   W   S

Map by Gene Thorp.

*   *   *

Late Saturday morning Washington trotted into Englishtown astride a white charger just sent to him as a gift from Governor Livingston of New Jersey. Horse and rider looked magnificent, as if assembled into a unified martial creature, although in a day the beautiful mount would be dead from the heat. His Excellency knew that danger lurked nearby. General Steuben and young John Laurens, scouting the enemy camp at his request, rode close enough "to fire a pistol at their horsemen whilst feeding their horses," as Steuben reported in a midday dispatch. Like poking a hornets' hive, this gesture provoked a furious chase by British dragoons, notwithstanding further blasts from the baron's enormous horse pistols. Steuben lost his cocked hat as he and Laurens hurdled a fence and galloped to safety.

Washington dashed off several official letters in Englishtown, then met Lee at his headquarters in the Village Inn, joined by Lafayette, Wayne, and other Continental officers. No one left the war council doubting that the commanding general wanted the enemy harassed early on Sunday morning. Yet he had issued no detailed, unambiguous edict; Lee, for one, considered any guidance to be discretionary, contingent on his best judgment about battlefield circumstances. Washington promised that the bulk of the army—more than seven thousand troops and most of Knox's artillery—would continue pressing forward to support Lee, then rode off to his temporary headquarters, four miles northwest, to make it so.

At five p.m., Lee gathered his senior lieutenants for a brief, cursory conference. Enemy strength and dispositions were "mere conjecture," he said, and therefore it was pointless to draft a battle plan. Further efforts to gather intelligence had come to naught—"the people here are inconceivable stupid," he complained—but he chose not to conduct his own reconnaissance, or question New Jersey militiamen familiar with the terrain, or summon Morgan and Dickinson for advice. He would improvise, trusting his own light-footed savvy. An accurate local map could have helped, but only the British seemed to have those.

Around midnight on Saturday, fearful that Clinton might slip away unbruised, Washington directed Hamilton—now back at his elbow—to order Lee to "detach a party of six or eight hundred men to lie very near the enemy as a party of observation" and to "skirmish with them so as to produce some delay." This attack would allow time for the bulk of Lee's vanguard "to come up." But precisely what should happen once they came up was unclear. A full-throated assault? A hit-and-run raid? An attack on Clinton's baggage train? Washington had long been deferential to Lee, who in the absence of an explicit command again assumed that the decision was his to make. After a courier brought the commander in chief's message to Englishtown, Lee, at around two a.m. on Sunday, instructed General Dickinson to push eight hundred Jersey militiamen nearer to the enemy for close observation. Lee also ordered Morgan to be prepared to strike Clinton's right rear flank "tomorrow morning." Assuming that this meant Monday rather than Sunday, Morgan kept his riflemen at their ease; they would not fire a shot in the Battle of Monmouth.

At first light on Sunday, Dickinson alerted both Washington and Lee that Clinton had broken camp: "$^1/_4$ past 4 o'clock a.m., June 28, 1778. The enemy are in motion, marching off. . . . They moved as early as 4 o'clock." Several thousand of Lee's Continentals now scurried about in Englishtown, shedding superfluous kit, dressing their lines, and bumping into one another in the morning twilight. Rum and rations had been issued, but there was no time for breakfast. Guides assigned to lead a fifteen-hundred-man vanguard disappeared, requiring a frantic search for replacements. Striding into the Village Inn for final instructions, Lafayette found Lee slumped in a chair, his eyes bleary and his face drawn, a dog at his feet. Not until seven a.m. did the column lurch forward, eastbound on the Monmouth road, muskets shouldered, a tawny nimbus of dust rising on the morning thermals.

Past the Tennent meetinghouse and a churchyard crowded with dead Presbyterians, they crossed the West Ravine, the wooden bridge bouncing beneath their heavy tread. Jewelweed, arrowvine, and purple-clustered ironweed grew tangled in the boggy branch below. The scold of catbirds and a rattle of insects rose from the thickets, and the first snicker of musketry sounded half a mile ahead, where Jersey militiamen had fired a long-range volley at redcoat pickets before haring west to join the approaching Continentals. General Wayne also tucked into the column, with more than five hundred men. Lee, who had heaved himself from his chair and onto a horse, now complained with exasperation at wild-eyed messengers who pounded up on lathered mounts to deliver breathless, contradictory reports. The enemy had vacated his camp. No, the enemy remained in strength around Monmouth Court House. A large enemy column was seen moving northeast toward Middletown. No, enemy troops were massing to attack. A redcoat detachment could be seen to the north. No—and this much was true—they were simply lost New Jersey militiamen looking for General Dickinson.

That gentleman himself appeared on the road to greet Lee just past the West Ravine. British troops remained in Monmouth, Dickinson insisted. This contradicted his written message several hours earlier, as Lee caustically pointed out. Tempers flared. The Continentals, Dickinson warned, were at risk of being pinned against the ravine, since the bridge was a bottleneck that would impede any retreat. "You," he added, "are in a perilous situation."

Lee harrumphed in vexation, then spurred his horse forward to see for himself. A distant dust cloud to the northeast seemed to confirm that Clinton was marching off. Lee urged the Continentals across a causeway spanning the Middle Ravine, then had them peel left away from the road toward Briar Hill. There a redcoat rear guard could be seen screening the Middletown road, which lay just beyond the rise. While Lafayette swung within a few hundred yards of the courthouse, Lee ordered Wayne to take charge of the lead regiments. The morning sun beat down like a mallet as the men fanned out across grain fields and through stands of birch, oak, and sugar maple on a front that widened to half a mile.

Clinton's departure from Monmouth had begun at first light amid whipcracks and teamster yawps. Knyphausen led the way with the vast baggage train, two British brigades, and most of his Hessians plodding toward Middletown, fifteen miles away and more than half the distance to Sandy Hook. Dragoons flanked the road for security, but because the procession soon stretched for more than five miles in dense, wooded terrain, they battled small bands of brazen Jersey militiamen darting out of the East Ravine to chafe the column and plunder a few wagons. "Swarms of Americans not over twenty to thirty paces away . . . killing men and horses," Captain Ewald wrote. "We were forced to fire on all sides." After loitering near the courthouse, Clinton ordered Cornwallis and the rest of the king's brigades to follow Knyphausen while he trailed behind with a rear guard of fifteen hundred men, including the Queen's Rangers, in their faded green uniforms, a light infantry regiment, and the 16th Light Dragoons, who eighteen months earlier had captured General Lee thirty-five miles north of here.

To their left—west—they soon spied Lee's force approaching Briar Hill in an untidy crescent. To discourage any additional insults to the column on the Middletown road, Clinton ordered dragoons to swoop forward with Lieutenant Colonel John Graves Simcoe, who had taken command of the Queen's Rangers at Germantown. The fearless, vainglorious son of a Royal Navy captain who had died during the siege of Quebec in 1759, Simcoe plunged down the high ground and through an orchard in pursuit of several militia horsemen, not realizing that they were decoys sent to gull the British into just such an impetuous dash. "For God's sake," a militia rider hollered, playing his part, "form, or we are cut to pieces!" Then, at forty yards' range, Continental musketmen under Colonel Richard Butler stepped from concealment in a tree line. Yellow flame spurted from a hundred muzzles, followed by a flat boom, and several British mounts abruptly "had no riders," a witness reported. A lead ball smashed Simcoe's arm, and another grazed his terrified horse, who carried him toward the British rear, both leaking blood. Butler's men huzzahed and surged forward with bayonets fixed until checked by a Royal Artillery cannonade that also ignited a barn. The conspicuous blaze only made the sweltering morning seem hotter.

Emboldened by the rout of his former captors, Lee now saw a chance to bag the British rear guard before Clinton's main force could save them. "My dear marquis," he told Lafayette, gesturing toward Simcoe's detachment, "I think those people are ours." By ten-thirty a.m., several Continental regiments had swung north to encircle Briar Hill. "By God, I will take them all," Lee told one colonel. When Dr. McHenry appeared during a reconnaissance ride, Lee added, "The enemy do not appear to well understand the roads." Impressed by Lee's "fixed and firm tone of voice and countenance," McHenry swung back to the west to tell the commander in chief that his vanguard had confronted roughly two thousand enemies and "expected to fall in with them" momentarily.

This pretty plan soon came apart, stitch by popped stitch. British cannon fire drove the encircling Continentals back into the woods, badly wounding a Connecticut colonel and killing a Rhode Island lieutenant. A miasma of confusion spread across the terrain, thick as dust and acrid as artillery smoke. The Continentals lacked signal flags for communication, and the battle clangor swallowed bugle notes and drum cadences. The absence of distinctive uniforms and regimental colors left Lee unclear about who was where; two of his aides' horses had been killed by heat or gunfire, and two others were jaded beyond mounting, so that orders had to be carried afoot. Some commanders were uncertain of Lee's intentions, since he had neglected to tell them of his encirclement improvisation. "Our men were formed piecemeal in front of the enemy and there appeared no general plan or disposition," John Laurens later wrote his father. "One order succeeded another with a rapidity and indecision calculated to ruin us."

Clinton also improvised, and now it fell hard on the Americans. Recognizing that Washington was apparently not yet near enough to reinforce Lee and that the broken ground here impeded rebel maneuver, the British commander also saw that the rebel right was vulnerable to being outflanked. He ordered Cornwallis to make an about-face and hurry back toward Monmouth Court House to counterattack with ten thousand men, almost double Lee's force. Grenadiers, guardsmen, cavalry, foot regiments, and light infantry swept down the road, two blood-red columns in the midday sun.

This "put us into the most dangerous situation," Lee later acknowledged. His troubles now worsened considerably. An American battery under Lieutenant Colonel Eleazar Oswald had traded fire with British gunners for much of the morning, suffering two crewmen dead, several wounded, two horses killed, and a gun disabled; his round shot expended, Oswald ordered the battery back toward the West Ravine to replenish his ammunition caissons from a supply wagon. In the center of the American line, General Scott watched this withdrawal, took counsel of his fears, and ordered his brigade to shift west in search of better ground. "We retired in great haste, but in good order," sixteen-year-old Barnardus Swartout, Jr., of the 2nd New York, told his journal. "The enemy pressed hard on our rear." Brigadier General William Maxwell, on Scott's left, also pulled back. As historian Christian McBurney later noted, neither brigadier asked permission.

Dumbfounded by this unauthorized withdrawal, Lee soon regained his tongue and "expressed in strong terms his disapprobation," an aide recalled, warning that this "would prove the ruin of the day." Retreat became infectious, as it often did. Abandoned on the far right with three isolated regiments, Lafayette saw half the British army bearing down on him and ordered his men back onto the Englishtown road. British artillerymen in white breeches and black spatterdashes unlimbered their guns and shot began to skip through the rebel ranks. Dead horses soon littered the landscape, their legs stiff and upright as if carved from wood. A 12-pound ball severely wounded a Massachusetts colonel across the shoulders and another blew through a corporal's knapsack, tearing him apart. "Never mind," his captain told horrified comrades. "He has paid his last debt."

A Rhode Island officer tried to steady his jittery men with sips of brandy. But as the blazing sun crossed the meridian, with Lee's reluctant consent the retreat became general. Regiments slid back toward the Middle Ravine as though the landscape had been lifted and tilted west. Some officers, including Steuben and Laurens, would report "great disorder"; Hamilton claimed that "even rout would hardly be too strong an expression." Yet most witnesses described a disciplined withdrawal at a walking pace—the crushing heat precluded celerity—even if anxious men involuntarily narrowed their shoulders and crouched low with furtive backward glances. Behind them came two columns of British guardsmen, grenadiers, and foot regiments, with cavalry and artillery carriages positioned between them. Hessian grenadiers trailed in reserve.

With their ammunition boxes refilled, Oswald's gunners took post near the Middle Ravine, momentarily checking the pursuers with grape and canister before crossing the causeway to unlimber again on higher ground. Clinton ordered No-Flint Grey to angle his brigade through the ironweed morass in hopes of seizing the West Ravine bridge, a mile ahead, an obvious point of danger for the rebels. Farther north, Brigadier General Sir William Erskine led a thousand Queen's Rangers and light infantry troops on a wide sweep to the right. Bullets nickered and whined, more rebel grapeshot shredded a cider orchard, and soldiers on both sides fell on their faces from heatstroke, without a murmur.

For a man struggling to save his command, his reputation, and perhaps his life, Lee seemed imperturbable as he issued orders and scouted the countryside for firing positions from which to halt the enemy advance. Only when he was challenged did his self-possession crack. Told that a subordinate colonel had authorized a further withdrawal, Lee confronted the recalcitrant with a brandished sword. "By God," he snapped, "you are not commanding officer here. I am."

Washington had arrived in Englishtown at midmorning on Sunday. While waiting for his troops to finish closing on the village, he ate a late breakfast and at eleven-thirty wrote a three-hundred-word dispatch to Congress. It read, in part:

> I am now here with the main body of the army and pressing hard to come up with the enemy. . . . We have a select and strong detachment more forward under the command of Major General Lee, with orders to attack their rear if possible. Whether the detachment will be able to come up with it is a matter of question.

The first hint of trouble came from a local refugee whose house had burned down the previous day and who now asserted that American troops were in retreat near Monmouth. Washington sent two aides to investigate. No sooner had he swung into the saddle himself than an initial clutch of stragglers came scuffing up the sandy road. A horseman among them pointed to a fifer who, he said, had claimed that the entire vanguard was fleeing westward. Washington ordered the hapless musician detained to keep the rumor from spreading, then touched his horse into a trot across the wooded ridge beyond the Tennent meetinghouse.

Now there could be no doubt. Hundreds of Continentals trudged toward the West Ravine, felty with dust, sweat beading on red faces that bore the same daunted countenances he had seen at Long Island, Kip's Bay, Brandywine, Germantown. "By God," a New Jersey regimental commander wailed, "they are flying from a shadow." Washington appeared "exceedingly alarmed," an aide-de-camp, Tench Tilghman, recorded, "finding the advance corps falling back upon the main body, without the least notice given him."

After crossing the West Ravine bridge, the commanding general trotted half a mile to a rise just south of the Monmouth road. There, at twelve forty-five p.m., he spied Lee. Riding up briskly, his own face darkening with anger, Washington snapped, "I desire to know, sir, what is the reason? Whence arises this disorder and confusion?" By Lee's own account, he expected "congratulation and applause" for extracting the vanguard from peril. "I confess," he later wrote, "I was disconcerted, astonished, and confounded by the words and manner in which His Excellency accosted me." Lee stammered, "Sir, sir . . ." Washington's tone sharpened: "What is it you have been about this day?"

Various embellished accounts from those who were not present would claim that Washington swore vividly, "till the leaves shook on the trees." In fact, his fury was evident without expletives. Lee sought to explain: how the intelligence had been contradictory, how the British strength had grown insuperable, how the retreat had begun "contrary to my intentions." General Scott, in particular, he said, had "quitted a very advantageous position without orders." Lee maintained that he had made the best of his predicament, avoiding pitched battle against a superior foe.

Washington would have none of it. "All this may be very true, sir," he said brusquely, by Lee's account, "but you ought not to have undertaken it unless you intended to go through with it." Lee should not have asked to command the detachment if he was reluctant to attack. Washington expected his orders "would have been obeyed." That a certain ambiguity marked those orders went unsaid. With that, he spurred his horse down a lane to the south, leaving Lee, dazed and flustered, in his dust.

Lieutenant Colonel Marinus Willett, a stalwart at Fort Stanwix the previous summer, wrote that the commander in chief "had a spy-glass in his hand. . . . He seemed to observe and know everything." Washington actually knew little except, as an aide now informed him, that redcoats were fifteen minutes away. He "was much surprised, chagrined, and disappointed," McHenry recorded. "The enemy were in full view & full march."

There was not an instant to lose. Taking two officers by the hand, Washington "told them how much depended on a moment's resistance." Orders flew. He instructed Knox to bring his field guns forward. Tilghman hurried north in search of coherent units to hold fast on the left flank; he soon found two regiments "in some disorder, the men exceeding heated and so distressed with fatigue they could scarcely stand," but others were in "tolerable good order." Wayne was to form a rear guard with six hundred Maryland, Virginia, and Pennsylvania troops in a copse called Point of Woods near the Middle Ravine, keeping the enemy "in play." Lee—forgiven for the moment—would organize defenses at a prominent hedgerow perpendicular to the road, half a mile to the west. "I will do everything in my power," Lee told Washington, according to Knox, "and Your Excellency may rely upon it that I myself will be one of the last men off the field." Hamilton suddenly appeared, assuring Lee with operatic fervor, "I will stay here with you, my dear general, and die with you. Let us all die here rather than retreat." Irked at yet another presumptuous inferior, Lee replied coolly, "I do not care how soon we die."

Washington hoped these expedients would buy time for the reinforcements commanded by Stirling and Greene to claim two good swatches of defensive ground: Perrine's Hill, just east of the meetinghouse, and Combs Hill, seven hundred yards to the south. "General Washington seemed to arrest fate with a single glance," Lafayette later wrote. Perhaps so, but he also tempted it. Enemy gunfire began to find the range as the commander in chief dashed forward, reined in his horse to study the landscape for a long moment, then dashed back. "The shot from the British artillery were rending up the earth all around him," wrote Joseph Plumb Martin. Surgeon William Read described seeing the commanding general standing in his stirrups, straining to see as junior officers urged him to find a safer vantage.

"The dust and smoke would sometimes so shut out the view that one could form no idea of what was going on," Read added, "the roar of the cannon, the crackling of musketry, [and] men's voices making horrible confusion." The afternoon temperatures climbed to ninety-six degrees Fahrenheit by one reading, ninety-eight by another. Men crawled on hands and knees to slurp from the stream trickling through the West Ravine. "Almost too hot to live in," Martin wrote.

As if to prove the point, without warning Washington's majestic gift horse staggered and fell dead, a white lump in the road. William Lee, His Excellency's manservant, soon appeared with a replacement, a chestnut blood mare with a flowing mane and a long tail. The battle went on.

Henry Clinton had not sought to give battle once his army was strung out on the Middletown road, but now that it was upon him he intended to win. Three battalions of guardsmen and grenadiers swarmed across the

Middle Ravine several hundred yards south of the road, then clambered up the far side at one-fifteen p.m. No sooner had they formed ranks than from the Point of Woods thicket on their right came a scalding volley and several dozen redcoats fell writhing on the ground, including Colonel Harry Trelawny, the 1st Guards commander and a future lieutenant general. In a frenzy, Anthony Wayne's ambushers tore open new cartridges with their teeth, then poked powder and ball down each barrel with metal ramrods. Some loosed a second volley before bolting through the woods and across a hayfield, pursued by enraged grenadiers and dragoons thundering in from the south, raised sabers glinting in the sun.

Clinton joined the chase, waggling his sword overhead. "Charge, grenadiers!" he cried. "Never heed forming!" Lieutenant Hale of the 45th Foot would write of being "astonished at seeing the commander of an army galloping like a Newmarket jockey at the head of a wing of grenadiers." From the hedgerow to the west, Lee and Lafayette watched Wayne's men run for their lives, the slow-footed cut down with sword slashes or bayonet thrusts. Knox stalked along his gun line, ordering 3- and 6-pounders to lash the pursuers with grape and case shot at ranges as close as forty yards. Rhode Island and New York Continentals added volley after volley until smoke lay like a filthy blanket over the hay stubble.

Wayne and his survivors skittered up the road and across the bridge before collapsing with tongues lolling on the edge of Perrine's Hill. In danger of being outflanked by dragoons on the right and guardsmen on the left, Lee ordered his field guns pulled back through gaps in the hedgerow. Infantrymen followed in good order, leapfrogging with the gunners until all but the dead, dying, and lame had crossed the West Ravine. "We were obliged to retreat," Knox said simply. Hamilton, Laurens, and Lieutenant Colonel Aaron Burr each had horses shot out from under them.

The 2nd Grenadiers followed on their heels, unaware that in the past two hours seven thousand Continentals with a dozen field guns had formed three defensive lines on Perrine's Hill under the command of General Lord Stirling. Vain, bald, and bibulous, "braver than wise" in Lafayette's estimation, Stirling had burned through an inherited fortune exceeding £100,000 by building a lavish New Jersey estate that included cherry trees imported from England, two thousand grapevines, gilded vanes, coach houses, and a rose garden. He had spent years and more money in a quixotic effort to claim the earldom of Stirling, a title recognized by his shoulder-shrugging American comrades even if rejected by Parliament. Burr asserted that the main task of the general's aide, the Virginia captain James Monroe, was "to fill his lordship's tankard and hear, with indications of admiration, his lordship's long stories about himself."

Yet Stirling's virtues, which included lupine ferocity and devotion to Washington, emerged most vividly in battle, whether at Long Island, at Brandywine, or now, on Perrine's Hill.

The grenadiers had advanced two hundred yards beyond the West Ravine when the 1st Pennsylvania Brigade and other sharpshooters posted along a fence on the lower slope unleashed a fusillade described by Lieutenant Hale as "the heaviest fire I have yet felt"; pinned flat by the blistering volleys, he paid a dollar to a teamster to creep on hands and knees to fill his canteen from the morass. Artillery and musketry killed a grenadier captain, shattered the right arm of another, and soon drove the redcoats back across the bridge to the hedgerow, leaving behind their commander, Lieutenant Colonel Henry Monckton, a viscount's son who had survived a grievous wound at Long Island but would not survive being drilled through the chest with grapeshot at Monmouth. Carried by rebels into the meetinghouse to die, Monckton was soon interred among the Presbyterians.

Clinton also probed Stirling's left flank with his light infantry and Scots regiments, but New Hampshire and Virginia Continentals bounded downhill, whooping and scrambling across split-rail fences to drive them back. As a lull momentarily settled over the battlefield, Lee—a spaniel capering at his side—again found Washington, to report that he had extracted his vanguard mostly intact. "How is it your pleasure that I should dispose of them?" he asked. The commanding general brusquely directed him to form a reserve in Englishtown. Lee rode back to the village in a "ruffled" state—his own adjective—while seeking reassurance from junior officers that he had been "cool and firm" in battle.

From his artillery train of forty-six pieces, Clinton summoned forward a dozen 6-pounders, two 12-pounders, and a pair of howitzers to unlimber between the Middle Ravine and the hedgerow. For more than two hours "the most terrible cannonade . . . ever heard," in a British officer's estimation, hammered Perrine's Hill—two or three rounds per minute from each gun in a plume of smoke and hellfire, balls screaming from the muzzles at fifteen hundred feet per second.

The rebels hammered back, with an aptitude for artillery that would long be a hallmark of American arms. From their high-ground emplacements, Knox's gunners pelted the hedgerow, guardsmen sheltering east of the bridge, and Grey's 3rd Brigade, scattered across a farm north of the Monmouth road. Added to this was a bombardment from Combs Hill, to the south, which Greene's division had managed to seize despite swampy, broken terrain. Four guns under the command of Lieutenant Colonel

Mauduit du Plessis, who had served so gallantly at Red Bank the previous fall, caught the enemy's left flank in a lacerating cross fire at a range of six hundred yards. Cornwallis sent a column to chivy the battery off the hill, but enfilade fire drove the redcoats back down the slope. "We gave the enemy a fine drubbing," a Pennsylvania soldier wrote his wife.

Hundreds of projectiles whizzed back and forth, forcing thousands of men to hug the earth. "If anything can be called musical where there is so much danger," wrote Lieutenant Colonel Henry Dearborn, "I think that was the finest music I ever heard." But the artillery duel dismounted no guns on either side and caused few casualties beyond a few men killed and a few others wounded, some from fence splinters. More horses were disemboweled, their legs poking skyward.

As the afternoon shadows began to stretch, Washington announced, "We will advance in our turn." Two modest infantry sorties encouraged Clinton to draw back. More than three hundred chosen men under Colonel Joseph Cilley of the 1st New Hampshire and Colonel Richard Parker of the 1st Virginia closed to within twenty yards of Grey's surprised Highlanders, driving them through an apple orchard and across the Middle Ravine. "They run off," Cilley wrote. "I killed a number on the field." At the same time Wayne led four hundred Pennsylvanians across the West Ravine bridge to attack grenadiers scattered behind the hedgerow and across the trampled hay meadow. "Steady, steady," Wayne told his men. "Wait for the word, then pick out the king birds." Three volleys pummeled the redcoats, but reinforcements from the 33rd Foot pushed the rebels back through the hedge and had begun to turn Wayne's flanks when another screeching barrage of case shot from Combs Hill halted the counterattack with the incivility of a slammed door. By seven p.m. American gunnery had "quailed them so much," by one Continental's account, that the British withdrew into a tight perimeter close to the courthouse where they had laagered the previous night.

The long summer day faded. In Englishtown, Steuben appeared with new orders from Washington: he was to relieve Lee, assembling three brigades from the reserve and quick-stepping to the meetinghouse, where they would bivouac before resuming the attack at dawn on Monday. Lee pronounced himself "tired out" and retreated to his quarters at the Village Inn after observing loudly that Washington was making a foolish tactical error in attacking an enemy so superior in cavalry. Still, he considered the day to have ended well enough. "To call the affair a complete victory would be a dishonorable gasconade," he wrote. But the battle had given the enemy "a very handsome check, which did the Americans honor."

*   *   *

Washington and Lafayette slept side by side on a cloak beneath a spreading oak. They woke at first light to find the enemy gone. A mile to the east, Clinton at ten p.m. had ordered his men to steal away, despite being "overpowered with fatigue," as he told Germain. By morning, Knyphausen's spearhead had reached defensible ground at Nut Swamp, near Middletown, thirteen miles from the battlefield.

The Americans pulled back to Englishtown, then set out northward at five p.m. on Monday. They moved slowly. Even unwounded men nursed bruised shoulders, from musket recoils, and powder burns on their hands and faces from firing pan sparks. In general orders, Washington ignored the day's shortcomings to congratulate "the army on the victory obtained over the arms of His Britannic Majesty." He also praised New Jersey militiamen for their "noble spirit," although Dickinson told him that once the gunfire had ceased, nearly all of his men had hurried home to tend their wheat crops. Continental troops were ordered to "appear as clean and decent as possible" for a service "in thanksgiving to the Supreme Disposer of human events for the victory . . . over the flower of the British troops." A chaplain wrote his wife, "It is glorious for America."

A burial detail of two hundred men in thirteen squads remained behind to collect the dead, who "lay in heaps like sheaves on a harvest field," according to Dr. Samuel Forman. Bloated corpses spoiled quickly in the heat, and "the stench from the woods was intolerable . . . they being filled with dead men and horses," wrote Lieutenant Colonel Samuel Smith. Pick-and-shovel detachments reported burying 217 British bodies—the enlisted dragged by their heels into common pits, while officers received a slightly more dignified interment. Surgeon Read found several dead redcoats mired to the waist in a bog, as well as an officer still breathing despite being nearly cut in half by a cannon shot; he leaned the moribund man against a tree trunk "that he might die easy."

Casualty estimates varied wildly, as usual. "The rebels have lost 2,500," Clinton's secretary insisted. "'Tis said Lee is killed, and a French general." Captain Ewald put the king's losses at two thousand, including deserters. The battle totals of dead, wounded, and missing likely were closer to five hundred for the British and Germans and four hundred for the Americans, including many sunstroke deaths on both sides. Among the British dead was Captain John Powell, commander of the 52nd Foot grenadiers and the regiment's fourth captain to die in action. "Well, I wonder who they'll get to accept our grenadier company now?" a drummer asked. "I'll be damned if I would." Reduced to fewer than a hundred men, the regiment would be sent home to England.

Some 150 British prisoners were marched to jail cells in Trenton. Still more German deserters skipped off to Philadelphia; Continental recruiters reportedly dressed some of them in fine togs to stroll through prisoner compounds with pretty women on their arms as a lure for more Hessian defections. Wounded redcoats had been left under truce flags at the Monmouth church, the courthouse, and in barns and private homes; this abandonment "for want of a sufficiency of wagons to bring them off" infuriated some British officers. Invalids from both armies were soon trundled to Nassau Hall, in Princeton, where the stacks of coffins kept near the entrance remained much in demand. Another typhus outbreak killed several patients each day and half the medical staff.

On July 1 the king's men trudged past Refugeetown, a hive of shanties tucked amid the cedars below the Sandy Hook lighthouse and occupied by runaway slaves, dispossessed white loyalists, and horse thieves. Dozens of Royal Navy warships and transports waited at anchor in New York's Lower Bay, after a becalmed twelve-day voyage from Philadelphia. Clinton reported 16,452 officers and men fit for duty, and possibly not one of them regretted leaving New Jersey. A *Jäger* captain who had survived dysentery, brutal combat, and killing heat wrote his brother, "I was forced to tussle for a fortnight against the man with the scythe until he was finally driven off." Lieutenant Heinrich von Feilitzsch told his diary, "Please, God, send us to Germany. The entire army is dissatisfied. . . . I will always hate this life."

A storm had ruptured the base of the Sandy Hook spit, opening a channel sixty yards wide and converting the peninsula into an island. Troops camped in the dunes to await construction of a bridge of boats across the gap. "We were so terribly bitten at night by mosquitoes and other kinds of vermin that we could not open our eyes for the swelling in our faces," Ewald recorded. On July 5 at four a.m., they marched in columns across the completed span, then broke up the bridge behind them to thwart pursuit. Horses and cattle swam the channel in droves of eight or ten tied together. Flatboats then shuttled the ranks from a beach near the lighthouse to offshore transports, which, in turn, carried them to encampments on Manhattan, Long, and Staten Islands. "What is intended to be done," wrote Lieutenant Loftus Cliffe upon reaching King's Bridge, "God only knows."

Clinton strode into his Manhattan headquarters at No. 1 Broadway and promptly rebuked his troops for ignoring repeated edicts against plundering. "The irregularity of the army during the march," he wrote in general orders, "reflected much disgrace." His own performance, he soon learned, would be widely praised at home. The *Morning Chronicle* detected "a great piece of generalship," while the *Morning Post* agreed that the "brilliant maneuver" did him "immortal honor . . . the happy presage of future victories." An inveterate pessimist, he ignored such balderdash, wondering whether he could hold both New York and Newport or would instead be consigned to a grim Nova Scotian winter under canvas in Halifax, a place so awash in bad liquor that "the business of one half of the town is to sell rum and the other half to drink it." Or so it was said.

He believed that if he'd had four more regiments or temperate weather he could have destroyed Lee's detachment and possibly the entire Continental Army. "To have gone near 100 miles without the loss of a single wagon is wonderful," he wrote his sisters. Yet even he "was near going raving mad with heat," which inflamed his old war wound. He continued:

> I will do the rebels justice to say it was well-timed. . . . With the thermometer at 96, when people fell dead in the street and even in their houses, what could be done at midday in a hot pine barren? . . . It breaks my heart that I was obliged under those cruel circumstances to attempt it.

America "possibly might have been recovered," he wrote. "As it is, I fear she will be lost." The Crown had conceded the loss of New England; now the middle colonies were also likely forfeit. "The sooner I get home the better," he added, "as I shall become totally useless here."

Washington allowed his army several days of recuperation in early July after their arrival in New Brunswick, described by one traveler as "a dismal town but pleasantly situated." The Continentals staged a rollicking Fourth of July celebration along the Raritan River, where a double line of infantrymen and cannoneers with green sprigs in their caps stretched for two miles down the banks. On signal, thirteen cannons fired a salute, followed by running fire of musketry and field guns, and three cheers for "perpetual and undisputed independence to the United States of America." This din could be heard by British troops swatting mosquitoes at Sandy Hook, twenty-four miles to the east. Fueled with a double allowance of rum, the Continentals again lurched northward, resting every other day before reaching White Plains, in Westchester County, where the army had encamped almost two years earlier. Washington asked Lieutenant Colonel Burr to "get all the intelligence you possibly can from the city of New York" regarding British intentions.

Years of fighting and killing remained, but for the rest of the war, no battle in the northern states would equal Monmouth in size or ferocity. Each adversary declared victory. The rebels cited heavy enemy casualties and American possession of the field; the British noted their largely unimpeded march across New Jersey. "Both parties boasted their advantages," wrote the author Mercy Otis Warren, "as is usual after an indecisive action." But the Americans stole a march in shaping public opinion with two quick dispatches from Washington and a flurry of blustery accounts from Hamilton, John Laurens, and other vassals, soon echoed in the newspapers. John Hancock declared that the battle had "ruined" the British, and Governor Livingston, who had been no closer to the gunfire than Trenton, claimed that Clinton had lost at least half his army. Congress quickly voted a formal thanks to the army for "gaining the important victory at Monmouth."

Much praise befell Washington. "I never saw the general to so much advantage," Hamilton wrote. "By his own good sense and fortitude he turned the fate of the day." McHenry told a friend on June 30, "He gave a new turn to the action. He retrieved what had been lost. He was always in danger." Certainly the commanding general and his army displayed admirable brio. "The corps of artillery have their full proportion of the glory of the day," Knox wrote his brother. To Lucy he added, "Upon the whole, it was very splendid." The Americans had fought well with bayonets as well as firelocks and field guns, demonstrating a discipline that reflected drillmaster Steuben's ministrations at Valley Forge. "They can't say we skulked in the bushes & fought like Indians," one officer declared.

Washington once again inflated enemy casualties, telling his brother that the march through New Jersey "has cost them at least 2,000 men." He made no mention of the confusion that left Morgan's riflemen out of the fight—"We are all very unhappy that we did not share in the glory," Morgan complained—or other tactical missteps, including his failure to issue more precise battle orders or keep the main army within closer supporting distance of Lee. The omission of public praise for his senior lieutenants especially irked Greene, still smoldering at the Brandywine snub.

Yet as Common Sense Paine would point out in *The American Crisis, Number VI*, despite an enormous expenditure of blood, time, and treasure, Britain now possessed not an acre of Continental America. Their occupation was limited to a few islands in New York and in Narragansett Bay— "holes and corners," in Paine's trenchant phrase. The irony was not lost on Washington. "After two years' maneuvering and undergoing the strangest vicissitudes that perhaps ever attended any one contest since the creation," Washington told a friend in Virginia, "both armies are brought back to the very point they set out from."

*   *   *

The guns might have gone silent, but a final casualty had yet to be tallied from Monmouth. In a volley of letters written while he was still brooding at the Village Inn, Charles Lee gave voice to his resentments and thereby unhorsed himself. The first, written to Washington on June 30, took offense at the commander in chief's "very singular expressions" during their stormy encounter on the battlefield on Sunday afternoon. "They implied that I was guilty either of disobedience of orders, of want of conduct, or want of courage," Lee wrote. "I have a right to demand some reparation for the injury committed." Without such redress, he intended to resign.

Washington replied immediately with a scathing retort, delivered by an aide: "You were guilty of a breach of orders and of misbehavior before the enemy . . . in not attacking them as you had been directed, and in making an unnecessary, disorderly, and shameful retreat." Lee later acknowledged being "thrown into a stupor" by this rebuke. "I read and read it over a dozen times." He then wrote again, misdating his letter June 28 and demanding "the opportunity of showing to America the sufficiency of her respective servants"—a public contest between himself and Washington, whom he accused of "tinsel dignity." In a third note, Lee requested that "I may be brought to a trial." Washington closed the exchange with a terse and final remark: "I have sent Colonel Scammel, the adjutant general, to put you in arrest."

Court-martial preparations were made on the march while both Lee and His Excellency's proxies solicited support in Congress and from the public. "A most hellish plan has been formed . . . to destroy forever my honor and reputation," Lee wrote Robert Morris. "General Washington had scarcely any more to do [at Monmouth] than to strip the dead." The trial opened at eight a.m. on July 4 in White Hall Tavern on Albany Street in New Brunswick, even as Continentals prepared their raucous celebration along the Raritan. General Stirling presided over a board that included four brigadiers and eight colonels assembled to hear three charges: disobedience of orders, misbehavior before the enemy by making an unwarranted retreat, and disrespect toward the commanding general in the correspondence of June 30. On and on it went for twenty-six sessions spread across nearly six weeks, the courtroom venue shifting repeatedly as the army made its way toward White Plains. Colonel John Lawrence, the Continental judge advocate, called twenty-eight witnesses for the prosecution. Hamilton conceded in his testimony that Washington's order "to have the enemy attacked on their march" was opaque enough to allow Lee "liberty to deviate" as necessary; while Lee had displayed "a certain indecision, improvidence, and hurry of spirits," he nonetheless "possessed himself and could not be said to have lost his senses."

Lee called thirteen witnesses, including his three aides: one had been studying for the Baptist ministry when the war began and the other two would become governors, one of Maryland, the other of Massachusetts. Their sympathetic testimony was supported by several artillery officers, including Knox, who told Lee, "I thought you perfectly master of yourself." Lee concluded the trial with a long, coherent closing argument, again asserting that Washington's orders "certainly implied a degree of discretionary power."

After three days of deliberation in a North Castle, New York, gristmill shaded by tall trees, on August 12 the board found Lee guilty on all counts and sentenced him to be suspended from the army for a year. Lafayette claimed the verdict met "universal approval," but that was untrue. Rush told John Adams, "I blush for my country," since Lee was "most unjustly condemned." Most historians would agree that Lee had been insubordinate if not insolent; a majority also concurred that the conviction for disobedience and battlefield misbehavior was unfair to the point of travesty. Yet it was the third charge—and his insistence on a public trial—that doomed him, forcing the board to choose between Lee and Washington.

Perhaps his case would have been strengthened had Clinton's exculpatory assessment of the battle's pivotal moment been available in 1778, rather than hidden in the British commander's papers until the twentieth century. As he wrote to Germain, the "whole flying army" was arrayed against the American vanguard, which had the ravine at its back; had Lee not retreated, his "whole corps would probably have fallen into the power of the king's army." In sum, Lee's generalship was deficient but not felonious; he had failed to scout the lay of the land, neglected to make a sensible plan, and displayed indecision. But as he belatedly recognized in a letter to a friend during the trial, "No attack it seems can be made on General Washington but it must recoil on the assailant. . . . I have been grossly, villainously dealt with." Congress eventually affirmed his conviction, narrowly, and Lee—"a blasted mortal," in his own description—made for Philadelphia in an effort to salvage his reputation.

Washington had not been required to testify at the court-martial and remained above the fray. By his account he "studiously declined expressing any sentiment of [Lee] or his behavior" during the trial. Yet another nettlesome rival had been dispatched, a harsh lesson to anyone inclined to challenge the commanding general's authority. He soon spoke of his former deputy in the past tense, telling Joseph Reed that "his temper and plans were too versatile & violent to attract my admiration."

Much remained of the fighting season, and Washington turned his attention to the next campaign. Good news found him as the army rambled north. A captured British victualler escorted into Boston carried 29,000 gallons of Madeira, and a butt—more than 150 gallons—was awaiting him at Fishkill. To replace the horse lost at Monmouth, an admirer sent him a nine-year-old chestnut "of most excellent qualities. He is not quite reconciled to the beat of drums, but [with] that he will soon be familiarized." Best of all, reports arrived of a French fleet approaching the American coast.

"The hand of Providence has been so conspicuous in all this," Washington wrote a friend in Virginia. "But it will be time enough for me to turn preacher when my present appointment ceases."

17.

———

Fortune Is a Fickle Jade

For more than a decade the lighthouse at Sandy Hook had loomed over the entrance to New York Harbor. One hundred and three feet tall and built of squared stones stacked in an octagon, it was capped with a seven-foot iron-and-glass lantern illuminated by forty-eight oil lamps. Rebel pillagers had made off with the copper lamps before the redcoats captured New York, two years earlier, but the British had installed improvised beacons while building a breastworks around the lighthouse and cutting cannon embrasures in the tower to discourage further raids. The keeper, by contract, was permitted to pasture two cows on Sandy Hook but prohibited from using the tower as a tavern.

At midday on July 11, British lookouts hoisted a red square above a blue ensign to signal an approaching enemy fleet. At two p.m. a dozen French two-decker warships escorted by several frigates dropped anchor in nine fathoms, four miles southeast of the Sandy Hook light. Those great splashes, and the flapping white banners embroidered with Bourbon fleurs-de-lis, signified the end of British naval superiority in American waters. With the sails furled, French naval officers crowded the rails, prepossessing in their dark blue collarless coats, cuffed and lined in red, with matching red waistcoats and breeches, a white cockade in each hat. After three months at sea since leaving Toulon, the fleet, carrying more than eleven thousand men, was desperate for water and fresh victuals; a detachment of 250 sailors and marines went ashore in small boats to buy greens and fill their kegs from farm wells. Others intercepted fishing smacks that were taking the day's catch to British tables in New York.

Standing on the quarterdeck of the ninety-gun flagship *Languedoc*, Admiral d'Estaing searched the shoreline with his glass for signs of the pilots Congress had promised. Tall and gangling—he was said to be six feet, two inches in peacetime but six feet four in battle—d'Estaing had large eyes under heavy brows and a long jawline sloping to a knobby chin. Now forty-nine, a native of Auvergne, like Lafayette, he had "the enthusiasm and the fire of a man of twenty," according to one shipmate, "profound in nothing but only superficial in everything," according to another. A schoolboy companion of Louis XVI's father, he later wrote sentimental poetry and tragic verse, notably *Les Thermopyles*, and squandered much of his wife's fortune on gambling and profligate living before they separated. He had begun his military career in the army, rising to brigadier general at age twenty-seven as a scrappy, inventive reformer and a deft intriguer at Versailles. Bayoneted and captured in India during the Seven Years' War, then released by the British from a Madras jail, he was subsequently accused of breaking his parole by again taking up arms against the Crown; a Royal Navy admiral vowed that if he caught d'Estaing he would "chain him upon the quarterdeck and treat him like a baboon." Captured once more, he was tossed into a Portsmouth prison cell. D'Estaing's reciprocal contempt for Britain ran so deep that upon being condemned to the guillotine during the Reign of Terror in 1794, he would tell the court, "When you have me beheaded, send my severed head to the English. They'll pay for it."

After the peace of 1763 he had shifted to *La Royale*, the French navy, an unusual but not unique metamorphosis. Despite no training as a sailor and little experience maneuvering a large fleet, he had been chosen the previous year as "vice admiral of the Asian and American seas." The appointment provoked skepticism if not scorn among habitually insubordinate French naval officers, who continued to call him *mon Général*. One junior captain referred to d'Estaing as "chicken-hearted and witless," while another told his mistress, "Imagine a sea general, the least of whose shortcomings is that he cannot sail." Authoritarian and short-tempered, "subject to violent spells of anger and impenetrable secrecy," the admiral so disdained advice that a subordinate "did not dare open his mouth when it was almost a crime even to think," an officer wrote. He had embarked a thousand soldiers in Toulon, presumably to enforce obeisance among his naval minions.

"Speed is the foremost of military virtues," d'Estaing once asserted. "To surprise is almost to have conquered." Yet the fleet had taken eighty-five days to reach the American seaboard from Toulon. Five weeks were spent simply clearing the Mediterranean. The admiral blamed "six different categories of speed" among the ships assigned to his expedition, but he had also chased stray merchantmen and practiced naval maneuvers in midocean. Had he made a typical summer crossing, in two months or so, he likely would have trapped and destroyed the smaller British fleet on the Delaware, leaving Clinton's garrison of twenty-four thousand troops marooned and starving in New York. Instead, the French arrived off Cape

May in early July to find that Admiral Howe had narrowly escaped up the coast from Philadelphia.

Even so, Congress welcomed d'Estaing with a letter notifying him that three vessels had been dispatched "with as much water as we can find casks for," as well as barreled flour and bread. Continental commissaries had been directed to collect vegetables and meat on the hoof at Shrewsbury, near Sandy Hook. Another twenty thousand barrels of flour would be provided later this year, despite an infestation of Hessian fly, a voracious pest that was devastating wheat, rye, and barley harvests from Maryland to North Carolina, causing bread prices to jump. Congress also recognized that this new alliance between a Roman Catholic monarchy and American Protestants historically hostile to Catholicism would require delicate diplomacy. Americans typically viewed the French as "light, brittle, queer-shapen mechanisms, only busy frizzling their hair and painting their faces, without faith or morals," one sardonic Frenchman observed. Already rumors were spreading that d'Estaing had transported a papal nuncio to America in order to organize Catholic parishes.

D'Estaing's orders, signed by the king, directed him to "begin hostilities when forty leagues west of Gibraltar." His campaign against the British had in fact begun when the French surprised the twenty-eight-gun frigate *Mermaid* on patrol in Delaware Bay, capturing her captain and crew on July 8 after she ran aground during a long chase. A new law in Versailles gave French sailors a bounty of six hundred livres per cannon for each enemy warship sunk or burned, and d'Estaing's men were keen for *le Général* to get on with it.

Sketchy reports in New York of a French fleet off the mid-Atlantic coast had been confirmed when the sloop *Zebra* arrived with news of a sure sighting a hundred miles south of Manhattan. Any hope that the flotilla was bound for Boston was dispelled by those anchor splashes off Sandy Hook on Saturday afternoon. Careful scrutiny of French gunports revealed that d'Estaing sported 854 cannons to 614 aboard the Royal Navy ships at New York, which comprised fifteen vessels, none carrying more than 64 guns and all "very indifferently manned owing to sickness." The French held an even greater advantage in the weight of metal: in addition to *Languedoc*, with her 90 guns, the fleet included an 80-gun warship, six 74s, three 64s, a 50, and various frigates. "I believe the war is over in this country," Captain William Dansey wrote his mother in Britain, "and we shall be wanted at home."

The British had one asset the French lacked: Admiral Richard Howe, the swashbuckler known as "Black Dick" for his swarthy complexion. "His abilities for carrying on war are not to be excelled," an admiring captain declared, while another wrote, "The greater his difficulties are, the more he seems to rise above them." A Jack Tar once observed, "I think we shall have a brush with the enemy this morning, for Black Dick was seen to smile." His virtues, as cited by the naval historian Alfred Thayer Mahan, included "firmness, endurance, uninterrupted persistence rather than celerity, [and] great professional skill ripened by constant reflection." Moreover:

> Howe exhibited an equable, unflagging energy, which was his greatest characteristic. . . . He was always on hand and always ready, for he never wearied, and he knew his business.

He had left Eton to go to sea in 1736, first in the merchant service after his father's premature death while governor of Barbados imperiled the family's finances. Joining the Royal Navy as an ordinary seaman in 1739, he became a midshipman a year later, then survived roaring seas off Cape Horn and bloody combat near Caracas before receiving command of the sloop *Baltimore* to hunt down Jacobites after Culloden. By 1760, according to one tally, he had fought in fifty-seven sea battles. Ashore at home, plagued by gout, he often took the waters at Bath, where he had his portrait painted by an ascendant artist named Thomas Gainsborough. He bought a country seat in Hertfordshire and a town house on Grafton Street in Mayfair; it had marble staircases, ornate plasterwork, and wrought-iron balustrades. George III called him his "trusty and well-beloved cousin."

Now more than midway through a six-decade career as one of Britain's greatest fighting sailors and naval innovators, Howe was deemed "a sober, even a somber man," taciturn as a stone, with "a very peculiar manner of explaining himself both in correspondence and conversation. But his mind was always clear." Known as "the sailor's friend" for his evident solicitude regarding life on the lower decks, he could also be punctilious and unsparing: when a court-martial the previous year had acquitted the officers and a gun crew aboard *Diamond* after the deaths of five men in a careless accident, Howe had twice reconvened the panel and threatened to remove from command any captain sitting in judgment who insisted on leniency.

With the French fleet approaching New York he wrote London in his bold, legible hand, the words evenly spaced, as if decades spent on a heaving warship had given him a preternatural equilibrium: "D'Estaing has begun to act hostilely. My motions must be regulated by circumstances." He invoked a Latin phrase attributed to Ovid—*finis coronat opus,* "the end crowns the work"—then got to work himself. From *Eagle*'s quarterdeck, thumbing through his salt-rimed signal book, he swiftly positioned his outgunned squadron by anchoring six warships in an arc along the edge of the channel leading through the Narrows to New York's Upper Bay. Each fitted springs on their cables, allowing them to swivel and fire repeated, concentrated broadsides eastward at any French ship making for the harbor. Three other vessels—*Preston*, *Phoenix*, and *Vigilant*—straddled the channel as a first line of defense, supported by four row galleys ready to harry the enemy before retreating into shoal water around Long Island. Howe personally sounded the channel, studying the New York tides and currents.

Should d'Estaing succeed in seizing Sandy Hook, he would place shore batteries on the spit, allowing him to drive away or destroy Howe's squadron, force entry into the harbor, and compel the garrison's surrender. In urgent notes to General Clinton, the admiral asked him to position field guns and fifteen hundred stalwart men on the Hook; this was done, with 18-pounders, howitzers, and four regiments entrenched below the lighthouse. Howe also strengthened his naval line by adding the storeship *Leviathan*, manned by merchant mariners and soon bristling with 32-pounders and lesser guns. To bolster other depleted crews, a thousand swabs volunteered from transports and victuallers. Eager grenadiers and light infantrymen cast lots to determine who would serve as marines. Some merchant sailors, disconsolate at being rejected as supernumeraries, hid in jolly boats shuttling to the Hook in a die-hard effort to join the defenses. One Scottish captain proposed converting his vessel into a fireship to ignite the French fleet. Other mariners slipped out to sea in shallops and yawls to warn inbound vessels of trouble at Sandy Hook or to watch for Foul-Weather Jack Byron, whose fleet from Plymouth was now overdue.

General Washington had big dreams. For the first time in more than three years of war he held the strategic initiative. From a temporary camp just west of the Hudson, he wrote d'Estaing on July 14, welcoming the fleet of "His Most Christian Majesty, our great ally. I congratulate you, sir." He regretted not being able to provide a precise count of British troops or warships in New York, "as they are constantly shifting their stations." But a spy in the city reported that an enemy supply convoy from Cork was expected soon, and "they are under great apprehension lest it should fall into your hands." The French arrival, he added, "makes me truly happy."

In "loose thoughts upon an attack of N. York," Washington privately envisioned joint Franco-American operations that included "destroying all the boats on Staten Island," sending French warships forty miles up the

Hudson to Haverstraw Bay, and "throwing troops over Harlem River" to seize the heights in upper Manhattan. More than 260 British merchantmen lay idle in New York Harbor, inviting French attack. "The present moment," Washington wrote, "is precious." He would send two of his trusted Francophone aides, Laurens and Hamilton, to the *Languedoc* as liaison officers, along with six pilots, fifty bullocks, two hundred sheep, and "a parcel of poultry." Lafayette sent his own jubilant greeting to d'Estaing on July 14, invoking their cherished Auvergne and condemning Britain—that "insolent nation"—while adding, "I know that you'll enjoy the pleasure of humiliating them. . . . May you start the major work that is their destruction!"

That major work was off to a fitful start. Still desperate for water—some French ships had less than a fortnight's supply—with scurvy and other diseases scourging the French crews, d'Estaing personally went ashore at the Shrewsbury estuary but found only hostile Quakers. "I began to think I would be the first victim of our difficulties," he later wrote. Instead the first victims were a marine officer and four seamen from the frigate *Aimable* who drowned in turbulent Jersey surf on July 15; two more drowned the next day when a sandbar stove in their dinghy while they were carrying mutton back to the fleet. More pleasing was the routine capture of insensible British merchantmen who blundered into the French cordon off Sandy Hook. At least twenty prizes were taken, including *Isabelle*, bound from Grenada with coffee and rum; the armed sloop *York*; a royal postal packet from England; and *Stanley*, an armed brig escorting five American prizes that anchored one night amid d'Estaing's fleet after mistaking it for a Royal Navy squadron. An agitated British officer decried "the worst of insults and mortifications—a British fleet blocked up by a squadron of Frenchmen! And in our own harbor! Vessels, bearing English colors, daily captured in our sight!"

D'Estaing soon realized that bulling his way past Howe's gauntlet into New York Harbor would be difficult, despite the superior French firepower. The harbor entrance had been described as "a seaman's purgatory": a wide approach channel from the open sea narrowed severely between Long Island and Sandy Hook, where it was obstructed by the East Bank, a treacherous sandbar lurking just below the surface. Large ships could enter the upper bay only one or two at a time on a favorable tide when the wind allowed pilots to steer west past the Hook and then north through the needle's-eye channel. Not only had British mariners sailed these waters for well over a century, Howe also benefited from *The Atlantic Neptune*, an Admiralty compendium of elegant copperplate charts and crow's-nest views of the American littoral, compiled by military cartographers with pilotage commentary on soundings and coastal mapping. D'Estaing, by contrast, was sailing half-blind despite efforts by the French navy to obtain charts and sheet maps of North America from London dealers, discreetly routed through neutral Ostend.

Worse yet, French ships of the line drew more water than their British counterparts. By one calculation, a sixty-four-gun French vessel required twenty-seven feet of clearance, compared to twenty-two feet for a similar Royal Navy ship. American pilots arriving aboard *Languedoc* with Hamilton reported that the bar was only twenty-three feet deep at the flood; a French lieutenant dispatched to make soundings found it to be just twenty to twenty-two feet during high water. D'Estaing offered "a recompense of fifty thousand crowns" to any doughty pilot who would guide him through but found no takers. A British grenadier wrote that d'Estaing "resolved not to let us out" while Howe—and hydrography—resolved "not to let him in." *Finis coronat opus.*

At nine a.m. on Wednesday, July 22, the French weighed anchor and swung wide of East Bank, gliding toward the Narrows channel. Spring tides and a favorable northeast wind would reportedly stack thirty feet of water over the bar by early afternoon. Howe's ships beat to quarters. Hundreds of bare feet slapped the decks as tars and proxy marines raced to their guns, sighting down the barrels when d'Estaing drew within three miles in attack formation. "The wind could not be more favorable for such a design," a British naval officer wrote. "It blew from the exact point by which he could attack us to the greatest advantage."

Then, a British captain recorded, "to our great surprise they came to anchor outside the bar." At three p.m., d'Estaing weighed again and sheared off. Bearing south, the fleet soon vanished over the horizon. "The French commander," Howe wrote, "has desisted." Some Royal Navy officers sneered at *l'Amiral's* reluctance to cross the bar "with his long-legged ships," but Commodore William Hotham was more sympathetic. "It would have been difficult," he told a friend. "It would have been playing a deep game, & I suppose [d'Estaing] thought it too hazardous."

"It is terrible to be within sight of your object and yet unable to attain it," d'Estaing wrote. The risk of running aground, the risk of being trapped within New York Harbor—Byron's fleet, he knew, was somewhere on the Atlantic—and the risk of failing in his first fleet command had all caused him to flinch. Another opportunity to destroy Howe's fleet went begging and, with it, the chance to scoop up Clinton's army. Through Hamilton, the admiral informed Washington that he would feint south until the trailing British advice boats fell away, then swing east toward Rhode Island. He asked that more pilots meet him there, with more water, more provisions, and an American host eager to help smash the British garrison at Newport.

Washington swallowed his disappointment. "I cannot forbear regretting that the brilliant enterprise which you at first meditated was frustrated by physical impossibilities," he wrote d'Estaing from White Plains, "but hope that something equally worthy of your sentiments is still in reserve for you."

After eighteen months of British occupation, Newport had grown accustomed to the calendrical rhythms of empire. Ships on the waterfront and gunners on high ground around the port fired salutes for the queen's birthday in January, the king's birthday in June, the anniversary of George's coronation in September, and on other imperial occasions. Victuallers, packets, and Royal Navy men-of-war flying British colors came and went from magnificent Narragansett Bay, an anchorage "safe from all winds," a German captain wrote. "Has room for 1,000 ships. . . . The shipyards extend from the middle of town down to Thames Street."

But war had lacerated Newport. The population of more than nine thousand had dropped by two-thirds, and a peacetime affluence derived from rum, shipping, smuggling, and slaving had vanished. "It has one long street, out of which run several lanes, the whole miserably paved and at this time extremely dirty," a British visitor wrote. Yankees complained of gardens looted, livestock filched, trees felled, and fences burned. "Last night a man was beat by Hessians," a diarist wrote. "It is now dangerous to walk the streets after dark." Residents needed British permission to hunt or fish. Those who complained too much found themselves confined with captured privateers aboard *Lord Sandwich*, a fetid prison ship previously known as *Endeavour* when she carried Captain Cook to the South Seas on his first voyage of discovery.

For several thousand of the king's men, Rhode Island life was agreeable enough, even if the garrison had to burn ten thousand cords of firewood in six months to cope with the harsh winters, requiring armed woodcutting expeditions to Long Island. Presbyterian and Baptist churches were seized for barracks, the pews yanked out like bad teeth. Block Island boats brought delectable wild ducks called redheads, and donated goods sent from England included gloves, shoes, tobacco, candles, and hog bristles. "The women are very beautiful and shapely," a Hessian private wrote, "almost like the gods in attractiveness." Perhaps too attractive: local physicians treated dozens of "sunburnt" soldiers—those, in a contemporary euphemism, afflicted with venereal maladies.

War was never far away. Britain occupied the two largest islands in the bay, Conanicut and Rhode Island, also known as Aquidneck; the latter sheltered Newport on its western shore and lent its name to the larger state, the rest of which rebels firmly held. Americans anchored their own prison ship, *Aurora*, outside Providence; another, near New London, Connecticut, was called *Retaliation* to make the point. British raiders periodically burned mills, houses, churches, and boats along Narragansett's north shore and brazenly sold plundered rings and necklaces on Newport streets. "The most effectual means of reducing the country to subjection is to burn and destroy everything the army can get at," Captain Frederick Mackenzie had told his diary in June. Expecting more trouble, in early July Clinton had sent five regiments of reinforcements—two thousand men—to Newport on eighteen ships, and the Royal Artillery positioned twenty more heavy guns to sweep entrances to the bay.

Trouble arrived on Wednesday, July 29, a fine day with a summer breeze from the southwest. At nine a.m. the ocean fog lifted to reveal a dozen ships of the line, four frigates, and several smaller escorts standing in for Narragansett Bay, "as sudden as if they had been brought to view by raising a curtain," an eyewitness recorded. Loyalist lookouts briefly, wishfully wondered if this was Admiral Howe's squadron. Then white Bourbon banners with fleurs-de-lis at the mastheads revealed them to be French warships, which soon anchored in a line abreast off Brenton Reef, five miles south of Newport.

Pandemonium swept the town. Two Hessian battalions and a loyalist regiment bolted from Conanicut Island to Aquidneck aboard a flotilla of rowboats and skiffs, abandoning their tents and baggage. Sweating troops manhandled some Conanicut field guns onto flatboats because "when fleeing," an Ansbach grenadier wrote, "oxen are too slow." Frigates on the bay warped close to shore batteries for protection, and storeships berthed along the Newport wharves to empty their holds onto a jumbled cavalcade of carts and wagons. Orders went out that no Royal Navy vessel should fall into French hands, so Jack Tars heaved their guns and ammunition ashore with block and tackle before preparing to scuttle each ship. Drovers herded cattle, sheep, and horses into the town from outlying farms, and a crier called for loyalist militiamen to appear under arms on the parade ground; some first buried their table silver and other household treasures. "The town," a diarist wrote, "appears in the greatest confusion."

John Laurens had galloped 160 miles from White Plains to Providence in barely two days, and a few hours after d'Estaing and his fleet appeared out of the mist, the aide-de-camp reached *Languedoc* from Point Judith with thirty pilots in eight whaleboats and a plan to capture Newport. At Washington's behest, he told *l'Amiral*, at least five thousand

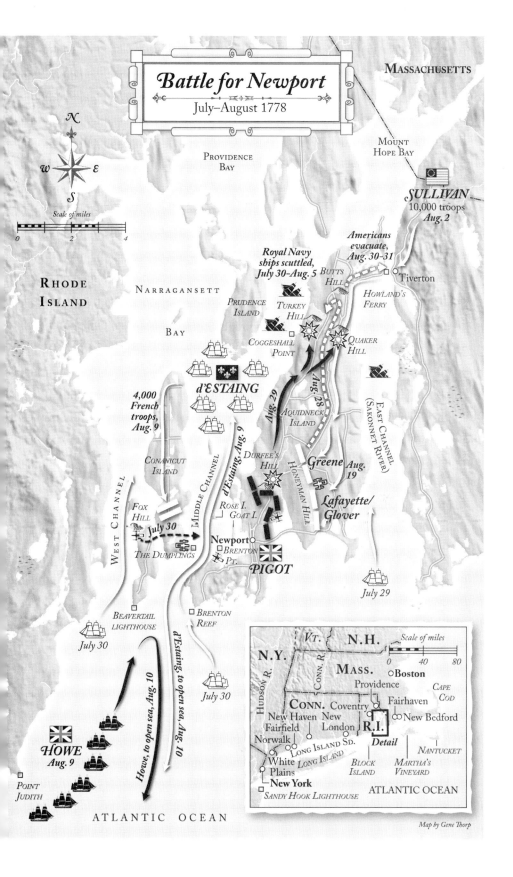

Battle for Newport
July–August 1778

MASSACHUSETTS

MOUNT
HOPE BAY

SULLIVAN
10,000 troops
Aug. 2

N
W + *E*
S

Scale of miles
0   2   4

PROVIDENCE
BAY

Americans
evacuate,
Aug. 30–31

Royal Navy
ships scuttled,
July 30–Aug. 5

BUTTS
HILL

Tiverton

HOWLAND'S
FERRY

RHODE
ISLAND

NARRAGANSETT

PRUDENCE
ISLAND

TURKEY
HILL

COGGESHALL
POINT

QUAKER
HILL

BAY

d'ESTAING

Aug. 29

Aug. 28

EAST CHANNEL
(SAKONNET RIVER)

4,000
French
troops,
Aug. 9

AQUIDNECK
ISLAND

CONANICUT
ISLAND

d'Estaing, Aug. 9

DURFEE'S
HILL

Greene Aug.
19

Lafayette/
Glover

WEST CHANNEL

MIDDLE CHANNEL

FOX
HILL

July 30

THE DUMPLINGS

ROSE I.
GOAT I.

HONEYMAN HILL

Newport
BRENTON
PT.

PIGOT

BEAVERTAIL
LIGHTHOUSE

July 30

BRENTON
REEF

July 29

d'Estaing, to open sea, Aug. 10

July 30

HOWE
Aug. 9

Howe, to open sea, Aug. 10

POINT
JUDITH

ATLANTIC   OCEAN

Detail inset

VT.   N.H.

Scale of miles
0   40   80

N.Y.

CONN. R.

MASS.

Boston

HUDSON R.

Providence

CAPE
COD

CONN.   Coventry

Fairhaven

New Haven   New
Fairfield   London

R.I.

New Bedford

Norwalk

LONG ISLAND SD.

Detail

NANTUCKET

White
Plains

LONG ISLAND

BLOCK
ISLAND

MARTHA'S
VINEYARD

New York

SANDY HOOK LIGHTHOUSE

ATLANTIC OCEAN

Map by Gene Thorp

New England militiamen had been summoned to Rhode Island. They were to be joined by Lafayette with two Continental brigades and another division led by Greene, now tramping east from Westchester County. This host would be commanded by Major General John Sullivan, whose equivocal earlier performances—at Canada, Long Island, Staten Island, and Brandywine—had been shrugged off; he was now the senior Continental officer in Rhode Island. "What a child of fortune," Greene had written him. "You are the first general that has ever had an opportunity of cooperating with the French forces. . . . Everything depends upon the success of this expedition. Your friends are anxious, your enemies are watching."

In a letter to d'Estaing from Sullivan carried by Laurens, the American general noted that Narragansett Bay could be entered through three channels: the East, Middle, and West. If French warships blockaded these entrances, Sullivan would continue amassing his army for a finishing blow against the enemy garrison. He had requested more artillery from Boston, as well as entrenching tools and surgeons "with instruments & every necessary for restoring broken limbs & raising men from the dead." Boat builders, carpenters, and Marblehead mariners were working through the night by lantern light to finish almost a hundred flatboats, each capable of carrying a hundred men, for an amphibious assault on Newport from both east and west.

D'Estaing agreed to Sullivan's plan, while pointing out that he was again desperate for fresh water and carried only enough provisions for twenty days. "Be kind enough to accept some pineapples and two barrels of fresh lemons," he wrote Sullivan, a magnanimous gesture given the scurvy plaguing *La Royale*. The admiral also noted the importance of suppressing British shore batteries ranging the anchorage. "To be fired on pointblank for a whole day without gaining anything is a sad position for a fleet," he added.

On the evening of July 29, two French frigates and a brig—the *Stanley*, captured from the British off Sandy Hook—sealed the East Channel. At dawn on Thursday, while the main fleet blockaded the Middle Channel, the fifty-gun *Sagittaire* and sixty-four-gun *Fantasque* forced the West Channel, trading blows with a pair of 24-pounders at Fox Hill on Conanicut Island before anchoring above the island with minor damage—"slight scratches," as Laurens told Washington. On orders from the British commander, the elfin, moonfaced Major General Robert Pigot, a survivor of Bunker Hill, gunners now abandoned Conanicut, spiking the guns on Fox Hill, shoving two more 24-pounders on their carriages into the sea, and blowing up a powder magazine. The Bourbon flag soon flew above the island—d'Estaing himself came ashore to reconnoiter—and French artillerists placed a battery on a steep granite promontory called the Dumplings, within range of Newport's harbor, a mile due east.

In the East Channel, with the French frigates drawing close early on Thursday afternoon, Royal Navy crews abandoned the fourteen-gun sloop *Kingfisher* and two row galleys, after setting fires in the holds. The sloop exploded in a geyser of planks, decking, and spars, then burned to the waterline; one galley, *Alarm*, "blew up and went to atoms," a witness wrote, raining debris on a nearby Hessian barracks. Matters now grew desperate for the king's men. Over the next several days, General Pigot and his naval commander, Captain John Brisbane, scuttled nine transports and the *Lord Sandwich* prison hulk to block approaches to Newport's waterfront. While d'Estaing waited for Sullivan to concentrate his forces north of Aquidneck, French cruisers captured a half dozen unwitting merchantmen carrying sugar, rum, coffee, limes, and turtle for the king's garrison. Another 245 prisoners joined the floating inmates aboard *Aurora*.

Worse was to come for the British at five a.m. on August 5 when *Fantasque* and *Sagittaire* raised anchor and glided northeast toward Prudence Island, followed by the sixty-four-gun *Protecteur*. Caught unawares, the frigate *Cerberus* ran aground before being set ablaze by the fleeing crew. A similar fate befell several of her sisters. *Orpheus* blew up near Coggeshall Point, on Aquidneck, with such violence that scorched books and Admiralty papers wafted to earth three miles from her burning corpse, including a page imprinted "*Orpheus*, Capt. Charles Hudson." *Lark*, carrying seventy-six barrels of gunpowder, detonated with particular force, setting fire to a house on the shoreline and spraying hot embers across the British fort at Butts Hill. *Juno* also detonated, as well as a galley named *Pigot* and two British transports. Pyres raged across the anchorage. "It was a most mortifying sight," Captain Mackenzie informed his diary. French warships even fired cannonballs at two officers from the 54th Foot, spotted bathing in the shallows. "We thought this action very inconsistent with French politeness," Mackenzie added.

A funereal pall from the burning hulks spread across the bay. In the greatest naval calamity for the Royal Navy in American waters during the war, the king, within a few days, had lost five frigates, two sloops, and three row galleys, plus at least a dozen transports or merchantmen sunk and ten others captured. American privateers darted around the wreckage, salvaging flotsam. The day was "much to be lamented by every lover of his country," a sailor from *Juno* wrote. More than a thousand Jack Tars, abruptly transformed into landsmen, had come ashore "without saving themselves a shirt," Mary Almy, a loyalist with six children, told her journal. The crews pitched sailcloth tents outside Newport. Mrs. Almy continued:

Every sailor was equipped with a musket that could get one. He that could not had a billet of wood, an old broom, or any club they could find. They took care to save a bottle of spirits, which they call "kill grief." . . . By dark the bottles were exhausted.

D'Estaing's arrival on the New England coast galvanized militia companies from Connecticut to New Hampshire. "The spirit, I assure you, is greater here than you ever saw it," Abigail Adams wrote a friend in Philadelphia. "Gentlemen of rank and fortune have joined that army in the capacity of volunteers, the spirit caught from town to town." John Hancock, now a militia major general, rode south to Rhode Island from Boston with six carriages hauling his military kit and a movable cellar of Madeira and French wines. Men who had been reluctant to leave their farms and shops now hoped to be in on the kill. "The fall of Newport will, in all human probability, terminate the war," wrote Brigadier General Jedediah Huntington of Connecticut.

Yet Sullivan struggled in early August to fashion a fighting force capable of overwhelming the enemy garrison. Supplies trickled in: two tons of gunpowder here, five tons of hard bread there, five hundred muskets, a few hundred barrels of flour, beef, and salt fish. He complained that a quarter cask of port sent to him personally "is so pricked that it is inferior to common cider." Whether callow militiamen could stand against the king's regulars remained uncertain, even when braced by Continentals. "All the tailors and apothecaries in the country must have been called out," a disdainful French officer wrote. "They were mounted on bad nags and looked like a flock of ducks in cross-belts." Sullivan initially believed that General Pigot commanded ten thousand troops—a third more than their actual number—and without doubt every passing day allowed the garrison to strengthen the artillery batteries and defensive works girdling Newport.

Greene arrived to command one wing of Sullivan's army after a brief stop in Coventry to see Caty and the two young children he hardly knew; this was his first return home in three years, excepting an hour in 1776 during the fast march from Boston to New York. Lafayette also arrived, bringing two thousand Continentals. Sullivan had proposed that d'Estaing feint toward Newport Harbor with the fleet, then land his four thousand troops on the western flank of upper Aquidneck near Coggeshall Point after the Americans attacked from the east, a pincer move that would trap the nearly eighteen hundred redcoats still entrenched north of Newport.

But d'Estaing balked at this subsidiary role, deeming it dishonorable— "militarily inadmissible"—to come ashore after the Americans. Not least of the admiral's concerns was his need to convert fourteen hundred sailors into infantrymen, since so many French soldiers were enfeebled by scurvy and other ills. Some French seamen had never held a firelock and were now binding cutlass blades to their musket barrels with tarred rope because of bayonet shortages.

Lafayette's overweening ambitions further complicated the battle plan. In their first meeting aboard *Languedoc*, he and d'Estaing chatted about the fine salmon fishing and their mutual friends at home in Auvergne. Lafayette privately urged the admiral to insist on a simultaneous attack with a combined Franco-American force led by the marquis, who envisioned a "decent crop of laurels" for himself. "It is not pleasant for some people to watch the best scenes in a play taken by foreign actors," he confided to *l'Amiral*. As Lafayette left the flagship to return to Providence, crewmen bellowed, *"Vive le Roi!"* "You know how to get everything going," d'Estaing had told him.

Lafayette's American comrades wondered whether Gallic pride and his personal vainglory now superseded "the general interest," as Laurens put it. Desperate to begin the assault, Sullivan agreed to loan Lafayette twelve hundred American troops; they would join French regiments attacking simultaneously from the west as Greene's legion struck from the east. As the last flatboats were caulked by candlelight in a Providence field, the commanding general postponed the attack once, then twice, cursing the "motley and disarranged chaos of militia," before selecting daybreak on Monday, August 10, for the hour of assault.

D'Estaing moved first, positioning his warships to provide more firepower for the Aquidneck landings. At three-thirty p.m. on Saturday, *Languedoc* and seven other ships of the line glided into the Middle Channel, two by two, the pairs separated by half a cable's length—a hundred yards—with only their topsails unfurled before a following wind from the south. Each vessel towed a launch and a dinghy on its port side, ready to intercept enemy fireships. A quartet of British 24-pounders began to roar at two miles' range from Brenton Point. White splashes leaped up around the ships; French gunners held their fire until edging closer, then answered with screaming broadsides of 24- and 36-pounders. Concussion ghosts rattled Newport windows, and the breeze tore dirty smoke from the muzzles after each salvo. With their gunports leering, *Languedoc* and the seventy-four-gun *Zélé* slid along Conanicut's eastern shoreline, taking fire from Goat and Rose Islands. The smack of iron against oak carried across the water to the six trailing ships, each embroiled in its own plangent, smoking war. "The echo of the guns down the bay had a very grand effect," Mackenzie wrote, "the report of each being repeated three or four times."

For seventy-five minutes British balls flew from Newport toward the ships, answered by French salvos into and over the town. "Six children hanging around me, the little girls crying out, 'Mama, will they kill us?'" wrote Mary Almy. "I call out for my children to run. . . . Women shrieking, the children falling down crying. . . . Fire and sword had come amongst us and famine was not far off." Nor was immolation. Captain Brisbane chopped down the masts of his own thirty-two-gun *Flora* and scuttled her, along with the sloop *Falcon*, by drilling large holes in their bottoms. The *Grand Duke of Russia*, a two-deck former East Indiaman, ran aground and was torched within twenty yards of the harbor wharves, threatening to set fire to the entire waterfront. Redcoats would finally beat out the flames at midnight. Pigot ordered twenty houses burned for better fields of fire beyond his outer redoubts; he also told outlying troops at the north end of Aquidneck to withdraw south toward Newport. By eight p.m. all sixty-seven hundred defenders were within the town's fortifications "like sheep in a pen," as a Hessian war diary acknowledged, waiting for the assault that each of the king's men now expected.

D'Estaing had anchored east of Conanicut, a mile above Newport's docks. *Languedoc*'s colors had been shot away, but damage to the eight ships of the line was minor—just a few dents, a few holes, and shredded rigging. As darkness settled over the bay, whaleboats, canoes, and other watercraft prepared to ferry four thousand French marines, soldiers, and those sailors with their improvised bayonets onto Conanicut to stage for Monday's attack across the channel to Aquidneck. Most of the men were wobbly, treading on solid ground for the first time in more than three months, and would need at least a day to regain their land legs.

They would not get a day. Some hardly got an hour. At midmorning on Sunday a courier from Sullivan reached d'Estaing on his quarterdeck. British deserters had reported Pigot's evacuation of his northern redoubts, and a patrol found only straw dummies dressed in red tunics defending Butts Hill, eight miles above Newport. Sullivan had ordered the flatboats massed along the mainland shoreline at Tiverton to immediately land his entire force, now ten thousand strong, on the northern tip of Aquidneck Island to seize the abandoned terrain before marching on Newport. The commanding general urged the French to cross the bay from Conanicut without delay to clasp hands with their American allies and seal General Pigot's fate.

That Sullivan had attacked a day early, although tactically sensible, infuriated d'Estaing and his lieutenants. Were the Americans intent on grabbing all the glory for themselves? Did they realize that French soldiers could hardly walk, much less fight? Was this any way to treat His Most Christian Majesty's armed forces? "This measure gave much umbrage to the French officers," John Laurens told his father. "They conceived their troops injured by our landing first, and talked like women disputing precedence in a country dance." D'Estaing composed himself, hushed his indignant subordinates, and at eleven-thirty ordered the unsteady assault force back into their boats to cross over to Aquidneck.

Unusually thick summer fog swaddled the Rhode Island coast this Sunday morning, as it had most mornings in recent weeks. "It was difficult to see fifty yards," Mackenzie wrote. "Everything was wetted by the fog as if there had been a heavy rain." As the mist finally burned off at one p.m., a sailor perched on *Languedoc*'s masthead spied a spatter of white dots approaching across the gray sea from the southwest. Telescopes on high ground in Newport soon made out thirty ships flying British colors. "The spirits of the whole garrison were at this period elevated to the highest pitch," Mackenzie wrote. A cry was heard in the street: "Lord Howe is coming with a fleet!"

Black Dick's signal book contained twenty-four combinations of drums, bells, and guns to prevent collisions while keeping a squadron intact in a heavy fog, and he had needed all two dozen in the passage from New York. He had hoped to be reinforced there by Foul-Weather Byron, but in late July the sixty-four-gun *Raisonnable* had arrived from Halifax to give harrowing details of "a terrible cyclone" that had bludgeoned the fleet after leaving Plymouth: winds boxed the compass and split sails, and mountainous seas broke green over the stern, flooding wardrooms and scattering ships across the North Atlantic. Unable to reach Sandy Hook aboard his injured *Princess Royal*, Byron instead limped into Halifax for refitting, eventually joined by other vessels from his squadron with a thousand broken spars and crews described as "very sickly."

After foul winds caused days of delay at New York, Howe's fleet finally weighed from Sandy Hook on Thursday, August 6, to confront *La Royale*, now known to be at Newport. Two more of Foul-Weather's ships had reached New York to join Howe, the fifty-gun *Centurion* and seventy-four-gun *Cornwall*. That helped to even the odds, giving the British almost 1,100 guns to d'Estaing's 956. Although the French still had more ships of the line—twelve versus eight—Howe commanded more frigates—twelve versus three—and had added three fireships, two bomb ketches, and several ancillary vessels. All now dropped anchor between Point Judith and the Beavertail Lighthouse, on the southern knob of Conanicut Island, just a few miles from the French.

"The surprise was complete," d'Estaing later wrote. "Nothing had announced it to me, not the least intelligence." For reasons unclear, not until two days after the British departed did Washington write *l'Amiral* from White Plains that Howe had "sailed out of the Hook with his whole fleet . . . supposed to be going to Rhode Island." With the Royal Navy parked outside the West Channel, d'Estaing ordered all French troops back aboard their ships, summoned his fleet captains to the *Languedoc* for orders, and wrote Sullivan that rather than risk a defensive battle in Narragansett's confined waters he intended to fight Howe on the open sea before returning to finish off Pigot at Newport. He would leave three French frigates and a brig behind in the East Channel.

At eight-thirty a.m. on Monday, with a four-knot wind shifting around to blow from the northeast, giving d'Estaing the weather gage, the admiral ordered his ships to cut their cables—leaving their anchors on the seafloor, marked with buoys—and head back out into the Atlantic. *Zélé* led under topsails, followed by *Tonnant*. D'Estaing "came firing through the harbor as if the very devil was in him," Mary Almy reported, "and our batteries returned his favors with a vengeance."

For more than an hour, shore guns and ships again traded brutish punches. "I am certain they did not fire less than 2,500 cannon shot," Mackenzie wrote of the French gunners. "Many of their shot fell into the town." Balls crashed through walls and bounded down cobbled lanes. Again civilians wailed in terror, "people scampering from the hills and running across the fields, children crying and women wringing their hands," a loyalist clergyman recorded. The British fire was "more considerable and better served than it had been the day before yesterday," Ensign Joseph Comte de Cambis wrote in his journal aboard *Languedoc*. French ships took a beating; the bodies of dead seamen tossed overboard would wash onto Rhode Island beaches for the next week.

Howe, meanwhile, had ordered his own fleet to weigh—cutting cables, unfurling sails, and making a course to the south while his smaller vessels headed back to New York, escorted by the frigate *Sphynx*. At eleven a.m., the French had cleared Brenton Point, and the last reverberations from the cannonade died away as d'Estaing urged on his ships in pursuit. "They crowded all the sail they could set, even to studding sails and royals," Mackenzie noted, "and stood directly for the British fleet." In Newport, redcoats and townsfolk alike gaped as the two flotillas disappeared from sight, less than five miles apart.

* * *

The stern chase continued through the night, stretching every stitch of canvas, and by first light on Tuesday pursuers and pursued stood eighty miles south of Newport. Ever wily, Howe almost imperceptibly altered his course during the day, degree by degree—sailing south by southwest, then southwest, then west, then northwest—so that by four p.m., in thickening weather, he had nearly regained the weather gage, which would allow him to unleash his three fireships, each now under tow by a frigate. Evidently oblivious to this stratagem, d'Estaing hugged the British rear like a hound baying after a fox, closing to within two miles as winds freshened and the Atlantic grew so feral that "we had sails dipping into the sea" to starboard, a lieutenant aboard *Languedoc* wrote. Even as he prepared for action, the French admiral signaled for all lower gunports to be closed against the mounting waves.

The gale—the Great Storm, as it would soon be known—struck full force at six p.m. with shrieking winds, horizontal rain, and terrifying seas. Howe had transferred his flag to the frigate *Apollo* for better mobility in the afternoon but now found himself unable to regain *Eagle*; the *Apollo* soon lost her main and mizzen topmasts, then her foremast before vanishing into the howling night with the fleet admiral lashed to the rudder head. *Cornwall* sprung her mainmast, *Raisonnable*'s bowsprit snapped off, *Roebuck* lost her mizzen top, and the fireship *Volcano* shipped so much water in her bow, with both pumps choked, that only a gallant tow from *Pearl* saved her.

It went worse for the French. A gust snapped the eighty-gun *Tonnant*'s mizzenmast, and another gust took the foremast. The seventy-four-gun *Marseillois* lost two of her three great sticks. *Languedoc* had spilled the wind from her sails and put the helm over hard to the southwest, but at three-thirty a.m. on Wednesday her bowsprit snapped, then the foremast, followed by the mainmast, and finally the mizzen. "In less than a quarter of an hour we no longer had any mast," an ensign told his journal. "We were as flat as a floating dock." Cannonballs broke free and rolled across the decks like iron marbles. Ax-swinging sailors hunched against the tempest as they hacked at the tangled heaps of canvas and cordage littered from forecastle to stern. Then, with a frightful crack, the rudder broke. "We were nothing but a floating mass," d'Estaing wrote, "supported by nothing, with no means to steer."

By Thursday afternoon, August 13, the seas and winds had subsided enough for the war to resume. When a strange man-of-war approaching the crippled *Languedoc* was ordered to show her colors, the fifty-gun

Renown hoisted a British white ensign, wore round the useless rudder, and poured three broadsides from pistol range down the flagship's length. As d'Estaing tossed his secret papers overboard, French sailors dragged half a dozen cannons to the stern and fought with enough desperation for *Renown* to draw back at nightfall. Early Friday several of *Languedoc*'s sisters appeared and chased the wolf away. Similar gunfights played out east of Cape May, including an apparent mismatch at point-blank range for ninety minutes between the seventy-four-gun *César* and the fifty-gun *Isis* that ended when the larger French ship broke off to run before the wind with a damaged rudder, fourteen dead, and thirty-nine wounded, including a flag captain whose arm had been ripped off above the elbow by a cannonball. The wounded captain, Joseph Louis, Chevalier de Raimondis, proclaimed himself "ready to lose his other arm in the cause of the Americans." *Isis*, though savagely mauled in her sails, masts, and rigging, returned to a hero's welcome in New York.

From *Roebuck*'s deck late on Thursday, Captain Andrew Snape Hamond saw the dismasted *Apollo* "rolling in the trough of the sea without a single stick standing." Edging up to the hulk in his cutter with a dozen seamen, Hamond found Howe "sitting by the rudder head to which he was lashed and the ship in deplorable condition . . . the sea running through and through the cabin." Black Dick, sodden but unperturbed, made his way to *Phoenix* and then to *Centurion* for the return voyage to Sandy Hook, where he hoped to find not only his scattered fleet but also the truant Admiral Byron.

D'Estaing also made his way to a safe haven. While carpenters set jury masts on several ships, the admiral shifted his flag to *Hector* until the emergency repairs were complete and then returned to *Languedoc*, which, despite her agony, had suffered only a single man killed and five wounded. On Monday, August 17, a week after bolting from Narragansett Bay, the battered French fleet slowly swayed north toward Newport. D'Estaing had little to say for himself except "I gave in to the desire to find the English."

"The most severe northeast storm I ever knew," as a militia artillery colonel and silversmith named Paul Revere told his wife from Rhode Island, had flattened cornfields, carried away tents, and ruined musket cartridges by the tens of thousands. "Found a haystack," a young army teamster reported. "Almost chilled to death. By and by the rain found the way to us and rained on us all night." Sullivan wrote the state's governor, "The situation of my army is now miserable beyond description."

He had planned to advance against Newport from the north on August 12, but not for another week did his sodden army on Aquidneck Island form a four-mile arc just northeast of the town along Honeyman Hill, led by Greene on the right and Lafayette on the left. By ten a.m. on August 19 a newly unlimbered pair of four-gun batteries had tossed more than three hundred screeching rounds into British lines. "The enemy dare not show their heads," Revere crowed. The incautious risked dismemberment, like the 54th Foot private who, with his wife and children looking on, abruptly lost a leg while mending his shoes. The Royal Artillery answered and an American chaplain near Lafayette told his diary, "Stood by the marquis when a cannonball passed between us. Was pleased with his firmness, but I found I had nothing to boast of my own."

Sullivan's pioneers had begun digging siege trenches, but they confronted a steep ravine, an abatis, enemy breastworks, and redoubts manned by six thousand men, as well as plunging artillery fire. Those defenses could be swept away by flanking naval gunfire from the East and Middle Channels, and like an answered prayer the French fleet suddenly appeared off Beavertail Lighthouse on Thursday morning, August 20, giving "universal joy in our army," as a Continental officer wrote.

Joy soon turned to ashes. D'Estaing put an officer ashore on Point Judith to report that five capital ships needed extensive repairs. At least part of Byron's fleet was now known to have joined Howe, and, *l'Amiral* wrote Sullivan, "Express orders I have from the king direct me in case of a superior force to retire to Boston." The American general immediately ordered Lafayette and Greene out to *Languedoc* on Friday morning.

After being piped aboard and picking their way past the stunted jury masts and cannon-splintered woodwork into the flag cabin, the two emissaries urged a weary d'Estaing to remain in Narragansett Bay for repairs while helping to force General Pigot's surrender, which surely would occur within forty-eight hours. The admiral vacillated, but when he convened his captains for advice, to a man they insisted on sailing for Boston, just over a hundred nautical miles around Cape Cod. Lafayette "did everything to prevail on the admiral to cooperate with us that man can do," Greene later told Washington. Greene himself wrote a measured, thirteen-paragraph remonstrance promising "every assistance in repairing your fleet" at Rhode Island and warning that a failure here "will produce a disagreeable impression respecting the alliance" and "produce great discontent and murmuring" about French constancy.

To no avail. The two generals returned to shore—Greene badly seasick—and *La Royale* vanished over the horizon on Saturday afternoon, eastbound, taking the trio of frigates from the East Channel and even evacuating the French field hospital on Conanicut. "The devil has got into the fleet," Greene wrote. Others were less charitable. "If the French fleet has a right to fight when they please and run when they please," an American major declared, "then I do not understand the alliance made with France." A Rhode Islander, congenitally suspicious of the French, told a friend, "The monsieurs have made a most miserable figure and are cursed by all ranks of people." An apoplectic Sullivan convened his war council to draw up a petulant, tactless protest. He listed nine reasons for denouncing a decision with "ruinous consequences" that also was "highly injurious to the alliance" and "derogatory to the honor of France." Laurens was packed off in a privateer to chase down the fleet and deliver this screed, but he soon returned without success. The protest was instead sent overland by courier to await d'Estaing in Boston.

Sullivan, an unlucky and mediocre general, now proved to be an abominable diplomat, despite Washington's request to cultivate "harmony and good agreement" with the French. In public orders on Monday, August 24, he decried "the sudden and unexpected departure of the French fleet" and urged his men to win for America "by our arms [that] which her allies refuse to assist in obtaining." To Congress he complained of "my inconstant ally," adding that "this movement has raised every voice against the French nation."

D'Estaing would deflect such prattle with wry forbearance. "General Sullivan has adopted towards me in his literary exchanges . . . the manner of a commander to his servant," he subsequently wrote. Lafayette, by contrast, responded to his commanding officer's fulminations with outrage. He had refused to sign the war council protest and now confronted Sullivan with such fury that his aide feared they were "almost on the point of fighting a duel." To d'Estaing the marquis wrote, "I told those gentlemen that my country was more dear to me than America, that whatever France did was always right." But he urged the admiral not to impute Sullivan's insolence to Washington or Congress, "the two great movers of all our undertakings." Sulking in his tent, he wrote a friend, "I begin to see that, seduced by a false enthusiasm, I made a mistake to leave everything and run to America."

Prodded by Washington to observe "cordiality," Sullivan apologized to both His Excellency and to Lafayette for his "struggles of passion" and publicly advised his army that "we ought not too suddenly censure" the French, despite having done precisely that himself. Delighted loyalists composed a street ballad: "D'Estaing scampers back to his boats, sir, / Each blaming the other / Each cursing his brother / And may they cut each other's throats, sir." But the contretemps soon subsided. At Sullivan's request, Lafayette raced off to Boston to mollify d'Estaing, covering more than sixty miles in seven hours. He was followed at a slower pace by Hancock, "gouty, aged, and infirm," in one officer's description.

The American bombardment of Newport continued apace, as General Glover replaced Lafayette in command of the left wing. "A soldier and two women were killed in the camp by the bursting of a bomb," a loyalist recorded in his diary. "A child was killed in its mother's lap by a cannonball." Mary Almy also noted "cartloads of wretched men brought in. . . . Every hospital is crowded." But Sullivan's tactical predicament at Newport worsened almost by the hour. Pigot's garrison had swung from gloom to jubilation as the French first returned, then decamped, prompting one emboldened Hessian to dismiss them as "nothing but frivolous and irresponsible dandies." Yankee militiamen, despondent in turn, had begun "to desert by shoals," Greene told Washington, reducing the American force by a third, to under eight thousand. "The disappointment," he wrote, "is vexatious and truly mortifying."

That disappointment soon deepened. Washington had positioned gallopers every twenty miles between White Plains and Providence to allow the delivery of military messages in forty-eight hours, and on the evening of August 24 a dispatch arrived from the commander in chief warning Sullivan that up to a hundred British ships had assembled in Long Island Sound, presumably to reinforce Rhode Island. At two p.m. on Thursday, August 27, a vanguard of three Royal Navy frigates anchored unimpeded before Newport to braying cheers from their besieged comrades. Sullivan convened his war council and agreed to fall back, on Friday evening, to more defensible ground around the former British earthworks at Butts Hill, on the northern tip of Aquidneck. Sergeant Ebenezer Wild of the 1st Massachusetts noted in his journal:

> At 8 o'clock we struck our tents & loaded our baggage in the most silent manner. About 9 o'clock we began our retreat. We marched with great silence.

At first light on Saturday, Captain Mackenzie climbed to a Newport rooftop and, as the morning brightened, "could plainly perceive that the rebels had struck their whole camp and marched off—hardly a man to be seen in their batteries or trenches." He hurried to inform Pigot in his headquarters. By six-thirty a.m. six thousand of the king's men had been called to arms and were wending north in three columns. Commanding three hundred men in the American forward pickets, John Laurens cantered about in a green coat, waving his sword and herding his troops back behind one stone wall after another.

Sullivan drew rein on Butts Hill, where he could see that his left wing was in danger of being outflanked on Quaker Hill, a 270-foot rise that loomed above the East Channel two miles to the south. He sent John Trumbull, a volunteer aide from Connecticut who one day would be a celebrated American artist, to warn the troops of their risk. Riding a strong bay and dressed in summer nankeen with a white handkerchief tied on his head to replace his lost hat, Trumbull passed a friend who had been shot through the abdomen. "He bid me a melancholy farewell," Trumbull later wrote, "and died before night." Pressing on through a spatter of grapeshot to reach Colonel Edward Wigglesworth, in command of Massachusetts Continentals, Trumbull pointed to blue-uniformed ranks marching in the distance. "Those are Germans," he advised. "They are moving to fall into your rear and intercept your retreat." Wigglesworth and his men scuttled back to Sullivan's main line of defense.

American sorties and well-served artillery slowed Pigot's thrust up the island. Murderous volleys at close range raked the 22nd Foot, which suffered thirteen killed and fifty-eight wounded during the melee; the regiment's commander, otherwise unscathed, acknowledged "a few shot through my waistcoat and coat." Late in the morning a small British squadron stood north in the Middle Channel, led by the twenty-gun *Sphynx* and the twenty-gun *Vigilant*, which had so unsparingly smashed Fort Mifflin on the Delaware the previous November. Broadsides lambasted the American right flank and rear, but to small effect among ranks dispersed behind trees and on commanding ground. On Greene's instruction, gunners at two p.m. wheeled three 18-pounders to earthen berms along the water; the return fire promptly hulled *Vigilant* three times with a gratifying crunch of splintered oak, forcing the ships to retreat toward Prudence Island, beyond cannon range.

Hessian attempts to turn the American right flank stalled at Durfee's Hill, where an earthworks redoubt was held by the 1st Rhode Island, "wild-looking men in their shirt-sleeves, and among them many Negroes," in one German description. This "colored regiment," "sable battalion," or "regiment of slaves" in fact included free blacks, Indians, and so-called mulattoes, as well as enslaved men who had been guaranteed emancipation in exchange for army duty, their owners handsomely compensated by Rhode Island's assembly. These Rhode Islanders were among some nine hundred black soldiers currently listed on Continental rolls—five thousand in total would serve during the war—often identified only as "a Negro man" or "Negro name unknown" or sometimes with a common surname: Scipio Negro, Cato Negro, Prince Negro. Some would amend their names to commemorate their new status, becoming Jeffrey Liberty or Ned Freedom. At Durfee's Hill, the Hessian commander wrote, "we found obstinate resistance" from black troops who fought with valor. Major Samuel Ward, the white commander of the 1st Rhode Island, reported that "a couple of the blacks were killed and four or five wounded, but none badly."

The right wing held, as had the left, and by midafternoon on this sweltering day Pigot had ordered his men to retreat back to high-ground breastworks at Quaker Hill and Turkey Hill, in some instances abandoning their dead and wounded. "I had the pleasure to see them run in worse disorder than they did at the battle of Monmouth," Greene told Washington. Pigot reported 260 casualties, including 38 dead; Sullivan tallied 211, with 30 dead. The brutality continued after the gunfire faded. Sergeant Wild described the capture of a former comrade in the 1st Massachusetts who had deserted during the British assault on Fort Montgomery in October. "We shot him in about an hour after we took him prisoner," Wild added.

"My whole army only seemed to want an opportunity of doing themselves & country honor," Sullivan wrote Washington. Yet he recognized his vulnerability in clinging to the northern nub of Aquidneck, particularly after reports arrived on Sunday of more enemy ships off Block Island, twenty-five miles southwest of Newport. At six p.m. he ordered all troops evacuated to the mainland that night. With the king's pickets less than two hundred yards away, Continentals and militiamen erected tents at dusk in a theatrical display of encampment, then struck them in the dark and slipped away to Howland's Ferry. Here boatmen from Salem, Marblehead, and other New England ports waited to transport the army and its kit the quarter mile across Sakonnet Channel to Tiverton. Lafayette arrived before midnight from Boston after another breakneck gallop, crestfallen at having missed the battle but now charged with bringing off the rear guard. By three a.m. on Tuesday, September 1, the island again belonged to the king. "Not a man was left behind," Sullivan claimed, "nor the smallest article lost."

The retreat was deft and timely. At seven a.m. on Monday, seventy Royal Navy ships, carrying General Clinton, General Grey, and forty-three hundred redcoats, rounded Point Judith. Three hours later the British commander strode into Newport "in a very ill humor," his mood soured by the contrary winds that had delayed him for three days in New York. His temper was not improved upon learning that the Americans had escaped inland, for which he unfairly blamed Pigot. Seething and vindictive, Clinton ordered punitive coastal raids "to convince these poor deluded people that that sort of war, carried to a greater extent and with more devastation, will sooner or later reduce them."

As the British general returned to New York aboard *Galatea*, No-Flint Grey and his despoilers sailed forty miles east to New Bedford and Fairhaven, where a "burning party" incinerated a hundred vessels, forty warehouses, and other flammables along six miles of the Acushnet River. On September 10 the marauders swung south to Martha's Vineyard, where affrighted islanders surrendered 388 firelocks, a couple dozen swords, and a drum. Grey's men destroyed a saltworks and sailed away with six thousand sheep, including one given as a bounty to each British officer for mutton chops.

An edict from Admiral Howe ordered the pillagers back to New York before more seaports could be put to the torch. "It is my wish," a Continental officer wrote, "that the fortune of war heave that rascal Grey into our hands that he should be burnt alive in a manner agreeable to Indian custom."

"Fortune is a fickle jade," Greene wrote Sullivan in October, "and often gives us a tumble when we least expect it." Both adversaries had found misfortune at Rhode Island. The British avoided another Saratoga but then missed opportunities to demolish both an American army and the French fleet. With remarkable alacrity, the Royal Navy repaired storm-damaged ships in New York to permit Howe's pursuit of d'Estaing; he arrived at the entrance to Boston Harbor on September 1, just two days behind the French. But d'Estaing had quickly positioned almost fifty guns and half a dozen mortars to cover the anchorage, thwarting any British attack. Howe weighed a day later and sailed back to New York, closing the naval campaign in North America for 1778.

American hopes at Newport had also come a cropper. "If the garrison of that place—consisting of near 6,000 men—had been captured," Washington wrote his brother John, "it would have given the finishing blow to British pretensions of sovereignty over this country." As usual, His Excellency put disappointment behind him and now concentrated on repairing relations with the French, who seemed intent on conducting their next campaign in the West Indies. "The whole continent sympathizes with you," Washington wrote d'Estaing, while also working to keep rumors of a Franco-American rupture out of the newspapers. Boston feted *l'Amiral* and his officers with one grand dinner at Hancock's mansion and a second, with twenty-three toasts, at Faneuil Hall; in search of a common language, some diners settled on Latin. Hancock gave d'Estaing a portrait of Washington, hung with ceremony aboard *Languedoc*. American officials also scraped together £35,000 to put the fleet in fighting trim, using spare masts that originally had been harvested in New England for the Royal Navy in the palmy days before the war.

D'Estaing maintained his aplomb, writing Sullivan, "If, during the coming centuries, we of America and France are to live in amity and confidence, we must banish recriminations and prevent complaints." Only in private dispatches to Versailles did he vent his frustration, telling the naval ministry, "All the news that General Washington passed on to me, with zeal and friendship, has always been late or false." Another blow to Franco-American amity occurred on September 8 when a violent dispute over bread rations at a Boston bakery led to the death of a French naval lieutenant who had once been chamberlain to the king's brother. The dead officer's body was carried through the streets by eight French sailors for burial in a King's Chapel crypt, and the state assembly voted to honor the man with an obelisk, which was finally dedicated in May 1917. Conrad-Alexandre Gérard, the foreign ministry deputy who had just arrived in Philadelphia as France's first ambassador, wrote Vergennes, "Unfortunately this is a nation of hotheads."

Admiral Byron's men-of-war continued to stagger into New York, "all their masts sprung, ships shattered, and above 1,200 men sick," a dispatch to Sandwich reported. Typhus had so enfeebled the crew aboard one seventy-four-gun ship that only eighty men were fully capable of duty. *Princess Royal* arrived on September 18 with a blue flag at the fore-topmast head, signifying that Foul-Weather Jack himself was aboard. The dismasted sixty-four-gun *Albion* had been blown to Lisbon and would not rejoin the fleet for another month. Still, the reinforcements strengthened the Royal Navy to the point that Washington wrote d'Estaing, "The present superiority of the enemy in naval force must for a time suspend all plans of offensive cooperation between us."

With this lull, Admiral Howe relinquished his command and sailed back to England on September 24. His grievances against the Admiralty included not getting a lucrative patronage job he coveted and a delayed promotion to vice admiral of the red squadron, a flag rank above white and blue. "I cannot cease to lament the public testimonies of their lordships' disesteem which I have experienced," he told Sandwich. But he was most offended by what he considered the government's shabby treatment of his brother William. "How exceedingly do I respect the Howe family for their love to each other," a friend wrote. To Britain's discredit, Howe would be succeeded as the North American naval commander by an unpopular incompetent, Vice Admiral James Gambier, described as an "old reptile" given to convulsions, bad nerves, and dispatches that began with maundering nonsense such as "Crippled and dying as I am."

Black Dick, in this most recent campaign, had saved his fleet, New York, Newport, and the king's army, "an achievement unsurpassed in the annals of naval defensive warfare," one naval historian concluded. These feats were all the more impressive since, according to Howe's final dispatch to the Admiralty, among ninety-two vessels on the North American station, only one of thirteen capital ships and seven of thirty-nine frigates were now fully "fit for sea." Another forty leased transport vessels needed extensive overhauls in Britain. Naval stores stockpiled in New York included almost three hundred watch glasses, twenty-three hundred blocks, barrels of pitch, tar, and turpentine, and spare sails ranging from flying jibs and staysails to mizzen and main courses. Yet that was simply not enough to sustain squadrons as roughly used as those sailing in American waters for the past three years.

In truth, the admiral's heart had never been given fully to this war. Amid the ovations at home he would also hear fatuous accusations that he and William were profiteers—supposedly prolonging the struggle in America to earn £100,000 each in annual spoils—or rebel sympathizers, a charge that would baffle Americans whose men were bayoneted, women raped, and towns burned. Both brothers had moments of deep ambivalence about waging a civil war against the colonists, but their field of battle in the coming years would shift to parliamentary hearings and drawing-room pleadings, with salvos of accusations, denials, and incendiary pamphlets flying through London. "The Howes are not in fashion," Walpole wrote, although in time fashions would change.

As for Rhode Island, it, too, had fallen from favor in London, since "all our batteries and an army of near 6,000 men could not prevent the French fleet going in and out of the harbor," as William Knox, the American Department undersecretary, wrote Germain in October. Major General Friedrich Wilhelm von Lossberg had observed from Newport, "Personally I do not see when the rebellion will come to an end. We have to deal with a whole continent, and as long as there is one person left, he will be a rebel with all his heart, even if he is not allowed to show it."

But for now he and his Hessians would be consigned to remain with their British comrades for another severe winter of scurvy, frostbite, and so much Narragansett snow that troops had to exit their quarters from second-floor windows. Lossberg would lament that he had "barley broth and not much else" to eat. As one of his men, Private Stephan Popp, subsequently wrote in December, "This year a hard fate was laid upon us."

18.

———⟡———

A Star and a Stripe from the Rebel Flag

Whenever General Clinton left the grand house at No. 1 Broadway, he was confronted by the empty plinth across the street where his monarch's equestrian statue had been yanked to the ground more than two years earlier by froward rebels. Often he also encountered supplicant loyalists outside the front door, plucking at his coattails and pleading for a favor, a dispensation, or just a moment of your time, Your Grace. To leave such cares behind, Clinton began stealing an hour or two to gallop up Broadway with his new aide-de-camp, Major John André. Sometimes they stopped at a handball court for a quick game or to play billiards in a tavern, then rode on to the Beekman mansion, the commanding general's country seat overlooking the East River, where the spy Nathan Hale had spent his final night on earth locked in the greenhouse before he was hanged.

"He flies about like an apparition," a British officer wrote after seeing Clinton race past one day. As the autumn days grew shorter and cooler, Clinton occasionally joined other officers in an afternoon steeplechase. "I saw him at 3 o'clock pass my window with several horsemen," the loyalist jurist William Smith, Jr., told his diary, "following a Hessian *Jäger* who dragged a bone pursued by a dog. All full speed over fences, through fields, etc. . . . What dissolute times!" Clinton's evenings were typically passed alone with Mary Baddeley or playing his violin with the chamber orchestra he had formed after spending £50 of Crown money on sheet music by Bach, Boccherini, and his beloved Haydn. The commanding general also paid £187 for a box at the Theatre Royal on John Street, refurbished with new lamps, upholstery, gilded ironwork, and a pit for a fourteen-piece ensemble that included a harpsichord and pianoforte. Twenty-one plays were scheduled for the coming season, with all roles taken by army and naval officers except for the occasional local actress paid a few guineas to play Mrs. Malaprop in *The Rivals* or Lady Teazle in *The School for Scandal*. "Clinton's Thespians" would take in £4,000 at the box office this year, all of it ostensibly to benefit war widows and orphans. But after deducting expenses for costumes, wigs, liquor, meals, and carriages to and from the theater for the players, only £140 remained for charity.

New York's population now exceeded thirty thousand, more than before the war, swollen by successive waves of loyalist refugees, escaped slaves, and almost twenty thousand royal troops—half of all those under Clinton's command from Nova Scotia to Florida. People lived atop one another in the crowded town. Few of the five hundred houses destroyed in the conflagration of September 1776 had been rebuilt, and recent fires had left even more people homeless. In early August a blaze ignited in a chandler's shop incinerated sixty structures—houses, shops, and warehouses—around Cruger's Wharf and Dock Street; British regulars trying to fight the flames were accused of impeding firemen and making things worse. Two days later lightning struck the sloop *Morning Star*, anchored on the East River with 240 barrels of gunpowder in her hold. The titanic detonation knocked pedestrians off their feet, set fire to another hundred buildings, damaged countless roofs, and, by one officer's account, shattered "almost every window in the town."

Even such acts of God came under suspicion in a town grown fluttery after d'Estaing's menacing appearances at Sandy Hook and Newport. Could the French be responsible? Or rebel saboteurs? Many fantastic rumors spread in grogshops and through the loyalist press, bellowed by criers at the corner of Wall and Queen Streets: that Catherine the Great was sending up to fifty thousand Cossacks from Russia to fight in America; that Congress intended to rescind the Declaration of Independence; that Washington had fathered bastard children and retired to his Virginia estates.

The Yankee alliance with Versailles spawned especially vivid fictions. It was said that French ships carried seventy thousand rosaries, three million consecrated wafers, tons of holy water, and chests laden with hair shirts and Catholic hymnals. It was said that Louis XVI would be crowned king of America, and that battalions of priest confessors, dancing masters, and friseurs garlanded with garlic and dried frogs were en route to America. It was said that rum would be banned in favor of French brandy, that Old South Meeting House in Boston was to become a popish cathedral, and that both the English language and trial by jury were to be abolished.

Clinton had greater worries than desiccated frogs, beginning with the security of New York. He expected d'Estaing's eventual return, and an artillery survey concluded that the defenses at Sandy Hook, Governors Island, and other key spots would need at least sixty heavy guns in total to fend off an assault. Washington's army lurked fifty miles north in Dutchess County, and rebel brigands infested Long Island around Bread and Cheese Hollow, where loyalists "are greatly exposed to the savage cruelty of these assassins," the *Royal Gazette* reported.

As he "ruminated with an aching heart on the blackness of the prospect before us," the lugubrious Clinton and his lieutenants took pains to assure loyal New Yorkers that Britain would not abandon the city as it had abandoned Boston and Philadelphia. Any hope for defeating the insurrection by force of arms depended on loyalist fervor, even if the commanding general had privately concluded that "provincials, if not sustained by regular troops, are not to be trusted." Where to find those regulars was among Clinton's greatest conundrums. Almost two-thirds of the British Army had already been deployed to North America, yet since the first gunshots at Lexington Common, three and a half years ago, at least nineteen thousand of the king's troops had been listed in regimental returns as dead, deserted, discharged, or captured. Thousands more would soon depart New York for the West Indies, Florida, and Georgia as part of the southern strategy concocted by the ministry the previous spring but delayed by the evacuation of Philadelphia and then by the lurking French.

"Clinton will do all that spirit and sense can do to remedy our evils, but human exertion is a limited thing," read an anonymous letter by a British officer recently published in the *Bath Chronicle*. "Every man we lose discourages his comrades." The losses certainly discouraged Clinton. So did the logistical burdens of waging expeditionary warfare three thousand miles from home. New Yorkers complained bitterly about soaring prices. Beef was up 50 percent this year alone; cheese had doubled and flour quadrupled. Civilians increasingly lived on rice, since even when flour was available they could not afford £4 per hundredweight. Army expenses now cost Clinton over £100,000 a month. Provisioning across the Atlantic remained hand-to-mouth at best, and every victualing convoy was at risk of capture by French cruisers. In the past three years, 229 provision ships had carried tens of thousands of tons of salt meat, flour, oatmeal, peas, and other staples across the sea, as well as war matériel. With the British now required to feed somewhere between forty thousand and fifty-six thousand soldiers, camp followers, and refugees in America—the precise number was bitterly disputed between Clinton's commissary and Lord North's Treasury—the demand had hardly diminished.

Food shortages had begun in the spring and would continue through the end of the year, exacerbated by enormous wastage in the transatlantic trade. That included a thousand tons of spoiled bread and rancid flour, leaky and short-weighted casks made from unseasoned wood, and inevitable administrative confusion—even a simple exchange of messages between London and New York took at least three months and sometimes six. Much shipping space was necessarily diverted to the six thousand tons of oats and even greater quantities of hay required annually from Britain to feed four thousand horses. The arrival of a victualing fleet in late August had staved off hunger, and perhaps even starvation, for both men and beasts. But provisions were already running low again, with the next convoy from Cork delayed until January. Clinton sent armed convoys from New York to Quebec and Halifax to beg for food.

"We have not at this time above twenty-four days' bread or flour," he wrote London. "I am sorry to say I am a little accustomed to this sort of neglect." Rations for both horses and Royal Navy tars would have to be cut by up to a third before Christmas. When the Treasury inquired yet again about gathering provisions in America, Commissary Daniel Wier tartly replied, "We have by no means a reasonable prospect of obtaining supplies of any kind or in any degree from this country. . . . I well know the enormous expense that attends the sending provisions from Europe." With winter approaching, the garrison in New York would also need seventy thousand cords of firewood and seventy-six tons of candles to heat and light five thousand barracks rooms.

Amid such worries, the king's men this fall notched several heartening military and naval successes. London had approved the use of loyalist privateers, and beginning in September more than a hundred letters of marque were issued for vessels sailing from New York. "Seamen of spirit who would prefer rich French prizes to piddling along shore in boats now have an opportunity to make their fortunes," a recruiting advertisement for a sixteen-gun ship promised. Loyalist women in New York even raised money to buy a privateer named the *Fair American*. Rebel commerce in Long Island Sound and around Rhode Island had been nearly annihilated, complementing an effective blockade farther south by Royal Navy frigates like *Perseus* and *Carysfort*, which this year had taken thirty-five prizes among them. Rebel and loyal privateers now traded ferocious beam-to-beam cannonades along the seaboard; gunners who exhausted their conventional ammunition reportedly loaded cannon barrels with scrap metal, crowbars, and in one case even the captain's speaking trumpet.

Ashore, regulars sprang several ambushes in New Jersey that left the Americans reeling and vengeful. In the small hours of September 28, British foragers commanded by No-Flint Grey and guided by loyalists surprised Colonel George Baylor's 3rd Continental Light Dragoons, known as Lady Washington's Horse, at their poorly guarded camp near the Hackensack River. Baylor, a Virginia planter and former Washington aide-de-camp, tried to conceal himself up a large Dutch chimney in his farmhouse headquarters but was bayoneted in the thigh and groin before escaping. Frenzied redcoats, heeding orders to "kill every one of them," slashed, stabbed, and clubbed for an hour, bayoneting some prisoners up to sixteen times, then robbing their victims' pockets by candlelight. A Continental surgeon later counted seventy dragoon casualties, nearly half the regiment, including sixteen dead and thirty-eight survivors who were marched off to New York as prisoners. "I saw a great deal of human misery," a New Jersey militiaman wrote after coming upon the scene. In his report to Washington, Baylor called the attack a "horrid massacre."

Two weeks later, sixteen British vessels led by the sloop of war *Zebra* sailed eighty miles down the New Jersey coast from Sandy Hook with three hundred regulars, marines, and loyalists under Captain Patrick Ferguson, the inventor of the breech-loading rifle, who had recovered from severe wounds suffered at Brandywine a year earlier. In an attack at Little Egg Harbor, described by Admiral Gambier as "a seminary for little rascally privateers," the raiders burned the hamlet of Chestnut Neck and thirty schooners, whaleboats, and rebel prizes before destroying three saltworks.

Prevented by contrary winds from returning immediately to New York, Ferguson and his men then rowed ten miles along the shoreline. Before dawn on October 15 they crossed a salt marsh to surprise a sleeping detachment commanded by Brigadier General Casimir Pulaski, a cavalry regiment that included Hungarian, French, Polish, and Italian volunteers. A Polish nobleman with extensive combat experience, Pulaski had fled his homeland under sentence of death after conspiring to kidnap his king for insufficiently resisting Russian aggression. Dispatched from Trenton to confront the British marauders at Little Egg Harbor but betrayed by deserters, Pulaski's Legion now paid in blood for failing to properly post sentinels. "We numbered their dead about fifty," Ferguson wrote Clinton after rowing back to his squadron. "It being a night attack, little quarter could of course be given, so that there are only five prisoners." As the *Annual Register* in London observed, "Civil wars are unhappily distinguished from all others by a degree of rancor in their prosecution."

Yet gratifying as such pinprick attacks might be, "these sort of things will never put an end to the war," a Scottish officer mused. Both Clinton and his government agreed. If the rebellion was to be throttled and the impertinent French vanquished, the moment had come for a new strategy in America.

*   *   *

On the afternoon of Sunday, November 8, Lieutenant Colonel Archibald Campbell, thickset and graying, climbed the broad front steps at No. 1 Broadway. One of the dozen servants working in the mansion met Campbell at the door with a respectful nod and led him to a spacious office where General Clinton and Admiral Gambier awaited him. After a brief greeting, Clinton told Campbell that he was to command a new expedition vital to the empire, then handed him official orders and £5,000 to cover expenses before leading him to the dining-room table.

"I found about twenty gentlemen in waiting, many of whom were merchants and strangers," Campbell recorded in his journal. A toast to the king's health "had scarce gone round," he added, "when Admiral Gambier filled a bumper and drank with an audible voice, 'Success to Colonel Campbell against the town of Savannah.' A general consternation ensued."

The southern campaign, long in gestation and long delayed, had begun. No one was more surprised than Campbell to find himself on Monday aboard the frigate *Phoenix*, anchored off Staten Island with a Royal Navy flotilla assigned—as his unsealed orders revealed—to free Georgia from rebel control as a first step before liberating Charleston, the Carolinas, and perhaps even Virginia. For this formidable task he now commanded just three thousand of the king's men, mostly Germans and loyalists, since British regulars were needed elsewhere. He was assured by Clinton's headquarters, a bit vaguely, that six thousand loyalists plus Indian allies waited to reinforce him in Georgia.

Colonel Campbell would eventually be honored as one of Britain's most distinguished generals, with burial next to Handel near Poets' Corner in Westminster Abbey. But the American war had so far brought him mostly misery and despair. Born in Inveraray to parents who had won prizes for spinning the most yarn in Scotland, he studied in Glasgow and then at the Royal Military Academy in Woolwich, joining the army as an engineer and earning plaudits against the French in the last war before being badly wounded at Quebec in 1759. After the peace he declined an offer to be chief engineer of Venice to take a similar post in Bengal, where he made a sufficient fortune with the East India Company to buy a Scottish estate and win a seat in Parliament. Back in uniform to fight the Americans, Campbell took command of a battalion in the 71st Foot, whose recruits were promised that "the lands of the rebels will be divided amongst you and every one of you become lairds." Instead, he and two hundred Highlanders sailed into Boston Harbor in June 1776 without realizing that Howe had abandoned the town three months earlier.

His first months as a prisoner of war were comfortable enough: he was attended by servants—including a shoemaker and a piper—and allowed such niceties as breakfast china, Westphalian hams, and drinkable porter. But cruel British treatment of captured Americans led Congress to adopt "principles of retaliation," which resulted in his confinement in a filthy Concord cell, a "loathsome black hole decorated with chains and iron rings," in his description. After two years of imprisonment, he was exchanged in May 1778 for the rebel Ethan Allen.

Now he was to win back at least part of what had been lost to the insurrection, albeit with only eight regiments and those loyalist legions supposedly awaiting his disgorgement onto the Georgia coast. Given the size and importance of his command, Campbell resented Clinton's refusal to promote him to brigadier general; in the rebel army, he complained, even "cobblers and blacksmiths" were lieutenant colonels. He was also appalled to find that the British Army seemed to have no reliable maps of Georgia, "nor any information of the roads, swamps, or creeks." Worse yet, no sooner had the expedition eased outside the Narrows to Sandy Hook on the evening of November 10 than a storm drove the transport *Betsey* aground, stranding much of his artillery in the surf and damaging several other vessels. This was followed by a foul wind that pinned the flotilla to the anchorage, first for a day, then for a week, then for a second week. The liberation of the American South was off to a slow start.

Day after day, Clinton waited in vain for word to reach No. 1 Broadway that Campbell had set sail. British military plans for the fall of 1778 were immensely complex, befuddling even some senior officers, and any delay threatened to disrupt the government's intricate timetable. The first component in the strategy, concocted by Germain and approved by North and King George in March, involved the West Indies. Five thousand regulars— ten regiments, plus artillery and engineers—had finally sailed from New York on November 4 under Major General Grant with orders to seize St. Lucia and threaten the French stronghold on Martinique, thirty miles north. Grant's force would greatly strengthen the feeble British presence in the Caribbean, now barely a thousand fit-for-duty men scattered on islands across twelve hundred miles, from Jamaica to Barbados. No foe was more fatal to redcoats than the West Indian climate, and London hoped for success before malaria, yellow fever, and other scourges inevitably thinned the ranks; each year disease killed on average more than one in ten British troops just during the voyage to the Caribbean. But such was the importance of King Sugar to the empire that dire mortality rates were accepted. Hessians, by treaty, were excused from service in the islands, and for good reason: of more than a thousand redcoats from the 79th Foot who would be sent to Jamaica, only eighteen survived to return home to Liverpool. Not one died in combat.

Also sailing from New York was Admiral Byron's reassembled fleet, which departed in late October with orders to keep d'Estaing bottled up in Boston. Predictably, a storm scattered Foul-Weather Jack's blockade, allowing the French to slip from the harbor and sail south through tempestuous seas for Martinique on the precise day that Grant sailed for St. Lucia on a parallel track. Neither expedition was aware of the other, but France had already reinforced its Caribbean colonies with eight thousand troops and had won the first victory in the islands. In September a two-thousand-man amphibious force aboard sloops and schooners from Martinique had swarmed onto Dominica, fifty miles north, easily capturing the British garrison of forty-one redcoats and a few local militia, plus 164 cannons and a fine anchorage. The war was quickly spreading into the West Indies.

As instructed by London, Clinton dispatched another three thousand troops to Pensacola and St. Augustine, the capitals of West and East Florida, respectively, and seven hundred to bolster Halifax, the Royal Navy's only substantial shipyard in the hemisphere. He even mustered three hundred invalids to reinforce Bermuda and the Bahamas. Yet the Georgia gambit remained Britain's best and perhaps only hope for regaining the initiative in America.

"Piecemeal reduction of separate colonies might achieve what the search for a single point of effort had failed to do," Germain wrote. Four-fifths of colonial exports before the war had come from the South, and seizing the southern states would deprive the Americans of tobacco, rice, indigo, and deerskins while providing the Royal Navy with ice-free harbors as well as timber, hemp, and other naval stores. Territory liberated by regulars could be defended and policed by loyalists, who would be armed, organized, and trained, allowing the army to advance north from Georgia to the Chesapeake. Moreover, as one loyalist wrote, "the poor slaves [will] be ready to rise upon their rebel masters" the instant the king's men appeared. Or so the government was assured by those with a vested interest in retrieving what they had lost, men like Sir James Wright, the exiled royal governor of Georgia, whose dispossessions included eleven plantations and more than five hundred slaves.

At last, after a sixteen-day delay, the gods relented, the winds at Sandy Hook swung round, and Colonel Campbell sailed off with his small host on November 27. Clinton remained behind, trying to put on a good face. "I discerned both firmness and diffidence in his conversation," William Smith, who saw him often, would tell his diary. "He smiled and was pleased, encouraged and discouraged by turns."

Yet having forfeited ten thousand troops—"the very nerves of this army"—to the government's disparate ventures, the commanding general gave voice to his despondence in official dispatches to London and notes to friends at home. This "dismemberment," he told Germain, was "fatal to the hopes of any future vigor in this army." The rump force of 13,661 rank and file remaining in New York and Newport—half of them German or armed loyalists—would be on "the most strict defensive," he added, and "you cannot wish me in the mortifying command of it." To Admiral Keppel he wrote, "To see such an army dissolve—and I fear to such little purpose—is heartbreaking." His duty, he told his cousin Newcastle, required him to tell the ministry "serious truths such as they are not used to." Privately he railed against the "imbecility on the side of Great Britain," then fell silent for long stretches. An officer in the headquarters considered Clinton "perplexed beyond words."

Clinton would never match the Howes for panache and popularity, yet as the year drew to a close, some subordinates found him ever more quarrelsome, isolated, and opaque. "Do not let anything be expected of me," he wrote, "shackled as I am." An aide, Lieutenant Colonel Stephen Kemble, described him as "despised and detested by the army," in part because of "his wavering, strange, mad behavior." Morale plummeted. "There is hardly one general officer who does not declare his intention of going home," Lieutenant Colonel Charles Stuart wrote his father, Lord Bute, the former prime minister. "The same with officers of all ranks."

Clinton was among them. He dispatched another staff assistant, Major Duncan Drummond, to London with a renewed petition to Germain requesting recall. He was reluctant to "remain a mournful witness of the debility of an army" and therefore asked the king's "gracious permission for resigning this command." He complained of shouldering "all the weight and responsibility of the American war" on behalf of a government that expected miracles from its field commanders. Should Britain lose the war, he no doubt would become a scapegoat, incurring "the undeserved censure of my country." This bleating cri de coeur, which Drummond delivered to the American secretary on November 29, was reinforced by Newcastle during an hour-long session with King George during which he sought to explain his cousin's misery.

Germain replied evenly on December 3 that His Majesty had "commanded me to acquaint you that he cannot at present comply with your request." Alas, Clinton was simply too valuable to the king and the kingdom. Nor could the ministry grant the commanding general's ancillary plea for at least temporary leave to return to England, given the number of other officers in America making similar entreaties. In a confidential aside two days later, Germain was more vehement. "Good God, Major Drummond," he told the courier. "Is it possible that Sir Henry Clinton can think of desiring to come home at this critical time, when without all manner of doubt this country looks upon him as the only chance we have of saving America?"

Savannah hardly seemed a prize worthy of imperial exertion. Flimsy wooden houses lined a sandy bluff overlooking rice fields and a muddy river. "The whole has a most wretched, miserable appearance," one visitor to the capital wrote. The peacetime population of 750 residents had swelled in recent years, and a few grace notes could be found amid the town's 450 ramshackle buildings, including a market, Governor Wright's forsaken mansion, and the filature, a factory where silkworm cocoons were stored and reeled into silk. Most of Georgia was thinly populated, except for the forty thousand souls—nearly half of them enslaved—living along the 120-mile Savannah River corridor that stretched northwest from the Atlantic to the frontier village of Augusta and provided a border with South Carolina.

American success against Britain in the South early in the war, including enemy defeats at Sullivan's Island, outside Charleston, and at Moore's Creek, in North Carolina, had resulted in both rebel insouciance and British neglect of the region for the subsequent two and a half years. Fewer than fifteen hundred Continental troops had been raised in Georgia and barely twice that number of militiamen. The state assembly focused more on enemies within than without, recently banishing more than a hundred citizens for alleged treason and seizing their property. Earlier this year a mob had ransacked the home of one loyalist, flinging his books into the Savannah River.

South Carolina's six Continental regiments remained at half strength despite offers of cash bonuses, land grants, and terms of service as short as two months. In a futile effort to fill the ranks, a "Vagrant Act" adopted in March by the state legislature required the forcible enlistment of "idle men, beggars, [and] strolling or straggling persons." For officers willing to serve, duty in the state was not arduous, although few lived as well as Captain Thomas Pinckney, whose family sent him brandy, turkeys, silk hats, cashmere waistcoats, mosquito netting, and a bathtub. Indiscipline had taken root among the bored rank and file, including the 2nd South Carolina Regiment, which in less than a year reported that 250 of 316 soldiers had been court-martialed for infractions ranging from desertion, insubordination, and sleeping on duty to selling government equipment and beating either their wives or someone else's wife.

Congress had given command of the Southern Department to Major General Robert Howe, known to friends as Bob, an affluent, convivial North Carolinian who had helped chase the royal governor from Virginia two years earlier. Educated in Europe, with a jaunty personal style marked by what one admirer called "stains of exquisite raillery," he was manifestly ill-suited for high command. A brief, disastrous expedition into Florida in May was notable not only for the lack of military success against British and loyalist adversaries—five hundred of Howe's troops died of malaria, yellow fever, or dysentery without fighting a single battle—but also for his decision to execute seven deserters, by hanging or firing squad, in a three-day punitive spree. Three months later, after squabbling incessantly with local officials, he fought a duel against Christopher Gadsden, a prominent political and military leader in Charleston, nicking Gadsden's ear with a pistol ball. Further bad behavior, particularly toward women, caused South Carolina and Georgia legislators to demand his removal from command. An acquaintance described him as "a horrid animal, a sort of woman-eater that devours everything that comes in his way and that no woman can withstand."

Congress had agreed to a recall, but the new Southern Department commander, Major General Benjamin Lincoln—recuperating from the gunshot wound to his leg at Saratoga fifteen months earlier—had yet to arrive. That left Bob Howe still in charge at Savannah when an enemy flotilla from New York appeared over the horizon and dropped anchor in seven fathoms just offshore on Wednesday, December 23.

Harrowing winter weather with squalls and waterspouts had turned Colonel Campbell's journey down the eastern seaboard into a four-week ordeal. "We had such violent storms that you could neither see nor hear," a Hessian officer recorded. "Trunks and portmanteaus were hurled helter-skelter. . . . The waves quarreled with each other as to which should break over or in the ship first." Even after reaching calm waters at the mouth of the Savannah River, some troops were wary of venturing into the Georgia wilderness. "Tigers, wolves, and bears prowl around the plantations," a worldly German captain assured his comrades, with "countless varieties of snakes, both venomous and harmless, as well as crocodiles and opossums."

A white flag with a red cross flapping from the *Phoenix* topgallant masthead—the signal to prepare for landing—put an end to such jabber.

Intelligence from loyalists and runaway slaves convinced Campbell that his three thousand invaders outnumbered rebel defenders at least two or three to one. Led by four shallow-draft men-of-war, including the redoubtable *Vigilant*, a convoy of troop transports eased up the Savannah River, each soldier carrying sixty musket rounds, two spare flints, and a day's rum ration. Rebel row galleys threw a few harmless shots and sculled upstream to safety. Continental artillery, poorly served and firing at a pointless range, also tossed a few balls into the river. An ebbing tide temporarily stranded several British ships on the mudflats, but at dawn on Tuesday, December 29, Campbell and his Highlander vanguard waded ashore at the Girardeau plantation, just east of Savannah, then marched—a bit wobbly on their sea legs—through dry rice paddies toward Brewton's Hill, a forty-foot bluff six hundred yards from the river. More regiments followed with horse-drawn field guns.

At a hundred yards' distance, the approaching Highlanders drew spattering fire from American skirmishers in farm buildings along the hillcrest. In a howling frenzy five hundred redcoats rushed forward, bayonets fixed. Another volley struck down nine of them, killing five, including a Highland captain, before the defenders fled "with precipitation by the back doors and windows," in Campbell's description. Several American officers on horseback approached just outside musket range, "using the most opprobrious and insulting language to the king's troops," then wheeled around and galloped back to the main rebel line, arrayed half a mile away on one of Governor Wright's erstwhile plantations.

General Howe recognized that he was overmatched. He had watched from Brewton's Hill as Royal Navy vessels anchored on the river and the enemy bridgehead spread across Girardeau's bottomland. There had been much talk in Savannah of building artillery batteries on high ground here and flooding the rice fields to canalize approaches to the town, but little had been done; the floodgates were in disrepair, and the fields remained dry. Howe's command included just 650 raw Continentals from Georgia and South Carolina, some armed with fowling pieces, plus a hundred or so badly equipped militiamen. Yet rather than retreat inland to wait for reinforcements that he knew had been dispatched from Charleston, Howe announced—with the unanimous concurrence of his war council—that he would defend Savannah "to the last." This poor decision, "the most ill-advised, rash opinion that possibly could be given," as a Continental general later called it, was now compounded by tactical ineptitude.

As Campbell could see after clambering up a tall tree at two p.m., the American line formed a shallow V half a mile southeast of town, with both ends anchored in swampy woodlands. At this moment an enslaved man identified in some accounts as Quamino Dolly, or simply Quash, appeared from Wright's plantation and offered to show the king's men an obscure trail "through the swamp upon the enemy's right" where Howe had neglected to post a flank guard, Campbell recorded. Without a moment to lose, six hundred light infantrymen and New York Volunteers filed off to the left, concealed by rising ground as they followed Quash. Campbell ordered a diversionary cannonade from his guns while another nine hundred Highlanders and Hessians swept from Brewton's Hill directly toward the American line.

Not until he heard the crackle of musketry in his rear did Howe recognize his full peril. Redcoats crossing broken ground from the right flank came "hopping over the little difficulties with great agility," an American officer reported, and the Georgia militia soon fled "in a very disorderly and irregular manner." By three p.m. Howe's line had disintegrated. "Their retreat," Campbell wrote, "was rapid beyond conception."

A Highland company seized fortifications in town overlooking the river and gave three lusty cheers from the parapet. Others chased the fleeing rebels past a local cemetery. "Follow me, soldiers," Howe was quoted as saying, "and I will conduct you to a safe retreat." Instead he led them to Musgrove Creek, swollen at flood tide. Those who could swim escaped with him; others drowned or cowered along the muddy bank, where pursuing redcoats fell on them with ferocity. "Plunging their bayonets into the sides of the unhappy wretches, they continued stabbing until, on withdrawing their blades, they tore out their victims' entrails," according to a French officer serving with the Americans. Someone waved a white rag, the rebels pleaded for mercy, and at length the killing stopped. Prisoners were pushed into a column and paraded past Colonel Campbell. As the sun dipped below the western horizon at five-thirty, the victors ignored their commander's injunction against looting. Highlanders and Hessians "ripped open feather beds, destroyed the public papers and records, and scattered everything about the streets," a loyalist woman wrote.

"The capital of Georgia fell into my hands before it was dark," Campbell reported. Eighty-three Americans had been killed, and thirty more were found floating facedown in the creek. Another 453 were captured, including thirty-eight officers. Howe fled into South Carolina with less than half his original force. The king's casualties numbered just twenty-six, among them seven dead. Most of Georgia's military stores were seized, including forty-eight cannons and almost a hundred barrels of gunpowder.

"We have lost the day," wrote John Houstoun, the American governor of Georgia, who was among those who escaped. A court-martial would later assess Howe's responsibility in that loss, but, in a decision of remarkable charity, it acquitted him with "the highest honor."

Some victors doubted Savannah's value as a prize. "The people here are sallow and in general disgusting," Lieutenant Colonel Stephen DeLancey, a New York loyalist, wrote his wife. "Their speech is so Negroish. . . . At what expense of life and happiness do we eat rice and sugar!" Loyalists with red ribbons dangling from their hats flocked into town from the countryside. Heeding Campbell's call for "well-disposed inhabitants" to unite under the king's standard, they received muskets and green riding vests trimmed in black before being pressed into militia duty. Campbell also sent out pickets to prevent the disaffected from carrying off their slaves. He offered a ten-guinea reward for every rebel official captured and two guineas for every foot soldier. Loyal divines were urged to preach "against rebellion and licentiousness" from their pulpits.

Word of Savannah's capture enthralled London. A jubilant George Germain ordered Governor Wright to sail promptly from England to resume his duties; other Georgia exiles were advised that their pension payments would stop, but that the government would foot the bill for passage home across the Atlantic. The glad tidings from Campbell coincided with welcome news from the Indian Ocean, where French commanders had surrendered Pondicherry after a brief naval battle and siege. Soon every French outpost in India would fall.

Better still, the British expedition from New York under General Grant had joined Rear Admiral Samuel Barrington in the West Indies to easily silence French shore batteries on the west coast of St. Lucia before putting ten regiments ashore in flatboats to complete the rout. Yet no sooner had Grant raised his flag over the abandoned governor's house than at three p.m. on December 14 a dozen French ships of the line, with ten frigates and twenty-nine transports, heaved into view in a great cloud of canvas. Having sailed from Boston and collected nine thousand troops from nearby Martinique, d'Estaing intended to capture the British islands of Barbados, Grenada, and St. Vincent—but only after trapping and destroying the interlopers at St. Lucia.

Outnumbered almost two to one in capital ships and outgunned by seven hundred cannons, Barrington barely had time to shoo his own transports inside the Grand Cul de Sac before anchoring eight men-of-war and his flagship, *Prince of Wales*, across the mouth of the bay and placing shore guns on the headlands. Aboard *Languedoc*, d'Estaing glided past the British fleet twice on December 15 for noisy but ineffectual exchanges of broadsides, then swung north five miles to disembark his regiments on the beach at Choc Bay. Seven thousand men hiked inland before surging in three columns on December 16 to confront sixteen hundred British defenders barricaded across a rocky peninsula at La Vigie. Caught in a murderous cross fire, the French were beaten back three times in three hours at a catastrophic cost of four hundred dead and eleven hundred wounded in what redcoats would soon dub the "Bunker Hill of the Caribbean." British losses were trifling, including thirteen killed in action.

Bloated French corpses carpeted La Vigie, putrefying in the tropical sun. D'Estaing reembarked his survivors on December 28 and sailed back to Martinique, giving up the fight as he had at New York and Newport. Barely a week later Admiral Byron arrived on station, delayed by mutinous weather, as usual, but soon to be reinforced with another squadron from England to give the Royal Navy at least twenty-one capital ships and unquestioned naval superiority in the West Indies. Britain would hold St. Lucia and its sheltered harbors for the rest of the war, although as reputedly the least healthy of the Leeward Islands. "No man would inhabit St. Lucia who could live anywhere else," a British major wrote his sister in England. Grant and his five thousand redcoats were supposed to return to Clinton's command in New York, but for now that move was postponed. In the next six months, eighteen hundred of those men would fall sick or die.

As for d'Estaing, he licked his new wounds and confessed in a dispatch to Versailles, "From failure to failure, from one misfortune to another."

At dawn on January 24, Colonel Campbell gave the nod and a thousand of his liberators started northwest up the Savannah River valley. Cavalry clopped two abreast on the hard-packed river road, followed by double files of infantrymen. Six stout wagons and a pair of tumbrels carried a month's worth of provisions, rum, and salt. He, too, had been reinforced in mid-January: the Swiss-born commander of British forces in Florida, Brigadier General Augustine Prévost—known as Old Bullet Head from a disfiguring wound to the face suffered in the Seven Years' War—had swept north from St. Augustine, bringing more than seven hundred additional redcoats and loyalist troops, plus a large contingent of loyal refugees who had been hiding in the south Georgia wilderness. "Prévost seems a worthy man, but too old & inactive for this service," Campbell wrote a government friend in London. "He will do in garrison, and I shall gallop with the light troop."

If not precisely galloping, Campbell's cavalcade moved with purpose and on February 1 seized mostly deserted Augusta, which he described as "straggling houses arranged in a long street parallel to the river." A British detachment marched on fifty miles to overrun several small stockades on the Georgia frontier, and carpenters built flatboats so troops could at least threaten rebels skulking across the Savannah River in the South Carolina uplands. Within ten days fourteen hundred loyalists had gathered in Augusta to swear allegiance to the king, to draw shoulder arms and ammunition, and to form twenty militia companies. Campbell wrote Germain that he was proud to be "the first British officer to rend a stripe and a star from the rebel flag of Congress."

Indeed he had. Georgia was no longer a state but had reverted to the status of a royal colony; it would remain under Crown authority for the duration. A Continental officer in South Carolina, Brigadier General William Moultrie, later estimated that the loss of Georgia and the empowerment of southern loyalists had extended the war by a year.

Yet the putative removal of stripe and star would not be so simple for the king's men. Campbell had expected six thousand loyalists to rally from the backcountry, fourfold more than actually appeared. He acknowledged that many were "a mere rabble of undisciplined freebooters"; some deserted as soon as they collected a firelock. A British engineer complained that "they could not be brought to any regularity. . . . They were mostly crackers." No Creek Indian allies rallied to the Union Jack, contrary to loyalist assurances. In New York, Clinton doubted that the achievement in Georgia inevitably presaged success farther north. "I have as yet received no assurances of any favorable temper in the province of South Carolina," he wrote Germain.

With supplies dwindling and a growing throng of armed rebels massing across the river, the loyalist militia quickly melted away. "I used every argument," Campbell reported, "but they were deaf to reason and left me to a man." At four a.m. on Sunday, February 14, he ordered his column back to Savannah. The occupation had lasted barely a fortnight. That same day, eight hundred Carolina loyalists who had crossed the Savannah River fifty miles north under Colonel James Boyd headed toward Augusta, unaware that the British force they intended to join was now retreating downriver. Shadowed by four hundred hell-bent rebel militiamen commanded by Colonel Andrew Pickens, Boyd broke camp Sunday morning with flags flying and drums beating and marched two miles along Kettle Creek, a swollen streamed in a dense thicket of hardwoods and southern conifers.

Although confronting twice his number, Pickens ordered two hundred rebels to pin down the loyalists with a frontal lunge toward a rocky hill overlooking the creek while two flanking detachments enveloped the enemy from right and left. Thick canebrakes entangled the flankers, and the alert Boyd ambushed Pickens at thirty yards' range from behind a deadfall along an old fence line. But the morning abruptly swung against the loyalists when Boyd fell mortally wounded by musketmen who had wriggled within his lines for a clear shot. Two hours after it began, the battle sputtered to a close with dispirited loyalists either captured, dead, or running for their lives.

Boyd, on his deathbed Sunday evening, reportedly asked Pickens to send his wife a brooch he had saved for her. Upon receiving this token from the grave, the widow insisted, "It's a lie. No damned rebel ever killed my husband." But kill him they had, and more than sixty others as well, at a cost of nine rebel dead. They also captured more than 150 of Boyd's men and six hundred horses in "the severest check and chastisement the Tories ever received in Georgia or South Carolina," Colonel Pickens declared.

This minor skirmish in the hinterland foretold the sort of war that would be fought for years to come in the American South: unsparing, cruel, and internecine. Seven loyalist prisoners taken at Kettle Creek were promptly hanged for looting during their march up. More than a hundred others were led in chains to Ninety Six, a South Carolina crossroads north of Augusta with twelve dwellings, a courthouse, and a jail. Here, before a jury chosen by Sheriff William Moore, they were prosecuted for treason. After trials that lasted for three weeks, half were released, fifty were convicted but reprieved, and another twenty-two were condemned and required to sign their own death warrants as rebels dug their graves and built a gallows within sight of the cells.

British officials threatened retaliation but feared a spiral of retribution that would fall hard on Burgoyne's imprisoned army, now held in Charlottesville. In the end, five loyalists were hanged at Ninety Six, along with two more in Charleston and a free black man in Orangeburg. Others received parole, with the proviso that certain death awaited those who again took up arms against the patriot cause. Sheriff Moore submitted a bill to the rebel government requesting reimbursement for the expense of confinements, trials, and executions, but as late as 1787 he would still be awaiting his money.

If Georgia was once again a royal colony, the campaign had exposed loyalist weakness in the backcountry without a permanent, stiffening force of British regulars. Many who wore red ribbons and swore fealty to the king now switched allegiance again.

As for Colonel Campbell, after assuring Clinton in a dispatch from Savannah that "we have nothing to fear at present from the rebels of Carolina," he sailed back to England aboard *Phoenix* in early March, his tour of duty in America ended. During a levee at St. James's Palace, the king invited him to kiss the royal hand as a reward for service to the Crown and as a gesture of His Majesty's approbation.

19.

⸻

The Uncertainty of Human Prospects

The curiously named Point No Point Road stretched straight as a gun-shot northeast of Philadelphia through fallow grain fields and barren fruit orchards dreaming of spring. Skim ice glistened on nearby Frankford Creek, and by three-thirty p.m. on Wednesday, December 23, long winter shadows stretched from the buttonwood and willow trees bracketing the road, as well as from the stone four-mile marker where two Continental Army comrades had agreed to try to kill each other.

At least seven duels had been fought in Philadelphia already this season. "The rage for dueling here has reached an incredible and scandalous point," Ambassador Gérard wrote Vergennes. "This license is regarded as the appendage of liberty." Article XI of Continental Army regulations forbade officers and enlisted men from issuing "a challenge to any person to fight," a prohibition too often ignored. In the past month, Major General Lee had shrugged off challenges from Generals Steuben and Wayne, but Lieutenant Colonel Laurens, outraged that Lee "had spoken of General Washington in the grossest and most opprobrious terms of personal abuse," had been more persistent in demanding satisfaction. Now the hour of reckoning had come round.

Lee arrived early at the four-mile stone, accompanied by Major Evan Edwards of the 11th Pennsylvania, a former aide who had agreed to be his second. In the four months since a court-martial had suspended him from duty for misbehavior at Monmouth, Lee had continued to argue his case publicly, privately, and through sympathetic surrogates. "I have been almost mobbed in defending you," Major Edwards recently informed him. "Ten thousand infamous lies have been spread." In a long defense published earlier this month in the *Pennsylvania Packet*, with footnotes and postscripts, Lee condemned Washington's flawed orders in New Jersey, blamed subordinates for "a most glorious opportunity lost," and suggested that the commander in chief held too much power for the country's good.

As usual, Washington declined to respond, while confidentially telling a friend that his former deputy "has most barefacedly misrepresented facts . . . to have the world believe that he was a persecuted man." Laurens refused to let the insults pass, and after a delay to allow Lee's recovery from a fall off his horse and a bad spell of gout, this remote dueling ground had been chosen.

Laurens arrived late with his own second, a fellow Washington aide-de-camp, Lieutenant Colonel Hamilton. After a perfunctory greeting, each duelist grasped a pistol and eyed his opponent as they moved apart on the vacant road. Lee suggested that they advance simultaneously, firing whenever it seemed proper. Laurens agreed, and they strode to within six paces of each other, pistols extended. Then flame spurted from the barrels and two sharp claps broke the morning calm as both squeezed the trigger at the same instant. Peering through the smoke at his still-standing opponent, Laurens began to reload. "You may fire at me all day if it will amuse you," Lee called, before buckling slightly at the knees and conceding that he had been shot.

The ball had grazed his right side, "carrying away some flesh and producing a considerable effusion of blood." As Laurens and the seconds stood gawking at the wound, Lee pronounced it trifling and proposed another volley. Hamilton and Edwards disagreed. Lee insisted. Unless the general was "influenced by motives of personal enmity," Hamilton said, honor had been satisfied; the affair should end. As the seconds stepped away to confer, the adversaries discussed their dispute in civil tones. Laurens repeated his accusation that "in contempt of decency and truth you have publicly abused General Washington." Lee countered that "every man has a right to give his sentiments freely of military characters." He "might perhaps do so again," but he had "always esteemed General Washington as a man."

With this meandering colloquy the confrontation was declared over, and all parties agreed to return to Philadelphia. "How handsomely the young fellow behaved," Lee reportedly mused as he watched Laurens vanish down the road. "I could have hugged him." His flesh wound healed, and the general soon retired to Prato Rio, his dilapidated farm in western Virginia, where he announced an intention to "learn to hoe tobacco." There he spent his days with his dogs and his grievances, "a pilgrim to all eternity," as he later wrote his sister, living in a barnlike house built of rough-cut limestone, without glass in the windows, the rooms delineated only by lines chalked across the floor. Although he talked of immigrating to Tuscany or Hungary, he rarely ventured far from home except to stay with friends and borrow money.

"From an income of near £1,000 a year, from my zeal for this country I am reduced . . . to absolute beggary," he wrote Robert Morris. Depressed and racked by gout, convinced that Washington partisans intended to assassinate him, he intensified his venomous attacks against Wayne, Sullivan, and particularly the commander in chief, whom he called a "bladder of emptiness and pride" and a "puffed-up charlatan . . . extremely prodigal of other men's blood." After renouncing future service to the cause in an intemperate message to Congress, he would be stripped of his commission and dismissed from the army in January 1780.

The final collapse of the man who had been but a heartbeat away from commanding the Continental Army came swiftly. He sold Prato Rio to settle £4,500 in debts, then took a dingy room at the Sign of the Conestoga, on High Street in Philadelphia. Plagued by old wounds, a lung ailment, and bad dreams, he drafted his will, asking not to be buried in a churchyard because "since I have resided in this country I have kept so much bad company while living that I do not choose to continue it when dead." During his final delirium on October 2, 1782, he would cry out, "Stand fast, my brave grenadiers." Moments later he crossed over. Friends removed Lee's body to City Tavern and collected $11 in donations for a mahogany coffin, which was then carried with military pomp to Christ Church. A throng of army officers, congressmen, and Philadelphia worthies attended the funeral, which included a reading of Psalm 39: "I will take heed to my ways that I sin not with my tongue." Despite his request, Lee was buried just outside the southwest door of the church, in consecrated ground. He was fifty years old.

"I can never mention General Lee," a Massachusetts artillery officer wrote, "without reflecting on the uncertainty of human prospects."

Summoned by Congress for consultations, Washington had arrived in Philadelphia on the evening of December 22, a day before the Point No Point duel. What he thought of the gunplay between his aide and his former deputy went unrecorded, but no doubt he felt a certain awkwardness, since he and Martha had accepted an invitation to stay in the Chestnut Street house of Henry Laurens, who had just yielded the presidency of Congress to John Jay of New York. His Excellency intended to linger in the city for only a few days before returning to his army, which had settled for the winter in a half dozen camps arrayed in an arc from northern New Jersey to the eastern rim of the Hudson Valley. In the event, he would remain in the town for six weeks. There was much work to be done and, as he wrote, "I shall have full employment during the winter to prepare for the campaign that follows it."

With the British long gone, he found Philadelphia again swarming with rebel gentry, artisans, and yeomen. Many loyalist properties and furnishings had been confiscated by the state and auctioned to buyers who for the first time in their lives enjoyed Chinese porcelain, Delft fireplace tiles, Chippendale furniture, and other grace notes; Joseph Galloway's house alone contributed brass candlesticks, silver teaspoons, and six mahogany tables. Merchants and journeymen who had fled the redcoat occupation returned to resume their trades; others arrived in hopes of sharing a resurgent prosperity. Staymaker Henry Hineman offered wares in the "approved French and English tastes." At the corner of Strawberry Alley, merchant John Levins sold Bengal and durant cloth, worsted knee garters, Congou tea in canisters, and good proof whiskey by the hogshead. The *Pennsylvania Packet* advertised the services of "Doctor Baker, a surgeon dentist from Williamsburg, in Virginia, who handles all disorders of the teeth. . . . He eradicates the scurvy, be it ever so bad."

Four newspapers soon vied for state and congressional printing contracts, subsidies that ensured their commitment to the cause. Together they answered the loyalist press in New York, which relentlessly attacked the American alliance with French Catholics in Versailles. Louis XVI was instead depicted as a rights-of-man champion, irrespective of his faith, an interpretation encouraged by Ambassador Gérard, who paid agents to write articles favorable to France. He routinely slipped almost $1,000 a year to the Reverend Samuel Cooper, a Franklin associate dubbed "Silver-Tongue Sam," who also wrote a long defense of Admiral d'Estaing's actions.

Yet prosperity was slow to return to Philadelphia. Before the war, a coaster carrying merchandise arrived in port almost daily; now it was closer to monthly. Royal Navy cruisers and loyalist privateers dominated the Delaware capes, paralyzing trade. Outbound merchantmen loitered on the river, hoping for a dark night, a thick fog, or an armed escort to run for the open sea, but at times only one vessel in seven escaped capture. "Goods are exceeding scarce here," a trader reported, "and will sell at any price a man's conscience will let him take."

The city of brotherly love had been transformed into a war capital. Pennsylvania Hospital pleaded for vinegar, lint and linen for bandages, and "humane, industrious women as nurses." Other Philadelphia women, including Franklin's daughter, Sally Bache, raised money to make more than two thousand shirts for soldiers. Carpenters' Hall served as an armory and a Continental Army depot. The city's armorers and smiths made gunlocks, barrels, bayonets, ramrods, and the "furniture" needed to assemble muskets. Munitions production surged, notably at a factory on

Fifth Street that had opened in August and would produce four million musket cartridges, more than half made by women, who each averaged 131 cartridges every working day. No one outdid Catherine Friend, who was credited with working 570 days in the complex and fabricating 211,300 cartridges herself.

After the British evacuation, Pennsylvania had adopted a repressive campaign against loyalist counterrevolutionaries. Militia in each Philadelphia neighborhood interrogated strangers, arresting "all persons of suspicious character." Mail was opened and subversive books that might "promote tumults" were banned. White adult males who refused to swear an oath of allegiance could lose the right to vote, hold office, serve on juries, transfer property, or bear arms. "Who hold a traitorous correspondence with the enemy?" a letter in the *Pennsylvania Packet* asked. "The Tories! Who daily send them intelligence? The Tories! Who dissuade men from entering the army? The Tories!"

Before the end of 1778, the state's Supreme Executive Council compiled a list of more than four hundred suspected traitors who "aided and assisted the enemy." Grand juries declined to indict some of the accused, or neighbors refused to testify against neighbors. Others on the list fled the state, even abandoning their families.

But beginning in September of this year, twenty-three men had been tried for treason; after hearing from more than four hundred witnesses, Philadelphia juries acquitted nineteen. Two of those convicted, Abraham Carlisle and John Roberts, both elderly Quakers, were sentenced to death for collaborating with the British, despite clemency petitions signed by seven thousand Philadelphians, including Continental officers and a majority of the jurors who'd found them guilty. On November 4 both marched to the scaffold on the Common with nooses around their necks. Tearful, kneeling supplications from Roberts's wife and ten children fell on deaf ears. "His behavior on the gallows did honor to human nature," a witness recorded. As for Carlisle, Elizabeth Drinker noted in her diary after visiting his house the night he died, "The body is brought home and laid out. Looks placid & serene. No marks of agony or distortion." He was interred in the Friends' burial ground as four thousand mourners walked in his cortege, more than a few troubled by the price of patriot vengeance.

This was Washington's fourth winter as commander in chief, and never had his countrymen held him in higher esteem. Babies were named for him, and the first public celebrations of his birthday would occur in February. The same month, a German-language almanac published in Lancaster described him as "father of the country." The Virginia House of Delegates in late November voted to send him "four of the finest geldings . . . as a small testimony of the gratitude of this state." Philadelphians also accorded him deference and high honors throughout his stay in their city. Carriages brought a parade of visitors to the Laurenses' front door, eager for a word with the general or at least a glimpse. Three hundred fellow Masons escorted "our illustrious brother, George Washington" to Christ Church in late December for a commemoration of Saint John the Evangelist, despite a blizzard that had virtually entombed the city in snow that week. He and Lady Washington were invited to dinners or soirees almost every evening, including a feast at Ambassador Gérard's residence on New Year's Eve and a dance at the mayor's house on January 6, the Washingtons' twentieth wedding anniversary.

The Supreme Executive Council requested a full-length portrait of His Excellency by Charles Willson Peale so "that the contemplation of it may excite others to tread in the same glorious and distinguished steps." Washington obliged, sitting for hours in late January after Peale made battlefield sketches at Trenton and Princeton to use those famous victories for a backdrop. The finished painting showed the commander in chief in his dark blue uniform with buff facings and azure rank sash. (Not for another six months would general officers wear stars on their epaulets.) He stood cross-legged in knee boots and spurs, with one hand resting on a cannon barrel, enemy battle flags at his feet, and prisoners shuffling past Nassau Hall in the distance. If his head seemed a bit too small, the torso too long, and the shoulders too narrow, his eyes were alert and knowing, the expression mettlesome, even jaunty. Billing almost £2,000 for the original, Peale would make at least nineteen oil copies, some with backgrounds depicting Monmouth or the French fleet. Gérard bought one to send to Louis XVI.

That countenance was a mask. "Our good general is in health but not happy," Greene had recently written a friend. "I can plainly see the marks of distress." This was the first time in three years that Washington had met with the entire Congress, and only a dozen of the forty-seven delegates from that last encounter remained in the national legislature. "Where are our men of abilities?" he wondered in a private note to George Mason, a fellow Virginian. "Why do they not come forth to save their country?" To another Virginia ally, Benjamin Harrison, he wrote on December 30, "Our affairs are in a more distressed, ruinous, & deplorable condition than they have been in since the commencement of the war."

Congress seemed petty and split into factions. "Much business of a trifling nature & personal concernment withdraws their attention from matters of great national moment at this critical period," Washington told

Mason. In a spasm of rectitude, Congress demanded the dismissal of any army officer "who shall act, promote, encourage, or attend any play or theatrical entertainment." Washington preferred to focus on the war: in the year just ended, the country had fought 155 naval and military engagements, about half the number from 1777, but casualties had been almost as high, including twelve hundred American battle deaths. Britain had evacuated Pennsylvania and New Jersey, yet strengthened the king's forces in Florida, Nova Scotia, and Quebec. Georgia might be slipping away. The British loss of Dominica had been offset by France's loss of the more valuable St. Lucia.

As he had at Valley Forge, Washington meticulously prepared for his many sessions with the congressmen. His first task was to throttle yet another proposal to invade Canada, drafted by Congress in October with Lafayette's tacit encouragement. The eight-page scheme would require snowshoes, moose skins, and most of the army. In mid-November Washington sent a five-thousand-word rebuttal, questioning the wisdom of marching thirteen thousand men through the northern wilderness on an expedition "infinitely too doubtful and precarious to justify the undertaking." He also privately warned that although Versailles had renounced any ambitions to reclaim Quebec as a colony, "Canada would be a solid acquisition to France. . . . No nation is to be trusted farther than it is bound by its interest." Congress reluctantly concurred, but not until January 1, after another week of Washington's personal exhortation, was the plan finally scuttled. Instead of leading a lunge into Canada, Lafayette would sail home to France with instructions to encourage his king to send another fleet and more troops to bolster the American cause. "The sails are just going to be hoisted," the marquis wrote Washington from the frigate *Alliance* in Boston Harbor on January 11. "Farewell, my dear general. I hope your French friend will ever be dear to you."

His Excellency now suggested to Congress three possible courses of action in the 1779 campaign: attack New York and Newport; dispatch an expedition against Fort Niagara, a British and loyalist stronghold on Lake Ontario; or keep the main army on the defensive—thus saving money—while striking predatory Iroquois tribes in the New York and Pennsylvania backcountry. Congress inclined to the third option, and in mid-January expanded Washington's authority by adding the Southern Department to his portfolio and giving him command over "military operations in all the departments in these states."

Yet Congress and the states seemed incapable of solving the country's most pernicious problems. The Articles of Confederation, a constitution intended to establish a "league of friendship," had been submitted to the states for ratification in late 1777. The document gave Congress the authority to make war and peace but no real ability to collect taxes, regulate commerce, or enforce its will over thirteen sovereign governments. Eleven states had signed the document, but Delaware and Maryland had balked because of claims made by seven of their sisters, based on old colonial charters and Indian treaties, of vast western lands that would give them great wealth and political power. Virginia alone claimed 230 million acres, a land grab that extended to the Pacific Ocean. Without unanimous approval, the constitution remained a dead letter, further hobbling Congress.

The war now cost the country more than $1 million a week, and no problem remained more vexing than the plummeting value of Continental currency. With little gold or silver mined in America for coinage, more emissions of paper bills—derided as "pasteboard dollars" or "rag money"—had been authorized in the past year, totaling $64 million; another $100 million would be printed in the coming year. But by early 1779, one paper dollar was worth twelve cents in specie. States printed bills in denominations as small as two cents, given the lack of small change in circulation. "We were, for years together, without seeing a single coin of the precious metals in circulation," Thomas Jefferson later wrote.

"Our money will soon be as useless as blank paper," Abigail Adams had warned her husband. Chronically short of cash, the army continued to issue promissory notes for confiscated supplies, eventually amounting to millions of dollars and largely worthless. Prices soared. A bushel of wheat that sold for 4 shillings in Philadelphia in 1776 would cost 150 shillings in May 1779. Major Ebenezer Huntington complained that his $50 monthly salary "will scarcely support me a week." Writing his father in Connecticut in late December he added:

We doubt the willingness of our countrymen to assist us. . . . Don't drive us to despair. We are now on the brink. Depend upon it, we cannot put up with such treatment any longer.

A British campaign of economic warfare added to Washington's worries. Enemy authorities encouraged counterfeiting, which contributed to the declining value of Continental currency. American officials warned that bogus bills could often be detected because they were printed on better paper and with finer engraving than legal tender. Counterfeit $30 bills spelled "Philadelphia" correctly, unlike the "Philadelpkia" that appeared on some genuine currency. "I hope to see him hanged," a New Hampshire official said of a local loyalist counterfeiter. "He has done more damage than ten thousand men could have done." Those caught passing phony money risked whipping, branding, having their ears cut off, or execution.

"Is there anything doing, or that can be done to restore the credit of our currency?" the commander in chief asked John Jay. "A wagonload of money will scarcely purchase a wagonload of provision." Such woes fell heaviest on supply officers. The price of certain staples—flour, beef, loaf sugar, molasses—had jumped 254 percent in December and continued to climb. Corn would rise almost 1,300 percent in 1779, despite fitful attempts in New England and elsewhere to impose price controls. By April a dozen eggs cost $18, a five-ounce gill of rum $2. Some farmers and merchants deliberately held provender off the market to drive up prices, infuriating Washington, who railed against "speculators, monopolizers, & all that tribe . . . preying upon our very vitals." "Intirely out of money," an army agent wrote. Another pleaded, "Money, money, money, for God's sake. . . . Send me what cash you can."

Quartermaster General Greene, whose expenditures had reached $32 million a year, calculated that to send the Continental camps three hundred barrels of flour a day and other supplies from a central magazine in Trenton required 840 wagons pulled by 3,360 draft horses at a cost of more than $500,000 a month. To provide sufficient winter forage for several thousand additional horses, the army dispersed them from Connecticut to Virginia; teamsters and cavalrymen received scythes to cut grass in the spring, when hay and oats would likely remain in short supply. Some congressmen questioned the 1 percent commission split by Greene and his two deputies on all department purchases. "I am drudging in an office from which I shall receive no honor and very few thanks," Greene snapped in reply. In early February he offered to forgo the commission in exchange for a straight annual salary of £3,000, paid in sterling; bereft of hard currency, Congress ignored the proposal. "This is a murmuring age," Greene wrote. "I am as willing to quit as to serve."

Infuriating shortages plagued the army, from thread and opium to blankets and hats, forcing Washington and Greene to spend countless hours negotiating with vendors, state officials, and the Board of War. "The states in general seem to have been for some time past in a profound sleep," Washington wrote General Lincoln. "They have been amusing themselves with idle dreams of peace, and have scarcely made any exertions for the war." In the last campaign nearly every tent had been ruined by storms or the soldiers' practice of building campfires too close to flammable canvas. Where to find more for the spring campaign? South Carolina agreed to provide ten thousand casks of rice as a substitute for wheat. But how, Greene wondered, to persuade victuallers sailing from the Low Country to run the gauntlet of enemy vessels "as thick upon the coast as grasshoppers?"

Thanks to French and New England clothing merchants, most Continental soldiers were now creditably uniformed. In mid-January Congress briefly considered adopting a different uniform color for each state—"there may be a difficulty in fixing upon thirteen colors," Washington said—before subsequently agreeing, after a lottery, that blue coats would go to North Carolina, Maryland, New Jersey, and New York troops while the rest would get brown, all with red facings. But where to find shoes, perpetually in short supply? Only seven thousand pairs could be found in stock, and a new factory north of Philadelphia employing captured British soldiers—former shoemakers by trade—would produce only a hundred pairs a month. Should the limited leather supplies be diverted to harnesses, bayonet belts, cartridge boxes, or footwear?

Almost as worrisome as the precipitous decline in the value of Continental currency was the loss of capable officers from the army. Washington continued to press Congress for better wages and a guarantee of lifetime half-pay for those willing to serve for the duration. "Officers cannot support themselves with their present pay," he warned. "Necessity will oblige them to leave the service." All too common was the letter from Lieutenant Colonel Henry Miller, a combat veteran who had joined the army in July 1775 but "cannot without material injury to my family continue any longer in the service." Washington replied with evident regret, "I always part reluctantly with the officer who, like you, has been early in the cause and borne his share of military danger and fatigue." Similar requests came from indispensable stalwarts like Brigadier General John Glover, who wrote Washington in January that his wife, Hannah, had died at age forty-five, leaving him with "my little flock" of eight children to care for. Congress granted him an indefinite furlough to return home to Massachusetts.

More than four thousand enlistments would expire before the spring. Soldiers who in mid-January still had not been paid since September were unlikely to reenlist, and promised bonuses of cash, land, and clothing failed to lure enough new volunteers. Maryland needed fourteen hundred men in the spring of 1779 to fill its Continental Army quota but got just six volunteers in the first three months of the year. Washington now believed that only compulsion could fill the Continental ranks. "The country has been already pretty well drained of that class of men whose tempers, attachments, and circumstances disposed them to enter permanently . . . into the army," he wrote.

Congress agreed, and in February asked most states to fulfill their quotas for Continental service by drafting militiamen, typically by pulling names from a hat. But many critical workers were exempt from military service. New York excused one miller per gristmill, five ironworkers per furnace, three munitions makers per powder mill, and a ferryman for every public river crossing. Boatbuilders, shoemakers, blacksmiths, and linen workers were also exempt in various states. Many Virginia planters who paid taxes on more than three slaves were considered vital to the war economy and excused from service.

In fact, no state disappointed Washington more than his native Virginia. Early in the war the commonwealth had provided from one-fifth to one-third of all Continental troops, but it now could be counted on for as few as one in ten, despite offering volunteers three hundred acres of frontier land, permanent exemption from poll taxes, half-pay for widows, and, eventually, a healthy young slave for "bound labor." The state finally imposed conscription—denounced by some Virginians as the "last of all oppressions"—but more than half of Virginia's counties failed to comply. Loudoun County, along the Potomac River, reported that it could not proceed with a draft because of "the violence and riotous behavior of the people." Virginia regiments increasingly comprised apprentices, indentured servants, and slaves who served as substitutes for their masters.

"A stupor seems to pervade our whole system," an exasperated Washington wrote his brother John. "The time is come when every man must put his shoulder to the wheel."

Inspector General von Steuben certainly had his brawny shoulder to the wheel. In February the baron delivered a thick manuscript to Washington composed of twenty-five chapters on topics ranging from drum calls, inspections, and courts-martial to troop movements, camp sanitation, and caring for the sick. Each chapter had been written in German, translated into French, then into bad English by the baron's secretary, before it was finally coaxed into fluent English by a literate American captain. The text included drawings by Captain Pierre Charles L'Enfant, an engineer who would one day design the spatial plan for the national capital, Washington, D.C. At heart, Steuben said, the manual was "a rhapsody," intended for an army officer "to gain the love of his men" through diligence, competence, and commitment among comrades. Fourteen pages detailed the responsibilities and duties for every rank from private to colonel.

Washington spent two weeks reading and editing what he titled *Regulations for the Order and Discipline of the Troops of the United States*. Publication was delayed by shortages of paper and ink, as well as a botched first set of copperplates; the only other copperplate printer in Philadelphia was busy churning out mountains of money for the Treasury. Surplus pages from the *Pennsylvania Magazine* were used for endpapers and flyleaves. The bookbinder had difficulty finding gold leaf to gild the page edges on leather-bound copies intended for Louis XVI, General Washington, and other select recipients. Steuben raged at every setback, but finally the printer delivered the initial fifteen hundred copies of what would soon be known as the "Blue Book," so called for the tint of the paper cover. As the official manual of the American army and state militias until the War of 1812, it would go through at least seventy-five editions. Congress, in gratitude, presented Steuben with two English saddle horses. His good humor restored, he would write in July, "What a beautiful, what a happy land this is! Without kings, without high priests, without idle barons. Here everyone is happy."

Not everyone. Although pleased with Steuben's work, Washington was frustrated and irritated at his own inability to penetrate British intentions, or even to provide d'Estaing with rudimentary intelligence about Royal Navy strength and movements. "The designs of the enemy, to me, are mysterious, indeed totally incomprehensible," he wrote Richard Henry Lee. The departure of expeditions from New York for the West Indies and Georgia explained reports that some regiments had been measured for lightweight linen clothing and were removing the heavy linings from their coats. But Clinton's overarching strategy remained opaque, particularly since "the Knight," as Washington disdainfully called him, seemed reluctant to confront the only thing holding the American cause together: the Continental Army.

Since taking command in 1775, Washington had served as his own intelligence chief, and his personal library included an English translation of Frederick the Great's *Military Instructions*, which advised, "Of spies, they are to be employed on every occasion." He also owned *Essays on the Art of War*, a translated French text that decreed, "A general should spare no trouble or expense to be well informed of everything that passes with the enemy. . . . Nothing is more absolutely necessary or more useful than spies." The commanding general paid $238 here and $500 there to informants, and authorized the "roasting" of suspicious loyalist mail over an open flame to reveal secret messages written in invisible ink. He personally drafted disinformation to feed enemy agents, including bogus claims that morale ran high in Continental ranks because officers "give them a great deal of rum and whiskey." Congress, this year, would provide him with two thousand guineas in precious hard currency to expand his espionage network.

Several subordinate Continental generals ran spy rings in New England with Washington's encouragement, but the most ambitious would operate in New York under his direct tutelage. To recruit and organize field agents, he chose a Long Island–born dragoon major with dark eyes, a wide forehead, and a harpoon nose. Benjamin Tallmadge had been such a prodigy as a young classics scholar that he was admitted to Yale at the age of twelve, although his father kept him home until he turned fifteen. Joining the army after a stint as a Connecticut school superintendent, he nursed a deep antipathy toward the British for two reasons: his closest friend had been the doomed Captain Nathan Hale, and an elder brother had died of mistreatment aboard a British prison ship after being captured during the Battle of New York.

Tallmadge adopted the nom de guerre "John Bolton," and two of his spies proved particularly indefatigable. In October 1778, Abraham Woodhull, a farmer on Long Island's north shore, had begun sending detailed dispatches by whaleboat across Long Island Sound to Tallmadge, a childhood friend, who then relayed them by dragoon courier to Washington's headquarters. Woodhull also acted as a conduit for reports from Robert Townsend, a Manhattan merchant who reportedly wrote an occasional loyalist philippic for the *Gazette* to mask his true allegiance. Given to depression and insomnia, Townsend was part owner of a coffee shop popular with the king's officers; he also moved easily through the baroque British bureaucracy in New York, which included, by one loyalist's description, "barrack masters, land commissioners, water commissaries, forage masters, cattle commissaries, cattle feeders, hay collectors, hay inspectors, hay weighers, wood inspectors, timber commissaries, board inspectors, refugee examiners, refugee provision providers" and a "train of clerks and deputy clerks." Woodhull and Townsend were known, respectively, as "Samuel Culper, Sr.," and "Culper, Jr.," their aliases a truncation of Culpeper, the Virginia town where Washington had worked as a seventeen-year-old surveyor.

Tallmadge devised a code using *Entick's Spelling Dictionary*, copies of which he gave to Washington and both Culpers. More than seven hundred common words were replaced with unique numbers: 72 for "British," 85 for "Congress," 305 for "imprudent," 633 for "time." Another fifty-three coded proper nouns included 711 for "Washington," 712 for "Henry Clinton," 727 for "New York," and 755 for "France." As another layer of security, this spring Washington began using an invisible ink discreetly sent to him by Sir James Jay, the brother of John Jay. A London physician and chemist who had been knighted by George III in 1763, Sir James had concocted two fluids: an agent, dubbed "stain" or "medicine," that could not be detected on paper until brushed with a liquid reagent, which Washington called "the counterpart." As a spymaster, the commanding general instructed his agents that "the ink is not easily legible unless it is on paper of a good quality."

Washington, Tallmadge, and their field operatives would exchange nearly two hundred missives over the next several years. While hardly as flamboyant as British spying on the American legation in Paris, the Culper ring for the rest of the war provided 711 with useful intelligence about 712 and the operations of the 72: unit strengths and garrison locations, ship movements from Britain and Ireland, sailing schedules, operations in Georgia, counterfeiting schemes, supply shortages. Although information about enemy movements sometimes arrived too late for effective countermeasures, Washington was grateful for what he called "intelligent, clear, and satisfactory" dispatches. He also recognized the enormous risks taken by spies operating undercover to help him see behind British lines. "We live in daily fear of death and destruction," Culper Sr. would write. "This, added to my usual anxiety, hath almost unmanned me."

Washington had arrived in Philadelphia to find Benedict Arnold, his military governor, utterly besotted. "I must tell you that Cupid has given our little general a more mortal wound than all the host of Britons could," Robert Morris's wife, Mary, told a friend. "Miss Peggy Shippen is the fair one." Just eighteen, she was the youngest daughter of a prominent lawyer with loyalist leanings who had declared, at the beginning of the war, that every "moderate thinking man" should "remain silent and inactive" for the duration. During the British occupation of her hometown, Peggy had been neither silent nor inactive. "We were all in love with her," one Royal Navy captain wrote, while another officer called her the most beautiful woman he had ever seen in England or America.

Arnold, a thirty-seven-year-old widower with three young boys at home in Connecticut under his sister's care, sent Peggy a bouquet of roses and jonquils a few weeks after taking command in Philadelphia. Two months later he wrote a love letter with passionate lines he copied from an earlier, unsuccessful infatuation. "Your charms have lighted up a flame in my bosom which can never be extinguished," he told her. "On you alone my happiness depends. . . . Will you doom me to languish in despair?" A frequent visitor to the three-story Shippen house on Fourth Street, Arnold also pressed his case with her father, who was skeptical of a firebrand soldier twice his daughter's age and crippled by war wounds and gout. "My public character is well-known," Arnold told Edward Shippen. "My private one is, I hope, irreproachable." He expected no dowry; his own fortune, if modest, should suffice "to make us both happy." By early February, they were engaged.

Washington was even more surprised to find Arnold embroiled in a bitter feud with the Pennsylvania authorities. Abiding by the commander in chief's edict "to preserve tranquility and order," Arnold treated loyalist and neutral Philadelphians with what he considered charitable moderation, even socializing with suspected collaborators. This "lenity" offended patriot radicals, particularly Joseph Reed, a slippery lawyer and former Washington aide who on December 1 had become president of the Supreme Executive Council and effectively the state's governor. "Reed was an ambitious man," a French observer wrote. "He had the soul of Cromwell." Arnold's high living—the mansion, the servants, the extravagant parties, the £5,602 in undocumented "table expenses"—also drew contempt and accusations of venality. When confronted by Reed on January 25, Arnold brusquely declared himself accountable only to Congress and Washington.

A week later Reed's board brought eight charges against Arnold, published in the *Pennsylvania Packet* and as a handbill. The alleged offenses ranged from oppressing "the faithful subjects of this state" to profiteering and using public wagons for the transport of private goods. "These are charges too absurd to deserve a serious answer," Brigadier General John Cadwalader wrote Greene. "They . . . can never injure the character of a man to whom his country is so much indebted." Yet they could, and did. A congressional investigating committee largely exonerated Arnold, but Reed threatened to block assistance to the Continental Army from Pennsylvania militiamen and teamsters so long as Arnold remained commandant in Philadelphia. The dispute became a sordid tussle between state and federal authorities, threatening to damage if not discompose the patriot cause. Reluctant to offend Pennsylvania, Congress recommended that Washington convene a court-martial to examine the accusations.

"I am heartily tired with my journey, and almost with human nature," Arnold wrote Peggy. In mid-March he would resign his post as military viceroy of Philadelphia, ostensibly "for the recovery of my health and wounds," while keeping his army commission. At about the same time, he reportedly borrowed £12,000 from a French shipping agent for the down payment on Mount Pleasant, "the most elegant seat in Pennsylvania," according to John Adams—a Georgian mansion with symmetrical pavilions, sweeping lawns, and a rooftop balustrade overlooking the Schuylkill, which he gave to Peggy as a wedding present. On April 8 they married in the drawing room of the Shippen house, where the groom, still using a cane, leaned on an orderly's arm for support.

Eighty-one generals would serve under Washington during the war, none more capable in combat than Arnold or more infernally tormented away from the battlefield. The commander in chief set a trial date for May 1, then postponed it repeatedly after difficulties with witnesses, board members, and the enemy. "Every officer in the army must feel himself injured by the cruel and unprecedented treatment I have met with from a set of scoundrels in office," Arnold wrote Washington. He seethed. He railed. His grievances festered, and he brooded over how to repair his hurt. In another wrathful letter to the commander in chief he added:

> If Your Excellency thinks me criminal, for heaven's sake let me be immediately tried and if found guilty executed. I want no favor. I only ask for justice. . . . I have nothing left but the little reputation I have gained in the army. Delay in the present case is worse than death.

"Peace and retirement are my ultimate aim," Washington had written shortly before arriving in Philadelphia. Neither would befall him for years to come, and only in a rare reverie could he see himself at ease under his vine and fig tree back at Mount Vernon. In February he finally disentangled himself from the city and returned to the field in northern New Jersey, depressed and exasperated by the countless cares he carried along. For the remainder of the winter he rented a merchant's house near the Raritan River, thirty miles southwest of New York and a short ride from the main Continental bivouacs around Middlebrook. His Excellency and Lady Washington occupied one bedroom on the second floor, while his aides piled into a second.

He restocked his camp equipment for another fighting season: quills, stationery, eighteen campstools, two traveling trunks, two dozen ivory-handled knives and forks, four tablecloths, "a set of queen's china," candle snuffers, and pickle plates. Also: a bearskin saddle cover, a copper urinal, and a refracting pocket telescope from John Dollond, a celebrated London optician. He decided against spending £750 on another traveling carriage for Martha but paid £38 to Philadelphia hatter Isaac Parish, who would make his hats for the next twenty years. An admirer in France sent him a hogshead of "the best Bordeaux claret, in bottles."

Another dreary winter passed slowly. "My horse died," Colonel Jeduthan Baldwin told his diary. "It snowed." A lieutenant in the 6th Maryland was dismissed from the service for "unofficer and ungentlemanlike conduct" in challenging a superior to a duel and for "playing ball with sergeants." Hunters prowled the woods, sending sled loads of venison to camp commissaries grateful for the meat.

On February 18, General Knox organized a celebration at the artillery park near Pluckemin to commemorate the first anniversary of the French alliance. Thirteen cannons fired a salute at four p.m., an army band played, and the guests—the Washingtons among seventy ladies and several hundred men—wandered through thirteen arches with illuminated paintings depicting scenes from the war: the first shots at Lexington; the burning of Charlestown, Falmouth, Norfolk, and Esopus; the triumph at Saratoga; and fallen martyrs, including Generals Warren, Montgomery, and Nash, receiving thanks in Elysium from Brutus, Cato, and others who had struggled against tyrants. A final arch imagined a future, peaceable America as "a rising empire," her rivers covered with merchant ships and new canals traversing the land. Dinner was followed by fireworks, and then, Knox wrote, "we danced all night."

They danced again to fiddle music later that month at the nearby Greene house, where Caty had just arrived from Rhode Island in a two-horse phaeton wearing a gold locket containing a miniature of Nathanael. Washington, always enchanted by the comely Mrs. Greene, danced with her for "upwards of three hours without once sitting down," as General Greene subsequently told a friend. In a rare display of ribald humor, His Excellency joked about having stolen her from her "Quaker preacher" husband.

Then the war returned. With it came worries about Arnold and Continental currency, about spies and the absent French fleet, about dwindling ranks and congressional dabblers, about Pennsylvania radicals and scant supplies and shoes, shoes, shoes.

Part Three

20.

———◆———

A Summons to the Queen's House

A flutter of flags aboard the one-hundred-gun *Britannia* in Portsmouth Harbour on Thursday, January 7, told a tale of the Royal Navy's dire disarray. At nine a.m. a Union Jack hoisted on the larboard mizzen shrouds and a royal standard displayed from the starboard mizzen announced that an admiral was about to be court-martialed. An hour later, a signal gun and another Union Jack hoisted at the fore-topmast head summoned senior officers to repair on board. Barges glided from the docks carrying the five admirals and eight captains who would try the case. More barges transported the accused fleet commander, Vice Admiral Keppel, and his subordinate accuser, Vice Admiral Palliser, to the man-of-war. By noon the board was sworn in and the grubby business had begun.

The inconclusive battle between French and British fleets at Ushant had been over for five months, but blood continued to flow. Anonymous accusations, evidently endorsed by Keppel, of his subordinate's craven disobedience during the battle had caused the enraged Palliser to charge his commanding officer with misconduct and neglect of duty at Ushant, capital offenses in the navy. After the Admiralty reluctantly agreed to a trial, the quarrel in recent weeks had spilled into Parliament, where Keppel, an aristocratic darling of the opposition, mustered a large, loud following eager to embarrass the government. As a lord commissioner of the Admiralty and a close ally of Sandwich, the first lord, Palliser made a convenient foil, and soon an arcane dispute about naval tactics devolved into a national referendum on the ministry's war policy. So intense was the hostility that *Victory* and *Formidable*, the two admirals' flagships, were ordered to anchor miles apart at Portsmouth for fear of "fatal consequences" if their crews met in the street.

No sooner had the court-martial convened aboard *Britannia* than it adjourned: an act of Parliament had provided a dispensation to move the proceedings ashore to the port governor's house, ostensibly in deference to

Keppel's fragile health. This, in effect, allowed the defendant to pack the courtroom with applauding sailors and a supportive retinue that included several dukes and opposition leaders like Charles Fox and Edmund Burke, who had traveled from London for the spectacle. The charges were read in five long paragraphs, including Palliser's accusation that the fleet admiral "did not cause the fleet to pursue the flying enemy [and] a most glorious opportunity was lost."

Sixty-three witnesses testified, almost half of them ship captains who had fought in the line at Ushant. "The passions beneath the smooth surface of eighteenth-century life welled up," one historian later wrote. "Tears were shed, witnesses were hissed, the deity was invoked. The court made no pretense of fairness." Keppel, in the dock, played to the cheering gallery, "frequently affecting to smile contempt and often bursting into coarse laughs of ridicule," according to a spectator. After five weeks of testimony, Keppel declared, in a closing statement, "I submit the whole to the wisdom and justice of this court." Of his acquittal there was no doubt: by now coffeehouse touts were refusing to take more bets on his certain vindication. On February 11, the court duly pronounced the charges "malicious and ill-founded." A phalanx of naval officers and noblemen carried Keppel on their shoulders, huzzahing as if he had vanquished the French fleet rather than his own government. They followed a band playing "See the Conquering Hero Comes" and "Rule, Britannia." The defendant soon reboarded *Victory* to again hoist his fleet admiral's flag.

At eight p.m. messengers reached London with news of the verdict, provoking celebratory gunfire, clanging bells, and fireworks. Rioters wearing blue cockades rampaged through the streets, and residents were advised to illuminate their front windows to acclaim Keppel's victory or risk vandalism. Palliser arrived from Portsmouth in a hired post chaise and narrowly eluded the mob, reportedly by disguising himself. He was burned in effigy on Tower Hill, and by three a.m. on Friday crowds had pushed past guards to ransack his Pall Mall house, making a pyre of the furniture in St. James's Square. More rioters smashed Lord Germain's windows and Lord North's in Downing Street before advancing on the Admiralty, burning sedan chairs parked out front and lifting the iron gates off their hinges. Sandwich and his longtime mistress, Martha Ray, fled in what was described as "a most manifest panic" through the rear garden to the safety of the Horse Guards.

The Keppel craze persisted, briefly. Taverns and seaport streets were renamed "Admiral Keppel," and when the conquering hero arrived in London on February 16, celebrants unhitched the horses to pull the coach themselves past Palliser's demolished house. Before he removed to Bath to take the waters, Keppel wrote a sanctimonious letter to the king, deriding the Admiralty and adding, "I am ready to quit my command today." This pleased the government immensely, and on March 18, in an order signed by Sandwich and other officials, Keppel was told, "You are hereby required and directed to strike your flag and come on shore." He would never serve at sea again.

As passions cooled and his reputation deflated, even Keppel's own political allies drew back. Palliser's career also was finished. He resigned various offices, including his seat in the Commons, then demanded another trial to clear his name. The court found his performance at Ushant "in many respects highly exemplary and meritorious," while noting that he ought to have informed Keppel forthrightly about "the disabled state" of his ship during the battle. Palliser was eventually appointed governor of Greenwich Hospital and settled into obscurity.

But damage had been done—to the government, to the navy, and particularly to the Channel fleet, the nation's primary bulwark against foreign attack. "The unhappy difference between Mr. Keppel and Sir Hugh Palliser has almost ruined the navy," Vice Admiral Sir George Rodney wrote. "Discipline in a very great measure is lost." Several of Keppel's captains resigned their commissions; desertion from the lower decks spiked. Hard feelings would linger for a generation. And now, with so many leaders disaffected or disgraced, the Admiralty found itself relying on untested or superannuated commanders in a time of great peril.

Sandwich, who followed the Keppel imbroglio as if his own fortunes depended on the outcome, had once asserted that any first lord who failed to maintain a navy capable of confronting the combined French and Spanish fleets deserved dismissal. Spain had not yet entered the war, but this remark was repeatedly hurled back at him by his adversaries who doubted the navy's strength against both Bourbon powers. Scurrilous accusations were also thrown at him. It was said that Sandwich had directed Palliser to deliberately disobey orders at Ushant; that he and Palliser, whose family had once been Catholic, were intent on overthrowing Protestantism; that he bullied Miss Ray, not only his mistress but mother to five of his children. A motion in the Commons to censure him narrowly failed in early March, 204 to 170, but he was well along toward becoming a national villain.

The first lord's promotion and patronage choices had alienated many influential Royal Navy officers, the sort described as being of "weight and property." Germain and his American Department remained implacably hostile, accusing him of poor judgment in deploying the navy and of failing to adequately support the army in America. Sandwich answered with a succinct riposte:

> Every expedition, in regard to its destination, object, force, and number of ships, is planned by the cabinet, and is the result of the collective wisdom of all His Majesty's confidential ministers. The first lord of the Admiralty is only the executive servant of these measures.

True enough. Despite the first lord's anxiety at leaving home waters vulnerable, a third of the British fleet was now in or headed to the West Indies, as directed by the cabinet and the king, a quadrupling of the force there a year earlier. No man had pressed for naval rearmament more ardently than Sandwich, despite North's persistent reluctance to shoulder the cost. The surge in shipyard construction in the past couple years would give the Royal Navy 90 ships of the line in service by July—two dozen more than a year earlier—and 314 vessels total, the largest number ever in commission. France had only 63 capital ships, although if Spain's were added, the Bourbon force came to 121. Britain would also send 2,600 privateers into Atlantic, Baltic, and Mediterranean sea-lanes to torment enemy shipping. Six thousand British merchant vessels, including ships leased from Germany, Holland, and elsewhere, helped sustain overseas trade and keep the kingdom affluent.

Problems undoubtedly persisted, as Sandwich acknowledged. Parliament this year would increase the number of seamen and marines manning the Royal Navy to seventy thousand. But of every three men aboard ship, one was sick, largely because press-gangs seized unhealthy swabs and confined them belowdecks, where they infected their crewmates. Sailor wastage remained staggering, with some sixty thousand lost through death, desertion, or discharge since 1774. Frigate shortages and dispersal of the battle fleets still prevented Britain from blockading French naval bases at Rochefort, Toulon, and Brest, which the Royal Navy had accomplished so effectively in the last war.

This spring, responsibility for transporting provisions abroad would shift from the Treasury to the Navy Board, despite Germain's prickly resentment at placing army victualing in the navy's hands. But with Crown forces now scattered around the globe, the cabinet agreed that only the navy had the expertise to feed more than sixty thousand mouths from Quebec and New York to Newport and Savannah, not to mention Jamaica, the Lesser Antilles, India, Gibraltar, and other posts.

All in all, Sandwich could make a fair claim to being one of Britain's most successful first lords of the eighteenth century. Yet he was said to be as unpopular with his admirals as Germain was with his generals. As the Keppel business boiled over, the king wondered whether the navy would be better served with new leadership. In a naval war, George told North, "it is highly advantageous to have in the cabinet a person able to plan the most effectual manner of conducting it." On February 5, North began discussions—"a vague, rambling conversation of more than two hours," as he told the king—with their preferred candidate: Admiral Howe, recently home from his brilliant stint on the North American station.

Several daunting obstacles stood between Black Dick and high office. The Howes had become divisive figures in a divisive war. "Half the town abhor them for going to America & the other half detest them for doing so little there," one member of Parliament observed. Moreover, the admiral had laid down several demands before he would take the post, including personal emolument, the rehabilitation of his brother (perhaps with a governorship somewhere), and the abnegation of Germain—the two men loathed each other and could hardly be in the same city, much less the same cabinet. North then asked the admiral whether he would instead take command of the rudderless Channel fleet, but this second proposal was met with the same thorny stipulations.

"He has added conditions that it would be disgraceful to grant," George wrote North on March 1. When the admiral supported motions in Parliament to censure Sandwich and blame the government for inadequate war preparations, George told North on March 9, "Lord Howe may now be ranked in opposition." As if he had suddenly seen the light, the king added, "I am clear Lord Sandwich fills the Admiralty much better than any other man in the kingdom would."

The Admiralty building was described by one critic as "a lasting reproach to our national want of taste." Massive, three stories, and wrapped in a U shape around a central courtyard, it dated to 1720 and was bereft of ornamentation except for four pillars propping up a Greek pediment. The ground floor featured the notorious Waiting Room, where half-pay naval officers loitered in bureaucratic purgatory in hopes of a posting. Up the broad staircase was the oak-paneled Board Room, with an enormous mahogany table and eight armchairs arranged beneath a white-and-gold ceiling. Carved wooden replicas of navigation instruments framed the large fireplace. A wall map of Great Britain included a rotating pointer linked to a weather vane on the roof so that Sandwich and his colleagues would know which way the wind was blowing.

Window glass smashed during the Keppel riot had been replaced and the unhinged gates reset when Martha Ray set out in a carriage from Sandwich's Admiralty apartments late on Wednesday afternoon, April 7. Dressed in a silk gown and diamond earrings, her dark hair piled high, she was in excellent spirits, having reportedly received a generous offer from an impresario for a season of singing onstage. Tonight, though, she would sit in the audience: after picking up a friend, the retired diva Caterina Galli, she headed for Covent Garden Theatre, where the five-hour program included a one-act French comic opera, Isaac Bickerstaff's three-act musical *Love in a Village*, and a two-act pantomime. When the two women emerged, just after eleven p.m., the street was swarming with linkboys, livery servants, and hackney coachmen, all garishly lighted by oil lamps suspended from arches in the piazza. Streetwalkers lingered in the shadows; Covent Garden had been described as "the great square of Venus," and "Drury Lane ague" was slang for syphilis.

Among the lurkers was twenty-six-year-old James Hackman, tall, thin, and garbed in clerical black. Sipping brandy in the Bedford Coffee House, Hackman had watched the departing crowd for the face of the woman who had obsessed him for three years, ever since he was first invited, as an ensign in the 68th Regiment of Foot, for a social visit to Hinchingbrooke, Lord Sandwich's country seat. Smitten by Martha yet spurned by her when he subsequently proposed marriage, he sold his commission and this spring had been ordained as a Church of England priest. Hackman's coat pocket contained two letters. One, sent to Martha but returned unopened, read, "Think of me and pity me. . . . Nothing can relieve me but death or you." The other, intended for his brother, explained, "I have strove against it as long as possible, but now it overpowers me."

She was about to climb into her carriage behind Signora Galli when Hackman tugged at the back of her gown, clapped the muzzle of a pistol against her forehead, and pulled the trigger. The ball blew through her brain and emerged below her left ear. He fired a second pistol at himself but only grazed his brow. Tumbling to the pavement, he beat his bleeding head with both gun butts, shrieking, "Kill me! Kill me! For God's sake, kill me!" He was subdued and marched into the Shakespeare's Head tavern, crowded with horrified actors and theater patrons. Bystanders carried Martha's limp, bloody body to an adjacent room.

Sandwich had just retired for the night when a messenger from Westminster's chief magistrate brought the fatal news to the Admiralty door. The first lord ran back upstairs carrying a guttering candle and flung himself on the bed. "Leave me a while to myself," he cried. "I could have borne anything but this." Upon hearing the tidings, Walpole wrote, "It would be foolish to repeat that we are a nation of lunatics, yet with so many outward and visible signs, can one avoid thinking so?"

Charged with "the willful murder of Martha Ray, spinster," Hackman elicited more sympathy than his victim from a British public often sentimental toward remorseful, tormented killers. "'Twas love, not malice, gave the direful wound," the *Gazetteer and New Daily Advertiser* assured its readers. In the dock at the Old Bailey with his head bandaged, Hackman told the court, "I stand here this day the most wretched of human beings, and confess myself criminal in a high degree." The jury agreed and pronounced him guilty without bothering to leave the courtroom for deliberations.

On April 19 Hackman was led to Newgate chapel for prayers, then into the prison yard, where witnesses, having paid a shilling for admission, watched him loaded, hatless and dressed in black, into the tumbrel. Balladeers outside peddled broadsides describing in fictitious detail the supposed love affair that had led to this day of reckoning. Escorted by constables as St. Sepulchre's bells tolled his final hour on this earth, Hackman climbed the scaffold at Tyburn, prayed for ten minutes, then let the handkerchief slip from his bound hands to signal his readiness to the hangman. His corpse was cut down after an hour and carted to Surgeon's Hall for dissection, as prescribed by the Murder Act of 1752. Soon enough, a Grub Street journalist published sixty-five forged letters that had supposedly passed between Hackman and Martha; the anthology, a complete fraud titled *Love and Madness*, became a bestseller and was used as a cudgel against Sandwich by his remorseless political opponents.

Others were more charitable. The king, although a bit prudish about the first lord's domestic arrangement with Miss Ray, nevertheless expressed sympathy for a man "robbed of all comfort in the world." On April 11, four days after the killing, he wrote Sandwich to say, "I am sorry Lord Sandwich has met with any severe blow of a private nature." The same day a motion in the House of Lords to remove Sandwich from his position caused the first lord to reply, "I am at present totally unfit for business of any kind." Yet on April 23, when the debate resumed, he defended himself with vigor and precision, reminding the peers that upon taking office in 1771 he had inherited a fleet "in a most deplorable state—the ships decaying and unfit for service, the storehouses empty, and a general despondency running through the whole naval department." He subsequently had imported five thousand Baltic masts to compensate for lost American timber, and had laid in extraordinary quantities of timber, tar, pitch, and iron. Another five thousand tons of hemp would arrive this year for the navy's ropemakers. The number of ships now in commission spoke for itself.

He was too savvy, too irreplaceable. The motion to remove him failed badly, seventy-eight votes to thirty-nine, a sharp defeat for the opposition. The first lord had been vindicated, for now, and even in his grief he again threw himself into the task of ensuring that Britain's wooden walls—the Royal Navy—could withstand the heaviest blows the nation's enemies could devise.

George's forty-first birthday was celebrated on June 4 with the usual odes, pealing bells, and cannon salutes. At a gala that night, the London *Evening Post* reported, "The king's dress, as is customary on his birthday, was exceedingly plain. His Majesty wore an unornamented green silk coat and a diamond-hilted sword. The queen was very superbly dressed. . . . On her head she carried nine very large jewels and a diamond crown of a beautiful form." Noblewomen attending the ball avoided His Majesty's displeasure by keeping all French silk and lace off their gowns. The evening featured the first official public duty of the sixteen-year-old Prince of Wales, who opened the dancing by joining the Duchess of Hamilton in a minuet. "Aye," his proud father was heard to murmur, "the ladies must take care of their hearts."

London's elite had recovered from both Martha Ray's murder and the death of the great actor, dramatist, and producer David Garrick. *The Camp: A Musical Entertainment*, his last project at Drury Lane, satirized British efforts to organize defenses against an imaginary Bourbon invasion of southern England. Before he passed, Garrick sent a friend his favorite theatrical prop, a sword inscribed with the Ghost's injunction from *Hamlet*: "Adieu, remember me!" He was remembered—at his Westminster funeral, Dr. Johnson stood by his grave in Poets' Corner "bathed in tears"—but the social season went on.

For the government, the year had already been difficult, and it was not yet half over. Rioters in Edinburgh and Glasgow protested reforms intended to ease the oppression of Roman Catholics. Other rioters in manufacturing towns objected to the introduction of Richard Arkwright's water frame, a machine that ostensibly threatened manual jobs by spinning cotton yarn while powered by a water wheel. An ugly, inconclusive parliamentary inquiry dragged on from April into June, pitting the Howe brothers against Germain. A parade of senior officers testified in the Commons, variously offering exoneration, condemnation, or simply bleak assessments of the rebellion. "There can be no hopes of conquering America, or of being a match for General Washington's force of arms, with the present force we have there," General Grey asserted. Germain defended the administration's "management of the American war," and again insisted that "a very considerable part, if not a majority of Americans, were friends to Great Britain." He suggested that the rebels, by their alliance with Versailles, had "become French and should in future be treated as Frenchmen."

No domestic worry nagged the king and the North ministry more than restive, economically depressed Ireland, which nursed more grievances against Britain than the American colonists ever had. Most Catholic land-owners had been supplanted by English Protestants: roughly 15 percent of the population now held power over the great majority. English law had wrecked much of Irish industry by prohibiting the export of woolen cloth, among other insults. Irish worshippers, whether Catholic or Calvinist, were oppressed by the Church of England; intractable priests were liable to imprisonment. The Irish Parliament was a tool of Anglo suzerainty. Wheat prices had rarely been lower this century or taxes higher, and the British embargo of American ports crushed Irish linen makers and encouraged smuggling. Army recruiting in Ireland had become so dismal that it was suspended. "We are all Americans here," an Irishman had written. In an attempt to tamp down Irish unrest, in the coming year Parliament would again consider trade concessions, despite the king's skepticism. Pointing to America, George told North, "England gained nothing by granting indulgence to her dependencies."

British diplomats in St. Petersburg, Berlin, Vienna, and other European capitals sought alliances without success. Sir Joseph Yorke, the king's ambassador to The Hague, wrote that much of Europe believed that "we are proud, full of our own importance, and that it will not be amiss if we are brought a little more upon a level with our neighbors." British pugnacity on the high seas toward ships suspected of carrying American or French contraband stoked European anger. Fifteen Swedish merchantmen had been seized by Royal Navy men-of-war, and in October alone forty-two Dutch vessels would be claimed as British prizes; although many were released with compensation paid to the owners, some were detained with their cargoes confiscated. Britain resorted to bribery, espionage, and other covert means to win friends abroad. A small volume in red morocco with gilt edges kept track of disbursements for "His Majesty's Secret and Special Service." But even the £238,098 spent in 1778 and 1779 would have limited efficacy. Britain remained alone.

Versailles happily posed as a defender of European neutrality even as Vergennes continued to coax Spain into the war. Despite setbacks at

Newport and St. Lucia, as well as in India, French warships had scored several heartening successes, capturing a number of British men-of-war in various oceans. The frigate *La Concorde* overpowered the Royal Navy's thirty-two-gun *Minerva* near Jamaica, killing her captain and first lieutenant. Early this year, French men-of-war seized forty British privateers and brought them into Brest and Lorient. Along the coast of West Africa, a French squadron destroyed British forts and commercial outposts, confiscating ivory, gold dust, and other plunder.

For months Spain had played a double game. If obligated by the *Pacte de Famille* of 1761 to aid France, King Charles III was not obligated to hurry. Born in Madrid, he had moved to Italy to assume the title of Duke of Parma; at eighteen he conquered the kingdom of Naples and then built a twelve-hundred-room palace at Caserta that rivaled Versailles in ostentation. In 1759 he inherited the Spanish throne and returned to his natal city, blundering onto the losing side in the Seven Years' War but eventually reforming Spain's economy. With skin tanned like saddle leather, Charles, it was said, hunted every day of the year except Good Friday, mended his own boots, and decorated his dining halls with tapestries by a favored artist, Francisco de Goya.

Madrid seethed at Anglo insults, including Britain's occupation of the former Spanish possessions of Gibraltar, Minorca, Florida, and Jamaica, each lost to British force of arms over the past century or so. But Spain hardly endorsed America's rebellion against a lawful monarch—surely a baleful example for Spanish colonies in the New World. Charles had also insisted that two treasure fleets return to Spain before he would risk war against the Royal Navy. Both a Veracruz silver convoy worth twenty-two million pesos and a second squadron from Buenos Aires were now back safely in home waters.

José Moñino, the Count Floridablanca, the able if bad-tempered Spanish foreign minister, had hinted as early as April 1778 that Spain might be willing to mediate the struggle between France and Britain. London initially snubbed him, but that fall, eager to delay Spain's entry into the war, George instructed his cabinet to play for time by pretending interest. "I have no doubt next spring Spain will join France," the king wrote, "but if we can keep her quiet till then I trust the British Navy will be in a state to cope with both nations." Spain covertly suggested that Britain could buy Spanish neutrality by ceding Gibraltar and Minorca. London flicked away the proposal with disdain; surrendering the two ports, a naval historian later wrote, "would have been a national disgrace and annihilated British trade in the Mediterranean." No negotiations would be possible, George declared, until French forces withdrew from America and Versailles halted all aid to the rebels.

So ended the cynical Spanish gambit and the equally cynical British response. London "must know that what we do not get by negotiation we know how to get with a club," Floridablanca wrote. On May 29 Sandwich ordered the Channel fleet to intercept any Spanish warship headed toward a rendezvous with the French and, if possible, to blockade Brest "without leaving Great Britain & Ireland exposed."

Unknown to Britain, the Bourbon powers had already agreed to make common cause. On April 12, France and Spain had signed a convention of war at Charles's summer residence in Aranjuez, south of Madrid. Although the terms would remain secret for years, the treaty called for a joint invasion of Britain and for the war to continue by land and sea until Spain regained Gibraltar. "If we're going to war against Englishmen," Floridablanca said, "we ought to do it as the Romans did it to the Carthaginians."

"The views and pretensions of Spain are gigantic," Vergennes had told Louis XVI, but "Your Majesty cannot alone long sustain a contest with the English on equal terms." Having failed to defeat Britain in a single campaign in 1778, France had no choice but to pay a high price for Spanish help. "From Spain," Vergennes added, "nothing is to be got for nothing." In addition to Gibraltar, Spain intended to reacquire Florida and Minorca and to evict English settlements from the Bay of Honduras, a threat to the silver, sugar, and timber trade.

"The Spaniards are a little like children," a French diplomat wrote. "They can be interested only by presenting shiny objects to their gaze," France had an eye on her own shiny objects: Versailles hoped to expel the British from Newfoundland, Senegal, and Dominica; to end British control over the port of Dunkirk; and to regain trading posts in India. Both agreed that America's westward expansion should halt at the Mississippi River. Spain would agree to a formal alliance with France but would not recognize American independence until Britain did. The United States would be kept in the dark about the details of this agreement: ostensibly France's ally, the Americans had neither consented to this extension of the war nor been informed of French concessions.

On June 16, the Spanish ambassador in London presented Lord North's government with a démarche of trumped-up accusations. Britain had rejected Madrid's mediation offers, the document charged, spurning Charles's friendship and a chance to restore peace in Europe. Britain had also insulted the Spanish flag, violated Spanish territories, illegally searched Spanish ships, incited Indian hostility against Spanish posts in Louisiana, and committed other "grievances so numerous, so weighty." A day later North delivered an English translation of this list of complaints to Parliament and announced that both countries had recalled their ambassadors. The Spanish diatribe, he added, was tantamount to a declaration of war. His Majesty and the government intended "to exert all the power and all the resources of the nation to resist and repel any hostile attempts of the court of Spain."

In barely a year, Britain had gone from battling a noxious insurrection on the edge of the earth to fighting a world war against two formidable European adversaries. Suddenly not only the empire was at stake but the kingdom's very existence. The crisis, the Duke of Richmond told his peers in the House of Lords, was "the most awful this country has ever experienced."

The Queen's House stood where, in 1609, James I had planted mulberry bushes in a futile effort to nurture a British silkworm industry. The worms died and no silk was spun—he had planted the wrong sort of mulberry—but a century later, the alluring tract on the western edge of St. James's Park provided the Duke of Buckingham with the site for a grand house of brick and stone, described by the author Daniel Defoe as "one of the greatest beauties of London, both by reason of its situation and its building." Allegorical statues of Equity, Liberty, and Truth lined the roof, hiding a lead cistern that held fifty tons of Thames water used to irrigate the gardens.

George III bought the estate in 1761 from Buckingham's heirs for £28,000 and deeded it to Charlotte, who gave birth to all but one of their fifteen children within the walls of what rightly became known as the Queen's House. George removed the rooftop figures and other baroque features, spending £73,000 on renovations to create a neoclassical palace with a sweep of iron rails and broad steps leading to a front door framed by fluted Corinthian pilasters and crowned with a pediment. Eventually it would include 775 rooms. Most critics opined that he had altered the place without improving it. If "dull, dowdy, and decent," as one visitor wrote, the house became a home, with cavorting princelings, a splendid music room—often alive with strains of Handel—and a nearby menagerie that sheltered a zebra, two elephants, and eighteen kangaroos.

George's greatest pride, his children excepted, was the quartet of libraries he assembled in the house with advice from the likes of Dr. Johnson. Over time he spent £120,000 for a collection that included a first edition of *Paradise Lost*, two hundred variants of the Bible, and several hundred books about the American colonies, none of which seemed to explain the current quagmire. The trove also held fifty thousand charts, prints, and drawings, including military maps more than six feet wide pertinent to the American war, which hung on mahogany stands. They allowed a man who had never ventured beyond southern England to study battlefields on the far side of the world.

George also commissioned the expatriate American artist Benjamin West to create seven historical "statement" paintings on themes of heroic sacrifice and wartime valor. They included *The Death of General Wolfe*, depicting the glorious capture of Quebec in 1759, and *The Departure of Regulus*, derived from Livy's account of a Roman consul whose certain death in Carthaginian captivity personified dedication and honor. The king never gazed at these canvases without feeling inspirited—now more than ever, when bookmakers in London offered even odds that Jamaica would fall to the Spanish this month, to be followed by other British possessions around the globe.

In a note to Sandwich dated June 17, and disclosing, as usual, his location and the precise time—"Queen's House, 6:08 p.m."—the king invoked "the vigor of mind shown by Queen Elizabeth and her subjects" in defeating the Spanish Armada in 1588. Three days later, at "35 minutes past 9 a.m.," he wrote, "Every man must do his utmost, and those who will not are neither made for the times nor can answer any other end but to clog the wheels of government." Without the courage and fortitude of a Wolfe or a Regulus, he foresaw a bleak future for his nation: the loss of the overseas colonies, which provided strength and wealth; the withering of British power; and mass emigration from the home islands, which would then be devoured by Bourbon wolves. "The die is now cast," he wrote, "whether this shall be a great empire or the least dignified of European states."

On Monday, June 21, George, in his own hand, wrote requests to North, Germain, Sandwich, and five other members of his cabinet to appear at the Queen's House at one p.m. As each drove up in his carriage, the king ushered them into the library, where he took a chair at the head of a large table. Not since Queen Anne early in the century had a monarch presided over a cabinet meeting, and for the first time in his reign George invited his ministers to sit down. So somber was His Majesty that Germain, who provided an account of the conclave, believed they all were about to be sacked.

For an hour the king spoke, not in a "formal harangue, but as a plain narrative." He reviewed events that had led to the American war, finding no fault with his own conduct except in permitting a change of ministers in 1765 and a repeal of the Stamp Act a year later, to which he "imputed all the subsequent misfortunes." He was grateful to North and the Treasury for finding means to finance the war, and to Sandwich "for the respectable footing he had put the navy upon." To command the king's forces in America, everyone in authority had approved sending Howe, Clinton, and Burgoyne—"the fittest men for the service in the army," as Germain had told the Commons. He counted on "the favor and protection of almighty God" against all enemies, and he resolved "to part with this life rather than suffer his dominions to be dismembered." It was his duty to his subjects and to the Almighty to keep the realm intact, this realm on which the sun never set, and he expected "firmness and support" from each minister.

With that, he fell silent. For ninety minutes his counselors discussed "the mode of increasing our strength by sea and land." Then they adjourned, striding out the grand front door and down the broad steps to their carriages, relieved to still have their jobs. At "6:02 p.m." George wrote Sandwich, "If others will not be active, I must drive." To North he added the hope that "everyone felt how I am interested in the present moment." He believed resolution was the greatest trait an Englishman could display, and he was resolved to stand fast "whilst any ten men in the kingdom will stand by me."

Would those ten include Germain and North? That remained to be seen. For eighteen months the king had expected the American secretary's resignation, particularly after the sudden death of his wife the previous January. "He has not been of use in his department," George complained, and Germain's squabbling with the Howes, with Clinton, and with General Carleton, in Canada, was unseemly. He had "contrived to lose the esteem and reliance of every description of men, civil or military, who are to serve with him or under him," wrote William Eden. Yet the widening of the war seemed to invigorate Germain, and to bring out the hard, resolved warlord the king so desperately sought. "There is a great deal due to us from fortune," he asserted, "and I hope our luck will turn before we are quite ruined." When Germain hinted to North that his resignation was indeed available for the asking, the prime minister ignored him for months, until finally replying that the king had "always appeared desirous of your lordship's continuance in your office."

As for North, his misery only deepened. His pleas for release from the yoke of office became ever more abject. "Let me not go to the grave with the guilt of having been the ruin of my king and country," he wrote George. "I have been miserable for ten years in obedience to Your Majesty's commands." At times he seemed paralyzed, incapable of taking decisions or arbitrating disputes. The government's majority in the Commons grew more tenuous. "There is no energy, damn him," a colleague complained. "Nothing can goad him forward." The king wheedled, pleaded, bullied. "No man has a right to talk of leaving me at this hour," he wrote. Given Spain's alliance with France, North's departure "would be highly unbecoming." To John Robinson, North's senior secretary at the Treasury, George wrote, "Mr. Robinson must today attempt his irksome part of rousing Lord North."

Matters had grown much worse four days before the Queen's House convocation when North's two-year-old son, Dudley, had died at Bushy Park, the family's country home. "I sincerely condole with you on the loss of your son," George wrote. "Had I known of his illness, I should not have omitted inquiring after him." The prime minister was "quite unhinged," noted Robinson, who routinely sent private dispatches to the king. The *St. James's Chronicle* reported that upon appearing in Parliament after the cabinet meeting, North "was observed to be under a remarkable dejection of spirits," having spent the morning with his inconsolable wife, who "has alternately fainted and been seized with violent convulsions." A heartless personal attack by the opposition on the Commons floor brought North to tears.

The fate of the monarchy and the nation would remain chained to an exhausted man with a broken heart, "the most altered man I ever saw in my life," in Robinson's telling. "He has not spirits to set to anything." George, baffled as always by those less stalwart than himself, wrote in July, "His conduct is inexplicable. Yet I will do all I can to push him on." In another note the king added, "There are many things about him I wish were changed, [yet] I don't know any who would do so well."

The country, meanwhile, braced for a wider war. "We could not conquer America when it stood alone," Walpole wrote a friend. "Then France supported it, and we did not mend the matter. To make it still easier, we have driven Spain into the alliance. Is this wisdom?" Yet a cocky pugnacity crept into the British press. The *General Evening Post* assured readers that Britain was prepared "to correct the insolence of the court of Spain," while the *Ipswich Journal* saw new opportunities for privateers, since "there is more to be got by a war with the Spaniards than the French." George encouraged national truculence. When Parliament adjourned for the summer on July 3, he promised the departing lawmakers that their Bourbon foes would "wish they had not, without provocation or cause of complaint, insulted the honor and invaded the rights of my crown."

With garrisons to man from Canada to Bengal, the king had agreed to create almost thirty new infantry and dragoon regiments and to double the number of militiamen. Recruiting parties marched through villages and shires with drums rattling, offering bounties of a guinea and a half, with a particular eye for weavers, shoemakers, and others displaced by what would come to be called the Industrial Revolution. Posters beckoned "gentlemen volunteers who have courage enough to fight for their country." New regulations also allowed enlistment of men younger and older than previous recruits—sixteen to fifty—as well as shorter, including hundreds under five feet, four inches, who were described by an inspecting officer as "very fine little fellows." Many of those raised for the Highland regiments spoke only a Scottish Gaelic dialect known as Erse.

By the end of 1779, the government hoped to have three hundred thousand men under arms, including regulars, foreign troops, seamen, marines, militia, and "Fencibles," home guard volunteers often commanded by professional officers. But volunteers alone would not fill the ranks. On Wednesday evening, June 30, troops from the Tower of London lined each side of the Thames "during the impress for seamen in order to prevent the escape of a single person," according to the *Bath Chronicle*. "The impress was so brisk that more than 1,000 men were procured." Simultaneous sweeps occurred "at all seaports," the newspaper added. "It is supposed that upwards of 10,000 have been impressed in that short space of time."

Not to be outdone, the army also used strong-arm tactics approved by Parliament to draft "incorrigible rogues" across Britain, as well as smugglers and other "idle and disorderly persons who could not . . . follow some lawful trade or employment." One skeptical officer noted that "all the thieves, pickpockets, and vagabonds in the environs of London, too lame to run away or too poor to bribe the parish officers, were apprehended and delivered over as soldiers." Many were handcuffed and held in London's Savoy Prison until the army could claim them; to forestall desertion, such conscripts often were assigned to remote, insalubrious posts like the West Indies, where they died in flocks.

Fewer than fifteen hundred conscripts would be forcibly dragooned in England and Wales from March to October, but, as intended, the press encouraged volunteers, who increased in number by a third after the measure was enacted. The king also pardoned a few hundred criminals on the condition that they join the army; those given the choice of jail or military service included horse thieves, poachers, bigamists, and at least one highwayman. Some men balked at enlistment under any circumstances, preferring self-maiming to conscription. An officer in Manchester, upon learning that a pair of conscripts had severed their own thumbs, inquired of the War Office, "Please inform me in what manner I am to deal with these two men."

To pay for this expanding military, in 1779 Parliament passed a 5 percent increase in customs and excise taxes on coal, malt, hops, and other products, and 15 percent on soap, candles, and leather. This provided for less than a fifth of additional wartime expenses, forcing North, who remained adept at raising money despite his mental turbulence, to borrow the balance. Overseas trade had dropped by a quarter since 1774, and bankruptcies had doubled. But good harvests, expanded European trade, and more than £100 million in military spending during the war helped buoy the British economy for those who made everything from uniform buttons and tartan cloth to cannons, cartridge boxes, and beer. With the country in such a frenzy of preparation, gaffes by the government were inevitable. A sequence of mistakes by various departments during the summer would result in perfidious France receiving seventeen tons of British copper—twenty thousand sheets—for sheathing French warships, sent from England via Ostend.

"The present contest with America I cannot help seeing as the most serious to which any country was ever engaged," George told North. Yet he nurtured hopes—or delusions—that the rebels had grown weary of war and, unless bolstered by another Bourbon fleet, "must sue for peace" this summer. "After that," he added, "I would show that the parent's heart is still affectionate to the penitent child." He also reminded Sandwich that "if we lose our sugar islands it will be impossible to raise money to continue the war." As for threats to the home islands, he wrote, "We must stretch every nerve to defend ourselves, and must run some risks." That threat loomed ever larger: spies in Paris sniffed out Bourbon planning for attacks on Portsmouth and Plymouth, with a possible diversionary assault against Ireland. In early July North sent this intelligence in a strongbox to the king, who admitted in reply that he had lost the "key to the box [and] was forced to send for a locksmith before I could open it." George considered distributing pikes to "the country people" for defense and providing firearms to miners in northeast England. This provoked skepticism from Edmund Burke, who asked, "What could a miserable rabble, armed with weapons not much better than pitchforks, do against the cannon, firelocks, and bayonets of regular and well-appointed troops?"

As an earnest of his personal commitment to defend the realm, George this summer sent his thirteen-year-old son, William, to join the Channel fleet aboard the ninety-eight-gun *Prince George*. The king helped assemble the boy's sea chest, including books on astronomy and algebra, Latin and French dictionaries, *The Elements of Navigation* by John Robertson, drawing paper, two uniforms, three dozen shirts, four hats, and two swords. "Dear William," he wrote in a farewell letter, "you are now launching into a scene of life where you may either prove an honor or a disgrace to your family." He recommended "the habitual reading of the holy scriptures," adding, "More obedience is necessary from you to your superiors in the navy, more politeness to your equals, and more good nature to your inferiors." He signed the note, "Your very affectionate father, George R."

And then George R. again summoned Benjamin West. In the subsequent full-length portrait, a jowly, blue-eyed George has discarded his crown and royal robes for a smartly tailored uniform, sash, knee boots, and spurs—remarkably similar to the costume Washington had worn while posing in Philadelphia earlier this year. In his hand he holds the plan of an army camp. The background includes troops from the 15th Light Dragoons, the *Royal George* firing a salute, and a groom in royal livery holding the king's charger, ready to give battle.

"I trust in the protection of the Almighty," he had written North in late June, "in the justness of the cause, the uprightness of my own intentions, and my determination to show my people that my life is always ready to be risked for their safety or prosperity."

21.

⸺⸱⸺

I Detest That Sort of War

Spring had begun badly for General Clinton and the king's men in America. The 82nd Foot was a new regiment, recruited in the Scottish Lowlands and sent first to Halifax before several companies were dispatched onward for duty in New York. As a convoy escorted by the forty-four-gun *Rainbow* rounded Cape Cod bound for Sandy Hook, a storm scattered the ships. The transport *Mermaid* ran aground and bilged on Barnegat Shoals, in southern New Jersey, at five a.m. on Monday, March 22. "Most of the people on board were obliged to take to the tops & shrouds, where many died with cold & others worn out with fatigue dropped into the sea & were drowned," a witness reported. Not for thirty-six hours did a rebel rescue boat arrive to find floating bodies and waves rolling across *Mermaid*'s quarterdeck. More than three-quarters of the 145 dead were grenadiers and light infantrymen from the 82nd; the rest included sailors, women, children, and the ship's captain. Forty-two frostbitten survivors were trundled into rebel captivity in Philadelphia.

This ghastly news reached New York at the end of the month as Clinton fretted over the fighting season ahead. Could the capture of Savannah be expanded into the Carolinas? Would the French return, this time with the Spanish confederates widely expected to join the war? Where were the seven thousand reinforcements his masters in London had promised him—aside from those floating facedown in the Atlantic—and the five thousand men under General Grant who were supposed to return to America from the West Indies? What about the fifteen hundred tons of promised camp equipment? The Royal Navy in North America was as debilitated and scattered as his army. A dispatch sent to Sandwich in mid-April described "the real state of the fleet in this country, not as they appear upon paper but as they truly are: weak, half-manned, and enfeebled by sickness. . . . There are a fourth part of the cruisers who are blown off their stations and of whom no account has been received for several months." A shortage of seamen might require laying up half the ships on the North American station.

Clinton rarely agreed with Lord Germain about anything, but on the urgency of fashioning American loyalists into a sizable fighting force he and the American secretary concurred. "Our utmost efforts will fail," Germain wrote him, "if we cannot find means to engage the people of America in support of a cause which is equally their own and ours." Yet precisely how to help the good Americans subdue the bad ones had bedeviled British commanders for four years. More than thirty thousand loyalists would fight for the king in fifty separate provincial corps during the war, but few significant military leaders ever emerged from their ranks. This winter Clinton had persuaded the government to encourage recruitment of loyalist officers by offering half-pay after retirement, benefits to those wounded, and higher rank status. But the "sovereign contempt" British regulars held for Americans, as the *Annual Register* indelicately put it, discouraged many otherwise willing to fight. As seen in Georgia and elsewhere, loyalists were also subjected "to the fury of their bitterest enemies," a British officer conceded, including branding on the forehead with "GR"—George Rex. "They hang the turbulent, imprison the dangerous, fine the wealthy," a loyalist clergyman wrote of rebel vigilantes.

Clinton had long stressed the exigency of gaining hearts and subduing minds in America. That required protecting civilians and preventing the worst excesses of soldier misbehavior. When six grenadiers from the 71st Foot were convicted in mid-February of plundering a Long Island family, he approved fifteen hundred lashes each for five of them and death for the sixth, who had broken down the farmhouse door. Yet many of his officers, the fire-and-sword men, recoiled at moderation toward the rebels. They admired the likes of General John Vaughan, who was known as "the cock of the ball" for incinerating Esopus during the Saratoga campaign. "We have been a little employed of late in burning and destroying," Major James Murray wrote his sister after the sacking of New Bedford in September. "We are in hopes that the fashion may take root."

On April 24, Germain's secret orders for the forthcoming campaign arrived on Clinton's desk at No. 1 Broadway, more than three months after they were written in London. The government recommended trying to bring Washington to "a general & decisive action," or at least bottling up the Continental Army in the Hudson Highlands to allow the restoration of civil government in New York. Two amphibious forces of four thousand men each, with naval support, should ravage enemy enclaves along the New England coast and Chesapeake Bay, pacifying the rebel littoral and emboldening loyalists. Sometime this spring—Germain was hazy on the precise date—sixty-six hundred reinforcements would indeed arrive, including Highlanders and twelve hundred Germans, along with enough muskets to arm ten thousand loyal provincials.

In a private reply to Germain, covered with ink blotches and smudges reflecting his agitation, Clinton wrote, "Your lordship only recommends. But by that recommendation you secure the right of blaming me if I should adopt other measures and fail. I do not wish to be captious, my lord." But captious he was, and quibbling, impertinent, and self-pitying. The government demanded more of "my debilitated army"—only nineteen thousand were fit for duty on the continent—than was ever asked of Howe with a much larger force. He insisted that the American secretary stop listening to the suggestions of "people who cannot be competent judges. . . . For God's sake, my lord, if you wish I should do anything, leave me to myself and let me adapt my efforts to the hourly change of circumstances." The destruction of Washington's army "has been the object of every campaign during this war," yet forcing the Americans to give battle was unlikely without "at least 30,000 men, and those British." He added:

> Since I am ordered to remain in the command, your lordship may depend, during this campaign, upon the most active exertions that my powers can supply. But I must lament that my happiness is sacrificed.

He further unburdened himself in letters home. To Major Drummond, the aide still loitering in London, he asked, "Where do these gentlemen get their information? . . . Don't let them deceive themselves." To Newcastle he complained of being away from "my motherless babes" for so many years. "I still hope this may be the last campaign. For me at least, it must," Clinton wrote. And to William Eden, who had become a confidant in the government, he warned, "If this cursed war goes on, great alterations must be made in the manner of conducting it."

With that, he turned back to the business at hand. He had long been skeptical of coastal raiding, writing, the previous fall, "'Tis a doubt with me whether that sort of war is worthy of a great nation." But even before Germain's dispatch arrived he had put in motion plans for a crushing blow to the south. Clinton would demonstrate that he, too, could be a fire-and-sword man.

Commodore Sir George Collier had served in American waters since 1776 and was the rare salt who found favor with Henry Clinton. A midshipman at age thirteen, a lieutenant at sixteen, and a captain at twenty-four, Collier had commanded a succession of frigates, earned a knighthood, and won literary laurels for his dramatic romance *Selima and Azor*—a retelling of *Beauty and the Beast*—which was produced at Drury Lane. He loathed American insurgents—"I see with indignation & concern the rebel colors"—and had captured the frigate *Hancock* in July 1777 before destroying thirty vessels along the Maine coast and seizing the privateers *Hammond* and *General Gates*. When the execrated Admiral Gambier was recalled to England in February, Collier took temporary command on the North American station, hoisting his broad pennant aboard the sixty-four-gun *Raisonnable.*

He soon persuaded Clinton that an attack on the Chesapeake offered many benefits to the Crown. Although British cruisers patrolled the bay, blockade-runners still infiltrated through to Norfolk and nearby harbors. Suffolk, twenty miles inland, had become a boomtown as the terminus of a fifty-mile wagon trail used by smugglers from Edenton, North Carolina. Before the war, fifty thousand tons of tobacco had been shipped annually from the Chesapeake to Britain; although all rebel exports had been severely curtailed, France continued to pay extravagant prices for American leaf, much preferred by French smokers to Ukrainian, Hungarian, and Corsican tobacco. Just two Beaumarchais vessels, *Le Fier Roderique* and *Lyon*, had collected two thousand hogsheads—a thousand tons—the previous summer. A violent blow would discourage this illicit trade and also force Virginia troops to defend their state, rather than reinforce either Washington's Continentals or rebel regiments in the Carolinas. Moreover, Virginia's two hundred thousand enslaved residents comprised 40 percent of all those in America; the appearance of British liberators could badly disrupt the state's plantation economy.

Clinton agreed to "a short and desultory invasion," lasting no more than a month. A flotilla of twenty-eight ships led by *Raisonnable* sailed from New York on May 5, carrying twenty-five hundred regulars under the command of Major General Edward Mathew, a veteran of Brandywine, Germantown, and Monmouth. "Uncommonly favorable" winds whisked them through the Virginia capes four days later. "The sight was beautiful," a British officer wrote, "and formed the finest regatta in the world."

As rebel coasters scattered in fright across the bay and into feeder creeks, *Raisonnable* anchored on May 9 at Hampton Roads, a vast harbor, where Collier shifted his flag to the smaller *Rainbow*. Pressing south up the Elizabeth River toward Portsmouth as far as the rising tide allowed, he and Mathew boarded the ship's barge a day later, escorted by the galley *Cornwallis* and several gunboats with 6- and 9-pounders jutting from their

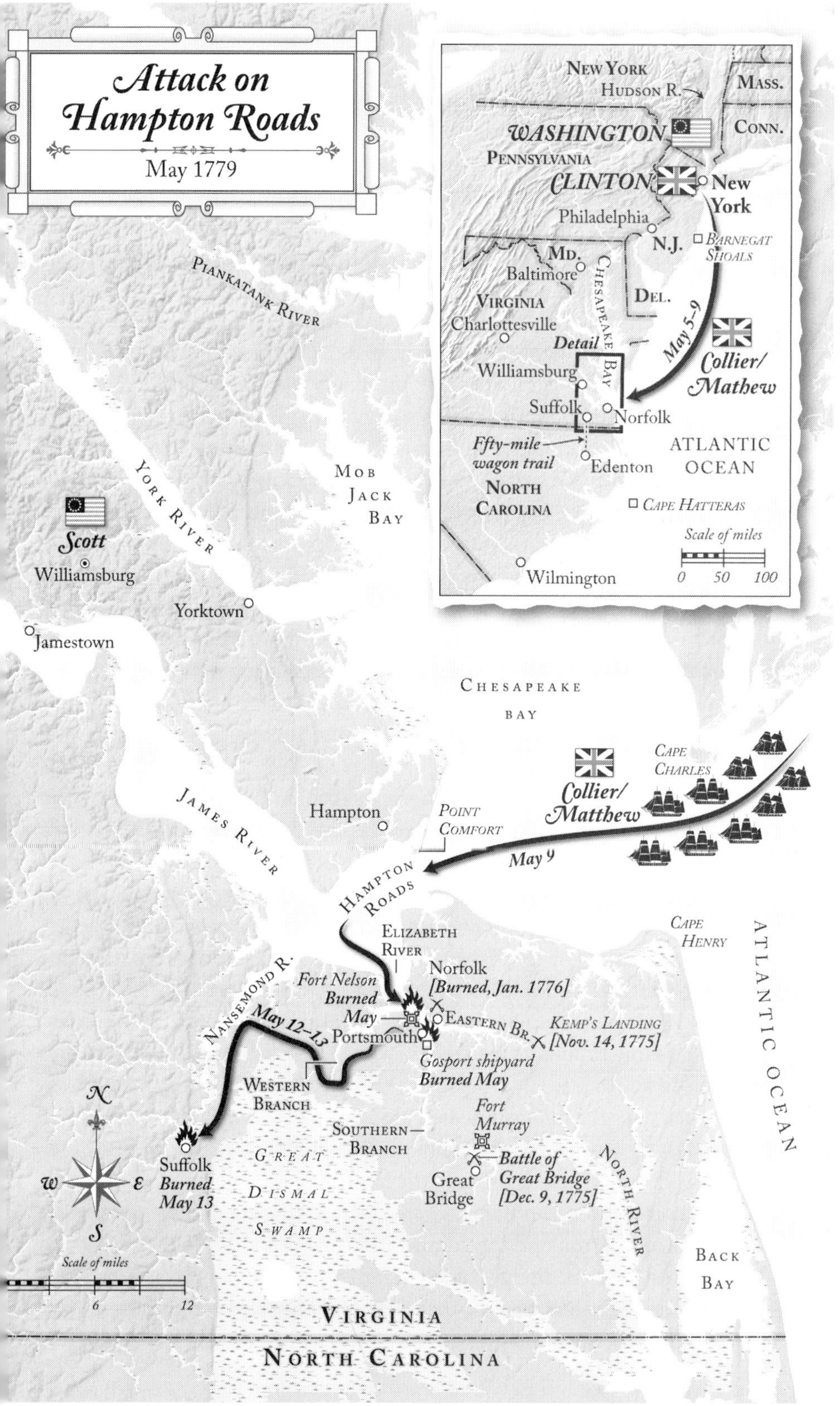

Attack on Hampton Roads
May 1779
NEW YORK
HUDSON R.
MASS.
CONN.
WASHINGTON
PENNSYLVANIA
CLINTON
New York
Philadelphia
N.J.
BARNEGAT SHOALS
MD.
Baltimore
CHESAPEAKE BAY
DEL.
VIRGINIA
Charlottesville
May 5–9
Detail
Collier/ Mathew
Williamsburg
Suffolk
Norfolk
Ffty-mile wagon trail
Edenton
ATLANTIC OCEAN
NORTH CAROLINA
CAPE HATTERAS
Scale of miles
0 50 100
Wilmington
PIANKATANK RIVER
YORK RIVER
MOB JACK BAY
Scott
Williamsburg
Yorktown
Jamestown
CHESAPEAKE BAY
CAPE CHARLES
Collier/ Matthew
JAMES RIVER
Hampton
POINT COMFORT
May 9
HAMPTON ROADS
ELIZABETH RIVER
CAPE HENRY
ATLANTIC OCEAN
NANSEMOND R.
Norfolk [Burned, Jan. 1776]
Fort Nelson Burned May
May 12–13
EASTERN BR.
KEMP'S LANDING [Nov. 14, 1775]
Portsmouth
Gosport shipyard Burned May
WESTERN BRANCH
Fort Murray
SOUTHERN BRANCH
N
W
E
S
Suffolk Burned May 13
GREAT DISMAL SWAMP
Battle of Great Bridge [Dec. 9, 1775]
Great Bridge
NORTH RIVER
BACK BAY
Scale of miles
6
12
VIRGINIA
NORTH CAROLINA

prows. An ecstasy of red and blue signal flags sent flatboats carrying assault troops to a glebe on the river's west bank before shuttling artillery carriages, horses, and more redcoats into the shallows. Bow ramps dropped to put them ashore almost dry-shod. A few cannonballs arced toward the invaders from Fort Nelson, a small redoubt with walls of timber and rammed earth fifteen feet thick. Then the 150-man rebel garrison fled inland to seek refuge in the Great Dismal Swamp, leaving the Stars and Stripes flying above the abandoned parapet.

Other American defenses were equally hapless. Virginia's feeble state navy put up no resistance and proved "unsuccessful beyond all my fears," wrote Jefferson, who would become the state's governor on June 1. Patrick Henry, in the final inglorious weeks of his own three-year governorship, failed to recognize the scope of the attack or call out the militia until it was too late. Brigadier General Scott, now commanding a Continental light infantry corps despite his dodgy performance at Monmouth, had orders to march to South Carolina but instead took post at Williamsburg, thirty miles up the James River, where he built breastworks and waited in vain for thousands of summoned militiamen who failed to show up. Virginia planters, required by law to remove the enslaved from proximity to enemy liberators, herded their chattel inland, a practice known as "running the Negroes."

The British rampaged without hindrance. Guardsmen marched eighteen miles through the night and at dawn on May 13 attacked Suffolk— "famous for their sedition," in Collier's assessment. Smoke and flame soon enshrouded the town. Other redcoats captured Portsmouth, then seized the shipyard at Gosport—the finest in America—and crossed the Elizabeth to occupy Norfolk, still charred from British and American arson three years earlier. Fleeing rebels set fire to *Virginia*, a newly built twenty-eight-gun frigate, as well as two French merchantmen loaded with baled goods and a thousand hogsheads of tobacco. Collier ordered *Rainbow* to take aboard loyalist refugees, runaway slaves, and deserters, who were to be fed the same rations as the frigate's crew. Rebel prisoners would receive two-thirds' allowance.

For ten days the raiders lingered around the lower bay, collecting cattle, horses, slaves, seventeen prize ships, and three thousand hogsheads of tobacco. Collier admitted to "some little irregularities," including the murder of several Frenchmen on their merchant vessels. Some loyalist houses also were burned in error, and the commodore sent a sloop laden with salt as a token of consolation, along with eight lambs to feed the infirm. Virginians would allege British atrocities, including the strangling of American sailors, gouging out eyes, and kidnapping women onto Royal Navy ships.

On May 16 Collier wrote Clinton that successes on the bay "infinitely exceed" even his highest hopes. Portsmouth was now a "secure asylum" with "an amazing quantity of fine seasoned oak timber"—five thousand wagonloads, plus a huge stockpile of masts, cordage, and other naval supplies. "This port," he added, "should remain in our hands." British occupation would halt all American trade in the Chesapeake, "distress the rebels exceedingly," and destroy "the sinews of the rebellion." He also had his eye not only on Williamsburg, the state capital, but several thousand British and Hessian prisoners from Burgoyne's army now held under light guard in Charlottesville, 160 miles to the northwest.

Clinton demurred. Without the promised reinforcements from Britain, New York remained vulnerable to Washington's Continentals. Rebel row galleys on the Chesapeake would soon threaten Collier's men-of-war in shoal water. The commodore ought "not burn his fingers" by overreaching. His orders were clear: the expedition was to return to Sandy Hook. "I still think all will go well," Clinton wrote. "But as I have often said, curse me if I know how." A disappointed Collier later conceded, "I then had no other alternative than to quit a place whose importance and utility stood higher in my opinion than almost any other in America."

The marauders collected as much timber, furniture, and livestock as their ships would carry, then lit a match. "The conflagration in the night appeared grand beyond description," a British officer recorded. Towering flames around Hampton Roads consumed the Gosport shipyard, the storehouses, the cranes, the smithies, Fort Nelson, pine masts, countless tons of oak planks and rope, eight thousand barrels of pitch, tar, and turpentine, and nine thousand barrels of salt pork intended for Washington's commissary. Flames also devoured 120 vessels, including, by Collier's count, fourteen-, eighteen-, and thirty-six-gun warships building on the stocks.

The squadron weighed and sailed out through the capes, carrying 90 loyalists and 518 liberated blacks, half of them women and children. Three days later, on May 29, Collier dropped anchor at New York. British battle casualties had amounted to two wounded; even Clinton found the results "beyond my most sanguine expectations." In a note to Germain, Collier wrote, "I may now say with some confidence that rebellion is thrown on its back, and that this campaign will be the last of this unnatural civil war."

To Sandwich on the same day he added, "I think Great Britain may now dictate her own terms to America."

Clinton now had the bit in his teeth. Even before Collier's return, he lunged up the Hudson with six thousand British and Hessian grenadiers, light infantry, and loyalist volunteers, leaving orders for the Virginia raiders to follow as soon as they threaded the Narrows into New York Bay. On May 31 a column under General Vaughan pushed up the east bank of the river toward Verplanck's Point. Clinton jumped to the western shore with three foot regiments and a hundred *Jäger*, burning a few houses and edging to within musket range of Stony Point, the rocky promontory where he had last set foot two years earlier during the capture of nearby Fort Montgomery. Rebel alarm signals echoed up the Hudson gorge—one gunshot for every five enemy vessels counted on the river. The small American garrison at Stony Point set fire to their new blockhouse, then scurried into the hills.

Fifty-eight grunting British gunners tied themselves into a rope harness under a bright moon to haul a 12-pounder to "the summit of this difficult rock," in Clinton's description. Others pushed from behind. At five a.m. on June 1 they opened fire across the Hudson at Fort Lafayette on Verplanck's Point, now invested by Vaughan's legion and further bombarded by a pair of row galleys. The defenders—a Continental captain with three lieutenants, seventy-one bedraggled men, and four shore guns—tossed their gunpowder into the river and surrendered after a two-hour negotiation, giving the British full possession of King's Ferry, the main rebel route from New England to New Jersey. "This little success was effected without the loss of a single man, and only one *Jäger* was wounded," Clinton wrote Germain.

He hoped that the loss of King's Ferry would draw Washington into the open from his Jersey stronghold near New Brunswick to confront the royal intruders. If reinforcements from Britain had reached New York, Clinton intended to push north another dozen miles to West Point, the dominant position in the Hudson Highlands. But for the moment he lacked sufficient strength, given the terrain in these harsh uplands. "No reinforcements arrived," he wrote Eden. "Good God! What could prevent the troops sailing in March or even in April?" As usual, his mood gyrated day by day. "He is only timid when he thinks ill, brave when he perceives hope of success," wrote William Smith, the loyalist jurist, who conferred with Clinton in late May. "Thinks Washington is distressed."

If not distressed, Washington surely was alarmed. After the long winter at Middlebrook, he broke camp on June 3, expecting the enemy to continue upriver toward West Point. "There is not a moment to be lost," he wrote. "Appearances grow more & more serious." As the Continental Army lumbered toward the Hudson, Greene warned that "the teams are failing and the wagons breaking hourly," not least because of overloading "with women and lazy soldiers." The commander in chief ordered the passengers to walk, placed his new headquarters in the village of New Windsor on June 21, and did the surveying himself for eight new redoubts and batteries to strengthen West Point's works at Forts Putnam and Arnold. He positioned eleven thousand men on either side of the river and braced for Clinton's attack.

No attack came. Scouts reported that a thousand British troops at Verplanck's and Stony Point had instead begun "to fortify with astonishing industry." A British officer now referred to the latter as "Little Gibraltar"; additional armament included cannons seized in the Chesapeake raid—each gun with three hundred rounds—and sixty thousand musket cartridges sent upriver from New York. To seize and secure the two outposts, Clinton had used at least a dozen square-rigged ships, three brigs, four schooners, six sloops, and innumerable smaller vessels and flatboats. Washington once again lamented the mobility that the Royal Navy's "canvas wings" allowed the enemy, "a source of much mischief & great perplexity to us," as he wrote his brother.

But he would not be baited into a pitched battle to recapture King's Ferry, even though the resultant detour now added an extra sixty miles to the journey of men and supplies from New England. "An attempt to dislodge them, from the natural strength of the positions, would require a greater force & apparatus than we are masters of," he wrote General Gates in mid-June. "All we can do is to lament what we cannot remedy."

If a sally up the Hudson would not entice Washington to give battle, perhaps the devastation of Connecticut coastal towns might. After returning to New York, Clinton approved another "desultory expedition," this one "to draw Mr. Washington from the strong post which he occupies in the mountains." Again low on provisions in New York, Clinton also intended to secure Long Island Sound against rebel "whale boats and other piratical craft" threatening supply convoys from Cork.

Major General William Tryon would wield the scourge this time. A British soldier for nearly three decades who had married a London heiress blessed with a £30,000 dowry, Tryon had demonstrated administrative competence and tact—first as royal governor of North Carolina, then, since 1771, as governor of New York. But insurrection made him surly, repressive, and widely despised. In a recent proposal to Germain he had suggested offering a £1,000 reward for each congressman and rebel governor delivered to the king's troops; he had also advocated transporting all captured Americans to English prisons and unleashing Indians "on the frontiers of the revolted colonies, unrestrained excepting to women and children." He deplored Clinton's "torpor" and over the past year had licensed nearly two hundred loyalist privateers out of New York with six thousand sailors in a retaliatory campaign of notable brutality that he deemed a "glorious success." Collier, on the contrary, advised the Admiralty this summer that Connecticut rebels had "impeded and almost totally destroyed the trade of His Majesty's faithful subjects passing through the Sound."

To make "impressions on the New England coast," twenty-six hundred regulars, Hessians, and a loyalist unit called the King's American Regiment embarked on Collier's transports. On July 3, with the commodore and Tryon aboard the twenty-gun *Camilla*, the flotilla sailed on the East River through Hell Gate, escorted by *Scorpion*, *Halifax*, *Hussar*, and other men-of-war. Tryon's avowed purpose was "a general terror and despondency"; when he asked Clinton for authority to burn rebel towns, the commanding general replied ambiguously, "I know you will if I don't forbid it." One of Clinton's favorite phrases was "*Je m'en lave les mains*"—I wash my hands of it. And now he washed his hands.

From *Camilla*, Tryon and Collier issued a menacing Fourth of July statement to "the inhabitants of Connecticut":

> We have hoped that you would recover from the phrenzy which has distracted this unhappy country. . . . Set the first example of returning to allegiance. Reflect on what gratitude requires of you.

At dawn on Monday, July 5, forty sails appeared off New Haven. As patriot alarm guns reverberated and drums beat to arms, boats shuttling from the ships deposited a thousand assault troops ashore west of town under Brigadier General George Garth and another eight hundred to the east with Tryon. All were reportedly "in the most malignant disposition." The Yale College president, Reverend Ezra Stiles, watched the landings through a telescope from the chapel steeple. "All then knew our fate," he would write. After bundling four of his daughters to safety north of town and sending the college records away with his son, Stiles rode off in a horse cart loaded with several beds and a hastily packed trunk.

The divinity professor Naphtali Daggett trotted on a black mare toward the approaching enemy, his gray hair flying and a fowling gun in the crook of his arm. Promptly slashed across the skull by a redcoat bayonet, Daggett was taken prisoner, beaten with muskets, and robbed of his tobacco box and silver shoe buckles. Others fared worse, according to depositions later sent to Washington. Charles Alling reported burying four men, including Captain John Gilbert, shot through the knee and clubbed to death; Asa

Todd, "pierced with a bayonet once through the head & twice through the body"; and Joseph Dorman, "killed with a large stone." Elisha Tuttle, described as mentally impaired, was mortally slashed with bayonets and had his tongue partly cut out. Abigail English found her husband, Benjamin, sitting at home in a blood-soaked chair with three bayonet wounds to the chest crying, "He has stabbed me! He has stabbed me!" After Sarah Townshend's husband was captured and forced onto a British ship, she took her three children and appealed for clemency to Collier, who allegedly looked at her youngest and said, "Are you willing it should be cut up and made a pie of?"

After a long afternoon and evening of plunder, the raiders marched back to their ships at sunrise on Tuesday morning, bent double beneath their swag. They offered freedom and employment to all enslaved blacks and left behind 150 men, some reportedly very drunk, to burn wharves, warehouses, and coastal vessels. Sporadic militia fire intensified to become "vigorous, incessant, & heavy," Stiles reported. The British rear guard carted their dead and wounded to the shoreline in five wagons, and the flotilla soon sailed west. Stiles tallied thirty-one Americans dead and several others mortally wounded. "This," he wrote, "is a taste of British clemency." Collier put the king's casualties in New Haven at fifty-six.

Twenty-five miles down the coast, Fairfield was next. At four a.m. on July 7, the muffled crack of alarm guns from Grover's Hill carried along the Sound. Fog concealed the squadron until midmorning as women, children, and aged men herded their livestock into the woods and hid the family silver in wells or the clefts of stone walls. Most local militiamen had marched to New Haven, but a few popped away with firelocks and fieldpieces—a "smart fire of musketry," Tryon later told Clinton. Landing parties strode along the beach and across the town green, scanning windows and rooftops for snipers. "The Hessians were first let loose for rapine and plunder," a resident wrote. "They robbed women of their buckles, rings, bonnets, aprons, and handkerchiefs." Others smashed mirrors, stoneware, and furniture, joined by loyalist gangs. "I escaped . . . and concealed myself in a wet ditch," reported Ann Nichols after her house was looted. Jane Buckley recounted milking her cow on the demand of thirsty redcoats, who then killed it.

An hour after sunset, a fire began to spread slowly from house to house. Much of the town still stood intact at dawn, but within two hours flames became general as *Jäger* and loyalist "burning parties" reduced almost two hundred structures to ash, including two churches, "which took fire unintentionally by the flakes from other buildings," Tryon insisted. John Sayre, an Anglican minister, outspoken loyalist, and town surgeon, wrote that "the ungovernable flames . . . in a few minutes left me with a family, consisting of my wife and eight children, destitute of food, house, and raiment."

After a quick detour across the Sound to replenish supplies at Huntington, on the north coast of Long Island, the expedition returned to Connecticut. On July 11 the raiders pounced on Norwalk. Just after sunset Tryon landed at Cow's Pasture, a peninsula on the east end of the harbor. The 54th Foot at first light swatted away rebel outposts and drove several hundred militia from Drummond Hill. By midmorning a second detachment to the west had captured the bridge over a salt creek. The militia fought back—Collier later complained to the Admiralty of rebel diehards "murdering the troops from the windows of houses after safeguards were granted them"—and now the town was doomed. The king's firebrands tossed torches into 252 structures, half of them houses, plus twenty whaleboats, two sawmills, two brigs on the stocks, and other vessels in the harbor, until Norwalk was a cauldron of flame and smoke. Several militiamen "were found with their skulls blowed off by muskets discharged into them after they were wounded," an American officer reported.

With Norwalk's immolation, Clinton recalled the raiders to New York and the British rampage ended. Three more American towns joined the lengthening list of those wrecked, ruined, or extirpated by the Crown. Coastal Connecticut had been particularly vulnerable, since many local men were scattered inland to help with the summer harvest and Continental troops near the coast had marched to the Hudson to counter Clinton's incursion there. "I can do little more than lament the depredations of the enemy at a distance," Washington wrote Connecticut's governor, Jonathan Trumbull, Sr., on July 12.

Collier assured the Admiralty that "the navigation of the Sound will be more clear for some time from the numerous pirates that infected it." Tryon estimated his casualties for the week at twenty killed, ninety-six wounded, and thirty-one missing. He acknowledged waging "desolation warfare" but pardoned himself out of "love of my country, my duty to the king, and the law of arms." Clinton voiced doubts about the raids he had approved, declaring, "I detest that sort of war." Such equivocation infuriated his subordinates. "It would seem as if Sir Henry wished the conflagrations, and yet not to be answerable for them," the jurist Smith told his diary on July 16. "Every place near the sea must dread a visit."

Washington had again refused to be lured into battle on the enemy's terms or to risk exposing the vital Hudson Highlands, which he called "the one essential point." But he fairly panted for revenge against the king's men. "Plundering and burning," he wrote John Jay in July, "appear to form a considerable part of their present system of war." As the flames finally subsided along the Connecticut coast, he added, "It seems to me high time to retaliate by destroying some of their towns."

Major Henry Lee III, a Virginia firebrand and cavalryman known as Light-Horse Harry, was said by one admirer to "have come out of his mother's womb a soldier." Only twenty-three, an accomplished student at the College of New Jersey, in Princeton, with a passion for Homer, Demosthenes, and Julius Caesar, he was a superb horseman who had earned his nickname battling British marauders around Philadelphia and in foraging sweeps during the Valley Forge winter. Washington praised his "gallant behavior" and offered him a position as an aide-de-camp. Lee declined, explaining, "I am wedded to my sword."

Light-Horse Harry had his own answer for British savagery, which he hoped would also deter Continental Army desertion. In a note to Washington on July 8, he proposed summary executions and public decapitations. Replying a day later, His Excellency firmly discouraged the "appearance of inhumanity," but it was too late. The previous night, Lee's troopers had captured three deserters near the Hudson and, with his permission, shot one of them, a corporal from Pennsylvania, cut off his head, and forced the other two to carry it on a pole through the camp before mounting the grisly trophy on a gallows.

"I fear it will have a bad effect both in the army and in the country," an appalled Washington wrote on July 10. "Have the body buried lest it fall into the enemy's hands." Lee voiced contrition but added, "From what I observe here, it has had a very immediate effect for the better on both troops & inhabitants."

Washington had already set his own retaliatory scheme in motion. To command a new light infantry brigade, he chose Anthony Wayne, who had recovered his reputation and self-possession since the debacle at Paoli two years earlier. If Brigadier General Wayne was "vain, impulsive, and given to hyperbole," in one biographer's assessment, and "more active and enterprising than judicious and cautious," as Washington acknowledged, those imperfect traits would serve him well in organizing the task at hand: the commander in chief had asked him to "dispossess" the British of Stony Point by capturing that Little Gibraltar.

Forty-six regiments contributed 1,350 men to Wayne's new elite corps, most of them from Connecticut, Pennsylvania, and Virginia. All were veterans, some with service dating to Bunker Hill. After conducting his own stealthy reconnaissance of Stony Point on July 6, Washington suggested

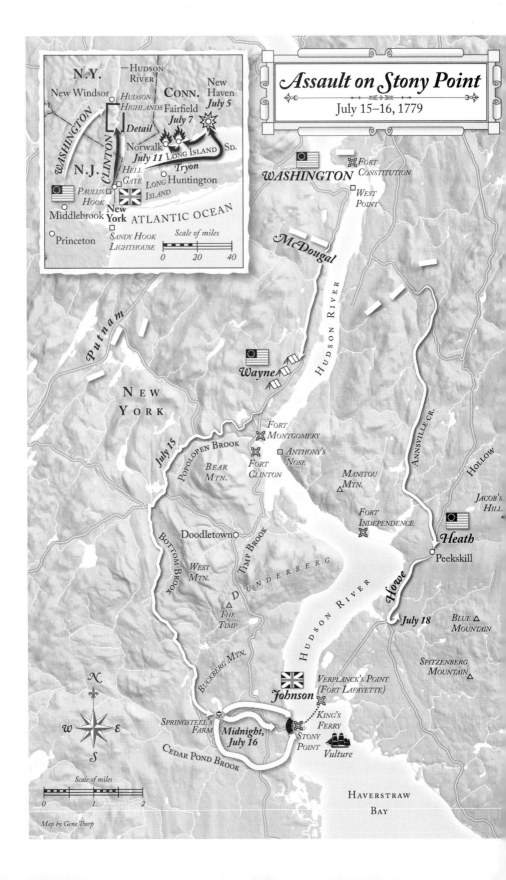

Assault on Stony Point

July 15–16, 1779

Map by Gene Thorp

Inset map:

N.Y.

New Windsor

HUDSON RIVER

HUDSON HIGHLANDS

Detail

CONN.

New Haven
July 5

Fairfield
July 7

WASHINGTON

CLINTON

Norwalk
July 11

LONG ISLAND SD.

Tryon

N.J.

HELL GATE

Long Huntington

PAULUS HOOK

New York

LONG ISLAND

Middlebrook

ATLANTIC OCEAN

Princeton

SANDY HOOK LIGHTHOUSE

Scale of miles

0   20   40

Main map:

WASHINGTON

FORT CONSTITUTION

WEST POINT

McDougal

HUDSON RIVER

Putnam

Wayne

NEW YORK

July 15

POPOLOPEN BROOK

FORT MONTGOMERY

ANTHONY'S NOSE

BEAR MTN.

FORT CLINTON

MANITOU MTN.

ANNSVILLE CR.

HOLLOW

JACOB'S HILL

FORT INDEPENDENCE

Heath

Peekskill

Doodletown

BOTTOM BROOK

WEST MTN.

TIMP BROOK

DUNDERBERG

THE TIMP

Howe

July 18

BLUE MOUNTAIN

HUDSON RIVER

BUCKBERG MTN.

SPITZENBERG MOUNTAIN

Johnson

VERPLANCK'S POINT (FORT LAFAYETTE)

KING'S FERRY

SPRINGSTEEL'S FARM

Midnight, July 16

STONY POINT

Vulture

N
W   E
S

CEDAR POND BROOK

Scale of miles

0   1   2

HAVERSTRAW BAY

that a small force of no more than two hundred troops might be able to seize the citadel in a sudden strike. Wayne disagreed. Only a brigade-sized assault had any chance. "I do not think a storm practicable," he told Washington. "But perhaps a surprise may be effected."

British deserters, American spies—including officers disguised in civilian togs who escorted farmwives selling garden greens and chickens to the Stony Point garrison—and Wayne's own surveillance revealed that Clinton had weakened the Hudson garrisons to reinforce his Connecticut expedition. Stony Point, a forty-acre knuckle of gneiss and granite, carved by glaciers and lapped on three sides by water, rose 150 feet above the river. British engineers had cleared fields of fire for eight hundred yards to the west and enclosed the earthen fort with two abatis—one of them still incomplete—fashioned from the sharpened boughs of apple trees clear-cut in a nearby orchard. Fifteen cannons stood in a flagstaff battery near the crown of the hill and behind a trio of twelve-foot-tall, V-shaped outworks called flèches. The garrison of 564 redcoats, commanded by Lieutenant Colonel Henry Johnson, was drawn mostly from the 17th Foot, veterans of battlefields from Long Island to Monmouth. Nearly all of the Royal Navy squadron had departed, leaving only the fourteen-gun sloop-of-war *Vulture* and a smaller vessel to shuttle between Stony Point and Verplanck's, fifteen hundred yards apart. "This post," a British officer had recently assured Clinton, "is perfectly quiet."

Washington urged Wayne to keep the enemy ignorant. Secrecy was paramount. "Knowledge of your intention, ten minutes previously obtained, blasts all your hopes," he warned. On Wednesday, July 14, he approved the attack for the following night, adding, "You are at liberty to choose between the different plans on which we have conversed." Wayne ordered the ranks to be "fresh shaved and powdered," and after company inspections on Thursday morning, eleven hundred men marched from Sandy Beach, below West Point, past the ruins of Fort Montgomery. Farmers detained along the route were pressed into service as guides, and Major Lee brought the latest intelligence gathered by his cavalry scouts. Swinging southwest, sweating like horses in the summer heat and silent but for their scuffing feet, the Continentals tramped single file for fourteen miles on a steep, rugged trace around Bear Mountain and the thousand-foot massif known as the Dunderberg.

At eight p.m., with the sun sinking, they halted at the remote farm of David Springsteel, barely a mile west of Stony Point. Officers distributed strips of white paper to be pinned to each hat as a recognition symbol. "The strictest silence must be observed," Wayne decreed. The men were to unload their muskets, placing their "whole dependence on the bayonet."

Wayne and other officers would carry only a spontoon, a short, wicked pike also considered a symbol of authority. Any soldier firing without orders or who "attempts to retreat one single foot" would be "instantly put to death by the officer next to him." But the first man to break into the enemy citadel would receive $500, authorized by General Washington. As the twilight faded from orange to magenta in the west, a cool north wind swept down the Hudson, chilling the men in their clammy uniforms. "I never came nearer perishing with cold in the middle of summer in all my life," one soldier would write.

Wayne crept forward for a final reconnaissance of the British works. He returned to the farm for a quick supper and to scribble a note to a family friend, asking him "to attend to the education of my little son & daughter" if he failed to survive the impending "scene of carnage." Ever melodramatic, Wayne added, "I am called to sup, but where to breakfast, either within the enemy's lines in triumph or in the other world?"

By nightfall on Thursday, July 15, the whistling wind was blowing hard enough that the eighty-eight British sentries posted around the western perimeter of Stony Point could no longer hear the ship's bells clanging aboard *Vulture*, now anchored in Haverstraw Bay to avoid being blown aground. Two grenadier companies from the 71st Foot had bivouacked with four 17th Foot companies along what the British called the Outer Works, leaving the rest of the garrison to occupy the Upper Works near the flagstaff, with its wildly flapping Union Jack. Shortly after midnight Lieutenant John Ross, commanding a thirty-man picket beyond the outer abatis, heard a single gunshot from a skittish sentry, who told others in the guard that he sensed intruders lurking in the marsh to the west. "I saw no enemy," Ross later wrote.

> The night being extremely dark and very windy made me suppose that what the men reported to have heard was occasioned by the wind rustling among the bushes. . . . I had hardly said this when I heard a volley of small arms. . . . I had just got within the works when I received the push of a bayonet from a man who knocked me down the hill with the butt end of his firelock.

Wayne had organized his attack into two columns on the left and right—north and south, respectively—with each led by a "forlorn hope" of twenty volunteers assigned to chop holes through the double abatis with axes. A third infantry detachment, the only troops allowed to fire their muskets, feinted in the middle. As a vanguard of 120 men on the left waded through a tidal slough around the enemy flank, British 3-pounders ripped the column with a rapid volley of nearly seventy grapeshot rounds that killed or wounded seventeen rebels in the forlorn hope. Torn, crumpled men lay tangled in the apple boughs. "The cannon was discharged so near my head it beat me back into the ditch," wrote Private Thomas Pope. "The report was so hard it disstroyed my hearing." But the column bulled through the barriers, and within twenty minutes, howling rebels—ghostly, muddy figures illuminated by British muzzle flashes—began climbing toward a howitzer battery on the fort's high ground, their bayonets pricking the night.

Led by Wayne, the right column waded waist-deep along the shore of Haverstraw Bay for two hundred yards to circumvent the outer abatis. At a gun battery below the flagstaff, a frantic 17th Foot captain pleaded with a Royal Artillery lieutenant, "For God's sake, why are not the artillery here made use of? The enemy are in the hollow and crossing the water!" Ammunition, however, had been locked in the powder magazine, and the barrels could not be depressed far enough to range the shoreline anyway. Attackers scrambled up the steep pitch from the river. They "cut and tore away the pickets," Major William Hull reported, "cleared the chevaux-de-frise at the sallyport, mounted the parapet, and entered the fort at the point of the bayonet."

Abruptly, Wayne pitched forward with a two-inch scalp wound from a stray bullet. Rising to a knee, his face masked in blood, he shouted, "Forward, my brave fellows, forward!" From above came an answering shout: "The fort's our own!" Lieutenant Colonel the Marquis de Fleury, who would split the $500 prize with his troops as the first men inside the works, ripped the British colors from their staff. "Considerable bayoneting," wrote Captain Henry Champion, "cleared the scene exactly at one o'clock."

In a two-sentence note to Washington dated "16th July 1779, 2 o'clock a.m.," Wayne wrote, "The fort & garrison . . . are ours. Our officers & men behaved like men who are determined to be free." He later added a postscript: "The pain I feel from a wound in my head prevents me from being particular."

The particulars emerged soon enough. American casualties included 15 dead and 80 wounded. The king's losses numbered 63 killed and 543 captured, among them dozens of women and children, plus 70 wounded soldiers. A few redcoats had escaped by swimming to the *Vulture*. The only officer to die from either side was Captain Francis Tew of the 17th Foot, who had survived wounds in Canada and the West Indies during the Seven Years' War but would not survive fratricidal fire from his own men at Stony Point.

"My astonishment could not but be extreme," Clinton wrote upon hearing of Little Gibraltar's loss. "This bold and well-combined attempt . . . was, I must confess, a very great affront to us." Major General James Pattison, now Clinton's subordinate as commandant of British forces in New York City, informed London that despite "this singular & unfortunate event . . . no instance of inhumanity was shown to any of the unhappy captives. No one was unnecessarily put to the sword or wantonly wounded."

The "perfection of discipline," as Greene called the assault, brought the Americans a windfall of fifteen brass guns, hundreds of muskets, twenty-nine thousand cartridges, tents, and even band instruments, including French horns, bassoons, and clarinets. The army purchased the trove for $159,000, and the prize money was apportioned by rank among the attackers, from $79 for each private to $1,420 for Wayne. A slave auction of three black boys seized in the fort was scheduled, then postponed; instead they were taken into domestic service by Continental officers. Five captured American deserters wearing uniforms of the 71st Foot were court-martialed, convicted, and hanged at the Stony Point flagstaff on July 18. Lieutenant Colonel Johnson, the garrison commander, would be exchanged, only to be captured again two years later at Yorktown.

Washington arrived at Stony Point on July 16, a few hours after receiving Wayne's two a.m. note. Accompanied by Steuben and surrounded by exultant soldiers, His Excellency was in a strutting mood. "I congratulate Congress upon our success," he wrote John Jay that morning. "The post was gained with but very inconsiderable loss on our part." Since before dawn, the captured guns had shelled the enemy garrison at Verplanck's Point, but a planned siege of Fort Lafayette was scuttled after delays in hauling heavy cannons and entrenching tools from West Point to the east side of the Hudson. By July 18, Washington had decided to abandon Stony Point once more. "Not less than 1,500 men would be requisite for its complete defense," he told Jay; this was more than he could spare, given continued Royal Navy mastery of the river and the persistent threat to West Point.

Continental troops blew apart the defensive works and evacuated the ground on July 19 just as fifty-eight British vessels with three regiments from New York hove into view on Haverstraw Bay. Clinton again seized

Stony Point, and again rebuilt the blockhouses, parapets, and gun batteries. But he, too, would soon find the cost of holding this stretch of the
Hudson beyond his means.

Further American raids revealed the vulnerability of isolated British
outposts. The boldest occurred on August 19 when the ubiquitous Light-
Horse Harry Lee led several hundred infantrymen and dismounted
dragoons twenty miles across the Hackensack River in a three a.m.,
bayonets-only attack against the British garrison at Paulus Hook, later
known as Jersey City. At a cost of only eight casualties, Lee and his men
broke through another double abatis, crossed a drawbridge, seized two
blockhouses and a barracks, and snatched 158 enemy prisoners before
narrowly eluding British pursuers.

"I was not very well pleased at this affront," Clinton wrote, "happening
so recently after the one at Stony Point." To a friend in Quebec he described
himself as "weak and miserable." *Laver les mains*, but even Clinton could
not wash his hands of such mishaps. Lieutenant Colonel Charles Stuart,
who had just returned to New York from England, described in a letter to
his father how Stony Point discomfited the commanding general. "He told
me with tears in his eyes that he was quite an altered man," Stuart wrote,
"that he felt himself incapable of his station." Stuart continued:

> "Believe me," he said, "my dear Colonel Stuart, I envy even that
> grenadier who is passing the door, and would exchange, with joy,
> situations. . . . Let me advise you never to take command of an army.
> I know I am hated, nay, detested in this army."

In October Clinton would order Stony Point forsaken for good rather
than risk another debacle. A small rebel detachment reoccupied the site
for the rest of the war.

Hardly a major battle, Stony Point nonetheless revived American spirits badly demoralized by the Connecticut and Chesapeake depredations—
spirits in need of lifting after four years of war, after the disappointing
French intercession, and after so much spilled blood. "Revenge becomes a
virtue," a Continental major told a friend. As Washington explained to
Congress, he had felt "the necessity of doing something to satisfy the expectations of the people and reconcile them to the defensive plan we are
obliged to pursue." His successful gamble, Jay told him, "has added another laurel to your wreath."

Ambassador Gérard wrote Steuben from Philadelphia that the exploit
would "much elevate the ideas of Europe about the military qualities of the

Americans." But Dr. Rush believed that the king's men had been schooled in a broader lesson. "You have taught our enemies that bravery, humanity, and magnanimity are the national virtues of the Americans," he told Wayne in August. "Britain, I hope, will soon enjoy the heroic pleasures of dying in the last ditch."

22.

——◦——

The Valley of Bones

A new, unlikely front had opened in the war for America on June 12 when five Royal Navy ships carried 640 redcoats, mostly Scots, from Halifax into Penobscot Bay, on the coast of Maine, 180 miles northeast of Boston. Their "Most Secret" orders from General Clinton were to build a fort and a naval base to attack New England privateers, disrupt the rebel timber and fish trade, and protect shipments of white pine masts from the north woods to British shipyards. London's larger ambition was to establish an entirely new colony, a scheme endorsed by William Knox, the American Department's undersecretary, with approval from Lords North and Germain. When eventually populated by loyalist refugees, "New Ireland" would block American territorial ambitions in Canada, provide the Church of England with another toehold in North America, and give the Crown a haven in the vast bay. Fed by nearly two hundred rivers and streams, Penobscot was said by one awed mariner to be "capable of containing all the navy in the world."

Two men led the expedition. Brigadier General Francis McLean, the sixty-two-year-old governor of Nova Scotia, had fought in nineteen major battles in Europe, Canada, and the West Indies before serving for fifteen years as a major general in Portuguese service, fortifying border towns against Spanish and French interlopers. His naval counterpart aboard the sloop-of-war *Albany* was Captain Henry Mowat, another Scot, who would spend thirty of his forty-four years in the king's service in North American waters; he had conducted extensive hydrological studies of the Maine coast. Mowat's vicious obliteration of Falmouth in October 1775 had unhoused two thousand men, women, and children at the beginning of winter and made him infamous throughout America—"an outrage exceeding in barbarity & cruelty every hostile act practiced among civilized nations," in Washington's contemptuous phrase.

For weeks soldiers from the 74th and 82nd Regiments cleared a site atop the Bagaduce Peninsula, a thickly wooded promontory on the eastern shore of Penobscot Bay. Five hundred local residents soon swore an "oath of allegiance and fidelity" to the Crown; many helped the troops begin construction of Fort George, a square, palisaded earthwork with corner bastions 160 feet above the bay and half a mile from the shoreline. Three gun batteries ranged the bay's entrance and protected the anchorage in a nearby cove. Four months' worth of provisions were muscled up the steep hillside and into the rude fort—"very laborious," McLean told Clinton. Mowat's men-of-war patrolled the coast, seeking suspicious vessels carrying papers claiming both American and British registries. The Royal Navy's presence emboldened loyalist raiders to attack rebel settlements in whaleboats and cutters, burning houses and shooting cattle. Day by day, New Ireland took shape as another outpost of empire.

Patriot leaders in Boston learned of the Penobscot intrusion in late June and swiftly planned a counterstroke to recapture Maine, which was still a province of Massachusetts. State officials authorized an expedition to "captivate, kill, or destroy the enemy's whole force, both by sea and land." They also imposed a forty-day embargo on merchant shipping, allowing the recruitment of enough sailors to man a squadron led by three Continental Navy vessels pressed into state service—the thirty-two-gun frigate *Warren*, the fourteen-gun brig *Diligent*, and the twelve-gun sloop *Providence*. In warehouses along Boston's wharves, quartermasters stockpiled small arms, field guns, kegged powder, fifty thousand extra cartridges, and victuals: nine tons of flour, ten tons of salt beef, and six hundred gallons of rum. To finance the mission, speculators bought shares in the plunder that would be reaped after routing the British invaders. Wary of Continental forces stealing their glory, New England organizers declined to notify either Congress or Washington of their stratagem, "reserving for their heads all the laurels to be derived from the anticipated conquest," as an early historian would write.

No man expected more laurels than Captain Dudley Saltonstall, who on July 2 was appointed commodore of the expedition. A thickset, hazel-eyed merchant ship master during the last war, he was among five original captains commissioned in the Continental Navy at the beginning of this one. Often irascible and overbearing, Saltonstall possessed a "rude, unhappy temper," according to John Paul Jones, who had served under him aboard the *Alfred* during a raid on the Bahamas three years earlier. A more forgiving officer found him to be "a sensible, indefatigable, morose man." Saltonstall's reputation had suffered after he eased the new frigate

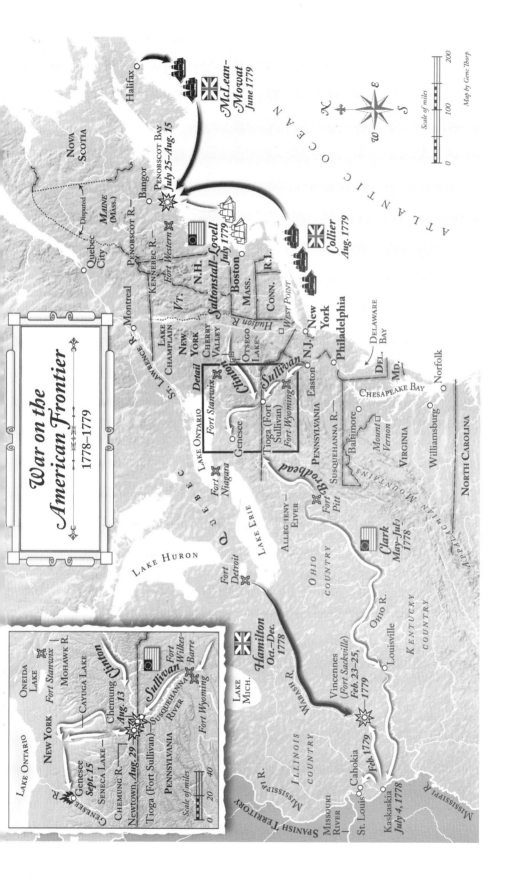

War on the
American Frontier
1778–1779

Map by Gene Thorp

Scale of miles
0   100   200

McLean–
Mowat
June 1779

Collier
Aug. 1779

Saltonstall–Lovell
July 1779

Penobscot Bay
July 25–Aug. 15

Halifax

NOVA
SCOTIA

Bangor

MAINE
(Mass.)

Penobscot R.

Fort Western

Quebec
City

Kennebec R.

Montreal

St. Lawrence R.

Lake
Champlain

VT.

N.H.

MASS.

Boston

CONN.

R.I.

West Point

New
York

N.J.

Philadelphia

Delaware
Bay

DEL.

MD.

Norfolk

Chesapeake Bay

Williamsburg

Mount
Vernon

VIRGINIA

NORTH CAROLINA

NEW
YORK

CHERRY
VALLEY

Otsego
Lake

Clinton

Sullivan

Detail

Fort Stanwix

Lake Ontario

Genesee

Tioga (Fort
Sullivan)

Fort Wyoming

Easton

PENNSYLVANIA

Susquehanna R.

Baltimore

Fort
Niagara

QUEBEC

Lake Erie

Alleg-heny
River

Broadhead

Fort
Pitt

OHIO
COUNTRY

APPALACHIAN MOUNTAINS

Fort
Detroit

LAKE HURON

Louisville

KENTUCKY
COUNTRY

OHIO R.

Hamilton
Oct.–Dec.
1778

Lake
Mich.

Wabash R.

Vincennes
(Fort Sackville)
Feb. 23–25,
1779

Clark
May–July
1778

ILLINOIS
COUNTRY

Feb. 1779

Cahokia

Louis.

St. Louis

Missouri
River

SPANISH TERRITORY

Kaskaskia
July 4, 1778

Mississippi R.

Mississippi R.

ATLANTIC OCEAN

ONEIDA
LAKE

Fort Stanwix

Mohawk R.

CAYUGA LAKE

Chemung
Aug. 13

Clinton

Fort
Wilkes-
Barre

Sullivan

NEW
YORK

Fort Western

Lake Ontario

Genesee
Sept. 15

Genesee R.

SENECA LAKE

Chemung R.

Newtown, Aug. 29

Tioga (Fort Sullivan)

PENNSYLVANIA

Susquehanna River

Fort Wyoming

Scale of miles
0   20   40

Trumbull from a shipyard down the Connecticut River only to find that she drew too much water to clear a sandbar in the river's mouth; there the ship sat for nearly three years until a more enterprising mariner figured out how to float her into Long Island Sound.

Militia forces bound for Maine would be commanded by Brigadier General Solomon Lovell, a gentleman farmer and local politician who had somehow earned a lustrous military reputation despite scant combat experience. Organizers hoped for fifteen hundred troops but enlisted fewer than a thousand, "a very inferior set of men, even for militia," according to one officer. A quarter of them, another officer reported, were "small boys and old men unfit for service." A shortage of firelocks also left some unarmed. Rounding out the expedition was Lieutenant Colonel Paul Revere with a hundred artillerymen, as well as nineteen black laborers—"to be employed on the fortifications"—and ten women with five children.

After a month of preparation, the largest American amphibious operation of the war set sail from Boston on Sunday, July 18. Thirty-nine vessels carried 344 carriage guns. The flotilla included the trio of Continental ships; the entire Massachusetts state navy, led by three fourteen-gun brigs; New Hampshire's sole warship, the twenty-gun *Hampden*; and a dozen privateers given aspirational names like *Tyrannicide* and *Vengeance*. Tucked among the men-of-war were twenty-one transports and storeships, including *Abigail*, *Hannah*, and two *Nancys*. A few other vessels joined the cavalcade as it beat north. After army and navy officers met for the first of countless conferences, Revere noted in his diary, "It was more like a meeting in the coffee house than a council of war. . . . After disputing about nothing two hours, it was broke up."

Entering Penobscot Bay at two p.m. on July 25, Saltonstall found the British alert and ready to fight, even if Fort George's walls remained so rudimentary that one defender reported he "could jump over them with a musket in each hand." With only fifty-six guns—barely a sixth the number carried by the American armada—Mowat moored his three sloops across the cove mouth; dodging the newcomers, the armed schooner *Rachel* sped south to summon help in New York. As *Abigail*, *Hannah*, and the other transports anchored half a mile inside the bay, five rebel warships stood in toward Mowat's little line, exchanging broadsides at long range until seven p.m., to small effect. When urged to press the attack, Saltonstall growled, "I am not going to risk my shipping in that damned hole."

Things went little better the next day. This time nine warships fired at Mowat's trio in a gaudy display of smoke and sound without getting close enough to draw much blood. At two-thirty p.m., two hundred American marines and artillerymen splashed onto Nautilus Island, south of the

Bagaduce Peninsula, chasing forty Royal Artillery gunners to the mainland. Revere's teams mounted two 18-pounders and a 12-pounder on high ground, but three attempts to land assault troops on the peninsula failed; during the final try a British cannonball flipped a flatbottom, drowning an American major and two privates. Puzzled by the confused rebel maneuvering and "random and irregular fires," Mowat slipped anchor to tuck his sloops closer to shore and await another attack.

That came at sunrise in swirling fog on Wednesday, July 28. At five-fifteen a.m. the privateers *Hunter* and *Sky-Rocket* opened fire with grape and solid shot on the west side of Dice Head, at the tip of the peninsula. Transports anchored just beyond musket range, and four hundred American marines and militiamen pushed ashore in small boats, braving plunging fire from redcoats atop the steep bluff. Marine Captain John Welsh fell dead, and thirty-three of his comrades would be killed or wounded. But other attackers scrambled up two crude trails and in twenty minutes reached the crest. "What a precipice we had ascended," General Lovell told his diary. "Almost perpendicular, & the men were obliged to pull themselves up by the twigs & trees." An enormous Union Jack floated above the fort ahead.

This would be the high-water mark of the American expedition. The British rear guard tumbled back into Fort George—"to my great astonishment," General McLean admitted—abandoning a three-gun battery as well as fifteen dead and eight captured. McLean prepared to strike his colors in capitulation, but General Lovell spared him the indignity. Rather than pressing the attack, the American commander ordered his men to dig in, and what might have been a swift, triumphant assault against an overmatched defender became a protracted, hapless siege.

For more than a fortnight, skirmishers traded potshots, gun crews lobbed cannonballs and mortar rounds at one another, and warships fired salvos at absurd ranges. With each passing day, the walls, abatis, and bastions at Fort George grew stouter. British fifers taunted the rebels by tootling "Yankee Doodle" from the parapet. At a war council aboard *Hazard* on August 7, thirteen senior officers voted to continue the siege; eight others, including Revere, disagreed, arguing that "should a superior fleet . . . arrive we should lose [our] whole fleet." American ordnance supplies dwindled until only a few 12-pounder powder cartridges remained and three-quarters of all small arms ammunition had been spent. Another war council on August 11 concluded that "nearly one-fourth of the army skulked out of the way." Saltonstall and Lovell bickered night and day. The ship's log aboard *Hunter* noted, "Three weeks have now elapsed since our siege began . . . in the course of which thirteen or fourteen councils of war have been held, resolving one day to attack and the next reversing their schemes."

At yet another conference, on Friday, August 13, fourteen officers again voted to hold fast. Ten others voted to evacuate Penobscot. With that, the talking shop closed down: at six p.m. the brig *Diligent* returned from a patrol with four pennants flying on her main topgallant, the signal for approaching enemy ships. As dusk settled over the sea, dozens of bone-white sails could be seen drifting through the Fox Islands, at the mouth of the bay. "British ships hove in sight," *Hunter* recorded in what would be the privateer's last log entry. "If the force should be superior, concluding to attempt an escape . . . or run the ships ashore and betake ourselves in the woods."

Upon sailing from Sandy Hook on August 3 after getting *Rachel*'s plea for assistance, Commodore Collier had been confined to his cabin aboard *Raisonnable* with such a debilitating fever that he briefly wondered if he was dying. Happily, the prospect of a sea fight against rebel infidels proved a tonic, and by the time his squadron pushed into Penobscot Bay on Saturday morning, August 14, he had recovered sufficiently to sit in a deck chair with a slight smile on his weathered face. His men-of-war included five frigates that had scourged the Chesapeake with him in May. Through a spyglass at eleven a.m. he saw rebel warships several miles ahead in a crescent formation, apparently "inclined to dispute the passage" up the bay, he recorded. "Their resolution, however, soon failed them . . . and an unexpected and ignominious flight took place." Collier ordered the signal hoisted for a general chase.

Alerted to the British approach, the Americans had begun striking their tents shortly after midnight before manhandling camp equipage and guns onto the transports. Yet the men were said to be "in an ungovernable state," with many militia melting into the woods before dawn on Saturday. In a final, pathetic conclave at midmorning, Saltonstall again polled his officers, to find them now unanimous in recommending a retreat north up the Penobscot River. When Captain Titus Salter asked Saltonstall for precise orders, he was advised that "we all must shift for ourselves."

Light airs persisted until early afternoon, becalming pursuers and pursued alike. With hawsers tied to the ships' bows, sailors in longboats, yawls, and launches put their backs into each stroke of their oars against the falling tide. Topmen rigged studding sails to catch the faintest puff. As a sea breeze at last picked up, filling Collier's sails first, Mowat's three sloops warped along the peninsula to embark McLean's light infantry before swaying into the bay. Bow chasers began to bark from nine Royal Navy pursuers. Great splashes leaped from the water around the rebel brigs, victuallers, and transports moving north, each unfurling every swatch of canvas that could be spread aloft.

At three p.m. a trio of rebel ships hauled round to the southwest in a bootless effort to escape down the bay's far shore. An hour later, chased by *Blonde* and *Galatea, Hunter* deliberately ran aground with every sail spread; fleeing sailors splashed through the shallows and into the woods, tossing a defiant musket shot or two over their shoulders as they ran. "She is a very fine ship of 18 guns," Collier wrote of his new prize, "and said to be the fastest sailing vessel in America." *Hampden*, the pride of New Hampshire and the only American ship to fire an answering salvo at the enemy that day, took several splintering shots to the hull before surrendering at five p.m. *Defence*, a new brig with sixteen 6-pounders, anchored in a shallow inlet, where her crew cracked open gunpowder kegs belowdecks, lit a fuse, and at midnight blew a hole in her keel. She settled on the bottom.

By Sunday morning the chase was well upriver, although hardly moving at more than a knot or two as the wind again faltered. "Us together with the *Virginia* and *Galatea* pursued the 21 sail of rebels & drove them before us without the return of a single shot," *Blonde*'s log recorded. "Most of them they set fire to, which obliged us to anchor." Collier, in his deck chair, found the rebel panic "highly picturesque." One by one the American vessels grounded and blossomed into flame. Fleeing sailors and militiamen clutched a few scraps of scavenged food as they straggled across the muddy banks and into the forest. In places where the river channel narrowed, the yards of larger British ships brushed tree limbs on both shores, forcing prudent captains to fall back downstream.

"To attempt to give a description of this terrible day is out of my power," Lovell wrote. "Transports on fire. Men-of-war blowing up . . . and as much confusion as can possibly be conceived." The chaos continued twenty-five miles inland near the future town of Bangor, where the Penobscot itself seemed to be in flames. Fire aboard *Black Prince* inadvertently spread to *Monmouth*. Some drifting vessels lacked boats to ferry their crews ashore. Sailors aboard *Hazard* heard pleas from two burning transports—"For God's sake, come and take us off!"—and officers in dinghies rowed from ship to blazing ship, plucking away survivors until only *Charming Sally* remained intact. Then she, too, became a pyre. A British courier traveled back to the bay with a four-word message entered in *Raisonnable*'s log: "The rebels all destroyed."

Collier scribbled a dispatch to Clinton: "We have taken, blown up, and destroyed them all, not even a single vessel escaping." The loss of twenty-one armed ships, brigs, and sloops, plus twenty-four transports and victuallers, was "not so great as the disgrace," an American officer conceded. Nearly five hundred rebels had been killed or captured at a cost to the Royal Navy of fourteen casualties, all on Mowat's sloops. Upon hearing the news in London, Walpole would write, "We have destroyed a whole navy of walnut shells."

Hundreds of survivors made their way south on foot. "Everyone was adrift in the wilderness," the historian George E. Buker would write. "There was no order, no command structure, no plan of action." Israel Trask, a crewman aboard *Black Prince*, carried away a slab of pork, a few biscuits, and a bottle of wine. "I escaped to the dense forest and traveled through the wilderness about three hundred miles," he later recorded. Revere and some of his gunners marched seventy miles to Fort Western, on the Kennebec River, where they bought a boat to sail back to Boston; he arrived on August 26, the first of the expedition's senior officers to return.

The returning refugees were greeted with anger and contempt. "A most miserable business, for which somebody ought to be hanged," the merchant Samuel A. Otis wrote General Greene. There would be no hanging, but an official investigation concluded that the expedition was, as one writer put it, "bad in conception, bad in preparation, bad in execution." Saltonstall, who was from Connecticut, became a useful scapegoat for Massachusetts officials, who concluded that "the principal reason for the failure was the want of proper spirit and energy on the part of the commodore." Court-martialed and cashiered from the Continental Navy, he eventually commanded the privateer *Minerva*, a sixteen-gun brig that preyed successfully on British shipping, including one captured cargo worth £80,000. Brigadier Lovell, who without doubt shared culpability, was exonerated by a board of inquiry, partly on the basis of his misleading, if not mendacious, testimony.

It fell harder on Revere, who was accused of "unsoldierlike behavior tending toward cowardice & disobedience." Relieved of command, he returned to his silversmithing and engraving but repeatedly demanded a court-martial, which, in 1782, finally acquitted him with honor. Massachusetts had indemnified privateer owners to encourage their participation in the expedition; now, having lost its modest navy and incurred debts exceeding £1 million, the state teetered on the edge of bankruptcy. Not for fourteen years would the national government reimburse Boston for some of its Penobscot expenses.

Commodore Collier soon sailed home, reaching Plymouth in late November after an absence from England of almost four years. He would eventually rise to the rank of vice admiral, despite feuds with Sandwich and others at the Admiralty. Collier had left his pugnacious mark on seven hundred miles of American seaboard, most recently in Maine, which remained a northern counterpart to Britain's southern foothold in Savannah. Loyalists flocked to Penobscot, some even returning from exile in Halifax and St. John. Britain would keep the outpost until 1784, when the garrison commander, after waiting in vain for someone from Massachusetts to take possession once the war had officially ended, simply burned Fort George and sailed away. New Ireland reverted to New England.

"This continent," Greene wrote Washington in the summer of 1779, "seems to be infested with enemies on every side." One challenge for America in claiming a vast frontier was the burden of defending it at every compass point against other claimants. If the British threat from the Atlantic was broad and obvious, war in the west was remote and obscure. Despite more than fifty thousand American pioneers crossing the Appalachians to settle the virgin lands beyond, London was determined to maintain sovereignty over the vast tract—roughly bounded by the Ohio and Mississippi Rivers and the Great Lakes—that the Crown had won from the French in the last war. In 1777, Germain had instructed the royal superintendent of Indian affairs at Fort Detroit, Lieutenant Governor Henry Hamilton, to mount raids with Indians and frontier loyalists, "exciting up an alarm upon the frontiers." The intent was "to divide the attention of the rebels . . . which cannot fail of weakening their main army." This, Germain added, "is the king's command."

In the subsequent two years, Hamilton, a Dublin-born former army major who became known as the "Hair-Buyer" for his alleged practice of paying for scalps, dispatched at least thirty-two war parties with hundreds of warriors as far south as Kentucky. The raids targeted isolated settlers, crops, and livestock—"the cattle came home with arrows sticking in them twelve inches," one farmer wrote—and forced pioneers to live "forted up" in crude stockades. "The Indians have done their duty perfectly," Hamilton reported in December 1777. "I cannot praise them enough." The following year he added that his warriors, exasperated at whites stealing their land, had already "brought in seventy-three prisoners alive . . . and 129 scalps." Among those captured was a frontiersman and militia officer named Daniel Boone; seized by Shawnees while on a salt-collecting expedition in February 1778, Boone was bundled off to Detroit, but eventually escaped to the South.

In 1777, Congress had planned an expedition of three thousand men to destroy the British headquarters at Detroit and secure the western frontier, but the scheme foundered on shortages of troops, money, and horses. Instead, a tall, sinewy redhead with a booming voice, a taste for strong drink, and eyes described as "black, penetrating, [and] sparkling" volunteered to help beat back imperial forces. Born near Charlottesville in 1752, George Rogers Clark had spent much of his adult life as a surveyor, hunter, and militia captain in Ohio and Kentucky. Clark had no use for the king's soldiers and even less for the king's Indians. "The same world will scarcely do for them and us," he declared. "To excel them in barbarity was and is the only way to make war upon Indians."

In December 1777, Clark had laid out a visionary plan in Williamsburg for several Virginia officials, including Jefferson and Patrick Henry, still governor at the time. By seizing the Illinois country bordering the Mississippi, he believed, he could also control the Ohio River valley, open trading routes to the Spanish in St. Louis and New Orleans, and discourage predatory Indian raids. With luck and sufficient firepower, he even hoped to march on Detroit, destroying British hegemony in what would be called the Old Northwest, much of which had been claimed by Virginia with the encouragement of land-hungry tidewater planters. Beguiled, Henry issued two sets of orders: a public directive for Clark, now commissioned a lieutenant colonel, to enlist a regiment to defend Kentucky, and private instructions, kept secret even from the Virginia assembly, to evict Britain from Illinois. The governor ordered Clark "to show humanity to such British subjects and other persons as fall in your hands," although those who stubbornly insisted on supporting the Crown "must feel the miseries of war."

In late June 1778, Clark and 179 volunteers floated down the Ohio River on flatboats, then marched overland—single file to minimize their tracks—to Kaskaskia, a vibrant trading town on the American Bottom, a crescent floodplain along the Mississippi, below the Spanish settlement at St. Louis. Surrounding the village and storming the small stockade on July 4, the intruders "in fifteen minutes had every street secured" without a shot fired, Clark reported. His news of a Franco-American alliance enchanted the residents, many of them French, who burst into song and offered welcoming bouquets. Clark sent a small contingent seventy miles north to Cahokia, where "every person appeared to be happy" and greeted the Americans as liberators. Clark also dispatched a compliant priest with a delegation to Vincennes, on the Wabash River, where the townsfolk promptly surrendered, renounced all "fidelity to George III," and swore allegiance to "the Republic of Virginia." A Union Jack flying above Fort Sackville—a trapezoidal, split-log stockade named to honor Lord Germain's ancestral family—was wrapped around a large stone and tossed into the river. Spectators shouted, "Long live the Congress!"

Lieutenant Governor Hamilton could hardly brook such disloyalty. With orders from Germain to "fill all the lower parts of the Ohio with bodies of savages . . . ready to fall upon the rebels," the Hair-Buyer marched south from Detroit. Covering six hundred miles in seventy-one days, he arrived at Vincennes on December 17 with 240 men, including 33 regulars from the 8th Foot, several militia companies, and some 70 Indians. A rebel captain with fewer than two dozen troops—the only remnant of Clark's force still holding Fort Sackville—quickly capitulated. Mutable residents again declared their allegiance to the king. Down came the Stars and Stripes; up went another Union Jack. Hamilton settled in for the winter, allowing most of his troops and Indian confederates to go home, except for the British regulars and three dozen loyal militiamen.

That proved a mistake. "Who knows what fortune will do for us?" Clark wrote Governor Henry from Kaskaskia on February 3, 1779. "Great things have been effected by a few men well-conducted." Without tents and in persistent winter rain, he then set off to the east with 130 men, half of them French volunteers. Despite "incredible difficulties far surpassing anything any of us had ever experienced," they traveled almost two hundred miles in nineteen days. Traversing icy bottomlands and wading chest-deep through rising floodwaters, they reached Vincennes with their colors flying at sunset on Tuesday, February 23.

Five minutes after evening candles were lighted, gunfire crackled outside Fort Sackville. "I heard the balls whistle [and] ordered the men to the blockhouses," Hamilton later recalled. Concealed in barns, houses, and a Catholic church, Clark's riflemen peppered the ten-foot palisade and gun embrasures through the night, dodging cannonballs fired by British gunners. Some marksmen crept to within thirty yards of the gate, taunting the garrison with catcalls and jeers. "Our troops grew warm and poured a heavy crossfire through every crack," Clark wrote. At eleven a.m. on Wednesday, the Americans sent a white-flag emissary to demand surrender; Hamilton declined "to be awed into any action unworthy of British subjects," while his regulars shouted, "God save the king!" But two hours later the lieutenant governor dispatched his own messenger to propose a three-day truce.

Clark had a dreadful answer. A small war party returning from a sortie into Kentucky blundered into town at two p.m. with whoops and celebratory gunfire, unaware of the American raiders. Clark's men raked the band with rifle fire, killing two and capturing or scattering the rest. Four trussed warriors were forced to sit in a circle a hundred yards outside Fort Sackville; while horrified defenders watched from the parapets, the doomed men sang an Ottawa death song before being hacked to death with tomahawks, one by one. The bodies were then scalped and tossed into the Wabash. Clark strolled to the gate, his hands and cheeks smeared with blood, to warn Hamilton that unless his garrison capitulated, every man inside could expect similar treatment.

At ten a.m. on Thursday, a disconsolate Hamilton wrote, "we marched out with fixed bayonets and the soldiers with their knapsacks. The colors had not been hoisted this morning that we might be spared the mortification of hauling them down." Clark's men raised their own flag, festooned British tents with the Indian scalps, renamed the stockade Fort Patrick Henry, and fired a thirteen-gun salute with the king's own cannon. Most of the garrison received parole, but Hamilton, by his own account, was "laid in irons and put into a place where the hogs had been kept." On March 8, the victors set out to travel seven hundred miles to Williamsburg, by boat and on foot, parading their captive through frontier settlements like a dancing bear.

They arrived in the Virginia capital on June 17. "On the general principle of national retaliation," as newly elected Governor Jefferson declared, Hamilton was deemed "a butcher of men, women, and children." Shackled with eighteen-pound fetters, he was consigned—"wet, jaded, and dispirited," in his description—to a dungeon cell shared with counterfeiters and deserters. Not until October 1780 would he be paroled to New York, before returning to England a year later.

Neither Clark nor any other rebel adventurer would oust the British from Detroit, and sanguinary raids by both sides continued in the outlands. But never again would Britain hold substantial territory on the Mississippi or its tributaries. A new patriot settlement built along the falls of the Ohio River was named Louisville to honor His Most Christian Majesty, the king of France, and the Illinois country beyond would remain an American dominion through the rest of the war. Major General Frederick Haldimand, the new British governor and commander in chief of Quebec, warned Lord Germain in September that the "unfortunate miscarriage of Lieutenant Governor Hamilton" jeopardized Britain's lucrative fur trade in "the Upper Country" around the Great Lakes and would have repercussions in the eastern theater of war.

"Retaining the Indians in our interest has been attended with a heavy expense," added Haldimand, a Swiss-born soldier of fortune who had joined the British Army in 1754. Britain, this year, would spend more than £25,000 on brass kettles, war paint, tobacco, blankets, gunpowder, and other gifts for the king's Indian allies in North America. Thousands also received British rations shipped up the St. Lawrence to Fort Niagara and other northern posts. Yet Haldimand doubted that loyalty could be bought forever. Despite "the amazing sums that have been expended," he told Germain, "it is much to be apprehended that our Indian allies have it in contemplation to desert us."

General Washington closely monitored developments in Georgia, on the Maine coast, and particularly in the Old Northwest, where he had long had both pecuniary and emotional interests. But no campaign preoccupied him more in 1779 than the army's push up the Susquehanna River into western New York, a punitive sally that became known as the Indian Expedition. Early in the war, Congress had encouraged Indian neutrality, addressing tribes as "brothers and friends" who should be unconcerned about "a family quarrel between us and Old England." Of the Six Nations making up the Iroquois Confederacy, who for centuries had lived between Lake Erie and the upper Hudson valley as perhaps the strongest native force on the continent, Washington had written in 1776, "We only desire that they will not fight against us."

Yet by mid-1779 neutrality was rare. Congress could not match British trade goods and other blandishments to buy Indian allegiance or complacence. White settlers continued to cut roads, clear fields, and build towns and mills. Border clashes in South Carolina had crushed the Cherokees and cowed other southern tribes. White retaliatory rage intensified after each frontier skirmish, including the infamous killing of Jane McCrea near Fort Edward in 1777. American militiamen murdered even Indian allies like White Eyes, a Delaware chief guiding a rebel expedition in November 1778, and Cornstalk, a Shawnee chief trying to negotiate a treaty when he was shot and mutilated. Franklin was later quoted as conceding that almost every war between Indians and whites was "occasioned by some injury of the latter towards the former." Pennsylvania and South Carolina offered up to $1,000 for each Indian scalp, regardless of age or gender, and many American whites shared George Rogers Clark's philosophy that the 150,000 natives east of the Mississippi should be consigned to a different world. Ezra Stiles, the Yale president, likened them in one sermon to the Canaanites of the Old Testament, who required extermination so that God's people could occupy the promised land.

The American war already had shattered the ancient Iroquois league in the promised land of New York. Four tribes—the Mohawk, Seneca, Cayuga, and Onondaga—continued to side with the British. Two others, the

Oneida and Tuscarora, mostly aligned with the Americans. Since the gory battle at Oriskany and Britain's failure to overrun Fort Stanwix two years earlier, the Mohawk region had remained violent and parlous. Raids by bloody-minded loyalists and their Iroquois allies against the New York and Pennsylvania borderlands outraged Congress; some delegates feared that army magazines in Carlisle were imperiled, and perhaps towns in New Jersey. It was claimed that Indians used dried strips of "pale skin" as currency.

Washington had first fought native tribes a quarter century earlier. He shared the present urgency of northern states to secure frontier villages and farmlands. Congress instructed him to organize a "chastisement of the savages" and appropriated $1 million for campaigns against the Iroquois and hostile tribes farther west. Given sweeping authority over strategy and tactics, His Excellency was told in mid-May 1779 to "consider yourself at liberty" to direct military operations "in such a manner as you may think expedient."

"The only certain way of preventing Indian ravages is to carry the war vigorously into their own country," Washington advised. For six months he had pondered how best to do precisely that. After first considering a winter campaign on snowshoes, he was persuaded by Greene and others that a violent blow in the summer, before the Iroquois harvested their corn, squash, and beans, would starve them into submission without requiring an American occupation force. The goal, the commander in chief told subordinates, was "to chastise and intimidate the hostile nations, to countenance & encourage the friendly ones, and to relieve our frontiers from the depredations." American troops were "to carry the war into the heart of the country of the Six Nations," he added, "destroy their next year's crops, and to do them every other mischief." Four thousand Continentals in four brigades would be led by some of the army's best generals, with much of the same artillery that had castigated the British so smartly at Monmouth.

In early July, as the Indian Expedition assembled along the Susquehanna in northeast Pennsylvania, no one could doubt that something awful had happened here a year earlier. Officers arriving at the hamlet of Wyoming—hardly more than seventy log cabins, a smokehouse, and a bakery—traveled in small groups down the riverbanks with cavalry escorts to view what a newspaper a few years earlier had deemed "the best and the pleasantest land we ever saw" but now was called the Valley of Bones. Decaying corpses, some of them badly charred, lay scattered across a two-mile stretch among ruined fields and burned homesteads. A chaplain described "a grave which contains seventy-five persons, and men's skulls which had been struck through with tomahawks." Lieutenant Colonel Henry Dearborn, a Saratoga veteran and future secretary of war, told his journal, "We found a great number of bones." A thousand pioneer families, many of them immigrants from Connecticut, had once raised grain, hemp, and flax for the Continental Army in this fertile valley; now it was largely peopled with wan widows and orphans. An army band gathered at one mass grave to play "Roslin Castle," a standard ballad at military funerals. "The devastations of war are not less conspicuous here than in any place in America," a surgeon from the 2nd New Jersey Regiment wrote.

Survivors told a lurid tale, all too familiar in the war's larger narrative. The previous July, twelve hundred Iroquois and New York loyalists—some thinly disguised as Indians—had attacked the seven scattered settlements in the Wyoming valley, each with its own modest fort. The marauders first murdered a dozen men and boys working in a field. Two stockades surrendered after being promised safe passage. But at Forty Fort—so named for the first forty Connecticut settlers in this place and midway between Fort Wyoming and Fort Wilkes-Barre—at two p.m. on July 3, 450 militiamen impetuously marched out to confront the invaders, their fifes and drums playing "St. Patrick's Day in the Morning." Unaware that they were badly outnumbered, the column blundered into an ambush. "Stand fast and the day is ours!" their commander called, but within half an hour they had been overrun. More than three hundred died, some of them tortured and most of them scalped. The rampage continued for several days, until all the palisaded forts, hundreds of houses, and every mill in the valley had been burned. Herds of sheep, swine, and horned cattle were driven off, along with human hostages. Survivors fled south and east in wagons, aboard rivercraft, or on foot in what became known as the "Great Runaway."

Atrocity stories soon spread, some invented, some true. "We deny any cruelties to have been committed at Wyoming either by whites or Indians," wrote Captain Walter Butler, a former Albany lawyer and loyalist militia officer known for brutality. "Not a man, woman, or child was hurt after the capitulation." Regardless, the season of internecine violence continued. Two months later, loyalists and Mohawk warriors led by Joseph Brant, an architect of the Oriskany slaughter, attacked German Flatts, New York, burning houses and barns and leaving more than seven hundred homeless. At Washington's direction, Continental detachments retaliated by burning Iroquois settlements, including Oquaga, described by one officer as "the finest Indian town I ever saw," with stone chimneys, glass windows, and shingled roofs. A particularly sanguinary raid hit Cherry Valley, an affluent Presbyterian village south of the Mohawk River. Indians, loyalists, and a few British officers led by Butler and Brant—who would soon receive a captain's commission from the king's government—attacked with fury on November 11. Burial parties counted thirty-three women, children, and civilian men slaughtered, along with sixteen Continental troops. Another forty were reportedly taken prisoner. "Such a shocking sight," Captain Benjamin Warren told his diary, "to see the husband mourning over his dead wife with four dead children lying by her side, mangled, scalped, and some their heads, some their legs and arms cut off."

To halt these depredations, or at least avenge them, Washington had chosen Major General John Sullivan to lead the Indian Expedition. Given yet another chance to redeem an uneven war record that stretched from Quebec to Rhode Island, Sullivan marshaled his force, amassed his supplies, and toiled over a thirty-page treatise intended "to prove the existence of a Supreme Being, the truth of the Bible, and that Jesus is the promised Messiah." A converted atheist, he now proselytized his men with scriptural justifications for unbridled retribution.

July 4, 1779, fell on a Sunday, so commemorations of the glorious Fourth were deferred until Monday. Sullivan organized a banquet for his officers on the east bank of the Susquehanna; the troops had built an eighty-foot bower of spruce and hemlock boughs, with a canvas marquee at either end. The first of thirteen toasts celebrated the spirit of 1776, followed by huzzahs for the United States, for "General Washington and the army," and for the king and queen of France. At length, as the bumpers were filled and refilled, an officer held up a pair of skulls. In unison the assembled comrades drank deeply to "civilization or death to all American savages."

Given the rare opportunity to design an offensive, Washington planned this campaign as meticulously as any during the entire war. While wintering with the main army in northern New Jersey he had gathered intelligence about roads, water routes, Iroquois villages, and other factors from scouts, trappers, missionaries, and frontiersmen. Compiling two lengthy surveys, he asked seventy-two questions, including "What number of warriors is supposed to be in the hostile tribes of the Six Nations?," "Can artillery be transported to their settlements?," and if the terrain was "hilly or level? Swampy or otherwise?"

He scrutinized lists of matériel sent to Sullivan: fifteen hundred felling axes, five hundred shovels, fifty scythes, and a thousand camp kettles, all boxed, labeled, and numbered. How many fish hooks would be needed? Quill pens? Horseshoes? In May he had ordered quartermasters to send another 3,160 pairs of coveralls, 2,100 shirts, and 2,000 pairs of spare shoes beyond the 7,400 pairs sent earlier. Commissaries were to organize a flotilla of rivercraft to transport three thousand barrels of flour and fifteen thousand gallons of rum, whiskey, and other spirits. The expedition would receive every map available, along with Oneida, Tuscarora, and Stockbridge guides. To decoy the enemy, a feigned assault on Quebec had been organized in New England with conspicuous fanfare.

Sullivan's objective in Iroquois country, Washington told him in excruciating detail, was "the total destruction and devastation of their settlements and the capture of as many prisoners of every age and sex as possible. It will be essential to ruin their crops." The intent was "terror." Drawing on his own checkered experience fighting native tribes, he advised attacking with "as much impetuosity, shouting, and noise as possible. . . . Rush on with the war whoop and fixed bayonet. Nothing will disconcert and terrify the Indians more than this."

To Washington's exasperation, the expedition dawdled near Fort Wyoming for five weeks while Sullivan demanded additional supplies. "I have not received the inkstands which I wish to have sent," he wrote, "with six good penknives." His public carping and a demand that the Board of War send a thousand additional muskets, a thousand more blankets, and another five thousand shirts drew a sharp rebuke from Philadelphia. The carping continued. Sullivan complained that a third of his salt meat was rancid, that much of his bread was moldy, and that only two hundred of the thousand promised cattle had arrived. He needed more than a thousand packhorses to advance beyond the Susquehanna, but how would he feed them? Moreover, the packsaddles were so shoddy the leather could be torn with a thumb and pinkie finger, and he lacked boatmen to man his Susquehanna bateaux, which had to be modified with rounded futtocks and keels to handle the river rapids. To John Jay he asserted, wrongly, that the enemy outnumbered him better than two to one.

"Great preparations and great exertions have been made to pave the way for your success," Greene assured him. Yet skepticism about Sullivan persisted in the high command. "He is in his usual pother," Lieutenant Colonel Hamilton observed. Behind Sullivan's back some officers derisively called him "the Duke de Sully." "I wish he may succeed better than heretofore," Greene wrote. "For although he has never met with any signal disgrace, he has not been remarkably fortunate in success."

Washington urged him to get moving. The delay "has filled me with inexpressible concern," he wrote Sullivan in early July. Surely no more than fifteen hundred foemen, Indian and white, would oppose the expedition; the Continental force would outnumber them three to one. "Hasten your operations with all possible dispatch," Washington commanded in another tart dispatch. "Disencumber yourself of every article of baggage and stores which is not necessary."

At length the tents were struck, the boats loaded, and the horses saddled. Junior officers offered a final toast, by name, to their wives and sweethearts, including Abby Wheeler, Minney Baldwin, and Phoebe Atwood. A preacher blessed the expedition with the words of Moses: "Come, go thou with us, and we will do thee good."

A single cannon shot from Fort Wyoming at noon on July 31 put the host in motion with drums, fifes, and unfurled flags. One hundred and twenty flatboats, propelled by boatmen with setting poles, carried supplies, baggage, and artillery northwest up the serpentine Susquehanna, past more charred homesteads. Within a mile of the river's east bank, on a muddy trail described as "most horridly rough," a vanguard of two dozen scouts and soldiers led three army brigades through soaring stands of black walnut and white oak, accompanied by twelve hundred packhorses and seven hundred lowing cattle in a procession that stretched for several miles. Black bears, deer, and wild turkeys ran before them in the bottomlands, and wolves howled at night from the river bluffs.

Eighty miles from Wyoming, just below the New York border, artillerymen scoured the shoreline with 6-pounders to drive away any Indian bushwhackers. Each regiment then waded waist-deep in swift water to cross to the river's west bank. Here at Tioga, on a triangular spit where the Chemung River spilled into the Susquehanna, soldiers built Fort Sullivan—a stockade and four blockhouses—and amused themselves by desecrating native graves.

The general himself led most of his force on a meandering overnight march twelve miles up a narrow Indian trace in hopes of catching the Iroquois village of Chemung asleep at dawn on August 13. Instead he found that it had been evacuated hours earlier. The Continentals burned several dozen houses and a chapel—"carefully attended it 'til consumed," one wrote—and "destroyed root and branch" forty acres of crops, including potatoes, pumpkins, and corn stalks eighteen feet high. "There is something so cruel in destroying the habitations of any people," Surgeon Jabez Campfield told his diary, "that I might say the prospect hurts my feelings."

The Indians had not gone far. Lured by stray gunshots from a distant ridge, a Continental advance guard under Brigadier General Edward Hand charged over Hog Back Hill into a single-volley ambuscade that left seven of them dead and thirteen wounded before Iroquois warriors vanished into the northern thickets. Some wounds were treated with a poultice of squirrel brains, tied on with the rodent's skin; the dead were lashed across those flimsy packsaddles and lugged back to Tioga for burial. Having failed to kill any Iroquois or take a single hostage, Sullivan wrote Washington, "I am much surprised that they did not make a greater opposition in defense of their town." Each officer was issued a quart of whiskey for his trouble—every enlisted man got half a pint—and the week's dour sermon at Fort Sullivan was drawn from Job: "O remember my life is wind. Mine eye shall see no more good."

On August 22 reinforcements arrived, as planned, in a fourth brigade. Brigadier General James Clinton, brother of the New York governor, had ascended the Mohawk with sixteen hundred men, crossed Otsego Lake, then descended the Susquehanna on more than two hundred bateaux. They were greeted by Sullivan with a thirteen-gun salute and musicians playing gaily. The expedition now numbered forty-five hundred men fit for duty. The "Succotash Campaign," as sardonic soldiers called this razing of Indian crofts, could begin in earnest, albeit two months behind schedule.

Forty villages would burn in the next three weeks as Sullivan led his army on a meandering anabasis across western New York around what would later be called the Finger Lakes. "Our march was very much impeded by the artillery & ammunition wagons," Colonel Dearborn noted in his diary on August 27. Dense woods and steep defiles reduced their progress to three miles on some days; streams swollen by thunderstorms swept away packhorses, baggage, flour, and ammunition. "In a word," a chaplain wrote, "the whole army was a perfect chaos."

Badly outnumbered and outgunned, the enemy gave battle only once. At eleven a.m. on Sunday, August 29, Continental scouts reported a long breastwork concealed by conifer branches across a hogback ridge above a bend in the Chemung River, a mile from the Indian village of Newtown. Bands of whooping warriors—"conspicuous from the quantity of paint they had on," an officer in the 11th Pennsylvania wrote—darted out of the fortification to fire wild volleys before retreating, in an obvious effort to entice an American attack. Estimating the Iroquois strength at fifteen hundred, Sullivan ordered his riflemen, field guns, and General Hand's troops to edge forward in a line of battle to fix the enemy frontally, while General Clinton and Brigadier General Enoch Poor led their brigades around the Indian left flank to block any retreat.

Sullivan overestimated his adversary's strength by a factor of two. Under the command of Lieutenant Colonel John Butler, the British Indian affairs agent in Niagara and a leader of the ruthless raid at Wyoming a year earlier, five hundred Seneca and Mohawk had joined two hundred loyalist militiamen and fifteen British regulars along the breastwork. Supported by his son Walter, Colonel Butler urged a retreat to better ground but "to no purpose," he later wrote. "The Indians were obstinately bent upon staying in the lines." That changed at one p.m., when the Continental cannonade began to batter the redoubt with round shot, grape, and even iron spikes. The defenders fell back, some galloping away in panic on their baggage horses and "leaving their kettles boiling over the fires," an American officer wrote.

Initially slowed by boggy ground, the eight flanking Continental regiments gave chase with fixed bayonets through pine and scrub oak uphill for two to three miles, sometimes fighting Indians "from tree to tree until they fled with the utmost precipitation, leaving their packs and blankets behind them," Clinton told his brother. As they ran they emitted "a most hideous yell, which resounded in the mountains." Panting in the summer heat, Continentals followed blood trails down to the Chemung, a soldier recalled, "anxious to extirpate those hell-hounds from off the face of the earth." But "fear had given them too great speed to be overtaken," Sullivan wrote Washington. A dozen bodies were found and scalped, and the next day two of the corpses were skinned from the hips down to make a macabre pair of boot leggings.

"The consequences of this affair will, I fear, be of the most serious nature," Colonel Butler wrote the British high command on August 31. For the Iroquois, the next fortnight proved grim. Sullivan's horde spent two days obliterating Newtown and burning 150 acres of what one soldier called "the best corn I ever saw." To make the expedition more nimble, Sullivan sent his heavy artillery back to Tioga, keeping only four brass 3-pounders and a howitzer. He also cut the rations for each man to a pound of flour and meat each day, advising them to live off the captured farm produce. Crossing a hemlock swamp near Seneca Lake in a "march as disagreeable as I have experienced, sometimes up to our knees in mud and mire," as Lieutenant William Barton told his diary, the troops fell on abandoned Catherine's Town so abruptly that they found corncobs roasting on the campfires. The village burned, and so did the next, and the next, and the next, notwithstanding an admonition written above one doorway: "He who destroys this house, his offspring shall suffer for it."

On September 13 Sullivan sent Lieutenant Thomas Boyd with twenty-six soldiers and an Oneida guide to scout the large Seneca village of Genesee, also known as Little Beard's Town, thirty miles south of Lake Ontario. The detachment had started back toward the main army when several hundred Indians and loyalists attacked. Eleven Continentals escaped, but Boyd and fifteen companions fought to the death with muzzle-to-muzzle ferocity. Sullivan and his column later discovered most of the bodies "in a small compass of ground," Lieutenant William McKendry noted in his journal. "They were all scalped and hacked with tomahawks." Boyd and Sergeant Michael Parker were found in abandoned Little Beard's Town—tongues ripped out, eyes gouged, intestines unspooled, noses and genitals severed, and "both of their heads cut off," McKendry recorded. "The lieutenant was all skinned, his back much bruised, his nails burnt out, and many stabs in his body. . . . Their bodies much eat by dogs." The corpses had been positioned to greet Continentals as they entered the town, a message from the Seneca that "they were not beaten and never would be," the historian Richard Berleth later concluded.

"Such is the barbarity of these savage Indians," a major in the 5th New Jersey wrote in his journal on September 14, adding, "This night we live sumptuously on beefsteak and potatoes." The next day the army razed the village and adjacent fields, using cornstalks for kindling to burn 128 houses. In a final spasm of violence before marching back into Pennsylvania, Sullivan sent incendiary columns down the shorelines of Cayuga and Seneca Lakes. "Destroyed about 1,500 peach trees, besides apple trees and other fruit trees," reported Sergeant Major George Grant of the 3rd New Jersey.

By late September the troops were back at Tioga, where they were greeted with news of Spain's entry into the war against Britain. "The evening was celebrated in our camp with much joy and gladness," a soldier wrote. Sullivan distributed an ox and five gallons of rum to the officers in each brigade. A *feu de joie* was fired "like a hallelujah," he reported, and the usual thirteen toasts raised, the last of which proclaimed, "May the enemies of America be metamorphosed into pack horses and sent on a western expedition against the Indians."

Great claims were made for the Indian Expedition's achievements. Chaplain Israel Evans assured the troops that they were "instruments in the hand of God," using fire and sword to spread the Christian gospel. "The whole country is totally destroyed for 150 miles in length and a considerable width," Colonel Israel Shreve told his wife. "The war cannot last long." Sullivan wrote Washington on September 28 that at a cost of fewer than forty Continental dead "there is not a single town left" and some 160,000 bushels of corn had been destroyed. With another two weeks of provisions, he added, he would have pressed on to Fort Niagara to overrun the British headquarters there. Washington congratulated Sullivan on his "complete and full success." Sullivan demolished the stockade at Tioga on October 3,

506 | *The Fate of the Day*

marched his army back to Wyoming, and, before the fates could again blemish his reputation, submitted his resignation from the army on grounds of ill health. Congress quickly accepted.

Subsequent estimates put the number of Iroquois killed by American troops during this fighting season at just under six hundred. A smaller expedition in western Pennsylvania, ordered by Washington, set out from Fort Pitt under Colonel Daniel Brodhead. These marauders destroyed ten additional native villages along the Allegheny River. By late September, five thousand Indian refugees from western New York and the Ohio Country had arrived at Fort Niagara; by one calculation, perhaps a thousand died of starvation, exposure, or disease in the brutal winter to come. Both the British supply system in Canada and royal relations with native tribes cracked under the strain. "Several chiefs came in lately and in council desired to know the reasons why the Great King, their Father, did not assist them in the time of their distress," Lieutenant Colonel Mason Bolton, the Niagara commander, wrote General Haldimand. "Their behavior altogether was different from what I had ever seen before." Spoliation of Iroquois lands, he added, "had been very rapidly effected by the rebels."

Yet the punitive marches failed to capture a single occupied village, and few Indian hostages were seized for negotiating leverage. "What have you to show for your exploits? Where are your prisoners?" Major Jeremiah Fogg asked in the last entry of the journal he kept during Sullivan's expedition. "The nests are destroyed, but the birds are still on the wing." Washington's failure to insist on Fort Niagara as a strategic objective left intact a stronghold and supply base for both the British and the Iroquois. The campaign, James Madison observed, "seems by its effects rather to have exasperated than to have terrified or disabled." If the Iroquois Confederacy was weakened, Indian rage only redoubled, and in February the first retaliatory raiders, wearing snowshoes, attacked the New York frontier. Oneida and Tuscarora villages were burned for collaborating with the Continentals. Within a year, by a British tally, more than two thousand warriors in fifty-nine war parties would destroy a thousand houses in New York, as well as barns and gristmills, capturing or killing three hundred whites.

Washington had hoped for a wrathful blow that made "the destruction of their settlements so final and complete as to put it out of their power to derive the smallest succor from them," as he wrote Sullivan in mid-September. Yet confrontations on the frontier would continue across the continent for the next century, and the army's violent subjugation of native tribes remained the task of white generations yet unborn. At a centennial commemoration of the Sullivan expedition in August 1879, another prominent Indian fighter, General William Tecumseh Sherman, told an assembled crowd of five thousand people, "Whenever men raise up their hands to oppose this great advancing tide of civilization, they must be swept aside—peacefully if possible, forcibly if we must."

Washington and his army had helped put that advancing tide in motion. It would remain part of His Excellency's legacy long after this war ended. "We called you Town Destroyer," a Seneca chief named Corn Planter wrote Washington in 1790. "And to this day when that name is heard, our women look behind them and turn pale, and our children cling close to the necks of their mothers."

23.

———◦———

Everything Is Now at Stake

From the moment Spain declared war in mid-June, Britain had braced for the Bourbon invasion that every Englishman knew was coming. More secret intelligence from the Continent informed King George of French and Spanish fleets converging, and of expeditionary armies assembling along the coast in Normandy and Brittany. "Great Britain and Ireland were never in such danger from foreign enemies," the Methodist divine John Wesley wrote a fellow preacher. "They are watching over us as a leopard over his prey."

Cries of "French dog!" and "French bastard!" could be heard in London streets, epithets hurled at foreign-looking tradesmen. Olive-skinned strangers arriving in English ports were challenged to "speak your damned French if you dare." One newspaper took cues from the king's belligerence in urging Britons to "fire your indignation at the thoughts of an invasion by the monsieurs of France." Yet anxiety also swept the land. "Never did a deeper political gloom overspread England," wrote Nathaniel Wraxall. "Despondency, consternation, and general dissatisfaction prevailed throughout the kingdom." An erroneous announcement during a church service that French troops were landing nearby triggered panic. Parishioners tumbled from their pews and ran squalling from the nave. "What a humiliating state is our country reduced to!" Captain John Jervis, aboard *Foudroyant*, wrote his sister.

Britain had a tradition of being unprepared for assaults on the home islands. A French threat during the Seven Years' War revealed that the forty-six guns at Pendennis Castle, intended to defend Falmouth and Cornwall Roads, were served by a master gunner who was more than ninety years old and supported by a single assistant. Perturbation now increased in southern England: a royal proclamation on July 9 ordered all horses and cattle along the coast driven inland to avoid capture. More orders went out to remove navigation buoys and beacons from the Thames, the Medway, Spithead, and Portsmouth Harbour. Lighthouses were to be extinguished, and Lord North on July 19 advised Sandwich to "employ every ship, frigate, sloop, cutter, [and] armed vessel that you can spare or hire to watch the narrow seas from the mouth of the Thames to Portsmouth." Sandwich agreed that "everything is now at stake."

A "scheme for defense of the coast," issued in August, directed all customs and excise craft to be "armed to the utmost" with swivels and deck guns. Yachts, dockyard boats, and post office packets were to be equipped under Royal Navy supervision with water casks, candles, hawsers—for towing disabled warships out of danger—and as many surgeon's mates as the Navy Board could find. All unemployed naval officers were to report for sea duty, and the king offered a twenty-shilling reward for information about any Royal Navy seaman hiding from service. Munitions workers in the Tower of London toiled even on Sundays; Walpole, after watching convoys of ammunition wagons rumble toward the coast, wrote, "Is it pleasant to know that the fate of one's country may be decided in a few weeks?" Cornish tin miners were sent to build fortifications in Plymouth, where a boom was begun across the port entrance, and trees were felled on Mount Edgcumbe to prevent enemy landing forces from staging there to attack the dockyards. North continually passed along tidbits of unconfirmed intelligence to the army high command in his barely legible scrawl, untidy with smeared ink and insertion carets. "Your army," he added, "should be in readiness to throw themselves between the Sussex coast and the capital."

That was easier commanded than effected. General Jeffrey Amherst, a capable soldier who had been appointed commander in chief of British forces for the emergency, found himself bombarded with pleas, requests, demands, and bright ideas. Exeter asked for carbines, the Isle of Wight needed cannons, Manchester wanted military kit of all sorts, and a former soldier suggested paying fifty thousand Moors to attack Spain with the aid of British artillery. Every southern port begged for combat troops, yet only twenty-one thousand regulars of all ranks could be found in England, bolstered by thirty thousand militiamen. Amherst dispatched a thin screen of dragoons to patrol the coasts of Kent and Sussex, while concentrating most forces closer to London to await developments. But hardly an armed yeoman could be found west of Plymouth; a single militia regiment defended all of Cornwall.

The king proposed "for each gentleman to mount himself and a servant properly armed with a broad sword and pistols to serve if an invasion should take place." Volunteer companies also answered the royal call, including such improbable warriors as London theater tradesmen recruited by playwright Richard Sheridan. Smugglers, said to be "accustomed to bad roads and night work," raised £1,500 and offered to form themselves into "a corps to serve His Majesty." Wesley approved a plan to "train a number of Methodists" as militiamen, and another ardent Englishman suggested raising a regiment of bankrupts. Efforts to recruit convicts from the Reading jail fell short—most preferred the security of their cells—but soon an estimated 150 militia companies with at least fifty volunteers each had formed across Britain. "Even this little quiet village is grown a camp," Walpole wrote from Strawberry Hill, his Gothic Revival estate southwest of London. "Servants are learning to fire all day long."

Alas, each hopeful bulletin seemed to be undercut by distressing news from elsewhere in the kingdom. Swansea, in Wales, reported on July 22 that "we have not a musket & bayonet in this town," adding that fifty brigands could easily incinerate the port. Two-thirds of the muskets carried by West Kent militiamen were defective. Sandwich pleaded for langrage shot to rip up enemy rigging but was told there was "none in store." After inspecting Plymouth, two generals informed the high command on July 29 that "there is no possibility of preventing an enemy in force from landing," notwithstanding the harbor boom; moreover, "if good things are expected of the artillery, we deceive ourselves." Amherst notified the Admiralty on August 24 that "the number of bays and length of coast will not admit of defenses being made to prevent an enemy from landing" on other shorelines too, particularly since "engineers are wanting everywhere. . . . The army has, at this time, only two." The nation's best hope against invaders, he wrote on September 6, might be a scorched-earth defense that turned southern England into a wasteland.

Two large camps now protected London: Coxheath, in Kent, and Warley, in Essex. The *London Chronicle* reported that the former was occupied by fifteen thousand armed men, commanded by the "flower of the nobility." Among the brightest blossoms were the Duke of Devonshire and his stylish duchess, Georgiana, who dressed *en militaire* in a tailored tunic over a tight dress while tromping ankle-deep in mud; their personal bivouac included a servants' hall, marquees with kitchens, and sleeping quarters appointed with oriental rugs and silver candlesticks. Officers fought sham battles by day—thousands of tourists came to watch—then went pheasant hunting before attending dress balls at night. At dawn on August 3, the military hive at Coxheath struck tents, loaded baggage, and marched five miles to East Malling Heath, where they pitched the tents, struck them again at five p.m., then marched back to Coxheath, reportedly "to perfect the men in the art of encamping." George visited these cantonments and others to present his hand for kissing by select officers and to be serenaded endlessly with "God Save the King." To North he voiced "thorough satisfaction at the manner in which I have been received by all ranks of people."

As captain general, His Majesty believed that the nation's destiny rested in large measure on his epauletted shoulders. The cabinet, according to a glum report from John Robinson, at the Treasury Board, was "totally disjointed. . . . All is confusion and each department blaming another." Naysayers lamented, as Walpole did on September 5, "to see England fallen so low. . . . No laws of gravitation could have thrown it so low in a century." North preferred to avert his eyes, telling his father, "I think the appearance of things not quite so threatening. They are however in a very ticklish situation."

Yet George, whose moral courage often expanded in proportion to Britain's peril, again invoked the "vigor of mind" and faith in divine providence that had saved the kingdom against the Spanish Armada in 1588. God, British fortitude, and, not least, the Royal Navy would rise to the occasion. "The officers and men of my fleet," the king declared, "will act with the ardor the times require."

For eighty years France and Spain had considered various schemes for assailing England. No sooner had the ink dried on the 1763 treaty ending the Seven Years' War than strategists had intensified planning for what Versailles now called "the Descent." An invasion blueprint drafted in 1765 that envisioned landings in Sussex followed by a march on London by sixty thousand men was pulled from the vault and dusted off, along with old sketches of the English coastline and twenty-two maps from a 1768 plan.

One French commander proposed seizing the Tower of London with a flying column to burn the armory and extract a ransom in gold and silver. But Vergennes was wary of alarming other European powers by humiliating Britain too abjectly. "While devoting our efforts to humbling England, we must carefully avoid giving any impression that we are seeking her destruction," he wrote. "She is necessary to the balance of Europe." He envisioned a day when British power might help restrain an ascendant Russia. Vergennes initially proposed a joint invasion of Ireland by thirty thousand troops—half French, half Spanish—to trigger an Irish insurrection and force London to negotiate a favorable peace. This found no favor in Madrid, where Charles III, reluctant to commit much of his weak army to a Gallic sideshow, wanted a quick war that could be won decisively in a single campaign. "Love for glory touches him," Floridablanca, the foreign minister, said of his monarch, "and he would like to make his reign worthy."

After a careful reconnaissance of fortifications in southern England, French and Spanish spies disguised as seamen reported that the defenses were weak and the garrisons undermanned at Portsmouth and adjacent Gosport. The Royal Navy now mustered ninety ships of the line world-wide, compared to sixty-three for France and fifty-eight for Spain. A united Bourbon fleet could overpower the Channel squadron, exposing English ports. A secret conference of Bourbon war planners in mid-June approved the final invasion scheme: once the combined armada routed the Royal Navy in British home waters, several hundred transports would ferry thirty thousand troops from western France to staging grounds on the Isle of Wight, ten miles south of Portsmouth. After destroying stockpiles of ship timber, grain, and flour, and capturing a British hospital with two thousand sick sailors, the invaders would cross the Solent to Gosport, bombard Portsmouth with mortars and artillery, and await the British surrender. Subsidiary raids could attack Bristol, Liverpool, and the huge depot at Cork, wreaking havoc and extracting ransom payments.

Once the English defenses collapsed, Madrid calculated, George III would trade Portsmouth for Gibraltar, which Britain had captured in 1704. Vergennes believed that the crushing blow would trigger financial panic in London, wrecking Britain's credit system, damaging the economy, and forcing George to negotiate an end to the war. Over this year and the last, France would spend more than three hundred million livres rebuilding the navy, fivefold the expenditure in 1777 and equivalent to three-quarters of the government's total annual revenue. The time had come, Vergennes declared, to snatch "the scepter of the seas which England has usurped." Now the spending, the sacrifice, and the scheming would pay off.

Charles III had insisted that his fleet return to Spanish ports by early September to avoid treacherous autumn weather in the English Channel. Yet delay upon delay put that schedule at risk. Three septuagenarians had been chosen to command the Descent, none of them celebrated for agility. Vice Admiral d'Orvilliers, who had led the French at Ushant, would command the combined fleet with his top Spanish deputy, Admiral Luis de Córdova y Córdova, now seventy-three and respected more for his piety than his seamanship. The ground forces staging in Brittany and Normandy were to be led by Lieutenant General Noël de Jourda, the Comte de Vaux, at seventy-four reputedly the oldest soldier in the French army. Vaux, who had worn a uniform since 1723, had once conquered Corsica in three months; now, hobbled by a chronic hernia, he was described by a French subordinate as "pedantic, dull, and second-rate." Apparently unconcerned,

British Home Waters

August–September 1779

Detail (inset):

SHETLAND Is.

Serapis escorting 40 British merchant ships from Denmark

PEARSON

Scarborough Castle

Serapis

7 p.m.

Bonhomme Richard

FLAMBOROUGH HEAD

JONES

10:30 p.m. Ships grappled, Serapis surrenders. Bonhomme Richard sinks, Sept. 25

Scale of miles
0   10   20

ORKNEY Is.

JONES
About
Aug. 31

HEBRIDES Is.

SCOTLAND

FIRTH OF FORTH

Leith
Edinburgh

ATLANTIC OCEAN

NORTH SEA

Bonhomme Richard defeats Serapis, Sept. 23–24, then sinks

Detail

Whitehaven

Scarborough Castle
FLAMBOROUGH HEAD

IRELAND

IRISH SEA

Liverpool   Manchester

Dublin

HUMBER R.

TEXEL ISLAND

GREAT

Oct. 3

ZUIDER ZEE

DINGLE PENINSULA

BRITAIN ENGLAND

Amsterdam

NETH.

WALES   THAMES R.   Warley
Woolwich   Essex

Cork

Swansea   Bristol

London

Coxheath

THE DOWNS

AUST.

Plymouth   Bath   Medway R.

EDDYSTONE ROCKS
Cornwall   Torbay Portsmouth
Falmouth   LIZARD
Penzance
LAND'S END
SCILLY ISLES   Aug. 11

July
4–14

Spithead
Sept. 3

SUSSEX

HARDY
Channel Fleet
Departed, June 16

NETH.

Armada recalled to Brest, Sept. 3

ATLANTIC OCEAN

Aug. 26

Aug. 31

Aug. 31

July 2

July 15–24

Le Havre   Rouen
Bayeux

CHANNEL ISLANDS   SEULLES

Paris

Two fleets briefly spot each other

USHANT ISLAND

Saint-Malo   RIVER

Army of Invasion   NORMANDY

Versailles

Aug. 6

Sept. 10

Brest

BRITTANY

Army of Invasion

FRANCE

N
W   E
S

Lorient

JONES
Departed, Aug. 14

D'ORVILLIERS/ CÓRDOVA
Bourbon fleet
French and Spanish fleets sailed
from northern Spain, July 30

BAY OF BISCAY

Scale of miles
0   100   200

Map by Gene Thorp

Louis XVI decreed from Versailles, "Your duty is to restore to the French flag the luster with which it once shone. Past misfortunes and faults must be buried out of sight."

Even as planners deliberated over the final invasion details, the Bourbon fleets were supposed to rendezvous off the northwest coast of Spain in mid-May, but Vergennes regretfully informed Madrid that d'Orvilliers had been delayed at Brest. Despite working Sundays and holidays, shipwrights were still refitting the flagship *Ville de Paris* to carry 104 guns instead of 90, the better to confront British three-deckers like *Victory*. More critically, the squadron was short four thousand sailors, forcing the admiral to draft soldiers and other landlubbers, said to include "weaklings, a great number of convalescents, and even sick men." On June 3, several weeks late, d'Orvilliers set sail across the Bay of Biscay with his advance squadron of more than forty ships; they arrived on June 10 at the Sisargas Islands, a small archipelago just west of Coruña.

Not a Spanish man-of-war could be seen. Admiral Córdova had also been plagued with difficulties: shortages of hemp, masts, and tar; rough seas at the Cádiz anchorage, in southern Spain, that delayed loading gunpowder into his holds; and such a grievous lack of experienced mariners that some officers hardly knew how to take a compass bearing. Moreover, the government was preoccupied with the assault of the British garrison at Gibraltar, which would begin in early July with a naval blockade and fourteen thousand Spanish troops digging siege trenches. When Córdova finally put to sea on June 23, ill winds along the coast of Portugal slowed progress to twenty miles a day. "At last, when we could hope to humiliate this proud rival," a French diplomat in Madrid wrote Vergennes about the British, "the elements rise up against us."

On July 23, with cannon salutes and much waving of caps and flags, the fleets converged. Now their real problems began. D'Orvilliers discovered that although French signal codes had been sent to Spain, they had not been translated, printed, or distributed to Spanish captains. Each set had to be copied by hand—"a vast writing of documents," by one account—which took a week. Having lingered off the Galician coast for a month and a half, the French ships had consumed half of their onboard provisions. Casks had grown so foul that drinking water was filtered through cloth three times to strain out the sludge. Haphazard loading in Brest meant that the fleet lacked medical stores, sufficient surgeons, and even lemons to combat scurvy. Sailors' bunks belowdecks, adjacent to pens of pigs, sheep, cows, and chickens, were alive with vermin.

Typhus and smallpox had appeared before the Spanish did, along with malaria, scurvy, and *flux intestinal*—perhaps dysentery combined with typhoid fever, which had raged in Brittany. By July 12, more than six hundred indisposed men had been removed from seven ships, including almost a hundred from *Ville de Paris* alone. Each day a frigate glided through the anchorage, taking off the sick and, soon enough, the dead. News of these difficulties reached Vergennes, who wrote, "Blackness overwhelms me. . . . Success seemed within our grasp."

On Friday, July 30, d'Orvilliers ordered all captains to make sail. The great flotilla began to beat northward: 150 vessels, including sixty-six capital ships carrying nearly five thousand guns, in a double column stretching from horizon to horizon, a force as large as *la felicissima armada*—the most fortunate fleet—which had set out for England from these very waters almost two centuries earlier.

If fearsome, the size of the force soon proved problematic, as d'Orvilliers recognized. Some lumbering Spanish ships had trouble keeping up. Men-of-war from both nations were integrated in five squadrons yet remained strangers. "We must center our hopes on bravery and firmness," d'Orvilliers wrote. "The combined fleet will be too numerous, and of too little experience to expect good maneuvering." Contrary winds beset the armada as it passed Ushant in mid-August, and resupply victuallers from Brest brought too little of everything, from food and medicines to spare anchors. Not enough pilots familiar with the English coast had been sent, provoking tart complaints from Admiral Córdova. Two-thirds of the French ships would soon run out of water. Worst of all for d'Orvilliers, his only son, a lieutenant aboard *Ville de Paris*, died in his arms, apparently of smallpox.

Broken with grief, the fleet admiral took a moment to compose a dispatch to Versailles. "The Lord took away all I had in the world," he wrote. "But he left me with the strength to finish this campaign."

Day after day, from first light to last, French sentries along the coasts of Brittany and Normandy searched the sea for the frigate that would bring Admiral d'Orvilliers's assurance that he now controlled the English Channel. Day after day, no such vessel appeared, and thirty-seven thousand impatient soldiers in what had been named the Army of Invasion consigned themselves to another hot summer night on the Continent. Fifty battalions of infantry had assembled, along with thirty-four hundred cavalrymen, five grenadier battalions, and twelve hundred artillerymen serving more than a hundred field guns. Five hundred barges and transports, laden with ammunition and provisions, bobbed at anchor in harbors and tidal estuaries, ready to carry the invaders across the Channel to the Isle of Wight to begin the Descent—but not until the Royal Navy threat had been neutralized.

Half the force encamped outside the Breton port of Saint-Malo, including some of the best troops in France, as well as young volunteers described by the French war office as "eager to be shot at." A regimental commander wrote Vergennes, "What a glorious opportunity you have given us. . . . Our children and our children's children will hold us up to execration if we fail to seize it." The author François-René de Chateaubriand, then ten years old and living in his family's turreted château in Combourg, would recall that "the tents, stacked arms, and picketed horses composed a beautiful scene, with the sea and ships, the wall, and far-off bell towers of the town."

A hundred miles to the northeast, the second encampment had sprung up between Le Havre and the ancient Norman town of Bayeux. Rows of tents stretched for miles along the Seulles River, each regiment denoted by brilliantly colored square flags with a central white cross evoking the venerated martyr Saint Denis, who was said to have carried his decapitated head in his own hands. Troops practiced embarking and disembarking and staged sham attacks for spectators, including fine ladies from Paris, who watched in comfort from reserved seats. Local aristocrats invited officers to supper in their manor houses and then to dance, if a bit awkwardly, in their knee boots. Supplies, guns, and remounts from across France poured into nearby Rouen, where workers toiled around the clock to make two million musket cartridges. General Vaux and his staff studied their maps, once again reviewing how eight thousand men shuttled from the Isle of Wight would land at Gosport and Portsea Island to bombard Portsmouth's dockyard, followed by seven thousand more storming the shingle beaches to attack the great port from the rear.

An ardent young officer wearing the uniform of a Continental Army major general was among those camped near Le Havre. "My heart yearns for the south wind that will bring Monsieur d'Orvilliers to us," the Marquis de Lafayette wrote Vergennes on August 13. "Here we are at last, on the threshold of great events." But the south wind brought only the scent of sun-scorched hay, and he, too, was left to study his maps and watch the mock battles while assuring Vergennes, "The thought of seeing England humiliated, crushed, makes me thrill with joy."

His return to France from America in late winter had been exceptionally fraught. After leaving Boston, the frigate *Alliance* had first survived a frightful storm off Newfoundland and then a plot by mutinous crewmen to kill the ship's officers and divert the vessel to Britain. An informant alerted Lafayette and others, who clapped the thirty-eight mutineers in irons before the ship safely reached Brest. Riding into Versailles to cheers in mid-February, he later recalled, "I had the honor of being consulted by all the ministers and, what was a great deal better, of being kissed by all the women." To the king, whose order he had ignored in bolting for America almost two years earlier, he wrote in late February, "The misfortune of having displeased Your Majesty produces such a deep sense of sorrow." Unmoved, Louis refused to see him and ordered Lafayette held under house arrest with Adrienne at the Hôtel de Noailles, his in-laws' magnificent palace on the rue Saint-Honoré.

That golden incarceration lasted but a week. Marie-Antoinette, who had given birth to a princess in December, asked him to ride with her in the Bois de Boulogne, a public sign of absolution. She also arranged for his purchase of a dragoon regiment for eighty thousand livres, which included a colonel's rank in the French army to complement his American commission. Louis soon invited him on hunts in the Marly Forest, and Lafayette received thunderous ovations at the opera and the Comédie-Française, where an improvised line delivered from the stage—"Behold this youthful courtier . . . his mind and soul inflamed"—drew an approving clamor from the audience. "I had left as rebel and fugitive," he wrote, "and returned in triumph as an idol."

He found a kindred spirit in the rebel idol Benjamin Franklin. Through the spring they commiserated and conspired together at Passy. "I admire much the activity of your genius," Franklin told him, "and the strong desire you have of being continually employed against our common enemy." With the French treaties ratified, Congress had decided that a single emissary to Versailles would suffice. John Adams and Arthur Lee packed up, and on March 23, Franklin, who had ordered a fine new vicuña coat for such occasions, appeared at the palace to bow three times before the king and present his credentials as the sole American plenipotentiary.

The previous day he and Lafayette had discussed a plan for the young Frenchman, in league with the intrepid John Paul Jones, to attack more British coastal towns on the Irish Sea. "Four or five thousand men, landing unexpectedly, might easily surprise and destroy or exact from them a heavy contribution, taking a part in ready money and hostages for the rest," Franklin told Lafayette. Liverpool alone would probably yield forty-eight million livres, and Bath another twelve million. As the expedition took shape in late April, Franklin wrote Captain Jones, "There is honor enough to be got for both of you."

Meanwhile, the minister plenipotentiary and Lafayette collected prints of "British cruelties," such as the burning of Esopus and Americans dying on prison ships, for a propaganda book to be published by Congress. Franklin also delivered to Versailles the latest American request for war matériel, a thirty-eight-page list that included blue uniform coats "covering the belly in cold or rainy weather," with buttons stamped "U.S.A."; five thousand light infantry caps and three thousand "narrowly brimmed" hats for wagoneers; five thousand watch coats "with large hoods"; fifty thousand goatskin knapsacks; clarinets, kettle drums, and other band instruments; five hundred dozen razors for enlisted men and a hundred dozen "best cast-steel" razors for officers; three hundred dozen flatiron candlesticks and japanned snuffers; and Indian trading goods, notably six thousand yards of purple calico, five hundred dozen silver crosses, and more than two tons of vermilion paint.

After initially approving the Irish Sea expedition, the French government abruptly insisted that it be postponed until after the assault on Portsmouth. Lafayette was ordered to join the Army of Invasion as an aide to the quartermaster general and a leader of the vanguard that would first set foot on British soil. And so he found himself in Normandy with an army poised to attack, telling Vergennes, "My blood is in fermentation." To Dr. Franklin he wrote, "We entirely depend on Mr. d'Orvilliers and his naval circumstances." Franklin sent him a sword of honor commissioned by Congress with an engraved scabbard depicting France crushing the British lion and scenes from Lafayette's battle exploits at Monmouth, Rhode Island, and on other fields. The hilt displayed his motto, *Cur non?* He vowed to plunge the blade "into the very heart of England."

But as the August days dwindled and summer slid toward a close, Lafayette and his comrades began to doubt that they would see any part of England. "Here our patience is giving out," an officer complained. "Time passes, the season advances, the officers are disgusted, the soldiers sick." Flour began to spoil, rats gnawed the tents, and horses suffered from the heat, despite sheds built as improvised stables. After two months of inaction in Brittany, an exasperated colonel wrote:

> My regiment would suffer less during a campaign. It is exhausted, divided, dilapidated, infected with scurvy, scabies, etc. All we are lacking is the plague. War itself would be less disagreeable than this.

George III was also impatient. "I sigh for an action," he wrote. The Channel fleet had put to sea in mid-June with twenty thousand men in thirty capital ships mounting twenty-five hundred guns. To the king's exasperation, a westerly gale in July had driven them all into Torbay, thirty miles east of Plymouth, without spotting the enemy. Had the "Grand Fleet," as some now called it, intercepted d'Orvilliers when he'd sailed from Brest, the French junction with the Spanish might have been thwarted. Instead, the vessels at Torbay replenished their supplies of beer and water—

collectively they consumed 150 tons daily—put sick sailors ashore, and resumed cruising toward the Isles of Scilly, southwest of Cornwall. "Over-caution is the greatest evil we can fall into," the king warned.

British naval strategy in home waters, devised by Sir Francis Drake two centuries earlier, required guarding the English Channel by stationing the main fleet to windward in the Western Approaches, a useful position for also protecting Ireland and threatening Brest. As the Admiralty received more intelligence of French invasion forces gathering near Saint-Malo and Le Havre, frigate squadrons took station in the Channel Islands and the Downs roadstead, at the edge of the North Sea, in hopes of intercepting enemy transports crossing from the Continent.

No Drake arose to command the Channel fleet. The uproar caused by the Keppel and Palliser courts-martial had so divided the navy that the government found few mariners of acceptable stature until the king finally settled on a man who had not been to sea in sixteen years. Admiral Sir Charles Hardy had served capably in the Seven Years' War, mostly as a second-in-command; since 1771 he had been governor of Greenwich Hospital, the Royal Navy's hostel for aged sailors. Affable, modest, and in poor health, Hardy had emerged from his slippered retirement to move into the fleet admiral's cabin aboard *Victory* earlier this year. One skeptical subordinate described him as "a man who never thinks beforehand and therefore is always under the confusion of a surprise when anything happens." Lord Germain commented with a smirk, "We have more reason to trust in Providence than in our admirals."

To help subdue the greatest threat to the nation since 1588, the Admiralty assigned Hardy an able deputy, Captain Richard Kempenfelt, a tall, stooped evangelical who wrote religious verse and was considered both the Royal Navy's preeminent intellectual and an expert on French naval tactics. Hardy would demonstrate unsuspected virtues, but he also displayed "the jealous obstinacy of a man unsure of himself," in the phrase of naval historian A. Temple Patterson. After serving at the fleet commander's elbow for several months, in midsummer Kempenfelt wrote the navy's comptroller, "There is a fund of good nature in the man, but not one grain of the commander in chief. . . . My God, what have your great people done by such an appointment?" Three days later Kempenfelt added, "An admiral who commands in chief should have the esteem, the respect, and the confidence of his officers. But our admiral fails in all these."

Even a Drake would have been confounded by the odds facing the Grand Fleet. Although reinforcement by the likes of *Resolution*, *Terrible*, and *Formidable* eventually gave Hardy forty-two ships of the line, upon putting to sea he was still outgunned roughly two to one by sixty-six

Bourbon vessels; having even five ships less than an opponent was widely considered fatal, given the larger fleet's ability to stretch the battle line and outflank an overmatched adversary. Several of the British vessels were also sufficiently decrepit to be classified "for summer service only," because they were unsafe in heaving winter seas. On the other hand, the Channel fleet had the advantage of experienced officers, mostly healthy crews, and seven nimble two-deckers with coppered bottoms. Bourbon captains also were vulnerable to the same fickle weather that had bedeviled the original armada, while Hardy, if necessary, could shelter in English harbors.

"I may appear strange," George wrote, "but I undoubtedly wish for the action and feel a confidence in the success that never attended any other event." At the king's insistence, new instructions to Hardy from the cabinet on July 29 confirmed that "the combined fleets of France and Spain have a design to invade the kingdom of Great Britain, or Ireland, or both" and to intercept British commercial convoys homebound from the West Indies. The fleet admiral was to straddle the Western Approaches and "not to leave your station." In a private note, Sandwich added, "I dread the thoughts of your coming into port. . . . Your enemies and mine are watching to take every advantage of us, and nothing can give them fairer ground than your coming home without having seen the enemy fled."

But another summer storm slapped the Grand Fleet eastward, and Hardy reported that for days his crews had clawed back down the Channel in an effort to at least again reach the Scilly Isles. Happier tidings arrived with reports that two vulnerable British merchant fleets had slipped into port. A Leeward Islands convoy worth £4 million came home safe on July 30, followed a week later by a convoy from Jamaica. Where the Bourbon armada had gone, no one could say.

That mystery was solved on Sunday, August 15, when a small squadron of Royal Navy reinforcements trying to reach Hardy spotted strange sails south of Penzance—first six capital ships, then eight, then suddenly more than sixty, "like a wood on the water," as a Jack Tar wrote. Narrowly escaping a stern chase, *Marlborough*'s captain scribbled a warning that the enemy fleet was "in the chops of the Channel," then sent it off with Lieutenant Sir Jacob Wheate aboard the fourteen-gun sloop *Cormorant*. Twenty hours after reaching Plymouth and setting out for London, Wheate hammered on Sandwich's door to warn that for the first time in living memory an enemy fleet controlled the English Channel.

* * *

At one p.m. on August 16, a sentinel on Maker Heights, above Plymouth, spied the armada through the offshore mists, "riding out the current at ebb tide, sails flattened to the mast in a dead calm," by one account. Panic began even before warning flags were fully hoisted, and panic grew worse when a distant rumble of cannon fire drifted over the port: the sixty-four-gun *Ardent*, mistaking the enemy for Hardy's fleet, missed a frantic recall signal from shore and sailed into the Bourbon anchorage, where she was abruptly pounded with broadsides by *Junon* and three other frigates. With five dead, eight wounded, and seawater gushing through her riddled hull, she soon struck her colors and would be taken into French service as *L'Ardent*.

"The consternation amongst all ranks here is not to be expressed," a doctor in Plymouth wrote. "Many families have already removed, and others are removing." As a French reconnaissance cutter eased to within two miles of shore, British officers argued over whether to sink vessels in the port entrance, finish the harbor boom, or prepare fireships. None of these measures was done quickly or well. Only three dozen superannuated gunners served Plymouth's two hundred guns, a parliamentary report would note, and they lacked wadding, rammers, sponges, and even musket flints. Some balls were too large for the barrels, and one officer had proposed using the British postal service to mail proper ammunition from the arsenal in Woolwich. The priceless dockyard could likely be captured in six hours, and "it would be impossible for us to fire ten shots at an enemy if it came," the garrison commander, Lieutenant General David Lindsay, advised the Admiralty shortly before pleading ill health to resign his post. Captain Paul Henry Ourry, the Plymouth port commissioner, wrote Sandwich, "I put the question to myself: shall I, Paul Ourry . . . set fire to the dockyard?" A galloper brought Sandwich's reply. "I think you rather despond too much," the first lord wrote. "I cannot think you in earnest when you talk of burning the dockyard." Sandwich also instructed the local naval commander to "give a little check to Mr. Ourry's military spirit."

"No news of Sir Charles Hardy," a Navy Board clerk wrote. "I am afraid our fate is sealed." Desolate rumors spread quickly through southern England. "It is supposed by this time [Plymouth] is reduced to ashes," the *Hampshire Chronicle* lamented. Walpole reported that the government issued frantic alarums "like a child that has set his frock on fire."

Only dimly aware of the fright he had struck along the English littoral, d'Orvilliers was preoccupied with his own difficulties. Informing Versailles in a dispatch on August 16 that he was "anchored in calm waters within sight of the tower of Plymouth," he also noted his tattered sails, his desperate shortage of water, and "this terrible epidemic which is weakening my ships." *L'Actif*'s captain this week reported 21 sailors dead and another 122 so incapacitated with "malignant fever" that the ship lacked enough healthy men at the capstan to weigh its largest anchor. Aboard *Auguste*, the enervated crew took an hour to brail the mainsail. On *Ville de Paris* alone the number of sick had swelled to three hundred, a quarter of the company, forcing d'Orvilliers to draft sailors from his frigates to keep the flagship and other depleted capital vessels in fighting trim. Unable to procure pilots familiar with this coastline, he had even tried without success to snatch men off local fishing boats.

"We are sailing as if at random, without knowledge of the dangers and currents of the coast," d'Orvilliers wrote. "The Spaniards are even more annoyed than we are." By the evening of Monday, August 16, rising winds forced him to shear off from the Plymouth anchorage for fear of being blown onto a lee shore. The armada ran west before the wind, and for the moment at least, the dockyard, port, and town would be spared.

Then, to d'Orvilliers's astonishment, the frigate *Terpsichore* brought new instructions from Versailles. Dated August 7, the orders advised the fleet admiral to forgo both the landings on the Isle of Wight and the attack at Portsmouth. The armada should instead descend on Falmouth, forty miles southwest of Plymouth, permitting General Vaux to land with much of his army from Saint-Malo and Le Havre, occupy Cornwall for the winter while supplied from Brest, then attack across southern England in the spring.

This asinine scheme, concocted by the impetuous Spanish ambassador in Versailles, had been accepted by the French government in confirmation of a courtier's observation that "our ministers have behaved like weak-minded people who never know what they want to do until the moment comes to do it." D'Orvilliers replied on August 20 that Falmouth Harbour was very small, strewn with rocks, and exposed to vicious winter winds; moreover, the British could bottle up Vaux's legions in the remote Cornwall peninsula indefinitely. Would it not be prudent for the expedition to return to Brest and try again next spring? At the moment, he added, "the condition of the navy alone—devastated by disease, without water and soon without food—makes it imperative to abandon it."

D'Orvilliers had assumed that the Channel fleet stood east of him, shielding Portsmouth. But on August 25 a passing vessel reported seeing Hardy in the Atlantic, a hundred miles west of the Scilly Isles. Summoning his senior captains to the flagship for a war council, d'Orvilliers saw a final chance to give battle on the open sea against a weaker opponent. A day later the wind shifted to come from the southwest, and on August 29 the

Royal Navy's *Cumberland* glimpsed a flotilla off Land's End—apparently a French resupply convoy looking for the armada—before losing it again in a fog bank. At dawn on August 31 the fleets at last spied each other off the Cornish coast, specks on opposite horizons. D'Orvilliers ordered a pursuit, but Hardy now had an inside track to the east and vanished in the mist, anchoring at eleven a.m. on September 1 off Eddystone Rocks, south of Plymouth.

"I shall do my utmost to draw them up Channel," Hardy wrote the Admiralty that day in a dispatch from *Victory*. The Bourbons had twenty more ships, but confronting them in narrower waters, with reinforcements and friendly ports at hand, would help balance the odds. D'Orvilliers indeed followed, his diseased squadrons straggling badly and slowed by the plodding Spanish, who were described by one contemptuous French officer as able "to overtake nothing and run away from nothing." The Admiralty urged every cutter, bumboat, and bark that could float to sail from southern harbors as fleet auxiliaries, including several unsound capital ships that gave the British forty-five ships of the line. "I think a battle is inevitable," Sandwich wrote Hardy on September 2, adding:

> I need not tell you that the eyes of all the world are upon you, and that no man in this kingdom ever had such an opportunity as yourself of serving his country. . . . Everything will go well when the day of decision comes, which I think is not far off.

But the fleet admiral had had enough. "In great want of water"—some ships were down to their bottom tier of casks—and with fevers spreading through his own crews, he swung into Spithead on Friday afternoon, September 3, and dropped anchor, bringing the confrontation to an end without the opposing fleets ever firing a shot at each other. Dejected British tars reportedly covered the figureheads on *Royal George* and *Victory* with jackets and hammocks to prevent them from witnessing what many considered a craven retreat. "O Britain!" a commentator wrote in the *Caledonian Mercury*. "Your grand fleet is chased into port and the whole island surrounded by the enemy's ships."

No one was more fretful than the king, who at midday on September 4 urged Sandwich to inspirit Hardy. "I am certain he must be eager to meet these faithless people," George wrote the first lord. "The enemy must not quit the Channel without having received hard blows." A day later Sandwich boarded *Victory* for a long conference with Hardy, even as more than eight hundred sick seamen from various ships were carried ashore to the hospital.

Hardy pledged to put back to sea as soon as possible, but Sandwich sent a glum message to the cabinet. "We have no one friend or ally to assist us," he wrote. "All those who ought to be our allies, except Portugal, act against us in supplying our enemies with the means of equipping their fleets." Lord North wrote an eight-page screed to General Amherst on square stationery, each ink-splotched page progressively more hysterical and less legible, noting that Hardy's retreat "left the west of England without any defense from the fleet." He urged "that every method is taken to move a part of the army to the western counties," then added, "The anxiety of my mind will not permit me to be silent."

In truth, the enemy no longer posed a threat to the west of England or any other part of the United Kingdom. An order dated September 3 from Sartine, the naval minister, had recalled d'Orvilliers to Brest, and even as Sandwich chivied the victualing office in Portsmouth to replenish Hardy's ships quickly, the Bourbon armada beat south past Ushant for home.

Illness was a way of life—and death—aboard ship in the age of sail. Of seventy thousand seamen in the Royal Navy this year, more than twenty-four thousand would sicken, a morbidity rate exceeding one-third. During the Seven Years' War, typhus and other diseases killed nearly half of the French mariners who sailed for Canada in 1757, and the survivors brought enough pathogens back to Brittany at the end of that year to also kill five thousand civilians. In the same bleak tradition, the ships that dropped anchor at Brest in mid-September bore eight thousand sick and dying French seamen, plus three thousand invalid Spaniards. So many corpses had been tossed overboard in English waters by the end of the voyage that residents of Cornwall and Devon supposedly would not eat fish for a month. The tally in Brest included 300 sick aboard both *Palmier* and *Destin*, 44 dead and 500 sick on *Augustus*, and, on *Ville de Paris*, 61 dead and 560 sick. Of those still alive upon reaching shore, "a great many perished in no time," a cadet from Picardy wrote. "I watched the covered wagons carrying the dead to their graves. They passed under my windows in a stream."

In the end, the Bourbon expedition had captured one Royal Navy man-of-war, a few supply vessels, and a thousand British seamen without setting foot on English soil. Sloppy and disjointed planning doomed the adventure, along with inadequate provisions, contrary winds, a lack of nautical charts, and confusion about the role of the Army of Invasion. "This is incredible," a French army commander wrote. "But then everything that has come out of Versailles for some time is incredible."

Hardy would not put to sea again until late October, and one newspaper proposed that he change his name to "Tardy." A great admiral might have exploited Bourbon weakness to win a sparkling victory; no one would confuse Hardy with the likes of Horatio Nelson, then a twenty-year-old frigate captain in the Caribbean. Yet his steadfast caution, aided by improvisation and luck, had turned away a prodigious foe and kept the Channel fleet intact to fight another day. For this achievement he received mostly scorn. "There is a special Providence for fools," Frederick the Great said of Britain's narrow escape. Walpole wrote, "Sir Charles Hardy is crowing upon what may very properly be called his own dunghill." Overworked and unsung by his countrymen, in less than a year he would be dead from an apoplectic fit.

Versailles proposed mounting another lunge at Cornwall, with fresh supplies and army troops serving as sailors on the diminished ships. But in early October a council of naval commanders rejected the plan, and General Vaux was ordered to close the camps at Le Havre and Saint-Malo, now rank with dysentery. Many senior officers returned to Paris, including Lafayette, who pestered the government to dispatch a war fleet and French troops across the Atlantic to "restore vigor to the American army." Córdova sailed for Spain in early November but left twenty capital ships to pass the winter in Brest, despite discord in the port between French and Spanish comrades. That mirrored bickering between the Bourbon regimes over responsibility for a fiasco that had cost more than one hundred million livres. Much opprobrium fell on d'Orvilliers, who was lampooned by cruel balladeers in Paris and was said by Córdova to be such a broken man that he could not sign his own letters. Still grieving for his lost son, he entered a monastery and eventually retired to Moulins, his native town in central France. It was left to Marie-Antoinette to provide the Descent's epitaph in a letter to her mother in mid-October:

> Our fleet was unable to find the English and did nothing at all. That is a wasted campaign which has cost a great deal of money. . . . The king lives with me in the most intimate way.

Across the Channel, disgruntlement quickly gave way to a resurgent swagger. Although Charles Fox, in the Commons, decried the government's "disgrace, misfortune, and calamity," a ditty from the new musical farce *Plymouth in an Uproar* proclaimed, "Let France and Spaniards vainly boast / No danger shall annoy our coast / While we've got a British Navy." The king urged "bold and manly efforts" in a counterblow, telling Sandwich, "I see the difficulties of the times. But I know nothing advantageous can be obtained without some hazard."

Lord North fairly crowed at the French retreat. "We have no reason to be dissatisfied at the event of their retiring," he wrote, "after their great preparations, their immense expenses, their boastings." In a note to Sandwich he added:

> One of the first things to be done after the departure of the combined fleets will be to send a squadron, or perhaps two, to look for Paul Jones and prevent the mischief he intends against the coasts of Great Britain and Ireland.

But where to find the mischievous Captain John Paul Jones? British intelligence had surmised during the summer that after a long hiatus in France, he was likely bound for British waters. A letter from Cork in the *Gazetteer and New Daily Advertiser* on September 13 reported him along the southern Irish shoreline. The *London Evening Post*, the same week, placed him "and his whole fleet at anchor in Bantry Bay," on the southwest tip of Ireland. Others claimed that he was carrying "combustibles" up the river Shannon to burn Limerick. Warnings from Whitehall advised northern ports to "be on your guard" against "Paul Jones, the pirate who infested the coast of Scotland last year."

This last was closer to the mark, for after sailing clockwise around Ireland and past the Hebrides, Orkneys, and Shetlands into the North Sea, on September 16 Jones and a small flotilla were advancing across the Firth of Forth, a wide estuary on the east coast of Scotland. British colors flew from their mastheads and, to further the ruse, some crewmen wore red coats or blue Royal Navy officer tunics with white facings and breeches. They were bound for Edinburgh, that haven of surgeons, goldsmiths, furriers, and philosophers on the firth's southern shore, and Leith, the city's adjacent port for the past five centuries. As concocted by Dr. Franklin and Minister Sartine after Lafayette left for Normandy, the Jones expedition was intended to divert British men-of-war from the Bourbon incursion in the south, to capture more enemy prisoners, and to spread havoc.

Jones was an eager accomplice. Since returning to France from his raid on Whitehaven and Belfast Lough aboard *Ranger* in the spring of 1778, he had spent a vexatious year trying to secure a man-of-war as large as his swashbuckling ambitions. He even complained to Louis XVI—in a letter he was persuaded not to send—of being "chained down to shameful inactivity." For the past seven months he had channeled his frustration by transforming, in the royal dockyard at Lorient, a nine-hundred-ton French merchantman formerly used for the China trade into *Bonhomme Richard*, a forty-gun frigate. If a sluggish sailor, *Richard* had certain grace notes, including giltwork, parquet decks, a spacious great cabin with drawing and dining rooms, a stern balcony with a gold balustrade, and timbers stout enough to withstand heavy blows from either the sea or enemy cannon fire. Jones painted the hull black to obscure the gun ports and outfitted her with twenty-eight 12-pounders, six 18-pounders, and six 8-pounders.

His 380 crewmen included more than a few described as "wretches picked up on the street." On board were Danish, Dutch, French, and Portuguese sailors, the latter permitted to bring along a statue of the Virgin Mary; 137 marines, mostly Irish mercenaries in French service; and a hundred or so Americans, most of them recently exchanged or escaped from British prisons and panting for revenge. Largely financed by the French government, the squadron also comprised the frigates *Alliance* and *Pallas*, the corvette *Vengeance*, a cutter, and two privateers. All subordinate captains were French mariners sworn into Continental service. "I intend," Jones told anyone who would listen, "to go in harm's way."

They had sailed from Lorient before dawn on August 14, just as the Bourbon armada appeared off Plymouth, and in the next month took seventeen prizes, notably the brig *Fortune*, carrying staves and whale oil from Newfoundland; the brigantine *Mayflower*, laden with butter and salt meat for London; and several colliers. Some were burned, some joined the squadron, and a few traveled back to France or into neutral ports with prize crews that reduced the company aboard *Richard* to 320 men. The cutter and privateers also fell away from the expedition. Jones displayed fine seamanship and a tempestuous disposition during the voyage, striking several froward subordinates "with his speaking trumpet over their heads," Midshipman Nathaniel Fanning recorded, and kicking a lieutenant who displeased him down a ladder before inviting the young officer to dine at the captain's table. "Thus it was with Jones," Fanning added, "passionate to the highest degree one minute, and the next ready to make a reconciliation." Relations were particularly fraught with Captain Pierre Landais of the *Alliance*, whose erratic, insolent behavior included twice vanishing from the formation for days on end.

Entering the Firth of Forth, Jones hoped "to teach the enemy humanity by some exemplary stroke of retaliation." Summoning his captains for a long, contentious conference, he proposed reducing Leith Harbour to ashes unless the town fathers paid £200,000 in sterling or silver plate. Brushing aside the officers' qualms at such a rash confrontation, he drafted a capitulation document for local magistrates. "I do not wish to distress the poor inhabitants," Jones wrote. "My intention is only to demand your contribution towards the reimbursements which Britain owes to much injured citizens of America."

The inhabitants were distressed anyway. Rumors of Jones's approach preceded him—"Where will the arch-pirate land?" Scots asked each other—and late on September 16 telescopes trained from the Edinburgh Castle ramparts detected the squadron near Kirkaldy, on the firth's north shore. British colors and red-coat disguises fooled no one. Drums pounded, pipes skirled, bells clanged, banks closed, and the castle portcullises slammed shut. After packing off their wives and children, tradesmen—some perhaps fortified with the rotgut liquor called Two Penny—marched to the waterfront carrying pikes, claymores, and fowling pieces. By September 17 the flotilla had edged past Inchkeith Rock with a clear view of Leith's docks, the castle on its volcanic bluff, and the stone buildings capped with wooden houses along the main street. A Presbyterian divine on the beach led his flock in prayers that "the piratical invader Paul Jones might be defeated."

That supplication was answered. As the tide turned, Jones was almost within cannon shot and preparing to send his ultimatum ashore when the wind shifted from northeast to southwest, quickly building force and capsizing a prize brig, whose crew narrowly avoided drowning. "A very severe gale of wind came on and . . . obliged us to bear away," Jones later wrote Franklin. "Therefore I gave up the project." *Bonhomme Richard* swung east and then south under short sail and pelting rain, followed by her sisters.

The cruise through the firth, if unsuccessful, further agitated Britons. On September 21 the *London Evening Post* declared Jones to be "here, there, and everywhere," and another newspaper warned that if more colliers were destroyed, "the price of coals will be enormous." Two pilots tricked by a false Union Jack into boarding *Richard* near the mouth of the Humber reported consternation in Yorkshire, with families along the coast burying their valuables willy-nilly and bolting inland. Still unaware of the Bourbon fiasco on the southern coast, Jones was eager for another sally; he proposed ransoming Newcastle upon Tyne, a coal-exporting capital, but his subordinate captains had had enough buccaneering and urged him to leave enemy waters before the Royal Navy appeared in strength.

As a compromise he ordered the flotilla to hunt for enemy merchantmen near Flamborough Head, a chalky, triangular promontory on England's northeast coast, eighty miles south of Newcastle. And there, at two-thirty p.m. on September 23, a calm, clear Thursday, he spotted the prey he had pined for: a convoy of more than forty brigantines, schooners, and other trading vessels, heavily laden with naval stores from the Baltics and now beating northeast in evident panic. Jones hoisted the signal to give chase.

In more than thirty years at sea for the Crown, Commodore Richard Pearson had sailed the world's oceans from Manila to Quebec, surviving ferocious storms, a French grapeshot wound in India, and the bad luck of having two high-ranking naval patrons die before they could secure promised commands for him. This year his fortunes seemed to improve: he was appointed captain of the *Serapis*, a fast new warship carrying forty-four guns, and then was assigned as commodore to escort the Baltic fleet across the North Sea from Denmark.

Upon approaching the Yorkshire coast on Thursday, Pearson spied a red flag atop Scarborough Castle, the signal for "enemy on our shores." A courier aboard a cutter brought warnings from a local magistrate that the freebooter Jones had been seen in these waters. At midday several frightened merchantmen in Pearson's charge rounded Flamborough Head, their topgallant sheets loosed and warning guns popping madly. By four p.m., from *Serapis*'s main deck, Pearson could make out a quartet of ships giving chase from the south, including three frigates. With a flutter of signal flags, he directed the convoy to huddle below the castle guns for protection. He then angled to intercept the approaching squadron, escorted by his sole Royal Navy consort, the twenty-gun sloop-of-war *Countess of Scarborough*. Pearson ordered his guns double-shotted, the ports triced up, and the lower sails furled on all three masts to improve visibility and lessen the risk of canvas catching fire during a fight. Powder monkeys carried cartridges from the orlop magazine to the two gun decks.

On light airs from the southwest, even with his studding sails and royals set, it took Captain Jones nearly four hours to close with the two British men-of-war cruising three miles off Flamborough Head between him and his prey. At five p.m. marine drummers tromped across *Richard*'s decks, beating to quarters. Forty-three sailors and marines scrambled onto platforms in the tops, armed with swivels, cohorns, shoulder arms, and a double allowance of grog. Gunners below loosened their carriage lashings. An hour later Jones ordered a combination of blue and yellow flags raised aloft to signal "form line of battle," instructions either missed or ignored by Captain Landais, aboard *Alliance*. The sun slid below the green hills to the west, further gentling the breeze. Twilight sifted over an indigo sea that barely whispered along the ships' hulls, and a brilliant harvest moon, two days shy of full, ascended through clouds bundled along the eastern horizon.

As the stranger flying a Union Jack approached within pistol shot of his port bow just before seven-thirty p.m., Pearson called out, "This is His Majesty's ship *Serapis*. What ship is that?" From the opposite quarterdeck a voice replied, "*Princess Royal*." Unpersuaded, Pearson bellowed, "Tell me instantly from whence you came and who you be, or I'll fire a broadside into you."

The stranger's Union Jack fluttered to the deck to be replaced in a trice by an American ensign with red, white, and blue stripes, and thirteen white stars in the canton. Almost simultaneously flame and smoke spurted from both ships, and with a shattering roar the great brawl began at point-blank range. Gun carriages lurched backward in recoil, checked by the breeching tackle as crews sponged the smoking barrels, loaded new cartridges and shot, then ran the guns out again for another volley. *Serapis* had immediate advantages, including more agile handling, greater weight of metal, and American misfortune when, during *Richard*'s second broadside, an old 18-pounder exploded, dismounting at least one other gun, killing or wounding thirty men, and forcing Jones to abandon his lower-deck battery. A *Serapis* broadside then knocked down almost half of the twenty French marines positioned on the exposed poop deck. The ghastly shrieks of men torn open added to the battle din.

Richard drew slightly ahead, allowing *Serapis* to cross her stern with a raking broadside of round shot and grape that shattered the great cabin with its gilded balcony. Iron balls tore through the length of the ship, splintering timbers and seamen alike. More broadsides followed, punching holes between wind and water; *Richard*'s carpenters tried to slow the gushing leaks with wooden plugs and tarred oakum. With a quarter of his crew dead or wounded, Jones maneuvered without success to come alongside *Serapis* to board her. But as Pearson swung sharply to port, his jib boom thrust across *Richard*'s poop and snagged the frigate's mizzen shrouds. A fluke on his starboard anchor also bit into *Richard*'s bulwark, like a barbed hook taking a fish. On Jones's command, barked from the quarterdeck, his sailors flung several dozen grappling hooks across the enemy's deck and into the rigging, lashing the vessels together in an embrace so tight—starboard to starboard, bow to stern, each ship pointing in the opposite direction—that the "muzzles of our guns touched each other's sides," Pearson later wrote. The commodore ordered his port anchor dropped in hopes of swinging clear, to no avail. As the yardarms entangled further, American marksmen shot down British tars trying to free their ship by cutting the grappling ropes. "We were on fire no less than ten or twelve times in different parts of the ship," Pearson recorded.

It was now after eight p.m. Hundreds of spectators lined the cliffs at Flamborough Head and along the beaches below, their lanterns "as thick as ever I saw lightning bugs," one sailor recalled. They gaped, slack-jawed, at molten flashes within the milky smoke that enveloped two ships "mortised together, snug as two logs in a woodpile," the naval historian Samuel Eliot Morison later wrote. With hull pressing hull and *Serapis* unable to open some of her starboard gunports, Pearson ordered them blown off with his own cannons fired from inside the gundeck. Relentless British broadsides then pummeled *Richard*, each salvo smashing holes through the frigate and shattering bulkheads. "*Richard*'s sides was shivered to pieces," an American crewman reported. To Jones "the scene was dreadful beyond the reach of language," as he would tell Franklin. *Serapis*'s 18-pounders had so hollowed out the interior of his ship that "during the last hour of combat the shot passed through both sides." A surgeon treating wounded men in the cockpit was said to be "bloody as a butcher," and his loblolly boy sanded the blood-slick deck to provide better footing. With *Richard*'s gunnery reduced to three 8-pounders firing from the quarterdeck, Jones ordered two of those cannons to rake the enemy with grape and canister while he personally aimed the third to repeatedly lash *Serapis*'s mainmast with double-headed shot.

The battle intensified with the abrupt appearance of *Alliance* around eight-thirty p.m. and again at ten to batter *Serapis* with broadsides while also hitting *Richard*, killing and wounding men on both ships, "to my utter astonishment," Jones wrote. Enraged, he would blame Captain Landais for reckless gunnery, if not purposeful malfeasance, although Landais and many of his crewmen swore in depositions that they aimed only at the British vessel, which had a bright yellow band painted around her hull. Jones hoisted three lanterns on a line from bow to stern as a recognition signal, even as an officer on a maintop platform pleaded with *Alliance*, as she drew near the second time, "I beg you will not sink us!" Among the victims of fratricidal fire on *Richard*'s forecastle was Midshipman Jonas Coran, who reportedly said with his dying breath, "*Alliance* has wounded me."

Each passing moment seemed to bring new threats. Sailors beat out fires with their jackets both belowdecks and in the tops. As water grew five feet deep in the hold, *Richard*'s master-at-arms released British prisoners at risk of drowning in the brig. Furious, Jones confronted them with a pistol and ordered them to man the three pumps still functioning. When a British boarding party appeared with cutlasses near the quarterdeck ladder, Jones and his seamen drove them back across the bulwarks to *Serapis* with pikes, firelocks, and shouted oaths. A panicky American gunner, convinced the ship was sinking, headed aft to strike the flag in surrender, until Jones knocked him unconscious with a pistol butt. And when Commodore Pearson, hopeful that the Americans were ready to capitulate, called out above the tumult, "Do you ask for quarter?," Jones scoffed. Various versions of his defiant reply would be attributed to him, including, almost half a century later, the exhilarating "I have not yet begun to fight." A week after the battle, Jones wrote Franklin only that he "answered him in the most determined negative." He later told Louis XVI that he had shouted, "I do not dream of surrendering, but I am determined to make you strike."

This he did, for at ten-fifteen p.m. fortune suddenly pivoted to favor the Americans. Sniping from *Richard*'s tops had driven most of *Serapis*'s sailors from her spars and weather deck when a seaman named William Hamilton, clutching a leather bucket of grenades and a live match, edged along a yardarm until he was directly above the British ship. Igniting the grenades one after another, he tossed them to the deck below and through an open hatch. A muffled detonation within *Serapis* was succeeded by several stupendous blasts: powder cartridges on the gun deck exploded, tossing heavy cannons from their carriages. Flames licked the inside of the gun deck, incinerating at least twenty men and chasing others through the ports and into the sea with their hair on fire and their lungs seared.

The British knew when they were beaten. The *Countess of Scarborough* had already surrendered to *Pallas*, after a two-hour pummeling that shredded her rigging, braces, and sails and dismounted seven guns. With his mainmast tottering, Commodore Pearson climbed to the taffrail and ripped the shredded red ensign from its staff. "Sir, I have struck," he called through his speaking trumpet. "I ask for quarter."

An American officer escorted him across the bulwarks to Captain Jones just before *Serapis*'s mainmast toppled over the side with a fearful crack, taking the mizzen topmast with it. As exhausted sailors with axes chopped at the tangled mass of rigging, spars, and grappling ropes to free the two ships from each other, Pearson surrendered his sword. His uniform stained with black powder, Jones invited him into the wreckage that had once been the great cabin. The two captains stood amid shattered glass and splintered wainscoting to share a glass of wine. When Pearson asked the nationality of *Richard*'s crew, Jones reportedly answered that many were American. "Very well," the commodore said. "It has been diamond cut diamond."

The diamonds had cut deep. Almost half of both crews were dead or injured—nearly three hundred casualties combined. Some burn victims aboard *Serapis* were found wearing "only the collars of their shirts" and were "burnt in such a shocking manner that the flesh of several of them dropped off from their bones and they died in great pain," Midshipman Fanning wrote. Others, he added, "had their legs or arms shot away, or the bones so badly fractured that they were obliged to suffer . . . amputation." Splash followed splash as the dead were committed to the sea.

Richard also was mortally hurt. Not until Friday morning were the last fires extinguished, including a blaze that came "within a few inches" of the powder magazine, Jones recorded. The rudder was all but blown away, along with the stern frame and transom. "The leak still gaining on us," an officer scribbled in the ship's log early Saturday, despite pumps, bailing buckets, and cannons tossed overboard to lighten the vessel. By nine a.m., water had reached the lower deck and Jones ordered all salvage crews evacuated, conceding "that it was impossible to prevent the good old ship from sinking. . . . A little after ten I saw with inexpressible grief the last glimpse of the *Bonhomme Richard*." Bow first she sank, colors still flying.

Serapis could still swim, and by one a.m. on Tuesday, September 28, with Jones now in command, the holes had been plugged and a mainmast jury-rigged. The battered squadron crept through squally weather across the North Sea, more than five hundred prisoners locked belowdecks, including some taken earlier in the cruise. Alerted in Spithead by the fleeing Baltic convoy, four Royal Navy frigates led by *Prudent*, a sixty-four-gun ship of the line, arrived off Flamborough Head to hunt down Captain Jones. He had hoped to reach the French port at Dunkirk, but his subordinate officers insisted on steering for the Dutch anchorage at Texel Island, more than a hundred miles closer. There they arrived on October 3; Jones, ever impatient, continued sixty miles up the shallow bay of the Zuiderzee to Amsterdam.

Although ostensibly neutral, Holland appreciated a naval hero and enjoyed tweaking the British, who, upon learning that Jones had eluded them again, demanded his arrest. Instead the Dutch were "overjoyed and mad to see the vanquisher of the English," reported a witness, who added, "They applaud him and bow down to his feet." Street balladeers sang his praises.

An American officer who carried Jones's dispatch to Passy informed him on October 9 that officials in France appeared "enchanted with your exploits. . . . Your combat of the 23rd places you in the rank of the greatest men, and immortalizes you." A week later Franklin sent Jones his own encomium. "Scarce anything was talked of at Paris and Versailles," he wrote, "but your cool conduct and persevering bravery."

London insisted that the tactical defeat at Flamborough Head was a strategic victory since the Baltic fleet had escaped. A court-martial eventually acquitted Captain Pearson of blame, and the king knighted him, leading Jones to quip, "Let me fight him again and I'll make him a lord." In the British imagination, the *Morning Post* admitted in October, "Paul Jones resembles a jack o' lantern to mislead our marines and terrify our coast. He is no sooner seen than lost." To recognize "the terror of the English," should he reappear in home waters, the *London Chronicle* advised readers that he wore "a Scotch bonnet edged with gold, is of middling stature, stern countenance, and swarthy complexion."

A British blockade of forty-two vessels, by Jones's count, kept him marooned in Holland for three months. But during a Christmas gale he snuck undetected into the North Sea aboard *Alliance* after relieving Captain Landais, that "malignant madman," of command. The frigate eluded the fleet at Spithead—"I had the pleasure of laughing at their expense," Jones wrote a friend—and, after an interim stop in northern Spain, reached Brittany unharmed. In Paris, Jones boasted, he was "feasted and caressed by all the world"—lionized by great men, pursued by beautiful women, and applauded in the street. A new ballet included a dancer dressed as *le capitaine Paul-Jones*. Marie-Antoinette invited him to escort her to the theater, and the king welcomed him to Versailles, presenting *Le Capitaine* with a gold-hilted sword and *l'Ordre du Mérite Militaire*.

A small, remote sea battle in a large war had become emblematic of indomitable American pluck. Jones would eventually cross the Atlantic westbound in the sixteen-gun *Ariel*, surviving an awful tempest, gunplay with a British privateer, and a mutiny before reaching Philadelphia and a triumphant homecoming. Congress later gave him command of *America*, a seventy-four-gun ship of the line under construction in New Hampshire, but she would not be finished until the war was all but over. He had fought his last battle under the Stars and Stripes.

Serapis, described by Jones as "the best ship I ever saw of the kind," was purchased by the French government and converted into a privateer for service in the Indian Ocean, where she was destroyed in an accidental fire near Madagascar. Not until 1848 would Congress resolve various disputes to pay $166,000 in prize money to descendants of the *Bonhomme Richard*'s crew, according to biographer Evan Thomas.

As for Jones, his hour done, he was fated to die not in a desperate battle on the high seas but in bed during a return to Paris, felled in 1792 by jaundice, nephritis, and bronchial pneumonia at age forty-five. He had once tried in verse to explain his turbulent, agonistic life, and unwittingly wrote his own epitaph:

> *Insulted freedom bled. I felt her cause*
> *And drew my sword to vindicate her laws.*
> *From principles, and not from vain applause*
> *I've done my best.*

24.

———◆———

The Greatest Event That Has Happened

At an unexpected moment in an unexpected place, forty-two French warships flying Bourbon fleurs-de-lis banners from their masts appeared off the Savannah River. In a quick sequence of bellicose splashes, they dropped anchor on September 8 and made ready to evict Britain from Georgia. Admiral d'Estaing—his jaw set and his eyes aglint aboard the flagship *Languedoc*—had returned to America.

Still seething over his failures at New York and Newport the previous summer, and at St. Lucia in December, d'Estaing was determined to make amends, exact revenge, and deliver a crushing blow to Britain before the month was over. Within hours after arriving on the coast, a French detachment prepared to cross the bar near Tybee Island into the river's mouth. They would escort longboats carrying seven hundred assault troops in crossbelts and tricorn hats as the vanguard of a larger force. D'Estaing intended to lead the attack on Savannah himself, confident that he could quickly wrest the town back from the British.

After eight convulsive months in the West Indies, in late June the admiral had received instructions from Versailles to return to Europe. But before sailing home he decided to head northwest from Cap-Haïtien on August 15, heeding pleas from Congress, from his erstwhile American comrades, and from French officials in Philadelphia to first divert to Georgia. Even Washington, usually fixated on New York, had endorsed a strike at Savannah as "promising more certain success" and "an object of the greatest magnitude."

"I would certainly have been declared a coward had I not attacked Savannah," d'Estaing later wrote. For the moment, his strength far exceeded anything Britain could assemble on the southern coast: he commanded twenty-two ships of the line, including *Fantasque*, *Robuste*, and *Hector*, as well as ten frigates, plus sundry schooners, cutters, transports, and barges.

The fleet carried four thousand troops, among them white volunteers from Guadeloupe, Martinique, and Haiti, and six hundred *Chasseurs Volontaires*, mostly free, property-owning men of color serving under white officers, except for a black colonel in command, Laurent-François Lenoir, the Marquis de Rouvray. Fleet officers included accomplished French men of letters—astronomers, inventors, hydrographers, and explorers. Among the most notable was the captain of the seventy-four-gun *Guerrier*, Louis-Antonine de Bougainville, famed for a treatise on integral calculus and as the author of *A Voyage Round the World*, an account of his three-year circumnavigation, the first by a French naval officer, during which he lent his name to a brilliant tropical flower.

Regardless of his strength, d'Estaing knew how fickle the gods of war could be. A storm a week earlier had damaged the rudders on seven ships, including *Languedoc*. Others had lost anchors or had their rigging shredded; three vessels were sent to Charleston to buy timber, cordage, and other matériel needed for repairs. His crews were also suffering. Many sailors had not been ashore since leaving Toulon seventeen months earlier, the better to thwart desertion. Scurvy was again pernicious, despite chaplains staging solemn processions across the deck in solicitation of good health. One officer, upon viewing men in a sick bay, noted "the marks of death painted on their faces." Provisions were mostly limited to salt meat and two-year-old bread so wormy that even the domestic animals penned below refused to eat it.

In a dispatch carried by d'Estaing's adjutant to Charleston, the admiral urged Continental Army and militia troops to march the hundred miles to Savannah as quickly as possible and then join him in encircling the British garrison; with hurricane season arriving, he intended to loiter along the coast for no more than a week. Speed and surprise were critical, although the admiral was vexed to learn that his arrival in Georgia had been reported in local newspapers. "The American gazettes are a terrible thing," he wrote. "As untruthful as the English papers, they are more impudent."

On Thursday, September 9, d'Estaing clambered onto the thirty-two-gun *Chimère* and with three other frigates glided easily across the bar into the Savannah River. Several British men-of-war—*Rose, Fowey, Germain*, and the galley *Comet*—threw a few cannonballs before quickly moving ten miles upriver on the tide, to Five Fathom Hole, an anchorage just below the town. A single British howitzer and a 24-pounder emplaced near the hundred-foot brick lighthouse on Tybee Island also fired several volleys, then fell silent. That evening d'Estaing transferred to a cutter with fifteen heavily armed comrades and went ashore. They found enemy works on the island abandoned and in flames.

After more French troops landed, the admiral returned to his cabin on *Languedoc* to finish planning the investment of Savannah, the next step in winning back Georgia. With a beachhead now on Tybee, men-of-war would press upriver to threaten the capital from the southeast while d'Estaing looped down the coast with twelve hundred men to land at Beaulieu, attacking from the south—ideally with the Americans arriving to share the glory. Naval subordinates remained wary of what they called this *"pousse-cailloux"*: a pebble-pushing foot soldier dressed up in an admiral's uniform. But all agreed that d'Estaing seemed a man possessed, "working night and day," an officer wrote, "sleeping only an hour after dinner, his head resting upon his hands, [or] sometimes lying down but without undressing."

Perhaps his luck was changing. After the calamity at St. Lucia, which had cost fifteen hundred French casualties, spring and summer in the Caribbean had favored France. D'Estaing's fleet at Martinique was reinforced three times, giving him a small but distinct advantage of twenty-five capital ships over the twenty-one under Foul-Weather Jack Byron, whose crews were plagued with sickness and dodgy provisioning. "The convoy has arrived," d'Estaing told Versailles after the third reinforcing squadron appeared in June. "These four words tell everything." With scarcely a shot fired, French forces that month captured St. Vincent, fifty miles south of St. Lucia. The small British garrison was said to have fewer than twenty barrels of gunpowder on the island.

D'Estaing then fixed his sights on Grenada, another eighty miles southwest and second only to Jamaica among British sugar producers. On July 2 he anchored with his entire fleet off the lower tip of the island, capturing a Royal Navy sloop and thirty rich merchantmen. Sword in hand and costumed in a scarlet uniform, the admiral led two thousand invaders ashore through thickets of giant ferns, shouting, *"Soldats en avant, suivez-moi!"* Forward, soldiers, follow me! Tropical birds rose in flapping, polychromatic clouds as French warships bombarded British defenses. Four hundred and sixty defenders, mostly luckless militia, surrendered the next day.

Alerted to this French insult but misinformed about the size of d'Estaing's host, Admiral Byron appeared close inshore at dawn on July 6 aboard the seventy-four-gun *Prince of Wales*, accompanied by his war fleet and more than two dozen troop and horse transports, victuallers, hospital ships, and ordnance vessels. As the French van sortied from St. George's harbor, Byron signaled "general chase" and then "engage" before belatedly realizing that he was outnumbered. The consequent melee started badly for the disorganized British. At seven a.m., *Prince of Wales, Boyne,* and *Sultan* were battered by the French line. Behind them the morning went even worse for *Cornwall, Grafton, Lion,* and *Fame*; all four soon dropped to leeward, crippled and adrift after being shot to splinters. Byron pulled away at noon to protect his transports, and d'Estaing, triumphant despite heavy casualties, soon swung back into the harbor of the island he now owned.

By one count, *Prince of Wales* had ninety-five holes in her hull, thoroughly perforated by some of the twenty thousand French cannonballs fired that day. *Monmouth* was dismasted. *Lion* lost both main and mizzen topmasts, with four shots in the bowsprit, her sails and rigging also rent. Half a dozen other capital ships sustained severe damage, particularly in the loss of "motive power"—spars and sails. Across the fleet, 183 men were dead and twice that number wounded. The Battle of Grenada, the naval historian Sam Willis would write, sounded "the death knell of British sea power in the Caribbean for 1779 [and] was the worst British naval defeat in ninety years." It was rumored that d'Estaing now sought pilots familiar with the reefs around Jamaica; Captain Horatio Nelson, then in charge of bolstering the island's defenses, speculated in a letter home that he soon might have to learn French. The six British regiments that were supposed to return to General Clinton in New York would remain in the Caribbean because, as General Grant wrote Germain in mid-July, "the islands must fall if they are not defended by strong garrisons." Byron limped to St. Kitts, where the fleet could undergo repairs; from there, he sailed home to England in ill health, his career at sea finished. "How different from the last war," a Royal Navy officer wrote, "when we were only accustomed to hear of victory."

Despite winning the day in Grenada, d'Estaing came in for caustic criticism. "Had our admiral's seamanship equaled his courage," a French captain complained, "we would not have allowed four dismasted ships to escape." British transports and storeships also got away. French casualties approached a thousand men killed and wounded. French shipping losses included most of the eleven vessels in an unlucky merchant convoy belonging to the front company Roderigue Hortalez & Cie, snapped up by nearby British cruisers at a cost to Monsieur Beaumarchais of two million livres.

Yet Britain had lost the richest island in the Lesser Antilles, causing d'Estaing to boast that George III would not have enough sugar "to sweeten his tea for breakfast by Christmas." British ports from Halifax to St. Augustine seemed vulnerable. When the news reached Versailles, Louis XVI ordered a *Te Deum* to give thanks for the victory; trophies taken from the

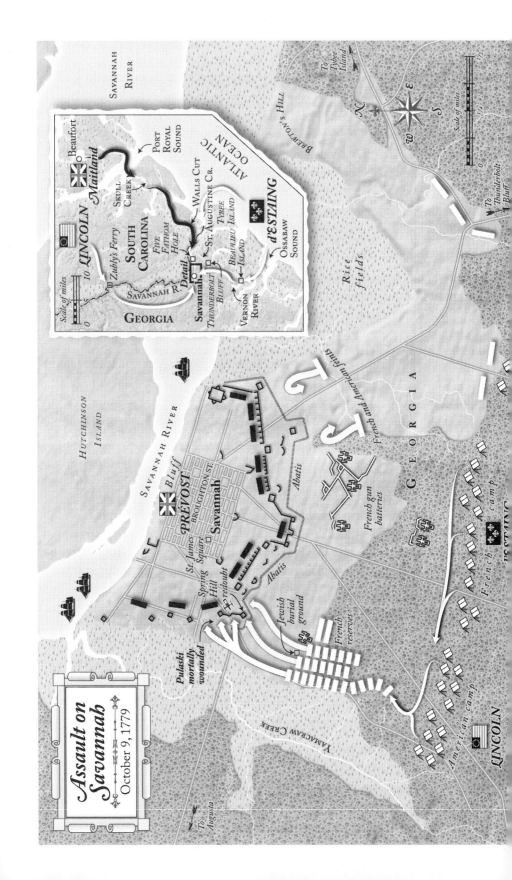

Assault on Savannah
October 9, 1779

Inset map:

Beaufort

LINCOLN
Maitland

SOUTH CAROLINA

Port Royal Sound

Skull Creek

Walls Cut

Five Fathom Hole

Zubly's Ferry

Savannah R.

GEORGIA

Detail

Savannah

St. Augustine Cr.

Thunderbolt Bluff

Tybee Island

Beaulieu Island

Vernon River

Ossabaw Sound

ATLANTIC OCEAN

d'ESTAING

Scale of miles 0 10

Brewton's Hill

To Tybee Island

Scale of miles

Main map:

SAVANNAH RIVER

HUTCHINSON ISLAND

SAVANNAH RIVER

Bluff

PREVOST

BROUGHTON ST.

Savannah

St. James Square

Spring Hill

Redoubt

Abatis

Abatis

Jewish burial ground

Pulaski mortally wounded

French reserves

French gun batteries

French and American feints

GEORGIA

YAMACRAW CREEK

To Augusta

French camp

d'ESTAING

American camp

LINCOLN

To Thunderbolt Bluff

To Tybee Island

Scale of miles

enemy were to be carried in a solemn procession and placed for public viewing at Les Invalides. Parisian hairdressers created two celebratory ladies' coiffures, one known as *Grenada*, featuring pomegranates and bright flowers, and another called *l'Amiral*, to honor d'Estaing personally. A miniature ship in full sail perched atop piled tresses, much like the *coiffure Belle Poule* a year earlier. Now it only remained for a final victory at Savannah to fully redeem *l'Amiral*'s reputation, repair strained Franco-American relations, and demolish the British southern strategy that was intended to tame the rebellion.

Warnings of the French arrival on the Georgia coast first reached Savannah in a frantic signal from atop the Tybee lighthouse before the shore guns there were spiked and the fortifications burned. The Royal Navy squadron retreating up the river brought further confirmation, along with navigation aids plucked from the channel to slow enemy pursuit. Little had been done to strengthen the capital's fortifications since its easy capture in December by the now-departed Lieutenant Colonel Campbell. Barely five hundred regulars manned a two-mile defensive line along the river bluff; recollecting how Savannah had been pillaged by redcoats and Hessians, the anxious defenders—and the four hundred women and children in the town—discussed in hushed tones whether the French were likely to put the garrison to the sword in retaliation. "We will defend ourselves as long as we can," the British commander, Brigadier General Prévost—Old Bullet Head—wrote in pleas for help sent to St. Augustine and New York. "If we are abandoned, it will be much the worse."

In his headquarters on Broughton Street, Prévost tried to make amends for eight months of indolence. Messengers hurried in and out, troops marched this way and that, and wagons carried black laborers with picks and shovels to the defensive lines, where they quickly expanded four earthen redoubts to fourteen, with breastworks, ditches, an abatis, and palisaded ramparts built under the direction of Captain James Moncrieff, a talented engineer. Some were slaves belonging to Governor James Wright, who had returned from London in July to reoccupy the official residence on St. James Square, if not all of his eleven plantations confiscated by the rebels. An estimated fifteen hundred of the enslaved had escaped bondage from rebel masters across Georgia this year, but runaways reclaimed by loyalists like Wright were still considered slaves who could be rented to the king's army. The British payroll in Savannah now listed 620 blacks, many of them newly liberated and earning a daily wage.

Blacks and whites alike burned buildings on the outskirts of town for better fields of fire. The overseer's house, a barn, and other structures from Wright's closest plantation were pulled down for bricks and planks to build platforms in fifteen batteries capable of mounting seventy-six cannons. Many of those guns were transferred from *Fowey, Rose, Crawford,* and other men-of-war. Sails became tents, cordage was made into gun wadding, and naval gunners came ashore as terrestrial artillerymen. Royal Navy marines joined redcoat grenadiers as soldiers in the 60th Foot.

There was not a moment to lose. A large American column from Charleston had crossed into Georgia at Zubly's Ferry, less than twenty miles north of Savannah. Shallow-draft French warships, eventually joined by American galleys, continued to press upriver from Tybee Island. D'Estaing and half a dozen ships had successfully sailed across Ossabaw Sound and up the Vernon River to Beaulieu, thirteen miles below Savannah, threatening the city's underbelly. By Wednesday, September 15, the admiral and 150 grenadiers appeared within a mile of the outer fortifications. Two thousand combat troops followed close behind.

On Thursday morning a French courier carrying a white flag rode to the British lines and delivered an ultimatum: "Count d'Estaing summons His Excellency General Prévost to surrender to the arms of the king of France"—*aux armes de Sa Majesté le Roi de France.* Prévost convened his anxious staff officers, then sent a reply asking for time to consult Governor Wright and requesting the precise conditions for capitulation, since "according to the rules of war the besieged & not the besiegers were to propose terms," as a British officer wrote.

At noon, as if by heavenly intercession, the vanguard of eight hundred mud-spattered reinforcements trudged up the river bluff, mostly Highlanders from the 71st Regiment with trademark red feathers in their caps. They were led by Lieutenant Colonel John Maitland, an earl's son who had lost his right arm to a French cannonball twenty years earlier. Maitland had proved his value in Georgia the previous spring by helping to ambush rebels at Brier Creek below Augusta; in fifteen minutes his troops had killed or wounded 150 and captured more than 200. Now he and his men had been summoned by Prévost from an outpost at Beaufort, thirty-five miles northeast on the South Carolina coast.

French and American commanders would later trade accusations over who had failed to keep Maitland bottled up in his isolated post. Regardless, the garrison had slipped across Port Royal Sound on a schooner, two galleys, canoes, and other small craft, then rowed down Skull Creek and, with guidance from two Gullah fishermen, through Walls Cut, an obscure tidal waterway reportedly known only to "bears, wolves, and runaway Negroes."

Dragging their boats through waist-deep sloughs, with the topgallants of French frigates visible in the distance, they edged past alligators basking on the banks to reach the Savannah River three miles from town. "Their arrival," Wright wrote, "brought inexpressible joy."

The garrison now included 2,360 defenders fit for duty, slightly more than half of them regulars and the rest sailors, loyalist militia, armed blacks, and Indians. Prévost sent a second note to d'Estaing, requesting a truce until Friday evening to further study the French surrender demand. "We asked twenty-four hours to consider," a British officer later wrote his family, "we having nothing in view but to steal time till we could be reinforced." D'Estaing, in a beneficent mood, readily agreed. When subordinates pointed out that the enemy was certainly entrenching if not growing stronger, he replied, "It is a matter of very little importance to me."

The admiral could afford to be nonchalant. Almost at the same hour that Maitland's brigade joined the defenders on Thursday, two thousand American reinforcements arrived to seal the cordon around the town and give d'Estaing nearly six thousand men in his siege force. The Americans had marched from Charleston into Georgia with rollicking high spirits in a column that included baggage and ammunition wagons, a few field guns, six understrength Continental regiments, and rebel militiamen armed with what one colonel described as "a medley of rifles, old muskets, & fowling pieces." Some carried only dry moss for ammunition wadding. South Carolina's social elite dominated the officer corps, including Lieutenant Colonel John Laurens, seconded from Washington's staff to bolster the southern front, and Brigadier General Andrew Williamson, a prominent planter whose entourage included three nephews and three sons-in-law. The march had fallen hard on loyalists along the route; their houses were pillaged, their horses and bondmen confiscated.

Leading this horde was the squat, rotund Major General Benjamin Lincoln, in his first field command since being shot in the right ankle at Saratoga two years earlier. Temperate, cautious, and pious, given to daily prayer and unsettled by profanity, Lincoln walked with a pronounced limp from a wound that continued to shed bone splinters. "I wish the Congress had fixed their minds on some other officer," he had told Washington after his appointment as commander of the Continental Army's Southern Department. A former Massachusetts farmer and maltster, Lincoln found southern politics as baffling as Congress's apparent indifference to his army. "I have met with almost every disappointment since I came into this department," he had written Washington earlier this year.

Virginia and North Carolina largely ignored him. South Carolina refused to conscript troops, preferring to offer volunteers one hundred acres and a slave as an ineffectual enticement to military service. Promised seven thousand Continentals plus state militia, he commanded fewer than a quarter that number and had been forced to ship fifteen hundred barrels of rice to Martinique to buy essential military stores on the French black market.

Now united, the allies eyed one another with curiosity and skepticism on Savannah's outskirts. French officers in royal blue coats and smart scarlet vests studied the unshaven Continentals, with their lank, tangled hair, and the Georgia militiamen in deerskin jackets and misshapen hats of felt, beaver, or straw. D'Estaing heartily welcomed the cavalry outriders on lathered horses led by Brigadier General Pulaski, the volatile Polish émigré who had been sent south after being surprised and routed at Little Egg Harbor the previous fall. But the admiral was unsure what to make of the hobbling Lincoln, who was as thick as he was tall, spoke with a stutter, and was possibly narcoleptic, as d'Estaing discovered when the general abruptly dozed off during a discussion of battle strategy. "He is not afraid of cannon fire," d'Estaing conceded, while a private French assessment concluded that "General Lincoln is an honest man, very touchy, punctilious, few ideas of his own but ready to adopt those which the first comer wishes to give him."

More than two mutually incomprehensible languages divided these armies. Not until the morning of Friday, September 17, did d'Estaing inform Lincoln in a casual note that the previous day he had demanded a British surrender to the forces of the king of France—with no mention of the Americans—and then agreed to a ceasefire. "I hope you approve the truce I have granted the enemy," he wrote. "It did not seem to be to be worth disturbing you about after the fatigue of the long march." Lincoln was surprised, his officers aghast. "My God! Whoever heard of anything like this before?" exclaimed Lieutenant Colonel Francis Marion, commanding the 2nd South Carolina Regiment. "First allow an enemy to entrench, and then fight him?" A French officer voiced suspicions that loyalist agents had infiltrated rebel militia companies, providing Prévost "the most exact account of all our operations." Any American soldier approaching French pickets without a written pass faced arrest; to prevent fistfights, Lincoln ordered the French camp off-limits to his troops.

Even before the truce expired at sunset on Friday, Prévost rejected d'Estaing's ultimatum, telling the admiral that "though we cannot look upon our post as absolutely inexpungible," Savannah "may and ought to be defended." His officers were puzzled by the French procrastination, wondering why they did not "storm and take this miserable sand pile with fixed bayonets," as one Hessian wrote. But what d'Estaing called the "doleful sight" of Maitland's final reinforcements striding into the jubilant British lines, which he watched with Lincoln from the crest of Brewton's Hill, persuaded the admiral that his only tactical options were to reduce the town with a methodical siege or sail away. "Laying siege to a fortified place defended by a force almost equal to the one attacking it would seem to be absolutely impossible," he later wrote. Even so, the recollection of the contempt he had incurred after abandoning New York and Newport prompted him to add that "London, America, and even Paris would have dishonored me" if he once again left the field.

Excavation began at seven p.m. on September 23, a quarter mile from the center of the British lines. "I began digging the trench with 300 workers," wrote Captain Antoine-François O'Connor, the French chief engineer. "During the night I dug a trench 206 yards long and started at the end of it a parallel trench 60 yards long which was only 300 yards away from [the British] works." While the Americans extended a line of log barricades east to the Savannah River, the monsieurs—as the British insisted on calling the French—could be heard "working like devils every night" to the west, serenaded by the trill of whippoorwills. At Thunderbolt, a new depot on St. Augustine Creek, French sailors disembarked thirty-five heavy mortars and cannons ranging from 6- to 18-pounders. Beneath live oaks and cypresses bearded with Spanish moss, carpenters built gun carriages with makeshift wheels sliced from the trunks of felled trees. "We shall be able to carry the place in a very few days," an American officer wrote a friend.

That optimism was misplaced. French troops received a bonus of a hundred crowns for each 18-pounder delivered to the four batteries under construction along the trenches. But heavy rains slowed the movement of the guns into the line, and although French men-of-war continued to edge up the Savannah River to bombard the town from the north, the British delayed the move by stretching a boom across the river and sinking vessels to obstruct the channel, including the frigate *Rose* and several transports.

At eight a.m. on September 24, a major in the 16th Foot led a redcoat detachment on a raid against an unfinished gun battery. Two French columns took the bait, chasing the British to their abatis with bayonets. "Three hundred men ambushed us when we least expected it," a French grenadier reported. "We pursued them back to their own lines [and] were exposed to grapeshot." Twenty British guns raked the pursuers, killing twenty-nine and wounding seventy-five. Prévost's casualties totaled twenty-one, including six dead, in the first substantial ground combat in America between France and Britain. After a brief truce to bury the corpses, skirmishing resumed on the river and along the siege lines. Aboard the *Guerrier*, a French naval cadet spoke for many of his disheartened comrades in describing the campaign as "an ill-conceived enterprise without anything in it for France."

A week later, the saps were at last dug, the batteries built, the guns unlimbered. On Saturday night, October 2, nine French mortars fired three hundred "firebombs"—incendiary rounds—into Savannah to terrify the town, followed at dawn by a full bombardment from thirty-seven allied cannons plus sixteen naval guns aboard two galleys and the sloop-of-war *La Truite*. Shells arced through the sky, trailing sparks from fuses set to crash through roofs, through floors, and into cellars before detonating. "It was believed the noise would intimidate the English and that they were only waiting for that to surrender," a French captain wrote.

No redcoat surrendered. The cannonade halted briefly at nine a.m., then resumed and lasted into Sunday night, by now answered salvo for salvo. That violent British riposte "did us much harm and killed many," a French officer wrote. "We were obliged to dig trenches hastily to cover our troops." D'Estaing's batteries, only a few hundred yards from the enemy guns, lacked the stout fortifications and embrasures protecting British crews, and the barrage killed the admiral's artillery commander. "We were exposed from the knees up," a French lieutenant complained.

Still the French bombardment persisted. More than a thousand shells and shot fell on Savannah in the next five days. "The town was torn to pieces," a British major wrote. "Nothing but shrieks from women and children to be heard." A young woman recalled ducking at each explosion "as if that could save me." Black children scooped sand to smother the fuses of undetonated rounds, then sold the inert shells and solid shot to British gunners for seven pence apiece. Some civilians sheltered below the river bluff among the fat wharf rats; others fled to the rice fields or to Hutchinson Island, where fifty-nine refugees jammed into a single barn. Prévost's wife and children remained in their house, propping feather beds against the windows and smothering any flames with wet blankets.

"Shells seemed to fall all around," wrote Georgia's former chief justice, whose quarters were pummeled. "There was not a single spot where the women and children could be put in safety." At midday on October 6, Prévost asked for a ceasefire to evacuate noncombatants from Savannah; d'Estaing and Lincoln refused, although the French, in a private apology to the British, later blamed the Americans for the decision. Prévost had already declined to allow rebel families trapped in the town to leave, including the wife and five children of Brigadier General Lachlan McIntosh, a tall, handsome Georgia planter who was Lincoln's deputy and a veteran of both Valley Forge and fighting on the western frontier. Only one uniformed defender was killed in the long bombardment, but some forty civilians died, most of them black.

"A mulatto man and three Negroes were killed in the lieutenant governor's cellar," wrote Governor Wright, who moved into a tent next to Colonel Maitland on the west side of the British encampment. "In the evening a house near the church was burned by a shell and seven Negroes lost their lives in it." A shell hit the jail, killing two men and wounding nine. "A poor woman with her infant in her arms were destroyed by a cannon ball," an officer wrote on October 7. "A more cruel war could not exist than this."

D'Estaing had told the Americans it would be "criminal" if he kept his troops in Georgia longer than eight days. They had now lingered for a month. The threat of hurricanes, of a surprise British naval attack, and of epidemical disease increased with each passing hour. The cannonade seemed hardly to have dented the enemy's works, and French artillery ammunition began to run short. The rebuilding of the damaged French rudders was nearly complete and, the admiral later wrote, "we were waiting for only a few hours of calm sea to mount them." As Versailles had directed, he must return home to refit the ships for next spring's campaign. General Lincoln observed that the admiral "appeared exceedingly anxious about his fleet."

Messages from the French anchorage along the coast had indeed grown frantic. Scurvy, dysentery, and other ills were killing thirty or more sailors a day. Fresh water was desperately short. Bread supplies were exhausted, forcing crews to eat rice, which they detested. *Le Magnifique* reportedly was sinking; "all the pumps set to work [can] scarcely keep her afloat," a dispatch advised. Other vessels were also in dire condition. The only good news from the fleet was the capture by *Sagittaire* of the fifty-gun *Experiment*, dismasted in a gale off Hilton Head while sailing from New York. She carried £30,000 sterling to pay the Savannah garrison, as well as two thousand barrels of flour, salt meat, and Brigadier General Garth, a despoiler of New Haven and Fairfield earlier this summer, who had been sent by Clinton to replace the exhausted Prévost.

Even without *Experiment's* provisions, d'Estaing guessed that the British had enough supplies to hold out for another two months. (In truth,

Prévost's commissaries had stockpiled flour to last until January and salt meat sufficient through March.) The sensible course was to abandon Georgia, the admiral wrote Versailles, but the Americans "never stopped begging, even demanding, our perseverance." Any attempt to overwhelm the defenders with a *coup de main* must happen soon.

On the morning of Friday, October 8, d'Estaing personally reconnoitered the British works. Deserters had reported weakness on the enemy's right flank near the Spring Hill redoubt, along marshy ground to the west where supposedly only loyalist militia faced the Americans. Perhaps this was the place to attack.

"It is more than probable that we shall be driven to the disagreeable necessity of storming," Major John Jones, an aide to General McIntosh, wrote his wife, Polly, who for safety had moved to South Carolina from their plantation below Savannah. "If it is my fate to survive this action, I shall. . . . [But] every soldier and soldier's wife should religiously believe in predestination." He asked that she send him "a pair of thick breeches, my blue coat, and three ruffled shirts," plus the enslaved Ishmael mounted on Black Sloven, his spare courser, since "I have sent home my English horse. He has been very sick." Polly wrote back, "I would to God this great affair was over, for oh how I dread it. . . . Do not run rashly into danger if you can avoid it. Consider you have two dear children and a wife whose happiness depends on yours."

After his reconnaissance ride, d'Estaing convened his senior commanders in a field tent and told them that he intended to attack the enemy right wing the next morning. This startling announcement found little favor. Catching Prévost off guard was imperative, but his troops seemed alert. Just today, Captain L'Enfant, the engineer, had led a five-man patrol forward in an effort to set fire to the British abatis; severely wounded by watchful sentries, L'Enfant would not walk again for months. Another French officer estimated that Savannah could not be taken with less than fifteen thousand "very good troops." Still others argued that any assault should target the enemy center or left wing since the ground there was firmer and much of the bombardment this week had fallen in those sectors. Of particular concern was d'Estaing's scheme to improvise shock battalions by peeling elite grenadier and light infantry companies away from their regiments. If new units were hastily assembled, many officers and men would be strangers to one another.

D'Estaing listened briefly to these objections before overruling his subordinates and ending the discussion. One officer wondered if the admiral intended to become a martyr for the American cause; another privately complained that his "haughty and vain character did not admit of advice."

Orders were quickly drafted. All troops were to be under arms with weapons inspected by midnight. The attack would start no later than four a.m. on Saturday, October 9, beginning with feints and deceptions, followed by a bayonet assault aimed at the Spring Hill bastion. "It is expressly forbidden on pain of death," d'Estaing declared, "to fire before the redoubt is carried. . . . Every soldier who breaks ranks to pillage shall be punished with death." All troops, French and American, would wear white cockades or paper scraps in their hats for mutual recognition.

D'Estaing acknowledged the difficulties of terrain, of an entrenched foe, and of a heterogeneous assault force drawn from two dissimilar armies. But, he added, "extreme bravery can conquer anything."

"To take them by surprise was the main point," the admiral later wrote. "In my eyes, everything depended on that." Yet there would be no surprise, and long before the day dawned the plan began to come unstitched. Three French columns of over a thousand men each were to move a mile northwest from their camp before four a.m., assembling five hundred yards from the British lines with two American columns falling in behind them. But the French arrived late, weary, and in disarray. Guides provided to lead the columns were too few and not "such masters of the ground as they ought to have been," an officer reported. An American sergeant from Charleston deserted during the night, providing Prévost with at least some details of d'Estaing's plan.

Worse, the feints were badly timed and virtually ignored by the British defenders. The sun would rise just before six-thirty that Saturday, but nautical twilight an hour earlier brightened the morning sufficiently for sentries to see twelve hundred American militiamen shuffling around for a feigned attack on the British far left. Redcoats on the parapet greeted them with a fusillade of long-range musketry, and a military band played "Come to the Maypole, Merry Farmers All" at a jaunty tempo. "Whether it was meant as a real attack or a feint is hard to determine," Lieutenant Colonel John Harris Cruger, a loyalist commander, wrote his family, "as under cover of a very thick fog they came on & went off." A brief bombardment from French guns and another tardy feint on the Savannah River proved equally ineffectual. "Day begins to dawn and we grow impatient," a French officer noted. The skirl of Highland bagpipes drifted from the British camp because, d'Estaing surmised, Prévost "wanted to remind us that his best troops were waiting for us."

The early light also revealed several thousand French soldiers, many in conspicuous long-tailed white army uniforms, milling along a tree line two hundred yards from the Spring Hill redoubt, which was occupied by a captain with just over a hundred defenders. Dismayed at the delay in forming his columns, d'Estaing ordered drummers to beat "advance at the double quick." Within moments the horde streamed north, shouting, "*Vive le roi! Vive le roi!*" "The grenadiers of Old France came on," the historian Alexander A. Lawrence later wrote, "white shadows that materialized out of the mist."

Firelocks winked along the parapet where British musketmen fired in volleys, punctuated by vivid yellow flame licking from British cannon muzzles in three batteries. "Disorder begins to prevail," a French diarist recorded. "We are crowded together and badly pressed. Two 18-pounder guns upon field carriages, charged with canister and placed at the head of the road, cause terrible slaughter." Near the van of the first column a musket ball grazed d'Estaing's right arm; he quickly fashioned a sling around his neck, then stood on a causeway waving his men on toward the redoubt. Grenadiers in the spearhead chopped at the abatis with hatchets, cutting holes wide enough for some brave souls to reach the smoke-shrouded fortifications, their heads bowed against sleeting grapeshot and scrap-metal langrage that reportedly included nails, bolts, and even old knife blades. A British galley anchored where Yamacraw Creek spilled into the Savannah swept the attackers with additional salvos, inflicting "frightful carnage," d'Estaing later reported.

Some troops scrambled into a ditch below the parapet but lacked ladders to climb out the far side. "Utmost confusion then reigned in this army," a French officer wrote. "All the detachments were mixed together." Captain Philippe Séguier de Terson later estimated that he and sixty men from different regiments lingered under fire for fifteen minutes between the abatis and the redoubt, awaiting reinforcements that never came. An artillery lieutenant added, "We took two steps forward and five backward, shouting all the time, 'Long live the king!'"

A few stalwarts managed to plant regimental flags on the parapets fronting the Spring Hill bastion. Those square damask swatches with a central white cross and exotic colors in the cantons briefly brightened the morning. "I believed the day was our own," wrote Colonel Curt von Stedingk, a Swedish baron fighting for France. But "a savage bayonet charge" wounded Stedingk, driving him and his comrades away. "Our people," he added, "were annihilated by crossfire." Colonel Arthur Dillon, an Irish nobleman also in the service of France, was driven back after briefly clinging to the fortifications with eighty red-jacketed men from his brigade. Enfilading fire from guns served by Royal Navy tars drove many French troops into Yamacraw Swamp, to the west, where they sheltered behind cypress stumps or lay flat in the mud. "Those who lost only their shoes," a lieutenant later observed, "were the most fortunate."

On the heels of the French, angling slightly to their left, came the Americans. Brigadier General Pulaski and his cavalry led the first column, cantering to the abatis with raised sabers. They got no farther: a grapeshot round the size of an egg slammed into Pulaski's groin above his right thigh, spilling him from the saddle. A fellow Pole found him on the ground bleeding badly and murmuring, "Jesus, Mary, Joseph." As Pulaski's horsemen reined in their wide-eyed, stamping mounts, six hundred Continental infantry and Charleston militiamen, led by Colonel Laurens, swept past them, hacking a narrow passage through the abatis and stumbling across the ditch to the rampart before musketry and oblique cannon fire brought them up short. Two color bearers managed to plant silk flags, one red and the other blue, on the parapet before the defenders sallied again. Hand-to-hand fighting with bayonets and musket butts routed the attackers "like a crowd leaving church," in the description of a French officer. Laurens, miraculously uninjured, reportedly flung his sword to the ground in frustration. The second American column fared no better. Two South Carolina regiments led by General McIntosh swerved around the redoubt, only to be scorched with grapeshot and driven into the Yamacraw morass. "Such a scene of confusion as there appeared is not often equaled," wrote Major Thomas Pinckney.

D'Estaing had been wounded a second time, this time by a bullet in the right calf, and his white uniform, already bloody from the gash to his arm, now was crimson. Whey-faced, grimacing in pain, he was bundled to the rear. Colonel Dillon, in command by default, ordered drummers to beat a general retreat. Prévost's aroused troops pursued the receding ranks, but French reserves posted with fieldpieces near the Jewish Burial Ground stood fast, driving them back. The shouting and the gunfire subsided; gray battle smoke slowly drifted into the heavens, like souls ascending. After stealing a final backward glimpse at the British lines, Major Pinckney reported that he found "not an assailant standing."

Captain O'Connor summarized the morning with admirable concision: "The action did not last longer than an hour. It was very violent."

"Such a sight I never saw before," Prévost's aide wrote. "The ditch was filled with dead. Many hung dead and wounded on the abatis." Another British officer noted, "For some hundred yards without the lines, the plain was strewed with mangled bodies." French guns resumed their cannonade that night "without any other effect than destroying the houses," a witness reported. On Sunday morning Prévost granted a six-hour truce requested by French and American emissaries to bury the dead.

The pick-and-shovel details would remain busy. Only at Bunker Hill, four years earlier, had one side incurred a comparable butcher's bill during a single day of bloodletting. The French officially reported 521 casualties, including 151 dead, although some officers believed the total of killed and wounded exceeded 800. American returns listed 234 casualties, but the figure certainly was higher. Prévost tallied 18 killed and 39 wounded among his defenders, plus one more casualty: the one-armed Colonel Maitland, who more than anyone had saved Savannah for the empire by his timely reinforcement of the garrison from Beaufort, collapsed in his quarters after the battle and died on October 22. Some said malaria killed him; a less generous commentator blamed "the habit of indulging himself freely with his glass."

"Of nine hundred choice troops I led into action, four hundred men and thirty-nine officers were dead or wounded," Colonel Stedingk subsequently wrote. British wagons hauled more than a hundred of the grievously injured attackers across the lines to avoid the burden of caring for them; they included the likes of Private John Looney, crippled by a ball in the left ankle that would plague him for the next forty-four years, until his lower leg was amputated and replaced with a wooden peg. The French and American officer corps had been particularly savaged. François, the Vicomte de Fontanges, who had been promoted from major to major general for this expedition, was severely wounded while covering the retreat. Lieutenant Louis de Saussure of the 3rd South Carolina was wounded, then died of lockjaw. Lieutenant Edward Lloyd, a South Carolina artilleryman, lost his right arm. Captain Samuel Warren was wounded twice and captured, losing his right leg. And Major John Jones, whose wife had implored him to be cautious, was killed instantly by a cannonball through the chest. He was dumped into a shallow trench and remained there until a determined friend exhumed his body to give him a decent burial in a deeper grave. Jones was thirty years old.

A surgeon who extracted the grapeshot orb from Pulaski's pelvis reported that he bore the pain "with inconceivable fortitude." Attended by French physicians, he was carried aboard the privateer brig *Wasp*, but gangrene set in and he apparently died before the vessel could sail for Charleston. "Pulaski has died as he lived—a hero but an enemy of kings," Stanislaw II, the Polish monarch, reportedly said upon hearing the news.

Some accounts claimed he was buried at sea, but the *Wasp*'s captain wrote General Lincoln that "I have brought him ashore and buried him" by torchlight in a wooden coffin made by the ship's purser, a former cabinet-maker. More than two centuries later, bones examined in a Savannah tomb were convincingly declared to be Pulaski's.

Litter bearers carried d'Estaing to the Thunderbolt waterside south of Savannah. Once again misfortune in America had "dealt some hard knocks," he acknowledged, telling his surgeon, "I have a deep wound which it is not in your power to cure." An American delegation urged that if the fleet must sail away, at least French army regiments should remain on the coast, perhaps after retreating overland to Charleston to recuperate and refit. Some French officers concurred, but at a war council on October 11 the admiral—flat on his back—insisted on returning home with his entire force. The long march to Charleston "would have meant more losses," he wrote. "Hundreds would have deserted."

Troops began trundling mortars and naval guns from the siege lines to lighters on St. Augustine Creek for ferrying to the ships. Under a "Convention of Retreat" drafted between d'Estaing and Lincoln on October 13, the allies agreed to part ways. The Americans would decamp first, making "as great a march as possible and leave the swamps between them and the English." A French rear guard would "secure the retreat of the Americans," a gesture Lincoln considered "new proof of the devotion of the French to the common cause."

Basking in a victory the British now called "the glorious Ninth of October," Prévost claimed, wishfully, that "mutual animosities" divided the French and American allies, who "were on the eve of cutting each other's throats." The truth was more nuanced. Lincoln regretted d'Estaing's imminent departure, telling a friend—also wishfully—that "could he have remained I see nothing which could have prevented our success." He wrote Congress that although "our disappointment is great . . . Count d'Estaing has undoubtedly the interest of America much at heart. . . . In our service he has bled. I feel much for him, for while he is suffering the distress of painful wounds, he has to combat chagrin." As for the defeat, "The causes of failure are such as attend the uncertain events of war."

D'Estaing compiled a catalog of American failings, some warranted, others unfair. "It is the nature of Americans to promise much and deliver little," he wrote. But in a dispatch to Versailles he also acknowledged, "I should have taken into account all possible mishaps." In the event, he proved to be an undistinguished, star-crossed battle commander: courageous and muddled on land, cautious and inexpert at sea. He took justifiable pride in leaving American waters without losing a ship and without the British capturing a single French gun as a trophy. Yet he was also leaving with more pain than acclaim. "Enterprising, bold even to temerity, all things appear possible to him," a French naval officer wrote. "[But] the sailors believe him inhuman. Many died upbraiding him with their misery, unwilling to pardon him."

More would die on the journey home. French medicos lacked linen to dress suppurating wounds, and ship captains were so desperate for fresh water that they filled their casks from the mouth of the brackish Savannah at low tide. Under a bright half-moon on the evening of October 18, Lincoln and his battered troops headed upriver to cross back into South Carolina at Zubly's Ferry. Unimpeded by redcoats, three rearguard French grenadier companies then rejoined their comrades at Thunderbolt. On October 20, sailors tied d'Estaing into an armchair before hoisting him with a rope and pulley to *Languedoc*'s deck, where he limped on crutches to his cabin. The fleet soon raised anchor to more baying from the crews of *"Vive le roi!"* A week later, delivering one last insult from the American littoral, a howling gale scattered the ships with seas described by the admiral as "higher than those I experienced off the Cape of Good Hope."

He found a chilly reception at Brest, but France would soon remember Grenada and forget Savannah. By the time d'Estaing reached Versailles, well-wishers on the street were strewing flowers before his carriage. He dined with the king and queen, his injured leg propped up on a stool that Marie-Antoinette herself adjusted for him. He could soon hobble about with help from a large cane. At the opera in Bordeaux, the audience cheered when a singer climbed up to d'Estaing's loge and placed a laurel crown, intended for a character in the drama, on the admiral's head instead.

France had provided America with war matériel, naval support, and six million livres, while guaranteeing the loan of another eight million and paying the interest accrued during the war. Now the sons of France had again paid in a harder currency. But d'Estaing's greatest contribution may have been in spooking the British, who feared further attacks on Jamaica, Halifax, or Rhode Island. With Spain in the war, General Clinton in late September proposed abandoning vulnerable Newport to concentrate his defenses at New York. The new Royal Navy commander on the North American station, Vice Admiral Marriot Arbuthnot, at first agreed— Narragansett Bay had "never been of the smallest use to the navy," he assured Clinton on October 6—then dithered over the decision before again concurring. The order was sent to evacuate what another admiral called "the best and noblest harbor in America."

On October 25, as d'Estaing was leaving the western Atlantic, seven thousand of the king's men and forty-six loyalist families hurried through Newport's streets to the docks, drums beating and flags flying. "Not a man or woman was allowed to look out of the windows, or to be on the street," a Hessian officer told his diary. A loyalist witness added, "The army and merchants are carrying their baggage as fast as possible. The whole town appears in one general confusion."

Flatboats shuttled the troops, loyalists, and sundry freed slaves across the bay to 120 transports guarded by half a dozen men-of-war. Ordnance officers also removed twenty brass fieldpieces, seventy-two iron guns, seventeen mortars, nine howitzers, and fifty-two horses. British firebrands raced around Newport with their fagots, burning artillery platforms, barracks, Long Wharf, Beavertail Lighthouse, and 160 houses. "It appeared as if the entire city had died," wrote Private Johann Döhla.

At eight p.m. the flotilla weighed anchor for New York. Eight hours later Rhode Island Continentals embarked at Rome Point, on the bay's western shore, before crossing to Conanicut Island and then to Newport, where, a rebel officer reported, "the inhabitants flocked in, in great multitudes." The redcoats, wrote General John Stark, were "gone, gone, gone!"

Where this war was headed, few British field officers could say. "We get up and we walk, we sit down, and we eat," Major James Murray told his sister. "We lie down and we sleep, and when we awake we find ourselves twenty-four hours nearer the end of our pilgrimage than we were the day before." Despite the forfeiture of Rhode Island and bleak news from the West Indies, the high command drew some optimism from the enemy's repulse in Georgia. The strategy of first snuffing out the insurrection in the southern colonies seemed ever more promising. "The spirit of rebellion is on the decline in South Carolina since the late defeat here," Governor Wright wrote Germain from Savannah on November 9. "And I doubt not but the country will be an easy conquest." Guns at the Tower of London would boom in celebration of the glorious Ninth. "It is the first time," declared General Grey, "I have seen daylight in this business."

Confirmation of the Georgia triumph reached New York via the privateer *Rosebud* on November 19. Within hours a *feu de joie* was organized, with thirteen regiments assembled on a parade ground near the Hudson. Batteries at Fort George on the southern tip of Manhattan fired a noisy salute, answered by the Paulus Hook garrison, across the river. Troops huzzahed until they grew hoarse, and illuminations brightened every house in town.

Clinton cheered with them, setting aside his usual dour skepticism. With the reinforcements newly arrived from Newport, he now could exploit the success in Georgia with an expedition that would finish crushing the rebellion in the South. "This," he wrote, "is the greatest event that has happened in the whole war."

39. A uniformed George III appears ready for battle as Britain's captain general in this portrait by the American artist Benjamin West, painted as the nation braced to oppose a Franco-Spanish invasion fleet in 1779. The king holds a document detailing his troop dispositions, while a liveried groom steadies the royal charger. The mounted officer closest to George is General Jeffrey Amherst, commander in chief of British land forces.

40. Queen Charlotte appears with thirteen of her eventual fifteen children in this Benjamin West painting, created as a companion piece to the 1779 portrait of the king. The south face of Windsor Castle appears in the background.

41. The Queen's House, later called Buckingham Palace, stood where James I in 1609 had planted mulberry bushes in a futile effort to nurture a British silkworm industry. George III in 1761 bought the fine house built on the site by the Duke of Buckingham and deeded it to Queen Charlotte. The king was particularly proud of the four libraries he assembled.

42. Lord George Germain served as secretary of state for the American Department and the king's most ardent warlord during the Revolution. A former army general, he had ascended to high office despite an earlier court-martial conviction for disobeying orders in battle. Fluent and meticulous in debate, Germain was also said to possess "an excess of dogmatic self-confidence, impatient of any plan but his own."

43. Frederick, Lord North, seen in this study for a portrait made around 1779, had served as prime minister since 1770, but had little appetite for waging war against the Americans. A colleague observed that he "only wanted one quality to make him a great and distinguished statesman—despotism and violence of temper."

44. The energetic, canny John Montagu, the Earl of Sandwich, had already served twice as first lord of the Admiralty when he took the post for a third time in 1771. As supervisor of the wartime Royal Navy, the western world's largest industrial organization, "no man in the administration was so much a master of the business, so quick, or so shrewd," an admirer wrote.

45. When mental illness incapacitated Sandwich's wife, he found a companion in Martha Ray, a mantua maker almost three decades his junior who eventually bore him nine children. In 1779, two years after this portrait was made, an obsessed suitor shot her dead as she emerged from a Covent Garden theater. Upon hearing the news, Sandwich cried, "I could have borne anything but this."

46. In spitting snow on December 19, 1777, Washington led nineteen thousand men into a dreary winter encampment at Valley Forge, a wooded uplands west of Philadelphia. A survey of the Continental Army revealed "the whole of them without watch coats, one-half without blankets, & more than a third without shoes, stockings, or breeches."

47. As surgeon general for the Continental Army's Middle Department, Dr. Benjamin Rush reported that when the troops moved into Valley Forge almost a third of them were sick. "A great majority of those who die under our hands perish with fevers caught in our hospitals," Rush added.

48. Baron Friedrich Wilhelm von Steuben professed to be a onetime aide-de-camp to Frederick the Great and a former Prussian lieutenant general when he arrived at Valley Forge in February 1778. Neither claim was true, but after quickly proving his value as a troop trainer, Steuben became a Continental major general and the army's inspector general. One private deemed him "the perfect personification of Mars."

49. Henry Laurens of South Carolina, once a partner in the largest slave-trading company in North America, succeeded John Hancock as president of the Continental Congress in 1777. A staunch supporter of Washington at a time when some Americans had begun to doubt the commanding general, Laurens also vigorously backed a military and diplomatic alliance with France.

50. Educated in Britain and Switzerland, Lieutenant Colonel John Laurens, Henry's son, served as both an aide to Washington and a combat leader. A committed abolitionist, young Laurens tried unsuccessfully to convince South Carolina planters to permit enslaved men to fight as American soldiers. "Your black air castle is blown up with contemptuous huzzahs," Henry told his son.

51. The fearless, vainglorious son of a Royal Navy captain, Lieutenant Colonel John Graves Simcoe at Germantown took command of the loyalist infantry regiment known as the Queen's Rangers. Early in the Battle of Monmouth in June 1778, he charged a detachment of American decoys before being wounded by a bullet to the arm.

52. After failing to penetrate British defenses protecting New York Harbor, a French fleet led by the ninety-gun flagship, *Languedoc,* sailed to Newport in July 1778 to collaborate with American forces besieging the enemy garrison there. A tremendous storm scattered the fleet, completely dismasting *Languedoc,* shown here under bombardment by the fifty-gun *Renown* until other French warships drove away the British frigate.

53. William Pitt, the Earl of Chatham and the preeminent architect of British victories in the Seven Years' War, was still widely revered in both Britain and America as "the Great Commoner." A movement to bring him back into the government had gained momentum, despite George III's resistance, when Chatham collapsed while giving a speech in the House of Lords on April 7, 1778. He died a month later.

54. This 1779 cartoon, captioned "an English jack-tar giving monsieur a drubbing," depicts a Royal Navy sailor beating a French nobleman while his dog attacks a French poodle.

55. Elected to the House of Commons at age nineteen, Charles James Fox became the undisputed leader of the opposition to Lord North's government despite a reputation for dissipation and spectacular gambling losses. "His conversation is like a brilliant player at billiards," one duchess recounted. "The strokes follow one another, piff, paff!"

56. Vice Admiral Charles Hector, the Count d'Estaing, commanded the French fleet sent to America to confront the Royal Navy in the summer of 1778. Formerly an army general, he had transferred to the navy despite no training as a sailor. "Imagine a sea general," one naval captain complained, "the least of whose shortcomings is that he cannot sail."

57. José Moñino, Count Floridablanca, the able if bad-tempered Spanish foreign minister, suggested that Britain could buy Madrid's neutrality by ceding Gibraltar and Minorca, notwithstanding Spain's obligation to support France under the so-called Bourbon "Family Compact." London "must know that what we do not get by negotiation we know how to get with a club," Floridablanca warned.

58. The waters around Ushant, a small, craggy island twenty miles off the western tip of Brittany, provided the setting in July 1778 for the first major sea battle between France and Britain during the American war. Inconclusive if violent, with twelve hundred casualties in the two fleets, the action stirred bitter controversy in the Royal Navy, including courts-martial and riots. "The times are fevered to a high degree," a British captain wrote.

59. "I am but an ordinary man," John Adams would write after arriving in Paris to bolster the American diplomatic delegation. "The times alone have destined me to fame." Referring to himself as "John Yankee," he found distrust and rancor between Benjamin Franklin and his fellow commissioner, Arthur Lee.

60. Despite not having been to sea in fifteen years, Vice Admiral Augustus Keppel was reputedly "well fitted to become the national hero" when selected to command the Royal Navy's Channel fleet in the confrontation against the French navy. This portrait by Sir Joshua Reynolds was painted shortly after Keppel's court-martial acquittal on charges that he had botched the battle of Ushant.

61. Continental Army officers staged recruiting rallies throughout the states, offering bonuses of cash, land, and clothing to those who would enlist. But severe shortfalls led to mandatory conscription, sometimes by pulling names from a hat.

62. After creditable service as an artillery officer, Lieutenant Colonel Alexander Hamilton joined Washington's staff as an aide-de-camp who was always ready to offer an opinion on strategic and tactical questions. The Continental Army, he had declared in July 1777, should "take advantage of favorable opportunities, and waste and defeat the enemy by piecemeal."

63. A charming, talented staff officer, newly promoted Major John André joined General Clinton's retinue as the commanding general's spymaster. In 1779, he opened a secret correspondence with an American general apparently willing to sell his services to the Crown—Benedict Arnold.

64. Known as "Foul-Weather Jack" for his propensity to attract gales at sea, Vice Admiral John Byron commanded a Royal Navy fleet sent to America to intercept a French expedition. His grandson, the poet George Gordon, Lord Byron, would immortalize him in *Don Juan,* writing, "He had no rest at sea, nor I on shore."

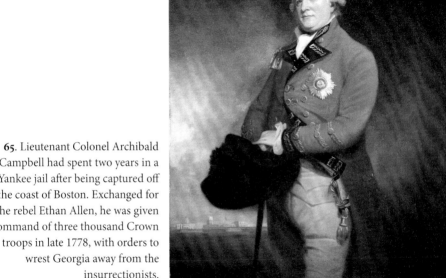

65. Lieutenant Colonel Archibald Campbell had spent two years in a Yankee jail after being captured off the coast of Boston. Exchanged for the rebel Ethan Allen, he was given command of three thousand Crown troops in late 1778, with orders to wrest Georgia away from the insurrectionists.

66. Commodore Sir George Collier had commanded a succession of Royal Navy frigates and won literary laurels as a playwright in London when he proposed a sweeping attack against rebel settlements in the lower Chesapeake Bay. As shipyards, naval stores, and houses were put to the torch in May 1779, "the conflagration in the night appeared grand beyond description," a British officer recorded.

67. The semiretired Vice Admiral Sir Charles Hardy had not been to sea in sixteen years, yet turmoil in the upper ranks caused the Royal Navy to appoint him commander in chief of the Channel fleet as a Franco-Spanish invasion force approached southern England. One skeptical subordinate described Hardy as "a man who never thinks beforehand and therefore is always under the confusion of surprise when anything happens."

68. Having first gone to sea at age thirteen from his native Scotland, John Paul Jones eventually was commissioned a captain in the fledgling Continental Navy and dispatched to France. Charmed by "the strange magnetism of his presence," Dr. Franklin ordered the young swashbuckler to wreak havoc "as you shall judge best for distressing the enemies of the United States."

69. As a Royal Navy officer, Captain Richard Pearson had sailed the world's oceans for three decades when he was given command of the fast new frigate *Serapis* and assigned to escort a large merchant convoy from the Baltic Sea to safe haven in England.

70. Jones's *Bonhomme Richard* and Pearson's *Serapis* fought to the death off the coast of Yorkshire under a full moon on September 23, 1779. Painted a year after the battle, this scene depicts the two ships trading blows while the Continental frigate *Alliance,* on the far right, fires into both of them. On the left, the British sloop-of-war *Countess of Scarborough* surrenders to the frigate *Pallas.*

71. Major General William Alexander, known as Lord Stirling because of his disputed claim to a Scottish earldom, was a bibulous spendthrift, "braver than wise" in one comrade's assessment. But his lupine ferocity was seen repeatedly in battles against the British at Long Island, Brandywine, Monmouth, and elsewhere.

72. Major Henry Lee III, a Virginia cavalryman known as Light-Horse Harry, was said to "have come out of his mother's womb a soldier." When given a chance to serve Washington as an aide-de-camp, he declined, explaining, "I am wedded to my sword."

73. A Polish nobleman who had fled his homeland after conspiring to kidnap his king, Brigadier General Casimir Pulaski commanded a Continental cavalry regiment that included volunteers from Hungary, Italy, France, and Poland.

74. A former New Hampshire lawyer, Major General John Sullivan "has his wants and he has his foibles," Washington conceded. But the commander in chief still chose him to lead a punitive expedition against Iroquois tribes in western New York.

75. Major General Benjamin Lincoln walked with a pronounced limp from a gunshot wound received at Saratoga when he was given command of the Continental Army's Southern Department. "I wish the Congress had fixed their minds on some other officer," he told Washington.

76. Major General Charles Cornwallis, in mourning after the death of his cherished wife, Jemima, returned from England to America to serve as deputy commander for the British expedition against Charleston. "I come to share fortunes with you," he wrote Henry Clinton, an old friend.

77. Vice Admiral Marriot Arbuthnot had been commander in chief of the Royal Navy's North American station for barely two months when he requested permission "to resign this command and return to England." Clinton, his army counterpart, denounced the admiral as "full of deceit and artifice."

78. British siege troops excavate approach trenches and artillery emplacements on Charleston Neck in this painting by Alonzo Chappel. The tall steeple of St. Michael's Church looms above the city in the distance, while on the left rebel defenders have scuttled a line of hulks to keep approaching Royal Navy warships out of the Cooper River.

79. The so-called Gordon Riots in London began as a protest against the expansion of political rights for Roman Catholics but soon metastasized into the most violent urban disturbance in British history. An estimated eight hundred to a thousand people died during the weeklong rampage in June 1780, including many looters shot by the king's troops, as depicted in this copperplate engraving of a confrontation in Broad Street.

25.

Eternity Is Nearer Every Day

The old wives claimed that a harsh winter was coming when woolly bear caterpillars displayed wide black rings, when geese breastbones grew thick and white, and when church weathervanes at noon on Saint Thomas's feast day showed wind blowing from the north. But no living American had ever experienced a winter like the one about to descend in the final weeks of 1779. Snow first fell on New York in early November, and Hudson River coves began to freeze a week later. Soon enough, blizzard would follow blizzard, and frigid temperatures would ice over every inlet, harbor, and sound on the Atlantic seaboard north of the Carolinas. Horse-drawn sleighs could travel atop the frozen Delaware River for thirty miles from Philadelphia to Trenton.

As the snow deepened, the Continental Army—perhaps eyeing those caterpillar rings—hurried into winter cantonments scattered across three states. Four Massachusetts brigades sheltered in the Hudson Highlands around West Point, five cavalry regiments camped in Connecticut and central New Jersey, and three infantry regiments protected the northern frontier from Fort Stanwix to Lake George. A troop of thirty army couriers took post between Williamsburg and the Hudson to carry dispatches for the high command.

But most of what one newspaper called "the Grand American Army" converged on familiar ground in northern New Jersey. Twenty miles west of New York City the terrain inclined almost imperceptibly except to a dray horse pulling a supply wagon or a man afoot shouldering a musket. On a wooded plateau beyond hills known as First and Second Mountains, Morristown was described by a visitor as "a very clever little village" of sixty houses, a courthouse on the green, and Presbyterian and Baptist churches with steeples that were said to give the place "a consequential look." Seven iron mines north of town yielded their ore, with forges, furnaces, and bloomeries nearby producing war matériel. Mills for lumber, grist, and gunpowder lined the Whippany River, and a sign in a general store offered "the highest prices for bee's wax and hog bristles."

The army had wintered here three years earlier, after the Battle of Princeton. That winter allowed a vital respite for the flickering American cause following repeated drubbings from the British around New York in 1776. Footsore and sickly, the Continentals spread enough disease from their encampment to kill a quarter of Morristown's population. The Presbyterian congregation alone counted sixty-eight smallpox deaths in 1777, and the meetinghouse, used as a hospital, had only just been reclaimed for godly purposes with a vinegar scrub and gunpowder burned to purify the nave.

Now, despite understandable local reluctance, the army was back. General Greene and his staff had searched the countryside for weeks, seeking a bivouac with adequate water, timber, and roads, as well as terrain rugged enough to discourage a surprise attack by British marauders marching from New York. "I have rode hot and cold, wet and dry, night and day in traversing the country in search of the most proper place for quartering the troops," Greene wrote a subordinate on November 28. In a note to Washington, still at West Point, he advised that "a very good position may be had at Jockey Hollow," four miles southwest of Morristown. Within days, eleven brigades and four artillery regiments began to descend on this remote place.

Two thousand acres of rolling woodland would be cleared to erect what one witness described as "a log-house city" of twelve hundred structures. Soldiers working in teams of twelve built notched-log shanties with clapboard roofs, clay chinking, bunks against three walls, and a chimney hearth along the fourth. Those who finished their hut first received two gallons of whiskey as a prize; those whose hut best resembled the model recommended by higher authority got four gallons. Each brigade occupied a swatch of hillside roughly three hundred yards deep by a hundred yards wide overlooking the parade ground. The early freeze impeded the sawmills cutting the boards needed for doors, bunks, and floors, and mud often froze before it could be daubed between the logs. The officers' huts were built last, leaving even colonels in tents during the frigid nights. But when the final brigade arrived in mid-December—New Jersey troops who had been fighting the Iroquois—some eleven thousand officers and men were settled around Morristown. "The encampments are exceedingly neat," the *New-Jersey Gazette* reported. "The huts are all of a size and placed in more exact order than Philadelphia."

Much had been learned about camp hygiene from the horrors of Valley Forge, and mortality at Jockey Hollow—fewer than a hundred dead in six months, despite the awful winter—would be twenty-fold lower. Even so, life at Morristown was miserable from the outset.

"Colder weather I never saw in this time of year," Lieutenant Erkuries Beatty of the 4th Pennsylvania wrote his brother in December. "What is worse than all, we scarcely got anything to eat." Crop failures had severely curtailed the fall harvest, and frozen streams prevented mills from grinding grain; some troops pounded flaxseed and corncobs together to make a crude bread flour. Emergency shipments of rice from Charleston via New England kept famine at bay for the moment, although British cruisers intercepted half of the victuallers.

Forage was so scarce that horses nibbled tree bark. The army counted fewer than five thousand blankets, and uniforms had grown so threadbare that some regimental officers were "ashamed to come out of their huts," General Stirling noted. Lieutenant Colonel Ebenezer Huntington of Connecticut added, "The men have suffered much without shoes and stockings, and working half-leg deep in snow. Poor fellows, my heart bleeds for them, while I damn my country as void of gratitude." A Massachusetts officer subsequently selected his own epitaph to be invoked if he did not survive the war: "I lived doubting, not dissolute. I die unresolved, not unresigned. Ignorance and error are incident to human nature."

The *Morning Chronicle and London Advertiser*, citing a spurious report from Boston, informed British readers that General Washington, "who had been ill for some time past, died at Philadelphia the 27th of November at one o'clock in the morning."

The same man, very much alive, arrived in Morristown on December 1 during a "severe storm of hail & snow," a Continental artillery lieutenant recorded. Swinging from the saddle and scraping the slush from his boots, Washington strode up four wide steps and through the front door of a bone-white Georgian mansion with a hipped roof and green shutters belonging to Theodosia Ford, the widow of a wealthy iron manufacturer. Despite His Excellency's efforts to be a gracious guest, Mrs. Ford hardly hid her dismay at this imposition: she would be consigned to two ground-floor rooms with her four children and domestic staff, while the general and his entourage—including staff officers, servants, and five aides—occupied the other six rooms as bedchambers and offices. Here on the village outskirts they would live cheek by jowl for the next seven months, as many as thirty people sleeping each night in what had abruptly become a very small house, sharing the same kitchen and trying not to trip over the pallets, fire buckets, and chamber pots.

The commander in chief took a second-floor bedroom with plaster walls, fourteen-inch-plank floors, and three windows facing the road. The room held a writing desk, a canopy bed, and a foot warmer near the fireplace. Two high-ceilinged rooms to the left of the center hall downstairs served as Washington's study and an officers' dining room, which also was used for military conferences. Seventy yards southeast of the house, the general's Life Guard, now expanded to 250 men uniformed in blue coats with red vests and black cocked hats, set to work building their own cabins in a meadow framed by towering oaks and maples.

This was Washington's fifth winter at war, and he had learned the virtues of endurance and makeshift comfort. His larder that December would include thirteen bushels of turnips, ham butts, nine dozen eggs, fifty-six quail, thirteen rabbits, a dozen geese, a dozen turkeys, and ten pounds of butter. To Robert Morris he wrote that he was "resolved to be equally contented with grog, should it even be made of New England rum & drank out of a wooden bowl, as the case has been." That said, a Spanish diplomat had sent him chocolate, a barrel of sherry, and a "small box of cigars of the Havana." Congress also provided two pipes of Madeira salvaged from a wreck at Little Egg Harbor, as well as eight pounds of green tea and twenty-four pounds of "curled hair" for mattress stuffing. As always, no distraction from his martial burdens pleased him more than a few moments stolen to correspond about Mount Vernon with Lund, his overseer. Washington hoped the locust trees along the north end of the manor house were trimmed, and that saplings had been planted along the millrace. Did other farmers in the neighborhood believe that grapevines, olive trees, or lemons would thrive in northern Virginia? (The answer came back: yes, no, and not without a greenhouse.)

Soon after arriving he ordered a four-horse coach built in Philadelphia for Martha, with "painting well done and in a tasty stile." Although delayed a week by deep snow, she reached the Ford mansion in late December and quickly recognized that "there was not much pleasure there," as she later wrote. "The poor general was so unhappy that it distressed me exceedingly." She did her best to make the crowded house a home, providing him with companionship, conjugal love, and private counsel.

There was much to make him unhappy. Another fighting season had ended. The year had seen 156 military and naval engagements in America, resulting in more than three thousand patriot battle casualties, exclusive of accidental injuries, desertions, and deaths from disease. Washington told Congress that "the enemy have wasted another campaign," yet few achievements could be claimed for his own cause other than some biffing with the Indians. D'Orvilliers's descent on southern England and d'Estaing's descent on Savannah had both ended badly. Washington in recent months had hoped for "one great stroke to finish the war," achieved by capturing the isolated British garrisons on Staten Island and at King's Ferry before trapping Clinton's army in New York with a siege force of thirty thousand men and French warships. But that ambition had evaporated with d'Estaing's departure for France, and if Britain's abandonment of Rhode Island was gratifying, it hardly dissolved his "impatience & anxiety."

He held no illusions that the forthcoming spring campaign was likely to be more promising. The future, Washington told a Virginia friend, loomed like "a wide and boundless field, puzzled with mazes and o'erspread with difficulties." Congress hoped to field an army of at least thirty-five thousand men in 1780, but filling the ranks with that number would be difficult; nearly six thousand enlistments were scheduled to expire in the next five months. Many officers had threatened to resign because, as an entreaty from a New York brigade lamented, the plummeting value of Continental currency "makes it altogether impossible for those of us who have families to afford them the smallest assistance." With Washington's tacit approval, twenty-seven generals—Greene, Knox, Sullivan, and Gates among them—sent Congress a petition, complaining that although generous land grants in exchange for service had been offered to Continental enlisted men and officers, from privates to colonels, no such emolument was available for general officers. The daily pay for a common laborer, they added, was now "twice the sum which a major general receives." Although in December a congressional committee proposed lifetime half-pay for generals and two to three thousand acres of land after the war, Congress ignored both the petition and the recommendation.

With officers bolting the army almost daily, Washington told Congress, "we are exceedingly deficient with respect to them and the service is suffering greatly for the want." Matériel shortages also plagued him. Paper had become so scarce that old tentage was sold to mills in hopes of getting a few reams in return. Salt for curing meat was now considered as valuable as gold or silver. Forage was so short that hundreds of army horses wintering in Pennsylvania had been driven into Philadelphia because farmers could no longer feed them. "Most of them," Greene warned, "will probably die in a few days for mere want of food."

Troops were as hard-pressed as the herds. "Our prospects are infinitely worse than they have been at any period of the war," Washington wrote Congress in December, "and unless some expedient can be instantly adopted, a dissolution of the army for want of subsistence is unavoidable." A day later he advised the states that his men had been "five or six weeks past on half-allowance, and we have not three days' bread. . . . Our magazines are absolutely empty everywhere." A bushel of wheat now cost $50, if it could be found, and Washington reported that "the soldiers eat every kind of horse food but hay."

Stealing from nearby farms by hungry troops became commonplace. "Mr. Thief stole my fowls," miller Benjamin Scudder recorded. Over the span of two weeks, he added, "Mr. Thief stole my pigs, 7 weeks old. . . . Mr. Thief stole my smoked meat out of the smokehouse." A sergeant wrote that his patrol happened upon a sheep and two turkeys who, "not being able to give the countersign," were "tried by fire and executed." To prevent the army from "becoming a band of robbers," Washington demanded frequent roll calls, nightly hut inspections, and floggings for plundering, despite one hundred lashes being the maximum allowed under the articles of war. "A night scarcely passes without gangs of soldiers going out of camp and committing every species of robbery, depredation, and the grossest personal insults," he fumed in general orders. "This conduct is intolerable and a disgrace to the army." The pilferage persisted anyway.

Much of the logistical burden fell on Quartermaster General Greene. "The distress of the army is very great," he wrote in early January. "God have mercy on us. We have little to hope and everything to fear." Farmers hid their provisions, repudiated their contracts, and refused any sale not paid in cash, of which the army had little. "I am so plagued for money," a deputy foragemaster complained, "that I am ashamed to set my head out of doors."

Greene commiserated. "We can no more support the army without cash than the Israelites could make bricks without straw," he told another officer. Local magistrates threatened commissary deputies with arrest; some forage officers were prosecuted after seizing fodder for army horses despite holding press warrants signed by Washington. One newspaper condemned quartermasters as "those greasy, money-making fellows," and Greene was personally accused of profiteering. In a letter to Congress he asked to resign his office and return to "the line of the army." The quartermaster's job, he added, is "injurious to my health, harassing to my mind, and opposed to my military pursuit." Congress ignored that request, too.

In mid-January, Washington and Greene devised a new army requisition scheme that met with grudging acceptance from New Jersey authorities. Each of the state's thirteen counties was given a quota—totaling twenty-two hundred head of cattle and twelve thousand bushels of grain—to be collected by a supply officer working with a local magistrate in exchange for promissory notes. The measure staved off starvation, if not hunger, at least for the moment. Furious as he was at any indiscipline in his ranks, Washington observed with some pride that "as an army they bore it with a most heroic patience."

"Money is justly considered the great sinew of war, and its want neces-sarily cramped all the military operations of the Americans," the shrewd Edmund Burke wrote in London for the *Annual Register* of 1779. A short-age of creditable money continued to be the root of all the evils afflicting the Continental Army. Through 1779, the war had cost $263 million by one calculation, and Congress continued to print money with such profli-gacy that the Treasury even hired one Henry Dawkins as a currency en-graver, after he finished serving a sentence for counterfeiting. But by early 1780 that currency had collapsed to one-fortieth of its face value: a dollar was worth $2^1/_2$ cents compared to a dollar early in the war, and the value plummeted further week by week. The states, unrestricted by Congress, also continued to print their own money—ultimately $210 million during the war, atop the $200 million in eleven emissions of Continental currency, as the economist Farley Grubb later documented. Those state emissions included six-hundred-dollar bills issued by North Carolina, where anyone speaking disrespectfully of the tender was deemed "an enemy to his coun-try." Congress lacked the authority to raise taxes and states lacked the po-litical courage, contributing barely $3 million to the national treasury as of September 1779.

Intensified British economic warfare contributed to American finan-cial woes. Loyalist purchasing agents worked the countryside around New York in what became known as the "London trade," buying provisions for General Clinton with sterling and other hard-currency specie to further diminish the foodstuffs available for Washington's men. Rebel privateers off Sandy Hook found bundles of counterfeit Continental cash aboard the captured British vessels *Blacksnake* and *Morning Star*, additional proof of efforts to undermine American finances. Congress offered a $2,000 reward for the identification of any counterfeiters, and American engravers used design elements they hoped would be difficult for forgers to replicate, in-cluding zodiacal symbols, umlauts, carets, Hebrew and Greek letters, and red ink. The counterfeiting continued apace.

By early 1780, Continental currency was fit "for little else but to make the tail of a paper kite," a Connecticut congressman wrote. Few farmers were willing to sell grain or livestock for a kite tail. Mercy Otis Warren, a Massachusetts woman of letters, considered dollars "immense heaps of paper trash." A published account claimed that dollars "are now used for papering rooms, lighting pipes, and other conveniences." Wages rose sharply, but hardly in step with the declining currency and soaring prices. Carpenters, wheelwrights, and other artificers typically were paid four dollars a day by late 1779—more than double what they'd earned at the beginning of the year—but the value of that daily wage had dropped to thirteen cents. "The present currency," the Board of War predicted, "will cease to be a medium of commerce."

In 1778 Congress had recommended that states abandon mandatory price controls as ineffective, but in November 1779, it suggested that controls be imposed again. New England governments, especially, adopted aggressive regulations to cap prices on everything from cheese and dunghill fowls to liver oil by the barrel. Wages were also capped for all trades, such as "sexton, for digging a grave for a grown person, usual guidance on the funeral and tolling the bell, nine shillings." Again the efforts proved unavailing if not counterproductive, partly because speculators purchased commodities in fixed-price states to sell in states without ceilings. Wheat purchased in New York for the maximum of $20 per bushel, for example, could be sold in Pennsylvania for $75.

As the currency's value declined, prices rose in a ruinous inflationary spiral. Beef in New England jumped from four cents a pound in 1777 to $1.69 by 1780; a bushel of Maryland wheat that sold for four shillings eight pence in late 1777 jumped to 150 shillings. Prices in Pennsylvania increased sevenfold in 1779. By January 1780, the army was paying double what it had paid for supplies three months earlier. "The times are growing worse from hour to hour," General Kalb wrote his wife from Morristown. "A hat costs four hundred dollars, a pair of boots the same. . . . Money scatters like chaff before the wind." He added that "an ordinary horse is worth $20,000. I say $20,000!"

Depreciation and inflation hit the poor and middling classes hardest, along with the soldiery. By the end of 1779, at least thirty food riots had occurred from Massachusetts to Maryland. An uprising in Philadelphia in October, fueled by economic grievances and intoxication, resulted in gunfire that killed half a dozen men and wounded more. "Every face wears the marks of fear and dejection," Dr. Rush wrote John Adams. Desperate civilian war workers throughout the states were said to be "transient, clamorous, ungovernable, and extortionate." In early spring Congress, also desperate, would try to stabilize the economy with assistance from the states by devaluing the Continental dollar at a rate of forty to one: forty old dollars would be exchanged for a new one that yielded 5 percent annual interest and could be redeemed after the war for Spanish-milled dollars, a stable specie. Six months earlier Congress had vowed to avoid such a "wanton violation of the public faith," but that pledge was tossed aside. Although the remedy eliminated much of the debt the government had incurred over the previous five years, it also wiped out the savings of countless Americans.

This scheme, too, would fail. By the end of the year a dollar would be worth a single penny and was no longer considered legal tender. "Some effectual measures must be taken to save our currency, save our army, and save our country," wrote Captain William Allen of the 2nd Rhode Island Regiment. A loyalist ridiculed the rebel predicament with a derisive couplet: "Mock money and mock states shall melt away / And the mock troops disband for want of pay."

Nearly five years had passed since Washington had last written in his personal diary, but on January 1 he resumed scribbling with a brief entry: "Clear, cold & freezing with little wind." This was followed a day later with "Very cold. About noon it began to snow & continued without intermission through the day & night." His troops made similar meteorological observations. "The weather was cold enough to cut a man in two," wrote Private Joseph Plumb Martin. During a snowstorm that lingered for several days, Martin reported that he had nothing to eat "except a little black birch bark which I gnawed off a stick. . . . I saw several of the men roast their old shoes and eat them." Major James Fairlie, a Steuben aide, wrote a friend on January 12, "Oh, my dear Charles, we have been almost starved. . . . During our hungry time, I eat several meals of dog and it relished very well."

Not once in January would the temperature rise above freezing. "Continewes exseading cold," wrote Silvanus Seely, a farmer and militia colonel. An army surveyor told a friend on January 10, "One of my ears froze hard as a pine knot." Surgeon's Mate Thacher noted that some troops were buried "like sheep in the snow," and Knox's men had to dig out their heavy guns to prevent ice from corrupting the barrels. Robert Hanson Harrison, the commander in chief's secretary, told the Continental clothier general that "the deficiency of shoes is so extensive that a great proportion of the army is totally incapable of duty and could not move on the most pressing exigency." Private Ebenezer Parkman, an artilleryman, wrote, "Time flies fast away. Eternity is nearer every day."

General and Mrs. Washington tried to keep up morale among the officers with "dancing assemblies" whenever the roads cleared sufficiently for a musical convocation. A few wives eventually joined their husbands in Morristown, including Lucy Knox; in the summer she had given birth to a daughter who died in infancy, prompting a bereft Henry to long for a day when "we shall sit down, free from the hurry, bustle, and impertinence of the world." Greene, also lonely, had written Caty in Rhode Island, "I am very impatient to hear from you. . . . If you love me, if you regard my peace and happiness, let me hear from you by every conveyance." She arrived in camp well advanced in her fourth pregnancy, and settled into Nathanael's quarters at Jacob Arnold's tavern on the village green.

Lieutenant Colonel Hamilton, living in the crowded aides' bunk room at the Ford mansion, was so obviously on the prowl for female companionship that Lady Washington named her lascivious tomcat "Hamilton." The previous spring Hamilton, who claimed that his motto was "All for love," had urged John Laurens to find him a wife in South Carolina. "She must be young, handsome (I lay most stress upon a good shape), sensible (a little learning will do), well bred," he wrote. "In politics I am indifferent what side she may be of. . . . She must believe in God and hate a saint." His prayers would be answered in early February when twenty-two-year-old Elizabeth Schuyler, one of General Schuyler's three daughters, arrived in Morristown to visit her uncle, Dr. John Cochran, the army's surgeon general, who occupied a white frame house a short walk from headquarters. "She is most unmercifully handsome and . . . has none of those petty affectations which are the prerogatives of beauty," wrote Hamilton, who had just turned twenty-three. "She has good nature, affability, and vivacity." Tench Tilghman, another aide, reported that "Hamilton is a gone man." In less than two months he and Eliza were engaged to be married.

Another visitor had come to Morristown, less auspiciously. Major General Arnold hobbled into the village just before Christmas with his hickory cane, as lithe and darkly handsome as ever in a blue-and-buff broadcloth uniform, appointed with a French sword knot and gold-braid epaulets once personally given to him by Washington as a token of admiration. He'd left Peggy in Philadelphia, pregnant with their first child and living in a modest house owned by her father on the corner of Sixth and High Streets; strapped for cash, Arnold had rented out Mount Pleasant, the mansion on the Schuylkill he bought for her as a wedding gift. The morning after his arrival he appeared in the low-ceilinged great room of the two-story Norris Tavern, where a dozen officers sat at a long wooden table. A stack of split logs blazed in the hearth. Here at ten a.m. his court-martial resumed, six months after it had been suspended in deference to more urgent army demands.

The trial board included three brigadiers—Knox among them—and eight colonels under the chairmanship of Major General Howe, who somehow remained in good odor despite his loss of Savannah a year earlier. The charges, brought by Arnold's relentless political enemies in Pennsylvania, had been narrowed to four misdemeanors allegedly committed while he was military governor in Philadelphia, notably profiteering and improper use of government property. For several days, witnesses appeared, testified under questioning from Colonel John Laurance, the judge advocate general, then stepped away to be succeeded by other witnesses. Arnold's cross-examinations were methodical, precise, and exculpatory. At the end of December, the court adjourned for more than two weeks, allowing the defendant time to prepare his own witnesses and compose a final statement of innocence.

Innocent he was not. Unknown to any patriot, the previous May Arnold had taken the first steps toward committing the most infamous act of treason in American history. Aggrieved, brooding, and in debt, he asserted during a circumspect conversation with a loyalist Philadelphia merchant named Joseph Stansbury that the war between Britain and America was "ruinous to both" and that he would welcome contact with General Clinton. Stansbury traveled secretly to New York, where he was escorted to the British headquarters at No. 1 Broadway. Here he met John André, impresario of the *Mischianza* spectacle in Philadelphia a year earlier, who would soon be assigned to serve as Clinton's deputy adjutant general and spymaster.

As directed by his commander, André opened a correspondence with Arnold that eventually led to an exchange of several dozen letters, most written in invisible ink or with a cipher keyed to volume 1 of *Blackstone's Commentaries* or Nathan Bailey's *Universal Etymological English Dictionary*. A sequence of three numbers indicated the page, the line, and the specific word in that line used to compose each message. Using the noms de guerre "Mr. A.G.," "Mr. Moore," and "Gustavus Monk," and almost certainly with Peggy's knowledge, Arnold soon passed along intelligence regarding the French alliance, the Sullivan expedition against the Iroquois, rebel hopes for financial assistance from the Dutch, and the weakness of General Lincoln's garrison in Charleston. To completely turn his coat, Arnold requested a payment of £10,000, "whether this contest is finished by sword or treaty." Clinton, for his part, wanted Arnold back in a field command, where he could do the most damage to the American cause. André, writing as "John Anderson," had urged him in June:

Accept a command, be surprised, be cut off. These things may happen in the course of maneuver, nor [would] you be censured or suspected.

A complete service of this nature, involving a corps of five or six thousand men, would be rewarded with twice as many thousand guineas.

In another note in late July, André had added, "We are thankful for the information transmitted and hope you will continue to give it as frequently as possible. Permit me to prescribe . . . procuring an accurate plan of West Point." The correspondence had then gone quiet, at least for the winter. "Arnold had named his price and Clinton had refused to meet it," the historian Carl Van Doren later wrote. But a channel for betrayal had been opened.

On January 21 in the Norris Tavern great room, Arnold finished calling the defense witnesses and gave his closing statement. "It is disagreeable to be accused," he told the court. When the war began, "I was in easy circumstances and enjoyed a fair prospect of improving them. I was happy in domestic connections and blessed with a rising family." Nevertheless, he continued:

> I sacrificed domestic ease and happiness to the service of my country. . . . I was one of the first that appeared in the field, and from that time to the present hour have not abandoned her service. . . . My time, my fortune, and my person have been devoted to my country in this war.

As his twelve judges listened closely, he noted his sword knot and epaulets, given to him by Washington with a note signed "sincerely and affectionately." His Excellency had specifically asked for Arnold as "an active, spirited officer" to check Burgoyne's progress down the Hudson from Ticonderoga. Arnold also produced encomiums from Congress praising his "gallant conduct" at Danbury and Saratoga. Again refuting the charges point by point, he concluded, "My conduct and character have been most unwarrantably traduced. . . . The charges brought against me are false, malicious, and scandalous." He limped from the tavern feeling a "pleasing anxiety," but confident of exoneration.

That confidence was misplaced. At eleven a.m. on January 26, the board acquitted him of two counts but convicted him of two others: improperly authorizing the *Charming Nancy*, a trading schooner in which he had a financial interest, to sail from Philadelphia with woolens, glass, loaf sugar, and other commodities regulated by Congress, and appropriating a dozen army wagons for his personal use. At least one board member wanted Arnold cashiered, but the majority cleared him of peculation and corrupt behavior. (Later investigation of the charges would in fact reveal substantial guilt.) The sentence amounted to a sharp slap on the wrist: "a reprimand from His Excellency, the commander in chief."

Stunned and furious—"A reprimand," he wrote Silas Deane. "For what?"—Arnold, in a bid for public sympathy, would ask Deane to have the court-martial record printed and circulated in both English and French. The Pennsylvania Supreme Executive Council, largely responsible for this prosecution, had second thoughts and wrote Congress that Arnold's "sufferings for and services to his country" should preclude "public censure." Congress swiftly approved the verdict anyway, and Washington, as instructed, rebuked Arnold in general orders for actions that were "imprudent and improper" and "peculiarly reprehensible," even as he acknowledged "an officer who has rendered such distinguished services to his country."

Later that winter, Arnold briefly toyed with the notion of joining the Continental Navy to command several hundred soldiers who, as marines, would be embarked on frigates for a swashbuckling springtime expedition, perhaps to the West Indies. Army pay had become all but worthless, and he apparently hoped for prize money from captured enemy merchantmen. But this scheme collapsed when Washington told the Board of Admiralty that the army could spare no troops for naval adventures.

Arnold shrugged, proposed taking a leave of absence, then changed his mind, writing General Schuyler, "Though attended with pain and difficulty, I wish to render my country every service in my power." A new plan had occurred to him, secretly suggested by André the previous summer. He would ask to return to the field as commanding general of the Highlands Department. Such a position would give him oversight of all defenses in the Hudson valley, including the bastion at West Point, the most vital fort in America. That, he believed, should be worth £10,000 of the king's gold.

Just beyond Morristown's eastern horizon, the king's army had also gone into winter quarters. On Manhattan Island, cantonments arose at Bloomingdale on the Hudson, at Marston's Wharf, and at McGowan's Pass. Hessian regiments settled around Harlem, in commandeered houses on the East River, at Cock Hill Fort, south of Spuyten Duyvil, and in the barracks at Fort Knyphausen—formerly Fort Washington. Soldiers also burrowed in on Staten Island and at Paulus Hook, above the Hudson River in New Jersey. Troops returning from Newport mostly laagered on Long Island. Captain John Peebles of the 42nd Foot described the winter camp built in Jamaica, near the island's western end: "each hut 24 feet by 12, to contain 12 men, the wall partly dug in the face of the hill and the rest made up of sod. The roof to be covered with cedar branches & thin sod. . . . One pane of glass to each hut."

Given the American surprise attack at Stony Point the previous summer, General Clinton decided that garrisons north of the Harlem River were too vulnerable. Demolition teams razed the batteries and redoubts around King's Bridge. Only Fort Number Eight was manned beyond the Harlem, and it was linked by ferry to Manhattan and within covering range of guns on Laurel Hill.

Four thousand reinforcements—half the number promised by Whitehall—had arrived from Britain in late summer. The voyage from Portsmouth, diverted and delayed by French cruisers, had taken five months to clear British waters and reach New York, by which time "malignant jail fever"—typhus—had ripped through passengers and crews. Sailors aboard one transport were so incapacitated that the commander of the 82nd Foot had been forced to take the helm in midocean. The reinforcements brought their contagion with them, Clinton wrote, and disease "soon spread itself among the rest of my army and sent six thousand of my best troops to hospital." Other fevers and dysentery—"a most invincible flux"—also raged, increasing the sick rolls to nine thousand men and filling barns, churches, and warehouses with ailing soldiers. Nearly every man in the 37th Foot was ill, thirty-five of them mortally; the 54th Foot, bivouacked on Long Island, suffered sixty-three deaths. "The season has been very unhealthy," the British paymaster, Robert Biddulph, wrote a friend. "Two-thirds of the army have been sick, the Guards excepted, who are almost constantly drunk." The city commandant, Major General Pattison, told London, "So sickly a time is not remembered in this country."

Ailments plaguing the Royal Navy also exacerbated other ills. A survey of *Rainbow, Romulus, Roebuck*, and *Renown* in late fall found "a great deficiency in point of seamen," with dozens who were invalids, landlubbers, or otherwise "perfectly useless." With Bourbon fleets threatening the home islands and British interests around the globe, only forty warships could be spared for the American seaboard, less than 10 percent of the navy's total strength, down from more than 40 percent in the summer of 1778. That might be enough to support the army, but it was not sufficient to secure the seas; rebel privateers preyed mercilessly on merchantmen and other vessels, including thirty "large trading ships from England loaded with salt provisions and cordage," Lieutenant Colonel Stuart wrote his father.

Worse still, the Admiralty had sent another dud to command the North American station. Vice Admiral Arbuthnot, who had brought the sickly convoy from Portsmouth, was sixty-seven years old, but his secretary took him to be seventy-five and another officer insisted that he was eighty. Smarmy with superiors, querulous with equals, and a bully to inferiors, he was described by the biographer William Willcox as "a pompous weathercock . . . by turns stubborn and vacillating, ebulliently overconfident and fearful. The only constants in his character were slowness to take responsibility and quickness to take alarm." Barely two months after reaching Sandy Hook, Arbuthnot wrote Sandwich from *Europe*, his sixty-four-gun flagship, and requested permission "to resign this command and return to England. . . . My feelings, my lord, are my own. I cannot help them."

New York remained a garrison town, under the heels of British military boots and without civilian courts, civil government, or elected officials. Clinton's ration summary for mid-December listed 34,299 men, 3,875 women, and 3,444 children; in addition to several thousand horses wintering on Long Island, the army also claimed 930 cattle and 1,019 sheep. The king's bureaucracy regulated every aspect of New York life, from grain and firewood prices to cartage fees by the mile: six shillings for a hogshead of rum or eight shillings for a load of hay. Brooklyn ferries could charge no more than two shillings for a horse, a penny for a rabbit, or sixpence for a man, a hog, a large looking glass, or a dead calf. Every house was required to keep two fire buckets, and "no corpse is to be buried in the yard of the meeting house." Auctioneers, boatmen, and various vendors needed licenses, and no stranger could set foot in New York without notifying the authorities. Commandant Pattison, warning that "many evils daily arise from the unlimited number of taverns and public houses," capped the number of grogshop licenses at two hundred, each subject to official approval. Hospital patients bought so much liquor that they would now be forced to wear an *H* on both sleeves, and barkeeps were forbidden to serve them.

Every New York male between sixteen and sixty was required to enroll in the militia, with exemptions granted for Quakers and four hundred firemen. This levy gave the city almost six thousand civilian defenders organized in companies like the King's Dockyard Volunteers and the Seamen's Ordnance Volunteers.

As the only viable sanctuary north of Savannah for runaway blacks and inveterate loyalists, New York grew more crowded by the week. "All Negroes that fly from the enemy's country are free," a British decree advised. "No person whatever can claim a right to them." In a proclamation printed in each issue of the *Royal Gazette* for three months, Clinton also promised freedom and job security for "every Negro who shall desert the rebel standard," although those captured while serving under arms in American ranks were to be sold into slavery. Clinton subsequently proposed "Freedom and a Farm," a program intended to settle freed blacks on confiscated rebel land. A 1779 census estimated that at least twelve hundred blacks had recently arrived in Manhattan, including runaways from New Jersey who had paddled makeshift rafts across the Hudson.

As for loyalists, in late October the patriot New York legislature had passed an act of attainder, confiscating the estates of fifty-nine landowners deemed "confirmed enemies" of the rebellion; those "adhering to the king" were also banished forever, on pain of death "without benefit of clergy" if they remained in the state. Hundreds of additional Tory properties would eventually be seized by "commissioners of sequestration." Many of the dispossessed fled to New York City, where they were welcomed by the Refugee Club, an association of militant exiles who met at Hicks's tavern to exchange grievances and plot their revenge. They were led by William Franklin, the estranged son of Benjamin and the former royal governor of New Jersey, who, after two years of harsh confinement in Connecticut, had been exchanged for the captured president of Delaware. Bitter and depressed at the death of his wife and the indifference of his father while he was in jail, Franklin advocated harsher treatment for American prisoners of war and remorseless violence to crush the rebellion.

Overcrowded, expensive, and surrounded by insurgents, New York was not a happy town. Petty corruption, spoliation, and other "shameful irregularities" by British and German garrison troops fueled resentment, as Pattison acknowledged. Judge Smith, although a confirmed loyalist, denounced redcoat authority as "military misrule." A British general told Parliament, "There was a great deal of plundering. . . . Naturally it would lose you friends and gain you enemies."

Much resentment was directed at Henry Clinton, who was "weak, irresolute, unsteady, vain" and advised by a "parcel of blockheads," in Governor Franklin's unsparing appraisal. Clinton wryly told a friend, "I am by no means the fashion here, with civil or military." His own troops, bored and discouraged, were indeed just as contemptuous. "Nothing surely can be more shameful than our perfect inactivity," an army surgeon wrote in a letter home. "It is unfortunately our fate to be commanded by a person that has no abilities to plan, nor firmness to execute the most trivial military operations."

That harsh judgment was wrong, and the commanding general would now prove it so. In mid-December a great bustle could be seen along the East River and across New York Bay as two expeditions began to convene. The first, with 130 ships, including the transports *Kingston*, *Polly*, and *Two*

Sisters, was a routine convoy returning to Britain. The destination of the second fleet remained secret, even as nine thousand troops, five thousand sailors, four hundred horses, ninety transports, and fourteen men-of-war assembled. Provisions sufficient for more than two months were winched into the holds, and ship captains received printed forms listing the proper signals to be transmitted by flags, lanterns, and guns. "Some think Rhode Island, some Boston is the object," Captain Peebles told his journal. "Others think it is only to be out of the way of the ice in North River."

In fact, as only Clinton and a few trusted lieutenants knew, the fleet's objective was Charleston. This voyage had been concocted in the spring after the initial capture of Savannah, then delayed for months, until the defeat of the Franco-American assault on Georgia and d'Estaing's departure from southern waters were confirmed. London believed this operation was of "vast importance," and the government expected great things in South Carolina. "The possession of Charleston would . . . be attended with the recovery of the whole of that province," Germain wrote Clinton, "and probably North Carolina would soon follow." The American secretary added, "Our cause is just, our councils firm and decided."

Clinton, for once, readily agreed. Not only would the seizure of Charleston prevent another rebel counterstroke in Georgia, but "the spirit of rebellion might be thoroughly subdued in the two Carolinas," he wrote, with British control of the South extended from Florida to at least Chesapeake Bay. That would severely truncate American pretensions. Charleston was a vital rebel port for both imports of smuggled war matériel and profitable exports of rice, indigo, and naval stores. Not least, Clinton had scores to settle: the humiliating repulse of Britain's assault under his command at Sullivan's Island, more than three years earlier, still rankled.

Yet doubts plagued him. With France and Spain in the war, the proportion of the British Army committed to fighting insurgents in North America had declined from almost two-thirds to less than a quarter. Convinced that Washington commanded sixty-five Continental regiments between West Point and Morristown—a substantial overstatement—Clinton felt obliged to leave at least twelve thousand troops to defend New York. This meant he was heading south with half the army manpower and a fleet one-third the size of the force under the Howe brothers when they sailed for Philadelphia in 1777. Opening a new front in South Carolina would disperse redcoats across this hemisphere more broadly than ever, from the seven thousand in Canada to the eight thousand in the West Indies, plus the four thousand still held in rebel prison camps from the Saratoga catastrophe.

If the southern strategy was to succeed, armed loyalists would have to turn out in greater numbers than the eight thousand enrolled in military units in 1779, only slightly more than the previous year. "So many attempts to raise men have totally failed," Clinton told Germain on December 15. "There is little encouragement to undertake anything more in this line." London continued to cling to what Clinton dismissed as "visionary hopes" for good Americans to subdue the bad ones. "I felt," the commanding general later wrote, "the tottering ground on which I stood."

Troops designated for Charleston began to embark in Brooklyn on December 20, despite frigid temperatures and ice that thickened by the hour. "Very cold business," Peebles wrote. "Some men frostbit, & two or three drowned." Hessian soldiers had initially been overjoyed to leave their miserable winter quarters for the vague hope of a warmer climate somewhere, but even before their ship left the harbor, two men froze to death belowdecks. "Many soldiers had frozen noses, hands, or ears," a private wrote. A German major complained that "the British are not keeping the transports in good repair and are overcrowding them." Captain Ewald settled aboard the transport *Pan* with eighty of his *Jäger*, then woke suddenly on December 23 to find that drift ice had severed the anchor chain. Floes on the flood tide pushed *Pan* onto the rocks near Hell Gate, tossing men to the deck and crushing the hull. Boatmen rowed the passengers and crew to shore—Ewald would transfer to the brigantine *Spring*—but their equipment and provisions were lost along with the ship. Six other vessels were also badly damaged by ice over the next three days and declared unfit for the open sea.

Clinton and his entourage strode from No. 1 Broadway on Christmas, boarded the horse transport *John*, and sailed to Sandy Hook, where they transferred to the forty-four-gun *Romulus*. The commanding general and Admiral Arbuthnot had already begun to bicker, communicating mostly by "peevish and petulant letters" and profanely denouncing each other to their respective staffs. Clinton blamed Arbuthnot, whom he described as "full of deceit and artifice," for excessive delays in leaving New York. The admiral complained tearfully that he was "tired to death by the general" and his "want of candor."

Only the presence of an old comrade, Major General Cornwallis, cheered Clinton. After departing America on emergency leave following the Battle of Monmouth, Cornwallis had reached home shortly before the death of his adored wife, Jemima. "This country has no charms for me," he had subsequently written Clinton from England. "Send for me and I will most readily come to you. . . . I come to share fortunes with you, but I will not let you desert me." In the late summer, Clinton, also a widower, had been delighted to welcome Cornwallis back to New York as his second-in-command. "How happy I am made by the return of Lord Cornwallis to this country," he wrote Germain. "To say truth, my lord, my spirits are worn out." Despite Cornwallis's plea not to be abandoned, Clinton had once again renewed his request to resign, proposing to turn the American war over to his deputy. And once again the gambit failed. "His Majesty is too well satisfied with your conduct," Germain told him, "to wish to see the command of his forces in any other hands."

On Sunday morning, December 26, Arbuthnot ordered the signal to set sail hoisted above *Europe*'s main deck. With a great winching of capstans and unsheeting of canvas, the expedition swayed into formation behind the thirty-two-gun *Perseus*. Victuallers, transports, single-masted horse carriers, and the remaining warships crowded on sail, 133 vessels in all. A single frigate remained behind in New York, where General Knyphausen took command in Clinton's absence.

"Fair weather, nothing remarkable," a British grenadier officer told his journal. Clinton was more expansive in a letter home to William Eden. "This is the most important hour Britain ever knew," he wrote. "If we lose it, we shall never see such another."

The fleet sailed in the nick of time. Hardly had the last ships vanished over the southern horizon than the protracted cold in New York turned murderous, with a low in the city of sixteen degrees below zero Fahrenheit. Twenty-seven snowfalls would be recorded around New York that winter, with the last of it not melting until May. "The snow was so deep that we could ride on the banks over the tops of the fences with horses and sleighs," a parson's son later wrote. The Hackensack, Passaic, and Raritan Rivers, in northern New Jersey, froze nearly to their bottoms, with ice eleven feet thick in places. "Almost all the wild beasts of the field and the birds of the air have perished with the cold," an American officer wrote.

By mid-January a two-ton cannon could be wheeled two thousand yards across the Hudson River ice from Manhattan to Paulus Hook, "an event unknown in the memory of man," Commandant Pattison wrote Germain. The *Royal Gazette* reported that three men walked twenty miles from Connecticut to Long Island across the frozen Sound. Eighty-six sleighs laden with provisions, each pulled by a pair of horses, traveled five miles across New York Bay from Fort George to Staten Island, escorted by a cavalry squadron. Farther south, the Chesapeake froze from Head of Elk to within twenty miles of the bay's mouth at Capes Charles and Henry, immobilizing ships for weeks. Carriages could cross from Maryland's Eastern Shore to Annapolis, a feat never imagined, much less witnessed. The James,

York, and Rappahannock Rivers in southern Virginia resembled glaciers more than tidal tributaries; the new privateer brig *Jefferson* was crushed by pack ice on the eve of her maiden voyage and sent to the bottom near Jamestown.

"The ink freezes in my pen," Judge Smith wrote in his New York town house in January. "I set before a large coal fire and within two feet of the grate, and yet am not comfortably warm. . . . We often hear of the deaths of the poor, frozen in their houses." Firewood grew so desperately scarce in New York that "sometimes the troops were obliged to eat their meat raw," paymaster Biddulph told his father. One woman reported paying a Spanish dollar for a single log. On orders from the high command, axmen felled all trees—sparing only fruit orchards—and various sailing vessels were chopped up for fuel. With the waters around Manhattan frozen solid for weeks, Generals Knyphausen and Pattison fretted incessantly over a sudden American attack across the ice. Three lights illuminated on a flagstaff and three sky rockets would warn of Continentals skating across the Hudson. Field guns remained loaded in the river batteries, Royal Navy seamen built an alarm post at Hay Wharf, and more loyalists willing to fight for the king received firelocks from the arsenal. Light fieldpieces were lashed to sleds as mobile artillery, and the guard was doubled each night at No. 1 Broadway and other headquarters. Not until a thaw in late February would soldiers be permitted to undress at night.

Such fears among the king's men were well-founded. Before dawn on Saturday, January 15, twenty-seven hundred Continentals from Morristown crossed the frozen Arthur Kill onto Staten Island with five hundred sleighs and sleds. General Lord Stirling's assault force trudged through waist-deep snow in two serpentine columns toward the British works on the island's northeast corner. Washington, who had provided the raiders with wool caps, mittens, and forty thousand musket cartridges, estimated the enemy garrison at a thousand men—roughly half their actual number. He hoped to capture most of them, along with droves of cattle and sheep, although Stirling had warned that "an attempt to surprise the enemy on Staten Island would have very little probability of success. They are as much upon their guard as they can be."

Stirling was correct. Deserters and loyalist informants alerted the redcoats, who retreated into fortifications protected by gun platforms and a ten-foot abatis coated in ice. Planks with nails driven through them had been concealed under the snow to cripple rebel horses. Stirling's men fired a few volleys and burned nine small vessels in the British anchorage, but by noon they had begun to build bonfires and dig burrows in the snow. After a bitter night, the invaders wheeled back toward New Jersey, shooed off by

British dragoons. They left behind more deserters, a few dead, and seventeen prisoners. "We found that one-third of our men's feet was froze," a Rhode Island officer recorded. Militiamen and Continentals alike looted farms and homesteads during the retreat—"necklaces off the ladies' necks, buckles from their shoes, shirts from men's backs." Ensign John Barr of the 4th New York added, "Our troops returned off the island with five hundred sleighloads of diverse articles."

Stirling's officers made fitful efforts to recover and return the booty. "It was a noble attempt," Greene said of the raid, "but a fruitless expedition." Joseph Lewis, one of the quartermaster general's deputies, was less indulgent. The raid "was expensive," Lewis wrote, "but answered no valuable purpose except to show the inclination of our inhabitants to plunder."

Repulse of the Staten Island marauders gave the high command in New York an additional reason to celebrate Queen Charlotte's birthday on January 18. A royal salute roared from Fort George at noon, answered with gusto from ships immobilized by harbor ice. General Tryon organized a dinner for senior officers, including two men captured at Saratoga who, with the permission of Congress, had just been released on parole: Major General Phillips, the British artillery chief, and Major General Riedesel, who commanded the Hessians. Many toasts were raised, including to "the most amiable, exemplary, and beloved princess upon earth": Charlotte. The afternoon passed, it was said, "with the most perfect hilarity."

Festivities resumed that evening with a ball at Hicks's tavern, where the newly painted public rooms were tricked out "with uncommon splendor and magnificence," as the *Royal Gazette* recorded. Above the main entrance a Doric pediment illuminated with colored lamps displayed full-length portraits of the king and queen in their royal robes beneath the motto BRITONS STRIKE HOME. At eight p.m. the honorary queen of the ball, bundled against the cold, stepped from a carriage and strolled inside on the arm of General Pattison to a fanfare from trumpets and kettledrums.

Seven months pregnant, Frederika Riedesel had also just been released from captivity with her husband and their three young daughters. Almost four years had passed since the undaunted baroness sailed from Germany; she and the girls had been in America so long that they spoke mostly English together. Since developing a taste for bear paws in the Hudson valley and watching the mortally wounded General Fraser die in her cabin after the defeat at Bemus Heights, she had eventually found herself with most of the captured army in the prison camp at Charlottesville. She learned to butcher pigs, sit on tree stumps in the absence of chairs, and avoid rattlesnakes. Thomas Jefferson's solicitude made confinement easier for the Riedesels. He sold them a piano from Monticello so she could sing her favorite Italian arias; he also commissioned a silversmith in Williamsburg to make her eight spoons. Now at liberty again in New York, if not yet free to return home, the family lived in a fine house appointed by Pattison with furniture and carpets confiscated from well-heeled rebels, although she was appalled at having to pay £10 for a cord of firewood.

Luminous and self-possessed as ever, she danced a minuet to open the ball. Country dances began at nine-thirty, and at midnight the company adjourned to supper at long tables strewn with artificial flowers and covered with nearly four hundred dishes. Seated under a canopy, the baroness was asked to represent Charlotte—another German—and give the first toast. "I was very much touched," she later wrote. The *Gazette* recorded that "the company retired about three o'clock in the morning, highly satisfied with the evening's entertainment."

Judge Smith grumbled that the four hundred guineas spent "would have been better laid out in fuel for the poor or in general charity to the plundered inhabitants of Staten Island." But a newspaper writer applauded "the most truly elegant ball and entertainment ever known on this side of the Atlantic." As for Frau Riedesel, she would give birth in early March to another girl. "I am fully satisfied if God but protects my four daughters," she wrote her mother. "We must leave all to God's will." The baron and baroness named the baby "America."

26.

————◆————

She Stoops to Conquer

One day after the British fleet left Sandy Hook for Charleston, the old gods rose from the deep. Storm followed storm with a ferocity that unnerved even master mariners. General Clinton, always prone to mal de mer, kept to his cabin aboard *Romulus*, bemoaning "the malevolence of the winds." A voyage that typically took ten days would last more than five weeks. "Terrible weather!" Captain Johann Hinrichs, a *Jäger* officer, told his diary. "Snow, rain, hail, foaming waves, and bitter cold."

"First the bow sank, then the stern, then a wave engulfed the ship," another Hessian diarist wrote on the third day at sea. "We all lay in our beds and, as one, lamented our fate." Even more crowded than usual because of the seven ice-damaged vessels left behind in New York, the transports pitched and rolled as men lashed themselves to bunks and bulkheads and vomited into their shoes. "The raging sea, the roaring of the wind, the shouts of the sailors, and the darkness of the night all contributed to make this moment so much the more terrible," a quartermaster aboard *Andrew* recorded on January 2. Mountainous waves slammed across the weather decks, sluicing seawater down the hatches to drench baggage, bedding, and passengers. Several German soldiers aboard *Apollo* were crushed to death in their bunks when the berths above them collapsed. No cook fires could be lighted, reducing meals for those with an appetite to weevily biscuits and rum. By January 4, only forty-eight ships remained in sight, the rest blown to the earth's edges. A Guards officer described life on a transport as "continued destruction in the foretops, the pox above-board, the plague between the decks, hell in the forecastle, the devil at the helm."

Tempestuous seas killed horses by the score, including ten belonging to General Cornwallis and his staff. Of thirty-one horses on one transport, just one survived. Shortages of forage and fresh water eventually forced grooms to toss many over the side. "Killed ten horses," Captain Archibald Robertson, a deputy quartermaster, wrote aboard *Briton*, "having only three bundles of hay left." Rebel privateers on the twenty-gun *Columbus* captured the sloop *Juno*, cut the throats of every horse, took a loyalist captain prisoner, then sent the vessel on its way. Rebels also captured *Swift*, carrying twenty-eight cavalry mounts, and *Rebecca*, with thirty-four more. By one count, the expedition would lose 223 animals, including nearly every dragoon and saddle horse, and all two dozen belonging to the Royal Artillery.

Of thirty-six days at sea, according to a lieutenant's log, the fleet endured twenty-five stormy days, thirteen of them with contrary winds. "Our sailors lost all heart and assured me in confidence that not one ship could withstand this terrible weather," Captain Ewald told his diary. "Here I thought to myself, 'O, miserable human being, why are you fearful?'" The toll among ships continued to mount in mid-January. Rolling seas "pooped us and stove in the stern window," wrote Captain Robertson. "We shipped a great deal of water. It was two feet deep in the cabin." The transport *Georgia*, carrying four light infantry companies, signaled distress at noon on January 16 as six feet of seawater filled the hold; all hands dived headfirst into rescue boats sent from two frigates before the ship sank behind them, her sails standing and standards flapping in the wind. The same day the man-of-war *Raisonnable* saved engineers and sailors from the foundering *Judith*, seen lying on her beam-ends in a "high, tumbling sea" with wreckage littering the waves. *Success Increase*, carrying part of the 33rd Foot and wallowing badly, then caught fire and lost her mainsail. *Swan* signaled distress and shifted all men to the hospital ship *Sally*, except for a detachment of brave men who remained at the pumps. "No job is more dangerous than that of a sailor in a storm," a grenadier observed in his journal.

No loss was more damaging to the expedition than the *Russia Merchant*. A loyalist privateer, *Lady Dunmore*, rescued the imperiled crew and eighty passengers, but the transport went down near Bermuda with much of Clinton's heavy artillery, ammunition, and four thousand muskets intended to arm southern loyalists. No ordeal exceeded that of *Anna*, dismasted in a collision shortly after leaving New York and taken under tow by *Renown*. The hawser parted, and *Anna*, carrying Hessian artillery and 250 souls reduced to eating pet dogs, drifted across the Atlantic for more than two months before the hulk washed ashore at St. Ives, on the north coast of Cornwall. Most of the German soldiers aboard would sail back to New York ten months later.

Each day at sea seemed to bring new perils, whether it was the shoals off Cape Hatteras—"deathly fear was to be seen in every face," a Hessian officer wrote—or an unintentional drift into the poorly charted Gulf Stream, which, to Clinton's fury, at times carried the fleet in the wrong direction. The transports *Diana* and *Silver Eel*, carrying five hundred men between them, ran out of bread and meat. On January 6 the *Margery* began rationing water to two quarts per man each day; two weeks later that was reduced to three pints. Another vessel was down to a daily allowance of a single pint. Some passengers, Captain Peebles noted, "like fools drink seawater."

On February 2, sixty-two vessels—less than half the fleet—dropped anchor within sight of Tybee Island, in the mouth of the Savannah River, the agreed rendezvous site before any advance on Charleston. More bedraggled stragglers arrived day by day; one transport's log estimated that the ship had traveled over eighteen hundred meandering miles since leaving New York, more than twice the usual sailing distance. A haggard Clinton, without even a horse to ride, admitted in a dispatch to Germain that the "very tedious voyage" had likely given rebel defenders time to bolster their fortifications along the South Carolina coast. With a half dozen ships still missing, including the *Russia Merchant*, the commanding general sent pleas to St. Augustine, the Bahamas, and various West Indies outposts for spare guns and artillery stores.

Clinton had intended to march overland to Charleston from Savannah, but a war council persuaded him to move the fleet closer to the city before opening his siege. He would avoid a frontal assault into the teeth of rebel defenses by outflanking and then encircling the city, exploiting British skill at amphibious operations demonstrated earlier at Long Island, Kip's Bay, and elsewhere. While a detachment of fourteen hundred men tramped toward Augusta as a feint, he ordered anchors weighed on February 9; two days later the vanguard crossed the bar into the North Edisto River, twenty-five miles southwest of Charleston. In a cold rain, flatboats carried grenadiers and light infantry onto Simmons Island that evening. Clinton followed on their heels, sheltering under a tree for a few hours' sleep.

More troops landed on February 12, as scouts pushed onto adjacent Johns Island. A staff officer in a whaleboat brought Clinton his camp bed, trunk, and a bag of gold. Loyalists and runaway slaves flocked to the invaders, offering Major André—part of the commanding general's retinue—intelligence about American troop and naval strength, as well as advice on where to find horses, sheep, and horned cattle. Word of the landings spread quickly in Charleston. "We are very much afraid of the British, who are on Johns Island," a local woman wrote in her journal on February 13. "People go out of town very fast."

If not fast, the British advance was relentless. The king's men waded waist-deep through salt marshes and coastal creeks, slashing at vines with their bayonets and firing muskets into the air when they got lost. "What a land to wage war in," Captain Hinrichs told his diary. Spanish moss lent "a very melancholy appearance" to the sea-island trees. In an inventive letter to his prince, Captain Ewald described "crocodiles sixteen feet long. The impassable woods are full of wolves and several species of venomous snakes." His Hessian comrades were beguiled by the bountiful oysters, yucca plants as tall as a man, pileated woodpeckers—"about as large as a medium-sized chicken"—and what they called "Virginia nightingales," the brilliant red northern cardinals, for which it was said English ladies would pay at least six guineas apiece. Foragers plundered local plantations, returning to camp with peddler's packs chock-full of candlesticks, salt cellars, salvers, butter boats, tea tongs, punch ladles, earrings, and opera glasses. "Living on the fat of the land," wrote Uzal Johnson, a loyalist physician, "the soldiers every side of us roasting turkeys, geese, fowls, ducks, pigs."

Clinton was chagrined to learn that the sixty-four-gun *Defiance* had bilged on a sandbar near Tybee on February 21. With nine feet of water in her hold, she soon broke up, and only a few 18-pounders could be salvaged from the gun decks. But three days later his army crossed the Stono River and soon possessed all of James Island. With his heavy artillery apparently lost, Clinton needed Royal Navy guns for a siege; Admiral Arbuthnot agreed to loan the army forty-five big guns, with a hundred round shot for each. The admiral balked at Clinton's request for double the number of shot, plus another 120 barrels of gunpowder, but the navy seconded several dozen gunnery officers from thirteen ships, plus 750 seamen and marines. The guns were lowered from *Europe* and *Raisonnable* into boats, rowed ashore, and—given the dearth of horses—dragged inland by teams of a hundred or more sweating, swearing men wearing rope harnesses.

Engineers under James Moncrieff, who had been promoted to major for his excellence in organizing Savannah's defenses the previous fall, built batteries with platforms and embrasures to hold the cannons. By March 12, Moncrieff had five guns emplaced at Fenwick's Point, across from the northern lip of James Island, capable of ranging both Charleston—just over a mile away—and any rebel man-of-war that ventured up the Ashley River, on the city's western flank. The American frigate *Queen of France* and other vessels soon abandoned the Ashley for safer waters in the Cooper River, to the east. The rebels had already evacuated Fort Johnson, a bastion on the northeastern tip of James Island overlooking the anchorage in Charleston Harbor, although a rebel cannonade kept Clinton from occupying the works in strength. War stocks poured into the British camp

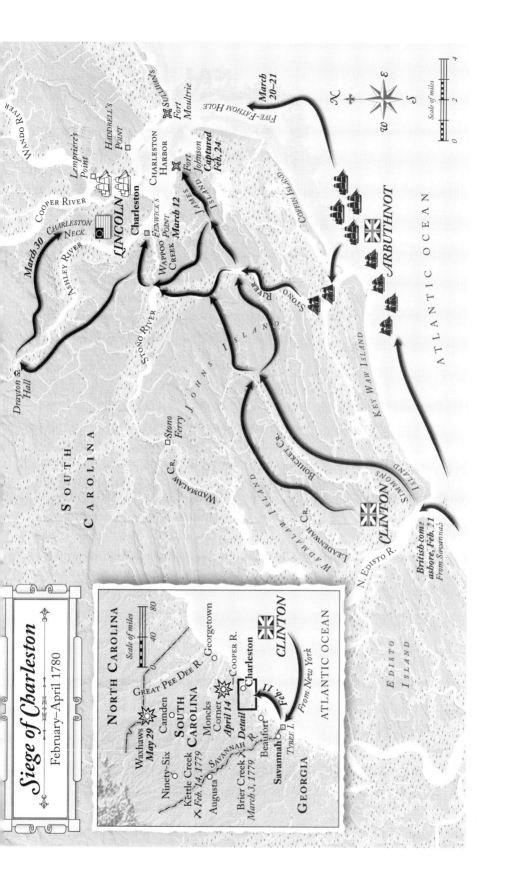

Siege of Charleston — February–April 1780

farther inland, and supply officers kept page after alphabetical page of accumulating matériel. Carriages, cartridges, cloths, coals. Flags, flax, flannel. Gauges, grease, and grates for heating shot.

Looking at Charleston through his spyglass for the first time since his repulse here in June 1776, Clinton could see pick-and-shovel teams working feverishly on the defensive fortifications. "One trench, one battery after another was thrown up," Hinrichs wrote. "Like mushrooms they sprang from the soil." An occasional cannonball arced across the Ashley from the American guns, to small effect. Cornwallis had led a detachment of *Jäger*, British grenadiers, and three foot regiments across Wappoo Creek, onto the South Carolina mainland, and skirmishing picked up. A British bayonet charge surprised eighty rebel militiamen, killing a captain and sixteen privates; an American ambush two days later killed three loyalist volunteers. Ewald described the capture of a wounded Virginia sergeant in a skirmish at a Hessian outpost. Told that the severe gash in his abdomen was fatal, "he quietly lay down like a brave man, clasping his hands, saying, 'Well, then. I die for my country and for its just cause.'" Ewald added that when the Virginian was offered a glass of wine, "he drank it down with relish and died like a man."

By late March, Clinton and much of his army had gathered around Drayton Hall, a plantation a dozen miles upstream on the south bank of the Ashley. Protected by armed galleys, they crossed the river in three waves aboard seventy-five flatboats and whalers, landing on the neck of land north of the city. "Spent the day in viewing Charleston," wrote Dr. Uzal Johnson, the loyalist medico. "Found it not a little like New York." Except for sporadic gunfire between American riflemen and *Jäger* marksmen, the crossing was unopposed. In an uncharacteristic burst of optimism, Clinton wrote Germain, "I entertain great hopes of success."

No one tracked Clinton's progress more closely than the man who every day since February had climbed to a perch near the pinnacle of the 186-foot steeple of St. Michael's Church, the most conspicuous landmark in Charleston. A Dutch-born printer and the town's postmaster, Peter Timothy had volunteered to watch the enemy army and send daily reports to General Lincoln, commander of the Southern Department and the senior Continental officer in the city. Bundled against the chill breeze, Timothy clambered up the rickety ladder, past the gravity-weight clock and eight large bells suspended from an oak frame in the loft. The octagonal white spire, rising through the cypress-shingle roof and capped with a gilded weather vane, was the first thing mariners saw when approaching the city; recently the St. Michael's vestry had painted it black in a futile effort to confound British navigators.

From this perch with his spyglass, Timothy had observed campfire smoke gradually spreading across Johns and then James Islands. He watched as enemy vessels edged along the coast and up the Stono, and made notes about the batteries building at Fenwick's Point and the guns— "each drawn by about 100 men"—manhandled into the embrasures along the Ashley. "Boats loaded with men, tools, tents, and casks crossed the river," he wrote in another dispatch. To the southeast, he saw Royal Navy sailors protected by gunboats sounding the bar east of James Island at the entrance to Charleston Harbor, despite harassment from the rebel brigs *Notre Dame* and *General Lincoln*. Three British frigates, a victualler, and a schooner had run aground on treacherous shoals in the inlet nearly four years ago, contributing to Britain's failure in that earlier assault. Clinton would not make the same mistake twice: soon a large white buoy could be seen, marking the channel entrance.

Even at high tide the narrow passage into the harbor offered barely twenty feet of clearance, so in mid-March tars lightened their drafts by hoisting cannons from the gun decks with block and tackle and ferrying them inshore. Leaving his ships of the line in deep water, Arbuthnot shifted his flag from *Europe* to *Roebuck* and, at seven a.m. on Monday, March 20, signaled for his smaller men-of-war to cross the bar on the spring flood tide. One by one they eased into the anchorage called Five-Fathom Hole— *Renown, Romulus, Richmond, Raleigh, Blonde, Virginia, Perseus.* By three p.m. on Tuesday, twenty-two enemy vessels had cleared the shoals to be reunited with their guns. "Joy to you, sir, to myself, and to us all upon your passage of that infernal bar," Clinton wrote Arbuthnot.

Outgunned and outmaneuvered, the small American squadron— including six frigates, the inaptly named munitions ship *Dove*, and the sloop-of-war *Ranger*, once commanded by Captain J. P. Jones—hoisted sail and eased farther up the Cooper River for sanctuary. Only the dilapidated and undermanned palmetto-log fort on Sullivan's Island stood between Charleston and headlong assault from the sea. That crude stronghold, now called Fort Moultrie, had also helped stymie the British in 1776, largely by surprising the attackers with its resilience and firepower. Clinton and the king's men clearly did not intend to be thwarted again.

All this Timothy watched from his aerie with fascination and alarm as the enemy's coils slowly tightened around the city. "Our naval department," he wrote as the American squadron drew back, "is feeble and unfertile." He detested the enemy, of course, but appreciated the martial pageant unfolding far below him on land and at sea. "They really make a most noble appearance," he would write, "and I could not help admiring the regularity and intrepidity with which they approached. . . . 'Tis pity they are not friends."

With the enemy almost at the gates, Benjamin Lincoln could be seen "on horseback from five in the morning until eight or nine each night, pushing on the works," one of his soldiers wrote. Occasionally the stout former farmer dismounted to swing a pick or grip a shovel, shoulder to shoulder with work gangs, both black and white. At dusk he hobbled on his bad ankle among pickets who scanned the perimeter for British infiltrators and bellowed "All is well" every fifteen minutes, cued on the quarter hour by a St. Michael's bell. By nine-thirty he was back in his headquarters for conferences, correspondence, and a snatch of sleep, careful not to violate his own curfew, announced by another toll of bells and the rattle of army drummers in the street. "Matters are fast ripening," Lincoln wrote Washington, "and will, I think, soon become very serious."

He felt overmatched, as he had at Savannah the previous fall. "I feel my own insufficiency and want of experience," he told the commander in chief. He regretted not having "your advice and direction," and confessed to being "greatly embarrassed to know what ground to occupy." With fewer than five thousand troops, a quarter of them impaired by illness or injury, Lincoln had chosen to hole up in Charleston rather than fight in the open against a ferocious foe with almost twice his strength. He expected a formal siege to begin any day and had ordered cattle, hogs, horses, and "every article which shall either nourish the enemy or facilitate their movements" to be swept from the countryside into town.

Wedged onto a peninsula between two rivers, the Ashley and the Cooper, Charleston had long been the most heavily fortified city in America. Lincoln's task now was to make it insuperable. For months work gangs had been repairing defenses outside the town, including Fort Moultrie and batteries at Haddrell's Point, across the Cooper. But Lincoln and the French engineers advising him realized that the greatest British threat would likely come from the northwest, in an overland attack down the neck against the city's rear. A seven-acre citadel, or "hornwork"—so called because two protruding half bastions resembled bull's horns—had been built just north of Boundary Street as the centerpiece of redans, redoubts, and a continuous parapet extending nearly a mile from river to river on the city's northern edge. Fitted with a new town gate, and the site of Lincoln's headquarters, the hornwork was hardened with tabby mortar made from crushed oyster shells, lime, sand, ash, and water; eighteen cannon embrasures perforated the wall. This citadel complemented a sixteen-gun redoubt on the southern tip of the peninsula and thirteen additional fortifications along the rivers, built with cypress piles, earth, and palmetto trunks. Altogether, more than eighty field guns, mortars, and a howitzer would sweep the Charleston neck: any attack from that vector would also have to fight through a thirty-foot ditch protected by a double abatis, a moat six feet deep—filled through sluices from a tidal creek—and hundreds of "wolf holes" embedded with sharp stakes. Wells were dug for drinking water.

"The works here are by no means completed," Lincoln wrote Washington, but if the defenses could be completed, he would consider the town "pretty safe." As a signal of American resolve, he hanged a man convicted of trying to pass intelligence to the British and left the body dangling in plain view of the enemy's lines.

The navy disappointed him, as it disappointed Peter Timothy. Lincoln had argued bitterly with Commodore Abraham Whipple, who, at Congress's direction, had sailed his squadron to Charleston but then declined to challenge the Royal Navy at the bar as pointless self-immolation. Instead, after his ships repaired on the tide up the Cooper, their guns were removed and distributed to batteries around the city. To barricade approaches to the river and discourage a British ascent, a brig was deliberately sunk in the channel opposite the Exchange—used as a custom house and meeting hall—followed by several other old vessels, after slaves weighted their hulls with brickbats. A dozen more derelicts were to be sunk in the channel near Sullivan's Island and entangled with four hundred fathoms of cable, three hundred fathoms of chain, and twenty-six anchors, but Whipple, concluding that the waters were too deep and the tides too strong, abandoned the effort. When Lincoln convened a war council of four generals and eighteen colonels to consider whether dilapidated Fort Moultrie should be evacuated or further reinforced, neither option was endorsed. Forty guns bristled from the works on Sullivan's Island, but they were manned by only two hundred of the estimated twelve hundred defenders required.

Lincoln peppered Governor John Rutledge with pleas for war matériel—ten tons of powder, fifteen tons of lead, gun flints, cordage—but what he most needed was manpower. Enlistments for North Carolina militiamen expired on March 24 and seven hundred promptly marched away, leaving behind another hundred or so comrades who agreed to tarry for three months in exchange for $50 and "a good suit of clothes." Dispatches from Lincoln and John Laurens in the late fall had persuaded Washington that, as he wrote, South Carolina was "in a more defenseless condition than I had even apprehended"; to bolster the garrison he dispatched a brigade of eight hundred Continentals from North Carolina and another seven hundred Virginians, who would not arrive from Morristown until April. "There never has been a time since the commencement of the present war when reinforcement was of like importance," Lincoln wrote Brigadier General William Woodford, the Virginia commander. "Leave your wagons and heavy luggage with your artillery . . . and move with the utmost dispatch to this place."

Most frustrating was the reluctance of South Carolinians to defend their own capital. Rutledge and several of his privy counselors had been prepared to surrender the city and proclaim the state's neutrality during a British raid a year earlier, until stouter patriots drove the redcoats away. Lincoln's engineers had recently requested sixteen hundred slaves as manual laborers, but fewer than half that number appeared; some masters were hesitant to lend their chattel, despite army patrols scouring nearby plantations for recalcitrants. Worse still was the refusal of the state's white militiamen to muster in Charleston, ostensibly because of a smallpox outbreak the previous fall; unlike northern states, South Carolina had been slow to adopt inoculation, and these cases were the city's first in sixteen years.

"Am much surprised to find the militia so unreasonable as to wish to avoid this town," Lincoln wrote his deputy, Brigadier General William Moultrie, who had led the successful defense of Sullivan's Island in 1776. "The safety of the town depends upon their coming to its assistance." Three thousand militia troops had been summoned, but Lincoln later estimated that only three hundred appeared from the backcountry. This contumacy incensed New England congressmen, already irked by the state's lukewarm support of the Continental Army and complaints of northern indifference. "The state of South Carolina have thought we neglected them," wrote James Lovell of Massachusetts. "We know they neglected themselves."

No less perplexing to Lincoln was the local penchant for delusion. Dr. David Ramsay pronounced the city defenses "strong," although as a precaution he sent $3,000 to his friend Dr. Rush in Philadelphia for safekeeping. Another Charlestonian assured his wife—who had fled the town—that "the lines may be now said in a great measure to be impregnable." Major Thomas Pinckney, the Oxford-educated scion of a wealthy planter family, wrote his sister from Fort Moultrie in late March that thousands of Continentals "are making forced marches to our assistance. . . . The Spanish fleet may come off our coast soon after our reinforcements come in." That would make Clinton's plight "truly deplorable," Pinckney added. "Indeed we have by the blessing of providence a very favorable prospect before us."

* * *

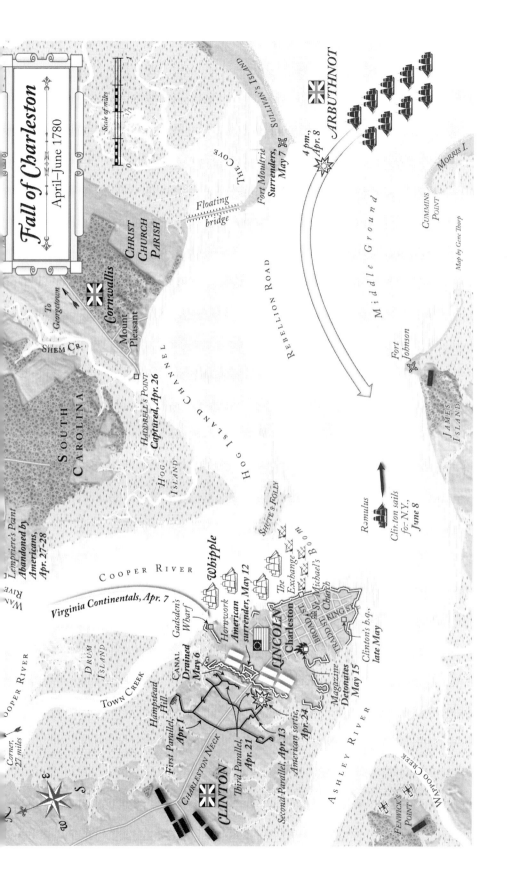

Fall of Charleston
April–June 1780

Scale of miles
0   ½   1

SULLIVAN'S ISLAND

THE COVE

Fort Moultrie
Surrenders,
May 7

Floating bridge

CHRIST CHURCH PARISH

CORNWALLIS

To Georgetown

Mount Pleasant

SHEM CR.

SOUTH CAROLINA

HADDRELL'S POINT
Captured, Apr. 26

HOG ISLAND

REBELLION ROAD

HOG ISLAND CHANNEL

SHUTE'S FOLLY

Middle Ground

Fort Johnson

JAMES ISLAND

MORRIS I.

CUMMINS POINT

Map by Gene Thorp

4 p.m.,
Apr. 8

ARBUTHNOT

Lempriere's Point
Abandoned by
Americans,
Apr. 27–28

WANDO RIVER

COOPER RIVER

Corner,
27 miles

COOPER RIVER

DRUM ISLAND

TOWN CREEK

Hampstead Hill

First Parallel,
Apr. 1

Virginia Continentals, Apr. 7

Whipple

Hornwork, May 12

Gadsden's Wharf

American surrender,
May 12

CANAL
Drained
May 6

CHARLESTON NECK

Second Parallel, Apr. 21

Third Parallel,
Apr. 21

American sortie,
Apr. 24

LINCOLN

The Exchange

Charleston

BROAD ST.

TRADD ST.

KING ST.

St. Michael's Church

St. Michael's Boom

Clinton's h.q.,
late May

Magazine
Detonates
May 15

Romulus

Clinton sails
for N.Y.,
June 8

ASHLEY RIVER

CLINTON

WAPPOO CREEK

FENWICK'S POINT

As a stranger in this strange land, the Massachusetts-born Lincoln was baffled by Charleston and the surrounding Low Country. With a population of roughly twelve thousand—half white and half enslaved black—this city, already the richest in America before the war, had thrived more than any other during the conflict, benefiting from high prices for indigo and rice, a brisk trade in Bermuda salt and privateering, and nimble blockade-runners who smuggled in arms, ammunition, and wares from Europe. Each June 28 local patriots celebrated the glorious repulse of Clinton and the Royal Navy at Sullivan's Island, four years earlier, with fireworks, a grand dinner in the statehouse, and bottomless toasts. To be sure, malaria, yellow fever, and other diseases kept mortality high and life short; only four of Henry Laurens's twelve children reached maturity. A "sea of flame" from a devastating fire in 1778 had incinerated 250 homes along Queen, Broad, and Tradd Streets—one of every six houses in the city—as well as seven thousand books, paintings, and scientific instruments in the town library and museum.

Yet Charleston retained much of its antebellum swank. The city "is beautiful beyond description," a visitor wrote. "The planters and merchants are rich and well-bred. The people are showy." Those showy people enjoyed horse races, concerts, and theater productions of Shakespeare and Oliver Goldsmith's *She Stoops to Conquer*. Gorgeous houses featured mahogany staircases and exquisite ironwork balconies, railings, and gates. With early spring now erupting along the coast, bluebells, dogwoods, periwinkles, and yellow jessamine vines bloomed in gardens across the city. A Charleston physician described the gentry as "absolutely above every occupation but eating, drinking, lolling, smoking, and sleeping, which five modes of action constitute the essence of their life."

Bondage made it all possible. Of one hundred thousand slaves in South Carolina—a fifth of all those in America—six thousand toiled in Charleston as the barbers, coachmen, washerwomen, cooks, cabinetmakers, and drudges who gave the town its sheen. Draconian slave laws, patterned after those of Barbados and Jamaica, kept the chattel mostly at heel and reflected the perpetual white dread of insurrection. "A man will shoot a Negro with as little emotion as he shoots a hare," a visitor from Boston wrote his brother in 1778. State law required all white men to carry a long gun or brace of pistols to church in case of an uprising. It was illegal to teach a slave to write; they could not own horses or boats, carry a drum, or use a firelock in the presence of a white man. Advertisements in the *South-Carolina Gazette* routinely announced such transactions as the "thirty valuable prime slaves" to be auctioned on twelve months' credit, including "a good cooper and five pair of good sawyers," or the estate sale of "seventeen valuable Negro slaves plus six head of oxen and four horses."

Congress had hoped that bondmen might prove the South's salvation. In March 1779, delegates in Philadelphia authorized South Carolina and Georgia to "take measures immediately for raising three thousand able-bodied Negroes . . . of standard size, not exceeding thirty-five years of age." Armed with muskets and commanded by white officers, these new black soldiers would receive $50 and freedom when peace returned, not unlike the "sable battalion" enlisted by Rhode Island. Each owner would collect $1,000 in compensation for every slave contributed to the cause.

This remarkable step toward emancipation had been conceived by John Laurens, whose education in England and Switzerland had imbued him with abolitionist notions, notwithstanding a father, Henry, whose former trading firm in Charleston had brokered the sale of more than ten thousand slaves—"the largest handler of slave cargoes in British North America," according to the historian Jack Rakove—and whose plantations still exploited hundreds. John argued that as "firm defender[s] of liberty," those "very blacks which have hitherto been regarded as our greatest weakness may be converted into our greatest strength." As part of "my black project," he proposed putting them in white uniforms with red facings, "a good contrast with the complexion of the soldier."

Henry, who implausibly claimed, "I abhor slavery," was skeptical that the enslaved would exchange the "comfortable" conditions of bondage for military service far from home. When Savannah fell, however, he agreed to endorse the plan in Congress. Washington, though dubious—"this is a subject that has never employed much of my thoughts," he wrote—did not oppose the congressional resolution. But South Carolina slave masters rejected it with fury. "The measure for embodying the Negroes," Dr. Ramsay recorded, "was received with horror by the planters, who figured to themselves terrible consequences." Lieutenant Governor Christopher Gadsden wrote Samuel Adams, "We are much disgusted here at Congress recommending us to arm our slaves. It was received with great resentment as a very dangerous and impolitic step." In August 1779, the state legislature disapproved the proposal by a vote of seventy-two to twelve. "Your black air castle," Henry wrote John, "is blown up with contemptuous huzzahs."

Rutledge still opposed the plan, yet with the king's men ever closer to encircling Charleston, Lincoln urged the governor to reconsider. "I think the measure of raising the black corps a necessary one," he wrote Rutledge in March, noting that in Savannah the British had demonstrated the utility of arming slaves. Although South Carolina had rejected the proposal in

August, he argued, "circumstances were different then. It was a providential measure. Now it is an absolutely necessary one." Moreover, he added ominously, the state's decision would "determine whether I stay in town or not." John Laurens, who had taken a seat in the state assembly while still on leave from Washington's staff, added his "harangues" to the debate, as he wrote Hamilton in Morristown.

To no avail. The state's privy council found the proposal "totally impracticable." An assembly committee recommended providing a thousand unarmed slaves for artillery crews, but legislators instead focused on compensating "sufferers"—plantation masters—whose slaves were killed or injured while performing manual labor for the state. In a note to his son, Henry Laurens noted how difficult it was "to persuade rich men to part willingly with the very source of their wealth and, as they suppose, tranquility."

Runaways continued to flock to the British, who posted placards across the Low Country encouraging defection. Blacks provided Clinton with intelligence and joined his foraging parties in rustling cattle and horses. Black labor also freed hundreds of redcoats from fatigue duty. As Peter Timothy could see from his church-spire perch, runaway slaves moved cannons and munitions around and, in early April, manhandled British gunboats across the neck on rollers, shifting them from the Ashley for eventual launching in the Cooper.

Disgusted at his compatriots' "supineness," John Laurens moved his regiment into the line near the hornwork and prepared to fight. He brought three family slaves with him—Stepney, Exeter, and Jacob—and put them to work with pioneer gangs strengthening the city's defenses.

At two p.m. on Friday, April 7, more than seven hundred long-striding Virginia Continentals clambered onto Gadsden's Wharf from schooners that had carried them down the Wando River and into the Cooper. Lusty cheers, pealing bells, and a thirteen-gun salute welcomed them. They wore "the appearance of what they are in reality—hardy veterans," one witness declared. The schooners soon sailed back up the Cooper, carrying townsfolk desperate to flee inland. General Clinton was among those pleased to hear of the reinforcements' arrival. "I rejoice at it," he wrote. "They will now defend their town, and when we take it, we shall take all in it."

The Virginians found a town besieged. With direction from Major Moncrieff and under the cover of darkness, fifteen hundred of the king's laborers had built three redoubts less than a thousand yards north of the rebel lines just outside the city limits. Zigzagging trenches down the neck led from the British rear to a parallel—a wide ditch—where assaulting infantry could soon gather. Work gangs had emplaced wooden blinds called mantelets—six feet high, sixteen feet long, and covered in earth—to shield the fortifications. Approach roads across boggy ground were corduroyed with pine trunks trimmed of branches. Two more crescent-shaped redoubts had also been raised, one along the Ashley and the other on Hampstead Hill near the Cooper. American field guns and the *Ranger* blistered the latter with at least two hundred rounds, until Moncrieff brought up a howitzer and a pair of 24-pounders to answer the enemy and drive off the sloop with a shot through her bow.

Just before four p.m. on Saturday, as fresh breezes blew from the southeast and a light rain fell, Arbuthnot, aboard *Roebuck*, abruptly weighed anchor to lead eight men-of-war and three transports from Five-Fathom Hole past the Middle Ground shoals to within eight hundred yards of Sullivan's Island. Some six thousand besieged Americans flocked to the city ramparts, hoping to see the squadron blown from the bay as it sailed beneath Fort Moultrie's guns, which guarded the only passage to Charleston's inner harbor. Sheets of fire spurted along the fort, answered with salvos from the passing ships. Nimble gunners sponged, loaded, and ran their pieces forward for another volley, their mouths opened wide to avoid ruptured eardrums from the concussion. Gray smoke soon swaddled both fort and fleet, a thick cloud brightened from within by twinkling muzzle flashes. Thudding cannonballs splintered both palmetto logs and oak hulls. "The fort was veiled in fire and smoke, and the roar of forty-three heavy guns resembled a terrible thunderstorm," Ewald wrote. "Only an English fleet can execute such a masterpiece."

For nearly ninety minutes the cannonade merged into one unbroken, maniacal clangor. "The admiral has received & returned the fire of Fort Moultrie and passed it without any apparent damage," a disconsolate Peter Timothy wrote from St. Michael's. That was incorrect, but not by much. *Richmond's* hull had been battered, her fore-topmast shot away, and a gun dismounted. *Renown* and the sloop *Sandwich*, bringing up the rear, took punishing fire, and a transport was abandoned and burned after running aground. Twenty-seven tars had been killed or wounded.

But the Royal Navy now commanded the Charleston roadstead, the waterfront, and the mouths of both rivers. On Sunday Clinton composed a note to Lincoln and sent a courier under a truce flag to the hornwork, warning the American commander of "havoc and devastation" unless the town capitulated. "An alternative is offered at this hour of saving lives and property," Clinton added. "But the same mild and compassionate offer can never be renewed."

Lincoln replied promptly. "Duty and inclination," he wrote, required resistance "to the last extremity." In the city at large, a willful bravado persisted. "The army and citizens are in high spirits," one rebel recorded, "and have no doubt of their being able to defend the city and make Sir Henry again give up the thought of taking it."

Yet Lincoln had doubts. On Thursday morning, April 13, he convened a war council in a large marquee near his headquarters and quickly outlined his predicament. Even with reinforcements from Virginia and North Carolina, the garrison was outnumbered two to one. As long as passage on the Cooper remained open, supplies could reach Charleston, but he had little hope of any "succor of consequence." Ammunition, gunpowder, and provisions would last weeks, not months. Governor Rutledge and several privy counselors had, with Lincoln's encouragement, stolen away this morning in hopes of rallying backcountry support. What, he asked, was the "propriety of evacuating the garrison?" One subordinate officer answered immediately that they should not wait "an hour longer."

Suddenly at ten a.m., before the conference ended, a stupendous artillery barrage opened from British batteries on the neck and across the Ashley. Lincoln and his lieutenants scattered as "balls flew through the streets," in one major's description. For fifteen hours the onslaught persisted, killing several women and children and setting houses ablaze with *feuerkugeln*—carcasses, or firebombs—from Hampstead Hill and naval guns. Royal Navy gunners cheered from the bay until an irate Clinton ordered that at least the incendiaries be halted, noting how "absurd, impolitic, and inhuman [it is] to burn a town you mean to occupy."

Even without carcasses, the greatest bombardment ever seen in America had begun in earnest, and more than six hundred guns from both sides rained shot and shell, night and day. Residents dug bombproofs in their cellars and piled dirt against house walls with an ear cocked for the whistle of cannonballs. Bar shot fired from British galleys made "a terrific clatter on the houses." The cannonade decapitated General Moultrie's aide, and also killed a man in bed and wounded the woman with him. A ball fired from James Island severed the marble right arm of the statue of William Pitt—holding the Magna Carta—erected in 1770 to commemorate the Great Commoner's role in repealing the Stamp Act. Shellfire riddled Henry Laurens's town house, puncturing the roof, shattering the mahogany stairs, and wrecking the kitchen, smokehouse, stable, garden wall, and counting-house.

The Americans answered as best they could. The British had opened a second parallel only nine hundred feet from the hornwork, and rebel gunners lacerated the earthworks; on April 15 Hinrich counted nineteen cannonballs, thirteen shells, and seventeen grapeshot rounds hitting the parallel. Rebel riflemen fired at any movement across the lines, terrorizing the shovelmen and shooting through the eye an incautious light infantryman who peeped over the trench wall. A ball aimed at *Comet*, on Wappoo Creek, carried away the right leg and left heel of the galley's master, provoking Arbuthnot to tell a subordinate that despite Clinton's avowed restraint, "I hope the general will burn their town. The sooner the better."

Yet trouble for Lincoln now came not from fire but from the sword. At three a.m. on April 14, a regiment of red-coated loyalists and dragoons in green tunics, riding from the west on whatever crowbait horses they had been able to buy or steal, approached Biggin Bridge, near Moncks Corner on the Cooper River, twenty-five miles north of Charleston. Known as the British Legion, they were led by Lieutenant Colonel Banastre Tarleton, the flamboyant son of a Liverpool merchant and the captor of General Lee in New Jersey more than three years earlier. Four hundred Continental cavalrymen had camped imprudently on the west side of the bridge, the only river crossing for six miles. They had just begun to stir when Tarleton ordered his legion to charge. The crack of an alarm pistol broke the morning calm, followed by the clatter of hooves. The attack, a rebel officer recalled, "was so sudden that although the horses were saddled & bridled, the men had not time to mount."

Pinned against the river, the American dragoons fled on foot through palmettos and sweet gums into a swamp. Enemy infantrymen sprinted across the bridge with bayonets held high to rout the North Carolina militiamen bivouacked on the east side. "Our whole army was cut to pieces, slaughtered and dispersed," a survivor wrote. Major Pierre-Jean François Vernier, commanding the remnant of Pulaski's Legion, was "mangled in the most shocking manner," including a sword gash across his skull; laid on a tavern table, where Tarleton's men pelted him with insults, he died a few hours later, cursing redcoats and loyalists alike. Other American casualties included three captains, a lieutenant, and ten privates killed, eighteen men wounded, and sixty-three captured. The raiders seized forty-two supply wagons, eighty-two dragoon mounts, more than a hundred dray horses, and five puncheons of rum—more than four hundred gallons. Two British foot regiments soon reinforced the bridge, severing the Cooper and further isolating Charleston. Barely two months into the campaign, the city's investment was nearly complete. A rebel defender in Charleston wrote on April 18 that General Clinton "moves with all the care and deliberation of an old Roman. . . . It seems to be the general opinion that we must at last succumb."

These pleasing developments should have gladdened the old Roman. They did not: the closer his army came to snapping shut the trap on Charleston's defenders, the more splenetic Clinton became. In early April he had begun to keep a battle journal, using a private code for particularly trenchant remarks—"blockhead" was a favorite epithet—and often scribbling with such vehemence that he neglected to sharpen his quill. While logging daily observations about his three a.m. inspection visits to the forward trenches and noting that "I run too much risk for my station," he also recorded his expanding contempt for Arbuthnot. Still irked at the fleet's errant drift into the Gulf Stream during the voyage from New York, he again condemned the admiral for declining to share more powder and ammunition with the army. "He forgets all he says and does, and talks nonsense," Clinton wrote. "I must ever be on my guard with this man." Even more aggravating was a timid reluctance by the navy to force the Cooper and finish the encirclement. Decrying Arbuthnot's indecision, Clinton told his journal, "In appearance we were the best of friends. But I am sure he is false as hell, and shall behave in consequence."

His growing disaffection with Cornwallis was even more venomous. As the siege intensified, Clinton accused his erstwhile friend of spreading rumors that he would soon succeed the commanding general, who was intent on returning to England. Cornwallis denied the charge "upon his honor"; wounded and exasperated, he then asked that he no longer be consulted on the army's war plans, ostensibly because he did not want the responsibility. André surmised that he in fact did not want the blame if things went awry. Regardless, Clinton would be on his own. "I can never be cordial with such a man," Clinton wrote.

Wary, cynical, and forlorn, he wanted Cornwallis out of sight. When twenty-five hundred reinforcements arrived from New York on April 18, Clinton put most of them under Cornwallis's command, ordered them to attack the remaining rebel fortifications east of the Cooper "in the manner most beneficial to the king's service," and then convinced himself that his deputy would botch the assignment. "I repent that I sent him," Clinton confided to his journal. "He will play me false."

During another war conference in the hornwork on Thursday evening, April 20, Lincoln again reviewed the American predicament with his lieutenants. Food and ammunition stocks were dwindling. The lower Cooper

River remained open, thanks to a large Continental gun battery at Lempriere's Point on the eastern shore. Consequently the road through Christ
Church Parish to the Santee River still provided an evacuation route,
should the Charleston garrison choose to flee by night. Enough boats had
been collected to cross the wide Cooper, although many of the three hundred men admitted to the hospital in April would have to be abandoned,
including sixty-three with gunshot wounds.

As Lincoln went through this bleak recitation, Lieutenant Governor
Gadsden barged into the meeting with four indignant members of the
privy council. They were "surprised and displeased," Gadsden snapped, at
the "thought of capitulation or evacuation." Even old women in Charleston
had become "so accustomed to the enemy's shot now that they traveled the
streets without fear or dread." South Carolina militiamen, Gadsden added,
were "willing to live upon rice alone rather than give up the town"—a ludicrous assertion, given the militia's craven reluctance to defend the city. As
recorded by Brigadier General Lachlan McIntosh, another councillor,
Thomas Ferguson, joined the tirade. The flotilla of boats assembled along
the Cooper had not gone unnoticed, Ferguson said. Should the Continentals decide to abandon the city, he vowed to "be among the first who would
open the gates for the enemy and assist them in attacking us before we got
aboard."

Rather than answer this shocking insolence by clapping the scoundrels
in irons, Lincoln meekly capitulated. It "is well not only to pay some, but
great attention to the advice of the citizen," he explained. On Friday, exhausted and resigned to a discreditable fate, the commanding general once
again convened his senior officers, who unanimously agreed that "before
our affairs become more critical," discussions with the British should resume. At eleven a.m. a courier carried a ceasefire flag and a proposal from
the hornwork: all Continental and militia troops would, within thirty-six
hours, withdraw from Charleston with their arms and artillery "to march
wherever General Lincoln may think proper." Civilian residents would be
given twelve months "to dispose of their effects," then leave town if they
chose. American vessels could also sail away.

Clinton replied with disdain. These preposterous terms, he said, "could
not be listened to." At ten-thirty p.m. British guns resumed the bombardment with more than eight hundred rounds, targeting the banks of the
Cooper to discourage evacuation. American gunners answered in kind. A
great roar again engulfed the Low Country.

By late April, British sappers had excavated most of a third parallel
within rifle range of the American defenses. Proximity increased danger
and misery for both lines. "The intolerable heat, the lack of good water,

and the billions of sandflies and mosquitoes make up the worst nuisance," Ewald wrote. Some rebel batteries ran short of ammunition and fired "ragged pieces of iron, broken bottles, old axes, gun barrels, tomahawks, etc.," a British captain in the 64th Foot recorded. Return fire from the besiegers grew vicious. "If a hat is tied up on a bayonet or ramrod for a few minutes, one or more balls from the Hessian *Jäger* would pass through it," wrote Joseph Manigault, a sixteen-year-old in the American garrison. After venturing into a forward redoubt, General Moultrie noted:

> An uncommon number of bullets whistled about me. . . . We were constantly skipping about to get out of the way of the shells thrown from their howitzers. They were not more than one hundred yards from our works, and throwing their shells in bushels.

The only rebel sally across the lines occurred at first light on April 24, when two hundred Virginia and South Carolina Continentals fell on the British right, surprising a work gang in the third parallel. "Damn me," a redcoat cried, "the rebels are here!" The attackers bayoneted fifteen men to death and dragged another dozen prisoners back to camp. "We were a little off our guard," a British officer told Clinton. Among the few American casualties was Captain Thomas Moultrie, the general's brother, shot dead during the raid and buried later that day in a churchyard on Cumberland Street.

At seven a.m. the following day the chief engineer of the Continental Army, Brigadier General Louis Duportail, slipped into Charleston under orders from Congress to evaluate the defenses "with all possible dispatch." Duportail subsequently told Washington, "I found the town in a desperate state, almost entirely invested by the British army and fleet." Twelve hundred enemy troops were now working night and day to finish the batteries along the second and third parallels. Royal Artillery gunners were bolstered by the arrival of another thousand barrels of gunpowder from New York, three thousand rounds of 24-pound shot from St. Augustine, and abandoned French cannons shipped from Savannah.

The American garrison was still only half the size required to defend the extensive perimeter. Each night, Lincoln set barrels of turpentine ablaze just beyond his lines to illuminate any sudden British attack. Only cowhide flaps over American gun embrasures prevented *Jäger* marksmen from shooting Continental gunners. Duportail estimated that enemy diggers would soon pierce the protective moat, draining the water at the rate of an inch every hour. "In a word," he concluded, "the fall of the town was unavoidable unless an army came to her assistance."

The encirclement was completed on April 28. Cornwallis's capture of the small battery at Haddrell's Point, just north of Fort Moultrie, exposed Colonel François de Malmédy, who held vital Lempriere's Point with three hundred Continental and North Carolina militia troops. Malmédy bolted across the Cooper to Charleston, and five hundred Royal Navy sailors landed on the point, seized half a dozen abandoned guns, and hoisted a large Union Jack. "We are now closely blocked up," Moultrie wrote. Benjamin Smith, a militia officer, told his wife in a letter on April 30, "Our affairs are daily declining and not a ray of hope remains. . . . The thirteen stripes will be leveled in the dust."

That was Clinton's intent, although he resisted suggestions from subordinates that the time was ripe for a full-throated assault on rebel lines. "The success of a storm is uncertain," he told his journal. "Our method is sure, though perhaps not so quick. But as there is no necessity for hurry, better proceed as we do." Keen to be in on the kill, Cornwallis wrote him, "I shall take it as a favor if you will let me be of the party. I can be with you in eight hours." Even as he hoped to avoid the bloodletting seen in Savannah, Clinton wrote back, "I begin to think these people will be blockheads enough to wait the assault. *Je m'en lave les mains.*" I wash my hands of it.

Like the siege itself, the end came in fits and starts. At eight a.m. on Sunday, May 7, the isolated garrison of 218 Continentals and militia at Fort Moultrie capitulated after being warned that those who resisted further would be put to the sword. The surrendered booty included forty-four cannons, fifty barrels of gunpowder, and forty thousand musket cartridges. In Charleston, American confidence sagged with the loss of the homely, valiant stronghold that had defeated the British four years earlier. "This fort by many people was reckoned impregnable," a sorrowful officer wrote.

The following morning, Clinton again summoned Lincoln to surrender. With a truce granted to discuss the issue, sixty-one senior American officers assembled in the hornwork to cast ballots. Forty-nine voted to offer capitulation terms; the other twelve—John Laurens among them—wanted to continue fighting. A draft proposal with a dozen articles was carried to Clinton and Arbuthnot, who revised the measures before returning the document. Lincoln rejected the revisions late Tuesday afternoon, May 9, not least because of the British insistence that captured militiamen be treated as prisoners of war before returning home on parole. Now thoroughly irked, Clinton denounced the American gambit as "utterly inadmissible. Hostilities will in consequence commence afresh at eight o'clock." Barrels of musket cartridges were trundled into the British trenches, where the besieging troops were told to shoot as much as they liked. Some Hessians inched to within thirty paces of the American parapet.

Church bells pealed as the bombardment resumed with redoubled intensity. "The rebels began with huzzahing and a violent cannonade from every gun they could fire, seemingly at random as if in a drunk frenzy," Captain Robertson wrote. The Royal Artillery answered with more than eight hundred rounds. Clinton abandoned his scruples about burning the town, and incendiary shells set fire to seven houses. "Cannonballs whizzing and shells hissing continually amongst us . . . like meteors crossing each other and bursting in the air," Moultrie reported. "It appeared as if the stars were tumbling down." More men died on both sides. But, he added, "it availed us nothing."

Charleston had had enough. "Militia abandon the lines" despite entreaties to stand fast, General McIntosh noted in his diary. A petition to Lincoln signed by more than a hundred civilians urged him to surrender "in this perilous situation"; other petitions endorsed by nearly six hundred South Carolina militiamen asked the same. At midafternoon on Thursday, May 11, a white flag appeared above the hornwork and a Continental officer stepped through the gate with a signed capitulation. Ewald accepted the letter, sent it to the rear, and ordered wine for the rebel courier. In his journal, Clinton wrote simply, "The place surrendered."

An eerie silence descended on Charleston, broken by birdsong and the shuffle of brogans as the king's army, at two p.m. on Friday, filed along the second parallel and the drained moat. Two companies of British and Hessian grenadiers then marched through the open gate to take possession of the hornwork. Oboists struck up "God Save the King." Lincoln emerged on horseback, accompanied by Moultrie on foot. They were trailed by artillerymen, then Carolina and Virginia Continentals.

"The rebels appeared thin, miserable, ragged, and very dirty," noted Lieutenant Christian Bartholomai, a *Jäger* officer. "Their officers appeared . . . each in a different colored uniform and with different facings, which gave the officers of their army the appearance of comedians about to commence a show." Brigadier General Alexander Leslie, the newly designated British military governor, asked Lincoln, "I take this, sir, to be your first division?" Lincoln replied, "This body, sir, contains my first and my last division. They are all the troops I have."

The surrender agreement permitted Continental drummers to beat a somber cadence, but Clinton denied Lincoln the honor of uncasing his colors or playing a British march. Rebel musicians settled instead for a Turkish ditty that Hessians dubbed "The Janissary March." As instructed, rank after rank stacked their arms between the two abatis. Militiamen were segregated from the Continentals and herded into a nearby pasture. A few defiant officers who shouted "Long live Congress!" were stripped of the swords and sidearms they had been permitted to retain. A Union Jack floated above the hornwork, saluted with twenty-one guns by the Royal Artillery, and three foot regiments moved forward to occupy the town. "It is the greatest and most humiliating misfortune of my life," young Laurens would write Washington.

"God was with us and preserved us," *Jäger* Captain Johann Hinrichs wrote his brother, "so that out of a million bullets, few did strike." Not everyone was preserved, of course, and more than a few bullets struck. The king's forces suffered 316 dead and wounded during the campaign. Lincoln counted fewer battle casualties—227—but the 5,610 men captured, by Clinton's tally, represented the greatest calamity of the war for the American cause. An entire army had been destroyed, and with it virtually all of the Virginia and Carolina Continental lines. The losses also included four hundred cannons, six thousand muskets, twenty-five tons of powder, and several dozen vessels, among them four frigates that were renamed, reflagged, and welcomed into the British fleet.

Under the surrender terms, militiamen were sent home on parole. But seven generals, three signers of the Declaration of Independence, and nearly three thousand Continentals were herded into camps. So many abruptly escaped that the British confined most enlisted men on iniquitous prison ships. Eight hundred would die in the next year; some five hundred others saved themselves by enlisting in the British Army and serving in the West Indies.

Three days after the surrender, another calamity struck Charleston. At one p.m. on May 15, a British work party tossed captured American weapons into a storehouse; a loaded musket went off, detonating two tons of barreled gunpowder. The blast demolished six buildings, including a poorhouse and a brothel. "The most dreadful cries arose from all sides of the city," wrote Ewald, who was a few blocks away. "We found some sixty people who were burnt beyond recognition, half-dead and writhing like worms." General Moultrie, detained nearby in the shadow of St. Michael's, described how "carcasses, legs, and arms were seen in the air. . . . One man was dashed with violence against the steeple of the new independent church." The imprint of his body could be seen for days.

Firelocks, ramrods, and bayonets rained onto rooftops. Three thousand muskets intended to arm backcountry loyalists were ruined. Severed limbs could be found more than five hundred yards from the detonation.

Estimates of the number killed ranged from a hundred to three hundred, including twenty-three British and Hessian soldiers. "Never in my life, as long as I have been a soldier," wrote Ewald, "have I witnessed a more deplorable sight."

A final, wretched episode in the Charleston campaign played out far from the city. Colonel Abraham Buford, a cavalryman and former hospital superintendent, having arrived too late to participate in Lincoln's doomed defense, now plodded north with 40 Virginia dragoons and 380 callow infantry recruits. They constituted the last Continental force at liberty in South Carolina, and General Cornwallis, alerted by loyalist spies, was bent on their destruction. He ordered Lieutenant Colonel Tarleton in pursuit with 270 cavalry and mounted infantry, some riding two to a horse. Covering more than a hundred miles in just over two days, despite horses and men collapsing in the heat, the pursuers caught their quarry on May 29 in a remote, hardscrabble woodland called the Waxhaws, just below the North Carolina border.

"You are now almost encompassed by a corps of seven hundred light troops on horseback," Tarleton wrote Buford in a hyperbolic surrender demand. "Earl Cornwallis is likewise within a short march with nine British battalions." If the Continentals failed to stack their arms in submission within an hour, "the blood be upon your head." Buford responded succinctly—"Sir, I reject your proposals"—then made two tactical mistakes: he ordered his baggage wagons and a pair of 6-pounder field guns to continue up the road, rather than forming a defensive breastworks, and he told his men not to fire until British attackers were within ten yards.

At three-thirty p.m., Tarleton's legion massed three hundred yards from the rebel line, then trotted forward before breaking into a full gallop to attack Buford's center and both flanks. The single point-blank volley from Continental muskets staggered the charge, but only for an instant. Some Americans threw down their weapons and raised their hands. Others fumbled to reload or broke for the rear. A bullet through the forehead brought down Tarleton's lathered horse, spilling the colonel to the ground and momentarily pinning him beneath the carcass. He soon regained his feet, but word passed from lip to ear that Tarleton had been killed, an affront that "stimulated the soldiers to a vindictive asperity not easily restrained," he later wrote. "Slaughter was commenced."

British dragoons wheeled through the terrified Continentals, hacking and thrusting. One lieutenant's "nose and lip were bisected obliquely and the lower jaw completely divided." Another soldier suffered twenty-two sword and bayonet wounds, including a fractured skull and the amputation of part of his right hand. They were among the lucky survivors. Within half an hour, 113 Americans sprawled dead in the dirt. Another 150 wounded lay bleeding or were carried off as prisoners. Farmers carted the injured to a log church with a straw floor; those tending their wounds included a woman named Elizabeth Hutchinson Jackson, who was accompanied by her thirteen-year-old son, Andrew. The future president later wrote that "none of the men had less than three or four, and some as many as thirteen gashes in them." Andrew Jackson would despise the British for the rest of his long life.

Few skirmishes in the war would be bloodier or more controversial than Waxhaws. One account claimed that British executioners had roamed the killing ground, "plunging their bayonets into all that exhibited any signs of life." Colonel Buford, who bolted to safety early in the attack, told Virginia legislators that many of his men were killed "after they had lain down their arms." Such accusations merged into an atrocity narrative of "unresisting Americans, praying for quarter [who] were chopped to pieces," as one historian wrote soon after the war, and the slaughter of helpless prisoners became known as "Tarleton's quarter." Soon Waxhaws turned into a rallying cry for vengeful rebels and foreshadowed the sanguinary war that would be fought across the American South in coming months by the likes of "Bloody Tarleton," as he was now called. Even Charles Stedman, a loyalist commissary for the British, wrote, "The virtue of humanity was totally forgot."

The unrepentant dragoon commander, who would be lionized at home as much as he was vilified in America, told Cornwallis bluntly, "They refused my terms." Along with the 6-pounders, wagons, and other plunder captured from the routed Continentals, the British seized three battle flags, including a bloodstained gold silk standard depicting thirteen silver stars and a beaver gnawing a palmetto tree above the motto PERSEVERANDO: "By persevering." More than two centuries later, the colors would be sold at auction for $5 million.

The war had shifted south, just as Britain intended. Charleston's fall was "a rude shock to the independence of America," a rebel prisoner wrote. That shock would be felt soon enough up the Atlantic seaboard. "Tis a severe stroke, but it is in vain to repine," Colonel Hamilton wrote from Morristown at the end of May. He hoped the loss would spur the country to greater exertions in the common cause. "But it must be confessed," he added, "if it is a blessing, 'tis a blessing in a very strange disguise."

"We are now thoroughly masters of South Carolina," Cornwallis declared. Clinton went even further in a letter to Newcastle. "Both the Carolinas," he wrote, "are conquered in Charleston." He chose the swift, twenty-gun *Perseus* to carry his ten-page account of the successful campaign to England. An American shipping agent in London would describe for John Adams how the news was received there:

> The people are absolutely mad with exultation. . . . Stocks have risen in consequence about 5 percent and everybody is buying. . . . The universal cry is that America is again ours. . . . They say that North Carolina will be certainly theirs . . . that Virginia will also be theirs. The joy of the king and court is visible to everyone. . . . Everything will be risked to carry on that war.

Within days Clinton and his lieutenants began transforming Charleston back into the stalwart outpost of empire it had once been. Redcoats claimed living quarters by chalking their names on the mansion doors of dispossessed rebels. For his headquarters, the commanding general took an exquisite brick Palladian house with a two-story portico on King Street near the tip of the peninsula. Nearby St. Michael's, which the rebels had separated from secular authority by an act of disestablishment, was again designated a pillar of the Anglican church, with a loyalist vicar imported from Savannah. On May 22, Clinton proclaimed that all "faithful and peaceable subjects" would receive the full protection of the king's army. Those suspected of incorrigible disloyalty, including the far-seeing Peter Timothy, were exiled to confinement in St. Augustine.

Among the thorny imperial matters to be resolved was what to do with the estimated twenty-five thousand runaway slaves who eventually sought sanctuary—a quarter of South Carolina's enslaved population and the largest exodus from bondage until the Civil War. So many streamed into Charleston that they were confined in a large sugar warehouse along the Ashley River. Political expediency compelled Clinton to return those claimed by loyalist masters, on the condition that they would not be punished. About eight hundred were employed repairing fortifications or cleaning streets, for which their owners collected eight pence a day for a common laborer and twice that for a skilled artificer. The enslaved belonging to "unfriendly persons" were considered public property—contraband—under the supervision of a commissioner of sequestered estates. Some were promised manumission at the end of the war in exchange for their toil, but Clinton's earlier pledge of freedom for "every Negro who shall desert the rebel standard" was hardly fulfilled. Moreover, a company of sixty-two black

Haitian soldiers who had fought for d'Estaing at Savannah before escorting wounded troops to Charleston was captured along with the rest of the garrison. The Haitians were then sold into slavery by the British.

Vast stocks of indigo, rice, and tobacco had been seized in the Low Country, much of which would now be exported to Britain. Settling into his role as a beneficent viceroy, Clinton paroled General Lincoln, who was allowed to sail to Philadelphia. Major André provided six dozen bottles of wine and ordered that "every comfort that can be given him be put on board." Lincoln's request for a congressional inquest to clear his name would never be granted, perhaps to the ultimate benefit of his reputation, given the indecision and pusillanimous deference to civilian demands that had marked his conduct in Charleston. Later in the year he would be exchanged for Generals Riedesel and Phillips.

Rebel militia garrisons surrendered in Camden, Beaufort, and other backcountry towns. Some militiamen reportedly handed over their officers as prisoners; others were said to have run for the hills to live with Catawba Indians. Rumors spread that Congress planned to cede the three southernmost states to Britain. Sixty miles northeast of Charleston, citizens in Georgetown submitted a petition to a redcoat detachment conceding that the American cause was lost and "we are therefore desirous of becoming British subjects."

To further pacify South Carolina, Clinton on June 1 offered pardons to those swearing allegiance to the Crown. Eager to avoid being pinned to a coastal enclave as Generals Thomas Gage and William Howe had been in Boston and New York, respectively, he seized market towns like Ninety-Six, 170 miles northwest of Charleston. Seventeen hundred troops also were dispatched to expand the Crown's occupation of Georgia. Before this fighting season ended, Clinton hoped to establish seaboard bastions as far north as Norfolk and then Baltimore, providing loyalist asylums and military redoubts. "The only thing in which we all agree," he wrote Cornwallis on June 1, "is that our next operation must be in [the] Chesapeake."

He further tightened his grip on June 3 with an edict requiring all citizens to assist the king's forces "whenever they shall be required in order to extirpate the rebellion." Those who refused to cooperate would be deemed enemies of the Crown. The time for neutrality in this war, for sitting on the fence, had ended. Everyone must "declare and evince his principles." Eventually Clinton would recognize that he had overplayed his hand. Partisans would exploit this autocratic decree, and grievances against a plundering, slave-freeing, bayonet-thrusting occupier smoldered. Many would swear allegiance and not mean it. The embers of rebellion were far from extinguished in the American South.

For now, Clinton nurtured his delusions. "I have the strongest reason to believe the general disposition of the people is to be not only friendly to the government, but forward to take up arms in support," he told Cornwallis. After all, fifteen hundred armed loyalists had offered their services to the British Army by the end of May. "There are few men in South Carolina," he wrote Germain, "who are not either our prisoners or in arms with us." The *Royal Gazette* trumpeted "the conquest . . . of that opulent, populous, and very important colony."

George III's birthday was celebrated in Charleston with unusual exuberance on June 4. Chimes played "God Save the King" beginning at six a.m. and continued all day. Bunting and flags adorned every ship in the harbor, and a grand salute at one p.m. echoed down the bay and up the peninsula. Magnolia blossoms the size of coffee saucers emitted "a most delicious odor," one lieutenant wrote. In the evening many a toast was lifted to the king's health, to the British Army, and to the "long life and never fading laurels of General Sir Henry Clinton."

A world that had wobbled badly now seemed so right, so rebalanced, that Clinton decided to return to New York. Unconfirmed reports had reached him that another French fleet might venture across the Atlantic, and he was needed up north. The government had finally authorized him to sail home on leave, but he had changed his mind. Victory was intoxicating. Although he was now "the most popular man in England," as one admirer asserted, he intended to see things through in America. Arbuthnot would accompany him to New York, although Clinton again privately lamented in his journal that the admiral "talks nonsense by the hour. . . . I have determined never to serve with such an old woman."

Eight thousand regulars and loyalist troops would remain in South Carolina, enough not only to hold the state but also to spread northward like a red ink stain. "I leave Lord Cornwallis here with a sufficient force to keep it against the world," he wrote Eden. The Charleston garrison would also retain 637 horses, 126 wagons, and, to arm more loyalists in North Carolina and Virginia, almost four thousand spare muskets, some of which "were saved out of the magazine that was blown up," Clinton wrote.

On Thursday, June 8, bargemen rowed him out to the *Romulus*. The ship's company stood at attention to welcome him aboard, perhaps with newfound respect for the conqueror of the biggest, richest city in the American South. Charleston had been, as the historian Carl P. Borick would write, "his greatest personal accomplishment and the largest British victory of the war." Across the anchorage, the fleet made ready. Forty-five hundred redcoats and Hessians who would go with him crowded the transport rails. Five hundred slaves selected to work as army pioneers in New York remained belowdecks.

As always, Clinton dreaded going to sea, even though this voyage in the summer sun would be far more tranquil than the dismal trip south six months earlier. He looked forward to being back in New York, back with Mrs. Baddeley, back with his violin and Haydn in the evenings, back to galloping up the post road with André in pursuit of an imaginary fox, and back to pursuit of that other fox, General Washington, in a personal confrontation now entering its sixth year.

Deckhands strained at the capstan to slowly weigh anchor. Topmen unbent the sails. Gulls screamed overhead as *Romulus* and her sisters glided past Sullivan's Island, where British colors floated above Fort Moultrie. Escorted by porpoises and pelicans, the ships eased across the bar before swinging north, and soon all that could be seen of Charleston was that slender black steeple above St. Michael's, pointing toward heaven.

Epilogue

The catastrophe began benignly enough. Sixty thousand protestors, angry that Parliament had expanded rights for Roman Catholics—partly in hopes that more would enlist in the beleaguered British Army—gathered in an open field south of the Thames late Friday morning, June 2, to air their displeasure. Shortly after noon, as the day grew sultry and heat lightning pricked the horizon, they crossed the river on Westminster, Blackfriars, and London Bridges with what one witness described as "a vulgar, furious zeal upon their countenances." Bagpipes skirled as they marched through the city eight abreast. Many wore their Sunday finest, singing Protestant hymns and carrying prayer books or NO POPERY signs. Most wore blue cockades as a badge of umbrage. By one account, "the better sort of tradesmen" had dominated the crowd across the bridges, but by the time the throng approached Palace Yard and the House of Commons, ruffians, inebriates, urchins, and every pickpocket in London had joined the protest.

Several burly men carried an enormous petition with 120,000 signatures or illiterate X's, demanding that Parliament rescind the Catholic Relief Act of 1778. Tailors had stitched the parchment sheets together and rolled them up like a rug. Bulling past the doorkeepers, protestors dumped the heavy scroll on the Commons floor. At two p.m., as unwitting lawmakers began to arrive for an afternoon session, blue banners waggled from Whitehall rooftops to signal the protestors below as to whether they should "applaud or abuse" the approaching coaches, Horace Walpole recorded. Those carrying suspected Catholic sympathizers were pelted with mud and excrement by a crush now grown bellicose. Members were "torn out of their chariots," Walpole added, and forced to don blue cockades while repeating, "No popery! No popery!"

The lord chief justice had the wig plucked from his head and all the windows of his coach broken. Lord Stormont, formerly ambassador to Versailles and now a secretary of state, was pelted and kicked, as plug-uglies bashed his carriage to splinters. Other peers had their gowns torn off, and the canonical robes of the archbishops of Canterbury and York were ripped; the bishop of London hid in a nearby house before disguising himself in a woman's dress to escape. Someone threw porter in the face of Lord Germain, who reportedly was treated "with great severity." Lord North's hat was snatched from his head and cut into souvenir pieces, which sold for a shilling each. "The tumult," Edward Gibbon wrote his wife, "has been dreadful." Yet even a historian celebrated for his grasp of imperial strife did not sense that he was witnessing the start of the most violent and protracted urban riots in British history.

The Relief Act was hardly a radical triumph of tolerance. Even now, with the country at war against Bourbon papists, no practicing Catholic could sit in Parliament, attend university, or serve as an army officer. Catholic church bells could not toll. The new law, passed without opposition two years earlier, removed prohibitions on Catholics buying or inheriting land in England, lifted the threat of life imprisonment for those who taught school, and permitted military recruits to swear allegiance to the Crown without renouncing their religion. But a recent proposal to extend the measures to Scotland had aroused what the *Annual Register* called "a furious spirit of bigotry and persecution," forcing Scottish Catholics to seek refuge in Edinburgh Castle.

This antagonism spread south, abetted by a fanatical incendiary named George Gordon, the dissolute youngest son of a duke. Thin and pale, with protruding blue eyes and lank red hair to his shoulders, Gordon, as a member of the Commons, routinely denounced both "the whore of Babylon"—the Roman Catholic church and its sympathizers—and "the mad, cruel, and accursed American war." To detractors he was "the lunatic apostle" and "Lord George Macbeth"; he preferred to consider himself "the people's pilot," or perhaps "the English Brutus." This Brutus had organized today's protest.

By midnight the mob, armed with hammers, crowbars, and torches, had moved from Parliament to the Sardinian embassy's Catholic chapel on Duke Street. The ambassador offered fifteen hundred guineas if the firebrands would spare the fine organ and a painting of Jesus. To no avail: both soon burned, along with the altar, vestments, and pews. Only a pair of chalices were saved. Then it was on to the Bavarian embassy chapel in Warwick Street, another Catholic church in Ropemakers' Alley, and the houses of Catholic brokers and manufacturers in Spitalfields.

"Here is a religious war added to all our civil and foreign wars," Walpole wrote a friend on Sunday. Yet the arson and mayhem had just begun, and more chapels burned in the following days. The fourteen thousand

Catholic families in London barricaded their doors; some flew blue flags, posted NO POPERY signs, or handed over a few coins to scowling extortionists who demanded money "for the true religion." Even Jews in Houndsditch scribbled "This house is true Protestant" on their shutters. Irishmen, presumed to be at least Catholic in spirit, risked assault in the street with bludgeons and knives. Edmund Burke, a Protestant Dubliner with a Catholic mother, abandoned his Charles Street home to take refuge with his wife in General Burgoyne's house. But religion had become a thin pretext for an uprising that was more revolutionary than theological, driven by lower-class resentments against "the gentleman, the manufacturer, the merchant, or the publican," as the historian George F. E. Rudé later wrote. "There lay a deeper social purpose: a groping desire to settle accounts with the rich, if only for a day."

London would not have a professional police force for another half century, and although some army and militia units had begun filtering into the city, General Amherst reported that with so many regiments deployed abroad, troops were hard to find. The cabinet dithered, and when Parliament warily reconvened on Tuesday, June 6, for the first time since Friday, the mob again waited in ambush. Sandwich was yanked from his coach and tossed to the ground, his cheek cut with a shard of broken glass before horse guards helped him escape back to the Admiralty.

The Portsmouth fleet was ordered to sea for fear that France would exploit the turmoil with another Descent. Gunsmiths padlocked their shops along the riverbank and hauled their stock into the Tower, where the drawbridges were then raised. Fearful Londoners fled what Samuel Johnson called "a time of terror" in the greatest exodus from the city since the bubonic plague epidemic of 1665. This "republican phrenzy" now targeted symbols of state authority. Lord Chief Justice Mansfield's house and priceless library in Bloomsbury Square burned, kindled with wood shavings and turpentine, as did the Bow Street house of Chief Magistrate Sir John Fielding, along with thirty years' worth of criminal records. Mobs sacked at least twenty crimping houses—taverns where unscrupulous publicans lured seamen in debt for delivery to navy press-gangs.

By Tuesday evening, rioters had begun to release criminals and debtors from virtually every cell in London, including Newgate, the city's largest prison. At eight p.m., thousands of men with sledgehammers and ladders swarmed around the massive stone complex, which had just been rebuilt and expanded. William Blake, a twenty-two-year-old engraver and aspiring poet, described "howlings & hissings, shrieks & groans & voices of despair" as attackers battered down the huge doors known as "the gates of Hell" before wrenching open the interior cells. Another poet, George

Crabbe, saw snaking lines of freed prisoners "conducted through the streets in their chains. Three of them were to be hanged on Friday." Rioters slurping from buckets of gin then set the place on fire and moved on with their fagots and tools to Fleet Prison, King's Bench Prison, New Gaol, and other penitentiaries, freeing hundreds of criminals and nearly two thousand debtors. London increasingly resembled "a city sacked and abandoned to a ferocious enemy," wrote Nathaniel Wraxall, who was reminded of Virgil's description of burning Troy. Tuesday, another witness declared, was "the most terrible night in the whole history of London."

In fact, Wednesday—Black Wednesday—was worse. More shops and houses burned, along with pubs in Whitechapel and the halfpenny tollbooths on Blackfriars Bridge. A large distillery in Holborn went up in flames, fueled by 120,000 gallons of gin in the cellar. Fire spread to more than twenty adjacent houses, "a pinnacle of flame resembling a volcano." Clerks at a bank in Fleet Street were issued ancient flintlocks, and their colleagues nearby at the Bank of England melted inkwells for casting in bullet molds. When rioters rushed the Royal Exchange, twenty were shot down by troops waiting with Brown Bess muskets.

By one count, thirty-six fires burned across London as the sun set. In Downing Street, grenadiers took post on the upper floors of North's house, ready to shoot from the windows. "It is now a real civil war," one Londoner wrote. "Heaven defend us all."

But the king was tired of waiting for both heaven and his government to intervene. "The tumult must be got the better of or it will encourage designing men to use it as a precedent for assembling the people on other occasions," George wrote. "Examples must be made." To discourage rioters from storming the Queen's House, three thousand troops now camped in the Buckingham gardens. The king strolled among the night watch with "easy affability" and personally ensured that the men had bedding straw and "a good allowance of wine and spirits." Couriers brought accounts of prisons overrun, of great houses sacked, of the royal print shop burned. "I fear without more vigor," George had written North on Tuesday night, "that this will not subside." A Guards captain observed, "I am persuaded that the king does not know what fear is."

George "was the first that recovered" from the panic and paralysis gripping the government, Dr. Johnson later asserted. Exasperated by "the great supineness of the civil magistrates," on Wednesday night the king summoned Attorney General Alexander Wedderburn and asked whether rioters "might legally be fired on by the military power" without a formal reading of the 1714 Riot Act, used to disperse illegal assemblies. Prodded by his monarch, Wedderburn agreed that deadly force was justified. "Then so let it be done," George ordered. A royal decree effectively authorized Amherst to impose martial law.

By Thursday more than eleven thousand troops filled the city. Tents covered Hyde Park and St. James's Park, giving "the whole metropolis a warlike appearance," a resident reported. Six regiments patrolled city streets, the army seized the Thames bridges, and now volleys of musketry greeted malefactors. "Near thirty persons were killed rioting in Fleet Street," Walpole wrote. Looters ransacking Broad Street houses were shot dead. After a brutal army assault on Blackfriars Bridge, corpses were fished from the river and laid in rows on Dung Wharf. Soldiers tore blue banners from houses and plucked blue cockades off hats and lapels. "We are at last pretty quiet," Lieutenant Colonel Charles Stuart wrote his family. "Yesterday the soldiers dealt death about pretty freely."

"The most horrid series of outrages that ever disgraced a civilized country," in James Boswell's estimation, sputtered to an end. Whitewash soon hid the bloodstains on the Bank of England's walls, and fresh dirt was shoveled over the gore spattering Blackfriars. An estimated 800 to 1,000 people had died in the week-long rampage, including 285 killed by Amherst's troops. Damage to the city would not be surpassed until the German bombing campaign—the Blitz—of 1940.

"I hope every means are taken to find out the movers and abettors of the horrid tumult we are now beginning to quell," George wrote North from the Queen's House on Friday, June 9. A handbill circulating through London claimed that the tumult had originated in Versailles. The *Morning Chronicle* went further by asserting that the disturbances were "carried on by French and American spies of inferior station." One magistrate suspected "lads well-trained by some of Dr. Franklin's people . . . and abetted by French money."

No evidence ever supported such allegations. Rather, deep-rooted prejudices, resentment at social inequities, a society disrupted by years of war, and intoxicated rage had combined to ignite what came to be known as the Gordon Riots. The "mischievous madman" himself, as Gibbon called George Gordon, was seized by horse guards at his house near Cavendish Square on Saturday afternoon. Following interrogation by North, Amherst, and other panjandrums, he was bundled into a closed hackney and escorted to the Tower by a regiment of dragoons, an infantry company, and three ranks of militiamen—"a more imposing military force," one witness noted, "than had attended Charles I on his way from St. James's Palace to the scaffold." But there would be no scaffold for Gordon: charged with high treason, after eight months in jail he was acquitted at trial and set free, thanks to a brilliant defense lawyer. "Our disgrace will be lasting," Gibbon told his wife, "and the month of June 1780 will ever be marked by a dark and diabolical fanaticism, which I had supposed to be extinct." Although Gordon went free, British justice fell hard on other accused rioters. Of nearly five hundred arrested, sixty-two were condemned to death and twenty-five ultimately hanged, including several sailors, a soldier, a bookbinder, a pencil maker, a blacksmith, and a prostitute.

Gallows appeared around the city, often at the scene of the crime, with the condemned escorted to the scaffold by hundreds of volunteer constables. Twelve thousand spectators swarmed onto Tower Hill to watch three executions there. A majority of all those hanged were reportedly under the age of eighteen. The youngest, "a slender lad" of fourteen named Richard Roberts, had weights inserted into his pockets as the noose was looped around his neck, "that he might sooner be out of pain." Of these young miscreants sent to their deaths, a witness reported, "I never saw children cry so."

If devastating to London, the riots proved a godsend to King George and the North government. Slow to act, the prime minister was nonetheless recognized as a bulwark against anarchy, a sober, trustworthy alternative to both hooligans and the opposition led by Charles Fox. "The governing class found itself faced with the nightmare of mob rule," the historian Ian R. Christie wrote. "There was a reknitting of the ranks in defense of the established order."

This revival of fortunes could not have been more timely for a tottering government beset by disgruntlement over the American war and by demands for lower taxes, broader Irish rights, election reform, and other fixes to the body politic. Even the monarchy and the king himself had increasingly come under attack, with a vitriol not heard in Parliament for generations. In a swipe at Germain and war policy, Burke and other reformers came within seven votes of abolishing the American secretary's position. And shortly before the Gordon rampage, the Commons approved a stunning rebuke to George in passing, by a vote of 233 to 215, a resolution declaring that "the power of the Crown has increased, is increasing, and ought to be diminished."

With the government now widely seen as a force for stability and the rule of law, the king could give his full attention to the war. He took heart from intercepted letters showing strains between France and America, and hints that Versailles fretted over the cost of fighting Britain. The happy news from Charleston, received in London a week after the riots, gladdened the kingdom and occasioned street celebrations described as "exuberant and wild," plus triple discharges of artillery and a *feu de joie* fired by troops still camped in Hyde Park. "I do believe that America is nearer coming into temper to treat than perhaps at any other period," the king wrote. Other providential tidings had also arrived that spring, disclosing the capture of twenty-two ships in a Spanish convoy, the defeat of a Spanish fleet off Portugal at Cape St. Vincent, and the successful arrival of a relief convoy at besieged Gibraltar, where the British garrison had been reduced to eating thistles and dandelions.

Not all the war news was heartening, of course. Britain remained friendless, as she had been since 1763. The most recent War Office returns showed that more than 10,000 British troops had died in North America and the West Indies since the troubles began; another 8,629 had been captured, 3,801 had deserted, and 3,885 had been discharged from the service for crippling wounds or other afflictions. Replacing those 26,000 casualties remained onerous.

George had now been king for twenty years, and Britain had been at war for nearly half of his reign. Obdurate optimism had seen him through, along with a resolute belief in his own righteousness. Others might quail; he would not. Conceding independence to America would plunge Britain into "a state of inferiority and consequently . . . into a very low class among the European states," he had recently reminded North. "I hope never to live to see that day." General Clinton's recent success, as well as loyalist assurances that they were gaining the upper hand in America, suggested that the rebels "must sue for peace this summer, if no great disaster befalls us."

The king's critics continued to question his judgment and his intransigence; some caricaturists had even begun depicting George as an oriental despot. But he believed that most Britons would stand by their monarch, their captain general. Future generations would surely recognize his patriotism, his good sense, his pure intentions. "However I am treated," he told North, "I must love this country."

The Continental Army and the American cause had survived the bitter winter, but spring revived old worries and brought new threats. In late May, a congressional committee reported that the army was "five months' pay in arrears . . . is without meat, and has been on half and on quarter allowances for some days past." More enlistments would soon expire, and few new recruits had arrived. Congress had provided each state with supply quotas for the next campaign, with beef, flour, salt, hay, and rum to be delivered to commissary magazines in exchange for future remuneration calculated in Spanish-milled dollars.

This makeshift arrangement already showed signs of collapse. Short-ages of food, clothing, and pay caused a Connecticut brigade—said to be "exasperated beyond endurance"—to mutiny in Jockey Hollow on May 25. Surrounded by armed Pennsylvania troops and ordered back to their huts, the mutineers were "dispersed without much difficulty," their colonel re-ported. But Washington told Congress that the brief uprising "has given me infinitely more concern than anything that has ever happened." Dire reports from Charleston only added to that anxiety, along with the realiza-tion that the Continental Navy, reduced to five vessels, had been all but obliterated. "In looking over the long list of vessels belonging to the United States, taken and destroyed . . . it is difficult to avoid tears," John Adams admitted.

"We are entered deeply in a contest on which our all depends," Hamil-ton wrote Greene as the apple trees blossomed in Morristown. "We must endeavor to rub through it." Rubbing through it had become the American way of war, an improvised skitter from one crisis to the next. Since 1775, the conflict had metastasized into something far bigger, bloodier, and more portentous than a revolt by disgruntled provincials on the edge of the world. Now fought on four continents and their adjacent seas, the war seemed likely to grow bigger still, perhaps drawing in the Netherlands, Sweden, Russia, and other European powers. Yet Americans "want to have the war carried on," Thomas Paine wrote in early June, "the Lord knows how." An indomitable persistence had survived another season, not in every patriot heart and not without despair, but in enough hearts and with enough hope to fight on. "I am persuaded things will come right in the end," Ebenezer Stanton, a Connecticut paymaster, wrote a friend from Morristown. "I could wish I had two lives to lose in defense of so glorious a cause. . . . I was free-born, and if I can support myself, I will stand or fall in defense of my country."

My country. That concept had taken root in the American seedbed, nurtured by a shared faith that this struggle, ostensibly about taxes, au-tonomy, and other parochial complaints, was ultimately about the chance to build both a new nation and a better world. "I was confirmed in the habit of considering America as my country and Congress as my govern-ment," wrote Captain John Marshall, a future chief justice, who had sur-vived Brandywine, Germantown, Monmouth, Valley Forge, and Stony Point. "I had imbibed these sentiments so thoroughly that they constituted a part of my being." Abigail Adams told her young son John Quincy, who had accompanied his father on another diplomatic trip to France, "These are the times in which a genius would wish to live. . . . Great necessities call out great virtues."

Faith in the future sustained an irrational optimism, despite all the obvious perils. Benjamin Franklin, upon learning of Charleston's fall, insisted that the city would prove a millstone around British necks, as Philadelphia had. Writing from Paris, he offered to give Washington, whom he called "one of the greatest captains of the age," a grand tour of European capitals once peace returned. "I must soon quit the scene," Franklin told him. "But you may live to see our country flourish, as it will amazingly and rapidly after the war is over." He compared America to "a field of young Indian corn" that, "by a thunder gust of violent wind, hail, & rain seemed to be threatened with absolute destruction. Yet the storm being past, it recovers fresh verdure, shoots up with double vigor, and delights the eye not of its owner only, but of every observing traveler."

Getting to that day, when the corn grew straight and tall, would depend on Washington's continued skill and luck as commander in chief. Providence "has always displayed its power and goodness when clouds and thick darkness seemed ready to overwhelm us," he wrote Lund, his overseer, in late May. The past two years had sharpened his abilities on and off the battlefield. Once prone to indecision, he was now decisive and confident in his generalship, just as he was meticulous and comprehensive as an administrator. A man who would never see those European capitals, notwithstanding Franklin's invitation, proved an exceptionally deft diplomat by integrating the French into his command and preventing ruptures with foreign friends. As a political general he remained peerless, nurturing strong alliances with Congress, state governments, and other civilian authorities, and outmaneuvering the likes of Charles Lee and Thomas Conway. A man who began the war as a relative novice with limited military experience had in five years become the unchallenged leader of a continental force holding the British empire at bay.

If at times stern and short-tempered, Washington continued to embody the classical virtues cherished by his countrymen, notably fortitude, prudence, temperance, and the subordination of private advantage to public benefit—"one steady line of conduct for the good of the great whole," as he put it. In his letter to Lund he elaborated: "You ask how I am to be rewarded for all this? There is one reward that nothing can deprive me of, and that is the consciousness of having done my duty with the strictest rectitude and most scrupulous exactness—and the certain knowledge that if we should ultimately fail in the present contest, it is not owing to the want of exertion in me."

In an era of great men, he already was in the front rank.

* * *

Washington had realized, to his mortification, that since Lafayette's departure for France in January 1779, "not one of the many letters which I have written to you since you left this continent had arrived safe," as he told the marquis in a note written from Morristown this March. He was therefore delighted when a courier galloped up to his headquarters at nine a.m. on Saturday, May 6, with a dispatch written "at the entrance of Boston harbor." Breaking the seal, Washington read:

> Here I am, my dear general. . . . I came from France on board of a frigate which the king gave me for my passage. I have affairs of the utmost importance that I should at first communicate to you alone. . . . [I] do assure you a great public good may derive from it. Lafayette.

Four days later Hamilton sent a note to General Steuben: "We have heard from the marquis. He will be here at dinner. Will you dine with us also? The general requests it." Escorted on the last leg of his journey by the commanding general's Life Guards, Lafayette and the cavalcade trotted up the long drive of the Ford mansion in bright sunshine to be greeted with cheers and clasped hands. "The marquis is in good health," an American major observed, "but I think not so fat as when he left us." Washington beamed, and by one account his "eyes filled with tears of joy."

Despite the jubilant welcome, Lafayette immediately recognized, as he later wrote, that "the condition of the army was very bad. There was no money. It had become impossible to recruit troops." After a celebratory dinner, Washington ushered the marquis into his study and shut the door. Lafayette's English was rusty from eighteen months of disuse, but he pulled out his orders from Vergennes and excitedly translated the momentous news: His Most Christian Majesty, Louis XVI, had agreed to send six ships of the line and other men-of-war to America with six thousand combat troops. The *Expédition Particulière* was now gathering in Brest under one of France's most experienced officers, Lieutenant General Jean-Baptiste Donatien de Vimeur, the Comte de Rochambeau. These reinforcements, to be placed under Washington's command, could be expected sometime in June.

Not since word of the Franco-American alliance reached Valley Forge, more than two years earlier, had His Excellency heard such galvanic news. After further discussion with the marquis, Washington summoned Greene and other senior commanders to discuss this astounding development. "The time slides away so fast," he told Lafayette. "Every moment is infinitely precious."

This was "the happiest opportunity we ever had to save ourselves"

Hamilton wrote Congress on Washington's behalf. "We must collect men, form magazines, and do a thousand things of as much difficulty as importance. . . . The fate of America is perhaps suspended on the issue." Provisions for the French must be stockpiled, and pilots positioned at Newport and Cape Henry, at the mouth of the Chesapeake, since the fleet's precise destination remained uncertain. Medicos would be needed to treat French troops suffering from scurvy and dysentery contracted during the long voyage. Horsemen were also needed as couriers, from southern Virginia to Rhode Island. More spies should be inserted into New York. To deceive the British, five hundred copies of a proclamation would be printed under Lafayette's name, urging Canadians to "renew their ancient friendship with France" by welcoming a French squadron that could be expected soon on the St. Lawrence River.

Washington began drafting his battle plans. In hopes of assembling an American army worthy of the French commitment, he would call for twenty-two thousand militiamen "well-armed and equipped" to join his Continentals, along with seven thousand horses and four hundred oxen. A successful assault on New York could end the war quickly, but he also considered attacks on enemy outposts at Halifax and Penobscot Bay. And, as he wrote Lafayette, if the French squadron of more than twenty warships now in the West Indies could be persuaded to sail north, "the most telling blow against England" might also be struck in Georgia and the Carolinas.

Between conferences with aides and lieutenants, Washington wrote scores of confidential letters to his generals, to French officials, to Congress, and to governors, urging heroic exertions "to bring out the resources of the country with vigor and decision."

"This is a decisive moment, one of the most—I will go further & say *the* most important America has ever seen," he declared in a letter to Pennsylvania authorities. "The court of France has made a glorious effort for our deliverance, and if we disappoint its intentions by our supineness, we must become contemptible in the eyes of all mankind."

There was not a moment to be lost.

Author's Note

Given the distracting inconsistency in eighteenth-century punctuation, spelling, capitalization, abbreviation, and grammar, I have corrected some of the more archaic or unorthodox extracts quoted from letters and other written sources. My intent is to improve accessibility and sense for a modern reader, while respecting the original meaning, language, and voice.

The abbreviated prefix *HMS*, for "His Majesty's Ship," was not in broad use until several years after the American Revolution ended. Therefore it does not appear in this account.

Money during the American Revolution remains a confusing if not stupefying subject. Beginning in 1775, Congress authorized the issue of Continental dollars, which by 1779 totaled $200 million but by war's end had become virtually worthless because of inflation—the rate reached 22 percent in 1777 alone—and depreciation. States also issued their own currency, variously denominated in pounds, shillings, pence, or dollars, and with fluctuating equivalences to the Continental dollar; for example, six Virginia shillings or eight New York shillings equaled a Continental.

The U.S. Department of Labor estimates that American prices have increased some 3,000 percent since the Revolution. Consequently, one Continental dollar in 1777 had the purchasing power equivalent to $29.63 in 2024.

The British pound sterling—twenty shillings to the pound, twelve pence to the shilling—remained largely stable through the war. A gold guinea coin—displaying George III in profile—was worth twenty-one shillings. For rough comparisons, £1 sterling equaled approximately five Continental dollars early in the war and $23^{1}/_{2}$ French livres. The dollar sign—$—was formally adopted in 1785, according to the U.S. Currency Education Program.

Notes

The following abbreviations appear in the endnotes and bibliography.

AA Peter Force, *American Archives* (series, volume, page; e.g., IV: 2, 630)
AFC L. H. Butterfield, ed., *Adams Family Correspondence*
AH Alexander Hamilton, including papers, FOL
AHR *American Historical Review*
AP Robert J. Taylor, ed., *The Adams Papers*, FOL
APS American Philosophical Society, Philadelphia
BA Benedict Arnold
BBSHS Bennington Battlefield State Historic Site, New York
BF Benjamin Franklin
BFTM *Bulletin of the Fort Ticonderoga Museum*
BSC Douglas R. Cubbison, *Burgoyne and the Saratoga Campaign: His Papers*
corr. correspondence
CtS Eric Schnitzer and Don Troiani, *Campaign to Saratoga—1777*
DAR K. G. Davies, ed., *Documents of the American Revolution, 1770-1783*
diss. dissertation
EPO Eric P. Olsen, historian, MNHP (monographs)
ES Eric Schnitzer, NPS ranger and historian, SNHP
f folio
fn footnote
FOL Founders Online, U.S. National Archives (papers of Adams, Franklin, Hamilton, Jay, Jefferson, Madison, Washington), https://founders.archives.gov
GSG George Sackville Germain papers, WLC
GW George Washington
HCP Henry Clinton papers, WLC
HDAR Hessian Documents of the American Revolution, Lidgerwood Collection, MNHP
HL Huntington Library, San Marino, California
JA John Adams
JAR *Journal of the American Revolution*, www.allthingsliberty.com
JLB Joseph Lee Boyle archive, VFNHP, provided to author (organized by AAA, BBB, etc.)
JMH *Journal of Military History*
JPJ Samuel Eliot Morison, *John Paul Jones: A Sailor's Biography*
JSHA *The Hessians: Journal of the Johannes Schwalm Historical Association*
LAC Library and Archives of Canada, Ottawa
LAAR Stanley J. Idzerda, ed., *Lafayette in the Age of the American Revolution: Selected Letters and Papers, 1776-1790*, vols. 1 and 2
LiA Louis Gottschalk, *Lafayette in America: 1777-1783*, 3 vols.
LOC Library of Congress, Washington, D.C.

LP Charles Lee, *The Lee Papers*, NYHS
MBSP Monmouth Battlefield State Park, New Jersey
MHQ Military History Quarterly
micro microfilm
MNHP Morristown National Historical Park, New Jersey
ms. manuscript
n note
n.d. no date
n.p. no place; not paginated
NDAR William Bell Clark, ed., *Naval Documents of the American Revolution*
NG Nathanael Greene
NPS National Park Service
NYHS New-York Historical Society, New York City
NYPL New York Public Library
PGW W. W. Abbot et al., eds. *The Papers of George Washington: Revolutionary War Series,*
   vols. 8–26
PH 19 The Parliamentary History of England, vol. 19
PMHB Pennsylvania Magazine of History and Biography
PNG Richard K. Showman, et al., eds., *The Papers of General Nathanael Greene*
PP G. R. Barnes and J. H. Owen, eds., *Sandwich The Private Papers of John, Earl of Sandwich,*
   First Lord of the Admiralty, 1771–82, 4 vols.
RA Royal Archives, Papers of George III, Windsor Castle, England
SNHP Saratoga National Historical Park
SoC Society of the Cincinnati, Washington, D.C.
s.p. self-published
SPBSHS Stony Point Battlefield State Historic Site, New York
TAR Henry Clinton, *The American Rebellion*
TBAC Rick Atkinson, *The British Are Coming*
T-P RC Thompson-Pell Research Center, Fort Ticonderoga, New York
TJ Thomas Jefferson
UK NA National Archives, Kew, U.K. (formerly Public Record Office)
VFHRR1 Wayne K. Bodle, "The Vortex of Small Fortunes: The Continental Army at Valley Forge,
   1777–1778," Valley Forge Historical Research Report, vol. 1
VFHRR2 Jacqueline Thibaut, "This Fatal Crisis: Logistics, Supply, and the Continental Army at
   Valley Forge, 1777–1778," Valley Forge Historical Research Report, vol. 2
VFHRR3 Jacqueline Thibaut, "In the True Rustic Order," Valley Forge Historical Research Report,
   vol. 3
VFNHP Valley Forge National Historical Park, including materials provided by ranger Jennifer
   Bolton and archivist Dona McDermott
WBW William B. Willcox collection, WLC
WLC William L. Clements Library, University of Michigan, Ann Arbor
WMQ William and Mary Quarterly

PROLOGUE

1   **As the Parisian:** Mercy-Argenteau, *Marie-Antoinette*, 3: 18–26; Manceron, *Age of the French*
   Revolution, 1: 411 (*half a million*); Bernier, *Secrets of Marie Antoinette*, 208–9; Schama, *Citi-*
   zens, 213–14 ("*Madame Deficit*").

1   **No matter:** "The Forum of Marie Antoinette," https://marie-antoinette.forumactif.org/
   (*spurs*); Bernier, *Secrets of Marie Antoinette*, 211 ("*telling the king*").

1   **The queen particularly:** Zweig, *Marie Antoinette*, 137 (*domino*); Castelot, *Queen of France*,
   136 (*coat of arms*); Bachaumont, *Marie-Antoinette, Louis XVI et la famille royale*, 100 (*stool*);
   Maugras, *The Duc de Lauzun and the Court of Marie Antoinette*, 88 ("*She fancied*"); Garrioch,

The Making of Revolutionary Paris (*the wellborn*); "The Forum of Marie Antoinette," https://marie-antoinette.forumactif.org/ (*"great ladies"*).

2 **Masked or unmasked:** Delalex, *A Day with Marie Antoinette,* 140 (*"so translucent"*); Delalex, *Un jour avec Marie-Antoinette,* 136, 142 (*jasmine*), 162 (*"music must be wrong"*); Fraser, *Marie Antoinette,* 121 (*"Goddess"*; the line is from the *Aeneid,* 1: 405).

2 **Some thought:** Bachaumont, *Marie-Antoinette, Louis XVI et la famille royale,* 101; Smythe, *The Guardian of Marie Antoinette,* 473 (*English noblemen*); *Les femmes de Versailles: Les beaux jours de Marie-Antoinette,* 220–21; Jusserand, "Our First Alliance," 518; Maugras, *The Duc de Lauzun and the Court of Marie Antoinette,* 78–84 (*all things English*); Zweig, *Marie Antoinette,* 138 (*"I am terrified"*).

2 **"My fate":** Hardman, *Marie-Antoinette,* xv, 21 (*"Madame"*), 32–33; Ferreiro, *Brothers at Arms,* 80; Delalex, *A Day with Marie Antoinette,* 31 (*sixteen thousand lanterns*); Darnton, *The Revolutionary Temper,* 123–25 (*"stigmatized"*); author visit, Versailles, May 29, 2022.

2 **Despite a lingering:** Hardman, *Marie-Antoinette,* xix (*German lessons*); Fraser, *Marie Antoinette,* 69 (*filbert nut*), 149–50 (*peignoir*); Delalex, *A Day with Marie Antoinette,* 115 (*Three times a year*); Zweig, *Marie Antoinette,* 131–32 (*Monsieur Léonard*).

3 **When Carnival at last:** Mercy-Argenteau, *Marie-Antoinette,* 3: 21 (*Shrove Tuesday*); Lemoine et al., *Versailles,* 74; author visit, Versailles, May 29, 2022; Garrioch, *The Making of Revolutionary Paris,* 262 (*effigy*); Smythe, *The Guardian of Marie Antoinette,* 474 (*"little amused"*).

3 **She returned to the palace:** author visit, Versailles, May 29, 2022; Castelot, *Queen of France,* 117 (*used stubs*); Delalex, *A Day with Marie Antoinette,* 57 (*Nineteen babies*); Dunlop, *Versailles,* 88 (*aqueduct*).

4 **All the while commissions:** Delalex, *A Day with Marie Antoinette,* 68, 80.

4 **As his vivacious, convivial:** Delalex, *A Day with Marie Antoinette,* 52; Hardman, *The Life of Louis XVI,* 25 (*"Exclaim, bawl out"*), 33; Farr, *Before the Deluge,* 45; Schama, *Citizens,* 58–59 (*garden sprinklers*).

4 **"My greatest fault":** Hardman, *The Life of Louis XVI,* 14–18 (*"full of dangers"*); Campan, *The Private Life of Marie Antoinette,* 149–50 (*Milton*); Hardman and Price, eds., *Louis XVI and the Comte de Vergennes,* 89 (*Charles I*).

4 **A fine equestrian:** Dunlop, *Versailles,* 168 (*189,251 birds*); Schama, *Citizens,* 54 (*128 horses*); Zweig, *Marie Antoinette,* 107–9 (*"Stag hunting"*); Nicolardot, ed., *Journal de Louis XVI,* n.p. (*240 livres*); Darnton, *The Revolutionary Temper,* 161 (*"the Desired"*).

5 **He was an accidental monarch:** "Louis XVI, 1754–1793," https://en.chateauversailles.fr/discover/history/great-characters/louis-xvi; Price, *The Road from Versailles,* 5; Schama, *Citizens,* 51 (*two occasions* and *"heretics"*); Padover, *The Life and Death of Louis XVI,* 83 (*scepter*); Hardman, *The Life of Louis XVI,* 90 (*scrofula*); Darnton, *The Revolutionary Temper,* 167.

5 **The second happy moment:** Schama, *Citizens,* 51, 55, 58; Price, *The Road from Versailles,* 5; Hardman, *The Life of Louis XVI,* 18, 27 (*first and only time*).

5 **Versailles had been the political:** Lemoine et al., *Versailles,* 17–18; Hardman, *The Life of Louis XVI,* 66–67 (*sedition*); Farr, *Before the Deluge,* 39; Castelot, *Queen of France,* 83 (*"fecal matter"*); Alsop, *Yankees at Court,* 122 (*proper hat*); Fraser, *Marie Antoinette,* 77–78 (*red wine*).

5 **"martyrs to decorum":** Farr, *Before the Deluge,* 39; Dunlop, *Versailles,* 170 (*"cleanly dressed"*); Delalex, *A Day with Marie Antoinette,* 84 (*forty dishes*); Lemoine et al., *Versailles,* 84; Ducros, *French Society in the Eighteenth Century,* 34–35.

6 **Even emptier ceremonies began:** author visit, Versailles, May 29, 2022; Maugras, *The Duc de Lauzun and the Court of Marie Antoinette,* 33; Hardman, *The Life of Louis XVI,* 66–67; Ducros, *French Society in the Eighteenth Century,* 30–34; Dunlop, *Versailles,* 166–67.

6 **Amid the relentless rituals:** Hardman, *The Life of Louis XVI,* 81–86 (*violent riots*).

6 **Of immediate concern was his nation's role:** McCusker and Menard, *The Economy of British America, 1607–1789,* 366; Coakley and Conn, *The War of the American Revolution,* 13–16; Corwin, "The French Objective in the American Revolution," 33+; Dull, *The French Navy and American Independence,* 17 (*40 percent of French imports*); Allison and Ferreiro, eds., *The*

American Revolution, 18; Bauer, "With Friends Like These," 664+ (*gold or silver mines*); Padover, *The Life and Death of Louis XVI,* 105n.

6 **In the past decade, French prosperity:** Ferling, ed., *The World Turned Upside Down,* 149; Eccles, *The French in North America, 1500–1783,* 266 (*"France possesses colonies"*).

7 **Losing the last war:** Allison and Ferreiro, eds., *The American Revolution,* 21; "France in the American Revolution," exhibition pamphlet, SoC, 2011–12, 6–7; Conway, *The War of American Independence 1775–1783,* 63; Werther, "Opposing the Franco-American Alliance," *JAR,* June 23, 2020 (*"first gunshot"*); Hardman, *Marie-Antoinette,* 64–65 (*Protestant banker*).

7 **Habitually cautious, Louis would move:** Van Doren, *Benjamin Franklin,* 573; Corwin, "The French Objective in the American Revolution," 33+; Hardman, *The Life of Louis XVI,* 112 (*million livres*), 117.

7 **Yet he knew:** Hardman, *The Life of Louis XVI,* 18 (*"humiliate"*).

7 **Since the end:** Van Tyne, *The War of Independence,* 457–58 (*500 guineas*); Echeverria, *Mirage in the West,* 20–21; Rodger, *The Command of the Ocean,* 411 (*French naval engineers*); Van Tyne, "French Aid Before the Alliance of 1778," 20+; Harris, *Industrial Espionage and Technology Transfer,* 128–29, 133 (*"live, travel, and bribe"*). A guinea coin was worth slightly more than £1.

7 **And all the while:** Martelli, *Jemmy Twitcher,* 108.

8 **When trumpets announced:** Alsop, *Yankees at the Court,* 83; Lemoine et al., *Versailles,* 27; Hoffman and Albert, eds., *Diplomacy and Revolution,* 79; Schoenbrun, *Triumph in Paris,* 152 (*rosewood desk*); Wharton, ed., "Attitude of France to the United States," *Revolutionary Diplomatic Correspondence of the United States,* 1:350 (*eight a.m.*); Hardman, *The Life of Louis XVI,* 104; Murphy, *Charles Gravier, Comte de Vergennes,* 215 (*"restless"*).

8 **A deft, loyal monarchist:** Murphy, *Charles Gravier, Comte de Vergennes,* 3, 166 (*two sons*), 345 (*"dissipations"*); Hoffman and Albert, eds., *Diplomacy and Revolution,* 79; Hardman, *The Life of Louis XVI,* 101 (*"woman of the people"*); Manceron, *Age of the French Revolution,* 2: 152; Hardman and Price, eds., *Louis XVI and the Comte de Vergennes,* xiv–xv; Alsop, *Yankees at the Court,* 82 (*"La Solitude"*).

8 **France did not wish:** Stoker et al., eds., *Strategy in the American War of Independence,* 144; Dull, *The French Navy and the Seven Years' War,* 253; Corwin, "The French Objective in the American Revolution," 33+ (*"right to influence"*); Meng, ed., *Despatches and Instructions of Conrad Alexandre Gérard, 1778–1780,* 71–75; Murphy, *Charles Gravier, Comte de Vergennes,* 235.

8 **Timing was critical:** Murphy, *Charles Gravier, Comte de Vergennes,* 220, 235, 242; Van Tyne, "Influence Which Determined the French Government to Make the Treaty with America, 1778," 528+ (*combined assault*).

9 **After pondering these complexities:** Ferreiro, *Brothers at Arms,* 95 (*"The time has come"*); Corwin, "The French Objective in the American Revolution," 33+ (*Peru and Mexico*). With Louis XVI's approval, the memo would be sent to Madrid on July 26 (Murphy, *Charles Gravier, Comte de Vergennes,* 244–45).

9 **Courage would be useless:** Corwin, "The French Objective in the American Revolution," 33+; Schama, *Citizens,* 55; Hardman, *The Life of Louis XVI,* 117 (*naval superiority*); Dull, *The French Navy and the Seven Years' War,* 113 (*English jails*), 170 (*cats*), 171 (*fir*).

9 **With Louis's wary support:** Murphy, *Charles Gravier, Comte de Vergennes,* 245 (*nearly tripled*); Lacour-Gayet, *La marine militaire de la France sous le règne de Louis XVI* (*100 million livres*); Martelli, *Jemmy Twitcher,* 108 (*"invasion of England"*); Dull, *The French Navy and American Independence,* 23; Hoffman and Albert, eds., *Diplomacy and Revolution,* 91–93; Willis, *The Struggle for Sea Power,* 208 (*Lavoisier*); Harris, *Industrial Espionage and Technology Transfer,* 250–52 (*Cannon production*); Volo, *Blue Water Patriots,* 66 (*Ten thousand*), 99.

9 **Improvements took root:** Miller, *Sea of Glory,* 326; Volo, *Blue Water Patriots,* 65, 98–99 (*extensive instruction*).

10 **Each month dockyards in Toulon:** Hoffman and Albert, eds., *Diplomacy and Revolution,* 94; Dull, *The Miracle of American Independence,* 78–79, 102–3 (*fifty-nine Spanish ships*); Murphy,

Charles Gravier, Comte de Vergennes, 220 (*"now has forty-two ships"*); Dull, *The French Navy and American Independence*, 83; Miller, *Sea of Glory*, 326 (*"tradition of victory"*).

10 **None of this went unseen:** Meng, ed., *Despatches and Instructions of Conrad Alexandre Gérard, 1778–1780*, 66–70; Wharton, ed., "Attitude of France to the United States," *Revolutionary Diplomatic Correspondence of the United States*, 1:343n; Miller, *Sea of Glory*, 257, 261.

10 **The task of protesting these insults:** Scott, *British Foreign Policy in the Age of the American Revolution*, 294–95; Alsop, *Yankees at the Court*, 80 (*"your conduct"*); Christie, *The End of North's Ministry, 1780–1782*, 6–7; Schiff, *A Great Improvisation*, 86 (*embalmed heart*).

10 **When Stormont complained:** Bemis, *The Diplomacy of the American Revolution*, 53–57; Black and Woodfine, eds., *The British Navy and the Use of Naval Power in the Eighteenth Century*, 174; Dull, *The French Navy and American Independence*, 75–76; Johnston, "American Privateers in French Ports, 1776–1778," 352+ (*disguising them*); Schiff, *A Great Improvisation*, 80 (*"unaccountable enthusiasm"*); Van Tyne, *The War of Independence*, 489; Clark, *Silas Deane*, 93 (*"He will lie"*).

11 **Stormont "has a talent":** Schiff, *A Great Improvisation*, 78–79; Dull, *The French Navy and American Independence*, 72–73 (*French ship of the line*).

11 **"If we are forced to make war":** Hardman, *The Life of Louis XVI*, 123.

11 **The lying, flattering, insincere:** Schiff, *A Great Improvisation*, 89–90 (*white barge*); Ferreiro, *Brothers at Arms*, 94; BF to Emma Thompson, Feb. 8, 1777, FOL (*"strong and hearty"*).

11 **The "fat old fellow":** Morgan, *Benjamin Franklin*, 35; author visit, Franklin Court and Franklin Museum, Philadelphia, Aug. 31–Sept. 3, 2021 (*lead type*); BF to Académie Royale des Sciences, Nov. 16, 1772, FOL; "A History of the Official American Presence in France," U.S. Department of State, n.d. (*Café de la Régence*); Wright, *Franklin of Philadelphia*, 270 (*"old peasant"*).

12 **Paris itself was a tonic:** Schiff, *A Great Improvisation*, 45 (*"prodigious mixture"*); Hussey, *Paris*, 166, 190 (*parasols*); Schama, *Citizens*, 181 (*Minstrels*).

12 **Each morning hundreds of wagons:** Popkin, ed., *Louis-Sébastien Mercier, Panorama of Paris*, 95 (*breasts bared*), 100, 132 (*"Here's your light"*); Lopez, *Mon Cher Papa*, 141 (*mineral water*); Alsop, *Yankees at Court*, 133n (*iron chairs*); Garrioch, *The Making of Revolutionary Paris*, 122 (*manures*), 206 (*witches*).

12 **Franklin was a frequent visitor:** Conway, *Footprints of Famous Americans in Paris*, 13; Alsop, *Yankees at Court*, 13; Echeverria, *Mirage in the West*, 31, 41; Schiff, *A Great Improvisation*, 81 (*Mexican cures*), 82 (*first daily newspaper*), 84–85 (Good Richard), "Poor Richard's Almanack," Benjamin Franklin Historical Society, http://www.benjamin-franklin-history.org/poor-richards-almanac/.

13 **Paris fully reciprocated:** Aldridge, *Franklin and His French Contemporaries*, 13 (*"human virtues"*); Lepore, *Book of Ages*, 83 (*son of a chandler*); Trevelyan, *The American Revolution*, 4:347 (*"America itself"*), 352 (*"People repeated"*).

13 **Demands for his image:** Conway, *Footprints of Famous Americans in Paris*, 10 (*150 engravings*); Schiff, *A Great Improvisation*, 88–89; Bailyn, *To Begin the World Anew*, 73–79, 84–85, 92; BF to Sarah Bache, June 3, 1779, FOL (*"clay medallion of me"*); Echeverria, *Mirage in the West*, 47 (*"Can he who has disarmed"*).

13 **He kept a hornbook:** JA, *Diary and Autobiography*, May 27, 1778, FOL; Lopez, *Mon Cher Papa*, 13 (*asparagus*), 22 (*"If you Frenchmen"*); Miller, *Triumph of Freedom, 1775–1783*, 360 (*"silent"*).

13 **In late February he had moved:** Lopez, *Mon Cher Papa*, 126; Schiff, *A Great Improvisation*, 50–51; Schaeper, *France and America in the Revolutionary Era*, 98–104; "Franklin's Home and Host in France," 741+; Van Doren, *Benjamin Franklin*, 639 (*lightning rod*); Lopez, *My Life with Benjamin Franklin*, 170 (*Strasbourg Cathedral*).

14 **Frugality, Franklin admitted:** Wright, *Franklin of Philadelphia*, 266; BF, agreement about board at Passy, Jan. 28, 1777, FOL; Van Doren, *Benjamin Franklin*, 650 (*coachman*); Schiff, *A Great Improvisation*, 90; Lopez, *Mon Cher Papa*, 131–32 (*a thousand bottles*); BF to Jane Mecom, Oct. 5, 1777, FOL (*"French cookery"*).

14 **In fact his household included:** BF to Jan Ingenhousz, Mar. 6, 1777, FOL (*"greatness of that loss"*).

14 **Life went on:** Lopez, *My Life with Benjamin Franklin*, 170 (*potato cultivation*); Schoenbrun, *Triumph in Paris*, 98, 114; Schiff, *A Great Improvisation*, 63.

14 **Occasionally he clambered into his coach:** Lopez, *My Life with Benjamin Franklin*, 62 (*French police*).

15 **"There hardly ever existed":** BF to David Hartley, Feb. 2, 1780, FOL; Ferling, *John Adams*, 197; Dull, "Franklin the Diplomat," 1+.

15 **In Paris he served:** Rose, "British Penetration of America's First Diplomatic Mission," 57+.

15 **In April the first ships:** Bob Ruppert, "America's First Black Ops," *JAR*, Sept. 5, 2017; Desmarais, *Washington's Engineer*, 211–12 (*sherry*); York, "Clandestine Aid and the American Revolutionary War Effort," 26+.

15 **Many more vessels were on the high seas:** Desmarais, *America's First Ally*, 6–11, 18–19 (*ten thousand uniforms*); BF and American commissioners to Jonathan Williams, Jr., Feb. 20 and 25, 1777; Jonathan Williams to commissioners, Mar. 4, 7, and 25, 1777, and commissioners contract for repair of arms, May 30, 1777, all FOL; Alsop, *Yankees at the Court*, 6, 61 (*tears painted*).

16 **Amsterdam had become:** Allison and Ferreiro, eds., *The American Revolution*, 164 (PRO LIBERTATE); Schoenbrun, *Triumph in Paris*, 86 (*Dutch gunpowder*); Edler, *The Dutch Republic and the American Revolution*, 40 (*rice barrels*); Albion and Pope, *Sea Lanes in Wartime*, 52 (*tobacco, indigo*); Van Alstyne, *Empire and Independence*, 84–85 (*"run the risk"*), 125 (*Spanish bankers*); Ferreiro, *Brothers at Arms*, 69 (*rebuffed Arthur Lee*), 215 (*quinine*); Bemis, *The Diplomacy of the American Revolution*, 90 (*powder from Mexico*).

16 **Versailles had rejected the American request:** Brands, *The First American*, 538 (*a million livres*); BF, American commissioners to Vergennes, Mar. 18, 1777, FOL (*British sugar islands*); Schoenbrun, *Triumph in Paris*, 116.

16 **Franklin shrugged off the rejections:** Clark, *Lambert Wickes*, 127–33 (Polly & Nancy); Miller, *Sea of Glory*, 285; Werther, "Captain Lambert Wickes and 'Gunboat Diplomacy, American Revolution Style,'" *JAR*, Jan. 3, 2019.

16 **Franklin dispatched Wickes again:** Clark, *Lambert Wickes*, 221–24, 233–36 (Burford); BF to Arthur Lee, Mar. 2, 1777, FOL (*brandy from Bristol*).

17 **Such rebel marauding:** Miller, *Sea of Glory*, 294–96 (*trade fair at Chester*); Scott, *British Foreign Policy in the Age of the American Revolution*, 252 (*"half war"*). *Reprisal* sank on October 1 (Daughan, *If By Sea*, 138; "Extract of a Letter from a Gentleman of This Place," *NDAR*, 10: 1009 [*gangway ladder*]).

17 **A gallant captain:** Miller, *Sea of Glory*, 296 (*"sea is overspread"*), 303; Lloyd, *The British Seaman*, 101–2 (*"brethren"*); Clowes, *The Royal Navy*, 4: 4, 100 (*Dublin and Penzance*); Black and Woodfine, eds., *The British Navy and the Use of Naval Power in the Eighteenth Century*, 185 (*Rarely did a day pass*); Allen, *A Naval History of the American Revolution*, 1: 234–36 (*Three brigantines*); Willis, *The Struggle for Sea Power*, 191 (*out of business* and Firth of Clyde).

17 **Franklin also found a worthy successor:** Fowler, *Rebels Under Sail*, 136–41; Neeser, ed., *Letters and Papers Relating to the Cruises of Gustavus Conyngham*, xxiii–xxx (Joseph), xlii (*"swag gering in"*); O'Shaughnessy, *The Men Who Lost America*, 332 (*two dozen Royal Navy warships*); Miller, *Sea of Glory*, 299–300 (*piratical cutthroat*).

18 **Supplicants by the hundreds:** Prelinger, "Benjamin Franklin and the American Prisoners of War in England During the American Revolution," 261+; Kirkland, ed., *Letters on the American Revolution*, 2: 44 (*"proposals of every kind"*); Brands, *Our First Civil War*, 258 (*"Our brandy"*); Clark, *Benjamin Franklin*, 359–60 (*twelve times in a minute*); Schiff, *A Great Improvisation*, 56 (*Trojan horse*); Nolan, "A British Editor Reports the American Revolution," 92+ (*"reflecting mirrors"*).

18 **More than four hundred volunteers:** Wright, *Franklin of Philadelphia*, 283 (*Capuchin monk* and *end of the war*); Ferreiro, *Brothers at Arms*, 141; Schiff, *A Great Improvisation*, 54–55 (*"bad poet"*); BF, American Commissioners to Committee of Secret Correspondence, Mar.

12–Apr. 9, 1777, FOL (*"fatigued with their applications"*); BF to Barbeu-Dubourg, after Oct. 2, 1777, FOL; Werther, "Volunteer Overload: Foreign Support of the American Cause Prior to the French Alliance," *JAR*, Sept. 8, 2020 (*eight-day period*); BF to James Lovell, Dec. 21, 1777, FOL (*"mere Caesars"*); Marquis de Brétigny to GW, Jan. 1, 1779, FOL (*Sevelinges*).

18 **Telling the truth:** Wright, *Franklin of Philadelphia*, 296 (*"only cunning"*); Schoenbrun, *Triumph in Paris*, 106, 110, 112 (*"ordered no prizes"*); Schiff, *A Great Improvisation*, 60 (*untruth*).

18 **In April, when Franklin wrote Lord Stormont:** BF, American Commissioners to Lord Stormont, Apr. 3, 1777 (*"no letters from rebels"*); Alsop, *Yankees at the Court*, 74 (stormonter); Isaacson, *Benjamin Franklin*, 340; Parton, *Life and Times of Benjamin Franklin*, 2: 228 (*"only a Stormont"*).

19 **"There is no little enemy":** BF to Joseph Priestly, Jan. 27, 1777, FOL (*"no cause but malice"*); Van Doren, *Benjamin Franklin*, 580 (*Gibbon*).

19 **Meanwhile he drew strength:** Wood, *The Americanization of Benjamin Franklin*, 190–92 (*"greatest revolution"*); Echeverria, *Mirage in the West*, viii (*"major events"*); American Commissioners to Committee for Foreign Affairs, May 25, 1777, FOL (*"take their own time"*); Wharton, ed., "Attitude of France to the United States," *Revolutionary Diplomatic Correspondence of the United States*, 1:369 (*"prancing"*).

19 **"We shall be stronger the next campaign":** BF to Joseph Priestley, Jan. 27, 1777, FOL; BF, American Commissioners to the Committee of Secret Correspondence, Mar. 12–Apr. 9, 1777, FOL (*"dignity and happiness"*).

19 **"Life is a kind of chess":** BF, "The Morals of Chess," before June 28, 1779, FOL; Lopez, *Mon Cher Papa*, 134–35 (*poor loser*).

20 **Three hundred miles southwest of Passy:** author visit, Musée National des Douanes and Musée des Beaux Arts, Bordeaux, June 2–3, 2022; East, *Business Enterprise in the American Revolutionary Era*; Desmarais, *America's First Ally*, 18–19, 26–27.

20 **On Wednesday, March 19:** LiA, 1: 94–95, 132–33 (*Roman Catholics*); Manceron, *Age of the French Revolution*, 1: 398–99; *LAAR*, 1: 37 (*"on business"*). Cap-Haïtien would later be in Haiti.

20 **A clerk recorded the older man's name:** Charavay, *Le Général La Fayette*, 8–10; Taafe, *Washington's Revolutionary War Generals*, 100 (*teetotaling*); Beakes, *De Kalb*, 26 (*eight-pointed cross*); Kapp, *The Life of John Kalb*, 4–7, 26–27, 37, 46–51, 81; Auricchio, *The Marquis Lafayette Reconsidered*, 33.

20 **His younger companion:** Charavay, *Le Général La Fayette*, 8–10; *LAAR*, 1: 28 (*"You will be astonished"*), 37, LiA, 1. 3 (*"baptized like a Spaniard"*), 91 (*"My zeal"*), 100; Elizabeth S. Kite, "Lafayette and His Companions on the 'Victoire,'" *Records of the American Catholic Historical Society of Philadelphia*, vol. 45, no. 1 (Mar. 1934): 1+; Unger, *Lafayette*, xvii (*among the wealthiest*).

21 **Their business in town concluded:** JA, *Diary and Autobiography*, Mar. 30, 1778, FOL (*farmers plowing, women hoeing*); Allison and Ferreiro, eds., *The American Revolution*, 146–50 (*Clary*); LiA, 1: 88 (*112,000 livres*); Charavay, *Le Général La Fayette*, 8n.

21 **He seemed an unlikely hero:** Auricchio, *The Marquis Lafayette Reconsidered*, xxi–xxii (*five feet, nine inches*), 22 (*"danced without grace"*); Thacher, *Military Journal*, 155–56 (*"nose large and long"*); author visit, Château Lafayette, Chavaniac, France, June 1, 2022 (*"smallness of his head"*); Charavay, *Le Général La Fayette*, 541–48 (*"nitwit," "idea of the century," "righter of wrongs"*); Unger, *Lafayette*, xxi (*"heroic character"*).

22 **He had been born in remote, rugged Auvergne:** author visit, Château Lafayette, Chavaniac, France, June 1, 2022 (*egalitarian bias*); Unger, *Lafayette*, 3–4; LiA, 1: 18 (*prize in Latin*), 22 (*Black Musketeers*); Auricchio, *The Marquis Lafayette Reconsidered*, 14 (*"desire to have a uniform"*).

22 **Misfortune made him a rich orphan:** Allison and Ferreiro, eds., *The American Revolution*, 143 (*three million livres*); LiA, 1: 22 (*120,000 livres*); Duncan, *Hero of Two Worlds*, 12–13 (*a thousand livres*); Auricchio, *The Marquis Lafayette Reconsidered*, 16–17 (*five daughters*); Maurois, *Adrienne*, 8 (*built with two wings*).

22   **Lafayette joined a Freemason lodge:** *LiA*, 1: 39-40 (*Metz*); Auricchio, *The Marquis Lafayette Reconsidered*, 26 (*avenge his father's death*).

22   **With the end of Carnival:** *LiA*, 1: 87-89; *LAAR*, 1: 23 (*"London is a delightful city"*); Memoirs, *Correspondence and Manuscripts of General Lafayette*, 1: 142 (*"desire to debase England"*); Craveri, *The Last Libertines*, 233 (*"to injure England"*).

23   **Then word had arrived from Bordeaux:** *LiA*, 1: 85 (Cur non?), 91.

23   **It was not to be quite so simple:** *LiA*, 1: 109-11, 98-99, 101 (lettre de cachet), 109 (*"harsh-ness"*).

23   **Hoisting himself onto *Victoire*'s main deck:** Unger, *Lafayette* (*"grief I was causing"*); Manceron, *Age of the French Revolution*, 1: 400; Zucker, *General De Kalb*, 110-12 (*"glorious weather"*); Kapp, *The Life of John Kalb*, 104; *LAAR*, 1: 147-48; Tower, *The Marquis de La Fayette in the American Revolution*, 1: 51 (*"avoid a rupture"*).

23   **Instead, on Friday, March 28:** Manceron, *Age of the French Revolution*, 1: 401-2; *LAAR*, 1: 32 (*"given my word"*).

24   **An assiduous contriver of his own myth:** *LiA*, 1: 111, 151-52; Schoenbrun, *Triumph in Paris*, 126 (*forbidden French officers*).

24   **As for the Noailles clan:** Manceron, *Age of the French Revolution*, 1: 395-96 (*"I was pregnant"*), 401-2 (*"I presented him"*); Unger, *Lafayette*, 27 (*"His age may excuse"*); Allison and Ferreiro, eds., *The American Revolution*, 149 (*some of Lafayette's elders*).

24   **On Monday, March 31:** Depeyre, "When *La Victoire* Carried the Hopes of Lafayette," 30+; *LiA*, 1: 113-14; Zucker, *General De Kalb*, 112-13; Kapp, *The Life of John Kalb*, 105; Beakes, *De Kalb*, 92 (*"This is the end"*).

24   **After three days of brooding:** *LiA*, 1: 114-18 (*"a short one indeed"*).

25   **Lafayette had nearly resigned himself:** *LAAR*, 1: 9-10; Duncan, *Hero of Two Worlds*, 44 (*All France wanted*); Zucker, *General De Kalb*, 114.

25   **He went. Boarding a chaise:** *LAAR*, 1: 9-10 (*disguised himself*); *LiA*, 1: 120-21; Unger, *Lafayette*, 28 (*innkeeper's daughter*); Kapp, *The Life of John Kalb*, 108 (*"the marquis has arrived"*).

25   **Lafayette wrote to the American diplomats:** *LiA*, 1: 122 (*"full of joy"*); *LAAR*, 1: 48-49 (*"Having to choose"*).

25   **On Sunday, April 20, *Victoire*:** Zucker, *General De Kalb*, 116 (*"state of enthusiasm"*); *LAAR*, 1: 10 (*blow up the ship*), 56-57 (*"The sea is so dismal"*).

25   **Rumors would arise:** *LiA*, 1: 104-5 (*"How I pity"*), 127-28 (*Providence*); BF, American Commissioners to Committee for Foreign Affairs, May 25, 1777, FOL (*"exceedingly beloved"*).

26   **Shipmates passed around:** Echeverria, *Mirage in the West*, 80-81; Tower, *The Marquis de La Fayette* (*"The happiness of America"*).

26   **Night fell. The darkened boat:** Unger, *Lafayette*, xix (*six hundred towns*).

1. THE MARCH OF ANNIHILATION

29   **A rattle of drums at four a.m.:** Lynn, ed., *An Eyewitness Account*, 57; Hadden, *A Journal Kept in Canada*, 80-81 (*"We are to contend for the king"*); BSC, 46-47, 51 (*eight thousand troops*).

29   **By five a.m., the sun:** Peckham, ed., *Sources of American Independence*, 1: 274-75; Lewis, *The Man Who Lost America*, 151-52; Hadden, *A Journal Kept in Canada*, 80 (*"music and drums"*).

29   **More than a hundred birch-bark canoes:** Hagist, ed., *A British Soldier's Story*, 33-34 (*twenty to thirty warriors*); Eelking and Rosengarten, *The German Allied Troops*, 54 (*vermilion paint*); Pettengill, ed., *Letters from America, 1776-1779*, 52 (*sheaths*); Griffith, *The War for American Independence*, 383 (*"arse clout"*).

30   **Arrayed across the mile-wide lake:** O'Shaughnessy, *The Men Who Lost America*, 148 (*"splendid regatta"*); Hamilton, *Fort Ticonderoga*, 191 (Royal George); James, *The British Navy in Adversity*, 57; Bellico, *Sails and Steam in the Mountains*, 140-41; Gadue, "The *Thunderer*, British Floating Gun-Battery on Lake Champlain," *JAR*, Apr. 4, 2019; Lender, *Fort Ticonderoga, the Last Campaign*, 82 (*133 naval guns*); *CtS*, 24 (*130 field cannons*); Peterson, *The Book of the Continental Soldiers*, 120 (*monogram*); Luzader, *Saratoga*, 45; Hadden, *A Journal Kept in Canada*, 80-84; O'Shaughnessy, *The Men Who Lost America*, 146 (*approached two thousand*).

30   **"It looked":** Hagist, ed., *A British Soldier's Story*, 34; Theobald, "Journal of the Hessen-Hanau

Erbprinz Infantry Regiment," 40+ (*"biting insect"*); Lewis, *The Man Who Lost America*, 140–41 (*cedar sap*).

30 **On the left, to the east:** Baer, *Hessians*, 1–2; Doblin and Lynn, "A Brunswick Grenadier with Burgoyne," 420+ (*ruling family*); Pettengill, ed., *Letters from America, 1776–1779*, 40–42 (*beaver tail*), 64. Since 1775, Karl Wilhelm Ferdinand had shared power with his father, Duke Karl I.

32 *Jäger* **scouts—professional hunters:** Kipping, *The Hessian View of America, 1776–1783*, 20 (*green coats*); Uhlendorf, trans. and annot., *Revolution in America*, 17–19; Arndt, "New Hampshire and the Battle of Bennington," 198+ (*"Chinese mandarin"*); Eelking and Rosengarten, *The German Allied Troops*, 27 (*American horses*); CtS, 114 (*waxed mustaches*), 123, 187, 198 (*spontoons*); Lynn, ed., *An Eyewitness Account*, 57 (*"large blisters"*).

32 **The Germans were led by:** Stone, ed., *Memoirs, and Letters and Journals of Major General Riedesel*, 1–6 (*conversational English*), 93 (*"will finish the war"*); Brown, *Baroness von Riedesel and the American Revolution*, xxvii (*"sent by Providence"*); Popp and Rosengarten, "Popp's Journal, 1777–1783," 25+ (*sworn allegiance*); Stone, *Journal of Captain Pausch*, 107 (*supercilious*); Snow, *1777*, 23 (*"Red Hazel"*).

32 **Those redcoats could now be seen:** CtS, 21 (*47th Regiment of Foot*), 162 (*felt caps*), 259; Hagist, *Noble Volunteers*, 143 (*two blankets*); John Downham, "The 47th (Lancashire) Regiment of Foot," https://www.lancashireinfantrymuseum.org.uk/47th-regiment; O'Shaughnessy, *The Men Who Lost America*, 145 (*thirty of whom*); Hadden, *A Journal Kept in Canada*, lvi (*full generals*).

32 **Squinting at both shorelines:** Lunt, *John Burgoyne of Saratoga*, 8–9 (*taught in Latin*), 13–14; Lewis, *The Man Who Lost America*, 6–16 (*on the Seine*).

33 **At last all was forgiven:** Mintz, *The Generals of Saratoga*, 11 (*diamond ring*); Lunt, *John Burgoyne of Saratoga*, 17–30, 40–41; Lewis, *The Man Who Lost America*, 28 (*war hero*).

33 **Burgoyne's ascent continued:** Lewis, *The Man Who Lost America*, 36–40, 47 (*East India Company*); Hargrove, *General John Burgoyne*, 44; Lunt, *John Burgoyne of Saratoga*, 60–61 (*Drury Lane*).

33 **As a military thinker:** Lunt, *John Burgoyne of Saratoga*, 107 (*"soldier's friend"*); O'Shaughnessy, *The Men Who Lost America*, 126–28 (*Irish Catholics*); Glover, *General Burgoyne in Canada and America*, 52 (*"thinking beings"*); Fuller, *British Light Infantry in the Eighteenth Century*, 112 (*"Never beat your men"*); Lunt, *John Burgoyne of Saratoga*, 32 (*"insight into the character"*).

33 **War with America brought new chances:** Lunt, *John Burgoyne of Saratoga*, 66 (*"too much indulgence"*); Billias, ed., *The Manuscripts of Captain Howard Vincente Knox*, 132–33; Germain to Carleton, Mar. 26, 1777, UK NA, CO 42/36, f 101 (*too passive*).

34 **Burgoyne had reappeared on the St. Lawrence:** Billias, ed., *The Manuscripts of Captain Howard Vincente Knox*, 132–33; Guy Carleton to George Germain, May 20, 1777, UK NA, CO 42/36, f 94 (*"every assistance"*); Reynolds, *Guy Carleton*, 116 (*"command it myself"*).

34 **"The king relies upon your zeal":** Germain to Carleton, Mar. 26, 1777, UK NA, CO 42/36, f 101; BSC, 150–52 (*"hourly before my eyes"*).

34 **"Thoughts" was bold, complex:** BSC, 32–36, 39, 42; Thomas, *Memoirs of the Marquis of Rockingham*, 330–31 (*studying his maps*); Clark, "Responsibility for the Failure of the Burgoyne Campaign," 542+ (*dismember the thirteen rebellious colonies*).

34 **Upon reaching Albany:** Germain to Carleton, Mar. 26, 1777, UK NA, CO 42/36, f 101; BSC, 191 (*"speedy junction"*); Brown, *The American Secretary*, 107–8 (*explicitly informed London*).

35 **With remarkable nonchalance:** Hargrove, *General John Burgoyne*, 121 (*"exceedingly satisfied"*).

35 **He had complaints, of course:** O'Shaughnessy, *The Men Who Lost America*, 145 (*eleven-thousand-man force*); Baer, *Hessians*, 144 (*only four hundred*); Burgoyne inquiry, *Parliamentary Register*, 12: 130–31 (*just 150*); Cruikshank et al., eds., *A History of the Organization, Development. . .*, 2: 40 (*"awkward, ignorant"*); Lanctôt, *Canada & the American Revolution, 1774–1783*, 164–66 (*monastery*); CtS, 27 (*"imbibed too much"*).

35 **He had ample artillery:** Lunt, *John Burgoyne of Saratoga*, 136 (*suspected a leak*), 140 (*124 rounds*); BSC, 89 (*eighteen tons*), 90 (*fourteen tons of forage*); Hamilton, *Fort Ticonderoga*, 203 (*eight hundred pounds*); Bowler, *Logistics and the Failure of the British Army in America*,

1775–1783, 227 (*1,125 carts*); Ferling, *Almost a Miracle*, 212 (*half would be completed*); Elting, *The Battles of Saratoga*, 22 (*green wood*); De Fonblanque, *Political and Military Episodes*, 242 (*"whole design"*).

36 **For all that, over the past two weeks:** O'Shaughnessy, *The Men Who Lost America*, 148; Baxter, *The British Invasion from the North*, 201 (*"With our glasses"*).

36 **Scouts had given Burgoyne sketches:** "Gen. Fraser's Account of Burgoyne's Campaign," 139+; Strach, "A Memoir of the Exploits of Captain Alexander Fraser," 164+; Burgoyne to W. Howe, July 2, 1777, GSG, vol. 6 (*"The army is in the fullest"*).

36 **No man standing on Ticonderoga's parapets:** Ketchum, *Saratoga*, 161 (*"scene thickens"*).

36 **For more than two decades a fortress:** author visit, Fort Ticonderoga, Sept. 28, 2021; Lender, *Fort Ticonderoga, the Last Campaign*, 62.

37 **Over the past two years the Americans:** Barbieri, "In Defense of Mount Independence"; "Mount Independence Research," https://historicsites.vermont.gov/mount-independence/research; Lender, *Fort Ticonderoga, the Last Campaign*, 62–63 (*"Great Bridge"*); Harte, *The River Obstructions of the Revolutionary War*, 31–32 (*double chain of iron links*); Furcron, "Mount Independence," 230+ (*"honor to the human mind"*).

37 **To command the "Gibraltar of the North":** Smith, ed., *The Life and Public Services of Arthur St. Clair*, 4–9 (*£14,000 dowry*); Ketchum, *Saratoga*, 115–16 (*quotations from Horace*).

37 **Ticonderoga horrified him:** Elting, *The Battles of Saratoga*, 12 (*powder magazines*); Hamilton, *Fort Ticonderoga*, 182 (*fourteen-gun schooner*); Gerlach, *Proud Patriot*, 235–36; Wilkinson, *Memoirs of My Own Times*, 166–77; Ketchum, *Saratoga*, 161 (*"so infested"*).

37 **Far worse was the shortage of men:** Cubbison, *"The Artillery Never Gained More Honour,"* 76; P. Schuyler to GW, Jan. 30, 1777, *PGW*, 8: 193 (*at least ten thousand*); Lender, *Fort Ticonderoga, the Last Campaign*, 27; P. Schuyler to GW, July 5, 1777, 10: 200n (*two thousand enlisted men*).

38 **Except for a few natty officers:** *CtS*, 37, 40 (*"none of the troops"*); Bush, *Revolutionary Enigma*, 110 (*bayonets*); Van Tyne, *The War of Independence*, 388 (*old books*); "The Trial of Major General St. Clair," 51–52 (*"languid"*), 59 (*almost to the lake*); St. Clair, *A Narrative*, 244 (*"scarcely within the reach"*); Morgan, "Arthur St. Clair's Decision to Abandon Fort Ticonderoga and Mount Independence," *JAR*, May 16, 2016 (*Some officers*).

38 **"I am in a situation":** Ryan, ed., *A Salute to Courage*, 80–81; St. Clair, *A Narrative*, 149 (*son*); "The Trial of Major General St. Clair," 22 (*"No army was ever"*).

38 **Now the wolf was at the door:** GW to Philip Schuyler, Mar. 12 and June 16, 1777, FOL; Gerlach, *Proud Patriot*, 212–17 (*Eight New England regiments*).

38 **On July 4:** Arthur St. Clair to GW, July 17, 1777, *PGW*, 10: 309 (*"mere boys"*); Ketchum, *Saratoga*, 169 (*"total defeat"*).

39 **"You may be sure":** Ebenezer Francis to Judith, July 3, 1777, T-P RC.

39 **An American bombardment of both wings:** Lynn, ed., *The Specht Journal*, 52; *BSC*, 265; Lender, *Fort Ticonderoga, the Last Campaign*, 90 (*blockhouses*); "A Journal of Carleton's and Burgoyne's Campaigns," part 2, 307+ (*Iroquois charge*); "Gen. Fraser's Account of Burgoyne's Campaign," 139+ (*"so much in liquor"*); "Diary of the Brunswick Troops in North America," HDAR, fiche 231–33, letter HZ-5; Kingsley et al., "German Auxiliaries Project," 28+ (*"Our people trip"*).

39 **A careful inspection with his spyglass:** De Fonblanque, *Political and Military Episodes*, 247 (*"military science"*); Davis, *Where a Man Can Go*, 2, 4, 16–17 (*appearance and temperament*); Ketchum, *Saratoga*, 135 (*fifteen canes*); Gadue, "The *Thunderer*, British Floating Gun-Battery on Lake Champlain," *JAR*, Apr. 4, 2019; Lynn, ed., *The Specht Journal*, 52 (*too unwieldy*).

39 **By the small hours of Saturday, July 5:** Sugar Loaf was later renamed Mount Defiance ("Gen. Fraser's Account of Burgoyne's Campaign," 139+); "A Turnbull Map of Fort Ticonderoga Rediscovered," *BFTM*, 129+ (*"Inaccessible Hill"*); Lender, *Fort Ticonderoga, the Last Campaign*, 56–57 (*too much hill*).

39 **At two p.m. a young British engineer:** author visit, Fort Ticonderoga, Sept. 28, 2021; Barbieri, "Guns on Mount Defiance," *JAR*, Sept. 26, 2021; Pownall and Almon, *The Remembrancer*, 350 (*"numbers counted"*); Hadden, *A Journal Kept in Canada*, 84 (*Four hundred*

axmen); Cubbison, *"The Artillery Never Gained More Honour,"* 78–79 (*"perpendicular ascent"*); Wright, "Some Notes on the Continental Army," 81+ (*ton and a half*); Thacher, *Military Journal*, 82 (*"decide our fate"*).

40 **In the event, that fate:** Johnson, "The Administration of the American Commissariat During the Revolutionary War," University of Pennsylvania, diss., 1941, 130 (*two-month provision*); Morgan, "Arthur St. Clair's Decision to Abandon Fort Ticonderoga and Mount Independence," *JAR*, May 16, 2016 (*appearance of redcoats*); "The Trial of Major General St. Clair," 53–55 (*"If he remained there"*).

40 **Quickly and unanimously:** council of war proceedings, Philip Schuyler to GW, July 14, 1777, FOL; Wickman, ed., " 'Breakfast on Chocolate': The Diary of Moses Greenleaf, 1777," 483+ (*four days' provisions*); Time and Date, https://www.timeanddate.com (*twilight faded*); BSC, 62–63; St. Clair, *A Narrative*, 91 (*payroll*); Ketchum, *Saratoga*, 181 (*"prudence, fortitude"*). Not yet a state, Vermont was commonly known at the time as the New Hampshire Grants.

40 **None of that obtained here:** Ketchum, *Saratoga* (*"greatest disorder"*); Kidder, *History of the First New Hampshire Regiment*, 28 (*"clothing chests"*); "The Trial of Major General St. Clair," 65–66 (*mob swept past*); Williams, *The Battle of Hubbardton*, 7 (*"Such a retreat"*).

41 **Fires broke out:** Baxter, ed., *The British Invasion from the North*, 206; Stanley, ed., *For Want of a Horse*, 116–17 (*"uncommon smoke"*); "Gen. Fraser's Account of Burgoyne's Campaign," 139+ (*Deserters at first light*); BSC, 269; Hargrove, *General John Burgoyne*, 14 (*"time to drink"*).

41 **By midmorning on Sunday, July 6:** "Gen. Fraser's Account of Burgoyne's Campaign," 139+; BSC, 267; Venter, *The Battle of Hubbardton*, 36–37 (*bakery and brewery*); Lynn, ed., *The Specht Journal*, 53–56 (*gold and silver thread*); "Diary of the Brunswick Troops in North America," HDAR, fiche 234, letter HZ-5 (*"privates in our army"*); "Journal of an Officer of the 47th Regiment of Foot," HL, mssHM 66, 51–55 (*£150,000*); "A Journal of Carleton's and Burgoyne's Campaigns," part 2, 307+ (*1,768 barrels*); Pownall and Almon, *The Remembrancer*, 355 (*salt*).

41 **A few shots from British gunboats:** BSC, 269–70 (*"great dexterity"*); Venter, *The Battle of Hubbardton*, 38–39 (*within half an hour*).

41 **Below Ticonderoga the water passage:** Ketchum, *Saratoga*, 222–23 (*Drowned Lands*); Palmer, *History of Lake Champlain*, 3 (*seventy-three families*); Cubbison, *The American Northern Theater Army in 1776*, 201–4 (*mosquito fleet*); Bird, *March to Saratoga*, 48–49.

42 **No sooner had the fugitives dropped anchor:** Thacher, *Military Journal*, 83–84 (*"Burgoyne himself"*).

42 **The schooner *Liberty*:** Cubbison, *"The Artillery Never Gained More Honour,"* 83; Venter, *The Battle of Hubbardton*, 39 (Enterprise); St. Clair, *A Narrative*, 94 (*fifteen tons*).

42 **Burgoyne's men took thirty prisoners:** BSC, 271; Weeden, "Diary of Enos Hitchcock, D.D., a Chaplain in the Revolutionary Army," 87+ (*walked all night*).

42 **In Skenesborough the fires:** Houlding and Yates, "Corporal Fox's Memoir of Service," 146+ (*grappling hooks*); Lynn, ed., *The Specht Journal*, 54 (*"country fair"*); John Pell, "Philip Skene of Skenesborough," *Quarterly Journal of the New York State Historical Association*, vol. 9, no. 1 (Jan. 1928): 27+; BSC, 203 (*"messengers of justice"*), 265 (*"king's service"*); Andrlik, *Reporting the Revolutionary War*, 216; Hargrove, *General John Burgoyne*, 142 (*Burgonius*).

42 **After a night's rest:** BSC, 272–73; Lynn, ed., *The Specht Journal*, 54; Kingsley, ed., "Letters to Lord Polwarth from Sir Francis-Carr Clerke," 393+ (*"British bayonet"*).

43 **General St. Clair and most of his disorderly:** author visit, signage, Hubbardton, Sept. 26, 2021; Duling, "Thomas Anburey at the Battle of Hubbardton," 1+; Williams, *The Battle of Hubbardton*, 9 (*some of his best Continental troops*). Massachusetts regiments were not officially designated by numbers until later in the war.

43 **The rearguard leader:** Luzader, *Saratoga*, 66 (*half-moon formation*); author visit, signage, Hubbardton, Sept. 26, 2021.

43 **The distant crackle of musketry:** Williams, *The Battle of Hubbardton*, 15 (*Sucker Brook*); Venter, *The Battle of Hubbardton*, 63 (*shavings of chocolate*); BSC, 271–72; "Gen. Fraser's Account of Burgoyne's Campaign," 139+ (*850 British soldiers* and *"most disaffected part"*); Corbett, *No Turning Point*, 115–16 (*Fraser*).

43 **The dim early light brightened:** Stephenson, *Patriot Battles*, 125–28 (*misfires*); author visit, signage, Hubbardton, Sept. 26, 2021 (*"Every man"*).

44 **Major Robert Grant of the 24th Foot:** author visit, signage, Hubbardton, Sept. 26, 2021 (*"showers of balls"*); Venter, *The Battle of Hubbardton*, 69 (*both eyes*), 91 (*"such a fire"*); Baxter, ed., *The British Invasion from the North*, 210; BSC, 69–70; "Diary of Joshua Pell, Junior, an Officer of the British Army in America, 1776–1777," 107+ (*under thirty yards*); Peckham, ed., *Sources of American Independence*, 1: 279; "Gen. Fraser's Account of Burgoyne's Campaign," 139+ (*at least two thousand*).

44 **The faint, familiar roar of battle:** Peckham, ed., *Sources of American Independence*, 1: 279; Riedesel to Erbprinz, July 10, 1777, "Hubbardton Battlefield," https://historicsites.vermont .gov/hubbardton-battlefield/research (*assumed that no British attack*); "Diary of the Bruns-wick Troops in North America," HDAR, fiche 235–37, letter HZ-5; Stone, ed., *Memoirs, and Letters and Journals of Major General Riedesel*, 116.

44 **The day turned:** BSC, 69–70 (*"Smoke was so thick"*); Wickman, ed., "'Breakfast on Chocolate': The Diary of Moses Greenleaf, 1777," 483+ (*"fatal wound"*); John Francis to GW, Mar. 15, 1780, FOL (*five children*).

46 **Alone or in small bands:** Venter, *The Battle of Hubbardton*, 103–4 (*"scatter and meet me"*); Wickman, ed., "'Breakfast on Chocolate': The Diary of Moses Greenleaf, 1777," 483+ (*"no blankets"*).

46 **The morning had proved dire:** CtS, 55–60. Battle accounts rarely agree on casualty figures. Another tally puts the Crown dead at 60 (Venter, *The Battle of Hubbardton*, 112–23 [*"born to be shot"*]). Kingsley, ed., "Letters to Lord Polwarth from Sir Francis-Carr Clerke," 393+; Bax-ter, ed., *The British Invasion from the North*, 246 (*Wolves*); "Hubbardton Battlefield," https:// historicsites.vermont.gov/hubbardton-battlefield/research (*bones littered*).

46 **The redcoats had "discovered that neither":** Duling, "Thomas Anburey at the Battle of Hub-bardton," 1+; Venter, *The Battle of Hubbardton*, 109 (*American prisoners*); Baxter, ed., *The British Invasion from the North*, 213 (*"very bad situation"*); "Diary of the Brunswick Troops in North America," HDAR, fiche 231–33, letter HZ-5 (*pelting rain*); Jones, *Plain Concise Practi-cal Remarks on the Treatment of Wounds and Fractures*, 26–28 (*two forefingers*); author visit, signage, Fort Ticonderoga, Aug. 18, 2015 (*pail of water*).

46 **"It happened in the most unfortunate place":** "Hubbardton Battlefield," https://historicsites .vermont.gov/hubbardton-battlefield/research; Kopperman, "The Numbers Game," 254+ (*"Capuchin friar"*); William Howe inquiry, *Parliamentary Register*, 12: 234 (*handbarrows*); At-kinson, "Some Evidence for Burgoyne's Expedition," 132 (*"removed on horseback"*).

47 **"Riedesel rages with anger":** "Hubbardton Battlefield," https://historicsites.vermont.gov/ hubbardton-battlefield/research.

47 **Fugitives from Ticonderoga:** Weeden, "Diary of Enos Hitchcock, D.D., a Chaplain in the Revolutionary Army," 87+ (*"Be not ye afraid"*).

47 **Such divine fortitude:** author visit, signage, Fort Edward, Sept. 26, 2021; "The History of Fort Edward," https://fortedward.net/about/history/ (*mills for lumber, grain*); P. Schuyler to GW, July 26–27, 1777, FOL (*crumbling palisade*).

47 **St. Clair arrived on July 12:** Smith, ed., *The Life and Public Services of Arthur St. Clair*, 425–26 (*"very happy"*); JA to Abigail Adams, Aug. 19, 1777, FOL (*"shoot a general"*); Arthur St. Clair to Congress, July 14, 1777, *Pennsylvania Packet*, July 22, 1777, 2 (*"saved a state"*); Philbrick, *Valiant Ambition*, 124–25 (*"load of obloquy"*).

48 **St. Clair's immediate superior:** Gerlach, *Proud Patriot*, 220–22, 228; Tuckerman, *Life of Gen-eral Philip Schuyler*, 133–36 (*embezzler*); Lossing, *Life and Times of Philip Schuyler*, 2: 219.

48 **"The spirit of malevolence":** P. Schuyler to GW, July 28, 1777, FOL; Elting, *The Battles of Saratoga*, 19 (*"crusty"*); Halsey, "General Schuyler's Part in the Burgoyne Campaign," 109+ (*ensnared in the violent dispute*); CtS, 35 (*New Hampshire Grants*); Commager and Morris, *The Spirit of 'Seventy-Six*, 569 (*"My crime"*).

48 **Wobbling between despair and defiance:** Gerlach, *Proud Patriot*, 260 (*felling axes*); Lossing, *Life and Times of Philip Schuyler*, 2: 242–65; Stone, *The Campaign of Lieut. Gen. John Bur-*

goyne, 29 (*jackstraws*); De Costa, *Notes on the History of Fort George*, 38 ("*nothing but a wilderness*"); P. Schuyler to GW, July 17, 1777, *PGW*, 10: 312 (*arrested loyalists*).

48 **A brigade of Continental reinforcements:** P. Schuyler to GW, July 14, 1777, *PGW*, 10: 280 ("*Several of these are Negroes*"); Gerlach, *Proud Patriot*, 263 (*country estate in Saratoga*); P. Schuyler to GW, July 18, 1777, *PGW*, 10: 325; HG to GW, Oct. 5, 1777, *PGW*, 11: 393n; Bush, *Revolutionary Enigma*, 123 (*hid their furniture*).

49 **Schuyler was gratified to hear:** P. Schuyler to GW, July 10, 21, 22, 1777, FOL; Lossing, *Life and Times of Philip Schuyler*, 2: 242 ("*gloomy aspect*").

49 **"If we act vigorously":** Gerlach, *Proud Patriot*, 269 ("*Greater misfortunes*").

49 **On Burgoyne's orders:** Lynn, ed., *The Specht Journal*, 56 ("*fortunate progress*"); CtS, 64–67 (*attacked near Fort Anne*); Hagist, *A British Soldier's Story*, 40 ("*a mighty torrent*"); Doblin, trans. and ed., "Journal of Lt. Colonel Christian Julius Prätorius," 67 ("*like the palm tree*"); Baxter, ed., *The British Invasion from the North*, 228 (*rattlesnakes*); Pettengill, ed., *Letters from America, 1776–1779*, 78 (*snake soup*), 186 (*kill with a glance*); Lynn, ed., *An Eyewitness Account*, 62 ("*color of the snake*").

49 **Pacing the fine parlor:** Luzader, *Saratoga*, 72–73, 76–78; BSC, 34–35; CtS, 74.

50 **Burgoyne chose both approaches:** Luzader, *Saratoga*, 83 (*forty-three field guns*); De Fonblanque, *Political and Military Episodes*, 267 ("*retrograde movement*"); BSC, 276 ("*more commodious*"). Another account puts the artillery train at 52 guns (Mackesy, *The War for America, 1775–1783*, 133).

50 **Advancing roughly a mile a day:** Pula, *Thaddeus Kościuszko*, 71 ("*meanest, worst*"), 72 ("*leitmotif*"), 73 ("*standing corn*"); *Gentleman's Magazine and Historical Chronicle, 1777*, vol. 47, 474 ("*thick as the lamps*"); BSC, 275 (*forty bridges*).

50 **American prisoners toiled:** Cubbison, *"The Artillery Never Gained More Honour,"* 94; Hadden, *A Journal Kept in Canada*, 102–5; Lanctôt, *Canada & the American Revolution, 1774–1783*, 165–66 (*already deserted*); CtS, 158, 314n (*general's baggage*); Mackesy, *The War for America, 1775–1783*, 113 (*a third of the horses*).

50 **In an eight-page letter:** Burgoyne to Germain, July 11, 1777, UK NA, CO 42/36 f 719.

50 **Burgoyne had also described for Germain:** Ibid.; BSC, 199–200; Lunt, *John Burgoyne of Saratoga*, 150 (*windy harangue*); Baer, *Hessians*, 148; CtS, 81 (*canoe flotilla*); Lynn, ed., *An Eyewitness Account*, 63 (*large chair*).

51 **"It may be permissible":** Lynn, ed., *An Eyewitness Account*, 64 (*barrel of rum*); Andrlik, *Reporting the Revolutionary War*, 222 (*medallions*).

51 **The killing began promptly:** Alexander, ed., "Diary of Captain Benjamin Warren on Battlefield of Saratoga," 201+ ("*eight killed*"); Reid, *Reminiscences of the Revolution*, 18–20 (*two graves*); CtS, 86; Honeyman, "The Indian Massacre of Jane McCrea in 1777," 250+; Holden, "Influence of Death of Jane McCrea on Burgoyne Campaign," 249; CtS, 81–86 (*chopped off* and *chintz gown*).

51 **If obscure in life:** Edgerton, "The Murder of Jane McCrea," 481+; Honeyman, "The Indian Massacre of Jane McCrea in 1777," 250+ (*Presbyterian divine*); Starbuck, "The Mystery of the Second Body," 1+; Griswold and Linebaugh, eds., *The Saratoga Campaign*, 131 (*petite*); CtS, 300n (*wedding dress*).

51 **The murder outraged Burgoyne:** Atkinson, "Some Evidence for Burgoyne's Expedition," 132+ ("*barbarities*"); Bradford, ed., "Lord Francis Napier's Journal of the Burgoyne Campaign," 285+ (*summoned several chiefs*); CtS, 86 (*put to death*); De Fonblanque, *Political and Military Episodes*, 258 ("*retire in a body*"); Luzader, *Saratoga*, 91 ("*total defection*").

52 **Burgoyne had intended:** Moore, *Diary of the American Revolution*, 1: 475–76 (*newspaper accounts*); Edgerton, "The Murder of Jane McCrea," 481+; Holden, "Influence of Death of Jane McCrea on Burgoyne Campaign," 249; Calloway, *The American Revolution in Indian Country*, 295 (*rage at the Indians*); Van Tyne, *The War of Independence*, 403–4 ("*counting the scalps*").

52 **As for Jenny McCrea, although buried:** Edgerton, "The Murder of Jane McCrea," 481+; "Jane McCrea," *BFTM*, 209+ ("*O cruel Britons!*").

52 **By late July, American troops had forsaken:** Alexander, ed., "Diary of Captain Benjamin

Warren on Battlefield of Saratoga," 201+ (*"dirty, hungry"*); BA to GW, July 27, 1777, *PGW*, 10: 434 (*"daily insulted"*); CtS, 71 (*"won I have on"* [McClure's spelling]).

52 On July 30, Burgoyne's advanced corps: "Journal of an Officer of the 47th Regiment of Foot," HL, mssHM 66, 78 (*on the heights*); Baxter, ed., *The British Invasion from the North*, 240 (*"tents were pitched"*); "A Journal of Carleton's and Burgoyne's Campaigns," part 2, 307+; Lynn, ed., *The Specht Journal*, 62 (*Raspberries*).

52 Departing rebels had smashed: Lynn, ed., *The Specht Journal*, 62; receipt, "Revolutionary War, British and Hessian Army, box 1," NYHS (*"one cow"*).

53 Burgoyne moved into a snug two-story house: Half a century later, memoirist Solomon Northup wrote *Twelve Years a Slave* in this house (author visit, signage, Fort Edward, Sept. 26, 2021). Lunt, *John Burgoyne of Saratoga*, 202; Lynn, ed., *An Eyewitness Account*, 66; Bradford, ed., "Lord Francis Napier's Journal of the Burgoyne Campaign," 285+ (*seven prisoners and four scalps*); Lynn, ed., *The Specht Journal*, 66 (*shoot absconders*).

53 "Our general is really a fine": "Gen. Fraser's Account of Burgoyne's Campaign," 139+ (*"lines of resistance"*); O'Shaughnessy, *The Men Who Lost America*, 150 (*another twenty hours*); CtS, 114; ES to author, Sept. 30, 2021 (*nearly a month*); BSC, 91 (*sixty-five carts*).

53 And then what?: Burgoyne to Germain, July 30, 1777, UK NA, CO 42/36, f 771 (*"total ignorance"* and *"act of desperation"*); Stone, ed., *Memoirs, and Letters and Journals of Major General Riedesel*, 136 (*told no one*); O'Shaughnessy, *The Men Who Lost America*, 152–53; Clinton, *The American Rebellion*, 70 (*expected to reach Albany*).

53 Except for two regiments: ES to author, July 2024; Stone, ed., *Memoirs, and Letters and Journals of Major General Riedesel*, 125 (*"march of annihilation"*).

54 A boy fleeing south with his father: Becker and Bloodgood, *The Sexagenary*, 73 (*"everyone for himself"*).

54 Some Americans wondered: Smith, ed., *Letters of Delegates to Congress, 1774–1789*, 7: 301; Weeden, "Diary of Enos Hitchcock, D.D., a Chaplain in the Revolutionary Army," 87+ (*cut her own throat*).

54 "The cursed war whoop": Upham, *Memoir of General John Glover of Marblehead*, 26 (*"strikes a panic"*); Ketchum, *Saratoga*, 279 (*"tired of marching"*).

54 On August 3, as the army's rear guard prepared: Kirkland, ed., *Letters on the American Revolution*, 2: 36 (*"Destruction & havoc"*); Gerlach, *Proud Patriot*, 289 (*"God only knows"*).

2. THIS CURSED, CUT-UP LAND

55 Two hundred miles downriver: Barck, *New York City During the War for Independence*, 76–78 (*above twelve thousand*).

55 Loyalists—called Tories: Stiles, *A History of the City of Brooklyn*, 1: 300 (*scarlet rags*); Davidson, *Propaganda and the American Revolution, 1763–1783*, 312 (Duty of Honoring); Chopra, *Unnatural Rebellion*, 78 (*Engravers, clockmakers*); Burrows and Wallace, *Gotham*, 183, 247; Barck, *New York City During the War for Independence*, 190 (*"Flying machines"*).

55 Hundreds of ships filled: Burrows and Wallace, *Gotham*, 124 (*fearnought jackets*); Carp, *Rebels Rising*, 64 (*every thirteen adult males*); Folsom, "The Battle of Hubbardton," 3+ (*"three bottle men"*); Barck, *New York City During the War for Independence*, 123 (*ivory combs*), 136–37 (*yellow flannels*); Stokes, *The Iconography of Manhattan Island, 1498–1909*, 5: 1059 (*"very elegant pictures"*); Hatch, *Major John André*, 127 (*"superfine broadcloths"*); CtS, 7 (Pocket Atlas).

56 British regulars had been posted here: Klein, "Why Did the British Fail to Win the Hearts and Minds of New Yorkers?," 357+; Rose, *Washington's Spies*, 144–45 (*redcoats drilled*); Jaffe, *New York at War*, 101 (*Rebels controlled*); "Journal of the Hon. Garrison-Regiment von Huyn," Lidgerwood Hessian Transcriptions, MNHP, 54 (*king's troops skittish*); Stiles, *A History of the City of Brooklyn*, 1: 304 (*whaleboats*); Münchhausen, *At General Howe's Side*, 13 (*fifty dragoons*); Anderson, *The Command of the Howe Brothers During the American Revolution*, 236 (*"All traveling"*).

56 Yet within the city a "Rule, Britannia": Tatum, ed., *The American Journal of Ambrose Serle*,

228; Münchhausen, *At General Howe's Side*, 13 (*four hundred vessels*), 24 (*Boats raced*); "Journal of the Hon. Garrison-Regiment von Huyn," Lidgerwood Hessian Transcriptions, MNHP, 67 (*celebratory musket fire*); Stokes, *The Iconography of Manhattan Island, 1498–1909*, 5: 1051 (*every house was illuminated*); Hagist, *Noble Volunteers*, 149 ("*knock-chops*"); Burrows and Wallace, *Gotham*, 247 (*cricket*); Barck, *New York City During the War for Independence*, 182–83 (*Ascot Heath*); Onderdonk, *Documents and Letters*, 142 ("*moderate war*").

56 **Martial law still prevailed:** Barck, *New York City During the War for Independence*, 54 (*no taxes*), 138 (*painted in red*); Onderdonk, *Revolutionary Incidents of Suffolk and Kings Counties*, 7–8 (*civil courts*); Klein, "Why Did the British Fail to Win the Hearts and Minds of New Yorkers?," 357+ (*no elections*); Valentine, *Manual of the Corporation of the City of New York*, 634 (*Any pub*), 648 ("*military execution*").

58 **No rules were enforced more rigorously:** Valentine, *Manual of the Corporation of the City of New York*, 635, 662 (*chimney inspections*); TBAC, 399; Burrows and Wallace, *Gotham*, 242 (*five hundred houses*); TBAC, 399; Schaukirk, "Occupation of New York City by the British," 418+ (*arsonists* and *Dutch churches*); Barck, *New York City During the War for Independence*, 84–86 (*400 percent*); Gruber, *The Howe Brothers and the American Revolution*, 191 (*seven or more*); Jones, *History of New York During the Revolutionary War*, 336; Gill and Curtis, eds., *A Man Apart*, 165 (*unburied rebels*).

58 **For many civilians, finding a decent place:** Gill and Curtis, eds., *A Man Apart*, 158 ("*dirty pot-house*"); Barck, *New York City During the War for Independence*, 80–82 (*Canvas Town*); Rose, *Washington's Spies*, 144–45 ("*Fireships*"); Lamb and Harrison, *History of the City of New York*, 2: 207 ("*highwaymen*").

58 **New York was also a haven:** Gruber, *The Howe Brothers and the American Revolution*, 197 (*£3 for defecting*); Loftus Cliffe to unknown, Mar. 5, 1777, Loftus Cliffe papers, WLC, box 1 ("*town swarms*"); Balderston and Syrett, eds., *The Lost War*, 122 ("*save our people*"), 140 (*twenty-five shillings*).

58 **Deserters and loyalists alike:** Onderdonk, *Documents and Letters*, 143 ("*100 acres of land*"); Klein, "Why Did the British Fail to Win the Hearts and Minds of New Yorkers?," 357+; Morison and Commager, *The Growth of the American Republic*, 199–200 (*more fighting men for loyalist units*); East and Judd, eds., *The Loyalist Americans*, 79 (*twenty-three thousand*).

59 **Two other groups crowded the city:** Chopra, *Unnatural Rebellion*, 144 (*16 percent*); Frey, *Water from the Rock*, 121–22 (*six pence* and *musket cartridges*); Jaffe, *New York at War*, 102 (*nurses, cooks*); Pybus, *Epic Journeys of Freedom*, 32 ("*Negro barracks*"); Burrows and Wallace, *Gotham*, 269 (*Negro Burial Ground*).

59 **Royal Navy raids along Chesapeake Bay:** Jaffe, *New York at War*, 102; Burrows and Wallace, *Gotham*, 248 (*ferry operators*); Schama, *Rough Crossings*, 112 ("*Ethiopian balls*").

59 **Even so, slaves belonging to New York:** Duncan, *History of the Royal Regiment of Artillery*, 1: 329 ("*Negro wench*"); Onderdonk, *Documents and Letters*, 134 ("*Negro boy*").

59 **The second group in New York:** Baer, *Hessians*, 1–2 (*More than eighteen thousand*); Burgoyne, trans. and ed., *A Hessian Officer's Diary of the American Revolution*, 112–77 (*causes of death*); Hoock, *Scars of Independence*, 202 (*prisoner farmhands*).

59 **Those who trudged across the East River:** Atwood, *The Hessians*, 212 ("*deserters of all nations*"); Kranish, *Flight from Monticello*, 106–7 (*haberdasher from Hannover*); Baer, *Hessians*, 74–75 (*horsewhips*).

60 **Some Hessians offered by their princes:** Atwood, *The Hessians*, 213 (*epilepsy*); Baer, *Hessians*, 43 ("*one eye*"); Syrett, *Shipping and the American War, 1775–1783*, 185 ("*places of repose*"), 191 (*killed at least 8 percent*); Town, *A Detail of Some Particular Services Performed in America*, 64 (*fireballs*); Pettengill, trans., *Letters from America, 1776–1779*, 163 (*linen hammock*); Uhlendorf, trans. and annot., *Revolution in America*, 11 ("*I never think*").

60 **"We have seen a true paradise":** Burgoyne, trans. and ed., *A Hessian Officer's Diary of the American Revolution*, 113; Pettengill, trans., *Letters from America, 1776–1779*, 164 (*sleep in a churchyard*); Londahl-Smidt, *German Troops in the American Revolution*, 1: 3 (*since 1715*);

Montross, *Rag, Tag and Bobtail*, 358 (*"confounded pride"*); Atwood, *The Hessians*, 152 (*"differing as we do"*); Uhlendorf, trans. and annot., *Revolution in America*, 8 (*more than a third*).

60 **For now these newcomers:** Döhla, *A Hessian Diary of the American Revolution*, 72 (*"only the vices"*).

61 **On Saturday, July 5:** Gill and Curtis, eds., *A Man Apart*, 174 (*three Royal Navy men-of-war*); Montrésor and Scull, "Journal of Captain John Montrésor," 393+ (*victuallers from Ireland*); Burrows and Wallace, *Gotham*, 251 (*eightfold*).

61 **The guns at Fort George boomed:** O'Shaughnessy, *The Men Who Lost America*, 215 (*old scar*); Lender and Stone, *Fatal Sunday*, 16 (*Coldstream Guards*). To save powder, Adm. Howe had ordered no salutes except for flag officers (Mackenzie, *Diary of Frederick Mackenzie*, 240).

61 **Peace in 1763 brought an opportunity:** Hagan and Roberts, eds., *Against All Enemies*, 23 (*Scipio, Marlborough*); *TBAC*, 254; *TAR*, xiv–xv (*his wife died*).

61 **The American war revived him:** O'Shaughnessy, "'To Gain the Hearts and Subdue the Minds,'" 199+; *TBAC*, 97, 366, 390, 334.

62 **As always with Clinton, insecurity:** Robson, *The American Revolution*, 136 (*morbid introspection*); Stuart-Wortley, ed., *A Prime Minister and His Son*, 154 (*"warm"*); Randall, *Benedict Arnold*, 461 (*"weathercock"*).

62 **Yet with few successful generals:** *TAR*, xxiv; Hargrove, *General John Burgoyne*, 105 (*"Burgoyne knew better"*); Willcox, "Too Many Cooks: British Planning Before Saratoga," 6+; Mackesy, *The War for America, 1775–1783*, 113 ; Eelking and Rosengarten, *The German Allied Troops in the North American War of Independence*, 92 (*fluency in German*); "Von Krafft's Journal," ix+ (*"Klington"*).

62 **He agreed but insisted on:** Clinton, Apr. 7, 1777, conversation with G. Germain, HCP, vol. 20, WLC (*"royal approbation"*); memo, Clinton-Harvey conversation, Apr. 1777, WBW (*"recompense for an injury"*); *TAR*, 59 (*Sullivan's Island*); *Public Advertiser*, Apr. 14, 1777, 4 (*touched him with a sword*); Huish, *Public and Private Life of His Late Excellent and Most Gracious Majesty, George the Third*, 375 (*"perfectly satisfied"*).

62 **An avid violinist:** Silverman, *A Cultural History of the American Revolution*, 371 (*fiddles and bass viols*); Ferling, *Winning Independence*, 84; Clinton, Apr. 7, 1777, conversation with G. Germain, HCP, vol. 20, WLC (*"Certainly no"*); Willcox, *Portrait of a General*, 139–40.

62 **The insurrectionists were said to be "deep into principles":** Ferling, ed., *The World Turned Upside Down*, 179 (*"principles"*), 181 (*four thousand*); *TBAC*, 254; O'Shaughnessy, *The Men Who Lost America*, 216 (*geographic warp*), 221; Christie, *Crisis of Empire*, 106.

63 **"Very sulkily I shall go":** Willcox, *Portrait of a General*, 142; Willcox, "British Strategy in America, 1778," 108 (*"neither esteem as an officer"*).

63 **General Sir William Howe, that very man:** Abbott, *New York in the American Revolution*, 208 (*No. 1 Broadway*); Duncan, *History of the Royal Regiment of Artillery*, 1: 332; Schenawolf, "Washington's New York City Headquarters—No. 1 Broadway," *Revolutionary War Journal*, July 9, 2013; Abbott, "The Neighborhoods of New York, 1760–1775," 47 (*Greek pediment*); Cunningham, *The Uncertain Revolution*, 166–67 (*"as grand as any"*); Stokes, *The Iconography of Manhattan Island, 1498–1909*, 1: 334.

63 **Dark and thickset, Howe looked the part:** Flavell, *The Howe Dynasty*, 207 (*twenty pages long*), 297 (*"a fine figure"*); Harris, *Brandywine*, 38 (*"Cleopatra"*); Jones, *History of New York During the Revolutionary War*, 171 (*"feasting, gunning"*); Henry Strachey to Jane Strachey, May 20, 1777, Strachey papers, WLC, box 1 (*grew envious*).

63 **Otherwise he was famously taciturn:** Flavell, *The Howe Dynasty*, 91 (*"silent"*); Billias, ed., *The Manuscripts of Captain Howard Vincente Knox*, 130 (*"not communicating"*); O'Shaughnessy, *The Men Who Lost America*, 83–84 (*119 British generals*).

64 **He had hoped to finish the war:** Howe inquiry, *Parliamentary Register*, 12: 330 (*forty-one thousand*); army strength reports, Aug. 1777, Lord Frederick North, box 2, WLC (*half of the king's land forces*); Flavell, *The Howe Dynasty*, 87 (*1762 at Havana*).

64 **"No man in the world":** Lundin, *Cockpit of the Revolution*, 318 (*"cut-up land"*); Mackesy, *The War for America, 1775–1783*, 152 (*missed opportunities*); "Extracts from the Letter Book of

Captain Johann Heinrichs [*sic*] of the Hessian *Jäger* Corps, 1778–1780," 137+ (*"no Caesar"*): *Report on the Manuscripts of Mrs. Stopford-Sackville*, 2: 70–71 (*"different scale"*); Conway, "From Fellow-Nationals to Foreigners," 89 (*"equivocal neutrality"*); *The Narrative of Lieut. Gen. Sir William Howe*, 2 (*"fewest blots"*).

64 **Howe and Clinton held three long conversations:** Willcox, *Portrait of a General*, 155 (*"raked over"*), 160 (*Frog's Neck*), 161 (*"wish to go home"*); memo, Clinton with W. Howe, July 6, 1777, WBW (*"never had agreed"*).

65 **But serve he must:** Graham, *The Royal Navy in the War of American Independence*, 8 (*eighty fighting ships*); Martelli, *Jemmy Twitcher*, 113–14 (*quarter of all British tars*); NDAR, 8: 1053 (*more than two hundred*); Gruber, *The Howe Brothers and the American Revolution*, 202–3; Miller, *Sea of Glory*, 194 (*one in nine*); Syrett, *The Royal Navy in European Waters*, 172n (*rare day*).

65 **Ashore the struggle was equally dire:** Schaukirk, "Occupation of New York City by the British," 418+ (*Washington had been killed*); Schechter, *The Battle for New York*, 278 (*"Lord Protector"*); Tatum, ed., *The American Journal of Ambrose Serle*, 203 (*"much agitated"*), 224 (*"caught him in tears"*); Fischer, *Washington's Crossing*, 352–59 (*thousand casualties*); Jeffrey A. Denman, "Fighting for Forage," 51+.

65 **The king himself encouraged:** Allen, *Tories*, 205–6 (*Danbury*); Dacus, "Again the Hero: David Wooster's Final Battle," *JAR*, Apr. 12, 2018; Lydenberg, ed., "Archibald Robertson's Diaries, 1762–1780," 283+ (*five thousand barrels*); Risch, *Supplying Washington's Army*, 148 (*tents*); Kwasny, *Washington's Partisan War, 1775–1783*, 124; Brumwell, *Turncoat*, 79 (*groin*).

65 **But the day had turned:** Fortescue, *The War of Independence*, 62; Lydenberg, ed., "Archibald Robertson's Diaries, 1762–1780," 283+; Philbrick, *Valiant Ambition*, 98 (*coat collar*); Murdoch, ed., *Rebellion in America*, 456 (*losses at 172*); Jonathan Trumbull, Sr., to GW, May 4, 1777, PGW, 9: 343n (*twice that*); Kwasny, *Washington's Partisan War, 1775–1783*, 123–26 (*"rascals are skulking"*).

66 **Ambushes, firefights, and raids:** Martin, *The Philadelphia Campaign, June 1777–July 1778*, 23–24 (*a thousand wagons*); Gerlach, ed., *New Jersey in the American Revolution, 1763–1783* (*dissident churches*); Owen, *The Revolutionary Struggle in New Jersey, 1776–1783*, 14–16; Wertenbaker, *Father Knickerbocker Rebels*, 129; Lengel, *General George Washington*, 216 (*only to lunge again*); Münchhausen, *At General Howe's Side*, 20; Ewald, *Diary of the American War*, 69 (*great arc*); Kemble, *The Kemble Papers*, 1: 452–55; PNG, 2: 107.

66 **Another month of the fighting season:** Buchanan, *The Road to Valley Forge*, 213 (*mid-November*); Gruber, *The Howe Brothers and the American Revolution*, 230 (*"I can scarce hear"*); Stevens's, no. 2066; Spring, *With Zeal and with Bayonets Only*, 129 (*"gnaw their own flesh"*).

66 **The forfeiture of the New Jersey granary:** Black and Woodfine, eds., *The British Navy and the Use of Naval Power in the Eighteenth Century*, 172; D. Chamier to Treasury, Mar. 31, 1777, UK NA, T 64/10, f 36–56 (*"no dependence"*); Syrett, *Shipping and the American War, 1775–83*, 77 (*six thousand vessels*), 243; Baker, *Government and Contractors*, 23 (*feeding 40,000*), 206–7; Bowler, *Logistics and the Failure of the British Army in America, 1775–1783*, 9 (*4,000 army horses*), 30, 67–69 (*purchased in Rhode Island* and *"perpetual harassment"*).

67 **Not since the time of the Romans:** D. Chamier to Treasury, Mar. 31, 1777, UK NA, T 64/10, f 36–56 (*"bad stuff"* and *350,000 gallons*); Baker, *Government and Contractors*, 120–21 (*iron hoop*).

67 **Nothing chafed the fraying relationship:** *The Narrative of Lieut. Gen. Sir William Howe*, 9–10 (*"finish the war"*); Coakley and Conn, *The War of the American Revolution*, 53 (*ten thousand up the Hudson*); Anderson, *The Command of the Howe Brothers During the American Revolution*, 217.

67 **Even before learning from London:** Coakley and Conn, *The War of the American Revolution*, 53 (*changed his mind*); Jackson, *With the British Army in Philadelphia, 1777–1778*, 3 (*overwhelmingly supportive*); Mackesy, *The War for America, 1775–1783*, 111–12 (*end the rebellion*).

67 **In his third plan, dated April 2:** Anderson, *The Command of the Howe Brothers During the*

American Revolution, 223 ("*abandon the Jerseys*"); *The Narrative of Lieut. Gen. Sir William Howe*, 12–15 ("*little assistance*"), 19–20 ("*surest road*"); Howe to Germain, Apr. 2, 1777, *Report on the Manuscripts of Mrs. Stopford-Sackville*, 2: 63–64 ("*my hopes of terminating*").

68 **London endorsed each scheme:** Brown, *The American Secretary*, 97 ("*entirely approves*"); Anderson, *The Command of the Howe Brothers During the American Revolution*, 228 ("*unhappy contest*"); Mackesy, *The War for America, 1775–1783*, 123 (*did not press the point*); Willcox, "Too Many Cooks: British Planning Before Saratoga," 6+ (*eight previous letters*).

68 **This muddle appalled Clinton:** Ketchum, *Saratoga*, 259–60 ("*totally disapprove*").

68 **To Howe he predicted:** *TAR*, 60–61 ("*miscarriage*"); Willcox, *Portrait of a General*, 153–55; Anderson, *The Command of the Howe Brothers During the American Revolution*, 265 ("*time of year*" and "*no rebellion*"); memo, Clinton conversation with G. Germain, Apr. 7, 1777, HCP, vol. 20, WLC ("*fool if he did*"); memo, Clinton conversation with W. Howe, July 8, 1777, WBW ("*same of Jersey*").

68 **Round and round they went:** *TAR*, 62 ("*oftener than was agreeable*").

69 **On July 14 American deserters:** Münchhausen, *At General Howe's Side*, 21; Taafe, *The Philadelphia Campaign, 1777–1778*, 45 (*well on its way*); Harris, *Brandywine*, 68 ("*no room to dread*"); Willcox, "Too Many Cooks: British Planning Before Saratoga," 6+ (*seven thousand men*); Clark, "Responsibility for the Failure of the Burgoyne Campaign," 542+.

69 **Clinton's pessimism now spiraled:** Willcox, *Portrait of a General*, 157 ("*murder us*"); McBurney, *Kidnapping the Enemy*, 108, 128–36; Joseph Spencer to GW, Aug. 15, 1777, FOL; Barton, *Narrative of the Surprize and Capture of Major-General Richard Prescott*, 10–14; Mackenzie, *Diary of Frederick Mackenzie*, 148–50 (*without a shot fired*); Dearden, *The Rhode Island Campaign of 1778*, 13; Dann, ed., *The Revolution Remembered*, 24 ("*let me get my clothes*").

69 **"Liable to General Howe's caprices":** Willcox, *Portrait of a General*, 158–59; memo, Clinton with W. Howe, July 8, 1777, WBW ("*false principles*"); Willcox, "Too Many Cooks: British Planning Before Saratoga," 6+ (*through the harsh winter*); Clinton to Harvey, July 11, 1777, WBW ("*as far as Albany*").

69 **Determined to stay busy:** Stokes, *The Iconography of Manhattan Island, 1498–1909*, 5: 1053 (*Morris mansion*); Kemble, *The Kemble Papers*, 125.

69 **Pulling out quill, ink, and paper:** Willcox, "Too Many Cooks: British Planning Before Saratoga," 6+ ("*deceive us all*" and "*ever so much inclined*"); *TAR*, 64–65.

70 **"Should I serve with him":** Willcox, *Portrait of a General*, 202.

70 **On July 16 General Howe:** Münchhausen, *At General Howe's Side*, 21 (*Fifty-six men*); Harris, *Brandywine*, 56, 58 ("*Lord knows*"), 60 ("*mysterious*"); Balderston and Syrett, eds., *The Lost War*, 138 (*recruited ship pilots*); Stuart-Wortley, *A Prime Minister and His Son*, 113 ("*What our chiefs think*").

70 **That evening, Howe's battle staff:** Münchhausen, *At General Howe's Side*, 21 (*white staterooms*); Henry Strachey to Jane Strachey, Sept. 1, 1777, Strachey papers, WLC, box 1 (*three cheers*); Gruber, ed., *John Peebles' American War, 1776–1782* (*manning the yards*); "Supernumeraries borne onboard the ships," July 7, 1777, UK NA, ADM 1/487, f 477 (*forty-one pilots*).

70 **For more than a week troops:** Harris, *Brandywine*, 56 (*four ferry landings*); W. Howe orderly book, July 3–12, 1777, WLC, box 1, folder 1; Kemble, *The Kemble Papers*, 1: 466 (*baggage to the beach*); Eller, ed., *Chesapeake Bay in the American Revolution*, 351–52 (*Manifests listed*); strength report, July 1, 1777, Richard and William Howe collection, WLC (*rank-and-file strength*); Seymour, ed., "A Contemporary British Account of General Sir William Howe's Military Operations in 1777," 69+ (*four pioneer companies*); Curtis, *The Organization of the British Army in the American Revolution*, 153 (*philamot yellow*).

70 **Twenty-three brigs, schooners, and sloops:** Eller, ed., *Chesapeake Bay in the American Revolution*, 351–52; Moomaw, "The Naval Career of Captain Hamond, 1775–1779," diss., 315 (*flatboats*); W. Howe orderly book, July 11, 1777, WLC, box 1, folder 1 ("*greatest care*"); Harris, *Brandywine*, 67 (*three hundred rounds*); Kemble, *The Kemble Papers*, 1: 458–63 (*Wills's Wharf*); "Invoices of Medicines, Instruments, and Materials," GSG, vol. 8 (*172 medications*).

71 **Red, white, yellow, blue, and striped signal pendants:** W. Howe orderly book, July 12, 1777, WLC, box 1, folder 1; Kemble, *The Kemble Papers*, 1: 473 (*summoning adjutants*); Uhlendorf,

trans. and annot., *Revolution in America*, 93 (*Fresh provisions dwindled*); Harris, *Brandywine*, 62 (*"waiting here so long"*); Kehoe, "A Military Guide: The British Infantry of 1775," 1974 (*"so many filthy heads"*); Murray, *Letters from America, 1773 to 1780*, 42 (*"only blessing"*).

71   **For several days the vessels caught:** Tatum, ed., *The American Journal of Ambrose Serle*, 239 (*wind came foul*); journal, *Eagle*, July 23, 1777, *NDAR*, 9: 318–20n; Lengel, *General George Washington*, 217 (*Rebel sentinels stared*); Martin, *The Philadelphia Campaign, June 1777–July 1778*, 31; Clowes, *The Royal Navy*, 3: 390 (*280 vessels*); Ewald, *Diary of the American War*, 72 (*led by the frigate* Liverpool); McGuire, *The Philadelphia Campaign*, 2: 277–79 (*"undescribably noble"*).

71   **As he watched the armada:** Willcox, *Portrait of a General*, 157 (*"It bears heavy"*); Clinton to Lord Percy, July 23, 1777, WBW (*"an end of British dominion"*).

72   **Just as Clinton had predicted:** Murray, *Letters from America, 1773 to 1780*, 47–48 (*"nothing new"*); Tatum, ed., *The American Journal of Ambrose Serle*, 241 (*"tossed about exceedingly"*); "The Journal of Ensign William, Viscount Cantelupe," Charles Grey, 1st Earl Grey, papers, July 28, 1777, University of Durham, U.K. (*signal guns fired*—with appreciation to author Thomas J. McGuire); Gill and Curtis, *A Man Apart*, 189 (*"The sea a-roaring"*).

72   **One hundred and fifty miles south:** Moomaw, "The Denouement of General Howe's Campaign of 1777," 498+ (*Hamond had been on station*); Moomaw, "The Naval Career of Captain Hamond, 1775–1779," diss., 314 (*counterfeit*); Benjamin Caldwell, R.N., to R. Howe, July 25, 1777, *NDAR*, 9: 338 (*"dying state"*); *NDAR*, 6: 973 (*"They seem to place"*).

72   **Shortly after dawn on Wednesday, July 30:** Moomaw, "The Denouement of General Howe's Campaign of 1777," 498+; Philbrick, *Valiant Ambition*, 22 (*white walls, mirrors*); Moomaw, "The Naval Career of Captain Hamond, 1775–1779," diss., 325 (*"every information"*).

73   **Relying on information received:** *The Narrative of Lieut. Gen. Sir William Howe*, 71 (*"difficult of navigation"*), 83 (*"never deceived me"*); Harris, *Brandywine*, 87 (*Reedy Island*); Moomaw, "The Naval Career of Captain Hamond, 1775–1779," diss., 322–23 (*"finer opportunity"*), 432–36 (*marching toward Wilmington*).

73   **General Howe listened intently:** "Narrative of Captain Andrew Snape Hamond," July 31, 1777, *NDAR*, 9: 364 (*"do great damage"*); *The Narrative of Lieut. Gen. Sir William Howe*, 24 (*"extremely hazardous"*).

73   **Asking Hamond to remain in the cabin:** Moomaw, "The Naval Career of Captain Hamond, 1775–1779," diss., 326 (*"without any molestation"*); Moomaw, "The Denouement of General Howe's Campaign of 1777," 498+ (*"no doubt"*).

73   **Certainly this plan surprised Captain Hamond:** Moomaw, "The Naval Career of Captain Hamond, 1775–1779," diss., 326–28 (*"great length of time"*); Moomaw, "The Denouement of General Howe's Campaign of 1777," 498+ (*"most hazardous"*); "Chesapeake Bay Facts," NPS, https://www.nps.gov/chba/learn/nature/nature.htm (*less than six feet*).

74   **An army quartermaster was summoned:** "Narrative of Captain Andrew Snape Hamond," July 31, 1777, *NDAR*, 9: 364 (*fourteen days* and *"from the beginning"*); Moomaw, "The Denouement of General Howe's Campaign of 1777," 498+ (*none of the forty-one pilots*).

74   **A decision had been made:** Harris, *Brandywine*, 90 (*flawed intelligence*); Moomaw, "The Naval Career of Captain Hamond, 1775–1779," diss., 444 (*fundamentally incorrect*).

74   **A signal gun barked from the *Eagle*:** Burgoyne, trans., *The Hesse-Cassel Mirbach Regiment in the American Revolution*, 15 (*telescopes*); Harris, *Brandywine*, 80 (*octagonal seventy-foot*); Moomaw, "The Naval Career of Captain Hamond, 1775–1779," diss., 335 (*By four p.m.*).

74   **William Howe chose not to inform London:** Howe inquiry, *Parliamentary Register*, 12: 99; Lundin, *Cockpit of the Revolution*, 310 (*"very secretive"*).

75   **Those who knew:** Tatum, ed., *The American Journal of Ambrose Serle*, 241 (*"The hearts of all men"*).

3. FELLOWS WILLING TO GO TO HEAVEN

76   **By midmorning even the shaded woodlands:** Pickering, *The Life of Timothy Pickering*, 151 (*"melting hot"*); JA to Abigail Adams, Aug. 13, 1777, *AFC*, FOL; author visit, Moland House Historic Farm, Little Neshaminy Creek, Aug. 31, 2021 (*orange jewelweed*); Jesberger, "Wash-

ington's Headquarters Along the Neshaminy," lecture, July 12, 2021; Davis, *History of Bucks County, Pennsylvania*, 2: 127 (*eleven thousand men*).

76　**For more than a month:** Rossman, *Thomas Mifflin and the Politics of the American Revolution*, 93 (*"wear out stockings"*); William S. Baker, "Itinerary of General Washington from June 15, 1775, to December 23, 1783," *PMHB*, vols. 14–15 (1890–91); John Hancock to GW, July 31, 1777, *PGW*, 10: 467n (*sailed south*); Ward, *Duty, Honor, or Country*, 92–93; Freeman, *George Washington: A Biography*, 4: 449 (*"field of conjecture"*).

76　**A report of the fleet dropping anchor:** Lengel, *General George Washington*, 218 (*men drowned*); Harris, *Brandywine*, 72 (*"Marching and countermarching"*).

77　**"We are yet entirely in the dark":** GW to I. Putnam, Aug. 7, 1777, *PGW*, 10: 546; GW to J. Hancock, Aug. 10, 1777, *PGW*, 10: 575; GW to A. Ward, Aug. 11, 1777, *PGW*, 10: 589 (*"as much puzzled"*).

77　**A week passed without further march orders:** Jesberger, "Washington's Headquarters Along the Neshaminy," lecture, July 12, 2021 (*musket racks* and *slaughter pens*); Bolton, *The Private Soldier Under Washington*, 151 (*grass-guard*); Buck, "Washington's Encampment on the Neshaminy," 275+ (*Presbyterian churchyard*).

77　**Martial noises filled the camp:** GW, general orders, June 6, 1777, *PGW*, 9: 614; Boulanger, Hathaway, and Gilbertson, "Mount Independence Chert: An Ancient and Revolutionary Stone," Mount Independence State Historic Site, 2005 (*knappers*); Silverman, *A Cultural History of the American Revolution*, 354 (*"God Save the Congress"*); Risch, *Supplying Washington's Army*, 344–45 (*"moral certainty"*); Ward, *Duty, Honor, or Country*, 109–10 (*"his testicles"*).

77　**"We have the most respectable body":** Drake, *Life and Correspondence of Henry Knox*, 42 (*"willing to go to heaven"*); *PGW*, 17: 536 (*Hate-evil*); JA to TJ, June 28, 1813, FOL.

78　**Knox and his fellow generals:** Peterson, *The Book of the Continental Soldiers*, 227, 242 (*cockades*); Jedidiah Huntington to Andrew Huntington, Aug. 12, 1777, JLB CCC (*"barefooted"*); Field, ed., *Diary of Colonel Israel Angell*, xii (*"ragged, lousy"*); GW to James Mease, July 18, 1777, *PGW*, 10: 322 (*"thin French pumps"*).

78　**As they formed ranks to practice:** McGuire, *Battle of Paoli*, 11 (*"blue sagathy"*); GW to James Mease, May 12, 1777, *PGW*, 9: 399 (*"destroying themselves"*); GW to James Mease, Apr. 17, 1777, *PGW*, 9: 195 (*scarlet coats*); Risch, *Supplying Washington's Army*, 285 (*cover the coats*).

78　**"We are well supplied":** Drake, *Life and Correspondence of Henry Knox*, 42; Brooks, *Henry Knox, a Soldier of the Revolution*, 94 (*"impiety"*); Ward, *George Washington's Enforcers*, 24 (*"swearing ways"*); White, "Standing Armies in Time of War," diss., 199 (*"horrid sins"*); Byrd, *Sacred Scripture, Sacred War*, 73 (*"Cursed be he"*); Jackson, *Valley Forge*, 167 (*Bibles*); Bolton, *The Private Soldier Under Washington*, 159.

79　**For now the army would enforce discipline:** Ward, *George Washington's Enforcers*, 35 (*number of lashes*); Davis, *History of Bucks County, Pennsylvania*, 2: 127 (*whipping post*); GW, general orders, Aug. 12, 1777, *PGW*, 10: 590; Gillard, "14 Colonial-Era Slang Terms to Work into Modern Conversation," Jan. 15, 2020 (*fishy*); "The Drinkers Dictionary," New England Historical Society, n.d., https://newenglandhistoricalsociety.com/call-someone-drunk-colonial-times-drinkers-dictionary/; Royster, *A Revolutionary People at War*, 75 (*wring-jaw cider*); Martin, *A Narrative of a Revolutionary Soldier*, 125–26 (*"the creature"*).

79　**Through "a signal act of mercy":** GW, general orders, Aug. 19, 1777, *PGW*, 11: 1; Buck, "Washington's Encampment on the Neshaminy," 275+ (*coat turned inside out*).

79　**The merciful George Washington occupied a two-story:** author visit, Moland House Historic Farm, Little Neshaminy Creek, Aug. 31, 2021 (*brown stone house*); Jesberger, "Washington's Headquarters Along the Neshaminy," lecture, July 12, 2021; Buck, "Washington's Encampment on the Neshaminy," 275+.

79　**Twenty-six months in command:** Henriques, *First and Always*, 5 (*"distinguish him to be a general"*); Chastellux, *Travels in North-America*, 139 (*"He is well-made"*); Martha Dangerfield Bland to friend, May 12, 1777, "Morristown 1777," MNHP chronology (*"throws off the hero"*); Kidd, *God of Liberty*, 125 (*legions of angels*).

80　**Some worried that he had grown:** Ferling, *The Ascent of George Washington*, 125–26 (*"ven-

eration"); JA to Abigail Adams, Oct. 26, 1777, FOL (*"We can allow"*); Thompson, *"The Only Unavoidable Subject of Regret,"* 43–44 (*"his wrath"*).

80 **"I never see that man laugh":** Thompson, *"The Only Unavoidable Subject of Regret,"* 47 (*"laughing inside"*); "Slavery," https://www.mountvernon.org/george-washington/slavery/; Reiss, *Medicine and the American Revolution,* 231 (*dental miseries*); Henriques, *First and Always,* 42 (*hippo ivory*); GW to Theodorick Bland, Aug. 15, 1786, FOL (*"better to go laughing"*).

80 **No one doubted that his journey:** Shreve, *Tench Tilghman,* 87 (*"weight of the whole war"*); Ferling, *The First of Men,* 263; GW to P. Schuyler, July 15, 1777, *PGW,* 10: 289–90 (*"stroke is severe"*).

81 **Washington could be impenetrably reserved:** Fraser, *The Washingtons,* 195 (*"dead eye"*); GW to John Thomas, July 23, 1777, FOL (*"all that is dear"*); Middlekauff, *Washington's Revolution,* 185–86; Ferling, *The First of Men,* 257 (*"slow in operation"*), 265 (*"great, manly"*); Higginbotham, ed., *George Washington Reconsidered,* 314 (*rectitude*); Wood, *The Idea of America,* 68 (*sacrifice self-interest*).

81 **"For attention to business":** Clarfield, *Timothy Pickering and the American Republic,* 46; Henriques, *First and Always,* 3–4 (*fencing lessons*); Lengel, ed., *A Companion to George Washington,* 363 (*three hundred letters*); Reiss, *Medicine and the American Revolution,* 231 (*malaria*).

81 **Like most mortals:** GW to Patrick Henry, Oct. 5, 1776, FOL (*"reputation to lose"*); GW to Continental Congress, June 16, 1775, *PGW,* 1: 1 (*"abilities & military experience"*); GW to John Parke Custis, Jan. 22, 1777, FOL (*"difficulties & perplexities"*).

82 **Washington would use more than a hundred names:** Lengel, ed., *A Companion to George Washington,* 563; GW, general orders, July 9, 1776, FOL (*"Christian soldier"*); GW to Robert Jackson, Aug. 2, 1755, FOL (*"uncertainty"*); Kowalski, *Revolutionary Spirits,* 68–69 (*"heights of greatness"*). Scholar David L. Preston observes that GW's rumination on "uncertainty" in 1755 may well be quoting a 1753 essay by Samuel Johnson. Note to author, July 22, 2024; for the essay, see https://www.johnsonessays.com/the-adventurer/no-108-on-the-uncertainty-of -human-things/.

82 **The road had surely been rough:** Peckham, ed., *The Toll of Independence,* 130 (*engagements*); Breen, *The Will of the People,* 30; Fischer, *Liberty and Freedom,* 145–48 (*a beaver*).

82 **Whatever the nation would become:** Bailyn, *The Ideological Origins of the American Revolution,* 304 (*a thousand pulpits*); Hagan and Roberts, eds., *Against All Enemies,* 28 (*busts*).

82 **His Excellency now believed:** GW to R. H. Lee, Apr. 24, 1777, *PGW,* 9: 256 (*"Her very existence"*); Higginbotham, ed., *George Washington Reconsidered,* 193 (*hundreds of letters*).

83 **He would continue to watch:** Weigley, *The American Way of War,* 20 (*"fatal stab"*); GW to John Hancock, Sept. 8, 1776, FOL (*"avoid a general action"*); AH to Hugh Knox, July 1–28, 1777, FOL (*"waste and defeat"*); GW to John Hancock, Dec. 16, 1776, FOL (*"respectable army"*). Hamilton's birth year has long been disputed (Chernow, *Alexander Hamilton,* 17).

83 **Of roughly two hundred thousand:** Millett, "Whatever Became of the Militia in the History of the American Revolution?," Georges Rogers Clark lecture, SoC, 1986 (*fought by militiamen alone*); Mackesy, "Could the British Have Won the War of Independence?," lecture, 1975; Kurtz and Hutson, eds., *Essays on the American Revolution,* 148.

83 **Washington never stopped carping:** Shy, *A People Numerous and Armed,* 237; GW to William Livingston, Jan. 24, 1777, FOL (*"lowest class"*); GW to Massachusetts General Court, July 9, 1776, FOL (*"more than competent"*); GW, general orders, Aug. 22, 1777, FOL (*"spirit and fortitude"*).

83 **Nudged by the commander in chief:** Martin and Lender, *A Respectable Army,* 7–9, 95; Lender and Stone, *Fatal Sunday,* 61 (*twenty-dollar bounty* and *738 officers and men*); Royster, *A Revolutionary People at War,* 131–32 (*seventy-six thousand*); "General officers' memorial to Congress," Nov. 15, 1779, JLB AAA (*hundred acres*); Pancake, *1777,* 78–79; Morrisey, *Monmouth Courthouse 1778,* 23–24; Wright, *The Continental Army,* 112 (*ten brigades*).

84 **This neat construct proved a pipe dream:** Ferling, *A Leap in the Dark,* 201 (*"going to be hanged"*); "'The pleasure of their number' 1778: Crisis, Conscription, and Revolutionary Soldiers' Recollections," 2: 1 (*"ruptures"*); Lerwill, "The Personnel Replacement System in the

United States Army," Aug. 1954 (*number that declined*); Royster, *A Revolutionary People at War*, 131; Resch and Sargent, eds., *War & Society in the American Revolution*, 14 (*half a million*).

84 **Moreover, this was an altered army:** Hoffman and Albert, eds., *Arms and Independence*, 122–24 (*propertied freeholders*); Countryman, *The American Revolution*, 141 (*returned to their farms*), 146; JA to Abigail Adams, Apr. 26, 1777, FOL (*"I am very mad"*).

84 **Instead the army increasingly derived:** Royster, *A Revolutionary People at War*, 129 (*landless young*); Martin and Lender, *"A Respectable Army,"* 90–98; Neimeyer, *America Goes to War*, 28 (*crop failures*), 123–24 (*$6.66*); Ruddiman, *Becoming Men of Some Consequence*, 7 (*one in five enlistees*); Spero and Zuckerman, eds., *The American Revolution Reborn*, 17 (*pension applications*); Chambers and Piehler, eds., *Major Problems in American Military History*, 82–83 (*more than ideology*).

84 **Several New England states this year:** Ferling, *The First of Men*, 199 (*conscription*); Higginbotham, *The War of American Independence*, 393 (*drawn from a hat*); Martin and Lender, *"A Respectable Army,"* 104; Hoffman and Albert, eds., *Arms and Independence*, 124 (*substitutes*); Karsten, ed., *The Military in America*, 72 (*40 percent*), 76 (*"mostly foreigners"*); Cox, *A Proper Sense of Honor*, 15 (*"arrested"*); Raphael, *A People's History of the American Revolution*, 79–80 (*"spunk of a louse"*).

85 **Still, the numbers fell short:** Wright, *The Continental Army*, 108 (*North Carolina regiments*), 110 (*seven to five*); Ryan, ed., *A Salute to Courage*, 77 (*2nd Maryland*); Resch and Sargent, eds., *War & Society in the American Revolution*, 109 (*barely 2,500*); GW to Patrick Henry, May 17, 1777, *PGW*, 9: 453n (*dozen regiments*).

85 **Desertion made things worse:** Gaines, *For Liberty and Glory*, 111 (*thwarting deserters*); Royster, *A Revolutionary People at War*, 133 (*five dollars for each absconder*); Turner, ed., *The Journal and Order Book of Captain Robert Kirkwood*, 78 (*"punished as soon"*); GW to John Hancock, Jan. 31, 1777, *PGW*, 8: 202 (*"shamefully reduced"*).

85 **For officers, the army remained:** Martin and Lender, *"A Respectable Army,"* 110 (*New Jersey officers*); Lapp, "Did They Really 'Take None but Gentlemen'?," 1239+ (*"deflected life"*).

85 **A Maryland colonel might grumble:** Royster, *A Revolutionary People at War*, 91 (*"perfect novices"*); EPO, "A Diverse Army," MNHP, 2020, 3–4 (*"Pumpkin Heads"*).

86 **"For posterity I bleed":** AA, 5: 2, 244; 2 Samuel 10:12 (*"Be of good courage"*).

86 **Washington had vowed "by every means":** GW to Robert Morris, Mar. 2, 1777, FOL; GW to Stirling, Jan. 19, 1777, FOL (*"unused to restraint"*); TBAC, 564.

86 **Keeping the army together:** Ruddiman, *Becoming Men of Some Consequence*, 61 (*face outward*); GW, general orders, June 12, 1777, 10: 6–8 (*"to sleep"*); GW, general orders, June 4, 1777, *PGW*, 9: 603 (*"music of the army"*); GW to Benjamin Tallmadge, Mar. 1, 1777, FOL (*near white*); GW, general orders, June 16, 1777, *PGW*, 10: 47–48 (*salutes*).

86 **There was more, always more:** GW, general orders, June 4, 1777, *PGW*, 9: 602 (*offal*); GW to Elizabeth Mallam Neil, Apr. 27, 1777, *PGW*, 9: 289 (*$50*); GW to Thomas Mifflin, Mar. 13, 1777, *PGW*, 8: 566–67 (*"U.S."*); Risch, *Supplying Washington's Army*, 355 (*"U.States"*); GW to W. Howe, June 10, 1777, *PGW*, 9: 661 (*prisoner exchange*); GW to Alexander Spotswood et al., Apr. 30, 1777, *PGW*, 9: 315 (*"sober, young, active"*); Ward, *George Washington's Enforcers*, 62–63 (*"some property"*); GW to Nathaniel Sackett, Apr. 8, 1777, *PGW*, 9: 95 (*"It runs in my head"*).

87 **An army needed maps:** Boan, "Mapmaking and the U.S. Army," 26+; Ruppert, "Robert Erskine, Surveyor-General of the Continental Army," *JAR*, Dec. 19, 2019 (*275 topographical*); Guthorn, *American Maps and Map Makers of the Revolution*, 17; Harley et al., *Mapping the American Revolutionary War*, 67–70; Hoffman and Albert, eds., *Arms and Independence*, 62; Rees, " 'The essential service he rendered. . . .' "; Christopher Ludwick, Superintendent of Bakers," vol. 9, no. 1 (*gingerbread*); Moore, *Diary of the American Revolution*, 447 (*thirteen white stars*); "History of the Treasury," https://home.treasury.gov/about/history-overview/history -of-the-treasury (*Hillegas*). The flag resolve was not published until Sept. 2, 1777.

87 **Dire shortages of guns and gunpowder:** Wright, *The Continental Army*, 103; Puls, *Henry Knox*, 84–85 (*powder laboratories*); Rosswurm, *Arms, Country, and Class*, 174 (*geometry*);

McKenney, *The Organizational History of Field Artillery, 1775–2003*, 9–12; Hoffman and Albert, eds., *Arms and Independence*, 57 (*aim at redcoat infantry*); GW to Richard Peters, June 30, 1777, *PGW*, 10: 154–55 (*"exceedingly heavy"*); McDonald, "French Firelocks in America Service: Markings on Continental Muskets," 2+.

87 **Every state except Delaware:** Bilby and Jenkins, *Monmouth Court House*, 169; Carp, *To Starve the Army at Pleasure*, 233 (*only a third*); William Heath to GW, Apr. 22, 1777, *PGW*, 9: 239n (*sloop* Republic); Desmarais, *America's First Ally*, 7 (*fifty tons from Nantes*); Reynolds, "Ammunition Supply in Revolutionary Virginia," 56+ (*powder brigs*).

88 **Washington also knew that the army's health:** Fried, *Rush*, 201–2; Hawke, *Benjamin Rush*, 192–93; Cutbush, *Observations on the Means of Preserving the Health of Soldiers and Sailors*, 337 (*close-cropped hair*).

88 **Among the most consequential decisions:** EPO, "'The Greatest of All Calamities': Smallpox & Morristown, 1777," n.p.; Gillett, *The Army Medical Department, 1775–1818*, 14; Fenn, *Pox Americana*, 32–33, 93–94; GW, general orders, May 26, 1776, FOL; "Morristown 1777," MNHP chronology (*"More frightful and pitiable"*).

88 **Pressed by both his medical staff and common soldiers:** GW to William Shippen, Jr., Feb. 6, 1777, *PGW*, 1:264 (*"more to dread"*); Thursfield, "Smallpox in the American War of Independence," 312+; Werther, "George Washington and the First Mandatory Immunization," *JAR*, Oct. 26, 2021; EPO, "'The Greatest of All Calamities': Smallpox & Morristown, 1777," n.p.

88 **Washington's abrupt conversion:** Wehrman, *The Contagion of Liberty*, 214, 218-24, 225-28 (*Mount Vernon*); GW to John Augustine Washington, June 1, 1777, PGW, 9: 586 (*"compel the masters"*).

89 **Throughout the spring and early summer:** Wehrman, *The Contagion of Liberty*, 218, 229 (*"constant pressure"*), 235–37; GW to Israel Putnam, June 17, 1777, *PGW*, 10: 62 (*"entirely clear"*).

89 **On Thursday morning, August 21:** GW, council of war, Aug. 21, 1777, *PGW*, 11: 20; author visit, Moland House Historic Farm, Little Neshaminy Creek, Aug. 31, 2021 (*Thirteen generals tromped*); Buck, "Washington's Encampment on the Neshaminy," 275+ (*"exceedingly impatient"*); Smith, *John Marshall*, 65 (*"markwiss"*).

89 **He had made landfall in South Carolina:** Unger, *Lafayette*, 30 (*fifty-four-day crossing*); Auricchio, *The Marquis Lafayette Reconsidered*, 41–42 (*"Nature adorns"*); *LiA*, 2: 37–38 (*"civilities and respect"*).

89 **"About eleven thousand men":** Unger, *Lafayette*, 41 (*"strange spectacle"*); NG to Caty Greene, Nov. 20, 1777, *PNG*, 2: 200 (*"sweet-tempered"*), Chernow, *Alexander Hamilton*, 96 (*"little whims"*); Auricchio, *The Marquis Lafayette Reconsidered*, 53 (*"intimate friend"*); Schama, *Citizens*, 32 (*Plutarch and Livy*).

90 **Washington had developed a fine disdain:** GW to J. Hancock, Feb. 11, 1777, *PGW*, 8: 305 (*"You cannot conceive"* and *"entirely useless"*); Werther, "Volunteer Overload," *JAR*, Sept. 8, 2020 (*"hungry adventurers"*); *LiA*, 2: 25 (*"spies in our camp"*).

90 **The matter had come to a head:** Freeman, *George Washington: A Biography*, 4: 422–23; Clary and Whitehorne, *The Inspectors General of the United States Army, 1777–1903*, 19–21 (*thirty duels*); Desmarais, *Washington's Engineer*, 4 (*metallurgy*); Callahan, *Henry Knox, General Washington's General*, 106–9; Hatch, *The Administration of the American Revolutionary Army*, 55–58; NG to J. Hancock, July 1, 1777, *PNG*, 2: 109–10; Smith, ed., *Letters of Delegates to Congress, 1774–1789*, 307 (*"displeasing"*); White, "Standing Armies in Time of War," diss., 218–22 (*ignored the demand*); Ferreiro, *Brothers at Arms*, 146 ("heureux accident"); Taafe, *Washington's Revolutionary War Generals*, 95–96 (*public expense*).

90 **Lafayette clearly seemed a different creature:** GW to Benjamin Harrison, Aug. 19, 1777, FOL (*"designs of Congress"*).

90 **The first question Washington put:** GW, council of war, Aug. 21, 1777, *PGW*, 11: 20 (*"most probable place"*); GW to John Hancock, July 25, 1777, FOL (*"amazing advantage"*); *Historical Anecdotes, Civil and Military*, 18 (*sailed to Bermuda*); GW to Horatio Gates, July 30, 1777, FOL (*"casting my eyes"*).

91 **The council unanimously concurred:** GW to Horatio Gates, Aug. 20, 1777, FOL.

91   **If this was so, he persisted:** GW, council of war, Aug. 21, 1777, FOL; GW to John Hancock, Aug. 21, 1777, *PGW*, 11: 21.

91   **"We have perhaps not a moment":** GW to John Hancock, Aug. 21, 1777, *PGW*, 11: 21; John Hancock to GW, Aug. 21, 1777, *PGW*, 11: 25 (*around Cape Charles*); GW, general orders, Aug. 22, 1777, *PGW*, 11: 30 (*"The army is to march"*); John Hancock to GW, Aug. 22, 1777, *PGW*, 11: 41 (*"two hundred sail"*).

91   **Aides settled the commanding general's account:** Jesberger, "Washington's Headquarters Along the Neshaminy," lecture, July 12, 2021 (*sweep up stragglers*).

91   **A sixteen-mile southward march:** GW, general orders, Aug. 23, 1777, fn, FOL; McGuire, *The Philadelphia Campaign*, 1: 123 (*"behaved civil"*).

92   **Certainly the moment was grave:** McGuire, *The Philadelphia Campaign*, 1: 124 (*biggest supply depot*); GW to John Hancock, Aug. 22, 1777, *PGW*, 11: 42.

92   **No doubt the war would grow darker:** GW to Israel Putnam, Aug. 22, 1777, *PGW*, 11: 46 (*"crush General Burgoyne"*).

92   **Gusty thunderstorms soaked the ranks:** JLB, "'Up to Our Knees in Mud for Four Days Past': The Weather and the Continental Army, August 1777–June 1778," Feb. 1998, n.p. (*lightning*); GW, general orders, Aug. 16, 1777, *PGW*, 10: 632–33 (*baggage wagons*); GW to John Hancock, Aug. 23, 1777, *PGW*, 11: 52 (*"some influence"*); Harris, *Brandywine*, 108 (*Front Street*).

92   **Washington led the column:** GW, general orders, Aug. 23, 1777, *PGW*, 11: 49–51 (*"without dancing"*); McGuire, *The Philadelphia Campaign*, 1: 131 (*Four hundred field musicians*).

92   **Across High Street they tramped:** Commager and Morris, eds., *The Spirit of 'Seventy-Six*, 650 (*"Thees and Thous"*); JA to Abigail Adams, Aug. 24, 1777, FOL (*"Much remains"*).

93   **For many of the rank and file:** Nash, *First City*, 45 (*"great and noble"*); Sullivan, *The Disaffected*, 12 (*fourth-largest*); Harris, *Brandywine*, 8 (*five thousand houses*); Albion and Pope, *Sea Lanes in Wartime*, 62–63 (*largest port*); author visit, New Market and Head House, Philadelphia, signage (*bear bacon*); Warner, *The Private City*, 16–17 (*seventy different trades*).

93   **At least a third:** Nash, *First City*, 60–61 (*women*); Bridenbaugh and Bridenbaugh, *Rebels and Gentlemen*, 363 (*Enlightenment*); Main, *The Social Structure of Revolutionary America*, 270 (*Not quite classless*).

93   **War now tested these admirable virtues:** Jackson, *With the British Army in Philadelphia, 1777–1778*, 277 (*thirty-eight thousand*); Tracy, *266 Days*, 8 (*downspouts*); Scharf and Westcott, *History of Philadelphia, 1609–1884*, 1: 339 (*Molesworth*), 343 (*invalids*); JA to Abigail Adams, Mar. 7, 1777, FOL (*"beetles"*); Larson, *The Trials of Allegiance*, 74 (*immense throng*); Reed, ed., *Life and Correspondence of Joseph Reed*, 2: 31–33 (*£50*); Allen, "Diary of James Allen," 287 (*loyalists stayed indoors*).

94   **New men-of-war stood:** Harris, *Brandywine*, 9 (*Old Swedes Church*); NDAR, 9: 277 (*"Frenchman born"*).

94   **The Pennsylvania assembly had passed a law:** Larson, *The Trials of Allegiance*, 76 (*renouncing allegiance*); Scharf and Westcott, *History of Philadelphia, 1609–1884*, 1: 343 (*Congress recommended*); Tracy, *266 Days*, 10; White, "Standing Armies in Time of War," diss., 230 (*"disposition inimical"*); Crane, ed., *The Diary of Elizabeth Drinker*, 63 (*"warm people"*); Allen, "Diary of James Allen," 293 (*"This civil war"*), 433 (*"Hard is the fate"*).

94   **Late in the morning Washington and his aides:** GW to John Hancock, Aug. 23, 1777, *PGW*, 11: 53n (*City Tavern*); GW, general orders, Aug. 23, 1777, FOL (*"not a woman"*); Taylor, *American Revolutions*, 201 (*"brows beady"*); Harris, *Brandywine*, 109 (*pontoon-and-plank*).

95   **Tomorrow the Continentals would march:** Godfrey, *The Commander-in-Chief's Guard*, 46 (*Wilmington*).

95   **None could be certain:** Pickering, *The Life of Timothy Pickering*, 153 (*"Having never been in action"*).

4. THINE ARROWS STICK FAST IN ME

96   **Omens had accumulated all summer:** Robertaccio, *Documents Relating to the Battle of Oriskany and the Siege of Fort Stanwix*, Utica, N.Y., Jan. 2013 (*$10*); Stone, *Life of Joseph Brant, Thayendanegea*, 1: 226 (*bullet in the back*); Bilharz, *Oriskany*, 40 (*men cutting sod*); Lowenthal,

ed., *Days of Siege*, 18 (*picking raspberries*); Glatthaar and Martin, *Forgotten Allies*, 156 (*Oneida scouts warned*).

96 **Only this forlorn outpost:** Gen. John Stanwix, who also built Fort Pitt in Pennsylvania, was lost at sea in 1766. "John Stanwix," NPS, https://www.nps.gov/people/general-john-stanwix .htm; author visit, Fort Stanwix, Sept. 29, 2021, signage (*slept sitting up*), details from Ranger Bill Sawyer (*Built for 400*).

97 **Colonel Peter Gansevoort:** Scott, *Fort Stanwix (Fort Schuyler) and Oriskany*, 90 (*tall, florid*); Glatthaar and Martin, *Forgotten Allies*, 151–52 (*worked tirelessly*); Stone, *The Campaign of Lieut. Gen. John Burgoyne*, 161–63 (*scraps of red cloth*); M. Willett to Horatio Gates, Aug. 1, 1777, NYHS, Horatio Gates papers, micro; Bilharz, *Oriskany*, 40 (*lead bullets*); author visit, Fort Stanwix, Sept. 29, 2021, signage (*"All my fear"*); Watt, *Rebellion in the Mohawk Valley*, 87 (*"I think myself as safe"*).

97 **At five p.m., as shadows stretched:** Willett, *A Narrative of the Military Actions of Colonel Marinus Willett*, 50; Robertaccio, *Documents Relating to the Battle of Oriskany and the Siege of Fort Stanwix*, 107 (*five bateaux*); Bilharz, *Oriskany*, 50.

97 **By Saturday morning Fort Stanwix:** author visit, Fort Stanwix, Sept. 29, 2021, signage; Berleth, *Bloody Mohawk*, 220 (*warriors*); CtS, 91 (*silver wheels*); Lowenthal, ed., *Days of Siege*, 28 (*bush to bush*); Robertaccio, *Documents Relating to the Battle of Oriskany and the Siege of Fort Stanwix*, 107 (*"horrid yelling"* and *killing one*).

97 **At three p.m. a British captain:** Luzader, *Saratoga*, 128; Watt, *Rebellion in the Mohawk Valley*, 130 (*"phrenzy"*).

97 **Here, then, was the other wing:** Bilharz, *Oriskany*, 50 (*sixteen-mile road*); Retzer and Barker, "The Hessen-Hanau Jägers," 35+ (*"tortured myself"* and *alder-leaf*).

98 **Brigadier General Barry St. Leger's orders:** BSC, 101 (*reach the Hudson*), 102 (*outpost in disrepair*), 185 (*"not to be imagined"*), 293 (*"most erroneous"*); Bilharz, *Oriskany*, 41–43; Boehlert, *The Battle of Oriskany and General Nicholas Herkimer*, 65 (*obsolete accounts*); author visit, Fort Stanwix, Sept. 29, 2021, signage (*paltry artillery*).

98 **St. Leger would have to rely:** Graymont, *The Iroquois in the American Revolution*, 120 (*"rum"*), 128 (*Great Peace*); Taylor, *The Divided Ground*, 96; author visit, Fort Stanwix, Sept. 29, 2021, signage (*Oneida and Tuscarora*).

98 **Perhaps St. Leger's most charismatic:** Jasanoff, *Liberty's Exiles*, 39 (*straddled two cultures*); Graymont, "Thayendanegea," *Dictionary of Canadian Biography*, vol. 5 (*"sprightly genius"*); Mintz, *Seeds of Empire*, 7 (*St. Mark*), 13–15 (*Boswell*); Graymont, *The Iroquois in the American Revolution*, 52–53; Taylor, *The Divided Ground*, 86 (*"conversed well"*).

100 **Now in his mid-thirties:** Taylor, *The Divided Ground*, 80 (*"lands & liberty"*); Watt, *Rebellion in the Mohawk Valley*, 134 (*eight hundred rebel militiamen*).

100 **After a quick conference, St. Leger detached:** author visit, Oriskany Battlefield State Historic Site, Sept. 29, 2021, signage; Boehlert, *The Battle of Oriskany and General Nicholas Herkimer*, 73 (*Place of Nettles*); Glatthaar and Martin, *Forgotten Allies*, 163–64 (*Cornplanter and Old Smoke*); Watt, *Rebellion in the Mohawk Valley*, 135 (*cold rations*); Retzer and Barker, "The Hessen-Hanau Jägers," 35+ (*"restrained"*).

100 **By midmorning on August 6:** Scott, *Fort Stanwix (Fort Schuyler) and Oriskany*, 205–8; author visit, Oriskany Battlefield State Historic Site, Sept. 29, 2021 (*purplestem aster*).

100 **They were led by a slender:** Siry, *Liberty's Fallen Generals*, 61–62; Scott, *Fort Stanwix (Fort Schuyler) and Oriskany*, 203 (*"every male person"*); Watt, *Rebellion in the Mohawk Valley*, 144 (*edge weapon*); Boehlert, *The Battle of Oriskany and General Nicholas Herkimer*, 17–18, 29, 37 (*rowed to church*); Bilharz, *Oriskany*, 55–56 (*Moneylending, portage services*).

101 **Herkimer preferred to speak German:** Berleth, *Bloody Mohawk*, 207 (*Dutch, French*); Scott, *Fort Stanwix (Fort Schuyler) and Oriskany*, 205 (*sixty Oneida warriors* and *"March on"*).

101 **The general and his vanguard:** Stone, *Life of Joseph Brant, Thayendanegea*, 1: 236 (*Two captains*); Berleth, *Bloody Mohawk*, 230 (*ball through the heart*); CtS, 98 (*ball clubs*); Robertaccio, *Documents Relating to the Battle of Oriskany and the Siege of Fort Stanwix*, 168 (*"Run, boys"*); Bilharz, *Oriskany*, 57 (*rear guard turned*); Retzer and Barker, "The Hessen-Hanau Jägers," 35+.

101 **Shouting orders in German:** Berleth, *Bloody Mohawk*, 231 (*six inches below*); Boehlert, *The Battle of Oriskany and General Nicholas Herkimer*, 93 (*tibia and fibula*).

102 **Fathers and sons died together:** Scott, *Fort Stanwix (Fort Schuyler) and Oriskany*, 220–21 (*muddy drinking water*).

102 **An abrupt, violent thunderstorm:** author visit, Oriskany Battlefield State Historic Site, Sept. 29, 2021, signage; Boehlert, *The Battle of Oriskany and General Nicholas Herkimer*, 92–96; Berleth, *Bloody Mohawk*, 231 (*canteens*).

102 **The butcher's bill was appalling:** Watt, *Rebellion in the Mohawk Valley*, 317–20; Mintz, *Seeds of Empire*, 36; Scott, *Fort Stanwix (Fort Schuyler) and Oriskany*, 225–27; Glatthaar and Martin, *Forgotten Allies*, 168; Berleth, *Bloody Mohawk*, 238 (*Seneca gauntlet*); author visit, Oriskany Battlefield State Historic Site, Sept. 29, 2021, signage (*"great mourning"*).

102 **The king's losses included:** Mintz, *Seeds of Empire*, 36 (*nine chiefs*); Stone, *The Campaign of Lieut. Gen. John Burgoyne*, 186–91; Bilharz, *Oriskany*, 63; Berleth, *Bloody Mohawk*, 206 (*"street brawler"*), 237; Retzer and Barker, "The Hessen-Hanau Jägers," 35+ (*"four to eight scalps"*); Werther, "Marinus Willett: The Exploits of an Unheralded War Hero," *JAR*, Sept. 20, 2022; author visit, Fort Stanwix, Sept. 29, 2021, signage (*twenty-one wagonloads*); Scott, *Fort Stanwix (Fort Schuyler) and Oriskany*, 188, 196 (*deerskins, brass kettles*); Lowenthal, ed., *Days of Siege*, 331 (*scalps believed*). Other estimates of Indian dead ran to nearly eighty.

103 **A final casualty from Oriskany:** Boehlert, *The Battle of Oriskany and General Nicholas Herkimer*, 122 (*thirty drops*).

103 **St. Leger resumed his siege:** Scott, *Fort Stanwix (Fort Schuyler) and Oriskany*, 238–39 (*candlelit dining room*), 247 (*"not the least effect"*); Watt, *Rebellion in the Mohawk Valley*, 133–34 (*"apples that children"*); Willett, *A Narrative of the Military Actions of Colonel Marinus Willett*, 50 (*wine, cheese*); Stone, *Life of Joseph Brant, Thayendanegea*, 1: 254 (*"blood will be on your head"*); Robertaccio, *Documents Relating to the Battle of Oriskany and the Siege of Fort Stanwix*, 65 (*enraged Indians*).

103 **By August 15, 137 cannonballs:** *CtS*, 107–9 (*"loudly scold"*); Lowenthal, ed., *Days of Siege*, 37 (*provisions shifted*), 39 (*two wells*); Bilharz, *Oriskany*, 64–65 (*siege trench*).

103 **The garrison's predicament had not gone:** Martin, *Benedict Arnold, Revolutionary Hero*, 363–64 (*Arnold volunteered*).

103 **Arnold was aware of the Oriskany calamity:** Wallace, *Traitorous Hero*, 124 (*five new major generals*); GW to R. H. Lee, Mar. 6, 1777, *PGW*, 8: 523 (*"spirited and sensible"*); GW to BA, Apr. 2, 1777, *PGW*, 9: 45–46 (*"strange mode"*); BA to GW, Mar. 26, 1777, FOL; BA to GW, Mar. 11, 1777, FOL.

104 **He quit, but held his resignation:** Malcolm, *The Tragedy of Benedict Arnold*, 182–84; BA to H. Gates, Aug. 21, 1777, in Lea, *A Hero and a Spy*, 253 (*"or no more"*).

104 **With militia reinforcements:** *CtS*, 143 (*fifteen hundred*); Bilharz, *Oriskany*, 65–66 (*"misty-minded"*); Watt, *Rebellion in the Mohawk Valley*, 243 (*clemency deal*).

104 **At dawn on Friday, August 22:** Glatthaar and Martin, *Forgotten Allies*, 175 (*panting Oneidas*).

104 **Weary of the ineffectual siege:** Retzer and Barker, "The Hessen-Hanau Jägers," 35+ (*"like cattle"*); *CtS*, 143–45 (*"huts and tents"*); Martin, *Benedict Arnold, Revolutionary Hero*, 366.

104 **A British deserter told Gansevoort:** *CtS*, 143 (*"great precipitation"*); Watt, *Rebellion in the Mohawk Valley*, 253 (*Indians dining*), 258–59 (*milch cows*).

105 **Informed by Gansevoort of the enemy's flight:** Scott, *Fort Stanwix (Fort Schuyler) and Oriskany*, 290 (*"I am at a loss"*); *CtS*, 146; Watt, *Rebellion in the Mohawk Valley*, 259 (*"dead had not been buried"*).

105 **Arnold's arrival at Stanwix:** Lowenthal, ed., *Days of Siege*, 51–52 (*thirteen cannons*); Bilharz, *Oriskany*, 64 (*"banditti of robbers"*).

105 **American sovereignty on the Mohawk:** Graymont, *The Iroquois in the American Revolution*, 148–49 (*Church of England chapel*); Taylor, *The Divided Ground*, 93 (*fled to Canada*).

105 **The Canada Army remained fifty miles north:** *BSC*, 313 (*"seventeen different nations"*); *CtS*, 112 (*nearly a month*).

106 **"It was often necessary":** *BSC*, 298; Bowler, *Logistics and the Failure of the British Army in America, 1775–1783*, 229–30 (*"mismanagement"*).

106 **A partial solution to the army's woes:** BSC, 299; Gabriel, *The Battle of Bennington*, 18; "Diary of the Brunswick Troops in North America," HDAR, fiche 180–93, letter HZ-5, 262 (*more than a thousand mounts*); Ketchum, *Saratoga*, 295–96 (*from corporal*); CtS, 119 ("*Lieutenant Colonel Baume*").

106 **Rather than heading northeast toward Manchester:** BSC, 304 ("*easy to surprise*"); Arndt, "New Hampshire and the Battle of Bennington," 198+; Luzader, *Saratoga*, 97; CtS, 115 (*a diversion*); author visit, BBSHS, Sept. 24, 2021, with ES; "Diary of the Brunswick Troops in North America," HDAR, fiche 180–93, letter HZ-5, 265.

106 **Riedesel, returning from an inspection trip:** "Diary of the Brunswick Troops in North America," HDAR, fiche 180–93, letter HZ-5, 265 ("*much astonished*"); Stone, ed., *Memoirs, and Letters and Journals of Major General Riedesel*, 129 ("*too great a distance*").

107 **Burgoyne brushed aside:** BSC, 299–300 ("*not to incur the danger*"); Arndt, "New Hampshire and the Battle of Bennington," 198+ ("*must be tied together*" and "*distinguish the good subjects*").

107 **On Wednesday, August 13, the expedition:** Lord, *War over Walloomscoick*, 27 ("*one-rod road*"); Mackesy, *The War for America, 1775–1783*, 133–34 (*saber scabbards*); Lynn, ed., *An Eyewitness Account of the American Revolution and New England Life*, 69 (*pumpkins*); BSC, 95 (*bells*); Hadden, *A Journal Kept in Canada and upon Burgoyne's Campaigns in 1776 and 1777*, 132 (*white paper strips*).

107 **Gallopers crisscrossed the countryside:** Spooner and Lansing, "Baum's Raid," 45+ ("*Prepare yourselves*"); Lord, *War over Walloomscoick*, 120 (*household duffle*); Gabriel, *The Battle of Bennington*, 87 ("*flight on horseback*").

107 **Burgoyne had apparently forgotten:** Corbett, *No Turning Point*, 201–2.

108 **John Stark and his New Hampshire regiment:** Kidder, *History of the First New Hampshire Regiment in the War of the Revolution*, 20–21 (*resigned*); Stark, *Memoir and Official Correspondence of Gen. John Stark*, 255 ("*noble disposition*"); Ketchum, *Saratoga*, 287 (*walked out of church*); Burns, "Massacre or Muster?," 133+ (*Tobago rum*).

108 **Just shy of forty-nine:** Stark, *Memoir and Official Correspondence of Gen. John Stark*, 11–14 (*torture by Indians*), 131n (*Charles XII*), 278 ("*quitted the army*"); Philbrick, *Valiant Ambition*, 133 ("*Stark chooses*"); Mattern, *Benjamin Lincoln and the American Revolution*, 44 ("*exceedingly soured*").

108 **Schuyler was shrewd enough:** Ketchum, *Saratoga*, 298 ("*private resentment*"); Arndt, "New Hampshire and the Battle of Bennington," 198+ (*repositioned his brigade*); Lunt, *John Burgoyne of Saratoga*, 198 (*flax shirts*), author visit, BBSHS, Sept. 24, 2021, with ES; CtS, 117 ("*make discoveries*") and (*lead bullets*); Arndt, "New Hampshire and the Battle of Bennington," 198+.

110 **Baum himself arrived in Cambridge:** "A Journal of Carleton's and Burgoyne's Campaigns," 2: 307+ ("*careful on my approach*"); Lord, *War over Walloomscoick*, 7 ("*head of a barrel*").

110 **Baum edged forward on Thursday, August 14:** Lord, *War over Walloomscoick*, 7 ("*very fine flour*"); author visit, BBSHS, Sept. 24, 2021, with ES.

110 **At noon the invaders reached:** Lord, *War over Walloomscoick*, 7.

110 **Still on the New York side of the border:** Lord, *War over Walloomscoick*, 47–48, 60–64 (*talus*); author visit, BBSHS, Sept. 24, 2021, signage ("*perfectly safe*"); Stark, *Memoir and Official Correspondence of Gen. John Stark*, 58 ("*enemy's temper*").

111 **Baum's men spent a wet, miserable night:** "Account of the Battle of Bennington, by Glich, a German Officer," 211+ ("*sense of impending danger*"); Lynn, ed., *An Eyewitness Account of the American Revolution and New England Life*, 71 ("*If this continues*").

111 **More militiamen had arrived:** Lord, *War over Walloomscoick*, 10 (*three-to-one advantage*); Ketchum, *Saratoga*, 303–4 (*pails of water*).

111 **From his command post on a hillside:** Stark, *Memoir and Official Correspondence of Gen. John Stark*, 61 (*abandoning their lines*); Gabriel, *The Battle of Bennington*, 22–25; "Diary of the Brunswick Troops in North America," HDAR, fiche 180–93, letter HZ-5, 269–71 (*distinguish the good Americans*).

111 **Two musket shots in rapid succession:** Dann, ed., *The Revolution Remembered*, 89; author

visit, BBSHS, Sept. 24, 2021, signage (*husks in their hats*); *CtS*, 125 (*"Our officers said"*), 127 (*"scattered"*).

112 **If brief, the assault was nasty:** Lord, *War over Walloomscoick*, 57–58 (*"turned by the bone"*); "Col. John Peters Autobiography used in his application for relief to the British government," June 5, 1786, https://www.uelac.org/Loyalist-Info/extras/Peters-John/John-Peters -bio-application-for-relief.pdf; "A Narrative of John Peters," Primary Sources Battle of Bennington, https://parks.ny.gov/documents/historic-sites/BenningtonBattlefieldLoyalist Sources.pdf.

112 **On Hessian Hill, the flankers:** author visit, BBSHS, Sept. 24, 2021, signage; "Account of the Battle of Bennington, by Glich, a German Officer," 211+ (*"sudden tramping"*); Dann, ed., *The Revolution Remembered*, 89 (*"The battle became general"*).

112 **One of the German 3-pounders:** Adrian B. Caruana, "Tin Case-Shot or Canister Shot in the 18th Century," https://www.militaryheritage.com/caseshot.htm; author visit, BBSHS, Sept. 24, 2021, with ES (*eighty yards* and *fight from horseback*); *CtS*, 123 (*ten rounds*); Lynn, ed., *An Eyewitness Account of the American Revolution and New England Life*, 71 (*"bullets went through"*).

112 **As the battle intensified:** "Account of the Battle of Bennington, by Glich, a German Officer," 211+ (*defenses seemed thinnest*); Luzader, *Saratoga*, 107; Weddle, *The Compleat Victory*, 248 (*"The bayonet, the butt"*); Cubbison, *"The Artillery Never Gained More Honour"* (*wounded above the eye*); Ketchum, *Saratoga*, 309 (*"no regular battle"*); Lord, *War over Walloomscoick*, 67 (*"I prayed the Lord"*); Lynn, ed., *An Eyewitness Account of the American Revolution and New England Life*, 72 (*"bullets were dreadful"*).

113 **Almost two hours into the battle:** *CtS*, 129 (*Stark advancing*); *BSC*, 311 (*draw their swords*); Lord, *War over Walloomscoick*, 70 (*swept downstream*); author visit, BBSHS, Sept. 24, 2021, with ES; Lynn, ed., *An Eyewitness Account of the American Revolution and New England Life*, 73 (*"completely naked"*).

113 **No sooner had the shooting ebbed:** *BSC*, 305 (*half a mile an hour*); *CtS*, 133 (*pair of 6-pounders*); Stone, ed., *Memoirs, and Letters and Journals of Major General Riedesel*, 256–59 (*greeted on the road*); Gabriel, *The Battle of Bennington*, 68 (*neglected to mention*).

113 **As the column plodded forward:** Ketchum, *Saratoga*, 315–16 (*white feathers*).

113 **I perceived a considerable number:** *BSC*, 307.

113 **Skene's horse fell dead:** *BSC*, 97; Dann, ed., *The Revolution Remembered*, 90–91; Stark, *Memoir and Official Correspondence of Gen. John Stark*, 130 (*"hottest engagement"*); Gabriel, *The Battle of Bennington*, 60 (*"flock of sheep"*), 62 (*"too hot to hold"* and *"fight on"*).

114 **Breymann had closed to within ninety yards:** author visit, BBSHS, Sept. 24, 2021, signage (*"with all speed"*); Ketchum, *Saratoga*, 317–18; Gabriel, *The Battle of Bennington*, 73 (*muzzle flashes*); *CtS*, 133–35.

114 **Surviving German gunners began creeping:** Stone, ed., *Memoirs, and Letters and Journals of Major General Riedesel*, 257 (*"horses either were dead"*); author visit, BBSHS, Sept. 24, 2021, signage (*slashed the traces*).

114 **Abandoning the cannons and their eight brass drums:** Pettengill, trans., *Letters from America, 1776–1779*, 91 (*flesh wound*); Arndt, "New Hampshire and the Battle of Bennington," 198+ (*"pursued them till dark"*); Ketchum, *Saratoga*, 318–19 (*"one hour longer"*); *BSC*, 307 (*Cambridge at midnight*).

114 **The Americans had won:** *BSC*, 98–99 (*undisputed*); Hamilton, *The Revolutionary War Lives and Letters of Lucy and Henry Knox*, 122 (*"bells were rung"*); Luzader, *Saratoga*, 113 (*belatedly reward*).

114 **Yet it was the small domestic stories:** Gabriel, *The Battle of Bennington*, 86 (*"very melancholy"* and *"Loving wife"*).

115 **More than half a century later:** Gabriel, *The Battle of Bennington*, 90 (*"crying for joy"*); "A Narrative of John Peters," Primary Sources Battle of Bennington, https://parks.ny.gov/ documents/historic-sites/BenningtonBattlefieldLoyalistSources.pdf; "Col. John Peters Autobiography used in his application for relief to the British government," June 5, 1786,

https://www.uelac.org/Loyalist-Info/extras/Peters-John/John-Peters-bio-application-for
-relief.pdf.

115 **Burgoyne would need them promptly:** Gabriel, *The Battle of Bennington*, 28; author visit, BBSHS, Sept. 24, 2021, signage (*207 dead*); Weddle, *The Compleat Victory*, 250–51 (*70 percent*); Strach, "A Memoir of the Exploits of Captain Alexander Fraser and His Company of British Marksmen, 1776–1777," part 2, 164+ (*all but exterminated*); CtS, 137 (*nine hundred swords*); Arndt, "New Hampshire and the Battle of Bennington," 198+ (*"caused us much damage"*).

115 **The battle's aftermath held the usual horror:** Ketchum, *Saratoga*, 324 (*"broken legs"*); Bolton, *The Private Soldier Under Washington*, 215 (*"with his left eye shot out"*); Scheer and Rankin, *Rebels and Redcoats*, 266 (*"dead in the woods"*).

116 **Women on the streets of Bennington:** Stark, *Memoir and Official Correspondence of Gen. John Stark*, 64; Spooner and Lansing, "Baum's Raid," 45+ (*two by two*); M'Alpine, *Genuine Narratives and Concise Memoirs*, 39 (*"tribes of vermin"*); Arndt, "New Hampshire and the Battle of Bennington," 198+; Lynn, ed., *An Eyewitness Account of the American Revolution and New England Life*, 74 (*fire through the door*).

116 **At three a.m. on August 17 couriers arrived:** Stone, ed., *Memoirs, and Letters and Journals of Major General Riedesel*, 130–33; Lunt, *John Burgoyne of Saratoga*, 202 (*new headquarters*).

116 **"Colonel Baum was induced to proceed":** Stone, ed., *Memoirs, and Letters and Journals of Major General Riedesel*, 272 (*"Breymann was very slow"*); BSC, 300, 301 (*"more than double to ours"*).

116 **In general orders, Burgoyne advised his troops:** Stanley, *For Want of a Horse*, 134 (*"chances of war"*); "Diary of the Brunswick Troops in North America," HDAR, fiche 180–93, letter HZ-5, 274 (*remaining on the Hudson*); Lynn, ed., *The Specht Journal*, 70 (*Madras*); Pettengill, trans., *Letters from America, 1776–1779*, 98–99 (*"pork at noon"*).

116 **Still, their objective lay near:** Pancake, *1777*, 139 (*"move on toward Albany"*).

117 **But his orders were clear:** De Fonblanque, *Political and Military Episodes . . . from the Life and Correspondence of the Right Hon. John Burgoyne*, 275 (*"force a junction"* and *"not at liberty"*).

5. A BARBAROUS BUSINESS IN A BARBAROUS COUNTRY

118 **The great British fleet:** Moomaw, "The Naval Career of Captain Hamond, 1775–1779," diss., 335–36 (*fair wind*); Harris, *Brandywine*, 98 (*a month on their ships*).

118 **"The weather is insufferably hot":** Whinyates, ed., *The Services of Lieut.-Colonel Francis Downman, R.A.*, 27; Tatum, *The American Journal of Ambrose Serle*, 244 (*"suffocating heat"*); Burgoyne, trans. and ed., *Diaries of Two Ansbach Jaegers*, 12 (*"misery and misfortune"*), 13 (*dozen cannonballs*).

118 **Where the bay was wide:** Tatum, ed., *The American Journal of Ambrose Serle*, 242 (*loamy whiffs*); Ewald, *Diary of the American War*, 74 (*Swans and sea eagles*); R. Howe to Admiralty, Aug. 28, 1777, UK NA, ADM 1/487, f 430 (*pilot vessels*); Laughton, ed., *The Naval Miscellany*, 1: 140 (*two cable lengths*); Eller, ed., *Chesapeake Bay in the American Revolution*, 364 (*only by day*); Miller, *Sea of Glory*, 242 (*Nine frigates*); Beatson, *Naval and Military Memoirs of Great Britain*, 6: 255 (*James River brig*).

119 **Thunderstorms "as has never been seen":** Harris, *Brandywine*, 105; Burgoyne, ed., *The Hesse-Cassel Mirbach Regiment in the American Revolution*, 80 (*"frightful thunder and lightning"*); Ewald, *Diary of the American War*, 72–74 (*ship's carpenter*); Münchhausen, *At General Howe's Side*, 23–24 (*igniting fires*); master's log, *Isis*, Aug. 24, 1777, UK NA, ADM 52/1809 (*burned the shrouds*); R. Howe to Admiralty, Aug. 28, 1777, UK NA, ADM 1/487, f 430 (*Isis limped*).

119 **Between tempests, some officers enjoyed:** L. Cliffe to brother, Oct. 24, 1777, Loftus Cliffe papers, WLC, box 1 (*"most beautiful bay"*); H. Strachey to Jane Strachey, Sept. 1, 1777, Henry Strachey papers, WLC, box 1 (*"healthy and merry"*).

119 **Alarm guns and signal fires:** Münchhausen, *At General Howe's Side*, 24 (*sell melons*); Burdick, *I Remain Your Friend*, 25 (*"mills useless"*), 32–33 (*Book of Sufferings*); Whinyates, ed., *The Services of Lieut.-Colonel Francis Downman, R.A.*, 28 (*"severe thrashing"*).

119 **If the voyage was hard on men:** Stevens, *On the Stowage of Ships and Their Cargoes*, 105 (*vin-*

egar); Curtis, *The Organization of the British Army in the American Revolution*, 126–27 (*heaved overboard*); JA to Abigail Adams, Aug. 29, 1777, FOL (*carcasses*); Uhlendorf, trans. and annot., *Revolution in America*, 98 (*170 horses*). Another German officer put the number of dead horses at four hundred (Harris, *Brandywine*, 116).

120 **The commanding general was often seasick:** H. Strachey to Jane Strachey, Sept. 1 and Oct. 27, 1777, Henry Strachey papers, WLC, box 1 (*"wooden cage"* and *"finished this year"*); *Report on the Manuscripts of Mrs. Stopford-Sackville*, 2: 66–67 (*"great degree diminished"*).

120 **Beginning at five a.m. on August 23:** Whinyates, ed., *The Services of Lieut.-Colonel Francis Downman, R.A.*, 29 (*admiral personally*); NDAR, 9: 810 (*hoisted his flag*); Taaffe, *The Philadelphia Campaign, 1777–1778*, 53 (*Turkey Point*); Ewald, *Diary of the American War*, 75 (*"boisterous shouts"*).

120 **Few residents could be found:** McGuire, *The Philadelphia Campaign*, 1: 135 (*"The women fled"*); Risch, *Supplying Washington's Army*, 208 (*Army storehouses*); Wilkin, *Some British Soldiers in America*, 227 (*hundred butts*); Taaffe, *The Philadelphia Campaign, 1777–1778*, 54 (*grain, sugar, and indigo*).

122 **Tents had been left aboard the ships:** Ewald, *Diary of the American War*, 78; McGuire, *The Philadelphia Campaign*, 1: 135–36 (*sixteen thousand cartridges*); Wilkin, *Some British Soldiers in America*, 228 (*"lived like beasts"*).

122 **Yet for all the hardships:** Hagist, *Noble Volunteers*, 112 (*"stroller, vagabond"*). See also Rick Atkinson, "Foreword," in Hagist, *Noble Volunteers*, xi–xiii.

122 **About half the enlisted troops:** Hagist, *Noble Volunteers*, 259 (*"glory of victory"*); Reid, *British Redcoat, 1740–1793*, 22 (*"master of his person"*); Curtis, *The British Army in the American Revolution*, 24–26 (*bought and sold*).

122 **Howe was determined to punish:** Tatum, *The American Journal of Ambrose Serle*, 246 (*"The Hessians are more infamous"*); Kemble, *The Kemble Papers*, 1: 483 (*five hundred lashes*); Stuart-Wortley, ed., *A Prime Minister and His Son*, 116 (*"irregularity"*); Hagist, *Noble Volunteers*, ms. (*"some lurking rebels"*); Gruber, ed., *John Peebles' American War, 1776–1782*, 129 (*"plunder on their backs"*); "André Memorial on Plundering," WBW, 1779 (*"lost two hundred men"*); McGuire, *The Philadelphia Campaign*, 1: 147–48 (*"barbarous"*).

123 **On Wednesday, September 3, the army:** Taaffe, *The Philadelphia Campaign, 1777–1778*, 55; L. Cliffe to brother, Oct. 24, 1777, Loftus Cliffe papers, WLC, box 1 (*two shirts*).

123 **Summer was gone:** Mowday, *September 11, 1777*, 17–19; Huth, "Letters from a Hessian Mercenary," 488+ (*"outcome will show"*).

123 **After a short, sharp scrap:** McGuire, *The Philadelphia Campaign*, 1: 140 (*leather aprons*); Montrésor and Scull, "Journal of Captain John Montrésor," 393+ (*"roads heavy"*); Lodge, ed., *Major André's Journal*, n.p. (*confiscate more livestock*); Burdick, *Revolutionary Delaware*, 77 (*amnesty offers*); Harris, *Brandywine*, 127 (*"neither friend nor foe"*).

123 **Howe soon recognized that he had:** Lodge, ed., *Major André's Journal*, n.p. (*"free and general pardon"*); *Report on the Manuscripts of Mrs. Stopford-Sackville*, 2: 75 (*"strongly in enmity"*); W. Howe to Germain, Aug. 30, 1777, GSG, vol. 6 (*"finished in time"*).

124 **For the moment the task:** Münchhausen, *At General Howe's Side*, 26 (*"this war"*).

124 **The elusive General Washington had spent:** Ecelbarger, "Washington's Head of Elk Reconnaissance," *JAR*, Apr. 16, 2020 (*Quaker Hill*); Harris, *Brandywine*, 119; "Now See Here," *MHQ*, 64 (*three-draw mahogany-and-brass*).

124 **Washington's army had nearly doubled:** Harris and Ecelbarger, "The Numerical Strength of George Washington's Army During the 1777 Philadelphia Campaign," *JAR*, Oct. 5, 2021; Lengel, *General George Washington*, 223–24 (*disappointed by the militia*); GW to John Dockery Thompson, Aug. 28, 1777, *PGW*, 11: 87n (*"all the rifles"*); Jameson, *The American Revolution Considered as a Social Movement*, 57 (Book of Martyrs); Leonard, "Paper as a Critical Commodity During the American Revolution," 488+ (*"literary ammunition"*).

124 **When the king's men began to move:** Lengel, *General George Washington*, 226; GW to William Maxwell, Sept. 2 and 3, 1777, FOL (*"how and where they lie"*); NG to Caty Greene, Sept. 10, 1777, *PNG*, 2: 155–56 (*"most distressing"*); GW, general orders, Sept. 5, 1777, *PGW*, 11: 147 (*"utterly undone"*).

125 **Howe refused, for the moment:** Harris, *Brandywine*, 143 (*"sedition & Presbyterian sermons"*), 147 (*Chads's*). The ford has had a variety of spellings, including "Chadds" in the twenty-first century.

125 **This rugged, vertical ground in Chester County:** Ashmead, *History of Delaware County, Pennsylvania*, 56 (*"amazing strong country"*); Robert Hanson Harrison to John Hancock, Sept. 10, 1777, *PGW*, 11: 182n; Walker, *Engineers of Independence*, 155 (*Continental geographer*); author visit, "Battle of Brandywine Driving Tour," July 10, 2021; Battle of Brandywine editorial note, *PGW*, 11: 187–93 (*twelve miles above Buffington's*).

125 **This was incorrect, but Washington:** Harris, *Brandywine*, 209, 448–49 (*seven hundred were mounted*).

126 **Washington placed his headquarters:** author visit, Benjamin Ring house and Gideon Gilpin house, Brandywine battlefield, July 10, 2021; https://www.mountvernon.org/preservation/collections-holdings/browse-the-museum-collections/object/w-473/#- (*long camp bed*); GW, general orders, Sept. 10, 1777, *PGW*, 11: 180; Robert Hanson Harrison to John Hancock, Sept. 10, 1777, *PGW*, 11: 182.

126 **Late in the afternoon of Wednesday, September 10:** Joab Trout, "A Sermon," broadside, LOC, https://www.loc.gov/resource/rbpe.17700300/; Mowday, *September 11, 1777*, 75–78 (*"doom of the British"*).

126 **Apples and peaches now ready:** Harris, *Brandywine*, 147–49 (*wood ash* and *Quakers*); McGuire, *The Philadelphia Campaign*, 1: 169 (*baking day*); Mowday, *September 11, 1777*, 54 (*expelled*); NG to Caty Greene, Sept. 14, 1777, *PNG*, 2: 163.

127 **Greene's division, the largest in the Continental Army:** Harris, *Brandywine*, 206; "The Battle of Brandywine," *PGW*, ed. note, 11: 187; author visit, Brandywine, July 10, 2021.

127 **Washington's right wing had been entrusted:** Pearce, ed., "Sullivan's Expedition to Staten Island in 1777," 167+ (*"insulting spectators"*); GW to John Hancock, June 17, 1776, FOL (*"foibles"*); Billias, ed., *George Washington's Generals and Opponents*, 152 (*"darts"*); J. Sullivan to GW, Aug. 7, 1777, *PGW*, 10: 547 (*"recover"*); GW to J. Sullivan, Mar. 15, 1777, *PGW*, 8: 580 (*"imaginary slights"*).

128 **A skeptical Dr. Benjamin Rush:** Nelson, *William Alexander, Lord Stirling*, 121 (*"weak, vain"*); Harris, *Brandywine*, 207–8 (*Brinton's Ford*).

128 **General Howe had placed his command post:** Harris, *Brandywine*, 217 (*twenty guineas*); Ewald, *Diary of the American War*, 83 (*captured Continentals*).

128 **At six a.m., General Knyphausen surged east:** Moss, "Patrick Ferguson and His Rifle," *JAR*, Dec. 13, 2018 (*British riflemen*); Lengel, *General George Washington*, 231–32.

128 **The weight of numbers soon told:** Dann, ed., *The Nagle Journal*, xvii, 6–7 (*"make them resolute"*); Harris, *Brandywine*, 237–39 (*cannon roars*).

128 **The Americans had reason to be pleased:** McGuire, *The Philadelphia Campaign*, 1: 175–76 (*six highly accurate rounds*); Peckham, ed., *Sources of American Independence*, 2: 287–89; Moss, "Patrick Ferguson and His Rifle," *JAR*, Dec. 13, 2018; Harris, *Brandywine*, 244; Wilkin, *Some British Soldiers in America*, 152–54.

128 **Still, Washington sat his horse:** Harris, *Brandywine*, 248 (*"merely to amuse"*).

129 **William Howe would not need:** Lengel, *General George Washington*, 231–33 (*eighty-two hundred men*).

129 **As the morning slipped past:** Harris, *Brandywine*, 247 (*"no enemy there"*); "The Battle of Brandywine," *PGW*, ed. note, 11: 187; GW to Theodorick Bland, Sept. 11, 1777, *PGW*, 11: 197 (*"earnestly entreat"*).

129 **Yet nothing was certain:** James Ross to GW, Sept. 11, 1777, *PGW*, 11: 196 (*"We are close"*); Harris, *Brandywine*, 255–56 (*sudden counterattack*); Sullivan to GW, Sept. 11, 1777, *PGW*, 11: 197 (*"heard nothing"*); McGuire, *The Philadelphia Campaign*, 1: 193 (*doubling back*).

130 **Howe had no such trickery in mind:** author visit, "Battle of Brandywine Driving Tour," July 10, 2021; Ewald, *Treatise on Partisan Warfare*, 1–2 (*left eye*); Fuller, *British Light Infantry in the Eighteenth Century*, 144 (*"Demoralize"*), 149 (*"fully secure"*); Ewald, *Diary of the American War*, 84 (*"A hundred men"*).

130 **As lathered teams pulled:** McGuire, *The Philadelphia Campaign*, 1: 199 (*twelve miles in eight*

hours); Harris, *Brandywine*, 269 (*"cheerful countenance"*); author visit, Birmingham Meeting House, Brandywine, July 10, 2021; Wildes, *Anthony Wayne*, 120–21 (*"much confusion"*).

130 **While many of his neighbors scattered:** Townsend, *Some Account of the British Army*, 21–25 (*"bright as silver"*).

131 **Washington had returned to his headquarters:** Theodorick Bland to GW, Sept. 11, 1777, *PGW*, 11: 198 (*"I have discovered"*); John Sullivan to GW, Sept. 11, 1777, *PGW*, 11: 198 (*"in the rear"*); Lengel, *General George Washington*, 236 (*uproar*); McGuire, *Battle of Paoli*, 14 (*"more surprised"*).

131 **His Excellency ordered his reserve divisions:** Harris, *Brandywine*, 268 (*"clouds of dust"*); McGuire, *The Philadelphia Campaign*, 1: 198–99 (*"I neither knew where"*).

131 **As regiments arrived from the Brandywine:** Harris, *Brandywine*, 275–76; McGuire, *The Philadelphia Campaign*, 1: 212 (*"final argument"*).

131 **And then the king's men were on them:** Harris, *Brandywine*, 267 (*Three columns*); McGuire, *The Philadelphia Campaign*, 1: 203 (*"scarlet clothing"*); Holmes, *Redcoat*, 4 (*brick dust*).

132 **A blood-smeared Dr. Rush:** Fried, *Rush*, 217 (*large pit*), 218 (*"heaviest firing"*); "Revolutionary Services of Captain John Markland," 102+ (*canteens*).

132 **The 170 men in the 3rd Virginia:** Smith: *John Marshall*, 58–60 (*"utter ruin"*); Dunkerly, *Decision at Brandywine*, 38–40; Lee, *Memoirs of the War of the Southern Department of the United States*, 1: 16 (*two bullets in his horse*).

132 **Scorching American fire forced:** Hagist, *Noble Volunteers*, ms. (*"learned from the rebels"*); Ewald, *Diary of the American War*, 85 (*"waved to me"*).

132 **Howe saw the same enemy disposition:** Harris, *Brandywine*, 273 (*nine thousand troops*), 283–84 (*"grand and noble sight"*); Urban, *Fusiliers*, 118 (*"Put on your caps"*); Wilkin, *Some British Soldiers in America*, 231 (*"three minutes of rapture"*).

134 **"The infantry that can load the fastest":** Stephenson, *Patriot Battles*, 128; Clay, *Staff Ride Handbook for the Saratoga Campaign*, 32 (*a third of battle casualties*); Hagist, *Noble Volunteers*, ms. (*quick and violent*); Simcoe, *A Journal of the Operations of the Queen's Rangers*, 60–63 (*"attention of his opponent"*); Spring, *With Zeal and with Bayonets Only*, 148–49 (*"English gallop"*); Harris, *Brandywine*, 295; McGuire, *The Philadelphia Campaign*, 1: 207 (*brass mitre caps*).

134 **"Now the battle began":** Brooks and Lear, "Extracts from the Journal of Surgeon Ebenezer Elmer of the New Jersey Continental Line," 103+; Holmes, *Redcoat*, 243 (*"first graze"*).

134 **When the enemy drew closer:** McGuire, *The Philadelphia Campaign*, 1: 226 (*grapeshot*), 235 (*"through Captain Stout"*); Harris, *Brandywine*, 286 (*"Cannons roaring"*); St. George, "The Actions at Brandywine and Paoli, Described by a British Officer," 368+ (*"most infernal fire"*).

134 **General Sullivan and his two Maryland brigades:** Harris, *Brandywine*, 273 (*fifty-three hundred men*), 288 (*Sullivan realized*); Anderson, *Personal Recollections of Captain Enoch Anderson*, 37 (*"word was again given"*).

135 **Sullivan's left proved even more:** Tacyn, "To the End," diss., 139–40 (*spraying the Marylanders*); Harris, *Brandywine*, 291–92 (*"We were in confusion"*); Mowday, *September 11, 1777*, 122–23 (*"in front and flank"*); McGuire, *The Philadelphia Campaign*, 1: 242 (*caromed among the branches*).

135 **The collapse of the American left:** McGuire, *The Philadelphia Campaign*, 1: 234 (*"the warmest"*); Harris, *Brandywine*, 312–14 (*"muzzle to muzzle"*); Hughes, *Firepower*, 27 (*fifteen hundred rounds*); *The British Military Library*, 1: 218, 308 (*"flutterings"*).

135 **Men fell, rose, and fell again:** Harris, *Brandywine*, 314 (*broke a collarbone*); author visit, Birmingham Hill, Brandywine, signage, July 10, 2021; Dunkerly, *Decision at Brandywine*, 55 (*Private John Francis*), 60, 74 (*upper teeth*).

136 **Despite Stirling's shouted encouragement:** Anderson, *Personal Recollections of Captain Enoch Anderson*, 37 (*"whipping and spurring"*); Mowday, *September 11, 1777*, 132 (*"broke and rallied"*); Lender and Martin, eds., *Citizen Soldier*, 127 (*"I was wounded"*); Ward, *Charles Scott and the "Spirit of '76,"* 36 (*streamed south*); Astronomical Applications Dept., U.S. Naval Observatory, https://aa.usno.navy.mil/data/RS_OneYear; Clark, "Diary of Joseph Clark, Attached to the Continental Army," 93+ (*"filled with smoke"*).

136 **Battered but not yet beaten:** author visit, Sandy Hollow, July 10, 2021; Unger, *Lafayette*, 43 (*sound of the guns*); Harris, *Brandywine*, 309–11 (*"dismounted and did his utmost"*).

136 **But more retreating men stumbled:** *LiA*, 2: 45 (*within twenty yards*); Harris, *Brandywine*, 309–11 (*"Confusion became extreme"*); *LAAR*, 1: 101 (*blood filled his boot*).

136 **Washington arrived at a gallop:** author visit, Birmingham Hill, signage, July 10, 2021; Lengel, *General George Washington*, 239 (*right wing collapse*); "The Battle of Brandywine," *PGW*, ed. note, 11: 187.

137 **Dusk began to sift over the landscape:** Ward, *Charles Scott and the "Spirit of '76,"* 37 (*formed a wedge*); Harris, *Brandywine*, 352–53; McGuire, *The Philadelphia Campaign*, 1: 255–57.

137 **"We had no sooner reached the hill":** Harris, *Brandywine*, 356; McGuire, *The Philadelphia Campaign*, 1: 259 (*seven officers*); "Memo: Battle of Brandywine, 11th Sept. 1777," APS, Feinstone Coll., #111 (*"our knees and bellies"*); McGuire, *The Philadelphia Campaign*, 2: 290–91; Taaffe, *The Philadelphia Campaign, 1777–1778*, 75.

137 **The light faded, transmuting men:** Ryan, ed., *A Salute to Courage*, 93 (*watched from horseback*); Lengel, *General George Washington*, 241 (*Greene's men*); NG to Henry Marchant, *PNG*, 2: 470 (*"upwards of a hundred"*).

137 **The battle ended:** Van der Oye, *Remembering Their Gallantry in Former Days*, 49 (*"much stained with blood"*); Harris, *Brandywine*, 325–32; Gara, *Queen's American Rangers*, 76 (*Seventy-two rangers*).

137 **Yet Knyphausen's weight of numbers:** McGuire, *The Philadelphia Campaign*, 1: 244–50; Harris, *Brandywine*, 328 (*"made a clear lane"*), 334 (*"near two rods"*).

138 **With their draft horses killed:** Dann, ed., *The Nagle Journal*, 10; Harris, *Brandywine*, 339 (*"many bodies crushed"*).

138 **"Our army was something broke":** Ryan, ed., *A Salute to Courage*, 93 (*"necessary to leave"*); Clark, "Diary of Joseph Clark, Attached to the Continental Army," 93+ (*"heart full of distress"*).

138 **"The rebels stood a considerable smart battle":** Lt. Gilbert Purdy diary, LAC, Z 20/C21/1975/U2; Inman, "George Inman's Narrative of the American Revolution," 237+ (*"able to sit down"*); L. Cliffe to brother, Oct. 24, 1777, Loftus Cliffe papers, WLC, box 1 (*"fatigues of this day"*).

138 **Little imagination was required:** Mackesy, *The War for America, 1775–1783*, 128–29 (*sabering*); Harris, *Brandywine*, 448–49 (*state of their mounts*); Spring, *With Zeal and with Bayonets Only*, 266, 270 (*failed to convert*); Scull, ed., "The Montrésor Journals," 130 (*"up the North River"*); Whinyates, ed., *The Services of Lieut.-Colonel Francis Downman, R.A.*, 34 (*"Washington is retiring"*).

139 **That seemed fair enough:** Ashmead, *History of Delaware County, Pennsylvania*, 64 (*move aside*); Dann, ed., *The Nagle Journal*, 9 (*"Coming to a well"*); diary of Sergeant Major John H. Hawkins, "Notes and Queries," *PMHB*, vol. 20 (1896): 420 (*"1 uniform coat"*); Freeman, *George Washington: A Biography*, 4: 484 (*red bandanna*).

139 **"The sun had for some time disappeared":** Harris, *Brandywine*, 366 (*proceeded in retiring*); Lengel, *General George Washington*, 241 (*wagons packed*); Kidder, *Crossroads of the Revolution*, 206 (*"53 hours after"*); Unger, *Lafayette*, 46 (*"Treat him"*); Clary, *Adopted Son*, 117, 468n; *LAAR*, 1: 108–10 (*"unpleasant consequences"*).

139 **Very early that Friday morning:** Chastellux, *Travels in North America*, 315n (*Chester*); Taaffe, *The Philadelphia Campaign, 1777–1778*, 73 (*combed for deserters*); Harris, *Brandywine*, 383 (*gill of rum* and *"washed clean"*).

139 **Once again Washington found himself:** Smith, ed., *Letters of Delegates to Congress, 1774–1789*, 7: 607 (*newly shod*); Freeman, *George Washington: A Biography*, 4: 484 (*blankets*); Pickering, *The Life of Timothy Pickering*, 1: 157.

140 **After reading the draft:** GW to John Hancock, Sept. 11, 1777, *PGW*, 11: 200 (*"in good spirits"*).

140 **The extent of those losses would take weeks:** Davies, ed., 14: 204 (*three hundred killed*); Lengel, *General George Washington*, 241–42; Harris, *Brandywine*, 368–69 (*eleven cannons*); Rees and McDonald, "'The Action was renewed with a very warm Cannonade,'" monograph, 45

(*"I still exist"*); Agnew and Howell, "A Biographical Sketch of Governor Richard Howell, of New Jersey," 221+ (*"think myself happy"*).

140 **At daybreak on September 12:** Kemble, *The Kemble Papers*, 1: 492–93 (*prowl the countryside*); author visit, MNHP museum, Ford mansion, Oct. 10, 2019 (*leather or lead bullets*); Dr. Barnabas Binney to Benjamin Lincoln, 1782, "Saving Soldiers: Medical Practice in the Revolutionary War," exhibition, Society of the Cincinnati, Washington, D.C., 2022; Townsend, *Some Account of the British Army*, 26 (*brass clamp*).

140 **At Howe's request, Washington sent:** Lengel, *General George Washington*, 244; Lodge, ed., *Major André's Journal*, n.p. (*Turk's Head*); Butterfield, ed., *Letters of Benjamin Rush*, 1: 154 (*"hate us in every shape"*).

141 **War in Chester County:** author visit, Gideon Gilpin house, Brandywine, July 10, 2021 (*four thousand fence rails*); "Battle of Brandywine Driving Tour," Brandywine Battlefield Park Associates and Pennsylvania Historical & Museum Commission (*five years would pass*).

141 **Brandywine justly burnished:** Münchhausen, *At General Howe's Side*, 32 (*only half of his troops*); Harris, *Brandywine*, 397 (*"Howe surely deserves great credit"*).

141 **As for the Americans:** Callahan, *Henry Knox*, 116 (*"most severe action"*); Watson and Hazard, *Annals of Philadelphia*, 2: 283 (*Indian Queen*).

141 **Some blamed Pennsylvania:** Pickering, *The Life of Timothy Pickering*, 1: 164 (*"constantly deserting"*); GW to Caesar Rodney, Sept. 24, 1777, FOL (*"conduct of the militia"*); Harris, *Brandywine*, 374 (*"scandal"*).

141 **Yet Congress found more fault:** Lender and Stone, *Fatal Sunday*, 33 (*"officers are incompetent"*); Commager and Morris, eds., *The Spirit of 'Seventy-Six*, 617–18 (*"fortune of the day"*); Hammond, *Letters and Papers of Major-General John Sullivan*, 1: 476 (*"ever my opinion"*); GW to J. Sullivan, Oct. 24, 1777, *PGW*, 11: 602 (*"I never blamed you"*).

142 **As was sometimes his wont:** GW, general orders, Sept. 13, 1777, FOL (*"enemy's loss"*); Lengel, *General George Washington*, 241 (*"worst battlefield performance"*); Kapp, *The Life of John Kalb, Major-General in the Revolutionary Army*, 127 (*"most amiable"*), 136 (*"absence of a navy"*).

142 **Good luck and an opponent's blunders:** McGuire, *Battle of Paoli*, 19 (*"panting"*); Harris, *Brandywine*, 394 (*"our solacing words"*); Mowday, *September 11, 1777*, 158–59 (*"ought to attack them"*).

142 **Perhaps the most lyrical exposition:** Wood, *Revolutionary Characters*, 209 (*"plain as the alphabet"*); Nelson, *Thomas Paine*, 113 (*foreign affairs*); Greene, *Understanding the American Revolution*, 291–92 (*"reverencing themselves"*); McGuire, *The Philadelphia Campaign*, 1: 271–72 (American Crisis).

143 **Paine closed with an admonition:** "The Crisis IV," https://www.gutenberg.org/files/3741/3741-h/3741-h.htm#link2H_4_0008.

6. THESE ARE DREADFUL TIMES

144 **Philadelphia took fright:** Tracy, *266 Days*, 19 (*"has invaded this state"*), 21 (*"every man"*); Jackson, *With the British Army in Philadelphia, 1777–1778*, 11 (*state library*); Scharf and Westcott, *History of Philadelphia, 1609–1884*, 1: 349 (Sturdy Beggar); Wallace, *An Old Philadelphian, Colonel William Bradford*, 156 (*"but little the worse"*).

144 **Even so, Congress ordered flour:** Mishoff, "Business in Philadelphia During the British Occupation, 1777–1778," 165+; Scharf and Westcott, *History of Philadelphia, 1609–1884*, 1: 349 (*boats shifted*), 350 (*Blankets, shoes*); Miller, ed., *The Selected Papers of Charles Willson Peale and His Family*, 1: 241 (*dismantled*); Jackson, *With the British Army in Philadelphia, 1777–1778*, 15, 16 (*tarred fagots*); Tracy, *266 Days*, 11 (*"Ran away on Sunday"*).

144 **Apprehension turned to panic:** Wallace, *An Old Philadelphian, Colonel William Bradford*, 154; AH to J. Hancock, Sept. 18, 1777, FOL (*"If Congress have not yet"*); Nelson, *Thomas Paine*, 114 (*"beautiful, still"*); Siebert, *The Loyalists of Pennsylvania*, 40 (*"most travelled"*); Wainwright and Fisher, "'A Diary of Trifling Occurrences,'" 448–49 (*"great knocking"*); McGuire, *Battle of Paoli*, 62 (*"Fright sometimes"*).

145 **"When morning came":** JLB, RRR (*Hamilton had misread*); McCullough, *John Adams*, 173 (*"partridges"*); Morton, "The Diary of Robert Morton," 1+ (*saddle*); Smith, ed., *Letters of Delegates to Congress, 1774–1789*, 7: 4 (*lottery tickets*); Robinson, "Continental Treasury Administration, 1775–1781," diss., 68 (*Lancaster*); Prowell, *History of York County, Pennsylvania*, 1: 290–91 (*sixpence*).

145 **As the government bustled west:** William R. Reynolds, "Securing the Bells," *JAR*, Dec. 7, 2023; "The Liberty Bell," NPS, https://www.nps.gov/inde/learn/historyculture/stories-liberty bell.htm; Jordan, "Bethlehem During the Revolution," part 2, 74 (*wagon broke down*); Liberty Bell Museum, http://en.wikipedia.org/wiki/Liberty_Bell_Museum; Harris, *Germantown*, 115–16. Northampton Towne was renamed Allentown. The original bell, cast in London, cracked and was recast. Later known as the Liberty Bell, it cracked again in 1846.

145 **The procession of refugees had just begun:** "Bethlehem Colonial History," https://bethlehem pa.org/about-bethlehem/history-of-bethlehem/ (*founded in 1741*); Jordan, "Bethlehem During the Revolution," part 1, 404.

146 **Sulfur and gunpowder were stored:** Prowell, *History of York County, Pennsylvania*, 1: 290–91 (*"much dirtied"*).

146 **Before long, nine hundred wagons:** Jordan, "Bethlehem During the Revolution," part 2, 74 (*"low women"*), and part 1, 405 (*"dreadful times"*); Allen, "Diary of James Allen, Esq., of Philadelphia," 426 (*Sun Inn*); JLB, BBB (*chained in pairs*); Prowell, *History of York County, Pennsylvania*, 1: 289 (*Moravian church*: Matthew 12:30).

146 **Broken boys from Brandywine:** "Bethlehem Colonial History," https://bethlehempa.org/about-bethlehem/history-of-bethlehem/ (*five hundred American soldiers*); "The Revolutionary War Burial Ground in Bethlehem," Mark Shaffer, Pennsylvania State Historic Preservation Office, Oct. 29, 2014, https://pahistoricpreservation.com/revolutionary-war-burial-ground-bethlehem/.

146 **Among the arriving invalids was Lafayette:** LiA, 49–50 (*Moravian brethren*); Jordan, "Bethlehem During the Revolution," part 2, 75 (*"very intelligent"*); Unger, *Lafayette*, 49 (*writing letters*); Auricchio, *The Marquis Lafayette Reconsidered*, 52–53 (*Greenland*).

146 **It was said that street minstrels:** Unger, *Lafayette*, 51 (*Voltaire*); LiA, 50 (*"make myself interesting"*).

147 **General Howe had loitered near Brandywine:** McGuire, *Battle of Paoli*, 35 (*"heaviest downpour"*), 37 (*"dye washed out"*); Drake, *Life and Correspondence of Henry Knox*, 50 (*"most terrible stroke"*); VFHRR2, 514 (*quarter million cartridges*).

147 **After missing an opportunity:** Montrésor and Scull, "Journal of Captain John Montrésor," vol. 6, no. 1, 34+ (*horseshoes*); JLB, RRR; McGuire, *Battle of Paoli*, 59–60 (*tomahawks, soap*); Roberts, *Napoleon: A Life*, 4–5 (*Il Babbù*).

147 **Washington ordered a countermove:** Dawson, *The Assault on Stony Point*, 11–14 (*"caged leopard"*); Michael Schellhammer, "The Nicknaming of General 'Mad' Anthony Wayne," in Andrlik et al., eds., *Journal of the American Revolution*, 1: 146 (*"Dandy"*); Billias, ed., *George Washington's Generals and Opponents*, 263 (*barber*); Wildes, *Anthony Wayne*, 99 (*lambskin breeches*); Irving, *The Life of George Washington*, 84 (*"fight as well as brag"* and *"sovereign contempt"*). Wayne did not pick up the sobriquet "Mad Anthony" until late in the war.

149 **Under a full harvest moon:** McGuire, *Battle of Paoli*, 64 (*Great Valley*); Wildes, *Anthony Wayne*, 126 (*ten fat cows*); GW to Anthony Wayne, Sept. 18, 1777, PGW, 11: 266; Lengel, *General George Washington*, 246–47 (*"harass & distress"*); McGuire, *The Philadelphia Campaign*, 1: 300 (*"cutting of the enemy's baggage"*).

149 **Early Friday morning, Wayne wrote:** Anthony Wayne to GW, Sept. 19, 1777, PGW, 11: 273 (*"too compact"*).

149 **Wayne was deluded:** Wildes, *Anthony Wayne*, 126 (*jammed cartridges*); McGuire, *Battle of Paoli*, 82 (*"only three miles"*).

150 **The Americans laagered in a rolling farm field:** author visit, Paoli battlefield, Aug. 31, 2021; signage (*Cromwell Pearce*).

150 **Wayne intended to pounce:** W. Smallwood to GW, Sept. 15, 1777, PGW, 11: 241–42n; An-

thony Wayne to GW, Oct. 22, 1777, *PGW*, 11: 582; McGuire, *Battle of Paoli*, 84 (*"Howe means to have us attacked"*).

150 **Darkness spread across the camp:** Lossing, *Pictorial Field-Book of the Revolution*, 370 (*wrapped their firelocks*); Stockwell, *Unlikely General*, 80 (*pulled out his watch*).

150 **Tall and spare, with a narrow chest:** Nelson, *Sir Charles Grey, First Earl Grey*, 28, 32, 37 (*"to a man, [are] against us"*), 73; Hatch, *Major John André*, 70–71.

150 **Grey had no hesitation:** McGuire, *Battle of Paoli*, 115 (*plaid kilts*); Bird, "Uniform of the Black Watch in America, 1776–1783," 171; author visit, Paoli battlefield, Aug. 31, 2021, signage (*Bear Road*); Pleasants, "The Battle of Paoli," 44+ (*remove the flint*); Lodge, ed., *Major André's Journal*, n.p. (*"By not firing"*).

151 **Wayne had deployed six picket posts:** McGuire, *Battle of Paoli*, 88, 96 (*videttes*); Hunter, *The Journal of Martin Hunter*, 31 (*vidette fired*); "The Actions at Brandywine and Paoli, Described by a British Officer," 368+.

151 **Grey's column followed:** McGuire, *Battle of Paoli*, 99–100 (*missing an eye*); "The Actions at Brandywine and Paoli, Described by a British Officer," 368+; Hunter, *The Journal of Martin Hunter*, 31 (*"Dash, light infantry!"*).

151 **Alerted by a galloping vidette:** McGuire, *Battle of Paoli*, 101 (*"I was waked"*); Futhey and Cope, *History of Chester County, Pennsylvania*, 85 (*"Up, men"*); McGuire, *Battle of Paoli*, 103 (*four gun carriages*).

151 **Wayne ordered two hundred men:** McGuire, *Battle of Paoli*, 104 (*"Stand like a brave soldier"*); "The Actions at Brandywine and Paoli, Described by a British Officer," 368+ (*"shrieks, groans, shouting"*).

152 **Five hundred baying light infantrymen:** McGuire, *Battle of Paoli*, 108; Hunter, *The Journal of Martin Hunter*, 31 (*"most dreadful scene"*).

152 **Some Continentals hid:** McGuire, *Battle of Paoli*, 109 (*"yells of hell"*), 115, 129 (*seventeen wounds*); Dann, ed., *The Revolution Remembered*, 149–50 (*"in sport"*); Stillé, *Major-General Anthony Wayne and the Pennsylvania Line in the Continental Army*, 100 (*"Give these assassins"*); author visit, Paoli battlefield, Aug. 31, 2021, signage (*bayoneted him*); Futhey and Cope, *History of Chester County, Pennsylvania*, 86 (*"annals of the age"*).

152 **Terrified men, some firing wildly:** author visit, Paoli battlefield, Aug. 31, 2021, signage (*lost a wheel*).

152 **Just west of the bloodletting at Paoli:** "William Smallwood (1732–1792)," Archives of Maryland, biographical series, https://msa.maryland.gov/megafile/msa/speccol/sc3500/sc3520/001100/001134/html/1134bio.html; Buchanan, *The Road to Valley Forge*, 261 (*"Many flung down"*); O'Donnell, *Washington's Immortals*, 154 (*Half of the Maryland brigade*).

153 **On Sunday morning, local farmers:** Futhey, "The Massacre of Paoli," 285+ (*scoop at puddles*); McGuire, *Battle of Paoli*, 185 (*long trench*).

153 **Captain André put total American casualties:** Hatch, *Major John André*, 77 (*"prodigious slaughter"*); W. Howe to GW, Sept. 21, 1777, FOL (*"lose no time"*); McGuire, *The Philadelphia Campaign*, 2: 298 (*"demolishes these people"*).

153 **Distracted if not demolished:** GW to John Augustine Washington, Oct. 18, 1777, FOL (*"proved our ruin"*).

153 **Before sunset on Monday:** Ecelbarger, "The Feint That Never Happened," *JAR*, Nov. 19, 2020 (*"fordable at almost any place"*); GW, council of war, Sept. 23, 1777, *PGW*, 11: 294n (*Fatland Ford*); W. Howe orderly book, Sept. 22, 1777, WLC, box 1, folder 1 (*"without firing a shot"*).

154 **As his foemen tramped east:** GW, council of war, Sept. 23, 1777, *PGW*, 11: 294 (*"barefooted"*); GW to John Hancock, Sept. 23, 1777, *PGW*, 11: 300 (*"Howe's situation in Philadelphia"*).

154 **The savagery of the Paoli massacre:** McGuire, *Battle of Paoli*, 140 (*"Bloodhounds"*), 169 (*"threaten retaliation"*).

154 **The long-suffering John Adams lamented:** JA *Diary and Autobiography*, Sept. 16, 1777, FOL (*"gloomy, dark"*); JA *Diary and Autobiography*, Sept. 21, 1777, FOL (*"Oh, heaven"*); GW, general orders, Oct. 11, 1777, *PGW*, 11: 480, 482n (*"highest honor"*); McGuire, *Battle of Paoli*, 183 (*"active, brave, and vigilant"*).

154 **On September 25, a mild, sunny Thursday:** Reed, *Campaign to Valley Forge*, 87 (*"no vio-*

lence"); McGuire, *The Surprise of Germantown*, 20 (*fence rails*); Taafe, *The Philadelphia Campaign, 1777–1778*, 90 (*three thousand*); McGuire, *The Philadelphia Campaign*, 2: 7 (*mustaches waxed*); McGuire, *Battle of Paoli*, 4 (NEC ASPERA TERRENT).

155 **On Friday, the city:** McGuire, *The Philadelphia Campaign*, 2: 6 (*boats on the Delaware*), 12 (*sixty-four steps*), 15–18; Wainwright and Fisher, "'A Diary of Trifling Occurrences,'" 450 (*ten a.m.*); Uhlendorf, trans. and annot., *Revolution in America*, 117; Jackson, *With the British Army in Philadelphia, 1777–1778*, 16 (*"God Save the King"*); Montrésor and Scull, "Journal of Captain John Montrésor," vol. 6, no. 1, 34+ (*"acclamation"*).

155 **Howe had ridden halfway to Philadelphia:** Münchhausen, *At General Howe's Side*, 36 (*Cornwallis take the honors*); McGuire, *Battle of Paoli*, 1–2 (*Palladian window*); Wainwright and Fisher, "'A Diary of Trifling Occurrences,'" 450 (*"wanton levity"*); Crane, ed., *The Diary of Elizabeth Drinker*, 63 (*"here are the English"*).

155 **Within hours they made the town:** Tracy, *266 Days*, 41 (*Bettering House*); Jackson, *With the British Army in Philadelphia, 1777–1778*, 18, 21 (*chalk marks*); Montrésor and Scull, "Journal of Captain John Montrésor," vol. 6, no. 1, 34+ (*eight shillings*); Scharf and Westcott, *History of Philadelphia, 1609–1884*, 1: 352 (*rewards*), 359 (*night watch*); Döhla, *A Hessian Diary of the American Revolution*, 65 (*also the weather*).

156 **An estimated twelve thousand Philadelphians:** Rosswurm, *Arms, Country, and Class*, 149 (*twice that number remained*); Scharf and Westcott, *History of Philadelphia, 1609–1884*, 1: 350–51 (*"joy in the countenances"*); Jackson, *With the British Army in Philadelphia, 1777–1778*, 17 (*needed the cells*), 120 (*stone walls*).

156 **Here, indeed, was the place to launch:** Klein, "An Experiment That Failed," 229+ (*"assist the good Americans"*); McGuire, *The Philadelphia Campaign*, 2: 27 (*"Here is more Toryism"*), 231–32 (*William Allen, Jr.*).

156 **Foremost among influential Philadelphia loyalists:** "Joseph Galloway," House Speaker Biographies, Pennsylvania House of Representatives, https://www.legis.state.pa.us/cfdocs/legis/SpeakerBios/SpeakerBio.cfm?id=90; Wood, *The Americanization of Benjamin Franklin*, 202 (*entrusted his papers*); Coleman, "Joseph Galloway and the British Occupation of Philadelphia," 281–82 (*"too valuable"*).

156 **Although Howe would eventually condemn Galloway:** *The Narrative of Lieut. Gen. Sir William Howe*, 41 (*"visionary"* and *£770*); Brands, *Our First Civil War*, 317 (*police supervisor*); Coleman, "Joseph Galloway and the British Occupation of Philadelphia," 272 (*scheme to kidnap*); Bakeless, *Turncoats, Traitors and Heroes*, 159 (*eighty agents*); Howe inquiry, *Parliamentary Register*, 12: 427 (*"four-fifths of the people"*); Langston, "'A Fickle and Confused Multitude': War and Politics in Revolutionary Philadelphia, 1750–1783," diss., 114 (*"Lucifer of earth"*).

157 **Yet Galloway and his masters in London:** Smith, *Loyalists and Redcoats*, ix–x (*political chimera*); Smith, "The American Loyalists," 259+ (*16 percent*); Brown, *The Good Americans*, 97 (*would fight for the Crown*); Taylor, *American Revolutions*, 181–82 (*loyalists would flee*); Eller, ed., *Chesapeake Bay in the American Revolution*, 386–87 (*"cut down alive"*).

157 **Loyalists lacked national leaders:** Nelson, *The American Tory*, 20, 40, 87–88 (*pockets of strength*).

157 **Local patriot agencies recruited soldiers:** Sabine, *The American Loyalists*, 81 (*a parent*); Van Tyne, *The Loyalists in the American Revolution*, 150 (*"rag money"*); Pancake, *1777*, 109 (*jailed without bond*).

158 **"In politics the middle way":** JA to Horatio Gates, Mar. 23, 1776, FOL; Taylor, *American Revolutions*, 225 (*"Liberty forever"*); Kidder, *Revolutionary Princeton 1774–1783*, 196 (*"unfeeling world"*); Higginbotham, *The War of American Independence*, 275–79 (*Judicial procedures*). Loyalists would be executed in every state except Georgia and New Hampshire, some without trial, occasionally by mobs (Ketchum, *Divided Loyalties*, 367).

158 **"A Tory is an incorrigible animal":** William Livingston to GW, Oct. 5, 1777, FOL; Jones, "'The rage of tory-hunting': Loyalist Prisoners, Civil War, and the Violence of American Independence," 719+ (*"drawn on a sled"* and *"emissaries of the enemy"*); Jones, *Captives of Liberty*, 120; Callahan, *Royal Raiders*, 196 (*enlisting Connecticut men*); Vaughn, "Moses Dunbar,

the Other Connecticut Man Hanged in the Revolution," n.p. (*offered to provide hemp*); Pond, *The Tories of Chippeny Hill, Connecticut*, 7 (*forced to sit beside him*).

158 **Brutal as Britain's treatment:** Jones, " 'The rage of tory-hunting': Loyalist Prisoners, Civil War, and the Violence of American Independence," 719+ (*few insurrectionists*); McDougall, *Freedom Just Around the Corner*, 264 (*"The cry was for liberty"*); Wallace, *An Old Philadelphian, Colonel William Bradford*, 145–54 (*"successful resistance"*); Bailyn, *The Ordeal of Thomas Hutchinson*, 385 (*"to stand by"*).

159 **General Howe had more immediate concerns:** Harris, *Germantown*, 133; R. Howe to Admiralty, Oct. 25, 1777, UK NA, ADM 1/488, f 72 (*early October*); Ewald, *Diary of the American War*, 97 (*strong drink*).

159 **American efforts to prevent British engineers:** Jackson, *With the British Army in Philadelphia, 1777–1778*, 19 (*"everything in your power"*); Jackson, *The Pennsylvania Navy, 1775–1781*, 124 (Fly); McGuire, *The Philadelphia Campaign*, 2: 32–34 (*into the Walnut Street jail*); Martin, *The Philadelphia Campaign*, 124–26 (*152 men*). *Delaware's* colors may have been sewn by a young Arch Street upholsterer, Elizabeth Griscom, better known by her married name, Betsy Ross; her husband, John Ross, also an upholsterer, had recently died in an accident. Several months earlier she had been paid £14 by the Navy Board to sew ships' jacks believed to have been a Stars and Stripes variant. The widow Ross would marry again, twice. Fischer, *Liberty and Freedom*, 159; Jackson, *The Pennsylvania Navy, 1775–1781*, 17; Boudreau, *Independence*, 251–54.

159 **In an hour, Hazelwood had lost:** author visit, Fort Mifflin, Mar. 21, 2022, signage and pamphlet (*flat-bottomed galleys*); Jackson, *The Pennsylvania Navy, 1775–1781*, 14–16 (*black and yellow*).

160 **Thomas Paine had read:** Nelson, *Thomas Paine*, 114 (*"bulb near the top"*); Coudray, "Observations on the Forts," 343+ (*French engineers favored*); Taafe, *The Philadelphia Campaign, 1777–1778*, 111 (*Delaware was narrowest*); Jackson, *With the British Army in Philadelphia, 1777–1778*, 26–27 (*two redcoat regiments*); Jackson, *The Pennsylvania Navy, 1775–1781*, 133–36 (*six muskets*).

160 **The two remaining river strongholds:** Waldo, "Valley Forge, 1777–1778," 301 (*"a burlesque"*); Lundin, *Cockpit of the Revolution*, 340 (*"the worst"*).

160 **Lieutenant Colonel Samuel Smith, ordered:** McGuire, *The Philadelphia Campaign*, 2: 137 (*"utmost confusion"*); Dorwart, *Fort Mifflin of Philadelphia*, 26–30 (*Invalid Corps*); author visit, Fort Mifflin, Mar. 21, 2022, signage and pamphlet (*muskrat holes* and *Montrésor*); Miller, *Sea of Glory*, 252 (*"cursed little mud island"*).

161 **The most formidable American defenses:** Jackson, *The Pennsylvania Navy, 1775–1781*, 353–58 (*Robert Smith*); Harte, *The River Obstructions of the Revolutionary War*, 3–5 (*£8,000*).

161 **Huge timbers formed frames:** Moomaw, "The Naval Career of Captain Hamond, 1775–1779," diss., 116–18; Jackson, *The Pennsylvania Navy, 1775–1781*, 358–63 (*iron spears*); TBAC, 359 (*wide, deep Hudson*); Harte, *The River Obstructions of the Revolutionary War*, 3–5 (*sworn to secrecy*); Taafe, *The Philadelphia Campaign, 1777–1778*, 111 (*triple row*); author visit, Fort Mifflin, Mar. 21, 2022, signage and pamphlet (*sixty tons*).

161 **These rebel nuisances:** author visit, Fort Mifflin, Mar 21, 2022, signage and pamphlet (*"stackadoes"*); "The Philadelphia Lazaretto: A Most Unloved Institution," Jim Byrne, Pennsylvania Center for the Book, 2010, https://pabook.libraries.psu.edu/literary-cultural-heritage-map-pa/feature-articles/philadelphia-lazaretto-most-unloved-institution.

161 **Upon reaching the Delaware with his fleet:** R. Howe to Admiralty, Oct. 25, 1777, UK NA, ADM 1/488, f 72 (*rows of stackadoes*); Mackey, *The Gallant Men of the Delaware River Forts, 1777*, 16–17 (*fire rafts*); Laughton, ed., *The Naval Miscellany*, 1: 152; Wallace, *An Old Philadelphian, Colonel William Bradford*, 172 (*back to Chester*); Balderston, "Lord Howe Clears the Delaware," 326+ (*no channels could be opened*).

161 **Food stocks in the city:** Morton, "The Diary of Robert Morton," 1+ (*hid their fences*); Gruber, ed., *John Peebles' American War, 1776–1782*, 139–40 (*"Much drunkenness"*); Wainwright and Fisher, " 'A Diary of Trifling Occurrences,' " 454 (*"Not a barrel"*).

162   **Reports of such difficulties:** GW to Philip Schuyler, Mar. 12, 1777, FOL (*"the loss of Philadelphia"*); GW to Thomas Wharton, Jr., Oct. 17–18, 1777, FOL (*"never remain"*).

7. BORN UNDER A FIERY PLANET

163   **The Continental Army collected itself:** GW to Alexander Mcdougall, Sept. 25, 1777, FOL; Brownlow, *A Documentary History of the Battle of Germantown*, 12 (*plundered fence rails*).

163   **While contemplating his next move, Washington:** *TBAC*, 493; "Charles Willson Peale," National Gallery of Art, https://www.nga.gov/collection/artist-info.1774.html; Evans, *Weathering the Storm*, 188 (*"residences of liars"*); Miller, ed., *The Selected Papers of Charles Willson Peale and His Family*, 1: 246–47 (*lead bullets*).

163   **No less belligerent:** GW, general orders, Oct. 3, 1777, *PGW*, 11: 375–77n; Harris and Ecelbarger, "The Numerical Strength of George Washington's Army During the 1777 Philadelphia Campaign," *JAR*, Oct. 5, 2021 (*sixteen thousand*); Harris, *Germantown*, 193 (*six divisions*); McGuire, *The Philadelphia Campaign*, 2: 49–52 (*subordinate generals*); Coakley and Conn, *The War of the American Revolution*, 58 (*strike simultaneously*).

164   **At noon on Friday, October 3:** McMichael, "Diary of Lieutenant James McMichael of the Pennsylvania Line, 1776–1778," 129+ (*invalids were carted*); McGuire, *The Philadelphia Campaign*, 2: 41–42 (*"land of the living"*); GW, general orders, Oct. 3, 1777, *PGW*, 11: 373 (*"Will you suffer"*).

164   **At six p.m., New Jersey and Maryland militiamen:** Harris, *Germantown*, 197, 254, 274 (*thirty-seven hundred*); "Col. John Eager Howard's Account of the Battle of Germantown," 314+ (*seven Maryland regiments*); Hammond, ed., *Letters and Papers of Major-General John Sullivan, Continental Army*, 1: 476 (*"very unjust"*); Whittemore, *A General of the Revolution*, 67–68.

164   **No men shared the commander in chief's:** Wildes, *Anthony Wayne*, 136 (*"Dawn is big"*).

164   **Founded a century earlier by Rhineland émigrés:** Harris, *Germantown*, 234–35 (*"quantity and perfection"*); Brownlow, *A Documentary History of the Battle of Germantown*, 7 (*vinegar house*).

166   **General Howe deliberately avoided:** Anderson, *The Command of the Howe Brothers During the American Revolution*, 290–91 (*"acknowledged superiority"*); W. Howe to Germain, Oct. 10, 1777, *DAR*, 14: 207 (*arranged ten regiments*).

166   **The king's men were aware:** St. George, "The Actions at Brandywine and Paoli, Described by a British Officer," 369+ (*"give no quarter"*); McGuire, *The Philadelphia Campaign*, 2: 58 (*"dispirited the enemy"*); Ewald, *Diary of the American War*, 396n (*"little credited"*); McGuire, *The Surprise of Germantown*, 36 (*lost rebel flanker*); William Scott, "The Battle of Germantown," APS, SMs Coll 9 (*Washington's entire army*); Lydenberg, ed., "Archibald Robertson's Diaries, 1762–1780," 283+.

166   **Yet if an alarm:** McGuire, *The Surprise of Germantown*, 36 (*"alert and accouter"*); W. Howe to Germain, Oct. 10, 1777, *DAR*, 14: 207 (*"immediately ordered"*); Brownlow, *A Documentary History of the Battle of Germantown*, 18 (*"We knew nothing"*); Ewald, *Diary of the American War*, 396n; Harris, *Germantown*, 263–64 (*"every sense of the word"*); Hunter, *The Journal of Martin Hunter*, 33 (*"the attack upon us"*).

166   **Swirling fog muted the first orange glow:** McGuire, *The Surprise of Germantown*, 40 (*bayonets and sabers*); William Scott, "The Battle of Germantown," APS, SMs Coll 9 (*fence rails*); McGuire, *The Philadelphia Campaign*, 2: 67 (*6-pounders*); Sullivan's account in GW to John Hancock, Oct. 5, 1777, fn, FOL.

167   **Sunrise at precisely six a.m.:** Ward, *Duty, Honor or Country*, 106 (*"horrid fog"*); Brownlow, *A Documentary History of the Battle of Germantown*, 22 (*through the wrist*); McGuire, *The Surprise of Germantown*, 40 (*Abraham Best*); McGuire, *The Philadelphia Campaign*, 2: 84–85 (*Nash*); Fried, *Rush*, 225 (*off a signpost*); Siry, *Liberty's Fallen Generals*, 79 (*left thigh*); Lambdin, "Battle of Germantown," 368+ (*"Never mind me"*).

167   **More Continentals pressed into the brawl:** L. Cliffe to brother, Oct. 24, 1777, Loftus Cliffe papers, WLC, box 1 (*"devil of a fire"*); Hunter, *The Journal of Martin Hunter*, 33–34 ("Blood-

hounds!"); Anderson, *Personal Recollections of Captain Enoch Anderson*, 45 (*"men were falling"*).

167 **At length the brag of a trumpet:** Hunter, *The Journal of Martin Hunter*, 34; Harris, *Germantown*, 276, 285 (*ten dead*); McGuire, *The Philadelphia Campaign*, 2: 71–72, 84 (*stabbing their gun-carriage horses*); Moorsom, ed., *Historical Record of the Fifty-Second Regiment*, 22 (*"great difficulty"*); Stillé, *Major-General Anthony Wayne and the Pennsylvania Line in the Continental Army*, 96 (*"rage and fury"*).

168 **An officer in the 10th Pennsylvania:** McGuire, *The Philadelphia Campaign*, 2: 72 (*"no quarter"*).

168 **In Beggarstown, a hamlet just north:** McGuire, *The Philadelphia Campaign*, 2: 74 (*rooftops*), 76 (*"great passion"*); Hunter, *The Journal of Martin Hunter*, 34 (*" 'Form! Form!' "*); Moorsom, ed., *Historical Record of the Fifty-Second Regiment*, 22 (*"felt pleased"*).

168 **Washington also felt pleased:** T. Pickering letter in "Judge Johnson and Count Pulaski," 425+ (*trailed Sullivan's division*); Martin, *A Narrative of a Revolutionary Soldier*, 63 (*driven back*); "Col. John Eager Howard's Account of the Battle of Germantown," 314+ (*drag ropes*); Tompkins, "Contemporary Account of the Battle of Germantown," 331 (*"midnight darkness"*); Sullivan's account in GW to John Hancock, Oct. 5, 1777, fn, FOL.

168 **Washington sent orders for General Lord Stirling's:** Harris, *Germantown*, 287, 289 (*"thick as the stones"*); Lacey, "Memoirs of Brigadier-General John Lacey, of Pennsylvania," 498+ (*"We had full possession"*).

169 **A mile and a half south:** author visit, Cliveden, Sept. 2, 2021, signage (*sculpted lions*); Van Doren, *In the Founders' Footsteps*, 106 (*twelve-over-twelve*); McGuire, *The Philadelphia Campaign*, 2: 83.

169 **Cliveden was the summer home:** Watson and Hazard, *Annals of Philadelphia*, 3: 167 (*"public liberty"*); author visit, Cliveden, Sept. 2, 2021, signage (*two hundred slaves*); Harris, *Germantown*, 450 (*opposed rebellion*); Larson, *The Trials of Allegiance*, 80 (*Union Iron Works*).

169 **The British now made good use:** Harris, *Germantown*, 323–24 (*only surviving heir*); McGuire, *The Surprise of Germantown*, 24–25 (*hole through one cheek*); TBAC, 547 (*Nassau Hall*).

169 **Fleeing redcoats warned:** McGuire, *The Philadelphia Campaign*, 2: 82–83 (*"tenable"*), 86; author visit, Cliveden, Sept. 2, 2021, signage (*U-shaped staircase*); Potts, ed., "Battle of Germantown from a British Account," 113 (*"sell themselves"*).

170 **Wayne's Pennsylvanians and Sullivan's Marylanders:** McGuire, *The Surprise of Germantown*, 53; McGuire, *The Philadelphia Campaign*, 2: 84; "Revolutionary Services of Captain John Markland," 102+ (*"much better"* and *"seemed to come in showers"*); "Lt. John Markland," State Society of the Cincinnati of Pennsylvania, https://pasocietyofthecincinnati.org/gallery_post/lt-john-markland/ (*slivers*); Harris, *Germantown*, 239 (*"brilliant & incessant"*).

170 **Washington and his staff halted on the high road:** McGuire, *The Philadelphia Campaign*, 2: 86 (*"Sullivan is throwing away"*); T. Pickering letter in "Judge Johnson and Count Pulaski," 425+ (*musket balls whizzing*); Martin, *The Philadelphia Campaign, June 1777–July 1778*, 107 (*carriage block*); Callahan, *Henry Knox, General Washington's General*, 123–24; Harris, *Germantown*, 289 (*"impossible to see"*).

171 **Squinting, they debated whether:** T. Pickering letter in "Judge Johnson and Count Pulaski," 425+ (*"fire on your flag"*); GW to J. Hancock, Oct. 5, 1777, PGW, 11: 399n (*eavesdropping junior officers*).

171 **Washington had no more experience:** T. Pickering letter in "Judge Johnson and Count Pulaski," 425+ (*volunteered to carry a truce flag*); McGuire, *The Philadelphia Campaign*, 2: 88 (*"Smith was brought back"*).

171 **Rebel soldiers had at last managed:** McGuire, *The Philadelphia Campaign*, 2: 86–87, 2: 89 (*stone urns*); McGuire, *The Surprise of Germantown*, 65 (*120 yards*), 66–69 (*tried to rehang the door*); Potts, ed., "Battle of Germantown from a British Account," 112+ (*blew Cliveden's front doors* and *shove chairs and tables*).

171 **But Wissahickon schist walls:** McGuire, *The Philadelphia Campaign*, 2: 90 (*"Hurrah to the

king!”); Ryan, ed., *A Salute to Courage*, 101 (*“My horse was shot”*). A town in Ohio would be named for Col. Dayton.

172 **Several officers now proposed:** Massey, *John Laurens and the American Revolution*, 76–77 (*armloads of straw*); Raphael, *Founders*, 319 (*spent ball*); McGuire, *The Surprise of Germantown*, 73 (*green sash* and *bayoneted in the mouth*); McGuire, *The Philadelphia Campaign*, 2: 93–94 (*would die the next day*).

172 **Continental artillery continued to rake:** Harris, *Germantown*, 344 (*five brigades*).

172 **Washington's plan at Germantown:** McGuire, *The Philadelphia Campaign*, 2: 97; McGuire, *The Surprise of Germantown*, 55 (*wrong turn*).

172 **Nonetheless, several thousand additional Continentals:** Martin, *A Narrative of a Revolutionary Soldier*, 63 (*“Our orders were not to fire”*); Harris, *Germantown*, 302–3 (*Luken's Mill*); McGuire, *The Philadelphia Campaign*, 2: 293 (*“fifty men”*).

173 **“The enemy were driven”:** Martin, *A Narrative of a Revolutionary Soldier*, 63 (*“left their kettles”*); Harris, *Germantown*, 308 (*“Victory was declaring”*).

173 **But victory could be capricious:** Harris, *Germantown*, 103 (*ten yards*); Lambdin, “Battle of Germantown,” 368+; McGuire, *The Philadelphia Campaign*, 2: 95 (*through a large window*); McGuire, *The Surprise of Germantown*, 76–77 (*firing round shot*).

173 **Disorder spiraled toward chaos:** Piecuch and Beakes, *“Cool Deliberate Courage”: John Eager Hower in the American Revolution*, 21; Ward, *Major General Adam Stephen and the Cause of American Liberty*, 185–86 (*fratricidal gunfight*); McGuire, *The Surprise of Germantown*, 80; McGuire, *The Philadelphia Campaign*, 2: 99; Harris, *Germantown*, 312; Stillé, *Major-General Anthony Wayne and the Pennsylvania Line in the Continental Army*, 97 (*“it was our own people”*).

173 **Major General Grey—the notorious “No-Flint”:** Tompkins, “Contemporary Account of the Battle of Germantown,” 331 (*crackling of thorns*); McGuire, *The Philadelphia Campaign*, 2: 104 (*Bethlehem*); Settle, “The Eastern Shore Battalion: The Story of the 9th Virginia Regiment,” *JAR*, Jan. 19, 2023; Watson and Hazard, *Annals of Philadelphia*, 2: 48 (*“well-blackened”*).

174 **By nine a.m. the American attack:** Harris, *Germantown*, 393 (*Uriah Forrest*); GW to W. Smallwood, Feb. 16, 1778, 565n (*back of his jawbone*); Sullivan's account, GW to J. Hancock, Oct. 5, 1777, fn, FOL (*“beg him to retire”*).

174 **That retreat had already started:** Pickering, *The Life of Timothy Pickering*, 1: 170 (*Half a dozen men*); Freeman, *George Washington: A Biography*, 4: 510–11 (*a flank turned*); Leake, *Memoir of the Life and Times of General John Lamb*, 183 (*“electrical shock”*); Lengel, *General George Washington*, 258 (*under the horses' bellies*); Tallmadge, *Memoir of Colonel Benjamin Tallmadge*, 31 (*“threw my squadron”*).

174 **Brigadier General James Agnew:** Hagist, *British Soldiers, American War*, 230 (*lower back* and *“a coffin made”*); Harris, *Germantown*, 355–56 (*Grumblethorpe*); McGuire, *The Philadelphia Campaign*, 2: 111–12 (*“could only turn his eyes”*).

175 **At Cliveden, Colonel Musgrave heard:** McGuire, *The Surprise of Germantown*, 88 (*fifes*); GW to John Hancock, Oct. 5, 1777, fn, FOL.

175 **General Lord Stirling's reserves:** Harris, *Germantown*, 379 (*held open*), 383 (*“hardly possible to catch”*); Lengel, *General George Washington*, 258–59 (*hasty retreat north*).

175 **General Cornwallis tried:** McGuire, *The Philadelphia Campaign*, 2: 75 (*“smoking their pipes”*); McGuire, *The Philadelphia Campaign*, 2: 121 (*“They took such care”*); Lambdin, “Battle of Germantown,” 368+ (*joined the chase*).

175 **Thomas Paine had followed the army:** Thomas Paine to BF, May 16, 1778, FOL (*“I met several of the wounded”*).

176 **By nine p.m. most rebel troops:** James McMichael account in GW to John Hancock, Oct. 5, 1777, fn, FOL; McMichael, “Diary of Lieutenant James McMichael of the Pennsylvania Line, 1776–1778,” 129+ (*“many fatigues”*); Martin, *A Narrative of a Revolutionary Soldier*, 68–69 (*“rank hold”*).

176 **Only now did many men realize:** Anderson, *Personal Recollections of Captain Enoch Ander-*

son, 47 (*"children of misfortune"*); Ryan, ed., *A Salute to Courage*, 103 (*"Got my breeches"*); "Journal of Capt. William Beaty, 1776–1781," 104+ (*"Some bad management"*).

176 **Once again every regiment was ordered:** George Weedon orderly book, Oct. 5, 1777, The Revolutionary City (*straggler lines*); Irving, *The Life of George Washington*, 3: 267 (*"Fortune smiled"*).

176 **On Sunday, October 5:** Ewald, *Diary of the American War*, 96 (*"counted seventy-five dead Americans"*); Lambdin, "Battle of Germantown," 368+ (*sightseers*); McGuire, *The Surprise of Germantown*, 87 (*a single pit*); Brownlow, *A Documentary History of the Battle of Germantown*, 61 (*"Pray now"*); Sargent, *The Life and Career of Major John André*, 113 (*"mothers' sons"*).

177 **Washington initially estimated:** GW to J. Hancock, Oct. 5, 1777, *PGW*, 11: 401n (*"upwards of three hundred"*); W. Howe to Germain, Oct. 10, 1777, *DAR*, 14: 207; McGuire, *The Philadelphia Campaign*, 2: 127–28 (*400 captured*), 133 (*two feather mattresses*); Harris, *Germantown*, 398 (*80 were killed*); Taaffe, *Washington's Revolutionary Generals*, 78 (*"brave, modest, sensible"*); McGuire, *The Surprise of Germantown*, 89–90 (*lock of his hair*); Quincy, *The Journals of Major Samuel Shaw*, 44 (*"Unrelenting war"*). Shaw would serve as the first U.S. consul to Canton.

177 **The usual agonies attended the wounded:** Rees, "'None of you know the hardships of a soldiers life . . . ,'" 9–10 (*"extracted four balls"*); *Pennsylvania Archives*, 2nd ser., 10: 235 (*John Geyer*).

177 **Uncovered, springless wagons hauled:** Hawke, *Benjamin Rush*, 208; Jordan, "Bethlehem During the Revolution," part 2, 75 (*"rags swarming with vermin"*); Gillett, *The Army Medical Department, 1775–1818*, 82 (*Single Brethren's House*), 88.

177 **British physicians converted:** McGuire, *The Philadelphia Campaign*, 2: 127 (*"long tables"*); Williams, "Independence and Early American Hospitals," 35+ (*basement cells*); Scharf and Westcott, *History of Philadelphia, 1609–1884*, 1: 359–60 (*sugar refinery* and *a half dollar per pound*).

178 **Dozens of captured Continental officers:** Burrows, *Forgotten Patriots*, 118–19 (*Golden Swan*); Board of General Officers to GW, June 28, 1779, FOL fn (*statehouse*); McGuire, *The Philadelphia Campaign*, 2: 223–24 (*windows had been nailed shut*); Scharf and Westcott, *History of Philadelphia, 1609–1884*, 1: 372 (*"villainous dog"*); Ryan, ed., *A Salute to Courage*, 105 (*"It swept off"*); Reiss, *Medicine and the American Revolution*, 183–88 (*typhus* and *ten of eleven surgeons*); Mitchell, *The Price of Independence*, 155 (*"languor of the whole body"*); author visit, Fort Ticonderoga, Sept. 28, 2021, medical exhibit (*gangrene*).

178 **One especially unfortunate prisoner:** Hagist, "Martin Hurley's Last Charge," *JAR*, Apr. 14, 2015 (*44th Foot*); McGuire, *The Philadelphia Campaign*, 2: 132 (*"enlisting with the rebels"*).

178 **General Howe's lieutenants were irate:** Morton, "The Diary of Robert Morton," 1+ (*"twelve miles round"*); "Estimate of damage done by the British in 1778 and 1777," Office of the Board of Revision of Taxes, The Revolutionary City (*119 Germantown houses*); Gruber, ed., *John Peebles' American War, 1776–1782*, 140 (*"most spirited"*); Münchhausen, *At General Howe's Side, 1776–1778*, 29 (*"very well planned"*).

179 **Not everyone conceded that:** Tyler, ed., "The Old Virginia Line in the Middle States During the American Revolution," 134 (*"drubbed"*); Ward, *Duty, Honor or Country*, 108 (*"So sportive is fortune"*).

179 **"Remember the mistakes":** Stephenson, *Patriot Battles*, 83; McGuire, *The Philadelphia Campaign*, 2: 78–80 (*desultory Pennsylvanians*); Harris, *Germantown*, 291–93 (*two-to-one advantage*); Lengel, *General George Washington*, 259; McGuire, *The Philadelphia Campaign*, 2: 105–8 (*"human heart"*). The unit, named for Queen Charlotte, had earlier been known as the "Queen's American Rangers" (Gara, *Queen's American Rangers*, 87).

179 **In a dispatch to the Massachusetts Council:** Puls, *Henry Knox*, 110 (*"America rises"*); Hamilton, *The Revolutionary War Lives and Letters of Lucy and Henry Knox*, 126–27 (*"God who orders all things"*).

179 **Paine confided to Franklin:** Thomas Paine to BF, May 16, 1778, FOL (*"at the same loss"*); Walker, *Engineers of Independence*, 182 (*"conquered General Howe"*).

179 **For a man proverbially incapable:** GW to John Hancock, Oct. 7, 1777, FOL (*"extreme haziness"* and *"tumult"*); Ferling, *The Ascent of George Washington*, 136 (*double if not triple*); GW, general orders, Oct. 5, 1777, FOL (*"they will remember"*); GW to John Augustine Washington, Oct. 18, 1777, *PGW*, 11: 552 (*"a bloody day"*).

180 **Beset by urgent army business:** GW to J. Hancock, Oct. 10–11, 1777, *PGW*, 11: 475 (*"Our distress"*); James Mease to GW, Nov. 4, 1777, *PGW* 12: 125n (*fifteen thousand coats*).

180 **"I have been a slave to the service":** GW to R. H. Lee, Oct. 16, 1777, FOL.

180 **The repulse at Germantown:** Brownlow, *A Documentary History of the Battle of Germantown*, 65 (*"miserable set"*); Fried, *Rush*, 226 (*"dirty, undisciplined"* and *"Be not deceived"*).

180 **But that was untrue:** JA to Abigail Adams, Oct. 7, 1777, *AFC*, FOL (*"Our people"*); Ward, *Major General Adam Stephen and the Cause of American Liberty*, 1–4 (*former British naval surgeon*), 142–43 (*gun factory*); Ward, *Charles Scott and the "Spirit of '76,"* 43 (*"cowardly sot"*); Harris, *Germantown*, 445 (*"unofficerlike behavior"*).

181 **The war moved on:** Lengel, *General George Washington*, 262 (*struck a medal*); McGuire, *The Philadelphia Campaign*, 2: 124 (*"glorious day"*); Lord Stirling to [Joseph Reed?], Oct. 5, 1777, JLB, AAA (*fine horse shot*); Nelson, *William Alexander, Lord Stirling*, 117 (*"enemy will find"*).

181 **That curious American buoyancy:** Harris, *Germantown*, 414 (*"Vengeance burns"*).

8. TO RISK ALL UPON ONE RASH STROKE

182 **Late summer in the Hudson valley:** "William Duer," *Appleton's Cyclopedia of American Biography*, 1900 ed., https://en.wfikisource.org/wiki/Appletons%27_Cyclop%C3%A6dia_of _American_Biography/Duer,_William; author visit, Duer house site, Fort Miller, Sept. 26, 2021, signage (*Four broad steps*); BSC, 205–6 (*two-story veranda*); Ketchum, *Saratoga*, 291 (*"first house"*).

182 **Camp social life was much enhanced:** Brown, trans., *Baroness von Riedesel and the American Revolution*, xxiv–xxix (*Tischbein*); Lina Sinnickson, "Frederika Baroness Riedesel," *PMHB*, vol. 30, no. 4 (1906): 385+; Willis, *The Struggle for Sea Power*, 179 (*nightcap*); Baer, *Hessians*, 215 (*Italian arias*); Stone, ed., *Memoirs, and Letters and Journals of Major General Riedesel*, 133 (*grilled bear*), 138 (*"never retreat"*); Frederika von Riedesel, *Letters and Journals Relating to the War*, 101 (*Cedar logs*); Lunt, *John Burgoyne of Saratoga*, 213 (*"The evening was spent"*); author visit, Patt Smyth house, Fort Edward, Sept. 26, 2021, signage (*"We passed"*).

183 **By mid-September the hour had approached:** Coakley and Conn, *The War of the American Revolution*, 61 (*"The great bulk"*); Commager and Morris, eds., *The Spirit of 'Seventy-Six*, 570; De Fonblanque, *Life and Correspondence of the Right Hon. John Burgoyne*, 274 (*"not half of them armed"*); O'Shaughnessy, *The Men Who Lost America*, 163 (*"time and patience"*).

183 **Except for the occasional bear paw:** "Orderly Book of Burgoyne's Army," T-P RC, FTA #4017 (*salt meat* and *three times a day* and *a thousand lashes* and *$20*); Stanley, *For Want of a Horse*, 137 (*shot*); CtS, 158 (*eighty warriors*); Hadden, *A Journal Kept in Canada*, lx; Stone, ed., *Memoirs, and Letters and Journals of Major General Riedesel*, 134 (*tribal harvests*), 137 (*fourteen thousand Americans*).

183 **Burgoyne would write that he never:** O'Shaughnessy, *The Men Who Lost America*, 152–53 (*"such a tract"* and *"winter there"*).

183 **Lack of reinforcements from Canada:** Reynolds, *Guy Carleton*, 118 (*"must be obeyed"*); Hadden, *A Journal Kept in Canada*, lx (*more than nine hundred men*); BSC, 108; De Fonblanque, *Life and Correspondence of the Right Hon. John Burgoyne*, 264 (*"situation a little difficult"*), 280 (*"drained the life blood"*).

184 **Burgoyne vowed to press on:** De Fonblanque, *Life and Correspondence of the Right Hon. John Burgoyne*, 276 (*"do not despond"*); "Diary of the Brunswick Troops in North America," Aug. 6, 1777, HDAR, fiche 180–93, HZ-5, 262 (*gaining ground*); ES to author, Oct. 2021 (*dysentery*); Lynn, ed., *The Specht Journal*, 74; Hadden, *A Journal Kept in Canada*, 140 (*rollers*); Curtis, *The Organization of the British Army in the American Revolution*, 142 (*extensive recaulking*); Howe inquiry, *Parliamentary Register*, 12: 173 (*four days' provisions*).

184 **Two-thirds of the Canada Army's big guns:** ES to author, Oct. 2021 (*left at Ticonderoga*);

Cubbison, *"The Artillery Never Gained More Honour,"* 102 (*"extremely formidable"*); Howe inquiry, *Parliamentary Register*, 12: 173 (*troubling worry*).

184 **High water from heavy rains:** Lynn, ed., *The Specht Journal*, 104 (*first bridge*), 124 (*Royal Navy*); *CtS*, 158–60.

184 **If some of the king's liege men:** Philbrick, *Valiant Ambition*, 117 (*"evil, mountainous"*); Kingsley, ed., "Letters to Lord Polwarth," 393+ (*"None but stupid mortals"*); Hibbert, *Redcoats and Rebels*, 184 (*"set our faces"*).

186 **Three days later, at seven:** *BSC*, 106–7; *CtS*, 160 (*float downriver*); Stone, ed., *Memoirs, and Letters and Journals of Major General Riedesel*, 139 (*"now cut off"*).

186 **The long column halted for the evening:** Stone, ed., *Memoirs, and Letters and Journals of Major General Riedesel*, 140 (*Fishkill*); WLC, https://quod.lib.umich.edu/e/ecco/004877784 .0001.000?rgn=main;view=fulltext; ES to author, July 2024 (*silver egg*); Howe inquiry, *Parliamentary Register*, 12: 93 (*"arrival at Albany"*); De Fonblanque, *Life and Correspondence of the Right Hon. John Burgoyne*, 280 (*"Success be ever with you"*).

186 **At noon on September 15:** Lynn, ed., *The Specht Journal*, 77 (*wheat and rye*); "Diary of the Brunswick Troops in North America," HDAR, fiche 180–93, HZ-5, Sept. 16, 1777 (*"saw nothing"*).

186 **On Wednesday morning, September 17:** Snow, *1777*, 71 (*three miles*); *BSC*, 108 (*Swords's House*); Stone, ed., *Memoirs, and Letters and Journals of Major General Riedesel*, 141 (*rebel camp sounds*); "Diary of the Brunswick Troops in North America," HDAR, fiche 180–93, HZ-5, 297, Sept 18, 1777 (*"Number 1"*).

187 **If uncertain of the precise disposition:** Hadden, *A Journal Kept in Canada*, 161 (*root for potatoes*); Wild, "Journal of Ebenezer Wild," 94; *CtS*, 163.

187 **Burgoyne was furious:** "Journal of an Officer of the 47th Regiment of Foot," HL, mssHM, 66; "Orderly Book of Burgoyne's Army," T-P RC, FTA #4017 (*"life of a soldier"*).

187 **After pummelings at Ticonderoga:** *CtS*, 149 (*the Sprouts*), 151 (*Ten Continental regiments*); Resch and Sargent, eds., *War & Society in the American Revolution*, 48–49 (*conch shell*); Buel, *Dear Liberty*, 127.

187 **Every day more armed New Englanders:** Ketchum, *Saratoga*, 344 (*"a man of war,"* Exodus 15:3).

187 **General Schuyler also was a man of war:** Gerlach, *Proud Patriot*, 273 (*"very mysterious"*); Lossing, *Life and Times of Philip Schuyler*, 2: 219 (*hollow cannonballs*), 306 (*"bent on your destruction"*); AH to Robert R. Livingston, Aug. 7, 1777, FOL (*"want of firmness"*).

188 **Schuyler advised Washington:** Philip Schuyler to GW, July 18, 1777, FOL (*"smiling"*); Bush, *Revolutionary Enigma*, 130 (*eleven states to one*); Lossing, *Life and Times of Philip Schuyler*, 2: 219 (*"Gates is the man"*).

188 **Gates appeared on the evening of August 19:** Gerlach, *Proud Patriot*, 301–3 (*Van Schaick Island*); Bush, *Revolutionary Enigma*, 133 (*"I have done all"*).

188 **Victory hardly seemed inevitable:** Luzader, *Saratoga*, 185 (*four brigades*), 189 (*twelve tons of lead*), 191 (*"not fit"*), 194 (*thirty barrels*); Nelson, "Legacy of Controversy," 41+ (*"as if by magic"*).

188 **As Samuel Adams observed:** Billias, ed., *George Washington's General and Opponents*, 80 (*"Granny"*), 90 (*"love of his soldiers"*); Nelson, *General Horatio Gates*, 5–6 (*"New Englander's hair"*); JLB, AAA (*"Bipeds"*); Corner, ed., *The Autobiography of Benjamin Rush*, 156 (*"world will do"* and *"abounded in anecdotes"*).

189 **Gates described himself:** Gates to Matthew Vishter, Oct. 4, 1777, Horatio Gates papers, NYHS, micro (*"grown old"*); Nelson, *General Horatio Gates*, 7–8 (*customs collector*), 28 (*financially strapped*); Mintz, *The Generals of Saratoga*, 40 (*gunshot wound to the chest*); Gates to Charles Mellish, July 21, 1772, University of Nottingham (U.K.) Manuscripts and Special Collections, Mellish Family Papers, Me C 29/2, courtesy of David L. Preston (*"diversified by care"*).

189 **He adored his adopted country:** Billias, ed., *George Washington's Generals and Opponents*, 83 (*"red-hot republican"*); Gates to Charles Mellish, Apr. 11, 1774, University of Nottingham (U.K.) Manuscripts and Special Collections, Mellish Family Papers, Me C 29/2, courtesy of

David L. Preston (*"such a fool"*); Nelson, *General Horatio Gates*, 76–77 (*dysentery*); GW to H. Gates, Mar. 10, 1777, *PGW*, 8: 548 (*"only means"*); Tuckerman, *Life of General Philip Schuyler*, 153 (*deserved better*).

189 **Not only did that army expand:** ES to author, Oct. 2021 (*combat experience*); author visit, John Neilson farm, SNHP, Sept. 25, 2021, and Sept. 13, 2024 (*riflemen*); Zambone, *Daniel Morgan*, 134; GW to George Clinton, Aug. 16, 1777, FOL (*"counterpoise"*); Posey, *General Thomas Posey*, 34–35 (*scalping knives*); Wright, "The Rifle in the American Revolution," 293+ (*two hundred yards*); Zambone, *Daniel Morgan*, 135 (*fewer than five hundred*); GW to Israel Putnam, Aug. 16, 1777, *PGW*, 10: 642 (*"a good purpose"*).

189 **Commanding this Detached Rifle Battalion:** ES to author, July 2024; Zambone, *Daniel Morgan*, 9–10 (*uncertain*), 32 (*bullet through the cheek*), 33 (*"From my youth"*), 37–43 (*horse thief*); Higginbotham, *Daniel Morgan, Revolutionary Rifleman*, 11–12 (*Abigail Curry*), 13–14 (*twenty-two times*); TBAC, 158 (*Quebec*); Callahan, *Daniel Morgan*, 45 (*"Exactly fitted"*).

190 **Meticulous tests made by British weapons experts:** Seymour, "A Chart Showing the Results of a 1779 Woolwich Ballistic Test," 373+ (*superior in accuracy*); Rogers, Seidule, and Watson, eds., *The West Point History of the American Revolution*, 106 (*oiled cloth patch*); Peterson, *The Book of the Continental Soldiers*, 40 (*octagonal*). Some of Morgan's riflemen carried round-barreled weapons that *could* carry a bayonet (author visit, SNHP, Sept. 25, 2021).

190 **To remedy these defects:** Brown and Peckham, eds., *Revolutionary War Journals of Henry Dearborn, 1775–1783*, 104; Wilkinson, *Memoirs of My Own Times*, 1: 230 (*"vigorous young men"*); GW to Richard Peters, June 20, 1777, *PGW*, 10: 88 (*five hundred spears*); Snow, *1777*, 91 (*enemy officers*).

190 **Another officer in Gates's ranks:** Ferreiro, *Brothers at Arms*, 124–25 (*Academy of Painting and Sculpture*); Trickey, "The Polish Patriot Who Helped Americans Beat the British," n.p. (*thwarted elopement*); Storozynski, *The Peasant Prince*, 2–12, 26 (*eleven different ways*); GW to Henry Laurens, Nov. 10, 1777, FOL (*"science & merit"*).

191 **Gates noticed:** Kajencki, *Thaddeus Kosciuszko*, 12 (*"improper places"*), 19 (*Sugar Loaf*); Storozynski, *The Peasant Prince*, 32–33 (*"shoe buckles"*); CtS, 153 (*better ground*).

191 **They found it three miles:** Griswold and Linebaugh, eds., *The Saratoga Campaign*, 197–202 (*Jotham Bemus*); Storozynski, *The Peasant Prince*, 32–33 (*"This is the spot"*).

191 **On Friday, September 12, the day:** Snow, *1777*, 24; CtS, 154 (*"to their eyes"*); Rogers, Seidule, and Watson, eds., *The West Point History of the American Revolution*, 105 (*"without reason"*); author visit, SNHP, Sept. 25, 2021, signage (*new tents*); Griswold and Linebaugh, eds., *The Saratoga Campaign*, 44 (*Twenty-two cannons*), 129 (*field hospital*); Starbuck, "The American Headquarters for the Battle of Saratoga," 16+ (*brass door handles*).

192 **Six hundred yards north, Arnold shared:** author visit, SNHP, Sept. 25, 2021 (*drafts and vermin*); Procknow, "Personal Honor and Promotion Among Revolutionary Generals and Congress," *JAR*, Jan. 23, 2018 (*seething*); Snow, *1777*, 46 (*new will*).

192 **Patrols captured a few careless infernals:** Wilkinson, *Memoirs of My Own Times*, 1: 237 (*sent to climb a tree*); Gates to Berkshire County committee et al., Sept. 17, 1777, Horatio Gates papers, NYHS, micro; Gates to Bennington Committee of Safety, Sept. 17, 1777, James S. Schoff Revolutionary War Collection, WLC (*"one rash stroke"*).

192 **The American ranks braced:** Michael Schellhammer, "Overlooked Hero: General John Glover," *JAR*, July 8, 2013; Upham, "A Memoir of Gen. John Glover, of Marblehead," 97+ (*"not blind"*).

192 **At dawn on Friday, September 19:** Wild, "Journal of Ebenezer Wild," 94 (*thick mist*); Glover, *General Burgoyne in Canada and America*, 186–87 (*"grasp with your hands"*); Griswold and Linebaugh, eds., *The Saratoga Campaign*, 41 (*fixed bayonets*); ES to author, Oct. 2021 (*knapsacks*); Hadden, *A Journal Kept in Canada*, 157–59 (*seventy round shot*).

193 **Burgoyne split the Canada Army:** "Diary of the Brunswick Troops in North America," HDAR, fiche 180–93, HZ-5, Sept. 19, 1777, 302–3 (*single hollow*); Stone, ed., *Memoirs, and Letters and Journals of Major General Riedesel*, 144 (*three columns*); Griswold and Linebaugh, eds., *The Saratoga Campaign*, 42–43 (*Great Ravine*).

193 **On the left, sixteen hundred:** Stone, ed., *Memoirs, and Letters and Journals of Major General*

Riedesel, 146 (*crackle of musket fire*); "Diary of the Brunswick Troops in North America," HDAR, fiche 180–93, HZ-5, Sept. 19, 1777, 302–3 (*eight hundred paces*); Lynn, ed., *The Specht Journal*, 79 (*cocked an ear*).

193 **Goaded by the aggressive Arnold:** *CtS*, 163 ("*observe their direction*"); Griswold and Linebaugh, eds., *The Saratoga Campaign*, 45–46 (*Gates had ordered*), 211; ES to author, July 2024 (*refugees*); "John Freeman and the Battle of Freeman's Farm," https://sites.rootsweb.com/~truax/freeman.html; author visit, SNHP, Sept. 25, 2021 and Sept. 13, 2024.

193 **A stupendous roar from several hundred:** Luzader, *Saratoga*, 234; Snow, *1777*, 95 (*wounded Major Forbes*).

194 **That was a mistake:** Wilkinson, *Memoirs of My Own Times*, 1: 238 (*turkey-call shell*).

194 **The battle was joined:** *CtS*, 170 (*Hamilton appeared*); Griswold and Linebaugh, eds., *The Saratoga Campaign*, 49 (*knapsacks, blankets*).

194 **The king's troops were abruptly intercepted:** Coffin, *The Lives and Services*, 85 (*Hampshire men*); *CtS*, 175–76 (*back into the underbrush*); Weddle, *The Compleat Victory*, 279–80; Griswold and Linebaugh, eds., *The Saratoga Campaign*, 49 (*reverse course*); Luzader, *Saratoga*, 240 (*more than two thousand*); Baxter, ed., *The British Invasion from the North*, 273–74 ("*explosion of fire*").

194 **A large share of the carnage:** Smith and Kiley, *An Illustrated Encyclopedia of Uniforms from 1775–1783*, 149 (*sagittal plume*); Money, *To the Right Honorable William Windham*, 13 ("*national weapon*"), 18–19 ("*first to fall*"); *CtS*, 180 ("*friends and enemies*").

195 **Much of the British fire flew high:** Luzader, *Saratoga*, 243 ("*rifle-barrel pieces*"); Snow, *1777*, 126 (*more than a third*); Smyth, *History of the XX Regiment, 1688–1888*, 86–87 (*twice wounded*); Cubbison, "*The Artillery Never Gained More Honour*," 112 (*thirty-six of forty-eight*); Hadden, *A Journal Kept in Canada*, 163; *CtS*, 176 (*hauled from the river road*).

195 **By four-thirty p.m. the fighting:** *CtS*, 181–82; Snow, *1777*, 116–20 (*nineteen privates*); Campbell, *Revolutionary Services and Civil Life of General William Hull*, 94–96 (*William Hull*); Ketchum, *Saratoga*, 364–66 (*bayonet charge*).

195 **The shadows grew long as Arnold rode:** Snow, *1777*, 116 (*gray charger*); *CtS*, 182 (*10th Massachusetts*); Snow, *1777*, 38 (*potential defensive line*).

195 **Arnold pressed his case:** Snow, *1777*, 121.

196 **Gates's usual amiability:** *CtS*, 182 ("*drew his sword*"), 316n; Snow, *1777*, 122 (*full gallop*).

196 **General Riedesel had no intention:** *CtS*, 190; Griswold and Linebaugh, eds., *The Saratoga Campaign*, 51–52; Snow, *1777*, 122 ("*Come to my assistance*").

196 **Within minutes, the German commander had:** Barker, "The Battles of Saratoga and the Kinderhook Tea Party," 25+ ("*bellowed one hurrah*"); Stone, ed., *Memoirs, and Letters and Journals of Major General Riedesel*, 150–51 ("*thinned down*").

196 **Brunswickers pressed forward:** "Diary of the Brunswick Troops in North America," HDAR, fiche 180–93, HZ-5, Sept. 19, 1777, 307–8 ("*war cries*"); Stone, *Journal of Captain Pausch*, 143 ("*drunk*").

197 **"The fire never ceased":** Boyle, "From Saratoga to Valley Forge," 237+ ("*seventy acres*"); BSC, 325 ("*masters of the field*"); Griswold and Linebaugh, eds., *The Saratoga Campaign*, 55 (*weaker strategically*).

197 **Fraser convinced Burgoyne:** Snow, *1777*, 147 (*postponed until three p.m.*); Alexander Scammell to Jonathan C. Chadbourn, Sept. 26, 1777, James S. Schoff Revolutionary War Collection, WLC ("*good bruising*").

197 **Some 150,000 lead bullets:** *CtS*, 19–93 (*fired by both sides* and "*Tell my uncle*"); Holmes, *Redcoat*, 258 (*opium*); O'Shaughnessy, *The Men Who Lost America*, 155–56 (*shared a grave*); *CtS*, 193 ("*bravery and fidelity*"); Weddle, *The Compleat Victory*, 284 (*566 men*). As usual, different accounts cite variable casualty figures.

197 **American battle losses totaled:** ES to author, July 2024 (*about 325*); Griswold and Linebaugh, eds., *The Saratoga Campaign*, 53 (*Almost thirty officers*); Snow, *1777*, 139 (*bounties paid*); Alexander, ed., "Diary of Captain Benjamin Warren on Battlefield of Saratoga," 201+ ("*cries and groans*" and "*drink in a spoon*"). Weddle put American casualties at 465 (*The Compleat Victory*, 284).

198 **Damaged redcoats were trundled:** Stone, *Journal of Captain Pausch*, 145 (*"unpleasant sight"*); Ketchum, *Saratoga*, 371 (*"professional improvement"*); Kidder, *History of the First New Hampshire Regiments in the War of the Revolution*, 21–24 (*eleven teeth*).

198 **"I trust we have convinced":** Brown and Peckham, eds., *Revolutionary War Journals of Henry Dearborn, 1775–1783*, 106–7 (*"will fight"*); John F. Luzader, "Preliminary Documentary Report on Benedict Arnold at Saratoga," Oct. 27, 1958, SNHP, 11; Griswold and Linebaugh, eds., *The Saratoga Campaign*, 55; *CtS*, 195 (*effective distance*); Luzader, *Saratoga*, 392.

198 **Gates later faced condemnation:** Luzader, *Saratoga*, 393 (*"complemented each other"*).

199 **The clang of picks, shovels:** Wilkinson, *Memoirs of My Own Times*, 1: 263; Snow, *1777*, 145–46; *BSC*, 115; Griswold and Linebaugh, eds., *The Saratoga Campaign*, 58 (*extended rectangle*), 83–88 (*river cobbles*); Luzader, *Saratoga*, 251–52.

199 **Yet as the days grew shorter:** Doblin and Lynn, "A Brunswick Grenadier with Burgoyne," 420+ (*"No vegetables"*); Baxter, ed., *The British Invasion from the North*, 281 (*"not buried deep enough"*).

199 **Since leaving Skenesborough in July:** "Sir Henry Clinton's Hourglass Cipher," http://cryptiana .web.fc2.com/code/hourglass.htm; Hibbert, *Redcoats and Rebels*, 189 (*"If you think 2,000 men"*).

200 **Burgoyne ordered a cannon crew:** Baxter, ed., *The British Invasion from the North*, 279 (*at midnight*); *BSC*, 315 (*"Do it"*).

200 **As rumors about this exchange:** Baxter, ed., *The British Invasion from the North*, 279 (*"It must be owned"*).

9. HOW ART THOU FALLEN

201 **The secret courier carrying Burgoyne's plea:** Clinton, *The American Rebellion*, 72–73 (*at least twelve thousand*); Hibbert, *Redcoats and Rebels*, 189; *BSC*, 313–17; *CtS*, 212. Burgoyne's message reached Clinton on September 29. Clinton's reply never reached Burgoyne.

201 **Not to Albany:** Mackesy, *The War for America, 1775–1783*, 137–38 (*just under seven thousand*).

201 **Reinforcements from Britain:** Clinton, *The American Rebellion*, 72 (*seventeen hundred troops*); *CtS*, 212 (*three thousand*); Beatson, *Naval and Military Memoirs of Great Britain*, 6: 230–34 (*tedious* and *flatboats, bateaux*).

202 **The abrupt appearance:** Mackesy, *The War for America, 1775–1783*, 138 (*bolted inland*).

202 **A band of Precambrian granite:** Diamant, *Bernard Romans*, 58–60 (*"majestic, solemn"*); council of general officers to GW, May 17, 1777, *PGW*, 9: 450–51 (*"enemy will not attempt"*).

202 **One proposal for clogging the Hudson:** Diamant, *Chaining the Hudson*, 90 (*roll boulders*), 92–106 (*sixty-five million gallons*); Ruttenber, *Obstructions to the Navigation of Hudson's River*, 71–85 (*snapped twice*).

202 **A third, smaller redoubt:** Ruttenber, *Obstructions to the Navigation of Hudson's River*, 86 (*"winter grain"*); Diamant, *Chaining the Hudson*, 106 (*two new frigates*); Daughan, *Revolution on the Hudson*, 175–76 (*launched at Peekskill*).

204 **None of this deterred Henry Clinton:** Beatson, *Naval and Military Memoirs of Great Britain*, 6: 234–35 (*daybreak on Monday*).

204 **Ferocious fighting spilled:** *CtS*, 217–21 (*Campbell was killed* and *"heaven was falling"*); GW to Israel Putnam, Oct. 19, 1777, FOL; George Clinton to GW, Oct. 9, 1777, *PGW*, 11: 453–57 (*six hundred defenders*); Irving, *The Life of George Washington*, 3: 224–28 (*bayonet thrust*).

204 **By eight p.m. the king's men:** *CtS*, 221 (*183 casualties* and *sixty-seven field guns*); Weddle, *The Compleat Victory*, 302–3 (*70 killed*); "Journal of the Honorable Hessian Infantry Regiment von Bose," HDAR, 18–20; *Diary of Samuel Richards*, 56 (*nearby pond*).

204 **The debacle continued on the river:** Diamant, *Chaining the Hudson*, 117 (*foul wind and an ebb tide* and *"pyramids of fire"*); Daughan, *Revolution on the Hudson*, 175–76 (Shark); George Clinton to GW, Oct. 9, 1777, *PGW*, 11: 453–57; Clinton, *The American Rebellion*, 75–76.

205 **A day later Royal Navy tars:** *CtS*, 26 (*severed the chain*); "Journal of the Honorable Hessian Infantry Regiment von Bose," HDAR, 20 (*Union Jack*).

205 **Henry Clinton took a moment:** *BSC*, 317 ("Nous y voilà"); ES to author, July 2024 (*Sergeant*

Daniel Taylor) BSC, 127–29; Nagy, *Invisible Ink*, 108–10 (*camlet coat*); Bakeless, *Turncoats, Traitors and Heroes*, 151–53.

205 **This buoyant epistle:** Nagy, *Invisible Ink*, 108–10 (*faded red coats*); Lossing, *Pictorial Field-Book of the Revolution*, 116; Pratt, "An Account of the British Expedition Above the Highlands of the Hudson River," 109+.

205 **A search disclosed:** Rose, *Washington's Spies*, 58 (*personal letters*); CtS, 322n (*tartar emetic*); Lossing, *Pictorial Field-Book of the Revolution*, 116 (*apple tree*); BSC, 128–29; Bakeless, *Turncoats, Traitors and Heroes*, 152–53 (*farewell letter*); Pratt, "An Account of the British Expedition Above the Highlands of the Hudson River," 109+ (*"gospel penitent"*).

205 **Unaware of this sad muddle:** Mackesy, *The War for America, 1775–1783*, 139–40; CtS, 224 (*six months of supplies*); Clinton, *The American Rebellion*, 79–80 (*Vaughan to continue north*); Willcox, "Too Many Cooks," 85 (*two thousand troops*).

206 **Led by the brig *Diligent*:** Pratt, "An Account of the British Expedition Above the Highlands of the Hudson River," 109+ (Friendship); Ruttenber, *Obstructions to the Navigation of Hudson's River*, 105–13 (*Murderer's Creek*); Schoonmaker, *The History of Kingston, New York*, 293; Diamant, *Chaining the Hudson*, 119 (*"ill-tempered"*); "Journal of the Honorable Hessian Infantry Regiment von Bose," HDAR, 21 (*intended to reach Albany*); Pownall and Almon, *The Remembrancer*, 5: 43 (*"a nursery"*).

206 **"We are hellishly frightened":** Kelly, "So Heavy a Trial," JAR, Sept. 4, 2014; Schoonmaker, *The History of Kingston, New York*, 296–301, 309 ("Loop, jongens"); Forsyth, "The Burning of Kingston by the British on October 16th, 1777," 62+ (*buried their china*); Pratt, "An Account of the British Expedition Above the Highlands of the Hudson River," 109+ (*fleet prison*); Jones, "'The rage of tory-hunting,'" 719 (*"fetid cesspits"*); Crary, ed., *The Price of Loyalty*, 204 (*Rondout Creek*).

206 **Ignoring a few wild shots:** Kelly, "So Heavy a Trial," JAR, Sept. 4, 2014 (*"I pray the Lord"*); Forsyth, "The Burning of Kingston by the British on October 16th, 1777," 62+ (*116 houses*); Lord Stirling to Robert Livingston, Oct. 30, 1777, JLB, AAA (*"piratical destroyer"*); Moore, *The Diary of the American Revolution, 1775–1781*, 259–60 (*"how art thou fallen,"* Isaiah 14:12).

207 **Vaughan reboarded *Friendship*:** Clinton, *The American Rebellion*, 79–80 (*pilots refused*); Kwasny, *Washington's Partisan War, 1775–1783*, 175–76 (*five thousand rebels*); CtS, 263 ("impractical").

207 **Moreover, Henry Clinton had directed:** Burgoyne, trans., *Journal of a Hessian Grenadier Battalion*, 78–79 (*sloop-of-war*); Clinton, *The American Rebellion*, 81 (*"without delay"*); Willcox, *Portrait of a General*, 189 (*"From my heart"*).

207 **Clinton pitied himself more:** Thomas, *Memoirs of the Marquis of Rockingham and His Contemporaries*, 2: 334–38 (*"stronger reasons"*); Fleming, "The Enigma of General Howe," n.p.; Clinton, *The American Rebellion*, 83–84 (*"obliged to submit"*).

207 **General Vaughan's expedition:** Ruttenber, *Obstructions to the Navigation of Hudson's River*, 86 (*Fort Vaughan*); Beatson, *Naval and Military Memoirs of Great Britain*, 6: 236 (*sent on to Gibraltar*).

207 **In early October the Canada Army:** Doblin, trans., *The Specht Journal*, 85 (*hoarfrost*); "Diary of the Brunswick Troops in America," HDAR, fiche 180–93, letter HZ-5, 323 (*Eight hundred wounded and ailing*); Kopperman, "The Numbers Game," 254+; Snow, *1777*, 161 (*bridge*), 210 (*spruce beer*); BSC, 131 (*emaciated horses*).

208 **Desertion grew so promiscuous:** CtS, 225 (*"keep close watch"*); Barker, "The Battles of Saratoga and the Kinderhook Tea Party," 25+; "Diary of the Brunswick Troops in America," HDAR, fiche 180–93, letter HZ-5, 323 (*snatching men*); BSC, 122 (*bonfires*), 123–24 (*"All is hostile"*).

208 **Burgoyne required all mariners:** Doblin, trans., *The Specht Journal*, 82–84 (*drill and Clinton was advancing*); "Diary of the Brunswick Troops in America," HDAR, fiche 180–93, letter HZ-5, 315–16 (*thousand trees*); author visit, Great Redoubt, SNHP, Sept. 25, 2021; BSC, 130 (*"fond of indulging"*).

208 **With food stocks down:** Doblin, trans., *The Specht Journal*, 86–89 (*a few pence*); BSC, 124.

208 **Riedesel and Phillips balked:** Stone, ed., *Memoirs, and Letters and Journals of Major General Riedesel*, 162 (*should retract*); Doblin, trans., *The Specht Journal*, 89–90.

208 **Burgoyne pondered the dilemma:** "Diary of the Brunswick Troops in America," HDAR, fiche 180–93, letter HZ-5, 331–32 (*"retrograde movement"*); CtS, 227 (*large reconnaissance force*), 323n; Doblin, trans., *The Specht Journal*, 89–90; BSC, 326 (*"any possible means"*).

210 **The next day, to boost morale:** Doblin, trans., *The Specht Journal*, 87 (*signal rockets*).

210 **Any potential retreat to the north:** Kingsley, "A German Perspective on the American Attempt," 5+; Cubbison, *"The Artillery Never Gained More Honour,"* 132–33; Kopperman, "The Numbers Game," 254+ (*malaria, dysentery*).

210 **More than twice that number:** Mattern, *Benjamin Lincoln and the American Revolution*, 1–3, 13, 19, 36 (*"excellent officer"*); Hoyt, "The Pawlet Expedition, September 1777," 69+ (*"one shift of clothes"*).

210 **The third detachment followed:** Pell, "John Brown and the Dash for Ticonderoga," 23+ (*"this man's God"*).

211 **At first light on September 18:** Cubbison, *"The Artillery Never Gained More Honour,"* 132 (*lobbed 12-pound balls*); Stone, *Journal of Captain Pausch*, 148–51; Kingsley, "A German Perspective on the American Attempt," 5+ (*overran the battery*); "Col. John Brown's Expedition Against Ticonderoga and Diamond Island, 1777," 284+ (*"out of their holes"*); Hamilton, *Fort Ticonderoga*, 218–19 (*Nearly three hundred*); Hoyt, "The Pawlet Expedition, September 1777," 69+ (*two hundred bateaux*).

211 **Good, if imperfect:** "Col. John Brown's Attack of September 1777 on Fort Ticonderoga," 208–9; "Col. John Brown's Expedition Against Ticonderoga and Diamond Island, 1777," 284+ (*"garrison entrusted"*); CtS, 203; Barbieri, "Brown's Raid on Ticonderoga and Mount Independence," JAR, Jan. 20, 2022; Venter, "Behind Enemy Lines," 12+.

211 **Yet the weeklong sequence of attacks:** "General Powell to Sir Guy Carleton," Sept. 23, 1777 (*two thousand troops*), Sept. 27, 1777 (*St. Leger finally arrived*); BFTM, vol. 7, no. 2 (July 1945): 32–34.

211 **News of the pummeling:** Mattern, *Benjamin Lincoln and the American Revolution*, 47 (*"universal joy"*); Snow, *1777*, 222 (*"risk all"*); Gates to Col. Bedel, Oct. 4, 1777, Horatio Gates papers, NYHS, micro (*"finishing stroke"*).

212 **During the fortnight since the Battle:** CtS, 204 (*Nearly thirteen thousand*); Luzader, *Saratoga*, 282; Wright, *The Continental Army*, 117; ES to author, July 2024 (*half of them militiamen*); Weddle, *The Compleat Victory*, 99 (*bivouac assignments*); Clay, *Staff Ride for the Saratoga Campaign*, 13–14 (*more than fifty regiments*); BSC, 117 (*Oneida and Tuscarora*); CtS, 206 (*red wool caps*); Boyle, "From Saratoga to Valley Forge," 237+ (*prisoners*); Snow, *1777*, 165 (*red or black*); "Journal of Oliver Boardman of Middletown," 223+ (*"hooting & hollowing"*); Baldwin, *The Revolutionary Journal of Col. Jeduthan Baldwin, 1775–1778*, 121 (*$20 bounty*).

212 **Commissary officers collected writing paper:** Horatio Gates to GW, Oct. 5, 1777, FOL, fn; GW to Horatio Gates, Sept. 24, 1777, FOL (*"if his services"*); Horatio Gates to GW, Oct. 5, 1777, FOL (*"most afraid of"*).

212 **The prospect of another bloody brawl:** "A Letter from Saratoga," 182 (*"Remember my love"*); "Captain Brooks and Captain Bancroft," 265+ (*"prepared for a better meeting"*); Raphael, *Founders*, 315 (*"happiest camp"*). Massachusetts Continental regiments had not yet formally adopted numerical designations.

212 **There were unhappy corners:** Martin, *Benedict Arnold, Revolutionary Hero*, 382 (*"genius of war"*); CtS, 207 (*Gates's dispatch*); Luzader, *Saratoga*, 260 (*"very high strain"*); Snow, *1777*, 189 (*petition*); BA to Gates, Sept. 23, 1777, Horatio Gates papers, NYHS, micro (*"designing villain"*).

213 **Congenitally thin-skinned, Arnold:** Luzader, *Saratoga*, 272 (*"spirit of jealousy"*); Martin, *Benedict Arnold, Revolutionary Hero*, 388 (*"fatigue of body"*); Ketchum, *Saratoga*, 390 (*"beyond reconciliation"*).

213 **Fortunately for the American cause:** CtS, 208 (*Arnold's division*); Gates to Matthew Vishter,

Oct. 4, 1777, Horatio Gates papers, NYHS, micro (*"a happy issue"*). Later assertions that Arnold was relieved or superseded are incorrect.

213 **Sunrise at five forty-four:** "Table of Sunrise/Sunset," Astronomical Applications Dept., U.S. Naval Observatory; *CtS*, 230 (*overnight showers*).

213 **Burgoyne and his generals:** Stone, *Journal of Captain Pausch*, 161 (*two hours in a tent*); Snow, *1777*, 235 (*no written orders*); *CtS*, 228 (*haversacks*).

213 **Three columns stepped off:** author visit, "Barber Wheatfield," SNHP, Sept. 25, 2021 and Sept. 13, 2024 (*"damned crooked road"*); *CtS*, 230 (*cutting the grain*).

214 **British grenadiers and light infantry sidled:** *CtS*, 228–29; author visit, "Barber Wheatfield," SNHP, Sept. 25, 2021 (*worm fence*); Snow, *1777*, 241 (*climbed to the roof*); Stone, *Journal of Captain Pausch*, 162–65 (*12-pounders*).

214 **Burgoyne sat his horse:** author visit, "Barber Wheatfield," SNHP, Sept. 25, 2021.

214 **A mile and a half south, Horatio Gates:** "Captain Brooks and Captain Bancroft," 265+ (*ox heart* and *"commence the attack"*); SNHP, signage, "John Neilson House."

214 **The *pock pock pock* of distant gunshots:** "Captain Brooks and Captain Bancroft," 265+ (*"Shall I go out"*); *CtS*, 230; Wilkinson, *Memoirs of My Own Times*, 1: 265–68 (*"begin the game"*); Snow, *1777*, 249 (*Spanish bay*). Historian Kevin J. Weddle notes that Wilkinson in his account essentially substitutes himself for Arnold (Weddle, *The Compleat Victory*, 317–18).

215 **The seven hundred men:** ES to author, July 2024; Brown and Peckham, eds., *Revolutionary War Journals of Henry Dearborn, 1775–1783*, 108 (*"got bewildered"*); *CtS*, 230–32 (*"file to the left"*).

215 **From the excited, wheezing pickets:** Nathanial Bacheller to Susanna, Oct. 9, 1777, ES to author, Oct. 2021 (*"late in the day"*); ES, lecture, George Washington Round Table of the American Revolution, Washington, D.C., Nov. 3, 2021.

215 **With Gates's permission, Arnold:** Snow, *1777*, 250–51; Griswold and Linebaugh, eds., *The Saratoga Campaign*, 64 (*Learned's brigade*), 215–16 (*scored the balls*).

216 **By four p.m. the fire:** *CtS*, 232–33 (*"violent and incessant"* and *6-pounders*); Snow, *1777*, 235 (*"all in hell"*); Stone, *Journal of Captain Pausch*, 168–71 (*blister any hand*).

216 **Captain John Money:** Money, *To the Right Honorable William Windham*, 12 (*"in a scarlet coat"*).

216 **Those red coats now fell:** Wilkinson, *Memoirs of My Own Times*, 1: 268 (*"like a torrent"*); "A Narrative of the Saratoga Campaign—Major General Henry Dearborn, 1815," 4+ (*found Captain Clerke*); Howe inquiry, *Parliamentary Register*, 12: 257.

216 **Overwhelmed grenadiers on the British left:** Wilkinson, *Memoirs of My Own Times*, 1: 270–71 (*"agonies"* and *"shot through both legs"*); Thorp, ed., *The Acland Journal*, xxv, 32 (*fifty guineas*).

217 **With rebels enveloping:** Snow, *1777*, 262–63 (*"draw as soon"*); BSC, 134; *CtS*, 238 (*rode toward the Hudson* and *"to save themselves"*); Stone, *Journal of Captain Pausch*, 166–67 (*"disorder"*), 173 (*"running pell-mell"*).

217 **General Fraser had lingered:** Snow, *1777*, 258–61 (*basswood tree*); *CtS*, 325n (*"pooh, he was gone"*); Harrington and Jordan, "The Other Mystery Shot of the American Revolution," 1037+; Snow, *1777*, 261 (*aide caught*).

217 **By five p.m. none of the king's men:** Griswold and Linebaugh, eds., *The Saratoga Campaign*, 64; Luzader, *Saratoga*, 285 (*Every field piece*); "Historical Handbook Number Four," SNHP, 1959, https://www.nps.gov/parkhistory/online_books/hh/4/hh4toc.htm; Snell, "A Report on the Balcarres and Breymann Redoubts," Feb. 2, 1949, SNHP, 9–25; author visit, Balcarres Redoubt, SNHP, Sept. 25, 2021; *CtS*, 238 (*camp followers scrambled*).

217 **The pursuing Americans "attacked":** Howe inquiry, *Parliamentary Register*, 12: 160 (*"as much fury"*); "The Decisive Moment, Breymann Redoubt," SNHP, https://www.nps.gov/places/the-decisive-moment-7-breymann-redoubt-continued.htm; "Baron Riedesel's Letter to Duke of Brunswick," Oct. 21, 1777, SNHP, 1–4; "Historical Handbook Number Four," SNHP, 1959, https://www.nps.gov/parkhistory/online_books/hh/4/hh4toc.htm; *CtS*, 241 (*unforgiving gunfire*).

218 **A better prospect lay:** Buell, ed., *The Memoirs of Rufus Putnam*, 68 (*5th and 6th Massachu-setts*); *CtS*, 239–40 (*poorly designed*); Morison, *The Oxford History of the American People*, 248 ("'*Come on, boys*'").

218 **Defenders fired one erratic volley:** "A Narrative of the Saratoga Campaign—Major General Henry Dearborn, 1815," 4+; Von Papet, "The Brunswick Contingent in America, 1776–1783," 218+ (*"constant tyrant"*); Doblin and Lynn, "A Brunswick Grenadier with Burgoyne," 433n.

218 **As a bellowing Arnold demanded:** "A Narrative of the Saratoga Campaign—Major General Henry Dearborn, 1815," 4+ (*"if he was badly wounded"*); Malony, "An Analysis of the Near-fatal Wound Suffered by Benedict Arnold at Saratoga," Friends of Saratoga Battlefield, n.p. (*Four agonizing days*); Ketchum, *Saratoga*, 403 (*onto a litter*); Luzader, *Saratoga*, 296 (*"gallant Major General Arnold"*).

218 **Darkness rolled over the battlefield:** "Journal of Oliver Boardman of Middletown," 223+ (*"Drove them"*); *CtS*, 245 (*road that angled*).

219 **"The fields are strowed":** Alexander, ed., "Diary of Captain Benjamin Warren on Battlefield of Saratoga," 201+; Stone, *Journal of Captain Pausch*, 174n (*skulls*), 176n (*woodcutters*).

219 **Northern Army casualties:** Griswold and Linebaugh, eds., *The Saratoga Campaign*, 66 (*about 150*); ES to author, July 2024 (*thirty of them officers*); Becker and Bloodgood, *The Sexagenary*, 96 (*"pale and lifeless"*); "Diary of Ezra Tilden," Gilder Lehrman Institute for American History, https://www.gilderlehrman.org/collection/glc01450004; Rees, "'I Extracted 4 balls by cutting,'" 7 (*"died of their wounds"*).

219 **Among the last Continental casualties:** Mattern, *Benjamin Lincoln and the American Revolu-tion*, 49 (*"checking and spurring"*); Trumbull, *Autobiography, Reminiscences and Letters of John Trumbull*, 307 (*"rascals have struck me"*).

219 **Three miles north, this new day:** Griswold and Linebaugh, eds., *The Saratoga Campaign*, 67 (*British losses*); Ketchum, *Saratoga*, 405 (*Germans counted*); Snow, *1777*, 280; Brown, trans., *Baroness von Riedesel and the American Revolution*, 51–53 (*"fatal ambition"*).

220 **Yes, he must:** Hadden, *A Journal Kept in Canada*, li (*"devoted to glory"*); Stone, ed., *Memoirs, and Letters and Journals of Major General Riedesel*, 168–69 (*"military funeral"*); Baxter, ed., *The British Invasion from the North*, 293 (*"big with the fate"*).

220 **"I never saw so affecting":** Howe inquiry, *Parliamentary Register*, 12: 257; "Gen. Fraser's Ac-count of Burgoyne's Campaign on Lake Champlain and the Battle of Hubbardton," 139+ (*"in-cessant cannonade"*).

220 **"Everything might go very badly":** Riedesel, *Letters and Journals Relating to the War of American Independence*, 104; Brown, trans., *Baroness von Riedesel and the American Revolu-tion*, 53–54 (*"calashes were ready"*); Snow, *1777*, 300.

220 **Americans swiftly overran:** *CtS*, 250 (*four hundred enemy*); Rees, "'I Extracted 4 balls by cut-ting,'" 8 (*"terribly mangled"*); Doblin, trans., *The Specht Journal*, 92; Snow, *1777*, 294–95 (*"I recommend them"*).

221 **A gray, wet dawn on Thursday:** Hagist, *British Soldiers, American War*, 208 (*seventy-two bar-rels*); BSC, 137 (*deserters*); Boyle, "From Saratoga to Valley Forge," 237+ (*with their wives*); Kidder, *History of the First New Hampshire*, 37 (*threw a wheel*); *CtS*, 251 (*gunpowder, flour*); Alexander, ed., "Diary of Captain Benjamin Warren on Battlefield of Saratoga," 201+ (*"Roads strowed"*).

221 **Early that evening the column closed:** BSC, 137; Doblin, trans., *The Specht Journal*, 94 (*St. Leger and hard freeze*); BSC, 329 (*shooting up bateaux*); Doblin and Lynn, "A Brunswick Gren-adier with Burgoyne," 420+ (*"Heavy hoarfrost"*).

221 **Burgoyne again moved into Schuyler's:** Griswold and Linebaugh, eds., *The Saratoga Cam-paign*, 150, 181–82 (*sawmills*); author visit, Schuyler house, SNHP, Sept. 25, 2021; BSC, 329 (*"escape as they could"*); Houlding and Yates, "Corporal Fox's Memoir of Service, 1766–1783," 146+; Hagist, *British Soldiers, American War*, 209 (*back to Saratoga*).

221 **Convinced that Gates intended:** Griswold and Linebaugh, eds., *The Saratoga Campaign*, 179 (*privy*); Hagist, ed., *A British Soldier's Story*, 53 (*"birds of prey"*).

222 **Thousands of American Continentals:** Ketchum, *Saratoga*, 412; Trumbull, *Autobiography*,

Reminiscences and Letters of John Trumbull, 301–3 ("*Brother Burgoyne*"); Brandow, *The Story of Old Saratoga and History of Schuylerville*, 133 (*small wooden house*); CtS, 253–55 (*jump the creek*); Luzader, *Saratoga*, 307–10; ES to author, July 2024 (*Generals Glover and John Nixon*); Stone, *The Campaign of Lieut. Gen. John Burgoyne*, 67n (*bone fragments*); Upham, *Memoir of General John Glover of Marblehead*, 31 ("*whole army*"); Buell, ed., *The Memoirs of Rufus Putnam*, 69.

222 **Even so, the Canada Army's predicament:** Snow, *1777*, 330–31 ("*bad as possible*"); Howe inquiry, *Parliamentary Register*, 12: 161 ("*discomposed*"); Baxter, ed., *The British Invasion from the North*, 304 ("*cattle began to die*"); Houlding and Yates, "Corporal Fox's Memoir of Service, 1766–1783," 146+ (*four biscuits*); Bradford, ed., "Lord Francis Napier's Journal of the Burgoyne Campaign," 285+.

222 **"All things in this camp":** "Victory Woods," SNHP, www.nps.gov/places/victory-woods.htm; CtS, 256 (*stinking cellar*); Brown, trans., *Baroness von Riedesel and the American Revolution*, 58 ("*Eleven cannonballs*"); Snow, *1777*, 320 (*other leg torn off*).

222 **Brother Burgoyne estimated:** BSC, 330 ("*extended three parts*").

223 **He listed five options:** "Minutes of Council of War," Oct. 12, 1777, DAR, 14: 212–14 ("*utmost secrecy*"); BSC, 343.

223 **Canada Army's last rations:** Doblin, trans., *The Specht Journal*, 96 ("*a certain joy*"); BSC, 344 ("*immediately discovered*"); Snow, *1777*, 341 ("*too late*").

223 **At seven p.m. on Monday:** BSC, 334–45 ("*full representation*").

223 **Burgoyne posed his final question:** Snow, *1777*, 347.

224 **Only sketchy details:** Luzader, *Saratoga*, 324 (*threat of Henry Clinton*); Snow, *1777*, 348; "George Williams," https://www.62ndregiment.org/George_Williams.htm (*ensign*).

224 **An eerie calm sifted over the river:** ES to author, July 2024 (*a ford near the creek's mouth*); Wilkinson, *Memoirs of My Own Times*, 1: 298 (*blindfolded*); BSC, 333 ("*superiority of your numbers*").

224 **The endgame at Saratoga had begun:** BSC, 341; CtS, 261 ("*capitulation*").

224 **Gates agreed, looking over his shoulder:** Snow, *1777*, 364 ("*stringent measures*"); BSC, 141–42, 341 (*thirteen clauses*).

224 **"The grand army":** Lunt, *John Burgoyne of Saratoga*, 271 ("*agreed to be*"); Stone, ed., *Memoirs, and Letters and Journals of Major General Riedesel*, 187 ("*most unfortunate man*"); Doblin, trans., *The Specht Journal*, 100 (*colors and tassels*); Hadden, *A Journal Kept in Canada*, 401 (*presented to George III*); CtS, 267–68 (*Thirty sets*); Cannon, *Historical Record of the Ninth*, 32–33 (*9th Foot*); ES to author, July 2024 (*distributed through the ranks*).

225 **As the morning fog burned:** Wild, "Journal of Ebenezer Wild," 66+; Stone, ed., *Memoirs, and Letters and Journals of Major General Riedesel*, 189–90 ("*like a dandy*"); ES to author, July 2024 (*already scratched his signature*); Snow, *1777*, 380 ("*convention signed*"); Smyth, *History of the XX Regiment, 1688–1888*, 91 ("*sobbed*"); Baxter, ed., *The British Invasion from the North*, 321 ("*ended all our hopes*").

225 **At ten-thirty a.m. the king's men:** CtS, 279 ("*stepping off*"); John Langdon to American commissioners, Oct. 29, 1777, FOL.

225 **A British officer wrote:** Stone, ed., *Memoirs, and Letters and Journals of Major General Riedesel*, 188 (*Fort Hardy*); John Langdon to American commissioners, Oct. 29, 1777, FOL; Fischer, *Liberty and Freedom*, 219 ("*lover's spell*").

225 **"The greatest conquest ever known":** Brown and Peckham, eds., *Revolutionary War Journals of Henry Dearborn, 1775–1783*, 111; Lowell, *The Hessians*, 169 (*more than 8,000 men*); Clay, *Staff Ride for the Saratoga Campaign*, 69; CtS, 269–72; Tallmadge, *Memoir of Colonel Benjamin Tallmadge*, 110 ("*strong & heavy*"); McGuire, *The Philadelphia Campaign*, 2: 213–15 ("*an acquisition*"); Wade and Lively, *This Glorious Cause*, 232 ("*fatiguing campaign*").

225 **So had Horatio Gates:** Pettengill, trans., *Letters from America, 1776–1779*, 113 (*gray strands*); CtS, 269–72; Wild, "Journal of Ebenezer Wild," 99; Pond, ed., "An Eye-Witness of Burgoyne's Surrender," 279 ("*No laughing*").

226 **Gates plucked the hat:** CtS, 269 ("*enterprise, courage, and perseverance*"); Lunt, *John Burgoyne of Saratoga*, 269–70 (*two glasses*).

226 **As the meal ended:** *CtS*, 269–72 (*"filled a bumper"*); ES to author, July 2024 (*sword in its scabbard*); Luzader, *Saratoga*, 332 (*half-pay major*); Miller, *Triumph of Freedom*, 214 (*"calamitous"*).

226 **At three-thirty p.m. the king's men:** Baldwin, *The Revolutionary Journal of Col. Jeduthan Baldwin, 1775–1778*, 125 (*"most agreeable sight"*); Hughes, "Note Relative to the Campaign Against Burgoyne," 265+ (*colors flying*); Doblin, trans., *The Specht Journal*, 101–2 (*gunners next to their guns*); Matthews and Wecter, *Our Soldiers Speak, 1775–1918*, 49 (*"perfectly quiet"*); Bradford, ed., "Lord Francis Napier's Journal of the Burgoyne Campaign," 285+ (*"greatest decency"*).

226 **By sunset the last echelons:** Thacher, *Military Journal*, 109 (*"reverse of fortune"*); Snow, *1777*, 379 (*"obstinate old slut"*).

227 **Thousands of prisoners crossed the Hudson:** Matthews and Wecter, *Our Soldiers Speak, 1775–1918*, 51 (*"full of troops"*); Upham, *Memoir of General John Glover of Marblehead*, 31 (*"foreign troops"*).

227 **Yankee families drove up:** JLB, AAA (*cartridge pouches*); Doblin, trans., *The Specht Journal*, 105 (*stole the wretched horses*); Billias, *General John Glover and His Marblehead Mariners*, 152–53 (*"sugar dolls"*); Loane, *Following the Drum*, 115 (*"sordid set"*); Hagist, "Notes on German Army Women," 20.

227 **Burgoyne and a score:** *BSC*, 143–44; Alexander J. Wall, "The Story of the Convention Army, 1777–1783," in *Narratives of the Revolution in New York*, 187; Thacher, *Military Journal*, 112 (*"ancient style"*); Lossing, *Life and Times of Philip Schuyler*, 2: 380 (*smoked tongue*); Lunt, *John Burgoyne of Saratoga*, 271 (*"the fate of war"*); "Schuyler Estate," SNHP, www.nps.gov/places/schuyler-estate.htm; author visit, Schuyler Mansion State Historic Site, Sept. 12, 2024, signage (*rhinestone buckles*).

227 **They left behind a town:** Thacher, *Military Journal*, 112–13; Huston, *Logistics of Liberty*, 102 (*tincture of myrrh*); Becker and Bloodgood, *The Sexagenary*, 96 (*"horror and sickness"*).

228 **Two American major generals lay:** Mattern, *Benjamin Lincoln and the American Revolution*, 51–53 (*youngest daughter*); "Letter from Dr. James Browne," *New England Historical and Genealogical Register*, vol. 18 (1864): 34 (*"abuses us"*); Martin, *Benedict Arnold*, 404–5 (*"damned nonsense"*).

228 **With the limb immobilized:** Malony, "An Analysis of the Near-fatal Wound Suffered by Benedict Arnold at Saratoga," Friends of Saratoga Battlefield, n.p. (*fracture box*); Thacher, *Military Journal*, 103 (*"very peevish"*); Palmer, *George Washington and Benedict Arnold*, 255–56 (*restore Arnold's seniority*); Martin, *Benedict Arnold*, 405 (*two inches*).

228 **"The malice of this man":** Philbrick, *Valiant Ambition*, 173.

228 **If Arnold was miserable:** Ferling, *Winning Independence*, 66 (*salutes*); Moore, *The Diary of the American Revolution, 1775–1781*, 2: 513–16 (*bonfires*); De Fonblanque, *Life and Correspondence of the Right Hon. John Burgoyne*, 257 (*"Burgoyne unmindful"*); Royster, *A Revolutionary People at War*, 267 (*"Burgoyne's Surrender"*); Diamant, *Chaining the Hudson*, 120 (*"damned rebel lie"*).

228 **Washington congratulated Gates:** GW to Gates, Oct. 30, 1777, FOL (*"signal success"*); Royster, *A Revolutionary People at War*, 176–77 (*"superintending Providence"*), 267 (*five-to-one*); Ferling, *Winning Independence*, 66 (*"Jack Brag"*).

229 **Loyalists stood with mouths agape:** Syrett, *Admiral Lord Howe*, 74 (*"Burgoyne's disaster"*); *Historical Anecdotes, Civil and Military*, 29 (*"blunders"*); Harcourt, *The Harcourt Papers*, 11: 224–25 (*"loss of his army"*); Nelson, *General Sir Guy Carleton, Lord Dorchester*, 123 (*"This unfortunate event"*).

229 **The strategy of using Canada as a springboard:** Cubbison, "The Artillery Never Gained More Honor," 138; Watt, *Rebellion in the Mohawk Valley*, 309 (*On November 8*); Skeffington Lutwidge to Guy Carleton, Nov. 4, 1777, *NDAR*, 10: 392 (*Flexible, Maria*).

229 **"We saw all the log houses":** Cubbison, "The Artillery Never Gained More Honour," 141; Kingsley, "A German Perspective on the American Attempt," 5+ (*forty-nine prisoners*); Willis, *The Struggle for Sea Power*, 188 (*struck a rock*); Skeffington Lutwidge to Guy Carleton, Nov. 4, 1777, *NDAR*, 10: 392 (*150 sick and wounded*); Doblin, trans., *The American Revolution, Garrison Life in French Canada and New York*, 86 (*"Carthage had probably not"*), 87 (*"drawings of hell"*).

230 **To evacuate the Convention Army:** Mackenzie, *Diary of Frederick Mackenzie*, 1: 243 (*two thousand barrels*); Boyd, *Elias Boudinot*, 46 (*better treatment*).

230 **Intent on forcing London to recognize:** Nelson, *General Horatio Gates*, 151–52 ("*explicit ratification*"); Jones, *Captives of Liberty*, 155–58; Knight, "Prisoner Exchange and Parole in the American Revolution," 201+; Wallace, *The Life of Henry Laurens*, 251 ("*our capacity*"); Mackenzie, *Diary of Frederick Mackenzie*, 1: 251 ("*breach of faith*").

230 **Yet bad faith cut:** GW to William Heath, Nov. 13, 1777, *PGW*, 12: 238–40n ("*keep the enemy ignorant*"); O'Malley, "1776—The Horror Show," *JAR*, Jan. 29, 2019; Knollenberg, *Washington and Revolution*, 141, 149–50; Jones, *Captives of Liberty*, 159, 165.

230 **The Americans indeed remained ignorant:** GW to Richard Henry Lee, Oct. 28, 1777, FOL ("*great precaution*"); Doblin and Lynn, "A Brunswick Grenadier with Burgoyne," 420+ (*every Thursday parading*); Pettengill, trans., *Letters from America, 1776–1779*, 132 ("*sad loneliness*"); William Heath to GW, Apr. 13, 1778, FOL (*almost £30,000*); Jones, *Captives of Liberty*, 171–73 (*threadbare uniforms*); "Journal of an Officer of the 47th Regiment of Foot," HL, mssHM 66.

231 **Here they would remain for years:** Frey, *The British Soldier in America*, 73 (*termites and rats*); O'Shaughnessy, *The Men Who Lost America*, 159 (*plantation houses*); Pettengill, trans., *Letters from America, 1776–1779*, 150–51 ("*Who would have expected*"); Brown, trans., *Baroness von Riedesel and the American Revolution*, xxxiv (*seeds and a piano*); Jonathan Clarke to Daniel Wier, June 16, 1779, Albemarle, Va., *Report on American Manuscripts in the Royal Institution of Great Britain*, vol. 1 (*eighty pipes*).

231 **John Burgoyne followed a different fate:** De Fonblanque, *Life and Correspondence of the Right Hon. John Burgoyne*, 316 ("*surrounded with enemies*"), 326 (*died on the battlefield*); *DAR*, 14: 237 ("*mind and body*"); Billias, ed., *George Washington's Generals and Opponents*, 177 ("*Had all my troops been British*").

231 **In truth, he was overmatched:** *BSC*, 356; Billias, ed., *George Washington's Generals and Opponents*, 185 ("*communication with the sea*").

231 **Upon arriving in Boston:** Heath, *Memoirs of Major-General Heath*, 126 ("*streets were filled*"); Lossing, *Pictorial Field-Book of the Revolution*, 25 ("*spectators*"); De Fonblanque, *Life and Correspondence of the Right Hon. John Burgoyne*, 326 ("*The value of life*"); Burgoyne to H. Laurens, Feb. 11, 1778, *BSC*, 351 ("*under God*"); Mackenzie, *Diary of Frederick Mackenzie*, 1: 266 (*without a farewell salute*); Hadden, *A Journal Kept in Canada*, 403 (Grampus). Queen Street became Court Street in 1788.

231 **He had predicted that:** Lunt, *John Burgoyne of Saratoga*, 274–76 ("*ministerial ingratitude*"), 298 (*ill health*); Murdoch, ed., *Rebellion in America*, 600 (*prisoner on parole*); "Parliament and the Howes," 128–29 (*waters at Bath*); O'Shaughnessy, *The Men Who Lost America*, 160 ("*suicide*"); Mackesy, *The War for America*, 238 (*Fort William*).

232 **In 1780 he would return:** Jesse, *Memoirs of King George the Third*, 3: 132–33 ("*most pleasing*"); De Fonblanque, *Life and Correspondence of the Right Hon. John Burgoyne*, 466n (*soon forgotten*); Lunt, *John Burgoyne of Saratoga*, 332 ("*scapegoat*"), from G. B. Shaw, "Notes to *The Devil's Disciple*."

232 **As for Saratoga:** Willcox, "Too Many Cooks," 89 ("*impropriety*"); Lengel, "From Defeat to Victory in the North: 1777–1778," n.p. (*shattered British pretensions*).

232 **"Thus ended a campaign":** Bradford, ed., "Lord Francis Napier's Journal of the Burgoyne Campaign," 285+ ("*more than mortals*").

10. THE ELEMENTS IN FLAMES

233 **Before dawn on Tuesday, October 21:** Kipping, *The Hessian View of America, 1776–1783*, 30 ("*C.E.U.*"); McGuire, *The Philadelphia Campaign*, 2: 163 ("*No fear*"); Fischer, *Washington's Crossing*, 56–57 (*overbearing*).

233 **He had pleaded for this chance:** *TBAC*, 513, 526–28 ("*disgrace*"); Stryker, *The Forts on the Delaware in the Revolutionary War*, 15 ("*Tell your general*"); Howe inquiry, *Parliamentary Register*, 12: 15–16 (*Howe relented*); Jackson, *With the British Army in Philadelphia, 1777–1778*, 63 (*three Hessian grenadier*), 92 (*below Chester*); McGuire, *The Philadelphia Campaign*, 2: 191 (*two hundred victuallers*).

233 **At sunrise, soldiers, horses:** Atwood, *The Hessians*, 123 (*fourteen flatboats*); "The Fort at Red Bank," https://friendsofredbank.weebly.com/the-story-of-the-battle-of-red-bank.html; Tatum, *The American Journal of Ambrose Serle*, 260 ("*They say*"). Cooper's Ferry became Camden.

234 **Regardless of the Canada Army's fate:** Mackesy, *The War for America, 1775–1783*, 130 (*Fourteen perimeter redoubts*); Seymour, ed., "A Contemporary British Account," 69+ (*from Germantown*); McGuire, *The Philadelphia Campaign*, 2: 144 (*eighteen thousand, plus twenty-five thousand*); Moomaw, "The Naval Career of Captain Hamond, 1775–1779," diss., 375 (*hundred-foot gap*); Mackey, *The Gallant Men of the Delaware River Forts, 1777*, 18 (*two strongholds*); Jackson, *The Pennsylvania Navy, 1775–1781*, 23–24 (Arnold *and* Putnam); court-martial records, John Vatas and Richard Blackmore, WO 71/84, ff. 355–97, UK NA ("*Come along*"); Whinyates, ed., *The Services of Lieut.-Colonel Francis Downman, R.A.*, 45.

234 **Such craven malfeasance:** Huth, "Letters from a Hessian Mercenary," 488+ ("*show us the way*"); Atwood, *The Hessians*, 164 (*barbers, and innkeepers*); McGuire, *The Philadelphia Campaign*, 2: 155 ("*made enemies*"); Retzer, trans., "The Philadelphia Campaign, 1777–1778," 1+ ("*improvise*"). Cornwallis told Parliament that Donop's attack orders were "entirely discretionary" (Howe inquiry, *Parliamentary Register*, 12: 15–16).

234 **The autumn sun had passed:** Atwood, *The Hessians*, 123 (*square formation*); "The Fort at Red Bank," https://friendsofredbank.weebly.com/the-story-of-the-battle-of-red-bank.html (*Buck Tavern*); Retzer, trans., "The Philadelphia Campaign, 1777–1778," 1+ ("*disquieted our march*").

236 **At midday the Germans reached Red Bank:** Jackson, *The Pennsylvania Navy, 1775–1781*, 176–77 (*howitzers*); McGuire, *The Philadelphia Campaign*, 2: 142, 157 ("*on their stomachs*"); Mackey, *The Gallant Men of the Delaware River Forts, 1777*, 25 (*hickory tree*); Ewald, *Diary of the American War*, 98 ("*assault stakes*").

236 **The gate was open:** "The Fort at Red Bank," https://friendsofredbank.weebly.com/the-story -of-the-battle-of-red-bank.html (*wash day*).

236 **War had come to the ninety-acre farm:** Mackey, *The Gallant Men of the Delaware River Forts, 1777*, 8; McGeorge, *Ann C. Whitall, the Heroine of Red Bank*, 3 ("*wicked world*").

236 **American soldiers had also brought:** "The Fort at Red Bank," https://friendsofredbank.weebly .com/the-story-of-the-battle-of-red-bank.html; McGeorge, *Ann C. Whitall, the Heroine of Red Bank*, 4 (*stockade timber*); Reed, *Campaign to Valley Forge*, 289 (*forty-seven sheep*); Chastellux, *Travels in North America*, 317n (*trees*); author visit, Fort Mercer, Red Bank, Mar. 21, 2022, signage (*fieldstone wing*); Safko, "The Whitall Family and the Battle of Red Bank," *JAR*, Oct. 1, 2019 ("*turned us out*").

237 **On Wednesday morning, October 22:** Jackson, *The Pennsylvania Navy, 1775–1781* ("*pleasant and fair*"); Reed, *Campaign to Valley Forge*, 289 (*twenty-one cows*); "The Fort at Red Bank," https://friendsofredbank.weebly.com/the-story-of-the-battle-of-red-bank.html (*tea table*).

237 **Contrary to Colonel Donop's delusion:** author visit, Fort Mercer, Red Bank, Mar. 21, 2022, signage (*had run ten miles*); Field et al., "The Diary of Colonel Israel Angel," *Primary Sources*, paper 2, http://digitalcommons.providence.edu/primary/2 ("*certain intelligence*"); Mackey, *The Gallant Men of the Delaware River Forts, 1777*, 25 (*fourteen field pieces*); Jackson, *The Pennsylvania Navy, 1775–1781*, 175; Catts et al., "'It Is Painful for Me to Lose So Many Good People,'" Gloucester County (N.J.) Department of Parks and Recreation, June 2017; Atwood, *The Hessians*, 124 (*flapping laundry*).

237 **Donop had also been misinformed:** GW to Christopher Greene, Oct. 8, 1777, *PGW*, 11: 437 ("*utmost importance*"); Walker, *Engineers of Independence*, 157 ("*Double-boarded walls*"); Catts et al., "'It Is Painful for Me to Lose So Many Good People,'" Gloucester County (N.J.) Department of Parks and Recreation, June 2017 (*a third of that* and *fire steps*); Atwood, *The Hessians*, 123; William Harcourt to father, Oct. 26, 1777, Harcourt, ed., *The Harcourt Papers*, 11: 221–23 ("*intelligence was bad*").

237 **Four hours after arriving in Red Bank:** Jackson, *With the British Army in Philadelphia, 1777–1778*, 64–65; Jackson, *The Pennsylvania Navy, 1775–1781*, 178; Field et al., "The Diary of Colonel Israel Angel," *Primary Sources*, paper 2, http://digitalcommons.providence.edu/ primary/2 (*cannon fire*).

238 **Donop waved off the doubters:** Williams, *Biography of Revolutionary Heroes*, 223 (*"soldiers of Congress"*); McGuire, *The Philadelphia Campaign*, 2: 160 (*"no quarter"*); Ewald, *Diary of the American War*, 98 (*"his compliments"* and *"good beating"*).

238 **Ten minutes later flame spurted:** Field et al., "The Diary of Colonel Israel Angel," *Primary Sources*, paper 2, http://digitalcommons.providence.edu/primary/2 (*Hessian gun line*); Taaffe, *The Philadelphia Campaign, 1777–1778*, 121 (*balls rained down*); McGuire, *The Philadelphia Campaign*, 2: 162 (*"gravel and dust"*); "The Fort at Red Bank," https://friendsofredbank .weebly.com/the-story-of-the-battle-of-red-bank.html; Greenman, *Diary of a Common Soldier in the American Revolution, 1775–1783*, 92 (*"rushed on"*); Ewald, *Diary of the American War*, 98–99 (Jäger *marksmen*); Burgoyne, trans., "Journal Kept by the Distinguished Hessian Field Jaeger Corps," part 1, 45+ (*flanks*); Carbone, *Nathanael Greene*, 80 (*"Fire low"*).

238 **Fascines filled the ditch:** Jackson, *The Pennsylvania Navy, 1775–1781*, 179–80 (*"Victoria!"*); "The Fort at Red Bank," https://friendsofredbank.weebly.com/the-story-of-the-battle-of-red -bank.html (*one another's shoulders*).

238 **Then hundreds of muskets appeared:** McGuire, *The Philadelphia Campaign*, 2: 164; McDonald, ed., "Thro Mud & Mire into the Woods," n.p. (*"smart fire"*); "The Fort at Red Bank," https://friendsofredbank.weebly.com/the-story-of-the-battle-of-red-bank.html (*speaking trumpets*).

238 **Caught in a cross fire:** Stryker, *The Forts on the Delaware in the Revolutionary War*, 18–19 (*heaps*); Jackson, *With the British Army in Philadelphia, 1777–1778*, 65; Lossing, *The Pictorial Field-Book of the Revolution*, 2: 290; Jackson, *The Pennsylvania Navy, 1775–1781*, 182–83 (*gun wadding* and *"thrashing them"*); Baer, *Hessians*, 248 (*"die or retire"*).

238 **Many died. Others retired:** Field et al., "The Diary of Colonel Israel Angel," *Primary Sources*, paper 2, http://digitalcommons.providence.edu/primary/2 (*"most precipitated"*); McGuire, *The Philadelphia Campaign*, 2: 164 (*"slawter"*), 165 (*"Both of his legs"*); Ewald, *Diary of the American War*, 98–99 (*dead near the gateposts*).

239 **While leading a patrol:** Chastellux, *Travels in North America*, 265 (*"revenge yourselves"*); Jackson, *The Pennsylvania Navy, 1775–1781*, 191; McGuire, *The Philadelphia Campaign*, 2: 167 (*"bustle and disorder"*); Martin, *A Narrative of a Revolutionary Soldier*, 73 (*tossed into a creek*); Ewald, *Diary of the American War*, 102 (*"four of my best friends"*); Whinyates, ed., *The Services of Lieut.-Colonel Francis Downman, R.A.*, 44 (*"This night's march"*).

239 **Those unable to hobble away:** Boyle, "'Up to Our Knees in Mud for Four Days Past,'" VFNHP, Feb. 1998, n.p. (*Skim ice*); McGuire, *The Philadelphia Campaign*, 2: 168 (*"I am content"*); Safko, "The Whitall Family and the Battle of Red Bank," *JAR*, Oct. 1, 2019 (*"no one else to blame"*).

239 **For the Royal Navy, worse was to come:** *NDAR*, 10: 339, 603, 607–10; Jackson, *With the British Army in Philadelphia, 1777–1778*, 59 (*Three ships had run aground*); "The Siege of Fort Mifflin," 82+ (*five hundred yards from Fort Mercer*); Mackey, *The Gallant Men of the Delaware River Forts, 1777*, 39.

240 **The sloop-of-war *Merlin*:** *NDAR*, 10: 603 (*"took the ground"* and *"hove without any effect"*). Mantua Creek was also known as Mud Creek.

240 **Dawn on Thursday brought Royal Navy:** R. Howe to Admiralty, Oct. 25, 1777, UK NA, ADM 1/488, f 72 (*guns blazing*); Jackson, *The Pennsylvania Navy, 1775–1781*, 195–97 (*heated shot* and *six dead*); Wallace, *An Old Philadelphian*, 188 (*"elements seemed to be"*).

240 **Captain Reynolds was pacing:** *NDAR*, 10: 603 (*"odd crackling"*); R. Howe to Admiralty, Oct. 25, 1777, UK NA, ADM 1/488, f 72 (*wads from her own guns*); Tatum, *The American Journal of Ambrose Serle*, 261 (*hammocks*); "Francis Reynolds-Moreton, 3rd Lord Ducie," https:// morethannelson.com (*barges and longboats*); McGeorge, *The Battle of Red Bank*, 10 (*seamen leaped*); Commager and Morris, eds., *The Spirit of 'Seventy-Six*, 633 (*"through every port"*).

240 **Just past noon the inferno:** H. Strachey to Jane Strachey, Oct. 27, 1777, Henry Strachey Papers, WLC, box 1 (*"Vesuvius"*); "The Fort at Red Bank," https://friendsofredbank.weebly.com/ the-story-of-the-battle-of-red-bank.html (*Washington's camp*); Thomas Paine to BF, May 16, 1778, FOL (*"like a pillar"*); R. Howe to Admiralty, Oct. 25, 1777, UK NA, ADM 1/488, f 72

(*Howe would obscure*); Montrésor and Scull, *Journal of Captain John Montrésor, PMHB*, vol. 6, no. 1: 34+ (*"sixty men perished"*); *NDAR*, 10: 603.

241 ***Roebuck*** **and *Isis* anchored:** Daniel Cunyngham Clymer to GW, Oct. 26, 1777, *PGW*, 12: 9 (*silver watches*); McGeorge, *The Battle of Red Bank*, 2 (*Daughters of the American Revolution*).

241 **In two days rebels had caused:** Mackey, *The Gallant Men of the Delaware River Forts, 1777*, 43; Stryker, *The Forts on the Delaware in the Revolutionary War*, 21 (*died during the return*); Retzer, trans., "The Philadelphia Campaign, 1777–1778," 1+ (*Two British regiments*); Münchhausen, *At General Howe's Side*, 41 (*thirty wagons*); Whinyates, ed., *The Services of Lieut.-Colonel Francis Downman, R.A.*, 44 (*"well thrashed"*).

241 **Hessian losses from Fort Mercer:** Jackson, *With the British Army in Philadelphia, 1777–1778*, 66 (*approached four hundred*); Ewald, *Diary of the American War*, 399n; "The Fort at Red Bank," https://friendsofredbank.weebly.com/the-story-of-the-battle-of-red-bank.html (*stripping the German dead*); McDonald, ed., "Thro Mud & Mire into the Woods," n.p. (*hardly keep up*); Greenman, *Diary of a Common Soldier in the American Revolution, 1775–1783*, 82 (*mass graves*); Atwood, *The Hessians*, 234 (*colonel and ninety-five others*); Retzer, trans., "The Philadelphia Campaign, 1777–1778," 1+ (*"writing with the left"*); author visit, Fort Mercer, Red Bank, Mar. 21, 2022, signage (*prayer books*); Johnson, ed., *The Journal and Biography of Nicholas Collin*, 241 (*"About 200 were lying"*).

242 **Colonel Donop was moved:** Retzer, trans., "The Philadelphia Campaign, 1777–1778," 1+ (*"finest saddle"*); McGuire, *The Philadelphia Campaign*, 2: 168 (*"a victim of my own ambition"*).

242 **He crossed over at eight-thirty p.m.:** Field et al., "The Diary of Colonel Israel Angel," *Primary Sources*, paper 2, http://digitalcommons.providence.edu/primary/2; McGuire, *The Philadelphia Campaign*, 2: 170–71 (*"with his ancestors"*); Mackey, *The Gallant Men of the Delaware River Forts, 1777*, 37 (*walking sticks*); Lossing, *The Pictorial Field-Book of the Revolution*, 2: 290 (*skull*).

242 **"How German bones are scattered":** Ewald, *Diary of the American War*, 128 (*fourteen thousand*), 195; Retzer, trans., "The Philadelphia Campaign, 1777–1778," 1+ (*linen pouches*); Atwood, *The Hessians*, 129 (*"lost our desire"*).

242 **The Whitall family reclaimed:** Greenman, *Diary of a Common Soldier in the American Revolution, 1775–1783*, 97n (*"conducting ye enemy"*); McDonald, ed., "Thro Mud & Mire into the Woods," n.p. (*dangled in their nooses*); author visit, Fort Mercer, Red Bank, Mar. 21, 2022, signage (*British foragers*).

242 **James and Ann would submit:** Chastellux, *Travels in North America*, 317n (£5,760); Safko, "The Whitall Family and the Battle of Red Bank," *JAR*, Oct. 1, 2019 (*never paid*).

243 **The disaster at Red Bank:** Montrésor and Scull, *Journal of Captain John Montrésor, PMHB*, vol. 6, no. 1: 34+ (*"army without provisions"*); Münchhausen, *At General Howe's Side, 1776–1778*, 42 (*"all perishing"*); Retzer, trans., "The Philadelphia Campaign, 1777–1778," 1+ (*"ability to make progress"*).

243 **The bombardment of Fort Mifflin began:** Montrésor and Scull, *Journal of Captain John Montrésor, PMHB*, vol. 6, no. 1: 34+ (*gusty rain*); Jackson, *With the British Army in Philadelphia, 1777–1778*, 75 (*eighty rounds*); Jackson, *The Pennsylvania Navy, 1775–1781*, 223 (*thirty-five wagons*), 238 (*"slight squeeze"*); Samuel Smith to GW, Nov. 10, 1777, FOL (*"laid open"*); GW to Samuel Smith, Nov. 12, 1777, FOL (*"last extremity"*).

243 **For now, autumn rains flooded:** Greenman, *Diary of a Common Soldier in the American Revolution, 1775–1783*, 84 (*two feet*); Samuel Smith to GW, Nov. 12, 1777, FOL (*striking Smith*); Jackson, *The Pennsylvania Navy, 1775–1781*, 239, 244 (*Simeon Thayer*); author visit, Fort Mifflin, Mar. 23, 2022, signage (*"utterly impossible"*); Mackey, *The Gallant Men of the Delaware River Forts, 1777*, 54–55 (*burned their hands*).

244 **But there was no dodging:** Martin, *A Narrative of a Revolutionary Soldier*, 80 (*"split like fish"*); Dorwart, *Fort Mifflin of Philadelphia*, 47–49 (*wet rawhides*), 55–57 (*seventy men killed*); author visit, Fort Mifflin, Mar. 23, 2022 (*graves scooped*); Martin, *A Narrative of a Revolutionary Soldier*, 77 (*wielded his cane*); Jackson, *The Pennsylvania Navy, 1775–1781*, 247 (*"rammed earth"*); Walker, *Engineers of Independence*, 171–72 (*"defend the ground"*).

244 **The end came a day later:** R. Howe to Admiralty, Apr. 23, 1777, UK NA, ADM 1/487, f 359 (Grand Duchess of Russia); Pickering, *The Life of Timothy Pickering*, 1: 181 (*bags of cotton*); Vigilant log, *NDAR*, 10: 467, 508 (*sloop* Fury); Moomaw, "The Naval Career of Captain Hamond, 1775–1779," diss., 373–74; McDonald, ed., "Thro Mud & Mire into the Woods," n.p. (*"Such a thunder"*).

244 **One Continental officer estimated:** Wallace, *An Old Philadelphian*, 211 (*in twenty minutes*); Greenman, *Diary of a Common Soldier in the American Revolution, 1775–1783*, 85 (*"almost impossible"*); "The Siege of Fort Mifflin," 82+; J. Hazelwood to Thomas Wharton, Jr., Dec. 1, 1777, *NDAR*, 10: 645+ (*almost forty sailors*).

244 **"The whole area of the fort":** Martin, *A Narrative of a Revolutionary Soldier*, 80; Wallace, *An Old Philadelphian*, 223 (*"lost a great many"*); Mackey, *The Gallant Men of the Delaware River Forts, 1777*, 54–55 (*forty volunteers*); Whinyates, ed., *The Services of Lieut.-Colonel Francis Downman, R.A.*, 50–52 (*"fort in flames"*).

245 **Daybreak on Sunday showed:** Montrésor and Scull, *Journal of Captain John Montrésor*, *PMHB*, vol. 6, no. 2: 189+ (*tore down the rebel colors*); Retzer, trans., "The Philadelphia Campaign, 1777–1778," 1+ (*two hundred*); Whinyates, ed., *The Services of Lieut.-Colonel Francis Downman, R.A.*, 52 (*"blood and brains"*); McGuire, *The Philadelphia Campaign*, 2: 211 (*"cutting up an ox"*).

245 **Still, a grudging admiration:** author visit, Fort Mifflin, Mar. 23, 2022, signage (*"defended it with a spirit"*); Wallace, *An Old Philadelphian*, 245 (*"as gallant"*).

245 **With the loss of Fort Mifflin:** Puls, *Henry Knox*, 113 (*two thousand*); Jackson, *The Pennsylvania Navy, 1775–1781*, 280 (*portable bridge*).

245 **At three o'clock the next morning:** Jackson, *The Pennsylvania Navy, 1775–1781*, 273 (*thirteen row galleys*); Taaffe, *The Philadelphia Campaign, 1777–1778*, 139 (*chased a schooner aground*); Clark, *Gallant John Barry, 1745–1803*, 133–35 (*xebecs* Repulse and Champion); McGuire, *The Philadelphia Campaign*, 2: 220 (*Another crowd*); Lundin, *Cockpit of the Revolution*, 370 (*flaming masts*); Münchhausen, *At General Howe's Side, 1776–1778*, 44 (*"beautiful fireworks"*).

246 **Howe completed the inferno:** Morton, "The Diary of Robert Morton," 1+ (*belonged to loyalists*); Siebert, *The Loyalists of Pennsylvania*, 54 (*from their rooftops*); Maj. Ichabod Burnett to unidentified, Nov. 30, 1777, JLB, BBB (*"ravages & burnings"*).

246 **On Sunday, November 23:** Mackey, *The Gallant Men of the Delaware River Forts, 1777*, 57–63; Moomaw, "The Naval Career of Captain Hamond, 1775–1779," diss., 373 (*sixty vessels rode*); Black and Woodfine, eds., *The British Navy and the Use of Naval Power in the Eighteenth Century*, 182 (*nearly two months*); Wallace, *An Old Philadelphian*, 226 (*"upwards of four hundred"*); Morton, "The Diary of Robert Morton," 1+ (*"power far inferior"*).

246 **As his army settled in around him:** Lawler, "The President's House in Philadelphia," 5+ (*fluted columns*); Flavell, *The Howe Dynasty*, 181 (*"greater compass"*); W. Howe to Germain, Oct. 22, 1777, GSG, vol. 6 (*"I am led to hope"*); W. Howe to Germain, Oct. 21, 1777, *Report on the Manuscripts of Mrs. Stopford-Sackville*, 2: 79–80 (*"no prospect"*); W. Howe to Gordon and Crowder, Oct. 26, 1777, *Report on American Manuscripts in the Royal Institution of Great Britain*, 1: 145 (*"extraordinary expenses"*). Later in the century both Presidents Washington and Adams would live in the house Howe had occupied.

246 **Until hearing a reply from his government:** Hatch, *Major John André*, 82 (*"only hardships"*); Stryker, *The Battle of Monmouth*, 18 (Bunch of Grapes); Jackson, *With the British Army in Philadelphia, 1777–1778*, 104 (French lessons), 216 (Moore's Alley).

247 **Officers hosted balls at City Tavern:** Hatch, *Major John André*, 86; Scharf and Westcott, *History of Philadelphia, 1609–1884*, 1: 371 (*Friendly Brothers*); Mishoff, "Business in Philadelphia During the British Occupation, 1777–1778," 174 (*dressing their hair*); Tracy, *266 Days*, 204 (*Southwark Theater*); Jackson, *With the British Army in Philadelphia, 1777–1778*, 200–202 (No One's Enemy); Sargent, *The Life and Career of Major John André*, 154 (*"uncommonly spirited"*); H. Strachey to Jane Strachey, Mar. 24, 1778, Henry Strachey Papers, WLC, box 1 (*in his stage box*).

247 **Hessian officers admired:** McCullough, *John Adams*, 79–81; Kipping, *The Hessian View of America, 1776–1783*, 16–17 (*"wide stone pavement"*); Sullivan, *The Disaffected*, 163 (*five thou-*

sand uniforms); Siebert, *The Loyalists of Pennsylvania*, 42–43; Jackson, *With the British Army in Philadelphia, 1777–1778*, 100; Nash, *First City*, 90 (*"every gallant hero"*). Estimates of loyalist recruits raised in Philadelphia range from less than seven hundred to about twice that.

247 **Even so, taverns echoed with the roar:** Silverman, *A Cultural History of the American Revolution*, 133–34 (*"Britons, Strike Home"* and *cricket bats*); Mishoff, "Business in Philadelphia During the British Occupation, 1777–1778," 170–73 (*"as much elegance"*); Andrlik, *Reporting the Revolutionary War*, 233 (*ivory forks, tea trays*); Tracy, *266 Days*, 197 (*"No questions"*).

247 **Auctions of household furniture:** Tracy, *266 Days*, 260 (*"a mulatto girl"*); Bowler, *Logistics and the Failure of the British Army in America, 1775–1783*, 72–73; Trevelyan, *The American Revolution*, 4: 353 (*"we are well-supplied"*).

248 **WH was not likely to forget:** Ewald, *Diary of the American War*, 111 (*every two days*); Oaks, "The City Under Military Occupation," in Morris and West, eds., *Essays on Urban America*, 32 (*night watch*); Sullivan, *The Disaffected*, 142 (*burglary, rape*); Crane, ed., *The Diary of Elizabeth Drinker*, 69 (*"sad times"*); Jackson, *With the British Army in Philadelphia, 1777–1778*, 150 (*"retailers of strong liquors"*).

248 **Ice had begun to obstruct:** Moomaw, "The Naval Career of Captain Hamond, 1775–1779," diss., 382–83; Whinyates, ed., *The Services of Lieut.-Colonel Francis Downman, R.A.*, 55 (*"We have dilly-dallied"*); Jackson, *With the British Army in Philadelphia, 1777–1778*, 160 (Juliana), 169–70 (*foraging expeditions*); Oaks, "The City Under Military Occupation," in Morris and West, eds., *Essays on Urban America*, 28 (*twenty-four tons*); Syrett, *Shipping and the American War, 1775–83*, 126.

248 **Food, ammunition, and blankets:** Bowler, *Logistics and the Failure of the British Army in America, 1775–1783*, 71 (*"We cannot with safety"*).

248 **With the fourth year of war:** McGuire, *The Philadelphia Campaign*, 2: 275 (*"folly & iniquity"*); Richard Fitzpatrick to brother, Jan. 31, 1778, JLB, BBB (*"more & more disgusted"*); Duncan, *History of the Royal Regiment of Artillery*, 1: 327–28 (*"All the efforts"*); James Pattison papers, Loyalist Collection, University of New Brunswick, https://loyalist.lib.unb.ca/node/4530.

249 **At six p.m. on December 11:** Lefkowitz, "French Adventurers, Patriots, and Pretentious Imposters," *JAR*, June 8, 2021 (*two bridges*); Wright, *The Continental Army*, 131 (*thirty-six wagons*); Brier, "They Passed This Way," VFNHP, Sept. 2002, 34–36 (*thirteenth crossing*); Waldo, "Valley Forge, 1777–1778," 305 (*at sunrise*); LiA, 2: 82 (*"way of danger"*); author visit, VFNHP, Sept. 1, 2021 (*four hundred women and children*); Harris and Ecelbarger, "A Reconsideration of Continental Army Numerical Strength at Valley Forge," *JAR*, May 18, 2021 (*nineteen thousand troops*); Harris and Ecelbarger, "The Numerical Strength of George Washington's Army During the 1777 Philadelphia Campaign," *JAR*, Oct. 5, 2021.

249 **"The leaves and ground were as wet":** Martin, *A Narrative of a Revolutionary Soldier*, 84–85 (*"curs"*); Waldo, "Valley Forge, 1777–1778," 306–7 (*"Poor food"*).

249 **Camp scuttlebutt swirled:** Duane, ed., *Extracts from the Diary of Christopher Marshall*, 143 (Howe), 152 (*deflowering virgins*), 167 (*Franklin had been assassinated*), 168 (*paving stones*); Sullivan, *The Disaffected*, 172, 177 (*fled France for Prussia*).

249 **Amid the lurid rumors:** JLB, AAA (*thirty tons of sulfur* and *wrap their bare feet*); GW, general orders, Nov. 22, 1777, *PGW*, 12: 344.

250 **Congress honored the victory at Saratoga:** Jackson, *Valley Forge*, 20 (*"thanksgiving and praise"*); Byrd, *Sacred Scripture, Sacred War*, 164 (*Moses at the Red Sea*); McDonald, ed., "Thro Mud & Mire into the Woods," n.p. (*"in the midst of thy camp"*); Martin, *A Narrative of a Revolutionary Soldier*, 87 (*tablespoon of vinegar*); Brown and Peckham, eds., *Revolutionary War Journals of Henry Dearborn, 1775–1783*, 118 (*"not in the grave"*).

250 **Where "thy camp" should be located:** Harley et al., *Mapping the American Revolutionary War*, 40 (*"primary studies"*); NG to GW, Dec. 3, 1777, *PNG*, 2: 237n (*imprudent*); Callahan, *Henry Knox, General Washington's General*, 131 (*"tranquility"*); GW to Joseph Reed, Dec. 2, 1777, *PGW*, 12: 500 (*Wilmington*); McGuire, *The Philadelphia Campaign*, 2: 266–67 (*Lancaster or Reading*); Lengel, *General George Washington*, 266 (*wanted the army interposed*).

250 **At ten a.m. on December 19:** Ecelbarger, "Permanent Losses and New Gains During the 1778 Valley Forge Encampment," *JAR*, Feb. 15, 2024 (*nineteen thousand*); Brier, "They Passed This

Way," VFNHP, Sept. 2002, 37 (*"The sun shone"*); Field et al., "The Diary of Colonel Israel Angel," *Primary Sources*, paper 2, http://digitalcommons.providence.edu/primary/2 (*"roads was excessive bad"*).

250 **Here then was Valley Forge:** author visit, VFNHP, Sept. 1, 2021; Trussel, *Birthplace of an Army*, 1 (*Mount Misery*).

251 **Washington had chosen this rugged place:** VFHRR3, 197 (*Three creeks*); VFHHR1, 74 (*Reading and Pottsgrove*); Brier, "They Passed This Way," VFNHP, Sept. 2002, 37 (*"The general seems resolved"*).

251 **Castrametation began in earnest:** Ecelbarger, "The First Four Days at Valley Forge," *JAR*, Dec. 8, 2022 (*fifteen brigade laagers*); Bodle, *The Valley Forge Winter*, 104–5 (*Timbering squads*).

251 **Yet Valley Forge was ghastly:** John Sullivan to GW, Dec. 1, 1777, FOL (*"without watch coats"*); GW to Henry Laurens, Dec. 23, 1777, FOL (*"unfit for duty"*); Freeman, *George Washington: A Biography*, 4: 570–71 (*"lousy"*); VFHRR2, 479 (*"the Meases"*).

251 **They were perishing of other afflictions:** Gillett, *The Army Medical Department, 1775–1818*, 80 (*three thousand patients*); Kidder, *Revolutionary Princeton 1774–1783*, 166–67; Butterfield, *Letters of Benjamin Rush*, 1: 175 (*"five thousand"*); Dec. 1777 sickness report, in Lesser, ed., *The Sinews of Independence* (*Almost a third*); B. Rush to GW, Dec. 26, 1777, FOL (*"A great majority"*); Martin, *A Narrative of a Revolutionary Soldier*, 97–98 (*sulfur*); Reiss, *Medicine and the American Revolution*, 199–201 (*"the itch"*); Grose, *A Classical Dictionary of the Vulgar Tongue*, n.p. (*Scotch fiddle*).

252 **Despite these troubles, Washington:** Ecelbarger, "The First Four Days at Valley Forge," *JAR*, Dec. 8, 2022 (*attack Philadelphia*); GW to Henry Laurens, Dec. 23, 1777, FOL; VFHRR2, 37 (*wagons and pull teams*); Risch, *Supplying Washington's Army*, 218–19 (*not a single cow*), 220 (*Warehouses*). Various sources have slightly different consumption figures.

252 **"His Excellency amazed":** Charles Stewart, Dec. 22, 1777, JLB, "My Last Shift Betwixt Us & Death," ms; John Chaloner to William Buchanan, Dec. 28, 1777, Ephraim Blaine letterbook, JLB, ms (*"language"*); Massey, *John Laurens and the American Revolution*, 87 (*"tears of blood"*).

252 **An urgent meeting of general officers:** Waldo, "Valley Forge, 1777–1778," 309 (*owls and crows*); Martin, *A Narrative of a Revolutionary Soldier*, 90 (*small pumpkin*); McDonald, ed., "Thro Mud & Mire into the Woods," n.p. (*ear of corn*); Ecelbarger, "The First Four Days at Valley Forge," *JAR*, Dec. 8, 2022 (*"Hunger will break"—Coriolanus*, I:1); GW to Henry Laurens, Dec. 23, 1777, FOL (*"capital change"*); VFHRR1, 142 (*"tottering"*).

253 **Earlier in the fall, Congress:** Tilley, *Journals of the Continental Congress, 1774–1789*, 9: 1014–15 (*"leaving such quantities"*); Spero and Zuckerman, eds., *The American Revolution Reborn*, 63 (*alienate*); John Chaloner to Thomas Wharton, Jr., Dec. 24, 1777, Ephraim Blaine letterbook, JLB, ms (*each brigade*); White, "Standing Armies in Time of War," diss., 241 (*seventy-mile radius*).

253 **"We have hardly been here":** Zucker, *General De Kalb, Lafayette's Mentor*, 166 (*"more severe"*); VFHRR2, 118 (*seven hundred head*); John Chaloner to Ephraim Blaine, Dec. 22, 1777, Ephraim Blaine letterbook, JLB, ms (*"fate of tomorrow"*).

253 **The holy day came and went:** Brown and Peckham, eds., *Revolutionary War Journals of Henry Dearborn, 1775–1783*, 119 (*"not so merry"*); McDonald, ed., "Thro Mud & Mire into the Woods," n.p. (*"Nothing remarkable"*); Peckham, ed., *The Toll of Independence*, 130 (*266 military engagements*).

253 **Yet the aggregate tally:** Weinman, "Oliver Reed: Letters of an American Soldier," *JAR*, Aug. 6, 2015 (*"Bone of your bone"*).

11. THE KING'S WAR

257 **War brought Britain's animal spirits:** Germain to W. Knox, Nov. [13?], 1777, William Knox papers, WLC, box 3 (*Brandywine*); Steuart, ed., *The Last Journals of Horace Walpole*, 2: 71 (*"transports of joy"*); Ritcheson, *British Politics and the American Revolution*, 231 (*"wild tumult"*).

257 **War was what great powers did:** Brewer, *The Sinews of Power*, 189 (*commercial wealth*); Schwartz, *Daily Life in Johnson's London*, 46 (*between 1695 and 1815*); George, *London Life in*

the Eighteenth Century, 269; Rudé, *Hanoverian London, 1714–1808*, 36 (*trade, banking, and insurance*); Miller, *Triumph of Freedom, 1775–1783*, 422 (*War contracts*); Warner, "Telescopes for Land and Sea," 33+ (*St. Paul's churchyard*); Clark, *British Opinion and the American Revolution*, 110 (*Poole*); Thomas, *Lord North*, 98 (*forty-six major contractors*). Britain was at war for 63 of those 120 years.

257 **Trade with rebellious America:** Clark, *British Opinion and the American Revolution*, 101 (*"orders from Russia"*), 108 (*English velvets*); Porter, *English Society in the Eighteenth Century*, 311–13 (*Pig-iron production*), 331 (*Arkwright's water frame*); Ackroyd, *Revolution*, 225 (*"running mad"*).

257 **The author Daniel Defoe:** Rudé, *Hanoverian London, 1714–1808*, 41 (*seven groups*); Lord Westcote to W. Knox, Aug. 17, 1777, in Billias, ed., *The Manuscripts of Captain Howard Vincente Knox*, 136 (*turtle and malmsey*); Flavell, *The Howe Dynasty*, 119 (*quarreled in French*); Picard, *Dr. Johnson's London*, 118 (*washing lace*); George, *London Life in the Eighteenth Century*, 309 (*Small Sums*).

258 **War came with costs:** Ackroyd, *Revolution*, 186 (*£8 of every £10* and *"the English are taxed"*); Clark, *British Opinion and the American Revolution*, 123–24 (*land tax*), 132 (*government debt*).

258 **But if thirteen Crown colonies:** Taylor, *American Revolutions*, 144 (*fourteen others*), 146 (*275,000 black slaves*); O'Shaughnessy, *An Empire Divided*, 58 (*Some 1,800*), 161 (*died of malnutrition*); Pancake, *This Destructive War*, 10 (*a hundred thousand hogsheads*); Carrington, *The British West Indies During the American Revolution*, 48 (*cane fields to cropland*).

258 **The sounds of imperium:** Picard, *Dr. Johnson's London*, 26 (*"By your leave"*), 125 (*strip-me-naked*); Rudé, *Hanoverian London, 1714–1808*, 36 (*two hundred thousand rural families*); Simpson, ed., *The Waiting City*, 81 (*forty-two markets*), 82 (*seven hundred thousand sheep and lambs*).

259 **Women sold milk from pails:** Picard, *Dr. Johnson's London*, 102–3 (*chalk and water*), 167 (*fried mice*), 168 (*powdered human skull*); Flavell, *When London Was Capital of America*, 125 (*dice boxes*), 211 (*royal proclamations*); Schwartz, *Daily Life in Johnson's London*, 18 (*"their defects"*).

259 **For every sound there was a sight:** George, *London Life in the Eighteenth Century*, 98 (*fresh air*); Besant, *London in the Eighteenth Century*, 359 (*Field of Forty Footsteps*); Schwartz, *Daily Life in Johnson's London*, 70 (*thirty rounds*), 101–2 (*Oxford Road*); Rudé, *Hanoverian London, 1714–1808*, 93 (*Bruising Peg*).

259 **The broad-shouldered town:** White, *A Great and Monstrous Thing*, 212–15 (*skinners, tanners*); Besant, *London in the Eighteenth Century*, 374 (*Bedlam*); Flavell, *When London Was Capital of America*, 93 (*"reproductive organ"*), 174–75 (*porcupines*); Norton, *The British-Americans*, 81 (*"Learned Pig"*); Damrosch, *The Club*, 67 (*Mrs. Salomon's Waxworks*), 190 (*Regan sobbed*).

260 **"When a man is tired of London":** George, *London Life in the Eighteenth Century*, 109; Porter, *English Society in the Eighteenth Century*, 99 (*world's suicide capital*).

260 **Dr. Johnson was contemptuous:** Damrosch, *The Club*, 303 (*"sulfurous vapor"*); Ferling, *Winning Independence*, 51 (*roughly fifteen thousand*); O'Shaughnessy, *An Empire Divided*, 158 (*twenty-five thousand hogsheads*), 213 (*"piracy and freebooting"*); Johnston, "American Privateers in French Ports, 1776–1778," 352+; McGrath, *Give Me a Fast Ship*, 157 (*28 percent*). In December 1777 the *General Advertiser* put war costs at over £30 million (Lutnick, *The American Revolution and the British Press, 1775–1783*, 121).

261 **Despite the distraction of porcupines:** Nelson, *The American Tory*, 154 (*Threadneedle*); Norton, *The British-Americans*, 156 (*how to spur the king's ministry*); Trevelyan, *The American Revolution*, ed. Morris, 265 (*"nobodies"*).

261 **Year by year, the civil war:** Plumb, *England in the Eighteenth Century*, 135 (*"From one end of North America"*); David McNaughton, "Richard Price," *Stanford Encyclopedia of Philosophy*, https://plato.stanford.edu/entries/richard-price/.

261 **No one asked more uncomfortable:** Toynbee, ed., *The Letters of Horace Walpole*, 10: 134 (*"people should never"*), 144 (*"Impatience is very high"*), 153 (*"Can you conquer"*); Jesse, *Mem-*

oirs of Celebrated Etonians, 2: 41 (*"long and slender"*); Whiteley, "Horace Walpole, Early American," 212+ (*"crossing a wet street"*); Coupland, *The American Revolution and the British Empire*, 10–12 (*"we shall molder"*).

262 **By custom and obligation:** Roberts, *The Last King of America*, 80 (*shaved himself*); Thackeray, *The Four Georges*, 111 (*carpet in his bedroom*); Ayling, *George the Third*, 182 (*"eating plain"*).

262 **Before noon he traveled:** Ayling, *George the Third*, 182 (*sedan chair*); Huish, *Public and Private Life of His Late Excellent and Most Gracious Majesty, George the Third*, 376 (*attacked*); *Annual Register 1777*, June 25, 1777 (*smashed the glass*); Namier, "King George III: A Study in Personality," 610+ (*more liked than loved*).

262 **Dressers, courtiers, and retainers:** Ayling, *George the Third*, 190 (*No one spoke*); Brooke, *King George III*, 309 (*"dangerous and faithless"*); Roberts, *The Last King of America*, 48 (*"I am born"*).

263 **In midafternoon the gilded:** *TBAC*, 164–66; Ehrman, *The Younger Pitt*, 1: 27 (*"insanitary"*); Marshall, *Dr. Johnson's London*, 115–17 (*House of Lords*).

263 **The king ascended a low platform:** Ehrman, *The Younger Pitt*, 1: 41 (*sinecures*); Roberts, *The Last King of America*, 69 (*placemen beholden*); Clark, *British Opinion and the American Revolution*, 233 (*privy purse*); Trevelyan, *The American Revolution*, ed. Morris, 429–30 (*no one kept a closer eye*); De Fonblanque, *Life and Correspondence of the Right Hon. John Burgoyne*, 237n (*Bench of Bishops*); Conway, *The British Isles and the War of American Independence*, 143 (*"put to the sword"*).

263 **The king's ministers had been of mixed:** Ritcheson, *British Politics and the American Revolution*, 216–17 (*"goodish news"*); *PH* 19, 354; Toynbee, ed., *The Letters of Horace Walpole*, 10: 152.

264 **George still regretted giving concessions:** Pares, *King George III and the Politicians*, 67–68 (*Stamp Act*); Fortescue, ed., *The Correspondence of King George the Third*, 3: 449 (*"great lenity"*), 450 (*"treat before winter"*); Hibbert, *George III*, 161 (*"majority of the people"*); Ayling, *George the Third*, 268–70 (*encouraging insurrections*); Thackeray, *The Four Georges*, 105 (*"flogged"*).

264 **Perched on his throne:** *PH* 19, 354–55 (*"our most serious attention"*).

264 **He paused, studying the script:** Van Alstyne, *Empire and Independence*, 133 (*eighty-five sailings*); Bemis, "Secret Intelligence, 1777: Two Documents," 244–45 (*three thousand barrels*); Trevelyan, *The American Revolution*, ed. Morris, 357 (*Dunkirk to Bayonne*); *PP Sandwich*, 1: 343–44 (*"arming and equipping"*).

265 **He stood and swept from the hall:** Ackroyd, *Revolution*, 232 (*"king's war"*); Black, *George III, America's Last King*, 118 (*Windsor uniform*).

265 **So much about this war baffled him:** Roberts, *The Last King of America*, 254 (*tenfold larger*). On December 3 the government put the total number of royal troops in North America at 55,095 (*PII* 19, 532).

265 **Rebellion posed the mortal threat:** Black, *George III, America's Last King*, 219–24 (*erasure*).

265 **There was nothing for it:** Fleming, *1776, Year of Illusions*, 73 (*"can do no wrong"*); Roberts, *The Last King of America*, 267 (*military band*); Donne, *The Correspondence of King George the Third to Lord North*, 2: 214 (*"Firmness"*).

265 **Wild rumors swept London:** Hutchinson, *The Diary and Letters of His Excellency Thomas Hutchinson, Esq.*, 148–50 (*Washington had died*), 161 (*Arnold had surrendered*); *St. James's Chronicle*, Jan. 2, 1777, in Lutnick, *The American Revolution and the British Press, 1775–1783*, 22 (*cannibalism*), 23 (*"motley medley"*), 103 (*converted to Quakerism*).

266 **Yet bad news traveled on long legs:** Fortescue, ed., *The Correspondence of King George the Third*, 3: 500 (*Red Bank debacle*), 503 (*"not without remedy"*); Steuart, ed., *The Last Journals of Horace Walpole*, 2: 80 (*"agonies"*); Gruber, *The Howe Brothers and the American Revolution*, 273.

266 **Finding that remedy would fall:** Scott, *British Foreign Policy in the Age of the American Revolution*, 259; Ritcheson, *British Politics and the American Revolution*, 234 (*"extricating this country"*).

266 **He had been through worse:** Marlow, *Sackville of Drayton*, 211 (*"no man better understood"*).

267 **A devoted husband with five children:** *TBAC*, 174–76 (*"Minden buggering hero"*); Cumberland, *Character of the Late Lord Viscount Sackville*, 4–5 (*"companions"*), 14 (*"such power of seeing"*); Mackesy, *The Coward of Minden*, 34 (*melancholy*); Guttridge, "Lord George Germain in Office, 1775–1782," 26 (*"dogmatic self-confidence"*).

267 **Appointed American secretary:** Wickwire, *British Subministers and Colonial America, 1763–1783*, 18 (*first among equals*); Mackesy, *The War for America, 1775–1783*, 154 (*"speak of nothing"*); Spector, *The American Department of the British Government, 1763–1782*, 91–94 (*oilskin*), 117 (*fleet commanders*), 124 (*"Secret and Confidential"*); Bellot, *William Knox*, 153–55; Lowell, *The Hessians*, 50–52 (*down the Rhine*); Eelking and Rosengarten, *The German Allied Troops in the North American War of Independence*, 143; R.J.B. Knight, "The Royal Navy's Recovery," in Andreopoulos and Selesky, eds., *The Aftermath of Defeat*, 17 (*speaking terms since 1758*); Roberts, *The Last King of America*, 283 (*British system that splintered*).

268 **Germain referred to himself:** Marlow, *Sackville of Drayton*, 2 (*"man-of-war"*), 87 (*bloody uniform*); O'Shaughnessy, *The Men Who Lost America*, 175–76 (*"whole power of the state"*); Brown, *The American Secretary*, 24 (*"riotous rabble"*); PH 19, 1397 (*"no longer as a child"*).

268 **Many sheets of foolscap:** Mackesy, *The Coward of Minden*, 34, 252; Brown, *The American Secretary*, 178–79 (*revolutionary ideology*); O'Shaughnessy, *The Men Who Lost America*, 192–93 (*never grasped*); Marlow, *Sackville of Drayton*, 188 (*no profit in negotiating*).

268 **He, more than anyone:** Willcox, "Too Many Cooks," 90; Pemberton, *Lord North*, 272; Spector, *The American Department of the British Government, 1763–1782*, 148–54 (*"Considerations"*); Bellot, *William Knox*, 155–56; Greene, "William Knox's Explanation for the American Revolution," 293+.

268 **Germain urged "Roman severity":** Guttridge, "Lord George Germain in Office, 1775–1782," 24; O'Shaughnessy, *The Men Who Lost America*, 175; Roberts, *The Last King of America*, 281 (*"our present confusion"*).

268 **On the afternoon of Wednesday, December 3:** Trevelyan, *The American Revolution*, ed. Morris, 396–97 (*"Hear him!"*).

269 **Germain rose to his feet:** PH 19, 533–34 (*"unhappy intelligence"*).

269 **Jaws dropped. Eyes widened:** *Gentleman's Magazine and Historical Chronicle*, 47: 608 (*"great consternation"*); Moore, *Diary of the American Revolution*, 526 (*"like so many bulldogs"*).

269 **Barré barked first:** PH 19, 532–41 (*"his own misconduct"*).

269 **The worst pummeling came:** Ayling, *Fox*, 55 (*"greatest genius"*); Trevelyan, *The American Revolution*, ed. Morris, 396 (*living aboard warships*); Trevelyan, *The Early History of Charles James Fox*, 300 (*Iliad* in Greek), 487 (*"whipping, spurring"*).

270 **Even adversaries acknowledged:** Trevelyan, *The Early History of Charles James Fox*, 475 (*"piff, paff!"*), 498 (*"what fire"*); Prior, *Memoir of the Life and Character of the Right Hon. Edmund Burke*, 1: 348 (*blue and buff*); Ayling, *Fox*, 49–50; Ketchum, *Saratoga*, 442 (*"ill-omened"*); Brown, *The American Secretary*, 131 (*"More blood!"*); Pemberton, *Lord North*, 274 (*"full feather"*).

270 **Parliament had been "imposed on":** PH 19, 532–41.

270 **Fox sat, his face flushed:** *TBAC*, 427 (*"home victorious"*).

270 **The search for scapegoats:** Ferling, ed., *The World Turned Upside Down*, 179 (*Parliament blamed ministers*); Lunt, *John Burgoyne of Saratoga*, 291–94; Lutnick, *The American Revolution and the British Press, 1775–1783*, 110 (*"lying prophet"*); Flavell, *The Howe Dynasty*, 280 (*"wished she was a man"*).

271 **Advent came and went:** Huish, *Public and Private Life of His Late Excellent and Most Gracious Majesty, George the Third*, 376 (*"I consider it impious"*).

271 **London merchants, ever hopeful:** Lutnick, *The American Revolution and the British Press, 1775–1783*, 127 (*resumption of trade*); Fortescue, *The War of Independence*, 98 (*Manchester*); Donne, *The Correspondence of King George the Third to Lord North*, 2: 97n (*Liverpool*), 118 (*"Perhaps the time"*).

271 **The confusion intensified when Lord Germain:** Kate Ravilious, "The Many Lives of an English Manor House," *Archaeology*, Jan.–Feb. 2016, https://www.archaeology.org/issues/199

-1601; Germain to W. Knox, Jan. 16, 1778, in Billias, ed., *The Manuscripts of Captain Howard Vincente Knox*, 141 (*"depressed by misfortunes"*).

271 **The king and Lord North privately hoped:** Shorto, *Revolution Song*, 325 (*"so many enemies"*); Suffolk to Germain, Jan. 20, 1778, *Report on the Manuscripts of Mrs. Stopford-Sackville*, 2: 91 (*"Avail yourself"*); Marlow, *Sackville of Drayton*, 199 (*"We can't go far"*); Dunelm, ed., *The Political Life of William Wildman, Viscount Barrington*, 197 (*"not equal"*); Mackesy, *The War for America, 1775–1783*, 180 (*Prince Ferdinand*); Hayter, ed., *An Eighteenth-Century Secretary at War*, 16 (*silver inkstands*).

272 **As Germain pondered his course:** Weddle, "'A Change of Both Men and Measures,'" 837+ (*Downing Street*); Smith, *The Early Career of Lord North the Prime Minister*, 278 (*tin hip tub*).

272 **In a spacious ground-floor room:** Fortescue, ed., *The Correspondence of King George the Third*, 4: 22 (*another thirty thousand*); Mackesy, *The War for America, 1775–1783*, 156 (*three or four thousand*); Weddle, "'A Change of Both Men and Measures,'" 837+ (*"As soon as France"*); NDAR, 11: 859 (*secret orders*); Sandwich to North, Dec. 8, 1777, *PP Sandwich*, 1: 328–34 (*"imminent danger"* and *"made it very difficult"*).

272 **More chin stroking:** Hibbert, *George III*, 156 (*"most striking proofs"* and *"single syllable"*); Ayling, *Fox*, 62.

273 **Frederick, Lord North, detested:** North to W. Knox, Oct. 7, 1777, in Billias, ed., *The Manuscripts of Captain Howard Vincente Knox*, 139 (*"more decisive turn"*); Butterfield, *George III, Lord North and the People, 1779–1780*, 19 (*depression, lassitude*); Smith, *The Early Career of Lord North the Prime Minister*, 254 (*Bushy Park*); Brooke, *King George III*, 186 (*"inclined to despond"*); TBAC, 18–19 (*friends since boyhood*).

273 **He was amiable, gracious:** Rodger, *The Insatiable Earl*, 322 (*"a first-class mind"*); Roberts, *The Last King of America*, 180–81 (*"untuneable voice"*); Glover, *General Burgoyne in Canada and America*, 18–19 (*"void of affectation"*).

273 **Among the prime minister's admirers:** Lutnick, *The American Revolution and the British Press, 1775–1783*, 108 (*"no reasonable man"*); Ho, "Edward Gibbon, Historian of the Roman Empire," https://www.his.com/~z/gibho1.html (*"register of the crimes"*); De Beer, *Gibbon and His World*, 72 (*civilization and barbarism*); Gibbon, *The Autobiography and Correspondence of Edward Gibbon*, 89–90 (*"spotless integrity"*); Trevelyan, *The American Revolution*, ed. Morris, 277 (*"King George in a fright"*).

274 **North was leader of the Commons:** Brooke, *King George III*, 196 (*"few constitutions"*); O'Shaughnessy, *The Men Who Lost America*, 72 (*Garter star*); Ayling, *George the Third*, 239–40 (*"took the trouble"*); Thomas, *Lord North*, 97 (*670 formal meetings*); Brewer, *The Sinews of Power*, 133 (*Bank of England and London financiers*); Ellis, *The Cause*, 198; González Encisco, *War, Power and the Economy*, 256; Watson, *The Reign of George III, 1760–1815*, 226 (*male servants*); Ellis, *His Excellency*, 111; Wickwire, *British Subministers and Colonial America, 1763–1783*, 14–15.

274 **"Curse his virtues":** Jesse, *Memoirs of Celebrated Etonians*, 2: 252 (*"undone"*—from *Cato, a Tragedy*, IV:iv); Robson, *The American Revolution*, 189 (*"love of indecision"*); Brooke, *King George III*, 196 (*bullying*); North to W. Knox, Oct. 7, 1777, William Knox papers, WLC, box 3 (*American geography*); Anson, ed., *Autobiography and Political Correspondence of Augustus Henry, Third Duke of Grafton, K.G.*, 303 (*ignorance*); Butterfield, *George III, Lord North and the People, 1779–1780*, 21 (*"prime minister"*); Rodger, *The Command of the Ocean*, 332 (*"violence of temper"*). "Good butcher" attributed to William Ewart Gladstone (https://libquotes .com/william-ewart-gladstone/quote/lbd9f7i).

274 **Good or otherwise, he was:** Ayling, *George the Third*, 255 (*"If £20,000 is necessary"*); Donne, *The Correspondence of King George the Third to Lord North*, 2: 82–83 (*"I love you"*); Roberts, *The Last King of America*, 325 (*secret service fund*).

275 **So he remained at the helm:** *Public Advertiser* (London), May 28, 1777 (*"weak old man"*); Whitely, *Lord North*, 170 (*"such obligations to the king"*).

275 **In late January, North had insisted to the Commons:** Lucas, *Lord North, Second Earl of Guilford, K.G., 1732–1792*, 2: 58 (*"constitutional war"*); Thomas, *Lord North*, 115–16 (*150-vote margin*); Murdoch, ed., *Rebellion in America*, 563 (*"church doors"*), 566.

275 **More alarming, "an approaching war":** North to George, Jan. 6, 1778, Fortescue, ed., *The Correspondence of King George the Third*, 4: 1–16; Lutnick, *The American Revolution and the British Press, 1775-1783*, 133 (*"perfidious Gaul"*), 135 (*"old arch-rebel"*), 147–48 (*Malabar coast*).

275 **Britain had no allies in Europe:** Christie, *Crisis of Empire*, 104; Murdoch, ed., *Rebellion in America*, 511 (*blockading French fleets*).

275 **Desperate times required:** PH 19, 762–67 (*"conciliatory propositions"*).

276 **North eased back onto his bench:** Murdoch, ed., *Rebellion in America*, 577 (*"dull, melancholy silence"*); Christie, *Crisis of Empire*, 103 (*concessions even exceeded*); Pemberton, *Lord North*, 279 (*"mortification"*).

276 **Fox popped to his feet:** PH 19, 767–72 (*"What reparation"*); Murdoch, ed., *Rebellion in America*, 578 (*"existence of the empire"*).

276 **Late in the evening the king wrote:** Donne, *The Correspondence of King George the Third to Lord North*, 2: 133 (*"I sincerely rejoice"*); "Parliament and the Howes," 87+ (*"without consulting me"*); Bellot, *William Knox*, 161 (*Germain's star*).

276 **The conciliation measures would continue:** Tuchman, *The March of Folly*, 219 (*"bundle of imbecility"*); O'Shaughnessy, *The Men Who Lost America*, 64 (*"ungrateful bastards"*); Walpole to Horace Mann, Feb. 18, 1778, from Sherman, "The View from Strawberry Hill" (*"one defect"*); Toynbee, ed., *The Letters of Horace Walpole*, 10: 191 (*"The nation has leaped"* and *"How one blushes"*).

277 **To this he would add:** Toynbee, ed., *The Letters of Horace Walpole*, 10: 270–72.

12. BLESSED IS HE THAT EXPECTS NOTHING

278 **The old arch-rebel had offered:** Schoenbrun, *Triumph in Paris*, 190 (Alceste), 191 (les Insurgents).

278 **French police lurking outside:** Schiff, *A Great Improvisation*, 100 (*"seems to have lost"*); Murphy, *Charles Gravier, Comte de Vergennes*, 246 (*captured Albany*); Murphy, "The Battle of Germantown and the Franco-American Alliance of 1778," 55+ (*Howe advanced*).

278 **A year had passed since his arrival:** NDAR, 11: 863 (*load of salt*), 11: 893 (Duchesse de Grammont); White, *The American Revolution in Notes, Quotes, and Anecdotes*, 45 (*"Blessed is he"*).

278 **On the morning of Thursday, December 4:** Wright, *Franklin of Philadelphia*, 275 (*Franklin called him Figaro* and *unless I bang it*); Lemaitre, *Beaumarchais*, 159–60 (*February 1775*), 215–18 (*scathing criticism*). *The Marriage of Figaro* would not be produced until 1784.

279 **An intriguer "with every finger":** Hardman and Price, eds., *Louis XVI and the Comte de Vergennes*, 45; TBAC, 471–74 (*rue Vieille du Temple*); Lemaitre, *Beaumarchais*, 226–27 (*bankrupt*), 231 (*small cargo of rice*); Ferreiro, *Brothers at Arms*, 107 (*five million livres' worth*); Kite, *Beaumarchais and the War of American Independence*, 141 (*received nothing*); Wharton, ed., "Attitude of France to the United States," in *The Revolutionary Diplomatic Correspondence of the United States*, 1: 374 (*a secret gift*); Rappleye, *Robert Morris*, 99 (*"one or two whores"*).

279 **As Figaro, his alter ego:** Kite, *Beaumarchais and the War of American Independence*, 27 (*"hasten to laugh"*), 125–27, 138 (*emergency subsidy*); Grendel, *Beaumarchais*, 192 (*"exhausted my money and credit"*).

280 **"Yes, sir," Austin replied:** "Memoir of Jonathan Loring Austin," 57+ (*"greater news"*); Murphy, *Charles Gravier, Comte de Vergennes*, 247 (*Germantown*); Schiff, *A Great Improvisation*, 110 (*"glorious news"*); Isaacson, *Benjamin Franklin*, 343 (*stock market investments*); Kite, *Beaumarchais and the War of American Independence*, 145 (*"charming news"*).

280 **Franklin and his colleagues composed:** Lee, *Life of Arthur Lee, LL.D.*, 357; Schoenbrun, *Triumph in Paris*, 166 (*"total reduction of the force"*); BF, American commissioners to Vergennes, Dec. 8, 1777, FOL (*"commerce, wealth"*); Murphy, "The Battle of Germantown and the Franco-American Alliance of 1778," 55+; Murphy, *Charles Gravier, Comte de Vergennes*, 248 (*permitted Howe*); Loménie, *Beaumarchais and His Times*, 300 (*"brave people"*).

280 **Word spread quickly among Parisians:** Schiff, *A Great Improvisation*, 111 (*"demonstrations of joy"*); Lopez, *Mon Cher Papa*, 36 (*"we share your joy"*).

280 **On December 6:** Meng, ed., *Despatches and Instructions of Conrad Alexandre Gérard*, 35–39

(*Alsatian lawyer*); Stinchcombe, *The American Revolution and the French Alliance*, 32; Conrad-Alexandre Gérard to BF, commissioners, Dec. 5, 1777, FOL (*"ability and resolution"*); Lee, *Life of Arthur Lee, LL.D.*, 357 (*three million livres*), 362 (*"prosperous state"*).

281 **"All this seems to bring us"**: Murphy, *Charles Gravier, Comte de Vergennes*, 250 (*"moment of crisis"*); Hardman, "Louis XVI and the War of American Independence," lecture, 2019 (*more than eighty of the largest*); Willis, *The Struggle for Sea Power*, 199 (*close to parity*); Schiff, *A Great Improvisation*, 112 (*"our friends"*); Corwin, *French Policy and the American Alliance of 1778*, 150–51; Van Tyne, "Influences Which Determined the French Government to Make the Treaty with America, 1778," 539 (*"more expedient"*); Hardman and Price, eds., *Louis XVI and the Comte de Vergennes*, 42 (*"Approuvé"*).

281 **But first, as Vergennes now told**: Corwin, "The French Objective in the American Revolution," 33+ (*twenty ships of the line*); Van Doren, *Benjamin Franklin*, 615 (*Pacte de Famille*); Meng, ed., *Despatches and Instructions of Conrad Alexandre Gérard*, 78–79 (*French and Spanish possessions*); Lee, *Life of Arthur Lee, LL.D.*, 362 (*Mississippi River*).

281 **The discussion ended with bows**: Meng, ed., *Despatches and Instructions of Conrad Alexandre Gérard*, 79 (*"if reconciliation with Britain"*).

282 **British officials had been steaming**: Ellis, *The Post Office in the Eighteenth Century*, 62–65 (*"Secret Office"*); Weber, *Masked Dispatches*, 49; Campbell-Smith, *Masters of the Post*, 80 (*Lombard Street*); Hemmeon, *The History of the British Post Office*, 46–47; Westley, "5 Things You Didn't Know About the Spying Army of the Post Office," *BBC History Magazine*, Oct. 15, 2014, n.p.

282 **This operation was financed**: Brooke, *King George III*, 209–10 (*bribes*); Wright, *Franklin of Philadelphia*, 289 (*bankers in Rotterdam*); Renaut, *L'Espionnage naval au XVIIIe siècle*, 70 (*agents in French ports*); Rose, "British Penetration of America's First Diplomatic Mission," 57+ (*"far better informed"*); Schaeper, *Edward Bancroft*, 24–25 (*flamboyant style*); Clark, *Benjamin Franklin*, 319 (*twenty identities*); Alsop, *Yankees at Court*, 96–97 (*cleverest man* and *"better than I"*).

282 **Wentworth's prize agent in Paris**: Schaeper, *Edward Bancroft*, 3–9 (*thousand or more slaves*), 31–35 (*dyes*).

282 **Silas Deane, who as a young Yale graduate**: Schaeper, *Edward Bancroft*, 48–53, 97 (*136 for Spain*), 124–25 (*Tuileries*), 163 (*£500 annual stipend*); Rose, "British Penetration of America's First Diplomatic Mission," 57+; Schoenbrun, *Triumph in Paris*, 127 (*"papers of the first consequence"*).

283 **"Three may keep a secret"**: BF, *Poor Richard, 1735: An Almanack*, FOL; BF to Juliana Ritchie, Jan. 19, 1777, FOL (*"I should blush"*); Rose, "British Penetration of America's First Diplomatic Mission," 57+ (*Joseph Hynson*); Lopez, *My Life with Benjamin Franklin*, 62; Schiff, *A Great Improvisation*, 73 (*blank paper*); Clark, *Lambert Wickes*, 355 (*"apparently stupid"*). Historian Thomas J. Schaeper argues that there is no evidence that intelligence from Bancroft "or any other informer led to the capture of a particular vessel" (Schaeper, *Edward Bancroft*, 146–47).

283 **A man pretending to be**: Schiff, *A Great Improvisation*, 73 (*hotel desk in Berlin*), 104–5 (*George Lupton*); James, *Silas Deane, Patriot or Traitor?*, 22 (*Nantes, Bordeaux*); Stevens's, 2: 171, 172, G. Lupton to W. Eden, June 11 and Aug. 20, 1777; Schoenbrun, *Triumph in Paris*, 128 (*Deane's closet*); Arthur Lee to JA, July 5, 1778, FOL; Hezekiah Ford to commissioners, June 25, 1778, FOL; Rose, "British Penetration of America's First Diplomatic Mission," 57+ (*Hezekiah Ford*); Potts, *Arthur Lee*, 201–5 (*John Thornton*); Haworth, "Frederick the Great and the American Revolution," 460+ (*sought Prussian support*); Lopez, *Mon Cher Papa*, 132–33 (*embezzling from him*).

284 **Damage from the intrusions**: Fortescue, *The Correspondence of King George the Third*, 3: 532 (*"entirely an American"*); Brooke, *King George III*, 210 (*"productions of untruths"*).

284 **The stockjobber appeared in Paris**: Augur, *The Secret War of Independence*, 254 (*Bathing Machine*), 256 (*"vain, desultory"*); Silas Deane papers, *Collections of the New-York Historical Society*, 1: ix–xii; James, *Silas Deane, Patriot or Traitor?*, 51–52 (*knighthoods, governorships*).

284 **Days passed. Wentworth was closely**: Kite, *Beaumarchais and the War of American Indepen-

dence, 149 (*"Be sure that the English"*); Van Doren, *Benjamin Franklin*, 592–93; Augur, *The Secret War of Independence*, 257 (*burned his secret papers*).

285 **"He said it was a very interesting":** Van Doren, *Benjamin Franklin*, 595 (*two hours*); P. Wentworth to W. Eden, Jan. 7, 1778, BF papers, FOL (*"never knew him so eccentric"*).

285 **Precisely as the tamer of lightning:** Lemoine et al., *Versailles*, 96–97 (*porphyry bust*); author visit, Versailles, May 29, 2022.

285 **In a reply received on December 31:** Dull, *The French Navy and American Independence*, 96; Corwin, *French Policy and the American Alliance of 1778*, 157–61 (*republican rebels*); Craveri, *The Last Libertines*, 57 (*"we are ready"*).

285 **This found no favor with Vergennes:** Christie, *Crisis of Empire*, 88 (*France would not alarm*); Patterson, *The Other Armada*, 37–38 (*"wildest folly"*); Stinchcombe, *The American Revolution and the French Alliance*, 33 (*protecting the weak*); Ferreiro, *Brothers at Arms*, 96–97 (*"Nothing can justify"*); Murphy, *Charles Gravier, Comte de Vergennes*, 252; Morison and Commager, *The Growth of the American Republic*, 1: 214 (*"glory and inestimable advantages"*).

286 **Louis listened, perhaps both to:** Hardman, *The Life of Louis XVI*, 124–25; Van Tyne, *The War of Independence: American Phase*, 499–500; Meng, ed., *Despatches and Instructions of Conrad Alexandre Gérard*, 81 (*twin treaties*); Stourzh, *Benjamin Franklin and American Foreign Policy*, 139 (*"Now or never"*).

286 **At six p.m. on January 8:** BF, "The American Commissioners' Interview on Jan. 8 with Gérard: Four Documents," FOL (*"very satisfied with each other"*).

286 **Louis wrote Charles III to explain:** Murphy, *Charles Gravier, Comte de Vergennes*, 250 (*"destruction of the army"*), 252 (*"supreme decision"*); Hardman, *The Life of Louis XVI*, 128 (*"given courage"*).

287 **On Friday evening, February 6:** Bache and Franklin, "Franklin's Ceremonial Coat," 444+ (*Manchester velvet*); TBAC, 29 (*Privy Council*); Van Doren, *Benjamin Franklin*, 596 (*"a little revenge"*).

287 **He disembarked from his coach:** Ferreiro, *Brothers at Arms*, 99 (*to have them copied*); U.S. Department of State, "A History of the Official American Presence in France," n.d. (*Hôtel de Coislin*). Some accounts place the signing in a French foreign ministry office, but a historical plaque on the Place de la Concorde locates it in Deane's apartment.

287 **The French had been remarkably generous:** Stinchcombe, *The American Revolution and the French Alliance*, 30; BF, "The Franco-American Treaty of Alliance," Feb. 6, 1778, FOL.

287 **"The treaties with France":** BF and Silas Deane to Congress, Feb. 8, 1778, FOL (*"magnanimity and goodness"*); BF, Commissioners to Committee for Foreign Affairs, Feb. 16, 1778, FOL (*"encourage other powers"*). Lee's name was omitted from the February 8 dispatch.

288 **Word of Lord North's conciliatory proposals:** BF and Silas Deane to Congress, Feb. 8, 1778, FOL; Schaeper, *Edward Bancroft*, 115 (*in less than three days*); Van Doren, *Benjamin Franklin*, 597.

288 **"Preparations for war are carried on":** BF and Silas Deane to Congress, Feb. 8, 1778, FOL; Dull, *The Miracle of American Independence*, 107 (*back from the West Indies*); Dull, *The French Navy and American Independence*, 101–2 (*leaves were canceled*); NDAR, 11: 987, 1009 (*"work must not"*), 1130 (*"pour vous seul"*); Van Tyne, *The War of Independence: American Phase*, 477–78 (*Matériel shipped to America*).

288 **With France hurtling toward:** Hoffman and Albert, eds., *Diplomacy and Revolution*, 138 (*"feeble confidence"*); Dull, *The French Navy and American Independence*, 103 (*Stormont was recalled*); Schiff, *A Great Improvisation*, 140 (*Hôtel des Deux-Ponts*); Maugras, *The Duc de Lauzun and the Court of Marie Antoinette*, 150 (*"those who have any claims"*).

289 **As for the Americans:** Schiff, *A Great Improvisation*, 132 (*"They play us off"*).

289 **On Friday morning, March 20:** Alsop, *Yankees at Court*, 109 (*Gardes Suisses*); Manceron, *Age of the French Revolution*, 2: 56 (*forty thousand livres*).

289 **Shortly before noon a procession:** Parton, *Life and Times of Benjamin Franklin*, 2: 311–13 (*separate vehicles*); Schoenbrun, *Triumph in Paris*, 182 (*"a fat head"*); Lopez, *Mon Cher Papa*, 179 (*"russet velvet coat"*), 183–84 (*"stocky farmer"*).

289 **Vergennes served a light meal:** BF, "The Presentation of the American Commissioners at Versailles: Two Accounts," Mar. 20, 1778, FOL; author visit, Versailles, May 29, 2022 (*two hundred clocks*); Ferreiro, *Brothers at Arms*, 99 (*"thirteen united provinces"*); Alsop, *Yankees at Court*, 110 (*king's bedchamber*).

290 **A carved allegory titled *France*:** Lemoine et al., *Versailles*, 93–94 (*died in this room*); Manceron, *Age of the French Revolution*, 2: 55 (*Vichy water*); BF, "The Presentation of the American Commissioners at Versailles: Two Accounts," Mar. 20, 1778, FOL (*"hair undressed"*).

290 **"Please assure Congress":** BF, "The Presentation of the American Commissioners at Versailles: Two Accounts," Mar. 20, 1778, FOL.

290 **Then they were done:** Thomas E. Kaiser, "John Hardman, *The Life of Louis XVI*," review, *Journal of Modern History*, 90: 1 (Mar. 2018): 199 (*the Silent King*); Padover, *The Life and Death of Louis XVI*, 113 (*"judged them free people"*); BF, "The Presentation of the American Commissioners at Versailles: Two Accounts," Mar. 20, 1778, FOL (*"you who discovered electricity"*); Hardman, *The Life of Louis XVI*, 130 (*"implacable war"*).

290 **Later Marie-Antoinette sent an invitation:** Parton, *Life and Times of Benjamin Franklin*, 2: 313 (*golden piles*); author visit, Versailles, May 29, 2022 (*straddled by women*); Lopez, *Mon Cher Papa*, 183–84 (*amused by his nickname*); Hardman, *Marie-Antoinette*, 59 (*180,000 livres*).

291 **"It looks as if our navy":** Bernier, *Secrets of Marie Antoinette*, 242–43 (*"soon be active"*), 243 (*"sleeps with me"*); Hardman, *Marie-Antoinette*, 58 (*this very night*); Antonia Fraser, *Marie Antoinette: The Journey*, 166–67; Manceron, *Age of the French Revolution*, 2: 60–61 (*a girl*).

13. THE VORTEX OF SMALL FORTUNES

292 **From the quartzite citadel:** Elliott, *Surviving the Winters*, 81 (*"grand city"*); author visit, Valley Forge, Sept. 1, 2021, signage (*five redoubts*); weather records, VFNHP (*ten days of falling snow*); Brier, "Tolerable Comfortable," VFNHP, 17 (*ten thousand cords*).

292 **Grunting men swung billhooks:** LiA, 2: 104 (*"dungeon cells"*); Brier, "Tolerable Comfortable," VFNHP, 7 (*oilcloth*); Huston, *The Sinews of War*, 59 (*oiled paper*); author visit, Valley Forge, Sept. 1, 2021, signage (*musket cartridge*).

292 **Muddy Forge, as soldiers called:** Pickering, *The Life of Timothy Pickering*, 1: 203; Jackson, *Valley Forge*, 48 (*old hats*); Cook, "Allan McLane, Unknown Hero of the Revolution," 74+ (*linen tablecloths*); Stryker, *The Battle of Monmouth*, 4 (*yoked themselves*); Mathews and Wecter, *Our Soldiers Speak, 1775–1918*, 55 (*"dreaded its ceasing"*).

293 **Surgeon Albigence Waldo recorded:** Waldo, "Valley Forge, 1777–1778," 299+ (*"All wet"* and *"frail, dying creature"*); GW to J. Cadwalader, Mar. 20, 1778, FOL fn (*Sixty soldiers a week*); author visit, Valley Forge, Sept. 1, 2021, signage; Ecelbarger, "Permanent Losses and New Gains During the 1778 Valley Forge Encampment," *JAR*, Feb. 15, 2024 (*two thousand or more*); Jackson, *Valley Forge*, 164–65 (*three to a grave*); Rees, "'None of you know the hardships of a soldiers life,'" n.d., 26 (*"the many deaths"*); Lapham, ed., *Elijah Fisher's Journal*, 7 (*"I gits better"*).

293 **The wonder was that any recovered:** McHenry, "John Morgan vs. William Shippen," *JAR*, Jan. 28, 2020 (*thirty-five hundred physicians*); Beck, *Medicine in the American Colonies*, 35 (*"bleeding, vomiting"*), 46 (*"death by physician"*); Wildes, *Valley Forge*, 184–85 (*burning gunpowder*); Hawke, *Benjamin Rush*, 27 (*rabbit fat*); Reiss, *Medicine and the American Revolution*, 188 (*20 percent*), 203 (*whirling a black cat*); Gillett, *The Army Medical Department, 1775–1818*, 14 (*"nihilism"*).

293 **Warm clothing would have helped:** Freeman, *George Washington: A Biography*, 4: 578 (*four thousand men*); Jackson, *Valley Forge*, 73–75 (*for each one hundred soldiers*); Rappleye, *Robert Morris*, 100; VFHRR2, 395 (*Ice on the Susquehanna*); Stillé, *Major-General Anthony Wayne and the Pennsylvania Line in the Continental Army*, 115 (*buttons*); T. Pickering to GW, Jan. 10, 1778, JLB, CCC (*219 former tailors*).

294 **Misery could be found in every corner:** Isaac How Davenport to James Davenport, Jan. 15, 1778, Museum of the American Revolution; "Historical Notes of Dr. Benjamin Rush, 1777,"

129+, JLB, CCC (*fifteen hundred*); *John Laurens*, 127 (*carcasses*); Mathews and Wecter, *Our Soldiers Speak, 1775–1918*, 60 ("*need not name*"); Boyle, "My Last Shift Betwixt Us & Death," VFNHP ms. (*250 wagons* and "*Not a candle*"); Selby, *The Revolution in Virginia, 1775–1783*, 176 (*most bountiful harvest*); Jameson, *The American Revolution Considered as a Social Movement*, 58–59 (*saltworks*); VFHRR2, 39.

294 **Resignations by army administrators:** Risch, *Supplying Washington's Army*, 39–40 (*Mifflin had quit*); Ferling, ed., *The World Turned Upside Down*, 100 (*wagonmaster general*); Carp, *To Starve the Army at Pleasure*, 44 (*thirty shillings a day*); VFHRR2, 47–48 ("*paralyzed*"), 90 ("*resigned repeatedly*").

295 **"What are Congress doing?":** Boyle, *Writings from the Valley Forge Encampment*, 1: 101; Carp, *To Starve the Army at Pleasure*, 44 ("*No person knows*"); William Duer to Francis Lightfoot Lee, Feb. 19, 1778, "Transportation," VFNHP, 91.

295 **"We should give much":** Gaston Marie Léonard Maussion de la Bastie to mother, Jan. 31, 1778, JLB, AAA.

295 **Yes, he did: hours, days, weeks:** GW to W. Smallwood, Feb. 16, 1778, FOL ("*Dr sr*").

295 **Washington had occupied thirty:** author visit, Moland House historic farm, Pa., Aug. 31, 2021, "Where George Washington Lodged," signage; author visit, Potts house, Valley Forge, Sept. 1, 2021, signage; "Washington's Headquarters," NPS, https://www.nps.gov/vafo/learn/historyculture/washingtons_headquarters.htm; "William (Billy) Lee," https://www.mountvernon.org/library/digitalhistory/digital-encyclopedia/article/william-billy-lee/; GW, general orders, Dec. 20, 1777, *PGW*, 12: 644n ("*pinched*").

296 **Martha Washington arrived at dusk:** Thane, *Washington's Lady*, 137–38 (*dried fruit*), 150 (*rum and well water*); Chernow, *Alexander Hamilton*, 131 (*short, plump*); Brady, *Martha Washington*, 118 (*third consecutive winter*); Martha Washington to Lucy Knox, May 1797, in Kaminski, ed., *The Founders on the Founders*, 526 ("*steady as a clock*"); *PNG*, 2: 54 ("*excessive fond*"); Fitzpatrick, ed., *George Washington's Accounts of Expenses*, 53 (*fifteen shillings*); W. Smallwood to GW, Feb. 15, 1778, FOL (*lemons*); GW to H. Gates, Feb. 27, 1778 (*writing paper*); J. Barry to GW, Apr. 6, 1778, FOL ("*best hair powder*").

296 **As always, the commanding general found:** GW to Lund Washington, Feb. 28, 1778, FOL ("*banished*"); Lund Washington to GW, Jan. 28 and Mar. 18, 1778, FOL (*Steady* and *oyster shells*); Lund to GW, Jan. 25, 1776, Mar. 4 and Mar. 11, 1778, FOL (*Silla*); GW to Lund, Apr. 3, 1779, FOL.

296 **Martha also paid $56:** Fraser, *The Washingtons*, 194 (*portrait and two miniatures*); Bill, *New Jersey and the Revolutionary War*, 69 (*a face aged*); GW to Continental Congress Camp Committee, Jan. 29, 1778, FOL (*fewer than six hundred*); *PNG*, 2: 301 ("*near a thousand*"); GW to Charles Lewis, Mar. 21, 1778, FOL ("*are we to quit?*").

296 **The fate of the army:** GW to William Buchanan, Feb. 7, 1778, FOL ("*fatal crisis*"); Gouverneur Morris to John Jay, Feb. 1, 1778, JLB, CCC ("*skeleton of an army*"); GW to William Buchanan, Feb. 7, 1778, FOL, 465n ("*most unhappy man*"); Charles Whittelsey to Wayhan Parks, Feb. 20, 1778, JLB, CCC ("*beef we draw*").

297 **The army was forced to rely:** Chernow, *Alexander Hamilton*, 107–8 ("*Exert yourself*"); *PNG*, 2: 293; Boyle, "My Last Shift Betwixt Us & Death," VFNHP ms. ("*Very disagreeable*").

297 **Greene, Wayne, and Captain Henry Lee:** GW to NG, Feb. 12, 1778, FOL fn ("*disbanding*"); NG to GW, Feb. 15, 1778, FOL ("*harden my heart*"); Herrera, "Foraging and Combat Operations at Valley Forge," 7+ ("*forage the country naked*"); Wildes, *Anthony Wayne*, 153 (*3,000 head*); Bodle, *The Valley Forge Winter*, 173 ("*vortex of small fortunes*").

297 **In trying to feed:** GW to Thomas Wharton, Jr., Feb. 12, 1778, FOL ("*dwindled away*"); Walter Stewart to GW, Jan. 18, 1778, FOL ("*eight or ten thousand*"); Bodle, *The Valley Forge Winter*, 174 (*sheep drover*), 215 ("*practicable*"); Ely and Jordan, *History of Bucks County, Pennsylvania*, 2: 128 (*own eggs*); GW to John Lacey, Jr., Mar. 20, 1778, and Lacey to GW, Mar. 21, 1778, FOL.

297 **Like most civil wars:** Bill, *New Jersey and the Revolutionary War*, 65 ("*Everywhere distrust*").

298 **In desperation, Washington in February:** VFHRR1, 233–34; *PNG*, 2: 309n ("*Nobody ever*

heard"); VFHRR1, 240 (*"line of splendor"*); Bodle, *The Valley Forge Winter*, 159 (*1 percent commission*); *PNG*, 2: 461–62 (*"no other man"*).

298 **He was precisely the right man:** *PNG*, 2: 140 (birthmark), 190 (*"fisty cuffing"*), 209 (*"cause is too important"*), 463–64n, 471 (*Brandywine*), 480 (*"book of fate"*); Carbone, *Nathanael Greene*, 6–7 (*"substance out of a book"*); *PNG*, 3: 510 (*"Human life is checkered"*).

298 **Not least among Greene's assets:** Stegeman and Stegeman, *Caty*, 51; Kapp, *The Life of Frederick William von Steuben*, 121 (*"handsome, elegant"*); Loane, *Following the Drum*, 57–58 (*violet eyes*); *PNG*, 2: 84 (*"mind and spell well"*), 85 (*"a blank in my heart"*).

299 **The new quartermaster soon recognized:** *PNG*, 2: 405 (*"out of order"*); *PNG*, 2: 554–57, appendix II (*dung forks, saddles*); *PNG*, 3: 480–87 (*eleven types of saws*); Greene, *The Life of Nathanael Greene*, 2: 52 (*taking office*), 55–57 (*equine mortality*).

299 **He organized a flotilla:** Bodle, *The Valley Forge Winter*, 190; Syrett, *Admiral Lord Howe*, 75 (*blockade duty*); *PNG*, 2: 319n (*supplies by water*); GW to George Baylor, Mar. 4, 1778, FOL (*"clean made"*); VFHRR2, 111 (*rice by the tierce*), 329 (*"drive as if the devil"*), 569–70 (*camp kettles*).

299 **Greene's desk at Moore Hall:** Golway, *Washington's General*, 194 (*tomahawks*); JLB, AAA (*Juniata*); Stapleton, "General Daniel Roberdeau and the Lead Mine Expedition, 1778–1779," 361+ (*experienced miners*); Hatch, *The Administration of the American Revolutionary Army*, 99 (*only thirteen hundred yards*); Risch, *Supplying Washington's Army*, 20 (*currency values*).

300 **But slowly the camp:** *PNG*, 2: 319 (*twenty-five hundred letters*), 422 (*"but a breakfast"*); Ferling, ed., *The World Turned Upside Down*, 108 (*three thousand agents*); H. Knox to GW, "Artillery Estimate for 1778," *PGW*, 12: 194–99 (*170 guns*); Joseph Watkins to GW, Mar. 12, 1778, JLB, AAA (*six thousand cartridges*).

300 **After Caty went home:** *PNG*, 2: 425 (*"I am here in the usual style"*).

300 **Another indispensable man arrived:** Lockhart, *The Drillmaster of Valley Forge*, 68 (*"illustrious stranger"*), 87 (*swagger stick*), 88 (*Mars*), 98 (*beaver bicorne*); Du Ponceau and Whitehead, "The Autobiography of Peter Stephen Du Ponceau," 189+ (*scarlet uniform* and *Azor*); Royster, *A Revolutionary People at War*, 213 (*Star of Fidelity*); Palmer, *General Von Steuben*, 4; Kapp, *The Life of Frederick William von Steuben*, 74–75.

301 **Washington trotted out to escort him:** John Sullivan to GW, Feb. 14, 1778, FOL (*nine-pillared bridge*); Ferreiro, *Brothers at Arms*, 151 (Flamand); Kapp, *The Life of Frederick William von Steuben*, 77–78 (*stupendous storm, three fires*); Whitridge, "Baron von Steuben: Washington's Drillmaster," 429+ (*mutineers were shot*); W. Heath to GW, Dec. 7, 1777, 12: 569n (*four thousand muskets*); Lockhart, *The Drillmaster of Valley Forge*, 52 (*"rhinoceros"*); Pettengill, trans., *Letters from America, 1776–1779*, 242 (*"five Negroes"*); Steuben to GW, Dec. 6, 1777, 12: 567n (*volunteer*); J. Laurens to Peter Du Ponceau, n.d., JLB, CCC (*find a dyer*); GW to Henry Laurens, Feb. 27, 1778, FOL (*"a man of military knowledge"*).

301 **In fact, he was not what he seemed:** Ferreiro, *Brothers at Arms*, 151; Kapp, *The Life of Frederick William von Steuben*, 57–60 (*captured by the Russians*), 63 (*"irreproachable conduct"*); Lockhart, *The Drillmaster of Valley Forge*, 5–14 (*Prussian army engineer*), 41–43 (*Beaumarchais*); Lockhart, "Steuben Comes to America," 26+ (Don Quixote); Clary and Whitehorne, *The Inspectors General of the United States Army, 1777–1903*, 33 (*honorific title*); Bell, "What Do We Know About Gen. de Steuben's Sexuality?" and "A Letter of Recommendation for the Baron de Steuben," *Boston 1775*, July 27 and 28, 2018 (*"taken familiarities"* and *"deliberate liar"*). In one memoir, Steuben claimed he left Prussian service to retire to his Swabian estate (Palmer, *General Von Steuben*, 86).

301 **Apparently unaware of the malfeasance:** BF to GW, Sept. 4, 1777, FOL (*"true zeal"*); Clary and Whitehorne, *The Inspectors General of the United States Army, 1777–1903*, 35 (*loss of his European income*); Steuben to AH, Jan. 27, 1790, FOL; "Report on the Memorial of Baron von Steuben," Mar. 29, 1790, FOL (*"obtained my pardon"*).

302 **That much, at least, was true:** Lockhart, *The Drillmaster of Valley Forge*, 77 (*Cervantes and Voltaire*); Kapp, *The Life of Frederick William von Steuben*, 130 (*smoked his pipe* and *"undertaken the discipline"*).

302 **No defect plagued the Continental Army:** Bodle, *The Valley Forge Winter*, 131 (*close-order drill*); Royster, *A Revolutionary People at War*, 218 (*"almost impossible to advance"*); Lockhart, *The Drillmaster of Valley Forge*, 102 (*120 paces*); Wright, *The Continental Army*, 141–42; VFHRR1, 345 (*"country dance"*); Clary and Whitehorne, *The Inspectors General of the United States Army, 1777–1903*, 42.

302 **American officers were astonished:** Royster, *A Revolutionary People at War*, 217 (*personally barking*); Clary and Whitehorne, *The Inspectors General of the United States Army, 1777–1903*, 37 (*"In our European armies"*); Du Ponceau and Whitehead, "The Autobiography of Peter Stephen Du Ponceau," 189+ (*"swear for me"*); Lockhart, *The Drillmaster of Valley Forge*, 103 (*"Goddamn!"*); Irving, *The Life of George Washington*, 3: 359 (*"curse dem no more"*); Echeverria, *Mirage in the West*, 86 (*"You say to your soldier"*).

303 **Steuben continued to dine often:** Clary and Whitehorne, *The Inspectors General of the United States Army, 1777–1903*, 42 (*pilfered muskets*); Du Ponceau and Whitehead, "The Autobiography of Peter Stephen Du Ponceau," 189+ (*"salamanders"*); EPO, "Chronology Morristown, Nov. 1779–December 1780" (*"Bang Stubang"* and *"needless to inform you"*); Kapp, *The Life of Frederick William von Steuben*, 139 (*major general's rank*).

303 **By the time Steuben confessed:** Massey, *John Laurens and the American Revolution*, 104 (*"sensible progress"*); Simms, ed., *The Army Correspondence of Colonel John Laurens*, 160 (*"exerting himself"*).

303 **On April 5 another poseur:** Patterson, *Knight Errant of Liberty*, 189–93; Lapham, ed., *Elijah Fisher's Journal*, 7–9 (*corporal and eight privates*); PNG, 2: 332 (*"best horses"*); Stryker, *The Battle of Monmouth*, 43n (*"All the music"*).

304 **Captivity had not improved:** Moore, *The Treason of Charles Lee*, ix–x (*"disagreeable"*); Thacher, *Military Journal*, 463 (*"real deformity"*); Mazzagetti, *Charles Lee*, 58 (*fox pelts*); Boudinot, *Exchange of Major-General Charles Lee*, 9–10 (*"looked as dirty"*).

304 **He would forever remain a riddle:** Mazzagetti, *Charles Lee*, 35 (*"vagabond"*); Papas, *Renegade Revolutionary*, 18 (*"most canine"*); Moore, *The Treason of Charles Lee*, 4 (*"born in the army"*); Paterson, *Knight Errant of Liberty*, 21 (*Latin, Greek*); Lender and Stone, *Fatal Sunday*, 106 (*Plutarch*); Murrin and Waldron, eds., *Conflict at Monmouth Court House*, 37–38 (*Polish major general*); Corner, ed., *The Autobiography of Benjamin Rush*, 156 (*"witty and brilliant"*); Bell, "Why Charles Lee Loved Dogs," *Boston 1775*, Sept. 19, 2014 (*"quadruped friends"*).

305 **"His brain was lucid":** Alden, *General Charles Lee*, 305; TBAC, 488, 502 (*character flaws*); Thacher, *Military Journal*, 458 (*"querulous clown"*).

305 **He disliked what he saw:** Boudinot, *Exchange of Major-General Charles Lee*, 11 (*"a sergeant's guard"*); Boyd, *Elias Boudinot, Patriot and Statesman, 1740–1821*, 54 (*fortress in Pittsburgh*); Patterson, *Knight Errant of Liberty*, 187 (*"row down the Ohio"*); LP, 387 (*"plan of defense"*), 392 (*lieutenant general*); Mazzagetti, *Charles Lee*, 150 (*"without me"*).

305 **Lee knew that skeptics in Congress:** Knollenberg, *Washington and the Revolution*, 191 (*nurtured doubts*); Lender, *Cabal!*, 30–31; Hawke, *Benjamin Rush*, 190–91; GW to Thomas Conway, Nov. 5, 1777, FOL (*"weak general"*); GW to Horatio Gates, Jan. 4, 1778, FOL; William Heath to GW, Apr. 26, 1777, FOL fn; Russell, "The Conway Cabal," 84+; Freeman, *George Washington: A Biography*, 4: 545 (*Horatio Gates*), 4: 548–49 (*"as unfortunate a measure"*); GW to R. H. Lee, Oct. 16, 1777, FOL; GW to H. Laurens, Jan. 2, 1778, FOL; Clary and Whitehorne, *The Inspectors General of the United States Army, 1777–1903*, 31 (*sweeping powers*); GW to William Gordon, Jan. 23, 1778, FOL; AH to George Clinton, Feb. 13, 1778, FOL (*"calumniator"*).

306 **Although Greene suspected a "cabal":** PNG, 2: 252–53; Simms, ed., *The Army Correspondence of Colonel John Laurens*, 104 (*"junto"*); Martin and Lender, *"A Respectable Army,"* 115; Massey, *John Laurens and the American Revolution*, 91–92; Lender and Stone, *Fatal Sunday*, 39–40 (*"tittle tattle"* and *"if he has an enemy"*); Ferling, *The First of Men*, 228; Horatio Gates to GW, Jan. 23, 1778, and Feb. 19, 1778, FOL; GW to Horatio Gates, Feb. 24, 1778, FOL (*"in silence"*); T. Conway to H. Laurens, May 18, 1778, Thomas Addis Emmet Collection, NYPL, EM. 8730 (*resignation*); Bill, *New Jersey and the Revolutionary War*, 69 (*"stopped his lying*

mouth"); Thomas Conway to GW, July 23, 1778, FOL (*"great and good man"*); Russell, "The Conway Cabal," 84+ (*recovered*); GW to Bryan Fairfax, Mar. 1, 1778, FOL. The duel was fought on July 4, 1778.

306 **Whether Charles Lee saw in this ruction:** Lee, "Scheme for Putting an End to the War," in *LP*, 363–65 (*"great desolation"*).

307 **In late 1776 Lee:** *TBAC*, 488 (*"kind of treason"*); Murrin and Waldron, eds., *Conflict at Monmouth Court House*, 43; Billias, ed., *George Washington's Generals and Opponents*, 40–41 (*hoped to mislead the Howes*). Several other Lee biographers reached the same conclusion about his betrayal. See McBurney, *General Washington's Nemesis*, 6, 19, 81, and Mazzagetti, *Charles Lee*, 140–43. George Moore, who discovered the document, ascribed to Lee "as wicked a spirit of treason as ever existed" (Moore, *The Treason of Charles Lee*, 95).

307 **For now, Lee headed west:** GW to Charles Lee, Apr. 22, 1778, FOL (*"congratulate you"*); H. Laurens to GW, Apr. 27, 1778, FOL (*"renounce, refuse, and abjure"*).

307 **Greening grass and the croak of frogs:** Henry Sewall diary, Apr. 23, 1778 (*apple blossoms*); Gruber, ed., *John Peebles' American War, 1776–1782*, 173; Prowell, *History of York County, Pennsylvania*, 1: 290–91 (*286 houses*); Wallace, *The Life of Henry Laurens*, 231–32 (*"small, inconvenient"*); Meade, *Patrick Henry, Practical Revolutionary*, 214 (*"worst roads"*); Pickering, *The Life of Timothy Pickering*, 1: 208 (*half a dollar*); Lender, *Cabal!*, 145 (*"no fine women"*).

307 **Printing money seemed to be:** Prowell, *History of York County, Pennsylvania*, 1: 301 (*once owned by Franklin*); "Hall & Sellers Press," https://www.hmdb.org/m.asp?m=4569; Newman, *The Early Paper Money of America*, 22 (*blue fibers*), 39 (*two witnesses* and *ornate hog*), 80 (*one in black ink*); Michael Hillegas to H. R. Purviance, Mar. 25, 1778, "Selected Letters of Michael Hillegas, Treasurer of the United States," 232+ (*Frankfort black*); James Abeel to NG, May 23, 1778, *PNG*, 2: 400n (*hire boys*); Wells, "Mind Your Business: Patriotic Mottoes & Emblems on Continental Currency," 38+ (*POST NUBILA PHOEBUS*).

308 **Printers could hardly meet the demand:** Timothy Pickering to Henry Hollingsworth, May 1, 1778, APS, Feinstone Coll., #1143 (*"'Tis impossible"*); Grubb, *The Continental Dollars*, 5; *LiA*, 343 (*$6 to a dollar in silver*); Louis Jordan, "Colonial Currency," University of Notre Dame, https://coins.nd.edu/colcurrency/index.html; Bullock, *The Finances of the United States from 1775 to 1789*, 123 (*taxation*); Gouge, *A Short History of Paper Money and Banking in the United States*, 27 (*"a wagonload of money?"*); James Abeel to NG, May 23, 1778, *PNG*, 2: 400 (*shears*).

308 **Since shortly after the first shots:** Dull, *The Miracle of American Independence*, 65–66 (*executive, legislative, and judicial*); Wallace, *The Life of Henry Laurens*, 241 (*"no frolickers"*), 277 (*"genius, insight"*); Bill, *New Jersey and the Revolutionary War*, 68 (*less than twenty*); Simner, "A Further Evaluation of the Carlisle Peace Commission's Initiative," *JAR*, Sept. 30, 2021 (*eighty-eight elected congressmen*); Rossie, *The Politics of Command in the American Revolution*, 137 (*"Debates were perplexed"*); Ferling, *A Leap in the Dark*, 229 (*"when it was ignorant"*); Stewart, *George Washington*, 243 (*253 in number*); Sumner, *The Financier and the Finances of the American Revolution*, 1: 7 (*$16.39 for ferry fees*); Smith, ed., *Letters of Delegates to Congress, 1774–1789*, 10: 20 (*"catch the bear"*).

308 **At three p.m. on Saturday, May 2:** Prowell, *History of York County, Pennsylvania*, 1: 314–15 (*cupola bell*); Ferreiro, *Brothers at Arms*, 101 (*on the Maine coast*); Harry Livingston to Walter Livingston, May 11, 1778, Livingston Papers, NYHS, box 4.

309 **Congress agreed, and unanimously ratified:** Chinard, ed., *The Treaties of 1778 and Allied Documents*, xv (*Three hundred copies*); *NDAR*, 12: 4 (*Six vessels*); Prowell, *History of York County, Pennsylvania*, 1: 314–15 (*$3,000*).

309 **The tidings triggered jubilation:** GW to Henry Laurens, May 1, 1778, FOL (*"heartfelt joy"*); GW to John Augustine Washington, Aug. 5–9, 1777, FOL (*"among those few"*); GW to Alexander McDougall, May 1, 1778, FOL (*"shake off"*); Gara, *Queen's American Rangers*, 123–26 (*Crooked Billet*); Jackson, *With the British Army in Philadelphia, 1777–1778*, 223–25; John Lacey, Jr., to GW, May 2, 1778, FOL (*"butchered"*); James Potter to GW, May 18, 1778, FOL (*buckwheat fire*); GW to John Lacey, Jr., May 3, 1778, FOL (*"permitting yourself"*).

309 **At nine a.m. on Wednesday, May 6:** Byrd, *Sacred Scripture, Sacred War*, 11 (*sixty were Roman Catholic*); Davidson, *Propaganda and the American Revolution, 1763–1783*, 378 (*God himself*).

309 **A cannon shot at ten-thirty:** VFHRR1, 398 (*"Triumph beamed"*); Greene, *The Life of Nathanael Greene*, 2: 71–75 (*"Long live"*); Royster, *A Revolutionary People at War*, 253 (*"your favorite Handel"*).

310 **"The officers of each brigade":** Miller, ed., *The Selected Papers of Charles Willson Peale and His Family*, 1: 273 (*"saluting him"*); Moore, *The Diary of the American Revolution, 1775–1783*, 302 (*"brilliancy and good order"*); Unger, *Lafayette*, 71–72 (*Tears streaked*); LAAR, 77 (*"My heart is tormented"*).

310 **The review ended, and the troops dispersed:** Chernow, *Washington: A Life*, 336 (*cricket*); Wildes, *Valley Forge*, 225 (*long bullet*); Freeman, *George Washington: A Biography*, 5: 1–2 (*"fat meat, strong wine"*); VFHRR1, 398 (*"greatest day ever"*); Greene, *The Life of Nathanael Greene*, 2: 71–75 (*"so radiant"*).

310 **He had survived the hardest season:** Kapp, *The Life of Frederick William von Steuben*, 138 (*"much blood"*); GW to Landon Carter, May 20, 1778, FOL (*"Providence has a just claim"*).

311 **A day after the Valley Forge merriment:** Mackesy, *The War for America, 1775–1783*, 213; Germain to Clinton, Mar. 21, 1778, "Secret Military Dispatches," Germain papers, WLC, vol. 18 (*"trusty"*); Germain to Clinton, Mar. 8, 1778, WLC, Germain papers, vol. 7 (*"power, reputation"*); Willcox, *Portrait of a General*, 202–5 (*"the best officer we have"*).

311 **Bearing it was not Clinton's forte:** Willcox, "British Strategy in America, 1778," 97+ (*"This command"* and *"certainly not desirable"*); Clark, "Responsibility for the Failure of the Burgoyne Campaign," 542+ (*self-exculpatory letters*); Wyatt and Willcox, "Sir Henry Clinton," 3+ (*peppered the ministry*); Willcox, ed., *The American Rebellion*, 85 (*"hopeless"*); O'Shaughnessy, *The Men Who Lost America*, 219 (*North had been skeptical*); Germain to Clinton, Aug. 5, 1778, NDAR, 13: 1123 (*"all the king's forces"*).

311 **Only love brightened his life:** Clinton notebook L, Aug. 6, 1794, and his will, Dec. 26, 1794, WBW (*"gain an inch"* and *"attached herself"*); Willcox, *Portrait of a General*, 198–99.

312 **Clinton had been ashore in Philadelphia:** NDAR, 13: 65 (*Commission for Quieting Disorders*); Marlow, *Sackville of Drayton*, 188–89; Germain to Clinton, Mar. 8, 1778, WLC, Germain papers, vol. 7 (*"no room to doubt"*).

312 **The second sheaf, marked "Most Secret":** Germain to Clinton, Mar. 21, 1778, "Secret Military Dispatches," WLC, Germain papers, vol. 18 (*"an immediate attack"*); Willcox, ed., *The American Rebellion*, 86 (*St. Augustine*).

312 **Finally, Germain continued, "it is":** Germain to Clinton, Mar. 21, 1778, "Secret Military Dispatches," WLC, Germain papers, vol. 18 (*"evacuate Philadelphia"*); Germain to Clinton, Mar. 8, 1778, WLC, Germain papers, vol. 7 (*"zeal and ability"*).

312 **"I am directed to evacuate":** Clinton memo, [May 1778?], WBW.

313 **At three-thirty p.m. on Monday, May 18:** Gruber, ed., *John Peebles' American War, 1776–1782*, 181–82; "Particulars of the Mischianza in America," 353+; André, "Major André's Account," 687+; Münchhausen, *At General Howe's Side*, 52 (*One hundred and eight musicians*); Jackson, *With the British Army in Philadelphia, 1777–1778*, 240 (*Near Market Place*); Moore, *The Diary of the American Revolution, 1775–1783*, 305–6.

313 **Here then was the *Mischianza*:** Hatch, *Major John André*, 98–105 (*"variety of entertainments"*); Shields and Teute, "The Meschianza: Sum of All Fêtes," 185+; Jackson, *With the British Army in Philadelphia, 1777–1778*, 241–45 (*medieval knights*); Irvin, "The Streets of Philadelphia," 7+; Colley, *Britons*, 150 (*lofty crusade*).

313 **At length the tournament ended:** Whinyates, ed., *The Services of Lieut.-Colonel Francis Downman*, 61 (*"anything so ridiculous"* and *"Thy laurels"*); Murdoch, ed., *Rebellion in America*, 624 (*firepots, rockets*).

313 **Supper was served at midnight:** Shields and Teute, "The Meschianza: Sum of All Fêtes," 185+ (*eighteen chandeliers* and *"magnificent"*); André, "Major André's Account," 687+ (*Negro slaves*); Sargent, *The Life and Career of Major John André*, 166 (*"fine green turtle"*).

314 **Skeptics disagreed. "Our enemies"**: Tatum, *The American Journal of Ambrose Serle*, 293; Hatch, *Major John André*, 104 (*"farce"*); Nash, *First City*, 99 (*"shameful scene"*); Weintraub, *Iron Tears*, 155 (*"dancing at a funeral"*).

314 **Hardly had the final toast**: Unger, *Lafayette*, 75–76 (*more than two thousand*); LiA, 2: 186–93; VFHRR1, 427–29; GW to Lafayette, May 18, 1778, *PGW*, 15: 151–54 (*"every possible precaution"*); H. Laurens to Cornelius Harnett, May 30, 1778, JLB, BBB (*before the dawdling redcoats could cinch*); Trussell, *Epic on the Schuylkill*, 45 (*"run very swift"*); Uhlendorf, trans. and annot., *Revolution in America*, 176 (*"fruitless march"*); Ambrose Serle, *American Journal*, JLB, BBB (*"follies and blunders"*).

314 **Barren Hill would be William Howe's**: "Particulars of the Mischianza in America," 353+ (*officers wept*); Uhlendorf, trans., *Revolution in America*, 173 (*nineteen-gun salute*); Wilkin, *Some British Soldiers in America*, 250 (*"a better general"*).

314 **Upon reaching England in early July**: Lutnick, "The American Victory at Saratoga," 103+ (*"Every error"*); Ferling, *Winning Independence*, 53–54 (*"brought home in chains"*); Allen, "Diary of James Allen, Esq.," 438 (*"His conduct has given"*).

315 **His battlefield successes at Long Island**: Gruber, *The Howe Brothers and the American Revolution*, 359–60 (*neglect of the loyalists*); Shy, "The American Revolution Today," lecture, 1974 (*plodding, pessimistic*); Anderson, *The Command of the Howe Brothers During the American Revolution*, 342 (*"The situation demanded"*).

315 **Before the competent man left**: Jackson, *With the British Army in Philadelphia, 1777–1778*, 231–34 (*Spanish olives* and *"very unenviable"*).

315 **The Commission for Quieting Disorders arrived**: Stryker, *The Battle of Monmouth*, 34 (*aboard the* Trident); Burdick, *Revolutionary Delaware*, 107 (*"fired several shots"*); Trevelyan, *The American Revolution*, 4: 365; "Commissioners for Quieting Disorders" to Germain, June 15, 1778, *DAR*, 15: 140 (*"most prejudicial"*); Lender and Stone, *Fatal Sunday*, 83–84 (*"ridicule, nullity"*); Charles Thomson to John Jay, Aug. 9, 1781, JLB, BBB (*four square miles*); Reed, *Life and Correspondence of Joseph Reed*, 1: 393 (*"nothing on a great scale"*), 1: 425–26 (*no one in London*).

315 **Carlisle, barely thirty years old**: Jesse, *Memoirs of King George the Third*, 196 (*Almack's gaming tables*); Thackeray, *The Four Georges*, 89 (*"scarcely crawl"*); Ferling, *Almost a Miracle*, 265 (*"bepowdered fop"*); Reed, *Life and Correspondence of Joseph Reed*, 1: 423 (*opera glasses*).

316 **Despite such ridicule, he**: Stryker, *The Battle of Monmouth*, 34 (*caressing her children*), 49 (*a kite*); Nathan R. Einhorn, "The Reception of the British Peace Offer," https://journals.psu.edu, 191+; Mackenzie, *Diary of Frederick Mackenzie*, 272 (*town hangman*); Conway, *The War of American Independence, 1775–1783*, 220 (*"Can they raise our cities"*); Commager and Morris, *The Spirit of 'Seventy-Six*, 694 (*dukedom*), 700 (*£10,000*); GW to H. Laurens, Apr. 18, 1778, FOL (*"poison the minds"*).

316 **"The common people hate us"**: Commager and Morris, *The Spirit of 'Seventy-Six*, 701; VFHRR1, 443–44 (*"derogatory"*); Simner, "A Further Evaluation of the Carlisle Peace Commission's Initiative," *JAR*, Sept. 30, 2021 (*"The great powers of Europe"*).

316 **So did the army**: Willcox, ed., *The American Rebellion*, 89 (*travel overland*); Mackesy, *The War for America, 1775–1783*, 214n (*thirty-four thousand people*); Clinton memo, [May 1778?], WBW ("Nous verrons").

317 **General Howe had intended to abandon**: Bodle, *The Valley Forge Winter*, 232 (*make peace*); Tatum, *The American Journal of Ambrose Serle*, 295 (*"Now a rope"*), 298–301 (*"distress of the inhabitants"*); Metzger, *The Prisoner in the American Revolution*, 159 (*toast and butter*); Balch, ed., *The Examination of Joseph Galloway, Esq.*, 34 (*offered passage*); Jackson, *With the British Army in Philadelphia, 1777–1778*, 259–60 (*Three thousand accepted*); Historical Manuscript Commission, *Report on the Manuscripts of Mrs. Stopford-Sackville*, "Deserters from the Rebels," Sept. 30, 1777, to June 17, 1778, 2: 100, 116 (*4,347*); Braisted, "The American Vicars of Bray," *JAR*, Nov. 3, 2015.

317 **By mid-June, hundreds of baggage wagons**: Morrissey, *Monmouth Courthouse 1778*, 33; Pattison to Board of Ordnance (U.K.), James Pattison papers, NYHS, May 22, 1778 (*forty-six field guns*); Lender and Stone, *Fatal Sunday*, 86–87 (*damaged cannons*); Uhlendorf, trans. and

annot., *Revolution in America*, 174, 182 (*Two dozen unfinished vessels*); Burgoyne, trans. and ed., *A Hessian Officer's Diary of the American Revolution*, 136 (*horse transports*); Baer, *Hessians*, 260–61 (*further defections*); Jackson, *With the British Army in Philadelphia, 1777–1778*, 144 (*Penrose Wharf*); Kemble, *The Kemble Papers*, 1: 152 (*Six hundred*), 593 (*Active and Webb*); Hagist, *Noble Volunteers*, 220 (*locked troops in their barracks*) and 234 (*"shameful inattention"*).

317 **Wheelbarrows, drays, and jolt-wagons:** Jackson, *With the British Army in Philadelphia, 1777–1778*, 257 (*"terror, hurry"*), 259–60 (*Reedy Island*); Simms, ed., *The Army Correspondence of Colonel John Laurens*, 176; Scharf and Westcott, *History of Philadelphia, 1609–1884*, 1: 385 (*auctioned their furniture*); Trevelyan, *The American Revolution*, 4: 370 (*purchased surreptitiously*); Mishoff, "Business in Philadelphia During the British Occupation, 1777–1778," 165+ (*£10,000 in unpaid debts*); Philemon Dickinson to GW, May 31, 1778, *PGW*, 15: 283 (*bobbing squadron of chairs*); Patterson, *Knight Errant of Liberty*, 202 (*"Imagine this river"*).

318 **An embittered, end-of-days mood:** "Von Krafft's Journal," ix+ (*"Everything in the rooms"*); Jackson, *With the British Army in Philadelphia, 1777–1778*, 174–75 (*"cruel and ridiculous"*); Sullivan, *The Disaffected*, 187 (*"pity us here"*); Wiener, "The Military Occupation of Philadelphia in 1777–1778," 310+ (*"comedy of errors"*); Sargent, *The Life and Career of Major John André*, 183 (*portrait of Franklin*); Hatch, *Major John André*, 107; Hart, "The Wilson Portrait of Franklin," 409+ (*ancestral seat*). The Franklin portrait was eventually returned to hang in the White House.

318 **On June 16, Clinton reported:** Clinton orders, June 16–17, 1778, Frederick Mackenzie papers, WLC, box 3, vol. E (*crossed the next day*).

318 **The last grenadiers and light infantry:** Jackson, *With the British Army in Philadelphia, 1777–1778*, 263 (*Gloucester Point*); *NDAR*, 13: 148 (Vigilant).

318 **"This morning when we arose":** Crane, ed., *The Diary of Elizabeth Drinker*, 77; Stryker, *The Battle of Monmouth*, 48 (*"They vanished"*).

318 **As Continental cavalrymen swept into town:** Du Ponceau and Whitehead, "The Autobiography of Peter Stephen Du Ponceau," 211 (*"Uncle Howe"*); Scharf and Westcott, *History of Philadelphia, 1609–1884*, 1: 385 (*the Dock Creek bridge*); Sargent, *The Life and Career of Major John André*, 185 (*British deserters*); Crane, ed., *The Diary of Elizabeth Drinker*, 77 (*"drawn swords"*).

318 **"I found many lean faces":** Miller, ed., *The Selected Papers of Charles Willson Peale and His Family*, 1: 277; Larson, *The Trials of Allegiance*, 108 (*six hundred houses*); Tracy, *266 Days*, 347 (*holes in floors*); Drake, *Life and Correspondence of Henry Knox*, 56 (*"Lucy and I went in"*).

319 **Fences, palings, and thousands of fruit trees:** Rosswurm, *Arms, Country, and Class*, 152; Jackson, *With the British Army in Philadelphia, 1777–1778*, 267 (*force Congress to reconvene*), 272–73 (*Every church*); author visit, Old Pine Street Church, signage and "Old Pine Conservancy" pamphlet, Sept. 2, 2021; Dorwart, *Invasion and Insurrection*, 149 (*Windsor chairs*); Larson, *The Trials of Allegiance*, 108 (*local college*); Prowell, *History of York County, Pennsylvania*, 1: 321 (*$45 to a bell ringer*); Mishoff, "Business in Philadelphia During the British Occupation, 1777–1778," 165+ (*"a Negro boy named Tony"*).

319 **The realization that the British:** Carp, *Rebels Rising*, 217 (*"some purification"*); Thompson, *Benedict Arnold in Philadelphia*, 42–43 (*one leg propped up* and *Slate Roof House*); Lossing, *The Pictorial Field-Book of the Revolution*, 2: 300–301 (*William Penn*).

319 **Arnold's arrival at Valley Forge:** Martin, *Benedict Arnold, Revolutionary Hero*, 423 (*"great joy"*); Malony, "An Analysis of the Near-fatal Wound Suffered by Benedict Arnold at Saratoga," Friends of Saratoga Battlefield (*special shoe*); Randall, *Benedict Arnold*, 417–18 (*"violent oppression"*); Thompson, *Benedict Arnold in Philadelphia*, 38 (*"support, maintain"*).

319 **Within hours of reaching Philadelphia:** Lawler, "The President's House in Philadelphia," 5+ (*martial law*); Irvin, "The Streets of Philadelphia," 7+ (*confiscate the property*); GW to BA, June 19, 1778, FOL (*"tranquility and order"*); "Proceedings of . . . the Trial of Major General Arnold, June 1, 1779," https://quod.lib.umich.edu/e/evans/N13495.0001.001/1.3.2?rgn=div2; view=fulltext (*closing all private shops* and *"much crowded with business"*).

320 **Twenty miles northwest of the city:** Bernardus Swartout, Jr., journal, June 19, 1778, Swartout papers, NYHS (*two a.m.*); GW to Philemon Dickinson, June 20, 1778, *PGW*, 15; 479 (*Coryell's*

Ferry); Harris and Ecelbarger, "A Reconsideration of Continental Army Numerical Strength at Valley Forge," *JAR*, May 18, 2021 (*more than sixteen thousand*); GW, council of war, June 17, 1778, *PGW*, 15: 414 (*seven questions*); Henry Knox to GW, June 18, 1778, FOL ("*most criminal*").

320 **"We shall proceed"**: GW to Henry Laurens, June 18, 1778, FOL; Rees, " 'Reach Coryels Ferry. Encamp on the Pennsylvania Side': The March from Valley Forge to Monmouth Courthouse, 18 to 28 June 1778" (*"whole army in motion"*).

14. I WOULD RATHER LOSE THE CROWN

321 **Englishmen went about their business**: *Gentleman's Magazine and Historical Chronicle*, vol. 48 (1778): 187–89 (*Blue Boar*).

321 **The confirmation of an American alliance**: Marshall, *The Making and Unmaking of Empires*, 358 (*"ancient, inveterate"*); Lutnick, *The American Revolution and the British Press*, 138 (*"Say, Yankees"*); Weintraub, *Iron Tears*, 157 (*"Rouse, Britain's"*); White, *A Great and Monstrous Thing*, 139 (*luxury trades*).

321 **A brushfire war in North America**: Fortescue, *The Correspondence of King George the Third*, 4: 54; Brooke, *King George III*, 187 (*"man of great abilities"*), 188–89 (*"capital punishment"*), 191 (*"go to the grave"*); Ayling, *George the Third*, 258–59 (*procrastination*); O'Shaughnessy, *The Men Who Lost America*, 66 (*"my own master"*).

322 **The king urged him to spend a restful week**: Black, *George III, America's Last King*, 238 (*"recruit your mind"*); Pemberton, *Lord North*, 290 (*"cast off his indecision"*); Brooke, *King George III*, 194 (*Cinque Ports*); Roberts, *The Last King of America*, 357–58 (*silver greyhound*).

322 **"Peace with America"**: Ayling, *George the Third*, 260; Fortescue, *The Correspondence of King George the Third*, 4: 56 (*greatest living Briton*); Black, *George III, America's Last King*, 233; McDougall, *Freedom Just Around the Corner*, 190 (*colonists as compatriots*); Roberts, *The Last King of America*, 172–73; Plumb, *England in the Eighteenth Century*, 113–14; Brown, *William Pitt, Earl of Chatham*, 411–12 (*bludgeoning the French*).

322 **His fame, eloquence, and effulgent patriotism**: Peters, *The Elder Pitt*, 236 (*"one great man"*); Black, *Pitt the Elder*, 297 (*from Parliament for two years*); Williams, *The Life of William Pitt, Earl of Chatham*, 2: 317–18 (*"dawn of joy"*); Jesse, *Memoirs of King George the Third*, 3: 145 (*public clamor*); Ayling, *The Elder Pitt*, 423; Peters, *The Elder Pitt*, 236 (*French dreaded*).

322 **So, too, did George III**: Peters, *The Elder Pitt*, Peters, *The Elder Pitt*, 237–38 (*more than any public figure*); Fortescue, *The Correspondence of King George the Third*, 3: 449 (*"specious words"*); Black, *Pitt the Elder*, 297 (*"imbecility, cruelty"*); Von Ruville, *William Pitt, Earl of Chatham*, 3: 324–26 (*"rapine and plunder"*); Kallich and MacLeish, eds., *The American Revolution Through British Eyes*, 107 (*"unjust in its principles"*); PH 19, 359–63 (*"If I were an American"*); Hibbert, *George III*, 155.

323 **No doubt Chatham had "the scent"**: Peters, *The Elder Pitt*, 223; Brown, *William Pitt, Earl of Chatham*, 390 (*"perfidious man"*); Donne, *The Correspondence of King George the Third to Lord North*, 2: 153–54 (*"Whilst any ten men"*).

323 **Both the upper galleries**: Marshall, *Dr. Johnson's London*, 117 (*drafty chamber*); Thomas, *Memoirs of the Marquis of Rockingham and His Contemporaries*, 2: 352 (*wrapped in flannels*); Brown, *William Pitt, Earl of Chatham*, 392–93 (*"looked like a dying man"*).

323 **Lord Chatham had endured debilitating**: Tuchman, *The March of Folly*, 161 (*schoolboy at Eton*); Ayling, *The Elder Pitt*, 417; Brown, *William Pitt, Earl of Chatham*, 385 (*"streak of frenzy"*); Roberts, *The Last King of America*, 172 (*hatch in the door*).

324 **He rose slowly, leaning on a crutch**: Von Ruville, *William Pitt, Earl of Chatham*, 3: 342 (*"stillness in the house"*); Ayling, *George the Third*, 261 (*aligned with the king*); Hibbert, *George III*, 159; Almon, *Anecdotes of the Life of the Right Hon. William Pitt, Earl of Chatham*, 2: 177–78 (*"let us fall like men"*).

324 **He sat down after ten minutes**: Von Ruville, *William Pitt, Earl of Chatham*, 3: 342–43 (*frown creasing his brow*); Jesse, *Memoirs of King George the Third*, 3: 183–84 (*reviving salts*).

324 **He was indeed dying**: Ehrman, *The Younger Pitt*, 1: 7–8 (*twenty-four bedrooms*); Ayling, *The Elder Pitt*, 425 (*Hector*).

324 **Parliament appropriated £20,000:** Ehrman, *The Younger Pitt,* 1: 19; Brown, *William Pitt, Earl of Chatham,* 394 (*single vote*); Jesse, *Memoirs of King George the Third,* 3: 190 (*"offensive measure"*); Gibbon, *The Autobiography and Correspondence of Edward Gibbon,* 258 (*"double odium"*); Trevelyan, *The American Revolution,* 4: 379 (*newspaper hirelings*).

325 **He lay in state at Westminster:** *Bath Chronicle,* June 11, 1778, 3 (*Painted Chamber*); Marshall, *Dr. Johnson's London,* 115–16 (*Spanish Armada*); Brown, *William Pitt, Earl of Chatham,* 394 (*Eight halberdiers*); Peters, *The Elder Pitt,* 226–35 (*"colors of popularity"*); Almon, *Anecdotes of the Life of the Right Hon. William Pitt, Earl of Chatham,* 2: 390 (*"height of prosperity"*); Ayling, *The Elder Pitt,* 426 (*seventy indigents*).

325 **Now he was gone:** Von Ruville, *William Pitt, Earl of Chatham,* 3: 344 (*"May not the political exit"*).

325 **George rarely traveled beyond:** Ayling, *George the Third,* 205 (*coal mine*); *London Gazette,* Apr. 25, 1778, 1 (Princess Augusta).

325 **Past Woolwich he sailed:** *London Gazette,* Apr. 25, 1778, 1 (*twenty-one guns*); White, *A Great and Monstrous Thing,* 219 (*Fifteen hundred workers*); Schama, *A History of Britain,* 2: 277 (Royal Charles).

326 **George was determined that no:** Lutnick, *The American Revolution and the British Press, 1775–1783,* 137 (Judas Maccabaeus), 140 (*French wines*); Brooke, *King George III,* 183 (*new regiments*); Curtis, *The Organization of the British Army in the American Revolution,* 75–77 (*fifteen thousand troops*); Conway, *The British Isles and the War of American Independence,* 118 (*"quite a military rage"*).

326 **After sailing three miles up the Medway:** "A Short History of Sheerness Dockyard," https://www.thehistorypress.co.uk/articles/a-short-history-of-sheerness-dockyard/; *London Gazette,* Apr. 25, 1778, 1 (*"inviolable attachment"*); *Public Advertiser* (U.K.), May 4, 1778, 2.

326 **An easterly breeze on Sunday:** Eastland and Ballantyne, *HMS Victory, First Rate 1765,* 16–17 (*"largest and finest ship"* and *four acres*), 41 (*octagonal lanterns*); captain's log, *Victory,* Apr.–May 1778, UK NA, ADM 51/1036 (*tarred the rigging*); Willis, *The Struggle for Sea Power,* 216 (*twenty-one tons*). *Victory,* which later served as Horatio Nelson's flagship at Trafalgar, had been largely built at the end of the Seven Years' War but remained "in ordinary"—reserve—for thirteen years, until completed in 1778 (author visit, HMS *Victory,* Portsmouth, June 2014).

327 **George adored this wooden world:** Keegan, *The Price of Admiralty,* 1–2 (*smells of pitch and tar*); Vale, "Pitch, Paint, Varnish and the Changing Color Schemes of Royal Navy Warships, 1775–1815," 30+ (*Venetian red* and *fish glue*); Brown, *Maritime Portsmouth,* 46 (*eight knots*); Miller, *Sea of Glory,* 221 (*"One hand for the ship"*); Lloyd, *The British Seaman,* 120, 248 (*nineteen shillings*).

327 **At length the king took his leave:** captain's log, *Victory,* Apr. 27, 1778, UK NA, ADM 51/1036 (*kissed the royal hand*); "A Short History of Sheerness Dockyard," https://www.thehistorypress.co.uk/articles/a-short-history-of-sheerness-dockyard/; *London Gazette,* Apr. 25, 1778, 1 (*£5 for every able seaman*); Black, *George III, America's Last King,* 236 (*"justness of my cause"*).

327 **No one was more pleased:** Roberts, *The Last King of America,* 229–30 (*tutorials in naval design*); Haas, "The Royal Dockyards," 191+ (*biggest employer*); Rodger, *The Wooden World,* 29 (*largest industrial organization*); Allison and Ferreiro, eds., *The American Revolution,* 36; PH 19, 378 (*"more than a match"*).

328 **"No man in the administration":** Syrett, *The Royal Navy in European Waters During the American Revolutionary War,* 12; Martelli, *Jemmy Twitcher,* 22 (*versifier in Greek and Latin*), 85–86 (*"both sides of the street"*); Joseph Highmore, "John Montagu, 4th Earl of Sandwich," 1740, National Portrait Gallery, London (*Turkish turban*); Levy, *Love & Madness,* 18 (*"jolly, hearty, lively"* and *"Beef and Liberty"*); O'Shaughnessy, *The Men Who Lost America,* 322 (*"never tell anyone"* and *Royal Academy of Arts*); Roberts, *The Last King of America,* 122–23 (*Antient Music*); Jesse, *Memoirs of Celebrated Etonians,* 2: 56 (*Memphis catacombs*), 82 (*kettledrums*).

328 **He had more experience than any other man:** *PP Sandwich,* xi–xiii (*third stint*); Rodger, *The Command of the Ocean,* 332 (*impoverished*); Mackesy, *The War for America, 1775–1783,*

10–11 (*seventeen seats*); Broomfield, "Lord Sandwich at the Admiralty Board," 7+ (*small but influential*); Rodger, *The Insatiable Earl*, 321 (*"a hard man to surprise"*).

328 **Some considered him a rascal:** Jesse, *Memoirs of Celebrated Etonians*, 2: 67 (*blasphemy*), 71–72 (*"Vices, more than years"*); Martelli, *Jemmy Twitcher*, 86 (*"ladies of pleasure"*); Brewer, *A Sentimental Murder*, 91 (*affair with his sister-in-law*); Rodger, *The Insatiable Earl*, 80 (*"I have never pretended"*), 320 (*"clerk-like knowledge"*).

329 **His wife, the daughter of an Irish viscount:** Martelli, *Jemmy Twitcher*, 25, 40 (*deportment, singing, French*); Rodger, *The Insatiable Earl*, 71–72 (*Windsor Castle*); Jesse, *Memoirs of Celebrated Etonians*, 2: 78–79 (*mantua maker*); Levy, *Love & Madness*, 23–24 (*five of whom survived*); Brewer, *A Sentimental Murder*, 15 (*"perpetual smile"*).

329 **From six a.m. until nightfall:** Martelli, *Jemmy Twitcher*, 18–19 (*sliced meat*); Sandwich inspection, 1775, UK NA, ADM 7/662, f 79 (*"My business"*); Knight, "The Royal Dockyards in England at the Time of the American War of Independence," diss., 19; Haas, "The Royal Dockyards," 191+ (*"never so much convinced"*).

329 **To build a durable fleet:** Haas, "The Royal Dockyards," 191+ (*green wood*); Sandwich inspection, 1775, UK NA, ADM 7/662, f 74–75; Enciso, *War, Power and the Economy*, 218 (*tar, iron, hemp*); Rodger, *The Command of the Ocean*, 372–74; Graham, *The Royal Navy in the War of American Independence*, 6 (*sticks from New England*); Mackesy, *The War for America, 1775–1783*, 166–70; Knight, *Portsmouth Dockyard Papers, 1774–1783*, 115 (*Riga and Gothenburg*); O'Shaughnessy, *The Men Who Lost America*, 324 (*James Cook*).

329 **At times he could be smug and prideful:** Sandwich dockyard inspection, 1773, UK NA, ADM 7/660, f 1–27; O'Shaughnessy, *The Men Who Lost America*, 327 (*"sound of cannon"*); R.J.B. Knight, "The Royal Navy's Recovery After the Early Phase of the American Revolutionary War," in Andreopoulos and Selesky, eds., *The Aftermath of Defeat*, 13–15 (*defeat at Saratoga*); timeline, Portsmouth Royal Dockyard Historical Trust, https://portsmouthdockyard .org (*almost four hundred vessels*); Graham, *The Royal Navy in the War of American Independence*, 9. Admiralty figures showed 256 ships at sea on January 1, 1778 (*PP Sandwich*, 1: 422).

330 **That would require all of the first lord's skill:** R.J.B. Knight, "The Royal Navy's Recovery After the Early Phase of the American Revolutionary War," in Andreopoulos and Selesky, eds., *The Aftermath of Defeat*, 12 (*quick, cheap war*); Martelli, *Jemmy Twitcher*, 110; Rodger, *The Insatiable Earl*, 236 (*frigates*), 237 (*full mobilization*); Syrett, *The Royal Navy in European Waters During the American Revolutionary War*, 3 (*entire cruiser strength*), 113; Marshall, ed., *The Oxford History of the British Empire*, 2: 181 (*dispersed*); O'Shaughnessy, *The Men Who Lost America*, 331 (*fleet was simply too small*).

330 **Shipyards had been ordered to pick up:** Knight, *Plymouth Dockyard Papers, 1774–1783*, 36–37 (*double shifts*); Knight, "The Royal Dockyards in England at the Time of the American War of Independence," diss., 69 (*Royal Navy stronger*); Rodger, *The Insatiable Earl*, 236 (*nine months to build*); R.J.B. Knight, "The Royal Navy's Recovery After the Early Phase of the American Revolutionary War," in Andreopoulos and Selesky, eds., *The Aftermath of Defeat*, 13–14 (*skilled shipwrights*), 17 (*squabbling among admirals*); Johnston, "American Privateers in French Ports, 1776–1778," 352+ (*733 merchant vessels*); Syrett, *Shipping and the American War, 1775–83* (*net losses would reach almost 2,400*).

330 **Manning the fleet remained particularly difficult:** Mackesy, *The War for America, 1775–1783*, 176 (*42,000 would desert*); Rodger, *The Command of the Ocean*, 318 (*"r"—for "run"*), 398–400 (*"birdcage-like space"*).

330 **Britain's traditional remedy for manpower:** Brunsman, *The Evil Necessity*, 55, 142–45; Syrett, *The Royal Navy in European Waters During the American Revolutionary War*, 20 (*on March 16*), 31 (*outbound sailings*); Lloyd, *The British Seaman*, 153 (Black Book), 291–92 (*Impress Service*); Masefield, *Sea Life in Nelson's Time*, 48–50 (*a third of a warship's company*); Bowler, *Logistics and the Failure of the British Army in America, 1775–1783*, 244 (*from army victualing vessels*); Syrett, *Shipping and the American War, 1775–83*, 222–23 (*immobilized*).

331 **Despite his bravado in assuring Parliament:** Syrett, *The Royal Navy in European Waters During the American Revolutionary War*, 21 (*"more than we are equal"*).

331 **Sandwich argued that Britain could:** Syrett, *The Royal Navy in European Waters During the American Revolutionary War*, 15; Miller, *Sea of Glory*, 329 (*enemy fleet was divided*).

331 **Abandoning America altogether to fight:** Syrett, "Home Waters or America?," 365+ (*"I can never sufficiently lament"*); PP Sandwich, 2: 35–37 (*twelve French capital ships*); Dudley W. Knox, "D'Estaing's Fleet Revealed," *U.S. Naval Institute Proceedings*, vol. 61, no. 2 (Feb. 1935): 161; Brown, "The Anglo-French Naval Crisis, 1778," 3+ (*"If we are not able to resist"*).

332 **The greater risk, Sandwich countered:** PP Sandwich, 2: 37–38 (*"our dilemma is very great"* and *"Philadelphia or New York"*).

332 **The decision was made:** Brown, *The American Secretary*, 163–65 (*Thirteen capital ships*); Brown, "The Anglo-French Naval Crisis, 1778," 3+ (*"convinced of the propriety"*).

332 **"Left the Queen's House":** Ayling, *George the Third*, 262 (*"Arrived at Portsmouth"*); *Public Advertiser*, May 4, 1778, 3 (*twelve miles per hour*); Fortescue, *The Correspondence of King George the Third*, 4: 125–26 (*three changes of horse teams*); George to Princes George and Frederick, May 3, 1778, George III, Private Papers, RA, GEO/MAIN/#41765 (*such heavy rain*); Huish, *Public and Private Life of His Late Excellent and Most Gracious Majesty, George the Third*, 377 (*Sandwich met him*).

333 **Five years had passed since George:** TBAC, 1–11; Hagist, *British Soldiers, American War*, 22 (*"rolled us down"*); Urban, *Fusiliers*, 175.

333 **Servants hauled several wagonloads:** *Public Advertiser*, May 2, 1778, 2 (*royal bed*); *Jackson's Oxford Journal*, May 9, 1778, 2; Brooke, *King George III*, 216 (*another £6,000*), 262 (*"queen of my heart"*); Namier, "King George III," 610+ (New Berlin Almanac); Thackeray, *The Four Georges*, 98–99 (*the king had winced*); Hibbert, *George III*, 96 (*jewelry, dogs, and snuff*); O'Shaughnessy, *The Men Who Lost America*, 44–45 (*"excellent qualities"*); Hadlow, *A Royal Experiment*, 284 (*"only of war"*).

333 **At three p.m. the king dined with Sandwich:** George to Princes George and Frederick, May 3, 1778, George III, Private Papers, RA, GEO/MAIN/#41765 (*"bad custom of toasting"*); *Gentleman's Magazine and Historical Chronicle*, vol. 48 (1778): 189 (*Spithead and St. Helen's Road*).

333 **By five p.m. he was in the dockyard:** *London Gazette*, May 5, 1778, 1 (*"Britons, Strike Home!"*); king's memorandum, in Fortescue, *The Correspondence of King George the Third*, 4: 127–31 (*Gun Wharf*); Lynn, ed., *The Specht Journal*, 12 (*House of Vulcan*); TBAC, 555–57 (*John the Painter*); Brown, *Maritime Portsmouth*, 18; Knight, *Portsmouth Dockyard Papers, 1774–1783*, 84 (*Ratcatchers set traps*), 116 (*38 tons of beer*). Provision amounts listed are for *Barfleur*, 98 guns, in 1779. SNHP has recently resumed using the structure's original name: the Light Infantry Redoubt, ES to author, July 2024.

334 **Nothing intrigued George more:** Cock, " 'The Finest Invention in the World,' " 446+; Willis, "Fleet Performance and Capability in the Eighteenth-Century Royal Navy," 372+ (*"design improvement of the century"*); Knight, "The Royal Dockyards in England at the Time of the American War of Independence," diss., 349 (*fifteen months*); Knight, "The Introduction of Copper Sheathing into the Royal Navy, 1779–1786," 299+ (Teredo navalis); Staniforth, "The Introduction and Use of Copper Sheathing," 21+.

334 **For centuries mariners had experimented:** "The Peak Years of British Copper Mining," Copper Development Association (*half of the world's copper*); Cock, " 'The Finest Invention in the World,' " 446+ (*late 1775*); Rodger, *The Command of the Ocean*, 344–45 (*gained a knot*); "Copper Sheathing," Wikipedia (*fifteen tons*); R.J.B. Knight, "The Royal Navy's Recovery After the Early Phase of the American Revolutionary War," in Andreopoulos and Selesky, eds., *The Aftermath of Defeat*, 21–23 (*within two years*). *Fox* would be captured again in September 1778, this time by the French (Winfield, *British Warships in the Age of Sail, 1714–1792*, 233).

334 **The king reboarded *Augusta*:** Perrin, ed., *The Keith Papers*, 1: 83 (*conserve powder*); King's memorandum, in Fortescue, *The Correspondence of King George the Third*, 4: 127–31; Huish, *Public and Private Life of His Late Excellent and Most Gracious Majesty, George the Third*, 378 (*Fifty yawls and barges*); *London Gazette*, May 5, 1778, 1 (Prince George); Martelli, *Jemmy Twitcher*, 134 (*"great alacrity"*).

335 **The monarch and his queen:** Roberts, *The Last King of America*, 347.

335 **"I know very well"**: George to Princes George and Frederick, May 3, 1778, George III, Private Papers, RA, GEO/MAIN/#41765 (*"best of my abilities"* and *"quicken the sailing"*); Roberts, *The Last King of America*, 347 (*"universal comfort"*).

335 **Yet the fleet did not sail**: Brown, "The Anglo-French Naval Crisis, 1778," 3+ (*"till further orders"*); Syrett, "Home Waters or America?," 365+.

335 **Finally on June 2 the frigate *Proserpine***: Miller, *Sea of Glory*, 331 (*"great press of sail"*).

335 **The fleet bound for America had assembled**: PP Sandwich, 2: 375, appendix B (*"put to sea"*); Clowes, *The Royal Navy*, 3: 394–95 (*two days of contrary winds*); John Byron to John Kendall, corr., HL, HM 64533 (*"lucky circumstance"*).

336 **That was unlikely**: Douglas, "John Byron," *Dictionary of Canadian Biography*, vol. 4 (*at age nine*); Byron, *The Narrative of the Honourable John Byron*, 11, 21, 236–46, 252–57 (*acclaimed narrative*); Layman, *The Wager Disaster*, 39, 53–55, 258 (*"boisterous elements"*); Ralfe, *The Naval Biography of Great Britain*, 1: 60, 71–74.

336 **That was sweet nonsense**: Hiscocks, "Hon. John Byron," http://morethannelson.com/officer/hon-john-byron/ (*more than seven feet tall*).

336 **The Romantic poet George Gordon**: Lord Byron, "Epistle to Augusta," 1830 (*"He had no rest at sea"*); Wheatley, ed., *The Historical and the Posthumous Memoirs of Sir Nathaniel William Wraxall, 1772–1784*, 1: 223 (*"unlucky planet"*); PP Sandwich, 2: 287 (*colossal gale*).

336 **The other British fleet, now preparing**: "Hon. Augustus Keppel 1st Viscount," https://morethannelson.com/officer/hon-augustus-keppel-1st-viscount-keppel/; *PP Sandwich*, 2: 191 (*"national hero"*); Willis, *The Struggle for Sea Power*, 217 (*fifteen years*); Syrett, *The Royal Navy in European Waters During the American Revolutionary War*, 24 (*"bad nerves"*).

337 **Between entertainments for the king and queen**: Keppel, *The Life of Augustus Viscount Keppel*, 2: 17–19 (*ransacked of sailors, sails*); Mackesy, *The War for America, 1775–1783*, 204 (*to outfit Byron's fleet*); Martelli, *Jemmy Twitcher*, 131 (*"If this fleet is soon"*); Rodger, *The Insatiable Earl*, 244 (*embarrassment of the government*).

337 **Regardless, the moment had come**: NDAR, 13: 869 (*appear the aggressor*); Lloyd, *The British Seaman*, 212 (*holystones shaped like Bibles*); captain's log, *Victory*, May 1778, UK NA, ADM 51/1036.

337 **By dusk England was a faint green**: Clowes, *The Royal Navy*, 13: 869 (*Twenty-one British ships*).

15. THE FRENCH FLAG IN ALL ITS GLORY

338 **No event in early 1778**: Ducros, *French Society in the Eighteenth Century*, 307 (*burned by the public hangman*); J. B. Shank, "Voltaire," *The Stanford Encyclopedia of Philosophy*, Summer 2022 ed. (*"Crush the infamy"*); Manceron, *Age of the French Revolution*, 1: 541 (*"king of thought"*), 559–60 (*ass's milk*); Gutman, *Mozart*, 407 (*kiss the horses*); *Annual Register 1778*, "Characters," 1 (*"breathe upon us"*); Brands, *The First American*, 564 (*fifty cups of coffee*).

338 **It was only fitting**: Schiff, *A Great Improvisation*, 136–37 (*"worthiest man"*); Isaacson, *Benjamin Franklin*, 354 (*"God and liberty"*); AP, Apr. 29, 1778, FOL (*"two aged actors"*); Commager and Morris, eds., *The Spirit of 'Seventy-Six*, 677–78 (*"embracing Sophocles"*); Schama, *Citizens*, 22 (*"die in peace"*).

339 **Franklin lived on, now allied**: Morgan, "The Puritan Ethic and the American Revolution," 3+ (*embezzlement*); Ferguson, *The Power of the Purse*, 89, 102–4 (*would spend years*); Abernethy, "Commercial Activities of Silas Deane in France," 477+; JA to Abigail Adams, Apr. 12, 1778, AFC, FOL (*thirteen toasts*); Ferling, *John Adams*, 203 (le fameux *Adams*); Levin, *Abigail Adams*, 106 (*nine p.m. on April 8*); McCullough, *John Adams*, 18 (*split his own firewood*), 192 (*join him in Passy*).

339 **"I am but an ordinary man"**: AP, Apr. 26, 1779, FOL; JA to James Warren, Aug. 4, 1778, FOL (*"John Yankee"*); Ellis, *Revolutionary Summer*, 13 (*Cicero* and *"His Rotundity"*); Ferling, *John Adams*, 169 (*"whole of a subject"*); Bailyn, *Faces of Revolution*, 9 (*"his prose the most alive"*); AP, diary, Jan. 1759, FOL (*"My motions"*); "About John and Abigail Adams," Massachusetts Historical Society, https://www.masshist.org/digitaladams/archive/index (*eleven hundred letters*); Abigail Adams to James Lovell, Dec. 15, 1777, FOL (*"cheerfully comply"*).

339 **For the moment, yes:** Ferling, *John Adams*, 203 (*"out of his element"*); Bailyn, "Butterfield's Adams," 238+ (*admired and despised*); AP, diary, June 7, 1778, FOL (*"too sublime"*); JA to Abigail Adams, June 3 and July 26, 1778, FOL (*"one great garden"*); JA to James Warren, Aug. 4, 1778, FOL (*"It is a rock"*); JA to Abigail Adams, July 26, 1778, FOL (*"like a schoolboy"*); AP, diary, Apr. 27, 1778, FOL (*read the text*).

340 **He was surprised to find turmoil:** JA to Samuel Adams, Aug. 7, 1778, FOL (*"ugly situation"*); Potts, *Arthur Lee*, 1 (*"the Wasp"*); AP, diary, Feb. 9, 1779, FOL (*"all men selfish"*); "The Railroading of Silas Deane," New England Historical Society, 2022, https://newenglandhistorical society.com/the-railroading-of-silas-deane-or-how-to-destroy-a-patriots-reputation-for-225 -years/; Drury, "The Rise and Fall of Silas Deane, American Patriot," Oct. 2, 2020, https:// connecticuthistory.org/the-rise-and-fall-of-silas-deane-american-patriot/; Lee, *Life of Arthur Lee, LL.D.*, 1: 16–17 (*graduate of Eton*); Alsop, *Yankees at the Court*, 88 (*"yellow skin, green eyes"*).

340 **With Deane's departure Lee concentrated:** Schiff, *A Great Improvisation*, 153 (*"most corrupt"*); Wood, *The Americanization of Benjamin Franklin*, 189 (*"concerned in the plunder"*); BF to Arthur Lee, Apr. 3, 1778, FOL (*"your sick mind"*); AP, diary, May 2, 1778, FOL (*"an umpire"*); JA to Samuel Adams, May 21, 1778, FOL (*"no books"*); JA to Richard Henry Lee, Aug. 5, 1778, FOL (*"more animosity"*).

340 **Adams, to be sure, disapproved:** McCullough, *John Adams*, 192–93; JA to Mercy Otis Warren, Dec. 18, 1778, FOL (*"passion for old age"*).

341 **His name was familiar:** JA to *Boston Patriot*, Nov. 8, 1810, FOL.

341 **But Adams wondered if Franklin:** Van Doren, *Benjamin Franklin*, 603 (*too indolent, too taciturn*); AP, diary, May 12, 1779, FOL (*"conjuror"*); JA to Samuel Adams, Dec. 7, 1778, FOL (*"loves his ease"*); JA to Elbridge Gerry, July 9, 1778, FOL (*"backstairs intrigues"*); Bailyn, "Butterfield's Adams," 238 (*secretary to spy*); extract of BF letter to Robert R. Livingston, July 22, 1783, FOL (*"out of his senses"*).

341 **Their mutual love of country:** JA to Samuel Adams, Dec. 7, 1778, FOL (*"as determined a soul"*).

341 **Abigail Adams would describe Captain John Paul Jones:** Abigail Adams to Elizabeth Cranch, Dec. 3, 1784, FOL (*"uncommon character"*); Thomas, *John Paul Jones*, 112 (*"The world lays all"*).

341 **The son of a gardener from Solway Firth:** *JPJ*, 3–9, 16 (*sentimental verse*), 70 (*epaulets*), 110 (*mother and sisters*), 111 (Pro Republica), 113 (*"illiterate"*); *TBAC*, 467–68.

342 **Dr. Franklin, charmed by:** Schiff, *A Great Improvisation*, 182 (*"strange magnetism"*); BF, American commissioners to J. P. Jones, Jan. 16–18, 1778, FOL (*"distressing the enemies"*); *JPJ*, 122–23 (*"sleeping dictionary"*); North to Sandwich, Mar. 3, 1778, *PP Sandwich*, 270 (*"will soon insult"*).

342 **"Fresh gales, close weather":** Thomas, *John Paul Jones*, 113 (*lead ballast*); *NDAR*, 12: 582 (*Union Jack*); *JPJ*, 106 (*superior Russian duck*), 113 (*"bone in her teeth"*).

342 **Those shabby fabrics were characteristic:** Chapelle, *The American Sailing Navy*, 56 (*political influence*), 61 (*shortage of shipwrights*); Toll, *Six Frigates*, 16 (*waited a year or more*); "The Continental Navy," https://revolutionarywar.us/continental-navy/ (*sixty-four vessels*); Volo, *Blue Water Patriots*, 44 (*thirteen hundred cannons* and *a tenth the number of guns*); Maclay, *A History of the United States Navy from 1775 to 1898*, 1: 94 (*almost seven thousand guns*); Dull, "Was the Continental Navy a Mistake?," 167+ (*Half of the new warships* and *two thousand American privateers*); Miller, *Sea of Glory*, 225 (Trumbull); Fowler, *Rebels Under Sail*, 244; Brewington, "The Designs of Our First Frigates," appendix B, 10+.

343 **This spring was particularly catastrophic:** Clark, *Gallant John Barry, 1745–1803*, 156 (*Narragansett Bay*); *JPJ*, 178–79; *NDAR*, 11: 544 (*"covered with parts of her"*); Clark, *Captain Dauntless*, 241–49 (*flotsam raft*); Miller, *Sea of Glory*, 322 (Ocracoke bar); Fowler, *Rebels Under Sail*, 119–20; McGrath, *Give Me a Fast Ship*, 208–13; Patton, *Patriot Pirates*, 110–11.

343 **"Our naval affairs have been":** Miller, *Sea of Glory*, 322; Lindsey, "Treatment of American Prisoners of War During the Revolution," 1+ (*filthy cells*); Matthews and Wecter, *Our Soldiers*

Speak, 1775–1918, 39–43; Herbert, *A Relic of the Revolution*, 212 (*"Rats have been eat"*); Cutter, "A Yankee Privateersman in Prison in England, 1777–1779," 174+ (*"forty days"* and *"American monsters"*). Forton and Mill Prisons eventually warehoused 2,300 Americans (Hoock, *Scars of Independence*, 231).

344 **Various retaliatory schemes had been proposed:** John Jay to Robert Morris, Aug. 23, 1777, in Kirkland, ed., *Letters on the American Revolution in the Library at "Karolfred,"* 1: 42 (*"burning of Liverpool"*); Biron, *Memoirs of the Duc du Lauzun*, 263 (*British commercial interests*); J. P. Jones to BF, American commissioners, Dec. 5, 1777, FOL (*"We cannot yet fight"*).

344 **Such a place lay in Whitehaven:** Sweetman, ed., *Great American Naval Battles*, 31–33; NDAR, 12: 596 (*each English ship burned*), 597 (*brimstone*); Thomas, *John Paul Jones*, 121–23 (*boat cloak*).

344 **The first apricot glow of dawn:** *JPJ*, 140–41 (*one another's shoulders*); Sweetman, ed., *Great American Naval Battles*, 31–33 (*"free with the liquor"*); NDAR, 12: 597 (*turncoat Irish seaman* and *"great violence"*).

345 **"Had it been possible":** Mahan, "John Paul Jones in the Revolution," 22+ (*"not a single ship"*); NDAR, 12: 592 (*"much alarmed"*); Seitz, *Paul Jones*, 5 (*"capital seaports"*), 17 (*"idiotism"*).

345 **No tocsin could reach St. Mary's Isle:** *JPJ*, 144–54 (*press-gang*); Sweetman, ed., *Great American Naval Battles*, 33 (*Countess of Selkirk*); NDAR, 12: 674 (*hostage to be exchanged*); De Koven, *The Life and Letters of John Paul Jones*, 1: 333 (*"plunder rather than honor"*); Thomas, *John Paul Jones*, 126–27 (*"horrid-looking wretches"*).

345 **Aboard *Drake*, Captain George Burdon:** *JPJ*, 157–60 (*"warm, close"* and *"very much galled"*); Thomas, *John Paul Jones*, 131–32 (*"Quarter!"*); NDAR, 12: 846 (*"low rigging much shattered"*).

346 **The *Morning Chronicle and London Advertiser*:** Lutnick, *The American Revolution and the British Press, 1775–1783*, 151 (*"intimidation"*); Zellers-Frederick, "A Chink in Britain's Armor," *JAR*, June 25, 2010 (*"stripped you naked"*); Nolan, "A British Editor Reports the American Revolution," 92+ (*"Impudence!"*).

346 **Bankers packed up their gold:** De Koven, *The Life and Letters of John Paul Jones*, 1: 288 (*stocks fell*); NDAR, 12: 505 (*quadrupled*); Seitz, *Paul Jones*, 20 (*"charge of powder"*); Zellers-Frederick, "A Chink in Britain's Armor," *JAR*, June 25, 2010 (*coalfields*); Trevelyan, *The American Revolution*, 4: 445 (*fighting bishop*); Philip Stephens, Admiralty, to Adm. Lord Shuldham, Aug. 8, 1778, NDAR, 14: 1127 (*"leaching grounds"*).

346 **"Not all their boasted navy":** Sweetman, ed., *Great American Naval Battles*, 34; De Koven, *The Life and Letters of John Paul Jones*, 1: 292 (*spooked their children*); *JPJ*, 163 (*"You have heard o' Paul Jones"*).

347 **Lionized in Paris, he became:** Schama, *Citizens*, 44 (La science); "Morin transcription of *La Science*," Historical Society of Pennsylvania, https://hsp.org/sites/default/files/legacy_files/migrated/findingaidam8085morin.pdf.

347 **Jones also sent the Countess of Selkirk:** NDAR, 12: 674 (*"soft persuasive arts"*); Sweetman, ed., *Great American Naval Battles*, 33 (*"citizen of the world"*); *JPJ*, 154 (*almost three thousand livres*); Toynbee, ed., *The Letters of Horace Walpole*, 10: 231n (*breakfast tea*).

347 **The French soon had their own hero:** Bickham, *Making Headlines*, 130 (*published tables*); Ferreiro, *Brothers at Arms*, 111 (*seen as an aggressor*); Murphy, *Charles Gravier, Comte de Vergennes*, 257 (*European sympathy*).

347 **After leaving Portsmouth, Admiral Keppel:** Mackesy, *The War for America, 1775–1783*, 207 (*seize any French cruiser*); Lloyd, *The British Seaman*, 238 (*powder monkeys*).

348 **The French scattered, but by six p.m.:** Winfield, *British Warships in the Age of Sail, 1714–1792*, 200 (Arethusa); Syrett, *The Royal Navy in European Waters During the American Revolutionary War*, 36–38 (Belle Poule); Pownall and Almon, *The Remembrancer*, 6: 231 (*de la Clocheterie*); captain's log, *Victory*, June 20, 1778, UK NA, ADM 51/1036 (*she required towing*); Hiscocks, "The Battle of Ushant," https://morethannelson.com/the-battle-of-ushant-27-july-1778-and-the-political-aftermath/; Clowes, *The Royal Navy*, 4: 14–15 (*45 dead*).

348 **A ten-gun French schooner was captured:** NDAR, 13: 986; Clowes, *The Royal Navy*, 4: 14–15 (Licorne, *also came to grief*).

348 **With nearly four dozen French sailors dead:** Pownall and Almon, *The Remembrancer*, 6: 231–32 (*pensions*); Lemaitre, *Beaumarchais*, 235 (*powdered curls*).

348 **"The insult done to my flag":** NDAR, 13: 986; Dull, *The French Navy and American Independence*, 120 (*make for the open sea*); James, *The British Navy in Adversity*, 81 (*renaissance of the French navy*); Patterson, *The Other Armada*, 28 (*since the reign of Louis XIV*); Hardman, *The Life of Louis XVI*, 135 (*a single campaign*); Ferreiro, *Brothers at Arms*, 111 (*Louis authorized*); Weddle, "'A Change of Both Men and Measures,'" 837+; Pownall and Almon, *The Remembrancer*, 6: 237 (*"the God of battles"*).

349 **From captured French officers:** Mackesy, *The War for America, 1775–1783*, 207 (*twenty-seven ships of the line*), 308–9 (*scorched-earth campaign*); Keppel to Sandwich, July 29, 1778, *PP Sandwich*, 2: 98–99.

349 **Sandwich hastened to Portsmouth:** Martelli, *Jemmy Twitcher*, 141 (*"Nothing has yet happened"*).

349 **On July 9, Keppel once again:** Martelli, *Jemmy Twitcher*, 141 (*twenty-four ships*).

349 **Keppel's Channel fleet by now:** Syrett, *The Royal Navy in European Waters During the American Revolutionary War*, 40–41 (*thirty ships of the line*); NDAR, 13: 869; Willis, *The Struggle for Sea Power*, 221 (*stretch for nine miles*); Manceron, *Age of the French Revolution*, 2: 24 (*"crabbed and despondent"*); Oliver Chaline, "Admiral Louis Guillouet, Comte d'Orvilliers," in R. Harding and A. Guimerá, eds., *Naval Leadership in the Atlantic World* (London: University of Westminster Press, 2017, 73–84). Three French ships of the line were considered unfit for battle (Clowes, *The Royal Navy*, 3: 413).

350 **Sartine, the naval minister, had told:** Willis, *The Struggle for Sea Power*, 221 (*"eyes of Europe"*); Manceron, *Age of the French Revolution*, 2: 16–17 (*unicorns, gargoyles*); Ferreiro, *Brothers at Arms*, 111 (*"show the French flag"*); Clowes, *The Royal Navy*, 3: 413 (*under propitious conditions*); Mahan, *The Major Operations of the Navies in the War of American Independence*, 107 (*"If I know him to be"*).

350 **Friday morning dawned with Keppel:** Syrett, *The Royal Navy in European Waters During the American Revolutionary War*, 40–41 (*French held the weather gage*); Mackesy, *The War for America, 1775–1783*, 210 (*1,950 guns*); Willis, "Fleet Performance and Capability in the Eighteenth-Century Royal Navy," 373+ (*"like a haystack"*).

350 **That opening came on Monday, July 27:** Blandemor, ed., *The Trial of the Honourable Augustus Keppel*, 125–27, 268–69; Hiscocks, "The Battle of Ushant," https://morethannelson.com/the-battle-of-ushant-27-july-1778-and-the-political-aftermath/; Dull, *The Age of the Ship of the Line*, 4–7 (*naval tactics had changed little*).

350 **Tempestuous seas and the French maneuver:** captain's log, *Victory*, June 20, 1778, UK NA, ADM 51/1036, July 27, 1778 (*"great confusion"*); Syrett, *The Royal Navy in European Waters During the American Revolutionary War*, 42 (*eleven-twenty a.m.*).

351 **Tongues of flame stabbed back and forth:** Glete, *Navies and Nations*, 1: 35 (*three hundred pounds or more*); Miller, *Sea of Glory*, 94–95 (*shredding sails, rigging*), 340 (*smoke swaddled*); Middlebrook, *Salisbury Connecticut Cannon*, 56 (*"Sponge the gun!"*); Volo, *Blue Water Patriots*, 138 (*three to five minutes*); Ropp, *War in the Modern World*, 72 (*under three hundred yards*); Clowes, *The Royal Navy*, 4: 97 (*weight of metal*); Toll, *Six Frigates*, 7–8 (*superior rate of fire*); Martelli, *Jemmy Twitcher*, 144 (*upward roll*).

351 **As the largest vessel in the Channel fleet:** Blandemor, ed., *The Trial of the Honourable Augustus Keppel*, 270–71 (*Victory's gunners held their fire*), 296 (*large hole through the mainmast*); Miller, *Sea of Glory*, 341–43 (*gaping wound in* Bretagne's *side*); Syrett, *The Royal Navy in European Waters During the American Revolutionary War*, 42–43 (*firing at six more enemy ships*); captain's log, *Victory*, June 20, 1778, UK NA, ADM 51/1036, July 28, 1778 (*"damaged in the rigging & sails"* and *eleven dead*).

351 **By one p.m. she had cleared the French line:** Balderston and Syrett, eds., *The Lost War*, 165 (*"a very heavy fire"*); captain's log, *Victory*, June 20, 1778, UK NA, ADM 51/1036, July 28, 1778; Syrett, *The Royal Navy in European Waters During the American Revolutionary War*, 43 (*took an hour to wear round*); Rodger, *The Insatiable Earl*, 238–39 (*signaling at sea*); Clowes,

The Royal Navy, 3: 420 (*Five British ships*); Hiscocks, "The Battle of Ushant," https://morethan nelson.com/the-battle-of-ushant-27-july-1778-and-the-political-aftermath/.

352 **Confusion now devolved into chaos:** "Sir Hugh Palliser," www.historyofparliament.org; Keppel, *The Life of Augustus Viscount Keppel*, 2: 179 (*arms chest exploded*); PP Sandwich, 2: 191–92.

352 **By four p.m. Keppel had managed to get:** Clowes, *The Royal Navy*, 3: 421 (*"only waiting for him"* and *"extraordinary—if not culpable"*); Mahan, *The Major Operations of the Navies in the War of American Independence*, 118 (*fretted and fumed*); Blandemor, ed., *The Trial of the Honourable Augustus Keppel*, 300–303 (*French lamps could be seen*); Miller, *Sea of Glory*, 343 (*decoys*); Willis, *The Struggle for Sea Power*, 222 (*twenty miles away*).

353 **No ships had been sunk or captured:** Syrett, *The Royal Navy in European Waters During the American Revolutionary War*, 44 (*inexperience*).

353 **If indecisive, the fray had hardly:** Clowes, *The Royal Navy*, 3: 422 (*161 dead*); Miller, *Sea of Glory*, 89 (*purser's glims*); Lloyd, *The British Seaman*, 263 (*stupefied with rum*).

353 **Each side claimed a victory:** Mackesy, *The War for America, 1775–1783*, 210 (*neither had won*); PP Sandwich, 2: 128 (*"That I have beat the French"* and *"crippled the fleet"*); Rodger, *The Command of the Ocean*, 337 (*"French behaved"*); Palliser to Sandwich, Aug. 10, 1778, *PP Sandwich*, 2: 142 (*seventy shot holes*); Balderston and Syrett, eds., *The Lost War*, 169 (*confused Royal Navy sister*).

353 **Even the king acknowledged:** George to Sandwich, Aug. 9, 1778, *PP Sandwich*, 2: 141 (*"great havoc"*); Knight, *Portsmouth Dockyard Papers, 1774–1783*, lvi (*short of skilled artificers*); Keppel, *The Life of Augustus Viscount Keppel*, 2: 57 (*"saved us twice"*); Rodger, *The Insatiable Earl*, 245 (*"out of our power"*).

354 **The first news of Ushant:** Oliver Chaline, "Admiral Louis Guillouet, Comte d'Orvilliers," in R. Harding and A. Guimerá, eds., *Naval Leadership in the Atlantic World* (London: University of Westminster Press, 2017, 73–84); Hardman, *The Life of Louis XVI*, 136 (*relieved Chartres of command*); Miller, *Sea of Glory*, 343–44 (*"unusual experience"*); Dull, *The Miracle of American Independence*, 111; Ferreiro, *Brothers at Arms*, 111 (*needed Spain's help*).

354 **Both fleets were patched up enough:** Mackesy, *The War for America, 1775–1783*, 211 (*Bay of Biscay*); Syrett, *The Royal Navy in European Waters During the American Revolutionary War*, 48 (*fourteen hundred sick sailors*); Keppel to Sandwich, Oct. 1, 1778, *PP Sandwich*, 2: 174 (*imperil naval operations*); Martelli, *Jemmy Twitcher*, 145 (*"afflicted with his disorder"*).

354 **Few shipboard maladies were as noxious:** Broomfield, "The Keppel-Palliser Affair, 1778–1779," 195+ (*anonymous article*).

354 **The controversy caught fire:** Hatch, ed., "Letters of Captain Sir John Jervis to Sir Henry Clinton, 1774–1782," 87+ (*"Terrible schisms"*).

16. FLYING FROM A SHADOW

356 **No place in America had been:** Bill, *New Jersey and the Revolutionary War*, 76–77 (*fourth time in eighteen months*); Murrin and Waldron, eds., *Conflict at Monmouth Court House*, 20 (*allegiances*); Bilby and Jenkins, *Monmouth Court House*, 126 (*"an enemy's country"*); Burgoyne, trans. and ed., *Diaries of Two Ansbach Jaegers*, 24 (*"careful of the farmers"*); Clark, "Diary of Joseph Clark," 93+ (*"Never did the Jerseys"*). By some counts, New Jersey provided as many full-time troops for the king as for Congress (Morrissey, *Monmouth Courthouse 1778*, 12).

356 **General Clinton's "noble little army":** Bodle, *The Valley Forge Winter*, 241; Lender and Stone, *Fatal Sunday*, 126–28 (*soldiers, armed loyalists, teamsters*); Stryker, *The Battle of Monmouth*, 89–90 (*"useless stuff"*); Stokes, *The Iconography of Manhattan Island, 1498–1909*, 5: 1068 (*"women of the army"*); D. Wier to Treasury, July 23, 1778, UK NA, T 64/114, f 67 (*provisions for sixteen more*); Hagist, ed., *A British Soldier's Story*, xxxii (*every third morning*); Rees, "'The load a soldier generally carries during a campaign,'" 5–7, 17 (*dipped in oil*); Martin, *A Narrative of a Revolutionary Soldier*, 107–8 (*cut from their flanks*). Recent scholarship has questioned Knyphausen's assertion of fifteen hundred wagons, with one calculation putting the

number "between 180 and 395"; see Wickersty, "Were There Really 1,500 British Wagons on the Road to Monmouth?," *JAR*, July 23, 2024.

357 **Rebels, in turn, "destroyed every bridge":** Stryker, *The Battle of Monmouth*, 55–56 (*"full corps"*); Inman, "George Inman's Narrative of the American Revolution," 237+ (*filled in wells*); Lender and Stone, *Fatal Sunday*, 137 (*stream sluices*); Morrissey, *Monmouth Courthouse 1778*, 35 (*"being Burgoyned"*); Bell, "Journal of Andrew Bell, Secretary of General Clinton," June 20, 1778, 15–16 (*"ran into the cellar"*); Zimmerman, "The Battle of Crosswicks," *JAR*, Aug. 4, 2022 (*eight hundred*); Kwasny, *Washington's Partisan War, 1775–1783*, 203–4; Uhlendorf, trans. and annot., *Revolution in America*, 184 (*six hours*).

357 **By June 25 the torrid summer heat:** Lender and Stone, *Fatal Sunday*, 155 (*"carried along with us"*); Ewald, *Diary of the American War*, 135 (*"lost over 60 men"*); Wilkin, *Some British Soldiers in America*, 258 (*"Such a march may I never"*).

357 **Desertion also thinned the ranks:** Berger, *Broadsides and Bayonets*, 115–16 (*eight hundred acres*); Boyle, *From Redcoat to Rebel*, 223–25 (*sold his musket*).

358 **Clinton discouraged such disloyalty:** Morrissey, *Monmouth Courthouse 1778*, 35 (*dangling*); Lender and Stone, *Fatal Sunday*, 149 (*still bleeding* and *estimated five hundred*).

358 **On Friday morning, June 26:** GW, general orders, June 25, 1778, FOL (*"remarkably bad"*); Stryker, *The Battle of Monmouth*, 89 (*Wrongly informed that General Gates*); Lender and Stone, *Fatal Sunday*, 154.

358 **By this decision, war sank its sharp talons:** Bell, "Journal of Andrew Bell, Secretary of General Clinton," June 27, 1778, 17 (*"They are determined"*).

358 **Monmouth consisted of little more:** author visit, MBSP, Aug. 31, 2021; Adelberg, *The American Revolution in Monmouth County*, 11 (*hundred bloody frays*), 19 (*Union saltworks*); Tiedemann et al., eds., *The Other Loyalists*, 55–56 (*"noted hanging place"*); Wroblewski, "Loyalist 'Banditti' of Monmouth County, New Jersey," *JAR*, June 10, 2021 (*"pack of kittens"*).

360 **Clinton's men also brought violence:** Krafft, "Von Krafft's Journal," ix+ (*"plundered by the English"*); Lender and Stone, *Fatal Sunday*, 144 (*"good deal of plundering"*), 214–16 (*looted farms*); Conway, *The War of American Independence, 1775–1783*, 52 (*"great irregularity"*); Uhlendorf, trans. and annot., *Revolution in America*, 185 (*"made the country people"*).

360 **On both Friday and Saturday nights:** Krafft, "Von Krafft's Journal," ix+ (*"got wet through"*); Clinton orders, June 27, 1778, Frederick Mackenzie papers, WLC, box 3, vol. E (*break camp at three a.m.*); Lender and Stone, *Fatal Sunday*, 157 (*"having a brush"*), 214–15 (*Elizabeth Covenhoven*).

360 **Even Washington was uncertain:** GW, general orders, June 21, 1778, *PGW*, 15: 483n (*Coryell's* and *"trouble, etc."*); GW general orders, June 22, 1778, *PGW*, 15; 492 (*"cold water"*); Holcomb, "Washington's Headquarters at Coryell's Ferry," 850+ (*cut-stone house*); VFHRR1, 357–58 (*"big with the fates"*).

361 **In their frayed shirts and threadbare breeches:** Huston, *The Sinews of War*, 24–25 (*one in five lacked shoes*); VFHRR1, 437 (*two thousand muskets*); Jackson, *Valley Forge*, 211 (*three petticoats*).

361 **Washington split the army into two wings:** Lender and Stone, *Fatal Sunday*, 161; GW, general orders, June 1, 1778, *PGW*, 15: 288 (*flank guards*); John Chaloner to Jeremiah Wadsworth, May 17, 1778, JLB, "My Last Shift Betwixt Us & Death," ms (*one hundred thousand rations*); Risch, *Supplying Washington's Army*, 107 (*two hundred thousand bushels*); PNG, 2: 446n (*latrines, firewood*).

361 **At nine a.m. on June 24:** Tatum, *The American Journal of Ambrose Serle*, 314 (*impossible to read*); Lender and Stone, *Fatal Sunday*, 89–90 (*Scotch Willie* and *"hanging on their flanks"*), 129 (*More than a thousand militiamen*).

362 **Here, Washington told his generals:** GW, council of war, June 24, 1778, FOL (*"Will it be advisable"*).

362 **In the crepuscular room:** Lender and Stone, *Fatal Sunday*, 174 (*"very eloquently"*); Stryker, *The Battle of Monmouth*, 76–77 (*full-fledged battle*); GW, council of war, June 24, 1778, FOL (*"bridge of gold"*).

362 **Washington adjourned the meeting:** Lender and Stone, *Fatal Sunday*, 176 (*"disgraceful"*); Lafayette to GW, June 24, 1778, FOL (*"all what I possess"*); NG to GW, June 24, 1778, FOL (*"If we suffer"*).

362 **No one was more agitated:** AH, "Eulogy on Nathanael Greene," July 4, 1789, FOL (*"imbecility"*); AH to Elias Boudinot, July 5, 1778, FOL (*"midwives"*).

362 **Lee's prudence was more sensible:** Lender and Stone, *Fatal Sunday*, 173 (*badly underestimated*); Ecelbarger, "Did Charles Lee Disobey George Washington's Attack Order at Monmouth?," *JAR*, Mar. 7, 2024 (*eighteen thousand*); GW to Daniel Morgan, June 24, 1778, FOL (*"as much annoyance"*); Zambone, *Daniel Morgan*, 174–75 (*Life Guard*).

363 **Washington chose Lafayette to lead:** GW to Lafayette, June 25, 1778, FOL (*"most effectual means"*); GW, general orders, June 25, 1778, FOL (*"in raptures"*).

363 **Less enraptured was Major General Lee:** Charles Lee to GW, June 25, 1778, FOL (*"odd appearance"*).

363 **Although Hamilton later denounced this gambit:** AH to Elias Boudinot, July 5, 1778, FOL (*"truly childish"*); Lender and Stone, *Fatal Sunday*, 187–88 (*prevailing conventions*); GW to Lee, June 26, 1778, FOL (*"every assistance"*); Lengel, *General George Washington*, 294–95 (*further enlarge the vanguard*).

364 **This solution may have been too clever:** Lafayette to GW, June 26, 1778, FOL (*"schort of provisions"*); AH to GW, June 26, 1778, FOL (*"extreme distress"*); Lafayette to GW, June 26, 1778, FOL (*"given up the project"*).

364 **This mare's nest awaited Lee:** Samuel Adams to Sally Preston Adams, July 19, 1778, APS, Feinstone Coll., #28 (*hemmed in by woodlands*); Lender and Stone, *Fatal Sunday*, 190 (*thirty-one infantry regiments*); Morrissey, *Monmouth Courthouse 1778*, 41 (*knew few of his subordinates*); Greenman, *Diary of a Common Soldier in the American Revolution, 1775–1783*, 121 (*huckleberry bushes*); Barnardus Swartout, Jr., journal, June 27, 1778, Swartout, Sr., papers, NYHS (*brush huts*); Patterson, *Knight Errant of Liberty*, 212 (*$30 for a drink*).

364 **Troops felled by the heat:** author visit, MBSP, Tennent meetinghouse, Aug. 31, 2021.

366 **Late Saturday morning Washington trotted:** Stryker, *The Battle of Monmouth*, 80–81 (*white charger*); Steuben to GW, June 27, 1778, FOL (*"fire a pistol"*); Lockhart, *The Drillmaster of Valley Forge*, 155 (*horse pistols*); Kapp, *The Life of Frederick William von Steuben*, 159 (*lost his cocked hat*).

366 **Washington dashed off several official letters:** Lender and Stone, *Fatal Sunday*, 190–91 (*Village Inn*), 234 (*more than seven thousand*); GW, general orders, June 27, 1778, FOL; Ecelbarger, "Did Charles Lee Disobey George Washington's Attack Order at Monmouth?," *JAR*, Mar. 7, 2024 (*four miles northwest*).

366 **At five p.m., Lee gathered:** Stryker, *The Battle of Monmouth*, 107 (*"mere conjecture"*); Charles Lee to GW, June 27, 1778, FOL (*"inconceivable stupid"*); Mazzagetti, *Charles Lee*, 164 (*He would improvise*).

366 **Around midnight on Saturday:** Lee court-martial proceedings (GW papers), July 4, 1778, FOL (*"detach a party"*); Ecelbarger, "Did Charles Lee Disobey George Washington's Attack Order at Monmouth?," *JAR*, Mar. 7, 2024 (*instructed General Dickinson*); Lender and Stone, *Fatal Sunday*, 194 (*"tomorrow morning"*).

367 **At first light on Sunday, Dickinson alerted:** Dickinson to GW, June 28, 1778, FOL (*"enemy are in motion"*); Barnardus Swartout, Jr., journal, June 28, 1778, Swartout, Sr., papers, NYHS (*Rum and rations*); Ecelbarger, "Did Charles Lee Disobey George Washington's Attack Order at Monmouth?," *JAR*, Mar. 7, 2024 (*search for replacements*); Lender and Stone, *Fatal Sunday*, 198 (*dog at his feet*).

367 **Past the Tennent meetinghouse:** author visit, MBSP, Tennent meetinghouse, Aug. 31, 2021; P. Dickinson to GW, June 28, 1778, *PGW*, 15: 573–76n; Lender and Stone, *Fatal Sunday*, 241 (*long-range volley*); Stryker, *The Battle of Monmouth*, 122–23 (*Jersey militiamen*).

367 **That gentleman himself appeared:** Alden, *General Charles Lee*, 214; Stryker, *The Battle of Monmouth*, 122–23 (*Tempers flared*); Lender and Stone, *Fatal Sunday*, 250 (*"perilous situation"*).

368 **Clinton's departure from Monmouth:** P. Dickinson to GW, June 28, 1778, *PGW*, 15: 573–

76n; Ewald, *Diary of the American War*, 136 (*"Swarms of Americans"*); Ritchie, ed., "A New York Diary of the Revolutionary War," 221+; Stryker, *The Battle of Monmouth*, 129–30; McBurney, *George Washington's Nemesis*, 130–33; Morrissey, *Monmouth Courthouse 1778*, 46–47 (*Queen's Rangers* and *16th Light Dragoons*).

368 **To their left—west—they soon spied:** Gara, *Queen's American Rangers*, 88 (*fearless, vainglorious*); Wilkin, *Some British Soldiers in America*, 90–92 (*siege of Quebec*); Simcoe, *A Journal of the Operations of the Queen's Rangers*, 41–42; Van der Oye, *Remembering Their Gallantry in Former Days*, 51 (*Royal Navy captain*), 55; Lender and Stone, *Fatal Sunday*, 259 (*"no riders"*); Bilby and Jenkins, *Monmouth Court House*, 194–96; Stryker, *The Battle of Monmouth*, 135 (*ball smashed Simcoe's arm*).

369 **Emboldened by the rout of his former captors:** P. Dickinson to GW, June 28, 1778, *PGW*, 15: 573–76n; McBurney, *George Washington's Nemesis*, 130–33; Lender and Stone, *Fatal Sunday*, 261 (*"those people are ours"*); Stryker, *The Battle of Monmouth*, 141 (*"take them all"* and *"understand the roads"*); Steiner, *The Life and Correspondence of James McHenry*, 19–20 (*"fixed and firm tone"*).

369 **This pretty plan soon came apart:** Lender and Stone, *Fatal Sunday*, 262 (*into the woods*), 265–66 (*uncertain of Lee's intentions*), 270 (*signal flags*); Stryker, *The Battle of Monmouth*, 134 (*wounding a Connecticut colonel*); "Proceedings of a General Court Martial," *LP*, 3: 156–58; Simms, ed., *The Army Correspondence of Colonel John Laurens*, 196 (*"men were formed piecemeal"*).

369 **Clinton also improvised, and now it fell:** Lender and Stone, *Fatal Sunday*, 264–65 (*ten thousand men*); Willcox, ed., *The American Rebellion*, 93–94; Morrissey, *Monmouth Courthouse 1778*, 49 (*two blood-red columns*).

370 **This "put us into the most dangerous situation":** Lender and Stone, *Fatal Sunday*, 262–63; Stryker, *The Battle of Monmouth*, 140, 155–57; Bilby and Jenkins, *Monmouth Court House*, 199; Alden, *General Charles Lee*, 217–19 (*round shot expended*); Ward, *Charles Scott and the "Spirit of '76,"* 49–50 (*took counsel of his fears*); Barnardus Swartout, Jr., journal, June 28, 1778, Swartout, Sr., papers, NYHS (*"retired in great haste"*); McBurney, *George Washington's Nemesis*, 133 (*asked permission*).

370 **Dumbfounded by this unauthorized withdrawal:** Lender and Stone, *Fatal Sunday*, 267–68 (*"expressed in strong terms"*); Stryker, *The Battle of Monmouth*, 149–50 (*Massachusetts colonel*), 158–59 (*"ruin of the day"*); "Captain Stephen Olney's Account," JLB (*"paid his last debt"*).

370 **A Rhode Island officer tried to steady:** Williams, *Biography of Revolutionary Heroes*, 244 (*brandy*); *LP*, 3: 95–96 (*"great disorder"*); Stryker, *The Battle of Monmouth*, 165 (*"rout would hardly be too strong"*); Lender and Stone, *Fatal Sunday*, 271–72 (*disciplined withdrawal*), 273–74 (*Hessian grenadiers trailed in reserve*).

371 **With their ammunition boxes refilled:** *LP*, 3: 157–58 (*Oswald's gunners*); Lender and Stone, *Fatal Sunday*, 274–75 (*Grey to angle his brigade*); author visit, MBSP, Aug. 31, 2021, signage.

371 **For a man struggling to save his command:** Lender and Stone, *Fatal Sunday*, 280 (*"you are not commanding officer"*).

371 **Washington had arrived in Englishtown at midmorning:** GW to Henry Laurens, June 28, 1778, FOL (*"I am now here with the main body"*).

371 **The first hint of trouble:** Stryker, *The Battle of Monmouth*, 175–76 (*American troops were in retreat*).

371 **Now there could be no doubt:** Freeman, *George Washington: A Biography*, 5: 27–28 (*sweat beading*); Stryker, *The Battle of Monmouth*, 177 (*"flying from a shadow"*); *LP*, 3: 79–82 (*"exceedingly alarmed"*). As a volunteer aide, Tilghman would not be commissioned with a lieutenant colonel's rank until 1780.

372 **After crossing the West Ravine bridge:** McBurney, "Did George Washington Swear at Charles Lee During the Battle of Monmouth?," *JAR*, Mar. 10, 2022; *LP*, 3: 191 (*"this disorder and confusion"* and *"I was disconcerted"*); Papas, *Renegade Revolutionary*, 251 (*"What is it"*).

372 **Various embellished accounts from those:** Lender and Stone, *Fatal Sunday*, 290 (*"the leaves shook"*); *LP*, 3: 191 (*"contrary to my intentions"*).

372 **Washington would have none of it:** Lender and Stone, *Fatal Sunday*, 289 (*"ought not to have undertaken"*); Shreve, *Tench Tilghman*, 105–6 (*"would have been obeyed"*); Bilby and Jenkins, *Monmouth Court House*, 205 (*should not have asked to command*); Lengel, *General George Washington*, 297–98 (*ambiguity*).

372 **Lieutenant Colonel Marinus Willett, a stalwart:** Willett, *A Narrative of the Military Actions of Colonel Marinus Willett*, 70 (*"know everything"*); McHenry, *Journal of a March, a Battle, and a Waterfall*, 6 (*"much surprised, chagrined"*); Ryan, *A Salute to Courage*, 129 (*"enemy were in full view"*).

372 **There was not an instant to lose:** McHenry, *Journal of a March, a Battle, and a Waterfall*, 6 (*"a moment's resistance"*); Shreve, *Tench Tilghman*, 106 (*"in some disorder"*); P. Dickinson to GW, June 28, 1778, *PGW*, 15: 573–76n (*Wayne was to form*); McBurney, *George Washington's Nemesis*, 144 (*six hundred*); Stillé, *Major-General Anthony Wayne and the Pennsylvania Line in the Continental Army*, 149–53 (*"in play"*); McBurney, "Did George Washington Swear at Charles Lee During the Battle of Monmouth?," *JAR*, Mar. 10, 2022 (*prominent hedgerow*); *LP*, 3: 114 (*"I will stay here with you"*), 3: 156 (*"everything in my power"*).

373 **Washington hoped these expedients would buy time:** *LAAR*, 2: 11 (*"seemed to arrest fate"*); Martin, *A Narrative of a Revolutionary Soldier*, 110–11 (*"rending up the earth"*).

373 **"The dust and smoke would sometimes":** Rees, "'I Extracted 4 balls by cutting in the opposite side,'" n.d.; Kipping, *The Hessian View of America, 1776–1783*, 20 (*ninety-six degrees*); Martin, *A Narrative of a Revolutionary Soldier*, 112 (*"almost too hot"*).

373 **As if to prove the point:** Stryker, *The Battle of Monmouth*, 201, 205 (*chestnut blood mare*).

373 **Henry Clinton had not sought to give battle:** McBurney, *George Washington's Nemesis*, 145–46 (*across the Middle Ravine*); Lender and Stone, *Fatal Sunday*, 302–3 (*several dozen redcoats*); Bilby and Jenkins, *Monmouth Court House*, 208 (*Trelawny*).

374 **Clinton joined the chase:** Wilkin, *Some British Soldiers in America*, 258 (*"Never heed"*); McBurney, *George Washington's Nemesis*, 148–49 (*as close as forty yards*).

374 **Wayne and his survivors skittered:** Lender and Stone, *Fatal Sunday*, 304–5; *LP*, 3: 157–58 (*"obliged to retreat"*); Chernow, *Alexander Hamilton*, 115 (*horses shot*).

374 **The 2nd Grenadiers followed on their heels:** author visit, MBSP, Perrine's Hill, Aug. 31, 2021; Martin, *The Philadelphia Campaign*, 238 (*"braver than wise"*); Nelson, *William Alexander, Lord Stirling*, 44 (*New Jersey estate*), 123 (*"his lordship's tankard"*); Lundin, *Cockpit of the Revolution*, 22–23 (*gilded vanes* and *earldom*); *TBAC*, 369–70.

375 **The grenadiers had advanced two hundred yards:** Lender and Stone, *Fatal Sunday*, 310–12 (*Monckton*); Wilkin, *Some British Soldiers in America*, 258 (*"heaviest fire"*), 261 (*paid a dollar*); Stryker, *The Battle of Monmouth*, 216–17 (*killed a grenadier captain*).

375 **Clinton also probed Stirling's left flank:** McBurney, *George Washington's Nemesis*, 154; Stryker, *The Battle of Monmouth*, 210 (*Continentals bounded downhill*); Lender and Stone, *Bloody Sunday*, 315 (*"How is it your pleasure"*), 316 (*"ruffled"*).

375 **From his artillery train of forty-six pieces:** Lender and Stone, *Fatal Sunday*, 320 (*dozen 6-pounders*); McBurney, *George Washington's Nemesis*, 154 (*"most terrible cannonade"*); Hughes, *British Smooth-Bore Artillery*, 33–35 (*fifteen hundred feet per second*).

375 **The rebels hammered back:** Wright, *The Continental Army*, 150; Weigley, *History of the United States Army*, 69 (*aptitude for artillery*); Lender and Stone, *Fatal Sunday*, 318–20; Stryker, *The Battle of Monmouth*, 211–13 (*enfilade fire*); author visit, MBSP, Aug. 31, 2021, signage (*"a fine drubbing"*).

376 **Hundreds of projectiles whizzed:** Brown and Peckham, eds., *Revolutionary War Journals of Henry Dearborn, 1775–1783*, 126–27 (*"finest music"*).

376 **As the afternoon shadows began to stretch:** Lender and Stone, *Fatal Sunday*, 336 (*"advance in our turn"*), 347 (*"quailed them"*); McBurney, *George Washington's Nemesis*, 155 (*four hundred Pennsylvanians*); Rees, "'None of you know the hardships of a soldiers life,'" n.d., 34–35 (*"They run off"*); Bilby and Jenkins, *Monmouth Court House*, 219; McBurney, "Did George Washington Swear at Charles Lee During the Battle of Monmouth?," *JAR*, Mar. 10, 2022 (*British withdrew*).

376 **The long summer day faded:** Stryker, *The Battle of Monmouth*, 225–26 (*assembling three bri-*

gades); Lockhart, *The Drillmaster of Valley Forge*, 162 (*"tired out"*); Steiner, *The Life and Correspondence of James McHenry*, 19–20 (*superior in cavalry*); Alden, *General Charles Lee*, 229; *LP*, 2: 452.

377 **Washington and Lafayette slept side by side:** Auricchio, *The Marquis Lafayette Reconsidered*, 71 (*on a cloak*); Stryker, *The Battle of Monmouth*, 225–26 (*spreading oak*), 227 (*Clinton at ten p.m.*); Clinton to Germain, July 5, 1778, *LP*, 2: 461 (*"overpowered"*).

377 **The Americans pulled back to Englishtown:** GW, general orders, June 29, 1778, FOL (*"noble spirit"*); Philemon Dickinson to GW, June 29 and 30, 1778, FOL (*hurried home*); GW, general orders, June 30, 1778, FOL (*"decent as possible"*); Lender and Stone, *Fatal Sunday*, 353 (*"glorious for America"*).

377 **A burial detail of two hundred men:** Bilby and Jenkins, *Monmouth Court House*, 225 (*"like sheaves"* and *dragged by their heels*); Lender and Stone, *Fatal Sunday*, 356 (*"stench from the woods"*), 362 (*"he might die easy"*).

377 **Casualty estimates varied wildly:** Bilby and Jenkins, *Monmouth Court House*, 222–25 (*"Lee is killed"*); Lender and Stone, *Fatal Sunday*, 366–69 (*two thousand*); P. Dickinson to GW, June 28, 1778, *PGW*, 15: 573–76n (*battle totals of dead*); Lengel, *General George Washington*, 304 (*sunstroke*); *DAR*, 13: 320, 15: 159; Moorsom, ed., *Historical Record of the Fifty-Second* Regiment, 23–24 (*"I wonder who they'll get"*).

378 **Some 150 British prisoners were marched:** Lender and Stone, *Fatal Sunday*, 356 (*jail cells in Trenton*), 364; Neimeyer, *America Goes to War*, 60 (*pretty women on their arms*); Gruber, ed., *John Peebles' American War, 1776–1782*, 194 (*truce flags*); Stryker, *The Battle of Monmouth*, 229 (*barns and private homes*); Ritchie, ed., "A New York Diary of the Revolutionary War," 221+ (*"want of a sufficiency of wagons"*); Kidder, *Revolutionary Princeton 1774–1783*, 205 (*coffins*).

378 **On July 1 the king's men:** Adelberg, *The American Revolution in Monmouth County*, 84 (*Refugeetown*); Tiedemann et al., eds., *The Other Loyalists*, 59 (*horse thieves*); Lender and Stone, *Fatal Sunday*, 378 (*becalmed twelve-day voyage*); Trevelyan, *The American Revolution*, 4: 371n (*16,452 officers and men*); "Extract from the Letter Book of Captain Johann Heinrichs of the Hessian *Jäger* Corps, 1778–1780," 137+ (*"forced to tussle"*); Burgoyne, ed., *Enemy Views*, 271 (*"send us to Germany"*).

378 **A storm had ruptured the base of the Sandy Hook:** Ewald, *Diary of the American War*, 137 (*"terribly bitten"*); Ritchie, ed., "A New York Diary of the Revolutionary War," 221+ (*broke up the bridge*); Lydenberg, ed., "Archibald Robertson's Diaries, 1762–1780," 283; Burgoyne, trans., *Defeat, Disaster and Dedication*, 109 (*droves of eight or ten*); Cliffe to unknown, July 5, 1778, Loftus Cliffe papers, WLC, box 1 (*"What is intended"*).

378 **Clinton strode into his Manhattan headquarters:** Clinton orders, July 5, 1778, Frederick Mackenzie papers, WLC, box 3, vol. E (*"much disgrace"*); Lutnick, *The American Revolution and the British Press, 1775–1783*, 119 (*"immortal honor"*); Mackesy, *The War for America, 1775–1783*, 221–22 (*winter under canvas*); Blatchford, *The Narrative of John Blatchford*, 10n (*"business of one half"*).

379 **He believed that if he'd had:** Clinton to sisters, July 6, 1778, WBW (*"To have gone near 100 miles"*); Willcox, ed., *The American Rebellion*, 94 (*"It breaks my heart"*).

379 **America "possibly might have been recovered":** Bilby and Jenkins, *Monmouth Court House*, 233–34; Clinton to sisters, Aug. 1, 1778, WBW (*"sooner I get home"*).

379 **Washington allowed his army several days:** John Berkenhout, "Journal of an Excursion from New York to Philadelphia in the Year 1778," GSG, vol. 8 (*"dismal town"*); GW, general orders, July 4, 1778, FOL (*"undisputed independence"*); Gruber, ed., *John Peebles' American War, 1776–1782*, 196 (*din could be heard*); Lender and Stone, *Fatal Sunday*, 370 (*resting every other day*); Lord Stirling to GW, July 2, 1778, FOL (*"get all the intelligence"*).

379 **Years of fighting and killing remained:** Lender and Stone, *Fatal Sunday*, 382 (*"boasted their advantages"*); Lengel, ed., *A Companion to George Washington*, 238 (*"ruined" the British* and *"important victory"*).

380 **Much praise befell Washington:** AH to E. Boudinot, July 5, 1778, FOL (*"so much advantage"*); Montgomery, "The Battle of Monmouth, as Described by Dr. James McHenry," 355+ (*"gave a*

new turn"); H. Knox to brother, July 3, 1778, JLB, AAA (*"full proportion"*); Brooks, *Henry Knox, a Soldier of the Revolution*, 121 (*"very splendid"*); Coakley and Conn, *The War of the American Revolution*, 66 (*fought well with bayonets*); Bilby and Jenkins, *Monmouth Court House*, 232 (*"can't say we skulked"*).

380 **Washington once again inflated enemy casualties:** GW to John Augustine Washington, July 4, 1778, *PGW*, 16: 26 (*at least 2,000 men*); Graham, *The Life of General Daniel Morgan*, 211 (*"very unhappy"*); Golway, *Washington's General*, 178–79 (*irked Greene*).

380 **Yet as Common Sense Paine would point out:** Davidson, "Whig Propagandists of the American Revolution," 442+ (*not an acre*); Paine, *The American Crisis, Number VI*, Oct. 20, 1778 (*"holes and corners"*); GW to Thomas Nelson, Jr., Aug. 20, 1778, FOL (*"strangest vicissitudes"*).

381 **The guns might have gone silent:** Charles Lee to GW, June 30, 1778 [misdated July 1], FOL (*"very singular"*).

381 **Washington replied immediately with a scathing:** GW to Lee, June 30, 1778, FOL (*"You were guilty"*); *LP*, 3: 206 (*"thrown into a stupor"*); Lee to GW, June 30, 1778, FOL (*"brought to a trial"*); GW to Lee, June 30, 1778, FOL (*"put you in arrest"*).

381 **Court-martial preparations were made:** McBurney, *George Washington's Nemesis*, 174 (*"A most hellish plan"*); GW to Lee, June 30, 1778, FOL fn; McBurney, *George Washington's Nemesis*, 181–82; Stryker, *The Battle of Monmouth*, 244 (*twenty-six sessions*); AH to Lord Stirling, July 14, 1778, FOL (*"indecision, improvidence"*); Chernow, *Alexander Hamilton*, 115–16; *LP*, 3: 8 (*"liberty to deviate"*).

382 **Lee called thirteen witnesses:** Alden, *General Charles Lee*, 236–37; *LP*, 3: 158 (*"master of yourself"*), 3: 175 (*"discretionary power"*).

382 **After three days of deliberation:** Patterson, *Knight Errant of Liberty*, 228 (*North Castle*), 235 (*"blush for my country"*); *LP*, 3: 208 (*guilty on all counts*); Thayer, *The Making of a Scapegoat*, 94; McBurney, *George Washington's Nemesis*, 203, 220, 230. The historian Gary Ecelbarger argues that Lee's incoherent battle plan ignored Washington's instructions enough to prove him guilty of disobeying orders ("Did Charles Lee Disobey George Washington's Attack Order at Monmouth?," *JAR*, Mar. 7, 2024).

382 **Perhaps his case would have been strengthened:** Fleming, "The 'Military Crimes' of Charles Lee," 12+ (*"whole flying army"*); Willcox, ed., *The American Rebellion*, 96 (*"into the power of the king's army"*); Reed, *Life and Correspondence of Joseph Reed*, 1; 369–70 (*"No attack it seems"*); Alden, *General Charles Lee*, 236–38, 249 (*"blasted mortal"*).

382 **Washington had not been required to testify:** GW to J. Reed, Dec. 12, 1778, FOL (*"temper and plans"*).

383 **Much remained of the fighting season:** John Brown to GW, July 9, 1778, FOL (*Madeira*); GW to Thomas Nelson, Jr., Aug. 20, 1778, FOL (*"excellent qualities"*).

383 **"The hand of Providence":** GW to Thomas Nelson, Jr., Aug. 20, 1778, FOL.

17. FORTUNE IS A FICKLE JADE

384 **For more than a decade the lighthouse:** "Sandy Hook Light," http://www.njlhs.org/njlight/sandy.html; Adelberg, "'So Dangerous a Quarter': The Sandy Hook Lighthouse During the American Revolution," *Keeper's Log* (Spring 1995): 10+.

384 **At midday on July 11:** Nagy, *Invisible Ink*, 240 (*red square*); Francis Barber to GW, July 13, 1778, FOL (*two p.m.*); "Journals of Henry Duncan, Captain, Royal Navy," in Laughton, ed., *The Naval Miscellany*, 1: 160; Schermerhorn, *American and French Flags of the Revolution, 1775–1783*, 107 (*white banners*); Christie, *Crisis of Empire*, 104 (*end of British naval superiority*); O'Beirne, *A Candid and Impartial Narrative of the Transactions of the Fleet*, 11 (*more than eleven thousand*); *NDAR*, 13: 342 (*dozen French two-decker*), 13: 359 (*fishing smacks*).

384 **Standing on the quarterdeck:** *NDAR*, 13: 3, 337 (*pilots*); Clary, *Adopted Son*, 202 (*six feet four in battle* and *brigadier general*); Jones, ed., *The Siege of Savannah in 1779*, 69–70 (*"enthusiasm and the fire"*); *LiA*, 2: 253 (*"profound in nothing"*); Doniol, *Histoire de la participation de la France*, 3: 175–76 (*schoolboy companion*); Colman-Maison, *L'amiral d'Estaing*, 30–48 (*breaking his parole*); Lawrence, *Storm over Savannah*, 9 (*his wife's fortune* and *"like a baboon"*);

Lacour-Gayet, *La marine militaire de la France sous le règne de Louis XVI*, 140 (*"When you have me beheaded"*). Ten guns had been added to *Languedoc* for this expedition (https://threedecks.org/index.php?display_type=show_ship&id=1964).

385 **After the peace of 1763:** James, *The British Navy in Adversity*, 90; Stoker et al., eds., *Strategy in the American War of Independence*, 147 (*"witless"*), 149 (*no training*); Manceron, *Age of the French Revolution*, 2: 137 (*"Asian and American seas"*), 154 (*"he cannot sail"*); LiA, 2: 253 (*skepticism if not scorn*); Merlant, *Soldiers and Sailors of France in the American War for Independence*, 59 (*"violent spells of anger"*); McBurney, *The Rhode Island Campaign*, 150–51 (*"a crime even to think"*); Doniol, *Histoire de la participation de la France,* 3: 183–84 (*thousand soldiers*).

385 **"Speed is the foremost":** Miller, *Sea of Glory*, 332 (*"To surprise"*); Dull, *The French Navy and American Independence*, 115 (*Five weeks*); Lacour-Gayet, *La marine militaire de la France sous le règne de Louis XVI*, 152 (*"six different categories"*); Dearden, *The Rhode Island Campaign of 1778*, 30 (*chased stray merchantmen*); Willcox, ed., *The American Rebellion*, 99 (*trapped and destroyed*); Lender and Stone, *Fatal Sunday*, 379 (*two months*); Mackesy, *The War for America, 1775–1783*, 217 (*twenty-four thousand troops*); Clowes, *The Royal Navy*, 3: 398.

386 **Even so, Congress welcomed d'Estaing:** Ballagh, ed., *The Letters of Richard Henry Lee*, 1: 23–25 (*"as much water"*); Selby, *The Revolution in Virginia, 1775–1783*, 181 (*twenty thousand barrels* and *Hessian fly*); Ashmead, *History of Delaware County, Pennsylvania*, 208; GW to H. Laurens, Oct. 29, 1778, FOL (*voracious pest*); Willis, *The Struggle for Sea Power*, 204 (*"busy frizzling their hair"*).

386 **D'Estaing's orders, signed by the king:** Clowes, *The Royal Navy*, 3: 394–95 (*"forty leagues west"*); NDAR, 13: 315, 397n, 560 (Mermaid); Willis, *The Struggle for Sea Power*, 231 (*six hundred livres per cannon*).

386 **Sketchy reports in New York of a French fleet:** O'Beirne, *A Candid and Impartial Narrative of the Transactions of the Fleet*, 10–11 (Zebra); Gruber, *The Howe Brothers and the American Revolution*, 305 (*bound for Boston*); Laughton, ed., *The Naval Miscellany*, 1: 104 (*854 cannons to 614* and *weight of metal*); NDAR, 13: 342 (*"indifferently manned"*); Clowes, *The Royal Navy*, 3: 399–400; Lender and Stone, *Fatal Sunday*, 376 (*"I believe the war is over"*).

386 **The British had one asset the French lacked:** NDAR, 6: 973 (*"His abilities"*); Willcox, *Portrait of a General*, 245 (*"The greater his difficulties"*); Thomas, *Memoirs of the Marquis of Rockingham and His Contemporaries*, 2: 359–65 (*"Black Dick was seen to smile"*); Mahan, *The Major Operations of the Navies in the War of American Independence*, 99–100 (*"firmness, endurance"*).

387 **He had left Eton to go to sea:** "Richard Howe, 1st Earl 4th Viscount," https://morethannelson.com/officer/richard-howe-1st-earl-4th-viscount/; Flavell, *The Howe Dynasty*, 15, 29–30 (*fifty-seven sea battles*), 78, 90, 93 (Gainsborough), 102 (*"well-beloved cousin"*).

387 **Now more than midway through:** TBAC, 383; O'Shaughnessy, *The Men Who Lost America*, 89–90 (*naval innovators*); Willcox, *Portrait of a General*, 252 (*"sober, even a somber man"*); Flavell, *The Howe Dynasty*, 15 (*"his mind was always clear"*), 90 (*"the sailor's friend"*); Laughton, ed., *The Naval Miscellany*, 1: 96–99 (Diamond).

387 **With the French fleet approaching:** R. Howe to William Eden, July 9, 1778, APS, Feinstone Coll., #561 (*"to act hostilely"*); R. Howe, signal book, WLC; Clowes, *The Royal Navy*, 3: 399–400 (*fitted springs*); Mackesy, *The War for America, 1775–1783*, 217; James, *The British Navy in Adversity*, 101; Hiscocks, "Lord Howe's Defence of New York, July 1778," https://morethannelson.com/lord-howes-defence-of-new-york-july-1778/.

388 **Should d'Estaing succeed in seizing Sandy Hook:** NDAR, 13: 392–93n, 445 (*compel the garrison's surrender*); O'Beirne, *A Candid and Impartial Narrative of the Transactions of the Fleet*, 12 (*shallops and yawls* and *cast lots*), 15 (*storeship* Leviathan); Laughton, ed., *The Naval Miscellany*, 1:160 (*32-pounders and lesser guns*); Ralfe, *The Naval Biography of Great Britain*, 1: 97 (*into a fireship*).

388 **General Washington had big dreams:** GW to d'Estaing, July 14, 1778, PGW, 16: 67 (*"I congratulate you"*); GW to d'Estaing, July 17, 1778, PGW, 16: 88 (*"truly happy"*).

388 **In "loose thoughts upon an attack":** GW to d'Estaing, July 14, 1778, PGW, 16: 68–69n; GW

to d'Estaing, July 14, 1778, *PGW*, 16: 71n (*"precious"*); GW to d'Estaing, July 17, 1778, *PGW*, 16: 88 (*Francophone aides*); GW to Jeremiah Wadsworth, July 15, 1778, *PGW*, 16: 81 (*"parcel of poultry"*); Lacour-Gayet, *La marine militaire de la France sous le règne de Louis XVI*, 157–58 (*"insolent nation"*).

389 **That major work was off to a fitful start:** *NDAR*, 13: 233 (*desperate for water* and *drowned in turbulent Jersey surf*); Freeman, *George Washington: A Biography*, 5: 49–50 (*"first victim"*); Allen, *A Naval History of the American Revolution*, 1: 329–30 (*twenty prizes*); *NDAR*, 13: 420 (Isabelle), 428 (York); Schecter, *The Battle for New York*, 314 (*five American prizes*); O'Beirne, *A Candid and Impartial Narrative of the Transactions of the Fleet*, 15–16 (Stanley), 20 (*"in our own harbor"*).

389 **D'Estaing soon realized that bulling:** Tilley, *The British Navy and the American Revolution*, 84 (*"seaman's purgatory"*); Harley et al., *Mapping the American Revolutionary War*, 88–92 (Ostend); "Utility of the *Atlantic Neptune*," LOC, https://www.loc.gov/resource/g3301pm .gan00003/?sp=3.

390 **Worse yet, French ships of the line:** Welle, "Revolutionary War Artillery in the South," 250+ (*required twenty-seven feet*); Clowes, *The Royal Navy*, 3: 401–2 (*twenty-three feet deep at the flood*); *NDAR*, 13: 446 (*twenty to twenty-two feet*); d'Estaing to GW, Aug. 3, 1778, FOL (*"fifty thousand crowns"*); Lender and Stone, *Fatal Sunday*, 379 (*"resolved not to let us out"*).

390 **At nine a.m. on Wednesday, July 22:** O'Beirne, *A Candid and Impartial Narrative of the Transactions of the Fleet*, 16 (*"wind could not be more favorable"*).

390 **Then, a British captain recorded:** Moomaw, "The Naval Career of Captain Hamond, 1775–1779," diss., 405 (*"to our great surprise"*); Mahan, *The Major Operations of the Navies in the War of American Independence*, 90 (*"has desisted"*); William Hotham to Charles Hotham Thompson, July 27, 1778, *NDAR*, 13: 529 (*"a deep game"*).

390 **"It is terrible to be within sight":** Unger, *Lafyette*, 80; AH to GW, July 20, 1778, FOL (*feint south*).

391 **Washington swallowed his disappointment:** GW to d'Estaing, July 22, 1778, FOL (*"brilliant enterprise"*).

391 **After eighteen months of British occupation:** Mackenzie, *Diary of Frederick Mackenzie*, 1: 184 (*coronation*), 237 (*queen's birthday*); Kipping, *The Hessian View of America, 1776–1783*, 16–20 (*"safe from all winds"*).

391 **But war had lacerated Newport:** Carp, *Rebels Rising*, 116–17 (*rum, shipping*), 225 (*dropped by two-thirds*); Tatum, *The American Journal of Ambrose Serle*, 271 (*"one long street"*); Neimeyer, "The British Occupation of Newport, Rhode Island, 1776–1779," 30+ (*"beat by Hessians"*); Johnson, *Occupied America*, 90 (*hunt or fish* and Lord Sandwich); McBurney, "British Treatment of Prisoners During the Occupation of Newport, 1776–1779," 1+ (Endeavour).

391 **For several thousand of the king's men:** Mackenzie, *Diary of Frederick Mackenzie*, 1: 408 (*ten thousand cords*), 433 (*redheads*); "Newport in the Hands of the British," 1+ (*pews yanked out*); "Journal of the Hon. Garrison-Regiment von Huyn," HDAR, 53 (*hog bristles*); Popp, *A Hessian Soldier in the American Revolution*, 11 (*"like the gods"*); Johnson, *Occupied America*, 2 (*physicians treated dozens*); Grose, *A Classical Dictionary of the Vulgar Tongue*, n.p. (*"sunburnt"*).

391 **War was never far away:** McBurney, "British Treatment of Prisoners During the Occupation of Newport, 1776–1779," 1+ (Aurora); Dearden, *The Rhode Island Campaign of 1778*, 25–27 (*British raiders*), 36 (*five regiments*); "Newport in the Hands of the British," 1+ (*plundered rings*); Mackenzie, *Diary of Frederick Mackenzie*, 1: 298 (*"most effectual means"*), 309–10 (*eighteen ships*), 318 (*twenty more heavy guns*).

392 **Trouble arrived on Wednesday, July 29:** Mackenzie, *Diary of Frederick Mackenzie*, 1: 319 (*dozen ships of the line*); John Laurens to GW, Aug. 4, 1778, FOL (*"raising a curtain"*); Almy, "Mrs. Almy's Journal," 17+ (*Howe's squadron*); Dearden, *The Rhode Island Campaign of 1778*, 48 (*off Brenton Reef*).

392 **Pandemonium swept the town:** Mackenzie, *Diary of Frederick Mackenzie*, 1: 319 (*rowboats and skiffs*); Walther, ed., "Diary of Johann Christoph Doehlemann," 11+ (*"oxen are too slow"*);

NDAR, 13: 549–52 (*no Royal Navy vessel*); Almy, "Mrs. Almy's Journal," 17+ (*buried their table silver*); "Newport in the Hands of the British," 1+ (*"greatest confusion"*).

392 **John Laurens had galloped 160 miles:** *NDAR*, 13: 508 (*thirty pilots*); Massey, *John Laurens and the American Revolution*, 115 (*barely two days*); J. Laurens to GW, July 25, 1778, FOL (*eight whaleboats*); Dearden, *The Rhode Island Campaign of 1778*, 35 (*five thousand New England militiamen*); NG to J. Sullivan, July 23, 1778, *PNG*, 2: 466 (*"child of fortune"*).

394 **In a letter to d'Estaing from Sullivan:** Sullivan to GW, July 26, 1778, FOL fn; Whittemore, *A General of the Revolution*, 89 (*"raising men from the dead"*); Greene to d'Estaing, Aug. 21, 1778, *PNG*, 2: 482n (*lantern light*).

394 **D'Estaing agreed to Sullivan's plan:** Johnson, "The Administration of the American Commissariat," diss., 141 (*provisions for twenty days*); Miller, *Sea of Glory*, 346 (*"pineapples"*); d'Estaing to GW, Aug. 3, 1778, FOL; Hammond, *Letters and Papers of Major-General John Sullivan*, 2: 151 (*"fired on pointblank"*). Sullivan personally visited *Languedoc* on July 30 (Whittemore, *A General of the Revolution*, 91).

394 **On the evening of July 29:** Whittemore, *A General of the Revolution*, 91 (*sealed the East Channel*); John Laurens to GW, Aug. 4, 1778, FOL (*"slight scratches"*); "Journal of the Hon. Garrison-Regiment von Huyn," HDAR, 89 (*abandoned Conanicut*); John Laurens to GW, Aug. 4, 1778, FOL; McBurney, *The Rhode Island Campaign*, 84–85 (*Dumplings*).

395 **In the East Channel, with the French frigates:** Mackenzie, *Diary of Frederick Mackenzie*, 1: 321 (*"went to atoms"*); *NDAR*, 13: 608 (Kingfisher); McBurney, *The Rhode Island Campaign*, 93–94 (*Captain John Brisbane*); Desmarais, *America's First Ally*, 85 (*245 prisoners*).

395 **Worse was to come for the British at five a.m.:** Mackenzie, *Diary of Frederick Mackenzie*, 1: 328–31 (*"most mortifying"* and *"very inconsistent"*).

395 **A funereal pall from the burning hulks:** Clowes, *The Royal Navy*, 3: 403 (*five frigates, two sloops*); *NDAR*, 13: 648 (*at least a dozen transports*); McBurney, *The Rhode Island Campaign*, 91–92 (*"much to be lamented"*), 95 (*greatest naval calamity*); "Journal of the Hon. Garrison-Regiment von Huyn," HDAR, 89 (*sailcloth tents*); Almy, "Mrs. Almy's Journal," 17+ (*"without saving themselves a shirt"* and *"kill grief"*).

396 **D'Estaing's arrival on the New England coast:** Abigail Adams to John Thaxter, Aug. 19, 1778, FOL (*"Gentlemen of rank"*); McBurney, *The Rhode Island Campaign*, 96–100 (*"terminate the war"*).

396 **Yet Sullivan struggled in early August:** McBurney, *The Rhode Island Campaign*, 100 (*"ducks in cross-belts"*), 105 (*"so pricked"*); Dearden, *The Rhode Island Campaign of 1778*, 49 (*Pigot commanded ten thousand*).

396 **Greene arrived to command one wing:** Thayer, *Nathanael Greene*, 252 (*brief stop in Coventry*); McBurney, *The Rhode Island Campaign*, 106–7 (*"militarily inadmissible"*); Tower, *The Marquis de La Fayette in the American Revolution*, 1: 456 (*binding cutlass blades*).

397 **Lafayette's overweening ambitions:** Manceron, *Age of the French Revolution*, 2: 82 (*salmon fishing*); Dearden, *The Rhode Island Campaign of 1778*, 67 (*"decent crop"*), 70 (*"best scenes"*); Auricchio, *The Marquis Lafayette Reconsidered*, 73 (*"You know how to get"*).

397 **Lafayette's American comrades wondered:** *LiA*, 2: 246 (*"the general interest"*); Dearden, *The Rhode Island Campaign of 1778*, 151–52 (*caulked by candlelight*); McBurney, *The Rhode Island Campaign*, 107 (*twelve hundred American troops*), 108 (*"chaos of militia"*); Whittemore, *A General of the Revolution* (*daybreak on Monday, August 10*).

397 **D'Estaing moved first:** *NDAR*, 13: 748 (*Goat and Rose Islands*), 752 (*Languedoc and seven other ships*), 774; Moore, *The Diary of the American Revolution, 1775–1781*, 323 (*two miles' range*); Mackenzie, *Diary of Frederick Mackenzie*, 1: 145 (*"echo of the guns"*).

398 **For seventy-five minutes British balls:** Almy, "Mrs. Almy's Journal," 17+ (*"will they kill us?"*); Neimeyer, "The British Occupation of Newport, Rhode Island, 1776–1779," 30+ (*"Fire and sword"*); McBurney, *The Rhode Island Campaign*, 110 (*drilling large holes*); Mackenzie, *Diary of Frederick Mackenzie*, 1: 340–41 (*torched within twenty yards*); *NDAR*, 13: 752 (*twenty houses burned*); "Journal of the Hon. Garrison-Regiment von Huyn," HDAR, 90 (*"sheep in a pen"*).

398 **D'Estaing had anchored east of Conanicut:** Dearden, *The Rhode Island Campaign of 1778*, 73 (*colors had been shot away*); McBurney, *The Rhode Island Campaign*, 112–13.

398 **They would not get a day:** McBurney, *The Rhode Island Campaign*, 112–13 (*straw dummies*); Clowes, *The Royal Navy*, 3: 403 (*ten thousand strong*); Whittemore, *A General of the Revolution*, 95 (*urged the French*).

399 **That Sullivan had attacked a day early:** Simms, ed., *The Army Correspondence of Colonel John Laurens*, 220 ("*in a country dance*"); Massey, *John Laurens and the American Revolution*, 116 ("*gave much umbrage*"); McBurney, *The Rhode Island Campaign*, 112–13.

399 **Unusually thick summer fog:** Mackenzie, *Diary of Frederick Mackenzie*, 1: 364 ("*difficult to see fifty yards*"); D'Estaing campaign journal, Aug. 9, 1778, Archives Nationales, naval archives, série B4, vol. 147, micro (*spatter of white dots*); Mackenzie, *Diary of Frederick Mackenzie*, 1: 341–42 ("*spirits of the whole garrison*"); "Journal of the Hon. Garrison-Regiment von Huyn," HDAR, 90 ("*Lord Howe is coming*").

399 **Black Dick's signal book:** R. Howe, signal book, WLC (*heavy fog*); *Princess Royal* journal, John Kendall corr., HL, HM 64533 ("*very sickly*"); Clowes, *The Royal Navy*, 3: 397 (*limped into Halifax*).

399 **After foul winds caused days of delay:** Moomaw, "The Naval Career of Captain Hamond, 1775–1779," diss., 409 (*Thursday, August 6*); Clowes, *The Royal Navy*, 3: 404 (*foul winds*); McBurney, *The Rhode Island Campaign*, appendix C, 234–36.

400 **"The surprise was complete":** Dearden, *The Rhode Island Campaign of 1778*, 79; GW to d'Estaing, Aug. 8, 1778, FOL ("*his whole fleet*"); GW to J. Laurens, Aug. 8, 1778, FOL; D'Estaing campaign journal, Aug. 9, 1778, Archives Nationales, naval archives, série B4, vol. 147, micro (*troops back aboard*); Syrett, *Admiral Lord Howe*, 83 (*risk a defensive battle*).

400 **At eight-thirty a.m. on Monday:** "Journal of le comte de Cambis," Aug. 10, 1778, *NDAR*, 13: 785 (*Zélé led under topsails*); Almy, "Mrs. Almy's Journal," 17+ ("*devil was in him*").

400 **For more than an hour, shore guns and ships:** "Newport in the Hands of the British," 1+ (*traded brutish punches*); McBurney, *The Rhode Island Campaign*, 120 ("*people scampering*"); "Journal of le comte de Cambis," Aug. 10, 1778, *NDAR*, 13: 785 ("*more considerable*"); Miller, *Sea of Glory*, 349 (*bodies of dead seamen*).

400 **Howe, meanwhile, had ordered his own fleet:** McBurney, *The Rhode Island Campaign*, 122 (*frigate* Sphynx); *Phoenix* journal, Aug. 10, 1778, *NDAR*, 13: 797 (*cutting cables, unfurling sails*); Mackenzie, *Diary of Frederick Mackenzie*, 1: 345 ("*crowded all the sail*").

401 **The stern chase continued through the night:** Gruber, *The Howe Brothers and the American Revolution*, 311–15 (*eighty miles south*); Moomaw, "The Naval Career of Captain Hamond, 1775–1779," diss., 409 (*south by southwest*); Laughton, ed., *The Naval Miscellany*, 1: 161–62 (*fireships*); journal of Lieutenant de Vaisseau Jean-Julien, chevalier Le Mauff, *NDAR*, 13: 806 ("*sails dipping*").

401 **The gale—the Great Storm:** O'Beirne, *A Candid and Impartial Narrative of the Transactions of the Fleet*, 32–34 (*transferred his flag*); Moomaw, "The Naval Career of Captain Hamond, 1775–1779," diss., 409–10 (*lashed to the rudder head*); Laughton, ed., *The Naval Miscellany*, 1: 162 (*main and mizzen topmasts*); *Volcano* journal, Aug. 12, *NDAR*, 13: 819, 837 (*tow from Pearl*).

401 **It went worse for the French:** McBurney, *The Rhode Island Campaign*, 125 (Tonnant's *mizzenmast*), 126–27 ("*floating dock*"); Doniol, *Histoire de la participation de la France*, 3: 453–54 (*bowsprit snapped* and "*nothing but a floating mass*"); *NDAR*, 13: 818. The ship's name is sometimes spelled *Marseillais*.

401 **By Thursday afternoon, August 13, the seas:** *NDAR*, 13: 846; O'Beirne, *A Candid and Impartial Narrative of the Transactions of the Fleet*, 34–35 (*three broadsides*), 36 (*sails, masts, and rigging*); McBurney, *The Rhode Island Campaign*, 128 (*secret papers overboard*); Clowes, *The Royal Navy*, 3: 409 (*larger French ship broke off*); NG to GW, Aug. 28–31, 1778, FOL fn; Heath, *Memoirs of Major-General William Heath*, 176 ("*his other arm*"); Dearden, *The Rhode Island Campaign of 1778*, 81–82 (*hero's welcome*).

402 **From *Roebuck*'s deck late on Thursday:** Moomaw, "The Naval Career of Captain Hamond,

1775–1779," diss., 410 (*"rolling in the trough"*); Willis, *The Struggle for Sea Power*, 245; Clowes, *The Royal Navy*, 3: 408 (*return voyage to Sandy Hook*).

402 **D'Estaing also made his way to a safe haven:** Dearden, *The Rhode Island Campaign of 1778*, 81 (*jury masts*); McBurney, *The Rhode Island Campaign*, 128 (*single man killed*); Lacour-Gayet, *La marine militaire de la France sous le règne de Louis XVI*, 168 (*"I gave in"*).

402 **"The most severe northeast storm":** Daughan, *If By Sea*, 179; Mackenzie, *Diary of Frederick Mackenzie*, 1: 350–52 (*carried away tents*); Hammond, *Letters and Papers of Major-General John Sullivan*, 2: 207–8, 211; Matthews and Wecter, *Our Soldiers Speak, 1775–1918*, 62 (*"Found a haystack"*); Whittemore, *A General of the Revolution*, 98 (*"miserable beyond description"*).

402 **He had planned to advance against Newport:** Whittemore, *A General of the Revolution*, 98 (*on August 12*); McBurney, *The Rhode Island Campaign*, 146 (*four-gun batteries* and *lost a leg*); Dearden, *The Rhode Island Campaign of 1778*, 98–99 (*"enemy dare not"* and *"Stood by the marquis"*).

403 **Sullivan's pioneers had begun digging:** Sullivan to H. Laurens, Aug. 16, 1778, in Moore, *Materials for History*, 120–23 (*six thousand men*); Field, ed., *Diary of Colonel Israel Angell*, 3.

403 **Joy soon turned to ashes:** Stinchcombe, *The American Revolution and the French Alliance*, 50–51 (*extensive repairs*); Mackesy, *The War for America, 1775–1783*, 219 (*part of Byron's fleet*); J. Sullivan to GW, Aug. 23, 1778, FOL fn (*"Express orders"*); NG to GW, Aug. 28–31, 1778, FOL (*"did everything to prevail"*); NG to d'Estaing, Aug. 21, 1778, *PNG*, 2: 480 (*"disagreeable impression"*).

403 **To no avail. The two generals returned:** "Journal of the Hon. Garrison-Regiment von Huyn," HDAR, 91 (*French field hospital*); Greene to Charles Pettit, Aug. 22, 1778, *PNG*, 2: 491 (*"devil has got"*); McBurney, *The Rhode Island Campaign*, 151–52 (*"right to fight"*); Dearden, *The Rhode Island Campaign of 1778*, 107 (*"a most miserable figure"*); "A Protest . . . to Count d'Estaing," Aug. 22, 1778, *PNG*, 2: 487 (*"ruinous consequences"*); John Sullivan to GW, Aug. 23, 1778, FOL fn.

404 **Sullivan, an unlucky and mediocre general:** "A Protest . . . to Count d'Estaing," Aug. 22, 1778, *PNG*, 2: 491 fn; GW to Sullivan, Sept. 1, 1778, FOL (*"harmony and good agreement"*); "A Protest . . . to Count d'Estaing," Aug. 22, 1778, *PNG*, 2: 490n (*"sudden and unexpected"*); Sullivan to H. Laurens, Aug. 16, 1778, in Moore, *Materials for History*, 120–23 (*"inconstant ally"*).

404 **D'Estaing would deflect such prattle:** Freeman, *George Washington: A Biography*, 5: 65–66 (*"commander to his servant"*); McBurney, *The Rhode Island Campaign*, 153 (*"fighting a duel"*); *LAAR*, 2: 139 (*"my country was more dear"*), 143 (*"two great movers"*); *LiA*, 2: 259 (*"I begin to see"*).

404 **Prodded by Washington to observe:** GW to J. Sullivan, Sept. 1, 1778, FOL (*"cordiality"*); J. Sullivan to GW, Sept. 3, 1778, FOL (*"passion"*); Dearden, *The Rhode Island Campaign of 1778*, 105 (*"suddenly censure"*); Davidson, *Propaganda and the American Revolution, 1763–1783*, 324 (*"cut each other's throats"*); *LiA*, 2: 263 (*in seven hours*); Fleury to d'Estaing, Aug. 8, 1778, *NDAR*, 13: 779 (*"gouty, aged"*).

405 **The American bombardment of Newport continued:** "Newport in the Hands of the British," 1+ (*"A soldier and two women"*); Wild, "Journal of Ebenezer Wild," 66+; Almy, "Mrs. Almy's Journal," 17+ (*"cartloads of wretched men"*); Walther, ed., "Diary of Johann Christoph Doehlemann," 11+ (*"irresponsible dandies"*); NG to GW, Aug. 28–31, 1778, FOL (*"desert by shoals"*); McBurney, *The Rhode Island Campaign*, 170, 242.

405 **That disappointment soon deepened:** Dexter, ed., *The Literary Diary of Ezra Stiles, D.D., LL.D.*, 2: 295 (*gallopers every twenty miles*); Dearden, *The Rhode Island Campaign of 1778*, 117 (*braying cheers*); Wild, "Journal of Ebenezer Wild," 66+ (*"At 8 o'clock we struck"*).

405 **At first light on Saturday:** Mackenzie, *Diary of Frederick Mackenzie*, 1: 380–81 (*"rebels had struck"*); McBurney, *The Rhode Island Campaign*, 173 (*three hundred men*).

406 **Sullivan drew rein on Butts Hill:** Trumbull, *Autobiography, Reminiscences and Letters of John Trumbull*, 51–52 (*"melancholy farewell"*), 53 (*"Those are Germans"*); McBurney, *The Rhode Island Campaign*, 185.

406 **American sorties and well-served artillery:** McBurney, *The Rhode Island Campaign*, 180, 186 (*"shot through my waistcoat"*), 189–90 (*hulled* Vigilant *three times*); Dearden, *The Rhode Island Campaign of 1778*, 124 (*small British squadron*); Vigilant log in Sullivan to GW, Aug. 29, 1778, FOL fn (*retreat toward Prudence Island*).

406 **Hessian attempts to turn the American right flank:** Geake, *From Slaves to Soldiers*, 40 (*compensated*), 58 (*"wild-looking men"* and *"couple of the blacks were killed"*); McBurney, "The Discovery of an Important Letter from a Soldier of the 1st Rhode Island Regiment," *JAR*, Apr. 14, 2021 (*"sable battalion"*); Dearden, *The Rhode Island Campaign of 1778*, xiv (*"regiment of slaves"*); Buskirk, *Standing in Their Own Light*, 101–3 (*guaranteed emancipation*); Neimeyer, *America Goes to War*, 75; Greenman, *Diary of a Common Soldier in the American Revolution, 1775–1783*, 102; Quarles, *The Negro in the Making of America*, 47–48; Risch, *Supplying Washington's Army*, 27 (*"Negro name unknown"*); Pybus, *Epic Journeys of Freedom*, 29 (*Scipio Negro*); Gilbert, *Black Patriots and Loyalists*, 107 (*Jeffrey Liberty*); McBurney, *The Rhode Island Campaign*, 187–88 (*"obstinate resistance"*). A return of Aug. 24, 1778, counted 755 blacks in fourteen brigades, exclusive of the 1st Rhode Island (Lengel, *General George Washington*, 317).

407 **The right wing held, as had the left:** NG to GW, Aug. 28–31, 1778, FOL (*"I had the pleasure"*); Sullivan to GW, Aug. 29 and 31, 1778, FOL fn; Dearden, *The Rhode Island Campaign of 1778*, 126 (*"shot him in about an hour"*).

407 **"My whole army only seemed to want":** Sullivan to GW, Aug. 29, 1778, FOL; Whittemore, *A General of the Revolution*, 107–8 (*ordered all troops evacuated*); Mackenzie, *Diary of Frederick Mackenzie*, 1: 387; *LiA*, 2: 266 (*arrived before midnight*); Pownall and Almon, *The Remembrancer*, 7: 110 (*"Not a man"*).

407 **The retreat was deft and timely:** Mackenzie, *Diary of Frederick Mackenzie*, 1: 389 (*seventy Royal Navy ships*); McBurney, *The Rhode Island Campaign*, 204 (*"very ill humor"*); Willcox, *Portrait of a General*, 251 (*"poor deluded people"*).

408 **As the British general returned:** Lodge, *Major André's Journal*, n.p. [Sept. 5, 1778] (*"burning party"*); Dearden, *The Rhode Island Campaign of 1778*, 128 (*New Bedford and Fairhaven*); Pownall and Almon, *The Remembrancer*, 7: 36–38 (*388 firelocks*); Mackenzie, *Diary of Frederick Mackenzie*, 1: 395.

408 **An edict from Admiral Howe ordered the pillagers:** Lodge, *Major André's Journal*, n.p. [Sept. 12, 1778]; Huntington, *Letters Written by Ebenezer Huntington During the American Revolution*, 74 (*"It is my wish"*).

408 **"Fortune is a fickle jade":** NG to J. Sullivan, Oct. 24, 1778, *PNG*, 3: 11; James, *The British Navy in Adversity*, 109 (*remarkable alacrity*); Moomaw, "The Naval Career of Captain Hamond, 1775–1779," diss., 413 (*Boston Harbor on September 1*); Clowes, *The Royal Navy*, 3: 409–11 (*almost fifty guns*).

408 **American hopes at Newport had also:** GW to John Augustine Washington, Sept. 23, 1778, FOL (*"finishing blow"*); Coakley and Conn, *The War of the American Revolution*, 66 (*campaign in the West Indies*); GW to d'Estaing, Sept. 11–12, 1778, FOL (*"whole continent sympathizes"*); Stinchcombe, *The American Revolution and the French Alliance*, 57 (*out of the newspapers*); Miller, *Sea of Glory*, 351 (*Latin*), 352 (*£35,000*); Dearden, *The Rhode Island Campaign of 1778*, 134–35; Unger, *Lafayette*, 86 (*portrait of Washington*); *TBAC*, 263 (*spare masts*).

409 **D'Estaing maintained his aplomb:** Freeman, *George Washington: A Biography*, 5: 75 (*"amity and confidence"*); Languedoc journal, Nov. 5, 1778, Archives Nationales, naval archives, série B4, vol. 141, f 241, micro (*"late or false"*); Stinchcombe, *The American Revolution and the French Alliance*, 59; McBurney, "Why Did a Boston Mob Kill a French Officer?," *JAR*, Oct. 23, 2014 (*dedicated in May 1917*); Fitz-Henry Smith, Jr., *The Memorial to the Chevalier de Saint-Sauveur*, 6, 16; Dearden, *The Rhode Island Campaign of 1778*, 135 (*"nation of hotheads"*).

409 **Admiral Byron's men-of-war continued to stagger:** Gambier to Sandwich, Sept. 6, 1778, *PP Sandwich*, 2: 309; O'Beirne, *A Candid and Impartial Narrative of the Transactions of the Fleet*, 52 (*only eighty men*); Mackenzie, *Diary of Frederick Mackenzie*, 1: 396 (Princess Royal); Syrett, *Admiral Lord Howe*, 81 (*blown to Lisbon*); GW to d'Estaing, Sept. 11–12, 1778, FOL (*"superiority of the enemy"*).

409 **With this lull, Admiral Howe relinquished:** Moomaw, "The Naval Career of Captain Hamond, 1775–1779," diss., 416; Broomfield, "Lord Sandwich at the Admiralty Board," 7+ (*"I cannot cease to lament"*); Atkinson, "Brothers in Arms," July 20, 2021, 14 (*"How exceedingly do I respect"*); "James Gambier," www://morethannelson.com/officer/james-gambier-1/ (*unpopular incompetent*); Gruber, *The Howe Brothers and the American Revolution*, 322 (*"old reptile"*); Billias, ed., *George Washington's Generals and Opponents*, 264–65 (*"Crippled and dying"*).

410 **Black Dick, in this most recent campaign:** Clowes, *The Royal Navy*, 3: 410–11; Mahan, *The Major Operations of the Navies in the War of American Independence*, 100 (*"achievement unsurpassed"*); O'Shaughnessy, *The Men Who Lost America*, 331 (*"fit for sea"*); "Navy-hired transports at New York," UK NA, ADM 1/488, f 479 (*forty leased transport vessels*); Naval stores in New York, Aug. 28, 1778, UK NA, ADM 1/488, f 463 (*three hundred watch glasses*); Syrett, *Shipping and the American War, 1775–83*, 218–19 (*squadrons as roughly used*).

410 **In truth, the admiral's heart:** Flavell, *The Howe Dynasty*, 264 (*£100,000 each*); W. Knox to Germain, Oct. 31, 1778, William Knox papers, WLC, box 4 (*rebel sympathizers*); Atkinson, "Brothers in Arms," July 20, 2021, 14 (*"not in fashion"*).

410 **As for Rhode Island, it, too, had fallen:** W. Knox to Germain, Oct. 31, 1778, William Knox papers, WLC, box 4 (*"all our batteries"*); Kipping, *The Hessian View of America, 1776–1783*, 33 (*"Personally I do not see"*).

410 **But for now he and his Hessians:** "Journal of the Hon. Garrison-Regiment von Huyn," HDAR, 102 (*second-floor windows*); Neimeyer, "The British Occupation of Newport, Rhode Island, 1776–1779," 30+ (*"barley broth"*); Popp, *A Hessian Soldier in the American Revolution*, 14 (*"a hard fate"*).

18. A STAR AND A STRIPE FROM THE REBEL FLAG

411 **Whenever General Clinton left the grand house:** Skemp, *William Franklin*, 228 (*supplicant loyalists*); Hatch, *Major John André*, 122 (*handball*); TBAC, 401 (*Nathan Hale*).

411 **"He flies about like an apparition":** Gruber, ed., *John Peebles' American War, 1776–1782*, 222; Sabine, ed., *Historical Memoirs of William Smith*, 2: 78–79 (*"pass my window"*); Silverman, *A Cultural History of the American Revolution*, 371 (*£50 of Crown money*), 374–76 (*"Clinton's Thespians"*); Cunningham, *The Uncertain Revolution*, 167 (*violin*); Brown, "A Note on British Military Theatre in New York at the End of the American Revolution," 177+ (*£187*); Barck, *New York City During the War for Independence*, 93 (*only £140*), 172–74 (*Twenty-one plays*); Dunlap, *History of the American Theatre*, 1: 93–94 (*a few guineas*), 102; Burrows and Wallace, *Gotham*, 247.

412 **New York's population now exceeded thirty thousand:** Burrows and Wallace, *Gotham*, 245; Lodge, *Major André's Journal*, n.p. (*Nova Scotia to Florida*); Barck, *New York City During the War for Independence*, 82 (*ignited in a chandler's shop*); Wertenbaker, *Father Knickerbocker Rebels*, 177–78 (*making things worse*); Ritchie, ed., "A New York Diary of the Revolutionary War," 221+ (*240 barrels*); Ewald, *Diary of the American War*, 143; Kemble, *The Kemble Papers*, 159 (*pedestrians off their feet*); Whinyates, ed., *The Services of Lieut.-Colonel Francis Downman, R.A.*, 72 (*"almost every window"*).

412 **Even such acts of God:** Ewald, *Diary of the American War*, 143; Dunlap, *History of the American Theatre*, 1: 92–93 (*bellowed by criers*); Nolan, "A British Editor Reports the American Revolution," 92+ (*Catherine the Great*); Burgoyne, trans. and ed., *Diaries of Two Ansbach Jaegers*, 50–51; Johnson, *Occupied America*, 143; Rose, *Washington's Spies*, 151 (*rescind the Declaration*); Uhlendorf, trans. and annot., *Revolution in America*, 248 (*retired to his Virginia estates*).

412 **The Yankee alliance with Versailles:** Rose, *Washington's Spies*, 152 (*seventy thousand rosaries* and *king of America*); Van Tyne, *The Loyalists in the American Revolution*, 154 (*hair shirts*), 156 (*dancing masters, and friseurs*); Davidson, *Propaganda and the American Revolution, 1763–1783*, 19–20 (*rum would be banned*).

412 **Clinton had greater worries:** Schecter, *The Battle for New York*, 328 (*d'Estaing's eventual return*); J. Pattison to H. Clinton, Sept. 17, 1778, James Pattison papers, NYHS (*sixty heavy guns*); Onderdonk, *Documents and Letters Intended to Illustrate the Revolutionary Incidents of Queens County*, 81 (*"savage cruelty"*).

413   As he "ruminated with an aching heart": Willcox, ed., *The American Rebellion*, 110; Chopra, *Unnatural Rebellion*, 104, 106 (*took pains*), 118–19 (*"if not sustained"*); Roberts, *The Last King*, 340 (*two-thirds of the British Army*); O'Shaughnessy, *The Men Who Lost America*, 214 (*"all that spirit and sense"*); *Bath* [England] *Chronicle*, Sept. 3, 1778, 2 (*"discourages his comrades"*); Conway, *The British Isles and the War of American Independence*, 26 (*at least nineteen thousand*). The war had claimed thousands of additional German casualties.

413   The losses certainly discouraged Clinton: Barck, *New York City During the War for Independence*, 100 (*229 provision ships*), 102–4 (*flour quadrupled*); "Proceedings of a Board of General Officers of the British Army at New York, 1781," 256 (*£100,000 a month*); Bowler, *Logistics and Failures of the British Army in America, 1775–1783*, 117–19, 123–24 (*risk of capture*); John Robinson to Daniel Wier, Oct. 31, 1778, UK NA, T 64/119, f 21–24 (*number was bitterly disputed*).

413   Food shortages had begun in the spring: Bowler, *Logistics and Failures of the British Army in America, 1775–1783*, 64 (*Quebec and Halifax*), 93 (*six thousand tons of oats*), 105 (*unseasoned wood*), 112–15 (*administrative confusion*), 258 (*at least three months*); Barck, *New York City During the War for Independence*, 105 (*victualing fleet in late August*); Mackesy, *The War for America, 1775–1783*, 223 (*delayed until January*).

414   "We have not at this time": Conway, *The War of American Independence, 1775–1783*, 53 (*"this sort of neglect"*); Kemble, *The Kemble Papers*, 167 (*cut by up to a third*); Daniel Wier to Treasury, n.d., UK NA, T 64/114 (*"We have by no means"*); Bowler, *Logistics and Failures of the British Army in America, 1775–1783*, 34 (*seventy thousand cords*); H. Clinton to Treasury, Aug. 4, 1778, UK NA, T 64/109, f 103 (*seventy-six tons*).

414   Amid such worries, the king's men this fall: Albion and Pope, *Sea Lanes in Wartime*, 39 (*"Seamen of sprit"*); Polf, *Garrison Town*, 40 (Fair American); Desmarais, *America's First Ally*, 80 (*thirty-five prizes*); Patton, *Patriot Pirates*, 45–46 (*speaking trumpet*).

414   Ashore, regulars sprang several ambushes: Israel Putnam to GW, Sept. 28, 1778, *PGW*, 17: 165, 173, 217, 456 (*poorly guarded camp*); Hoock, *Scars of Independence*, 250–63 (*"kill every one of them"*); Stryker, *The Massacre near Old Tappan*, 3–10; Braisted, *Grand Forage 1778*, 112 (*"human misery"*); George Baylor to GW, Oct. 19, 1778, FOL (*"horrid massacre"*).

415   Two weeks later, sixteen British vessels: Lord Stirling to GW, Oct. 7 and 22, 1778, *PGW*, 17: 300n, 532n; Gambier to Sandwich, Oct. 23, 1778, *PP Sandwich*, 2: 324 (*"seminary"*).

415   Prevented by contrary winds from returning: Kemp, *"A Nest of Rebel Pirates,"* 47–50; Kajencki, *Casimir Pulaski*, 64 (*Hungarian, French*), 84–91; Owen, *The Revolutionary Struggle in New Jersey, 1776–1783*, 26; Heston, *South Jersey*, 1: 229–31 (*"only five prisoners"*), 2: 767–68; Murdoch, *Rebellion in America*, 667 (*"Civil wars are unhappily distinguished"*).

415   Yet gratifying as such pinprick attacks: Peckham, ed., *Sources of American Independence*, 2: 290 (*"never put an end"*).

416   On the afternoon of Sunday, November 8: Cunningham, *The Uncertain Revolution*, 167 (*dozen servants*); Campbell, *Journal of an Expedition Against the Rebels*, 4–5 (*£5,000*).

416   "I found about twenty gentlemen": Campbell, *Journal of an Expedition Against the Rebels*, 4–5.

416   The southern campaign, long in gestation: Bellot, *William Knox*, 163–64; Piecuch, *Three Peoples, One King*, 125–27; Campbell, *Journal of an Expedition Against the Rebels*, 7 (*six thousand loyalists*).

416   Colonel Campbell would eventually be honored: "Sir Archibald and Sir James Campbell," https://www.westminster-abbey.org/abbey-commemorations/commemorations/sir-archibald-and-sir-james-campbell; McGeachy, "The American War of Lieutenant Colonel Archibald Campbell," n.p. (*most yarn*); Hagist, *Noble Volunteers*, 111 (*"lands of the rebels"*); *TBAC*, 318; Walcott, *Sir Archibald Campbell of Inverneill*, 13–22, 25 (*into Boston Harbor*).

416   His first months as a prisoner of war: Walcott, *Sir Archibald Campbell of Inverneill*, 25 (*shoemaker and a piper* and *"principles of retaliation"*); W. Howe to GW, Feb. 27, 1777, *PGW*, 8: 453n (*"loathsome black hole"*).

417   Now he was to win back at least part: J. Pattison to Lord Townshend, Dec. 18, 1778, James Pattison papers, NYHS (*stranding much of his artillery*); Coleman, *The American Revolution*

in Georgia, 1763–1789, 121 (*damaging several other vessels*); Campbell, *Journal of an Expedition Against the Rebels*, 10–11 (*then for a second week*), 31 (*no reliable maps* and *"roads, swamps, or creeks"*), 37 (*"cobblers and blacksmiths"*). Campbell paid himself a brigadier's salary for five months, but after an audit in 1809 his estate was required to repay the money (Campbell, *Journal of an Expedition Against the Rebels*, 103n).

417 **Day after day, Clinton waited in vain:** GW to R. H. Lee, Sept. 23, 1778, FOL fn (*immensely complex*); Willis, *The Struggle for Sea Power*, 256 (*barely a thousand*); Mackesy, *The War for America, 1775–1783*, 229n, 526 (*more than one in ten*); O'Shaughnessy, *The Men Who Lost America*, 194 (*only eighteen survived to return home*); Frey, *The British Soldier in America*, 37.

418 **Also sailing from New York was Admiral Byron's:** GW to H. Gates, Oct. 24, 1778, FOL; GW to Charles Scott, Oct. 27, 1778 (*bottled up in Boston*); Mackenzie, *Diary of Frederick Mackenzie*, 1: 418, 432; Clowes, *The Royal Navy*, 428–29 (*Neither expedition was aware*); Willis, *The Struggle for Sea Power*, 256 (*eight thousand troops*); Carrington, *The British West Indies During the American Revolution*, 98 (*swarmed onto Dominica*); James, *The British Navy in Adversity*, 113 (*164 cannons and a fine anchorage*).

418 **As instructed by London, Clinton dispatched:** H. Clinton to Germain, Oct. 8, 1778, *DAR*, 15: 209 (*Pensacola and St. Augustine* and *seven hundred to bolster Halifax*); Willcox, ed., *The American Rebellion*, 111 (*Bermuda and the Bahamas*). The two Floridas were administratively divided at the Apalachicola River.

418 **"Piecemeal reduction of separate colonies":** *PNG*, 4: 3–4 (*"single point of effort"*); Rogers et al., eds., *The West Point History of the American Revolution*, 147 (*Four-fifths of colonial exports*); Frey, *Water from the Rock*, 68–69 (*eleven plantations*), 79–80 (*tobacco, rice, indigo*); Miller and Kirkland, "A Backcountry Loyalist Plan to Retake Georgia and the Carolinas, 1778," 207+ (*timber, hemp* and *"the poor slaves"*); "Plan for Carrying on the War in America," n.d., William Knox papers, WLC, box 9 (*to the Chesapeake*); Crow and Tise, *The Southern Experience in the American Revolution*, 159 (*loyalists, who would be armed*); Stan Deaton, "James Wright (1716–1785)," *New Georgia Encyclopedia*, https://www.georgiaencyclopedia .org/.

418 **At last, after a sixteen-day delay:** Campbell, *Journal of an Expedition Against the Rebels*, 10; Coleman, *The American Revolution in Georgia, 1763–1789*, 121 (*November 27*); Calhoon, *The Loyalists in Revolutionary America, 1760–1781*, 379 (*"both firmness and diffidence"*).

419 **Yet having forfeited ten thousand troops:** H. Clinton to Germain, Oct. 8, 1778, *DAR*, 15: 209 (*"very nerves"* and *"mortifying command of it"*); Conway, *The War of American Independence, 1775–1783*, 108 (*"fatal to the hopes"*); Willcox, ed., *The American Rebellion*, 106–7 (*"strict defensive"*), 112 (*"imbecility"*); Willcox, "British Strategy in America, 1778," 97+ (*"see such an army dissolve"*); O'Shaughnessy, *The Men Who Lost America*, 223 (*"serious truths"*); Stuart-Wortley, ed., *A Prime Minister and His Son*, 133 (*"perplexed beyond words"*).

419 **Clinton would never match the Howes:** Mackesy, *The War for America, 1775–1783*, 222 (*"shackled as I am"*); Schecter, *The Battle for New York*, 329 (*"despised and detested"*); Stuart-Wortley, ed., *A Prime Minister and His Son*, 139 (*"hardly one general officer"*).

419 **Clinton was among them:** Willcox, *Portrait of a General*, 261 (*renewed petition*); H. Clinton to Germain, Oct. 8, 1778, WBW (*"gracious permission"*); Willcox, ed., *The American Rebellion*, 106–7 (*"weight and responsibility"*), 116 (*"undeserved censure"*); Duncan Drummond to H. Clinton, Dec. 17, 1778, WBW (*Newcastle*).

419 **Germain replied evenly on December 3:** Germain to H. Clinton, Dec. 12, 1778, WBW (*"cannot at present comply"*); Willcox, ed., *The American Rebellion*, 107 (*similar entreaties*); Duncan Drummond to H. Clinton, Dec. 5, 1778, WBW (*"Good God"*).

420 **Savannah hardly seemed a prize worthy:** Bain, ed., "The Siege of Charleston," 478+ (*"most wretched"*); Lawrence, *Storm over Savannah*, 2 (*silkworm cocoons*); Hayes, ed., *A Gentleman of Fortune*, 2: 164n; Pancake, *This Destructive War*, 30 (*forty thousand souls*).

420 **American success against Britain in the South:** Dorney, "A Demographic View of the Georgia Continental Line and Militia," *JAR*, Feb. 23, 2022 (*Fewer than fifteen hundred*); Piecuch, *Three Peoples, One King*, 96, 117 (*flinging his books*).

420 **South Carolina's six Continental regiments:** Edgar, *Partisans & Redcoats*, 42–43 (*two*

months); Fraser, "Reflections of 'Democracy' in Revolutionary South Carolina," 202+ (*"Vagrant Act"* and *cashmere waistcoats* and *250 of 316 soldiers*); Pinckney and Cross, "Letters of Thomas Pinckney, 1775–1780," 19+.

421 **Congress had given command of the Southern Department:** Lawrence, "General Robert Howe and the British Capture of Savannah in 1778," 303+ (*"exquisite raillery"*); Lumpkin, *From Savannah to Yorktown*, 27 (*five hundred of Howe's troops*); Cox, *A Proper Sense of Honor*, 112 (*execute seven deserters*); Wilson, *The Southern Strategy*, 67 (*"woman-eater"*), 69 (*Gadsden's ear*).

421 **Congress had agreed to a recall:** Wilson, *The Southern Strategy*, 69–71 (*yet to arrive*); Campbell, *Journal of an Expedition Against the Rebels*, 16 (*seven fathoms*).

421 **Harrowing winter weather with squalls:** J. J. Matthaeus to "your most serene highness," Jan. 16, 1779, HDAR, Von Trümbach Regiment corr., 11–12 (*waterspouts*); Coleman, *The American Revolution in Georgia, 1763–1789*, 121; Pettengill, trans., *Letters from America, 1776–1779*, 199–200 (*"We had such violent storms"*); Uhlendorf, trans. and ed., *The Siege of Charleston*, 155 (*"Tigers, wolves, and bears"*).

421 **A white flag with a red cross:** Campbell, *Journal of an Expedition Against the Rebels*, 18 (*white flag with a red cross* and *sixty musket rounds*); Coleman, *The American Revolution in Georgia, 1763–1789*, 121 (*two or three to one*); Mary Granger, ed., "Savannah River Plantations," Georgia Historical Society (1947): 46.

422 **At a hundred yards' distance:** Campbell, *Journal of an Expedition Against the Rebels*, 23 (*"back doors"*), 24 (*"insulting language"*).

422 **General Howe recognized that he was overmatched:** Lawrence, "General Robert Howe and the British Capture of Savannah in 1778," 303+ (*floodgates* and *just 650*); Moultrie, *Memoirs of the American Revolution*, 1: 253 (*"most ill-advised"*).

422 **As Campbell could see after clambering:** Martin and Harris, *Savannah 1779*, 37–44 (*Quamino Dolly*); Lawrence, *Storm over Savannah*, 4 (*Quash*); Campbell, *Journal of an Expedition Against the Rebels*, 26–28 (*"upon the enemy's right"*); Wilson, *The Southern Strategy*, 73–76.

423 **Not until he heard the crackle of musketry:** Lawrence, "General Robert Howe and the British Capture of Savannah in 1778," 303+ (*"hopping over"*); Campbell, *Journal of an Expedition Against the Rebels*, 26–28 (*"rapid beyond conception"*); Martin and Harris, *Savannah 1779*, 40.

423 **A Highland company seized fortifications:** Campbell, *Journal of an Expedition Against the Rebels*, 27–28 (*lusty cheers*); Lawrence, "General Robert Howe and the British Capture of Savannah in 1778," 303+ (*"safe retreat," "victims' entrails,"* and *"ripped open feather beds"*).

423 **"The capital of Georgia fell into my hands":** Campbell, *Journal of an Expedition Against the Rebels*, 28 (*"before it was dark"*).

423 **"We have lost the day":** Lawrence, "General Robert Howe and the British Capture of Savannah in 1778," 303+ (*"highest honor"*).

424 **Some victors doubted Savannah's value:** Crary, ed., *The Price of Loyalty*, 273 (*"people here are sallow"*); Piecuch, *Three Peoples, One King*, 134 (*"well-disposed inhabitants"*); Pettengill, trans., *Letters from America, 1776–1779*, 204 (*green riding vests*); Campbell, *Journal of an Expedition Against the Rebels*, 34 (*"against rebellion"*), 37–40 (*ten-guinea reward*).

424 **Word of Savannah's capture enthralled London:** Campbell, *Journal of an Expedition Against the Rebels*, 109n (*ordered Governor Wright*); Piecuch, *Three Peoples, One King*, 135 (*pension payments would stop*); Dull, *The French Navy and American Independence*, 124 (*welcome news from the Indian Ocean*).

424 **Better still, the British expedition from New York:** Clowes, *The Royal Navy*, 429 (*west coast of St. Lucia*); Charles Stuart to Capt. Boyne, Jan. 8–Feb. 3, 1779, PP Sandwich, 2: 344–45 (*ten regiments*); James, *The British Navy in Adversity*, 118–19 (*collected nine thousand*); Miller, *Sea of Glory*, 392–94.

424 **Outnumbered almost two to one in capital ships:** James, *The British Navy in Adversity*, 118–19 (*surging in three columns*); Miller, *Sea of Glory*, 392–94 (*four hundred dead*); Conway, *The War of American Independence, 1775–1783*, 135–36 (*"Bunker Hill"*).

425 **Bloated French corpses carpeted:** Graham, *The Royal Navy in the War of American Independence*, 12 (*twenty-one capital ships*); Dull, *The French Navy and American Independence*, 159;

PP *Sandwich*, 1: 326 (*rest of the war*); Murray, *Letters from America, 1773 to 1780*, 63 (*"No man would inhabit"*); Miller, *Sea of Glory*, 394 (*eighteen hundred*).

425   **As for d'Estaing:** James, *The British Navy in Adversity*, 118–19 (*"From failure to failure"*).

425   **At dawn on January 24, Colonel Campbell gave the nod:** Pancake, *This Destructive War*, 32–33 (*a thousand of his liberators*); Ferling, *Winning Independence*, 112 (*Old Bullet Head*); Piecuch, *Three Peoples, One King*, 134–35 (*south Georgia wilderness*); Campbell, *Journal of an Expedition Against the Rebels*, 48 (*Six stout wagons*), 102n (*"too old & inactive"*).

425   **If not precisely galloping:** Piecuch, *Three Peoples, One King*, 137–38 (*fourteen hundred loyalists*); Campbell, *Journal of an Expedition Against the Rebels*, 54 (*"straggling houses"*), 41–42 (*"first British officer"*). Several versions of this boast exist (O'Shaughnessy, *The Men Who Lost America*, 223, and Mackesy, *The War for America, 1775–1783*, 234).

426   **Indeed he had. Georgia was no longer a state:** Edgar, *Partisans & Redcoats*, 44 (*royal colony*); Bragg, *Crescent Moon over Carolina*, 106–7 (*by a year*).

426   **Yet the putative removal of stripe and star:** Crow and Tise, *The Southern Experience in the American Revolution*, 181 (*"mostly crackers"*); Piecuch, *Three Peoples, One King*, 136 (*"no assurances"*), 139 (*No Creek Indian allies*).

426   **With supplies dwindling:** Pancake, *This Destructive War*, 33 (*"deaf to reason"*); Davis, "Battle of Kettle Creek," *New Georgia Encyclopedia*, https://www.georgiaencyclopedia.org/articles/history-archaeology/battle-of-kettle-creek/; Davis and Thomas, "Kettle Creek," Georgia Department of Natural Resources, 36–37 (*drums beating*).

427   **Boyd, on his deathbed Sunday evening:** Davis and Thomas, "Kettle Creek," Georgia Department of Natural Resources, 43 (*"No damned rebel"*); Martin and Harris, *Savannah 1779*, 51; Pancake, *This Destructive War*, 33; "Kettle Creek Battlefield," inventory nomination form, National Register of Historic Places, 1975; Davis and Thomas, "Kettle Creek," Georgia Department of Natural Resources, 39 (*six hundred horses*); Piecuch, *Three Peoples, One King*, 139 (*"severest check"*).

427   **This minor skirmish in the hinterland foretold:** Piecuch, *Three Peoples, One King*, 140 (*Seven loyalist prisoners*); Davis, "The Loyalist Trials at Ninety Six in 1779," 172+ (*Sheriff William Moore*); Lambert, *South Carolina Loyalists in the American Revolution*, 84 (*sign their own death warrants*).

427   **British officials threatened retaliation:** Lambert, *South Carolina Loyalists in the American Revolution*, 84 (*five loyalists were hanged at Ninety Six*); Davis, "The Loyalist Trials at Ninety Six in 1779," 172+ (*as late as 1787*). Different accounts give different figures for the number executed (Martin and Harris, *Savannah 1779*, 51).

427   **If Georgia was once again a royal colony:** Piecuch, *Three Peoples, One King*, 140 (*switched allegiance again*); Campbell, *Journal of an Expedition Against the Rebels*, 74 (*"nothing to fear"*), 79 (*kiss the royal hand*).

19. THE UNCERTAINTY OF HUMAN PROSPECTS

428   **The curiously named Point No Point Road:** AH and Evan Edwards, "Account of a Duel," Dec. 24, 1778, FOL.

428   **At least seven duels had been fought:** Massey, *John Laurens and the American Revolution*, 128–29; Gérard de Rayneval to Vergennes, Jan. 17, 1779, in Durand, ed., *New Materials for the History of the American Revolution*, 187 (*"rage for dueling"*); Article XI, JLB, DDD (*"a challenge"*); Steuben to C. Lee, Dec. 2, 1778, in Kirkland, ed., *Letters on the American Revolution*, 2: 57; Brumwell, *George Washington*, 345 (*Lee*); GW, general orders, Dec. 23, 1778, *PGW*, 18: 491n (*"grossest and most opprobrious"*).

428   **Lee arrived early at the four-mile stone:** Fleming, "The 'Military Crimes' of Charles Lee," 12+ (*"almost mobbed"*); GW to Joseph Reed, Dec. 12, 1778, FOL (*"most barefacedly"*); Massey, *John Laurens and the American Revolution*, 125–26 (*fall off his horse*).

429   **Laurens arrived late with his own second:** Graydon, *Memoirs of His Own Time*, 323; AH and Evan Edwards, "Account of a Duel," Dec. 24, 1778, FOL; Patterson, *Knight Errant of Liberty*, 242 (*"You may fire at me"*).

429   **The ball had grazed his right side:** Graydon, *Memoirs of His Own Time*, 324 (*"effusion of*

blood"); "Narrative of a Duel Between General Lee and Colonel Laurens," *LP*, 3: 285 (*"motives of personal enmity"*); "Account of a Duel Between Major General Charles Lee and Lieutenant Colonel John Laurens," AH, FOL, Dec. 24, 1778 (*"might perhaps do so again"*).

429 **With this meandering colloquy:** Simms, ed., *The Army Correspondence of Colonel John Laurens*, 39 (*"How handsomely"*); "General Charles Lee House, 'Prato Rio,'" National Register of Historic Places; Fleming, "The 'Military Crimes' of Charles Lee," 12+ (*"hoe tobacco"*); Billias, ed., *George Washington's Generals and Opponents*, 46 (*"pilgrim"*); Papas, *Renegade Revolutionary*, 283 (*borrow money*).

429 **"From an income of near £1,000":** Patterson, *Knight Errant of Liberty*, 252 (*"absolute beggary"*), 254 (*"bladder of emptiness"*); Alden, *General Charles Lee*, 288 (*dismissed from the army*), 297 (*"charlatan"*).

430 **The final collapse of the man:** Patterson, *Knight Errant of Liberty*, 279 (*Sign of the Conestoga*); Mazzagetti, *Charles Lee*, 207 (*"so much bad company"*); Patterson, *Knight Errant of Liberty*, 279–80 (*"take heed to my ways"*); Alden, *General Charles Lee*, 299 (*southwest door*).

430 **"I can never mention General Lee":** Quincy, *The Journals of Major Samuel Shaw*, 56.

430 **Summoned by Congress for consultations:** GW, general orders, Dec. 23, 1778, *PGW*, 18: 491n; Fraser, *The Washingtons*, 209 (*Chestnut Street house*); Schechter, *The Battle for New York*, 321 (*half dozen camps*); Huggins, *Washington's War, 1779*, 15 (*arrayed in an arc*); GW to John Augustine Washington, Nov. 26, 1778, FOL (*"full employment"*).

431 **With the British long gone:** Evans, *Weathering the Storm*, 188, 236–37 (*Delft fireplace tiles*); Silverman, *A Cultural History of the American Revolution*, 367; Sargent, *The Life and Career of Major John André*, 121; "Revolutionary War Forfeited Estates, 1779," Pennsylvania Historical & Museum Commission, http://www.phmc.state.pa.us/portal/communities/documents/1776-1865/revolutionary-war-forfeited-estates.html (*Galloway's house*); Mishoff, "Business in Philadelphia During the British Occupation, 1777–1778," 165+; *Pennsylvania Packet*, July 28, 1778, 1 (*Bengal and durant*), Feb. 4, 1779, 1 (*"eradicates the scurvy"*).

431 **Four newspapers soon vied:** Stinchcombe, *The American Revolution and the French Alliance*, 113 (*rights-of-man champion*), 119–24 (*"Silver-Tongue Sam"*).

431 **Yet prosperity was slow to return:** Doerflinger, *A Vigorous Spirit of Enterprise*, 204 (*closer to monthly*); Albion and Pope, *Sea Lanes in Wartime*, 64 (*"exceeding scarce"*).

431 **The city of brotherly love:** Mishoff, "Business in Philadelphia During the British Occupation, 1777–1778," 165+ (*"industrious women"*); Blanco, "American Army Hospitals in Pennsylvania During the Revolutionary War," 347+; Nash, *First City*, 97–98 (*two thousand shirts*); Smith, *Manufacturing Independence*, 83–84 (*four million*), 87 (*Catherine Friend*); Toogood, "Independence Mall, the Eighteenth Century Development," NPS, 21–25.

432 **After the British evacuation:** Dorwart, *Invasion and Insurrection*, 151–52 (*"suspicious character"*); Moore, *The Diary of the American Revolution*, 365 (*"Who hold a traitorous"*).

432 **The state's Supreme Executive Council:** Langston, "'A Fickle and Confused Multitude,'" diss., 162 (*more than four hundred*); Rosswurm, *Arms, Country, and Class*, 154 (*"aided and assisted"*); Sullivan, *The Disaffected*, 207–8 (*declined to indict*); Heidler and Heidler, eds., *Daily Lives of Civilians in Wartime Early America*, 37 (*abandoning their families*).

432 **But beginning in September of this year:** Larson, *The Trials of Allegiance*, 223 (*acquitted nineteen*); Sullivan, *The Disaffected*, 216 (*seven thousand Philadelphians*); Walker, "Life of Margaret Shippen, Wife of Benedict Arnold," 257+ (*Continental officers*); Brown, *The Good Americans*, 139 (*"behavior on the gallows"*); Crane, ed., *The Diary of Elizabeth Drinker*, 82 (*"body is brought home"*); Balch, ed., *The Examination of Joseph Galloway, Esq.*, 78n (*wife and ten children* and *four thousand mourners*).

432 **This was Washington's fourth winter:** Royster, *A Revolutionary People at War*, 257 (*celebrations of his birthday*); Ellis, *The Cause*, 164–65 (*"father of the country"*); GW to Benjamin Harrison, Dec. 18–30, 1778, *PGW*, 18: 447n (*"geldings"*); Freeman, *George Washington: A Biography*, 91–92 (*parade of visitors*); GW, general orders, Dec. 28, 1778, *PGW*, 18: 519n (*"illustrious brother"*); Lord Stirling to GW, Dec. 30, 1778, *PGW*, 18: 539n (*Gérard's residence*); GW, general orders, Jan. 6, 1779, *PGW*, 18: 583n (*anniversary*).

433 **The Supreme Executive Council requested:** GW to Pennsylvania General Assembly, Jan. 20, 1779, *PGW*, 19: 44n (*"may excite others"*); Silverman, *A Cultural History of the American Revolution*, 361 (*nineteen oil copies*); Richardson et al., *Charles Willson Peale and His World*, 57–59 (*stars on their epaulets* and *Gérard bought one*).

433 **That countenance was a mask:** NG to Alexander McDougall, Nov. 8, 1778, *PNG*, 3: 48; Ferling, *Almost a Miracle*, 347 (*only a dozen*); GW to George Mason, Mar. 27, 1779, FOL (*"Where are our men"*); GW to Benjamin Harrison, Dec. 18–30, 1778, *PGW*, 18: 447 (*"distressed, ruinous"*).

433 **Congress seemed petty and split:** Freeman, *George Washington: A Biography*, 83 (*"act, promote, encourage"*); Peckham, ed., *The Toll of Independence*, 130 (*155 naval and military engagements*); Mackesy, *The War for America, 1775-1783*, 69 (*more valuable St. Lucia*).

434 **As he had at Valley Forge:** *LAAR*, 2: 206–7n (*another proposal to invade Canada*); Committee for Foreign Affairs to GW, Oct. 27, 1778, FOL (*eight-page scheme*); GW to Jacob Bayley, Sept. 26, 1778, FOL (*snowshoes*); Jacob Bayley to GW, Nov. 5, 1778, *PGW*, 18: 45 (*moose skins*); GW to Henry Laurens, Nov. 11, 1778, FOL (*"doubtful and precarious"*); Lanctôt, *Canada & the American Revolution, 1774-1783*, 178 (*Versailles had renounced*); GW to Henry Laurens, Nov. 14, 1778, FOL (*"No nation is to be trusted"*); Unger, *Lafayette*, 89–91; Franklin et al. to Vergennes, Jan. 1, 1779, in Wharton, *The Revolutionary Diplomatic Correspondence of the United States*, 3: 3–5; Lafayette to GW, Jan. 11, 1779, *PGW*, 18: 615 (*"ever be dear"*).

434 **His Excellency now suggested to Congress:** Huggins, *Washington's War, 1779*, 18–19 (*three possible courses*); Freeman, *George Washington: A Biography*, 93 (*"military operations"*).

434 **Yet Congress and the states seemed incapable:** Articles of Confederation, U.S. National Archives, https://www.archives.gov/milestone-documents/articles-of-confederation; Alden, *The American Revolution*, 174–76; Lepore, *These Truths*, 114; Countryman, *The American Revolution*, 179–80; Werther, "The Articles of Confederation and Western Expansion," *JAR*, June 14, 2022 (*230 million acres*); Selby, *The Revolution in Virginia, 1775-1783*, 142 (*claims made by seven*). Maryland would not ratify the articles until March 1781.

435 **The war now cost the country:** Ferguson, *The Power of the Purse*, 28–30 (*more than $1 million a week*); Grubb, *The Continental Dollar*, 15, 30–31, 246; Newman, *The Early Paper Money of America*, 15 (*"rag money"*); Bolles, *The Financial History of the United States from 1774 to 1789*, 69–70 (*$64 million*); Carp, *To Starve the Army at Pleasure*, 104; Bullock, *The Finances of the United States from 1775 to 1789*, 129–30 (*worth twelve cents*); Newman, *The Early Paper Money of America*, 14 (*lack of small change*); Thomas Jefferson to George Hammond, May 29, 1792, FOL (*"without seeing a single coin"*).

435 **"Our money will soon be as useless":** Abigail Adams to JA, Sept. 10, 1777, FOL; Ferguson, *The Power of the Purse*, 60–61 (*promissory notes*); Carp, *To Starve the Army at Pleasure*, 106 (*150 shillings in May 1779*); Huntington, *Letters Written by Ebenezer Huntington During the American Revolution*, 77–78 (*"scarcely support me"*); McBurney, "Mutiny!," 47+ (*"cannot put up with such treatment"*).

435 **A British campaign of economic warfare:** Scheer and Rankin, *Rebels and Redcoats*, 303 (*better paper*); *Pennsylvania Packet*, July 22, 1777, 3 (*finer engraving*); Scott, *Counterfeiting in Colonial America*, 254–55; Scott, "A British Counterfeiting Press in New York Harbor, 1776," 117+; Cumming and Rankin, *The Fate of a Nation*, 229 (*"Philadelpkia"*); Brown, *The Good Americans*, 88 (*"hope to see him hanged"*); Scott, "New Hampshire Tory Counterfeiters Operating from New York City," 31+.

436 **"Is there anything doing":** GW to John Jay, Apr. 23, 1779, FOL; Rosswurm, *Arms, Country, and Class*, 168 (*254 percent*), 172; Foner, *Tom Paine and Revolutionary America*, 161 (*1,300 percent*); McBurney, "Mutiny!," 47+ (*dozen eggs*); Hoffman and Albert, eds., *Arms and Independence*, 157 (*off the market*); Johnson, "The Administration of the American Commissariat," diss., 160; GW to Lund Washington, May 29, 1779, FOL (*"speculators, monopolizers"*); Carp, *To Starve the Army at Pleasure*, 70 (*"Intirely out of money"*).

436 **Quartermaster General Greene, whose expenditures:** NG to John Jay, Feb. 15, 1779, *PNG*, 3: 256n (*$32 million* and *1 percent commission*); "Estimate of Teams Required," *PNG*, 3: 19–22

(*840 wagons*); Risch, *Supplying Washington's Army*, 112 (*Connecticut to Virginia*), 113 (*scythes*); Golway, *Washington's General*, 198 (*salary of £3,000*); NG to Griffin Greene, Mar. 4, 1779, *PNG*, 3: 329 (*"murmuring age"*).

436 **Infuriating shortages plagued the army:** GW to Board of War, Oct. 18, 1778, FOL (*blankets*); Risch, *Supplying Washington's Army*, 289, 293–96; GW to B. Lincoln, July 30, 1779, FOL (*"profound sleep"*); Jeremiah Wadsworth to NG, Jan. 2, 1779, *PNG*, 3: 134 (*"grasshoppers"*).

437 **Thanks to French and New England clothing merchants:** GW to Congress, Jan. 23, 1779, *PGW*, 19: 55 (*"fixing upon thirteen colors"*); GW to George Measam, Oct. 28, 1778, FOL (*blue coats*); Risch, *Supplying Washington's Army*, 295–96 (*Only seven thousand pairs*); Rees, "'A Quantity of Public Leather . . . Made Up into Shoes,'" n.p. (*former shoemakers*); GW to George Measam, Oct. 14, 1778, FOL (*limited leather supplies*).

437 **Almost as worrisome as the precipitous decline:** Freeman, *George Washington: A Biography*, 12 (*half-pay*); GW to Congress, *PGW*, 19: 39 (*"cannot support themselves"*); GW to Henry Miller, Dec. 18, 1778, *PGW*, 18: 454 (*"I always part reluctantly"*); John Glover to GW, Jan. 28, 1779, FOL (*"my little flock"*); Upham, *Memoirs of General John Glover of Marblehead*, 36 (*furlough*); Billias, *General John Glover and His Marblehead Mariners*, 178.

437 **More than four thousand enlistments would expire:** Freeman, *George Washington: A Biography*, 81; Pierce, Jr., to GW, Jan. 21, 1779, *PGW*, 19: 49–50 (*not been paid since September*); Tacyn, "'To the End': The First Maryland Regiment and the American Revolution," diss., 204–5 (*just six*); GW to Congress, Jan. 29, 1778, FOL (*"pretty well drained"*).

438 **Congress agreed, and in February asked:** Heidler and Heidler, eds., *Daily Lives of Civilians in Wartime Early America*, 40 (*drafting militiamen*); Higginbotham, *The War of American Independence*, 309 (*exempt from military service*); Kranish, *Flight from Monticello*, 127 (*more than three slaves*).

438 **In fact, no state disappointed Washington more:** Selby, *The Revolution in Virginia, 1775–1783*, 131 (*one-fifth to one-third*), 136 (*"violence and riotous behavior"*); Bushman, *The American Farmer in the Eighteenth Century*, 233–34 (*healthy young slave*); Van Buskirk, *Standing in Their Own Light*, 64; Bolton, *The Private Soldier Under Washington*, 60–61; Heidler and Heidler, eds., *Daily Lives of Civilians in Wartime Early America*, 42 (*half of Virginia's counties*); McDonnell, *The Politics of War*, 261, 337 (*apprentices, indentured servants*); Kranish, *Flight from Monticello*, 127 (*"last of all oppressions"* and *slaves who served as substitutes*).

438 **"A stupor seems to pervade":** GW to John Augustine Washington, May 12, 1779, *PGW*, 20: 460–62.

438 **Inspector General von Steuben certainly had:** Royster, *A Revolutionary People at War*, 220 (*"rhapsody"*); Sculley, *Contest for Liberty*, 37 (*private to colonel*).

439 **Washington spent two weeks reading and editing:** Lockhart, *The Drillmaster of Valley Forge*, 205 (*shortages of paper and ink*); Wright, *The Continental Army*, 142; Kapp, *The Life of Frederick William von Steuben*, 217 (*copperplate printer*), 219 (*gold leaf*); *Regulations for the Order and Discipline of the Troops of the United States*, www.AmericanRevolutionInstitute.org (*botched first set* and *War of 1812* and Pennsylvania Magazine); Clary and Whitehorne, *The Inspectors General of the United States Army, 1777–1903*, 49 (*seventy-five editions*); Pettengill, trans., *Letters from America, 1776–1779*, 245 (*"What a beautiful"*).

439 **Not everyone. Although pleased with Steuben's work:** GW to R. H. Lee, Sept. 23, 1778, FOL (*"designs of the enemy"*); Stirling to GW, Oct. 8, 1778, FOL (*linen clothing*); GW to Joseph Reed, Dec. 12, 1778, *PGW*, 18: 396 (*"the Knight"*); GW to H. Laurens, Oct. 3, 1778, FOL.

439 **Since taking command in 1775:** Hagist, "How to Be a Revolutionary War Spy Master," *JAR*, Apr. 12, 2018 (*"employed on every occasion"*); Fitzpatrick, ed., *George Washington's Accounts of Expenses*, 43 (*paid $238*); Israel Shreve to GW, May 26, 1779, *PGW*, 20: 637n; GW to William Maxwell, May 6, 1779, *PGW*, 20: 349n (*"rum and whiskey"*); John Jay to GW, May 4, 1779, *PGW*, 20: 320.

440 **Several subordinate Continental generals:** editorial note, GW espionage operations, *PGW*, 22: 42–45; Tallmadge, *Memoir of Colonel Benjamin Tallmadge*, 8 (*admitted to Yale*); Weber, *Masked Dispatches*, 29–30; Rose, *Washington's Spies*, 43 (*British prison ship*), 48, 71–72.

440 **Tallmadge adopted the nom de guerre:** GW to Benjamin Tallmadge, Mar. 21, 1779, *PGW*, 19: 561–63n; Bleyer, "George Washington's Culper Ring," *JAR*, June 3, 2021; Schellhammer, "Abraham Woodhull: The Spy Named Samuel Culper," *JAR*, May 19, 2014; Bakeless, *Turncoats, Traitors and Heroes*, 228 (*philippic for the* Gazette); Rose, *Washington's Spies*, 75 (*Culpeper*), 161 (*"train of clerks and deputy clerks"*).

440 **Tallmadge devised a code:** Tallmadge to GW, July 25, 1779 (*seven hundred common words*); Rose, *Washington's Spies*, 107–10 (*"stain"*), 124 (Entick's Spelling Dictionary); John Jay to GW, Nov. 19, 1778, *PGW*, 18: 209n (*"medicine"*); Pennypacker, *General Washington's Spies on Long Island and in New York*, 31–36, 51–52 (*"counterpart"*), 58–59 (*"paper of a good quality"*).

441 **Washington, Tallmadge, and their field operatives would exchange:** Bleyer, "George Washington's Culper Ring," *JAR*, June 3, 2021 (*nearly two hundred missives*); Pennypacker, *General Washington's Spies on Long Island and in New York*, 63–64, 68–69, 72–73 (*"intelligent, clear, and satisfactory"*); GW, enclosure, Samuel Culper to Benjamin Tallmadge, Jan. 22, 1779, *PGW*, 19: 101–2n (*sailing schedules*); Rose, *Washington's Spies*, 167 (*sometimes arrived too late*); Schellhammer, "Abraham Woodhull: The Spy Named Samuel Culper," *JAR*, May 19, 2014 (*"daily fear"*).

441 **Washington had arrived in Philadelphia:** Shields and Teute, "The Meschianza: Sum of All Fêtes," 185+ (*"Cupid"*); Brandt, *The Man in the Mirror*, 155 (*"moderate thinking man"*); Malcolm, *The Tragedy of Benedict Arnold*, 248 (*"We were all in love"*).

441 **Arnold, a thirty-seven-year-old widower:** Thompson, *Benedict Arnold in Philadelphia*, 58 (*roses and jonquils*); Brandt, *The Man in the Mirror*, 156–57 (*unsuccessful infatuation*); GW to Benedict Arnold, Mar. 28, 1780, FOL fn (*"Your charms"*); Malcolm, *The Tragedy of Benedict Arnold*, 249 (*"My public character"*); Jacob and Case, *Treacherous Beauty*, 85 (*engaged*).

442 **Washington was even more surprised:** Irving, "The Streets of Philadelphia," 7+ (*suspected collaborators*); Martin, *Benedict Arnold, Revolutionary Hero*, 427; Siebert, *The Loyalists of Philadelphia*, 69 (*"lenity"*); Randall, *Benedict Arnold*, 437 (*"soul of Cromwell"*); BA, table expenses, Apr. 1, 1779, APS, Feinstone Coll., #1818 (*£5,602*); BA to GW, Mar. 19, 1779, FOL.

442 **A week later Reed's board brought eight charges:** Irving, "The Streets of Philadelphia," 7+ (*handbill*); Philbrick, *Valiant Ambition*, 231–33; Pownall and Almon, *The Remembrancer*, 349–51 (*"faithful subjects"*); John Cadwalader to NG, Dec. 5, 1778, *PNG*, 3: 103 (*"charges too absurd"*); Benedict Arnold to GW, Apr. 18, 1779, *PGW*, 20: 112n (*largely exonerated*); Randall, *Benedict Arnold*, 443 (*block assistance*); Brumwell, *Turncoat*, 150 (*sordid tussle*).

442 **"I am heartily tired":** Martin, *Benedict Arnold, Revolutionary Hero*, 428; BA to GW, Mar. 19, 1779, FOL (*"health and wounds"*); JA, *Diary and Autobiography*, Sept. 25, 1775, FOL (*"most elegant seat"*); Lea, *A Hero and a Spy*, 324; Brandt, *The Man in the Mirror*, 176 (*drawing room*). Different figures are given for the Mount Pleasant purchase price (Jacob and Case, *Treacherous Beauty*, 89; Brandt, *The Man in the Mirror*, 173; Thompson, *Benedict Arnold in Philadelphia*, 82–83; Philbrick, *Valiant Ambition*, 234–35).

443 **Eighty-one generals would serve under Washington:** "George Washington & His Generals," SOC exhibition, Feb. 2009–Jan. 2010; BA to GW, Apr. 18, 1779, *PGW*, 20: 112 (*"Every officer in the army"*); BA to GW, May 5, 1779, *PGW*, 20: 327 (*"thinks me a criminal"*).

443 **"Peace and retirement are my ultimate":** GW to Joseph Reed, Dec. 12, 1778, FOL; Freeman, *George Washington: A Biography*, 94 (*depressed and exasperated*); GW, general orders, Feb. 6, 1779, *PGW*, 19: 134–35n (*house near the Raritan*).

443 **He restocked his camp equipment:** GW, general orders, Sept. 12, 1778, *PGW*, 16: 578n (*copper urinal*); GW to John Cox, Jr., Oct. 4, 1778, FOL (*pocket telescope*); John Mitchell to GW, Nov. 3, 1778, *PGW*, 18: 34 (*bearskin saddle cover*); GW to John Mitchell, Feb. 17, 1779, *PGW*, 19: 222–23n (*his hats*); John Grizzage Frazer to GW, Dec. 20, 1778, *PGW*, 18: 473 (*"best Bordeaux"*).

444 **Another dreary winter passed slowly:** Baldwin, *The Revolutionary Journal of Col. Jeduthan Baldwin, 1775–1778*, Jan. 5, 1779, 142 (*"My horse died"*); GW, general orders, Apr. 14, 1779, *PGW*, 20: 56 (*"playing ball"*); Thayer, *Nathanael Greene*, 263 (*venison*).

444 **On February 18, General Knox organized:** Greene, *The Life of Nathanael Greene*, 2: 162

(*French alliance*); GW to William Maxwell, Feb. 16, 1779, *PGW*, 19: 211–14n (*"rising empire"*); Drake, *Life and Correspondence of Henry Knox*, 60–61 (*"danced all night"*).

444 **They danced again to fiddle music:** Thayer, *Nathanael Greene*, 263–64 (*two-horse phaeton*); Stegeman and Stegeman, *Caty*, 69 (*"upwards of three hours"*).

20. A SUMMONS TO THE QUEEN'S HOUSE

447 **A flutter of flags aboard the one-hundred-gun *Britannia*:** "Hon. Augustus Keppel, 1st Viscount," https://morethannelson.com/officer/hon-augustus-keppel-1st-viscount-keppel/; Blandemor, ed., *The Trial of the Honourable Augustus Keppel*, 1–2 (*five admirals and eight captains*); Thomas, *Memoirs of the Marquis of Rockingham and His Contemporaries*, 2: 368 (*larboard mizzen shrouds*).

447 **The inconclusive battle between French and British fleets:** Rodger, *The Insatiable Earl*, 246–47; Mackesy, *The War for America, 1775–1783*, 243 (*anchor miles apart*); Martelli, *Jemmy Twitcher*, 164 (*"fatal consequences"*).

447 **No sooner had the court-martial convened:** Keppel, *The Life of Augustus Viscount Keppel*, 2: 181 (*pack the courtroom*); Blandemor, ed., *The Trial of the Honourable Augustus Keppel*, 3–4 (*"did not cause the fleet"*).

448 **Sixty-three witnesses testified:** Blandemor, ed., *The Trial of the Honourable Augustus Keppel*, xi (*almost half of them ship's captains*); Mahan, *The Major Operations of the Navies in the War of American Independence*, 117 (*fought in the line*); Mackesy, *The War for America, 1775–1783*, 242 (*"Tears were shed"*); Martelli, *Jemmy Twitcher*, 156 (*"affecting to smile"*); "Sir Thomas Pye," https://morethannelson.com/officer/sir-thomas-pye/; Blandemor, ed., *The Trial of the Honourable Augustus Keppel*, 377 (*"I submit the whole"*); Bickham, *Making Headlines*, 131 (*refusing to take more bets*); Keppel, *The Life of Augustus Viscount Keppel*, 2: 183–87 (*reboarded Victory*); Rodger, *The Insatiable Earl*, 249 (*"Conquering Hero"*); PP Sandwich, 2: 194–97.

448 **At eight p.m. messengers reached London:** Besant, *London in the Eighteenth Century*, 480 (*celebratory gunfire*); Hibbert, *George III*, 215 (*blue cockades*); Toynbee, ed., *The Letters of Horace Walpole*, 10: 375–78 (*hired post chaise*), 381–83; Martelli, *Jemmy Twitcher*, 159 (*disguising himself*); Keppel, *The Life of Augustus Viscount Keppel*, 2: 191 (*effigy on Tower Hill*); Clowes, *The Royal Navy*, 3: 425 (*ransack his Pall Mall house*); Donne, *The Correspondence of King George the Third to Lord North*, 2: 228n (*North's in Downing Street*); Rudé, *Hanoverian London, 1714–1808*, 219–20 (*gates off their hinges*); Jesse, *Memoirs of King George the Third*, 3: 217–19 (*"manifest panic"*).

448 **The Keppel craze persisted, briefly:** Rodger, *The Command of the Ocean*, 338; Ayling, *George the Third*, 262; Keppel, *The Life of Augustus Viscount Keppel*, 2: 225 (*"ready to quit"*), 228 (*"strike your flag"*).

449 **As passions cooled and his reputation deflated:** Rodger, *The Insatiable Earl*, 251; PP Sandwich, 2: 221 (*demanded another trial*); Keppel, *The Life of Augustus Viscount Keppel*, 2: 238 (*"disabled state"*); Mackesy, *The War for America, 1775–1783*, 243 (*Greenwich Hospital*).

449 **But damage had been done:** Syrett, *The Royal Navy in European Waters During the American Revolutionary War*, 59 (*"almost ruined the navy"*); Mackesy, *The War for America, 1775–1783*, 243 (*captains resigned*); Rodger, *The Command of the Ocean*, 338 (*for a generation*); Miller, *Sea of Glory*, 345 (*great peril*). Keppel would return to become first lord in 1782 (Clowes, *The Royal Navy*, 3: 426).

449 **Sandwich, who followed the Keppel imbroglio:** Patterson, *The Other Armada*, 90 (*deserved dismissal*); Rodger, *The Insatiable Earl*, 246 (*overthrowing Protestantism*); Levy, *Love & Madness*, 21–25, 30 (*bullied Miss Ray*); Thomas, *Lord North*, 116 (*204 to 170*); Martelli, *Jemmy Twitcher*, 164 (*national villain*).

449 **The first lord's promotion and patronage:** Broomfield, "Lord Sandwich at the Admiralty Board," 7+ (*"weight and property"*); Bellot, *William Knox*, 151, 162 (*implacably hostile*); Martelli, *Jemmy Twitcher*, 182–83 (*"Every expedition, in regard to its destination"*).

450 **True enough. Despite the first lord's anxiety:** O'Shaughnessy, *The Men Who Lost America*, 328–29 (*90 ships of the line*), 342–43 (*a third of the British fleet*); Patterson, *The Other Armada*,

87 (*North's persistent reluctance*); Dull, *The Miracle of American Independence*, 111 (*two dozen more* and *the Bourbon force came to 121*); Martelli, *Jemmy Twitcher*, 183–84 (*314 vessels total*); Allison and Ferreiro, eds., *The American* Revolution, 40 (*2,600 privateers*); Syrett, *Shipping and the American War, 1775–1783*, 77 (*Six thousand British merchant vessels*). Including those in reserve or out of commission, the number of British vessels reached 432 (Allen, *A Naval History of the American Revolution*, 1: 363–64).

450 **Problems undoubtedly persisted:** Syrett, *The Royal Navy in European Waters During the American Revolutionary War*, 66 (*of every three men aboard ship*); Dull, *The French Navy and the Seven Years' War*, 136 (*so effectively*); Allison and Ferreiro, eds., *The American Revolution*, 58 (*Rochefort, Toulon, and Brest*); Conway, "British Mobilization in the War of American Independence," 58+ (*sixty thousand lost*). The figure goes through 1780.

450 **This spring, responsibility for transporting provisions:** Syrett, *Shipping and the American War, 1775–1783*, 136–37 (*Germain's prickly resentment*), 139 (*sixty thousand mouths*).

450 **All in all, Sandwich could make a fair claim:** Ayling, *George the Third*, 263; Black, *George III, America's Last King*, 237 (*"highly advantageous"*); Gruber, *The Howe Brothers and the American Revolution*, 333–34 (*"vague, rambling conversation"*).

451 **Several daunting obstacles stood:** Flavell, *The Howe Dynasty*, 322 (*"Half the town abhor them"*); Rodger, *The Insatiable Earl*, 256–57 (*laid down several demands*).

451 **"He has added conditions":** Rodger, *The Insatiable Earl*, 251 (*"Sandwich fills the Admiralty"*); Gruber, *The Howe Brothers and the American Revolution*, 336 (*censure Sandwich*); Flavell, *The Howe Dynasty*, 312 (*"ranked in opposition"*).

451 **The Admiralty building was described:** George, *London Life in the Eighteenth Century*, 187 (*"lasting reproach"*); Tilley, *The British Navy and the American Revolution*, 44 (*rotating pointer*).

452 **Window glass smashed during the Keppel riot:** Levy, *Love & Madness*, 1–3 (*set out in a carriage*), 6 (*linkboys, livery servants*); Martelli, *Jemmy Twitcher*, 170 (*generous offer*); Brewer, *A Sentimental Murder*, 18 (Love in a Village); Damrosch, *The Club*, 71 (*"great square of Venus"*).

452 **Among the lurkers:** Levy, *Love & Madness*, 39, 44, 49–50, 62 (*ordained*); Brewer, *A Sentimental Murder*, 20 (*"Think of me"*); "Trial of James Hackman," Old Bailey Proceedings Online, https://www.oldbaileyonline.org/browse.jsp?div=t17790404-3 (*"overpowers me"*).

452 **She was about to climb into her carriage:** Levy, *Love & Madness*, 6–9 (*"Kill me!"*).

452 **Sandwich had just retired:** Levy, *Love & Madness*, 12 (*fatal news*); Martelli, *Jemmy Twitcher*, 169–70 (*"Leave me a while"*); Toynbee, ed., *The Letters of Horace Walpole*, 10: 402 (*"nation of lunatics"*).

453 **Charged with "the willful murder":** "Trial of James Hackman," Old Bailey Proceedings Online, https://www.oldbaileyonline.org/browse.jsp?div=t17790404-3 (*"criminal in a high degree"*); Levy, *Love & Madness*, 73 (*"'Twas love, not malice"*); Martelli, *Jemmy Twitcher*, 173 (*without bothering to leave the courtroom*).

453 **On April 19 Hackman was led:** Levy, *Love & Madness*, 133–38 (Balladeers), 139 (Surgeon's Hall); Brewer, *A Sentimental Murder*, 152 (*forged letters*), 156; "James Hackman," https://everything2.com/?node=James+Hackman#google_vignette (*Murder Act* and *cudgel against Sandwich*).

453 **Others were more charitable:** Mackesy, *The War for America, 1775–1783*, 283 (*"robbed of all comfort"*); Knight, "New England Forests and British Seapower," 221+ (*Baltic masts*); PP Sandwich, 2: 249 (*"blow of a private nature"*), 257 (*"totally unfit"*), 259 (*"most deplorable state"*), 262 (*five thousand tons of hemp*).

454 **He was too savvy, too irreplaceable:** PP Sandwich, 2: 255 (*sharp defeat*).

454 **George's forty-first birthday was celebrated:** Trevelyan, *The American Revolution*, 4: 432–33 (*"The king's dress"*); Huish, *Public and Private Life of His Late Excellent and Most Gracious Majesty, George the Third*, 392–93 (*French silk* and *"ladies must take care"*).

454 **London's elite had recovered:** Damrosch, *The Club*, 191 (*"remember me"*), 192 (*"bathed in tears"*).

454 **For the government, the year had already been difficult:** Jesse, *Memoirs of King George the*

Third, 3: 232 (*Arkwright's water frame*); Mackesy, *The War for America, 1775–1783*, 244 (*Howe brothers against Germain*); Gruber, *The Howe Brothers and the American Revolution*, 338–45; Howe inquiry, *Parliamentary Register*, 12: 23 (*"no hopes of conquering America"*), 273–74 (*"management"*); *The Parliamentary History of England*, 19: 1397 (*"become French"*).

455 **No domestic worry nagged the king:** Watson, *The Reign of George III, 1760–1815*, 221–23; Damrosch, *The Club*, 299–300 (*15 percent of the population*); Miller, *Triumph of Freedom, 1775–1783*, 412–14; Mackesy, *The War for America, 1775–1783*, 305 (*Wheat prices*); Whiteley, *Lord North*, 177; James Pattison to "Maj. Gen. Cleaveland," May 3, 1779, "Official Letters of Major General James Pattison," 49 (*recruiting in Ireland*); Gilmour, *Riot, Risings and Revolution*, 343–44 (*"all Americans here"*); Coupland, *The American Revolution and the British Empire*, 123–24 (*"gained nothing"*).

455 **British diplomats in St. Petersburg:** Scott, *British Foreign Policy in the Age of the American Revolution*, 265 (*sought alliances*), 282 (*Swedish merchantmen*), 286–87 (*forty-two Dutch vessels*); Patterson, *The Other Armada*, 79 (*"we are proud"*); Laprade, ed., *Parliamentary Papers of John Robinson, 1774–1784*, 147–49.

455 **Versailles happily posed as a defender:** Clowes, *The Royal Navy*, 4:18–19; Winfield, *British Warships in the Age of Sail, 1714–1792*, 190 (*La Concorde*); Desmarais, *America's First Ally*, 96 (*ivory, gold dust*), 97–100 (*forty British privateers* and Minerva).

456 **For months Spain had played a double game:** Ferreiro, *Brothers at Arms*, 77–78 (*Duke of Parma* and *Goya*); Manceron, *Age of the French Revolution*, 1: 535 (*hunted every day*).

456 **Madrid seethed at Anglo insults:** Mackesy, *The War for America, 1775–1783*, (*Gibraltar, Minorca, Florida*); Willis, *The Struggle for Sea Power*, 280–81; Comte de Montmorin to Vergennes, Feb. 22, 1780, Archives Diplomatiques, vol. 597, f 361 (*hardly endorsed America's rebellion*); Morris, *The Peacemakers*, 17; Ferreiro, *Brothers at Arms*, 113–14 (*twenty-two million pesos*).

456 **José Moñino, the Count Floridablanca, the able:** Corwin, *French Policy and the American Alliance of 1778*, 181 (*snubbed him*), 183 (*until French forces withdrew*); Ferreiro, *Brothers at Arms*, 113 (*"I have no doubt"*); Murphy, *Charles Gravier, Comte de Vergennes*, 264–65; Allison and Ferreiro, eds., *The American* Revolution, 36 (*"national disgrace"*); Dull, *The French Navy and American Independence*, 130–31.

457 **So ended the cynical Spanish gambit:** Bemis, *The Diplomacy of the American Revolution*, 78 (*"with a club"*); Sandwich to Charles Hardy, May 29, 1779, UK NA, ADM 2/1336, f 23–28 (*"Great Britain & Ireland exposed"*). Adm. Sir Charles Hardy was still struggling to get his fleet out of Portsmouth.

457 **Unknown to Britain, the Bourbon powers:** Murphy, *Charles Gravier, Comte de Vergennes*, 269, 276–77 (*convention of war*); Hardman, *The Life of Louis XVI*, 139 (*joint invasion*); Del Perugia, *La tentative d'invasion de l'Angleterre de 1779*, 25 (*"as the Romans did"*).

457 **"The views and pretensions of Spain":** Murphy, *Charles Gravier, Comte de Vergennes*, 267; Phillips, *The West in the Diplomacy of the American Revolution*, 96–102 (*France had no choice*); Corwin, *French Policy and the American Alliance of 1778*, 192 (*"nothing is to be got"*); Ferreiro, *Brothers at Arms*, 86 (*silver, sugar*), 114 (*Florida and Minorca*); Dull, *The French Navy and American Independence*, 143 (*Bay of Honduras*); Hardman, *The Life of Louis XVI*, 139.

457 **"The Spaniards are a little like children":** Corwin, *French Policy and the American Alliance of 1778*, 161, 193 (*would not recognize American independence*); Ferreiro, *Brothers at Arms*, 115 (*Mississippi River*); Dull, *The French Navy and American Independence*, 143 (*Senegal* and *trading posts in India*); Hardman, *The Life of Louis XVI*, 139; Chávez, *Spain and the Independence of the United States*, 133; Bemis, *The Diplomacy of the American Revolution*, 86 (*neither consented*).

457 **On June 16, the Spanish ambassador:** Bemis, *The Diplomacy of the American Revolution*, 85–87; *Parliamentary Register*, 12: 446 (*"grievances so numerous"* and *"resist and repel"*).

458 **In barely a year, Britain had gone:** Ferreiro, *Brothers at Arms*, 115 (*world war*); Butterfield, *George III, Lord North and the People, 1779–1780*, 42 (*"most awful"*).

458 **The Queen's House stood where, in 1609:** "Royal Residences: Buckingham Palace" (*silkworm*

industry); Rinder, "Buckingham Palace and Its Site," 3+ (*"one of the greatest beauties"*); "Westminster: Buckingham Palace," British History Online (*Equity, Liberty and Truth*); Picard, *Dr. Johnson's London*, 51 (*cistern*).

458 **George III bought the estate in 1761:** Rinder, "Buckingham Palace and Its Site," 3+ (*Queen's House*); Black, *George III, America's Last King*, 175 (*£73,000 on renovations*); "Royal Residences: Buckingham Palace" (*775 rooms*); "Westminster: Buckingham Palace," British History Online (*"dull, dowdy"*); Hibbert, *George III*, 67 (*strains of Handel*); Roberts, *The Last King of America*, 78 (*kangaroos*).

458 **George's greatest pride, his children excepted:** Rinder, "Buckingham Palace and Its Site," 3+ (*the likes of Dr. Johnson*); Roberts, *The Last King of America*, 90 (Paradise Lost); " 'George III's Collection of Military Maps' Published Online," Royal Collection Trust, press release, Jan. 29, 2020 (*fifty thousand charts, prints*); author visit, Royal Library map room, Windsor Castle, Apr. 2016.

459 **George also commissioned the expatriate:** Black, *George III, America's Last King*, 167 (Departure of Regulus); Roberts, *The Last King of America*, 192 (*"statement" paintings*); O'Shaughnessy, *An Empire Divided*, 189 (*Jamaica would fall*).

459 **In a note to Sandwich dated June 17:** *PP Sandwich*, 3: 20 (*"vigor"*), 25 (*"clog the wheels"*); Miller, *Triumph of Freedom, 1775–1783*, 405–6 (*"die is now cast"*).

459 **On Monday, June 21, George, in his own hand:** *PP Sandwich*, 3: 25 (*appear at the Queen's House*); Billias, ed., *The Manuscripts of Captain Howard Vincente Knox*, 260–61; O'Shaughnessy, *The Men Who Lost America*, 35 (*Not since Queen Anne*). Germain gave the account to Knox.

459 **For an hour the king spoke:** Billias, ed., *The Manuscripts of Captain Howard Vincente Knox*, 260–61 (*"all the subsequent misfortunes"*).

460 **With that, he fell silent:** Butterfield, *George III, Lord North and the People*, 44 (*"mode of increasing"*); *PP Sandwich*, 3: 26 (*"I must drive"*); O'Shaughnessy, *The Men Who Lost America*, 36 (*"any ten men"*).

460 **Would those ten include Germain and North?:** Butterfield, *George III, Lord North and the People*, 28 (*"not been of use"*); Guttridge, "Lord George Germain in Office, 1775–1782," 23+ (*"contrived to lose the esteem"*); Brown, *The American Secretary*, 147 (*resolved warlord*); Germain to W. Knox, July 27, 1778, in Billias, ed., *The Manuscripts of Captain Howard Vincente Knox*, 145 (*"great deal due to us"*); Marlow, *Sackville of Drayton*, 199–200 (*"appeared desirous"*).

460 **As for North, his misery:** Miller, *Triumph of Freedom, 1775–1783*, 407 (*"go to the grave"*), 409 (*"no energy, damn him"*); Mackesy, *The War for America, 1775–1783*, 245–46 (*seemed paralyzed*); Black, *George III, America's Last King*, 175 (*"No man has a right"*); Pemberton, *Lord North*, 295 (*"highly unbecoming"*); Ayling, *George the Third*, 266 (*"rousing Lord North"*).

461 **Matters had grown much worse:** Donne, *The Correspondence of King George the Third to Lord North*, 2: 257–58 (*"sincerely condole"*); Butterfield, *George III, Lord North and the People*, 46 (*"quite unhinged"*); *The Parliamentary History of England*, 20: 927 (*brought North to tears*), 953n (*"dejection of spirits"*).

461 **The fate of the monarchy and the nation:** Mackesy, *The War for America, 1775–1783*, 265 (*"conduct is inexplicable"*), 303; O'Shaughnessy, *The Men Who Lost America*, 34 (*"I wish were changed"*), 66 (*"most altered man"*).

461 **The country, meanwhile, braced for a wider war:** Walpole to countess of Ailesbury, July 10, 1779, https://www.bookrags.com/ebooks/4919/205.html#gsc.tab=0; Bickham, *Making Headlines*, 136–37 (*"correct the insolence"*); Huish, *Public and Private Life of His Late Excellent and Most Gracious Majesty, George the Third*, 393 (*"insulted the honor"*).

461 **With garrisons to man from Canada to Bengal:** Conway, *The War of American Independence, 1775–1783*, 46 (*almost thirty*); *The Parliamentary History of England*, 20: 915 (*double the number of militiamen*); Ferling, ed., *The World Turned Upside Down*, 173 (*a guinea and a half*); Hagist, *Noble Volunteers*, 178 (*"gentlemen volunteers"*), 180 (*"very fine little fellows"*)," 181 (*Erse*).

462 **By the end of 1779, the government hoped:** *The Parliamentary History of England*, 20: 920

(*three hundred thousand men under arms*); *Bath Chronicle*, July 1, 1779, 2 ("*impress was so brisk*").

462 **Not to be outdone, the army also:** Curtis, *The Organization of the British Army in the American Revolution*, 56–58 ("*disorderly persons*"), 59–60 ("*rogues*"); Hagist, *British Soldiers, American War*, 154 ("*thieves, pickpockets*"); Ferling, ed., *The World Turned Upside Down*, 172 (*insalubrious posts*).

462 **Fewer than fifteen hundred conscripts:** Hagist, *Noble Volunteers*, 185 (*encouraged volunteers*), 187 (*at least one highwayman*); Conway, "Recruitment of Criminals into the British Army, 1775–81," 46+ (*pardoned a few hundred*); Holmes, *Redcoat*, 139 (*horse thieves*); Conway, *The War of American Independence, 1775–1783*, 36 (*self-maiming*); Urban, *Fusiliers*, 174 ("*Please inform me*").

463 **To pay for this expanding military:** Robson, *The American Revolution, in Its Political and Military Aspects*, 148 (*customs and excise taxes*); Conway, *The British Isles and the War of American Independence*, 54 (*less than a fifth*), 70 (*Overseas trade*), 77–79 (*beer*), 94 (*bankruptcies*); Wickwire, *British Subministers and Colonial America, 1763–1783*, 165 (*seventeen tons of British copper*).

463 **"The present contest with America":** Donne, *The Correspondence of King George the Third to Lord North*, 2: 252–54 ("*most serious*"), 267 ("*parent's heart*"), 270 ("*send for a locksmith*"); Marshall, *The Making and Unmaking of Empires*, 363 ("*our sugar islands*"); Mackesy, *The War for America, 1775–1783*, 263 ("*stretch every nerve*"); Patterson, *The Other Armada*, 100 (*Portsmouth and Plymouth*); Conway, "The Recruitment of Criminals into the British Army, 1775–81," 46+ ("*miserable rabble*").

463 **As an earnest of his personal commitment:** George III, Private Papers, RA, GEO/MAIN, #16147 (Elements of Navigation), and George R. to Prince William, June 13, 1779, #16158 ("*you are now launching*").

464 **And then George R. again summoned:** "George III (1738–1820)," Royal Collection Trust, https://www.rct.uk/collection/405407/george-iii-1738-1820.

464 **"I trust in the protection":** Black, *George III, America's Last King*, 240 ("*justness of the cause*").

21. I DETEST THAT SORT OF WAR

465 **Spring had begun badly for General Clinton:** Ritchie, ed., "A New York Diary of the Revolutionary War," 2: 401+ ("*Most of the people*"); Town, *A Detail of Some Particular Services Performed in America*, 72; Hagist, "James Gilmour, 82nd Regiment, survives a shipwreck," blog post, Apr. 6, 2014, https://redcoat76.blogspot.com/2014/04/james-gilmour-82nd-regiment-survives_6.html (*floating bodies*).

465 **This ghastly news reached New York:** Willcox, ed., *The American Rebellion*, 118–19 (*seven thousand reinforcements*); Mackesy, *The War for America, 1775–1783*, 260 (*fifteen hundred tons*); Town, *A Detail of Some Particular Services Performed in America*, 72–73 (*debilitated*); George Collier to Sandwich, Apr. 19, 1779, *PP Sandwich*, 3: 127 ("*as they truly are*"); Collier to Germain, Apr. 19, 1779, Historical Manuscripts Commission, *Report on the Manuscripts of Mrs. Stopford-Sackville*, 2: 125 (*half the ships*).

466 **Clinton rarely agreed with Lord Germain:** Brown, *The Good Americans*, 98 (*fifty separate provincial corps*), 117 ("*sovereign contempt*"), 121 ("*bitterest enemies*"), 123–24 ("*hang the turbulent*"), 137 ("*GR*"); Smith, *Loyalists and Redcoats*, 124 ("*Our utmost efforts will fail*").

466 **Clinton had long stressed the exigency:** Hagist, *Noble Volunteers*, 173 (*fifteen hundred lashes*); Conway, "To Subdue America," 381+ ("*cock of the ball*"); Murray, *Letters from America, 1773 to 1780*, 61 ("*burning and destroying*").

466 **On April 24, Germain's secret orders:** Germain to H. Clinton, Jan. 23, 1779, WLC, Germain papers, "Secret Military Dispatches," vol. 18 ("*decisive action*" and *sixty-six hundred reinforcements*); Germain to North, Jan. 11, 1779, WLC, Germain papers, vol. 9; Willcox, ed., *The American Rebellion*, 399.

467 **In a private reply to Germain:** Willcox, ed., *The American Rebellion*, 407 ("*secure the right of blaming me*" and "*debilitated army*"); Clinton to Germain, May 22, 1779, *DAR*, 17: 129 ("*leave*

me to myself "); Willcox, ed., *The American Rebellion*, 119 (*"at least 30,000 men"*); Clinton to Germain, May 14, 1779, WBW (*"object of every campaign"* and *"my happiness is sacrificed"*).

467 **He further unburdened himself in letters home:** Clinton to Drummond, Mar. 1–2, 1779, WBW (*"get their information"*); Willcox, *Portrait of a General*, 270 (*"motherless babes"*); Clinton to Newcastle, June 18, 1779, WBW (*"last campaign"*); Clinton to Eden, [July?], 1779, WBW (*"cursed war"*).

467 **With that, he turned back to the business:** Willcox, "British Strategy in America, 1778," 97+ (*"worthy of a great nation"*).

467 **Commodore Sir George Collier had served:** Willis, *The Struggle for Sea Power*, 328 (*"I see with indignation"*); "Collier, Sir George," *Dictionary of National Biography, 1885–1900* (Selima and Azor); "Sir George Collier," https://morethannelson.com/officer/sir-george-collier/; Town, *A Detail of Some Particular Services Performed in America*, 72–73 (*temporary command*).

468 **He soon persuaded Clinton:** Selby, *The Revolution in Virginia, 1775–1783*, 179 (*Suffolk*), 180–81 (*two thousand hogsheads*); Price, *France and the Chesapeake*, 2: 681 (*fifty thousand tons*), 689, 719 (*Ukrainian, Hungarian*); Willcox, *Portrait of a General*, 275 (*Virginia troops*); Morison and Commager, *The Growth of the American Republic*, 1: 244 (*two hundred thousand enslaved*).

468 **Clinton agreed to a "short and desultory invasion":** Clinton to Germain, May 5, 1779, WBW (*no more than a month*); Hamilton, *The Origin and History of the First or Grenadier Guards*, 237 (*Edward Mathew*); Collier to Germain, May 22, 1779, *DAR*, 17: 131 (*"Uncommonly favorable"*); Kranish, *Flight from Monticello*, 115 (*"finest regatta"*).

468 **As rebel coasters scattered in fright:** captain's log, *Raisonnable*, May 8–10, 1779, UK NA, ADM 51/763 (*smaller* Rainbow); "Collier-Mathew Raids," American Revolution Podcast, Oct. 10, 2021, https://blog.amrevpodcast.com/2021/10/arp221-collier-mathew-raids.html; Town, *A Detail of Some Particular Services Performed in America*, 76–78 (*galley* Cornwallis); Willis, *The Struggle for Sea Power*, 125 (*Bow ramps*); Lee, *Memoirs of the War in the Southern Department of the United States*, 1: 96–98 (*Great Dismal Swamp*).

470 **Other American defenses were equally hapless:** Meacham, *Thomas Jefferson*, 129 (*"beyond all my fears"*); Kranish, *Flight from Monticello*, 116 (*failed to recognize the scope*); Ward, *Charles Scott and the "Spirit of '76,"* 70 (*Williamsburg*); Quarles, *The Negro in the Making of America*, 55 (*"running the Negroes"*).

470 **The British rampaged without hindrance:** Hamilton, *The Origin and History of the First or Grenadier Guards*, 237 (*marched eighteen miles*); Town, *A Detail of Some Particular Services Performed in America*, 79–81 (*"famous for their sedition"*); Collier to Capt. Kendall, *Rainbow*, May 13, 1779, HL, John Kendall corr., letterbook vol. 1, HM 64532 (*refugees, runaway slaves*).

470 **For ten days the raiders lingered:** Frey, "Between Slavery and Freedom," 375+ (*three thousand hogsheads*); Town, *A Detail of Some Particular Services Performed in America*, 82–83 (*eight lambs*); Selby, *The Revolution in Virginia, 1775–1783*, 206 (*gouging out eyes* and *"little irregularities"*); Kranish, *Flight from Monticello*, 116.

471 **On May 16 Collier wrote Clinton:** Collier to Clinton, May 16, 1779, WBW (*"infinitely exceed"* and *"sinews of the rebellion"*); Collier to Sandwich, June 15, 1779, *PP Sandwich*, 3: 132 (*"amazing quantity"*); Kranish, *Flight from Monticello*, 115–16 (*masts, cordage*), 117 (*Charlottesville*).

471 **Clinton demurred. Without the promised reinforcements:** Clinton to unknown, May 19, 1779, WBW (*"burn his fingers"* and *"all will go well"*); Collier to Germain, June 15, 1779, Historical Manuscripts Commission, *Report on the Manuscripts of Mrs. Stopford-Sackville*, 2: 128 (*"no other alternative"*).

471 **The marauders collected as much timber:** Richard Parker to NG, May 27, 1779, *PNG*, 3: 89; Kranish, *Flight from Monticello*, 117–18 (*"conflagration"*); Town, *A Detail of Some Particular Services Performed in America*, 79 (*warships building*), 80 (*eight thousand barrels of pitch*); Eller, *Chesapeake Bay in the American Revolution*, 38. The 137 lost vessels included 17 sailed away by the British (Selby, *The Revolution in Virginia, 1775–1783*, 208).

471 **The squadron weighed and sailed out:** Kranish, *Flight from Monticello*, 118 (*90 loyalists*); Pybus, "Jefferson's Faulty Math," 243+ (*half of them women and children*); Selby, *The Revolution in Virginia, 1775–1783*, 205 (*two wounded*); Willcox, ed., *The American Rebellion*, 123 (*"sanguine expectations"*); Collier to Germain, June 15, 1779, Historical Manuscripts Commission, *Report on the Manuscripts of Mrs. Stopford-Sackville*, 2: 129 (*"rebellion is thrown"*).

471 **To Sandwich on the same day:** *PP Sandwich*, 3: 132.

471 **Clinton now had the bit in his teeth:** William De Hart to GW, May 30, 1779, *PGW*, 20: 692–93n (*lunged up the Hudson*); GW to John Jay, June 6, 1779, FOL, 21: 4n, 89; "Governor Geo. Clinton's Original Official Records," Mar. 10, 1779, HL, HM 630 (*one gunshot for every five enemy vessels*).

472 **Fifty-eight grunting British gunners:** J. Pattison to Lord Viscount Townshend, June 9, 1779, "Official Letters of Major General James Pattison," 73 (*into a rope harness*); GW, general orders, June 1, 1779, FOL fn (*"difficult rock"* and *"This little success"*).

472 **He hoped that the loss of King's Ferry:** Willcox, ed., *The American Rebellion*, 125 (*draw Washington*); Huggins, *Washington's War, 1779*, 90; William De Hart to GW, May 30, 1779, *PGW*, 20: 692–93n (*to West Point*); Johnston, *The Storming of Stony Point*, 55 (*"No reinforcements arrived"*); Sabine, ed., *Historical Memoirs of William Smith*, 2: 110 (*"He is only timid"*), 114 (*"Washington is distressed"*).

472 **If not distressed, Washington surely was alarmed:** William De Hart to GW, May 30, 1779, *PGW*, 20: 692–93n (*to continue upriver*); GW to Henry Champion, Sr., June 4, 1779, FOL, 21: 51 (*"not a moment to be lost"*); GW to J. Sullivan, June 4, 1779, FOL, 21: 65 (*"more and more serious"*); NG to GW, June 6, 1779, FOL, 21: 88 (*"teams are failing"*); Huggins, *Washington's War, 1779*, 92 (*eight new redoubts and batteries*).

473 **No attack came. Scouts reported:** author visit, SPBSHS, Oct. 4, 2019; "Stony Point Battlefield," state pamphlet (*"Little Gibraltar"*); Pattison to H. Clinton, June 7, 1779, "Official Letters of Major General James Pattison," 70–71 (*three hundred rounds*); GW to John Jay, June 6, 1779, *PGW*, 21: 154; GW, general orders, June 1, 1779, FOL fn; GW to John Augustine Washington, June 20, 1779, FOL (*"astonishing industry"* and *"source of much mischief"*).

473 **But he would not be baited:** Willcox, ed., *The American Rebellion*, 125 (*sixty miles*); GW to Horatio Gates, June 11, 1779, FOL (*"An attempt to dislodge them"*).

473 **If a sally up the Hudson:** Johnston, *The Storming of Stony Point*, 56–57 (*"desultory expedition"*); Pownall and Almon, *The Remembrancer*, 8: 362 (*"draw Mr. Washington"*); Willcox, ed., *The American Rebellion*, 128–29.

473 **Major General William Tryon would wield the scourge:** "William Tryon," https://en.wikisource.org/wiki/1911_Encyclop%C3%A6dia_Britannica/Tryon,_William; "William Tryon," https://www.nps.gov/people/william-tryon.htm; Sabine, ed., *Historical Memoirs of William Smith*, 2: 59 (*$1,000 reward*), 93 (*"torpor"*); W. Tryon to Germain, Dec. 24, 1778, *DAR*, 15: 296 (*"unrestrained excepting to women"*); Chopra, *Unnatural Rebellion*, 127 (*six thousand sailors*); *DAR*, 17: 19–20 (*"glorious success"*); GW to Jonathan Trumbull, Sr., July 7, 1779, FOL fn (*"almost totally destroyed"*).

474 **To make "impressions on the New England coast":** Sabine, ed., *Historical Memoirs of William Smith*, 2: 93; Allen, *Tories*, 302 (*King's American Regiment*); GW to Jonathan Trumbull, Sr., July 7, 1779, FOL fn; Pownall and Almon, *The Remembrancer*, 8: 355 (Scorpion, Halifax, Hussar); Pancake, *This Destructive War*, 17 (*"terror and despondency"*); Ferling, *Winning Independence*, 154 (*"I know you will"*); Willcox, *Portrait of a General*, 280 (*wash my hands*).

474 **From *Camilla*, Tryon and Collier issued:** Samuel Holden Parsons to GW, July 14, 1779, FOL fn (*"recover from the phrenzy"*).

474 **At dawn on Monday, July 5:** Dexter, ed., *The Literary Diary of Ezra Stiles, D.D., LL.D.*, 2: 352–57 (*"knew our fate"*); Buel, *Dear Liberty*, 190–91 (*a thousand assault troops*); Moore, *The Diary of the American Revolution, 1775–1781*, 375 (*"malignant disposition"*).

474 **The divinity professor Naphtali Daggett trotted:** Gipson, *American Loyalist*, 364–67 (*fowling gun*); Samuel Holden Parsons to GW, July 31, 1779, FOL fn (*Daggett was taken prisoner* and *"cut up and made a pie of?"*). Daggett preceded Stiles as Yale's president.

475 **After a long afternoon and evening:** Samuel Holden Parsons to GW, July 14, 1779, FOL fn

(*offered freedom*); Dexter, ed., *The Literary Diary of Ezra Stiles, D.D., LL.D.*, 2: 359 (*"British clemency"*); Pownall and Almon, *The Remembrancer*, 8: 355 (*king's casualties*).

475   **Twenty-five miles down the coast, Fairfield:** Samuel Holden Parsons to GW, July 10, 1779, FOL; Stephen St. John to GW, July 9, 1779, FOL fn (*Grover's Hill*); Allen, *Tories*, 304 (*clefts of stone walls*); Pownall and Almon, *The Remembrancer*, 8: 362 (*"smart fire"*); Samuel Holden Parsons to GW, July 31, 1779, FOL fn (*"Hessians were first let loose"* and *"wet ditch"*).

475   **An hour after sunset, a fire began:** Buel, *Dear Liberty*, 191–92 (*almost two hundred structures*); Tryon to Clinton, July 20, 1779, in Willcox, ed., *The American Rebellion*, 414 (*"took fire unintentionally"*); Griffin, "Plight of the Loyalist Refugees of Lloyd's Neck, Long Island," *JAR*, Feb. 20, 2020 (*"ungovernable flames"*).

476   **After a quick detour across the Sound:** Pownall and Almon, *The Remembrancer*, 8: 355 (*"murdering the troops"*), 363 (*Drummond Hill*); Buel, *Dear Liberty*, 194 (*Cow's Pasture*); Samuel Holden Parsons to GW, July 11, 1779, FOL fn (*"skulls blowed off"*).

476   **With Norwalk's immolation, Clinton recalled:** GW to Jonathan Trumbull, Sr., July 7, 1779, FOL fn (*summer harvest*), and July 12, 1779, FOL (*"lament the depredations"*); Buel, *Dear Liberty*, 192–96.

476   **Collier assured the Admiralty:** GW to Jonathan Trumbull, Sr., July 7, 1779, FOL fn (*"numerous pirates"*); Pownall and Almon, *The Remembrancer*, 8: 364–65 (*Tryon estimated his casualties*); Allen, *Tories*, 307 (*"desolation warfare"*); Tryon to H. Clinton, July 20, 1779, *DAR*, 17: 162–65 (*"love of my country"*); Pancake, *This Destructive War*, 17 (*"I detest that sort of war"*); Sabine, ed., *Historical Memoirs of William Smith*, 2: 137 (*"wished the conflagrations"*).

476   **Washington had again refused to be lured:** GW to Jonathan Trumbull, Sr., July 12, 1779, FOL; GW to John Jay, July 9, 1779, FOL (*"Plundering and burning"*); GW to John Jay, July 13, 1779, FOL (*"high time"*).

477   **Major Henry Lee III, a Virginia firebrand:** Hall, "An Irregular Reconsideration of George Washington and the American Military Tradition," 986 (*"mother's womb"*); Piecuch and Beakes, *"Light Horse Harry" Lee in the War for Independence*, 5–7 (*Homer, Demosthenes*); Herrera, " 'The zealous activity of Capt. Lee,' " 9+ (*"gallant behavior"*); Ferling, *The First of Men*, 274 (*"wedded to my sword"*). A future Virginia governor, Lee was the father of Robert E. Lee.

477   **Light-Horse Harry had his own answer:** GW to Henry Lee, July 9, 1779, FOL (*"inhumanity"*); EPO, "Off with His Head," n.d. (*three deserters*); Piecuch and Beakes, *"Light Horse Harry" Lee in the War for Independence*, 29–30 (*trophy on a gallows*).

477   **"I fear it will have a bad effect":** GW to Henry Lee, July 10, 1779, FOL (*"body buried"*); Henry Lee to GW, July 11, 1779, FOL (*"immediate effect"*).

477   **Washington had already set his own:** Billias, ed., *George Washington's Generals and Opponents*, 261 (*"vain, impulsive"*); Loprieno, *The Enterprise in Contemplation*, 10 (*"more active and enterprising"*); GW to A. Wayne, July 1, 1779, FOL.

477   **Forty-six regiments contributed 1,350 men:** Johnston, *The Storming of Stony Point*, 69 (*Lexington and Bunker Hill*); Stillé, *Major-General Anthony Wayne and the Pennsylvania Line in the Continental Army*, 184 (*Connecticut, Pennsylvania*); GW to John Jay, July 22, 1779, FOL fn (*stealthy reconnaissance*); GW to A. Wayne, July 10, 1779, FOL (*small force*); A. Wayne to GW, July 3, 1779, FOL (*"perhaps a surprise"*).

479   **British deserters, American spies:** Commager and Morris, eds., *The Spirit of 'Seventy-Six*, 723 (*officers disguised*); Lengel, "Bayonets at Midnight," HistoryNet, November 5, 2009, https://www.historynet.com/bayonets-at-midnight-the-battle-of-stony-point/ (*weakened the Hudson garrisons*); Dawson, *The Assault on Stony Point*, 39 (*gneiss and granite*); *Narratives of the Revolution in New York*, 280–81; Pattison to H. Clinton, June 7, 1779, "Official Letters of Major General James Pattison," 70 (*two abatis*); author visit, SPBSHS, Oct. 4, 2019, signage, fort model (*flèches*); Loprieno, *The Enterprise in Contemplation*, 7 (*Henry Johnson*), 13–14; Pattison to H. Clinton, June 9, 1779, "Official Letters of Major General James Pattison," 71 (*"perfectly quiet"*).

479   **Washington urged Wayne to keep the enemy:** GW to A. Wayne, July 10, 1779, FOL (*"Knowledge of your intention"*); GW to A. Wayne, July 14, 1779, FOL (*"You are at liberty"*); Stillé, *Major-General Anthony Wayne and the Pennsylvania Line in the Continental Army*, 192, 209;

Loprieno, *The Enterprise in Contemplation*, 20 (*fourteen miles*); A. Wayne to GW, July 15, 1779, FOL.

479 **At eight p.m., with the sun sinking:** *South of the Mountains*, Rockland County (N.Y.) Historical Society, vol. 25, no. 3 (July–Sept. 1981): 1; Peterson, *The Book of the Continental Soldiers*, 99–100 (*spontoon*); A. Wayne to GW, "Plan of Attack, July 15, 1779," FOL (*"strictest silence"* and *"instantly put to death"*); GW to John Jay, July 21, 1779, FOL; Loprieno, *The Enterprise in Contemplation*, 21 (*"perishing with cold"*).

480 **Wayne crept forward:** Stillé, *Major-General Anthony Wayne and the Pennsylvania Line in the Continental Army*, 192 (*"I am called to sup"*).

480 **By nightfall on Thursday, July 15:** Loprieno, *The Enterprise in Contemplation*, 20 (*eighty-eight British sentries*), 25–26 (*"The night being extremely dark and very windy"*), 70 (*ship's bells*).

480 **Wayne had organized his attack into two columns:** author visit, SPBSHS, Oct. 4, 2019, signage, information from Michael J. F. Sheehan, senior historian (*seventeen rebels in the forlorn hope*); A. Wayne to GW, July 17, 1779, FOL; Thomas Pope, pension application R8326, Feb. 6, 1822, https://revwarapps.org/r8326.pdf (*"beat me back"*).

481 **Led by Wayne, the right column waded:** Loprieno, *The Enterprise in Contemplation*, 27–29 (*"For God's sake"* and *barrels could not be depressed*); Campbell, *Revolutionary Services and Civil Life of General William Hull*, 163 (*"cut and tore away the pickets"*).

481 **Abruptly, Wayne pitched forward:** Stillé, *Major-General Anthony Wayne and the Pennsylvania Line in the Continental Army*, 196 (*"Forward, my brave fellows"*); Dawson, *The Assault on Stony Point*, 51 (*Rising to a knee*); Campbell, *Revolutionary Services and Civil Life of General William Hull*, 163 (*"fort's our own"*); A. Wayne to GW, July 17, 1779, FOL; Loprieno, *The Enterprise in Contemplation*, 31–32 (*ripped the British colors*); author visit, SPBSHS, Oct. 4, 2019, signage (*"Considerable bayoneting"*).

481 **In a two-sentence note to Washington:** A. Wayne to GW, July 16, 1779, FOL (*"determined to be free"*); A. Wayne to GW, July 16, 1779, FOL (*"The pain I feel"*).

481 **The particulars emerged soon enough:** Huggins, *Washington's War, 1779*, 98–100; GW to Goose Van Schaick, July 22, 1779, FOL (*sixty-three killed*); GW to William Woodford, July 22, 1779, FOL fn; author visit, SPBSHS, Oct. 4, 2019, signage (*swimming to the* Vulture); Loprieno, *The Enterprise in Contemplation*, 31 (*Francis Tew*).

482 **"My astonishment could not but be":** Huggins, *Washington's War, 1779*, 101–2; Willcox, ed., *The American Rebellion*, 133 (*"very great affront"*); GW to A. Wayne, July 1, 1779, FOL fn (*"singular & unfortunate"*); Pattison to Lord Viscount Townshend, July 26, 1779, "Official Letters of Major General James Pattison," 96 (*"no instance of inhumanity"*).

482 **The "perfection of discipline":** Wildes, *Anthony Wayne*, 197, 199 (*into domestic service*); GW to John Jay, July 22, 1779, FOL fn (*French horns*); EPO, "The Plunder & Prizes of Stony Point," n.d. (*three black boys*); Loprieno, *The Enterprise in Contemplation*, 37 (*hanged at the Stony Point flagstaff*), 47 (*prize money*), 81 (*exchanged, only to be captured again*).

482 **Washington arrived at Stony Point:** Kapp, *The Life of Frederick William von Steuben*, 229 (*exultant soldiers*); GW to John Jay, July 16, 1779, FOL (*"I congratulate Congress"*); GW to John Jay, July 22, 1779, FOL (*"Not less than 1,500 men"*); GW to A. Wayne, July 1, 1779, FOL fn.

482 **Continental troops blew apart:** Richard Butler to GW, July 19, 1779, FOL (*British vessels*); Sheehan, "Stony Point: The Second Occupation, July–October 1779," *JAR*, Apr. 21, 2020 (*rebuilt the blockhouses*).

483 **Further American raids revealed:** Henry Lee to GW, Aug. 22, 1779, FOL; Piecuch and Beakes, *"Light Horse Harry" Lee in the War for Independence*, 35–49 (*158 enemy prisoners*); Morison and Commager, *The Spirit of 'Seventy-Six*, 726–77; Owen, *The Revolutionary Struggle in New Jersey, 1776–1783*, 25–26.

483 **"I was not very well pleased":** Piecuch and Beakes, *"Light Horse Harry" Lee in the War for Independence*, 47; Johnston, *The Storming of Stony Point*, 93 (*"weak and miserable"*); Stuart-Wortley, ed., *A Prime Minister and His Son*, 149 (*"He told me with tears"*).

483 **In October Clinton would order:** Loprieno, *The Enterprise in Contemplation*, 57–58 (*rest of the war*).

483 **Hardly a major battle, Stony Point nonetheless:** Quincy, *The Journals of Major Samuel Shaw*, 62 (*"Revenge becomes"*); GW to John Jay, July 22, 1779, FOL (*"doing something"*); John Jay to GW, July 27, 1779, FOL (*"laurels"*).

483 **Ambassador Gérard wrote Steuben:** Kapp, *The Life of Frederick William von Steuben*, 230 (*"much elevate"*); Butterfield, ed., *Letters of Benjamin Rush*, 1: 237 (*"You have taught our enemies"*).

22. THE VALLEY OF BONES

485 **A new, unlikely front had opened:** Francis McLean to H. Clinton, June 26, 1779, *Report on American Manuscripts in the Royal Institution of Great Britain*, 1: 458–60 (*five Royal Navy ships*); Norton, "The Penobscot Expedition," 1+ (*640 redcoats*); Duncan, *Coastal Maine*, 229 (*timber and fish*); Daughan, *If By Sea*, 192 (*white pine masts*); Clinton, *The American Rebellion*, 134–35, 419–20; Spector, *The American Department of the British Government, 1768–1782*, 136 (*"New Ireland"*); Spector, "The Case of New Ireland—Not Meant to Be," *JAR*, Sept. 17, 2024; Holton, *Liberty Is Sweet*, 379 (*give the Crown a haven*); Goold, "Captain Henry Mowat's Account," 46+ (*"all the navy"*). Britain's colonial plan fell short in Maine but succeeded in New Brunswick.

485 **Two men led the expedition:** Buker, *The Penobscot Expedition*, 6 (*nineteen major battles*); Wickwire, "McLean, Francis," *Dictionary of Canadian Biography*, vol. 4, http://www.biographi.ca/en/bio/mclean_francis_4E.html; *TBAC*, 136–39 (*Falmouth*); GW to John Hancock, Oct. 24, 1775, FOL (*"barbarity & cruelty"*).

485 **For weeks soldiers from the 74th and 82nd Regiments:** Francis McLean to H. Clinton, June 26 and Aug. 23, 1779, *Report on American Manuscripts in the Royal Institution of Great Britain*, 1: 458–60 (*"very laborious"*), 2: 14; Buker, *The Penobscot Expedition*, 13–15 (*Three gun batteries*); Albion and Pope, *Sea Lanes in Wartime*, 59 (*American and British registries*); Duncan, *Coastal Maine*, 228 (*shooting cattle*).

486 **Patriot leaders in Boston learned:** Maine broke free of Massachusetts with statehood in 1820. Shaw, "Penobscot Assault—1779," 83+ (*"captivate, kill"*); Norton, "The Penobscot Expedition," 1+ (*embargo*); Symonds, "The American Naval Expedition to Penobscot, 1779," 64+ (*fifty thousand extra cartridges*); Duncan, *Coastal Maine*, 229 (*nine tons of flour*); Buker, *The Penobscot Expedition*, 24 (*"reserving for their heads"*).

486 **No man expected more laurels:** Norton, "The Penobscot Expedition," 1+ (*thickset*); Buker, *The Penobscot Expedition*, 19–22 (*"rude, unhappy"* and *"morose"*).

488 **Militia forces bound for Maine:** Buker, *The Penobscot Expedition*, 19 (*gentleman farmer*); Shaw, "Penobscot Assault—1779," 83+ (*scant combat experience*); Allen, *A Naval History of the American Revolution*, 2: 421–22 (*"very inferior"*); Forbes, *Paul Revere and the World He Lived In*, 355 (*"small boys"*); Goss, *The Life of Colonel Paul Revere*, 2: 326 (*"employed on the fortifications"*).

488 **After a month of preparation:** Daughan, *If By Sea*, 192; Miller, *Sea of Glory*, 413 (*The flotilla included*); Buker, *The Penobscot Expedition*, 31 (*"coffee house"*).

488 **Entering Penobscot Bay at two p.m.:** Shaw, "Penobscot Assault—1779," 83+ (*"jump over"*); Symonds, "The American Naval Expedition to Penobscot, 1779," 64+ (*fifty-six guns*); Buker, *The Penobscot Expedition*, 15 (Rachel *sped south*), 37–40 (*"that damned hole"*).

488 **Things went little better the next day:** Buker, *The Penobscot Expedition*, 39–40 (*flipped a flat-bottom*); Miller, *Sea of Glory*, 414; Shaw, "Penobscot Assault—1779," 83+ (*"random and irregular"*).

489 **That came at sunrise in swirling fog:** Buker, *The Penobscot Expedition*, 42–44; Symonds, "The American Naval Expedition to Penobscot, 1779," 64+ (Hunter *and* Sky-Rocket); Shaw, "Penobscot Assault—1779," 83+ (*thirty-three of his comrades*); Cecere, "The Penobscot Expedition of 1779," *JAR*, Aug. 8, 2019 (*"What a precipice"*); Duncan, *Coastal Maine*, 230.

489 **This would be the high-water mark:** McLean to Germain, Aug. 26, 1779, in Clinton, *The American Rebellion*, 419 (*"astonishment"*); Shaw, "Penobscot Assault—1779," 83+ (*fifteen dead*); Buker, *The Penobscot Expedition*, 45 (*strike his colors*).

489 **For more than a fortnight:** Pownall and Almon, *The Remembrancer*, 8: 357; Buker, *The*

Penobscot Expedition, 56 (*"Yankee Doodle"*), 64–65 (*"superior fleet"*); Shaw, "Penobscot Assault—1779," 83+ (*"skulked"*); Symonds, "The American Naval Expedition to Penobscot, 1779," 64+ (*"Three weeks have now elapsed"*).

490 **At yet another conference, on Friday, August 13:** Symonds, "The American Naval Expedition to Penobscot, 1779," 64+ (*"British ships hove in sight"*).

490 **Upon sailing from Sandy Hook:** Collier to H. Clinton, Aug. 19, 1779, *Report on American Manuscripts in the Royal Institution of Great Britain*, 2: 12; Pownall and Almon, *The Remembrancer*, 8: 352–53 (*"inclined to dispute"*); Willcox, ed., *The American Rebellion*, 416–17 (*"ignominious flight"*).

490 **Alerted to the British approach:** Norton, "The Penobscot Expedition," 1+ (*"ungovernable state"*); Buker, *The Penobscot Expedition*, 77–79 (*retreat north* and *"shift for ourselves"*).

490 **Light airs persisted until early afternoon:** captain's log, *Raisonnable*, Aug. 14–15, 1779, UK NA, ADM 51/763 (*longboats, yawls*); Buker, *The Penobscot Expedition*, 80 (*filling Collier's sails first*).

491 **At three p.m. a trio of rebel ships:** Duncan, *Coastal Maine*, 232 (*only American ship to fire*); captain's log, *Raisonnable*, Aug. 14–15, 1779, UK NA, ADM 51/763 (Hunter); Pownall and Almon, *The Remembrancer*, 8: 352–53 (*"fastest sailing vessel"* and *settled on the bottom*); Buker, *The Penobscot Expedition*, 82–83 (*a new brig*).

491 **By Sunday morning the chase:** Allen, *A Naval History of the American Revolution*, 2: 433 (*"Us together with the* Virginia"); Town, *A Detail of Some Particular Services Performed in America*, 110 (*"picturesque"*), 111 (*brushed tree limbs*).

491 **"To attempt to give a description":** Miller, *Sea of Glory*, 417; Buker, *The Penobscot Expedition*, 93 (*"take us off"*); captain's log, *Raisonnable*, Aug. 20, 1779, UK NA, ADM 51/763 (*"rebels all destroyed"*).

491 **Collier scribbled a dispatch to Clinton:** Collier to H. Clinton, Aug. 19, 1779, *Report on American Manuscripts in the Royal Institution of Great Britain*, 2: 12 (*"We have taken"*); Buker, *The Penobscot Expedition*, 95 (*twenty-one armed ships*); Miller, *Sea of Glory*, 417 (*"as the disgrace"*); Norton, "The Penobscot Expedition," 1+ (*Nearly five hundred rebels*); Pownall and Almon, *The Remembrancer*, 8: 354 (*fourteen casualties*); Toynbee, ed., *The Letters of Horace Walpole*, 11: 27 (*"walnut shells"*).

492 **Hundreds of survivors made their way south:** Buker, *The Penobscot Expedition*, 99 (*"adrift"* and *"through the wilderness"*); Forbes, *Paul Revere and the World He Lived In*, 358 (*Fort Western*).

492 **The returning refugees were greeted:** Samuel A. Otis to NG, Aug. 30, 1779, *PNG*, 3: 347 (*"ought to be hanged"*), 348n (*"bad in conception"*); Miller, *Sea of Glory*, 417 (*"want of proper spirit"*); Forbes, *Paul Revere and the World He Lived In*, 360 (*cargo worth £80,000*); Buker, *The Penobscot Expedition*, 115 (*misleading, if not mendacious*).

492 **It fell harder on Revere:** Goss, *The Life of Colonel Paul Revere*, 2: 337 (*"cowardice & disobedience"*); Forbes, *Paul Revere and the World He Lived In*, 365 (*court-martial*), 389–90; Buker, *The Penobscot Expedition*, 113 (*fourteen years*), 146–48 (*acquitted him with honor*); PNG, 3: 347–48 (*debts exceeding £1 million*); Bourne, "The Penobscot Fiasco," *American Heritage*, n.p. (*bankruptcy*).

492 **Commodore Collier soon sailed home:** Town, *A Detail of Some Particular Services Performed in America*, 110 (*Plymouth in late November*); "Sir George Collier," https://morethannelson.com/officer/sir-george-collier/; Duncan, *Coastal Maine*, 233 (*Halifax and St. John*); PNG, 3: 347–48n (*until 1784*).

493 **"This continent," Greene wrote:** NG to GW, May 31, 1779, FOL; Calloway, *The American Revolution in Indian Country*, 19 (*fifty thousand American pioneers*); Barnhart, ed., *Henry Hamilton and George Rogers Clark in the American Revolution*, 13; Peckham, *The War for Independence*, 106 (*"exciting up an alarm"*); Bowler, *Logistics and the Failure of the British Army in America, 1775–1783*, 230 (*"divide the attention"*); Allen, *Tories*, 272 (*"king's command"*). The American population was doubling every quarter century (Kurtz and Hutson, eds., *Essays on the American Revolution*, 298).

493 **In the subsequent two years, Hamilton:** Griffin, *American Leviathan*, 87 (*"arrows sticking in them"*); Sterner, *Till the Extinction of This Rebellion*, 8 (*"perfectly"*); Allen, *Tories*, 273 ("129

scalps"); Neimeyer, *America Goes to War*, 99; Dann, ed., *The Revolution Remembered*, 281–82 (*salt-collecting*); Peckham, *The War for Independence*, 106 (*bundled off to Detroit*).

493 **In 1777, Congress had planned an expedition:** James, ed., *George Rogers Clark Papers, 1771–1781*, xlvii (*scheme foundered*); Nester, *George Rogers Clark*, 5–6 (*taste for strong drink*); Cumming and Rankin, *The Fate of a Nation*, 249 ("*black, penetrating*"); Dotson, ed., *America Rebels*, 267–69 (*surveyor*); Alden, *The South in the Revolution, 1763–1789*, 283; Calloway, *The American Revolution in Indian Country*, 48 ("*excel them in barbarity*"). Clark's younger brother, William, would later lead a Corps of Discovery expedition to the Pacific with Meriwether Lewis.

494 **In December 1777, Clark had laid out:** Selby, *The Revolution in Virginia, 1775–1783*, 189–91; Meade, *Patrick Henry, Practical Revolutionary*, 173–75 (*two sets of orders*); James, ed., *George Rogers Clark Papers, 1771–1781*, lvii (*commissioned a lieutenant colonel*); Raphael, *Founders*, 341–42 (*secret even from the Virginia assembly*); Sterner, *Till the Extinction of This Rebellion*, 14 ("*show humanity*").

494 **In late June 1778, Clark and 179 volunteers:** Alden, *The South in the Revolution, 1763–1789*, 284 (*flatboats*); James, ed., *George Rogers Clark Papers, 1771–1781*, lxiii (*single file to minimize their tracks*); Sterner, *Till the Extinction of This Rebellion*, 11, 30 (*American Bottom*); Hammon and Taylor, *Virginia's Western War, 1775–1786*, 76–78 ("*every street secured*"); Commager and Morris, eds., *The Spirit of 'Seventy-Six*, 1040 (*burst into song*); Cumming and Rankin, *The Fate of a Nation*, 251 ("*appeared to be happy*"); James, ed., *George Rogers Clark Papers, 1771–1781*, 56 ("*Republic of Virginia*" and "*Long live*"); Griffin, *American Leviathan*, 143 (*wrapped around a large stone*).

495 **Lieutenant Governor Hamilton could hardly brook:** Griffin, *American Leviathan*, 127–28 ("*fill all the lower parts*"); Peckham, *The War for Independence*, 108; James, ed., *George Rogers Clark Papers, 1771–1781*, lxxi (*in seventy-one days*); Sterner, *Till the Extinction of This Rebellion*, 72–76 (*240 men*), 85 (*fewer than two dozen*), 112–15; Cumming and Rankin, *The Fate of a Nation*, 252; Selby, *The Revolution in Virginia, 1775–1783*, 194; Alden, *The South in the Revolution, 1763–1789*, 286 (*Vincennes on December 17*); Nester, *George Rogers Clark*, 145 (*his regulars*).

495 **That proved a mistake:** Commager and Morris, eds., *The Spirit of 'Seventy-Six*, 1043 ("*Who knows what fortune*"); Selby, *The Revolution in Virginia, 1775–1783*, 195 ("*incredible difficulties*"); Huston, *Logistics of Liberty*, 214–17 (*icy bottomlands*); James, ed., *George Rogers Clark Papers, 1771–1781*, 140–42.

495 **Five minutes after evening candles:** "Report by Lieut.-Governor Henry Hamilton," July 6, 1781, in *Report on the Manuscripts of Mrs. Stopford-Sackville*, 2: 223–48 ("*heard the balls whistle*"); Dotson, ed., *America Rebels*, 283 ("*Our troops grew warm*"); Barnhart, ed., *Henry Hamilton and George Rogers Clark in the American Revolution*, 181 ("*God save the king!*"); James, ed., *George Rogers Clark Papers, 1771–1781*, 145 (*three-day truce*).

495 **Clark had a dreadful answer:** English, *Conquest of the Country Northwest of the River Ohio, 1778–1783*, 1: 334; Sterner, *Till the Extinction of This Rebellion*, 116–17 (*blundered into town*); Commager and Morris, eds., *The Spirit of 'Seventy-Six*, 1050 (*Ottawa death song*); Haffner, ed., "British Prisoner of War in the American Revolution," 17+ (*hacked to death*); "Report by Lieut.-Governor Henry Hamilton," July 6, 1781, in *Report on the Manuscripts of Mrs. Stopford-Sackville*, 2: 223–48 (*tossed into the Wabash*).

496 **At ten a.m. on Thursday, a disconsolate Hamilton:** Cumming and Rankin, *The Fate of a Nation*, 254 ("*spared the mortification*"); English, *Conquest of the Country Northwest of the River Ohio, 1778–1783*, 1: 334–49; "Report by Lieut.-Governor Henry Hamilton," July 6, 1781, in *Report on the Manuscripts of Mrs. Stopford-Sackville*, 2: 223–48 (*with the Indian scalps* and "*laid in irons*"); Sterner, *Till the Extinction of This Rebellion*, 121 (*Fort Patrick Henry*).

496 **They arrived in the Virginia capital:** TJ to William Phillips, July 22, 1779, FOL ("*general principle*"); Allen, *Tories*, 274 ("*butcher of men*"); Barnhart, ed., *Henry Hamilton and George Rogers Clark in the American Revolution*, 203 ("*wet, jaded*"); "Report by Lieut.-Governor Henry Hamilton," July 6, 1781, in *Report on the Manuscripts of Mrs. Stopford-Sackville*, 2: 223–48 (*England a year later*).

496 **Neither Clark nor any other rebel:** Griffin, *American Leviathan*, 146–47 (*from Detroit*); Peckham, *The War for Independence*, 109 (*sanguinary raids*); Hammon and Taylor, *Virginia's Western War, 1775–1786*, 100–101 (*His Most Christian Majesty*); Alden, *The South in the Revolution, 1763–1789*, 286 (*an American dominion*); Frederick Haldimand to Germain, Sept. 13, 1779, UK NA, CO 42/39 f 234 (*"unfortunate miscarriage"*).

496 **"Retaining the Indians in our interest":** Frederick Haldimand to Germain, Sept. 13, 1779, UK NA, CO 42/39 f 234 (*"heavy expense"* and *"amazing sums"*); Baker, *Government and Contractors*, 200 (*more than £25,000*); Bowler, *Logistics and the Failure of the British Army in America, 1775–1783*, 232 (*British rations*).

497 **General Washington closely monitored developments:** Ferling, ed., *The World Turned Upside Down*, 117 (*"brothers and friends"*); GW to Joseph Johnson, Feb. 20, 1776, FOL (*"We only desire"*).

497 **Yet by mid-1779 neutrality was rare:** Calloway, *The American Revolution in Indian Country*, 31 (*British trade goods*); Graymont, *The Iroquois in the American Revolution*, 112–13; *TBAC*, 344 (*crushed the Cherokees*); Taylor, *American Revolutions*, 260 (*White Eyes*); Calloway, *The Indian World of George Washington*, 265 (*mutilated*); Hemmis, "Under the Banner of War," *JAR*, Mar. 29, 2022 (*Cornstalk*); Calloway, *The American Revolution in Indian Country*, 293 (*"occasioned by some injury"*); Bruce, *Benjamin Franklin Self-Revealed*, 2: 155; Taylor, *American Revolutions*, 258 (*up to $1,000*); Davis, "The Employment of Indian Auxiliaries in the American War," 709+ (*150,000 natives*); Byrd, *Sacred Scripture, Sacred War*, 5 (*Canaanites*) (See Deuteronomy 20:16–17.)

497 **The American war already had shattered:** Bilharz, *Oriskany*, 41; Calloway, *The American Revolution in Indian Country*, 34 (*Oneida and Tuscarora*); Dorwart, *Invasion and Insurrection*, 157 (*magazines in Carlisle*). An analysis in December 2015 of one such sample of "pale skin" showed it to be cowhide (curatorial note, Luke Swatland collection, HL, HM 72607).

498 **Washington had first fought native tribes:** *PNG*, 3: xiii (*urgency*); John Jay to GW, Feb. 26, 1779, FOL fn (*"chastisement"*); Calloway, *The Indian World of George Washington*, 244 (*$1 million*); John Jay to GW, May 10, 1779, FOL (*"consider yourself at liberty"*).

498 **"The only certain way of preventing":** GW to Henry Laurens, Nov. 16, 1778, *PGW*, 18: 169; Huggins, *Washington's War, 1779*, 76–77; Ferling, ed., *The World Turned Upside Down*, 123; NG to GW, Jan. 5, 1779, *PNG*, 3: 144–45 (*violent blow in the summer*); GW to Horatio Gates, Mar. 6, 1779, *PGW*, 19: 377 (*"chastise and intimidate"*); Lengel, *General George Washington*, 311 (*four thousand Continentals*); Berleth, *Bloody Mohawk*, 276 (*artillery*).

498 **In early July, as the Indian expedition:** Jordan, "Adam Hubley, Jr.," 1: 129+ (*seventy log cabins*); Mintz, *Seeds of Empire*, 54 (*"best and the pleasantest"*); Berleth, *Bloody Mohawk*, 275 (*Valley of Bones*); Hoock, *Scars of Independence*, 276 (*Decaying corpses*); "The Revolutionary War Diary of Chaplain Andrew Hunter," July 8, 1779, n.p. (*"grave which contains"*); Brown and Peckham, eds., *Revolutionary War Journals of Henry Dearborn, 1775–1783*, 157–59 (*"great number of bones"*); Tiedemann et al., *The Other Loyalists*, 143–45; Callahan, *Royal Raiders*, 164–65 (*flax for the Continental Army*); Jordan, "Adam Hubley, Jr.," 1: 129+ (*widows and orphans*); Silverman, *A Cultural History of the American Revolution*, 357 (*"Roslin Castle"*); Cook, ed., *Journals of the Military Expedition of Major General Sullivan*, 81 (*"devastations of war"*).

499 **Survivors told a lurid tale:** The number of attackers varies. Koehler, "Hostile Nations," 427+ (*thinly disguised*); Tiedemann et al., *The Other Loyalists*, 143 (*seven scattered settlements*); John Butler to Lt. Col. Bolton, July 8, 1778, in Willcox, ed., *The American Rebellion*, 386–87 (*most of them scalped* and *sheep, swine, and horned cattle*); Williams, *Year of the Hangman*, 117 (*a dozen men and boys*), 121–24 (*"St. Patrick's Day"*), 138 (*"Great Runaway"*).

499 **Atrocity stories soon spread:** Howard Swiggett, *War Out of Niagara: Walter Butler and the Tory Rangers*, 135; Berleth, *Bloody Mohawk*, 261; Graymont, *The Iroquois in the American Revolution*, 179 (*seven hundred homeless*), 187 (*Cherry Valley*); Calloway, *The American Revolution in Indian Country*, 124 (*"finest Indian town"*); Calloway, *The Indian World of George Washington*, 245 (*glass windows*); Swiggett, *War Out of Niagara*, 144–56 (*taken prisoner*); Tay-

lor, *The Divided Ground*, 94 (*captain's commission*); Tiedemann et al., *The Other Loyalists*, 146 (*thirty-three women, children*); Berleth, *Bloody Mohawk*, 268–71; Werther, "Walter Butler," *JAR*, Aug. 25, 2022; Alexander, ed., "Diary of Captain Benjamin Warren at Massacre of Cherry Valley," 377+ (*"shocking sight"*).

500 **To halt these depredations:** Whittemore, *A General of the Revolution*, 127 (*thirty-page treatise*); Mintz, *Seeds of Empire*, 97–98 (*converted atheist*).

500 **July 4, 1779, fell on a Sunday:** Brown and Peckham, eds., *Revolutionary War Journals of Henry Dearborn, 1775–1783*, 159 (*thirteen toasts*); Hoock, *Scars of Independence*, 276 (*"General Washington and the army"*); Mintz, *Seeds of Empire*, 98 (*"civilization or death"*).

500 **Given the rare opportunity to design an offensive:** Calloway, *The Indian World of George Washington*, 216–17 (*as meticulously*); *PGW*, 19: xxix–xxx; Flick, ed., "New Sources on the Sullivan-Clinton Campaign in 1779," 185+ (*seventy-two questions*); "Questions and Answers," *PGW*, 19: 690 (*"What number of warriors"*).

500 **He scrutinized lists of matériel sent to Sullivan:** NG to GW, Mar. 2, 1779, *PNG*, 3: 326–27 (*felling axes*); Schuyler to GW, Mar. 1–7, 1779, *PGW*, 19: 315–16 (*fish hooks*); Hammond, *Letters and Papers of Major-General John Sullivan*, 3: 24 (*2,100 shirts*), 39 (*rum, whiskey*), 40 (*2,000 pairs of shoes*); GW to Board of War, Aug. 21, 1779, *PGW*, 22: 196n; "Headnote on the Sullivan Expedition," *PNG*, 4: 22–27n (*every map available*); Ryan, ed., *A Salute to Courage*, 161 (*Stockbridge guides*); GW to H. Gates, Mar. 6, 1779, *PGW*, 19: 378 (*assault on Quebec*); *Narratives of the Revolution in New York*, 315 (*fanfare*).

501 **Sullivan's objective in Iroquois country:** GW to J. Sullivan, May 31, 1779, *PGW*, 20: 716–19 (*"total destruction"* and *"war whoop"*).

501 **To Washington's exasperation, the expedition:** J. Sullivan to NG, May 12, 1779, *PNG*, 4: 27 (*"inkstands"*); Board of War to GW, May 24, 1779, *PGW*, 20: 595 (*thousand additional muskets*); GW to Board of War, Aug. 21, 1779, FOL (*five thousand shirts*); Fischer, *A Well-Executed Failure*, 114 (*rounded futtocks and keels*), 118 (*a third of his salt meat*); Whittemore, *A General of the Revolution*, 126 (*only two hundred*); Robert L. Hooper, Jr., to NG, May 15, 1779, *PNG*, 4: 31 (*more than a thousand packhorses*); Richard Claiborne to NG, May 18, 1779, *PNG*, 4: 43 (*packsaddles were so shoddy*).

501 **"Great preparations and great exertions":** NG to J. Sullivan, *PNG*, 4: 175–76, 177n (*"your success"* and *"Duke de Sully"*); AH to NG, May 22, 1779, FOL (*"usual pother"*); NG to Jeremiah Wadsworth, Apr. 14, 1779, *PNG*, 3: 403 (*"I wish he may succeed"*).

501 **Washington urged him to get moving:** GW to J. Sullivan, July 1, 1779, FOL (*"inexpressible concern"*); Whittemore, *A General of the Revolution*, 133 (*three to one*); GW to J. Sullivan, July 29, 1779, FOL (*"Hasten your operations"*).

502 **At length the tents were struck:** Cook, ed., *Journals of the Military Expedition of Major General Sullivan*, 82 (*Abby Wheeler*); Bolton, *The Private Soldier Under Washington*, 160 (*"go thou with us"*).

502 **A single cannon shot from Fort Wyoming:** Whittemore, *A General of the Revolution*, 132 (*at noon on July 31*); Brown and Peckham, eds., *Revolutionary War Journals of Henry Dearborn, 1775–1783*, 168–69 (*"horridly rough"* and *black walnut*); Mintz, *Seeds of Empire*, 103 (*twelve hundred packhorses*); "The Revolutionary War Diary of Chaplain Andrew Hunter," Aug. 1779, n.p. (*bears, deer, and wild turkeys*); Cook, ed., *Journals of the Military Expedition of Major General Sullivan*, 5.

502 **Eighty miles from Wyoming:** Jordan, "Adam Hubley, Jr.," 1: 129+ (*scoured the shoreline*); Whittemore, *A General of the Revolution*, 135 (*waded waist-deep*); Hardenbergh et al., *Narratives of Sullivan's Expedition, 1779*, 72 (*four blockhouses*); Graymont, *The Iroquois in the American Revolution*, 204 (*desecrating native graves*).

502 **The general himself led most of his force:** Flick, ed., "New Sources on the Sullivan-Clinton Campaign in 1779," 265+ (*"root and branch"*); Graymont, *The Iroquois in the American Revolution*, 204 (*forty acres*); Bolton, *The Private Soldier Under Washington*, 198 (*"There is something so cruel"*).

502 **The Indians had not gone far:** "The Revolutionary War Diary of Chaplain Andrew Hunter,"

Aug. 13, 1779, n.p. (*stray gunshots*); Bernardus Swartout, Jr., journal, Aug. 13, 1779, NYHS (*ambuscade*); Cook, ed., *Journals of the Military Expedition of Major General Sullivan*, 125 (*Hog Back Hill*); Dann, ed., *The Revolution Remembered*, 296 (*squirrel brains*); J. Sullivan to GW, Aug. 15, 1779, FOL (*"I am much surprised"*); Hardenbergh et al., *Narratives of Sullivan's Expedition, 1779*, 29n (*quart of whiskey*); Jordan, "Adam Hubley, Jr.," 2: 279+ (*"my life is wind,"* Job 7: 7).

503 **On August 22 reinforcements arrived:** Hardenbergh et al., *Narratives of Sullivan's Expedition, 1779*, 64 (*crossed Otsego Lake*); *The Orderly Book of Capt. Leonard Bleeker*, 111–13n; Simms, *History of Schoharie County and Border Wars of New York*, 299 (*two hundred bateaux*); Calloway, *The Indian World of George Washington*, 250–51 (*forty-five hundred men*); Hardenbergh et al., *Narratives of Sullivan's Expedition, 1779*, 143–44 (*"Succotash Campaign"*).

503 **Forty villages would burn:** Whittemore, *A General of the Revolution*, 147 (*next three weeks*); Brown and Peckham, eds., *Revolutionary War Journals of Henry Dearborn, 1775–1783*, 176 (*"very much impeded"*); Cook, ed., *Journals of the Military Expedition of Major General Sullivan*, 7 (*swept away packhorses*); Mintz, *Seeds of Empire*, 133–34 (*"perfect chaos"*).

503 **Badly outnumbered and outgunned:** The site was just south of the current town of Elmira. Whittemore, *A General of the Revolution*, 138–39 (*village of Newtown*); Hardenbergh et al., *Narratives of Sullivan's Expedition, 1779*, 41–43; Jordan, "Adam Hubley, Jr.," 2: 279+ (*"the quantity of paint"*); Cook, ed., *Journals of the Military Expedition of Major General Sullivan*, 127 (*effort to entice*); J. Sullivan to GW, Sept. 28, 1779, FOL (*fifteen hundred*); Whittemore, *A General of the Revolution*, 140–41 (*Indian left flank*).

503 **Sullivan overestimated his adversary's strength:** Whittemore, *A General of the Revolution*, 141 (*factor of two*); Bowler and Wilson, "Butler, John," *Dictionary of Canadian Biography*, vol. 4 (*agent in Niagara*); Flick, ed., "New Sources on the Sullivan-Clinton Campaign in 1779," 265+ (*"no purpose"* and *"obstinately bent"*); Graymont, *The Iroquois in the American Revolution*, 212 (*baggage horses*); Bernardus Swartout, Jr., journal, Aug. 29, 1779, NYHS (*"kettles boiling"*).

504 **Initially slowed by boggy ground:** Brown and Peckham, eds., *Revolutionary War Journals of Henry Dearborn, 1775–1783*, 177–78; Hardenbergh et al., *Narratives of Sullivan's Expedition, 1779*, 41–45 (*two to three miles*); Van Wyck, ed., "Autobiography of Philip Van Cortlandt," 278+; Commager and Morris, eds., *The Spirit of 'Seventy-Six*, 1017 (*"tree to tree"*); Kidder, *History of the First New Hampshire Regiment in the War of the Revolution*, 51 (*"hideous yell"*); J. Sullivan to GW, Aug. 30, 1779, FOL (*"fear had given them"*); Flick, ed., "New Sources on the Sullivan-Clinton Campaign in 1779," 265+ (*"hell-hounds"*); Cook, ed., *Journals of the Military Expedition of Major General Sullivan*, 8 (*boot leggings*).

504 **"The consequences of this affair":** Flick, ed., "New Sources on the Sullivan-Clinton Campaign in 1779," 265+; Adamiak, "The 1779 Sullivan Campaign," https://www.varsitytutors.com/earlyamerica/early-america-review/volume-3/1779-sullivan-campaign; J. Sullivan to GW, Sept. 28, 1779, FOL (*sent his heavy artillery*); Cook, ed., *Journals of the Military Expedition of Major General Sullivan*, 8 (*"march as disagreeable"*), 476 (*"He who destroys"*).

504 **On September 13 Sullivan sent:** Little Beard's Town was near today's Leicester, New York. "General Sullivan's Report," Sept. 30, 1779, in Cook, ed., *Journals of the Military Expedition of Major General Sullivan*, 301 (*Thomas Boyd with twenty-six soldiers*); "Revolutionary War Diary of Chaplain Andrew Hunter," Sept. 13–14, 1779, n.p. (*eyes gouged*); Brown and Peckham, eds., *Revolutionary War Journals of Henry Dearborn, 1775–1783*, 186–88 (*tongues ripped out*); Simms, *History of Schoharie County and Border Wars of New York*, 308–13; J. Sullivan to GW, Sept. 28, 1779, FOL; Hardenbergh et al., *Narratives of Sullivan's Expedition, 1779*, 128 (*"The lieutenant was all skinned"*); Berleth, *Bloody Mohawk*, 283 (*"were not beaten"*).

505 **"Such is the barbarity":** Cook, ed., *Journals of the Military Expedition of Major General Sullivan*, 48 (*"we live sumptuously"*); J. Sullivan to GW, Sept. 28, 1779, FOL; Bernardus Swartout, Jr., journal, Sept. 15, 1779, NYHS; Hardenbergh et al., *Narratives of Sullivan's Expedition, 1779*, 80–81 (*"Destroyed about 1,500 peach trees"*).

505 **By late September the troops were back:** Cook, ed., *Journals of the Military Expedition of Major General Sullivan*, 13 (*"like a hallelujah"*); Hardenbergh et al., *Narratives of Sullivan's Expedition, 1779*, 60 (*"metamorphosed into pack horses"*).

505 **Great claims were made for the Indian Expedition's:** Kidd, *God of Liberty*, 125–26 (*"instruments in the hand"*); Thompson, *Israel Shreve*, 62 (*"The whole country is totally destroyed"*); J. Sullivan to GW, Sept. 28, 1779, FOL (*"not a single town left"*); GW, general orders, Oct. 17, 1779, FOL (*"full success"*); Whittemore, *A General of the Revolution*, 150 (*resignation*).

506 **Subsequent estimates put the number of Iroquois killed:** Calloway, *The Indian World of George Washington*, 255 (*ten additional native villages*); Koehler, "Hostile Nations," 427+ (*under six hundred*); Graymont, *The Iroquois in the American Revolution*, 218–19; Cook, ed., *Journals of the Military Expedition of Major General Sullivan*, 302–3; Hemmis, "Under the Banner of War," *JAR*, Mar. 29, 2022 (*Fort Pitt*); Koehler, "Hostile Nations," 427+ (*perhaps a thousand*); Calloway, *The American Revolution in Indian Country*, 33; *Narratives of the Revolution in New York*, 326; Syrett, *Shipping and the American War, 1775–1783*, 171 (*supply system in Canada*); Flick, ed., "New Sources on the Sullivan-Clinton Campaign in 1779," 265+ (*"Several chiefs came in"* and *"very rapidly effected"*).

506 **Yet the punitive marches failed:** Whittemore, *A General of the Revolution*, 148 (*"nests are destroyed"*), 149 (*"rather to have exasperated"*); Fischer, *A Well-Executed Failure*, 194 (*failure to insist on Fort Niagara*); Lengel, *General George Washington*, 312–13 (*Indian rage*); Graymont, *The Iroquois in the American Revolution*, 224 (*snowshoes*); Calloway, *The Indian World of George Washington*, 257 (*a thousand houses*); *Narratives of the Revolution in New York*, 328.

506 **Washington had hoped for a wrathful blow:** GW to John Sullivan, Sept. 15, 1779, FOL (*"final and complete"*); Fischer, *A Well-Executed Failure*, 192 (*"Whenever men raise up"*).

507 **Washington and his army had helped put:** Seneca chiefs to GW, Dec. 1, 1790, FOL (*"Town Destroyer"*).

23. EVERYTHING IS NOW AT STAKE

508 **From the moment Spain declared war, in mid-June:** Fortescue, ed., *The Correspondence of King George the Third*, 4: 388–401; Willis, *The Struggle for Sea Power*, 293 (*"never in such danger"*).

508 **Cries of "French dog!":** Flavell, *When London Was Capital of America*, 165 (*"your damned French"*); Willis, *The Struggle for Sea Power*, 293 (*"fire your indignation"*); Wheatley, ed., *Memoirs of Sir Nathaniel William Wraxall, 1772–1784*, 1: 219 (*"political gloom"*); Keppel, *The Life of Augustus Viscount Keppel*, 2: 244 (*tumbled from their pews*); Clowes, *The Royal Navy*, 3: 445 (*"humiliating state"*).

508 **Britain had a tradition of being unprepared:** Lunt, *John Burgoyne of Saratoga*, 28–29 (*forty-six guns at Pendennis*); Clowes, *The Royal Navy*, 3: 445 (*horses and cattle*); Syrett, *The Royal Navy in European Waters During the American Revolutionary War*, 76; Knight, *Portsmouth Dockyard Papers, 1774–1783*, 92–93 (*navigation buoys*); North to Sandwich, July 18, 1779, *PP Sandwich*, 3: 48 (*"employ every ship, frigate"*); Sandwich to North, Oct. 15, 1778, *PP Sandwich*, 2: 179 (*"now at stake"*).

509 **A "scheme for defense of the coast":** Admiralty board meetings, Aug. 18 and 19, 1779, UK NA, ADM 3/89 (*candles*); "August 1779. Scheme for defense of the coast," *PP Sandwich*, 3: 52; comptroller to Sandwich, Sept. 1, 1779, *PP Sandwich*, 3: 87 (*hawsers*); *Caledonian Mercury*, Aug. 14, 1779 (*twenty-shilling reward*); Toynbee, ed., *The Letters of Horace Walpole*, 9: 16 (*"pleasant to know"*); Miller, *Sea of Glory*, 404 (*Cornish tin miners*); *Gentleman's Magazine and Historical Chronicle*, 49: 422 (*Mount Edgcumbe*); *PP Sandwich*, 3: 38 (*trees were felled*); North to Amherst, July [19?], 1779, UK NA, WO 34/116, f 112–16 (*"Your army"*).

509 **That was easier commanded than effected:** Patterson, *The Other Armada*, 121 (*fifty thousand Moors*); Amherst corr., UK NA, WO 24/231, f 196 (*Isle of Wight*), f 254 (*Exeter*), f 258 (*Manchester*); Mackesy, *The War for America, 1775–1783*, 290 (*twenty-one thousand regulars*); Ruppert, "France and Spain Invade England—Almost," *JAR*, Jan. 30, 2020 (*single militia regiment*).

509 **The king proposed "for each gentleman":** Butterfield, *George III, Lord North and the People, 1779–1780*, 54 (*"properly armed"*), 55 (*"train a number of Methodists"* and *150 militia companies*); William Campbell to Amherst, July 25, 1779, UK NA, WO 34/116, f 163 (*"corps to serve His Majesty"*); Patterson, *The Other Armada*, 112 (*bankrupts*), 117 (*"bad roads and night work"*); Morris, *The Peacemakers*, 32 (*Reading jail*); Toynbee, ed., *The Letters of Horace Walpole*, 9: 18 (*"Even this little quiet village"*).

510 **Alas, each hopeful bulletin:** G. R. Jones to Amherst, July 22, 1779, UK NA, WO 34/116, f 183 (*"we have not a musket"*); Patterson, *The Other Armada*, 123 (*West Kent militiamen*); Amherst to Sandwich, Sept. 8, 1779, UK NA, WO 24/231, f 267 (*"none in store"*); Lindsay to Amherst, June 22, 1779, UK NA, WO 34/115, f 195 (*"no possibility"*); William Beford to Amherst, June 22, 1779, UK NA, WO 34/115 f 116 (*"we deceive ourselves"*); Amherst to Monckton, Aug. 24, 1779, UK NA,WO 24/231, f 196 (*"only two"*); Amherst to Haviland, Sept. 6, 1779, UK NA, WO 24/231, f 220 (*scorched-earth*).

510 **Two large camps now protected London:** Foreman, *The Duchess*, 62 (*"flower of the nobility"*), 63 (*oriental rugs*); "Homeland Defense: Protecting Britain During the American War," SoC (*thousands of tourists*); Hunter, *The Journal of Martin Hunter*, 46 (*pheasant hunting*); Gentleman's *Magazine and Historical Chronicle*, 49: 420 (*"perfect the men"*); Holt, *The Public and Domestic Life of His Late Most Gracious Majesty, George the Third*, 1: 223 (*"God Save the King"*); *Caledonian Mercury*, Oct. 5, 1778, 2–3; *Jackson's Oxford Journal*, Oct. 3, 1778, 1; Black, *George III, America's Last King*, 234 (*"thorough satisfaction"*).

511 **As captain general, His Majesty believed:** Butterfield, *George III, Lord North and the People, 1779–1780*, 60–61 (*"totally disjointed"*); Toynbee, ed., *The Letters of Horace Walpole*, 9: 20 (*"England fallen so low"*); North and Hughes, "Lord North's Correspondence, 1766–1783," 218+ (*"appearance of things"*).

511 **Yet George, whose moral courage often:** Rodger, *The Insatiable Earl*, 259–60 (*Britain's peril*); Ayling, *George the Third*, 273 (*"vigor of mind"*); Pares, *King George III and the Politicians*, 69 (*"act with the ardor"*).

511 **For eighty years France and Spain:** Mackesy, *The War for America, 1775–1783*, 279–80 (*various schemes*); Manceron, *Age of the French Revolution*, 2: 155 (*"the Descent"*); Patterson, *The Other Armada*, 7 (*blueprint drafted in 1765*); Lopez, *My Life with Benjamin Franklin*, 102 (*sketches of the English coastline*).

511 **One French commander proposed seizing the Tower:** Patterson, *The Other Armada*, 14 (*gold and silver*), 227 (*"While devoting our efforts"*); Dull, *The Age of the Ship of the Line*, 103 (*ascendant Russia*); Murphy, *Charles Gravier, Comte de Vergennes*, 268 (*invasion of Ireland*); Dull, *The French Navy and American Independence*, 129; Dull, *The Miracle of American Independence*, 112 (*quick war*); Dull, "Mahan, Sea Power, and the War for American Independence," 59+ (*single campaign*); Del Perugia, *La tentative d'invasion de l'Angleterre de 1779*, 63n (*"Love for glory"*).

512 **After a careful reconnaissance of fortifications:** Patterson, *The Other Armada*, 50 (*Bristol, Liverpool*), 55–56 (*defenses were weak*), 58 (*thirty thousand*); Ferreiro, *Brothers at Arms*, 182–83 (*garrisons undermanned*); Dull, *The Age of the Ship of the Line*, 103–4 (*ninety ships of the line*); Murphy, *Charles Gravier, Comte de Vergennes*, 269 (*Isle of Wight*); Manceron, *Age of the French Revolution*, 2: 173 (*two thousand sick sailors*); Mackesy, *The War for America, 1775–1783*, 279–80 (*Subsidiary raids*).

512 **Once the English defenses collapsed:** Patterson, *The Other Armada*, 58 (*for Gibraltar*); Hardman, *The Life of Louis XVI*, 121 (*more than three hundred million livres*), 140; BF to Committee for Foreign Affairs, May 26, 1779, FOL fn (*three-quarters*); Morris, *The Peacemakers*, 27 (*"scepter of the seas"*). The French government's revenue for 1779 was about four hundred million livres. Much of the naval spending was incurred as debt (Dull, *The French Navy and American Independence*, 135).

512 **Charles III had insisted that his fleet:** Dull, *The French Navy and American Independence*, 148 (*by early September*); Mackesy, *The War for America, 1775–1783*, 280 (*treacherous autumn weather*); Morris, *The Peacemakers*, 29; Martelli, *Jemmy Twitcher*, 195–96 (*piety*); Patterson, *The Other Armada*, 151–52 (*hernia*); Maugras, *The Duc de Lauzun and the Court of*

Marie Antoinette, 184 (*"pedantic, dull"*); Martelli, *Jemmy Twitcher*, 109 (*"Your duty is to restore"*). D'Orvilliers was a few months shy of seventy.

514 **Even as planners deliberated over:** Ferreiro, *Brothers at Arms*, 183 (*delayed*); Patterson, *The Other Armada*, 68 (*"weaklings"*); Dull, *The French Navy and American Independence*, 144–46; Del Perugia, *La tentative d'invasion de l'Angleterre de 1779*, 88; Mackesy, *The War for America, 1775–1783*, 280 (*several weeks late*).

514 **Not a Spanish man-of-war could be seen:** Patterson, *The Other Armada*, 62–63 (*take a compass bearing*); Dull, *The French Navy and American Independence*, 149; Chávez, *Spain and the Independence of the United States*, 139–40 (*fourteen thousand Spanish troops*); Morris, *The Peacemakers*, 31 (*Córdova finally put to sea*); Montmorin to Vergennes, July 23, 1779, Archives Diplomatiques, Fonds Administration Centrale, 5. Affaires politiques, série 37CP, Espagne, Paris, vol. 594, f 464 (*"the elements rise up"*).

514 **On July 23, with cannon salutes:** Clowes, *The Royal Navy*, 3: 444 (*distributed to Spanish captains*); Patterson, *The Other Armada*, 68 (*even lemons*); Del Perugia, *La tentative d'invasion de l'Angleterre de 1779*, 88; Manceron, *Age of the French Revolution*, 2: 175 (*"vast writing"*), 176 (*strain out the sludge* and *adjacent to pens*); Mackesy, *The War for America, 1775–1783*, 280–81 (*consumed half of their onboard provisions*).

514 **Typhus and smallpox had appeared:** Manceron, *Age of the French Revolution*, 2: 174 (flux intestinal); Patterson, *The Other Armada*, 162 (*more than six hundred*), 165 (*"Blackness overwhelms me"*); Del Perugia, *La tentative d'invasion de l'Angleterre de 1779*, 97 (*a hundred from* Ville de Paris); Murphy, *Charles Gravier, Comte de Vergennes*, 277 (*taking off the sick*).

515 **On Friday, July 30, d'Orvilliers ordered:** *PP Sandwich*, 3: 6 (*beat northward*); *JPJ*, 191–92 (*five thousand guns*); Ruppert, "France and Spain Invade England—Almost," *JAR*, Jan. 30, 2020 (*double column*); "The History of the Spanish Armada," Royal Museums Greenwich (la felicissima armada).

515 **If fearsome, the size of the force:** James, *The British Navy in Adversity*, 178 (*"center our hopes"*); Patterson, *The Other Armada*, 167 (*too little of everything*); Chevalier, *Histoire de la marine française pendant la guerre de l'indépendance américaine*, 169–70 (*pilots*); Ruppert, "France and Spain Invade England—Almost," *JAR*, Jan. 30, 2020 (*out of water*); Morris, *The Peacemakers*, 31 (*died in his arms*).

515 **Broken with grief:** Chevalier, *Histoire de la marine française pendant la guerre de l'indépendance américaine*, 165–66 (*"The Lord took away"*).

515 **Day after day, from first light to last:** Dumas, *Memoirs of His Own Time*, 1: 17 (*searched the sea*); Ferreiro, *Brothers at Arms*, 186 (*Army of Invasion*); Ruppert, "France and Spain Invade England—Almost," *JAR*, Jan. 30, 2020 (*Fifty battalions of infantry*); Del Perugia, *La tentative d'invasion de l'Angleterre de 1779* (*more than a hundred field guns*); Patterson, *The Other Armada*, 149–51, 155 (*Five hundred barges and transports*); Manceron, *Age of the French Revolution*, 2: 180–81 (*bobbed at anchor*).

516 **Half the force encamped outside the Breton port:** Maugras, *The Duc de Lauzun and the Court of Marie Antoinette*, 184 (*"eager to be shot at"*); Patterson, *The Other Armada*, 153 (*"glorious opportunity"*); Manceron, *Age of the French Revolution*, 2: 170–71 (*"tents, stacked arms"*).

516 **A hundred miles to the northeast:** author visit, Normandy, June 2014, signage, "The Vaussieux Camp" (*along the Seulles River*); Maugras, *The Duc de Lauzun and the Court of Marie Antoinette*, 186 (*fine ladies from Paris*); Patterson, *The Other Armada*, 155 (*Rouen*); Ruppert, "France and Spain Invade England—Almost," *JAR*, Jan. 30, 2020 (*eight thousand men shuttled*).

516 **An ardent young officer:** Manceron, *Age of the French Revolution*, 2: 172–73 (*"My heart yearns"*); Morris, *The Peacemakers*, 28 (*"seeing England humiliated"*).

516 **His return to France from America:** *LAAR*, 2: 225–28 (*mutinous crewmen*), 232 (*"sense of sorrow"*); Unger, *Lafayette*, 93–94 (*in irons*); Tower, *The Marquis de La Fayette in the American Revolution*, 56 (*"I had the honor"*); Maurois, *Adrienne*, 75 (*house arrest*).

517 **That golden incarceration lasted but a week:** *LAAR*, 2: 226; Auricchio, *The Marquis Lafayette Reconsidered*, 80 (*dragoon regiment*); Unger, *Lafayette*, 94 (*"rebel and fugitive"*), 97–98 (*"youthful courtier"*).

517 **He found a kindred spirit:** BF to Lafayette, Mar. 22, 1779, FOL (*"strong desire"*); Schiff, *A Great Improvisation*, 208 (*bow three times*).

517 **The previous day he and Lafayette had:** BF to Lafayette, Mar. 22, 1779, FOL (*"Four or five thousand"*); BF to J. P. Jones, Apr. 27, 1779, FOL (*"honor enough"*).

517 **Meanwhile, the minister plenipotentiary and Lafayette:** "List of prints to illustrate British cruelties," May 1779, FOL fn [vol. 29]; Lafayette to BF, July 12, 1779, FOL; author visit, Benjamin Franklin Museum, Philadelphia, Mar. 22, 2022 (*thirty-eight-page list*).

518 **After initially approving the Irish Sea expedition:** Lafayette to GW, Oct. 7, 1779, FOL (*leader of the vanguard*); *Memoirs, Correspondence and Manuscripts of General Lafayette*, 1: 296 (*"fermentation"*); Lafayette to BF, July 12, 1779, FOL (*"entirely depend"*); Schama, *Citizens*, 42–43 (*"the very heart of England"*).

518 **But as the August days dwindled:** Del Perugia, *La tentative d'invasion de l'Angleterre de 1779*, 142 (*began to doubt*); Martelli, *Jemmy Twitcher*, 196–97 (*"our patience"*); Patterson, *The Other Armada*, 155 (*rats gnawed the tents*); Craveri, *The Last Libertines*, 195 (*"My regiment would suffer"*).

518 **George III was also impatient:** Mackesy, *The War for America, 1775–1783*, 286 (*"I sigh"*); PP *Sandwich*, 3: 35–36 (*twenty thousand men*), 59 (*150 tons daily*); Patterson, *The Other Armada*, 171–72 (*into Torbay*); Clowes, *The Royal Navy*, 3: 447 (*French junction with the Spanish*); Ruppert, "France and Spain Invade England—Almost," *JAR*, Jan. 30, 2020; Mackesy, *The War for America, 1775–1783*, 284 (*"greatest evil"*).

519 **British naval strategy in home waters:** Marshall, ed., *The Oxford History of the British Empire*, 2: 174 (*Western Approaches*); Mackesy, *The War for America, 1775–1783*, 287 (*frigate squadrons took station*).

519 **No Drake arose to command:** Rodger, *The Insatiable Earl*, 257 (*second-in-command*); Hiscocks, "The Channel Fleet Retreat—August 1779," blog post, Nov. 24, 2016 (*Greenwich Hospital*); Patterson, *The Other Armada*, 178 (*"never thinks beforehand"*); Mackesy, *The War for America, 1775–1783*, 288 (*"more reason to trust in Providence"*).

519 **To help subdue the greatest threat:** "Richard Kempenfelt," https://morethannelson.com/officer/richard-kempenfelt/ (*religious verse*); Patterson, *The Other Armada*, 199 (*"jealous obstinacy"*); "Sir Charles Hardy," https://www.historyofparliamentonline.org/volume/1754-1790/member/hardy-sir-charles-1714-80 (*"fund of good nature"*); James, *The British Navy in Adversity*, 174 (*"An admiral who commands"*).

519 **Even a Drake would have been confounded:** PP *Sandwich*, 3: 51; Rodger, *The Insatiable Earl*, 257–58 (*stretch the battle line*); Andreopoulos and Selesky, eds., *The Aftermath of Defeat*, 11 (*"summer service only"*); Dull, *The French Navy and American Independence*, 158 (*mostly healthy*); "Ships Under Command of Sir Charles Hardy That Are Coppered," July 1779, in Fortescue, ed., *The Correspondence of King George the Third*, 4: 401; Mackesy, *The War for America, 1775–1783*, 286 (*shelter in English harbors*).

520 **"I may appear strange":** Mackesy, *The War for America, 1775–1783*, 288; PP *Sandwich*, 3: 6 (*"combined fleets of France and Spain"*), 55 (*"I dread the thoughts"*).

520 **But another summer storm slapped the Grand Fleet:** Charles Hardy to Admiralty, Aug. 6, 1779, UK NA, ADM 1/95, f 406 (*clawed back down*); Hiscocks, "The Channel Fleet Retreat—August 1779," blog post, Nov. 24, 2016 (*worth £4 million*); Clowes, *The Royal Navy*, 3: 445 (*convoy from Jamaica*).

520 **That mystery was solved on Sunday, August 15:** Patterson, *The Other Armada*, 181 (*"wood on the water"* and *Jacob Wheate*); Mackesy, *The War for America, 1775–1783*, 289 (*controlled the English Channel*).

521 **At one p.m. on August 16:** Morris, *The Peacemakers*, 36 (*"riding out the current"*); Hiscocks, "The Channel Fleet Retreat—August 1779," blog post, Nov. 24, 2016 (*pounded with broadsides*); Winfield, *British Warships in the Age of Sail, 1714–1792*, 100 (*L'Ardent*).

521 **"The consternation amongst all ranks here":** Coupland, *The American Revolution and the British Empire*, 26–27 (*"families have already removed"*); Morris, *The Peacemakers*, 36–37 (*sink vessels* and *"fire ten shots"*); *The Parliamentary History of England*, 20: 1068–76 (*super-*

annuated gunners); Keppel, *The Life of Augustus Viscount Keppel*, 2: 245 (*too large for the barrels*); Morris, *The Peacemakers*, 36–37; Hiscocks, "The Channel Fleet Retreat—August 1779," blog post, Nov. 24, 2016 (*pleading ill health*); *PP Sandwich*, 3: 67 ("*set fire to the dockyard?*"), 67–69 ("*despond too much*"), 71 ("*a little check*"), 74 (*fireships*). The boom was completed on August 24.

521 **"No news of Sir Charles Hardy":** Mackesy, *The War for America, 1775–1783*, 293–94 ("*our fate is sealed*"); Patterson, *The Other Armada*, 183 ("*reduced to ashes*"); Whiteley, "Horace Walpole, Early American," 212+ ("*set his frock*").

521 **Only dimly aware of the fright:** Manceron, *Age of the French Revolution*, 2: 179 ("*anchored in calm waters*"); James, *The British Navy in Adversity*, 180–82 ("*this terrible epidemic*"); Lacour-Gayet, *La marine militaire de la France sous le règne de Louis XVI*, 281 ("*malignant fever*"); Chevalier, *Histoire de la marine française pendant la guerre de l'indépendance américaine*, 172n (*brail the mainsail*); Ferreiro, *Brothers at Arms*, 188 (*draft sailors from his frigates*).

522 **"We are sailing as if at random":** Lacour-Gayet, *La marine militaire de la France sous le règne de Louis XVI*, 275 ("*Spaniards are even more annoyed*").

522 **Then, to d'Orvilliers's astonishment:** Lacour-Gayet, *La marine militaire de la France sous le règne de Louis XVI*, 273–74 (Terpsichore); Clowes, *The Royal Navy*, 3: 447 (*forgo both the landings*); Martelli, *Jemmy Twitcher*, 201; Allison and Ferreiro, eds., *The American Revolution*, 70–71; Mackesy, *The War for America, 1775–1783*, 181 (*descend on Falmouth*).

522 **This asinine scheme:** Patterson, *The Other Armada*, 205 (*Spanish ambassador*), 206 (*next spring*); James, *The British Navy in Adversity*, 182 ("*our ministers have behaved*"); Ruppert, "France and Spain Invade England—Almost," *JAR*, Jan. 30, 2020 (*winter winds*); Mackesy, *The War for America, 1775–1783*, 294–95; Martelli, *Jemmy Twitcher*, 201–2 ("*condition of the navy*").

522 **D'Orvilliers had assumed that the Channel fleet:** Ruppert, "France and Spain Invade England—Almost," *JAR*, Jan. 30, 2020 (*on August 25 a passing vessel*); Patterson, *The Other Armada*, 194–95 (*resupply convoy*), 196 (*dawn on August 31*); Martelli, *Jemmy Twitcher*, 202; Hiscocks, "The Channel Fleet Retreat—August 1779," blog post, Nov. 24, 2016 (*off the Cornish coast*); *PP Sandwich*, 3: 7–8; Ruppert, "France and Spain Invade England—Almost," *JAR*, Jan. 30, 2020 (*Eddystone Rocks*).

523 **"I shall do my utmost":** Charles Hardy to Admiralty, Sept. 1, 1779, UK NA, ADM 1/95, f 410; Miller, *Sea of Glory*, 407 ("*overtake nothing*"); George to Sandwich, Sept. 2, 1779, *PP Sandwich*, 3: 85; Mackesy, *The War for America, 1775–1783*, 295 (*unsound capital ships*); Sandwich to Hardy, Sept. 2, 1779, *PP Sandwich*, 3: 88–89 ("*eyes of the world*").

523 **But the fleet admiral had had enough:** James, *The British Navy in Adversity*, 185–86 (*ever firing a shot*); Patterson, *The Other Armada*, 202 (Royal George); Miller, *Sea of Glory*, 407 (*prevent them from witnessing*); Hiscocks, "The Channel Fleet Retreat—August 1779," blog post, Nov. 24, 2016 (*craven retreat*); *Caledonian Mercury*, Sept. 27, 1779 ("*Your grand fleet*").

523 **No one was more fretful than the king:** *PP Sandwich*, 3: 92–93 ("*these faithless people*"); Patterson, *The Other Armada*, 203 (*Sandwich boarded* Victory).

524 **Hardy pledged to put back to sea:** Black and Woodfine, eds., *The British Navy and the Use of Naval Power in the Eighteenth Century*, 149 ("*We have no one friend*"); North to Amherst, Sept. 5, 1779, UK NA, WO 34/118, f 61 ("*left the west of England*").

524 **In truth, the enemy no longer posed a threat:** Ruppert, "France and Spain Invade England—Almost," *JAR*, Jan. 30, 2020; Patterson, *The Other Armada*, 211.

524 **Illness was a way of life—and death:** Dull, *The French Navy and the Seven Years' War*, 80–81 (*kill five thousand civilians*); Patterson, *The Other Armada*, 210 (*eight thousand sick and dying* and *eat fish*); Allison and Ferreiro, eds., *The American Revolution*, 71 (*three thousand invalid Spaniards*); H. Butterfield, *George III, Lord North, and the People, 1779–80*, 66n; Chevalier, *Histoire de la marine française pendant la guerre de l'indépendance américaine*, 171–72 (Palmier *and* Destin); Ruppert, "France and Spain Invade England—Almost," *JAR*, Jan. 30, 2020 (Augustus); *JPJ*, 192 (*61 dead*); Manceron, *Age of the French Revolution*, 2: 181 ("*a great many perished*").

524 **In the end the Bourbon expedition:** Morris, *The Peacemakers*, 41 (*"This is incredible"*).

525 **Hardy would not put to sea again:** Patterson, *The Other Armada*, 202 (*"Tardy"*); Morris, *The Peacemakers*, 40 (*"special Providence"* and *"his own dunghill"*); "Sir Charles Hardy," https://morethannelson.com/officer/sir-charles-hardy/ (*apoplectic fit*).

525 **Versailles proposed mounting another lunge:** Lacour-Gayet, *La marine militaire de la France sous le règne de Louis XVI*, 289; Patterson, *The Other Armada*, 226; Morris, *The Peacemakers*, 41 (*rank with dysentery*); Unger, *Lafayette*, 103 (*"restore vigor"*); *PP Sandwich*, 3: 9 (*pass the winter in Brest*); Del Perugia, *La tentative d'invasion de l'Angleterre de 1779*, 161–62n (*discord in the port*); Montmorin to Vergennes, Sept. 27, 1779, Archives Diplomatiques, Fonds Administration Centrale, 5. Affaires politiques, série 37CP, Espagne, Paris, vol. 595, f 441 (*sign his own letters*); Patterson, *The Other Armada*, 211 (*retired to Moulins*); Bernier, *Secrets of Marie Antoinette*, 282 (*"unable to find the English"*).

525 **Across the Channel, disgruntlement quickly gave way:** Roberts, *The Last King of America*, 371 (*"disgrace, misfortune"*); Lutnick, *The American Revolution and the British Press, 1775–1783*, 155 (*"vainly boast"*); Rodger, *The Insatiable Earl*, 271 (*"bold and manly"*).

526 **Lord North fairly crowed at the French retreat:** *PP Sandwich*, 3: 97 (*"no reason to be dissatisfied"*).

526 **But where to find the mischievous:** Seitz, *Paul Jones*, 32 (*Irish shoreline*); Callo, *John Paul Jones, America's First Sea Warrior*, 82–83 (*"Bantry Bay"*); Thomas, *John Paul Jones*, 172 (*"combustibles"*); Amherst to Lt. Gen. Adam Gordon, Sept. 3, 1779, UK NA, WO 23/231, f 235 (*"on your guard"*).

526 **This last was closer to the mark:** Boudriot, *John Paul Jones and the Bonhomme Richard*, 97 (*Royal Navy officer tunics*); Barnes, ed., *Fanning's Narrative*, 30–31; Gilkerson, *The Ships of John Paul Jones*, 34–36 (*white facings*); Isaacson, *Benjamin Franklin*, 389–90; *JPJ*, 191; De Koven, *The Life and Letters of John Paul Jones*, 1: 402. Leith Harbour was granted to Edinburgh by King Robert I in 1329 (Arnot, *The History of Edinburgh*, 570).

526 **Jones was an eager accomplice:** Allen, *A Naval History of the American Revolution*, 2: 441 (*vexatious year*); *JPJ*, 177 (*"chained down"*); De Koven, *The Life and Letters of John Paul Jones*, 1: 387 (*"chained down"*); Schaeper, *John Paul Jones and the Battle of Flamborough Head*, 70 (*dockyard at Lorient*); Gilkerson, *The Ships of John Paul Jones*, 32 (*spacious great cabin*); Thomas, *John Paul Jones*, 151–52 (*giltwork, parquet decks*).

527 **His 380 crewmen included more than a few:** *JPJ*, 193 (*"wretches"*); Gilkerson, *The Ships of John Paul Jones*, 34–36 (*Irish mercenaries*); *JPJ*, 197 (*Danish, Dutch, French*); Matthews and Wecter, *Our Soldiers Speak, 1775–1918*, 44; J. P. Jones to BF, Oct. 3, 1779, FOL; Sweetman, ed., *Great American Naval Battles*, 34 (*squadron also comprised*); *JPJ*, 182 (*"harm's way"*).

527 **They had sailed from Lorient before dawn:** J. P. Jones to BF, Oct. 3, 1779, FOL; *JPJ*, 209–16 (Mayflower); Maclay, *A History of the United States Navy from 1775 to 1898*, 1: 114 (*320 men*), 115; Barnes, ed., *Fanning's Narrative*, 24 (*"speaking trumpet"*), 28 (*"Thus it was with Jones"*); Schaeper, *John Paul Jones and the Battle of Flamborough Head*, 38–40, 53–54. Franklin accused Landais of being "so imprudent, so litigious and quarrelsome" (BF to Pierre Landais, Mar. 12, 1780, FOL).

527 **Entering the Firth of Forth, Jones:** De Koven, *The Life and Letters of John Paul Jones*, 1: 439 (*"teach the enemy humanity"*); Allen, *A Naval History of the American Revolution*, 2: 453 (*"do not wish to distress"*); Sands, ed., *Life and Correspondence of John Paul Jones*, 172 (*"demand your contribution"*).

528 **The inhabitants were distressed anyway:** *JPJ*, 218 (*Drums pounded, pipes skirled*); "John Paul Jones and the Building of the Leith Fort," *Georgian Edinburgh* (blog), Feb. 3, 2012 (*castle portcullises*);"History of Edinburgh," Civitatis Edinburgh, https://www.introducingedinburgh.com/history#; Sands, ed., *Life and Correspondence of John Paul Jones*, 176n (*"piratical invader"*).

528 **That supplication was answered:** Barnes, ed., *Fanning's Narrative*, 32 (*wind shifted from northeast*); J. P. Jones to BF, Oct. 3, 1779, FOL (*"gave up the project"*).

528 **The cruise through the firth, if unsuccessful:** Thomas, *Memoirs of the Marquis of Rocking-*

ham and His Contemporaries, 2: 382 (*agitated Britons*); Callo, *John Paul Jones, America's First Sea Warrior*, 82–83 ("*here, there*"), 87 ("*price of coals*"); J. P. Jones to BF, Oct. 3, 1779, FOL fn; Maclay, *A History of the United States Navy from 1775 to 1898*, 1: 114 (*Two pilots tricked*).

528   **As a compromise he ordered the flotilla:** Gilkerson, *The Ships of John Paul Jones*, 43 (*at two-thirty p.m.*); J. P. Jones to BF, Oct. 3, 1779, FOL (*convoy*); Middlebrook, ed., *The Log of the* Bon Homme Richard, 45–46 (*give chase*).

529   **In more than thirty years at sea for the Crown:** "Sir Richard Pearson," https://morethan nelson.com/officer/sir-richard-pearson/ (*Manila to Quebec*); Walsh, *Night on Fire*, 9 (*French grapeshot*); *JPJ*, 226–27. Jones, who later commanded *Serapis*, wrote that she had ports for fifty-two guns but mounted forty-four (J. P. Jones to BF, Feb. 12, 1780, FOL).

529   **Upon approaching the Yorkshire coast:** Thomas, *John Paul Jones*, 179 ("*enemy on our shores*"); Sweetman, ed., *Great American Naval Battles*, 35–36 (*cutter brought warnings* and Countess of Scarborough); Walsh, *Night on Fire*, 25 (*sails furled*), 26 (*double-shotted*).

529   **On light airs from the southwest:** *JPJ*, 228 (*nearly four hours* and "*form line of battle*"); Barnes, ed., *Fanning's Narrative*, 35 (*double allowance*).

530   **As the stranger flying a Union Jack:** Richard Pearson account, Oct. 6, 1779, in *Annual Register 1779*, 309–12 ("Princess Royal"); Mahan, "John Paul Jones in the Revolution," 204+ (*within pistol shot*); Thomas, *John Paul Jones*, 182–83 ("*What ship is that?*"); Middlebrook, ed., *The Log of the Bon Homme Richard*, 45–46 ("*Tell me instantly*").

530   **The stranger's Union Jack fluttered to the deck:** Gilkerson, *The Ships of John Paul Jones*, 43 (*red, white, and blue stripes*), 45 (*killing or wounding thirty*); *JPJ*, 229–31; Walsh, *Night on Fire*, 40 (*half of the twenty French marines*). Jones initially believed that two guns had exploded (J. P. Jones to BF, Oct. 3, 1779, FOL).

530   *Richard* **drew slightly ahead:** Gilkerson, *The Ships of John Paul Jones*, 45 (*cross her stern*); Thomas, *John Paul Jones*, 184; Callo, *John Paul Jones, America's First Sea Warrior*, 89 (*grappling hooks*); Richard Pearson account, Oct. 6, 1779, in *Annual Register 1779*, 309–12 ("*muzzles of our guns*" and "*on fire no less than ten or twelve times*").

531   **It was now after eight p.m.:** Thomas, *John Paul Jones*, 189 (*spectators lined the cliffs*); Walsh, *Night on Fire*, 51–52; Perry, *Reminiscences of the Revolution*, 40–41 ("*shivered to pieces*"), 42 ("*lightning bugs*"); *JPJ*, 233 ("*mortised together*"); McGrath, *Give Me a Fast Ship*, 308 ("*bloody as a butcher*"); J. P. Jones to BF, Oct. 3, 1779, FOL ("*dreadful beyond language*" and *he personally aimed*).

531   **The battle intensified with the abrupt appearance:** J. P. Jones to BF, Oct. 3, 1779, FOL ("*utter astonishment*"); J. P. Jones to BF, Oct. 3, 1779, FOL fn; Gilkerson, *The Ships of John Paul Jones*, 48–50; *JPJ*, 234–35; Allen, *A Naval History of the American Revolution*, 2: 463 (*three lanterns*); Walsh, *Night on Fire*, 76 ("*beg you will not sink us*"); Thomas, *John Paul Jones*, 190 ("Alliance has wounded me"); "*Bonhomme Richard* (Frigate) 1779," Naval History and Heritage Command. Historian Thomas J. Schaeper makes a good case for the fratricidal fire being accidental (Schaeper, *John Paul Jones and the Battle of Flamborough Head*, 44–51; see also affidavit from *Alliance* crew, Oct. 21, 1779, HL, HM 1589).

531   **Each passing moment seemed to bring:** Barnes, ed., *Fanning's Narrative*, 45 (*beat out fires*); Thomas, *John Paul Jones*, 190–93 (*British boarding party*); Sweetman, ed., *Great American Naval Battles*, 41 (*pistol butt*), 43 (*versions of his defiant reply*); Lewis, "'I Have Not Yet Begun to Fight,'" 229+ ("*most determined negative*" and "*I do not dream*").

532   **This he did, for at ten-fifteen p.m.:** *JPJ*, 236 (*edged along a yardarm*); Thomas, *John Paul Jones*, 194 (*lungs seared*); Walsh, *Night on Fire*, 71 (*into the sea*).

532   **The British knew when they were beaten:** *Caledonian Mercury*, Oct. 16, 1779 (*dismounted seven guns*); McGrath, *Give Me a Fast Ship*, 306 ("*Sir, I have struck*").

532   **An American officer escorted him:** J. P. Jones to BF, Oct. 3, 1779, FOL; Gilkerson, *The Ships of John Paul Jones*, 51 (*glass of wine*); De Koven, *The Life and Letters of John Paul Jones*, 1: 462 ("*diamond cut diamond*").

533   **The diamonds had cut deep:** Callo, *John Paul Jones, America's First Sea Warrior*, 93 (*nearly three hundred casualties*); Richard Pearson account, Oct. 6, 1779, in *Annual Register 1779*,

309–12; *JPJ*, 244; Thomas, *John Paul Jones*, 197 (*"only the collars"*); Barnes, ed., *Fanning's Narrative*, 58–59 (*"dropped off from their bones"*).

533 **Richard also was mortally hurt:** McGrath, *Give Me a Fast Ship*, 208–9; J. P. Jones to BF, Oct. 3, 1779, FOL (*"within a few inches"*); Appendix A, log book, John Paul Jones Cottage Museum (*"still gaining"*); Mahan, "John Paul Jones in the Revolution," 204+ (*Bow first*).

533 **Serapis could still swim:** Barnes, ed., *The Logs of the* Serapis, Alliance, Ariel, 25–27 (*jury-rigged*); Callo, *John Paul Jones, America's First Sea Warrior*, 101 (*led by* Prudent); Allen, *A Naval History of the American Revolution*, 2: 481 (*Dunkirk*); J. P. Jones to BF, Oct. 11, 1779, FOL fn. The prisoners were to be exchanged for French captives held by the British (J. P. Jones to BF, Dec. 13, 1779, FOL).

533 **Although ostensibly neutral, Holland appreciated:** Scott, *British Foreign Policy in the Age of the American Revolution*, 295–96 (*demanded his arrest*); Thomas, *John Paul Jones*, 202 (*"overjoyed"*); *JPJ*, 247 (*balladeers*); De Koven, *The Life and Letters of John Paul Jones*, 1: 475 (*"enchanted with your exploits"*); BF to J. P. Jones, Oct. 15, 1779, FOL (*"your cool conduct"*).

534 **London insisted that the tactical defeat:** Sweetman, ed., *Great American Naval Battles*, 42 (*"Let me fight him again"*); Miller, *Sea of Glory*, 386 (*"jack o'lantern"*); Seitz, *Paul Jones*, 106 (*"Scotch bonnet"*).

534 **A British blockade of forty-two vessels:** J. P. Jones to BF, Jan. 16, 1780, FOL fn; Thomas, *John Paul Jones*, 210 (*"pleasure of laughing"*), 215 (*"feasted and caressed"*); Fraser, *Marie Antoinette*, 171 (*new ballet*); Sweetman, ed., *Great American Naval Battles*, 43 (*Marie-Antoinette invited him*). Landais would eventually be stripped of both his American and his French naval commissions (Norton, "The Revolutionary War's Most Enigmatic Naval Captain: Pierre Landais," *JAR*, July 17, 2018).

534 **A small, remote sea battle in a large war:** The warship *America* was ultimately given to France as a gesture of appreciation and to replace a French vessel destroyed while entering Boston Harbor (*JPJ*, 317, 328).

534 **Serapis, described by Jones:** J. P. Jones to BF, Nov. 29, 1779, FOL (*"best ship I ever saw"*); J. P. Jones to BF, June 23, 1780 fn; Winfield, *British Warships in the Age of Sail, 1714–1792*, 178; Thomas, *John Paul Jones*, 23 (*prize money to descendants*).

535 **As for Jones, his hour done:** *JPJ*, 404; Thomas, *John Paul Jones*, 219 (*"Insulted freedom bled"*).

24. THE GREATEST EVENT THAT HAS HAPPENED

536 **At an unexpected moment in an unexpected place:** Lawrence, *Storm over Savannah*, 4 (*forty-two French warships*).

536 **Still seething over his failures:** Jones, ed., *The Siege of Savannah in 1779*, 13 (*seven hundred assault troops*).

536 **After eight convulsive months in the West Indies:** Dull, *The French Navy and American Independence*, 161 (*return to Europe*); GW to Gouverneur Morris, May 8, 1779 (*"more certain success"*); GW to Conrad-Alexandre Gérard, May 1, 1779, FOL; John Jay to GW, May 10, 1779, FOL.

536 **"I would certainly have been declared":** Merlant, *Soldiers and Sailors of France in the American War for Independence*, 88; Jones, ed., *The Siege of Savannah in 1779*, 12 (*twenty-two ships of the line*); Tucker, *Brothers in Liberty*, 91 (*property-owning*); Davis, "Black Haitian Soldiers at the Siege of Savannah," *JAR*, Feb. 22, 2021 (*Lenoir, the Marquis de Rouvray*); "African Americans and Native Americans of the Revolutionary War Era Who Should Be Better Remembered," *JAR*, Feb. 15, 2022; A. Hamilton to Steuben, March 27, 1794, FOL; Allison and Ferreiro, eds., 188–90; Lawrence, *Storm over Savannah*, 6–7 (*hydrographers*); Taillemite, "Bougainville, Louis-Antoine de," *Dictionary of Canadian Biography*, vol. 5; d'Estaing to GW, Sept. 17, 1778, FOL fn (*circumnavigation*).

537 **Regardless of his strength, d'Estaing knew:** Willis, *The Struggle for Sea Power*, 313–14 (*rudders on seven ships*); Lawrence, *Storm over Savannah*, 14 (*"marks of death"*); Jones, ed., *The Siege of Savannah in 1779*, 62 (*so wormy*).

537 **In a dispatch carried by d'Estaing's adjutant:** Massey, *John Laurens and the American Revolution*, 144 (*no more than a week*); Mackesy, *The War for America, 1775–1783*, 277; d'Estaing

comment in O'Connor siege journal, Oct. 22, 1779, Archives Nationales, navy archives, série B4, d'Estaing corr., vol. 142, micro, f 156 (*"American gazettes"*).

537 **On Thursday, September 9, d'Estaing clambered:** Jones, ed., *The Siege of Savannah in 1779*, 13 (*Five Fathom Hole*); "Tybee Island Lighthouse," https://www.lighthousefriends.com/light .asp?ID=322; "Inventory of Historic Light Stations," https://irma.nps.gov/DataStore/ Reference/Profile/2299727; Lawrence, *Storm over Savannah*, 109–10.

538 **After more French troops landed:** Lawrence, *Storm over Savannah*, 7 (*"working night and day"*), 44 (*"pousse-cailloux"*).

538 **Perhaps his luck was changing:** James, *The British Navy in Adversity*, 144–46 (*"convoy has arrived"*); Clowes, *The Royal Navy*, 434 (*St. Vincent*); O'Shaughnessy, *An Empire Divided*, 169–79 (*twenty barrels*).

538 **D'Estaing then fixed his sights on Grenada:** O'Shaughnessy, " 'If Others Will Not Be Active, I Must Drive,' " 1+ (*second only to Jamaica*); Clowes, *The Royal Navy*, 434 (*thirty rich merchantmen*); Willis, *The Struggle for Sea Power*, 306 ("Soldats, en avant"); Conway, *The War of American Independence, 1775–1783*, 136–37; Manceron, *Age of the French Revolution*, 2: 143 (*Tropical birds*); Mackesy, *The War for America, 1775–1783*, 273. D'Estaing intended to attack Barbados, but contrary winds sent him to Grenada.

538 **Alerted to this French insult:** Ralfe, *The Naval Biography of Great Britain*, 1: 78–79 (*misinformed*); James, *The British Navy in Adversity*, 151–53 (*"general chase"*); Clowes, *The Royal Navy*, 436–37 (Prince of Wales, Boyne); William Cornwallis, *Lion*, to Peter Parker, July 26, 1779, UK NA, ADM 1/241, f 297 (*protect his transports*).

539 **By one count, *Prince of Wales* had ninety-five holes:** O'Shaughnessy, *An Empire Divided*, 171; Ralfe, *The Naval Biography of Great Britain*, 1: 81 (Monmouth *was dismasted*); William Cornwallis, *Lion*, to Peter Parker, July 26, 1779, UK NA, ADM 1/241, f 297 (*four shots in the bowsprit*); Mahan, *The Major Operations of the Navies in the War of American Independence*, 137 (*"motive power"*); James, *The British Navy in Adversity*, 153 (*183 men were dead*); Mackesy, *The War for America, 1775–1783*, 273 (*six British regiments*), 274 (*around Jamaica*); Conway, *The War of American Independence, 1775–1783*, 136–37 (*"islands must fall"*); Willis, *The Struggle for Sea Power*, 309–10 (*"death knell"*), 310–11 (*learn French* and *"How different"*).

539 **Despite winning the day in Grenada:** James, *The British Navy in Adversity*, 153 (*"seamanship equaled his courage"*); Mahan, *The Major Operations of the Navies in the War of American Independence*, 137 (*French casualties*); Loménie, *Beaumarchais and His Times*, 312 (*two million livres*); Lemaître, *Beaumarchais*, 252.

539 **Yet Britain had lost the richest island:** O'Shaughnessy, *An Empire Divided*, 170 (*"sweeten his tea"*); *Caledonian Mercury*, Oct. 4, 1779 (Te Deum); Schoenbrun, *Triumph in Paris*, 251 (*Grenada* and *l'Amiral*).

541 **Warnings of the French arrival:** "An English Journal of the Siege of Savannah in 1779," 12+ (*Tybee lighthouse*); Pownall and Almon, *The Remembrancer*, 9: 68; Lawrence, *Storm over Savannah*, 25 (*"If we are abandoned"*).

541 **In his headquarters on Broughton Street:** author visit, Savannah, Nov. 14–15, 2019, signage (*breastworks, ditches*); Lawrence, *Storm over Savannah*, 2 (*St. James Square*), 110; Swisher, *The Revolutionary War in the Southern Back Country*, 14; Deaton, "James Wright, 1716–1785," *New Georgia Encyclopedia* (*eleven plantations*); Martin and Harris, *Savannah 1779*, 70. Historian Sylvia Frey estimated that as many as five thousand Georgia slaves escaped bondage, but Cassandra Pybus put the figure at about one-third that number (Schama, *Rough Crossings*, 97–98; Pybus, "Jefferson's Faulty Math," 243+).

542 **Blacks and whites alike burned buildings:** "Account of the Siege of Savannah from a British Source," 129+ (*fifteen gun batteries*); "An English Journal of the Siege of Savannah in 1779," 12+ (*guns were transferred*); Pownall and Almon, *The Remembrancer*, 9: 68–70 (*Sails became tents*).

542 **On Thursday morning a French courier:** Lawrence, *Storm over Savannah*, 23 (aux armes de Sa Majesté); Pownall and Almon, *The Remembrancer*, 9: 72–73 (*"summons His Excellency"*); Cruger, "The Siege of Savannah, 1779," 489+ (*"the rules of war"*).

542 **At noon, as if by heavenly intercession:** Lawrence, *Storm over Savannah*, 4, 17–18 (*red feathers*); Sisken and Sisken, "A Wonderful Revolutionary Letter," https://njpostalhistory.org/february12featuredcover.html; Martin and Harris, *Savannah 1779*, 52–53.

542 **French and American commanders would later trade:** Swisher, *The Revolutionary War in the Southern Back Country*, 94–95 (*Walls Cut*); Schama, *Rough Crossings*, 98 (*"bears, wolves"*); Wilson, *The Southern Strategy*, 144–45 (*Dragging their boats*); Lawrence, *Storm over Savannah*, 31, 33–34 (*"inexpressible joy"*).

543 **The garrison now included 2,360 defenders:** Lawrence, *Storm over Savannah*, 36 (*half of them regulars*); Wright diary, included in letter to Germain, Nov. 5, 1779, *Collections of the Georgia Historical Society*, vol. 3 (1873): 267; Cruger, "The Siege of Savannah, 1779," 489 (*"to steal time"*); Mattern, *Benjamin Lincoln and the American Revolution*, 82 (*"very little importance"*). Other sources put the British manpower total somewhat higher (Martin and Harris, *Savannah 1779*, 23–24).

543 **The admiral could afford to be nonchalant:** Lawrence, *Storm over Savannah*, 14–15 (*Andrew Williamson*), 16 (*"medley of rifles"*), 39–40; Piecuch, *Three Peoples, One King*, 146 (*fallen hard on loyalists*).

543 **Leading this horde was the squat, rotund:** Billias, ed., *George Washington's Generals and Opponents*, 199 (*unsettled by profanity*); Lincoln to GW, Oct. 24, 1778, FOL (*"I wish the Congress"*); Lincoln to GW, Jan. 5–6, 1779, FOL (*"every disappointment"*); Mattern, *Benjamin Lincoln and the American Revolution*, 68 (*ignored him*); Mattern, *Benjamin Lincoln and the American Revolution*, 77 (*rice to Martinique*).

544 **Now united, the allies eyed one another:** Lawrence, *Storm over Savannah*, 16 (*deerskin jackets*), 34 (*dozed off*), 125n (*"an honest man, very touchy"*); Mattern, *Benjamin Lincoln and the American Revolution*, 3, 13 (*narcoleptic*), 83–84 (*"cannon fire"*).

544 **More than two mutually incomprehensible languages:** d'Estaing to Lincoln, Sept. 17, 1779, Thomas Addis Emmet Collection, NYPL, EM. 7422; Lawrence, *Storm over Savannah*, 40 (*"I hope you approve"*), 48 (*written pass*); Rankin, *Francis Marion*, 35 (*"Whoever heard"*); Piecuch, *Three Peoples, One King*, 148 (*"the most exact account"*); Mattern, *Benjamin Lincoln and the American Revolution*, 83 (*off-limits*).

544 **Even before the truce expired at sunset:** Martin and Harris, *Savannah 1779*, 73 (*"ought to be defended"*); Walker, *Engineers of Independence*, 265 (*"Laying siege"*); Lawrence, *Storm over Savannah*, 34 (*"doleful sight"*), 39–40 (*"miserable sand pile"* and *"Paris would have dishonored"*).

545 **Excavation began at seven p.m.:** Walker, *Engineers of Independence*, 265 (*"I began digging the trench"*); Prévost to Clinton, Nov. 2, 1779, in Willcox, ed., *The American Rebellion*, 432; Kennedy, ed. and trans., *Muskets, Cannon Balls, & Bombs*, 125 (*makeshift wheels*); Lawrence, *Storm over Savannah*, 41 (*"working like devils"*), 42 (*"very few days"*).

545 **That optimism was misplaced:** Lawrence, *Storm over Savannah*, 41 (*a hundred crowns*); Wilson, *The Southern Strategy*, 149 (*frigate Rose*).

545 **At eight a.m. on September 24:** Prévost, "Journal of the Siege of Savannah in 1779," 259+ (*six dead*); Kennedy, ed. and trans., *Muskets, Cannon Balls, & Bombs*, 15–16 (*"Three hundred men ambushed"*); Wilson, *The Southern Strategy*, 151 (*Twenty British guns* and *first substantial ground combat*); Walker, *Engineers of Independence*, 266 (*killing twenty-nine*); "An English Journal of the Siege of Savannah in 1779," 12+ (*truce to bury the corpses*); Lawrence, *Storm over Savannah*, 48 (*"ill-conceived enterprise"*).

546 **A week later, the saps were at last dug:** Willcox, ed., *The American Rebellion*, 432 (*thirty-seven allied cannons*); Moultrie, *Memoirs of the American Revolution*, 2: 36 (*sixteen naval guns*); Walker, *Engineers of Independence*, 267–68 (*three hundred "firebombs"*); Meyronnet, "Meyronnet de Saint-Marc's Journal," 255+ (*sloop-of-war La Truite*); Wilson, *The Southern Strategy*, 153–54 (*"noise would intimidate"*).

546 **No redcoat surrendered:** Hayes, ed., *A Gentleman of Fortune*, 2: 113 (*halted briefly at nine a.m.*); Kennedy, ed. and trans., *Muskets, Cannon Balls, & Bombs*, 33 (*"from the knees up"*).

546 **Still the French bombardment persisted:** Lawrence, *Storm over Savannah*, 52 (*"town was torn"*), 53 (*"could save me"*); Johnston, *Recollections of a Georgia Loyalist*, 57 (*seven pence*), 58–60 (*wet blankets*).

546 **"Shells seemed to fall":** Moore, *Diary of the American Revolution*, 2: 223–31 (*"not a single spot"*); Prévost, "Journal of the Siege of Savannah in 1779," 259+ (*blamed the Americans*); "Gen. Lachlan McIntosh (1727–1806)," Georgia Historical Society; Jackson, *Lachlan McIntosh and the Politics of Revolutionary Georgia*, 6, 7, 92, 94, 98; Mattern, *Benjamin Lincoln and the American Revolution*, 84–85 (*forty civilians*); "Account of the Siege of Savannah from a British Source," 135 (*"mulatto man"*); Lawrence, *Storm over Savannah*, 51–52 (*"A poor woman"*).

547 **D'Estaing had told the Americans:** Lawrence, *Storm over Savannah*, 44 (*began to run short*), 60 (*"criminal"*); Kennedy, ed. and trans., *Muskets, Cannon Balls, & Bombs*, 64 (*"a few hours of calm sea"*); Mattern, *Benjamin Lincoln and the American Revolution*, 83 (*"exceedingly anxious"*).

547 **Messages from the French anchorage:** Clinton to Treasury, Dec. 11, 1779, UK NA, T 64/109, f 243 (*£30,000*); Lawrence, *Storm over Savannah*, 58 (*Scurvy, dysentery* and *rice*); Meyronnet, "Meyronnet de Saint-Marc's Journal," 255+ (*"keep her afloat"*).

547 **Even without *Experiment*'s provisions:** Kennedy, ed. and trans., *Muskets, Cannon Balls, & Bombs*, 64; Walker, *Engineers of Independence*, 269 (*two months*); Lawrence, *Storm over Savannah*, 47 (*"never stopped begging"*), 57 (*sufficient through March*).

548 **On the morning of Friday, October 8:** Walker, *Engineers of Independence*, 269 (*personally reconnoitered*); Lawrence, *Storm over Savannah*, 60 (*only loyalist militia*).

548 **"It is more than probable":** White, *Historical Recollections of Georgia*, 535–36 (*"predestination"*), 537 (*"I would to God"*).

548 **After his reconnaissance ride:** Lawrence, *Storm over Savannah*, 61 (*"very good troops"*), 103 (*L'Enfant*); Wilson, *The Southern Strategy*, 157 (*enemy center or left wing*), 159–60 (*shock battalions*); Meyronnet, "Meyronnet de Saint-Marc's Journal," 255+ (*strangers to one another*).

548 **D'Estaing listened briefly to these objections:** Lawrence, *Storm over Savannah*, 61–63 (*"haughty and vain"*).

549 **Orders were quickly drafted:** "Siege of Savannah: General Orders of the Count d'Estaing," 548+ (*"expressly forbidden"* and *paper scraps*).

549 **D'Estaing acknowledged the difficulties:** Lawrence, *Storm over Savannah*, 61–63 (*"extreme bravery"*).

549 **"To take them by surprise":** Lawrence, *Storm over Savannah*, 65, 69–70 (*"masters of the ground"*); Walker, *Engineers of Independence*, 269–70; author visit, Savannah, Nov. 14–15, 2019, signage; Moultrie, *Memoirs of the American Revolution*, 2: 41–42 (*details of d'Estaing's plan*); Jones, ed., *The Siege of Savannah in 1779*, 31n (*American sergeant*).

549 **Worse, the feints were badly timed:** https://www.timeanddate.com/sun/usa/savannah?month=10&year=1779 (*six-thirty*); Lawrence, *Storm over Savannah*, 77 (*"Come to the Maypole"*); Cruger, "The Siege of Savannah, 1779," 489+ (*"real attack or a feint"*); "Memorial of John Harris Cruger of New York," Feb. 9, 1784, http://www.royalprovincial.com/military/mems/ny/clmcrug.htm; Swisher, *The Revolutionary War in the Southern Back Country*, 101–4; Elliott, "'The Greatest Event That Has Happened the Whole War,'" University of Georgia, 27 (*tardy feint*); Wilson, *The Southern Strategy*, 162 (*"Day begins to dawn"*); Kennedy, ed. and trans., *Muskets, Cannon Balls, & Bombs*, 73 (*"best troops were waiting"*).

549 **The early light also revealed:** Martin and Harris, *Savannah 1779*, 19, 78–79; Wilson, *The Southern Strategy*, 162 (*"double quick"*); Lawrence, *Storm over Savannah*, 71 (*"grenadiers of Old France"*).

550 **Firelocks winked along the parapet:** Jones, ed., *The Siege of Savannah in 1779*, 31–32 (*"Disorder begins to prevail"*); Wilson, *The Southern Strategy*, 173 (*knife blades*); Lawrence, *Storm over Savannah*, 72 (*"frightful carnage"*).

550 **Some troops scrambled into a ditch:** Hayes, ed., *A Gentleman of Fortune*, 2: 116–17 (*lacked ladders*); Kennedy, ed. and trans., *Muskets, Cannon Balls, & Bombs*, 20 (*sixty men*), 37 (*"took two steps forward"*).

550 **A few stalwarts managed to plant:** Prévost, "Journal of the Siege of Savannah in 1779," 259+ (*plant regimental flags* and *Royal Navy tars*); Lawrence, *Storm over Savannah*, 71–72 (*"day was our own"*); Benson, *American Swedish Historical Foundation Yearbook*, 34; Elliott, "'The

Greatest Event That Has Happened the Whole War,' " 26; Kennedy, ed. and trans., *Muskets, Cannon Balls, & Bombs*, 37 (*"who lost only their shoes"*).

551 **On the heels of the French:** Kajencki, *Casimir Pulaski*, 163 (*spilling him from the saddle*); Jones, ed., *The Siege of Savannah in 1779*, 35 (*"Jesus, Mary, Joseph"*); author visit, Spring Hill redoubt, Savannah, Nov. 14–15, 2019, signage; Martin and Harris, *Savannah 1779*, 80–81; Kennedy, ed. and trans., *Muskets, Cannon Balls, & Bombs*, 37 (*"like a crowd leaving church"*); Lawrence, *Storm over Savannah*, 76–77 (*flung his sword*); Hough, *The Siege of Savannah*, 168 (*scorched with grapeshot*); Wilson, *The Southern Strategy*, 168–69 (*Yamacraw morass*); Garden, *Anecdotes of the Revolutionary War*, 24–26; Massey, *John Laurens and the American Revolution*, 147 (*"scene of confusion"*).

551 **D'Estaing had been wounded a second time:** Wilson, *The Southern Strategy*, 169 (*white uniform, already bloody*); Hough, *The Siege of Savannah*, 168 (*"not an assailant standing"*).

551 **Captain O'Connor summarized the morning:** Walker, *Engineers of Independence*, 270 (*"very violent"*).

551 **"Such a sight I never":** Lawrence, *Storm over Savannah*, 80 (*"ditch was filled with dead"*); Elliott, " 'The Greatest Event That Has Happened the Whole War,' " 39 (*"plain was strewed"*); Edward L. Hayward to John Laurens, Dec. 1779, in Moore, *Materials for History*, 161–73 (*"without any other effect"*); "Francis Rush Clark's Narration of Occurrences," Oct. 9, 1779, APS, Feinstone Coll., box 35, #2338 (*bury the dead*).

552 **The pick-and-shovel details would remain busy:** Lawrence, *Storm over Savannah*, 80–81, 105 (*"habit of indulging"*); Swisher, *The Revolutionary War in the Southern Back Country*, 106 (*exceeded 800*); Wilson, *The Southern Strategy*, 170 (*234 casualties*), 176 (*malaria*); "Maitland, Hon. John (1732–79)," https://www.historyofparliamentonline.org/volume/1754-1790/member/maitland-hon-john-1732-79. Two centuries after his death, Maitland's bones would be repatriated to his native Scotland. British casualties at Bunker Hill exceeded 1,000, including 226 dead (*TBAC*, 110).

552 **"Of nine hundred choice troops":** Lawrence, *Storm over Savannah*, 73; Prévost, "Journal of the Siege of Savannah in 1779," 259+ (*grievously injured attackers*); Elliott, " 'The Greatest Event That Has Happened the Whole War,' " 31 (*John Looney*), 32 (*Edward Lloyd*), 34–35 (*Vicomte de Fontanges*); GW to George Clinton, Oct. 1, 1779, FOL fn (*major to major general*); White, *Historical Recollections of Georgia*, 537 (*exhumed his body*).

552 **A surgeon who extracted the grapeshot:** Kajencki, *Casimir Pulaski*, 163 (*"fortitude"*), 165–66 (*"brought him ashore"*); Wroblewski, "Casimir Pulaski and the Threat to the Upper Delaware River Valley," *JAR*, May 13, 2020 (*"died as he lived"*).

553 **Litter-bearers carried d'Estaing:** Lawrence, *Storm over Savannah*, 88 (*"hard knocks"*), 90–91 (*American delegation*); Merlant, *Soldiers and Sailors of France in the American War for Independence*, 88 (*"I have a deep wound"*); Meyronnet, "Meyronnet de Saint-Marc's Journal," 255+ (*war council on October 11*); Kennedy, ed. and trans., *Muskets, Cannon Balls, & Bombs*, 74 (*"would have deserted"*).

553 **Troops began trundling mortars and naval guns:** "Convention of Retreat from Before Savannah," Oct. 13, 1779, Thomas Addis Emmet Collection, NYPL, EM. 7505 (*"as great a march"* and *"new proof of the devotion"*).

553 **Basking in a victory the British now called:** Prévost, "Journal of the Siege of Savannah in 1779," 259+ (*"cutting each other's throats"*); Lincoln to Everard Meade, Nov. 1, 1779, Thomas Addis Emmet Collection, NYPL, EM. 7459 (*"prevented our success"*); Billias, ed., *George Washington's Generals and Opponents*, 201 (*"disappointment is great"*); Kennedy, ed. and trans., *Muskets, Cannon Balls, & Bombs*, 120 (*"causes of failure"*).

553 **D'Estaing compiled a catalog:** Kennedy, ed. and trans., *Muskets, Cannon Balls, & Bombs*, 55 (*"promise much"*), 70 (*"all possible mishaps"*); Stoker et al., eds., *Strategy in the American War of Independence*, 151 (*without losing a ship*); d'Estaing dispatch, Dec. 5, 1779, Archives Nationales, navy archives, série B4, d'Estaing corr., vol. 142, micro, f 124 (*single French gun*); Jones, ed., *The Siege of Savannah in 1779*, 69–70 (*"Enterprising, bold"*).

554 **More would die on the journey home:** Jones, ed., *The Siege of Savannah in 1779*, 67 (*filled their casks*); Mattern, *Benjamin Lincoln and the American Revolution*, 86 (*Zubly's Ferry*); Ken-

nedy, ed. and trans., *Muskets, Cannon Balls, & Bombs*, 23 (*three rearguard French grenadier companies*); Lawrence, *Storm over Savannah*, 95–97 (*"Cape of Good Hope"*).

554 **He found a chilly reception at Brest:** Lawrence, *Storm over Savannah*, 95–97 (*strewing flowers*); Merlant, *Soldiers and Sailors of France in the American War for Independence*, 89–90; Bachaumont, *Marie-Antoinette, Louis XVI et la famille royale*, 183–84 (*his injured leg*); JA to Samuel Cooper, Feb. 23, 1780, FOL (*laurel crown*). For helping Louis XVI try to escape during the French Revolution, d'Estaing was sent to the guillotine in April 1794, during the Reign of Terror.

554 **France had provided America with war matériel:** Stinchcombe, *The American Revolution and the French Alliance*, 88 (*another eight million*); Willcox, *Portrait of a General*, 291 (*abandoning vulnerable Newport*); Arbuthnot to Clinton, Oct. 6, 1779, in Willcox, ed., *The American Rebellion*, 424 (*"smallest use"*); Clowes, *The Royal Navy*, 443 (*"best and noblest"*).

555 **On October 25, as d'Estaing was leaving:** Ephraim Bowen to NG, Oct. 26, 1779, *PNG*, 4: 498n; "Journal of the Hon. Garrison-Regiment von Huyn," Oct. 25, 1779, Lidgerwood Hessian Transcriptions, HDAR (*drums beating*); Eelking and Rosengarten, *The German Allied Troops in the North American War of Independence*, 101 (*"Not a man or woman"*); "Newport in the Hands of the British," 1+ (*"The army and merchants"*).

555 **Flatboats shuttled the troops, loyalists:** "Journal of the Hon. Garrison-Regiment von Huyn," Oct. 25, 1779, Lidgerwood Hessian Transcriptions, HDAR (*120 transports*); Pattison to the Board of Ordnance, Nov. 7, 1779, "Official Letters of Major General James Pattison," 133 (*twenty brass fieldpieces*); Neimeyer, "The British Occupation of Newport, Rhode Island, 1776–1779," 30+ (*"entire city had died"*).

555 **At eight p.m. the flotilla weighed anchor:** "Newport in the Hands of the British," 1+; Field, ed., *Diary of Colonel Israel Angell*, 87 (*"flocked in"*); McBurney, "British Treatment of Prisoners During the Occupation of Newport, 1776–1779," 1+ (*"gone, gone, gone!"*).

555 **Where this war was headed, few:** Murray, *Letters from America, 1773 to 1780*, 63 (*"We get up and we walk"*); Wright to Germain, Nov. 9, 1779, *Collections of the Georgia Historical Society*, vol. 3 (1873), 271 (*"spirit of rebellion"*); Toynbee, ed., *The Letters of Horace Walpole, Fourth Earl of Orford*, 11: 81 (*Tower of London*); Piecuch, *Three Peoples, One King*, 172 (*"daylight"*).

555 **Confirmation of the Georgia triumph:** Ritchie, ed., "A New York Diary of the Revolutionary War," 2: 401+ (*privateer Rosebud*); Burgoyne, trans. and ed., *A Hessian Officer's Diary of the American Revolution*, 169 (*illuminations brightened every house*).

556 **Clinton cheered with them:** Willcox, ed., *The American Rebellion*, 149 (*"greatest event"*).

25. ETERNITY IS NEARER EVERY DAY

557 **The old wives claimed that a harsh winter:** Cunningham, *The Uncertain Revolution*, 100 (*geese breastbones*). St. Thomas's day, previously Dec. 21, was changed to July 3 in 1969.

557 **As the snow deepened:** *PGW*, 24: xxv (*winter cantonments*); GW to NG, Jan. 27, 1780, *PGW*, 24: 284n (*thirty army couriers*).

557 **But most of what one newspaper called:** "Chronology Morristown," EPO, Nov. 17, 1779 (*"Grand American Army"*); NG to James Abeel, Nov. 4, 1779, *PNG*, 5: 14n (*First and Second Mountains*); Scheer and Weigley, *Morristown*, 33–34 (*"clever little village"*); Martha Dangerfield Bland to friend, May 12, 1777, in "Morristown 1777," EPO (*"consequential look"*); Smith, *Winter at Morristown*, 5 (*"highest prices"*).

558 **The army had wintered here three years earlier:** author visit, Ford mansion, MNHP museum, Oct. 10, 2019 (*kill a quarter*); Scheer and Weigley, *Morristown*, 38 (*sixty-eight smallpox deaths*); "Churches Used, Abused & Burned During the American Revolution," EPO, Mar. 2022, 2–3 (*vinegar scrub*).

558 **Now, despite understandable local reluctance:** NG to John Cox, Nov. 28, 1779, *PNG*, 5: 122 (*"I have rode"*); NG to GW, Nov. 27, 1779, FOL (*"very good position"*): *PGW*, 24: xxv (*four artillery regiments*).

558 **Two thousand acres of rolling woodland:** author visit, MNHP museum, Oct. 10, 2019 (*"loghouse city"*); Elliott, *Surviving the Winters*, 131 (*two gallons of whiskey*); "Weather & the Environment, 1779–1780," EPO, 2020 (*freeze impeded the sawmills*); author visit, Jockey Hollow,

Oct. 10, 2019 (*fighting the Iroquois*); "Chronology Morristown," EPO, Dec. 14, 1779 (*mud often froze*), Dec. 16–18, 1779 ("*exceedingly neat*"), Dec. 31, 1779 (*eleven thousand*).

558 **Much had been learned about camp hygiene:** Scheer and Weigley, *Morristown*, 59 (*fewer than a hundred*).

559 **"Colder weather I never saw":** GW to NG, Nov. 30, 1779, FOL fn; Lengel, *General George Washington*, 319 (*Crop failures*); Heidler and Heidler, eds., *Daily Lives of Civilians in Wartime Early America*, 52 (*flaxseed and corncobs*); PNG, 3: xiv (*rice from Charleston*).

559 **Forage was so scarce:** "Chronology Morristown," EPO, Dec. 14, 1779 (*tree bark*); GW to Samuel Huntington, Nov. 18, 1779, FOL (*fewer than five thousand blankets*); GW to John Augustine Washington, June 6–July 6, 1780, FOL; Nelson, *William Alexander, Lord Stirling*, 154 ("*ashamed to come out*"); Ford, ed., *Correspondence and Journals of Samuel Blachley Webb*, 2: 231–32 ("*suffered much*"); Benjamin West to Samuel West, July 1779, James S. Schoff Revolutionary War Coll., WLC ("*lived doubting*"). This epitaph is on the tomb of John Sheffield, Duke of Buckingham, in Westminster Abbey.

559 **The *Morning Chronicle and London Advertiser*, citing:** Miller, *The American Revolution*, 11 ("*ill for some time*").

559 **The same man, very much alive:** "Chronology Morristown," EPO, Dec. 1, 1779 ("*severe storm*"); GW to NG, Nov. 30, 1779, FOL fn (*hardly hid her dismay*); Smith, *Winter at Morristown*, 21–22 (*two ground-floor rooms*); author visit, Ford mansion, MNHP museum, Oct. 10, 2019 (*chamber pots*).

560 **The commander in chief took a second-floor bedroom:** author visit, Ford mansion, MNHP museum, Oct. 10, 2019 (*fourteen-inch-plank floors*); blueprints, Col. Jacob Ford, Jr., house, Morristown, Historical American Buildings Survey, U.S. Department of Interior; Godfrey, *The Commander-in-Chief's Guard*, 71 (*southeast of the house*).

560 **This was Washington's fifth winter at war:** Ferling, *The First of Men*, 276 (*thirteen bushels of turnips*); GW to R. Morris, Feb. 4, 1780, PGW, 24: 375 ("*contented with grog*"); Juan de Miralles to GW, May 22, 1779, PGW, 20: 579n ("*cigars of the Havana*"); John Mitchell to GW, Feb. 17, 1780, PGW, 24: 497n ("*curled hair*"); GW to Lund, Apr. 3, 1779, PGW, 19: 735 (*locust trees*); GW to Philip Mazzei, July 1, 1779, PGW, 21: 319 (*not without a greenhouse*).

560 **Soon after arriving he ordered:** Cunningham, *The Uncertain Revolution*, 145 ("*tasty stile*"); GW, general orders, Feb. 16, 1780, PGW, 24: 484–85n; "Martha Washington's Winter Vacation, 1779–1780," MNHP (*delayed a week*); Fraser, *The Washingtons*, 228 ("*not much pleasure there*").

560 **There was much to make him unhappy:** Peckham, ed., *The Toll of Independence*, 130 (*156 military and naval engagements*); GW to Benjamin Harrison, Oct. 25, 1779, FOL ("*enemy have wasted*"); "Editorial Note," PGW, 22: 594–601n ("*one great stroke*" and "*impatience & anxiety*"); Horatio Gates to GW, Oct. 8, 1779, FOL.

561 **He held no illusions:** GW to Benjamin Harrison, Oct. 25, 1779, FOL ("*wide and boundless*"); Wright, *The Continental Army*, 154 (*at least thirty-five thousand*); NG to John Cox, Nov. 28, 1779, PNG, 5: 122n (*six thousand enlistments*); petition, New York brigade officers, Feb. 1, 1780, Bernardus Swartout, Sr., papers, NYHS ("*altogether impossible*"); JLB, AAA ("*twice the sum*"); "General officers' memorial to Congress," Nov. 15, 1779, PNG, 5: 73–77n (*three thousand acres*).

561 **With officers bolting the army:** GW to Committee on Reducing the Army, Jan. 23, 1780, PGW, 24: 221 ("*exceedingly deficient*"); Morgan Lewis to NG, Nov. 21, 1779, PNG, 5: 106n (*salt*); NG to Joseph Reed, Mar. 30, 1780, PNG, 5: 484 ("*die in a few days*"); NG to GW, Mar. 31, 1780, PNG, 5: 486–88.

561 **Troops were as hard-pressed as the herds:** GW to Samuel Huntington, Dec. 15, 1779, FOL ("*infinitely worse*"); GW, circular to the states, Dec. 16, 1779, FOL ("*absolutely empty*"); Smith, *Winter at Morristown*, 13 (*wheat now cost $50*); GW to Philip Schuyler, Jan. 30, 1780, FOL ("*horse food*").

562 **Stealing from nearby farms:** "Chronology Morristown, Nov. 1779–December 1780," EPO, Apr. 6, 1780 ("*Mr. Thief*"); Risch, *Supplying Washington's Army*, 191–92 ("*countersign*"); GW,

general orders, Dec. 29, 1779, FOL (*"band of robbers"*); GW to Lewis Nicola, Feb. 5, 1780, *PGW*, 24: 386–87 (*one hundred lashes being the maximum*); GW, general orders, *PGW*, 24: 299 (*"A night scarcely passes"*); Freeman, *George Washington: A Biography*, 5: 144 (*pilferage*).

562 **Much of the logistical burden:** NG to Jeremiah Wadsworth, Jan. 5, 1780, *PNG*, 5: 236 (*"distress of the army"*); Carp, *To Starve the Army at Pleasure*, 93 (*"plagued for money"*).

562 **Greene commiserated. "We can no more":** NG to John Cox, Nov. 28, 1779, *PNG*, 5: 123; Risch, *Supplying Washington's Army*, 52 (*officers were prosecuted*); Carp, *To Starve the Army at Pleasure*, 101 (*"greasy, money-making"*); NG to Samuel Huntington, Dec. 12, 1779, *PNG*, 5: 164–68n (*"line of the army"* and *profiteering*).

562 **In mid-January, Washington and Greene devised:** Circular to the New Jersey Magistrates, Jan. 7, 1780, *PGW*, 24: 49, 52n (*twenty-two hundred head of cattle*); Lengel, *General George Washington*, 320; Scheer and Weigley, *Morristown*, 62–63; GW to P. Schuyler, Jan. 30, 1780, *PGW*, 24: 334 (*"as an army"*).

563 **"Money is justly considered":** *Annual Register . . . 1779*, 180; Ferguson, *The Power of the Purse*, 28–29 (*$263 million*); Newman, *The Early Paper Money of America*, 16 (*one-fortieth of its face value*), 22 (*Henry Dawkins*); Bleeker, *The Order Book of Capt. Leonard Bleeker*, 27n (*2^1/$_2$ cents*); Robinson, *Continental Treasury Administration, 1775–1781*, 77–78 (*states, unrestricted by Congress*); Mitchell, *The Price of Independence*, 91 (*$210 million*); Newman, *The Early Paper Money of America*, 23 (*six-hundred-dollar bills*); Risch, *Supplying Washington's Army*, 229 (*lacked the political courage*); Harlow, "Aspects of Revolutionary Finance, 1775–1783," 46+ (*"enemy to his country"* and *barely $3 million*). Farley Grubb notes that many higher figures exist for the amount of Continental money printed, but he persuasively puts the amount at just under $200 million (Grubb, *The Continental Dollar*, 199, 243–46).

563 **Intensified British economic warfare:** Smith, *Winter at Morristown*, 14 (*"London trade"*); Scott, *Counterfeiting in Colonial America*, 255 (Blacksnake *and* Morning Star); Hatfield, "Faking It," *JAR*, Oct. 7, 2015 (*$2,000 reward*); Newman, *The Early Paper Money of America*, 27 (*umlauts, carets*).

563 **By early 1780, Continental currency:** Taylor, *American Revolutions*, 196 (*"paper kite"*); Risch, *Supplying Washington's Army*, 229 (*kite tail*); Nash, *The Unknown American Revolution*, 309 (*"paper trash"*); Newman, *The Early Paper Money of America*, 16 (*"papering rooms"*); William M. Betts to NG, Nov. 3, 1779, *PNG*, 5: 10–11n (*thirteen cents*); Freeman, *George Washington: A Biography*, 5:133 (*"medium of commerce"*).

564 **In 1778 Congress had recommended that states:** Miller, *Triumph of Freedom, 1775–1783*, 443 (*sold in Pennsylvania for $75*), 444, 464 (*imposed again*); Breen, *The Will of the People*, 187 (*dunghill fowls*), 188 (*"sexton"*); Harlow, "Aspects of Revolutionary Finance, 1775–1783," 59.

564 **As the currency's value declined:** Heidler and Heidler, eds., *Daily Lives of Civilians in Wartime Early America*, 51 (*Beef in New England jumped*); Conway, *The War of American Independence, 1775–1783*, 165 (*sevenfold*); Kapp, *The Life of John Kalb, Major-General in the Revolutionary Army*, 183 (*"times are growing worse"*); Scheer and Weigley, *Morristown*, 63 (*"ordinary horse"*).

564 **Depreciation and inflation hit the poor:** Mitchell, *The Price of Independence*, 106 (*poor and middling classes*); Heidler and Heidler, eds., *Daily Lives of Civilians in Wartime Early America*, 53 (*thirty food riots*); Miller, ed., *The Selected Papers of Charles Willson Peale and His Family*, 5: 79–81; Reader, "Fort Wilson," *Encyclopedia of Greater Philadelphia*, https://philadelphiaencyclopedia.org/essays/fort-wilson/; Diestelow, "The Fort Wilson Riot and Pennsylvania's Republican Formation," *JAR*, Feb. 28, 2019; Smith, *James Wilson, Founding Father, 1742–1798*, 131–39; Alexander, "The Fort Wilson Incident of 1779," 580+; Butterfield, ed., *Letters of Benjamin Rush*, 1: 240 (*"fear and dejection"*); Miller, *Triumph of Freedom, 1775–1783*, 445 (*"transient, clamorous"*); Harlow, "Aspects of Revolutionary Finance, 1775–1783" (*forty to one*); Scheer and Weigley, *Morristown*, 63 (*5 percent annual interest*); Charles Pettit to NG, Mar. 17, 1780, *PNG*, 5: 462–63n (*Spanish-milled dollars*); Rappleye, *Robert Morris*, 211 (*"wanton violation"*); Chernow, *Alexander Hamilton*, 137 (*wiped out the savings*).

565 **This scheme, too, would fail:** Charles Pettit to NG, Mar. 17, 1780, *PNG*, 5: 462–63n (*a single*

penny); Grubb, *The Continental Dollar*, 175 (*legal tender*); "Chronology Morristown, Nov. 1779–December 1780," Jan. 5, 1780, EPO (*"Some effectual measures"*); Alden, *The American Revolution*, 221 (*"Mock money"*).

565 **Nearly five years had passed since Washington:** Jackson, ed., *The Diaries of George Washington*, 3: 340–47 (*"Clear, cold"*); Martin, *A Narrative of a Revolutionary Soldier*, 147–48 (*"cut a man in two"*); Ryan, ed., *A Salute to Courage*, 178 (*"meals of dog"*).

565 **Not once in January:** Smith, *Winter at Morristown*, 11; Puls, *Henry Knox*, 141 (*dig out their heavy guns*); GW to James Wilkinson, Dec. 19, 1779, FOL fn; "Chronology Morristown, Nov. 1779–December 1780," EPO, Jan. 10, 1780 (*"pine knot"*), Jan. 14, EPO (*"exseading cold"*), Jan. 31 (*"Eternity is nearer"*).

565 **General and Mrs. Washington tried to keep up morale:** Smith, *Winter at Morristown*, 19 (*"dancing assemblies"*); Hamilton, *The Revolutionary War Lives and Letters of Lucy and Henry Knox*, 150 (*"hurry, bustle, and impertinence"*); NG to Caty, Sept. 4, 1779, *PNG*, 4: 361 (*"If you love me"*); Carbone, *Nathanael Greene*, 122 (*Jacob Arnold's tavern*).

566 **Lieutenant Colonel Hamilton, living in the crowded:** Chernow, *Alexander Hamilton*, 126 (*lascivious tomcat*); McDonald, *Alexander Hamilton, a Biography*, 5 (*"All for love"*); AH to John Laurens, Apr. 1779, FOL (*"She must be young"*); author visit, Campfield house, Morristown, Oct. 10, 2019 (*Elizabeth Schuyler*); AH to Margarita Schuyler, Feb. 1780, FOL (*"unmercifully handsome"*); Chernow, *Alexander Hamilton*, 129 (*"a gone man"*); Flexner, *The Young Hamilton*, 280.

566 **Another visitor had come to Morristown:** Philbrick, *Valiant Ambition*, 259; Lea, *A Hero and a Spy*, 324 (*modest house*), 363–64 (*split logs*); GW, general orders, Dec. 21, 1779, FOL (*Norris Tavern*).

566 **The trial board included three brigadiers:** Wallace, *Traitorous Hero*, 186 (*Howe*); "Proceedings of . . . the Trial of Major General Arnold, June 1, 1779," n.p. (*four misdemeanors*).

567 **Innocent he was not:** Van Doren, *Secret History of the American Revolution*, 196 (*"ruinous"*); Lea, *A Hero and a Spy*, 334–35 (*Stansbury traveled secretly*).

567 **As directed by his commander, André:** Schopieray, "The Treasonous Correspondence of Benedict Arnold," lecture, Dec. 9, 2020 (*several dozen letters*); Van Doren, *Secret History of the American Revolution*, 205–7 (*"Accept a command, be surprised"*), 208–9 (*"Gustavus Monk"*), 210 (*"by sword or treaty"*), 216; Philbrick, *Valiant Ambition*, 244–45 (*Lincoln's garrison*).

568 **In another note in late July, André:** Van Doren, *Secret History of the American Revolution*, 212 (*"thankful for the information"*), 214 (*"named his price"*), 453.

568 **On January 21 in the Norris Tavern great room:** "Proceedings of . . . the Trial of Major General Arnold, June 1, 1779," n.p. (*"disagreeable to be accused"*).

568 **As his twelve judges listened closely:** "Proceedings of . . . the Trial of Major General Arnold, June 1, 1779," n.p. (*"My conduct and character"*); Randall, *Benedict Arnold*, 492 (*"pleasing anxiety"*).

568 **That confidence was misplaced:** Martin, *Benedict Arnold, Revolutionary Hero*, 428; "Proceedings of . . . the Trial of Major General Arnold, June 1, 1779," n.p. (*convicted him*); Van Doren, *Secret History of the American Revolution*, 173–74 (*glass, loaf sugar*); Van Wyck, ed., "Autobiography of Philip Van Cortlandt, Brigadier-General in the Continental Army," 278+ (*wanted Arnold cashiered*).

569 **Stunned and furious:** Van Doren, *Secret History of the American Revolution*, 251 (*"For what?"*); Brumwell, *Turncoat*, 193 (*"sufferings for"*); GW, general orders, Apr. 6, 1780, FOL (*"imprudent and improper"*).

569 **Later that winter, Arnold briefly toyed:** BA to GW, Mar. 6, 1780, FOL (*springtime expedition*); Van Doren, *Secret History of the American Revolution*, 252–53; GW to Board of Admiralty, Mar. 15, 1780, FOL.

569 **Arnold shrugged, proposed taking a leave:** Van Doren, *Secret History of the American Revolution*, 257–58 (*"pain and difficulty"*).

569 **Just beyond Morristown's eastern horizon:** Ewald, *Diary of the American War*, 158 (*cantonments arose*); Griffin, " 'To Huts': British Winter Cantonments Around New York City," *JAR*, Feb. 25, 2019.

570 **Given the American surprise attack:** Schwab, *The Revolutionary History of Fort Number Eight*, 44–48 (*razed the batteries*).

570 **Four thousand reinforcements:** Willcox, *The American Rebellion*, 140–41 (*arrived from Britain* and *forced to take the helm*); Hagist, *Noble Volunteers*, 118 (*five months*) and 142–43 (*nearly every man in the 37th Foot*); Syrett, *Shipping and the American War, 1775–83*, 190 (*"spread itself"*); "Journal of the Honorable Hessian Infantry Regiment von Bose," Dec. 25, 1779–Apr. 14, 1780 (*dysentery*); Lidgerwood Hessian Transcriptions, HDAR; Willcox, *Portrait of a General*, 284; Clinton memo, Dec. 12, 1779, WBW (*nine thousand men*); Gruber, ed., *John Peebles' American War, 1776–1782*, 291 (*barns*); Sabine, ed., *Historical Memoirs of William Smith*, 2: 178 (*churches*); Biddulph, "Letters of Robert Biddulph, 1779–1783," 87+ (*"constantly drunk"*); Pattison to Lord Viscount Townshend, Sept. 25, 1779, in "Official Letters of Major General James Pattison," 119 (*"So sickly a time"*).

570 **Ailments plaguing the Royal Navy:** John Kendall to M. Arbuthnot, Nov. 11, 1779, Kendall corr., vol. 1, HL, HM 64532 (*"great deficiency"*); Mackesy, *The War for America, 1775–1783*, 339 (*forty warships*); O'Shaughnessy, *The Men Who Lost America*, 224 (*less than 10 percent*); Stuart-Wortley, ed., *A Prime Minister and His Son*, 157 (*"large trading ships"*).

570 **Worse still, the Admiralty had sent:** Billias, ed., *George Washington's Generals and Opponents*, 267–68 (*bully to inferiors*); Willcox, *Portrait of a General*, 284–85 (*eighty* and *"weathercock"*); *PP Sandwich*, 3: 139 (*"resign this command"*).

571 **New York remained a garrison town:** Klein, "Why Did the British Fail to Win the Hearts and Minds of New Yorkers?," 357+ (*without civilian courts*); Daniel Weir to Treasury, Dec. 12, 1779, UK NA, T 64/ 114, f 223 (*34,299 men*), f 31 (*horses wintering*); police orders, James Pattison papers, NYHS, Mar. 5, 1779 (*"no corpse is to be buried"*); *Narratives of the Revolution in New York*, 230 (*Auctioneers, boatmen*); Valentine, *Manual of the Corporation of the City of New York*, 666 (*two shillings for a horse*), 688 (*"many evils"*); Pattison order to "Col. De Bishausen," May 28, 1780, "Official Letters of Major General James Pattison," 398 (*both sleeves*).

571 **Every New York male between sixteen and sixty:** Barck, *New York City During the War for Independence*, 78 (*Quakers and four hundred firemen*), 199 (*six thousand civilian defenders*).

571 **As the only viable sanctuary:** police orders, June 7, 1779, James Pattison papers, NYHS (*"All Negroes that fly"*); Pownall and Almon, *The Remembrancer*, 8: 367 (*"every Negro who shall desert"*); O'Shaughnessy, *The Men Who Lost America*, 227; Frey, *The British Soldier in America*, 18 (*sold into slavery*); Gilbert, *Black Patriots and Loyalists*, 121 (*"Freedom and a Farm"*); Egerton, *Death or Liberty*, 89 (*twelve hundred blacks*).

572 **As for loyalists, in late October the patriot New York:** Ketchum, *Divided Loyalties*, 366 (*act of attainder*); Williams, "New York Transformed," diss., 229–30 (*"confirmed enemies"* and *"commissioners of sequestration"*); Hall, *Philipse Manor Hall at Yonkers, N.Y.*, 156 (*"adhering to the king"*); Burrows, *Forgotten Patriots*, 142 (*Refugee Club*); Skemp, *William Franklin*, 225 (*president of Delaware*), 231 (*remorseless violence*).

572 **Overcrowded, expensive, and surrounded:** "Official Letters of Major General James Pattison," 275 (*"irregularities"*); Sabine, ed., *Historical Memoirs of William Smith*, 2: viii (*"military misrule"*); Klein, "Why Did the British Fail to Win the Hearts and Minds of New Yorkers?," 357+ (*"plundering"*).

572 **Much resentment was directed at Henry Clinton:** Skemp, *William Franklin*, 234–35 (*"parcel of blockheads"*); Clinton to [Keppel?], [Nov. ?] 1779, WBW (*"no means the fashion"*); Conway, *The War of American Independence, 1775–1783*, 114 (*"perfect inactivity"*).

572 **That harsh judgment was wrong:** Borick, *A Gallant Defense*, 23–24; *Narratives of the Revolution in New York*, 302 (*130 ships*); Burgoyne, trans., *Journal of Hessian Grenadier Battalion*, 90 (*routine convoy*); Borick, *A Gallant Defense*, 23; O'Shaughnessy, *The Men Who Lost America*, 230 (*nine thousand troops, five thousand sailors*); Uhlendorf, trans. and ed., *The Siege of Charleston*, 106–7 (*more than two months*); Gruber, ed., *John Peebles' American War, 1776–1782*, 316 (*"Some think Rhode Island"*).

573 **In fact, as only Clinton:** Mackesy, *The War for America, 1775–1783*, 278 (*d'Estaing's departure*); Germain to Clinton, Sept. 27, 1779, *DAR*, 17: 223 (*"vast importance"*); Willcox, ed., *The*

American Rebellion, 423 (*"possession of Charleston"*); *Report on the Manuscripts of Mrs. Stopford-Sackville*, 2: 136 (*"Our cause is just"*).

573 **Clinton, for once, readily agreed:** Clinton to Eden, Aug. 22, 1779, WBW (*counterstroke in Georgia*); Willcox, *The American Rebellion*, 151 (*"spirit of rebellion"*); Willis, *The Struggle for Sea Power*, 347–48 (*vital rebel port*).

573 **Yet doubts plagued him:** Mackesy, *The War for America, 1775–1783*, 524–25 (*less than a quarter*); Willcox, *The American Rebellion*, 152 (*leave at least twelve thousand*); Clinton to Eden, Oct. 10, 1779, WBW (*half the army manpower*); "English Forces in America, 1779," *Report on the Manuscripts of Mrs. Stopford-Sackville*, 2: 153 (*disperse redcoats*).

573 **If the southern strategy was to succeed:** *DAR*, 17: 19 (*"So many attempts"*); Willcox, *The American Rebellion*, 155 (*"visionary hopes"* and *"tottering ground"*).

574 **Troops designated for Charleston:** journal, George Philip Hooke, Dec. 20, 1779, WLC, M-1239 (*embark in Brooklyn*); Gruber, ed., *John Peebles' American War, 1776–1782*, 317 (*"cold business"*); Ewald, *Diary of the American War*, 190 (*miserable winter quarters*), 191 (*tossing men to the deck*); Burgoyne, ed., *Enemy Views*, 349–55 (*"frozen noses"*); Uhlendorf, trans. and annot., *Revolution in America*, 323 (*"British are not keeping"*); Willcox, ed., *The American Rebellion*, 438 (*damaged by ice*).

574 **Clinton and his entourage strode:** Bain, ed., "The Siege of Charleston," 478+ (*horse transport John*); Arbuthnot to Capt. Elphinstone, n.d., in Clinton's journal of Charleston siege, WBW (*delays in leaving New York*); Stuart-Wortley, ed., *A Prime Minister and His Son*, 160–61 (*"peevish and petulant," "deceit,"* and *"tired to death"*).

574 **Only the presence of an old comrade:** Willcox, *Portrait of a General*, 281 (*"no charms"*); Willcox, ed., *The American Rebellion*, 417 (*"How happy I am made"*); Clinton to Eden, Aug. 22, 1779, WBW (*request to resign*). Written in London on November 4, 1779, the reply from Germain rejecting this resignation plea did not reach Clinton until March 1780. Ross, ed., *Correspondence of Charles, First Marquis Cornwallis*, 1: 42 (*"too well satisfied"*).

575 **On Sunday morning, December 26, Arbuthnot ordered:** Ewald, *Diary of the American War*, 192–93 (*133 vessels*); Willcox, *Portrait of a General*, 301 (*single frigate*).

575 **"Fair weather, nothing remarkable":** journal, George Philip Hooke, Dec. 26, 1779, WLC, M-1239; Willcox, *Portrait of a General*, 295 (*"most important hour"*).

575 **The fleet sailed in the nick of time:** "The Hard Winter Summarized," EPO, Apr. 2022 (*sixteen degrees below zero*); author visit, Ford mansion, MNHP museum, Oct. 10, 2019 (*Twenty-seven snowfalls*); GW to NG, Nov. 30, 1779, *PNG*, 5: 139n (*not melting until May*); Cunningham, *The Uncertain Revolution*, 102 (*Hackensack, Passaic, and Raritan*); Smith, *Winter at Morristown*, 27 (*eleven feet thick*); Lengel, *General George Washington*, 319 (*"beasts of the field"*).

575 **By mid-January a two-ton cannon:** "Official Letters of Major General James Pattison," 152 (*"memory of man"*); Stokes, *The Iconography of Manhattan Island, 1498–1909*, 5: 1102 (*three men walked*); Arthur St. Clair to GW, Feb. 7, 1780, *PGW*, 24: 405n (*Eighty-six sleighs*); "The Hard Winter Summarized," EPO, Apr. 2022 (*pulled by a pair of horses*); Eller, ed., *Chesapeake Bay in the American Revolution*, 44 (*within twenty miles*); Jackson, ed., *The Diaries of George Washington*, 3: 340 (*Chesapeake froze*); William Finnie to NG, Jan. 15, 1780, *PNG*, 5: 273 (*brig Jefferson*); Brumwell, *Turncoat*, 187 (*near Jamestown*).

576 **"The ink freezes in my pen":** Sabine, ed., *Historical Memoirs of William Smith*, 2: 211 (*"grate"*), 214 (*"deaths of the poor"*), 232 (*sparing only fruit orchards*); Biddulph, "Letters of Robert Biddulph, 1779–1783," 87+ (*"eat their meat raw"*); Wertenbaker, *Father Knickerbocker Rebels*, 184–85 (*single log*); "Official Letters of Major General James Pattison," 146–52 (*firelocks from the arsenal*); Simco, *A Journal of the Operations of the Queen's Rangers*, 90 (*undress at night*).

576 **Such fears among the king's men:** "Chronology Morristown, Nov. 1779–December 1780," EPO, Jan. 15, 1780 (*five hundred sleighs*); Stirling to GW, Jan. 16, 1780, FOL; "William Alexander's (Lord Stirling) Raid of Staten Island, January 14–15, 1780," blog post, Sept. 9, 2019; GW to Stirling, Jan. 13 and 14, 1780, *PGW*, 24: 109 (*forty thousand musket cartridges*), 137 (*mittens*); "Instructions for Attack on Staten Island," Jan. 12, 1780, *PGW*, 24: 113 (*a thousand

men); Smith, *Winter at Morristown*, 24 (*half their actual number*); Stirling to GW, Jan. 13, 1780, FOL (*"an attempt to surprise"*).

576 **Stirling was correct. Deserters and loyalist informants:** Stirling to GW, Jan. 16, 1780, FOL fn; Nelson, *William Alexander, Lord Stirling*, 152 (*ten-foot abatis* and *nine small vessels*); Simcoe, *A Journal of the Operations of the Queen's Rangers*, 81 (*nails*); Stirling to GW, Jan. 16, 1780, *PGW*, 24: 161–63n (*bonfires*); Morris, *Morris's Memorial History of Staten Island*, 1: 232–34; Greenman, *Diary of a Common Soldier in the American Revolution, 1775–1783*, 167 (*"feet was froze"*); "Chronology Morristown, Nov. 1779–December 1780," EPO, Jan. 15, 1780 (*"necklaces off the ladies' necks"*); Smith, *Winter at Morristown*, 24 (*"five hundred sleighloads"*).

577 **Stirling's officers made fitful efforts:** Stirling to GW, Jan. 16, 1780, FOL; Ferling, *Winning Independence*, 185 (*"noble attempt"*); "Chronology Morristown, Nov. 1779–December 1780," EPO, Jan. 15, 1780 (*"no valuable purpose"*).

577 **Repulse of the Staten Island marauders:** Moore, *The Diary of the American Revolution, 1775–1781*, 405–6 (*royal salute*); *Narratives of the Revolution in New York*, 301 (*released on parole*); Stokes, *The Iconography of Manhattan Island, 1498–1909*, 5: 1101 (*"most amiable"*); Barck, *New York City During the War for Independence*, 181–82 (*"perfect hilarity"*). Although Queen Charlotte's birthday was May 19, it was celebrated in January to provide some separation from the king's birthday, in early June.

577 **Festivities resumed that evening:** Moore, *The Diary of the American Revolution, 1775–1781*, 405–6 (*BRITONS STRIKE HOME*); Brown, trans., *Baroness von Riedesel and the American Revolution*, 100 (*trumpets and kettledrums*).

577 **Seven months pregnant, Frederika Riedesel:** Baer, *Hessians*, 215 (*spoke mostly English and Italian arias*); Brown, trans., *Baroness von Riedesel and the American Revolution*, xxxiv (*eight spoons*), 100–105 (*£10 for a cord*); Kranish, *Flight from Monticello*, 107–8.

578 **Luminous and self-possessed as ever:** Schecter, *The Battle for New York*, 331 (*nearly four hundred dishes*); Brown, trans., *Baroness von Riedesel and the American Revolution*, 100 (*"very much touched"*); Moore, *The Diary of the American Revolution, 1775–1781*, 405–6 (*"retired about three o'clock"*).

578 **Judge Smith grumbled that:** Sabine, ed., *Historical Memoirs of William Smith*, 2: 217; Stokes, *The Iconography of Manhattan Island, 1498–1909*, 5: 1101 (*"better laid out"* and *"truly elegant"*); Brown, trans., *Baroness von Riedesel and the American Revolution*, xxxvi (*"America"*), 203 (*"protects my four daughters"*).

26. SHE STOOPS TO CONQUER

579 **One day after the British fleet left Sandy Hook:** Ferling, *Winning Independence*, 192 (*"malevolence of the winds"*); Uhlendorf, trans. and ed., *The Siege of Charleston*, 125 (*"Terrible weather!"*).

579 **"First the bow sank, then the stern":** Burgoyne, ed., *Enemy Views*, 351–53; Borick, *A Gallant Defense*, 23–24, 26 (*seven ice-damaged vessels*); "Journal of the Hon. Garrison-Regiment von Huyn," Lidgerwood Hessian Transcriptions, HDAR, 122 (*"raging sea"*); Baer, *Hessians*, 320–21 (*crushed to death*); Syrett, *Shipping and the American War, 1775–1783*, 182–83 (*"destruction in the foretops"*).

579 **Tempestuous seas killed horses:** Bain, ed., "The Siege of Charleston," 478+ (*General Cornwallis*), 481 (*cut the throats*); Bass, *The Green Dragoon*, 72 (*just one survived*); Borick, *A Gallant Defense*, 26 (*over the side*); Lydenberg, ed., "Archibald Robertson," 283+ (*"Killed ten horses"*); Knight, *War at Saber Point*, 83 (Rebecca), 84 (*223 animals*); Pattison to Board of Ordnance, Mar. 25, 1780, "Official Letters of Major General James Pattison," 158 (*nearly every dragoon and saddle horse*).

580 **Of thirty-six days at sea:** Burgoyne, trans. and ed., *Diaries of Two Ansbach Jaegers*, 104 (*twenty-five stormy days*); Ewald, *Diary of the American War*, 194 (*"Here I thought"*); Lydenberg, ed., "Archibald Robertson," 283+ (*"pooped us"*); Uhlendorf, trans. and ed., *The Siege of Charleston*, 127 (*four light infantry companies*), 129 (*remained at the pumps*); "Journal of the Hon. Garrison-Regiment von Huyn," Lidgerwood Hessian Transcriptions, HDAR, 123 (*six*

feet of seawater); Baer, *Hessians*, 320–21 (*sails standing*); Gruber, ed., *John Peebles' American War, 1776–1782*, 326 (*"tumbling sea"*); Bain, ed., "The Siege of Charleston," 478+; journal, George Philip Hooke, Jan. 16, 1780, WLC, M-1239 (*wreckage*); Burgoyne, trans., *Journal of a Hessian Grenadier Battalion*, 95 (Sally and *"No job is more dangerous"*).

580 **No loss was more damaging:** Uhlendorf, trans. and ed., *The Siege of Charleston*, 221 (*four thousand muskets*); Baer, *Hessians*, 320–21 (*eating pet dogs*); Edwards and Shepperson, eds., *Scotland, Europe and the American Revolution*, 52–54 (*at St. Ives*); Eelking and Rosengarten, *The German Allied Troops in the North American War of Independence*, 105 (*ten months later*). Another source called the rescue vessel the *Lord Dunmore* (Bain, ed., "The Siege of Charleston," 485).

580 **Each day at sea seemed to bring new perils:** Willcox, ed., *The American Rebellion*, 159 (*wrong direction*); Edwards and Shepperson, eds., *Scotland, Europe and the American Revolution*, 52–53 (*Gulf Stream*), 54 (*"drink seawater"*); Borick, *A Gallant Defense*, 29 (Diana *and* Silver Eel); journal, George Philip Hooke, Jan. 20, 1780, WLC, M-1239 (*three pints*).

581 **On February 2, sixty-two vessels:** Uhlendorf, trans. and ed., *The Siege of Charleston*, 23 (*Tybee Island*), 25 (*ships still missing*), 140–41 (*eighteen hundred meandering miles*); O'Shaughnessy, *The Men Who Lost America*, 230 (*without even a horse*); Clinton to Germain, Mar. 9, 1780, *DAR*, 18: 53 (*"very tedious"*); Willcox, ed., *The American Rebellion*, 160 (*St. Augustine, the Bahamas*). The city was officially called Charles Town until 1783.

581 **Clinton had intended to march overland:** B. Lincoln to GW, Feb. 11–12, 1780, *PGW*, 24: 441n (*move the fleet closer*); *TBAC*, 361, 389 (*amphibious operations*); Willcox, ed., *The American Rebellion*, 160 (*toward Augusta*). Simmons Island was renamed Seabrook Island in the nineteenth century.

581 **More troops landed on February 12:** Bain, ed., "The Siege of Charleston," 478+ (*camp bed and where to find horses*); McCowen, *The British Occupation of Charleston, 1780–82*, 100 (*slaves flocked*); "Extracts from the Journal of Mrs. Gabriel (Ann Ashby) Manigault, 1754–1781," S.C. Historical Society, ms. collection, College of Charleston Library, Feb. 15, 1780 (*"very fast"*).

581 **If not fast, the British advance:** Borick, *A Gallant Defense*, 30 (*slashing at vines*); Uhlendorf, trans. and ed., *The Siege of Charleston*, 29 (*"full of wolves"*); Jones, "The 1780 Siege of Charleston as Experienced by a Hessian Officer," 2: 63 (*"Virginia nightingales"*); Ewald, *Diary of the American War*, 197 (*six guineas*); Saberton, ed., *The Cornwallis Papers*, 25–26 (*opera glasses*); "Memorandum of Occurrences During the Campaign, 1780," Uzal Johnson journal, S.C. Historical Society, ms. collection, College of Charleston, Mar. 16, 1780 (*"fat of the land"*).

582 **Clinton was chagrined to learn:** Bain, ed., "The Siege of Charleston," 478+ (*nine feet of water in her hold*); B. Lincoln to GW, Feb. 11–12, 1780, *PGW*, 24: 441n (*crossed the Stono*); M. Arbuthnot to Germain, May 15, 1780, *Report on the Manuscripts of Mrs. Stopford-Sackville*, 2: 162 (*forty-five heavy guns* and *750 seamen*); Willcox, ed., *The American Rebellion*, 438–39 (*120 barrels*); Perrin, ed., *The Keith Papers*, 1: 152 (*officers from thirteen ships*); Willis, *The Struggle for Sea Power*, 352 (*rope harnesses*).

582 **Engineers under James Moncrieff:** Uhlendorf, trans. and ed., *The Siege of Charleston*, 206–9 (Queen of France); Borick, *A Gallant Defense*, 44, 63–64 (*Fort Johnson*), 65 (*five guns emplaced*); "return of ordnance and stores," May 2, 1780, HCP, vol. 96, WLC (*Carriages, cartridges*).

584 **Looking at Charleston through his spyglass:** Uhlendorf, trans. and ed., *The Siege of Charleston*, 211 (*"Like mushrooms"*); "Memorandum of Occurrences During the Campaign, 1780," Uzal Johnson journal, S.C. Historical Society, ms. collection, College of Charleston, Mar. 18, 1780 (*eighty rebel militiamen*); Ewald, *Diary of the American War*, 214 (*"he quietly lay down"*).

584 **By late March, Clinton and much of his army:** Willcox, ed., *The American Rebellion*, 162–63 (*Drayton Hall*); Borick, *A Gallant Defense*, 102–3 (*seventy-five flatboats*); "Memorandum of Occurrences During the Campaign, 1780," Uzal Johnson journal, South Carolina Historical Society, ms. collection, College of Charleston, Mar. 29, 1780 (*"like New York"*); Clinton to Germain, Mar. 9, 1780, *DAR*, 18: 53 (*"hopes of success"*).

584 **No one tracked Clinton's progress more closely:** *TBAC*, 323 (*most conspicuous*); King, "Peter Timothy," *South Carolina Encyclopedia*, https://www.scencyclopedia.org/sce/entries/timothy -peter/; author visit, St. Michael's Church, Mar. 14, 2014; Williams, *St. Michael's*, 24, 44 (*painted it black*), 148–49 (*cypress-shingle roof*).

585 **From this perch with his spyglass:** Peter Timothy journal, South Carolina Historical Society Archives, College of Charleston Library, 43/2249, Mar. 26, 1780 ("*each drawn*"); B. Lincoln to Abraham Whipple, Feb. 28, 1780, Thomas Addis Emmet Collection, NYPL, EM. 7723 (Notre Dame); *TBAC*, 334–39 (*run aground*); Borick, *A Gallant Defense*, 78 (*white buoy*), 107 ("*loaded with men, tools*").

585 **Even at high tide the narrow passage:** B. Lincoln to GW, Mar. 24, 1780, FOL fn (*twenty-two enemy vessels*); Borick, *A Gallant Defense*, 81–85 ("*Joy to you*").

585 **All this Timothy watched from his aerie:** Peter Timothy journal, South Carolina Historical Society Archives, College of Charleston Library, 43/2249, Apr. 2, 1780 ("*feeble*"), Apr. 8, 1780 ("'*Tis pity*").

586 **With the enemy almost at the gates:** Borick, *A Gallant Defense*, 47 (*army drummers*), 91 ("*All is well*"); Billias, ed., *George Washington's Generals and Opponents*, 200 (*swing a pick*); B. Lincoln to GW, Feb. 11–12, 1780, *PGW*, 24, 440 ("*fast ripening*").

586 **He felt overmatched:** B. Lincoln to GW, Jan. 23, 1780, *PGW*, 24: 235 ("*insufficiency*"); Mattern, *Benjamin Lincoln and the American Revolution*, 99 (*twice his strength*); Borick, *A Gallant Defense*, 53 (*fight in the open*), 54 ("*every article*").

586 **Wedged onto a peninsula between two rivers:** *TBAC*, 327; Fraser, *Charleston! Charleston!*, 158–59 (*Haddrell's Point*); Clinton, "Sir Henry Clinton's 'Journal of the Siege of Charleston, 1780,' " 147+ (*from the northwest*); Butler, "Demolition by Neglect in the 1720s: Forsaking Charleston's Earthen Fortifications," *Rediscovering Charleston's Colonial Fortifications* (blog), Oct. 17, 2023, https://walledcitytaskforce.org/ ("*hornwork*"); Rogers, *Charleston in the Age of the Pinckneys*, 59 (*new town gate*); Borick, *A Gallant Defense*, 116; author interview, Nic Butler, public historian, Charleston County Library, Mar. 2014 ("*wolf holes*"); Walker, *Engineers of Independence*, 273 (*Wells*).

587 **"The works here are by no means":** B. Lincoln to GW, Feb. 11–12, 1780, *PGW*, 24: 440n; B. Lincoln to GW, Dec. 23, 1779, FOL ("*pretty safe*"); Borick, *A Gallant Defense*, 93–94 (*left the body dangling*).

587 **The navy disappointed him:** Borick, *A Gallant Defense*, 44 (*manned by only two hundred*), 72 76 (*declined to challenge*); Fowler, *Rebels Under Sail*, 110 (*sailed his squadron to Charleston*); B. Lincoln to GW, Mar. 24, 1780, FOL (*guns were removed*); Baldwin, "Diary of Events in Charleston, S.C.," 77+ (*brickbats*); Abraham Whipple et al., to John Rutledge and B. Lincoln, Mar. 11, 1780, Thomas Addis Emmet Collection, NYPL, EM. 7723 (*four hundred fathoms* and *twenty-six anchors*); A. Lincoln war council, Thomas Addis Emmet Collection, NYPL, EM. 7667 (*neither option*).

587 **Lincoln peppered Governor John Rutledge:** Mattern, *Benjamin Lincoln and the American Revolution*, 90 (*ten tons of powder*); Baldwin, "Diary of Events in Charleston, S.C.," 77+ ("*good suit of clothes*"); GW to Samuel Huntington, Nov. 29, 1779, FOL ("*defenseless condition*"); B. Lincoln to GW, Feb. 22, 1780, *PGW*, 24: 545; B. Lincoln to William Woodford, Mar. 17, 1780, APS, Feinstone Coll., #815 ("*never has been a time*").

588 **Most frustrating was the reluctance:** McCrady, *The History of South Carolina in the Revolution, 1775–1780*, 367–76 (*prepared to surrender*); Wilson, *The Southern Strategy*, 109–11; [Laumoy ?] to B. Lincoln, Mar. 8, 1780, Thomas Addis Emmet Collection, NYPL, EM. 7551 (*sixteen hundred slaves*); Mattern, *Benjamin Lincoln and the American Revolution*, 71–72 (*state's neutrality*), 91 (*Three thousand militia*), 96 (*fewer than half*); McCowen, *The British Occupation of Charleston, 1780–82*, 98 (*army patrols*); Fenn, *Pox Americana*, 117 (*smallpox outbreak*); Wehrman, *The Contagion of Liberty*, 242 (*sixteen years*).

588 **"Am much surprised to find":** Moultrie, *Memoirs of the American Revolution*, 2: 54–55; Borick, *A Gallant Defense*, 119 (*only three hundred*). Mattern, *Benjamin Lincoln and the American Revolution*, 90 ("*neglected themselves*"). Another estimate put the number of militia in Charleston at a thousand by late March (Wilson, *The Southern Strategy*, 205).

588 **No less perplexing to Lincoln:** Borick, *A Gallant Defense*, 94 (*$3,000* and *"impregnable"*); Cross and Pinckney, "Letters of Thomas Pinckney, 1775–1780," 224+ (*"forced marches"*).

590 **As a stranger in this strange land:** *TBAC*, 323 (*richest in America*); Montross, *Rag, Tag and Bobtail*, 357 (*thrived more*); Nadelhaft, *The Disorders of War*, 48–49 (*high prices for indigo*); Rogers, *Charleston in the Age of the Pinckneys*, 10, 109 (*seven thousand books*); Johnson, "A Frenchman Visits Charleston in 1777," 88+ (*fireworks*); Wallace, *The Life of Henry Laurens*, 59 (*only four*); Fraser, *Charleston! Charleston!*, 157 (*"sea of flame"*); Clark, *Captain Dauntless*, 227–29.

590 **Yet Charleston retained much:** McCowen, *The British Occupation of Charleston, 1780–82*, 112 (She Stoops to Conquer); Massey, *John Laurens and the American Revolution*, 12 (*"eating, drinking"*).

590 **Bondage made it all possible:** Morison and Commager, *The Growth of the American Republic*, 1: 244 (*a fifth of all those*); Harris, *The Hanging of Thomas Jeremiah*, 29 (*barbers, coachmen*); Quarles, *The Negro in the Making of America*, 40 (*Barbados and Jamaica*); Benjamin West to Samuel West, July 23, 1778, James S. Schoff Revolutionary War Collection, WLC (*"shoot a Negro"*); Van Buskirk, *Standing in Their Own Light*, 28–29 (*illegal to teach a slave to write*); *South-Carolina Gazette and Country Journal*, July 7 and 17, 1777, 3 (*"thirty valuable"* and *"seventeen valuable"*).

591 **Congress had hoped that bondmen:** H. Laurens to GW, Mar. 16, 1779, *PGW*, 19: 503n (*"take measures immediately"*); Rakove, *Revolutionaries*, 232 (*"standard size"* and *$1,000*); Van Buskirk, *Standing in Their Own Light*, 156–57 (*$50 and freedom*).

591 **This remarkable step toward emancipation:** Massey, *John Laurens and the American Revolution*, 93–94 (*abolitionist notions*); Rakove, *Revolutionaries*, 205 (*"largest handler"*); Van Buskirk, *Standing in Their Own Light*, 156 (*"firm defender[s]"*); Massey, *John Laurens and the American Revolution*, 140 (*"greatest weakness"*); Simms, ed., *The Army Correspondence of Colonel John Laurens*, 120 (*"good contrast"*).

591 **Henry, who implausibly claimed:** Maslowski, "National Policy Toward the Use of Black Troops in the Revolution," 1+ (*"I abhor"*); Piecuch, *Three Peoples, One King*, 121 (*"comfortable"*); Henry Laurens to GW, Mar. 16, 1779, FOL (*agreed to endorse*); GW to Henry Laurens, Mar. 20, 1779, FOL (*"much of my thoughts"*); David Ramsay to William Henry Drayton, Sept. 1, 1779, in Gibbes, *Documentary History of the American Revolution, 1776–1782*, 121 (*"received with horror"*); Massey, *John Laurens and the American Revolution*, 140 (*"much disgusted"*), 143 (*"black air castle"*).

591 **Rutledge still opposed the plan:** Maslowski, "National Policy Toward the Use of Black Troops in the Revolution," 1+ (*"measure of raising"*); Piecuch, *Three Peoples, One King*, 214 (*Savannah*); Van Buskirk, *Standing in Their Own Light*, 163 (*"circumstances were different"*); Mattern, *Benjamin Lincoln and the American Revolution*, 92–93 (*"determine whether I stay"*); Rakove, *Revolutionaries*, 235 (*"harangues"*).

592 **To no avail. The state's privy council:** Mattern, *Benjamin Lincoln and the American Revolution*, 92–93 (*"totally impracticable"*); Rakove, *Revolutionaries*, 238 (*artillery crews*); Massey, *John Laurens and the American Revolution*, 155–56 (*"sufferers"*); Maslowski, "National Policy Toward the Use of Black Troops in the Revolution," 1+ (*"persuade rich men"*).

592 **Runaways continued to flock to the British:** Piecuch, *Three Peoples, One King*, 216–17 (*from fatigue duty*); Burgoyne, trans., *Journal of a Hessian Grenadier Battalion*, 125 (*British gunboats*).

592 **Disgusted at his compatriots' "supineness":** Massey, *John Laurens and the American Revolution*, 156, 159 (*Stepney, Exeter*).

592 **At two p.m. on Friday, April 7:** Borick, *A Gallant Defense*, 130 (*"hardy veterans"*); "Journal of the Siege of Charleston," WBW, n.d. (*"I rejoice"*).

592 **The Virginians found a town besieged:** Borick, *A Gallant Defense*, 121–23 (*mantelets*); Uhlendorf, trans. and ed., *The Siege of Charleston*, 45 (*24-pounders*), 233–35 (*fifteen hundred of the king's laborers*).

593 **Just before four p.m. on Saturday:** Bain, ed., "The Siege of Charleston," 478+ (*within eight hundred yards*); Borick, *A Gallant Defense*, 133–34 (*breezes blew from the southeast*); Jones, "The 1780 Siege of Charleston as Experienced by a Hessian Officer," 2: 63+ (*flocked to the city*

ramparts); Burgoyne, trans., *Journal of a Hessian Grenadier Battalion*, 124 (*twinkling muzzle flashes*); Ewald, *Diary of the American War*, 226 (*"veiled in fire and smoke"*).

593 **For nearly ninety minutes the cannonade:** Borick, *A Gallant Defense*, 133 (*"admiral has received"*), 134 (Richmond's *hull*).

593 **But the Royal Navy now commanded:** B. Lincoln to GW, Apr. 9, 1780, FOL; Borick, *A Gallant Defense*, 136–37 (*"havoc and devastation"*).

594 **Lincoln replied promptly:** Borick, *A Gallant Defense*, 138 (*"Duty and inclination"*); McCowen, *The British Occupation of Charleston, 1780–82*, 5 (*"in high spirits"*).

594 **Yet Lincoln had doubts:** Borick, *A Gallant Defense*, 139 (*"succor of consequence"* and *"an hour longer"*).

594 **Suddenly at ten a.m.:** Borick, *A Gallant Defense*, 139 (*"balls flew"*); Bragg, *Crescent Moon over Carolina*, 172 (*fifteen hours*); Jones, "The 1780 Siege of Charleston as Experienced by a Hessian Officer," 2: 63+ (*feuerkugeln*); Allardyce, *Memoir of the Honourable George Keith Elphinstone, K.B.*, 45 (*setting houses ablaze*); Clinton, "Sir Henry Clinton's 'Journal of the Siege of Charleston, 1780,'" 147+ (*"absurd, impolitic"*).

594 **Even without carcasses the greatest bombardment:** Weller, "Revolutionary War Artillery in the South," 2: 377+ (*greatest bombardment* and *bombproofs*); Uhlendorf, trans. and ed., *The Siege of Charleston*, 47 (*"terrific clatter"*); Borick, *A Gallant Defense*, 164 (*killed a man in bed*); Moultrie, *Memoirs of the American Revolution*, 2: 64 (*decapitated*); Smith, "Wilton's Statue of Pitt," *South Carolina Historical and Genealogical Magazine*, vol. 15, no. 1 (Jan. 1914): 18+; Raphael, *Founders*, 356 (*Laurens's town house*).

595 **The Americans answered as best they could:** Bragg, *Crescent Moon over Carolina*, 173 (*second parallel*); Uhlendorf, trans. and ed., *The Siege of Charleston*, 251 (*on April 15 Hinrich*); Borick, *A Gallant Defense*, 165 (*through the eye*); Perrin, ed., *The Keith Papers*, 1: 167 (*"burn their town"*).

595 **Yet trouble for Lincoln now came:** Hayes, ed., *A Gentleman of Fortune*, 3: 63–67; Tarleton, *A History of the Campaigns of 1780 and 1781*, 15–17 (*Moncks Corner*); TBAC, 503 (*flamboyant son*); Harris and Baxley, "Tarleton Tightens the Noose Around Charleston Neck," 1+ (*"so sudden"*).

595 **Pinned against the river:** Harris and Baxley, "Tarleton Tightens the Noose Around Charleston Neck," 1+ (*"cut to pieces"*); Buchanan, *The Road to Guilford Courthouse*, 63 (*"mangled"*); Tarleton, *A History of the Campaigns of 1780 and 1781*, 15–17 (*severing the Cooper*); Wheeler, *Voices of 1776*, 369 (*"an old Roman"*).

596 **These pleasing developments should have:** Clinton, "Sir Henry Clinton's 'Journal of the Siege of Charleston, 1780,'" 147+ (*"blockhead"* and *"too much risk"*); Willcox, *Portrait of a General*, 311 (*"talks nonsense"*); Willcox, ed., *The American Rebellion*, 164 (*"on my guard"*), 166 (*"false as hell"*).

596 **His growing disaffection with Cornwallis:** Willcox, ed., *The American Rebellion*, 184 (*André surmised*); "Journal of the Siege of Charleston," WBW, n.d. (*"upon his honor"*).

596 **Wary, cynical, and forlorn:** Clinton to Cornwallis, Apr. 23, 1780, Saberton, ed., *The Cornwallis Papers*, 12 (*"most beneficial"*); Willcox, ed., *The American Rebellion*, 167 (*"play me false"*).

596 **During another war conference in the hornwork:** Borick, *A Gallant Defense*, 167 (*stocks were dwindling*); David Oliphant, monthly medical report, Apr. 1–May 1, 1780, Thomas Addis Emmet Collection, NYPL, EM. 6515 (*gunshot wounds*).

597 **As Lincoln went through this bleak recitation:** Borick, *A Gallant Defense*, 169 (*"without fear or dread"*); Mattern, *Benjamin Lincoln and the American Revolution*, 102 (*"open the gates"*).

597 **Rather than answer this shocking insolence:** McCrady, *The History of South Carolina in the Revolution, 1775–1780*, 512–13; Higgins, ed., *The Revolutionary War in the South*, 128 (*"advice of the citizen"*); B. Lincoln, council of officers, Apr. 20–21, 1780, Thomas Addis Emmet Collection, NYPL, EM. 7713 (*"more critical"*); Borick, *A Gallant Defense*, 171–72 (*"dispose of their effects"*).

597 **Clinton replied with disdain:** Borick, *A Gallant Defense*, 173 (*"could not be listened to"* and *more than eight hundred rounds*).

597 **By late April, British sappers:** Bain, ed., "The Siege of Charleston," 478+ (*"ragged pieces of iron"*); Moultrie, *Memoirs of the American Revolution*, 2: 83 (*"uncommon number of bullets"*).

598 **The only rebel sally across the lines:** McCrady, *The History of South Carolina in the Revolution, 1775–1780*, 482 (*Virginia and South Carolina Continentals*); Mattern, *Benjamin Lincoln and the American Revolution*, 104 (*"Damn me"*); Borick, *A Gallant Defense*, 178 (*"off our guard"*); Bragg, *Crescent Moon over Carolina*, 178 (*Thomas Moultrie*).

598 **At seven a.m. the following day:** GW to Samuel Huntington, Mar. 27, 1780, FOL (*"all possible dispatch"*); Louis Duportail to GW, May 17, 1780, FOL (*"desperate state"*); Uhlendorf, trans. and ed., *The Siege of Charleston*, 75 (*Twelve hundred enemy troops*); Pattison to Board of Ordnance, Mar. 25, 1780, "Official Letters of Major General James Pattison," 158 (*thousand barrels of gunpowder*); Jones, "The 1780 Siege of Charleston as Experienced by a Hessian Officer," 2: 63+ (*French cannons*); Bain, ed., "The Siege of Charleston," 478+ (*24-pound shot*).

598 **The American garrison was still only half:** Borick, *A Gallant Defense*, 180 (*turpentine*); Uhlendorf, trans. and ed., *The Siege of Charleston*, 271 (*cowhide flaps*), 273 (*inch every hour*); Duportail to Congress, May 17, 1780, in Walker, *Engineers of Independence*, 277 (*"fall of the town"*).

599 **The encirclement was completed on April 28:** Harris and Baxley, "Tarleton Tightens the Noose Around Charleston Neck," *Southern Campaigns of the American Revolution*, 1+; Moultrie, *Memoirs of the American Revolution*, 2: 64 (*"closely blocked up"*); Hough, *The Siege of Charleston*, 83; Borick, *A Gallant Defense*, 194 (*"thirteen stripes"*).

599 **That was Clinton's intent:** Clinton, "Sir Henry Clinton's 'Journal of the Siege of Charleston, 1780,'" 147+ (*"success of a storm"*); Clinton to Cornwallis, May 6, 1780, Saberton, ed., *The Cornwallis Papers*, 19 (*"blockheads enough"*).

599 **Like the siege itself, the end came:** "Memorandum of Occurrences During the Campaign, 1780," Uzal Johnson journal, S.C. Historical Society, ms. collection, College of Charleston, May 7, 1780 (*Fort Moultrie*); Mattern, *Benjamin Lincoln and the American Revolution*, 106 (*"impregnable"*).

599 **The following morning, Clinton again summoned:** Borick, *A Gallant Defense*, 209 (*sixty-one senior American*); Carl Borick to author, June 13, 2024 (*British insistence*); Clinton to B. Lincoln, May 9, 1780, Thomas Addis Emmet Collection, NYPL, EM. 7634 (*"utterly inadmissible"*); Jones, "The 1780 Siege of Charleston as Experienced by a Hessian Officer," 2: 63+ (*Barrels of musket cartridges*); Ewald, *Diary of the American War*, 237 (*thirty paces*).

600 **Church bells pealed as the bombardment resumed:** Lydenberg, ed., "Archibald Robertson," 283+ (*"rebels began with huzzahing"*); Borick, *A Gallant Defense*, 214 (*more than eight hundred rounds*); Uhlendorf, trans. and ed., *The Siege of Charleston*, 85 (*seven houses*); Mattern, *Benjamin Lincoln and the American Revolution*, 106–7 (*"Cannonballs whizzing"*); Moultrie, *Memoirs of the American Revolution*, 2: 96 (*"stars were tumbling"*).

600 **Charleston had had enough:** Louis Duportail to GW, May 17, 1780, FOL fn (*"Militia abandon"*); petition to B. Lincoln, May 10, 1780, Thomas Addis Emmet Collection, NYPL, EM. 7625 (*"perilous situation"*); Borick, *A Gallant Defense*, 216 (*nearly six hundred*); Ewald, *Diary of the American War*, 237 (*ordered wine*); Clinton, "Sir Henry Clinton's 'Journal of the Siege of Charleston, 1780,'" 147+ (*"The place surrendered"*).

600 **An eerie silence descended:** Uhlendorf, trans. and ed., *The Siege of Charleston*, 291 (*"God Save the King"*); Borick, *A Gallant Defense*, 219 (*Moultrie on foot*); Burgoyne, trans. and ed., *Diaries of Two Ansbach Jaegers*, 145 (*"thin, miserable, ragged"*); Mattern, *Benjamin Lincoln and the American Revolution*, 107 (*"all the troops I have"*).

600 **The surrender agreement permitted Continental drummers:** Jones, "The 1780 Siege of Charleston as Experienced by a Hessian Officer," 2: 63+ (*"Janissary March"*); Burgoyne, trans. and ed., *Diaries of Two Ansbach Jaegers*, 146–47 (*swords and sidearms*); Uhlendorf, trans. and ed., *The Siege of Charleston*, 88 (*"Long live Congress!"*); John Laurens to GW, May 25, 1780, FOL (*"most humiliating"*).

601 **"God was with us":** "Extracts from the Letter Book of Captain Johann Heinrichs [sic] of the Hessian *Jäger* Corps, 1778–1780," 137+ (*"a million bullets"*); Borick, *A Gallant Defense*, 222 (*316 dead and wounded*); H. Clinton to Germain, June 4, 1780, Germain papers, WLC, vol. 12

(*5,610 men captured*); Mattern, *Benjamin Lincoln and the American Revolution*, 108 (*four hundred cannons*); Moultrie, *Memoirs of the American Revolution*, 2: 106–7 (*twenty-five tons of powder*); Wilson, *The Southern Strategy*, 234–35 (*renamed, reflagged*).

601 **Under the surrender terms:** Willcox, ed., *The American Rebellion*, 171 (*seven generals*); Reiss, *Medicine and the American Revolution*, 260 (*Eight hundred would die*); Harris and Baxley, "Tarleton Tightens the Noose Around Charleston Neck," 1+ (*enlisting*); Ferling, *Winning Independence*, 206–7. The captured signers, militia officers who were eventually jailed in St. Augustine, were Thomas Heyward, Jr., Edward Rutledge, and Arthur Middleton (Carl Borick to author, June 13, 2024).

601 **Three days after the surrender:** Burgoyne, trans. and ed., *Diaries of Two Ansbach Jaegers*, 150–51 (*brothel*); Moultrie, *Memoirs of the American Revolution*, 2: 105–6 ("*legs, and arms were seen*").

601 **Firelocks, ramrods, and bayonets rained:** Uhlendorf, trans. and ed., *The Siege of Charleston*, 299; Wilson, *The Southern Strategy*, 235 (*Three thousand muskets*); Parker, *Parker's Guide to the Revolutionary War in South Carolina* (*more than five hundred yards*); Joshua Shepherd, "A Melancholy Accident: The Disastrous Explosion at Charleston," Aug. 5, 2015, *JAR*.

602 **A final, wretched episode in the Charleston campaign:** *PGW*, 13: 576n, FOL (*hospital superintendent*); Wilson, *The Southern Strategy*, 254 (*380 callow infantry recruits*); O'Shaughnessy, *The Men Who Lost America*, 257 (*two to a horse*); Willcox, ed., *The American Rebellion*, 176 (*just over two days*); Tarleton, *A History of the Campaigns of 1780 and 1781*, 27–28 (*horses and men collapsing*).

602 **"You are now almost encompassed":** Bass, *The Green Dragoon*, 79 ("*nine British battalions*"); B. Tarleton to A. Buford, May 29, 1780, Thomas Addis Emmet Collection, NYPL, EM. 9069 ("*upon your head*"); Tarleton, *A History of the Campaigns of 1780 and 1781*, 30 (*within ten yards*).

602 **At three-thirty p.m., Tarleton's legion:** Saberton, ed., *The Cornwallis Papers*, 35 (*bullet through the forehead*); Tarleton, *A History of the Campaigns of 1780 and 1781*, 30 ("*Slaughter was commenced*").

602 **British dragoons wheeled through:** McCrady, *The History of South Carolina in the Revolution, 1775–1780*, 522 ("*nose and lip*"); Harris, "Massacre at Waxhaws," 1+ (*twenty-two sword and bayonet wounds*); Meacham, *American Lion*, 11 ("*none of the men*"); James, *The Life of Andrew Jackson*, 19–20; Knight, *War at Saber Point*, 102–3 (*despise the British*).

603 **Few skirmishes in the war:** Commager and Morris, eds., *The Spirit of 'Seventy-Six*, 1112 ("*plunging their bayonets*"); Knight, *War at Saber Point*, 97 ("*after they had lain down*"); Lynch and Piecuch, "Debating Waxhaws," *JAR*, Aug. 7, 2013 ("*chopped to pieces*"); Wilson, *The Southern Strategy*, 259 ("*virtue of humanity*"). An analysis of Revolutionary War pension applications found that many survivors from Buford's command suffered defensive wounds to the hands and arms, suggesting they had no weapons (Harris, "What Can Pension Applications Contribute to Understanding the Battle of the Waxhaws and Other Events of the Revolutionary War?," 6, and Samuel Gilmore pension application, Nov. 24, 1811, https://revwarapps.org/VAS391.pdf). Harris puts Buford's contingent at approximately 350 American soldiers, and the number of wounded and captured at "a little over 200" (Harris, "American Soldiers at the Battle of Waxhaws," Pension Statements and Rosters, Aug. 11, 2021, https://revwarapps.org/b221.pdf). The historian John Buchanan also rejects assertions that only a few of Tarleton's men participated in the slaughter (*The Road to Charleston*, 21–22).

603 **The unrepentant dragoon commander:** Bass, *The Green Dragoon*, 81–82 ("*refused my terms*"); Richard Pyle, "Sotheby's Auctions Rare Revolutionary War Flags," Associated Press, June 14, 2006; John Knight, "Four Battle Flags of the Revolution," *JAR*, Aug. 27, 2019.

603 **The war had shifted south:** Rankin, *North Carolina in the American Revolution*, 32 ("*rude shock*"); AH to Marquis de Barbé-Marbois, May 31, 1780, FOL ("*a severe stroke*").

604 **"We are now thoroughly masters":** Rogers, Seidule, and Watson, eds., *The West Point History of the American Revolution*, 158 ("*of South Carolina*"); Borick, *A Gallant Defense*, 230 ("*Both the Carolinas*"); Allardyce, *Memoir of the Honourable George Keith Elphinstone, K.B.*, 48 (*20-gun Perseus*); Thomas Digges to JA, July 12, 1780, FOL ("*absolutely mad*"). Clinton's dispatch

was printed in a special edition of the *London Gazette* on June 15 (*Report on American Manuscripts in the Royal Institution of Great Britain*, 2: 122).

604 **Within days Clinton and his lieutenants:** Biddulph, "Letters of Robert Biddulph, 1779–1783," 87+ (*chalking their names*); Williams, *St. Michael's*, 40 (*loyalist vicar*); Smith, *Loyalists and Redcoats*, 130–31 (*"faithful and peaceable"*). The Miles Brewton house still stands (https://www.scpictureproject.org/charleston-county/miles-brewton-house.html). Forbidden to return to Charleston, Timothy drowned in a shipwreck in 1782 (King, "Peter Timothy," https://www.scencyclopedia.org/sce/entries/timothy-peter/).

604 **Among the thorny imperial matters:** Schama, *Rough Crossings*, 105 (*twenty-five thousand runaway slaves*); Neimeyer, *America Goes to War*, 80; Fraser, *Charleston! Charleston!*, 164 (*sugar warehouse*); McCowen, *The British Occupation of Charleston, 1780–82*, 100 (*not be punished*), 101–2 (*"unfriendly persons"*); Pybus, "Jefferson's Faulty Math," 243+ (*"every Negro"*); Davis, "Black Haitian Soldiers at the Siege of Savannah," *JAR*, Feb. 22, 2021 (*sold into slavery*).

605 **Vast stocks of indigo, rice, and tobacco:** McCowen, *The British Occupation of Charleston, 1780–82*, 80–81; J. André to unknown, June 3, 1780, Thomas Addis Emmet Collection, NYPL, EM. 7672 (*"every comfort"*); GW to Samuel Huntington, July 10, 1780, FOL fn; Mattern, *Benjamin Lincoln and the American Revolution*, 112–13 (*never be granted*); Borick, *A Gallant Defense*, 224 (*exchanged*).

605 **Rebel militia garrisons surrendered:** Edgar, *Partisans & Redcoats*, 53 (*Camden, Beaufort* and *"desirous of becoming"*); Rankin, *Francis Marion*, 48–49 (*Catawba Indians* and *cede the three southernmost*).

605 **To further pacify South Carolina:** O'Shaughnessy, *The Men Who Lost America*, 231 (*offered pardons*); Ferling, *Winning Independence*, 208 (*asylums and military redoubts*); Saberton, ed., *The Cornwallis Papers*, 61 (*"we all agree"*).

605 **He further tightened his grip on June 3:** Miller, *The American Revolution*, 15 (*"extirpate the rebellion"*); Edgar, *Partisans & Redcoats*, 55 (*"declare and evince"* and *overplayed his hand*); Borick, *A Gallant Defense*, 238, 242 (*far from extinguished*).

606 **For now, Clinton nurtured his delusions:** Borick, *A Gallant Defense*, 234 (*"strongest reason to believe"*); H. Clinton to Germain, June 4, 1780, Germain papers, WLC, vol. 12 (*"few men in South Carolina"*); McCowen, *The British Occupation of Charleston, 1780–82*, 11 (*"opulent, populous"*).

606 **George III's birthday was celebrated:** "Diary of Lieut. Anthony Allaire," in Draper, *King's Mountain and Its Heroes*, 496 (*"delicious odor"*); Hough, *The Siege of Charleston*, 185 (*"long life"*).

606 **A world that had wobbled badly:** O'Shaughnessy, *The Men Who Lost America*, 232 (*to sail home*); Ferling, *Winning Independence*, 207 (*"most popular man"*); Clinton, "Sir Henry Clinton's 'Journal of the Siege of Charleston, 1780,'" 147+ (*"talks nonsense"*).

606 **Eight thousand regulars and loyalist troops:** Wilson, *The Southern Strategy*, 265; Willcox, *Portrait of a General*, 319–20 (*"keep it against the world"*); "Drivers, Horses, and Wagons," June 1, 1780, William Dalrymple papers, NYHS, folder 1 (*637 horses*); Saberton, ed., *The Cornwallis Papers*, 57 (*"saved out of the magazine"*).

606 **On Thursday, June 8, bargemen rowed:** Tarleton, *A History of the Campaigns of 1780 and 1781*, 32 (Romulus); Borick, *A Gallant Defense*, 239 (*"greatest personal accomplishment"*); Willcox, ed., *The American Rebellion*, 191 (*Forty five hundred redcoats*); Frey, *Water from the Rock*, 124 (*Five hundred slaves*). Tarleton mistakenly dates Clinton's departure as June 5.

EPILOGUE

608 **The catastrophe began benignly enough:** Besant, *London in the Eighteenth Century*, 486 (*Sixty thousand protestors*); Fraser, *The King and the Catholics*, 9 (*heat lightning*); Gilmour, *Riots, Risings and Revolution*, 346 (*enlist*), 349 (*"vulgar, furious zeal"*); Rudé, "The Gordon Riots," 93+ (*"better sort"*); Hibbert, *King Mob*, 46 (*ruffians, inebriates*).

608 **Several burly men carried:** Hibbert, *King Mob*, 45 (*Tailors had stitched*); Toynbee, *The Letters*

of Horace Walpole, 11: 189 (*"applaud or abuse"*); Steuart, ed., *The Last Journals of Horace Walpole,* 2: 306 (*"torn out"*); *Gentleman's Magazine and Historical Chronicle,* vol. 49, 266 (*"No popery"*).

608   **The lord chief justice had the wig:** Hibbert, *King Mob,* 47–48 (*windows of his coach*); Jesse, *Memoirs of King George the Third,* 3: 255 (*in a woman's dress*); Haywood and Seed, eds., *The Gordon Riots,* 2–3 (*"great severity"*); Gibbon, *The Autobiography and Correspondence of Edward Gibbon,* 265 (*"The tumult"*); Colley, *Britons,* 339.

609   **The Relief Act was hardly a radical triumph:** Roberts, *The Last King of America,* 350 (*sit in Parliament*); Fraser, *The King and the Catholics,* 4–5 (*army officer* and *Catholic church bells*); Gilmour, *Riots, Risings and Revolution,* 345–46 (*"bigotry and persecution"*).

609   **This antagonism spread south:** Fraser, *The King and the Catholics,* 6 (*"whore of Babylon"*), 7 (*"mad, cruel"* and *"George Macbeth"*); Ackroyd, *Revolution,* 238 (*"English Brutus"*).

609   **By midnight the mob, armed:** Hibbert, *King Mob,* 59–60 (*altar, vestments*); Haywood and Seed, eds., *The Gordon Riots,* 148 (*fifteen hundred guineas*); Toynbee, *The Letters of Horace Walpole,* 11: 189 (*pair of chalices*); Rudé, "The Gordon Riots," 93+ (*Catholic brokers*).

609   **"Here is a religious war":** Toynbee, *The Letters of Horace Walpole,* 11: 191; Rudé, *Hanoverian London, 1714–1808,* 7 (*fourteen thousand Catholic families*); Gilmour, *Riots, Risings and Revolution,* 352–53; White, "The Gordon Riots, 1780," www.londonhistorians.org, 1+ (*"true religion"*); Haywood and Seed, eds., *The Gordon Riots,* 107 (*"true Protestant"*); "Burke, Edmund (1729–1797)," in Cousin, *A Short Biographical Dictionary of English Literature,* https:// gutenberg.org/cache/epub/13240/pg13240-images.html; Rudé, "The Gordon Riots," 93+ (*"the gentleman, the manufacturer"*).

610   **London would not have a professional police force:** "Metropolitan Police," https://www .parliament.uk/about/living-heritage/transformingsociety/laworder/policeprisons/overview/ metropolitanpolice/; Hibbert, *King Mob,* 77 (*cheek cut*), 102 (*troops were hard to find*); Jesse, *Memoirs of King George the Third,* 3: 270–77.

610   **The Portsmouth fleet was ordered to sea:** Wilson, *The Tower of London,* 220 (*drawbridges*); Gilmour, *Riots, Risings and Revolution,* 367 (*"time of terror"*); Haywood and Seed, eds., *The Gordon Riots,* 125 (*"republican phrenzy"*); Rudé, "The Gordon Riots," 93+ (*Mansfield's house*); White, "The Gordon Riots, 1780," www.londonhistorians.org, 1+ (*criminal records*); Davis, ed., *Crowd Actions in Britain and France from the Middle Ages to the Modern World,* 132 (*crimping houses*).

610   **By Tuesday evening, rioters had begun to release criminals:** Rudé, "The Gordon Riots," 93+ (*nearly two thousand debtors*); Ackroyd, *Revolution,* 238–39 (*"howlings & hissings"* and *"gates of Hell"*); Hibbert, *King Mob,* 86 (*"conducted through the streets"*); Wheatley, ed., *The Historical and the Posthumous Memoirs of Sir Nathaniel William Wraxall, 1772–1784,* 1: 235 (*"sacked and abandoned"*); Besant, *London in the Eighteenth Century,* 489 (*"most terrible night"*). In 1841 Charles Dickens wrote a vivid, fictionalized account of the Newgate attack in *Barnaby Rudge.*

611   **In fact, Wednesday—Black Wednesday:** Rudé, "The Gordon Riots," 93+ (*120,000 gallons*); Wheatley, ed., *The Historical and the Posthumous Memoirs of Sir Nathaniel William Wraxall, 1772–1784,* 1: 233 (*"pinnacle of flame"*); Roberts, *The Last King of America,* 383 (*melted inkwells*).

611   **By one count, thirty-six fires:** Wheatley, ed., *The Historical and the Posthumous Memoirs of Sir Nathaniel William Wraxall, 1772–1784,* 1: 238–39 (*grenadiers took post*); Stuart-Wortley, ed., *A Prime Minister and His Son,* 194 (*"a real civil war"*).

611   **But the king was tired of waiting:** Ayling, *George the Third,* 181 (*"The tumult"*); Rait, *Royal Palaces of England,* 353 (*"easy affability"*); Huish, *Public and Private Life of His Late Excellent and Most Gracious Majesty, George the Third,* 411 (*"wine and spirits"*); Stormont to George, June 7, 1780, in Fortescue, *The Correspondence of King George the Third,* 5: 76 (*royal print shop*); Roberts, *The Last King of America,* 382 (*"without more vigor"*), 386 (*"what fear is"*).

611   **George "was the first that recovered":** Roberts, *The Last King of America,* 386; George to North, June 5, 1780, in Fortescue, *The Correspondence of King George the Third,* 5: 73 (*"great*

supineness"); Huish, *Public and Private Life of His Late Excellent and Most Gracious Majesty, George the Third*, 411 (*"let it be done"*). The Riot Act was repealed in 1973 ("1714 Riot Act," UK Parliament).

612 **By Thursday more than eleven thousand:** Holmes, *Redcoat*, 72; de Castro, *The Gordon Riots*, 197 (*"warlike appearance"*); *Gentleman's Magazine and Historical Chronicle*, vol. 49, 295 (*Six regiments*); Steuart, ed., *The Last Journals of Horace Walpole*, 2: 311 (*"Near thirty persons"*); White, *A Great and Monstrous Thing*, 541 (*Broad Street houses*); Hibbert, *King Mob*, 127 (*Dung Wharf*); Jesse, *Memoirs of King George the Third*, 3: 278 (*tore blue banners*); Stuart-Wortley, ed., *A Prime Minister and His Son*, 187 (*"at last pretty quiet"*).

612 **"The most horrid series of outrages":** Damrosch, *The Club*, 170; Jesse, *Memoirs of King George the Third*, 3: 279 (*Whitewash soon hid*); Gilmour, *Riots, Risings and Revolution*, 370 (*eight hundred to a thousand*); de Castro, *The Gordon Riots*, 236 (*285 killed by Amherst's troops*); Fraser, *The King and the Catholics*, 1 (*the Blitz*).

612 **"I hope every means are taken":** George to North, June 9, 1780, in Fortescue, *The Correspondence of King George the Third*, 5: 79; Lutnick, *The American Revolution and the British Press, 1775–1783*, 161 (*"French and American spies"*); Davis, ed., *Crowd Actions in Britain and France from the Middle Ages to the Modern World*, 137 (*"lads well-trained"*). London's population was roughly 750,000.

612 **No evidence ever supported:** Weintraub, *Iron Tears*, 239 (*seized by horse guards*); Wilson, *The Tower of London*, 220 (*closed hackney*); Gibbon, *The Autobiography and Correspondence of Edward Gibbon*, 266 (*"disgrace will be lasting"*); Haywood and Seed, eds., *The Gordon Riots*, 205–6 (*sixty-two were condemned*), 219 (*a bookbinder*). Gordon converted to Judaism, learned Hebrew, underwent circumcision, and changed his name to Israel Abraham Gordon. But he again found himself in the dock, this time on charges of libeling various high personages including, improbably, Marie-Antoinette. Convicted and jailed in the rebuilt Newgate Prison, he died of typhus at the age of forty-one. Madame Tussaud later re-created him, in wax, in a vivid tableau of his cell that titillated visitors to her museum (Watson, *The Reign of George III, 1760–1815*, 239; Hibbert, *King Mob*, 180–85; Fraser, *The King and the Catholics*, 13; de Castro, *The Gordon Riots*, 243–46).

613 **Gallows appeared around the city:** Haywood and Seed, eds., *The Gordon Riots*, 210 (*Twelve thousand spectators*); Gilmour, *Riots, Risings and Revolution*, 372 (*under the age of eighteen*); Roberts, *The Last King of America*, 385 (*"out of pain"*); Holmes, *Redcoat*, 72 (*"never saw children"*).

613 **If devastating to London:** Rudé, "The Gordon Riots," 93+ (*proved a godsend*); Christie, *The End of North's Ministry, 1780–1782*, 24 (*"mob rule"*).

613 **This revival of fortunes:** Black, *George III, America's Last King*, 242–43 (*disgruntlement*); Ayling, *George the Third*, 282 (*within seven votes*); O'Shaughnessy, *The Men Who Lost America*, 37 (*233 to 215*); Plumb, *England in the Eighteenth Century*, 139 (*"ought to be diminished"*).

613 **With the government now widely seen:** Watson, *The Reign of George III, 1760–1815*, 215–16 (*intercepted letters*); Piecuch, *Three Peoples, One King*, 180–81 (*"exuberant and wild"*); McCowen, *The British Occupation of Charleston, 1780–82*, 10 (*triple discharges*); Clark, *British Opinion and the American Revolution*, 248 (*"coming into temper"*); Mackesy, *The War for America, 1775–1783*, 322–23 (*Spanish convoy* and *Cape St. Vincent*); Drinkwater, *A History of the Late Siege of Gibraltar*, 81 (*thistles*); Spinney, *Rodney*, 312–13.

614 **Not all the war news was heartening:** Watson, *The Reign of George III, 1760–1815*, 240 (*friendless*); JLB, BBB, "From *The Gentleman's Mag.* Apr. 1781, reprinted *Connecticut Journal*, January 31, 1782" (*War Office returns*).

614 **George had now been king for twenty years:** Fortescue, *The Correspondence of King George the Third*, 5: 30 (*"inferiority"*), 57 (*"sue for peace"*).

614 **The king's critics continued to question:** O'Shaughnessy, "'If Others Will Not Be Active, I Must Drive,'" 1+ (*despot*); Fortescue, *The Correspondence of King George the Third*, 5: 30 (*"I must love"*).

614 **The Continental Army and the American cause:** GW to Committee at Headquarters, May 25, 1780, *PGW*, 26: 166–69n (*"in arrears"*); Samuel Huntington to GW, Feb. 29, 1780, *PGW*,

24: 597–99n (*quotas*); NG to GW, Mar. 8–12, 1780, *PNG*, 5: 454n; Johnson, "The Administration of the American Commissariat During the Revolutionary War," diss., 164 (*Spanish-milled dollars*).

615 **This makeshift arrangement already showed:** Return Jonathan Meigs to GW, May 26, 1780, FOL (*"exasperated"*); GW to Samuel Huntington, May 27–28, 1780, FOL (*"more concern"*); Miller, *Sea of Glory*, 423 (*reduced to five vessels*); Toll, *Six Frigates*, 18.

615 **"We are entered deeply in a contest":** AH to NG, May 15–16, 1780, *PNG*, 5: 559 (*"rub through it"*); White, "Standing Armies in Time of War," diss., 295 (*"want to have the war"*); Ryan, ed., *A Salute to Courage*, 181 (*"I am persuaded"*).

615 *My country. That concept had taken root:* Smith, *John Marshall*, 4–5 (*"I was confirmed"*); McCullough, *John Adams*, 226 (*"These are the times"*).

616 **Faith in the future sustained:** Schiff, *A Great Improvisation*, 246 (*millstone*); BF to GW, Mar. 5, 1780, FOL (*"soon quit the scene"*).

616 **Getting to that day, when the corn:** GW to Lund Washington, May 19, 1780, FOL (*"displayed its power"*); Huggins, *Washington's War, 1779*, 148 (*prone to indecision*), 153; Lengel, ed., *A Companion to George Washington*, 252–53 (*deft diplomat*).

616 **If at times stern:** GW to John Armstrong, May 18, 1779, FOL (*"one steady line"*); GW to Lund Washington, May 19, 1780, FOL (*"You ask how"*).

617 **Washington had realized, to his mortification:** GW to Lafayette, Mar. 18, 1780, FOL (*"many letters"*); Lafayette to GW, Apr. 27, 1780, FOL (*"Here I am"*).

617 **Four days later Hamilton sent a note:** AH to Steuben, May 10, 1780, FOL (*"Will you dine"*); EPO, "Chronology Morristown, Nov. 1779–December 1780," May 10, 1780 (*bright sunshine*); Lafayette to GW, Apr. 27, 1780, FOL fn (*"not so fat"*); Unger, *Lafayette*, 114–15 (*"tears of joy"*).

617 **Despite the jubilant welcome:** Unger, *Lafayette*, 114 (*"condition of the army"*); Lafayette to GW, Apr. 27, 1780, FOL fn (*six ships of the line*).

617 **Not since word of the Franco-American alliance:** GW to Lafayette, May 19, 1780, FOL (*"time slides away"*).

617 **This was "the happiest opportunity":** AH to James Duane, May 14, 1780, FOL; GW to Lafayette, May 19, 1780, FOL (*"ancient friendship"*).

618 **Washington began drafting his battle plans:** GW, "Circular to the States," June 2, 1780, *PGW*, 26: 288 (*"well-armed"*); GW to James Duane, May 13, FOL fn (*Halifax*); GW to Lafayette, May 16, 1780, FOL fn (*"telling blow"*); GW to Joseph Jones, May 14, 1780, *PGW*, 26: 16–17 (*"vigor and decision"*). Congress had earlier promised Versailles an American army of at least twenty-five thousand men (Gottschalk, *Lafayette and the Close of the American Revolution*, 82–85).

618 **"This is a decisive moment":** GW to Joseph Reed, May 28, 1780, *PGW*, 26: 221.

Sources

BOOKS

Abbot, W. W., et al., eds. *The Papers of George Washington: Revolutionary War Series*. Vols. 8–26. Charlottesville: University Press of Virginia, 1998–2018.

Abbott, Wilbur C. *New York in the American Revolution*. New York: Charles Scribner's Sons, 1929.

Ackroyd, Peter. *Revolution: The History of England, from the Battle of the Boyne to the Battle of Waterloo*. New York: St. Martin's Press, 2016.

Adelberg, Michael S. *The American Revolution in Monmouth County*. Charleston, S.C.: History Press, 2010.

Albion, Robert Greenhalgh, and Jennie Barnes Pope. *Sea Lanes in Wartime: The American Experience, 1775–1942*. New York: W. W. Norton, 1942, and Hamden, Conn.: Archon Books, 1968.

Alden, John Richard. *The American Revolution, 1775–1783*. New York: Harper Torchbooks, 1962.

———. *General Charles Lee: Traitor or Patriot?* Baton Rouge: Louisiana State University Press, 1951.

———. *The South in the Revolution, 1763–89*. Baton Rouge: Louisiana State University Press, 1957.

Aldridge, Alfred Owen. *Franklin and His French Contemporaries*. New York: New York University Press, 1957.

Allardyce, Alexander. *Memoir of the Honourable George Keith Elphinstone, K.B.* Edinburgh: William Blackwood, 1882.

Allen, Gardner W. *A Naval History of the American Revolution*. 2 vols. Boston: Houghton Mifflin, 1913.

Allen, Thomas B. *Tories: Fighting for the King in America's First Civil War*. New York: Harper, 2011.

Allison, David K., and Larrie D. Ferreiro, eds. *The American Revolution: A World War*. Washington, D.C.: Smithsonian Books, 2018.

Almon, J. *Anecdotes of the Life of the Right Hon. William Pitt, Earl of Chatham*. Vol. 2. Dublin: P. Wogan, 1792.

Alsop, Susan Mary. *Yankees at the Court: The First Americans in Paris*. Garden City, N.Y.: Doubleday, 1982.

Anderson, Enoch. *Personal Recollections of Captain Enoch Anderson*. Edited by Henry Hobart Bellas. Wilmington, Del.: Historical Society of Delaware, 1896.

Anderson, Fred. *Crucible of War: The Seven Years' War and the Fate of Empire in British North America, 1754–1766*. New York: Vintage, 2001.

Anderson, Troyer Steele. *The Command of the Howe Brothers During the American Revolution*. Cranbury, N.J.: Scholar's Bookshelf, 2005.

André, John. *Major André's Journal*. Tarrytown, N.Y.: William Abbatt, 1930.

Andreopoulos, George J., and Harold E. Selesky, eds. *The Aftermath of Defeat: Societies, Armed Forces, and the Challenge of Recovery*. New Haven, Conn.: Yale University Press, 1994.

Andrlik, Todd. *Reporting the Revolutionary War*. Naperville, Ill.: Sourcebooks, 2012.

Andrlik, Todd, Hugh T. Harrison, and Don N. Hagist, eds. *Journal of the American Revolution*. Vol. 1. Yellow Springs, Ohio: Ertel Publishing, 2013.

Annual Register, or a View of the History, Politics, and Literature for the Year 1778. London: J. Dodsley, 1779.

Annual Register, or a View of the History, Politics, and Literature for the Year 1779. Second edition. London: J. Dodsley, 1786.

Anson, William R., ed. *Autobiography and Political Correspondence of Augustus Henry, Third Duke of Grafton, K.G.* London: John Murray, 1898.

Arnold, Catharine. *City of Sin: London and Its Vices.* London: Simon & Schuster, 2010.

Arnot, Hugo. *The History of Edinburgh.* Edinburgh: W. Creech, 1779.

Ashmead, Henry Graham. *History of Delaware County, Pennsylvania.* Philadelphia: L. H. Everts, 1884.

Atkinson, Richard. *Mr. Atkinson's Rum Contract: The Story of a Tangled Inheritance.* London: 4th Estate, 2021.

Atkinson, Rick. *The British Are Coming: The War for America, Lexington to Princeton, 1775–1777.* New York: Henry Holt, 2019.

Atwood, Rodney. *The Hessians: Mercenaries from Hessen-Kassel in the American Revolution.* Cambridge, U.K.: Cambridge University Press, 1980.

Augur, Helen. *The Secret War of Independence.* New York: Duell, Sloan and Pearce, 1955.

Auricchio, Laura. *The Marquis Lafayette Reconsidered.* New York: Vintage Books, 2014.

Ayer, A. J. *Thomas Paine.* Chicago: University of Chicago Press, 1988.

Ayling, Stanley. *The Elder Pitt.* New York: David McKay, 1976.

——. *Fox: The Life of Charles James Fox.* London: John Murray, 1991.

——. *George the Third.* New York: Knopf, 1972.

Bachaumont, Louis Petit de. *Marie-Antoinette, Louis XVI et la famille royale.* Paris: Frédéric Henry, 1866.

Baer, Friederike. *Hessians: German Soldiers in the American Revolutionary War.* New York: Oxford University Press, 2022.

Bailyn, Bernard. *Faces of the Revolution.* New York: Knopf, 1990.

——. *The Ideological Origins of the American Revolution.* Cambridge, Mass.: Belknap, 1992.

——. *The Ordeal of Thomas Hutchinson.* Cambridge, Mass.: Belknap Press, 1974.

——. *To Begin the World Anew.* New York: Vintage, 2004.

Bakeless, John. *Turncoats, Traitors and Heroes.* New York: Da Capo, 1998.

Baker, Norman. *Government and Contractors: The British Treasury and War Supplies, 1775–1983.* London: Athlone, 1971.

Balch, Thomas, ed. *The Examination of Joseph Galloway, Esq., by a Committee of the House of Commons.* Philadelphia: Seventy-Six Society, 1855.

——, ed. *Papers Relating Chiefly to the Maryland Line During the Revolutionary War.* Philadelphia: Seventy-Six Society, 1857.

Balderston, Marion, and David Syrett, eds. *The Lost War: Letters from British Officers During the American Revolution.* New York: Horizon Press, 1975.

Baldwin, Jeduthan. *The Revolutionary Journal of Col. Jeduthan Baldwin, 1775–1778.* Edited by Thomas Williams Baldwin. Bangor, Me.: The De Burians, 1906.

Ballagh, James Curtis, ed. *The Letters of Richard Henry Lee.* Vol. 1. New York: Macmillan, 1911.

Barck, Oscar. *New York City During the War for Independence.* New York: Columbia University Press, 1931.

Barnes, G. R., and J. H. Owen, eds. *The Private Papers of John, Earl of Sandwich, First Lord of the Admiralty, 1771–82.* 4 vols. London: Navy Records Society, 1932–38.

Barnes, John S., ed. *Fanning's Narrative.* New York: Naval Historical Society, 1912.

——, ed. *The Logs of the Serapis, Alliance, Ariel.* New York: Naval History Society, 1911.

Barnhart, John D., ed. *Henry Hamilton and George Rogers Clark in the American Revolution.* Crawfordsville, Ind.: R. E. Banta, 1951.

Barrow, John. *The Life of Richard Earl Howe, K.G.* London: John Murray, 1838.

Barton, William. *Narrative of the Surprize and Capture of Major-General Richard Prescott.* Windsor, Vt.: W. Spooner, 1821.

Bass, Robert D. *The Green Dragoon: The Lives of Banastre Tarleton and Mary Robinson.* Orangeburg, S.C.: Sandlapper, 1973.

Baxter, James Phinney, ed. *The British Invasion from the North.* Albany, N.Y.: Joel Munsell's Sons, 1887.

Beakes, John. *De Kalb: One of the Revolutionary War's Bravest Generals.* Berwyn Heights, Md.: Heritage Books, 2019.

Beatson, Robert. *Naval and Military Memoirs of Great Britain.* Vol. 6. London: Longman, Hurst, Rees, and Orme, 1804.

Beck, John B. *Medicine in the American Colonies.* Albany, N.Y.: Horn & Wallace, 1850.

Becker, John P., and S. Dewitt Bloodgood. *The Sexagenary, or Reminiscences of the American Revolution.* Albany, N.Y.: J. Munsell, 1866.

Bellico, Russell P. *Sails and Steam in the Mountains.* Fleischmanns, N.Y.: Purple Mountain Press, 2001.

Bellot, Leland J. *William Knox: The Life & Thought of an Eighteenth-Century Imperialist.* Austin: University of Texas Press, 1977.

Bemis, Samuel Flagg. *The Diplomacy of the American Revolution.* Bloomington: Indiana University Press, 1957.

Benson, Adolph B. *American Swedish Historical Foundation Yearbook.* Philadelphia: 1957.

Berger, Carl. *Broadsides and Bayonets: The Propaganda War of the American Revolution.* Philadelphia: University of Pennsylvania Press, 1961.

Bernier, Olivier. *Secrets of Marie Antoinette.* Garden City, N.Y.: Doubleday, 1985.

Berleth, Richard. *Bloody Mohawk.* Delmar, N.Y.: Black Dome, 2010.

Besant, Walter. *London in the Eighteenth Century.* London: Adam & Charles Black, 1902.

Bickham, Troy. *Making Headlines: The American Revolution as Seen Through the British Press.* DeKalb: Northern Illinois University Press, 2009.

Bilby, Joseph G., and Katherine Bilby Jenkins. *Monmouth Court House: The Battle That Made the American Army.* Yardley, Pa.: Westholme, 2010.

Bilharz, Joy. *Oriskany: A Place of Great Sadness.* Boston: National Park Service, 2009.

Bill, Alfred Hoyt. *New Jersey and the Revolutionary War.* New Brunswick, N.J.: Rutgers University Press, 1972.

Billias, George Athan. *General John Glover and His Marblehead Mariners.* New York: Henry Holt, 1960.

———, ed. *George Washington's Generals and Opponents.* New York: Da Capo, 1994.

———, ed. *The Manuscripts of Captain Howard Vincente Knox.* Boston: Gregg Press, 1972.

Bird, Harrison. *March to Saratoga: General Burgoyne and the American Campaign, 1777.* New York: Oxford University Press, 1963.

———. *Navies in the Mountains: The Battles on the Waters of Lake Champlain and Lake George, 1609–1814.* New York: Oxford University Press, 1962.

Biron, Armand-Louis de Gontaut. *Memoirs of the duc de Lauzun.* Translated by Jules E. Méras. New York: Sturgis & Walton, 1912.

Black, Jeannette D., and William Greene Roelker, eds. *A Rhode Island Chaplain in the Revolution: Letters of Ebenezer David to Nicholas Brown, 1775–1778.* Providence: Rhode Island Society of the Cincinnati, 1949.

Black, Jeremy. *George III, America's Last King.* New Haven, Conn.: Yale University Press, 2008.

———. *Pitt the Elder.* Cambridge, U.K.: Cambridge University Press, 1992.

Black, Jeremy, and Philip Woodfine, eds. *The British Navy and the Use of Naval Power in the Eighteenth Century.* Leicester, U.K.: Leicester University Press, 1988.

Blandemor, Thomas, ed. *The Trial of the Honourable Augustus Keppel.* Portsmouth, U.K.: J. Wilkes, Breadhower and Peadle, 1779.

Blatchford, John. *The Narrative of John Blatchford.* Edited by Charles I. Bushnell. New York: privately printed, 1865.

Bleeker, Leonard. *The Order Book of Capt. Leonard Bleeker.* New York: Joseph Sabin, 1865.

Bodle, Wayne. *The Valley Forge Winter: Civilians and Soldiers in War.* University Park: Pennsylvania State University Press, 2004.

Boehlert, Paul A. *The Battle of Oriskany and General Nicholas Herkimer*. Charleston, S.C.: History Press, 2013.

Bolles, Albert S. *The Financial History of the United States, from 1774 to 1789*. New York: D. Appleton, 1892.

Bolton, Charles Knowles. *The Private Soldier Under Washington*. New York: Charles Scribner's Sons, 1902.

Borick, Carl P. *A Gallant Defense: The Siege of Charleston, 1780*. Columbia: University of South Carolina Press, 2012.

Boudinot, Elias. *Exchange of Major-General Charles Lee*. Edited by William S. Baker. Philadelphia: J. B. Lippincott, 1891.

Boudreau, George W. *Independence: A Guide to Historic Philadelphia*. Yardley, Pa.: Westholme, 2012.

Boudriot, Jean. *John Paul Jones and the Bonhomme Richard*. Translated by David H. Roberts. Annapolis, Md.: Naval Institute Press, 1987.

Bowen, Catherine Drinker. *John Adams and the American Revolution*. Boston: Little, Brown, 1950.

Bowler, R. Arthur. *Logistics and the Failure of the British Army in America, 1775–1783*. Princeton, N.J.: Princeton University Press, 1973.

Boyd, George Adams. *Elias Boudinot, Patriot and Statesman, 1740–1821*. New York: Greenwood, 1969.

Boyle, Joseph Lee. *From Redcoat to Rebel: The Thomas Sullivan Journal*. Bowie, Md.: Heritage Books, 1997.

———. *Writings from the Valley Forge Encampment of the Continental Army, December 19, 1777–June 19, 1778*. Vol. 1. Westminster, Md.: Heritage Books, 2007.

Brady, Patricia. *Martha Washington: An American Life*. New York: Viking, 2005.

Bragg, C. L. *Crescent Moon over Carolina: William Moultrie and American Liberty*. Columbia: University of South Carolina Press, 2013.

Braisted, Todd W. *Grand Forage 1778: The Battleground Around New York City*. Yardley, Pa.: Westholme, 2016.

Brands, H. W. *The First American: The Life and Times of Benjamin Franklin*. New York: Anchor Books, 2002.

———. *Our First Civil War: Patriots and Loyalists in the American Revolution*. New York: Doubleday, 2021.

Brandow, John Henry. *The Story of Old Saratoga and History of Schuylerville*. Albany, N.Y.: Fort Orange Press, 1900.

Brandt, Clare. *The Man in the Mirror: A Life of Benedict Arnold*. New York: Random House, 1994.

Breen, T. H. *American Insurgents, American Patriots: The Revolution of the People*. New York: Hill and Wang, 2010.

———. *The Will of the People: The Revolutionary Birth of America*. Cambridge, Mass.: Belknap Press, 2019.

Brewer, John. *A Sentimental Murder: Love and Madness in the Eighteenth Century*. New York: Farrar, Straus and Giroux, 2004.

———. *The Sinews of Power: War, Money, and the English State, 1688–1783*. Cambridge, Mass.: Harvard University Press, 1990.

Bridenbaugh, Carl. *Cities in Revolt: Urban Life in America, 1743–1776*. London: Oxford University Press, 1971.

Bridenbaugh, Carl, and Jessica Bridenbaugh. *Rebels and Gentlemen: Philadelphia in the Age of Franklin*. New York: Oxford University Press, 1962.

The British Military Library. 2 vols. London: Richard Phillips, 1801–4.

Brooke, John. *King George III*. London: Constable, 1985.

Brookhiser, Richard. *Alexander Hamilton, American*. New York: Touchstone, 2000.

Brooks, Noah. *Henry Knox, a Soldier of the Revolution*. New York: G. P. Putnam's Sons, 1900.

Brown, Gerald Saxon. *The American Secretary: The Colonial Policy of Lord George Germain, 1775–1778*. Ann Arbor: University of Michigan Press, 1963.

Brown, Lloyd A., and Howard H. Peckham, eds. *Revolutionary War Journals of Henry Dearborn, 1775–83*. New York: Da Capo, 1971.

Brown, Marvin L., Jr., trans. *Baroness von Riedesel and the American Revolution*. Chapel Hill: University of North Carolina Press, 1965.

Brown, Paul. *Maritime Portsmouth: A History and Guide*. Stroud, U.K.: Tempus, 2005.

Brown, Peter Douglas. *William Pitt, Earl of Chatham: The Great Commoner*. London: George Allen & Unwin, 1978.

Brown, Wallace. *The Good Americans: The Loyalists in the American Revolution*. New York: William Morrow, 1969.

Brownlow, Donald Grey. *A Documentary History of the Battle of Germantown*. Germantown, Pa.: Germantown Historical Society, 1955.

Bruce, William Cabell. *Benjamin Franklin Self-Revealed*. Vol. 2. New York: G. P. Putnam's Sons, 1917.

Brumwell, Stephen. *George Washington: Gentleman Warrior*. New York: Quercus, 2013.

———. *Turncoat: Benedict Arnold and the Crisis of American Liberty*. New Haven, Conn.: Yale University Press, 2018.

Brunsman, Denver. *The Evil Necessity: British Naval Impressment in the Eighteenth-Century Atlantic World*. Charlottesville: University of Virginia Press, 2013.

Buchanan, John. *The Road to Charleston*. Charlottesville: University of Virginia Press, 2019.

———. *The Road to Guilford Courthouse: The American Revolution in the Carolinas*. New York: John Wiley, 1997.

———. *The Road to Valley Forge*. Hoboken, N.J.: John Wiley & Sons, 2004.

Buel, Richard, Jr. *Dear Liberty: Connecticut's Mobilization for Revolutionary War*. Middletown, Conn.: Wesleyan University Press, 1980.

———. *In Irons: Britain's Naval Supremacy and the American Revolutionary Economy*. New Haven, Conn.: Yale University Press, 1998.

Buell, Rowena, ed. *The Memoirs of Rufus Putnam*. Boston: Houghton Mifflin, 1903.

Buker, George E. *The Penobscot Expedition: Commodore Saltonstall and the Massachusetts Conspiracy of 1779*. Camden, Me.: Down East Books, 2015.

Bullock, Charles J. *The Finances of the United States from 1775 to 1789*. Madison: University of Wisconsin, 1895.

Bunker, Nick. *An Empire on the Edge: How Britain Came to Fight America*. New York: Vintage, 2015.

Burdick, Kim Rogers. *I Remain Your Friend: Daniel Byrnes, a Quaker in the Revolutionary Era*. Newark, Del.: Hale Byrnes House, 2011.

———. *Revolutionary Delaware: Independence in the First State*. Charleston, S.C.: History Press, 2016.

Burgoyne, Bruce E., trans. *Defeat, Disaster and Dedication: The Diaries of the Hessian Officers Jakob Piel and Andreas Wiederhold*. Bowie, Md.: Heritage Books, 1996.

———, trans. and ed. *Diaries of Two Ansbach Jaegers: Lieutenant Heinrich Carl Philipp von Feilitzsch and Lieutenant Christian Friedrich Bartholomai*. Westminster, Md.: Heritage Books, 2007.

———, ed. *Enemy Views: The American War as Recorded by the Hessian Participants*. Bowie, Md.: Heritage Books, 1996.

———, trans. *The Hesse-Cassel Mirbach Regiment in the American Revolution*. Bowie, Md.: Heritage Books, 1998.

———, trans. and ed. *A Hessian Officer's Diary of the American Revolution*. Bowie, Md.: Heritage Books, 1994.

———, trans. *Journal of a Hessian Grenadier Battalion*. Edited by Marie E. Burgoyne. Westminster, Md.: Heritage Books, 2005.

Burrows, Edwin G. *Forgotten Patriots*. New York: Basic Books, 2008.

Burrows, Edwin G., and Mike Wallace. *Gotham: A History of New York City to 1898*. New York: Oxford University Press, 2000.

Bush, Martin H. *Revolutionary Enigma*. Port Washington, N.Y.: Ira J. Friedman, 1969.

Bushman, Richard Lyman. *The American Farmer in the Eighteenth Century: A Social and Cultural History*. New Haven, Conn.: Yale University Press, 2018.

Butterfield, H. *George III, Lord North and the People, 1779–1780*. London: G. Bell and Sons, 1949.

Butterfield, L. H., ed. *Adams Family Correspondence*. Vols. 1 and 2. New York: Athenaeum, 1965.

———, ed. *Diary & Autobiography of John Adams*. 4 vols. New York: Athenaeum, 1964.

———, ed. *Letters of Benjamin Rush*. Vol. 1. Princeton, N.J.: Princeton University Press, 1951.

Byrd, James P. *Sacred Scripture, Sacred War: The Bible and the American Revolution*. New York: Oxford University Press, 2017.

Byron, John. *The Narrative of the Honourable John Byron*. London: S. Baker and G. Leigh, 1768.

Calhoon, Robert McCluer. *The Loyalists in Revolutionary America, 1760–1781*. New York: Harcourt Brace Jovanovich, 1973.

Callahan, North. *Daniel Morgan: Ranger of the Revolution*. New York: Holt, Rinehart and Winston, 1961.

———. *Henry Knox, General Washington's General*. New York: A. S. Barnes, 1958.

———. *Royal Raiders: The Tories of the American Revolution*. Indianapolis: Bobbs-Merrill, 1963.

Callo, Joseph. *John Paul Jones, America's First Sea Warrior*. Annapolis, Md.: Naval Institute Press, 2006.

Calloway, Colin G. *The American Revolution in Indian Country*. Cambridge, U.K.: Cambridge University Press, 1996.

———. *The Indian World of George Washington*. New York: Oxford University Press, 2018.

Campan, Jeanne Louise Henriette. *The Private Life of Marie Antoinette*. Vol. 1. London: Richard Bentley and Son, 1883.

Campbell, Archibald. *Journal of an Expedition Against the Rebels of Georgia in North America*. Edited by Colin Campbell. Augusta, Ga.: Richmond County Historical Society, 1981.

Campbell, Maria. *Revolutionary Services and Civil Life of General William Hull*. New York: D. Appleton, 1848.

Campbell-Smith, Duncan. *Masters of the Post: The Authorized History of the Royal Mail*. London: Penguin, 2012.

Carbone, Gerald M. *Nathanael Greene: A Biography of the American Revolution*. New York: Palgrave Macmillan, 2010.

Carp, Benjamin L. *Rebels Rising: Cities and the American Revolution*. New York: Oxford University Press, 2007.

Carp, E. Wayne. *To Starve the Army at Pleasure: Continental Army Administration and American Political Culture, 1775–1783*. Chapel Hill: University of North Carolina Press, 1984.

Carrington, Selwyn H. H. *The British West Indies During the American Revolution*. Dordrecht, Netherlands: Foris Publications, 1988.

Castelot, André. *Queen of France: A Biography of Marie Antoinette*. Translated by Denise Folliot. New York: Ishi Press, 2009.

Chambers, John Whiteclay II, and G. Kurt Piehler, eds. *Major Problems in American Military History*. Boston: Houghton Mifflin, 1999.

Chapelle, Howard I. *The American Sailing Navy*. New York: Konecky & Konecky, 1949.

Charavay, Étienne. *Le général La Fayette, 1757–1834*. Paris: Au Siège de la Société, 1898.

Chastellux, François-Jean de. *Travels in North-America*. London: G.G.J. and J. Robinson, 1787.

Chávez, Thomas E. *Spain and the Independence of the United States: An Intrinsic Gift*. Albuquerque: University of New Mexico Press, 2002.

Chernow, Ron. *Alexander Hamilton*. New York: Penguin, 2005.

———. *Washington: A Life*. New York: Penguin, 2011.

Chevalier, Édouard. *Histoire de la marine française pendant la guerre de l'indépendance américaine*. Paris: Hachette, 1877.

Chinard, G., ed. *The Treaties of 1778 and Allied Documents*. Baltimore: Johns Hopkins Press, 1928.

Chopra, Ruma. *Unnatural Rebellion: Loyalists in New York City During the Revolution*. Charlottesville: University of Virginia Press, 2013.

Christie, Ian R. *Crisis of Empire: Great Britain and the American Colonies, 1754–1783*. New York: W. W. Norton, 1967.

———. *The End of North's Ministry, 1780–1782*. London: Macmillan, 1958.

Clarfield, Gerard H. *Timothy Pickering and the American Republic*. Pittsburgh: University of Pittsburgh Press, 1980.

Clark, Dora Mae. *British Opinion and the American Revolution*. New York: Russell & Russell, 1966.

Clark, George L. *Silas Deane: A Connecticut Leader in the American Revolution*. New York: G. P. Putnam's Sons, 1913.

Clark, Ronald W. *Benjamin Franklin: A Biography*. New York: Random House, 1983.

Clark, William Bell. *Captain Dauntless: The Story of Nicholas Biddle of the Continental Navy*. Baton Rouge: Louisiana State University Press, 1949.

———. *Gallant John Barry, 1745–1803*. New York: Macmillan, 1938.

———. *George Washington's Navy*. Baton Rouge: Louisiana State University Press, 1960.

———. *Lambert Wickes: Sea Raider and Diplomat*. New Haven, Conn.: Yale University Press, 1932.

Clark, William Bell, et al., eds. *Naval Documents of the American Revolution*. 13 vols. Washington, D.C.: Government Printing Office, 1964–2005.

Clary, David A. *Adopted Son: Washington, Lafayette, and the Friendship That Saved the Revolution*. New York: Bantam Books, 2007.

Clary, David A., and Joseph W. A. Whitehorne. *The Inspectors General of the United States Army, 1777–1903*. Washington, D.C.: U.S. Army, 1987.

Clay, Steven E. *Staff Ride Handbook for the Saratoga Campaign, 13 June to 8 November 1777*. Fort Leavenworth, Kan.: Combat Studies Institute Press, 2018.

Clinton, Henry. *The American Rebellion*. Edited by William B. Willcox. New Haven, Conn.: Yale University Press, 1954.

Clowes, William Laird, Sr. *The Royal Navy: A History from the Earliest Times to the Present*. Vols. 3 and 4. London: Sampson Low, 1898–99.

Coakley, Robert W., and Stetson Conn. *The War of the American Revolution*. Washington, D.C.: Center of Military History, 1974.

Coffin, Charles. *The Life and Services of Major General John Thomas*. New York: Egbert, Hovey & King, 1845.

Coleman, Kenneth. *The American Revolution in Georgia, 1763–1789*. Athens: University of Georgia Press, 1958.

Colley, Linda. *Britons: Forging the Nation, 1707–1837*. New Haven, Conn.: Yale University Press, 2012.

Colman-Maison, Jean Joseph Robert. *L'amiral d'Estaing*. Paris: Calmann-Lévy, 1910.

Commager, Henry Steele, and Richard B. Morris, eds. *The Spirit of 'Seventy-Six*. Edison, N.J.: Castle Books, 2002.

Conlin, Jonathan. *Tales of Two Cities: Paris, London, and the Birth of the Modern City*. Berkeley, Calif.: Counterpoint, 2013.

Conway, John Joseph. *Footprints of Famous Americans in Paris*. New York: John Lane, 1912.

Conway, Stephen. *The British Isles and the War of American Independence*. Oxford, U.K.: University Press, 2003.

———. *The War of American Independence, 1775–1783*. London: Edward Arnold, 1995.

Cook, Frederick, ed. *Journals of the Military Expedition of Major General Sullivan*. Auburn, N.Y.: Knapp, Peck & Thompson, 1887.

Corbett, Theodore. *No Turning Point: The Saratoga Campaign in Perspective*. Norman: University of Oklahoma Press, 2012.

Corner, George W., ed. *The Autobiography of Benjamin Rush*. Princeton, N.J.: Princeton University Press, 1948.

Corwin, Edward S. *French Policy and the American Alliance of 1778*. Princeton, N.J.: Princeton University Press, 1916.

Countryman, Edward. *The American Revolution*. New York: Hill and Wang, 1994.

———. *A People in Revolution*. New York: W. W. Norton, 1989.

Coupland, R. *The American Revolution and the British Empire*. New York: Russell & Russell, 1965.

Cox, Caroline. *A Proper Sense of Honor: Service and Sacrifice in Washington's Army.* Chapel Hill: University of North Carolina Press, 2004.

Crane, Elaine Forman, ed. *The Diary of Elizabeth Drinker.* Philadelphia: University of Pennsylvania Press, 2010.

Crary, Catherine S. *The Price of Loyalty: Tory Writings from the Revolutionary Era.* New York: McGraw-Hill, 1973.

Craveri, Benedetta. *The Last Libertines.* Translated by Aaron Kerner. New York: New York Review of Books, 2016.

Crow, Jeffrey J., and Larry E. Tise, eds. *The Southern Experience in the American Revolution.* Chapel Hill: University of North Carolina Press, 1978.

Cruikshank, Ernest, et al., eds. *A History of the Organization, Development and Services of the Military and Naval Forces of Canada.* Vol. 2. Ottawa: Historical Section, General Staff, 1919.

Crytzer, Brady J. *Hessians.* Yardley, Pa.: Westholme, 2015.

Cubbison, Douglas R. *"The Artillery Never Gained More Honour": British Artillery in the 1776 Valcour Island and 1777 Saratoga Campaigns.* Fleischmanns, N.Y.: Purple Mountain Press, 2007.

———. *The American Northern Theater Army in 1776.* Jefferson, N.C.: McFarland, 2010.

———. *Burgoyne and the Saratoga Campaign: His Papers.* Norman, Okla.: Arthur H. Clark, 2012.

Cumberland, Richard. *Character of the Late Lord Viscount Sackville.* London: C. Dilly, 1785.

Cumming, William P., and Hugh F. Rankin. *The Fate of a Nation.* London: Phaidron, 1975.

Cunningham, John T. *The Uncertain Revolution: Washington & the Continental Army at Morristown.* West Creek, N.J.: Cormorant, 2007.

Cunningham, Peter, ed. *The Letters of Horace Walpole.* Vol. 6. London: Richard Bentley and Son, 1891.

Curtis, Edward E. *The Organization of the British Army in the American Revolution.* Gansevoort, N.Y.: Corner House Historical Publications, 1998.

Cutbush, Edward. *Observations on the Means of Preserving the Health of Soldiers and Sailors.* Philadelphia: Thomas Dobson, 1808.

Damrosch, Leo. *The Club: Johnson, Boswell, and the Friends Who Shaped an Age.* New Haven, Conn.: Yale University Press, 2019.

Dann, John C., ed. *The Nagle Journal: A Diary of the Life of Jacob Nagle, Sailor, from the Year 1775 to 1841.* New York: Weidenfeld and Nicolson, 1988.

———, ed. *The Revolution Remembered.* Chicago: University of Chicago Press, 1980.

Darnton, Robert. *The Revolutionary Temper: Paris, 1748–1789.* New York: W. W. Norton, 2024.

Daughan, George C. *If By Sea: The Forging of the American Navy, from the American Revolution to the War of 1812.* New York: Basic Books, 2008.

———. *Revolution on the Hudson.* New York: W. W. Norton, 2016.

Davidson, Philip. *Propaganda and the American Revolution, 1763–1783.* New York: W. W. Norton, 1973.

Davies, K. G., ed. *Documents of the American Revolution, 1770–1783.* 21 vols. Shannon: Irish University Press, 1972–81.

Davis, Michael T., ed. *Crowd Actions in Britain and France from the Middle Ages to the Modern World.* New York: Palgrave Macmillan, 2015.

Davis, Robert P. *Where a Man Can Go: Major General William Phillips, British Royal Artillery, 1731–1781.* Westport, Conn.: Greenwood Press, 1999.

Davis, William W. H. *History of Bucks County, Pennsylvania.* Vol. 2. New York: Lewis Publishing, 1905.

Dawson, Henry B. *The Assault on Stony Point.* Morrisania, N.Y.: New-York Historical Society, 1863.

Deane, Silas. *Collections of the New-York Historical Society for the Year 1886.* Deane Papers. Vol. 1. New York: NYHS, 1887.

Dearden, Paul F. *The Rhode Island Campaign of 1778: Inauspicious Dawn of Alliance.* Providence: Rhode Island Publications Society, 1980.

De Beer, Gavin. *Gibbon and His World.* New York: Viking, 1968.

De Castro, J. Paul. *The Gordon Riots.* London: Oxford University Press, 1926.

De Costa, B. F. *Notes on the History of Fort George.* New York: J. Sabin & Sons, 1871.

De Fonblanque, Edward Barrington. *Political and Military Episodes . . . from the Life and Correspondence of the Right Hon. John Burgoyne*. London: Macmillan, 1876.

De Koven, Anna. *The Life and Letters of John Paul Jones*. 2 vols. London: T. W. Laurie, 1913.

Delalex, Hélène. *A Day with Marie Antoinette*. Translated by Barbara Mellor. Paris: Flammarion, 2015.

———. *Un jour avec Marie-Antoinette*. Paris: Flammarion, 2015.

Del Perugia, Paul. *La tentative d'invasion de l'Angleterre de 1779*. Paris: Presses Universitaires de France, 1939.

Desmarais, Norman. *America's First Ally: France in the Revolutionary War*. Philadelphia: Casemate, 2019.

———. *Washington's Engineer: Louis Duportail and the Creation of an Army Corps*. Guilford, Conn.: Prometheus Books, 2021.

Dexter, Franklin Bowditch, ed. *The Literary Diary of Ezra Stiles, D.D., LL.D.* Vol. 2. New York: Charles Scribner's Sons, 1901.

Diamant, Lincoln. *Bernard Romans: Forgotten Patriot of the American Revolution*. Harrison, N.Y.: Harbor Hill Books, 1985.

———. *Chaining the Hudson: The Fight for the River in the American Revolution*. New York: Fordham University Press, 2004.

Diary of Samuel Richards, Captain of Connecticut Line War of the Revolution, 1775–1781. Philadelphia: published by his great grandson, 1909.

Doblin, Helga, trans. *The American Revolution, Garrison Life in French Canada and New York*. Edited by Mary C. Lynn. Westport, Conn.: Greenwood Press, 1993.

Doerflinger, Thomas M. *A Vigorous Spirit of Enterprise: Merchants and Economic Development in Revolutionary Philadelphia*. Chapel Hill: University of North Carolina Press, 1986.

Döhla, Johann Conrad. *A Hessian Diary of the American Revolution*. Edited and translated by Bruce E. Burgoyne. Norman: University of Oklahoma Press, 1990.

Doniol, Henri. *Histoire de la participation de la France à l'établissement des Étas-Unis d'Amérique*. 6 vols. Paris: Imprimerie Nationale, 1886–99.

Donne, W. Bodham, ed. *The Correspondence of King George III to Lord North*. Vol. 2. London: John Murray, 1867.

Donoghue, Norman E., II. *Prisoners of Congress: Philadelphia's Quakers in Exile, 1777–1778*. University Park, Pa.: Pennsylvania State University Press, 2023.

Dorson, Richard M., ed. *America Rebels: Narratives of the Patriots*. Greenwich, Conn.: Fawcett Premier, 1966.

Dorwart, Jeffery M. *Fort Mifflin of Philadelphia: An Illustrated History*. Philadelphia: University of Pennsylvania Press, 1998.

———. *Invasion and Insurrection: Security, Defense, and War in the Delaware Valley, 1621–1815*. Newark: University of Delaware Press, 2008.

Drake, Francis S. *Life and Correspondence of Henry Knox*. Boston: Samuel G. Drake, 1873.

Draper, Lyman Copeland. *King's Mountain and Its Heroes*. New York: Dauber & Pine, 1929.

Drayton, John. *Memoirs of the American Revolution*. 2 vols. Charleston, S.C.: A. E. Miller, 1821.

Drinkwater, John. *A History of the Late Siege of Gibraltar*. London: T. Spilsbury, 1786.

Duane, William, ed. *Extracts from the Diary of Christopher Marshall*. Albany, N.Y.: Joel Munsell, 1877.

Ducros, Louis. *French Society in the Eighteenth Century*. Translated by W. de Geijer. London: G. Bell and Sons, 1926.

Duer, William Alexander. *The Life of William Alexander, Earl of Stirling*. New York: Wiley & Putnam, 1847.

Dull, Jonathan R. *The Age of the Ship of the Line: The British & French Navies, 1650–1815*. Lincoln: University of Nebraska Press, 2009.

———. *A Diplomatic History of the American Revolution*. New Haven, Conn.: Yale University Press, 1985.

———. *The French Navy and American Independence*. Princeton, N.J.: Princeton University Press, 1975.

———. *The French Navy and the Seven Years' War*. Lincoln: University of Nebraska Press, 2005.

———. *The Miracle of American Independence*. Lincoln, Neb.: Potomac Books, 2015.

Dumas, Mathieu. *Memoirs of His Own Time*. Vol. 1. Philadelphia: Lea & Blanchard, 1839.

Duncan, Francis. *History of the Royal Regiment of Artillery*. Vol. 1. London: John Murray, 1879.

Duncan, Mike. *Hero of Two Worlds: The Marquis de Lafayette in the Age of Revolution*. New York: Public Affairs, 2021.

Duncan, Roger F. *Coastal Maine: A Maritime History*. Woodstock, Vt.: Countryman Press, 2002.

Dunelm, S., ed. *The Political Life of William Wildman, Viscount Barrington*. London: Payne and Foss, 1815.

Dunkerly, Robert M. *Decision at Brandywine: The Battle on Birmingham Hill*. Yardley, Pa.: Westholme, 2021.

Dunlap, William. *History of the American Theater*. 2 vols. London: Richard Bentley, 1833.

Dunlop, Ian. *Versailles*. New York: Taplinger Publishing, 1970.

Durand, John, ed. *New Materials for the History of the American Revolution*. New York: Henry Holt, 1889.

East, Robert Abraham. *Business Enterprise in the American Revolutionary Era*. New York: AMS Press, 1969.

East, Robert Abraham, and Jacob Judd, eds. *The Loyalist Americans: A Focus on Greater New York*. Tarrytown, N.Y.: Sleepy Hollow Restorations, 1975.

Eastland, Jonathan, and Iain Ballantyne. *HMS Victory, First Rate 1765*. Annapolis, Md.: Naval Institute Press, 2011.

Eccles, W. J. *The French in North America, 1500–1783*. Markham, Ontario: Fitzhenry & Whiteside, 1998.

Echeverria, Durand. *Mirage in the West: A History of the French Image of American Society to 1815*. Princeton, N.J.: Princeton University Press, 1968.

Edgar, Walter. *Partisans & Redcoats: The Southern Conflict That Turned the Tide of the American Revolution*. New York: Perennial, 2003.

Edler, Friedrich. *The Dutch Republic and the American Revolution*. Baltimore: Johns Hopkins Press, 1911.

Edwards, Owen Dudley, and George Shepperson, eds. *Scotland, Europe and the American Revolution*. New York: St. Martin's, 1976.

Eelking, Max von, and Joseph George Rosengarten. *The German Allied Troops in the North American War of Independence*. Driffield, U.K.: Leonaur, 2012.

Egerton, Douglas R. *Death or Liberty: African Americans and Revolutionary America*. New York: Oxford University Press, 2011.

Ehrman, John. *The Younger Pitt*. Vol. 1. *The Years of Acclaim*. Bury St. Edmunds, U.K.: Anchor Press, 1984.

Einstein, Lewis. *Divided Loyalties: Americans in England During the War of Independence*. London: Cobden-Sanderson, 1933.

Eller, Ernest McNeill, ed. *Chesapeake Bay in the American Revolution*. Centreville, Md.: Tidewater, 1981.

Elliott, Steven. *Surviving the Winters: Housing Washington's Army During the American Revolution*. Norman: University of Oklahoma Press, 2021.

Ellis, Joseph J. *The Cause: The American Revolution and Its Discontents, 1773–1783*. New York: Liveright, 2021.

———. *Founding Brothers: The Revolutionary Generation*. New York: Knopf, 2001.

———. *His Excellency: George Washington*. New York: Vintage, 2004.

———. *Revolutionary Summer: The Birth of American Independence*. New York: Knopf, 2013.

Ellis, Kenneth. *The Post Office in the Eighteenth Century*. London: Oxford University Press, 1969.

Elting, John R. *The Battles of Saratoga*. Monmouth Beach, N.J.: Philip Freneau Press, 1977.

Enciso, A. González. *War, Power and the Economy: Mercantilism and State Formation in 18th-Century Europe*. London: Routledge, 2019.

English, William Hayden. *Conquest of the Country Northwest of the River Ohio, 1778–1783*. Vol. 1. Indianapolis: Bowen-Merrill, 1897.

Evans, Elizabeth. *Weathering the Storm: Women of the American Revolution*. New York: Charles Scribner's Sons, 1975.

Ewald, Johann. *Diary of the American War: A Hessian Journal*. Edited and translated by Joseph P. Tustin. New Haven, Conn.: Yale University Press, 1979.

———. *Treatise on Partisan Warfare*. Translated and edited by Robert A. Selig and David Curtis Skaggs. New York: Greenwood Press, 1991.

Farr, Evelyn. *Before the Deluge: Parisian Society in the Reign of Louis XVI*. London: Peter Owen, 1994.

Les femmes de Versailles: Les beaux jours de Marie-Antoinette. Paris: E. Dentue, 1882.

Fenn, Elizabeth A. *Pox Americana: The Great Smallpox Epidemic of 1775–82*. New York: Hill and Wang, 2002.

Ferguson, E. James. *The Power of the Purse: A History of American Public Finance, 1776–1790*. Chapel Hill: University of North Carolina Press, 1961.

Ferling, John. *Almost a Miracle: The American Victory in the War of Independence*. New York: Oxford University Press, 2009.

———. *The Ascent of George Washington*. New York: Bloomsbury Press, 2009.

———. *The First of Men: A Life of George Washington*. New York: Oxford University Press, 2010.

———. *John Adams: A Life*. New York: Oxford University Press, 2010.

———. *A Leap in the Dark: The Struggle to Create the American Republic*. New York: Oxford University Press, 2005.

———. *Winning Independence: The Decisive Years of the Revolutionary War, 1778–1781*. New York: Bloomsbury, 2021.

———, ed. *The World Turned Upside Down: The American Victory in the War of Independence*. New York: Greenwood Press, 1988.

Ferreiro, Larrie D. *Brothers at Arms: American Independence and the Men of France and Spain Who Saved It*. New York: Vintage, 2016.

Field, Edward, ed. *Diary of Colonel Israel Angell*. Providence, R.I.: Preston and Rounds, 1899.

Fischer, David Hackett. *Liberty and Freedom*. New York: Oxford University Press, 2005.

———. *Washington's Crossing*. New York: Oxford University Press, 2004.

Fischer, Joseph R. *A Well-Executed Failure: The Sullivan Campaign Against the Iroquois, July–September 1779*. Columbia: University of South Carolina Press, 1997.

Fitzgerald, Percy. *The Good Queen Charlotte*. London: Downey, 1899.

Fitzpatrick, John C., ed. *George Washington's Accounts of Expenses*. Boston: Houghton Mifflin, 1917.

Flavell, Julie. *The Howe Dynasty*. New York: Liveright, 2021.

———. *When London Was Capital of America*. New Haven: Yale University Press, 2010.

Fleming, Thomas. *1776, Year of Illusions*. Edison, N.J.: Castle Books, 1996.

Flexner, James Thomas. *The Young Hamilton*. Boston: Little, Brown, 1978.

Foner, Eric. *Tom Paine and Revolutionary America*. New York: Oxford University Press, 1976.

Forbes, Esther. *Paul Revere and the World He Lived In*. Boston: Houghton Mifflin, 1999.

Force, Peter, ed. *American Archives*. Series 4 and 5. Washington, D.C.: M. St. Clair Clarke and Peter Force, 1837–53.

Ford, Worthington Chauncey, ed. *Correspondence and Journals of Samuel Blachley Webb*. Vols. 1 and 2. New York [Lancaster, Pa.: Wickersham Press], 1893.

Foreman, Amanda. *The Duchess*. New York: Random House, 2008.

Fortescue, J. W., ed. *The Correspondence of King George the Third*. Vols. 3 and 4. London: Macmillan, 1928.

———. *A History of the British Army*. Vol. 3. London: Macmillan, 1911.

———. *The War of Independence: The British Army in North America, 1775–1783*. London: Greenhill, 2001.

Fowler, William M., Jr. *Rebels Under Sail: The American Navy During the Revolution*. New York: Charles Scribner's Sons, 1976.

Fraser, Antonia. *The King and the Catholics: England, Ireland, and the Fight for Religious Freedom, 1780–1829*. New York: Doubleday, 2018.

————. *Marie Antoinette: The Journey*. New York: Anchor Books, 2002.

Fraser, Flora. *The Washingtons*. New York: Knopf, 2015.

Fraser, Walter J., Jr. *Charleston! Charleston!: The History of a Southern City*. Columbia: University of South Carolina Press, 1991.

Freeman, Douglas Southall. *George Washington: A Biography*. Vols. 4 and 5. New York: Charles Scribner's Sons, 1951 and 1952.

Frey, Sylvia R. *The British Soldier in America*. Austin: University of Texas Press, 1981.

————. *Water from the Rock: Black Resistance in a Revolutionary Age*. Princeton, N.J.: Princeton University Press, 1992.

Fried, Stephen. *Rush: Revolution, Madness, and the Visionary Doctor Who Became a Founding Father*. New York: Crown, 2018.

Fuller, J.F.C. *British Light Infantry in the Eighteenth Century*. London: Hutchinson, 1925.

Futhey, J. Smith, and Gilbert Cope. *History of Chester County, Pennsylvania*. Philadelphia: Louis H. Everts, 1881.

Gabriel, Michael P. *The Battle of Bennington: Soldiers & Civilians*. Charleston, S.C.: History Press, 2014.

Gaines, James R. *For Liberty and Glory: Washington, Lafayette, and Their Revolutions*. New York: W. W. Norton, 2007.

Gara, Donald J. *The Queen's American Rangers*. Yardley, Pa.: Westholme, 2015.

Garden, Alexander. *Anecdotes of the Revolutionary War*. Charleston, S.C.: A. E. Miller, 1828.

Garrioch, David. *The Making of Revolutionary Paris*. Berkeley: University of California Press, 2004.

Geake, Robert A. *From Slaves to Soldiers: The 1st Rhode Island Regiment in the American Revolution*. Yardley, Pa.: Westholme, 2016.

The Gentleman's Magazine and Historical Chronicle. Vols. 47–50. London: F. Jeffries, 1777–80.

George, M. Dorothy. *London Life in the Eighteenth Century*. New York: Harper & Row, 1964.

Gerlach, Don R. *Proud Patriot: Philip Schuyler and the War of Independence, 1775–1783*. Syracuse, N.Y.: Syracuse University Press, 1987.

Gerlach, Larry R., ed. *New Jersey in the American Revolution, 1763–1783: A Documentary History*. Trenton, N.J.: New Jersey Historical Commission, 1975.

Gibbes, R. W. *Documentary History of the American Revolution, 1776–1782*. New York: D. Appleton, 1857.

Gibbon, Edward. *The Autobiography and Correspondence of Edward Gibbon*. London: Alex. Murray & Son, 1869.

Gilbert, Alan. *Black Patriots and Loyalists*. Chicago: University of Chicago Press, 2013.

Gilkerson, William. *The Ships of John Paul Jones*. Annapolis, Md.: U.S. Naval Academy Museum, 1987.

Gill, Harold B., Jr., and George M. Curtis, III, eds. *A Man Apart: The Journal of Nicholas Cresswell, 1774–1781*. Lanham, Md.: Lexington Books, 2009.

Gillett, Mary C. *The Army Medical Department, 1775–1818*. Washington, D.C.: U.S. Army, 1981.

Gilmour, Ian. *Riot, Risings and Revolution: Governance and Violence in Eighteenth-Century England*. London: Hutchinson, 1992.

Gipson, Lawrence Henry. *American Loyalist: Jared Ingersoll*. New Haven, Conn.: Yale University Press, 1971.

Glatthaar, Joseph T., and James Kirby Martin. *Forgotten Allies: The Oneida Indians and the American Revolution*. New York: Hill and Wang, 2006.

Glete, Jan. *Navies and Nations: Warships, Navies and State Building in Europe and America, 1500–1860*. Vol. 1. Stockholm: Almqvist & Wiksell International, 1993.

Glover, Michael. *General Burgoyne in Canada and America*. London: Gordon & Cremonesi, 1976.

Godfrey, Carlos E. *The Commander-in-Chief's Guard*. Washington, D.C.: Stevenson-Smith, 1904.

Golway, Terry. *Washington's General: Nathanael Greene and the Triumph of the American Revolution*. New York: Owl, 2006.

González Ensisco, A. *War, Power and the Economy: Mercantilism and State Formation in 18th-Century Europe*. London: Routledge, 2019.

Gordon, John W. *South Carolina and the American Revolution: A Battlefield History*. Columbia: University of South Carolina Press, 2003.

Goss, Elbridge Henry. *The Life of Colonel Paul Revere*. 2 vols. Boston: Joseph George Cupples, 1891.

Gottschalk, Louis. *Lafayette in America: 1777–1783*. 3 vols. Arveyres, France: L'Esprit de Lafayette Society, 1975.

Gouge, William M. *A Short History of Paper Money and Banking in the United States*. Philadelphia: T. W. Ustick, 1833.

Graham, Gerald S. *The Royal Navy in the War of American Independence*. London: Her Majesty's Stationery Office, 1976.

Graham, James. *The Life of General Daniel Morgan*. New York: Derby & Jackson, 1856.

Graydon, Alexander. *Memoirs of His Own Time: With Reminiscences of the Men and Events of the Revolution*. Edited by John Stockton Littell. Philadelphia: Lindsay & Blakiston, 1846.

Graymont, Barbara. *The Iroquois in the American Revolution*. Syracuse, N.Y.: Syracuse University Press, 1972.

Greene, George Washington. *The Life of Nathanael Greene*. Vol. 2. New York: Hurd and Houghton, 1871.

Greene, Jack P. *Understanding the American Revolution: Issues and Actors*. Charlottesville: University Press of Virginia, 1998.

———, ed. *The American Revolution: Its Character and Limits*. New York: New York University Press, 1987.

Greenman, Jeremiah. *Diary of a Common Soldier in the American Revolution, 1775–1783*. Edited by Robert C. Bray and Paul E. Bushnell. DeKalb: Northern Illinois University Press, 1978.

Greenwood, Isaac J., ed. *The Revolutionary Services of John Greenwood*. New York: De Vinne Press, 1922.

Grendel, Frédéric. *Beaumarchais: The Man Who Was Figaro*. New York: Thomas Y. Crowell, 1977.

Griffin, Patrick. *American Leviathan: Empire, Nation, and Revolutionary Frontier*. New York: Hill and Wang, 2008.

Griffith, Samuel B., II. *The War for American Independence*. Urbana: University of Illinois Press, 2002.

Griswold, William A., and Donald W. Linebaugh, eds. *The Saratoga Campaign: Uncovering an Embattled Landscape*. Hanover, N.H.: University Press of New England, 2016.

Grose, Francis. *A Classical Dictionary of the Vulgar Tongue*. London: Hooper and Wigstead, 1797.

Grubb, Farley. *The Continental Dollar: How the American Revolution Was Financed with Paper Money*. Chicago: University of Chicago Press, 2023.

Gruber, Ira D. *Books and the British Army in the Age of the American Revolution*. Chapel Hill: University of North Carolina Press, 2010.

———. *The Howe Brothers and the American Revolution*. Chapel Hill: University of North Carolina Press, 1972.

———, ed. *John Peebles' American War, 1776–1782*. Far Thrupp, U.K.: Army Records Society, 1998.

Guthorn, Peter J. *American Maps and Map Makers of the Revolution*. Monmouth Beach, N.J.: Philip Freneau Press, 1966.

Gutman, Robert W. *Mozart: A Cultural Biography*. San Diego: Harvest Book, 1999.

Hadden, James M. *A Journal Kept in Canada and upon Burgoyne's Campaign in 1776 and 1777*. Edited by Horatio Rogers. Albany, N.Y.: Joel Munsell's Sons, 1884.

Hadlow, Janice. *A Royal Experiment: The Private Life of King George III*. New York: Henry Holt, 2014.

Hagan, Kenneth J., and William R. Roberts, eds. *Against All Enemies: Interpretations of American Military History from Colonial Times to the Present*. New York: Greenwood Press, 1986.

Hagist, Don N. *British Soldiers, American War: Voices of the American Revolution*. Yardley, Pa.: Westholme, 2012.

———, ed. *A British Soldier's Story: Roger Lamb's Narrative of the American Revolution*. Baraboo, Wis.: Ballindalloch Press, 2004.

———. *Noble Volunteers: The British Soldiers Who Fought the American Revolution.* Yardley, Pa.: Westholme, 2020 (read in manuscript).

Hale, Edward E., and Edward E. Hale, Jr. *Franklin in France.* Boston: Roberts Brothers, 1887.

Hall, Edward Hagaman. *Philipse Manor Hall at Yonkers, N.Y.* New York: American Scenic and Historic Preservation Society, 1912.

Hamilton, Edward P. *Fort Ticonderoga: Key to a Continent.* Boston: Little, Brown, 1964.

Hamilton, F. W. *The Origin and History of the First or Grenadier Guards.* Vol. 2. London: John Murray, 1874.

Hamilton, Phillip. *The Revolutionary War Lives and Letters of Lucy and Henry Knox.* Baltimore: Johns Hopkins University Press, 2017.

Hammon, Neal, and Richard Taylor. *Virginia's Western War, 1775–1786.* Mechanicsburg, Pa.: Stackpole Books, 2002.

Hammond, Otis G. *Letters and Papers of Major-General John Sullivan, Continental Army.* 3 vols. Concord, N.H.: New Hampshire Historical Society, 1930–39.

Harcourt, Edward William, ed. *The Harcourt Papers.* 14 vols. Oxford, U.K.: printed for private circulation by James Parker and Co., 1880–1905.

Hardenberg, John L., William McKendry, William Elliott Griffis, and Simon L. Adler. *Narratives of Sullivan's Expedition, 1779.* Driffield, U.K.: Leonaur, 2010.

Hardman, John. *The Life of Louis XVI.* New Haven, Conn.: Yale University Press, 2016.

———. *Marie-Antoinette: The Making of a French Queen.* New Haven, Conn.: Yale University Press, 2021.

Hardman, John, and Munro Price, eds. *Louis XVI and the Comte de Vergennes: Correspondence, 1774–1787.* Oxford, U.K.: Voltaire Foundation, 2018.

Hargrove, Richard J., Jr. *General John Burgoyne.* Newark: University of Delaware Press, 1983.

Harley, J. B., Barbara Bartz Petchenik, and Lawrence W. Towner. *Mapping the American Revolutionary War.* Chicago: University of Chicago Press, 1978.

Harris, J. R. *Industrial Espionage and Technology Transfer: Britain and France in the Eighteenth Century.* London: Routledge, 2017.

Harris, J. William. *The Hanging of Thomas Jeremiah.* New Haven, Conn.: Yale University Press, 2009.

Harris, Michael C. *Brandywine: A Military History of the Battle That Lost Philadelphia but Saved America, September 11, 1777.* El Dorado Hills, Calif.: Savas Beatie, 2014.

———. *Germantown: A Military History of the Battle for Philadelphia, October 4, 1777.* El Dorado Hills, Calif.: Savas Beatie, 2020.

Harte, Charles Rufus. *The River Obstructions of the Revolutionary War.* Hartford: Connecticut Society of Civil Engineers, 1946.

Hatch, Louis Clinton. *The Administration of the American Revolutionary Army.* New York: Longmans, Green, 1904.

Hatch, Robert McConnell. *Major John André: A Gallant in Spy's Clothing.* Boston: Houghton Mifflin, 1986.

Hayter, Tony, ed. *An Eighteenth-Century Secretary at War: The Papers of William, Viscount Barrington.* London: Bodley Head, 1988.

Haywood, Ian, and John Seed, eds. *The Gordon Riots: Politics, Culture and Insurrection in Late Eighteenth-Century Britain.* Cambridge, U.K.: Cambridge University Press, 2014.

Hawke, David Freeman. *Benjamin Rush: Revolutionary Gadfly.* Indianapolis: Bobbs-Merrill, 1971.

Hayes, John T., ed. *A Gentleman of Fortune: The Diary of Baylor Hill, First Continental Light Dragoons, 1777–1781.* 3 vols. Fort Lauderdale, Fla.: Saddlebag Press, 2002.

Heath, William. *Memoirs of Major-General William Heath.* Edited by William Abbatt. New York: William Abbatt, 1901.

Heidler, David S., and Jeanne T. Heidler, eds. *Daily Lives of Civilians in Wartime Early America.* Westport, Conn.: Greenwood, 2007.

Hemmeon, J. C. *The History of the British Post Office.* Cambridge, Mass.: Harvard University, 1912.

Henriques, Peter R. *First and Always: A New Portrait of George Washington.* Charlottesville: University of Virginia Press, 2020.

Herbert, Charles. *A Relic of the Revolution*. Boston: Charles H. Peirce, 1847.

Heston, Alfred M. *South Jersey: A History, 1664–1924*. 4 vols. New York: Lewis Historical Publishing, 1924.

Hibbert, Christopher. *George III: A Personal History*. New York: Basic Books, 1998.

———. *King Mob: The Story of Lord George Gordon and the Riots of 1780*. Gloucestershire, U.K.: Sutton Publishing, 2004.

———. *Redcoats and Rebels*. New York: W. W. Norton, 2002.

Higginbotham, Don. *Daniel Morgan, Revolutionary Rifleman*. Chapel Hill: University of North Carolina Press, 1961.

———, ed. *George Washington Reconsidered*. Charlottesville: University of Virginia Press, 2001.

———. *The War of American Independence: Military Attitudes, Policies, and Practice, 1763–1789*. Boston: Northeastern University Press, 1983.

Higgins, W. Robert, ed. *The Revolutionary War in the South: Power, Conflict, and Leadership*. Durham, N.C.: Duke University Press, 1979.

Historical Anecdotes, Civil and Military. London: J. Bew, 1779.

Historical Manuscripts Commission. *Report on the Manuscripts of Mrs. Stopford-Sackville, of Drayton House, Northamptonshire*. Vol. 2. Hereford, U.K.: His Majesty's Stationery Office, 1910.

Hoffman, Ronald, and Peter J. Albert, eds. *Arms and Independence: The Military Character of the American Revolution*. Charlottesville: University Press of Virginia, 1984.

———, eds. *Diplomacy and Revolution: The Franco-American Alliance of 1778*. Charlottesville: University Press of Virginia, 1981.

Holmes, Richard. *Redcoat: The British Soldier in the Age of the Horse and Musket*. New York: HarperCollins, 2002.

Holt, Edward. *The Public and Domestic Life of His Late Most Gracious Majesty, George the Third*. Vol. 1. London: Sherwood, Neely, and Jones, 1820.

Holton, Woody. *Liberty Is Sweet: The Hidden History of the American Revolution*. New York: Simon & Schuster, 2021.

Hoock, Holger. *Scars of Independence: America's Violent Birth*. New York: Crown, 2017.

Hough, Franklin Benjamin. *The Siege of Charleston*. Albany, N.Y.: J. Munsell, 1867.

———. *The Siege of Savannah*. Albany, N.Y.: J. Munsell, 1866.

Houlding, J. A. *Fit for Service: The Training of the British Army, 1715–1795*. Oxford, U.K.: Clarendon Press, 1981.

Huteland, Otto. *Westchester County During the American Revolution, 1775–1783*. White Plains, N.Y.: Westchester County Historical Society, 1926.

Huggins, Benjamin Lee. *Washington's War, 1779*. Yardley, Pa.: Westholme, 2018.

Hughes, B. P. *British Smooth-Bore Artillery*. London: Arms and Armour Press, 1969.

———. *Firepower: Weapons Effectiveness on the Battlefield, 1630–1850*. New York: Sarpedon, 1997.

Huish, Robert. *Public and Private Life of His Late Excellent and Most Gracious Majesty, George the Third*. London: Thomas Kelly, 1821.

Hunter, Martin. *The Journal of Gen. Sir Martin Hunter*. Edinburgh: Edinburgh Press, 1844.

Huntington, Ebenezer. *Letters Written by Ebenezer Huntington During the American Revolution*. New York: Charles Frederick Heartman, 1914.

Hussey, Andrew. *Paris: The Secret History*. New York: Bloomsbury, 2007.

Huston, James A. *The Logistics of Liberty*. Newark: University of Delaware Press, 1991.

———. *The Sinews of War: Army Logistics, 1775–1953*. Washington, D.C.: U.S. Army, 1988.

Hutchinson, Peter Orlando. *The Diary and Letters of His Excellency Thomas Hutchinson, Esq.* Boston: Houghton Mifflin, 1886.

Idzerda, Stanley J., ed. *Lafayette in the Age of the American Revolution: Selected Letters and Papers, 1776–1790*. Vols. 1 and 2. Ithaca, N.Y.: Cornell University Press, 1977.

Irving, Washington. *The Life of George Washington*. Vol. 3. New York: G. P. Putnam, 1856.

Isaacson, Walter. *Benjamin Franklin: An American Life*. New York: Simon & Schuster, 2003.

Jackson, Donald. *The Diaries of George Washington*. Vol. 3. Charlottesville: University Press of Virginia, 1978.

Jackson, Harvey H. *Lachlan McIntosh and the Politics of Revolutionary Georgia*. Athens: University of Georgia Press, 2003.

Jackson, John W. *The Pennsylvania Navy, 1775–1781: The Defense of the Delaware*. New Brunswick, N.J.: Rutgers University Press, 1974.

———. *Valley Forge: Pinnacle of Courage*. Gettysburg, Pa.: Thomas Publications, 1992.

———. *With the British Army in Philadelphia, 1777–1778*. San Rafael, Calif.: Presidio Press, 1979.

Jacob, Mark, and Stephen H. Case. *Treacherous Beauty*. Guilford, Conn.: Lyons Press, 2012.

Jaffe, Steven H. *New York at War*. New York: Basic Books, 2012.

James, Coy Hilton. *Silas Deane, Patriot or Traitor?* East Lansing: Michigan State University Press, 1975.

James, James Alton, ed. *George Rogers Clark Papers, 1771–1781*. Springfield: Illinois State Historical Library, 1912.

James, Marquis. *The Life of Andrew Jackson*. Indianapolis: Bobbs-Merrill, 1938.

James, W. M. *The British Navy in Adversity*. London: Longmans, Green, 1926.

Jameson, J. Franklin. *The American Revolution Considered as a Social Movement*. Princeton, N.J.: Princeton University Press, 1969.

Jasanoff, Maya. *Liberty's Exiles: The Loss of America and the Remaking of the British Empire*. London: HarperPress, 2011.

Jensen, Merrill. *The Founding of a Nation: A History of the American Revolution, 1763–1776*. New York: Oxford University Press, 1968.

Jesse, John Heneage. *Memoirs of Celebrated Etonians*. Vol. 2. London: Richard Bentley and Son, 1875.

———. *Memoirs of the Life and Reign of King George the Third*. Vol. 3. Boston: L. C. Page, 1902.

Johnson, Amandus, ed. and trans. *The Journal and Biography of Nicholas Collin*. Philadelphia: New Jersey Society of Pennsylvania, 1936.

Johnson, Donald F. *Occupied America: British Military Rule and the Experience of Revolution*. Philadelphia: University of Pennsylvania Press, 2020.

Johnston, Elizabeth Lichtenstein. *Recollections of a Georgia Loyalist*. Edited by Arthur Wentworth Eaton. New York: Bankside Press, 1901.

Johnston, Henry P. *The Storming of Stony Point*. New York: James T. White, 1900.

Jones, Charles C., Jr., ed. *The Siege of Savannah in 1779*. Albany, N.Y.: Joel Munsell, 1874.

Jones, John. *Plain Concise Practical Remarks on the Treatment of Wounds and Fractures*. Philadelphia: Robert Bell, 1776.

Jones, T. Cole. *Captives of Liberty: Prisoners of War and the Politics of Vengeance in the American Revolution*. Philadelphia: University of Pennsylvania Press, 2020.

Jones, Thomas. *History of New York During the Revolutionary War*. 2 vols. Edited by Edward Floyd de Lancey. New York: New York Historical Society, 1879.

Kajencki, Francis Casimir. *Casimir Pulaski: Cavalry Commander of the American Revolution*. El Paso, Tex.: Southwest Polonia Press, 2001.

———. *Thaddeus Kosciuszko: Military Engineer of the American Revolution*. El Paso, Tex.: Southwest Polonia Press, 1998.

Kallich, Martin, and Andrew MacLeish, eds. *The American Revolution Through British Eyes*. New York: Harper & Row, 1962.

Kaminski, John P., ed. *The Founders on the Founders: Word Portraits from the American Revolutionary Era*. Charlottesville: University of Virginia Press, 2008.

Kapp, Friedrich. *The Life of Frederick William von Steuben*. New York: Mason Brothers, 1859.

———. *The Life of John Kalb, Major-General in the Revolutionary Army*. New York: Henry Holt, 1884.

Karsten, Peter, ed. *The Military in America: From the Colonial Era to the Present*. New York: Free Press, 1986.

Keegan, John. *The Price of Admiralty: The Evolution of Naval Warfare from Trafalgar to Midway*. New York: Penguin, 1990.

Kemble, Stephen. *The Kemble Papers: Journals of Lieut.-Col. Stephen Kemble, 1773–1789*. Vol. 1. New York: New-York Historical Society, 1883.

Kemp, Franklin W. *A Nest of Rebel Pirates*. Batsto, N.J.: Batsto Citizens Committee, 1966.

Kennedy, Benjamin, ed. and trans. *Muskets, Cannon Balls, & Bombs: Nine Narratives of the Siege of Savannah in 1779*. Savannah, Ga.: Beehive Press, 1974.

Keppel, Thomas. *The Life of Augustus Viscount Keppel*. Vol. 2. London: Henry Colburn, 1842.

Ketchum, Richard M. *Divided Loyalties*. New York: Henry Holt, 2002.

———. *Saratoga: Turning Point of America's Revolutionary War*. New York: Owl Books, 1999.

Kidd, Thomas S. *God of Liberty: A Religious History of the American Revolution*. New York: Basic Books, 2010.

Kidder, Frederic. *History of the First New Hampshire Regiment in the War of the Revolution*. Albany, N.Y.: Joel Munsell, 1868.

Kidder, William L. *Crossroads of the Revolution: Trenton, 1774–1783*. Lawrence Township, N.J.: Knox Press, 2017.

———. *Revolutionary Princeton, 1774–1783*. Lawrence Township, N.J.: Knox Press, 2017.

Kipping, Ernst. *The Hessian View of America, 1776–1783*. Monmouth Beach, N.J.: Philip Freneau Press, 1971.

Kirkland, Frederic R., ed. *Letters on the American Revolution in the Library at "Karolfred."* Vol. 1. Philadelphia: privately printed, 1941.

———. *Letters on the American Revolution in the Library at "Karolfred."* Vol. 2. New York: Coward-McCann, 1952.

Kite, Elizabeth S. *Beaumarchais and the War of Independence*. 2 vols. Boston: Gorham Press, 1918.

Knight, John. *War at Saber Point: Banastre Tarleton and the British Legion*. Yardley, Pa.: Westholme, 2020.

Knight, R.J.B. *Portsmouth Dockyard Papers, 1774–1783: The American War*. Portsmouth, U.K.: City of Portsmouth, 1987.

Knollenberg, Bernhard. *Washington and the Revolution: A Reappraisal*. New York: Macmillan, 1940.

Kowalski, Gary. *Revolutionary Spirits: The Enlightened Faith of America's Founding Fathers*. New York: BlueBridge, 2008.

Kranish, Michael. *Flight from Monticello: Thomas Jefferson at War*. New York: Oxford University Press, 2010.

Krebs, Daniel. *A Generous and Merciful Enemy: Life for German Prisoners of War During the American Revolution*. Norman: University of Oklahoma Press, 2013.

Kurtz, Stephen G., and James H. Hutson, eds. *Essays on the American Revolution*. Chapel Hill: University of North Carolina Press, 1973.

Kwasny, Mark V. *Washington's Partisan War, 1775–1783*. Kent, Ohio: Kent State University Press, 1996.

Lacour-Gayet, Georges. *La marine militaire de la France sous le règne de Louis XVI*. Paris: Editions Teissèdre, 2007.

Lamb, Martha J., and Mrs. Burton Harrison. *History of the City of New York: Its Origin, Rise, and Progress*. 3 vols. New York: A. S. Barnes, 1877–96.

Lambert, Robert Stansbury. *South Carolina Loyalists in the American Revolution*. Columbia: University of South Carolina Press, 1987.

Lanctôt, Gustave. *Canada & the American Revolution, 1774–1783*. Translated by Margaret M. Cameron. Cambridge, Mass.: Harvard University Press, 1967.

Lapham, William B., ed. *Elijah Fisher's Journal*. Augusta, Me.: Badger and Manley, 1880.

Laprade, William Thomas, ed. *Parliamentary Papers of John Robinson, 1774–1784*. London: Royal Historical Society, 1922.

Larson, Carlton F. W. *The Trials of Allegiance: Treason, Juries, and the American Revolution*. New York: Oxford University Press, 2019.

Laughton, John Knox, ed. *The Naval Miscellany*. Vol. 1. London: Navy Records Society, 1902.

Lawrence, Alexander A. *Storm over Savannah*. Savannah, Ga.: Tara Press, 1979.

Layman, C. H. *The Wager Disaster: Mayhem, Mutiny and Murder in the South Seas*. London: Uniform Press, 2015.

Lea, Russell M. *A Hero and a Spy: The Revolutionary War Correspondence of Benedict Arnold*. Westminster, Md.: Heritage Books, 2008.

Leake, Isaac Q. *Memoir of the Life and Times of General John Lamb.* Albany, N.Y.: Joel Munsell, 1850.

Leamon, James S. *Revolution Downeast: The War for American Independence in Maine.* Amherst: University of Massachusetts Press, 1993.

Lee, Charles. *The Lee Papers.* 4 vols. New York: New-York Historical Society, 1872–75.

———. *Memoirs of the War in the Southern Department of the United States.* Vol. 1. Philadelphia: Bradford and Inskeep, 1812.

Lee, Henry. *Memoirs of the War in the Southern Department of the United States.* Vol. 1. Philadelphia: Bradford and Inskeep, 1812.

Lee, Richard Henry. *Life of Arthur Lee, LL.D.* Vol. 1. Boston: Wells and Lilly, 1829.

Lemaitre, Georges. *Beaumarchais.* New York: Knopf, 1949.

Lemoine, Pierre, et al. *Versailles: Château, Estate, Collections.* Versailles, France: Château de Versailles, n.d.

Lender, Mark Edward. *Cabal! The Plot Against General Washington.* Yardley, Pa.: Westholme, 2019.

———. *Fort Ticonderoga, the Last Campaign: The War in the North, 1777–1783.* Yardley, Pa.: Westholme, 2022.

Lender, Mark Edward, and Garry Wheeler Stone. *Fatal Sunday: George Washington, the Monmouth Campaign, and the Politics of Battle.* Norman: University of Oklahoma Press, 2016.

Lender, Mark Edward, and James Kirby Martin, eds. *Citizen Soldier: The Revolutionary War Journal of Joseph Bloomfield.* Yardley, Pa.: Westholme, 2018.

Lengel, Edward G. *General George Washington: A Military Life.* New York: Random House, 2005.

———, ed. *A Companion to George Washington.* Chichester, U.K.: Wiley-Blackwell, 2012.

Lepore, Jill. *Book of Ages: The Life and Opinions of Jane Franklin.* New York: Knopf, 2013.

———. *These Truths: A History of the United States.* New York: W. W. Norton, 2018.

Lesser, Charles H., ed. *The Sinews of Independence: Monthly Strength Reports of the Continental Army.* Chicago: University of Chicago Press, 1976.

Levin, Phyllis Lee. *Abigail Adams: A Biography.* New York: St. Martin's Griffin, 2001.

Levy, Martin. *Love & Madness: The Murder of Martha Ray, Mistress of the Fourth Earl of Sandwich.* New York: William Morrow, 2004.

Lewis, Paul. *The Man Who Lost America: A Biography of Gentleman Johnny Burgoyne.* New York: Dial Press, 1973.

Lloyd, Christopher. *The British Seaman.* Rutherford, N.J.: Fairleigh Dickinson University Press, 1970.

Loane, Nancy K. *Following the Drum: Women at the Valley Forge Encampment.* Lincoln, Neb.: Potomac Books, 2020.

Lockhart, Paul. *The Drillmaster of Valley Forge: The Baron de Steuben and the Making of the American Army.* New York: HarperCollins, 2008.

Lodge, Henry Cabot, ed. *Major André's Journal.* Boston: Bibliophile Society, 1903.

Loménic, Louis de. *Beaumarchais and His Times.* Translated by Henry S. Edwards. New York: Harper & Brothers, 1857.

Londahl-Smidt, Donald M. *German Troops in the American Revolution.* Vol. 1., *Hessen-Cassel.* Oxford, U.K.: Osprey, 2021.

Longmore, T. *A Treatise on Gunshot Wounds.* Philadelphia: J. B. Lippincott, 1862.

Lopez, Claude-Anne. *Mon Cher Papa: Franklin and the Ladies of Paris.* New Haven, Conn.: Yale University, 1990.

———. *My Life with Benjamin Franklin.* New Haven, Conn.: Yale University Press, 2000.

Loprieno, Don. *The Enterprise in Contemplation: The Midnight Assault of Stony Point.* Westminster, Md.: Heritage Books, 2004.

Lord, Philip, Jr. *War over Walloomscoick: Land Use and Settlement Pattern on the Bennington Battlefield, 1777.* Albany, N.Y.: New York State Museum Bulletin No. 473, 1989.

Lorenz, Lincoln. *John Paul Jones: Fighter for Freedom and Glory.* Annapolis, Md.: United States Naval Institute, 1943.

Lossing, Benson J. *The Life and Times of Philip Schuyler.* 2 vols. New York: Sheldon, 1860 and 1873.

———. *The Pictorial Field-Book of the Revolution.* Vol. 2. New York: Harper & Brothers, 1852.

Lowell, Edward J. *The Hessians*. New York: Harper & Brothers, 1884.

Lowenthal, Larry, ed. *Days of Siege: A Journal of the Siege of Fort Stanwix in 1777*. N.p.: Eastern National, 1983.

Lucas, Reginald. *Lord North, Second Earl of Guilford, K.G., 1732-1792*. 2 vols. London: Arthur L. Humphreys, 1913.

Lumpkin, Henry. *From Savannah to Yorktown: The American Revolution in the South*. New York: Paragon House, 1987.

Lundin, Leonard. *Cockpit of the Revolution: The War for Independence in New Jersey*. Princeton: Princeton University Press, 1940.

Lunt, James. *John Burgoyne of Saratoga*. New York: Harcourt Brace Jovanovich, 1975.

Lutnick, Solomon. *The American Revolution and the British Press, 1775-1783*. Columbia: University of Missouri Press, 1976.

Luzader, John F. *Saratoga: A Military History of the Decisive Campaign of the American Revolution*. New York: Savas Beatie, 2008.

Lynn, Mary C., ed. *An Eyewitness Account of the American Revolution and New England Life: The Journal of J. F. Wasmus, German Company Surgeon, 1776-1783*. Translated by Helga Doblin. Westport, Conn.: Greenwood Press, 1990.

———, ed. *The Specht Journal: A Military Journal of the Burgoyne Campaign*. Translated by Helga Doblin. Westport, Conn.: Greenwood Press, 1995.

Mackenzie, Frederick. *Diary of Frederick Mackenzie*. Vol. 1. Cambridge, Mass.: Harvard University Press, 1930.

Mackesy, Piers. *The Coward of Minden: The Affair of Lord George Sackville*. New York: St. Martin's Press, 1979.

———. *The War for America, 1775-1783*. Lincoln: University of Nebraska Press, 1993.

Mackey, Harry D. *The Gallant Men of the Delaware River Forts, 1777*. Philadelphia: Dorrance, 1973.

Maclay, Edgar Stanton. *A History of the United States Navy from 1775 to 1898*. Vol. 1. New York: D. Appleton, 1898.

Mahan, Alfred Thayer. *The Major Operations of Navies in the War of American Independence*. 1913; repr. Hamburg, Germany: Tradition, 2006.

Main, Jackson Turner. *The Social Structure of Revolutionary America*. Princeton, N.J.: Princeton University Press, 1970.

Malcolm, Joyce Lee. *The Tragedy of Benedict Arnold: An American Life*. New York: Pegasus Books, 2018.

M'Alpine, John. *Genuine Narratives and Concise Memoirs*. Greenock, U.K.: W. M'Alpine, 1780.

Manceron, Claude. *Age of the French Revolution*. Vol. 1, *Twilight of the Old Order, 1774-1778*. Translated by Patricia Wolf. New York: Touchstone, 1989.

———. *Age of the French Revolution*. Vol. 2. *The Wind from America, 1778-1781*. Translated by Nancy Amphoux. New York: Touchstone, 1989.

Mansfield, Harvey C., Jr., ed. *Selected Letters of Edmund Burke*. Chicago: University of Chicago Press, 1984.

Marlow, Louis. *Sackville of Drayton*. Totowa, N.J.: Rowman and Littlefield, 1973.

Marshall, Dorothy. *Dr. Johnson's London*. New York: John Wiley & Sons, 1968.

Marshall, P. J. *The Making and Unmaking of Empires*. New York: Oxford University Press, 2009.

———. *The Oxford History of the British Empire*. Vol. 2, *The Eighteenth Century*. New York: Oxford University Press, 2001.

Martelli, George. *Jemmy Twitcher: A Life of the Fourth Earl of Sandwich, 1718-1792*. London: Jonathan Cape, 1962.

Martin, David G. *The Philadelphia Campaign, June 1777-July 1778*. Cambridge, Mass.: Da Capo, 2003.

Martin, James Kirby. *Benedict Arnold, Revolutionary Hero*. New York: New York University Press, 2000.

Martin, James Kirby, and David L. Preston, eds. *Theaters of the American Revolution*. Yardley, Pa.: Westholme, 2017.

Martin, James Kirby, and Mark Edward Lender. *A Respectable Army: The Military Origins of the Republic, 1763-1789*. Wheeling, Ill.: Harlan Davidson, 1982.

Martin, Joseph Plumb. *A Narrative of a Revolutionary Soldier*. New York: Signet Classics, 2010.

Martin, Scott, and Bernard Harris. *Savannah 1779: The British Turn South*. Oxford, U.K.: Osprey, 2017.

Masefield, John. *Sea Life in Nelson's Time*. Annapolis, Md.: Naval Institute Press, 2002.

Massey, Gregory D. *John Laurens and the American Revolution*. Columbia: University of South Carolina Press, 2015.

Mattern, David B. *Benjamin Lincoln and the American Revolution*. Columbia: University of South Carolina Press, 1998.

Matthews, William, and Dixon Wecter. *Our Soldiers Speak, 1775–1918*. Boston: Little, Brown, 1943.

Maugras, Gaston. *The Duc de Lauzun and the Court of Marie Antoinette*. London: Osgood, McIlvaine, 1896.

Maurois, André. *Adrienne: The Life of the Marquise de La Fayette*. Translated by Gerard Hopkins. New York: McGraw-Hill, 1961.

May, Henry F. *The Enlightenment in America*. New York: Oxford University Press, 1976.

Mazzagetti, Dominick. *Charles Lee: Self Before Country*. New Brunswick, N.J.: Rutgers University Press, 2013.

McBurney, Christian. *George Washington's Nemesis: The Outrageous Treason and Unfair Court-Martial of Major General Charles Lee During the Revolutionary War*. El Dorado Hills, Calif.: Savas Beatie, 2020.

———. *Kidnapping the Enemy: The Special Operations to Capture Generals General Lee and Richard Prescot*. Yardley, Pa.: Westholme, 2014.

———. *The Rhode Island Campaign*. Yardley, Pa.: Westholme, 2011.

McCowen, George Smith, Jr. *The British Occupation of Charleston, 1780–82*. Columbia: University of South Carolina Press, 1972.

McCrady, Edward. *The History of South Carolina in the Revolution, 1775–1780*. New York: Macmillan, 1901.

McCullough, David. *John Adams*. New York: Simon & Schuster, 2001.

McCusker, John J., and Russell R. Menard. *The Economy of British America, 1607–1789*. Chapel Hill: University of North Carolina Press, 1991.

McDonald, Forrest. *Alexander Hamilton, a Biography*. New York: W. W. Norton, 1982.

McDonnell, Michael. *The Politics of War: Race, Class and Conflict in Revolutionary Virginia*. Chapel Hill: University of North Carolina Press, 2007.

McDougall, Walter A. *Freedom Just Around the Corner: A New American History, 1585–1828*. New York: HarperCollins, 2004.

McGeorge, Isabella G. *Ann C. Whitall, the Heroine of Red Bank*. Woodbury, N.J.: Gloucester County Historical Society, 1904.

McGeorge, Wallace. *The Battle of Red Bank*. Camden, N.J.: [Sinnickson Chew, printers,] 1905.

McGrath, Tim. *Give Me a Fast Ship: The Continental Navy and America's Revolution at Sea*. New York: NAL Caliber, 2014.

McGuire, Thomas J. *Battle of Paoli*. Mechanicsburg, Pa.: Stackpole, 2006.

———. *The Philadelphia Campaign*. Vol. 1, *Brandywine and the Fall of Philadelphia*. Mechanicsburg, Pa.: Stackpole, 2014.

———. *The Philadelphia Campaign*. Vol. 2, *Germantown and the Roads to Valley Forge*. Mechanicsburg, Pa.: Stackpole, 2007.

———. *The Surprise of Germantown, or the Battle of Cliveden, October 4th, 1777*. Gettysburg, Pa.: Thomas Publications, 1994.

McHenry, James. *Journal of a March, a Battle, and a Waterfall*. [Greenwich? Conn.]: privately printed, 1945.

Meacham, Jon. *American Lion: Andrew Jackson in the White House*. New York: Random House, 2008.

———. *Thomas Jefferson: The Art of Power*. New York: Random House, 2012.

Meade, Robert Douthat. *Patrick Henry, Practical Revolutionary*. Philadelphia: J. B. Lippincott, 1969.

Memoirs, Correspondence and Manuscripts of General Lafayette. Vol. 1. London: Saunders and Otley, 1837.

Meng, John J., ed. *Despatches and Instructions of Conrad Alexandre Gérard, 1778–1780*. Baltimore: Johns Hopkins Press, 1939.

Mercy-Argenteau, Florimond de. *Marie-Antoinette. Correspondance secrète entre Marie-Thérèse et le comte de Mercy-Argenteau*. 3 vols. Paris: Firmin Didot, 1874.

Merlant, Joachim. *Soldiers and Sailors of France in the American War for Independence*. Translated by Mary Bushnell Coleman. New York: Charles Scribner's Sons, 1920.

Metzger, Charles H. *The Prisoner in the American Revolution*. Chicago: Loyola University Press, 1971.

Middlebrook, Louis F. *Salisbury Connecticut Cannon: Revolutionary War*. Salem, Mass.: Newcomb & Gauss, 1935.

———, ed. *The Log of the Bon Homme Richard*. Mystic, Conn.: Marine Historical Assoc., 1936.

Middlekauff, Robert. *The Glorious Cause: The American Revolution, 1763–1789*. New York: Oxford University Press, 2005.

———. *Washington's Revolution: The Making of America's First Leader*. New York: Vintage, 2016.

Miller, Elizabeth R. *The American Revolution: As Described by British Writers and* The Morning Chronicle and London Advertiser. Bowie, Md.: Heritage Books, 1991.

Miller, John C. *Triumph of Freedom, 1775–1783*. Boston: Little, Brown, 1948.

Miller, Lillian B., ed. *The Selected Papers of Charles Willson Peale and His Family*. Vols. 1 and 5. New Haven, Conn.: Yale University Press, 1983 and 2000.

Miller, Nathan. *Sea of Glory: A Naval History of the American Revolution*. Charleston, S.C.: Nautical & Aviation Publishing, 1974.

Mintz, Max M. *The Generals of Saratoga: John Burgoyne & Horatio Gates*. New Haven, Conn.: Yale University Press, 1990.

———. *Seeds of Empire: The American Revolutionary Conquest of the Iroquois*. New York: New York University Press, 1999.

Mitchell, Broadus. *The Price of Independence: A Realistic View of the American Revolution*. New York: Oxford University Press, 1974.

Money, John. *To the Right Honorable William Windham, on a Partial Reorganization of the British Army*. London: T. Egerton, 1799.

Montross, Lynn. *Rag, Tag and Bobtail: The Story of the Continental Army, 1775–1783*. New York: Harper & Brothers, 1952.

Moore, Frank. *The Diary of the American Revolution*. 2 vols. New York: Charles Scribner, 1860.

———. *The Diary of the American Revolution, 1775–1781*. Edited by John Anthony Scott. New York: Washington Square Press, 1968.

———. *Materials for History*. New York: Zenger Club, 1861.

Moore, George H. *The Treason of Charles Lee*. New York: Charles Scribner, 1860.

Moore, Howard Parker. *A Life of General John Stark of New Hampshire*. Boston: Spaulding-Moss, 1949.

Moorsom, W. S., ed. *Historical Record of the Fifty-Second Regiment (Oxfordshire Light Infantry)*. London: R. Bentley, 1860.

Morgan, Edmund S. *Benjamin Franklin*. New Haven, Conn.: Yale University Press, 2002.

———. *The Birth of the Republic, 1763–89*. Chicago: University of Chicago Press, 2013.

Morison, Samuel Eliot. *John Paul Jones: A Sailor's Biography*. New York: Time, 1964.

———. *The Oxford History of the American People*. New York: Oxford University Press, 1965.

Morison, Samuel Eliot, and Henry Steele Commager. *The Growth of the American Republic*. Vol. 1. New York: Oxford University Press, 1965.

Morris, Ira K. *Morris's Memorial History of Staten Island*. Vol. 1. New York: Memorial Publishing, 1898.

Morris, Margaret Francine, and Elliott West, eds. *Essays on Urban America*. Austin: University of Texas Press, 1975.

Morris, Richard B. *The Peacemakers: The Great Powers and American Independence*. New York: Harper Torchbooks, 1970.

Morrissey, Brendan. *Monmouth Courthouse 1778: The Last Great Battle in the North*. Botley, U.K.: Osprey, 2004.

Moultrie, William. *Memoirs of the American Revolution.* Vols. 1 and 2. New York: David Long-worth, 1802.

Mowday, Bruce E. *September 11, 1777: Washington's Defeat at Brandywine Dooms Philadelphia.* Shippensburg, Pa.: White Mane Books, 2002.

Mullin, Gerald W. *Flight and Rebellion: Slave Resistance in Eighteenth-Century Virginia.* New York: Oxford University Press, 1974.

Münchhausen, Friedrich Ernst von. *At General Howe's Side, 1776–1778.* Translated by Ernst Kipping and Samuel Stelle Smith. Monmouth Beach, N.J.: Philip Freneau Press, 1974.

Murdoch, David H., ed. *Rebellion in America: A Contemporary British Viewpoint, 1765–1783.* Santa Barbara, Calif.: Clio Books, 1979.

Murphy, Orville T. *Charles Gravier, Comte de Vergennes: French Diplomacy in the Age of Revolution, 1719–1787.* Albany: State University of New York Press, 1982.

Murray, James. *Letters from America, 1773–1780.* Edited by Eric Robson. New York: Barnes and Noble, 1951.

Murray, John, ed. *The Autobiographies of Edward Gibbon.* London: John Murray, 1897.

Murrin, Mary R., and Richard Waldron, eds. *Conflict at Monmouth Court House.* Trenton: New Jersey Historical Commission, 1984.

Nadelhaft, Jerome J. *The Disorders of War: The Revolution in South Carolina.* Orono: University of Maine at Orono Press, 1981.

Nagy, John A. *Invisible Ink: Spycraft of the American Revolution.* Yardley, Pa.: Westholme, 2011.

Namier, Lewis. *England in the Age of the American Revolution.* London: Macmillan, 1974.

The Narrative of Lieut. Gen. Sir William Howe. London: H. Baldwin, 1781.

Narratives of the Revolution in New York. New York: New-York Historical Society, 1975.

Nash, Gary B. *First City: Philadelphia and the Forging of Historical Memory.* Philadelphia: University of Pennsylvania Press, 2006.

———. *The Unknown American Revolution: The Unruly Birth of Democracy and the Struggle to Create America.* New York: Viking, 2005.

Neeser, Robert Wilden, ed. *Letters and Papers Relating to the Cruises of Gustavus Conyngham.* New York: Naval History Society, 1915.

Neimeyer, Charles Patrick. *America Goes to War: A Social History of the Continental Army.* New York: New York University Press, 1996.

Nelson, Craig. *Thomas Paine: Enlightenment, Revolution, and the Birth of Modern Nations.* New York: Viking, 2006.

Nelson, Paul David. *General Horatio Gates, a Biography.* Baton Rouge: Louisiana State University Press, 1976.

———. *General Sir Guy Carleton, Lord Dorchester.* Madison, N.J.: Fairleigh Dickinson University Press, 2000.

———. *Sir Charles Grey, First Earl Grey: Royal Soldier, Family Patriarch.* Madison, N.J.: Fairleigh Dickinson University Press, 1996.

———. *William Alexander, Lord Stirling.* Tuscaloosa: University of Alabama Press, 1987.

Nelson, William H. *The American Tory.* Boston: Beacon Press, 1968.

Nester, William R. *George Rogers Clark: "I Glory in War."* Norman: University of Oklahoma Press, 2012.

Nevins, Allan. *The American States During and After the American Revolution, 1775–1789.* New York: Macmillan, 1924.

Newman, Eric P. *The Early Paper Money of America.* Iola, Wis.: Krause Publications, 2008.

Nicolardot, Louis, ed. *Journal de Louis XVI.* Paris: E. Dentu, 1873.

Norton, Mary Beth. *The British-Americans: The Loyalist Exiles in England, 1774–1789.* Boston: Little, Brown, 1972.

O'Beirne, Thomas Lewis. *A Candid and Impartial Narrative of the Transactions of the Fleet, Under the Command of Lord Howe.* London: J. Almon, 1779.

O'Shaughnessy, Andrew Jackson. *An Empire Divided: The American Revolution and the British Caribbean.* Philadelphia: University of Pennsylvania Press, 2000.

———. *The Men Who Lost America: British Leadership, the American Revolution and the Fate of the Empire.* New Haven, Conn.: Yale University Press, 2013.

Onderdonk, Henry, Jr. *Documents and Letters Intended to Illustrate the Revolutionary Incidents of Queens County*. New York: Leavitt, Trow, 1846.

——. *Revolutionary Incidents of Suffolk and Kings Counties*. New York: Leavitt, 1849.

Owen, Lewis F. *The Revolutionary Struggle in New Jersey, 1776–1783*. Trenton: New Jersey Historical Commission, 1975.

Padover, Saul K. *The Life and Death of Louis XVI*. London: Alvin Redman, 1963.

Paine, Thomas. *Common Sense, The Rights of Man, and Other Essential Writings of Thomas Paine*. New York: Meridian, 1984.

Palmer, Dave R. *George Washington and Benedict Arnold: A Tale of Two Patriots*. Washington, D.C.: Regnery, 2006.

——. *George Washington's Military Genius*. Washington, D.C.: Regnery, 2012.

Palmer, John McAuley. *General Von Steuben*. New Haven, Conn.: Yale University Press, 1937.

Palmer, Peter S. *History of Lake Champlain, from Its First Exploration by the French in 1609, to the Close of the Year 1814*. Albany, N.Y.: J. Munsell, 1866.

Pancake, John S. *This Destructive War: The British Campaign in the Carolinas, 1780–1782*. Tuscaloosa: University of Alabama Press, 2003.

——. *1777: The Year of the Hangman*. Tuscaloosa: University of Alabama Press, 1992.

Papas, Phillip. *Renegade Revolutionary: The Life of General Charles Lee*. New York: New York University Press, 2014.

Pares, Richard. *King George III and the Politicians*. London: Oxford University Press, 1953.

Parker, John C., Jr. *Parker's Guide to the Revolutionary War in South Carolina*. West Conshohocken, Pa.: Infinity Publishing, 2013.

The Parliamentary History of England. Vols. 19 and 20. London: T. C. Hansard, 1814.

Parliamentary Register. Vol. 12. London: John Stockdale, 1802.

The Parliamentary Register, or History of the Proceedings and Debates of the House of Lords. Vol. 2. London: J. Almon, 1775.

Parton, James. *Life and Times of Benjamin Franklin*. 2 vols. Boston: Ticknor and Fields, 1867.

Patterson, A. Temple. *The Other Armada: The Franco-Spanish Attempt to Invade Britain in 1779*. Manchester, U.K.: Manchester University Press, 1960.

Patterson, Samuel White. *Knight Errant of Liberty: The Triumph and Tragedy of General Charles Lee*. New York: Lantern Press, 1958.

Patton, Robert H. *Patriot Pirates: The Privateer War for Freedom and Fortune in the American Revolution*. New York: Pantheon, 2008.

Peckham, Howard H., ed. *Sources of American Independence: Selected Manuscripts from the Collections of the William L. Clements Library*. 2 vols. Chicago: University of Chicago Press, 1978.

——, ed. *The Toll of Independence: Engagements & Battle Casualties of the American Revolution*. Chicago: University of Chicago Press, 1974.

——. *The War for Independence: A Military History*. Chicago: University of Chicago Press, 1970.

Pemberton, W. Baring. *Lord North*. London: Longmans, Green, 1938.

Pennsylvania Archives. Vol. 10, 2nd serial. Harrisburg: Clarence M. Busch, 1896.

Pennypacker, Morton. *General Washington's Spies on Long Island and in New York*. Brooklyn, N.Y.: Long Island Historical Society, 1939.

Perrin, W. G., ed. *The Keith Papers: Selected from the Letters and Papers of Admiral Viscount Keith*. Vol. 1. London: Navy Records Society, 1927.

Perry, Ichabod. *Reminiscences of the Revolution*. Lima, N.Y.: Daughters of the American Revolution, 1915.

Peters, Marie. *The Elder Pitt*. London: Longman, 1998.

Peterson, Harold L. *The Book of the Continental Soldiers*. Harrisburg, Pa.: Promontory Press, 1968.

Pettengill, Ray W., trans. *Letters from America, 1776–1779: Being Letters of Brunswick, Hessian, and Waldeck Officers with the British Armies During the Revolution*. Boston: Houghton Mifflin, 1924.

Philbrick, Nathaniel. *Valiant Ambition: George Washington, Benedict Arnold, and the Fate of the American Revolution*. New York: Viking, 2016.

Phillips, Paul Chrisler. *The West in the Diplomacy of the American Revolution*. New York: Russell & Russell, 1913.

Picard, Liza. *Dr. Johnson's London: Life in London, 1740–1770*. London: Phoenix, 2003.

Pickering, Octavius. *The Life of Timothy Pickering*. Vol. 1. Boston: Little, Brown, 1867.

Piecuch, Jim. *Three Peoples, One King: Loyalists, Indians, and Slaves in the Revolutionary South, 1775–1782*. Columbia: University of South Carolina Press, 2008.

Piecuch, Jim, and John H. Beakes, Jr. *"Cool Deliberate Courage": John Eager Howard in the American Revolution*. Charleston, S.C.: Nautical and Aviation Publishing, 2009.

———. *"Light Horse Harry" Lee in the War for Independence*. Charleston, S.C.: Nautical and Aviation Publishing, 2013.

Plumb, J. H. *England in the Eighteenth Century*. London: Penguin, 1950.

———. *The First Four Georges*. Glasgow: Fontana/Collins, 1976.

Polf, William A. *Garrison Town: The British Occupation of New York City, 1776–1783*. Albany, N.Y.: New York State American Revolution Bicentennial Commission, 1976.

Pond, E. Le Roy. *The Tories of Chippeny Hill, Connecticut*. New York: Grafton Press, 1909. http://anglicanhistory.org/usa/tories/chapter7.html.

Popkin, Jeremy D., ed. *Louis-Sébastien Mercier, Panorama of Paris*. University Park: Pennsylvania State University Press, 2003.

Popp, Stephan. *A Hessian Soldier in the American Revolution*. Translated by Reinhart J. Pope. n.p.: private printing, 1953.

Porter, Roy. *English Society in the Eighteenth Century*. New York: Penguin, 1990.

Posey, John Thornton. *General Thomas Posey: Son of the American Revolution*. East Lansing: Michigan State University Press, 1992.

Potts, Louis W. *Arthur Lee: A Virtuous Revolutionary*. Baton Rouge: Louisiana State University Press, 1981.

Pownall, Thomas, and John Almon. *The Remembrancer, or Impartial Repository of Public Events*. Vols. 5–9. London: J. Almon, 1778–79.

Preston, David L. *Braddock's Defeat: The Battle of the Monongahela and the Road to the Revolution*. New York: Oxford University Press, 2015.

Price, Jacob M. *France and the Chesapeake: A History of the French Tobacco Monopoly, 1674–1791*. 2 vols. Ann Arbor: University of Michigan Press, 1973.

Price, Munro. *Preserving the Monarchy: The Comte de Vergennes, 1774–1787*. Cambridge, U.K.: Cambridge University Press, 2004.

———. *The Road from Versailles: Louis XVI, Marie Antoinette, and the Fall of the French Monarchy*. New York: St. Martin's Griffin, 2004.

Prior, James. *Memoir of the Life and Character of the Right Hon. Edmund Burke*. Vol. 1. London: Baldwin, Cradock, and Joy, 1826.

Prowell, George R. *History of York County, Pennsylvania*. Vol. 1. Chicago: J. H. Beers, 1907.

Pula, James S. *Thaddeus Kościuszko, the Purest Son of Liberty*. New York: Hippocrene, 1999.

Puls, Mark. *Henry Knox: Visionary General of the American Revolution*. New York: Palgrave Macmillan, 2008.

Pybus, Cassandra. *Epic Journeys of Freedom: Runaway Slaves of the American Revolution and Their Global Quest for Liberty*. Boston: Beacon Press, 2006.

Quarles, Benjamin. *The Negro in the Making of America*. New York: Collier Books, 1968.

Quincy, Josiah. *The Journals of Major Samuel Shaw*. Boston: William Crosby and H. P. Nichols, 1847.

Rait, R. S. *Royal Palaces of England*. New York: James Pott, 1911.

Rakove, Jack. *Revolutionaries: A New History of the Invention of America*. Boston: Houghton Mifflin Harcourt, 2010.

Ralfe, James. *The Naval Biography of Great Britain*. Vol. 1. London: Whitmore & Fenn, 1828.

Ramsay, David. *The History of the American Revolution*. Vol. 2. Philadelphia: R. Aitken, 1789.

Randall, Willard Sterne. *Benedict Arnold: Patriot and Traitor*. New York: William Morrow, 1990.

———. *A Little Revenge: Benjamin Franklin and His Son*. Boston: Little, Brown, 1984.

Rankin, Hugh F. *Francis Marion: The Swamp Fox*. New York: Thomas Y. Crowell, 1973.

———. *North Carolina in the American Revolution*. Raleigh, N.C.: North Carolina Department of Cultural Resources, 1996.

Ranlet, Philip. *The New York Loyalists*. Knoxville: University of Tennessee Press, 1986.

Raphael, Ray. *The First American Revolution: Before Lexington and Concord*. New York: New Press, 2002.

———. *Founders: The People Who Brought You a Nation*. New York: New Press, 2009.

———. *A People's History of the American Revolution: How Common People Shaped the Fight for Independence*. New York: Perennial, 2002.

Rappleye, Charles. *Robert Morris: Financier of the American Revolution*. New York: Simon & Schuster, 2011.

Reed, John F. *Campaign to Valley Forge*. Union City, Tenn.: Pioneer Press, 1980.

Reed, William B., ed. *Life and Correspondence of Joseph Reed*. 2 vols. Philadelphia: Lindsay and Blakiston, 1847.

Reid, Arthur. *Reminiscences of the Revolution, or Le Loup's Bloody Trail*. Utica, N.Y.: Roberts, 1859.

Reid, Stuart. *British Redcoat, 1740–1793*. Botley, U.K.: Osprey, 1999.

Reiss, Oscar. *Medicine and the American Revolution*. Jefferson, N.C.: McFarland, 1998.

Renaut, Francis Paul. *L'Espionnage naval au XVIIIe siècle. Le Secret Service de l'Amirauté britannique au temps de la guerre d'Amérique, 1776–1783*. Paris: Editions du Graouli, 1936.

Report on American Manuscripts in the Royal Institution of Great Britain. Vol. 1. London: His Majesty's Stationery Office, 1904.

Resch, John, and Walter Sargent, eds. *War & Society in the American Revolution*. DeKalb: Northern Illinois University Press, 2007.

Reynolds, Paul R. *Guy Carleton: A Biography*. New York: William Morrow, 1980.

Richardson, Edgar P., Brooke Hindle, and Lillian B. Miller. *Charles Willson Peale and His World*. New York: Harry N. Abrams, 1982.

Riedesel, Frederika von. *Letters and Journals Relating to the War of American Independence and the Capture of the German Troops at Saratoga*. Translated by Claus Reuter. Scarborough, Ontario: German-Canadian Museum, n.d.

Risch, Erna. *Supplying Washington's Army*. Washington, D.C.: U.S. Army, 1986.

Ritcheson, Charles R. *British Politics and the American Revolution*. Norman: University of Oklahoma Press, 1954.

Roberts, Andrew. *The Last King of America: The Misunderstood Reign of George III*. New York: Viking, 2021.

———. *Napoleon: A Life*. New York: Penguin, 2015.

Robinson, Edward Forbes. *Continental Treasury Administration, 1775–1781: A Study in the Financial History of the American Revolution*. Madison: University of Wisconsin, 1969.

Robson, Eric. *The American Revolution, in Its Political and Military Aspects, 1763–1783*. New York: W. W. Norton, 1966.

Rodger, N.A.M. *The Command of the Ocean: A Naval History of Britain, 1649–1815*. London: Penguin Books, 2006.

———. *The Insatiable Earl: A Life of John Montagu, 4th Earl of Sandwich, 1718–1792*. London: HarperCollins, 1993.

———. *The Wooden World: An Anatomy of the Georgian Navy*. New York: W. W. Norton, 1996.

Rogers, Clifford J., Ty Seidule, and Samuel J. Watson, eds. *The West Point History of the American Revolution*. New York: Simon & Schuster, 2017.

Rogers, George C., Jr. *Charleston in the Age of the Pinckneys*. Columbia: University of South Carolina Press, 1980.

Ropp, Theodore. *War in the Modern World*. Baltimore: Johns Hopkins University Press, 2000.

Rose, Alexander. *Washington's Spies: The Story of America's First Spy Ring*. New York: Bantam, 2007.

Ross, Charles, ed. *The Correspondence of Charles, First Marquis Cornwallis*. Vol. 1. London: John Murray, 1859.

Rossie, Jonathan Gregory. *The Politics of Command in the American Revolution*. Syracuse, N.Y.: Syracuse University Press, 1975.

Rossman, Kenneth R. *Thomas Mifflin and the Politics of the American Revolution*. Chapel Hill: University of North Carolina Press, 1952.

Rosswurm, Steven. *Arms, Country, and Class: The Philadelphia Militia and the "Lower Sort" During the American Revolution, 1775–1783*. New Brunswick, N.J.: Rutgers University Press, 1987.

Royster, Charles. *A Revolutionary People at War: The Continental Army and American Character, 1775–1783*. Chapel Hill: University of North Carolina Press, 1979.

Ruddiman, John A. *Becoming Men of Some Consequence: Youth and Military Service in the Revolutionary War*. Charlottesville: University of Virginia Press, 2014.

Rudé, George. *Hanoverian London, 1714–1808*. Thrupp, U.K.: Sutton Publishing, 2003.

Ruttenber, E. M. *Obstructions to the Navigation of Hudson's River*. Albany, N.Y.: J. Munsell, 1860.

Ruville, Albert von. *William Pitt, Earl of Chatham*. Vol. 3. Translated by H. J. Chaytor. London: William Heinemann, 1907.

Ryan, Dennis P., ed. *A Salute to Courage: The American Revolution as Seen Through Wartime Writings of Officers of the Continental Army and Navy*. New York: Columbia University Press, 1979.

Saberton, Ian, ed. *The Cornwallis Papers: The Campaigns of 1780 and 1781*. Vol. 1. Uckfield, England: Naval & Military Press, 2010.

Sabine, Lorenzo. *The American Loyalists*. Boston: Charles C. Little and James Brown, 1847.

Sabine, William H. W., ed. *Historical Memoirs of William Smith*. 2 vols. New York: New York Times, 1969–71.

Sands, Robert C., ed. *Life and Correspondence of John Paul Jones*. New York: A. Chandler, 1830.

Sargent, Winthrop. *The Life and Career of Major John André, Adjutant-General of the British Army in America*. Boston: Ticknor and Fields, 1861.

Schaeper, Thomas J. *Edward Bancroft: Scientist, Author, Spy*. New Haven, Conn.: Yale University Press, 2011.

———. *France and America in the Revolutionary Era: The Life of Jacques-Donatien Leray de Chaumont, 1725–1803*. Providence, R.I.: Berghahn Books, 1995.

———. *John Paul Jones and the Battle of Flamborough Head: A Reconsideration*. New York: Peter Lang, 1989.

Schama, Simon. *Citizens: A Chronicle of the French Revolution*. New York: Vintage Books, 1990.

———. *A History of Britain*. Vol. 2, *The Wars of Britain, 1603–1776*. New York: Hyperion, 2001.

———. *Rough Crossings: Britain, the Slaves and the American Revolution*. New York: HarperCollins, 2007.

Scharf, J. Thomas, and Thompson Westcott. *History of Philadelphia, 1609–1884*. Vol. 1. Philadelphia: L. H. Everts, 1884.

Schecter, Barnet. *The Battle for New York: The City at the Heart of the American Revolution*. London: Pimlico/Random House, 2003.

Scheer, George F., and Hugh F. Rankin. *Rebels and Redcoats*. Cleveland: World Publishing, 1957.

Scheer, George F., and Russell F. Weigley. *Morristown: A History and Guide*. Washington, D.C.: U.S. Department of the Interior, 1983.

Schermerhorn, Frank Earle. *American and French Flags of the Revolution, 1775–1783*. Philadelphia: Pennsylvania Society of Sons of the Revolution, 1948.

Schiff, Stacy. *A Great Improvisation: Franklin, France, and the Birth of America*. New York: Henry Holt, 2006.

Schnitzer, Eric, and Don Troiani. *Campaign to Saratoga—1777*. Guilford, Conn.: Stackpole, 2019.

Schoenbrun, David. *Triumph in Paris: The Exploits of Benjamin Franklin*. New York: Harper & Row, 1976.

Schoonmaker, Marius. *The History of Kingston, New York*. New York: Burr Printing, 1888.

Schwab, John Christopher. *The Revolutionary History of Fort Number Eight*. New Haven, Conn.: privately printed, 1897.

Schwartz, Richard B. *Daily Life in Johnson's London*. Madison: University of Wisconsin Press, 1983.

Scott, H. M. *British Foreign Policy in the Age of the American Revolution*. Oxford, U.K.: Clarendon Press, 1990.

Scott, John Albert. *Fort Stanwix (Fort Schuyler) and Oriskany*. Rome, N.Y.: Rome Sentinel, 1927.

Scott, Kenneth. *Counterfeiting in Colonial America*. Philadelphia: University of Pennsylvania Press, 2000.

Sculley, Seanegan P. *Contest for Liberty: Military Leadership in the Continental Army, 1775–1783*. Yardley, Pa.: Westholme, 2019.

Seitz, Don C. *Paul Jones: His Exploits in English Seas During 1778–1780*. New York: E. P. Dutton, 1917.

Selby, John E. *The Revolution in Virginia, 1775–1783*. Williamsburg, Va.: Colonial Williamsburg Foundation, 2007.

Shorto, Russell. *Revolution Song: A Story of American Freedom*. New York: W. W. Norton, 2018.

Showman, Richard K., et al., eds. *The Papers of General Nathanael Greene*. 13 vols. Chapel Hill: University of North Carolina Press, 1976–2005.

Shreve, L. G. *Tench Tilghman: The Life and Times of Washington's Aide-de-Camp*. Centreville, Md.: Tidewater, 1982.

Shy, John. *A People Numerous and Armed: Reflections on the Military Struggle for American Independence*. Ann Arbor: University of Michigan Press, 2010.

Siebert, Wilbur H. *The Loyalists of Pennsylvania*. Columbus: Ohio State University, 1920.

Silverman, Kenneth. *A Cultural History of the American Revolution*. New York: Columbia University Press, 1987.

Simcoe, John Graves. *A Journal of the Operations of the Queen's Rangers*. Exeter, U.K.: printed for the author, 1789.

Simms, Jeptha R. *History of Schoharie County and Border Wars of New York*. Albany, N.Y.: Munsell & Tanner, 1845.

Simms, W. M. Gilmore, ed. *The Army Correspondence of Colonel John Laurens*. New York: Bradford Club, 1867.

Simpson, Helen, ed. *The Waiting City: Paris 1782–88*. Philadelphia: J. B. Lippincott, 1933.

Siry, Steven E. *Liberty's Fallen Generals: Leadership and Sacrifice in the American War of Independence*. Washington, D.C.: Potomac Books, 2012.

Skemp, Sheila L. *William Franklin: Son of a Patriot, Servant of a King*. New York: Oxford University Press, 1990.

Smith, Charles Daniel. *The Early Career of Lord North the Prime Minister*. London: Athlone Press, 1979.

Smith, Charles Page. *James Wilson, Founding Father, 1742–1798*. Chapel Hill: University of North Carolina Press, 1956.

Smith, Jean Edward. *John Marshall: Definer of a Nation*. New York: Henry Holt, 1996.

Smith, Paul H. *Loyalists and Redcoats: A Study in British Revolutionary Policy*. Chapel Hill: University of North Carolina Press, 1964.

Smith, Paul H., ed. *Letters of Delegates to Congress, 1774–1789*. 26 vols. Washington, D.C.: Library of Congress, 1976.

Smith, Robert F. *Manufacturing Independence: Industrial Innovation in the American Revolution*. Yardley, Pa.: Westholme, 2016.

Smith, Samuel Stelle. *Winter at Morristown, 1779–1780: The Darkest Hour*. Monmouth Beach, N.J.: Philip Freneau Press, 1979.

Smith, William Henry, ed. *The Life and Public Services of Arthur St. Clair*. Vol. 1. Cincinnati: Robert Clarke, 1882.

Smyth, B. *History of the XX Regiment, 1688–1888*. London: Simpkin, Marshall, 1889.

Smythe, Lillian C. *The Guardian of Marie Antoinette: Letters from the Comte de Mercy-Argenteau*. Vol. 2. London: Hutchinson, 1902.

Snow, Dean. *1777: Tipping Point at Saratoga*. New York: Oxford University Press, 2016.

Sparks, Jared, ed. *The Diplomatic Correspondence of the American Revolution*. Vol. 1. Boston: N. Hale and Gray & Bowen, 1829.

Spector, Margaret Marion. *The American Department of the British Government, 1768–1782.* New York: Columbia University Press, 1940.

Spero, Patrick, and Michael Zuckerman, eds. *The American Revolution Reborn*. Philadelphia: University of Pennsylvania Press, 2016.

Spring, Matthew H. *With Zeal and with Bayonets Only: The British Army on Campaign in North America, 1775–1783*. Norman: University of Oklahoma Press, 2008.

Spinney, David. *Rodney*. London: George Allen & Unwin, 1969.

St. Clair, Arthur. *A Narrative*. Philadelphia: Jane Aitken, 1812.

Stanley, George F. G., ed. *For Want of a Horse.* Sackville, New Brunswick: Tribune Press, 1961.

Stark, Caleb. *Memoir and Official Correspondence of Gen. John Stark.* Concord, N.H.: G. Parker Lyon, 1860.

Stegeman, John F., and Janet A. Stegeman. *Caty: A Biography of Catharine Littlefield Greene.* Athens: University of Georgia Press, 1985.

Steiner, Bernard C. *The Life and Correspondence of James McHenry.* Cleveland: Burrows Brothers, 1907.

Stephenson, Michael. *Patriot Battles: How the War of Independence Was Fought.* New York: Harper, 2008.

Sterner, Eric. *Till the Extinction of This Rebellion: George Rogers Clark, Frontier Warfare, and the Illinois Campaign of 1778–1779.* Yardley, Pa.: Westholme, 2024.

Steuart, A. Francis, ed. *The Last Journals of Horace Walpole, During the Reign of George III from 1771–1783.* Vol. 2. London: John Lane, 1910.

Stevens, Benjamin Franklin, ed. *General Sir William Howe's Orderly Book.* London: Benjamin Franklin Stevens, 1890.

Stevens, Benjamin Franklin. *B. F. Stevens's Facsimiles of Manuscripts in European Archives Relating to America, 1773–1783.* 25 vols. London: Malby & Sons, 1889–98.

Stevens, Robert White. *On the Stowage of Ships and Their Cargoes.* Plymouth, U.K.: Stevens, 1858.

Stewart, David O. *George Washington: The Political Rise of America's Founding Father.* New York: Dutton, 2021.

Stiles, Henry. *A History of the City of Brooklyn.* 2 vols. Brooklyn: published by subscription, 1867.

Stillé, Charles J. *Major-General Anthony Wayne and the Pennsylvania Line in the Continental Army.* Philadelphia: J. B. Lippincott, 1893.

Stinchcombe, William C. *The American Revolution and the French Alliance.* Syracuse, N.Y.: Syracuse University Press, 1969.

Stockwell, Mary. *Unlikely General: "Mad" Anthony Wayne and the Battle for America.* New Haven, Conn.: Yale University Press, 2018.

Stoker, Donald, Kenneth J. Hagan, and Michael T. McMaster, eds. *Strategy in the American War of Independence: A Global Approach.* London: Routledge, 2011.

Stokes, I. N. Phelps. *The Iconography of Manhattan Island, 1498–1909.* 6 vols. New York: Robert H. Dodd, 1915–28.

Stone, William L., [Jr.]. *The Campaign of Lieut. Gen. John Burgoyne and the Expedition of Lieut. Col. Barry St. Leger.* Albany, N.Y.: Joel Munsell, 1877.

———. *Journal of Captain Pausch.* Albany: N.Y.: Joel Munsell's Sons, 1886.

———. trans. *Letters of Brunswick and Hessian Officers During the American Revolution.* Albany, N.Y.: Joel Munsell's Sons, 1891.

———, ed. *Memoirs, and Letters and Journals of Major General Riedesel.* Translated by Max von Eelking. Albany, N.Y.: J. Munsell, 1868.

Stone, William L., [Sr.]. *Life of Joseph Brant, Thayendanegea.* 2 vols. New York: Alexander V. Blake, 1838.

Storozynski, Alex. *The Peasant Prince: Thaddeus Kosciuszko and the Age of Revolution.* New York: St. Martin's Griffin, 2010.

Stourzh, Gerald. *Benjamin Franklin and American Foreign Policy.* Chicago: University of Chicago Press, 1954.

Stryker, William S. *The Battle of Monmouth.* Princeton, N.J.: Princeton University Press, 1927.

———. *The Forts on the Delaware in the Revolutionary War.* Trenton, N.J.: John L. Murphy, 1901.

———. *The Massacre near Old Tappan.* Trenton, N.J.: Naar, Day and Naar, 1882.

Stuart-Wortley, Mrs. E. [Violet], ed. *A Prime Minister and His Son: From the Correspondence of the Third Earl of Bute, and of Lt.-General the Hon. Sir Charles Stuart.* New York: E. P. Dutton, 1925.

Sullivan, Aaron. *The Disaffected: Britain's Occupation of Philadelphia During the American Revolution.* Philadelphia: University of Pennsylvania Press, 2019.

Sumner, William Graham. *The Financier and the Finances of the American Revolution.* Vol. 1. New York: Dodd, Mead, 1891.

Sweetman, Jack, ed. *Great American Naval Battles.* Annapolis, Md.: Naval Institute Press, 1998.

Swiggett, Howard. *War Out of Niagara: Walter Butler and the Tory Rangers.* New York: Columbia University Press, 1933.

Swisher, James K. *The Revolutionary War in the Southern Back Country.* Gretna, La.: Pelican Publishing, 2012.

Syrett, David. *Admiral Lord Howe.* Annapolis, Md.: Naval Institute Press, 2006.

———. *The Royal Navy in American Waters, 1775–1783.* Aldershot, England: Scholar Press, 1989.

———. *The Royal Navy in European Waters During the American Revolutionary War.* Columbia: University of South Carolina Press, 1998.

———. *Shipping and Military Power in the Seven Years War.* Exeter, U.K.: University of Exeter Press, 2008.

———. *Shipping and the American War, 1775–1783: A Study of British Transport Organization.* London: University of London, Athlone Press, 1970.

Syrett, Harold C., ed. *The Papers of Alexander Hamilton.* Vols. 1 and 2. New York: Columbia University Press, 1961.

Taaffe, Stephen R. *The Philadelphia Campaign, 1777–1778.* Lawrence: University Press of Kansas, 2003.

———. *Washington's Revolutionary War Generals.* Norman: University of Oklahoma Press, 2019.

Tallmadge, Benjamin. *Memoir of Colonel Benjamin Tallmadge.* New York: Gilliss Press, 1904.

Tarleton, Banastre. *A History of the Campaigns of 1780 and 1781.* London: T. Cadell, 1787.

Tatum, Edward H., Jr., ed. *The American Journal of Ambrose Serle.* San Marino, Calif.: Huntington Library, 1940.

Taylor, Alan. *American Revolutions: A Continental History, 1750–1804.* New York: W. W. Norton, 2016.

———. *The Divided Ground: Indians, Settlers, and the Northern Borderlands of the American Revolution.* New York: Knopf, 2006.

———. *The Internal Enemy: Slavery and War in Virginia, 1772–1832.* New York: W. W. Norton, 2014.

Taylor, Robert J., et al., eds. *Papers of John Adams.* 17 vols. Cambridge, Mass.: Harvard University Press, 1977–2014.

Thacher, James. *Military Journal, During the American Revolutionary War.* Hartford, Conn.: Silas Andrus & Son, 1854.

Thackeray, William Makepeace. *The Four Georges.* London: Blackie & Son, n.d.

Thane, Elswyth. *Washington's Lady.* New York: Dodd, Mead, 1960.

Tharp, Louis Hall. *The Baroness and the General.* Boston: Little, Brown, 1962.

Thayer, Theodore. *The Making of a Scapegoat: Washington and Lee at Monmouth.* Port Washington, N.Y.: Kennikat Press, 1976.

———. *Nathanael Greene: Strategist of the American Revolution.* New York: Twayne Publishers, 1960.

Thomas, Evan. *John Paul Jones: Sailor, Hero, Father of the American Navy.* New York: Simon & Schuster, 2003.

Thomas, George. *Memoirs of the Marquis of Rockingham and His Contemporaries.* Vol. 2. London: Richard Bentley, 1852.

Thomas, P.D.G. *The House of Commons in the Eighteenth Century.* Oxford, U.K.: Clarendon Press, 1971.

Thomas, Peter D. G. *Lord North.* New York: St. Martin's, 1976.

Thompson, Mary V. *"The Only Unavoidable Subject of Regret": George Washington, Slavery, and the Enslaved Community at Mount Vernon.* Charlottesville: University of Virginia Press, 2019.

Thompson, Ray. *Benedict Arnold in Philadelphia.* Fort Washington, Pa.: Bicentennial Press, 1975.

Thompson, William Y. *Israel Shreve, Revolutionary War Officer.* Ruston, La.: McGinty Trust Fund Publication, 1979.

Thorp, Jennifer D., ed. *The Acland Journal: Lady Harriet Acland and the American War.* Winchester, U.K.: Hampshire County Council, 1993.

Tiedemann, Joseph S., Eugene R. Fingerhut, and Robert W. Venables, eds. *The Other Loyalists: Ordinary People, Royalism, and the Revolution in the Middle Colonies, 1763–1787.* Albany, N.Y.: State University of New York Press, 2009.

Tilley, John A. *The British Navy and the American Revolution.* Columbia: University of South Carolina Press, 1987.

Tilley, S. D., et al., eds. *Journals of the Continental Congress, 1774–1789.* 34 vols. Washington, D.C.: Government Printing Office, 1904–37.

Toll, Ian W. *Six Frigates: The Epic History of the Founding of the U.S. Navy.* New York: W. W. Norton, 2008.

Tower, Charlemagne. *The Marquis de La Fayette in the American Revolution.* Vol. 1. Philadelphia: J. B. Lippincott, 1901.

Town, Ithiel. *A Detail of Some Particular Services Performed in America.* New York: G. F. Hopkins, 1835.

Townsend, Joseph. *Some Account of the British Army.* Philadelphia: Townsend Ward, 1846.

Toynbee, Paget, ed. *The Letters of Horace Walpole, Fourth Earl of Orford.* Vols. 10 and 11. Oxford: Clarendon Press, 1904.

Tracy, Michael W. *266 Days: Eye-witness Accounts of the British Occupation of Philadelphia.* Minneapolis: Mill City Press, 2015.

Trevelyan, George Otto. *The American Revolution.* Edited by Richard B. Morris. New York: David McKay, 1964.

———. *The American Revolution.* Vol. 4. *Saratoga ad Brandywine, Valley Forge, England and France at War.* London: Longmans, Green, 1912.

———. *The Early History of Charles James Fox.* London: Longmans, Green, 1880.

Trumbull, John. *Autobiography, Reminiscences and Letters of John Trumbull.* New York: Wiley and Putnam, 1841.

Trussell, John B. B., Jr. *Birthplace of an Army: A Study of the Valley Forge Encampment.* Harrisburg, Pa.: Pennsylvania Historical and Museum Commission, 1976.

———. *Epic on the Schuylkill.* Harrisburg, Pa.: Pennsylvania Historical and Museum Commission, 1992.

Tuchman, Barbara W. *The March of Folly: From Troy to Vietnam.* New York: Ballantine Books, 1985.

Tucker, Phillip Thomas. *Brothers in Liberty: The Story of the Free Black Haitians Who Fought for American Independence.* Lanham, Md.: Stackpole, 2023.

Tuckerman, Bayard. *Life of General Philip Schuyler.* New York: Dodd, Mead, 1904.

Uhlendorf, Bernhard A., trans. and annot. *Revolution in America: Confidential Letters and Journals, 1776–1784, of Adjutant General Major Baurmeister of the Hessian Forces.* New Brunswick, N.J.: Rutgers University Press, 1957.

———, trans. and ed. *The Siege of Charleston.* Ann Arbor: University of Michigan Press, 1938.

Upham, William P. *Memoir of General John Glover of Marblehead.* Salem, Mass.: Charles W. Swasey, 1863.

Urban, Mark. *Fusiliers: The Saga of a British Redcoat Regiment in the American Revolution.* New York: Walker, 2008.

Unger, Harlow Giles. *Lafayette.* Hoboken, N.J.: John Wiley & Sons, 2002.

Valentine, D. T. *Manual of the Corporation of the City of New York.* New York: Edmund Jones, 1863.

Van Alstyne, Richard W. *Empire and Independence: The International History of the American Revolution.* New York: John Wiley & Sons, 1967.

Van Buskirk, Judith L. *Standing in Their Own Light: African American Patriots in the American Revolution.* Norman: University of Oklahoma Press, 2018.

Van der Oye, David Schimmelpenninck. *Remembering Their Gallantry in Former Days: A History of the Queen's York Rangers.* Toronto: Double Dagger Books, 2010.

Van Doren, Adam. *In the Founders' Footsteps: Landmarks of the American Revolution.* Boston: Godine, 2022.

Van Doren, Carl. *Benjamin Franklin.* New York: Book-of-the-Month-Club, 1980.

———. *Secret History of the American Revolution.* New York: Viking, 1941.

Van Tyne, Claude Halstead. *The War of Independence: American Phase.* Boston: Houghton Mifflin, 1929.

———. *The Loyalists in the American Revolution*. New York: Macmillan, 1902.

Venter, Bruce M. *The Battle of Hubbardton*. Charleston, S.C.: History Press, 2015.

Volo, James M. *Blue Water Patriots: The American Revolution Afloat*. Lanham, Md.: Rowman & Littlefield, 2007.

Wade, Herbert T., and Robert A. Lively. *This Glorious Cause: The Adventures of Two Company Officers in Washington's Army*. Princeton, N.J.: Princeton University Press, 1958.

Walcott, Charles H. *Sir Archibald Campbell of Inverneill*. Boston: Beacon Press, 1898.

Walker, Paul K. *Engineers of Independence: A Documentary History of the Army Engineers in the American Revolution, 1775–1783*. Washington, D.C.: Office of the Chief of Engineers, 1981.

Wallace, David Duncan. *The Life of Henry Laurens*. New York: G. P. Putnam's Sons, 1915.

Wallace, John William. *An Old Philadelphian, Colonel William Bradford, the Patriot Printer of 1776*. Philadelphia: Sherman, 1884.

Wallace, Willard M. *Traitorous Hero: The Life and Fortunes of Benedict Arnold*. New York: Harper & Brothers, 1954.

Walsh, John Evangelist. *Night on Fire*. New York: McGraw-Hill, 1978.

Ward, Christopher. *The War of the Revolution*. New York: Skyhorse, 2011.

Ward, Harry M. *Charles Scott and the "Spirit of '76."* Charlottesville: University Press of Virginia, 1988.

———. *Duty, Honor or Country: General George Weedon and the American Revolution*. Philadelphia: American Philosophical Society, 1979.

———. *George Washington's Enforcers: Policing the Continental Army*. Carbondale: Southern Illinois University Press, 2006.

———. *Major General Adam Stephen and the Cause of American Liberty*. Charlottesville: University Press of Virginia, 1989.

Warner, Sam Bass, Jr. *The Private City: Philadelphia in Three Periods of Its Growth*. Philadelphia: University of Pennsylvania Press, 1987.

Watson, J. Steven. *The Reign of George III, 1760–1815*. London: Clarendon Press, 1960.

Watson, John F., and Willis P. Hazard. *Annals of Philadelphia, and Pennsylvania, in the Olden Time*. 3 vols. Philadelphia: Edwin S. Stuart, 1891.

Watt, Gavin K. *Rebellion in the Mohawk Valley: The St. Leger Expedition of 1777*. Toronto: Dundurn Group, 2002.

Weber, Ralph E. *Masked Dispatches: Cryptograms and Cryptology in American History, 1775–1900*. Washington, D.C.: National Security Agency Center for Cryptologic History, 2013.

Weddle, Kevin J. *The Compleat Victory: Saratoga and the American Revolution*. New York: Oxford University Press, 2021.

Wehrman, Andrew M. *The Contagion of Liberty: The Politics of Smallpox in the American Revolution*. Baltimore: Johns Hopkins University Press, 2022.

Weigley, Russell F. *History of the United States Army*. Bloomington: Indiana University Press, 1984.

Weigley, Russell F., ed. *Philadelphia: A 300-Year History*. New York: W. W. Norton, 1982.

Weintraub, Stanley. *Iron Tears: America's Battle for Freedom, Britain's Quagmire*. New York: Free Press, 2005.

Wertenbaker, Thomas Jefferson. *Father Knickerbocker Rebels: New York City During the Revolution*. New York: Cooper Square Publishers, 1969.

Wharton, Francis, ed. *The Revolutionary Diplomatic Correspondence of the United States*. Vols. 1–3. Washington D.C.: Government Printing Office, 1889.

Wheatley, Henry B., ed. *The Historical and the Posthumous Memoirs of Sir Nathaniel William Wraxall, 1772–1784*. Vol. 1. London: Bickers & Son, 1884.

Whinyates, F. A., ed. *The Services of Lieut.-Colonel Francis Downman, R.A.* Woolwich, U.K.: Royal Artillery Institution, 1898.

White, George. *Historical Recollections of Georgia*. New York: Pudney & Russell, 1855.

White, Jerry. *A Great and Monstrous Thing: London in the Eighteenth Century*. Cambridge, Mass.: Harvard University Press, 2013.

White, Lee M. *The American Revolution in Notes, Quotes, and Anecdotes*. Fairfax, Va.: L. B. Prince, 1975.

Whiteley, Peter. *Lord North: The Prime Minister Who Lost America.* London: Hambledon Press, 1996.

Whittemore, Charles P. *A General of the Revolution: John Sullivan of New Hampshire.* New York: Columbia University Press, 1961.

Wickwire, Franklin B. *British Subministers and Colonial America, 1763–1783.* Princeton, N.J.: Princeton University Press, 1966.

Wickwire, Franklin, and Mary Wickwire. *Cornwallis: The American Adventure.* Boston: Houghton Mifflin, 1970.

Wiencek, Henry. *An Imperfect God: George Washington, His Slaves, and the Creation of America.* New York: Farrar, Straus and Giroux, 2003.

Wildes, Harry Emerson. *Anthony Wayne: Trouble Shooter of the American Revolution.* New York: Harcourt, Brace, 1941.

Wilkin, W. H. *Some British Soldiers in America.* London: Hugh Rees, 1914.

Wilkinson, James. *Memoirs of My Own Times.* Vol. 1. Philadelphia: Abraham Small, 1816.

Willcox, William B., ed. *The Papers of Benjamin Franklin.* Vols. 21–23. New Haven, Conn.: Yale University Press, 1978–83.

———. *Portrait of a General: Sir Henry Clinton in the War of Independence.* New York: Knopf, 1964.

Willett, William M. *A Narrative of the Military Actions of Colonel Marinus Willett.* New York: G. & C. & H. Carvill, 1831.

Williams, Basil. *The Life of William Pitt, Earl of Chatham.* Vol. 2. London: Longmans, Green, 1914.

Williams, Catherine R. *Biography of Revolutionary Heroes.* New York: Wiley & Putnam, 1839.

Williams, George W. *St. Michael's: Charleston, 1751–1951.* Columbia: University of South Carolina Press, 1951.

Williams, Glenn F. *Year of the Hangman: George Washington's Campaign Against the Iroquois.* Yardley, Pa.: Westholme, 2006.

Williams, John. *The Battle of Hubbardton.* Vermont Division for Historic Preservation, 1988.

Willis, Sam. *The Struggle for Sea Power: A Naval History of American Independence.* London: Atlantic Books, 2015.

Wilson, David K. *The Southern Strategy: Britain's Conquest of South Carolina and Georgia, 1775–1780.* Columbia: University of South Carolina Press, 2008.

Wilson, Derek. *The Tower of London: A Thousand Years.* London: Allison & Busby, 1998.

Winfield, Rif. *British Warships in the Age of Sail, 1714–1792.* Barnsley, U.K.: Seaforth, 2007.

Wood, Gordon S. *The Americanization of Benjamin Franklin.* New York: Penguin, 2005.

———. *The Creation of the American Republic 1776–1787.* Chapel Hill: University of North Carolina Press, 1998.

———. *The Idea of America.* New York: Penguin, 2012.

———. *The Radicalism of the American Revolution.* New York: Vintage, 1993.

———. *Revolutionary Characters.* New York: Penguin, 2007.

Wright, Esmond. *Franklin of Philadelphia.* Cambridge, Mass.: Belknap Press, 1997.

Wright, Robert K., Jr. *The Continental Army.* Washington, D.C.: U.S. Army, 1983.

Zambone, Albert Louis. *Daniel Morgan: A Revolutionary Life.* Yardley, Pa.: Westholme Publishing, 2018.

Zucker, A. E. *General De Kalb, Lafayette's Mentor.* Chapel Hill: University of North Carolina Press, 1966.

Zweig, Stefan. *Marie Antoinette.* Translated by Eden and Cedar Paul. London: Pushkin Press, 2010.

PERIODICALS

Abbott, Carl. "The Neighborhoods of New York, 1760–1775." *New York History,* vol. 55, no. 1 (Jan. 1974): 35+.

Abernethy, Thomas P. "Commercial Activities of Silas Deane in France." *AHR,* vol. 39, no. 3 (Apr. 1934): 477+.

"Account of the Battle of Bennington, by Glich, a German Officer Who Was in the Engagement, Under Col. Baum." *Collection of the Vermont Historical Society,* vol. 1 (1870): 211+.

"Account of the Siege of Savannah, from a British Source." *Collections of the Georgia Historical Society,* vol. 5, no. 1 (1901): 129+.

"African Americans and Native Americans of the Revolutionary War Era Who Should Be Better Remembered." *JAR*, Feb. 15, 2022.

Adelberg, Michael S. " 'So Dangerous a Quarter': The Sandy Hook Lighthouse During the American Revolution." *Keeper's Log* (Spring 1995): 10+.

Agnew, Daniel, and Richard Howell. "A Biographical Sketch of Governor Richard Howell, of New Jersey." *PMHB*, vol. 22, no. 2 (1898): 221+.

Alexander, David E., ed. "Diary of Captain Benjamin Warren on Battlefield of Saratoga." *Journal of American History*, vol. 3, no. 2 (1909): 201+.

———, ed. "Diary of Captain Benjamin Warren at Massacre of Cherry Valley." *Journal of American History*, vol. 3, no. 3 (1909): 377+.

Alexander, John K. "The Fort Wilson Incident of 1779." *WMQ*, vol. 34, no. 4 (Oct. 1974): 580+.

Allen, James. "Diary of James Allen, Esq., of Philadelphia, Counsellor-at-Law, 1770–1778." 3 parts. *PMHB*, vol. 9, no. 2 (July 1885), no. 3 (Oct. 1885), no. 4 (Jan. 1886): 176+ (continuous pagination).

Almy, Mary. "Mrs. Almy's Journal." *Newport Historical Magazine*, vol. 1 (1880–81): 17+.

André, John. "Major André's Account." *Century*, vol. 47 (1894): 687+.

Applegate, Howard Lewis. "Remedial Medicine in the American Revolutionary Army." *Military Medicine* (June 1961): 451+.

Arndt, Karl J. R. "New Hampshire and the Battle of Bennington: Colonel Baum's Mission and Bennington Defeat as Reported by a German Officer Under General Burgoyne's Command." *Historical New Hampshire*, vol. 32 (Winter 1977): 198+.

Atkinson, C. T. "Some Evidence for Burgoyne's Expedition." *Journal of the Society for Army Historical Research*, vol. 26, no. 108 (Winter 1948): 132+.

Atkinson, Rick. "Brothers in Arms." *New York Times Book Review*, July 20, 2021, 14.

Bache, Richard Meade, and Benjamin Franklin. "Franklin's Ceremonial Coat." *PMHB*, vol. 23, no. 4 (1889): 444+.

Baker, William S. "Itinerary of General Washington from June 15, 1775, to December 23, 1783." *PMHB*, vols. 14–15 (1890–91).

Bailyn, Bernard. "Butterfield's Adams: Notes for a Sketch." *WMQ*, vol. 19, no. 2 (Apr. 1962): 238+.

Bain, James, Jr., ed. "The Siege of Charleston: Journal of Captain Peter Russell, December 25, 1779, to May 2, 1780." *AHR*, vol. 4, no. 3 (Apr. 1889): 478+.

Balderston, Marion. "Lord Howe Clears the Delaware." *PMHB*, vol. 96, no. 3 (July 1972): 326+.

Baldwin, Samuel. "Diary of Events in Charleston, S.C., from March 20th to April 20th, 1780." Edited by A. B. Thompson. *Proceedings of the New Jersey Historical Society*, vol. 2, no. 2 (1847): 771.

"Bamford's Diary: The Revolutionary Diary of a British Officer." *Maryland Historical Magazine*, vol. 27, no. 3 (Sept. 1932): 240+.

Barbieri, Michael. "Brown's Raid on Ticonderoga and Mount Independence." *JAR*, Jan. 20, 2022.

———. "Guns on Mount Defiance." *JAR*, Sept. 26, 2021.

———. "In Defense of Mount Independence." *JAR*, July 27, 2021.

Barker, Thomas M. "The Battles of Saratoga and the Kinderhook Tea Party: The Campaign Diary of a Junior Officer of Baron Riedesel's Musketeer Regiment in the 1777 British Invasion of New York." *JSHA*, vol. 9 (2006): 25+.

Bauer, Jean. "With Friends Like These: John Adams and the Comte de Vergennes on Franco-American Relations." *Diplomatic History*, vol. 37, no. 4 (2013): 664+.

Becker, Ann M. "Smallpox in Washington's Army." *JMH*, vol. 68, no. 2 (Apr. 2004): 381+.

Bell, Andrew. "Journal of Andrew Bell, Secretary of General Clinton." *Proceedings of the New Jersey Historical Society*, vol. 6 (1853), 15+.

Bemis, Samuel Flagg. "Secret Intelligence, 1777: Two Documents." *Huntington Library Quarterly*, vol. 24, no. 3 (May 1961): 233+.

Biddulph, Violet. "Letters of Robert Biddulph, 1779–1783." *AHR*, vol. 29, no. 1 (Oct. 1923): 87+.

Bird, Harrison K. "Uniform of the Black Watch in America, 1776–1783." *Journal of the American Military History Foundation*, vol. 2, no. 3 (Fall 1938): 171+.

Blanco, Richard L. "American Army Hospitals in Pennsylvania During the Revolutionary War." *Pennsylvania History*, vol. 48, no. 4 (Oct. 1981): 347+.

Bleyer, Bill. "George Washington's Culper Spy Ring: Separating Fact from Fiction." *JAR*, June 3, 2021.

Boan, Matthew T. "Mapmaking and the U.S. Army." *Army History* (Spring 2021): 26+.

Bourne, Russell. "The Penobscot Fiasco." *American Heritage*, vol. 25, no. 6 (Oct. 1974), https://www.americanheritage.com/penobscot-fiasco#.

Boyle, Joseph Lee. "From Saratoga to Valley Forge: The Diary of Lt. Samuel Armstrong." *PMHB*, vol. 121, no. 3 (July 1997): 237+.

Bradford, S. Sydney, ed. "A British Officer's Revolutionary War Journal, 1776–1778." *Maryland Historical Magazine*, vol. 56, no. 2 (June 1961): 150+.

———. "Lord Francis Napier's Journal of the Burgoyne Campaign." *Maryland Historical Magazine*, vol. 57, no. 4 (Dec. 1962): 285+.

Braisted, Todd W. "The American Vicars of Bray." *JAR*, Nov. 3, 2015.

Brewington, M. V. "The Designs of Our First Frigates." *American Neptune*, vol. 8 (Jan. 1948): 10+.

Brooks, John Nixon, and Tobias Lear. "Extracts from the Journal of Surgeon Ebenezer Elmer of the New Jersey Continental Line, Sept. 11–19, 1777." *PMHB*, vol. 35, no. 1 (1911): 103+.

Broomfield, J. H. "The Keppel-Palliser Affair, 1778–1779." *Mariner's Mirror*, vol. 47, no. 3 (Aug. 1961): 195+

———. "Lord Sandwich at the Admiralty Board: Politics and the British Navy, 1771–1778." *Mariner's Mirror*, vol. 51, no. 1 (Feb. 1965): 7+.

Brown, Gerald S. "The Anglo-American Naval Crisis, 1778: A Study of Conflict in the North Cabinet." *WMQ*, third series, vol. 13, no. 1 (Jan. 1956): 3+.

Brown, Jared A. "A Note on British Military Theatre in New York at the End of the American Revolution." *New York History*, vol. 62, no. 2 (Apr. 1981): 177+.

Buck, William J. "Washington's Encampment on the Neshaminy." *PMHB*, vol. 1, no. 3 (1877): 275+.

Burgoyne, Bruce E., trans. "Journal Kept by the Distinguished Hessian Field Jaeger Corps During the Campaigns of the Royal Army of Great Britain in North America." 2 parts. *JSHA*, vols. 3 and 4 (1987–88): 45+ and 23+.

Burns, Brian. "Massacre or Muster? Burgoyne's Indians and the Militia at Bennington." *Proceedings of the Vermont Historical Society*, vol. 45, no. 3 (Summer 1977): 133+.

Cecere, Michael. "The Penobscot Expedition of 1779." *JAR*, Aug. 8, 2019.

Clark, Jane. "Responsibility for the Failure of the Burgoyne Campaign." *AHR*, vol. 35, no. 3 (Apr. 1930): 542+.

Clark, Joseph. "Diary of Joseph Clark, Attached to the Continental Army." *Proceedings of the New Jersey Historical Society*, vol. 7 (1855): 93+.

Clinton, Henry. "Sir Henry Clinton's 'Journal of the Siege of Charleston, 1780.'" Edited by William T. Bulger. *South Carolina Historical Magazine*, vol. 66, no. 3 (July 1965): 147+.

Cock, Randolph. "'The Finest Invention in the World': The Royal Navy's Early Trials of Copper Sheathing." *Mariner's Mirror*, vol. 87, no. 4 (2001): 446+.

Coffin, Charles Carleton. "Diary of Capt. Peter Kimball, 1776." *Granite Monthly* (Mar. 1881): 230+.

Coleman, John M. "Joseph Galloway and the British Occupation of Philadelphia." *Pennsylvania History*, vol. 30, no. 3 (July 1963): 272+.

"Col. John Brown's Attack of September 1777 on Fort Ticonderoga." *BFTM*, vol. 11, no. 4 (July 1964): 208–9.

"Col. John Brown's Expedition Against Ticonderoga and Diamond Island, 1777." *New England Historical and Genealogical Register*, vol. 74 (Oct. 1920): 284+.

"Col. John Eager Howard's Account of the Battle of Germantown." *Maryland Historical Magazine*, vol. 4 (1909): 314+.

"Colonel Brooks and Captain Bancroft." *Proceedings of the Massachusetts Historical Society*, vol. 3 (1855–58): 265+.

Conway, Stephen. "British Mobilization in the War of American Independence." *Historical Research*, vol. 72, no. 177 (Feb. 1999): 58+.

———. "From Fellow-Nationals to Foreigners: British Perceptions of the Americans, Circa 1739–1783." *WMQ*, third series, vol. 59, no. 1 (Jan. 2002): 65+.

———. "The Politics of British Military and Naval Mobilization, 1775–1783." *English Historical Review*, vol. 112, no. 449 (Nov. 1997): 1179+.

——— . "To Subdue America: British Army Officers and the Conduct of the Revolutionary War." *WMQ*, third series, vol. 43, no. 3 (July 1986): 381+.

Conway, Stephen R. "The Recruitment of Criminals into the British Army, 1775–1781." *Bulletin of the Institute of Historical Research*, vol. 58 (1985): 46+.

Cook, Fred J. "Allan McLane, Unknown Hero of the Revolution." *American Heritage*, vol. 7, no. 6 (Oct. 1956): 74+.

"Correspondence of the Brothers Joshua and Jedidiah Huntington During the Period of the American Revolution." *Collections of the Connecticut Historical Society*, vol. 20 (1923).

Corwin, Edward S. "The French Objective in the American Revolution." *AHR*, vol. 21 (1915–16): 33+.

Coudray, Philippe Charles Tronson du. "Observations on the Forts Intended for the Defense of the Two Passages of the River Delaware." *PMHB*, vol. 24, no. 3 (1900): 343+.

Cross, Jack L., and Thomas Pinckney. "Letters of Thomas Pinckney, 1775–1780." *South Carolina Historical Magazine*, vol. 58, no. 1 and no. 4 (Jan. and Oct. 1957): 19+ and 224+.

Cruger, John Harris. "The Siege of Savannah, 1779." *Magazine of American History*, vol. 2 (1878): 489+.

Curtis, Edward E. "The Provisioning of the British Army in the Revolution." *Magazine of History*, vol. 18 (Jan.–June 1914): 240+.

Cutter, William Richard. "A Yankee Privateersman in Prison in England, 1777–1779." *New-England Historical and Genealogical Register* (Apr. 1876): 174+.

Dacus, Jeff. "Again the Hero: David Wooster's Final Battle." *JAR*, Apr. 12, 2018.

Davidson, Philip G. "Whig Propagandists of the American Revolution." *AHR*, vol. 39, no. 3 (Apr. 1934): 442+.

Davis, Andrew McFarland. "The Employment of Indian Auxiliaries in the American War." *English Historical Review*, vol. 2, no. 8 (Oct. 1887): 709+.

Davis, Robert Scott. "Black Haitian Soldiers at the Siege of Savannah." *JAR*, Feb. 22, 2021.

Davis, Robert Scott, Jr. "The Loyalist Trials at Ninety Six in 1779." *South Carolina Historical Magazine*, vol. 80, no. 2 (Apr. 1979): 172+.

Denman, Jeffrey A. "Fighting for Forage." *MHQ*, vol. 26, no. 3 (Spring 2014): 51+.

Depeyre, Michel. "When *La Victoire* Carried the Hopes of Lafayette." *Le Fil*, no. 25 (Apr. 2013): 30+.

"The Deputy Adjutant General's Orderly Book." *BFTM*, vol. 3, no. 2 (July 1933): 88+.

"Diary of Joshua Pell, Junior, an Officer of the British Army in America, 1776–1777." *Magazine of American History*, vol. 2, part 1 (1878): 107+.

"Diary of Rev. Benjamin Boardman." Massachusetts Historical Society, *Proceedings* (May 1892), 400+.

Diestelow, Kevin. "The Fort Wilson Riot and Pennsylvania's Republican Formation." *JAR*, Feb. 28, 2019.

Doblin, Helga B., trans. and ed. "Journal of Lt. Colonel Christian Julius Prätorius." *BFTM*, vol. 15, no. 3 (Winter 1991): 62+.

Doblin, Helga B., and Mary C. Lynn. "A Brunswick Grenadier with Burgoyne: The Journal of Johann Bense, 1776–1783." *New York History*, vol. 66, no. 4 (Oct. 1985): 420+.

Dorney, Douglas R., Jr. "A Demographic View of the Georgia Continental Line and Militia: 1775–1783." *JAR*, Feb. 23, 2022.

Duling, Ennis. "Thomas Anburey at the Battle of Hubbardton: How a Fraudulent Source Misled Historians." *Vermont History*, vol. 78, no. 1 (Winter–Spring 2010): 1+.

Dull, Jonathan R. "Franklin the Diplomat: The French Mission." *Transactions of the American Philosophical Society*, new series, vol. 72, no. 1 (1982): 1+.

——— . "Mahan, Sea Power, and the War for American Independence." *International History Review*, vol. 10, no. 1 (Feb. 1988): 59+.

——— . "Was the Continental Navy a Mistake?" *American Neptune*, vol. 44, no. 3 (Summer 1984): 167+.

Du Ponceau, Peter Stephen, and James L. Whitehead. "The Autobiography of Peter Stephen Du Ponceau." *PMHB*, vol. 63, no. 2 (Apr. 1939): 189+.

Ecelbarger, Gary. "Did Charles Lee Disobey George Washington's Attack Order at Monmouth?" *JAR*, Mar. 7, 2024.

———. "The Feint That Never Happened: Unheralded Turning Point of the Philadelphia Campaign." *JAR*, Nov. 19, 2020.

———. "The First Four Days at Valley Forge." *JAR*, Dec. 8, 2022.

———. "Permanent Losses and New Gains During the 1778 Valley Forge Encampment." *JAR*, Feb. 15, 2024.

———. "Washington's Head of Elk Reconnaissance: A New Letter (and an Old Receipt)." *JAR*, Apr. 16, 2020.

Edgerton, Samuel Y., Jr. "The Murder of Jane McCrea: The Tragedy of an American *Tableau d'Histoire*." *Art Bulletin*, vol. 47, no. 4 (Dec. 1965): 481+.

Edwards, William Waller. "Morgan and His Riflemen." *WMQ*, vol. 23, no. 2 (Oct. 1914): 73+.

"An English Journal of the Siege of Savannah in 1779." *Historical Magazine*, vol. 8 (1864): 12+.

"Extracts from the Letter Book of Captain Johann Heinrichs [*sic*] of the Hessian *Jäger* Corps, 1778–1780." *PMHB*, vol. 22, no. 2 (1898): 137+.

Farmer, Edward G. "Skenesborough: Continental Navy Shipyard." U.S. Naval Institute, *Proceedings*, vol. 90 (Oct. 1964): 160+.

Fenn, Elizabeth A. "Biological Warfare in Eighteenth-Century North America: Beyond Jeffrey Amherst." *Journal of American History*, vol. 86, no 4 (Mar. 2000): 1552+.

Fleming, Thomas. "The Enigma of General Howe." *American Heritage*, vol. 15, no. 2 (Feb. 1964), https://www.americanheritage.com/enigma-general-howe.

———. "The 'Military Crimes' of Charles Lee." *American Heritage*, vol. 19, no. 3 (Apr. 1968): 12+.

Flick, A. C. "New Sources on the Sullivan-Clinton Campaign in 1779." 2 parts. *Quarterly Journal of the New York State Historical Association*, vol. 10, no. 3 and no. 4 (July and Oct. 1929): 185+ and 265+.

Folsom, William R. "The Battle of Hubbardton." *Vermont Quarterly*, vol. 20, no. 1 (Jan. 1952): 3+.

Forsyth, Mary Isabella. "The Burning of Kingston by the British on October 16th, 1777." *Proceedings of the New York State Historical Association*, vol. 11 (1912): 62+.

"Franklin's Home and Host in France." *Century Magazine*, vol. 35 (1888): 741+.

Fraser, Walter J., Jr. "Reflections of 'Democracy' in Revolutionary South Carolina: The Composition of Military Organizations and the Attitudes and Relationships of the Officers and Men, 1775–1780." *South Carolina Historical Magazine*, vol. 78, no. 3 (July 1777): 202+.

Freehling, William W. "The Founding Fathers and Slavery." *AHR*, vol. 77, no. 1 (Feb. 1972): 81+.

Frey, Sylvia R. "Between Slavery and Freedom: Virginia Blacks in the American Revolution." *Journal of Southern History*, vol. 49, no. 3 (Aug. 1983): 375+.

Furcron, Thomas B. "Mount Independence." *BFTM*, vol. 9, no. 4 (Winter 1954): 230+.

Futhey, J. Smith. "The Massacre of Paoli." *PMHB*, vol. 1, no. 3 (1877): 285+.

Gadue, Michael. "The *Thunderer*, British Floating Gun-Battery on Lake Champlain," *JAR*, Apr. 4, 2019.

"Gen. Fraser's Account of Burgoyne's Campaign on Lake Champlain and the Battle of Hubbardton." *Proceedings of the Vermont Historical Society*, Oct. 18 and Nov. 2, 1898: 139+.

"General Daniel Morgan: An Autobiography." *Historical Magazine*, 2nd series, vol. 9, no. 6 (June 1871): 379+.

"General Powell to Sir Guy Carleton." *BFTM*, vol. 7, no. 2 (July 1945): 30+.

Gerlach, Don R. "Philip Schuyler and 'the Road to Glory': A Question of Loyalty and Competence." *NYHS Quarterly*, vol. 49, no. 4 (Oct. 1965): 341+.

Goold, Nathan. "Captain Henry Mowat's Account." *Magazine of History*, vol. 3 (1910): 46+.

Greene, Jack P. "William Knox's Explanation for the American Revolution." *WMQ*, vol. 30, no. 2 (Apr. 1973): 293+.

Griffin, David M. "Plight of the Loyalist Refugees of Lloyd's Neck, Long Island." *JAR*, Feb. 20, 2020.

———. " 'To Huts': British Winter Cantonments Around New York City." *JAR*, Feb. 25, 2019.

Gruber, Ira D. "Lord Howe and Lord George Germain: British Politics and the Winning of American Independence." *WMQ*, third series, vol. 22, no. 2 (Apr. 1965): 225+.

Guttridge, George H. "Lord George Germain in Office, 1775–1782." *AHR*, vol. 33, no. 1 (Oct. 1927): 23+.

Haas, James M. "The Royal Dockyards: The Earliest Visitations and Reform, 1749–1778." *Historical Journal*, vol. 13, no. 2 (1970): 191+.

Haffner, Gerald O., ed. "A British Prisoner of War in the American Revolution: The Experiences of Jacob Schieffelin from Vincennes to Williamsburg, 1779–1780." *Virginia Magazine of History and Biography*, vol. 86, no. 1 (Jan. 1778): 17+.

Hagist, Don N. "How to Be a Revolutionary War Spy Master." *JAR*, Apr. 12, 2018.

———. "Notes on German Army Women." *Brigade Dispatch*, vol. 32, no. 2 (Summer 2002): 20.

Hall, John W. "An Irregular Reconsideration of George Washington and the American Military Tradition." *JMH*, vol. 78, no. 3 (July 2014): 961+.

Halsey, Francis Whiting. "General Schuyler's Part in the Burgoyne Campaign." *Proceedings of the New York State Historical Association*, vol. 12 (1913): 109+.

Harlow, Ralph Volney. "Aspects of Revolutionary Finance, 1775–1783." *AHR*, vol. 35, no. 1 (Oct. 1929): 46+.

Harrington, Hugh T. "Charles Willson Peale's 'Riffle with a Telescope to It.'" *JAR*, July 10, 2013.

Harrington, Hugh T., and Jim Jordan. "The Other Mystery Shot of the American Revolution: Did Timothy Murphy Kill British Brigadier General Simon Fraser at Saratoga?" *JMH*, vol. 74, no. 4 (Oct. 2010): 1037+.

Harris, C. Leon. "Massacre at Waxhaws: The Evidence from Wounds." *Southern Campaigns of the American Revolution*, vol. 11, no. 21 (May 2016): 1+.

———. "What Can Pension Applications Contribute to Understanding the Battle of the Waxhaws and Other Events of the Revolutionary War?" *Southern Campaigns of the American Revolution*, vol. 10, no. 2 (summer 2014): 6+.

Harris, C. Leon, and Charles B. Baxley. "Tarleton Tightens the Noose Around Charleston Neck." *Southern Campaigns of the American Revolution*, vol. 18, no. 2 (Nov. 29, 2021): 1+.

Harris, Michael C., and Gary Ecelbarger. "The Numerical Strength of George Washington's Army During the 1777 Philadelphia Campaign." *JAR*, Oct. 5, 2021.

———. "A Reconsideration of Continental Army Numerical Strength at Valley Forge." *JAR*, May 18, 2021.

Hart, Charles Henry. "The Wilson Portrait of Franklin: Earl Grey's Gift to the Nation." *PMHB*, vol. 30, no. 4 (1906): 409+.

Hatch, Marie Martel, ed. "Letters of Captain Sir John Jervis to Sir Henry Clinton, 1774–1782." *American Neptune*, vol. 7 (Apr. 1947): 87+.

Hatfield, Stuart. "Faking It: British Counterfeiting During the American Revolution." *JAR*, Oct. 7, 2015.

Haworth, Paul Leland. "Frederick the Great and the American Revolution." *AHR*, vol. 9, no. 3 (Apr. 1904): 460+.

Hemmis, Timothy C. "Under the Banner of War: Frontier Militia and Uncontrolled Violence." *JAR*, Mar. 29, 2022.

Herrera, Ricardo A. "Foraging and Combat Operations at Valley Forge." *Army History* (Spring 2011): 7+.

———. "'The zealous activity of Capt. Lee': Light-Horse Harry Lee and *Petite Guerre*." *JMH*, vol. 79, no. 1 (Jan. 2015): 9+.

Hillegas, Michael. "Selected Letters of Michael Hillegas, Treasurer of the United States." *PMHB*, vol. 29 (1905): 232+.

Holcomb, Richmond. "Washington's Headquarters at Coryell's Ferry." *Proceedings of the New Jersey Historical Society*, new series, vol. 11, no. 2 (Apr. 1926): 850+.

Holden, James Austin. "Influence of Death of Jane McCrea on Burgoyne Campaign." *Proceedings of the New York State Historical Association*, vol. 12 (1913): 249+.

Honeyman, A. Van Doren. "The Indian Massacre of Jane McCrea in 1777." *Somerset County Historical Quarterly*, vol. 7 (1918): 250+.

Houlding, J. A., and G. Kenneth Yates. "Corporal Fox's Memoir of Service, 1766–1783: Quebec, Saratoga, and the Convention Army." *Journal of the Society for Army Historical Research*, vol. 68, no. 275 (Autumn 1990): 146+.

Hoyt, Edward A. "The Pawlet Expedition, September 1777." *Vermont History*, vol. 75, no. 2 (Summer–Fall 2007): 69+.

Hughes, J. M. "Notes Relative to the Campaign Against Burgoyne." *Proceedings of the Massachusetts Historical Society*, vol. 3 (1855–58): 265+.

Huth, Hans. "Letters from a Hessian Mercenary." *PMHB*, vol. 62, no. 4 (Oct. 1938): 488+.

Inman, George. "George Inman's Narrative of the American Revolution." *PMHB*, vol. 7, no. 3 (1883): 237+.

Irvin, Benjamin H. "The Streets of Philadelphia: Crows, Congress, and the Political Culture of Revolution, 1774–1783." *PMHB*, vol. 129, no. 1 (Jan. 2005): 7+.

"Jane McCrea." *BFTM*, vol. 2, no. 6 (July 1932): 209+.

Johnson, Elmer Douglas. "A Frenchman Visits Charleston in 1777." *South Carolina Historical and Genealogical Magazine*, vol. 52, no. 2 (Apr. 1951): 88+.

Johnston, Ruth Y. "American Privateers in French Ports, 1776–1778." *PMHB*, vol. 53, no. 4 (Oct. 1929): 352+.

Jones, George Fenwick. "The 1780 Siege of Charleston as Experienced by a Hessian Officer." *South Carolina Historical Magazine*, vol. 88, nos. 1 (Jan. 1987) and 2 (Apr. 1987): 22+ and 63+.

Jones, T. Cole. " 'The rage of tory-hunting': Loyalist Prisoners, Civil War, and the Violence of American Independence." *JMH*, vol. 81, no. 3 (July 2017): 719+.

Jordan, John W. "Adam Hubley, Jr. Lt. Colo. Com. 11th Pennsylvania Regiment, His Journal." 2 parts. *PMHB*, vol. 33, no. 2 and 3 (1909): 129+and 279+.

———. "Bethlehem During the Revolution: Extracts from the Diaries in the Moravian Archives at Bethlehem, Pennsylvania." *PMHB*, vol. 12, no. 4 (1888): 385+ and vol. 13, no. 1 (1889): 71+.

"Journal of Capt. William Beaty, 1776–1781." *Maryland Historical Magazine*, vol. 3, no. 2 (June 1908): 104+.

"A Journal of Carleton's and Burgoyne's Campaigns." 2 parts. *BFTM*, vol. 11, nos. 5 and 6 (Dec. 1964 and Sept. 1965): 235+ and 307+.

"Journal of Oliver Boardman of Middletown: 1777, Burgoyne's Surrender." *Collections of the Connecticut Historical Society*, vol. 7 (1899): 223+.

"Judge Johnson and Count Pulaski." *North American Review*, vol. 23 (1826): 425+.

Jusserand, J. J. "Our First Alliance." *National Geographic*, vol. 31 (Jan.–June 1917): 518+.

Kelly, Jack. "So Heavy a Trial: The Burning of New York's First Capital." *JAR*, Sept. 4, 2014.

Kepner, Frances Reece, ed. "Notes and Documents: A British View of the Siege of Charleston, 1776." *Journal of Southern History*, vol. 2, no. 1 (Feb. 1945): 93+.

Kingsley, Ronald F. "A German Perspective on the American Attempt to Recapture the British Forts at Ticonderoga and Mount Independence on September 18, 1777." Translation by Helga Doblin. *Vermont History*, vol. 67, nos. 1 and 2 (Winter–Spring 1999): 5+.

———. "Letters to Lord Polwarth from Sir Francis-Carr Clerke, Aide-de-Camp to General John Burgoyne." *New York History*, vol. 79, no. 4 (Oct. 1998): 393+.

Kingsley, Ronald F., Harvey Alexander, and Eric Schnitzer. "German Auxiliaries Project: The Incursion to Mount Independence." *JSHA*, vol. 8 (2005): 28+.

Kite, Elizabeth S. "Lafayette and His Companions on the 'Victoire.' " *Records of the American Catholic Historical Society of Philadelphia*, vol. 45, no. 1 (Mar. 1934): 1+.

Klein, Milton M. "An Experiment That Failed: General James Robertson and Civil Government in British New York, 1779–1783." *New York History*, vol. 61, no. 3 (July 1980): 229+.

———. "Why Did the British Fail to Win the Hearts and Minds of New Yorkers?" *New York History*, vol. 64, no. 4 (Oct. 1983): 357+.

Knight, Betsy. "Prisoner Exchange and Parole in the American Revolution." *WMQ*, vol. 48, no. 2 (Apr. 1991): 201+.

Knight, R.J.B. "The Building and Maintenance of the British Fleet During the Anglo-French Wars, 1688–1815." *Les Marines de Guerre Européennes*: 38–39.

———. "The Introduction of Copper Sheathing into the Royal Navy, 1779–1786." *Mariner's Mirror*, vol. 59 (1973): 299+.

———. "New England Forests and British Seapower: Albion Revised." *American Neptune*, vol. 46, no. 4 (Fall 1986): 221+.

Koehler, Rhiannon. "Hostile Nations: Quantifying the Destruction of the Sullivan-Clinton Genocide of 1779." *American Indian Quarterly*, vol. 42, no. 4 (Fall 2018): 427+.

Kopperman, Paul. "The Numbers Game: Health Issues in the Army That Burgoyne Led to Saratoga." *New York History*, vol. 88, no. 3 (Summer 2007): 254+.

Krafft, John Charles Philip von. "Von Krafft's Journal." Edited by Thomas H. Edsall. *Collections of the New-York Historical Society* (1882): ix+.

Krebs, Daniel. "Useful Enemies: The Treatment of German Prisoners of War During the American War of Independence." *JMH*, vol. 77, no. 1 (Jan. 2013): 9+.

Lacey, John. "Memoirs of Brigadier-General John Lacey, of Pennsylvania." *PMHB*, vols. 25–26, nos. 4, 1, and 2 (1901–1902): 498+, 101+, and 265+.

Lambdin, Alfred C. "Battle of Germantown." *PMHB*, vol. 1, no. 4 (1877): 368+.

Lapp, Derrick E. "Did They Really 'Take None but Gentlemen'?: Henry Hardman, the Maryland Line, and a Reconsideration of the Socioeconomic Composition of the Continental Officer Corps." *JMH*, vol. 78, no. 4 (Oct. 2014): 1239+.

Laughton, John Knox, ed. "Journals of Henry Duncan, Captain, Royal Navy, 1776–1782." *The Naval Miscellany*, vol. 1, *Publications of the Navy Records Society*, 20 (1902): 111+.

Lawler, Edward, Jr. "The President's House in Philadelphia: The Rediscovery of a Lost Landmark." *PMHB*, vol. 126, no. 1 (Jan. 2002): 5+.

Lawrence, Alexander A. "General Robert Howe and the British Capture of Savannah in 1778." *Georgia Historical Quarterly*, vol. 36, no. 4 (Dec. 1952): 303+.

Lefkowitz, Arthur S. "French Adventurers, Patriots, and Pretentious Imposters in the Fight for American Independence." *JAR*, June 8, 2021.

Leonard, Eugenie Andruss. "Paper as a Critical Commodity During the American Revolution." *PMHB*, vol. 74, no. 4 (Oct. 1950): 488+.

"Letter from Dr. James Browne." *New England Historical and Genealogical Register*, vol. 18 (1864): 34.

"A Letter from Saratoga." *BFTM*, vol. 6, no. 6 (July 1943): 182.

Lewis, Charles Lee. "'I Have Not Yet Begun to Fight.'" *Mississippi Valley Historical Review*, vol. 29, no. 2 (Sept. 1942): 229+.

Lindsey, William R. "Treatment of American Prisoners of War During the Revolution." *Emporia State Research Studies*, vol. 22, no. 1 (Summer 1973): 5+.

Lockhart, Paul. "Steuben Comes to America." *MHQ*, vol. 22, no. 2 (Winter 2010): 26+.

Lossing, Benson J. "Washington's Life Guard." *Historical Magazine*, vol. 2, no. 5 (May 1858): 129+.

Lutnick, Solomon. "The American Victory at Saratoga: A View from the British Press." *New York History*, vol. 44, no. 2 (Apr. 1963): 103+.

Lydenberg, Harry Miller, ed. "Archibald Robertson: His Diaries and Sketches in America, 1762–1780." *Bulletin of The New York Public Library*, vol. 37, no. 11 (Nov. 1933): 283+.

Lynch, Wayne, and Jim Piecuch. "Debating Waxhaws: Was There a Massacre?" *JAR*, Aug. 7, 2013.

Mahan, A. T. "John Paul Jones in the Revolution." *Scribner's*, vol. 24 (July and Aug. 1898): 22+ and 204+.

Martin, Asa E. "American Privateers and the West Indies Trade." *AHR*, vol. 39 (July 1934): 700+.

Maslowski, Pete. "National Policy Toward the Use of Black Troops in the Revolution." *South Carolina Historical Magazine*, vol. 73, no. 1 (Jan. 1972): 1+.

McBurney, Christian M. "British Treatment of Prisoners During the Occupation of Newport, 1776–1779: Disease, Starvation and Death Stalk the Prison Ships." *Newport History*, vol. 79, no. 263 (Fall 2010): 1+.

———. "Did George Washington Swear at Charles Lee During the Battle of Monmouth?" *JAR*, Mar. 10, 2022.

———. "The Discovery of an Important Letter from a Soldier of the 1st Rhode Island Regiment." *JAR*, Apr. 14, 2021.

———. "Mutiny! American Mutinies in the Rhode Island Theater of War, Sept. 1778–July 1779." *Rhode Island History*, vol. 69, no. 2 (Summer–Fall 2011): 47+.

McDonald, Bob. "French Firelocks in America Service: Markings on Continental Muskets." *Brigade Dispatch*, vol. 33 (Autumn 2003): 2+.

McGeachy, Robert A. "The American War of Lieutenant Colonel Archibald Campbell." *Early American Review*, vol. 5, http://www.earlyamerica.com/early-america-review/volume-5/the-american-war-of-lieutenant-colonel-archibald-campbell/.

McHenry, Justin. "John Morgan vs. William Shippen: The Battle That Defined the Continental Medical Department." *JAR*, Jan. 28, 2020.

McMichael, James. "Diary of Lieutenant James McMichael, of the Pennsylvania Line, 1776–1778." *PMHB*, vol. 16, no. 2 (July 1892): 129+.

"Memoir of Jonathan Loring Austin." *Boston Monthly Magazine*, vol. 2, no. 11 (July 1826): 57+.

Meng, John J. "A Footnote to Secret Aid in the American Revolution." *AHR*, vol. 43, no. 4 (July 1938): 791+.

Meyronnet de Saint-Marc Fauris, Joseph-Philippe-Auguste de. "Meyronnet de Saint-Marc's Journal." *New-York Historical Society Quarterly*, vol. 35 (July 1952): 255+.

Miller, Randall M., and Moses Kirkland. "A Backcountry Loyalist Plan to Retake Georgia and the Carolinas, 1778." *South Carolina Historical Magazine*, vol. 75, no. 4 (Oct. 1974): 207+.

Mishoff, Willard O. "Business in Philadelphia During the British Occupation, 1777–1778." *PMHB*, vol. 61, no. 2 (Apr. 1937): 165+.

Montgomery, Thomas Harrison. "The Battle of Monmouth, as Described by Dr. James McHenry." *Magazine of American History* (June 1879): 355+.

Montrésor, John, and G. D. Scull. "Journal of Captain John Montrésor." *PMHB*, vol. 5, no. 4 (1881): 393+; vol. 6, no. 1, no. 2, and no. 3 (1882): 34+, 189+, and 284+.

Moomaw, W. H. "The Denouement of General Howe's Campaign of 1777." *English Historical Review*, vol. 79, no. 312 (June 1964): 498+.

Morgan, Edmund S. "The Puritan Ethic and the American Revolution." *WMQ*, vol. 24, no. 1 (Jan. 1967): 3+.

Morgan, Ron. "Arthur St. Clair's Decision to Abandon Fort Ticonderoga and Mount Independence." *JAR*, May 16, 2016.

Morton, Robert. "The Diary of Robert Morton." *PMHB*, vol. 1, no. 1 (1877): 1+.

Moss, Matthew. "Patrick Ferguson and His Rifle." *JAR*, Dec. 13, 2018.

Murphy, Orville T. "The Battle of Germantown and the Franco-American Alliance of 1778." *PMHB*, vol. 82, no. 1 (Jan. 1958): 55+.

Namier, Lewis. "King George III: A Study in Personality." *History Today*, vol. 3, no. 1 (Jan. 1953): 610+.

"A Narrative of the Saratoga Campaign—Major General Henry Dearborn, 1815." *BFTM*, vol. 1, no. 5 (Jan. 1929): 4+.

Neimeyer, Charles P. "The British Occupation of Newport, Rhode Island, 1776–1779." *Army History* (Winter 2010): 30+.

Nelson, Paul David. "Legacy of Controversy: Gates, Schuyler, and Arnold at Saratoga, 1777." *Military Affairs*, vol. 37, no. 2 (Apr. 1973): 41+.

Neville, Gabriel. "The Continental Dollar: How the American Revolution Was Financed with Paper Money." *JAR*, Jan. 29, 2024.

"Newport in the Hands of the British: A Diary of the Revolution." *Historical Magazine*, vol. 4, no. 1 (Jan. 1860): 1+.

Nolan, J. Bennett. "A British Editor Reports the American Revolution." *PMHB*, vol. 80, no. 1 (1956): 92+.

North, Lord, and Edward Hughes. "Lord North's Correspondence, 1766–83." *English Historical Review*, vol. 62, no. 243 (Apr. 1947): 218+.

Norton, Louis Arthur. "The Penobscot Expedition: A Tale of Two Indicted Patriots." *The Northern Mariner*, vol. 16, no. 4 (Oct. 2006): 1+.

———. "The Revolutionary War's Most Enigmatic Naval Captain: Pierre Landais." *JAR*, July 17, 2018.

"Official Letters of Major General James Pattison." *Collections of the New-York Historical Society for the Year 1875.*

O'Malley, Brian P. "1776—The Horror Show." *JAR*, Jan. 29, 2019.

O'Shaughnessy, Andrew Jackson. "'If Others Will Not Be Active, I Must Drive': George III and the American Revolution." *Early American Studies*, vol. 2, no. 1 (Spring 2004): 1+.

———. "'To Gain the Hearts and Subdue the Minds of America': General Sir Henry Clinton and the Conduct of the British War for America." *Proceedings of the American Philosophical Society*, vol. 158, no. 3 (Sept. 2014): 199+.

"Parliament and the Howes." *Proceedings of the Massachusetts Historical Society*, third series, vol. 44 (Oct. 1910–June 1911): 87+.

"Particulars of the Mischianza in America." *Gentleman's Magazine*, vol. 48 (1778): 353+.

Pearce, Steward, ed. "Sullivan's Expedition to Staten Island in 1777." *PMHB*, vol. 3, no. 2 (1879): 167+.

Peckham, Howard H. "Independence: The View from Britain." *Proceedings of the American Antiquarian Society*, vol. 85, part 2 (1976): 387+.

Pell, Robert T. "John Brown and the Dash for Ticonderoga." *BFTM*, vol. 2, no. 1 (Jan. 1930): 23+.

Pleasants, Henry, Jr. "The Battle of Paoli." *PMHB*, vol. 72, no. 1 (Jan. 1948): 44+.

Pond, Nathan G., ed. "An Eye-Witness of Burgoyne's Surrender." *Magazine of American History*, vol. 29 (Jan.–June 1893): 279+.

Popp, Stephan, and Joseph G. Rosengarten. "Popp's Journal, 1777–1783." *PMHB*, vol. 26, no. 1 (1902): 25+.

Potts, William J., ed. "Battle of Germantown from a British Account." *PMHB*, vol. 11, no. 1 (1887): 112+.

Pratt, George W. "An Account of the British Expedition Above the Highlands of the Hudson River." *Collections of the Ulster Historical Society*, vol. 1 (1860): 109+.

Prelinger, Catherine M. "Benjamin Franklin and the American Prisoners of War in England During the American Revolution." *WMQ*, third series, vol. 32, no. 2 (Apr. 1975): 261+.

Prévost, Augustine. "Journal of the Siege of Savannah in 1779." *Publications of the Southern History Association*, vol. 1 (1897): 257+.

"Proceedings of a Board of General Officers of the British Army at New York, 1781." *Collections of the New-York Historical Society*, 1916.

Procknow, Gene. "Personal Honor and Promotion Among Revolutionary Generals and Congress." *JAR*, Jan. 23, 2018.

Pybus, Cassandra. "Jefferson's Faulty Math: The Question of Slave Defections in the American Revolution." *WMQ*, third series, vol. 62, no. 2 (Apr. 2005): 243+.

Ranlet, Philip. "British Recruitment of Americans in New York During the American Revolution." *Military Affairs*, vol. 48, no. 1 (Jan. 1984): 26.

Ravilious, Kate. "The Many Lives of an English Manor House." *Archaeology*, Jan.–Feb. 2016, https://www.archaeology.org/issues/199-1601.

Rees, John U. "'The essential service he rendered to the army . . .': Christopher Ludwick, Superintendent of Bakers." *Food History News*, vol. 9, no. 1 (Summer 1997) and vol. 17, no. 1 (Summer 2005).

Retzer, Henry J., trans. "The Philadelphia Campaign, 1777–1778: Letters and Reports from the von Jungkenn Papers," part 1. Edited by Donald M. Londahl-Smidt. *JSHA*, vol. 6, no. 2 (1998): 1+.

Retzer, Henry J., and Thomas M. Barker. "The Hessen-Hanau Jägers, the Siege of Fort Stanwix and the Battle of Oriskany: The Diary of First Lieutenant Philipp Jakob Hildebrandt." *JSHA*, vol. 14 (2012): 35+.

"Revolutionary Services of Captain John Markland." *PMHB*, vol. 9, no. 4 (Apr. 1885): 102+.

Reynolds, Donald E. "Ammunition Supply in Revolutionary Virginia." *Virginia Magazine of History and Biography*, part 1, vol. 73, no. 1. (Jan. 1965): 56+.

Riedel, Stefan. "Edward Jenner and the History of Smallpox and Vaccination." Baylor University Medical Center, *Proceedings*, vol. 18, no. 1 (Jan. 2005): 21+.

Rinder, Frank. "Buckingham Palace and Its Site." *Argosy*, vol. 74 (Apr. 1901): 3+.

Ritchie, Carson I. A., ed. "A New York Diary of the Revolutionary War." 2 parts. *New-York Historical Society Quarterly*, vol. 50, no. 3 (July 1966): 221+, and no. 4 (Oct. 1966): 401+.

Rose, P. K. "British Penetration of America's First Diplomatic Mission." *Studies in Intelligence*, vol. 41, no. 4 (1997): 57+.

Rudé, George F. E. "The Gordon Riots: A Study of the Rioters and Their Victims." *Transactions of the Royal Historical Society*, vol. 6 (1956): 93+.

Ruppert, Bob. "America's First Black Ops." *JAR*, Sept. 5, 2017.

———. "France and Spain Invade England—Almost." *JAR*, Jan. 30, 2020.

———. "Robert Erskine, Surveyor-General of the Continental Army." *JAR*, Dec. 19, 2019.

Rush, Benjamin. "Historical Notes of Dr. Benjamin Rush, 1777." *PMHB*, vol. 27, no. 2 (1903): 129+.

Russell, Preston. "The Conway Cabal." *American Heritage*, vol. 46, no. 1 (Feb.–Mar. 1995): 84+.

Safko, Gregory. "The Whitall Family and the Battle of Red Bank." *JAR*, Oct. 1, 2019.

Schaukirk, Ewald Gustav. "Occupation of New York City by the British." *PMHB*, vol. 10, no. 4 (Jan. 1887): 418+.

Schellhammer, Michael. "Abraham Woodhull: The Spy Named Samuel Culper." *JAR*, May 19, 2014.

Schenawolf, Harry. "Battle of Red Bank, Oct. 22, 1777." *Revolutionary War Journal*, Aug. 21, 2013, http://www.revolutionarywarjournal.com/battle-of-red-bank/.

Scott, Kenneth. "A British Counterfeiting Press in New York Harbor, 1776." *NYHS Quarterly*, vol. 39, no. 2–3 (Apr.–July 1955): 117+.

———. "New Hampshire Tory Counterfeiters Operating from New York City." *NYHS Quarterly*, vol. 34, no. 1 (Jan. 1950): 31+.

Scull, G. D., ed. "The Montresor Journals." NYHS, *Collections* (1881): 1+.

Settle, John. "The Eastern Shore Battalion: The Story of the 9th Virginia Regiment." *JAR*, Jan. 19, 2023.

Seymour, Joseph. "A Chart Showing the Results of a 1779 Woolwich Ballistic Test." *Military Collector & Historian*, vol. 65, no. 4 (Winter 2013): 373+.

Seymour, Robert Francis, ed. "A Contemporary British Account of General Sir William Howe's Military Operations in 1777." *Proceedings of the American Antiquarian Society* (Apr. 1930): 69+.

Shaw, Henry I., Jr. "Penobscot Assault—1779." *Military Affairs*, vol. 17, no. 2 (Apr. 1953): 83+.

Sheehan, Michael J. F. "Stony Point: The Second Occupation, July–October 1779." *JAR*, Apr. 21, 2020.

Shields, David S., and Frederika J. Teute. "The Meschianza: Sum of All Fêtes." *Journal of the Early American Republic*, vol. 35, no. 2 (Summer 2015): 185+.

"The Siege of Fort Mifflin." *PMHB*, vol. 11, no. 1 (Apr. 1887): 82+.

"Siege of Savannah: General Orders of the Count d'Estaing." *Magazine of American History*, vol. 2, part 1 (1878): 548+.

Simner, Marvin L. "A Further Evaluation of the Carlisle Peace Commission's Initiative." *JAR*, Sept. 30, 2021.

Sinnickson, Lina. "Frederika Baroness Riedesel," *PMHB*, vol. 30, no. 4 (1906): 385+.

Sisken, Ed, and Jean Sisken. "A Wonderful Revolutionary Letter." *New Jersey Postal History Journal*, Feb. 2012, https://njpostalhistory.org/february12featuredcover.html.

Smith, D. E. Huger. "Wilton's Statue of Pitt." *South Carolina Historical and Genealogical Magazine*, vol. 15, no. 1 (Jan. 1914): 18+.

Smith, Paul H. "The American Loyalists: Notes on Their Organization and Numerical Strength." *WMQ*, third series, vol. 25, no. 2 (Apr. 1968): 259+.

Spooner, Paul, and Amy E. Lansing. "Baum's Raid." *Quarterly Journal of the New York Historical Association*, vol. 9, no. 1 (Jan. 1928): 45+.

Staniforth, Mark. "The Introduction and Use of Copper Sheathing—A History." *Bulletin of the Australian Institute of Maritime Archaeology*, vol. 9, no. 1 (1985): 21+.

Stapleton, Darwin H. "General Daniel Roberdeau and the Lead Mine Expedition, 1778–1779." *Pennsylvania History*, vol. 38, no. 4 (Oct. 1971): 361+.

St. George, Richard. "The Actions at Brandywine and Paoli, Described by a British Officer." *PMHB*, vol. 29 (1905): 368+.

Starbuck, David R. "The American Headquarters for the Battle of Saratoga." *Northeast Historical Archaeology*, vol. 17, no. 2 (1988): 16+.

———. "The Mystery of the Second Body." *Plymouth Magazine*, vol. 28, no. 1 (Spring–Summer 2013): 1+.

Strach, Stephen G. "A Memoir of the Exploits of Captain Alexander Fraser and His Company of British Marksmen, 1776–1777." Part 2. *Journal of the Society for Army Historical Research*, vol. 63, no. 255 (Autumn 1985): 164+.

Symonds, Craig L. "The American Naval Expedition to Penobscot, 1779." *Naval War College Review*, vol. 24, no. 6 (Apr. 1972): 64+.

Syrett, David. "Home Waters or America? The Dilemma of British Naval Strategy in 1778." *Mariner's Mirror*, vol. 77, no. 4 (1991): 365+.

Theobald, Philipp. "Journal of the Hessen-Hanau Erbprinz Infantry Regiment," vol. 7, no. 1: 40+.

Thursfield, Hugh. "Smallpox in the American War of Independence." *Annals of Medical History*, 3rd series, vol. 2, no. 4 (July 1940): 312+.

Tompkins, Hamilton B. "Contemporary Account of the Battle of Germantown." *PMHB*, vol. 11, no. 3 (Oct. 1887): 330+.

"The Trial of Major General St. Clair, August 1778." *Collections of the New-York Historical Society*, vol. 13 (1880): 1+.

Trickey, Erick. "The Polish Patriot Who Helped Americans Beat the British." *Smithsonian*, Mar. 8, 2017, https://www.smithsonianmag.com/history/polish-patriot-who-helped-americans-beat -british-180962430/.

"A Turnbull Map of Fort Ticonderoga Rediscovered." *BFTM*, vol. 13, no. 2 (June 1971): 129+.

Tyler, Lyon G., ed. "The Old Virginia Line in the Middle States During the American Revolution." *Tyler's Quarterly*, vol. 12, no. 1 (July 1930): 1+.

Upham, William P. "A Memoir of Gen. John Glover, of Marblehead." *Historical Collections of the Essex Institute*, vol. 5, no. 3 (June 1863): 97+.

Vale, Brian. "Pitch, Paint, Varnish and the Changing Color Schemes of Royal Navy Warships, 1775–1815." *Mariner's Mirror*, vol. 106, no. 1 (Feb. 2020): 30+.

Van Tyne, C. H. "French Aid Before the Alliance of 1778." *AHR*, vol. 31, no. 1 (Oct. 1925): 20+.

———. "Influence Which Determined the French Government to Make the Treaty with America, 1778." *AHR*, vol. 21, no. 3 (Apr. 1916): 528+.

Van Wyck, Pierre C. "Autobiography of Philip Van Cortlandt, Brigadier-General in the Continental Army." *Magazine of American History*, vol. 2, part 1 (1878): 278+.

Venter, Bruce M. "Behind Enemy Lines: Americans Attack Burgoyne's Supply Line." *Patriots of the American Revolution* (May–June 2015): 12+.

Von Papet, Frederick Julius. "The Brunswick Contingent in America, 1776–1783." *PMHB*, vol. 15, no. 2 (1891): 218+.

Wainwright, Nicholas B., and Sarah Logan Fisher. "'A Diary of Trifling Occurrences': Philadelphia, 1776–1778," *PMHB*, vol. 82, no. 4 (Oct. 1958): 411+.

Waldo, Albigence. "Valley Forge, 1777–1778: Diary of Surgeon Albigence Waldo, of the Connecti-cut Line." *PMHB*, vol. 21, no. 3 (1897): 299+.

Walker, Lewis Burd. "Life of Margaret Shippen, Wife of Benedict Arnold." *PMHB*, vol. 24, no. 3 (1900): 257+.

Walther, Karl, ed. "Diary of Johann Christoph Doehlemann, Grenadier Company, Ansbach Regi-ment, March 1777 to September 1778." Translated by Henry J Retzer. *ISHA*, vol. 11 (2008): 11+.

Warner, Deborah Jean. "Telescopes for Land and Sea." *Rittenhouse*, vol. 12, no. 2 (1998): 33+.

Weddle, Kevin J. "'A Change of Both Men and Measures': British Reassessment of Military Strategy After Saratoga, 1777–1778." *JMH*, vol. 77, no. 3 (July 2013): 837+.

Weeden, William B., ed. "Diary of Enos Hitchcock, D.D., a Chaplain in the Revolutionary Army." *Publications of the Rhode Island Historical Society*, new series, vol. 7 (1899): 87+.

Weinman, Erin. "Oliver Reed: Letters of an American Soldier." *JAR*, Aug. 6, 2015.

Weller, Jac. "Revolutionary War Artillery in the South." *Georgia Historical Quarterly*, vol. 46, nos. 3 and 4 (Sept. 1962 and Dec. 1962): 250+ and 377+.

Wells, Jim. "Mind Your Business: Patriotic Mottoes & Emblems on Continental Currency." Paper Money, *The Numismatist*, Oct. 2019, 38+.

Werther, Richard J. "The Articles of Confederation and Western Expansion." *JAR*, June 14, 2022.

———. "Captain Lambert Wickes and 'Gunboat Diplomacy, American Revolution Style.'" *JAR*, Jan. 3, 2019.

———. "The Case of New Ireland—Not Meant to Be." *JAR*, Sept. 17, 2024.

———. "George Washington and the First Mandatory Immunization." *JAR*, Oct. 26, 2021.

———. "Marinus Willett: The Exploits of an Unheralded War Hero." *JAR*, Sept. 20, 2022.

———. "Opposing the Franco-American Alliance: The Case of Anne-Robert Jacques Turgot." *JAR*, June 23, 2020.

———. "Volunteer Overload: Foreign Support of the American Cause Prior to the French Alli-ance." *JAR*, Sept. 8, 2020.

———. "Walter Butler: The Dastardly Loyalist." *JAR*, Aug. 25, 2022.

Westley, Megan. "5 Things You Didn't Know About the Spying Arm of the Post Office." *BBC History Magazine*, Oct. 15, 2014, https://www.historyextra.com/membership/5-things-you-didnt-know-about-the-secret-spying-arm-of-the-post-office/.

Whiteley, Emily Stone. "Horace Walpole, Early American." *Virginia Quarterly Review*, vol. 7, no. 2 (Spring 1931): 212+.

Whiteley, W. H. "The British Navy and the Siege of Quebec, 1775–76." *Canadian Historical Review*, vol. 61, no. 1 (1980): 3+.

Whitridge, Arnold. "Baron von Steuben: Washington's Drillmaster." *History Today*, vol. 26, no. 7 (July 1976): 429+.

Wickersty, Jason R. "Were There Really 1,500 British Wagons on the Road to Monmouth?" *JAR*, July 23, 2024.

Wickman, Donald. "The Diary of Timothy Tuttle." *New Jersey History*, vol. 113, nos. 3–4 (Fall–Winter 1995): 61+.

Wickman, Donald H., ed. "'Breakfast on Chocolate': The Diary of Moses Greenleaf, 1777." *BFTM*, vol. 15, no. 6 (1997): 483+.

Wiener, Frederick Bernays. "The Military Occupation of Philadelphia in 1777–1778." *Proceedings of the American Philosophical Society*, vol. 111, no. 5 (Oct. 16, 1967): 310+.

Willcox, William B. "British Strategy in America, 1778." *Journal of Modern History*, vol. 19, no. 2 (June 1947): 97+.

———. "Too Many Cooks: British Planning Before Saratoga." *Journal of British Studies*, vol. 2, no. 1 (Nov. 1962): 6+.

Wild, Ebenezer. "Journal of Ebenezer Wild." *Proceedings of the Massachusetts Historical Society*, second series, vol. 6 (1890–91): 66+.

Williams, William H. "Independence and Early American Hospitals, 1751–1812." *JAMA*, vol. 236, no. 1 (July 5, 1976): 35+.

Willis, S.B.A. "Fleet Performance and Capability in the Eighteenth-Century Royal Navy." *War in History*, vol. 11, no. 4 (Nov. 2004): 373+.

Wright, John W. "The Rifle in the American Revolution." *American Historical Review*, vol. 29, no. 2 (Jan. 1924): 293+.

———. "Some Notes on the Continental Army." *WMQ*, 2nd series, vol. 11, no. 2 (Apr. 1931): 81+.

Wroblewski, Joeseph E. "Casimir Pulaski and the Threat to the Upper Delaware River Valley." *JAR*, May 13, 2020.

———. "Loyalist 'Banditti' of Monmouth County, New Jersey: Jacob Fagan and Lewis Fenton." *JAR*, June 10, 2021.

Wyatt, Frederick, and William B. Willcox. "Sir Henry Clinton: A Psychological Exploration in History." *WMQ*, third series, vol. 16, no. 1 (Jan. 1959): 3+.

York, Neil L. "Clandestine Aid and the American Revolutionary War Effort." *Military Affairs*, vol 43, no. 1 (Feb. 1979): 26+.

Young, Henry J. "Treason and Its Punishment in Revolutionary Pennsylvania." *PMHB*, vol. 90, no 3 (July 1966): 287 | .

Zellers-Frederick, Andrew A. "A Chink in Britain's Armor: John Paul Jones's 1778 Raid on White-haven." *JAR*, June 25, 2019.

Zimmerman, Colin. "The Battle of Crosswicks: Prelude to Monmouth." *JAR*, Aug. 4, 2022.

EIGHTEENTH-CENTURY PERIODICALS CITED

British: *Adams's Weekly Courant*; *Bath Chronicle*; *Caledonian Mercury*; *Cumberland Chronicle*; *Cumberland Packet and Whitehaven Advertiser*; *Gazetteer and New Daily Advertiser*; *General Advertiser and Morning Intelligencer*; *General Evening Post*; *Gentleman's Magazine*; *Hampshire Chronicle*; *Ipswich Journal*; *Jackson's Oxford Journal*; *Lloyd's Evening Post*; *London Chronicle*; *London Courant*; *London Evening Post*; *London Gazette and New Daily Advertiser*; *Morning Chronicle and London Advertiser*; *Morning Post and Daily Advertiser*; *Public Advertiser*; *Public Ledger*; *Stamford Mercury*; *St. James's Chronicle*

American: *New-Jersey Gazette*; *New York Gazette*; *New York Journal*; *New York Packet*; *Pennsylva* *nia Evening Post; Pennsylvania Journal; Pennsylvania Ledger; Pennsylvania Packet; Providence Ga-zette; Royal Gazette; Royal Pennsylvania Gazette; South-Carolina Gazette and Country Journal; Virginia Gazette* (various editions)

MANUSCRIPTS, COLLECTIONS, AND ARCHIVES

American Philosophical Society, Philadelphia
Archives Diplomatiques, Paris
Archives Nationales, Paris
Benjamin Franklin Museum, Philadelphia
David Center for the American Revolution (now within the American Philosophical Society), Philadelphia
Firestone Library, Princeton University, New Jersey
Founders Online, U.S. National Archives and Records Administration, Washington, D.C.
Georgian Papers, Royal Archives, Windsor Castle, U.K.
Gilder Lehrman Institute of American History, New York City
Hessian Documents of the American Revolution and Hessian Transcriptions, Lidgerwood Collec-tion, Morristown, New Jersey
Historical Society of Pennsylvania, Philadelphia
Huntington Library, San Marino, California
Library and Archives Canada, Ottawa
Library of Congress, Washington, D.C.
Loyalist Collection, University of New Brunswick, Canada
Massachusetts Historical Society, Boston
Morristown National Historical Park, New Jersey
Museum of the American Revolution, Philadelphia
National Archives, Kew, U.K.
National Museum of the Royal Navy, Portsmouth, U.K.
New-York Historical Society, New York City
New York Public Library, Thomas Addis Emmet Collection and Bancroft Collection
Papers of George Washington, University of Virginia, Charlottesville
The Revolutionary City, https://therevolutionarycity.org/
Saratoga National Historical Park, Saratoga, N.Y.
Society of the Cincinnati, Washington, D.C.
South Carolina Historical Society, manuscript collection, Addlestone Library, College of Charleston
St. Eustatius Historical Foundation Museum, Oranjestad, St. Eustatius
Thompson-Pell Research Center, Fort Ticonderoga, New York
University of Nottingham (U.K.), Manuscripts and Special Collections
U.S. Army Military History Institute, Army Heritage and Education Center, Carlisle, Pennsylvania
Valley Forge National Historical Park, Pennsylvania
William L. Clements Library, University of Michigan, Ann Arbor

DOCTORAL DISSERTATIONS

Hast, Adele. "Loyalism in Revolutionary Virginia: The Norfolk Area and the Eastern Shore." Uni-versity of Iowa (1979).
Johnson, Victor Leroy. "The Administration of the American Commissariat During the Revolu-tionary War." University of Pennsylvania (1941).
Knight, Roger John Beckett. "The Royal Dockyards in England at the Time of the American War of Independence." University of London (1972).
Langston, Paul. "'A Fickle and Confused Multitude': War and Politics in Revolutionary Philadel-phia, 1750–1783." University of Colorado (2006).
Moomaw, W. Hugh. "The Naval Career of Captain Hamond, 1775–1779." University of Virginia (1955).
Robinson, Edward Forbes. "Continental Treasury Administration, 1775–1781: A Study in the Fi-nancial History of the American Revolution." University of Michigan (1970).

Tacyn, Mark Andrew. "To the End: The First Maryland Regiment and the American Revolution." University of Maryland, College Park (1999).

White, John Todd. "Standing Armies in Time of War: Republican Theory and Military Practice During the American Revolution." George Washington University (1978).

Williams, Colin Jay. "New York Transformed: Committee, Militias, and the Social Effects of Political Mobilization in Revolutionary New York." University of Alabama (2013).

MISCELLANY

"About John and Abigail Adams." Massachusetts Historical Society, https://www.masshist.org/digital adams/archive/index.

Adamiak, Stanley J. "The 1779 Sullivan Campaign," https://www.varsitytutors.com/earlyamerica/ early-america-review/volume-3/1779-sullivan-campaign.

"Archives of Maryland Online." *Maryland Gazette Collection*, http://msa.maryland.gov/megafile/ msa/speccol/sc4800/sc4872/001282/html/m1282-1168.html.

"Articles of Confederation." Milestone Documents, U.S. National Archives, https://www.archives .gov/milestone-documents/articles-of-confederation.

"Baron Riedesel's Letter to Duke of Brunswick," Oct. 21, 1777. SNHP.

"Battle of Brandywine Driving Tour." Brandywine Battlefield Park Associates and Pennsylvania Historical & Museum Commission.

Bell, J. L. "A Letter of Recommendation for the Baron de Steuben." *Boston 1775*, July 28, 2018, https://boston1775.blogspot.com.

———. "What Do We Know About Gen. de Steuben's Sexuality?" *Boston 1775*, July 27, 2018, https://boston1775.blogspot.com.

———. "Why Charles Lee Loved Dogs." *Boston 1775*, Sept. 19, 2014, https://boston1775.blogspot .com.

Bell, John. "On the Nature and Cure of Gun-Shot Wounds." *The British Military Library*, vol. 1.

"Bethlehem Colonial History." https://bethlehempa.org/about-bethlehem/history-of-bethlehem/.

Bodle, Wayne K. "The Vortex of Small Fortunes: The Continental Army at Valley Forge, 1777–1778." Valley Forge Historical Research Report, vol. 1, VFNHP, May 1980.

"*Bonhomme Richard* (Frigate) 1779." Naval History and Heritage Command, https://www.history .navy.mil/research/histories/ship-histories/danfs/b/bonhomme-richard-frigate-i.html.

Boulanger, Matthew, Allen Hathaway, and Elsa Gilbertson. "Mount Independence Chert: An Ancient and Revolutionary Stone." Mount Independence State Historic Site, 2005.

Bowler, R. Arthur, and Bruce G. Watson. "Butler, John." *Dictionary of Canadian Biography*, vol. 4, https://www.biographi.ca/en/bio/butler_walter_4E.html.

Boyle, Joseph Lee. "'My Last Shift Betwixt Us & Death': The Ephraim Blaine Letterbook, 1777–1778." VFNHP, ms.

———. "'Up to Our Knees in Mud for Four Days Past': The Weather and the Continental Army, August 1777–June 1778." VFNHP, Feb. 1998.

Brier, Marc A. "They Passed This Way." VFNHP, Sept. 2002.

———. "Tolerable Comfortable: A Field Trial of a Recreated Soldier Cabin at Valley Forge." VFNHP, Aug. 1, 2004.

"Burke, Edmund (1729–1797)." John W. Cousin, *A Short Biographical Dictionary of English Literature*. London: J. M. Dent, 1910, https://gutenberg.org/cache/epub/13240/pg13240-images.html.

Burt, A. L. "Guy Carleton, Lord Dorchester, 1724–1808." Ottawa: Canadian Historical Association Booklets, no. 5, 1968.

Butler, Nic. "Demolition by Neglect in the 1720s: Forsaking Charleston's Earthen Fortifications." *Rediscovering Charleston's Colonial Fortifications* (blog), Oct. 17, 2023, https://walledcitytask force.org/.

Catts, Wade P., et al. "'It Is Painful for Me to Lose So Many Good People': Report of an Archeological Survey at Red Bank Battlefield Park (Fort Mercer)." Gloucester County (N.J.) Department of Parks and Recreation, June 2017.

Cohn, Michael. "Fortification of New York During the Revolutionary War, 1776–1782." New York City Archeological Group, 1962.

"Collier, Sir George." *Dictionary of National Biography*, https://en.wikisource.org/wiki/Dictionary
_of_National_Biography,_1885-1900/Collier,_George.

"Collier-Mathew Raids." American Revolution Podcast, Oct. 10, 2021, https://blog.amrevpodcast
.com/2021/10/arp221-collier-mathew-raids.html.

"Complete Sun and Moon Data for One Day." U.S. Naval Observatory, http://aa.usno.navy.mil/
data/docs/RS_OneDay.php.

"The Continental Navy." https://revolutionarywar.us/continental-navy/.

Davis, Robert S., Jr., and Kenneth H. Thomas, Jr. "Kettle Creek: The Battle of the Cane Brakes."
Georgia Department of Natural Resources, 1975, https://dlg.usg.edu/record/dlg_ggpd_s-ga
-bn200-pp6-bm1-b1974-bk4#text.

Davis, Robert Scott. "Battle of Kettle Creek." *New Georgia Encyclopedia*, https://www.georgia
encyclopedia.org/articles/history-archaeology/battle-of-kettle-creek/.

Deaton, Stan. "James Wright (1716–1785)." *New Georgia Encyclopedia*, https://www.georgia
encyclopedia.org/.

"The Decisive Moment, Breymann Redoubt." SNHP, https://www.nps.gov/places/the-decisive
-moment-7-breymann-redoubt-continued.htm.

Delaware River Basin Commission. River mileage system, http://www.state.nj.us/drbc/basin/river/.

Douglas, W.A.B. "John Byron." *Dictionary of Canadian Biography*, vol. 4. University of Toronto,
1979, https://www.biographi.ca/en/bio/byron_john_4E.html.

Drury, David. "The Rise and Fall of Silas Deane, American Patriot." Oct. 2, 2020, https://connecticut
history.org/the-rise-and-fall-of-silas-deane-american-patriot/.

Elliott, Rita F. " 'The Greatest Event That Has Happened the Whole War': Archaeological Discovery
of the Spring Hill Redoubt, Savannah, Georgia." Department of Anthropology, University of
Georgia, report no. 13453, 2011.

Emerick, Paige. "Royalty on the Road: Insights into the Royal Visits of George III and George IV."
Georgian Papers Programme, 2019, https://georgianpapers.com/2021/05/21/royalty-on-the
-road-insights-into-the-royal-visits-of-george-iii-and-george-iv/.

"Extracts from the Journal of Mrs. Gabriel (Ann Ashby) Manigault, 1754–1781." South Carolina
Historical Society, manuscript collection, College of Charleston Library.

Field, Edward, Israel Angel, and Norman Desmarais. "The Diary of Colonel Israel Angel." *Primary
Sources*, paper 2, http://digitalcommons.providence.edu/primary/2.

"The Fort at Red Bank." https://friendsofredbank.weebly.com/the-story-of-the-battle-of-red-bank
,html.

"The Forum of Marie Antoinette." https://marie-antoinette.forumactif.org/.

"France in the American Revolution." Exhibition pamphlet, SoC, 2011–12.

"Francis Reynolds-Moreton, 3rd Lord Ducie." https://morethannelson.com.

"Francis Rush Clark's Narration of Occurrences Relative to His Majesty's Provision Train in North
America." APS, Feinstone Coll., box 35, #2338.

"Galloway, Joseph." *Biographical Directory of the United States Congress*, http://bioguide.congress
.gov/scripts/biodisplay.pl?index=G000026.

"George Washington & His Generals." SoC exhibition, Feb. 2009–Jan. 2010.

"George III (1738–1820)." Royal Collection Trust, https://www.rct.uk/collection/405407/george-iii
-1738-1820.

"George Williams." https://www.62ndregiment.org/George_Williams.htm.

"General Charles Lee House, 'Prato Rio.' " National Register of Historic Places, https://npgallery
.nps.gov/GetAsset/f8e4dd27-0115-4e4c-b159-60af9defb45c.

"Gen. Lachlan McIntosh (1727–1806)." Georgia Historical Society, https://georgiahistory.com/
ghmi_marker_updated/gen-lachlan-mcintosh-1727-1806/.

"Gold State Coach." Royal Collection Trust, www.royalcollection.org.uk/collection/5000048/gold
-state-coach.

Graymont, Barbara. "Thayendanegea." *Dictionary of Canadian Biography*, vol. 5, https://www
.biographi.ca/en/bio/thayendanegea_5E.html.

Hagist, Don N. "James Gilmour, 82nd Regiment, survives a shipwreck." Blog post, Apr. 6, 2014,
https://redcoat76.blogspot.com/2014/04/james-gilmour-82nd-regiment-survives_6.html.

"Hall & Sellers Press." https://www.hmdb.org/m.asp?m=4569.

Hardman, John. "Louis XVI and the War of American Independence." George Rogers Clark lecture, Society of the Cincinnati, 2019.

Harris, C. Leon. "American Soldiers at the Battle of Waxhaws." Pension Statements and Rosters, Aug. 11, 2021, https://revwarapps.org/b221.pdf.

Hiscocks, Richard. "The Battle of Ushant." https://morethannelson.com/the-battle-of-ushant-27-july-1778-and-the-political-aftermath/.

———. "The Channel Fleet Retreat—August 1779." Blog post, Nov. 24, 2016, https://morethannelson.com/channel-fleet-retreat-august-1779/.

———. "Lord Howe's Defence of New York, July 1778." https://morethannelson.com/lord-howes-defence-of-new-york-july-1778/.

"Historical Handbook Number Four." SNHP, 1959, https://www.nps.gov/parkhistory/online_books/hh/4/hh4toc.htm.

"The History of Fort Edward." https://fortedward.net/about/history/.

"A History of the Official American Presence in France." U.S. State Department, n.d.

"The History of the Spanish Armada." Royal Museums Greenwich, https://www.rmg.co.uk/stories/topics/spanish-armada-history-causes-timeline.

"History of the Treasury." https://home.treasury.gov/about/history-overview/history-of-the-treasury.

"Homeland Defense: Protecting Britain During the American War." SoC exhibition, Oct. 2014–Mar. 2015.

"Hon. Augustus Keppel 1st Viscount." https://morethannelson.com/officer/hon-augustus-keppel-1st-viscount-keppel/.

"Hon. John Byron." https://morethannelson.com/officer/hon-john-byron/.

"Inventory of Historic Light Stations." https://irma.nps.gov/DataStore/Reference/Profile/2299727.

"James Gambier." www://morethannelson.com/officer/james-gambier-1/.

"James Hackman." https://everything2.com/?node=James+hackman#google_vignette.

Jesberger, Michael. "Washington's Headquarters Along the Neshaminy: The August Encampment of 1777." Lecture, July 12, 2021, online.

"John Freeman and the Battle of Freeman's Farm." https://sites.rootsweb.com/~truax/freeman.html.

"John Paul Jones and the Building of the Leith Fort." *Georgian Edinburgh* (blog), Feb. 3, 2012, https://georgianedinburgh.blogspot.com/2012/02/john-paul-jones-and-building-of-leith.html.

Jordan, Louis. "Colonial Currency." University of Notre Dame, https://coins.nd.edu/colcurrency/index.html.

"Journal of an Officer of the 47th Regiment of Foot." HL, mssHM 66.

Kehoe, Vincent J-R. "A Military Guide: The British Infantry of 1775." Society for the Preservation of Colonial Culture, 1974.

"Kettle Creek Battlefield." Inventory nomination form, National Register of Historic Places, 1975.

King, Martha J. "Peter Timothy." *South Carolina Encyclopedia*, https://www.scencyclopedia.org/sce/entries/timothy-peter/.

Lengel, Edward G. "Bayonets at Midnight: The Battle of Stony Point." HistoryNet, November 5, 2009, https://www.historynet.com/bayonets-at-midnight-the-battle-of-stony-point/.

———. "From Defeat to Victory in the North: 1777–1778." Ms. to author, 2013.

Lerwill, Leonard L. "The Personnel Replacement System in the United States Army." Department of the Army, Aug. 1954.

"The Liberty Bell." NPS, https://www.nps.gov/inde/learn/historyculture/stories-libertybell.htm.

"Life Guards." *Digital Encyclopedia of George Washington*, http://www.mountvernon.org/digital-encyclopedia/article/life-guards/.

Log book. John Paul Jones Cottage Museum, https://johnpauljonesmuseum.com/wp-content/uploads/2019/02/bhrlog.pdf.

Mackesy, Piers. "Could the British Have Won the War of Independence?" Lecture, Clark University, Worcester, Mass., Sept. 1975.

"Maitland, Hon. John (1732–79)." https://www.historyofparliamentonline.org/volume/1754-1790/member/maitland-hon-john-1732-79.

Malony, William J. "An Analysis of the Near-fatal Wound Suffered by Benedict Arnold at Saratoga." Friends of Saratoga Battlefield, http://friendsofsaratogabattlefield.org/an-analysis-of-the-near -fatal-wound-suffered-by-benedict-arnold-at-saratoga/.

"Martha Washington's Winter Vacation, 1779–1780." MNHP, https://www.nps.gov/morr/learn/ historyculture/martha-washington-s-winter-vacation-1779-1780.htm#:~:text=General%20 Washington%20had%20to%20send,Mansion%20on%20December%2031%2C%201779.

McDonald, Bob, ed. "Thro Mud & Mire into the Woods: The 1777 Continental Army Diary of Sergeant John Smith, First Rhode Island Regiment." American Antiquarian Society, from VFNHP.

McGeachy, Robert A. "The American War of Lieutenant Colonel Archibald Campbell." *Early America Review*, vol. 5, https://www.varsitytutors.com/earlyamerica/early-america-review/ volume-5/the-american-war-of-lieutenant-colonel-archibald-campbell.

"Memo: Battle of Brandywine, 11th Sept. 1777." APS, Feinstone Collection, #111.

"Memorandum of Occurrences During the Campaign, 1780." Uzal Johnson journal, South Carolina Historical Society, manuscript collection, College of Charleston.

"Memorial of John Harris Cruger of New York," Feb. 9, 1784. http://www.royalprovincial.com/ military/mems/ny/clmcrug.htm.

"Metropolitan Police." https://www.parliament.uk/about/living-heritage/transformingsociety/law order/policeprisons/overview/metropolitanpolice/.

"Miles Brewton house." https://www.scpictureproject.org/charleston-county/miles-brewton-house .html.

Millett, Allan R. "Whatever Became of the Militia in the History of the American Revolution?" George Rogers Clark lecture, SoC, 1986.

"Morin Transcription of *La Science*." Historical Society of Pennsylvania, https://hsp.org/sites/ default/files/legacy_files/migrated/findingaidam8085morin.pdf.

"Mount Independence Research." https://historicsites.vermont.gov/mount-independence/research.

"The Old Exchange & Provost Dungeon." http://oldexchange.org/history/.

Olsen, Eric P. "Churches Used, Abused & Burned During the American Revolution." MNHP, Mar. 2022.

Osman, Julia. "From Greatest Enemies to Greatest Allies: France and America in the War for Independence." Lecture, 4th Annual Conference on the American Revolution, Mar. 2015, Williamsburg, Va.

Paine, Thomas. *The American Crisis, Number VI*, Oct. 20, 1778. https://www.gutenberg.org/ files/3/41/3/41-h/3741-h.htm#link2H_1_0010.

"The Peak Years of British Copper Mining." Copper Development Association, Inc., 2013, https:// copper.org/education/history/60centuries/raw_material/thepeak.php#:~:text=The%20hey %2Dday%20of%20British,the%20bulk%20coming%20from%20Cornwall.

"Poor Richard's Almanack." Benjamin Franklin Historical Society, http://www.benjamin-franklin -history.org/poor-richards-almanac/.

Pope, Thomas. Pension application. R8326, Feb. 6, 1822. Southern Campaigns American Revolution Rension Statements & Rosters, https://revwarapps.org/r8326.pdf.

"Proceedings of . . . the Trial of Major General Arnold, June 1, 1779." https://quod.lib.umich.edu/e/ evans/N13495.0001.001/1:3.2?rgn=div2;view=fulltext.

Purdy, Lt. Gilbert, diary, LAC, Z 20/C21/1975/U2 (courtesy of Thomas J. McGuire).

"The Railroading of Silas Deane." New England Historical Society, 2022, https://newengland historicalsociety.com/the-railroading-of-silas-deane-or-how-to-destroy-a-patriots-reputation -for-225-years/.

Reader, David. "Fort Wilson." *Encyclopedia of Greater Philadelphia*, https://philadelphiaencyclopedia.org/essays/fort-wilson/.

Rees, John U. " 'I Extracted 4 balls by cutting in the opposite side from where they went in . . . ': Miscellaneous Accounts of Continental Army Surgeons and Surgeon's Mates." https://www.scribd .com/doc/236104178/John-U-Rees-author-s-articles-only-World-of-the-Common-Soldier/.

———. " 'The load a soldier generally carries during a campaign . . . ': The British Soldier's Burden in the American War for Independence." https://www.scribd.com/document/335479170/The

-load-a-soldier-generally-carries-during-a-campaign-The-British-Soldier-s-Burden-in-the
-American-War-for-Independence.

———. "'None of you know the hardships of a soldiers life . . . ': Service of the Connecticut
Regiments of Maj. Gen. Alexander McDougall's Division, 1777–1778." https://www.scribd
.com/doc/236104178/John-U-Rees-author-s-articles-only-World-of-the-Common-Soldier.

———. "'The pleasure of their number,' 1778: Crisis, Conscription, and Revolutionary Soldiers'
Recollections." https://www.scribd.com/document/126069484/First-Part-The-pleasure-of-their
-number-1778-Crisis-Conscription-and-Revolutionary-Soldiers-Recollections-A-Preliminary
-Study-Part-I-Filling.

———. "'A Quantity of Public Leather . . . Made Up into Shoes and Accoutrements': Soldiers, Prisoners, and Deserters at the Continental Manufactory in Philadelphia." https://www.scribd
.com/doc/306876120/A-quantity-of-public-leather-made-up-into-shoes-and-accoutrements
-Soldiers-Prisoners-and-Deserters-at-the-Continental-Manufactory-in-Philadel.

———. "'Reach Coryels Ferry. Encamp on the Pennsylvania side': The March from Valley Forge to
Monmouth Courthouse, 18 to 28 June 1778." https://www.academia.edu/4595041/_Endnotes
_Reach_Coryels_ferry_Encamp_on_the_Pennsylvania_side_The_March_from_Valley_Forge
_to_Monmouth_Courthouse_18_to_28_June_1778.

Rees, John U., and Bob McDonald. "'The Action was renewed with a very warm Cannonade':
New Jersey Officer's Diary, 21 June 1777 to 31 August 1778." https://www.scribd.com/doc/
216378254/The-Action-was-renew-d-with-a-very-warm-Canonade-New-Jersey-Officer-s-Diary
-21-June-1777-to-31-August-1778.

"Regulations for the Order and Discipline of the Troops of the United States, by Friedrich Wilhelm
Steuben," American Revolution Institute, https://www.americanrevolutioninstitute.org/master
piecesin-detail/steuben-regulations/.

"The Revolutionary War Diary of Chaplain Andrew Hunter." https://revwar75.com/library/bob/
HunterDiaries2.htm.

"Revolutionary War Forfeited Estates, 1779." Pennsylvania Historical & Museum Commission,
http://www.phmc.state.pa.us/portal/communities/documents/1776-1865/revolutionary-war
-forfeited-estates.html.

"Richard Howe, 1st Earl 4th Viscount." https://morethannelson.com/officer/richard-howe-1st
-earl-4th-viscount/.

"Richard Kempenfelt." https://morethannelson.com/officer/richard-kempenfelt/.

"River Mileage System." Delaware River Basin Commission, https://www.nj.gov/drbc/basin/river
-mileage-sys.html.

Robertaccio, Joseph. "Documents Relating to the Battle of Oriskany and the Siege of Fort Stanwix."
3rd ed., Jan. 2013, https://www.fort-plank.com/ORISKANY_Robertaccios_Notes_Updated
.pdf.

"Royal Residences: Buckingham Palace." https://www.royal.uk/royal-residences-buckingham-palace
#:~:text=George%20III%20bought%20Buckingham%20House,15%20children%20were%20
born%20there.

"Sandy Hook Light." New Jersey Lighthouse Society, http://www.njlhs.org/njlight/sandy.html.

Schaffer, Mark. "The Revolutionary War Burial Ground in Bethlehem." Pennsylvania State Historic
Preservation Office, Oct. 29, 2014, https://pahistoricpreservation.com/revolutionary-war
-burial-ground-bethlehem/.

Schenawolf, Harry. "Washington's New York City Headquarters, No. 1 Broadway." *Revolutionary War
Journal,* July 9, 2013, http://www.revolutionarywarjournal.com/washingtons-headquarters/.

Schnitzer, Eric. Lecture, George Washington Round Table of the American Revolution, Washington, D.C., Nov. 3, 2021.

Schopieray, Cheney. "The Treasonous Correspondence of Benedict Arnold." Lecture, Dec. 9, 2020,
WLC.

Scott, William. "The Battle of Germantown." APS, SMs Coll 9.

"1714 Riot Act." UK Parliament, https://www.parliament.uk/about/living-heritage/transforming
society/electionsvoting/newport-rising/1839-newp-ris/riot-act-1714/.

Sewall, Henry, diary. Ms. from *Maine Farmer,* 1872 (courtesy of William M. Ferraro).

Seymour, Joseph. Lecture, U.S. Army National Guard historian. SoC, Jan. 16, 2015.

Shank, J. B. "Voltaire." *The Stanford Encyclopedia of Philosophy*, Summer 2022 ed., https://plato.stanford.edu/archives/sum2022/entries/voltaire/.

Sherman, William Thomas. "The View from Strawberry Hill: Horace Walpole and the American Revolution." http://gunjones.com/.

"A Short History of Sheerness Dockyard." https://www.thehistorypress.co.uk/articles/a-short-history-of-sheerness-dockyard/.

Shy, John W. "The American Revolution Today." Harmon Memorial Lecture, U.S. Air Force Academy, 1974.

"Sir Archibald and Sir James Campbell." https://www.westminster-abbey.org/abbey-commemorations/commemorations/sir-archibald-and-sir-james-campbell.

"Sir Charles Hardy." https://www.historyofparliamentonline.org/volume/1754-1790/member/hardy-sir-charles-1714-80.

"Sir George Collier." https://morethannelson.com/officer/sir-george-collier/.

"Sir Richard Pearson." https://morethannelson.com/officer/sir-richard-pearson/.

"Sir Thomas Pye." https://morethannelson.com/officer/sir-thomas-pye/.

Smith, Fitz-Henry, Jr. *The Memorial to the Chevalier de Saint-Sauveur.* Proceedings of the Bostonian Society, 1918.

Snell, Charles W. "A Report on the Balcarres and Breymann Redoubts." SNHP, Feb. 2, 1949.

Taillemite, Étienne. "Bougainville, Louis-Antoine de." *Dictionary of Canadian Biography*, vol. 5, https://www.biographi.ca/en/bio/bougainville_louis_antoine_de_5E.html.

Thompson, Mary V. "As If I Had Been a Very Great Somebody." Lecture, Nov. 9, 2002, Mount Vernon, http://catalog.mountvernon.org/cdm/ref/collection/p16829coll4/id/2.

Thibaut, Jacqueline. "This Fatal Crisis: Logistics, Supply, and the Continental Army at Valley Forge, 1777–1778." Valley Forge Historical Research Report, vol. 2, VFNHP, 1979.

———. "In the True Rustic Order." Valley Forge Historical Research Report, vol. 3. VFNHP, 1979.

"Thomas Jefferson, a Brief Biography." https://www.monticello.org/site/jefferson/thomas-jefferson-brief-biography.

Toogood, Anna Coxe. "Independence Mall, the Eighteenth Century Development." NPS, 2004.

"Tybee Island Lighthouse." https://www.lighthousefriends.com/light.asp?ID=322.

"Utility of the *Atlantic Neptune*." LOC, https://www.loc.gov/resource/g3301pm.gan00003/?sp=3.

Vaughn, Thomas. "Moses Dunbar, the Other Connecticut Man Hanged in the Revolution." New England Historical Society, n.d., http://www.newenglandhistoricalsociety.com/moses-dunbar-connecticut-man-hanged-revolution/.

Washington's camp bed. Mount Vernon, https://emuseum.mountvernon.org/objects/807/field-bedstead.

"Westminster: Buckingham Palace." British History Online, https://www.british-history.ac.uk/old-new-london/vol4/pp61-74.

White, Jerry. "The Gordon Riots, 1780." London Historians, Oct. 2011, file:///C:/Users/lratk/Downloads/Gordon%20Riots%201780.pdf.

Wickwire, Franklin B. "McLean, Francis." *Dictionary of Canadian Biography*, vol. 4, https://www.biographi.ca/en/bio/mclean_francis_4E.html.

"William Alexander's (Lord Stirling) Raid of Staten Island, January 14–15, 1780." *The Revolutionary War on Staten Island* (blog), Sept. 9, 2019, https://revolutionarywarstatenisland.com/2019/09/09/william-alexanders-lord-stirling-raid-of-staten-island-january-14-15-1780/.

"William Smallwood (1732–1792)." Archives of Maryland, biographical series, https://msa.maryland.gov/megafile/msa/speccol/sc3500/sc3520/001100/001134/html/1134bio.html.

"William Tryon." https://www.nps.gov/people/william-tryon.htm.

"The Wreck of the *HMS Somerset* (III)." NPS, Cape Cod National Seashore, n.d., https://www.nps.gov/caco/learn/historyculture/upload/Somersetrack.pdf.

Acknowledgments

The second volume of the Revolution Trilogy is now complete, but only because of the generous assistance, expertise, and encouragement of many people. I am again indebted to a hundred or more archivists, historians, curators, and librarians at two dozen institutions, as well as a number of knowledgeable readers.

Mount Vernon is an exemplary seat of scholarship as well as George Washington's Virginia home, and I'm grateful for the support of Douglas Bradburn, the president and CEO. Thanks, too, to Patrick Spero, the former executive director of the George Washington Presidential Library, and to both his predecessor, Kevin Butterfield, and his successor, Lindsay M. Chervinsky, as well as to Stephen A. McLeod, director of library programs; Julie Coleman Almacy, vice president of media and communications; and the Mount Vernon Ladies' Association, including the regent, Margaret Hartman Nichols, and her colleagues.

At the remarkable William L. Clements Library on the University of Michigan campus, I thank Paul J. Erickson, the director; Cheney J. Schopieray, the curator of manuscripts; Clayton Lewis, the former curator of graphics materials; Terese Murphy, the head of reader services; and Jayne Ptolemy, the assistant curator of manuscripts. I again spent many productive hours in the library of the Society of the Cincinnati in Washington, D.C., for which I'm grateful to the former director Ellen McCallister Clark and research services librarian, Rachel Nellis.

The New-York Historical Society has been a splendid resource, and I thank Louise Mirrer, the president and CEO; Dale Gregory, the former vice president of public programs; Alexander Kassl, the former director of public programs; and, in the Patricia D. Klingenstein Library, manuscripts librarian Erin Weinman and reference librarians Mariam Touba and Jill Reichenbach. At the American Philosophical Society in Philadelphia, I thank Michael Miller, Sabrina Bocanegra, and their colleagues; the society now houses the David Center for the American Revolution, and I appreciate the help of Meg McSweeney, the former chief operating officer, and librarian Katherine A. Ludwig. At the Huntington Library in San Marino, California, my thanks to Jazmin Rew-Pinchem of reader services and the staff of the Munger Research Center.

I'm grateful to the staff of the National Archives, at Kew, in the United Kingdom, and to the Georgian Papers Programme at Windsor Castle, where, as a fellow in April 2016, I sharpened my sense of George III, his family, and his reign.

In Charleston, South Carolina, I thank Carl P. Borick, director of the Charleston Museum; C. J. Cantwell and Edward Jackson for their insights into St. Michael's Church; Nic Butler, public historian at Charleston County Public Library; and Winfred B. "Bo" Moore, Jr., former dean of humanities and social sciences at the Citadel. Particular thanks to David L. Preston, the General Mark W. Clark Distinguished Professor of History, also at the Citadel. Thanks, too, to Karen Stokes, archivist at the South Carolina Historical Society Archive, in Addlestone Library at the College of Charleston.

At Saratoga National Historical Park, ranger and historian Eric Schnitzer, whose knowledge about the battles there and throughout the northern campaign is unequaled, was generous enough to show me the lay of the land over the course of two days. I have profited immensely from his many years of deep research. I also thank David Pitlyk, historic site assistant at Bennington Battlefield State Historic Site in Walloomsac, New York, and the Friends of the Bennington Battlefield. At Valley Forge National Historical Park, I'm grateful to Rose Fennell, the superintendent; to archivist Dona M. McDermott; and to ranger Jennifer K. Bolton, who gave me a tour of the encampment in September 2021. I'm particularly grateful to former VFNHP historian Joseph Lee Boyle, who shared with me his vast archive of Valley Forge material.

At Morristown National Historical Park, I thank Thomas E. Ross, the superintendent; Jude M. Pfister, chief of cultural resources; Sarah E. Minegar, archivist and museum educator; and Eric P. Olsen, ranger and historian, whose many astute monographs were exceptionally helpful. Thanks also to Philip W. Gaffney, president emeritus of the Washington Association of New Jersey, and to James Amemasor, research specialist at the New Jersey Historical Society.

At the Georgia Historical Society in Savannah, I thank W. Todd Groce, the president and CEO; Walter M. "Sonny" Deriso, the former board chairman; Christy M. Crisp, director of programs; and most especially senior historian Stan Deaton, along with society colleagues Laura Garcia-Culler and Patricia Meagher. At the Château Lafayette in Chavaniac, France, my thanks to Claire Pratviel, *chargée de mission Grands Projets*, and her colleagues Aude Guerin and Flore Bédoussac. My thanks also to the staff of the Château de Versailles, including the guides who showed me the king's private apartments. At the Papers of George Washington project at the University of Virginia, I thank William M. Ferraro, research associate professor and managing editor; Benjamin Lee Huggins, research associate professor and associate editor; and their former colleague Edward G. Lengel.

At the Thompson-Pell Research Center at Fort Ticonderoga, New York, I'm grateful to curator Matthew Keagle and to Miranda Peters, vice president of collections and digital production. My thanks to Michael J. F. Sheehan, senior historian at Stony Point Battlefield State Historic Site in New York; to ranger William Sawyer at Fort Stanwix National Monument in Rome, New York; and to Beth Beatty, executive director of Fort Mifflin on the Delaware in Philadelphia, and her colleagues Connor Duffy and Matt Muto.

Thanks to Tom Snow for a tour of Cliveden—the Benjamin Chew House—in Germantown, Pennsylvania; to James J. Holmberg, curator of collections at the Filson Historical Society in Louisville, Kentucky; and to Ross Mulcare, former associate archivist at the Harvard University Archives. I thank the American Battlefield Trust for their fine work and support, particularly David N. Duncan, the president; Garry Adelman, the chief historian; and Kristopher White, the deputy director of education. Thanks also to filmmaker Ken Burns and his associates at Florentine Films—Sarah Botstein, David Schmidt, and Geoffrey C. Ward—for their encouragement as we pursue our respective projects on the Revolution.

In Carlisle, Pennsylvania, the U.S. Army Heritage and Education Center has been a welcoming home away from home for a quarter century, and I thank past and current staff members, including Richard L. Baker, Greta Braungard, Stephen Bye, Conrad C. Crane, Clifton Hyatt, David A. Keough, Kate C. Lemay, Michael E. Lynch, Geoffrey S. Mangelsdorf, Justine E. Melone, Tom Puffenbarger, and Jessica J. Sheets. At the adjacent U.S. Army War College, I thank the commandant, Major General David C. Hill; his predecessors, Major General John S. Kem and Major General Stephen J. Maranian; and particularly my friend and former teaching collaborator, retired Colonel Charles D. Allen.

The National World War II Museum in New Orleans is dedicated to a different war, as I was in a previous trilogy, but this great institution has continued to encourage and embrace me even after I've decamped to an earlier century. I'm grateful to Stephen Watson, the president and CEO, and his predecessor, Gordon H. "Nick" Mueller, now president emeritus, and their colleagues.

I thank Richard D. Brown, professor emeritus at the University of Connecticut; Richard Colton, historian and historic weapons supervisor at the Springfield Armory National Historical Site; Paul James deGategno, professor emeritus of English, Pennsylvania State University at Brandywine; Philippe Étienne, the former ambassador of France to the United States; Roger Knight, for his insights into the eighteenth-century Royal Navy; Zach Launey, president of NRVPC, and his colleagues for corralling misbehaving electrons; Gary Mortensen, president of Stoller Family Estate, in Dayton, Oregon; Julia Osman of Mississippi State University, for help with French archival sources; and the piano virtuoso Jeffrey Siegel, for his assistance in re-creating Paris in the spring of 1778, when one visitor to the city was Wolfgang Amadeus Mozart.

Thanks also to Charles Baxley; Carl M. Dozier; Steven E. Elliott; Don N. Hagist; Cherel Henderson; Martin R. Howard; Ross and Margaret Irvin; Hank Keirsey; Jason Liebman; William J. Longan, Jr.; Christian McBurney; Thomas J. McGuire; Linda Snow McLoon; E. Jerome Melson; Antony Page; Wayne R. Reynolds and Catherine B. Reynolds; retired Colonel James T. Roberts, USA; David Rubenstein; the late Stephen Rubin; Gregory W. Wendt; and Roger S. Williams.

I'm deeply grateful to my friends Bob Woodward and Elsa Walsh for helping to launch volume 1 of this trilogy, and to Sir Max Hastings and his wife, Penny, for their extraordinarily generous hospitality and friendship in London and Berkshire.

In researching this book I had invaluable help from Joseph Balkoski, former director of the Maryland Museum of Military History in Baltimore, and from my former *Washington Post* colleague Lucy Shackelford, who also tracked down most of the illustrations displayed in these pages. I couldn't ask for more resourceful, diligent comrades. In Paris, I thank Fabienne Chamelot for her assistance in researching French archives and in translating French texts. Master cartographer and military historian Gene Thorp, president of Cartographic Concepts, Inc., created the exceptional maps for this volume, as he has for five previous books of mine.

I was fortunate to have seven accomplished historians read all or portions of the manuscript: Joseph Balkoski, Carl P. Borick, Stan Deaton, David L. Preston, Barnet Schecter, Eric Schnitzer, and Ty Seidule. Their expertise and encouragement made this a better book; any errors of fact or interpretation are solely my responsibility.

This is the eighth book, spanning nearly forty years, for which I've had the priceless collaboration of my longtime editor and friend, John Sterling, and my longtime agent and friend, Rafe Sagalyn. For the eighth time, I thank them publicly and profusely. Thanks, too, to others on the team at

Crown Publishing and at Penguin Random House: Nihar Malaviya, David Drake, Gillian Blake, Annsley Rosner, Julie Cepler, Dyana Messina, Chris Brand, Christine Tanigawa, Andrea Lau, Natalie Blachere, Mason Eng, Amy Li, Jess Scott, and Isabela Alcantara. I'm again grateful to copy editor Bonnie Thompson for her sharp eyes and impeccable rigor, to copy editor Robin Slutzky, to proofreader Chuck Thompson, and to publicist Elizabeth Shreve for her exceptional efforts to promote the Revolution Trilogy.

It would all be pointless without my family, and my deepest gratitude goes to Jane, Rush, Sarah, J.P., Jessica, and the grandchildren who have joined our tribe since the publication of *The British Are Coming*, and who are properly positioned in the dedication of this book.

Index

Page numbers in *italics* refer to maps.

Abigail (American transport), 488
Acland, John, 216
Active (British warship), 316
act of attainder, 572
Adams, Abigail, 339, 341, 396, 435, 615
Adams, John, 48, 80, 84, 93, 146, 154, 158,
    339–41, 517
Adams, John Quincy, 339, 615
Adams, Samuel, 146, 180, 188
Addison, Joseph, 274
Admiralty building (British), 451–52
Aetna (British warship), 240
African Americans, 59. *See also* slaves and
    slavery
Agnew, James, 137, 174–75
Aimable (French frigate), 389
Aitken, James (John the Painter), 334
Albany (British sloop-of-war), 484
Albany, New York, 227–28
Albion (British ship), 409
Alden, John Richard, 305
Alexander, Charles, 159
Alexander, William. *See* Stirling, William
    Alexander, Lord
Allen, Ethan, 417
Allen, James, 146, 314–15
Allen, John, 51, 94
Allen, William, 565
Allen, William, Jr., 156
Alliance (French frigate), 516, 530, 531, 534
Alling, Charles, 474
Almy, Mary, 395–96, 398, 400, 405
America (Continental ship), 316, 534
American colonies. *See also specific colonies*
    celebration in, 444
    currency in, 307–8, 435–36, 563–65
    depreciation in, 564
    faith in, 616
    French support of, 11, 281, 289, 290, 309,
        444, 555–56, 617–18

inflation in, 435, 436, 564
loyalist support in, 157–58
map of, *28*
metaphors for, 82
my country viewpoint in, 615
price control in, 564
rebellion of, 8
treaty with France and, 9, 287–88
wages in, 564
war costs to, 435, 563
war viewpoint in, 615
American prisoners of war
    allowance of, 470
    exchange proposal regarding, 18, 86, 230, 346
    freedom for, 211
    in Indian Expedition, 493, 500
    labor of, 50
    movement of, 42, 46
    in New York, 127
    officers as, 605
    in Philadelphia, 156
    treatment of, 53, 153, 230, 231, 343, 415,
        572, 577
    victory announcement to, 228
    in Walnut Street jail, 178, 317
American spies, 163, 252, 439–40, 441, 479,
    612, 618
Amherst, Jeffrey, 509
Amphitrite (British ship), 87
Amsterdam, 16
Anderson, Enoch, 135, 167
Anderson, Troyer Steele, 315
André, John, 123, 151, 153, 246–47, 313–14,
    318, 411, 567–68, 581, 605
Andrew, Alexander, 175
Andrew Doria (American warship), 245, 579
Angell, Israel, 250
Anna (British vessel), 580
Apollo (British frigate), 401, 579
approach to Monmouth, 358–60, *359*
Arbuthnot, Marriot, 555–56, 570–71, 574, 575,
    582, 585, 593, 606

Ardent (British ship), 521
Arethusa (British warship), 348
Ariel (British ship), 534
Arkwright, Richard, 257, 454
Armstrong, John, 141
Armstrong, Samuel, 197, 250
Army of Invasion, 515, 518, 524
Arnold (American battery), 234
Arnold, Benedict
    acquittal of, 568
    anger of, 104
    in Battle of Saratoga at Freeman's Farm,
        189–98
    in Battle of Saratoga at Bemus Heights,
        214–18
    at Battle of Valcour Bay, 1776, 30, 41
    characteristics of, 218
    charges against, 442
    Charming Nancy (schooner) and, 568–69
    court-martial of, 566–67, 568
    criticism of, 210
    at Danbury, Connecticut, battle, 65–66
    feud of, 442
    at Fort Stanwix, 103–5
    Horatio Gates and, 198–99, 212–13
    on Indian tribe attacks, 52
    injuries to, 218, 228
    intelligence passing by, 567–68
    leadership of, 49, 65–66, 103–4, 189,
        319–20, 443
    malice of, 228
    oath of, 319
    Peggy Shippen and, 441–42, 443
    resignation of, 442–43
    at Skenesborough, 41–42
    treason by, 567
    in Valley Forge, 319
    will of, 192
Articles of Confederation, 434–35
articles of convention, 224
assault on Savannah, *540,* 541–52, 553–55,
    560 61
assault on Stony Point, *478,* 479–84
The Atlantic Neptune, 389–90
attack at Paoli, *148,* 151–53
attack on Hampton Roads, 468, *469,* 470–71
Atwood, Phoebe, 502
Augusta (British warship), 239–41, 326
Augusta, Georgia, 425–26
Augustus (ship), 524
Aurora (British frigate), 392
Austin, Jonathan, 280

Bache, Benjamin Franklin, 14
Bache, Sally, 431

Bacheller, Nathanial, 212, 215
Baddeley, Mary O'Callaghan, 311–12
Bahamas, 418
Bailyn, Bernard, 339
Baker, Doctor, 431
Balcarres Redoubt, 217, 218
Baldwin, Jeduthan, 226, 444
Baldwin, Minney, 502
Balfour, Nesbit, 318
Bancroft, Edward, 282–83, 284
Bancroft, James, 212
Barbados, 424
The Barber of Seville (Beaumarchais), 279
Barré, Isaac, 269
Barren Hill, 314–15
Barrington, Samuel, 424
Barrington, William, 272
Bartholomai, Christian, 600
Barton, William, 69, 504
Battle for Newport, 391–400, *393, 399,* 401,
    403–8
Battle for the Delaware. *See* Delaware, Battle
    for the
Battle for the Hudson Highlands, *203,* 204,
    206, 208
Battle of Bennington, 108–9, *109,* 110–16
Battle of Brandywine. *See* Brandywine, Battle
    of
Battle of Bunker Hill, 552
Battle of Germantown. *See* Germantown,
    Battle of
Battle of Grenada, 538–39
Battle of Hubbardton, 43–47, *45*
Battle of Minden, 267
Battle of Monmouth. *See* Monmouth, Battle of
Battle of Oriskany, *99,* 101–3
Battle of Saratoga. *See* Saratoga, Battle of
Battle of Saratoga at Bemus Heights, *209,* 210,
    211, 212, 213–14, 215–17
Battle of Ushant, 349–53, 354
Baum, Friedrich, 106, 110, 116, 218
Baurmeister, Carl, 314, 360
Baylor, George, 414–15
Bay of Honduras, 457
Bean, Benjamin, 111
Beatty, Erkuries, 559
Beatty, William, 176
Beaumarchais (Pierre-Augustin Caron),
    279–80, 282
Bell, Andrew, 357
Belle Poule (French frigate), 348
Bemus, Jotham, 191
Bennington, Battle of, 106–7, 108–9, *109,*
    110–16
Bense, Johann, 199

Bermuda, 418
Best, Abraham, 167
Bethlehem, Pennsylvania, 145–46
Betty (British ship), 16
Bibliothèque Nationale, 12–13
Biddulph, Robert, 570, 576
Bigelow, Timothy, 212
Biggin Bridge, 595
Billias, George Athan, 231
Billingsport, 160, 161
Birmingham Meeting House, 130, 132, 140
Black Dick (American ship), 159–60
Black Dick"s signal book, 399. *See also* Howe,
    Richard, Viscount
Black Prince (American ship), 491
blacks. *See* African Americans; slaves and
    slavery
Black Watch (Highland Scots), 150–51
Black Wednesday, 611
Blake, Thomas, 40–41
Blake, William, 610
Bland, Theodorick, 129, 131
Blonde (British ship), 491
Bloomfield, Joseph, 136, 139
Boardman, Oliver, 218
Bolton, Mason, 506
Bonaparte, Napoleon, 21
bondmen, 591
Bonhomme Richard (American frigate), 347,
    527, 528, 529–32, 533, 535
Book of Martyrs (Foxe), 124
Boone, Daniel, 493
Bordeaux, France, 20
Borick, Carl P., 606
Boston
    artillery from, 394
    conditions of, 231
    d'Estaing in, 408, 418
    escort into, 383
    evacuation from, 230
    expenses of, 492
    flotilla to, 386
    Old South Meeting House in, 412
    ration dispute in, 409
    report from, 559
Boswell, James, 260, 328, 612
Boudinot, Elias, 304
Bourbon War, 344–46, 347, 348–53
Bowater, Edward, 352
Boyd, James, 426, 427
Boyd, Thomas, 504–5
Boyne (British ship), 539
Braddock, Edward, 189
Brady, John, 135–36
Brandywine, Battle of

blame in, 141
British movement in, 129, 131, 132, *133*,
    134, 137–38
British post in, 128
British strategy for, 125, 128–29
casualties in, 128, 132, 134, 135–36, 137,
    139, 140
Continental movement in, 134–35, 137, 138,
    139
Continental post in, 127
Continental strategy for, 125
ending of, 137
Great Post Road in, 127
leadership of, 127
map of, *121, 133*
planning for, 120
start of, 128
topography of, 125
weaponry in, 134
Brant, Joseph (Thayendanegea), 98, 100,
    499–500
Bretagne (French ship), 288, 350, 351
Brétigney, Marquis de, 18
Breymann, Heinrich, 113, 114, 218
Breymann"s Redoubt, 218
Brisbane, John, 395, 398
Britannia (British brig), 70, 447
British Army, *See also* British Army units, *and*
    specific battles, and locations
    ambush on, 186
    Americans as against, 124
    American slaves in, 592
    booths of, 155
    booty of, 147, 225, 471, 475
    casualties of, 46, 49, 66, 102, 105, 112, 115,
        137, 140, 152, 167, 168, 177, 180, 186,
        195, 197, 204, 216, 217, 219, 229–30, 241,
        260, 357, 375, 377, 406, 407, 413, 422,
        423, 425, 471, 475, 476, 481–82, 483, 552,
        614
    celebration of, 556–57, 577
    challenges of, 116
    defections in, 316
    description of, 30, 32, 130–31
    deserters of, 50, 104–5, 208, 357–58, 482,
        548
    desertion by, 104–5, 208, 213, 221, 318, 330,
        426, 450, 479, 614
    disease in, 116, 570
    diversion of, 97–98
    encampment of, 569–70
    evacuation of, 229–30
    expansion of, 461–63
    flaws of, 195
    food of, 183

British Army *(cont'd)*
  Indian tribes allied with, 29, 39, 50–51, 98,
    499, 502–3, 504, 506
  instructions for, 312
  intelligence of, 422, 463, 508
  morale of, 66, 419
  movement of, 70–71, 76, 91, 123, *148,*
    154–55, 186–87, 201, 221, 356
  in Philadelphia, 155–56, 246–47, 316–18, 431
  physicians in, 140
  plans of, 70, 417, 418
  plundering by, 360
  prisoners from, 378, 427
  professions of, 122
  punishment in, 122–23
  recruitment and enlistment strategies of, 58,
    60, 122, 157–58, 271, 461–63, 571, 608
  reinforcements for, 201–2, 570
  retreat of, 104–5
  road building by, 50
  social life of, 182
  soldier treatment in, 33
  supplies and rations for, 66–67, 192–93, 199,
    208, 243, 356, 413, 414, 450, 496–97, 571
  support for, 157
  surrender of, *209,* 225–27
  treatment of American prisoners by, 158–59
  uniform of, 216
  war council options of, 223
  weaponry of, 30, 70–71, 184, 192, 195, 217,
    473, 542, 582
British Army units
  British Legion, 595
  Foot Regiments, 4th (King's Own), 137, 173;
    5th, 137, 167–68; 8th, 495; 9th, 42–43, 49,
    194, 225; 10th, 234; 16th, 545; 17th, 137,
    480, 481; 20th, 195; 22nd, 406; 24th, 194,
    214, 217; 28th, 358; 33rd, 376, 580; 37th,
    570; 40th, 169; 42nd, 150–51; 46th, 137;
    47th, 32, 221, 222; 52nd, 154, 167,
    377–78; 53rd, 211, 222; 54th, 395, 570;
    55th, 167–68; 60th, 542; 62nd, 194, 197,
    222; 64th, 135, 137; 71st, 123, 466, 480,
    482, 542; 74th, 484–85; 79th, 326, 417–18;
    82nd, 465, 484–85
  Grenadiers, 32, 234; 2nd, 374–75
  Gunners, 234
  Highlanders, 422
  King's American Regiment, 474
  Light Dragoons, 32, 111, 357; 16th, 138,
    150–51, 368; 17th, 207
  Light Infantry, 217
  Queen's Rangers, 137, 357, 368, 371
  Royal Artillery, 32, 134, 137, 155, 159, 192,
    195, 210, 220, 325, 369, 580, 598, 600

British home waters, *513*
British Parliament, 263, 269–71, 272–73, 275,
  312, 323–24, 608–11
  House of Commons, 268–71, 324–25
British prisoners of war, 16, 144, 174, 212, 227,
  378, 395, 471, 531–32
British Royal Navy, *See also specific battles,*
  locations, and ships
  casualties of, 241, 330, 348, 351–52, 353,
    389, 395, 401, 450, 465, 492, 521, 524,
    531, 533, 539, 570, 582, 585
  copper use by, 334
  defense of, 346, 388
  desertion in, 330
  disarray of, 447
  disease in, 524
  division in, 519
  dockyard of, 326, 329, 332–33, 334, 521
  in English Channel, 523
  evacuation of, 230
  failures of, 521
  fleet of, 30, 70–71, 72–73, 118–19, 159–60,
    230, 272, 326, 329, 330, 332, 334, 343,
    349, 350, 399–400, 425, 450, 473, 512,
    519–20, 570 (*See also specific vessels*)
  growth of, 450
  home waters strategy of, 519
  industry of, 327–28
  movement of, 335–36, 337, 415, 421, 450,
    490–91, 572–73
  patrol of, 17
  peril to, 239–40
  prisoners of, 531–32
  provisions for, 418
  recruitment strategies of, 462
  strategies of, 334
  supplies for, 450, 581
  wages in, 327
  war preparations of, 509
  weaponry of, 350, 388, 542, 582
  weather challenges of, 520, 579–81
British spies, 10, 90, 282, 314, 358, 368, 463, 602
Briton (British ship), 579–80
Brodhead, Daniel, 506
Brooks, John, 214–15
Brown, John, 210
Browne, Dr. James, 228
Brunswickers, 196, 217
Buchanan, William, 294
Buckley, Jane, 475
Buford, Abraham, 602
Buker, George E., 492
Bunker Hill, Battle of, 552
Burdon, George, 345–46
Burford (British warship), 17

Burgoyne, John
  on ambush, 186
  on American military, 39, 183
  battle flags of, 224–25
  on Battle of Bennington, 110
  in Battle of Saratoga, 197
  in Battle of Saratoga at Bemus Heights, 213, 216–17
  on Canada Army, 105, 183–84
  on capitulation, 223
  challenges of, 116–17
  criticism of, 208, 211, 229
  death of, 232
  description of, 53
  dethroning of, 232
  evacuation of, 230, 231–32
  family of, 34
  on fate of war, 227
  on Fort Ticonderoga, 36
  on Fraser, 220
  headquarters of, 42, 53, 182
  on Indian ambush, 51–52
  leadership of, 33–34, 35, 116, 200, 208, 210
  morale of, 231
  negotiations by, 224
  overview of, 32–33
  planning by, 49–50, 53
  as playwright, 232
  on provisions, 106
  at 'Schuyler's country house, 221, 227
  surrender of, 226, 269
  war council of, 223
Burke, Edmund, 269, 275, 353, 447, 563, 610
Burr, Aaron, 374, 379
Butler, John, 503–4
Butler, Reverend John, 263
Butler, Richard, 369
Butler, Thomas, 297
Butler, Walter, 499–500, 504
Byron, John, 335–36, 399, 403, 418, 538–39

Cadwalader, John, 306, 442
Cahokia, 494
Cambis, Joseph Comte de, 400
Campbell, Archibald, 416–17, 421, 423, 424, 425–26, 427, 541
Campbell, Mungo, 204
Campfield, Jabez, 502
Canada Army (British)
  in Battle of Saratoga, 193, 197
  casualties of, 219, 222
  challenges of, 105
  description of, 35
  extraction of, 229
  as independent command, 183
  instructions regarding, 183–84
  leadership of, 34–35
  morale of, 223
  movement of, 199, 220
  population of, 225
  strength of, 69
  supplies and provisions for, 205–6, 207–8
  treaty of convention and, 225
  weaponry of, 35–36, 184
Canadian prisoners of war, 212
Carleton (British warship), 30, 41, 211
Carleton, Guy, 33–34, 183
Carlisle, Abraham, 432
Carlisle, Frederick Howard, Lord, 312, 315–16
Carnival, 1, 3
Carysfort (British ship), 414
Case, Wheeler, 52
Castleton, 43
castrametation, 250, 251
Catholicism, 386, 608, 609–10
Catholic Relief Act, 608, 609
Cayuga Indians, 98, 497
Centurion (British warship), 307
Cerberus (British warship), 395
Chads's Ford, 125, 127, 129, 137
Champion (xebecs), 245
Champion, Henry, 481
Charing Cross, 259
Charles III, King of Spain, 281, 286, 456, 511, 512, 514
Charleston, South Carolina
  British attacks in, 602–3
  British landings at, 581–82
  casualties in, 601–2
  celebration in, 606
  defenses of, 586–87, 588
  description of, 590
  destruction in, 206, 590, 594–95, 600, 601–2
  detonation calamity in, 601–2
  economic conditions of, 590
  encirclement of, 599
  fall of, 590–601
  garrison in, 606
  importance of, 573
  plans regarding, 573–74
  siege of, 582, 583, 584–86, 587
  slavery in, 590–91, 604–5
  surrender of, 600
  transformation of, 604
Charlotte (Queen of England), 333, 334
Charming Nancy (British ship), 568–69
Chasseurs Volontaires, 537
Chateaubriand, Vicomte de, 21
Chatfield, Jesse, 214
Chatham, William Pitt, Earl of, 321–25

Chatham dockyard, 326
Cherokee Indians, 497
Cherry Valley, 499–500
Chesapeake Bay, 59, 65, 74, 91, 118, 119, 466, 573
chevaux-de-frise (stackadoes), 161, 233, 234, 239, 240, 246, 248
Chew, Benjamin, 169
Christie, Ian R., 613
Cilley, Joseph, 194, 376
citadel, in Charleston, South Carolina, 586–87
City Tavern (Philadelphia), 94–95
Clark, Daniel, 198
Clark, Ebenezer, 101
Clark, George Rogers, 494, 495, 497
Clark, Joseph, 356
Clark, Peter, 112, 115–16
Clary (Continental ship), 21
Clement, William, 112
Clerke, Sir Francis Carr, 43, 184, 186, 216
Cliffe, Loftus, 58, 119, 138, 167, 378
Clinton, Fort, 204, 207, 224
Clinton, George, 202, 205
Clinton, Henry
    on assault on Stony Point, 482
    on attack at Jersey City, 483
    background of, 61
    in Battle for Newport, 407–8
    in Battle for the Hudson Highlands, 204
    in Battle of Monmouth, 367–71, 373–75, 377, 378–79
    Benedict Arnold and, 567–68
    capitulation terms of, 599
    celebration of, 557
    characteristics of, 62, 311, 419, 596
    in Charleston, South Carolina, 573–74, 604, 606–7
    concerns of, 465–66, 467, 472
    Cornwallis and, 574–75, 596
    criticism of, 572–73
    declaration demands of, 605–6
    despondence of, 69
    encouragement from, 199–200
    in fall of Charleston, 593, 595, 596, 597, 599, 600–601
    at Fort Montgomery, 205
    free time of, 411–12
    on Germain's orders, 467
    home of, 69
    instructions to, 312
    knighting of, 62
    lament of, 207
    leadership of, 23, 61, 62, 69, 201–2, 205–6, 207, 311, 314, 417, 418, 466, 468, 473, 570, 581

    love of, 311–12
    at Monmouth Court House, 358–60
    morale of, 418–20, 574–75
    movement of, 471–72, 574
    as musician, 62
    on Negroes, 571–72
    in New York City, 61, 63, 412–13
    orders to, 331
    pardons from, 605
    on Penobscot Bay, Maine, 484
    plans of, 68, 555–56, 581
    praise for, 378–79
    on Royal Navy movement, 581
    on Saratoga campaign, 232
    at siege of Charleston, 584
    at Stony Point, 482–83
    travels of, 315
    on the war, 72
    on the weather, 579
    William Howe and, 64–65, 69–70
Clinton, James, 204, 503
Cliveden (Benjamin Chew house) (Germantown, Pennsylvania), 169, 171–72, 173, 175, 176–77
Clocheterie, Jean Isaac Chadeau de la, 348
Clowes, William Laird, 352
Cochran, Dr. John, 566
Coercive Acts of 1774, 275–76
Collier, Sir George, 467–68, 470–71, 474, 476, 490, 491–93
Collin, Nicholas, 241, 298
Columbus (American ship), 580
Comet (British galley), 240, 537, 595
Commager, Henry Steele, 58
Commission for Quieting Disorders, 312, 315
Company of Marksmen, 115
Conanicut, 391–92
Conciliatory Acts, 312, 315
Condorcet, Marquis de, 13
Congress
    authority from, 253, 308
    challenges of, 434–35
    Conciliatory Act rejection by, 315
    on Continental Army, 83–84
    factions in, 433–34
    fleet decisions by, 342–43
    general appointing by, 104
    military decisions of, 437, 561
    price control and, 564
    requests to, 295
    on slavery, 591
    sovereignty recognition demand by, 230
    state ceding by, 605
    treaty delivery to, 308–9
    war challenges of, 295

Congress (Continental frigate), 204
Connecticut, control of, 56
conscription, 84–85, 330–31, 462–63
Constitution, Fort, 202, 204
Continental Army, *See also* Continental Army
    regiments, *and specific battles, and specific*
    locations
  ailment treatments in, 293
  booths of, 150
  booty of, 241
  bravery of, 77–78, 164
  bridge destruction by, 357
  casualties of, 66, 82, 102, 115, 128, 132, 140,
    152, 153, 176–77, 180, 197–98, 204, 241,
    251–52, 253, 343, 370, 375, 377, 407, 415,
    423, 481, 505, 551, 552, 558–59, 577, 584,
    595, 598, 601, 602–3, 615
  celebration of, 228, 309–10, 379, 505
  challenges of, 40, 52
  conditions of, 77–78, 249, 251, 292–94, 297,
    305, 361, 364
  confiscation by, 297
  conscription in, 84–85
  criticism of, 141–42
  as deep into principles, 62
  demographics of, 78
  desertion by, 48, 58, 85, 230, 231, 317, 560
  desertion in, 85
  discipline in, 79
  disease in, 252, 558
  encampment of, 557–59
  enlistees in British Army from, 601
  enlistments in, 437–38
  espionage in, 439–41
  fatigue of, 176
  flag of, 87
  fleeing by, 40, 43
  fleet of, 87–88, 342–43
  foreign help to, 264–65
  foreign officers of, 90
  forming of, 83–84
  at Fort Ticonderoga, 37–38, 39–40
  growth of, 124
  intelligence of, 584–85
  limitations of, 38
  maps for, 87
  military training of, 302
  money shortage and, 563–64
  morale of, 54, 66, 78–79, 84, 249, 396, 561,
    565–66
  movement of, 73, 76, 91–92, 95, *148,* 187,
    249, 250, 320
  mutiny of, 615
  officers in, 85, 561
  in Philadelphia, 92–93

  physicians in, 293
  policies of, 86–87
  population of, 224
  positions in, 86
  prisoners from, 42, 50, 343–44, 601
  provisions of, 120, 122
  recruitment of, 84, 543–44, 561, 614
  Regulations for the Order and Discipline of
    the Troops of the United States for, 439
  religion in, 79
  resignations in, 294
  retreat of, 423
  review of, 309–10
  as rubbing through it, 615
  shock troops of, 363
  sickness and death of, 77, 88
  Southern Department of, 421, 543–44
  strength of, 73, 117
  structure of, 300, 361–62
  supplies and provisions for, 87, 188, 192,
    252, 253, 294, 297, 299–300, 361, 396,
    436–37, 500–501, 559, 561–63, 615
  threats to, 614
  uniforms of, 78, 293–94, 437, 517–18
  victories of, 114–15
  war council of, 154
  weaponry of, 38, 87, 124, 134, 146, 160, 190,
    217, 300, 375, 422, 431–32
Continental Army regiments
  3rd Continental Light Dragoons (Lady
    Washington's Horse), 414–15
  Connecticut, 215
  Life Guard, 363
  Maryland, 1st, 135; 2nd, 135; 4th, 160; 6th,
    444
  Massachusetts, 215; 5th, 218; 6th, 218; 8th,
    194; 10th, 195
  New Hampshire, 215–16; 1st, 194, 376; 3rd,
    194, 215
  New Jersey, 3rd, 136
  New York, 215
  Pennsylvania, 1st, 151, 375
  Rhode Island, 1st, 237, 406–7; 2nd, 237
  South Carolina, 420; 2nd, 420–21
  Virginia, 1st, 376; 3rd, 132
Continental Navy. *See also specific battles;*
    specific vessels
  casualties of, 489, 492
  fleet of, 488, 492
  internal conflicts in, 489–90
  morale of, 490, 615
  movement of, 488, 490–91, 529–30, 533,
    587
  retreat of, 492
  supplies for, 486

Continental Navy *(cont'd)*
  weaponry of, 486, 488
  weather impacts on, 580
Continental Navy Board, 450
Convention Army, 230–31
Convention of Retreat, 554
Conway, Thomas, 305–6
Conyngham, Gustavus, 17
Cook, James, 329
Cooper, Reverend Samuel, 431
copper, function of, 334
Córdova y Córdova, Luis de, 512, 514
Corn Planter (Seneca chief), 507
Cornstalk (Shawnee chief), 497
Cornwall (British ship), 401, 539
Cornwall, England, 525
Cornwallis (British galley), 468, 470
Cornwallis, Charles Earl
  at Battle of Brandywine, 132
  at Battle of Germantown, 175
  at Battle of Monmouth, 368–71
  Clinton and, 574–75
  criticism of, 596
  description of, 131–32
  on fall of Charleston, 604
  leadership of, 123, 131–32, 147, 155, 245
  on loss, 229
  at Monmouth Court House, 358–60
  at siege of Charleston, 584
  weather effects on, 119
costumes, function of, 1
coucher, 6
Coudray, Philippe Charles Tronson du, 90
counterfeiting, 435–36, 563. *See also* currency
Covenhoven, Elizabeth, 360
Covent Garden Theatre, 452
Cox, John, 164
Crabbe, George, 610–11
Crooked Billet, 309
Crosswicks Creek, 357
Cruger, John Harris, 549
Cumberland (British ship), 523
Cunningham, William, 178
currency, 307–8, 435–36, 563–65
Curry, Abigail, 190
Custis, John Parke, 81–82

Daggett, Naphtali, 474
Danbury, Connecticut, 65
Dansey, William, 70, 386
Davenport, Isaac Howe, 294
Dawkins, Henry, 563
Dayton, Elias, 171–72
Deane, Silas, 15, 19, 90, 279, 282–83, 284, 287, 339, 340, 569

Deane, Simeon, 308–9
Dearborn, Henry
  on artillery, 376, 503
  on battle, 198, 215, 225, 250
  on Benedict Arnold, 218
  on casualties, 499
  on Christmas, 253
  leadership of, 190, 194, 216
Defence (American brig), 491
Defiance (British vessel), 582
Defoe, Daniel, 257–58, 458
DeLancey, Stephen, 424
Delaware, 435
Delaware (frigate), 159, 245
Delaware, Battle for the
  British military movement in, 245
  casualties in, 238–39
  Continental ruse regarding, 237
  at Fort Mifflin, 243–45
  intelligence regarding, 237
  map of, *235*
  origin of, 234, 236
  overview of, 238, 240–41
  weather conditions for, 239–40, 245
Delaware River, 73, 76, 233, 248, 249
deserters/desertion
  British, 104–5, 208, 213, 221, 318, 330, 426, 450, 479, 614
  by Canadian laborers, 50
  Continental, 48, 58, 85, 230, 231, 317, 560
  German, 357–58, 378
  Hessian, 59–60, 317, 357–58, 378
  in New York, 58
  prevention of, 35, 49, 53, 176, 183, 477, 537
  punishment for, 79, 85, 421, 482
  rewards for, 94
d'Estaing, Charles Hector, Count
  in assault on Savannah, 542, 544, 545, 546, 547–49, 550, 551, 554–55
  attack of, 390
  in Battle for Newport, 394, 396–97, 398, 399–400, 401, 402, 403–10
  characteristics of, 384–85
  criticism of, 539
  injuries of, 551
  leadership of, 332, 385, 386, 389–90, 396, 409, 424–25, 536, 544, 560–61
  morale of, 425, 553, 555
  at Savannah, 537–38
  support for, 555
  welcoming of, 389
Destin (French ship), 524
Detroit, Michigan, 493–94
The Devil's Disciple (Shaw), 232
Diana (British warship), 581

Dickinson, Philemon, 362, 363, 366–68
Digby, William, 52, 194, 199, 200, 220, 222, 225
Diligent (American brig), 206, 486
Dillon, Arthur, 550, 551
disease
  in British Army and Royal Navy, 116, 417, 524, 570
  in Continental Army, 252, 558
  dysentery, 514
  in French military, 515–16, 523, 524, 537, 547, 618
  in German mercenaries, 210
  malaria, 514
  mortality and, 590
  scabies, 252
  scurvy, 184, 514
  smallpox, 88–89
  typhus, 514
Döhla, Johann, 556
Dollond, John, 443
Dolly, Quamino (Quash), 423
Dolphin (sloop), 16–17
Dominica, 418, 457
Donop, Carl Emil Ulrich von, 123, 233–34, 237–38, 239, 242
Dorman, Joseph, 475
d'Orvilliers, Comte de (Louis Guillouet). *See* Guillouet, Louis (Comte d'Orvilliers)
Dovegat, 186
Downman, Francis, 118, 138–39, 239, 241, 244–45, 248, 313
Drake (British ship), 345
Drake, Sir Francis, 519
Drayton, William Henry, 315
Drayton Hall, 584
Drinker, Elizabeth, 155, 248, 318, 432
Drowned Lands, 41
Drummond, Duncan, 419
Duchesse de Grammont (British ship), 278
Dudley, Banks, 136
Duke of Devonshire, 510
Dunbar, Moses, 158
Du Ponceau, Peter, 302–3
Duportail, Louis, 598
Dutch West Indies, 16. *See also* West Indies
dysentery. *See also* disease

Eagle (British warship), 70, 71, 74, 118, 120, 387–88, 401
Eden, William, 263, 315, 460
Edward (British brig), 72
Edward, Fort, 47, 49, 52–53, 221
Edwards, Evan, 428
Elmer, Ebenezer, 134

emancipation, 591
England. *See* Great Britain
English, Abigail, 475
English, Benjamin, 475
English Channel, 347, 519, 520, 521
Enterprise (British sloop-of-war), 42
Erskine, Robert, 87, 125
Erskine, Sir William, 371
Esopus (Kingston), 206, 224
espionage
  American, 163, 252, 439–40, 441, 479, 618
  Benjamin Franklin and, 283
  British, 10, 90, 282, 314, 358, 368, 463, 602
  example of, 283–85
  George III, King of England on, 284
  near Valley Forge, 314
  from prisoners, 36
  Spanish, 512
  tactics for, 439–41
  Washington on, 439–40, 441
Europe (British vessel), 582
Evans, Chaplain Israel, 80, 505
Ewald, Johann
  in Battle of Brandywine, 137
  on Battle of Germantown, 176–77
  on Battle of Monmouth, 368, 377
  on casualties, 239, 357
  on Charleston destruction, 601–2
  on conditions, 378
  in fall of Charleston, 593, 597–98
  on German casualties, 242
  on Hessians, 59–60
  leadership of, 130, 236
  retreat of, 132
  ship damage to, 574
  at siege of Charleston, 584
  on South Carolina, 582
  on the weather, 580

Fair American (British privateer), 414
Fairfield, Connecticut, 475–76
Fairlie, James, 565
Falcon (British warship), 398
fall of Charleston. *See also* Charleston, South Carolina
  Biggin Bridge in, 595
  booty from, 599
  British position in, 595, 597–98, 599
  capitulation terms of, 599
  casualties in, 595, 598, 601
  Continental Navy position in, 592
  effects of, 603–4
  encirclement in, 599
  map of, *589*
  overview of, 590–601

fall of Charleston *(cont'd)*
 proposal regarding, 597
 redoubts in, 592–93
 Royal Navy position in, 593–94
 war council regarding, 594, 596–97
Falmouth, attack on, 206, 522
Fame (British ship), 539
Family Compact, 8
Fanning, Nathaniel, 527, 533
Fantasque (French ship), 394, 395
Fatland Ford, 153, 251
Feilitzsch, Heinrich, 378
Fenton, Lewis, 360
Ferguson, Patrick, 128, 415
Ferguson, Thomas, 597
Fielding, Sir John, 610
fireworks tragedy, Paris, 2
Firth of Forth, 526, 527–28
Fisher, Elijah, 293
Fisher, John, 358
Fisher, Sarah Logan, 145, 155, 162
Fishkill, 222
Fitzpatrick, Richard, 166, 248
Flamand (French ship), 301
Flamborough Head, 529–32, 534
Fletcher, Ebenezer, 44
Fleury, Marquis de (François Louis Teisseydre),
 244, 481
Florida, 312, 457. *See also specific locations*
Floridablanca, José Moñino, Count, 456–57
Fly (British sloop), 159
Fogg, Jeremiah, 506
Fontages, François, Vicomte de, 552
Forbes, Gordon, 193
Ford, Hezekiah, 283–84
Ford, Theodosia, 559
Forman, Dr. Samuel, 377
Formidable (French ship), 352, 354, 447,
 519–20
Forrest, Uriah, 174
Fort Clinton, 204, 207, 224
Fort Constitution, 202, 204
Fort Edward, 47, 49, 52–53, 221
Fort George, 486, 489, 556, 577
Fort Hardy, 225
Fort Johnson, 582
Fort Lafayette, 472
Fort Mercer, 160, 233, 234, 236–38, 241, 242,
 245–46. *See also* Delaware, Battle for the
Fort Mifflin, 160, 234, 240, 243–45
Fort Montgomery, 202, 204, 207, 224
Fort Moultrie, 585, 587, 593, 599
Fort Nelson, 470
Fort Niagara, 506
Fort Number Eight, 570

Fort Sackville, 494–96
Fort Stanwix (Fort Schuyler), 96, 97, 98, *99*,
 101–2, 103–4
Fort Sullivan, 502
Fort Ticonderoga, New York
 abandonment of, 229
 booty from, 41
 British control of, 41
 British movement to, 29–30
 Continental Army at, 39–40
 defense of, 211
 description of, 36–37
 fall of, 69
 Great Bridge of, 37, 41
 lessons from, 187–88
 limitations of, 37
 military presence at, 37–38
Fortune (British merchant sloop), 527
Fort Wyoming, 501
Forty Fort, 499
Foudroyant (British ship), 354–55
Fowey (British ship), 537
Fox (British frigate), 334
Fox, Charles James, 269–70, 276, 447, 525, 613
Foxe, John, 124
Fox Indians, 50–51
France
 American support by, 11, 281, 289, 290, 309,
  444, 555–56, 617–18
 American view of, 386
 assistance from, 264–65
 Britain *versus*, 6, 7, 8
 British military spying by, 7–8
 celebrations in, 280, 541
 colonialism of, 418, 424
 convention of war with Spain and, 457
 criticism of, 525–26
 as enemy, 262–63
 espionage in, 7–8, 283–84
 Family Compact and, 8
 Franco-American alliance and, 281, 285, 309
 intelligence from, 331–32, 342
 prosperity of, 6–7
 reforms of, 7
 in Seven Years' War, 6, 47, 258, 508, 524
 threat from, 272, 275
 treaty with America and, 9, 287–88
 war strategies of, 511–12
 weaponry of, 15–16, 249–50
Francis, Ebenezer, 38–39, 44
Francis, John, 135
François de Noailles, Jean Paul, 22
Franklin, Benjamin
 on America, 616
 as author, 11–12

at Bibliothèque Nationale, 12–13
characteristics of, 11, 13, 14–15, 285, 287, 289
criticism of, 340–41
on diplomacy, 19
as diplomat, 11–19
Edward Bancroft and, 283
espionage and, 283–85
fame of, 341
family of, 14
on France, 14
French support for, 289
as gunrunner, 15
in Hôtel de Valentinois (Paris), 14
on John Paul Jones, 342
Lafayette and, 26, 517
leadership of, 161, 275, 278
Louis XVI and, 290
Marie-Antoinette and, 290–91
navy organization of, 16
in Paris, 12, 278
on Philadelphia, 280
Poor Richard's Almanack, 13, 19
popularity of, 13, 18
portrait of, 318
on prisoner exchange, 18–19
as radicalized, 15
report from, 280
retirement of, 616
on Steuben, 301–2
surveillance of, 278
Voltaire and, 338
on war, 15, 19, 288
war request of, 517–18
Franklin, William, 14, 356, 572
Franklin, William Temple, 14
Fraser, Simon, 43, 46, 193, 210, 217, 219–20
Frederick the Great, 60, 85, 134, 267, 525
Freedom (French ship), 17
Freedom and a Farm program, 572
Freeman, John, 193
Freeman's Farm, *185,* 193, 197. *See also* Battle of Saratoga
French and Indian War (Seven Years' War), 6, 47, 258, 508, 524
French Army, 288, 289, 335, 347, 425, 545–46, 551, 552, 618
French Navy. *See also specific battles; specific vessels*
advantages of, 386
in Battle of Ushant, 349–53
battle plans of, 618
casualties of, 348, 353, 389, 401, 522, 531, 538, 539, 545–46, 551, 555
challenges of, 521–22, 523

Chasseurs Volontaires in, 537
confusion of, 350–51
criticism of, 525–26
disease in, 523, 524, 537, 547
diversity of, 537
encampment of, 516
flags of, 529–30
fleet of, 9–10, 349, 350, 399–400, 424, 450, 512, 536–37, 547
flotilla of, 523
in Georgia, 536
movement of, 385–86, 528
overview of, 9–10, 15, 17
personnel of, 537
reinforcement of, 538
renaissance of, 348–49
at Sandy Hook, 384
successes of, 455–56
supplies for, 386
Washington's strategy regarding, 388–89
weather effects on, 537
French spies, 512, 612
Friedrich, Landgraf, II, 242
Friend, Catherine, 432
Friendship (British transport), 206, 207
Fury (British sloop), 244

Gadsden, Christopher, 421, 591, 597
Gage, Elizabeth, 115
Gainsborough, Thomas, 387
Galatea (British ship), 491
Galli, Caterina, 452
Galloway, Joseph, 156, 316
Gambier, James, 409, 415
Gansevoort, Peter, 97, 102–3
Garrick, David, 33, 454
Garth, George, 474, 547
Gates (American vessel), 42
Gates, Horatio
Arnold and, 198–99, 212–13, 218
background of, 189
in Battle of Saratoga, 198–99
in Battle of Saratoga at Bemus Heights, 212, 214–15
at British surrender, 225–27
congratulations to, 228–29
criticism of, 198–99
description of, 188–89
election of, 188
headquarters of, 191–92
leadership of, 190, 222, 306
negotiations with, 224
General Evening Post (newspaper), 461
General Gates (American privateer), 468
General Montgomery (American frigate), 204

Genessee (Little Beard's Town), 504–5
George, Fort, 486, 489, 556, 577
George III, King of England
    address of, 264–65
    on Americans, 264
    on British home waters, 520
    celebration for, 454, 606
    in Chatham, 326
    criticism of, 613, 614
    on defense of London, 510–11, 611–12
    description of, 262, 454
    on espionage, 284
    on Germain, 271
    leadership of, 265, 459–60, 461–62, 464
    on Lord Chatham, 322–23
    on Lord North, 274–75, 276, 325
    marriage of, 333
    morale of, 271, 323, 518, 523, 614
    pardoning by, 462–63
    in Parliament, 263, 264–65
    popularity of, 335
    possessions of, 458–59
    powers of, 262–63
    Queen's House of, 458–59
    on rioting, 611
    on Sandwich, 451
    son of, 463–64
    on Spanish negotiations, 456–57
    travels of, 262, 325–26, 332–35
    on *Victory* (ship), 326–27
    war news to, 266
    on war with America, 463
    on war with France, 326, 349
Georgetown, South Carolina, 605
Georgia, *See also specific battles, locations,* 420,
    421–22, 423, 425–26, 605
Georgia (British transport vessel), 580
Gérard, Conrad-Alexandre, 280–81, 286, 287,
    409, 428, 483–84
Germain (British man-of-war), 537
Germain, George Sackville, Lord
    accusations of, 270
    on the American war, 454–55
    on British plans, 418, 466
    Clinton and, 575
    concerns regarding, 460
    description of, 266–67
    dispatch from, 120
    grief of, 271
    home of, 23
    hostility of, 449–50
    in House of Commons, 269
    leadership of, 266, 267, 419–20, 460, 466–67,
        493
    on Lord North, 276

    as man of war, 268
    meeting of, 459–60
    on military proposal, 68
    on reconciliation, 312
    on Savannah, 424
    violence to, 609
    on war, 331–32
German mercenaries. *See also* Hessians
    in Battle for the Delaware, 234, 236
    in Battle of Saratoga, 196
    casualties of, 115, 219, 238–39, 241, 242, 260
    deserters of, 357–58, 378
    diseases in, 210
    leadership of, 32
    in New York City, 59
    opening of Delaware River by, 233–34
    in Philadelphia, 247
    reputation of, 233
    surrender of, 227
German prisoners of war, 116, 212
Germantown, Battle of
    aftermath of, 176–79
    British withdrawal in, 167–68, 169–70, 174
    casualties in, 167, 168, 174, 176–77, 180
    Cliveden house in, 171–72, 173, 175, 176–77
    element of surprise in, 166
    fatigue from, 176
    fog in, 166–67, 179–80
    lessons from, 178–79
    map of, *165*
    operatory in, 177–78
    overview of, 166–67, 172–76
    planning for, 172–73
Germantown, Pennsylvania, 163–66, 169,
    171–72, 173, 175, 176–77, 178–79
Geyer, John, 177
Geyer, Mary, 177
Gibbon, Edward, 19, 273–74, 325, 609, 612–13
Gibraltar, 614
Gilbert, John, 474
Gilmore, William, 107
Gilpin, Gideon, 141
Glover, John, 192, 222, 227, 405, 437
Golden Swan, 178
Gordon, George, 336, 609, 612–13
Gordon Riots, 608–13
Grafton (British ship), 539
Grand Duchess of Russia (Vigilant) (British
    warship), 244
Grand Duke of Russia (British ship), 398
Grant, George, 505
Grant, James, 119, 417, 424
Grant, Robert, 44
Great Britain
    allies of, 275

black viewpoint regarding, 59
casualties of, 614
Catholic Relief Act in, 608, 609
dishevelment in, 271–72
empire of, 6–7
foreign mail operation of, 282
France *versus*, 6, 7, 8
as friendless, 614
government instability in, 613–14
impressment method of, 10
intelligence of, 264, 331–32, 526
invasion of, 325–26, 511–12
invasion plans of, 511–12
map of, *28, 513*
marine panic in, 17
panic in, 346
prosperity in, 257–58
retaliation schemes against, 344
rioting in, 454
secret service fund of, 282
taxation in, 258, 463
trade with, 257, 271, 463, 563
vulnerability of, 539, 541
war costs to, 258, 268, 496–97
war news in, 266
war opinions in, 261, 264, 275, 276–77
war practices of, 257
war preparations in, 508–10
Great Redoubt, 208, 218, 220–21
Great Runaway, 499
Great Storm, 401, 402
Greene, Caty, 298–99, 300, 444, 566
Greene, Christopher, 237, 238, 245
Greene, George Washington, 298 99
Greene, Martha Washington, 298–99
Greene, Nathanael
    on assault on Stony Point, 472, 482
    in Battle for Newport, 394, 396, 403–4, 405,
        406, 408
    at Battle of Brandywine, 136–37
    in Battle of Monmouth, 375
    characteristics of, 298–99
    concerns of, 125, 250, 380, 436–37, 472–73,
        493, 498, 561–62, 577
    division of, 127
    family of, 566
    on fortune, 408
    home of, 444
    lament of, 298
    leadership of, 89, 127, 129, 297, 298,
        299–300, 361, 362, 394, 558, 561, 617
    on Martha Washington, 296
    on morale, 433
    observations of, 249
    as officer, 85

on Quakers, 127
on raid, 577
on success, 501
on supply shortages, 561, 562
on Washington, 433
Greenleaf, Moses, 46
Green Mountain Boys, 114, 229
Gregg, William, 108, 110
Grenada, 424, 538
Grenada, Battle of, 538–39
Grey, Charles, 150–51, 173–74, 408, 414,
    454
Greyhound (British frigate), 311
Grubb, Farley, 563
Guadeloupe, 6
Guillouet, Louis (Comte d'Orvilliers)
    challenges of, 514, 521–22
    on Falmouth Channel, 522–23
    as hero, 354
    leadership of, 349–50, 352, 512, 515, 523,
        560–61
    morale of, 525
    movement of, 354
    orders to, 524
gunpowder industry, 9, 16

Hackensack River, 414–15
Hackman, James, 452–53
Hagist, Don N., 122
Haines, Thomas, 198
hairstyles, features of, 3
Haldimand, Frederick, 496–97
Hale, Nathan, 411
Hale, William, 120, 122, 132, 374, 375
Hall of Mirrors, 3
Hamilton, Alexander
    in Battle of Brandywine, 136–37
    in Battle of Monmouth, 373, 374, 381-382
    in Battle of Saratoga, 194
    dispatch from, 144–45
    at duel, 429
    on fall of Charleston, 603
    on French support, 617–18
    Lafayette and, 89–90, 617
    leadership of, 83, 124, 171, 362, 389
    morale of, 615
    on Philip Schuyler, 188
    relationships of, 566
    on Washington, 380
Hamilton, Helen, 345
Hamilton, Henry, 493, 495, 496
Hamilton, James, 223
Hamilton, William, 532
Hammond (American privateer), 468
Hamond, Andrew Snape, 72, 73–74, 118, 402

Hampden (American warship), 488, 491
Hampton Roads, attack on, 468, *469,* 470–71
Hancock (American frigate), 468
Hancock, John, 144–45, 146, 380, 396, 408
Hand, Edward, 502
Handel, George Friederich, 326
Hannah (American transport), 488
Harcourt, William, 229
Hardi (French ship), 16
Hardy, Fort, 225
Hardy, Sir Charles, 519–20, 523–24, 525
Hargreaves, James, 257
Harris, Michael C., 74
Harrison, Benjamin, 433
Harrison, Robert Hanson, 565
Hartley, Thomas, 150
Harvey, Edward, 35
Harvey, Stephen, 197
Haudenosaunee, *See* Iroquois
Hay, Samuel, 152
Hayes, John McNamara, 46–47
Hazel, Red, 44
Hazelwood, John, 159, 244, 245
Hazen, Moses, 129
Head of Elk, 120, 122
Heath, William, 231
Hector (British ship), 402
The Heiress (Burgoyne), 232
Hellcat (American fireship), 240
Henry, Patrick, 81, 85, 470
Herkimer, Nicolas, 101–2
Herrick, Samuel, 111, 112
Hessians. *See also* German mercenaries
    in Battle for Newport, 406, 407
    in Battle of Brandywine, 136
    blame to, 122–23
    desertion by, 59–60, 317, 357–58, 378
    Henry Clinton and, 62
    Jäger, 32, 130, 132, 138, 214, 238, 472
    Mirbach Regiment, 241
    movement of, 474
    in New Haven, Connecticut, 475
    as prisoners of war, 144, 471
    recruitment of, 60
    on South Carolina, 582
    toward Fort Ticonderoga, 30
Highland Scots (Black Watch), 150–51
Hillegas, Michael, 87
Hineman, Henry, 431
Hinrichs, Johann, 579, 582, 584, 601
Hitchcock, Enos, 47
Hodgkins, Joseph, 225
Holland, 533–34
hornwork, 586–87
horses, 119–20, 294, 579–80

Hôtel de Valentinois (Paris), 13–14
Hotham, Commodore William, 390
House of Vulcan, 334
Houstoun, John, 423–24
Howard, Henry, 271
Howe, George, 64
Howe, Richard, Viscount
    in Battle for Newport, 399, 400, 401
    as Black Dick, 387, 402, 410, 451
    characteristics of, 386–87
    demands of, 451
    grievances of, 409
    leadership of, 65, 387–88
    popularity of, 451
    signal book of, 399
Howe, Robert, 421, 422, 424, 566–67
Howe, William
    admonition for, 143
    on attack at Paoli, 153–54
    at Barren Hill, 314–15
    in Battle for the Delaware, 240, 245–46
    in Battle of Brandywine, 125, 128, 129, 130,
        132, 141
    in Battle of Germantown, 166, 178–79
    on Canadian Army, 69
    characteristics of, 63–64, 74, 315
    criticism of, 123–24, 138, 234, 315
    encouragement from, 186
    grief of, 64
    Henry Clinton and, 64–65, 69–70
    home of, 63
    injuries of, 249
    on Joseph Galloway, 156–57
    leadership of, 34–35, 64, 66, 72, 74, 120, 123,
        153, 245–46, 314
    morale of, 246
    movement of, 147, 154–55
    in Philadelphia, 156, 246, 248
    plans of, 67–68, 69, 73–74, 230, 316
    praise for, 141, 314–15
    request to, 306–7
    on the war, 64
Howell, Dr. Lewis, 132
Hubbardton, Battle of, 43–47, *45*
Hubley, Adam, Jr., 131, 142
Hudson Highlands, 202, 476–77
Hudson Highlands, Battle for the, *203,* 204,
    206, 208
Hudson River (North River), 184, 186, 202,
    222, 471–72
Hudson Valley, *31*
Hull, William, 195, 481
Humpton, Richard, 151
Hunter (American privateer), 489, 491
Hunter, Martin, 152, 154, 166, 168

Huntington, Ebenezer, 435, 559
Huntington, Jedediah, 251, 396
Hurley, Ensign Martin, 178
Hynson, Joseph, 283

Illinois country, 494, 496
India, 457
Indian Expedition, 497, 498–507
Indians, 50–51, 53, 493, 497, 502–3, 506. *See also specific tribes*
Industrial Revolution, 462
inflation, 435, 436, 564
Inflexible (British warship), 30, 36, 41
Ipswich Journal (newspaper), 461
Ireland, 264, 346, 455, 463, 511, 546
Irish Sea expedition, 517–18
Iroquois (Haudenosaunee), 29, 39, 50–51, 98, 499, 502–3, 504, 506
Iroquois Confederacy, 497
Irvine, Andrew, 152
Isabelle (British ship), 389
Isis (British warship), 119, 241, 244

Jackson, Andrew, 603
Jackson, Elizabeth Hutchinson, 603
Jack Tars, 70, 234, 392, 395
James Island, 585
Jamison, John, 129
Jay, John, 436
Jay, Sir James, 441
Jefferson, Thomas, 13, 435, 470, 578
Jenny Hamilton (ship), 119
Jersey (American gundalow), 30
Jersey City, New Jersey, 483
Jervis, John, 354–55, 508
Jews, defense of, 610
John Neilson house, 192
Johns, Henry, 247
Johns Island, 581
Johnson, Dr. Uzal, 584
Johnson, Fort, 582
Johnson, Henry, 479, 482
Johnson, Samuel, 257, 260, 610
Johnson, Uzal, 582
Johnstone, George, 315
Jones, John, 548, 552
Jones, John Paul
    attack from, 344–46
    background of, 341–42
    characteristics of, 341, 346–47, 527
    complaints of, 526–27
    crewmen of, 527
    death of, 535
    fame of, 346–47
    in Firth of Forth, 527–28

in France, 534
leadership of, 517, 526–30, 531–32
movement of, 533, 534
on naval battle, 531
on Saltonstall, 486
support for, 533–34
Jones, Thomas, 63
Joseph (British brig), 17
Joslin, Joseph, 294
Jourda, Noël de (Comte de Vaux), 512, 516, 522, 525
Jouy, Anne-Louise Brillon de, 280
Judas Maccabaeus (Handel), 326
Judith (British vessel), 580
Juliana (British ship), 248
Juno (British sloop), 395, 580
Junon (French frigate), 521

Kalb, Baron Johann de, 20, 23, 24, 142, 253, 564
Kaskaskia, Illinois, 494
Kellogg, Sally, 115
Kemble, Stephen, 419
Kempenfelt, Richard, 519
Keppel, Augustus
    acquittal of, 448
    background of, 336–37
    court-martial of, 447–48
    criticism of, 354–55
    on the French, 353
    leadership of, 347–48, 352
    morale of, 354
    movement of, 347, 349
    popularity of, 448–49
    resignation of, 449
Kettle Creek, Georgia, 426–27
Kingfisher (British warship), 395
King's Ferry, 472, 473
Kingston (Esopus), 206, 224
Kingston, Robert, 224
Kirby, Ephraim, 168
Knight's Wharf, 313
Knox, Henry
    in Battle of Germantown, 170–71, 179
    in Battle of Monmouth, 375
    celebration of, 444
    concerns of, 147
    on Continental Army, 77–78, 141
    family of, 565–66
    leadership of, 78–79, 87, 89, 362
    as officer, 85
    orders to, 372
    on Washington, 380
Knox, Lucy, 114, 565–66
Knox, William, 410, 484

Knyphausen, Wilhelm von
  in Battle of Brandywine, 128, 137
  in Battle of Germantown, 166
  in Battle of Monmouth, 368–71, 377
  concerns of, 243, 576
  leadership of, 123, 147, 575
  at Monmouth Court House, 358–60
Koch, Adam, 135
Kościuszko, Thaddeus, 190–91
Kromma Kill, 186

Lacey, John, 168, 297
La Concorde (French frigate), 456
L'Actif (sixty-four-gun), 521, 522
Lady Dunmore (British vessel), 580
Lady Elizabeth (British ship), 278
Lady Washington (American galley), 206
Lafayette, Fort, 472
Lafayette, Gilbert du Motier, Marquis de
  as adventurer, 21–26
  in Army of Invasion, 518
  background of, 22
  in Battle for Newport, 394, 396–97, 403–4,
    407
  in Battle of Brandywine, 136
  Benjamin Franklin and, 517
  in Bethlehem, 146
  on British casualties, 516
  celebration of, 310
  characteristics of, 21, 26, 90
  concerns regarding, 23
  on Continental Army conditions, 617
  on d'Estaing, 389
  estate of, 22
  honor to, 516–17, 518
  on *La Victoire*, 23–24
  leadership of, 89–90, 361, 362, 363–64
  marriage of, 22, 24
  movement of, 525, 526
  praise for, 146–47
  retirement of, 434
  Washington and, 617
Lamar, Marien, 152
Lamb, Roger, 30, 195, 221–22
Landais, Pierre, 527, 530, 531, 534
Languedoc (British ship), 397–98, 401–2,
    424–25, 536, 537
Lark (British ship), 395
La Royale (French ship), 403–4
Laurance, John, 567
Laurens, Henry
  in Battle of Monmouth, 374
  concerns of, 253, 310–11
  family of, 590
  on fear, 145

home of, 594
  leadership of, 306, 308
  on slavery, 591
  on treaty, 230
  Washington and, 309, 430
Laurens, John
  in assault on Savannah, 543, 551
  in Battle for Newport, 397, 399, 404, 405
  concerns of, 147, 252
  duel of, 370, 428–29
  emancipation an, 591
  horse of, 374
  leadership of, 172, 306, 366, 369, 380, 389,
    392–93, 394, 587
  on slavery, 592
  on Steuben, 303
  on success, 309
La Victoire (French ship), 21, 23, 25
Lavoisier, Antoine, 9
Lawrence, Alexander A., 550
Lawrence, John, 381
Lear, William, 152
Learned, Ebenezer, 215
Le Brune (French ship), 278
Lee (American sloop), 30
Lee, Arthur, 15, 16, 279, 283–84, 287, 340, 517
Lee, Charles
  background of, 304–5
  in Battle of Monmouth, 366–68, 369,
    372–73, 376, 381
  characteristics of, 304–5
  court-martial of, 381–82
  criticism of, 428–29
  death of, 430
  duel of, 428
  leadership of, 305, 361, 362, 363, 364
  morale of, 429–30
  oath of, 307
  release of, 303–4
  secret of, 306–7
  Washington and, 372, 381, 382–83
Lee, Henry, III (Light-Horse Harry), 171, 297,
    477, 483
Lee, Richard Henry, 180, 307, 340, 439
Lee, William, 295
Le Magnifique (French ship), 547
Lender, Mark Edward, 358
L'Enfant, Pierre Charles, 438, 548
Lengel, Edward G., 142
Lenoir, Laurent-François (Marquis de
    Rouvray), 537
Léonard, Monsieur, 3
Leslie, Alexander, 600
lever, description of, 6
Leviathan (German ship), 388

Levins, John, 431
Lewis, Joseph, 577
Lexington (American brig), 16–17
Liberty (American schooner), 42
Licorne (French frigate), 348
Lincoln, Benjamin
  in assault on Savannah, 543, 544, 545, 547,
    555
  capitulation terms to, 599
  on Charleston, South Carolina, 587
  Convention of Retreat and, 553
  description of, 210
  in fall of Charleston, 590, 594, 596–97,
    600–601
  injuries of, 219, 228
  leadership of, 210, 213, 421
  parole of, 605
  on shortages, 436–37
  at siege of Charleston, 586–88
Lindsay, Alexander, 46, 217
Lindsay, David, 521
Lion (British ship), 539
Little Egg Harbor, 415
Liverpool (British frigate), 71, 244
Livingston, Henry B., 54
Livingston, William, 158
Lloyd, Edward, 552
Lloyd's Evening Post (newspaper), 266
London
  Black Wednesday in, 611
  celebrations in, 613–14
  conditions of, 259
  defense of, 610, 611–12
  description of, 259–60
  destruction in, 610–11, 612
  entertainment in, 260
  Frenchmen in, 321
  government instability in, 613–14
  hangings in, 613
  prejudices in, 612
  protection for, 510
  protesting and rioting in, 448, 608–11
  supplies and provisions in, 258–60
  violence in, 608–10
  war opinions in, 260
  war rumors in, 265–66
London Advertiser (newspaper), 559
Long Island Sound, 473
Looney, John, 552
The Lord of the Manor (Burgoyne), 232
Lord Sandwich (British ship), 391
Loring, Elizabeth, 63
Lossberg, Friedrich Wilhelm von, 410
Louis, Joseph (Chevalier de Raimondis), 402
Louisville, Kentucky, 496

Louis XIV (King of France), 5
Louis XV (King of France), 2
Louis XVI (King of France)
  as accidental monarch, 5
  on America, 290
  celebration by, 539, 541
  characteristics of, 4
  coronation of, 5
  coucher of, 6
  decisions of, 7, 24
  decree from, 514
  dining by, 5–6
  as king, 6
  lever of, 6
  as "Louis the Desired," 4
  Marie-Antoinette as compared to, 4
  military buildup of, 9
  Pacte de Famille and, 281
  palace of, 289–90
  rituals of, 6
  social activities of, 1
  support from, 617
  treaty request to, 280
  war declaration by, 348–49
  war preparations of, 288
  on war with England, 11, 286
Lovell, James, 307, 588
Lovell, Solomon, 488, 491, 492
Lowther, William, 259
loyalists. *See also* British Army; British Royal
  Navy; specific persons
  defense of, 56
  description of, 55
  expectations of, 124, 157
  as farmers, 119
  intelligence of, 106, 207, 439–40, 576, 602
  lack of leadership of, 157
  living in America, 157–58
  in New York City, 55, 56
  as prisoners, 146, 427, 470
  as privateers, 414, 474
  property confiscation of, 431
  as purchasing agents, 563
  as raiders, 358, 360
  as refugees, 247, 412, 485
  strength of, 62
  weaknesses of, 427
  women as, 414
Ludwick, Christopher, 87
Ludwig, Philip, 170
Luzader, John F., 199

Mackenzie, Frederick, 230, 392, 395, 399, 400,
  405
Mackesy, Piers, 267

Madison, James, 506
Mahan, Alfred Thayer, 387
The Maid of the Oaks (Burgoyne), 33
Maine, 486. *See also specific locations*
Maitland, John, 542, 545, 552
malaria. *See also* disease
Malmédy, François de, 599
Malone, John, 136
Manigault, Joseph, 598
Mansfield, Lord Chief Justice, 610
Margery (British vessel), 581
Maria (British warship), 30, 211
Maria Theresa, 1
Marie-Antoinette, Queen of France
    bedchamber of, 3
    Benjamin Franklin and, 290–91
    at the Carnival, 1
    characteristics of, 2, 3, 290–91, 339–40
    criticism of, 2
    dining by, 5–6
    on French campaign, 525
    invitation from, 290–91
    John Paul Jones and, 534
    Louis XVI as compared to, 4
    as "Madame Deficit," 1
    marriage of, 2
    on misfortune, 2
    orders from, 517
    palace of, 3–4
    possessions of, 2–3
    as queen, 2–3
    social activities of, 1
Marie-Thérèse Charlotte (princess of France),
    291
Marion, Francis, 544
Markland, John, 170
The Marriage of Figaro (Beaumarchais), 279
Marseillois (French ship), 401
Marshall, John, 615
Marshall, Thomas, 132
Martha (British ship), 118
Martha's Vineyard, 408
Martin, Joseph Plumb, 172–73, 243, 244, 249,
    373, 565
Martinique, 6, 417
Maryland, 85, 435, 437, 564
Mason, George, 315, 433
Massachusetts, 48, 230
Massachusetts (American ship), 17
Mathew, Edward, 468
Mathews, George, 174
Mauduit du Plessis, Thomas-Antoine de, 172,
    237, 239, 242, 375–76
Mauroy, Marquis de, 25
Maxwell, William, 125, 127, 361, 362, 370

Mayflower (brigantine), 527
McBurney, Christian, 370
McClure, James, 52
McCrea, Jane, 51–52, 497
McGuire, Thomas J., 174
McHenry, Dr. James, 320, 363, 369, 372, 380
McIntosh, Lachlan, 547, 551, 597
McKendry, William, 505
McLean, Francis, 484, 489
McMichael, James, 176
Mease, James, 251
Medicinal Compound, 259
medicos, work of, 46
Medows, William, 135
Mellen, Thomas, 114
Mercer, Fort, 160, 233, 234, 236–38, 241, 242,
    245–46. *See also* Delaware, Battle for the
Mercure (French ship), 87
Merlin (British sloop-of-war), 240
Mermaid (British transport), 386, 465
Mifflin, Fort, 160, 234, 240, 243–45
Mifflin, Thomas, 294
Mill, John Stuart, 21
Miller, Henry, 437
Miller, John, 123
Minden, Battle of, 267
Minerva (American privateer), 492
Minerva (British thirty-two-gun), 456
Minorca, 457
Mischianza, 313–14
Mohawk Indians, 98, 101, 105, 497
Molesworth, James, 93–94
monarchs, overview of, 1–4. *See also specific*
    persons
Monckton, Henry, 375
Moncrieff, James, 541, 582, 592
Money, John, 216
Monmouth (British ship), 491, 539
Monmouth, approach to, 358–60, *359*
Monmouth, Battle of
    British movement in, 368–71, 374
    casualties of, 369, 375, 377, 380
    combat in, 368–71, 374–76
    Continental battle plans for, 360–64,
        372–73
    Continental challenges in, 369, 370
    Continental movement in, 377
    Continental retreat in, 374–75
    effects of, 379–80
    map of, *365*
Monmouth Court House, 358–60
Monroe, James, 139, 374
Montagu, John, 266
Montgomery, Fort, 202, 204, 207, 224
Montgomery, Richard, 114

Montrésor, John, 123, 125, 138, 155, 160, 161, 243, 318
Monument Hill, 44
Moore, Sheriff William, 427
Moore Hall, 299–300
Moravians, 145–46
Morgan, Daniel, 85, 189–90, 363, 366–68
Morison, Samuel Eliot, 58, 531
Morning Chronicle (newspaper), 559
Morning Post (newspaper), 266
Morning Star (American sloop), 412
Morris, Gouverneur, 297, 307
Morris, James, 178
Morris, Robert, 144
Morristown, New Jersey, 557–58, 559–60
Morton, Robert, 246
Moultrie, Fort, 585, 587, 593, 599
Moultrie, Thomas, 598
Moultrie, William, 426, 588
Mount Hope, 39
Mount Independence, 41, 229
Mount Joy, 251
Mount Pleasant, 443
Mount Vernon, 296
Moutray, John, 266
Mowat, Henry, 484, 488
Münchhausen, Friedrich Ernst von, 124, 149, 179, 243, 245
Mure, Son & Atkinson, 67
Murray, David, 10
Murray, James, 71, 72, 466, 556
Museum of Anatomy (London), 260
Musgrave, Thomas, 151, 169–70

Nagle, Jacob, 139
Napier, Lord, 226, 232
Nash, Francis, 167, 175–76, 177, 179
Nassau Hall, Princeton, 378
Nelson, Fort, 470
Nelson, Horatio, 525, 539
New England Coffee House, 261
Newfoundland, 457
Newgate Prison, London, 610–11
New Hampshire, 108
New Haven, Connecticut, 474–75
New Ireland, 484, 493
New Jersey, 66, 84–85, 356
Newport, Battle for, 391–400, *393*, 399, 401, 403–8
Newport, Rhode Island, 391, 556
New York, *31*, 34–35, 85, 158, 438, 506
New York City
    act of attainder in, 572
    British control of, 56, 412–13
    British evacuation of, 417–18

conditions of, 412, 413, 572
defense of, 576
demographics of, 59–60
deserters in, 58
fire in, 58
food shortages in, 413–14
as garrison town, 571
housing shortage in, 58
loyalists in, 55, 56
map of, *57*
martial law in, 56
merchandise for, 55–56
Negroes in, 571–72
population of, 55, 412
rebel assault threat in, 229
slavery in, 59
in winter of 1779-1780, 575–76
New York Harbor, 47, 201, 307, 384, 389
New York Packet (newspaper), 206
Niagara, Fort, 506
Nichols, Ann, 475
Nichols, Benjamin, 111, 112
Ninety Six, 427
Nixon, John, 222
Noailles, Adrienne de (Lafayette's wife), 22–26, 89–90, 139, 146, 292, 310, 517
Nonsuch (British ship), 71
Norfolk, Virginia, 206
North, Lord Frederick
    on America, 263
    criticism of, 276
    description of, 273–74
    on English Channel, 524, 526
    George III's pleas to, 325
    grief of, 461
    leadership of, 269, 274, 450–51
    meeting of, 272, 459–60
    misery of, 460–61
    morale of, 273, 321
    proposals of, 315
    on rioting, 613
    speech of, 275–76
    suggestions of, 323
    wages to, 274–75
    on war, 330
North American Theater, 28
North Carolina, 85
Northern Army, 212, 219, 249
Norwalk, Connecticut, 476
Number Eight, Fort, 570
Nymphe (British frigate), 288

O'Connor, Antoine-François, 545, 551
officers, requirements for, 33
Ohio River valley, 494

Old Northwest, 494
Old Pine Street Church (Philadelphia), 319
Olney, Stephen, 238
Oneida Indians, 98, 212, 498, 506
"one-rod road," defined, 107
Onondaga Indians, 98, 497
Oquaga, 499
Orpheus (British warship), 395
O'Shaughnessy, Andrew Jackson, 260
Oswald, Eleazar, 370
Otis, Samuel A., 492
Ottawa Indians, 50–51
Otto, Dr. Bodo, 293
Ourry, Henry, 521

Pacte de Famille, 281
Paine, Thomas, 142–43, 145, 160, 175–76, 179,
    241, 380, 615
Pallas (British ship), 348
Palliser, Sir Hugh, 352, 354, 447–48, 449
Palmier (British ship), 524
Pan (British transport), 574
Paoli, attack at, *148,* 151–53
Paoli, Pasquale, 147
Paoli Tavern, 147
Papet, Julius, 218
Paris, 2, 12, 280, 283–84. *See also specific
    locations*
Parker, Michael, 505
Parker, Richard, 376
Parkman, Ebenezer, 565
Patterson, A. Temple, 519
Pattison, James, 248–49, 482, 570, 576
Päusch, Georg, 196, 198, 216, 217
Peale, Charles Willson, 163, 296, 310, 318, 319,
    433
Pearce, Cromwell, 150
Pearl (British warship), 244, 401
Pearson, Richard, 529, 530–31, 534
Peebles, John, 123, 162, 360, 569–70, 573, 574,
    581
Pennsylvania, 141, *148, 432,* 564. *See also
    specific locations; specific locations*
Pennsylvania Journal (newspaper), 144
Penobscot Bay, Maine, 484–85, 488–90, 492,
    493
Pensacola, Florida, 418
Perrine's Hill, 375–76
Perseus (British frigate), 414
Peters, Ann, 115
Peters, John, 112
Philadelphia. *See also* Brandywine, Battle of;
    Delaware, Battle for the
    British arrival in, 155–56, 246–47
    capture of, 280

    chevaux-de-frise at (stackadoes), 161, 233,
        234, 239, 240, 246, 248
    conditions in, 161–62
    Continental Army in, 92–93
    counterfeiting in, 435–36
    defense of, 159, 161
    description of, 93–94
    destruction in, 318–19
    duels in, 428
    entertainment in, 247
    evacuation of, 144–45, 156, 312, 316–18, 431
    forts at, 160
    hospitals in, 178
    military population in, 234
    Old Pine Street Church in, 319
    order in, 319–20
    plans to capture, 120
    supplies in, 248
    trade in, 247–48
    uprising in, 564
    as war capital, 431–32
    war plans regarding, 67–68, 73–74
Phillips, William, 39, 47, 50, 208, 214, 217, 222,
    223, 230, 577, 605
Phoenix (British warship), 416, 421–22
Pickens, Andrew, 426–27
Pickering, Timothy, 81, 129, 139–40, 141, 142,
    170–71, 179, 308
Pigot (British hospital ship), 395
Pigot, Robert, 394, 407
Pinckney, Thomas, 420, 551, 588
Plymouth, England, 510
Pointer, Thomas, 53
Point No Point duel, 428–30
Polly & Nancy (British ship), 16
Pondicherry, 424
Poor, Enoch, 192, 293–94, 503
Poor Richard's Almanack (Franklin), 13, 19
Pope, Thomas, 481
Popp, Stephan, 410
Porcupine (British sloop), 312
port of Dunkirk, 457
Portsmouth, England, 258, 266, 301, 332–35,
    337, 343, 347, 349, 354, 355, 385, 447–48,
    463, 509, 512, 516, 518, 522, 524, 570
Portsmouth, Virginia, 470, 471
Portugal, 275
Potts, Isaac, 295
Poughkeepsie, New York, 206
pousse-cailloux, 538
Powell, Henry Watson, 210, 211
Powell, John, 377–78
Prechtel, Johann Ernst, 60
Prescott, Richard, 69, 303
press-gang, 330–31

Prévost, Augustine, 425, 541, 542, 545–47, 552, 554
Price, Richard, 261
Priestley, Joseph, 19
Prince George (British ship), 335
Prince of Orange (British ship), 17
Prince of Wales (British flagship), 424, 538, 539
Princess Royal (British warship), 409, 530
prisoners of war
  American, 18, 42, 46, 50, 53, 86, 127, 153, 156, 178, 211, 228, 230, 231, 317, 343, 415, 470, 493, 500, 572, 577, 605
  bounty for, 212
  British, 16, 144, 174, 212, 227, 378, 395, 471, 531–32
  Canadian, 212
  exchange proposal regarding, 18, 86, 230, 346
  German, 116, 212
  Hessian, 144, 471
  intelligence from, 36
  in London, 611
  loyalist, 146, 427, 470
  as taken by Indians, 53
Proserpine (French frigate), 335
Protecteur (French ship), 395
Protestantism, 455
providence, 616
Providence (American sloop), 486
Providence Increase (British brigantine), 67
Prudent (British frigate), 533
Pulaski, Casimir, 415, 544, 551, 552–53
Putnam (American battery), 234
Putnam, Israel "Old Put," 207

Quakers, 93, 94, 127, 141, 389, 432
Queen of France (American frigate), 582
Queen's Grove, 3
Queen's House, 262, 266, 458–59, 611

Rachel (American schooner), 488
Rainbow (British ship), 465, 468, 470
Raisonnable (British ship), 401, 468, 470, 491, 582
Rakove, Jack, 591
Ramsay, Dr. David, 588, 591
Randolph (American frigate), 343
Randolph, Edward, 151
Ranger (British warship), 342–43, 344, 345, 346
rattlesnakes, 49
Ray, Martha, 448, 452–53
Read, William, 373
Rebecca (British ship), 580
rebellion, significance of, 265

Red Bank, 160, 233, 236, 237, 241–42, 243, 245. *See also* Fort Mercer
Reed, Joseph, 315, 442
Reed, Oliver, 253–54
Refugeetown, 378
Regulations for the Order and Discipline of the Troops of the United States, 439
Renown (British ship), 401–2, 580, 593
Reprisal (American warship), 16, 17
Republic (sloop), 87
Repulse (xebec), 245
Resolution (British ship), 519–20
Retaliation (American schooner), 392
Revenge (British schooner), 17, 42
Revere, Paul, 488, 489, 492
Reynolds, Francis, 240
Rhode Island, 391–92, 410
Richmond (British ship), 593
Riedesel, Frederika Charlotte von, 182–83, 208, 219–20, 222, 227, 577–78
Riedesel, Friedrich Adolph
  on American withdrawal, 53
  anger of, 47
  background of, 32
  in Battle of Saratoga, 196
  on Canada Army, 186
  on change of plans, 106–7
  concession of, 224
  on Fraser, 220
  leadership of, 46, 208, 577
  plea for, 44
  proposal by, 106
  surrender of, 226
  war council of, 223
rifle, American, 190
Ring, Benjamin, 126
Roberts, John, 432
Roberts, Richard, 613
Robertson, Archibald, 579–80, 600
Robinson, John, 461, 511
Robinson, Leonard, 112–13
Roderigue Hortalez & Cie, 279
Rodger, N.A.M., 328
Rodney, Sir George, 449
Roebuck (British warship), 72, 240, 241, 244, 402
Romney, George, 100
Romulus (British ship), 579, 606–7
Rose (British warship), 537
Ross, James, 129
Ross, John, 480
Royal Arms Factory, 16
Royal Charles (British ship), 326
Royal Convert (British ship), 30
Royal Gazette (newspaper), 265–66

Royal George (British frigate), 30, 36, 41, 523
Rudd, Sarah, 107
Rudé, George F. E., 610
running the Negroes, 470. *See also* slaves and
  slavery
Rush, Benjamin, 80, 128, 140, 251–52, 319,
  339, 382, 484, 564
Russia Merchant (British ship), 580, 581
Rutledge, John, 587, 591, 594

Sacket, Nathaniel, 86–87
Sackville, Fort, 494–96
Sagittaire (French ship), 394, 395
Sally (British hospital ship), 580
Salter, Titus, 490
Saltonstall, Dudley, 486, 487, 490, 492
Sandwich (British ship), 335, 593
Sandwich, John Montagu, 4th Earl of
  on Americans, 329–30
  background of, 328
  on Battle of Ushant, 354
  characteristics of, 328–29
  on dismissal, 449
  on English Channel conflict, 523
  fleeing by, 448
  on the French, 272
  grief of, 452–53
  hostility toward, 449–50
  leadership of, 453, 457
  marriage of, 329
  meeting of, 459–60
  morale of, 523–24
  strategy of, 335
  unpopularity of, 450–51
  violence against, 610
  on war, 331, 332
  war preparations of, 509
  work of, 327–28, 329, 330
Sandy Hollow, 136
Sandy Hook, 71, 358, 378–79, 388, 389, 394,
  399, 412–13
Sandy Hook lighthouse, 378, 384
Saratoga, Battle of
  battle cries in, 196
  beginnings of, 193–94
  at Bemus Heights, *209*, 210, 211, 212,
    213–14, 215–17
  blame in, 268
  British flaws in, 195
  British movement in, 192, 193, 196, 199
  casualties in, 193–95, 197–98
  celebration following, 250
  changing hands in, 195–96
  Continental status in, 189, 191–92
  length of, 197

  map of, *185*
  Northern Army placement in, 191
  spread of, 195
  weather for, 192
Saratoga, New York, 186, 221, 224
Sartine, Gabriel de, 288
Saussure, Louis de, 552
Savannah, assault on, *540*, 541–52, 553–55,
  560–61
Savannah, Georgia, 420, 422–23, 424, 426,
  536–38, 541–42, 545, 546. *See also* assault
  on Savannah
Sayre, John, 475–76
scalping, 51, 52, 53, 96, 183, 198, 493, 497
Scammell, Alexander, 194, 197
Scarborough Castle, 529
Schnitzer, Eric H., 197
Schuyler, Elizabeth, 566
Schuyler, Hanjost, 104
Schuyler, Philip, 48, 52, 81, 103, 108, 187–88,
  227
Schuylkill, 153, 154
Scott, Charles, 363, 370, 470
Scudder, Benjamin, 562
scurvy, 184. *See also* disease
Seely, Silvanus, 565
Seneca Indians, 98, 101, 102, 497
Senegal, 457
Sensible (French frigate), 309
Serapis (British warship), 529, 530–31, 532,
  533, 534–35
Serle, Ambrose, 66, 75, 123, 314
Sevelinges, Charles François, 18
Seven Years' War (French and Indian War), 6,
  47, 258, 508, 524
Shark (British ship), 204–5
Shaw, George Bernard, 232
Sherburne, Edward, 172
Sheridan, Richard, 509
Sherman, William Tecumseh, 507
Shippen, Edward, 442
Shippen, Peggy, 441–42, 443
Shreve, Israel, 134, 505
siege of Charleston, 582, *583*, 584–86, 587. *See
  also* Charleston, South Carolina
Silver Eel (British transport vessel), 581
Simcoe, John Graves, 368–69
Sisargas Islands, 514
Skene, Philip, 42, 113
Skenesborough, 41–42
Sky-Rocket (American privateer), 489
slaves and slavery, 59, 590–92, 604–5
smallpox, 88–89. *See also* disease
Smallwood, William, 152–53, 156, 179
Smith, John, 238, 253

Smith, Robert, 161
Smith, Samuel, 54, 160, 243, 377
Smith, William (Pickering deputy), 171
Smith, William, Jr. (judge), 411, 418, 472, 576, 578
Somerset (British warship), 244
South Carolina, 158, 497, 544, 582, 587–88, 591–92. *See also specific locations*
Southwark Theater (Philadelphia), 247
Spain
  British fear regarding, 508–9
  British insults to, 457–58
  convention of war with France and, 457
  double game of, 456
  Family Compact and, 8
  as mediator, 456–57
  threat from, 275
  treaty rejection by, 285–86
  war entry of, 505
  war strategies of, 511–12
  war viewpoint of, 456
Spanish Navy, 10, 512, 514–15, 520, 523, 525–26, 614
Spanish spies, 512
Spear, Joseph, 130
Sphynx (British warship), 118–19, 406
spies. *See* espionage
sporting events, 56
Springsteel, David, 479–80
Springsteen, Caspar, 59
Sprouts, 187
spruce beer, 184, 207
Stamp Act crisis, 264
Stanislaw II, 552
Stanley (British brig), 389, 394
Stanley, Charlotte, 33, 34
Stansbury, Joseph, 567
Stanton, Ebenezer, 615
Stanwix, Fort (Fort Schuyler), 96, 97, 98, 99, 101–2, 103–4
Stark, John, 108, 110–15, 555
Staten Island, 576–77
St. Augustine, Florida, 418
St. Clair, Arthur, 37, 38, 40, 47–48, 213
Stedingk, Curt, 550, 552
Stedman, Charles, 603
Stephen, Adam, 131, 173, 180–81
Steuben, Baron Friedrich Wilhelm von, 300–301, 302–3, 309–10, 362, 366, 376, 438–39
Stewart, Charles, 252
St. George, Richard, 154
Stiles, Reverend Ezra, 474, 475, 497
Stirling, William Alexander, Lord, 135, 136, 168, 175, 206, 361, 362, 374–75, 576–77

St. Leger, Barrimore, 34, 98, 100, 105
St. Lucia, 6, 312, 417, 425, 538
St. Michael's Church, 584–85
Stone, Gary Wheeler, 358
Stone, John Hoskins, 135
Stone, Nicholas, 222
Stony Point, assault on, *478,* 479–84
Stormont, David Murray, Lord, 10–11, 17, 18–19, 25, 278, 288–89, 608–9
Strachey, Henry, 119, 120, 240, 306
Strolling Players, 247
Stuart, Charles, 123, 238, 419, 483, 570, 612
Sturdy Beggar (American ship), 144
St. Vincent, 424
Success Increase (British ship), 580
Succotash Campaign, 503
Suffolk, Virginia, 470
Sugar Loaf, 39
Sullivan, Fort, 502
Sullivan, John, 127–28
  in Battle for Newport, 394, 396, 397, 404, 406, 407, 408
  in Battle of Brandywine, 135
  criticism of, 141–42
  in Indian Expedition, 500, 501, 503, 504–5
  leadership of, 127–28, 129
  orders to, 170
  resignation threat from, 90
Sultan (British ship), 539
Sun Inn (Bethlehem, Pennsylvania), 146
surgeries, process of, 140
Surprize (British ship), 17
Swan (British ship), 580
Swartout, Barnardus, Jr., 370
Swift (British ship), 580
Swords's House, 186

Tallmadge, Benjamin, 174, 440–41
Tarleton, Banastre, 595, 602
Tars, Jack, 234
Taylor, Daniel, 205
Teisseydre, François Louis (Marquis de Fleury), 244, 481
Terpsichore (British frigate), 522
Terrible (British ship), 519–20
Terson, Philippe Séguier, 550
Tew, Francis, 482
Thacher, James, 198, 226, 228, 305
Thames (British ship), 72
Thayer, Simeon, 243
Thomas, Evan, 535
Thomas, Margaret, 295
Thompson (collier), 344–45
Thornton, John, 283–84
Thunderer (British gunboat), 30, 229–30

Ticonderoga, Fort. *See* Fort Ticonderoga, New York

Tilden, Ezra, 219

Tilghman, Tench, 80–81, 372–73, 566

Timothy, Peter, 584–86, 592, 593

Tims, John, 157

Tioga, 505

Tischbein, Johann, 182, 233

tobacco trade, 468

Todd, Asa, 474–75

Todd, Jonathan, 177

Tonnant (French ship), 401

Tories, description of, 158

Tory Redoubt, 110, 111

Townsend, Joseph, 130, 131–32, 140

Townsend, Robert, 440

Townshend, Sarah, 475

Trask, Israel, 492

treason, 158, 307, 420, 427, 432, 567, 612

Treat, Samuel, 243

treaties, description of, 287

treaty of amity and commerce, 287–88, 309

treaty of convention, 225

Trelawny, Harry, 374

Trevanion, Sophia, 336

Trevelyan, George Otto, 159

Trident (British ship), 315

Trout, Reverend Joab, 126

Trumbull (American ship), 42, 343, 486, 488

Trumbull, John, 406

Trumbull, Joseph, 294

Tryon, William, 65, 473–74, 577

Tuscarora Indians, 98, 212, 498, 506

Tuttle, Elisha, 475

Twiss, William, 39–40

Tybee Island, Georgia, 537, 581

typhus, 514. *See also* disease

Tyrannicide (American privateer), 17, 488

United States. *See* American colonies

Ushant, Battle of, 349–53, 354

Ushant island, 349

Vagrant Act, 420

Valley Forge, 147, 250–51, 292–93, 296–97, 299, 307, 309–10, 320

Van Doren, Carl, 568

Van Zandt, Jacobus (George Lupton), 283

Varnum, James Mitchell, 252

Vaughan, John, 204, 206–7, 466, 472

Vaux, Jourda, Noël de, Comte de, 512, 516, 522, 525

Vengeance (American privateer), 488

Vergennes, Charles Gravier, comte de, 8, 9, 10, 11, 281, 284, 285–87, 288, 457

Vermont, 45

Vernier, Pierre-Jean François, 595

Versailles, 5–6, 8, 14, 22, 281, 285, 289–91, 359, 516–17, 522, 534, 539

Victory (British warship), 326–27, 329, 337, 351, 352, 447, 523

videttes, role of, 151

La Vigie, 425

Vigilant (British ship), 406, 422

Ville de Paris (French ship), 288, 524

Vimeur, Jean-Baptiste Donatien de (Comte de Rochambeau), 617

Vincennes, 494–95

Virgil, 2

Virginia, 85–86, 158, 438, 468, 470

Viviers, Anne, 8

Volcano (British fireship), 240, 401

Voltaire (François-Marie d'Arouet), 338–39

Vulcan (British fireship), 71

Vulture (British ship), 480

wages, capping of, 564

Waldo, Dr. Albigence, 249, 293

Wallace, Dr. James, 179

Walloomsac River, 110

Walnut Street jail, 178, 317

Walpole, Horace

  on America, 461

  on England, 511, 521

  grief of, 452–53

  on Hardy, 525

  home of, 261, 510

  on the Howes, 410

  on the king, 266

  on petition, 608

  on religious war, 609

  on rioting, 612

  on the Royal Navy, 492, 509

  on Sandwich, 328

  on war, 261–62, 273, 277

Ward, Samuel, 407

Warner, Seth, 43, 46, 114

War on the American Frontier

  casualties at, 489, 492, 495–96

  combat start of, 488–90

  at Fort Sackville, 494–96

  Indian attacks in, 497

  Indian Expedition in, 497, 498–507

  locations of, 493

  map of, *487*

  at Nautilus Island, 488–89

  in Ohio River valley, 494–95

  raids in, 493

  ship movement to, 488

  Washington's strategy regarding, 498

Warren (American frigate), 486
Warren, Benjamin, 198, 219, 500
Warren, Mercy Otis, 380, 563–64
Warren, Samuel, 552
Washington (American brig), 30
Washington (British brig), 41
Washington, George
  on Army conditions, 561–63
  on assault on Stony Point, 479, 482, 483
  at Battle of Brandywine, 125–26, 128–30, 131, 136–37, 139–40, 142
  in Battle of Germantown, 170, 172–73, 179–80, 280
  in Battle of Monmouth, 366–68, 376, 377
  battle plans of, 618
  on Benedict Arnold, 104
  on British attacks, 476–77
  on British movement, 77, 90–91
  celebration of, 228–29
  challenges of, 81
  characteristics of, 79–81, 142, 366, 372, 616
  at City Tavern (Philadelphia), 94–95
  concerns of, 153, 472–73
  on Congress, 433–34, 437
  Congressional concerns regarding, 305–6
  on Continental Army conditions, 252–53
  criticism of, 142, 305–6, 409, 507
  on desertion, 85
  in Englishtown, 371
  on enlistments, 437–38
  on espionage, 439–40, 441
  failures of, 125–26, 179–80
  on foreign officers, 90
  on Fort Mercer, 237
  on Great Britain, 82–83
  headquarters of, 124, 126
  home of, 79, 295, 443–44, 559–60
  influence to, 85
  on intelligence, 314
  at Iron Hill, 124
  on Iroquois Confederacy, 497
  Lafayette and, 617
  leadership of, 66, 76–77, 86, 88–90, 92, 125, 147, 149, 154, 163–64, 252, 298, 306, 320, 360–63, 372, 383, 405, 434, 439–40, 443, 477, 479, 616
  Lee and, 372, 381, 382–83
  legacy of, 507
  on management, 230
  on the militia, 83
  mission of, 82
  morale of, 439, 560–61, 615
  in Morristown, 559–60
  Mount Vernon and, 296
  movement of, 124–25, 360
  pardoning by, 79, 310
  in Philadelphia, 154, 162, 430–32
  pleas of, 295
  popularity of, 432–33
  portrait painting of, 163, 296, 433
  praise for, 306, 380, 616
  on providence, 616
  on *Regulations for the Order and Discipline of the Troops of the United States,* 439
  religious beliefs of, 82
  reputation of, 81–82
  rumors regarding, 65
  on Steuben, 301
  strategies of, 388–89, 405, 434
  support for, 80, 616
  Valley Forge and, 251
  on war with Indians, 498
  on the weather, 565
Washington, Lund, 296
Washington, Martha, 296, 310, 430, 560
Waxhaws, 603
Waxworks, 260
Wayne, Anthony
  acquittal of, 154
  at assault on Stony Point, 479–81
  on Battle of Germantown, 176
  at Battle of Monmouth, 367–68
  in Battle of Monmouth, 376
  characteristics of, 149
  demands of, 295
  on disease, 251
  home of, 147
  injuries of, 173
  leadership of, 89, 127, 138, 150, 151, 153, 297, 363, 477, 479
  morale of, 164
  orders to, 373
  on war, 168
weather
  for American military, 92
  at approach to Monmouth, 360
  on the Atlantic Ocean, 579–81
  at Battle for Newport, 399, 401
  at Battle of Bennington, 110–11
  at Battle of Saratoga, 192
  in Birmingham, 321
  conditions of, 72
  description of, 118, 147
  French navy and, 537
  thunderstorms in, 119
  winter of 1779-1780, 557–59, 565, 574, 575–76
Webb (hospital transport), 316
Webb, Charles, 181
Wedderburn, Alexander, 611–12

Wedgwood, Josiah, 261
Weedon, George, 167, 173, 179
Welch's Tavern, 128
Welsh, John, 489
Wentworth, Paul, 282–83, 284–85
Wesley, John, 508, 510
West, Benjamin, 459, 464
West Indies, 258, 260–61, 417, 425, 450
Wheate, Sir Jacob, 520
Wheeler, Abby, 502
Wheeler, Hannah, 115
Whipple, Abraham, 587
Whitall, James and Ann, 236, 239, 242
Whitall, Job, 242
White, John, 172
White Eyes (Delaware chief), 497
Whitehaven, England, 344–45
Wickes, Lambert, 16
Wier, Daniel, 248, 414
Wigglesworth, Edward, 406
Wild, Ebenezer, 405
Wilkes, John, 158–59
Wilkinson, James, 213, 216
Willcox, William, 64, 571
Willett, Marinus, 102–3, 372

William, Prince (future William IV), 463–64
Williams, William, 54
Williamson, Andrew, 543
Williamson, Daniel, 297
Willis, Sam, 539
Wilson, Benjamin, 318
Wilson, James, 151
Winnebago, 50–51
Witherspoon, James, 167
Witherspoon, John, 167
Woodford, William, 173, 588
Woodhull, Abraham, 440
Woodruff, Samuel, 219
Wooster, David, 65
Wraxall, Nathaniel, 336, 508, 611
Wright, Governor James, 424, 541, 543, 547

Yale College, 474
Yeldall, Dr. Anthony, 247
York (British sloop), 389
York, Pennsylvania, 307–8
Yorke, Sir Joseph, 455

Zebra (British sloop), 386
Zélé (French ship), 397–98, 400

About the Author

RICK ATKINSON is the #1 *New York Times* bestselling author of seven previous works of history, including *The Long Gray Line*, the Liberation Trilogy (*An Army at Dawn*, *The Day of Battle*, and *The Guns at Last Light*), and *The British Are Coming*, the first volume of the Revolution Trilogy. He has won numerous awards, including Pulitzer Prizes for history and journalism.